P9-CCC-578

# MARKETING THEORY:

## Classic and Contemporary Readings


Jagdish N. Sheth
Brooker Professor of Research
Graduate School of Business
University of Southern California

Dennis E. Garrett
Assistant Professor of Business Administration
University of Oklahoma


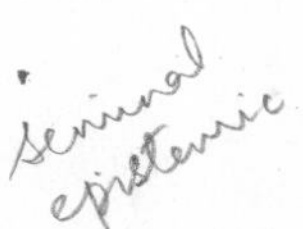

S25

Published by

**SOUTH-WESTERN PUBLISHING CO.**

CINCINNATI WEST CHICAGO, IL DALLAS PELHAM MANOR, NY LIVERMORE, CA

ISBN: 0-538-19253-4

Library of Congress
Catalog Card Number: 85-73301

1 2 3 4 5 6 7 FG 2 1 0 9 8 7 6
Printed in the United States of America

# PREFACE

Since its inception as an academic discipline in the early years of the 20th century, marketing has passed through several distinct eras in which certain topics dominated scholarly thought. In the 1980s the subject that is sparking the greatest interest among leading marketing scholars is the development of marketing theory. We can point to three broad motivations for this emergence of marketing theory as the current critical issue for discussion.

First, throughout the years marketing practitioners and marketing academicians have been inextricably linked in their efforts to determine more effective methods for bridging the gap between producers and consumers in the marketplace. Marketing practitioners, especially in the United States, are now facing increasingly competitive environments, both domestically and internationally, in which rival companies from foreign countries often enjoy cost and quality advantages. To address this problem, marketing practitioners are looking to their counterparts in academe to develop stronger and more applicable theories of marketing. Without sufficient theoretical guidance, the effectiveness and efficiency of marketing practice can deteriorate to unacceptable levels.

Second, marketing as a profession and an academic discipline has an image problem that must be corrected. Unfortunately, marketing is sometimes perceived as a second-rate discipline that survives only by borrowing theories from other more-established disciplines, such as psychology and sociology. Indeed, a sizable number of marketing professors received their doctorates in these other fields, and many of the references cited in marketing journal articles are from literature in these fields. Similarly, marketing practitioners still suffer from the stereotype held by many consumers that marketers are merely manipulative advertisers or greedy salespeople trying to take advantage of unsuspecting consumers. The public's misperception of marketing is colored to some extent by marketing's limited success in solving certain social problems, such as consumer safety and consumer education. The accuracy of these images of marketing is certainly debatable. However, if marketing hopes to eliminate any remaining vestiges of these negative stereotypes, stronger theories of marketing must be developed to enable marketing to stand as an independent scholarly discipline that is capable of addressing society's needs.

Third, in the past two decades marketing scholars have become enamored with sophisticated methodological techniques, particularly multivariate statistics. As a result, some critics now suggest that "the tail has begun to wag the dog." In short, marketing has become overly concerned with the technical complexity and correctness of research projects and less concerned with the theoretical framework that should be the foundation for the methodology. Thus, marketing practitioners increasingly complain that scholarly articles are becoming unreadable and bereft of managerial implications. Our attention must be directed to the development of more-credible marketing theories and, at the same time, more-sophisticated methodological procedures.

One of the most noticable features of *Marketing Theory: Classic and Contemporary Readings* is a heavy reliance on the lessons that the past can teach present-day theorists. We strongly believe that the development of marketing theory is facilitated as the history of marketing is better understood and appreciated. Thus, a sample of the earliest writings in each major school of thought is presented. In many cases the reader will probably be intrigued by the wisdom expressed by these early marketing scholars.

The breadth of coverage is another feature of this book. As noted earlier, marketing has borrowed heavily from a variety of disciplines. To convey this diversity, we have included articles from 11 distinct schools of marketing thought that have generated substantial interest during the history of marketing's theoretical development. If a general theory of marketing is ever going to be created, these diverse schools of thought must somehow be integrated into an inclusive framework that satisfactorily copes with their heterogeneity.

Finally, theory has both form and content. Although we stress the content dimension of marketing theory, as expressed in the 11 schools of thought presented, we also want to emphasize that marketing theory must meet certain rigorous standards. Therefore, sections are included that discuss the requirements of theory and science. These sections should be particularly appealing to students of marketing theory because these issues are currently being actively debated in the leading marketing journals.

*Jagdish N. Sheth*
*Dennis E. Garrett*

# CONTENTS

# PART ONE
# Theoretical Foundations

As a discipline, marketing addresses three broad questions: What is the nature and scope of marketing? Is marketing a science? What criteria should we use to judge marketing as a discipline?

The nature and scope of marketing is a relatively new issue. At one time, it appeared clear that marketing was a subset of economic activities that a firm performed well past the production and manufacturing stages. Marketing was limited to distribution activities, whether those activities were performed by the manufacturer or by middlemen, such as wholesalers and retailers. Indeed, marketing was viewed as a value-added function, supporting the primary functions of production and manufacturing.

Today the nature and scope of marketing is not as clearly defined. This is because we have broadened the marketing horizons. First, marketing is no longer considered merely a postmanufacturing process. Modern marketing is said to include preproduction processes because everything in business begins and ends with customer satisfaction. This new concept has produced some ambiguity and organizational conflicts, especially between engineering and marketing. Modern marketing has also broadened its horizons to include all exchanges of value not just economic exchanges. In other words, marketing is considered relevant to political voting and public services, which are free to the end users. This shift to include nonprofit services such as education, public health, and parks and recreation facilities, has created both excitement and uneasiness. Finally, marketing has been extended to intangible and perishable services, such as repair, maintenance, banking, insurance, and communication.

It is surprising to note that most of the boundary expansions of marketing have resulted in limiting our perception of marketing to selling and promotion. For example, although we are broadening our horizons to nonprofit or public services, we still often think of marketing as only advertising, selling, and promotion.

The second question encountered by marketing as a discipline is whether it is or can be a science. Some experts believe that to be a science, marketing must have either laws or law-like generalizations similar to those in physics and chemistry. Since we really do not have such laws, it is very difficult, if not impossible, to generate blueprints with which to replicate some success again and again. To that extent, marketing is not a science, nor can it ever be. In this view, marketing is much more an art in the sense that by trial and error it is possible to create acceptable outputs, such as paintings or gourmet meals. Furthermore, there may be thousands of artisans and cooks, but only a few great artists or master chefs. However, other experts believe that marketing *is* a science. The problem lies much less in the applications of scientific thinking than in the dynamic environment in which marketing is practiced.

The third challenge facing marketing as a discipline is the identification of criteria by which to judge it. On the one hand, we can take the metatheory approach and examine marketing in terms of the philosophy of science. In that case, such criteria as structure, scope, testability, empirical support, simplicity, and relevance become important. Of course, it is possible to debate what specific metatheory criteria are useful for marketing.

On the other hand, we can ignore scientific criteria as a basis on which to judge marketing as a discipline. For example, marketing can be judged from a moral viewpoint, one that mandates what marketing should be rather than what it is in practice. This viewpoint is not unusual in other areas of social science, such as clinical, religious, family, or political practice.

Part One of this book is devoted to addressing these issues. We have consciously attempted not to provide any hint as to our own personal feelings on these matters. These views are as emotional as those of politics and religion. They are often anchored to one's upbringing and prior education. Why should we claim to have an answer when no one really knows the answer?

# SECTION A
# Scope of Marketing

There is a growing debate about the nature and scope of marketing. The debate is focused on the following questions: What are the boundaries of marketing applications? Is marketing a useful consideration for nonprofit organizations and regulated public services such as electricity, gas, and water? Some scholars believe that the fundamental axioms of marketing, such as the exchange of values, are broad enough to encompass virtually all human interactions. Others argue that if marketing is so broadly defined that it encompasses all human behavior, it is likely to loose its identity as a distinct field of inquiry. Perhaps the best compromise is to limit marketing to exchange transactions that do have economic value. This limitation excludes friendship, charity, gifts and other noneconomic exchanges of values.

Second, can we develop a universal theory of marketing that can cover all areas of application? Most scholars tend to believe that such a grand theory is both impossible and impractical. As evidence of this, they cite failed attempts in sociology and buyer behavior studies. They recommend that marketing scholars develop separate theories for each domain of marketing, such as consumer, industrial, services, and international marketing. This, of course, presumes that the context is more important than the concept in theory development. It also supposes that in our theory construction we need to be more observant of the realities of a specific context.

There are some scholars who do believe in the grand theory of marketing. We have included a sample of their work in this book. Once again, it may be more pragmatic to allow each context-driven theory to develop and then to attempt an integration by using some bridging concepts.

Finally, what unique concepts should we use to define marketing as a distinct discipline? In other words, how do we distinguish ourselves from social psychology, economics, and consumer behavior disciplines? This is probably the hardest question to answer. The basic concept of exchange of values is common to so many disciplines that it blurs rather than distinguishes marketing from other disciplines.

Exchange of values focuses on the *agents* (middlemen) of marketing, the *activities* (functions), or the *objects* (products) of marketing. Earlier schools have used this focus in order to distinguish marketing from other disciplines. The jury is still out, and we really don't know what is likely to be an accepted framework to define marketing as a distinct discipline.

# 1 —— A Generic Concept of Marketing

***Philip Kotler***

Reprinted from *Journal of Marketing*, published by the American Marketing Association, Vol. 36 (April 1972), pp. 46-54. Reprinted by permission.

One of the signs of the health of a discipline is its willingness to reexamine its focus, techniques, and goals as the surrounding society changes and new problems require attention. Marketing has shown this aptitude in the past. It was originally founded as a branch of *applied economics* devoted to the study of distribution channels. Later marketing became a *management discipline* devoted to engineering increases in sales. More recently, it has taken on the character of an *applied behavioral science* that is concerned with understanding buyer and seller systems involved in the marketing of goods and services.

The focus of marketing has correspondingly shifted over the years. Marketing evolved through a *commodity focus* (farm products, minerals, manufactured goods, services); an *institutional focus* (producers, wholesalers, retailers, agents); a *functional focus* (buying, selling, promoting, transporting, storing, pricing); a *managerial focus* (analysis, planning, organization, control); and a *social focus* (market efficiency, product quality, and social impact). Each new focus had its advocates and its critics. Marketing emerged each time with a refreshed and expanded self-concept.

Today marketing is facing a new challenge concerning whether its concepts apply in the nonbusiness as well as the business area. In 1969, this author and Professor Levy advanced the view that *marketing is a relevant discipline for all organizations insofar as all organizations can be said to have customers and products*.[1] This "broadening of the concept of marketing" proposal received much attention, and the 1970 Fall Conference of the American Marketing Association was devoted to this theme.

Critics soon appeared who warned that the broadening concept could divert marketing from its true purposes and dilute its content. One critic did not deny that marketing concepts and tools could be useful in fund raising, museum membership drives, and presidential campaigns, but he felt that these were extracurricular applications of an intrinsical business technology.[2]

Several articles have been published which describe applications of marketing ideas to nonbusiness areas such as health services, population control, recycling of solid wastes, and fund raising.[3] Therefore, the underlying issues should be reexamined to see whether a more generic concept of marketing can be established. This author concludes that the traditional conception of marketing would relegate this discipline to an increasingly narrow and pedestrian role in a society that is growing increasingly post-industrial. In fact, this article will argue that the broadening proposal's main weakness was not that it went too far but that it did not go far enough.

This article is organized into five parts. The first distinguishes three stages of consciousness regarding the scope of marketing. The second presents an axiomatic treatment of the generic concept of marketing. The third suggests three useful marketing typologies that are implied by the generic concept of marketing. The fourth describes the basic analytical, planning, organization, and control tasks that make up the logic of marketing management. The fifth discusses some interesting questions raised about the generic concept of marketing.

## Three Stages of Marketing Consciousness

Three different levels of consciousness can be distinguished regarding the boundaries of marketing. The present framework utilizes Reich's consciousness categories without his specific meanings.[4] The traditional consciousness, that marketing is essentially a business subject, will be called *consciousness one*. Consciousness one is the most widely held view in the mind of practitioners and the public. In the last few years, a marketing *consciousness two* has appeared among some marketers holding that marketing is appropriate for all organizations that have customers. This is the thrust of the original broadening proprosal and seems to be gaining adherents. Now it can be argued that even consciousness two expresses a limited concept of marketing. One can propose *consciousness three* that holds that marketing is a relevant subject for all organizations in their relations with all their publics, not only customers. The future character of marketing will depend on the particular consciousness that most marketers adopt regarding the nature of their field.

### Consciousness One

Consciousness one is the conception that marketing is essentially a business subject. It maintains that marketing is concerned with *sellers, buyers,* and *"economic" products and services*. The sellers offer goods and services, the buyers have purchasing power and other resources, and the objective is an exchange of goods for money or other resources.

The core concept defining marketing consciousness one is that of *market transactions*. A market transaction involves the transfer of ownership or use of an economic good or service from one party to another in return for a payment of some kind. For market transactions to occur in a society, six conditions are necessary: (1) Two or more parties; (2) a scarcity of goods; (3) concept of private property; (4) one party must want a good held by another; (5) the "wanting" party must be able to offer some kind of payment for it; and (6) the "owning" party must be willing to forego the good for the payment. These conditions underlie the notion of a market transaction, or more loosely, economic exchange.

Market transactions can be contrasted with nonmarket transactions. Nonmarket transactions also involve a transfer of resources from one party to another, *but without clear payment by the other.* Giving gifts, paying taxes, receiving free services are all examples of nonmarket transactions. If a housekeeper is paid for domestic services, this is a market transaction; if she is one's wife, this is a nonmarket transaction. Consciousness one marketers pay little or no attention to nonmarket transactions because they lack the element of explicit payment.

## Consciousness Two

Consciousness two marketers do not see *payment* as a necessary condition to define the domain of marketing phenomena. Marketing analysis and planning are relevant in all organizations producing products and services for an intended consuming group, whether or not payment is required.

Table 1 lists several nonbusiness organizations and their "products" and "customer groups." All of these products, in principle, can be priced and sold. A price can be charged for museum attendance, safe driving lessons, birth conrol information, and education. The fact that many of these services are offered "free" should not detract from their character as products. A product is something that has value to someone. Whether a charge is made for its consumption is an incidental rather than essential feature defining value. In fact, most of these social goods are "priced," although often not in the normal fashion. Police services are paid for by taxes, and religious services are paid for by donations.

Each of these organizations faces marketing problems with respect to its product and customer group. They must study the size and composition of their market and consumer wants, attitudes, and habits. They must design their products to appeal to their target markets. They must develop distribution and communication programs that facilitate "purchase" and satisfaction.

**TABLE 1. Some Organizations and Their Products and Customer Groups**

| *Organization* | *Product* | *Customer Group* |
|---|---|---|
| Museum | Cultural appreciation | General public |
| National Safety Council | Safer driving | Driving public |
| Political candidate | Honest government | Voting public |
| Family Planning Foundation | Birth control | Fertile public |
| Police department | Safety | General public |
| Church | Religious experience | Church members |
| University | Education | Students |

They must develop customer feedback systems to ascertain market satisfaction and needs.

Thus consciousness two replaces the core concept of *market transactions* with the broader concept of *organization-client transactions*. Marketing is no longer restricted only to transactions involving parties in a two-way exchange of economic resources. Marketing is a useful perspective for any organization producing products for intended consumption by others. *Marketing consciousness two states that marketing is relevant in all situations where one can identify an organization, a client group, and products broadly defined.*

## Consciousness Three

The emergence of a marketing consciousness three is barely visible. Consciousness three marketers do not see why marketing technology should be confined only to an organization's transactions with its client group. An organization—or more properly its management—may engage in marketing activity not only with its customers but also with all other publics in its environment. A management group has to market to the organization's supporters, suppliers, employees, government, the general public, agents, and other key publics. *Marketing consciousness three states that marketing applies to an organization's attempts to relate to all of its publics, not just its consuming public.* Marketing can be used in multiple institutional contexts to effect transactions with multiple targets.

Marketing consciousness three is often expressed in real situations. One often hears a marketer say that his real problem is not *outside marketing* but *inside marketing*; for example, getting others in his organization to accept his ideas. Companies seeking a preferred position with suppliers or dealers see this as a problem of marketing themselves. In addition, companies try to market their viewpoint to congressmen in Washington. These and many other examples suggest that marketers see the marketing problem as extendding far beyond customer groups.

The concept of defining marketing in terms of *function* rather than *structure* underlies consciousness three. To define a field in terms of function is to see it as a process or set of activities. To define a field in terms of structure is to identify it with some phenomena such as a set of institutions. Bliss pointed out that many sciences are facing this choice.[5] In the field of political science, for example, there are those who adopt a structural view and define political science in terms of political institutions such as legislatures, government agencies, judicial courts, and political parties. There are others who adopt a functional view and define political science as the study of *power* wherever it is found. The latter political scientists study power in the family, in labor-management relations, and in corporate organizations.

Similarly, marketing can be defined in terms of functional rather than structural considerations. Marketing takes place in a great number of situations, including executive recruiting, political campaigning, church membership drives, and lobbying. Examining the marketing aspects of these situations can yield new insights into the generic nature of marketing. The payoff may be higher than from continued concentration in one type of structural setting, that of business.

It is generally a mistake to equate a science with a certain phenomenon. For example, the subject of *matter* does not belong exclusively to physics, chemistry, or biology. Rather physics, chemistry, and biology are logical systems that pose different questions about matter. Nor does *human nature* belong exclusively to psychology, sociology, social psychology, or anthropology. These sciences simply raise different questions about the same phenomena. Similarly, traditional business subjects should not be defined by institutional characteristics. This would mean that finance deals with banks, production with factories, and marketing with distribution channels. Yet each of these subjects has a set of core ideas that are applicable in multiple institutional contexts. An important means of achieving progress in a science is to try to increase the generality of its concepts.

Consider the case of a hospital as an institution. A production-minded person will want to know about the locations of the various facilities, the jobs of the various personnel, and in general the arrangement of the elements to produce the product known as health care. A financial-minded person will want to know the hospital's sources and applications of funds and its income and expenses. A marketing-minded person will want to know where the patients come from, why they appeared at this particular hospital, and how they feel about the hospital care and services. Thus the phenomena do not create the questions to be asked; rather the questions are suggested by the disciplined view brought to the phenomena.

What then is the disciplinary focus of marketing? The core concept of marketing is the *transaction. A transaction is the exchange of values between two parties.* The things-of-values need not be limited to goods, services and money; they include other resources such as time, energy, and feelings. Transactions occur not only between buyers and sellers, and organizations and clients, but also between any two parties. A transaction takes place, for example, when a person decides to watch a television program; he is exchanging his time for entertainment. A transaction takes place when a person votes for a particular candidate; he is exchanging his time and support for expectations of better government. A transaction takes place when a person gives money to a charity; he is exchanging money for a good conscience. *Marketing is specifically concerned with how transactions are created, stimulated, facilitated, and valued.* This is the generic concept of marketing.

## The Axioms of Marketing

The generic concept of marketing will now be more rigorously developed. Marketing can be viewed as a *category of human action* distinguishable from other categories of human action such as voting, loving, consuming, or fighting. As a category of human action, it has certain characteristics which can be stated in the form of axioms. A sufficient set of axioms about marketing would provide unambiguous criteria about what marketing is, and what it is not. Four axioms, along with corollaries, are proposed in the following section.

Axiom 1. *Marketing involves two or more social units, each consisting of one or more human actors.*

Corollary 1.1. The social units may be individuals, groups, organizations, communities, or nations.

Two important things follow from this axiom. First, marketing is not an activity found outside of the human species. Animals, for example, engage in production and consumption, but do not engage in marketing. They do not exchange goods, set up distribution systems, and engage in persuasive activity. Marketing is a peculiarly human activity.

Second, the referent of marketing activity is another social unit. Marketing does not apply when a person is engaged in an activity in reference to a *thing* or *himself*. Eating, driving, and manufacturing are not marketing activities, as they involve the person in an interactive relationship primarily with things. Jogging, sleeping, and daydreaming are not marketing activities, as they involve the person in an interactive relationship primarily with himself. An interesting question does arise as to whether a person can be conceived of marketing something to himself, as when he undertakes effort to change his own behavior. Normally, however, marketing involves actions by a person directed toward one or more other persons.

Axiom 2. *At least one of the social units is seeking a specific response from one or more other units concerning some social object.*

Corollary 2.1. The social unit seeking the response is called the *marketer*, and the social unit whose response is sought is called the *market*.

Corollary 2.2. The social object may be a product, service, organization, person, place, or idea.

Corollary 2.3. The response sought from the market is some behavior toward the social object, usually acceptance but conceivably avoidance. (More specific descriptions of responses sought are purchase, adoption, usage, consumption, or their negatives. Those who do or may respond are called buyers, adopters, users, consumers, clients, or supporters.)

Corollary 2.4. The marketer is normally aware that he is seeking the specific response.

Corollary 2.5. The response sought may be expected in the short or long run.

Corollary 2.6. The response has value to the marketer.

Corollary 2.7. *Mutual marketing* describes the case where two social units simultaneously seek a response from each other. Mutual marketing is the core situation underlying bargaining relationships.

Marketing consists of actions undertaken by persons to bring about a response in other persons concerning some specific social object. A social object is any entity or artifact found in society, such as a product, service, organization, person, place, or idea. The marketer normally seeks to influence the market to accept this social object. The notion of marketing also covers attempts to influence persons to avoid the object, as in a business effort to discourage excess demand or in a social campaign designed to influence people to stop smoking or overeating.[6] *The marketer is basically trying to shape the level and composition of demand for his product.* The marketer undertakes these influence actions because he values their consequences. The market may also value the consequences, but this is not a necessary condition for defining the occurrence of marketing activity. The marketer is normally conscious that he is attempting to influence a market, but it is also possible to interpret as marketing activity cases where the marketer is not fully conscious of his ends and means.

Axiom 2 implies that ''selling'' activity rather than ''buying'' activity is closer to the core meaning of marketing. The merchant who assembles goods for the purpose of selling them is engaging in marketing, insofar as he is seeking a purchase response from others. The buyer who comes into his store and pays the quoted price is engaging in buying, not marketing, in that he does not seek to produce a specific response in the seller, who has already put the goods up for sale. If the buyer decides to bargain with the seller over the terms, he too is involved in marketing, or if the seller had been reluctant to sell, the buyer has to market himself as an attractive buyer. The terms ''buyer'' and ''seller'' are not perfectly indicative of whether one, or both, of the parties are engaged in marketing activity.

Axiom 3. *The market's response probability is not fixed.*

Corollary 3.1. The probability that the market will produce the desired response is called the *market's response probability*.

Corollary 3.2. The market's response probability is greater than zero; that is, the market is capable of producing the desired response.

Corollary 3.3. The market's response probability is less than one; that is, the market is not internally compelled to produce the desired response.

Corollary 3.4. The market's response probability can be altered by marketer actions.

Marketing activity makes sense in the context of a market that is free and capable of yielding the desired response. If the target social unit *cannot respond* to the social object, as in the case of no interest or no resources, it is not a market. If the target social unit *must respond* to the social object, as in the case of addiction or perfect brand loyalty, that unit is a market but there is little need for marketing activity. In cases where the market's response probability is fixed in the short run but variable in the long run, the marketer may undertake marketing activity to prevent or reduce the erosion in the response probability. Normally, marketing activity is most relevant where the market's response probability is less than one and highly influenced by marketer actions.

Axiom 4. *Marketing is the attempt to produce the desired response by creating and offering values to the market.*

Corollary 4.1. The marketer assumes that the market's response will be voluntary.

Corollary 4.2. The essential activity of marketing is the creation and offering of value. Value is defined subjectively from the market's point of view.

Corollary 4.3. The marketer creates and offers value mainly through configuration, valuation, symbolization, and facilitation. (Configuration is the act of designing the social object. Valuation is concerned with placing terms of exchange on the object. Symbolization is the association of meanings with the object. Facilitation consists of altering the accessibility of the object.)

Corollary 4.4. *Effective marketing* means the choice of marketer actions that are calculated to produce the desired response in the market. *Efficient marketing* means the choice of *least cost* marketer actions that will produce the desired response.

Marketing is an approach to producing desired responses in another party that lies midway between *coercion* on the one hand and *brainwashing* on the other.

Coercion involves the attempt to produce a response in another by forcing or threatening him with agent-inflicted pain. Agent-inflicted pain should be distinguished from object-inflicted pain in that the latter may be used by a marketer as when he symbolizes something such as cigarettes as potentially harmful to the smoker. The use of agent-inflicted pain is normally not a marketing solution to a response problem. This is not to deny that marketers occasionally resort to arranging a ''package of threats'' to get or keep a customer. For example, a company may threaten to discontinue purchasing from another company if the latter failed to behave in a certain way. But normally, marketing consists of noncoercive actions to induce a response in another.

Brainwashing lies at the other extreme and involves the attempt to produce a response in another by profoundly altering his basic beliefs and values. Instead of trying to persuade a person to see the social object as serving his existing values and interests, the agent tries to shift the subject's values in the direction of the social object. Brainwashing, fortunately, is a very difficult feat to accomplish. It requires a monopoly of communication channels, operant conditioning, and much patience. Short of pure brainwashing efforts are attempts by various agents to change people's basic values in connection with such issues as racial prejudice, birth control, and private property. Marketing has some useful insights to offer to agents seeking to produce basic changes in people, although its main focus is on creating products and messages attuned to existing attitudes and values. It places more emphasis on preference engineering than attitude conditioning, although the latter is not excluded.

The core concern of marketing is that of producing desired responses in free individuals by the judicious creating and offering of values. The marketer is attempting to get value from the market through offering value to it. The marketer's problem is to create attractive values. Value is completely subjective and exists in the eyes of the beholding market. Marketers must understand the market in order to be effective in creating value. This is the essential meaning of the marketing concept.

The marketer seeks to create value in four ways. He can try to design the social object more attractively (configuration); he can put an attractive terms on the social object (valuation); he can add symbolic significance in the social object (symbolization); and he can make it easier for the market to obtain the social object (facilitation). He may use these activities in reverse if he wants the social object to be avoided. These four activities have a rough correspondence to more conventional statements of marketing purpose, such as the use of product, price, promotion, and place to stimulate exchange.

The layman who thinks about marketing often overidentifies it with one or two major component activities, such as facilitation or symbolization. In *scarcity economies,* marketing is often identified with the facilitation function. Marketing is the problem of getting scarce goods to a marketplace. There is little concern with configuration and symbolization. In *affluent economies,* marketing is often identified with the symbolization function. In the popular mind, marketing is seen as the task of encoding persuasive messages to get people to buy more goods. Since most people resent persuasion attempts, marketing has picked up a negative image in the minds of many people. They forget or overlook the marketing work involved in creating values through configuration, valuation, and facilitation. In the future post-industrial society concern over the quality of life becomes paramount, and the public understanding of marketing is likely to undergo further change, hopefully toward an appreciation of all of its functions to create and offer value.

## Typologies of Marketing

The new levels of marketing consciousness make it desirable to reexamine traditional classifications of marketing activity. Marketing practitioners normally describe their type of marketing according to the *target market* or

**FIGURE 1. An Organization's Publics**

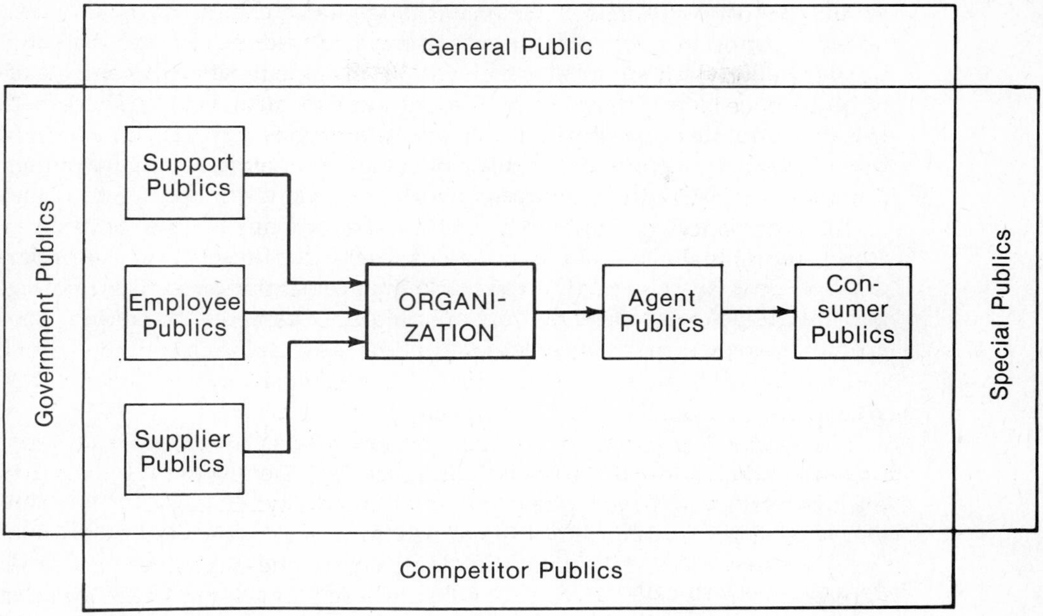

*product*. A *target-market classification* of marketing activity consists of consumer marketing, industrial marketing, government marketing, and international marketing.

A *product* classification consists of durable goods marketing, nondurable goods marketing, and service marketing.

With the broadening of marketing, the preceding classifications no longer express the full range of marketing application. They pertain to business marketing, which is only one type of marketing. More comprehensive classifications of marketing activity can be formulated according to the *target market, product,* or *marketer*.

## Target Market Typology

A *target-market classification* of marketing activity distinguishes the various *publics* toward which an organization can direct its marketing activity. *A public is any group with potential interest and impact on an organization.* Every organization has up to nine distinguishable publics (Figure 1). There are three *input publics* (supporters, employees, suppliers), two *output publics* (agents, consumers), and four *sanctioning publics* (government, competitors, special publics, and general public). The organization is viewed as a resource conversion machine which takes the resources of supporters (e.g., stockholders, directors), employees, and suppliers and converts these into products that go directly to consumers or through agents. The organizations's basic input-output activities are subject to the watchful eye of sanctioning publics such as government, competitors, special publics, and the general public. All of these publics are targets for organizational marketing activity because of their potential impact on the resource converting efficiency of the organization. Therefore, a *target-market classification* of marketing activity consists of supporter-directed marketing, employee-directed marketing, supplier-directed marketing, agent-directed marketing, consumer-directed marketing, general public-directed marketing, special public-directed marketing, government-directed marketing, and competitor-directed marketing.

## Product Typology

A typology of marketing activity can also be constructed on the basis of the *product* marketed. Under the broadened concept of marketing, the product is no longer restricted to commerical goods and services. An organization can try to market to a public up to six types of products or social objects. A product classification of marketing consists of goods marketing, service marketing, organization marketing, person marketing, place marketing, and idea marketing.

Goods and service marketing, which made up the whole of traditional marketing, reappear in this classification. In addition, marketers can specialize the marketing of organizations (e.g., governments, corporations, or universities), persons (e.g., political candidates, celebrities), places (e.g., real estate developments, resort areas, states, cities), and ideas (e.g., family planning, Medicare, anti-smoking, safe-driving).

## Marketer Typology

A typology can also be constructed on the basis of the *marketer,* that is, the organization that is carrying on the marketing. A first approximation would call for distinguishing between business and nonbusiness organization marketing. Since there are several types of nonbusiness organizations with quite different products and marketing tasks, it would be desirable to build a marketer classification that recognizes the different types of organizations. This leads to the following classifications: Business organization marketing, political organization marketing, social organization marketing, religious organization marketing, cultural organization marketing, and knowledge organization marketing.

Organizations are classified according to their primary or formal character. Political organizations would include political parties, government agencies, trade unions, and cause groups. Social organizations would include service clubs, fraternal organizations, and private welfare agencies. Religious organizations would include churches and evangelical movements. Cultural organizations would include museums, symphonies, and art leagues. Knowledge organizations would include public schools, universities, and research organizations. Some organizations are not easy to classify. Is a nonprofit hospital a business or a social organization? Is an employee credit union a political or a social organization? The purpose of the classification is primarily to guide students of marketing to look for regularities that might characterize the activities of certain basic types of organizations.

In general, the purpose of the three classifications of marketing activity is to facilitate the accumulation of marketing knowledge and its transfer from one marketing domain to another. Thus political and social organizations often engage in marketing ideas, and it is desirable to build up generic knowledge about idea marketing. Similarly, many organizations try to communicate a program to government authorities, and they could benefit from the accumulation of knowledge concerning idea marketing and government-directed marketing.

## Basic Tasks of Marketing Management

Virtually all persons and organizations engage in marketing activity at various times. They do not all engage in marketing, however, with equal skill. A distinction can be drawn between *marketing* and *marketing management*. *Marketing* is a descriptive science involving the study of how transactions are created, stimulated, facilitated, and valued. *Marketing management* is a normative science involving the efficient creation and offering of values to stimulate desired transactions. Marketing management is essentially a disciplined view of the task of achieving specific responses in others through the creation and offering of values.

Marketing management is not a set of answers so much as an orderly set of questions by which the marketer determines what is best to do in each situation. Effective marketing consists of intelligent analyzing, planning, organizing, and controlling marketing effort.

The marketer must be skilled at two basic analytical tasks. The first is *market analysis*. He must be able to identify the market, its size and location, needs and wants, perceptions and values. The second analytical skill is *product analysis*. The marketer must determine what products are currently available to the target, and how the target feels about each of them.

Effective marketing also calls for four major planning skills. The first is *product development*, i.e., configuration. The marketer should know where to look for appropriate ideas, how to choose and refine the product concept, how to stylize and package the product, and how to test it. The second is *pricing*, i.e., valuation. He must develop an attractive set of terms for the product. The third is *distribution*, i.e., facilitation. The marketer should determine how to get the product into circulation and make it accessible to its target market. The fourth is *promotion*, i.e., symbolization. The marketer must be capable of stimulating market interest in the product.

Effective marketing also requires three organizational skills. The first is *organizational design*. The marketer should understand the advantages and disadvantages of organizing market activity along functional, product, and market lines. The second is *organizational staffing*. He should know how to find, train, and assign effective co-marketers. The third is *organizational motivation*. He must determine how to stimulate the best marketing effort by his staff.

Finally, effective marketing also calls for two control skills. The first is *market results measurement*, whereby the marketer keeps informed of the attitudinal and behavioral responses he is achieving in the marketplace. The second is *marketing cost measurement*, whereby the marketer keeps informed of his costs and efficiency in carrying out his marketing plans.

## Some Questions About Generic Marketing

The robustness of the particular conception of marketing advocated in this article will be known in time through testing the ideas in various situations. The question is whether the logic called marketing really helps individuals such as educational administrators, public officials, museum directors, or church leaders to better interpret their problems and construct their strategies. If these ideas are validated in the marketplace, they will be accepted and adopted.

However, academic debate does contribute substantially to the sharpening of the issues and conceptions. Several interesting questions have arisen in the course of efforts by this author to expound the generic concept of marketing. Three of these questions are raised and discussed below.

1. *Isn't generic marketing really using influence as the core concept rather than exchange?*

   It is tempting to think that the three levels of consciousness of marketing move from *market transactions* to *exchange* to *influence* as the succeeding core concepts. The concept of influence undeniably plays an important role in marketing thought. Personal selling and advertising are essentially influence efforts. Product design, pricing, packaging, and distribution planning make extensive use of influence considerations. It would be too general to say, however, that marketing is synonymous with interpersonal, intergroup, or interorganizational influence processes.

   Marketing is a particular way of looking at the problem of achieving a valued response from a target market. It essentially holds that exchange values must be identified, and the marketing program must be based on these exchange values. Thus the anticigarette marketer analyzes what the market is being asked to give up and what inducements might be offered. The marketer recognizes that every action by a person has an opportunity cost. The marketer attempts to find ways to increase the person's perceived rate of exchange between what he would receive and what he would give up in *freely* adopting that behavior. The marketer is a specialist at understanding human wants and values and knows what it takes for someone to act.

2. *How would one distinguish between marketing and a host of related activities such as lobbying, propagandizing, publicizing, and negotiating?*

   Marketing and other influence activities and tools share some common characteristics as well as exhibit some unique features. Each influence activity has to be examined separately in relation to marketing. *Lobbying*, for example, is one aspect of government-directed marketing. The lobbyist attempts to evoke support from a legislator through offering values to the legislator (e.g., information, votes, friendship, and favors). A lobbyist thinks through the problem of marketing his legislation as carefully as the business marketer thinks through the problem of marketing his product or service. *Propagandizing* is the marketing of a political or social idea to a mass audience. The propagandist attempts to package the ideas in such a way as to constitute values to the target audience in exchange for support. *Publicizing* is the effort to create attention and interest in a target audience. As such it is a tool of marketing. *Negotiation* is a face-to-face mutual marketing process. In general, the broadened concept of marketing underscores the kinship of marketing with a large number of other activities and suggests that marketing is a more endemic process in society than business marketing alone suggests.

3. *Doesn't generic marketing imply that a marketer would be more capable of managing political or charitable campaigns than professionals in these businesses?*

   A distinction should be drawn between marketing as a *logic* and marketing as a *competence*. Anyone who is seeking a response in another would benefit from applying marketing logic to the problem. Thus a company treasurer seeking a loan, a company recruiter seeking a talented executive, a conservationist seeking an antipollution law, would all benefit in conceptualizing their problem in marketing terms. In these instances, they would be donning a marketer's hat although they would not be performing as professional marketers. A professional marketer is someone who (1) regularly works with marketing problems in a specific area and

(2) has a specialized knowledge of this area. The political strategist, to the extent he is effective, is a professional marketer. He has learned how to effectively design, package, price, advertise, and distribute his type of product in his type of market. A professional marketer who suddenly decides to handle political candidates would need to develop competence and knowledge in this area just as he would if he suddenly decided to handle soap or steel. Being a marketer only means that a person has mastered the logic of marketing. To master the particular market requires additional learning and experience.

## Summary and Conclusion

This article has examined the current debate in marketing concerning whether its substance belongs in the business area, or whether it is applicable to all areas in which organizations attempt to relate to customers and other publics. Specifically, *consciousness one marketing* holds that marketing's core idea is *market transactions,* and therefore marketing applies to buyers, sellers, and commercial products and services. *Consciousness two marketing* holds that marketing's core idea is *organization-client transactions,* and therefore marketing applies in any organizations that can recognize a group called customers. *Consciousness three marketing* holds that marketing's core idea is *transactions,* and therefore marketing applies to any social unit seeking to exchange values with other social units.

This broadest conception of marketing can be called *generic marketing.* Generic marketing takes a functional rather than a structural view of marketing. Four axioms define generic marketing. *Axiom 1:* Marketing involves two or more social units. *Axiom 2:* At least one of the social units is seeking a specific response from one or more other units concerning some social object. *Axiom 3:* The market's response probability is not fixed. *Axiom 4:* Marketing is the attempt to produce the desired response by creating and offering values to the market. These four axioms and their corollaries are intended to provide unambiguous criteria for determining what constitutes a marketing process.

Generic marketing further implies that marketing activity can be classified according to the *target market* (marketing directed to supporters, employees, suppliers, agents, consumers, general public, special publics, government, and competitors); the *product* (goods, services, organizations, persons, places, and ideas); and the *marketer* (business, political, social, religious, cultural, and knowledge organizations).

Marketers face the same tasks in all types of marketing. Their major analytical tasks are *market analysis* and *product analysis*. Their major planning tasks are *product development, pricing, distribution,* and *promotion*. Their major organizational tasks are *design, staffing,* and *motivation*. Their major control tasks are *market results measurement* and *marketing cost measurement*.

Generic marketing is a logic available to all organizations facing problems of market response. A distinction should be drawn between applying a marketing point of view to a specific problem and being a marketing professional. Marketing logic alone does not make a marketing professional. The professional also acquires competence, which along with the logic, allows him to interpret his problems and construct his marketing strategies in an effective way.

## ENDNOTES


1. Philip Kotler and Sidney J. Levy, "Broadening the Concept of Marketing," *Journal of Marketing*, Vol. 33 (January, 1969), pp. 10-15.
2. David Luck, "Broadening the Concept of Marketing—Too Far," *Journal of Marketing*, Vol. 33 (July, 1969), pp. 53-54.
3. *Journal of Marketing*, Vol. 35 (July, 1971).
4. Charles A. Reich, *The Greening of America* (New York: Random House, 1970).
5. Perry Bliss, *Marketing Management and the Behavioral Environment* (Englewood Cliffs, N.J.: Prentice-Hall, Inc., 1970), pp. 106-108,119-120.
6. See Philip Kotler and Sidney J. Levy, "Demarketing, Yes, Demarketing," *Harvard Business Review*, Vol. 49 (November-December, 1971), pp. 71-80.

# 2 —— The Nature and Scope of Marketing

*Shelby D. Hunt*

Reprinted from *Journal of Marketing*, published by the American Marketing Association, Vol. 40 (July 1976), pp. 17-28. Reprinted by permission.

During the past three decades, two controversies have overshadowed all others in the marketing literature. The first is the "Is marketing a science?" controversy sparked by an early *Journal of Marketing* article by Converse entitled "The Development of a Science of Marketing."[1] Other prominent writers who fueled the debate included Bartels, Hutchinson, Baumol, Buzzell, Taylor, and Halbert.[2] After raging throughout most of the '50s and '60s, the controversy has sinced waned. The waning may be more apparent than real, however, because many of the substantive issues underlying the marketing science controversy overlap with the more recent "nature of marketing" (broadening the concept of marketing) debate. Fundamental to both controversies are some radically different perspectives on the essential characteristics of both *marketing* and *science*.

The purpose of this article is to develop a conceptual model of the scope of marketing and to use that model to analyze (1) the approaches to the study of marketing, (2) the "nature of marketing" controversy, and (3) the marketing science debate. Before developing the model, some preliminary observations on the controversy concerning the nature of marketing are appropriate.

## The Nature of Marketing

What is marketing? What kinds of phenomena are appropriately termed *marketing phenomena*? How do marketing activities differ from nonmarketing activities? What is a marketing system? How can marketing processes be distinguished from other social processes? Which institutions should one refer to as marketing institutions? *In short, what is the proper conceptual domain of the construct labeled "marketing"?*

The American Marketing Association defines marketing as "the performance of business activities that direct the flow of goods and services from producer to consumer or user."[3] This position has come under attack from various quarters as being too restrictive and has prompted one textbook on marketing to note: "Marketing is not easy to define. No one has yet been able to formulate a clear, concise definition that finds universal acceptance."[4]

Although vigorous debate concerning the basic nature of marketing has alternately waxed and waned since the early 1900s, the most recent controversy probably traces back to a position paper by the marketing staff of the Ohio State University in 1965. They suggested that marketing be considered "the process in a society by which the demand structure for economic goods and services is anticipated or enlarged and satisfied through the conception, promotion, exchange, and physical distribution of goods and services."[5] Note the the conspicuous absence of the notion that marketing consists of a set of *business activities* (as in the AMA definition). Rather, they considered marketing to be a *social process*.

Next to plunge into the semantical battle were Kotler and Levy. Although they did not specifically propose a new definition of marketing, Kotler and Levy in 1969 suggested that the concept of marketing be broadened to include nonbusiness organizations. They observed that churches, police departments, and public schools have products and customers, and that they use the normal tools of marketing mix. Therefore, Kotler and Levy conclude that these organizations perform marketing, or at least marketing-like, activities. Thus,

> the choice facing those who manage nonbusiness organizations is not whether to market or not to market, for no organization can avoid marketing. The choice is whether to do it well or poorly, and on this necessity the case for organizational marketing is basically founded.[6]

In the same issue of the *Journal of Marketing*, Lazer discussed the changing boundaries of marketing. He pleaded that: "What is required is a broader perception and definition of marketing than has hitherto been the case—one that recognizes marketing's societal dimensions and perceives of marketing as more than just a technology of the firm."[7] Thus, Kotler and Levy desired to broaden the notion of marketing by including not-for-profit organizations, and Lazer called for a definition of marketing that recognized the discipline's expanding societal dimensions.

Luck took sharp issue with Kotler and Levy by insisting that marketing be limited to those business processes and activities that ultimately result in a *market* transaction.[8] Luck noted that even thus bounded, marketing would still be a field of enormous scope and that marketing specialists could still render their services to nonmarketing causes. Kotler and Levy then accused Luck of a new form of myopia and suggested that, "The crux of marketing lies in a *general ideal of exchange* rather than the narrower thesis of market transactions."[9] They further contended that defining marketing "too narrowly" would inhibit students of marketing from applying their expertise to the most rapidly growing sectors of the society.

Other marketing commentators began to espouse the dual theses that (1) marketing be broadened to include nonbusiness organizations, and (2) marketing's societal dimensions deserve scrutiny. Thus, Ferber prophesied that marketing would diversify into the social and public policy fields.[10] And Lavidge sounded a similar call to arms by admonishing marketers to cease evaluating new products solely on the basis of whether they *can* be sold. Rather, he suggested, they should evaluate new products from a societal perspective, that is, *should* the product be sold?

> The areas in which marketing people can, and must, be of service to society have broadened. In addition, marketing's functions have been broadened. Marketing no longer can be defined adequately in terms of the activities involved in buying, selling, and transporting goods and services.[11]

The movement to expand the concept of marketing probably became irreversible when the *Journal of Marketing* devoted an entire issue to marketing's changing social/environmental role. At that time, Kotler and Zaltman coined the term *social marketing*, which they defined as "the design, implementation and control of programs calculated to influence the acceptability of social ideas and involving considerations of product planning, pricing, communication, distribution, and marketing research."[12] In the same issue, marketing technology was applied to fund raising for the March of Dimes, health services, population problems, and the recycling of solid waste.[13] Further, Dawson chastised marketers for ignoring many fundamental issues pertaining to the social relevance of marketing activities:

> Surely, in these troubled times, an appraisal of marketing's actual and potential role in relation to such [societal] problems is at least of equal importance to the technical aspects of the field. Yet, the emphasis upon practical problem-solving within the discipline far outweighs the attention paid to social ramifications of marketing activity.[14]

Kotler has since reevaluated his earlier positions concerning broadening the concept of marketing and has articulated a "generic" concept of marketing. He proposes that the essence of marketing is the *transaction*, defined as the exchange of values between two parties. Kotler's generic concept of marketing states: "Marketing is specifically concerned with how transactions are created, stimulated, facilitated and valued."[15] Empirical evidence indicates that, at least among marketing educators, the broadened concept of marketing represents a *fait accompli*. A recent study by Nichols showed that 95% of marketing educators believed that the scope of marketing should be broadened to include nonbusiness organizations. Similarly, 93% agreed that marketing goes beyond just economic goods and services, and 83% favored including in the domain of marketing many activities whose ultimate result is not a market transaction.[16]

Although the advocates of extending the notion of marketing appear to have won the semantical battle, their efforts may not have been victimless. Carman notes that the definition of marketing plays a significant role in directing the research efforts of marketers. He believes that many processes (e.g., political processes) do not involve an exchange of values and that marketing should not take such processes under its "disciplinary wing."[17]

Bartels has also explored the so-called identity crises in marketing and has pointed out numerous potential disadvantages to broadening the concept of marketing. These *potential* disadvantages include (1) turning the attention of marketing researchers away from important problems in the area of physical distribution, (2) emphasizing methodology rather than substance as the content of marketing knowledge, and (3) an increasingly esoteric and abstract marketing literature. Bartels concluded: ''If 'marketing' is to be regarded as so broad as to include both economic and noneconomic fields of application, perhaps marketing as originally conceived will ultimately reappear under another name.''[18]

Similarly, Luck decries the ''semantic jungle'' that appears to be growing in marketing.[19] Citing conflicting definitions of *marketing* and *social marketing* in the current literature, Luck suggests that this semantic jungle has been impeding the efforts of marketers to think clearly about their discipline. He has challenged the American Marketing Association to create a special commission to clear up the definitional problems in marketing. Finally, a recent president of the American Marketing Association set the development of a consistent standard definition of marketing as a primary goal of the association.[20]

Three questions appear to be central to the ''nature [broadening the concept] of marketing'' controversy. First, what kinds of phenomena and issues *do* the various marketing writers perceive to be included in the scope of marketing? Second, what kinds of phenomena and issues *should* be included in the scope of marketing? Third, how can marketing be defined to both systematically encompass all the phenomena and issues that should be included and, at the same time, systematically exclude all other phenomena and issues? That is, a good definition of marketing must be both properly inclusive and exclusive. To rigorously evaluate these questions requires a conceptual model of the scope of marketing.

## The Scope of Marketing

No matter which definition of marketing one prefers, the scope of marketing is unquestionably broad. Often included are such diverse subject areas as consumer behavior, pricing, purchasing, sales management, product management, marketing communications, comparative marketing, social marketing, the efficiency/productivity of markeing systems, the role of marketing in economic development, packaging, channels of distribution, marketing research, societal issues in marketing, retailing, wholesaling, the social responsibility of marketing, international marketing, commodity marketing, and physical distribution. Though lengthy, this list of topics and issues does not exhaust the possibilities. Not all writers would include all the topics under the general rubric of marketing. The point deserving emphasis here, however, is that different commentators on marketing would *disagree* as to which topics should be excluded. The disagreement stems from fundamentally different perspectives and can best be analyzed by attempting to develop some common ground for classifying the diverse topics and issues in marketing.

The most widely used conceptual model of the scope of marketing is the familiar "4 Ps" model popularized by McCarthy in the early '60s.[21] The model is usually represented by three concentric circles. The inner circle contains the consumer, since this the focal point of marketing effort. The second circle contains the marketing mix ("controllable factors") of price, place, promotion, and product. Finally, the third circle contains the uncontrollable factors of political and legal environment, economic environment, cultural and social environment, resources and objectives of the firm, and the existing business situation. As is readily apparent, many of the subject areas previously mentioned have no "home" in the 4 Ps model. For example, where does social marketing or efficiency of marketing systems or comparative marketing belong?

During a presentation at the 1972 Fall Conference of the American Marketing Association, Kotler made some observations concerning the desirability of classifying marketing phenomena using the concepts of *micro, macro, normative,* and *positive*.[22] These observations spurred the development of the conceptual model detailed in Table 1. The schema proposes that all marketing phenomena, issues, problems, models, theories and research can be categorized using the three categorical dichotomies of (1) profit sector/nonprofit sector, (2) micro/macro, and (3) positive/normative. The three categorical dichotomies yield 2 × 2 × 2 = 8 classes or cells in the schema. Thus, the first class includes all marketing topics that are micro-positive and in the profit sector. Similarly, the second class includes all marketing activities that are micro-normative and in the profit sector, and so on throughout the table.

Some definitions are required to properly interpret the schema presented in Table 1. *Profit sector* encompasses the study and activities or organizations or other entities whose stated objectives include the realization of profit. Also applicable are studies that adopt the *perspective* of profit-oriented organizations. Conversely, *nonprofit* sector encompasses the study and perspective of all organizations and entities whose stated objectives do not include the realization of profit.

The *micro/macro* dichotomy suggests a classification based on the level of aggregation. *Micro* refers to the marketing activities of individual units, normally individual organizations (firms) and consumers or households. *Macro* suggests a higher level of aggregation, usually marketing systems or groups of consumers.

The *positive/normative* dichotomy provides categories based on whether the focus of the analysis is primarily descriptive or prescriptive. *Positive* marketing adopts the perspective of attempting to describe, explain, predict, and understand the marketing activities, processes, and phenomena that actually exist. This perspective examines *what is*. In contrast, normative marketing adopts the perspective of attempting to prescribe what marketing organizations and individuals ought to do or what kinds of marketing systems a society ought to have. That is, this perspective examines what *ought to be* and what organizations and individuals *ought to do*.

## ANALYZING APPROACHES TO MARKETING

An examination of Table 1 reveals that most of the early (circa 1920) approaches to the study of marketing reside in cell 3: profit sector/macro/positive. The institutional, commodity, and functional approaches analyzed existing (positive) business activities (profit sector) from a marketing systems (macro) perspective. However, not all the early marketing studies were profit/macro/positive. Weld's 1920 classic *The Marketing of Farm Products* not only examined existing distribution systems for farm commodities, but also attempted to evaluate such normative issues as: "Are there too many middlemen in food marketing?"[23] Thus, Weld's signally important work was both profit/macro/positive and profit/macro/normative. Similarly, the Twentieth Century Fund study *Does Distribution Cost Too Much?* took an essentially profit/macro/normative perspective.[24] Other important works that have combined the profit/macro/positive and the profit/macro/normative perspectives include those of Barger, Cox, and Borden.[25]

Although the profit/micro/normative (cell 2) orientation to marketing can be traced at least back to the 1920s and the works of such notables as Reed and White,[26] the movement reached full bloom in the early 1960s under proponents of the *managerial approach* to marketing, such as McCarthy.[27] The managerial approach adopts the perspective of the marketing manager, usually the marketing manager in a large manufacturing corporation. Therefore, the emphasis is micro and in the profit sector. The basic question underlying the managerial approach is: "What is the optimal marketing mix?" Consequently, the approach is unquestionably normative.

During the middle 1960s, writers such as Lazer, Kelley, Adler, and Fisk began advocating a *systems approach* to marketing.[28] Sometimes the systems approach used a profit/micro/normative perspective and simply attempted to apply to marketing certain sophisticated optimizing models (like linear and dynamic programming) developed by the operations researchers. Other writers used the systems approach in a profit/macro/positive fashion to analyze the complex interactions among marketing institutions. Finally, some used the systems approach in a profit/macro/normative fashion:

> The method used in this book is called the general systems approach. In this approach the goals, organization, inputs, and outputs of marketing are examined to determine how efficient and *how effective marketing is*. Constraints, including competition and government, are

**TABLE 1. The Scope of Marketing**

<table>
<tr><th></th><th></th><th>Positive</th><th>Normative</th></tr>
<tr><td rowspan="2">Profit Sector</td><td>Micro</td><td>(1) Problems, issues, theories, and research concerning:<br>a. Individual consumer buyer behavior<br>b. How firms determine prices<br>c. How firms determine products<br>d. How firms determine promotion<br>e. How firms determine channels of distribution<br>f. Case studies of marketing practices</td><td>(2) Problems, issues, normative models, and research concerning how firms should:<br>a. Determine the marketing mix<br>b. Make pricing decisions<br>c. Make product decisions<br>d. Make promotion decisions<br>e. Make packaging decisions<br>f. Make purchasing decisions<br>g. Make international marketing decisions<br>h. Organize their marketing departments<br>j. Plan their marketing strategy<br>k. Apply systems theory to marketing problems<br>l. Manage retail establishments<br>m. Manage wholesale establishments<br>n. Implement the marketing concept</td></tr>
<tr><td>Macro</td><td>(3) Problems, issues, theories, and research concerning:<br>a. Aggregate consumption patterns<br>b. Institutional approach to marketing<br>c. Commodity approach to marketing<br>d. Legal aspects of marketing<br>e. Comparative marketing<br>f. The efficiency of marketing systems<br>g. Whether the poor pay more<br>h. Whether marketing spurs or retards economic development<br>i. Power and conflict relationships in channels of distribution<br>j. Whether marketing functions are universal<br>k. Whether the marketing concept is consistent with consumers' interests</td><td>(4) Problems, issues, normative models, and research concerning:<br>a. How marketing can be made more efficient<br>b. Whether distribution costs too much<br>c. Whether advertising is socially desirable<br>d. Whether consumer sovereignty is desirable<br>e. Whether stimulating demand is desirable<br>f. Whether the poor should pay more<br>g. What kinds of laws regulating marketing are optimal<br>h. Whether vertical marketing systems are socially desirable<br>i. Whether marketing should have special social responsibilities</td></tr>
</table>

| | | | |
|---|---|---|---|
| Nonprofit Sector | Micro | (5) Problems, issues, theories, and research concerning:<br>a. Consumers' purchasing of public goods<br>b. How nonprofit organizations determine prices<br>c. How nonprofit organizations determine products<br>d. How nonprofit organizations determine promotion<br>e. How nonprofit organizations determine channels of distribution<br>f. Case studies of public goods marketing | (6) Problems, issues, normative models, and research concerning how nonprofit organizations *should*:<br>a. Determine the marketing mix (social marketing)<br>b. Make pricing decisions<br>c. Make product decisions<br>d. Make promotion decisions<br>e. Make packaging decisions<br>f. Make purchasing decisions<br>g. Make international marketing decisions (e.g., CARE)<br>h. Organize their marketing efforts<br>i. Control their marketing efforts<br>j. Plan their marketing strategy<br>k. Apply systems theory to marketing problems |
| | Macro | (7) Problems, issues, theories, and research concerning:<br>a. The institutional framework for public goods<br>b. Whether television advertising influences elections<br>c. Whether public service advertising influences behavior (e.g., "Smokey the Bear")<br>d. Whether existing distribution systems for public goods are efficient<br>e. How public goods are recycled | (8) Problems, issues, normative models, and research concerning:<br>a. Whether society should allow politicians to be "sold" like toothpaste<br>b. Whether the demand for public goods should be stimulated<br>c. Whether "low informational content" political advertising is socially desirable (e.g., ten-second "spot" commercials)<br>d. Whether the U.S. Army should be allowed to advertise for recruits |

also studied because they affect both the level of efficiency and the kinds of effects obtained.[29]

During the late 1960s, the *environmental approach* to marketing was promulgated by writers such as Holloway, Hancock, Scott, and Marks.[30] This approach emphasized an essentially descriptive analysis of the environmental constraints on marketing activities. These environments included consumer behavior, culture, competition, the legal framework, technology, and the institutional framework. Consequently, this approach may be classified as profit/macro/positive.

Two trends are evident in contemporary marketing thought. The first is the trend toward *social marketing* as proposed by Kotler, Levy, and Zaltman[31] and as promulgated by others.[32] Social marketing, with its emphasis on the marketing problems of nonprofit organizations, is nonprofit/micro/normative. The second trend can be termed *societal issues*. It concerns such diverse topics as consumerism, marketing and ecology, the desirability of political advertising, social responsibility, and whether the demand for public goods should be stimulated.[33] All these works share the common element of *evaluation*. They attempt to evaluate the desirability or propriety of certain marketing activities or systems and, therefore, should be viewed as either profit/macro/normative or nonprofit/macro/normative.

In conclusion, it is possible to classify all the approaches to the study of marketing and all the problems, issues, theories, models, and research usually considered within the scope of marketing using the three categorial dichotomies of profit sector/nonprofit sector, positive/normative, and micro/macro. This is not meant to imply that reasonable people cannot disagree as to which topics should fall within the scope of marketing. Nor does it even imply that reasonable people cannot disagree as to which cell in Table 1 is most appropriate for each issue or particular piece of research. For example, a study of the efficiency of marketing systems may have *both* positive and normative aspects; it may both *describe* existing marketing practices and *prescribe* more appropriate practices. Rather, the conceptual model of the scope of marketing presented in Table 1 provides a useful framework for analyzing fundamental differences among the various approaches to marketing and, as shall be demonstrated, the nature of marketing and marketing science controversies.

## Analyzing the Nature of Marketing and Marketing Science

The previous discussion on the scope of marketing now enables us to clarify some of the issues with respect to the "nature [broadening the concept] of marketing" controversy and the "Is marketing a science?" debate. Most marketing practitioners and some marketing academicians perceive the entire scope of marketing to be profit/micro/normative (cell 2 of Table 1).

That is, practitioners often perceive the entire domain of marketing to be the analysis of how to improve the decision-making processes of marketers. This perspective is exemplified by the definition of marketing Canton has suggested[34] and, somewhat surprisingly, by the definition proffered by Kotler in the first edition of *Marketing Management*: ''Marketing is the analyzing, organizing, planning, and controlling of the firm's customer-impinging resources, policies, and activities with a view to satisfying the needs and wants of chosen customer groups at a profit.''[35]

Most marketing academicians would chafe at delimiting the entire subject matter of marketing to simply the profit/micro/normative dimensions. Most would, at the very least, include all the phenomena, topics, and issues indicated in the top half of Table 1 (that is, cells 1 through 4). Kotler and others now wish to include in the definition of marketing *all* eight cells in Table 1.

Other fields have experienced similar discipline-definitional problems. Several decades ago, a debate raged in philosophy concerning the definition of philosophy and philosophy of science. Some philosophers chose a very narrow definition of their discipline. Popper's classic rejoinder should serve to alert marketers to the danger that narrowly circumscribing the marketing discipline may trammel marketing inquiry:

> ... the theory of knowledge was inspired by the hope that it would enable us not only to know more about knowledge, but also to contribute to the advance of knowledge—of scientific knowledge, that is.... Most of the philosophers who believe that the characteristic method of philosophy is the analysis of ordinary language seem to have lost this admirable optimism which once inspired the rationalist tradition. Their attitude, it seems, has become one of resignation, if not despair. They not only leave the advancement of knowledge to the scientists: they even define philosophy in such a way that it becomes, by definition, incapable of making any contribution to our knowledge of the world. The self-mutilation which this so surprisingly persuasive definition requires does not appeal to me. There is no such thing as an essence of philosophy, to be distilled and condensed into a definition. *A definition of the word ''philosophy'' can only have the character of a convention, of an agreement; and I, at any rate, see no merit in the arbitrary proposal to define the word ''philosophy'' in a way that may well prevent a student of philosophy from trying to contribute,* qua *philosopher, to the advancement of our knowledge of the world.*[36]

Four conclusions seem warranted. First, definitions of the nature of marketing differ in large part because their authors perceive the total scope of marketing to be different portions of Table 1. Second, there is a growing consensus that the total scope of marketing should appropriately include all eight cells of Table 1. Third, it may be very difficult to devise a definition of marketing that would both systematically *include* all eight cells of Table 1 and, at the same time, systematically *exclude* all other phenomena. Especially difficult will be the task of including in a single definition both the normative dimensions of the *practice* of marketing and the positive dimensions of the *discipline* or *study* of marketing.

The fourth conclusion deserves special emphasis and elaboration. There is now a consensus among marketers that most nonprofit organizations, such as museums, zoos, and churches, engage in numerous activities (pricing, promoting, and so forth) that are very similar to the marketing activities of their profit-oriented cousins. There is also consensus that marketing procedures that have been developed for profit-oriented organizations are equally applicable to nonprofit concerns. These are the two major, substantive issues involved in the debate over the nature (broadening the concept) of marketing. On these two issues there now exists substantial agreement.

The remaining two points of *disagreement* among marketers concerning the nature of marketing are minor when compared to the points of agreement. Issue one is essentially whether the activities of nonprofit organizations should be referred to as *marketing* activities or *marketing-like* activities. Given the agreement among marketers concerning the two previously cited substantive issues, the problem of distinguishing between marketing activities and marketing-like activities must be considered trivial to the extreme. The second issue on which disagreement exists concerns developing a definition of marketing. Although certainly nontrivial in nature, on this issue marketers would be well advised to take a cue from the discipline of philosophy, which has been around much longer and has yet to develop a consensus definition. That is, the discipline of marketing should not be overly alarmed about the difficulty of generating a consensus *definition* of marketing as long as there appears to be a developing consensus concerning its total *scope*.

The preceding analysis notwithstanding, there does remain a major, unresolved, substantive issue concerning the nature of marketing. Although *marketers* now recognize that nonprofit organizations (1) have marketing or marketing-like problems, (2) engage in marketing or marketing-like activities to solve these problems, and (3) can use the marketing policies, practices, and procedures that profit-oriented organizations have developed to solve marketing problems, we must candidly admit that most *nonmarketers* have yet to perceive this reality. Sadly, most administrators of nonprofit organizations and many academicians in other areas still do not perceive that many problems of nonprofit organizations are basically marketing in nature, and that there is an extant body of knowledge in marketing academia and a group of trained marketing practitioners that can help resolve these problems. Until administrators of nonprofit organizations perceive that they have marketing problems, their marketing decision making will inevitably suffer. Thus, the major *substantive* problem concerning broadening the concept of marketing lies in the area of *marketing* marketing to nonmarketers.

## Is Marketing a Science?

Returning to the "Is marketing a science?" controversy, the preceding analysis suggests that a primary factor explaining the nature of the controversy is the widely disparate notions of marketing held by the participants. The common element shared by those who hold that marketing is not (and cannot) be a science is the belief that the entire conceptual domain of marketing is cell 2: profit/micro/normative. Hutchinson clearly exemplifies this position:

> There is a real reason, however, why the field of marketing has been slow to develop an unique body of theory. It is a simple one: marketing is not a science. It is rather an art or a practice, and as such much more closely resembles engineering, medicine and architecture than it does physics, chemistry or biology. The medical profession sets us an excellent example, if we would but follow it; its members are called "practitioners" and not scientists. It is the work of physicians, as it is of any practitioner, to apply the findings of many sciences to the solution of problems.... It is the drollest travesty to relate the scientist's search for knowledge to the market research man's seeking after customers.[37]

If, as Hutchinson implies, the entire conceptual domain of marketing is profit/micro/normative, then marketing is not and (more importantly) probably *cannot* be a science. If, however, the conceptual domain of marketing includes both micro/positive and macro/positive phenomena, then marketing *could* be a science. That is, if phenomena such as consumer behavior, marketing isntitutions, marketing channels, and the efficiency of systems of distribution are included in the conceptual domain of marketing (and there appears to be a consensus to so include them), there is no reason why the study of these phenomena could not be deserving of the designation *science*.

Is marketing a science? Differing perceptions of the scope of marketing have been shown to be a primary factor underlying the debate on this question. The second factor contributing to the controversy is differing perceptions concerning the basic nature of science, a subject that will now occupy our attention.

### The Nature of Science

The question of whether marketing is a science cannot be adequatly answered without a clear understanding of the basic nature of science. So, what is a science? Most marketing writers cite the perspective proposed by Buzzell. A science is:

> ... a classified and systematized body of knowledge,... organized around one or more central theories and a number of general

> principles, ... usually expressed in quantitative terms, ... knowledge which permits the prediction and, under some circumstances, the control of future events.[38]

Buzzell then proceeded to note that marketing lacks the requisite central theories to be termed a science.

Although the Buzzell perspective on science has much to recommend it, the requirement ''organized around one or more central theories'' seems overly restrictive. This requirement confuses the *successful culmination* of scientific efforts with *science itself*. Was the study of chemistry not a science before discoveries like the periodic table of elements? Analogously, would not a pole vaulter still be a pole vaulter even if he could not vault fifteen feet? As Homans notes, ''What makes a science are its aims, not its results.''[39] The major purpose of science is to discover (create? invent?) laws and theories to explain, predict, understand, and control phenomena. Withholding the label *science* until a discipline has ''central theories'' would not seem reasonable.

The previous comments notwithstanding, requiring a science to be organized around one or more central theories is not completely without merit. There are strong *honorific* overtones in labeling a discipline a science.[40] These semantical overtones are so positive that, as Wartofsky has observed, even areas that are nothing more than systematized superstition attempt to usurp the term.[41] Thus, there are treatises on such subjects as the ''Science of Numerology'' and the ''Science of Astrology.'' In part, the label *science* is conferred upon a discipline to signify that it has ''arrived'' in the eyes of other scientists, and this confirmation usually occurs only when a discipline has matured to the extent that it contains several ''central theories.''[42] Thus, chronologically, physics achieved the status of science before psychology, and psychology before sociology. However, the total conceptual content of the term *science* is decidely not just honorific. Marketing does not, and should not, have to wait to be knighted by others to be a science. How, then, do sciences differ from other disciplines, if not by virtue of having central theories?

Consider the discipline of chemistry—unquestionably a science. Chemistry can be defined as ''the science of substances—their structure, their properties, and the reactions that change them into other substances.''[43] Using chemistry as an illustration, three observations will enable us to clarify the distinguishing characteristics of sciences. First, a science must have a distinct subject matter, a set of real-world phenomena that serve as a focal point for investigation. The subject matter of chemistry is *substances*, and chemistry attempts to understand, explain, predict, and control phenomena related to substances. Other disciplines, such as physics, are also interested in substances. However, chemistry can meaningfully lay claim to being a separate science because physics does not *focus on* substances and their reactions.

What is the basic subject matter of marketing? Most marketers now perceive the ultimate subject matter to be the *transaction*. Some subscribe to the *narrower thesis of marketing* and wish to delimit the basic subject matter to the *market* transaction. Others propose the *liberalized thesis of marketing* and wish to include within the subject matter of marketing all transactions that involve any form of *exchange of values* between parties.

Harking back to the chemistry analogue, marketing can be viewed as the *science of transactions*—their structure, their properties, and their relationships with other phenomena. Given this perspective, the subject matter of marketing would certainly overlap with other disciplines, notably economics, psychology, and sociology. The analysis of transactions is considered in each of these disciplines. Yet, only in marketing is the transaction the focal point. For example, transactions remain a tangential issue in economics, where the primary focus is on the allocation of scarce resources.[44] Therefore, the first distinguishing characteristic is that any science must have a distinct subject matter. Given that the *transaction* is the basic subject matter of marketing, marketing would seem to fulfill this requirement. Note that this conclusion is *independent* of whether one subscribes to the narrower or more liberal thesis of marketing.

A distinct subject matter alone is not sufficient to distinguish sciences from other disciplines, because all disciplines have a subject matter (some less distinct than others). The previously cited perspective of chemistry provides a second insight into the basic nature of science. Note the phrase, "their structure, their properties, and their reactions." Every science seeks to describe and classify the structure and properties of its basic subject matter. Likewise, the term *reactions* suggests that the phenomena comprising the basic subject matter of chemistry are presumed to be systematically interrelated. Thus, another distinguishing characteristic: *Every science presupposes the existence of underlying uniformities or regularities among the phenomena that comprise its subject matter. The discovery of these underlying uniformitites yields empirical regularities, lawlike generalizations (propositions), and laws.*

Underlying uniformities and regularities are necessary for science because (1) a primary goal of science is to provide responsibly supported explanations of phenomena,[45] and (2) the scientific explanation of phenomena requires the existence of laws or lawlike generalizations.[46] Uniformities and regularities are also a requisite for theory development since theories are systematically related sets of statements, *including some lawlike generalizations*, that are empirically testable.[47]

The basic question for marketing is not whether there presently exist several "central theories" that serve to unify, explain, and predict marketing phenomena, as Buzzell suggests. Rather, the following should be asked: "Are there underlying uniformities and regularities among the phenomena comprising the subject matter of marketing?" This question can be answered affirmatively on two grounds—one *a priori* and one empirical. Marketing is a discipline that investigates human behavior. Since numerous uniformities and regularities have been observed in other behavioral sciences,[48] there is no *a priori* reason for believing that the subject matter of marketing will be devoid of uniformities and regularities. The second ground for believing that the uniformities exist is empirical. The quantity of scholarly research conducted on marketing phenomena during the past three decades probably exceeds the total of *all* prior research in marketing. Substantial research has been conducted in the area of channels of distribution. Also, efforts in the consumer behavior dimension of marketing have been particulary prolific. Granted, some of the research has been less than profound, and the total achievements may not be commensurate with the efforts expended. Nevertheless, who can deny that *some* progress has been made or that *some* uniformities have been identified? In short, who can deny that there exist uniformities and regularities interrelating the subject matter of marketing? I, for one, cannot.

The task of delineating the basic nature of science is not yet complete. Up to this point we have used chemistry to illustrate that all sciences involve (1) a distinct subject matter and the description and classification of that subject matter, and (2) the presumption that underlying the subject matter are uniformities and regularities that science seeks to discover. The chemistry example provides a final observation. Note that "chemistry is the *science* of.... "This suggests that sciences can be differentiated from other disciplines by the method of analysis. At the risk of being somewhat tautologous: sciences employ a set of procedures commonly referred to as the scientific method. As Bunge suggests, "No scientific method, no science."[49] The historical significance of the development and acceptance of the method of science cannot be overstated. It has been called "the most significant intellectual contribution of Western civilization."[50] Is the method of science applicable to marketing?.

Detailed explication of the scientific method is beyond the the scope of this article and is discussed elsewhere.[51] Nevertheless, the cornerstone requirement of the method of science must be mentioned. The word *science* has its origins in the Latin verb *scire,* meaning "to know." Now, there are many ways *to know* things. The methods of tenacity, authority, faith, intuition, and science are often cited.[52] The characteristic that separates scientific knowledge from other ways to "know" things is the notion of *intersubjective certification*.

Scientific knowledge, in which theories, laws, and explanations are primal, must be *objective* in the sense that its truth content must be *intersubjectively certifiable*.[53] Requiring that theories, laws and explanations be empirically testable ensures that they will be intersubjectively certifiable since different (but reasonably competent) investigators with differing attitudes, opinions, and beliefs will be able to make observations and conduct experiments to ascertain their truth content. "Science strives for objectivity in the sense that its statements are to be capable of public tests with results that do not vary essentially with the tester."[54] Scientific knowledge thus rests on the bedrock of empirical testability.

There is no reason whatsoever to presume that the scientific method of analysis is any less appropriate to marketing phenomena than to other disciplines. Similarly, scholarly researchers in marketing, although sometimes holding rather distorted notions concerning such topics as the role of laws and theories in research, seem to be at least as technically proficient as researchers in other areas. Finally, although some marketing researchers continue to cite ''proprietary studies'' as evidentiary support for their positions, the extent of this practice is now extremely small.

In summary, sciences (1) have a distinct subject matter drawn from the real world which is described and classified, (2) presume underlying uniformities and regularities interrelating the subject matter, and (3) adopt intersubjectively certifiable procedures for studying the subject matter. This perspective can be appropriately described as a consensus composite of philosophy of science views on science.[55] For example, Wartofsky suggests that a science is

> ... an organized or systematic body of knowledge, using general laws or principles; that it is knowledge about the world; and that it is that kind of knowledge concerning which universal agreement can be reached by scientists sharing a common language (or languages) and common criteria for the *justification* of knowledge claims and beliefs.[56]

## Is Marketing a Science? A Conclusion

The scope of the area called marketing has been shown to be exceptionally broad. Marketing has micro/macro dimensions, profit sector/nonprofit sector dimensions, and positive/normative dimensions. Reasonable people may disagree as to which combination of these dimensions represents the *appropriate* total scope of marketing, although a consensus seems to be developing to include all eight cells in Table 1. If marketing is to be restricted to *only* the profit/micro/normative dimension (as many practioners would view it), then marketing is not a science and could not become one. All sciences involve the explanation, prediction, and understanding of phenomena.[57] These explanations and predictions frequently serve as useful guides for developing normative decision rules and normative models. Such rules and models are then *grounded* in science.[58] Nevertheless, any discipline that is *purely* evaluative or prescriptive (normative) is not a science. At least for marketing academe, restricting the scope of marketing to its profit/micro/normative dimension is unrealistic, unnecessary, and, without question, undesirable.

Once the appropriate scope of marketing has been expanded to include at least some *positive* dimensions (cells 1, 3, 5, and 7 in Table 1), the explanation, prediction, and understanding of these phenomena could be a science. The question then becomes whether the study of the positive dimensions of marketing has the requisite characteristics of a science. Aside from the strictly honorific overtones of *nonmarketers* accepting marketing as a science, the substantive characteristics differentiating sciences from other disciplines have been shown to be (1) a distinct subject matter drawn from the real world and the description and classification of that subject matter, (2) the presumption of underlying uniformities and regularities interrelating the subject matter, and (3) the adoption of the method of science for studying the subject matter.

The *positive* dimensions of marketing have been shown to have a subject matter properly distinct from other sciences. The marketing literature is replete with description and classification. There have been discoveries (however tentative) of uniformities and regularities among marketing phenomena. Finally, although Longman deplores "the rather remarkable lack of scientific method employed by scientists of marketing,"[59] researchers in marketing are at least as committed to the method of science as are researchers in other disciplines. Therefore, the study of the *positive* dimensions of marketing can be appropriately referred to as *marketing science*.

## ENDNOTES

1. Paul D. Converse, "The Development of a Science of Marketing," *Journal of Marketing*, Vol. 10 (July 1945), pp. 14-23.
2. Robert Bartels, "Can Marketing Be a Science?" *Journal of Marketing*,Vol. 15 (January 1951), pp. 319-328; Kenneth D. Hutchinson, "Marketing as a Science: An Appraisal," *Journal of Marketing* , Vol. 16 (January 1952), pp. 286-293; W.J. Baumol, "On the Role of Marketing Theory," *Journal of Marketing*, Vol. 21 (April 1957), pp. 413-419; Robert D. Buzzell, "Is Marketing a Science?" *Harvard Business Review,* Vol. 41 (January-February 1963), pp. 32-48; Weldon J. Taylor, "Is Marketing a Science? Revisited," *Journal of Marketing*, Vol. 29 (July 1965), pp. 49-53; and M. Halbert, *The Meaning and Sources of Marketing Theory* (New York: McGraw-Hill Book Co., 1965).
3. Committee on Terms, *Marketing Definitions: A Glossary of Marketing Terms* (Chicago: American Marketing Assn., 1960).
4. Stewart H. Rewoldt, James D. Scott, and Martin R. Warshaw, *Introduction to Marketing Management* (Homewood, Ill.: Richard D. Irwin, 1973), p. 3.
5. Marketing Staff of the Ohio State University, "Statement of Marketing Philsosophy," *Journal of Marketing*, Vol. 29 (January 1965), pp. 43-44.
6. Philip Kotler and Sidney J. Levy, "Broadening the Concept of Marketing,"*Journal of Marketing*, Vol. 33 (January 1969), p. 15.
7. William Lazer, "Marketing's Changing Social Relationships,"*Journal of Marketing*, Vol. 33 (January 1969), p. 9.
8. David Luck, "Broadening the Concept of Marketing—Too Far," *Journal of Marketing*, Vol. 33 (July 1969), p. 54.
9. Philip Kotler and Sidney Levy, "A New Form of Marketing Myopia: Rejoinder to Professor Luck," *Journal of Marketing*, Vol. 33 (July 1969), p. 57.
10. Robert Ferber, "The Expanding Role of Marketing in the 1970's," *Journal of Marketing*, Vol. 34 (January 1970), pp. 29-30.

11. Robert J. Lavidge, "The Growing Responsibilities of Marketing," *Journal of Marketing*, Vol. 34 (Janaury 1970) p. 27.
12. Philip Kotler and Gerald Zaltman, "Social Marketing: An Approach to Planned Social Change," *Journal of Marketing*, Vol. 35 (July 1971), p. 5.
13. *Journal of Marketing*, Vol. 35 (July 1971): William A. Mindak and H. Malcolm Bybee, "Marketing's Application to Fund Raising," pp. l3-18; Gerald Zaltman and Ilan Vertinsky, "Health Services Marketing: A Suggested Model," pp. 19-27; John U. Farley and Harold J. Leavit, "Marketing and Population Problems," pp. 28-33; and William G. Zinkmund and William J. Stanton, "Recycling Solid Wastes: A Channels-of-Distribution Problem," pp. 34-39.
14. Leslie Dawson, "Marketing Science in the Age of Aquarius," *Journal of Marketing*, Vol. 35 (July 1971), p. 71.
15. Philip Kotler, "A Generic Concept of Marketing," *Journal of Marketing*, Vol. 36 (April 1972), p. 49.
16. William G. Nichols, "Conceptual Conflicts in Marketing," *Journal of Economics and Business*, Vol. 26 (Winter 1974), p. 142.
17. James M. Carman, "On the Universality of Marketing," *Journal of Contemporary Business*, Vol. 2 (Autumn 1973), p. 14.
18. Robert Bartels, "The Identity Crisis in Marketing," *Journal of Marketing*, Vol. 38 (October 1974), p. 76.
19. David J. Luck, "Social Marketing: Confusion Compounded," *Journal of Marketing*, Vol. 38 (October 1974), pp. 2-7.
20. Robert J. Eggert, "Eggert Discusses Additional Goals for His Administration, Seeks Help in Defining Marketing," *Marketing News*, September 15, 1974.
21. E. J. McCarthy, *Basic Marketing* (Homewood, Ill.: Richard D. Irwin, 1960).
22. These observations were apparently extemporaneous since they were not included in his published paper: Philip Kotler, "Defining the Limits of Marketing," in *Marketing Education and the Real World*, Boris W. Becker and Helmut Becker, eds, (Chicago: American Marketing Assn., 1972).
23. L. D. H. Weld, *The Marketing of Farm Products* (New York: Macmillan, 1920).
24. Paul W. Stewart, *Does Distribution Cost Too Much?* (New York: Twentieth Century Fund, 1939).
25. Harold Barger, *Distribution's Place in the Economy Since 1869* (Princeton: Princeton University Press, 1955); Reavis Cox, *Distribution in a High Level Economy* (Englewood Cliffs, N.J.: Prentice-Hall, 1965); and Neil Borden, *The Economic Effects of Advertising* (Chicago: Richard D. Irwin, 1942).
26. Virgil Reed, *Planned Marketing* (New York: Ronald Press, 1930): and P. White and W. S. Hayward, *Marketing Practice* (New York: Doubleday, Page & Co., 1924).
27. Same reference as note 21.
28. William Lazer and Eugene Kelley, "Systems Perspective of Marketing Activity," in *Managerial Marketing: Perspectives and Viewpoints,* rev. ed. (Homewood, Ill.: Richard D. Irwin, 1962); Lee Adler, "Systems Approach to Marketing," *Harvard Business Review*, Vol. 45 (May-June, 1967); and George Fisk, *Marketing Systems: An Introductory Analysis* (New York: Harper & Row, 1967).
29. Fisk, same reference as note 28, p. 3.

30. Robert J. Holloway and Robert S. Hancock, *The Environment of Marketing Behavior* (New York: John Wiley & Sons, 1964); Robert J. Holloway and Robert S. Hancock, *Marketing in a Changing Environment* (New York: John Wiley & Sons, 1968); and Richard A. Scott and Norton E. Marks, *Marketing and Its Environment* (Belmont: Wadsworth, 1968).
31. Kotler and Levy, same reference as note 6; Kotler and Zaltman, same reference as note 12; and Kotler, same reference as note 15.
32. Mindak and Bybee, same reference as note 13; Farley and Leavitt, same reference as note 13; Carman, same reference as note 17; and Donald P. Robin, "Success in Social Marketing," *Journal of Business Research*, Vol. 3 (July 1974), pp. 303-310.
33. Lazer, same reference as note 7; Dawson, same reference as note 14; David S. Aaker and George Day, *Consumerism* (New York: Free Press, 1971); Norman Kangun, *Society and Marketing* (New York: Harper & Row, 1972); Frederick E. Webster, Jr., *Social Aspects of Marketing* (Englewood Cliffs, N.J.: Prentice-Hall, 1974); Reed Moyer, *Macro-Marketing* (New York: John Wiley & Sons, 1972); John R. Wish and Stephen H. Gamble, *Marketing and Social Issues* (New York: John Wiley & Sons, 1971); Ross L. Goble and Roy Shaw, *Controversy and Dialogue in Marketing* (Englewood Cliffs, N.J.: Prentice-Hall, 1975); Ronald R. Gist, *Marketing and Society* (New York: Holt, Rinehart & Winston, 1971); and William Lazer and Eugene Kelley, *Social Marketing* (Homewood, Ill.: Richard D. Irwin, 1973).
34. Irving D. Canton, "A Functional Definition of Marketing," *Marketing News*, July 15, 1973.
35. Philip Kotler, *Marketing Management* (Englewood Cliffs, N.J.: Prentice-Hall, 1967), p. 12.
36. Karl R. Popper, *The Logic of Scientific Discovery* (New York: Harper & Row, 1959), p. 19. [Emphasis added.]
37. Hutchinson, same reference as note 2.
38. Buzzell, same reference as note 2, p. 37.
39. George C. Homans, *The Nature of Social Science* (New York: Harcourt, Brace & World, 1967), p. 4.
40. Ernest Nagel, *The Structure of Science* (New York: Harcourt, Brace & World, 1961), p. 2.
41. Marx W. Wartofsky, *Conceptual Foundations of Scientific Thought* (New York: Macmillan Co., 1968), p. 44.
42. Thomas S. Kuhn, *The Structure of Scientific Revelations* (Chicago: University of Chicago Press, 1970), p. 161.
43. Linus Pauling, *College Chemistry* (San Francisco: W. H. Freeman & Co., 1956), p. 15.
44. Richard H. Leftwich, *The Price System and Resource Allocation* (New York: Holt, Rinehart & Winston, 1966), p. 2.
45. Same reference as note 40, p. 15.
46. Carl G. Hempel, *Aspects of Scientific Explanation* (New York: Free Press, 1965), pp. 354-364.
47. Richard S. Rudner, *The Philosophy of Social Science* (Englewood Cliffs, N.J.: Prentice-Hall, 1966), p. 10; and Shelby D. Hunt, "The Morphology of Theory and the General Theory of Marketing," *Journal of Marketing*, Vol. 35 (April 1971), pp. 65-68.

48. Bernard Berelson and Gary Steiner, *Human Behavior: An Inventory of Scientific Findings* (New York: Harcourt, Brace & World, 1964).
49. Mario Bunge, *Scientific Research I: The Search for System* (New York: Springer-Verlag, 1967), p. 12.
50. Charles W. Morris, "Scientific Empiricism," in *Foundations of the Unity of Science*, Vol. 1, Otto Newrath, Rudolf Carnap and Charles Morris, eds, (Chicago: University of Chicago Press, 1955), p. 63.
51. Shelby D. Hunt, *Marketing Theory: Conceptual Foundation of Research in Marketing* (Columbus, Ohio: Grid Publishing Co., 1976).
52. Morris R. Cohen and Ernest Nagel, *Logic and the Scientific Method* (New York: Harcourt, Brace & World, 1934), p. 193.
53. Same reference as note 36, p. 44.
54. Carl G. Hempel., "Fundamentals of Concept Formation in Empirical Science," in *Foundations of the Unity of Science*, Vol. 2, Otto Newrath, ed. (Chicago: University of Chicago Press, 1970), p. 695.
55. See, for example: Nagel, same reference as note 40, p. 4; May Brodbeck, *Readings in the Philosophy of the Social Sciences* (New York: Macmillan Co., 1968), pp. 1-11; Richard B. Braithwaite, *Scientific Explanation* (Cambridge: Cambridge University Press, 1951), pp. 1-21; B. F. Skinner, *Science and Human Behavior* (New York: Macmillan Co., 1953), pp. 14-22; Rudner, same reference as note 47, pp. 7-9; Abraham Kaplan, *The Conduct of Inquiry* (Scranton, Pa.: Chandler Publishing Co., 1964), p. 32; Popper, same reference as note 36, pp. 44-48; and Hempel, same reference as note 54, p. 672.
56. Same reference as note 41, p. 23
57. Nagel, same reference as note 40, p. 15; Henry E. Kyburg, Jr., *Philosophy of Science* (New York: Macmillan Co., 1968), p. 3; Carl G. Hempel, "The Theoretician's Dilemma," in *Aspects of Scientific Explanation* (New York: Free Press, 1965), p. 173; and Nicholas Rescher, *Scientific Explanation* (New York: Free Press, 1970), p. 4.
58. Mario Bunge, *Scientific Research II: The Search for Truth* (New York: Springer-Verlag, 1967), p. 132.
59. Kenneth A. Longman, "The Management Challenge to Marketing Theory," in *New Essays in Marketing Theory,* George Fisk, ed. (Boston: Allyn & Bacon, 1971), p. 10.

## ACKNOWLEDGEMENT

The author wishes to gratefully acknowledge the constructive criticisms of earlier drafts of this article by Professors George W. Brooker and John R. Nevin, both of the University of Wisconsin-Madison.

# 3 —— The Social Disorder of the Broadened Concept of Marketing

*Gene R. Laczniak, Ph.D. and*
*Donald A. Michie, Ph.D.*

*Journal of Academy of Marketing Science,* Vol. 7, No. 3 (Summer 1979), pp. 214-231. Reprinted by permisson.

Recently, the controversy concerning the scope of marketing has abated somewhat as growing numbers of marketers have come to accept the broadened concept of marketing. For example:

a. Hunt has been recognized (with the 1976 Harold H. Maynard Award) for his classificational schema—the Three Dychotomies Model—which positions the discipline as having macro-micro, positive-normative and profit-nonprofit dimensions (17).
b. Shuptrine and Osmanski have traced the meaning of marketing to its present expanded domain (42).
c. Nickels has found that most marketing educators believe marketing appropriately includes numerous nonbusiness activities (34).
d. Takas, a businessman, has written that increasingly broadened horizons for the marketing practitioner are inevitable (48).

In short, broadened marketing is almost a *fait accompli,* explained in most recent textbooks as being rooted in the generic concept of *exchange*—the premise initially advanced by Kotler and Levy (21, 23, 28). The contemporary view of marketing therefore goes far beyond the traditional conception, articulated by Luck and others, which held marketing to involve *business* activities central to *market* transactions (29, 30). In contrast, the essence of broadened marketing concerns any free exchange between two parties and holds that ''marketing is specifically concerned with how transactions are created, stimulated, facilitated and valued''(22).

Given the emerging consensus about the nature of marketing, this article analyzes the broadened concept of marketing in terms of its implications for social order. The authors maintain the widespread acceptance and practice of broadened marketing has the potential to diminish social order and ultimately damage the reputation of the discipline of marketing. This is not to say broadened marketing will undermine the entire social fabric. Rather, there are certain marketing-like practices which are occuring with growing frequency in the society. They may also bring about some major changes. The purpose of this paper is to pinpoint their nature and to argue that from the viewpoint of the marketing professional they are best *not* defined as *marketing*. By examining broadened marketing from the perspective of social order, some needed theoretical support is also provided for a recent article by Arndt which questions the expansion of marketing (2). Further some specific reservations are added to those initially expressed by Tucker (51).

## The Importance of Social Order in Society

Social order refers to the long run homeostasis which must exist between social phenomena—ideas, practices, organizations—and the society of which they are part. When a phenomenon has social order it is unambiguous; that is, it is widely recognized as having a defined place, role or function in the society (based on 11, 13, 50). In fact, the general concept of order is fundamental to the maintenance of any system. The behavior of celestial bodies is ordered by the principles of physics. The plant and animal kingdom possess a definite ecological order (20). Human behavior too seems to be ordered by the end result of a chain of concepts including values, attitudes, culture, previous behavior and other causal factors, although the precise interrelationship of these elements has yet to be discovered (26, 53). Order is essential to society (13).

What are the tenets of social order? Volumes have been written on this topic, but some generalizations have emerged (20). At the most fundamental level, *language serves to transmit order*. That is, order is implicit in the definitions of the words with which we choose to communicate. Segerstedt said it well: "When a word is defined, the meaning of the word is stated. Definitions of scientific terms consequently must be explanations of the meanings of terms... we must remember that a word has meaning only in a language system—people using that language behave in a certain way toward the object, as the object is perceived as equipped with certain properties" (40). The point is that human behavior, and therefore social order, is determined by the meaning and properties of the concept under scrutiny and that as one learns a concept's meaning, his behavior is likely to reflect that interpretation (8). Thus, social order is partially dependent upon an existing language system which is composed of concepts having precise definitions. Simply put, stable social systems—those having social order—place a premium upon assuring that communication in the system is unambiguous.

The above point, that precise meaning is the highest form or ordering (20), is more than just an arcane pontification. For example, some economists argue that one major reason why it is so difficult to convince the general public that the nation should switch from a "growth" to a "steady-state" economy is because of the positive connotation of the term "growth" (7). Similarly, one reason it has taken so long to repeal "fair trade" laws (resale price maintenance) is that it was psychologically difficult for many individuals to take a position against something so beneficial sounding as "fair trade.'' In summary, while disorderliness or ambiguity may provide satisfaction, pleasure and interest in the realm of art, literature or the cinema, major scientific or social concepts *(e.g. velocity, democracy, marketing)* demand precise definitions for the purpose of enhancing social order.

On a more pragmatic level, order in the society is dependent upon the *efficient interaction of social institutions*. Talcott Parsons, the eminent sociologist, was an eloquent spokesman for this point of view. His views have received wide support (18, 32, 43, 44, 55). Parsons identified four institutional functions which were central in the maintenance of social order (35, 36).

1. Goals had to be set and institutions (such as government) had to be formulated in order to attain them.
2. Values inherent in the society had to be maintained and perpetuated. Institutions such as religious organizations, universities and the family provided this needed ''pattern maintenance.''
3. An *integrative* function which would systematically allocate the society's benefits among the public was necessary. Traditionally, this meant some type of judicial institution.
4. An adaptaive function (i.e., an *economic* institution) to efficiently manage the social system's resources was essential.

Taken together, these four requirements suggest that social order is preserved by institutional direction and control over certain essential functions. Harmonious interactions of necessary institutions each performing required functions produce social order (54, 15).

Parsons and others have also warned that for such social systems to be responsive to the needs and welfare of its members, *institutional power and responsibility* had to *be balanced* (36, 12). In other words, the accountability for particular actions taken in a social system falls to those having power to cause the actions to be in initiated. As one philosopher put it: ''The demand of the law in a well ordered society is that responsibility shall lie where the power of decision lies. Where that demand is met, men have legal order; where it is not, they have only the illusion of one'' (49). Writers have also noted that in the long run, social systems where power and responsibility are not in balance will eventually be shaken, then reconstituted, and will move to equilibrium (10). In other words, power and responsibility are fastened together, in the long run, by an iron law.

In summary then, social order is based upon and depends on the following:

1. **Definitional specificity:** definitions in the language system which clearly specify the nature (meaning) of a concept and communicate the activities within its scope;
2. **Institutional specialization:** the division of essential tasks among appropriate institutions—including institutions which provide the *adaptive* and *integrative functions.*

3. **Equated power and responsibility:** social systems where the power and responsibility of institutions are in balance.

## Marketing's Traditional Role in Social Systems

Previous discussion has identified the economic function as one prerequisite in the orderly maintenance of a social system. That is, viable social systems require economic institutions to manage the development of their physical resources. This is what Parsons called the adaptive function. Historically, the task of marketing has been to efficiently distribute economic goods and services throughout the country. Marketing has served primarily as a subsystem in the provision of this economic function. This view is consistent with the initial development of marketing as a formal field of study. It is rooted in the application of economics to the distributive process by institutional economists who believed this to be a neglected aspect of economic analysis (3). Over the years, the domain of marketing management has expanded in order to integrate marketing related factors more effectively into the firm, but it has, until recently, been limited to *managerial* considerations influencing *marketplace* transactions by businesses. The expansion of marketing which had occured until recently, was premised on the notion that if marketing were more integrated in the thinking of the firm (e.g., the marketing concept, marketing research), the distribution of goods and services would be more efficient.

The question which must be raised is: has the historical concept of marketing been consistent with social order and does the broadened marketing concept threaten to diminish social order?

## Traditional and Broadened Marketing Compared

To address this issue it becomes necessary to evaluate both the traditional and broadened concepts of marketing with respect to their impact on the three dimensions of social order.

### Definitional Specificity

Denotatively, traditional marketing is perhaps best represented by the definition of marketing sanctioned by the American Marketing Association. It states that marketing is ''the performance of business activities that direct the flow of goods and services by producers to consumers'' (7). What are the conceptual implications of this definition? First, the definition serves to circumscribe the nature of marketing to managerial activities stemming from market transactions (producer/middleman/consumer exchange). Second, the definition serves to limit the scope of marketing to the ''profit sector'' half of Hunt's classificational schema (17). In other words, marketing's purview is within the business system and consequently, like the business system in total, is primarily a subsystem of the economic function, although like any sophisticated subsystem, marketing draws some of its content from other basic fields. This traditional definition of marketing is forthright and unambiguous. It clearly communicates the jurisdiction of marketing. A manager knows that he cannot be doing ''marketing'' unless he is part of a business firm performing activities that facilitate economic transactions

Broadened marketing, in contrast, suggests that marketing is a universal concept. Kotler says, ''marketing is a human activity directed at satisfying human need and wants'' (22). All that is required for marketing to occur are two persons able to communicate and deliver, each having something of value to exchange freely. Staudt, Taylor and Bowersox state:''... there is a universality to the application of marketing functions wherever there is an interface'' (45). Hunt has observed that a distinction between marketing and marketing-like activities must be considered trivial (17).

What are the implications of this broadened concept of marketing? First and foremost, it places diverse activities such as campaign speeches, marriage and vows and the solicitation of a prostitute in the domain of marketing (See Figure 1). Each of these situations meets Kotler's criteria for a marketing transaction. Exchange freely occurs between two parties—each with

**FIGURE 1. A Sampling of Activities Within the Domain of Broadened Marketing**

- The exchange of wedding vows
- The Strategic Arms Limiation Talks (SALT) between the U.S. and the Soviet Union
- Plea bargaining by an alleged felon turned State's witness
- The solicitation of a prostitute
- The Behavior Modification "chip system" in the State Mental Hospital
- A political candidate pledging labor reform in order to receive a union's endorsement
- A plenary indulgence granted by the Church in exchange for the performance of a novena
- A phone call
- The pass of a baton in an Olympic relay race
- The bidding process in a game of Bridge

something of value to deliver whether it be a political platform for a vote, fidelity for fidelity or money for sex. The *scope* of marketing is so extensive that it occurs almost everywhere, including such mundane instances as when a parent offers a child a cookie in exchange for good behavior. Thus, the *nature* of marketing conceivably involves the facilitation of activities such as political ''stumping,'' aspects of courtship, and even pimping. Everyone is a ''marketer,'' because virtually everyone engages in some social transactions. Social order is not served in that the definition of marketing is so broad as to render distinctions between marketing and any free mutual exchange among persons as meaningless. As Figure 1 suggests, current definitions of broadened marketing conceivabley subsume a vast terrain of human interactions.

### Institutional Specialization

Traditional marketing is consistent with social order in that it is clearly a subsystem of a necessary primary function (economics). Figure 2A is a depiction of the discipline of marketing as it has been traditionally conceived. It has basically applied economics but also borrows generously from the behavioral sciences, law and mathematics. The point is that since traditional marketing is primarily a subsystem of economics, we can rightfully look to *economic* criteria in order to assess whether traditional marketing is being

**FIGURE 2A. One Perspective of the Composition of Traditional Marketing**

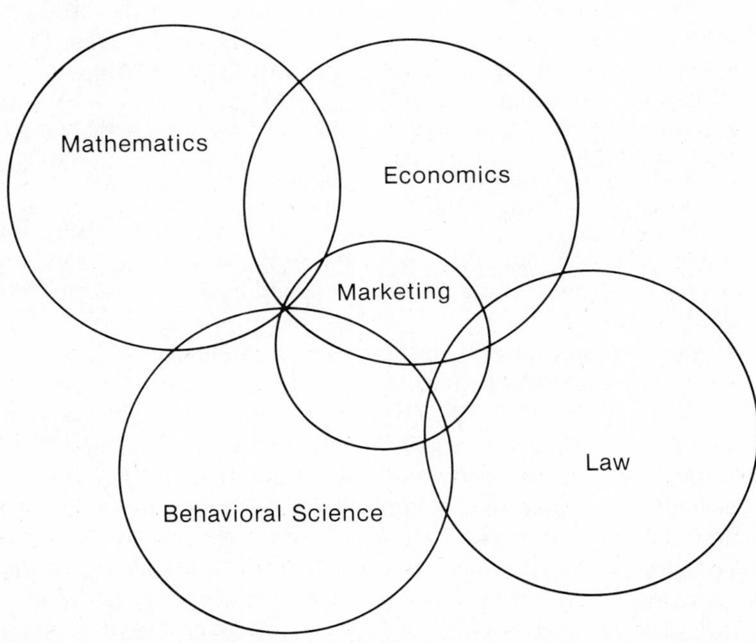

conducted efficiently. In practice, this evaluation may be difficult and measures of marketing efficiency such as *value added* at the *macro* level and the *marketing audit* at the *micro* level, are demonstrably crude. Most experts agree that marketing managers need to make a greater commitment to refining these evaluative tools. Nevertheless, there is little debate that traditional marketing practices should be analyzed with respect to economic performance standards—subject of course to social constraints, such as the law, which are provided by the social system's *integrative function* (to again use Parson's terminology). Thus, the role of traditional marketing in a social system is ordered in that marketing practices are constrained by the actions of other institutions, such as government and the economic market place. In addition, marketing is evaluated by criteria stemming from the essential (adaptive) function of which it is a part—economics.

Broadened marketing on the other hand, as a universal concept, with its boundaries encompassing the vast terrain of human exchange does not suggest any specific evaluative mechanism. The broadened definition of marketing paints the field as a giant discipline which encompasses substantial portions of other areas of study (see Figure 2B). Clearly, economic criteria are inappropriate in examining the role of marketing in the diffusion of a political personality, a religious belief or a controversial social organization, since social consequences far outweigh any economic considerations. How then should such marketing practices be evaluated? Theoretically, any concept should be evaluated according to the criteria of the *primary* function of which it is part (25). That is, evaluational standards should be based upon the function or purpose the object of evalaution serves. For example, the actions of a politician are constrained by a code of behavior based upon the Constitution; if that most basic code is violated the individual can be removed (directly or indirectly) from power because his primary service function is not being properly discharged. The Watergate affair vividly demonstrates this.

Significantly, the broadened perspective of marketing does not define the discipline of marketing as a part of any social institution or primary social function. Rather, marketing is perceived as a fundamental human interaction itself. Traditional fields of business specialization such as accounting, finance, personnel and production management make no such universal claims. Yet curiously, marketing, a field without trained specialists at the PH.D. level until the 1940s, purports to be the fountainhead of a fundamental human activity not previously identified for purposes of analysis. Marketing alone, among the specializations in business, stipulates that its activity permeates basic human exchanges. Interestingly, few academics outside the field of marketing would recognize such universality. The public does not. The fact that only marketers assert this expanded view of their field could be dismissed as egotistic arrogance if not for a third disturbing factor. When the broadened concept of marketing is applied in various instances, power and responsibility are not in balance. This consideration is treated below.

**FIGURE 2B. Broadened Marketing: A Perspective**

## Equated Power and Responsibility

Marketing as traditionally practiced has never been a bastion of ethical propriety (47). Theoretically, however, the checks and balances necessary to provide the impetus for equated power and responsibility are present. As historically conceived, marketing is part of the business system which in turn, is the major executing force of the economic function. The business system draws its license from an implicit ''social contact'' which exists between the business system and society (19, 46). This social contact is one of tradition and convention rather than one which is specified in writing. Society's benefit from the contract is that business system will provide the goods and services society needs. Marketing's major role in this delivery process was discussed earlier. Business' reward for providing this economic service is the potential of profit.

A major aspect of this business-society relationship is that society retains enough mechanisms (e.g., governmental action) to assure that the powerful actions of business are tempered by responsible behavior (15, 54). Society, through government, draws its ultimate justification as "controlling partner" from the words of the founding fathers which gave government the "right to regulate commerce" as specified in Article 1, Secton 8 of the U.S. Constitution. Over time, the courts have held that this phrase gives society the ability to regulate business in the pulic interest in any manner it sees fit, subject to a proper legal procedure. In other words, social order is served because legal mechanisms exist to assure a balance of power and responsibility in business decisions. Marketing falls within this jurisdiction.

Other less specific mechanisms, beyond the law, are also operative to achieve a relatively close balance between marketing power and responsibility. For example, in the largest corporations—and therefore those likely exercising the most power—the majority of the marketing executives have had training in the study of marketing. Thus, they bring to their job a degree of professionalism that formal study in marketing management and business administration instills. This professionalism, embodied partially in the marketing concept, as well as corporate codes of ethics and other industry standards for socially responsible behavior provide constraints which usually prevent gross power-responsibility imbalance.

However, in the broadened approach to marketing, a workable framework to insure that the balance of power and responsibility exists is very difficult to identify. When marketing is broadly defined few of the participants engaging in marketing have had formal training in the field of marketing and therefore lack the consequent professionalism this might instill. Even when professional marketers "practice" outside the business system, complications are likely. One aspect of the broadened perspective, social marketing (the marketing of people, organizations and ideas), serves to illustrate this point vividly (24).

Consider the broad application of sophisticated marketing methods to the dissemination of ethically charged ideas such as neofascism, euthanasia, pornographic entertainment, gay rights and other controversial concepts. The "marketing of ideas" is a major dimension of broadened marketing. Certainly the application of marketing-like analysis would make the presentation of such ideas more persuasive and palatable. Indeed the right to promulgate controversial ideas is protected in our society by the first amendment to the Constitution. The normative questions become: what responsibility do the marketers of these ideas bear if they are accepted by the general public as a result of the persuasive way marketing techniques permit them to be presented? What level of responsibility is it desirable for the marketers to assume?

Regarding the first question, marketers of social ideas have a convenient dodge to avoid assuming any responsibility. They can (and sometimes do) argue that they have simply helped a sender of a message more effectively ''encode'' his communication to his intended receivers by applying marketing expertise to a given situation. If society suffers because some members of the population accept a controversial and ultimately dysfunctional message, the marketer is not to blame since the only role served by marketing was to help the sender of a message exercise his right of free speech. Stated another way, marketing merely facilitated an intellectual exchange but in no way coerced the parties into a meeting of the minds.

The defense is unsatisfactory because it can be logically argued that the application of marketing techniques to a controversial situation provided the balance of communicative power to culminate a successful transaction. If no responsibility for subsequent events is accepted by the marketer in cases of broadened marketing, accountability breaks down and the power-responsibility equation is not in balance. It should be added however, that in the long run the general public will perceive the power of marketing in contributing to the success of certain communication campaigns, and will call for marketers to be held proportionately responsible. This is the ''iron law'' alluded to earlier which balances power and responsibility.

It is also worth mentioning that some writers have noted that marketers selling traditional economic goods also attempt to avoid responsibility (6, 14). For example Lavidge and others write that too many marketers ask regarding their product, ''*Can* it be sold?'' rather than ''*Should* it be sold?'' (29). It is true that among business marketers there are some crooks, pitchmen, hawkers and cheats. Nevertheless, the mechanisms to maintain social order are present because government can and does impose constraints on business practices. The advances of consumerism in the past fifteen years are testimony to this. However, when someone ''markets'' an idea, the first amendment limits the level of restraint which is possible (52).

## Broadened Marketing and the Social System

The continued application of systematic managerial thinking to situations outside the business sector is inevitable. Clearly, the methods of analysis used in management in general and marketing in particualr can make a valuable contribution to the efficient operation of diverse activities such as political campaigns, hospitals, charitable organizations, performing arts companies and so forth. The current involvement of persons with formal training in marketing in these areas verifies the benefits which are possible. But the question at issue is whether such applications should be defined as marketing? That is, is it beneficial for the field of marketing to expand its scope beyond business activities facilitating economic transactions? Should the application of marketing-like methods and marketing-like thinking outside the business system be called ''marketing''?

In our view, it should not. It is undesirable because the implications of the calculus discussed previously lead to the following observations:

a. Broadened marketing is defined so universally as to not suggest any functional standards by which its efficiency might be measured. Economic and legal criteria alone are definitely not a sufficient standard by which to evaluate the appropriateness and effectiveness of marketing outside the business sector. In the realm of broadened marketing, judging what distinguishes ''good'' marketing from ''bad'' marketing in terms of social necessity or morality becomes as difficult as attempting to define the elusive ''public good.''
b. Responsibility for the consequences of broadened marketing can be denied by arguing that marketing concerns itself with the exchange *process*, not the *content* of the exchange. This results in a situation where responsibility does not lie where the locus of power is to be found (i.e., with the marketing practitioner). Thus, the earlier discussed prerequisite of social order is undetermined.
c. If marketing practitioners choose to accept responsibility for their involvement outside the business sector, the field of marketing is claiming expertise in areas which exceed the scope of almost any other institution. Is marketing so basic and marketers so secure as to desire this responsiblity? If marketing denies responsibility for its action when problems and abuses occur, the public will eventually perceive the shaping role of marketing in the social arena *and severely regulate it*. Social complications caused by dysfunctional transactions will hurt the reputation of marketers in the eyes of the public. Many bright young persons may shy away from careers in marketing. Furthermore, any regulations generated to cope with *social* marketing or other forms of broadened marketing will likely be applied to traditional marketing as well. Alternatively, if the field of marketing succeeds in convincing the public that the domain of marketing rightly involves all transactions, the discipline of marketing is asking to play the role of a symbolic Atlas with the weight of the world upon its theoretical shoulders.

## AN ALTERNATIVE SCENARIO: DISORDER → SOCIAL INTERVENTION → SOCIAL ORDER

Broadened marketing seems destined to be increasingly accepted by marketing professionals as specifying the ''true'' domain of the field of marketing. Is it irrevocable then that events must culminate in the severe regulation of marketing practices suggested earlier? Will marketing professionals be discredited in the public's eyes due to abuses in the practice of social marketing? Must the "social disorder" scenario detailed above inevitably occur? Probably. But not necessarily, for the following reason.

Much of the previous analysis is based upon Parsonian structural sociology (35, 36, 37). A common general criticism of this school of thought has been its tendency toward equilibrium (or static) analysis without sufficient concern for the dynamics of social change (4, 5, 31, 39). Thus, while it can be argued (as was done above) that broadened marketing does not meet Parson's criteria of social order thereby causing dysfunctions for marketing and society to occur, an alternative and more dynamic interpretation of recent events is also possible.

Initially, the widespread application of broadened marketing may cause some problems and negative reactions as posited in this paper. But in the main, the public may come to believe that the application of marketing methods to public's health care, culture, social organizations and other nontraditional areas holds more social benefits than costs. Consequently, policy makers and other decision makers could take rapid steps to intervene upon the budding social disorders wrought by broadened marketing. Specifically, various social interventions may be used to (a) help balance power and responsibility when broadened marketing, especially social marketing is practiced; (b) assure the presence of specialized instituions (e.g. public review boards) to oversee broadened marketing; (c) resolve the lack of definitional specificity associated with broadened marketing.

In short, such a series of social interventions suggests that the evolution of broadened marketing might be more dynamic than the Parsonian framework would predict. In particular, while broadened marketing may be viewed as causing some momentary disturbances in the social system (disorder), the society may be flexible enough to interject social mechanisms (such as requiring increased professionalism by marketers) which will modify the existing state of affairs and culminate in a restored social order. This dynamic interpretation of events is no doubt forecast by some members of the marketing profession. However, if it is to materialize, considerable thought must be given *now* to the nature of these social interventions. Failing this, the social disorder predicted by the Parsonian framework may be unerringly accurate.

## Conclusion

Every branch of specialists tends to see the world from its own perspective and it is a natural manifestation of the self to do so. Thus, marketers wish to see the domain of marketing as including all human transactions. In doing so, the principles of social order are violated. Marketing becomes the ultimate illustration of empire building. As it is presently evolving, marketing is defined so broadly as to barely differentiate it from a multiplicity of human behaviors; it circumscribes so large a terrain as to place it beyond the perimeter of any of the traditional functions in a social system; and it is claimed to be so applicable and universal as to aspire to a role in the social system where the power of the discipline could be so great that it is tempting to avoid responsibility for some of the social changes it could cause. If abuses in the practice of broadened marketing occur, the repuation of marketing practitioners will steadily erode in the eyes of the public.

Marketers should take enough pride in the scope of traditional marketing. Marketing is a powerful force in society and essential to the business system. Traditional marketing bears an important responsibility in the social system. The activities of traditional marketing are now narrow. Marketers use the tools of classical economics, mathematics, social science and many other fields of study to bring about the essential and efficient exchange of goods and services. Just as marketing borrows concepts from other disciplines and applies them to its task, marketing perspectives and methods can be borrowed fruitfully by non-profit organizations and individuals! But before we place these applications within the strict domain of marketing and call them our children, the discipline of marketing should think long and carefully about what is required of a responsible parent.

## REFERENCES


1. Andreason, Alan R. and Best, Arthur. "Consumers Complain—Does Business Respond?" *Harvard Business Review*, (July-August 1977), 93-100.
2. Arndt, Johan. "How Broad Should the Marketing Concept Be?" *Journal of Marketing*, (January 1978), 101-103.
3. Bartels, Robert. *The History of Marketing Thought*, 2nd Edition. Columbus, Ohio; Grid, Inc., 1976, 21-29.
4. Boskoff, Alvin. "Functional as a Source of a Theoretical Repertory and Research Tasks in the Study of Special Change," G.K. Zollochan and Walter Hirsh (eds.) *Explorations in Social Change*. New York: Houghton Mifflin, 1964, 224.
5. Boskoff, Alvin, "Social Change: Major Problems in the Emergence of Theoretical and Research Tool", Howard Becker and A. Boskoff (eds.). *Modern Sociological Theory*. New York: Dryden Press 1967. 263-266.
6. Clausen, Earl A. "Marketing Ethics and the Consumer," *Harvard Business Review* (January-February 1967), 97-86.
7. Committee on Terms. *Marketing Definitions: A glossary of Marketing Terms*. Chicago: American Marketing Association, 1960.
8. Cooley, C. H. *Human Nature and the Social Order*. New York: Schocken Bocks, 1964, XVIII-XIX.
9. Daly, Herman E. *Steady State Economics*. San Francisco: W. H. Freeman and Co., 1977, Chapter 5.
10. Davis, Keith and Robert L. Blomstrom. *Business and Society: Environment and Responsibility*, 3rd Edition. New York: McGraw Hill, 1975, 47-53.

11. Frank Lawrence K. "What is Social Order?" *The American Journal of Sociology* Vol. XLIX (July-May 1943,44), 470-479.
12. Frankel, Charles, *The Case for Modern Man*. New York: Harper and Row, 1955, 203.
13. Geigen, Theodor. *On the Social Order and Mass Society*. Chicago: The University of Chicago Press, 1969.
14. Greenland, Leo. "Advertisers Must Stop Conning Consumers," *Harvard Business Review* (July-August 1974), 18-28 +.
15. Hiller, E. T. *The Nature and Basis of Social Order*. New Haven Conn.:Col lege and University Press, 1966, 42, 128-149.
16. Horton, John. "Order and Conflict Theories of Social Problems As Competing Ideologies," *American Journal of Sociology* Vol. LXXI, No. 6 (May 1966), 701-713.
17. Hunt, Shelby D. "The Nature and Scope of Marketing," *Journal of Marketing*, 40 (July, 1976), 19-24.
18. Jacobson, A.L. "A Theoretical and Empirical Analysis of Social Change and Conflict," Herman Turk and Richard L. Simpson (eds.) *Institutions and Social Exchange*. New York: Bobbs-Merrill Company, Inc., 344-360.
19. Kern, Robert R. "The Supervision of the Social Order," *The American Journal of Sociology* Vol. XXIV, No. 3 (November 1918), 260-288.
20. Klapp, Orrin E. *Models of Social Order*. Palo Alto, Calif.: National Press Books, 1973, 4, 8, 295.
21. Kotler, Philip and Levy, Sidney J. "Broadening the Concept of Marketing" *Journal of Marketing* 33 (January 1969) 10-15.
22. Kotler, Philip. "A Generic Concept of Marketing," *Journal of Marketing*, 36 (April 1972). 49
23. Kotler, Philip and Sidney Levy. "A New Form of Marketing Myopia: Rejoiner to Professor Luck," *Journal of Marketing*, 33 (July 1959),57.
24. Kotler, Philip and Gerald Zaltman. "Social Marketing: An Approach to Plan ned Social Change," *Journal of Marketing* (July 1971), 3-12.
25. Kunket, John H. *Society and Economic Growth*. New York: Oxford University Press, 1970, 185.
26. Landis, P.H. *Social Control*. Chicago: Lippincott, 1956, 25-26.
27. Lavidge, Robert J. "The Growing Responsibilities of Marketing,'" *Journal of Marketing* (January 1970), 25-28.
28. Levy, Sidney J. "Macology 101 or the Domain of Marketing" K. L. Bernhardt (Ed.) *Marketing: 1776-1976 and Beyond*. 1976 Educator's Proceedings. Chicago: American Marketing Association. 1976, 577-581.
29. Luck, David. "Broadening the Concept of Marketing—Too Far," *Journal of Marketing*, 33 (July 1969), 54.
30. Luck, David. " Social Marketing: Confusion Compounded," *Journal of Marketing*, 38 (October 1974), 2-7.
31. Maciver, Robert M. *Social Causation*. Boston: Ginn and Company. 1942. 27.
32. Martel, Martin U. "Academia Praecox: The Aims, Merits and Scope of Parson's Multisystemic Language Rebellion," Herman Turk and Richard L. Simpson (Eds). *Institutions and Social Exchange*. New York: Bobbs-Merrill Company, Inc., 1971, 175-211.
33. Mueldei, Walter G. *Foundations for a Responsible Society*, New York: Abingdon Press, 1956, 23, 129.

34. Nickels, William G. "Conceptual Conflicts in Marketing," *Journal of Economics and Business*, 26 (Winter 1974), 142.
35. Parsons, Talcott. *The Social System*. Glencoe, Illinois: The Free Press. 1951.
36. Parsons, Talcott. *The System of Modern Societies*. Englewood Cliffs. N.J.: Prentice Hall, Inc., 1971, 6, 10-12.
37. Parsons, Talcott and Edward A. Shils & (Eds.) *Toward a General Theory of Action*. Cambridge, Mass.: Harvard University Press, 1951, l07.
38. Prince, Henry Samuel, *The Social System*. Toronto, Canada: The Ryerson Press, 1958, 41-44.
39. Schneider, Louis. *Classical Theories of Social Change*. Morristown, N.J.: General Learning Press, 1976.
40. Segerstedt, Torgny. *Some Notes on Definitions in Empirical Science*. Uppsela: Alingrist and Widsedls, 1957, 3.
41. Shils, Edward. "Charisma, Order and Status," *American Sociological Review* Vol. 30, No. 2 (April 1965), 199-213.
42. Shuptrine, F. Kelly and Frank A. Osmanski. "Marketing's Changing Role: Expanding or Contracting," *Journal of Marketing* (April 1975), 58-66.
43. Simpson, Richard L. *Imperative Control, Associationalism and the Moral Order*. New York: Bobbs-Merrill Company, Inc., 1971, 253-271.
44. Smelsen, Neil J. *Social Change in the Industrial Revolution. Chicago*: University of Chicago Press, 1959.
45. Staudt, Thomas A., Donald A. Taylor and Donald J. Bowersox. *A Managerial Introduction to Marketing*, 3rd Edition. Englewood Cliffs, N.J.: Prentice Hall, Inc., 1976, 557.
46. Stiener, George A. *Business and Society*, 2nd Edition. New York: Random House, 1975, 8.
47. Stiener, Robert L. "The Prejudice Against Marketing," *Journal of Marketing* (July 1976), 138.
48. Takas, Andrew. "Societal Marketing: A Businessman's Perspective," *Journal of Marketing*, 38 (October 1974), 5.
49. Taylor, John F. A. "Is The Corporation Above the Law?" *Harvard Business Review* (March-April 1956), 126.
50. Tucker, W. T. "Future Directions in Marketing Theory," *Journal of Marketing*, 38 (April 1974) 30-35.
51. Tinberger, Jan (Coordinator). *RIO: Reshaping the International Order*. New York: E.P. Dutton Co., Inc., 1976, 4.
52. Turerk, David G. *The Political Economy of Advertising*. Washington, D.C.: American Enterprise Institute for Public Policy Research, 1978, 44.
53. Watkins, C. Ken. *Social Control*. New York: Longman Press, 1975, 6.
54. Weber, Max. *The Theory of Social Organization*. New York: The Free Press, 1947, 143-163.
55. White, Winston. *Beyond Conformity*. New York: The Free Press, 1961. 70-100.

## ACKNOWLEDGEMENT

Special thanks to J. Howard Westing of the University of Wisconsin-Madison and Richard P. Bagozzi of the University of California-Berkeley for commenting on portions of this manuscript. Neither necessarily shares the philosophical orientation expressed in this paper but both contributed greatly to improving the clarity of expression.

# SECTION B
# Requirements of Marketing Theory

There has been a growing interest in establishing a set of metatheory, or scientific criteria for evaluating and generating marketing theory. This reflects a growing interest in the philosophy of science issues in marketing. Although there are several alternative paradigms for marketing considerations, marketing has limited itself to the traditional notions of the philosophy of science. These include a focus on description, explanation, and relevance.

Description relates to the reality dimension. In other words, is it possible to test the theory and to obtain empirical evidence that validates the outcomes of the theory? In marketing it seems that unless we demonstrate some empirical basis for the theory (case study, casual observation, past evidence, or actual testing), the theory is labeled at best a speculation.

Explanation refers to the organization dimension of the theory. In other words, how good a theory is depends on the deductive logic and consistency with which the constructs of the theory are organized and specified as rationale or explanation for the phenomenon described in the theory. The key issues in explanation are lack of alternative explanations and consistency among the constructs chosen by the theory. Marketing, like many social sciences, seems to have many explanations for the same phenomenon. A number of alternative explanations can be offered for the same observation. These alternatives result in a sense of plurality that is often frustrating.

The final area is relevance. Relevance refers to the richness and simplicity of the theory. If a theory can explain all types of marketing phenomena with only a handful of constructs, it is best from the relevance point of view. For example, cognitive dissonance theory in psychology, offered by Leon Festinger, is often considered very relevant because it explains a large domain of human behavior with a very basic proposition of cognitive consistency. Similarly, perceived risk theory, proposed by Raymond Bauer, is also considered very relevant in consumer behavior because it tends to describe and explain much of buying behavior with a simple construct.

The following three papers discuss these philosophy of science issues as they apply to marketing.

# 4 —— The Requirements for Theory in Marketing

*Michael H. Halbert*

Reprinted from *Theory in Marketing*, published by the American Marketing Association, edited by Cox, Alderson, and Shapiro (1964), pp. 17-36. Reprinted by permission.

In any examination of the organized behavior system we called civilizations, we can observe some people devoted to reflection on the nature and operation of various activities of such systems. These people are often distinguished from those more active in the conduct of affairs by calling the first group, thinkers, and the second group, doers. It is abundantly clear, however, that in many areas of human activity, developments occur without any serious attempt to be reflective about their origins, their current activities, and their possible future. The greatest periods of culture growth have not necessarily coincided with the periods of greatest reflection. If we look at the current state of marketing activity and marketing thought, two apparently incongruous pictures appear. In the world as a whole and in the United States particularly, marketing is flourishing. It is growing and changing more quickly than perhaps any other institution of the society and rapidly increasing its impact on the total economic system. As an activity, then, marketing is both dynamic and progressive.

But when we look at the development and the present state of marketing theory the picture is just the reverse. From the point of view of the aid that theory can furnish to the practitioner, marketing has very little to offer. From the viewpoint of the established sciences, marketing has no theory that is defensible on the grounds of its logical consistency, philosophic adequacy, or experimental foundation. Why is it that we have and can have a marketing practice that is highly successful without an equally successful development of marketing theory? Before we can develop the requirements for theory in marketing we must look at the way the grounds differ for developing a practice as opposed to developing a theory adequate to explain that practice.

In every culture studied by anthropologists or historians, some form of exchange has existed. That exchange should develop is predetermined by two factors that are to be found in any organized human society—specialization and motivation. Not only are productive skills an objective of specialization within a culture, so also is specialization in resources and specialization in wants and desires. When specialization is coupled with motivation, exchange naturally occurs. Anything so vital a part of society tends to become institutionalized, acculturated, and ritualized. This is borne out by anthropological studies in which every culture examined shows some ritualistic aspects associated with the problems and practices of exchange. In fact, in early societies most of the exchange structure was integrated with the religious and other ritualistic aspects of the system. There is also good reason to believe that exchange of goods between tribes had its origin in a practice designed as a symbolic guarantee that the tribes were at peace rather than as a method of trading surpluses for mutual satisfaction and use. As man increased his ability to produce more finely differentiated means for the satisfaction of his wants and desires, the importance of the exchange function in culture increased until at the present time we have in many parts of the world cultures that could be described as marketing societies rather than as agricultural or manufacturing societies.

But to do a thing well it is not necessary to have an adequate theory of how it is done. Many people eat well without being nutritionists; men learned to see long before they learned the theory of optics; women had babies before they had obstetricians. The two necessary conditions for the development of a theory are the need for it (either for practical reasons or for intellectual satisfaction) and the availability of the techniques to develop the theory. The practice of marketing has attracted many able, competent, and highly motivated men who serve as marketing executives and marketing managers. These men realize that their marketing activities are growing more and more difficult as the complexity of the marketing environment increases and as the commitment to marketing alternatives becomes more binding for longer periods of time and involves larger and larger proportions of the total corporate assets. Thus, each of these men begins to develop marketing theory for himself.

In general the marketing executive or manager does not call it marketing theory. While he is concerned with gaining a practical understanding of how his system works, this concern is manifested in finding rules of thumb and immediate guides to action; his "theory" is implicit rather than explicit. His motivation is intensely practical and directed towards the performance of an almost impossible task. He needs ways of thinking about this task that tend to make it manageable and that enable him to relate his experience in past situations to his current problems. It is this kind of theory development that supports the notion that experience is the best teacher. Yet to learn from experience one must have a framework of concepts within which to interpret past events; otherwise experience cannot be relevant and nothing can be learned from it.

At the same time that the pressure for more adequate theory in marketing develops from the people who operate the marketing system, a parallel pressure for the development of theory is generated by the force of intellectual curiosity. Every large segment of human activity has been subjected to an attempt to organize it on the part of people with theoretical interests.

The extent to which this attempt is successful usually depends upon the availability of appropriate analytic and conceptual techniques, upon the total amount of manpower and intelligence devoted to the effort, and upon the cooperation of the operating system being studied. In the current case for marketing theory it appears that the conditions are more favorable than they have ever been in the past for the emergence of a more definitive science in marketing. More and more, intellectually curious people are studying the business system and the marketing part of that system. More and more, they are given adequate opportunities, adequate cooperation, and adequate support.

The purpose of the theorizer is to understand the phenomenon he investigates. Since understanding is a communicative process, especially so in science, the theorist would like to develop concepts about which he can talk in such a way that a great deal can be explained with a few concepts and that the confusing world of appearances can be reduced to an orderly world of understandable relationships among definable entities. Thus, the conventional theorist is motivated more by his dislike of confusion than by his desire to improve the operation of the system while the practical operating marketing man is motivated by his need for improved practice rather than by his intellectual desire to order his world. But each needs the other, and it often turns out that the theorist is an intensely practical, down-to-earth researcher, while the pragmatically oriented practitioner is concerned with concepts, theories, definitions, and relationships as much as his more theoretical counterpart. The theoretician needs data from operating systems. He needs a laboratory from the real world to experiment in, to check his hypotheses, and to validate his theories.

The main concern of this essay, then, is with the requirements for theory in marketing. This task presupposes some description of what is meant by theory (in marketing or other disciplines) and a statement of where marketing theory currently stands. Accordingly, one finds discussed in the remaining sections of this essay—

1. The meaning of theory as used in this chapter, including the place of observation and measurement in theory.
2. The contributions which marketing and other fields (e.g., business, law, economics, the behavioral and methodological sciences) have made to what currently exists as marketing theory.
3. The requirements which continued developments in marketing theory will have to meet.

## THE MEANING OF THEORY

Like all abstractions, the word "theory" has been used in many different ways, in many different contexts, at times so broadly so as to include almost all descriptive statements about a class of phenomena, and at other times so narrowly as to exclude everything but a series of terms and their relationships that satisfy certain logical requirements. We shall want to take a somewhat middle position here and say that at the very least a theoretical statement within the domain or framework of marketing must do more than merely describe the phenomena being observed. Even here, though, we must be careful, for to describe implies to have observed, and to have observed implies a choice as to which aspects of the marketing world should be chosen for observations.

Also implied in any description are choices of what the measurements or classifications used in the descriptions were. All of these are decisions which are based ultimately on a theory or a set of theories that explain what it is important to observe and report about marketing phenomena. Thus, the process of observation or recording or description cannot be divorced from the process of theory construction.

Perhaps more important to our present viewpoint, however, is the notion that we cannot accent the somewhat arbitrary, slightly naive descriptions of scientific method that lay out a sequence including observation, the construction of hypotheses, and theory development, as though theory were the end product of this process rather than an integral and necessary part of each phase of it. This is all by way of emphasizing the distinction between implicit and explicit theory.

Even in the simple recording of a sale of any company's product, there is implicit not only a theory that describes what a sale is, who the parties to the sale are, and what the price is, but the much more pervasive background theory that tells us why it is worth using up company resources to record the sale at all. If it should be recorded, then *how* it should be recorded implies what future operations are to be performed on the data, and this in turn implies knowing the information requirements for managerial decisions and, ultimately, policy decisions. The often heard complaint of analysts or executives that "the data weren't recorded in a way that makes such and such an analysis or decision possible" is an illustration of the awkward results of being implicit instead of explicit about the requirements of the information. Therefore, we shall constrain our discussion of theory at this point to explicit theory.

It is in this sense that a theory must be more than just a recording of observations or the results of an analysis performed upon such data; it must also be more than just a set of definitions and logical operations that can be performed on the definitions. There must be the complete statement of the operational or "semantic" relations between the terms in the definitions and the behaviors in the real world to which the definitions refer.

One of the most common definitions of theory is an explanation of a set of phenomena. But explanation involves people (data don't explain themselves). Why would anyone *want* to explain a set of phenomena? Why, to *use* the explanation, of course—to use it in making decisions, perhaps for the most basic of research needs, perhaps for the most pressing of practical reasons. A theory, then, must include an explanation of its own uses; that is, how one can make decisions with it. Thus (ideally) a theory exists for a set of phenomena when all of the possible decisions to be made involving those phenomena can be explained. These explanations must fit all possible individuals who make these decisions, and the fitting must be satisfactory to the theorist involved.

The inclusion of "must be satisfactory to the theorist" leads to rather interesting consequences. The emphasis on the relation of theory to decision making implies that people are a part of any theory and that the purpose of the development of theory is not to explain and to understand the physical world as separated and apart from human interests and human endeavor, but rather that any adequate notion of theory must include the behavior of people who are operating on the class of phenomena about which the theory is constructed. Thus, if one wishes to find out about the theory of metals, one observes people behaving with metals and asks them to explain the decisions they are making. Those people who can explain most adequately have the best theories of metals, and one usually expects to find them in scientific research laboratories. Following the same line of reasoning, if one wishes to find out about theories of marketing, one observes people making decisions about marketing phenomena, be they buyers or sellers, executives or manufacturers, business or government policy makers. Here we run into what at first looks like an anomaly, for we do not always find the most adequate explanations of the decisions made about marketing in our universities and academic circles.

The more adequately developed the theory of an area is, the more likely we are to find a professional, academic class concerned with this theory. In mathematics, astronomy, chemistry, physics, etc., we expect to find (and do find) the most adequate explanations for the decisions made about these areas in our better universities; yet in most of the business disciplines and in many of the social and behavioral disciplines it is at least as likely that adequate explanations for decision making will be found among the better practitioners (and the more thoughtful and reflective ones) as it is that they will be found in universities or in academic research areas.

This is by no means a criticism of academia; it rather reflects the state of theory development in these areas. If marketing is to develop and proceed as a science in future years, we can confidently expect the development and presence of marketing theory in the university circles to increase very rapidly and to take its expected and respected place among the other scientific disciplines in academic circles. That this is not yet the case merely provides us with a challenge for the future. The interest exists; the practice of marketing goes on and provides the resources wherewith to develop a theory.

## The Present State of Marketing Theory

The current state of marketing theory reflects not only the contributions of marketing practitioners and theorists but borrowings from other disciplines as well, e.g., (a) business, law, and economics; (b) the social and behavioral sciences; and (c) the formal or methodological sciences. Marketing, however, has no recognized central theoretical basis such as exists for many other disciplines, notably the physical sciences and, in some cases, the behavioral sciences. This lack of a conceptual foundation for marketing can be seen most clearly in an analysis of the course materials in the marketing curricula of the graduate schools of business in this country. In a survey recently completed by the Marketing Science Institute it is worthwhile noting that out of the 158 curricula surveyed, in which 140 references are used, only 31 of the references can be classified as dealing with marketing theory to any significant degree. This does not reflect a lack of interest in theory on the part of the academicians, but rather a lack of available material for the teaching of marketing theory—material that meets the academic and scientific requirements for such an undertaking.

Such a condition is not surprising in light of the point of view developed in the first section of this chapter. Since marketing has been considered by our culture primarily as an art or technique rather than as a science, most of the formal content that current marketing *has* collected has been derived from other areas rather than being original with marketing.

If we are to examine the rest of organized science for the current basis of marketing theory, in which particular directions shall we search? This depends, of course, on the object of the search. Science is a complicated activity, and there are many different ways of classifying its total content. The classification scheme used here is in terms of the different levels of generality of the material.

### Content

The *content* material of a science consists of the observations, measurements, and descriptions of the phenomena studied. These are usually called facts or data to distinguish them from theories, although this distinction is not as clear as one might think.

### Techniques

The second kind of borrowing that marketing can expect from other areas is the borrowing of *techniques*. Broadly speaking these are the ways of generating the content material just described. Techniques include both the process of measurement and analysis. Moreover, many techniques arising in other fields must be modified and adapted before they are suited to marketing. The questionnaire from psychology and public opinion polls has had extensive development by market researchers, and is more useful than when it was first borrowed. Conversely, many of the early difficulties with motivation research were due to the attempt to use the techniques of clinical psychology without modification or adaptation to the requirements of marketing.

### Concepts

The third class of material that comprises a science consists of the concepts, theories, and generalized ideas that form the abstract but essential element which distinguishes a science from an art or practice. Content is concerned with "what"; technique is concerned with "how"; concept is concerned with "why." The borrowing of concepts from another science is extremely dangerous, but can be extremely productive. The literature of marketing, of the other business disciplines, of the social and behavioral sciences, and of the management and methodological sciences was examined to see what it offered in terms of relevant content, technique, and concept. Table 1 puts in perspective the kinds of material we can expect to borrow from the various fields of study.

**TABLE 1. Contributions of Various Sciences and Disciplines to a Science of Marketing***

| | *Type of Contribution* | | |
|---|---|---|---|
| ***Science or Discipline Area*** | ***Content*** | ***Technique*** | ***Concept*** |
| Marketing | Major | minor | |
| Business disciplines | Major | minor | |
| Behavioral sciences | minor | Major | minor |
| Methodological sciences | | minor | Major |

*The entries in the table are to suggest the relative importance of the current potential of each scientific area for the content, the techniques, or the concepts of an emerging science of marketing.

While marketing theory, as currently constituted, does include the concepts of such noted scholars as Alderson, Converse, and Aspinwall, it can be noted from Table 1 that the major contribution of marketing as a discipline to marketing as a science has been in the area of content. We shall wish to examine next the contributions which other fields of study have made (and appear likely to make in the future) to theory in marketing.

## The Business Disciplines, Law and Economics

The business disciplines are the first group to be reviewed for potential contributions to marketing theory. It is no surprise that their literature, as well as that of marketing, consists mostly of content and not technique or concept. The relevant books, articles, and speeches are mostly concerned with the operation of various aspects of the business system and not with the theoretical aspects of that operation. Taken as a group, business disciplines supply guidelines on how to recognize a problem when it exists, and what kinds of data are useful in helping to solve the problem. In many cases, the writings also supply a recommended solution. In law and in economics things are a bit different. Both of these areas have a long history, and each has developed its philosophers and theoreticians.

Most of the other areas of business, however, are in no better state than marketing with respect to having a basic conceptual or theoretical framework. If we may distinguish between a discipline and a science on the grounds that a discipline has techniques and a science has theories, then we must go further and say that techniques supply answers to questions and theories supply criteria by which answers are to be judged.

For example, in the area of real estate management there is an extensive literature on how to locate a suburban shopping area and on the evaluation of specific urban sites for specific types of business enterprises. These prescriptions, however, are developed from an analysis of experience and a history of similar situations on which data are available. Few of the writers claim that their advice is deduced from general theories of real estate; rather, it is induced from a careful analysis of experience. There is much practical value in borrowing the techniques and content of the business disciplines, but since these disciplines are themselves lacking established theoretical bases it is not surprising that looking for marketing *theory* in an area that has little enough of its own is unfruitful.

There is a well-developed body of literature concerning the philosophy of law, but its theoretical content is related more to sociology and political science than it is to marketing. Those writings in law which deal with the aspect of legal impingement on marketing do so in general with a rather superficial bow to the notion that the function of law is to enforce the will of society on the recalcitrant few. Thus, there is seen in antitrust discussion some confusion as to what the will of society is. The interpretation of some cases suggests that it is to protect consumers from the evil effects of monopoly power. Other cases and their interpretation suggest that it is to protect some business enterprises from their more successful competitors.

Perhaps the most fundamental idea from legal philosophy that has applicability to marketing theory is that in a society where men are motivated by their own diverse desires, the function of law is to provide a structure that permits maximum attainment of individual desires with minimum infringement on another's ability to attain his desires.

Economics has a longer history than most of the other business disciplines and has a well-developed body of economic theory. Much of this theory has found its way into marketing, and concepts of price elasticity, of market equilibrium, and of economies of scale are familiar to most marketers. The concept of economic man has been of great value to marketing but has also had some unfortunate consequences. But many of the most pressing problems in marketing develop from exactly those aspects of the system that economic theory has chosen to ignore.

This choice on the part of economists was quite conscious and deliberate, for if they did not make these simplifying assumptions, they could not have developed the great wealth of material that has been so useful to date. Economic man is assumed to have full and complete information about the decision under consideration. In classical economics when the problem of price equilibrium is being considered, it is assumed that all customers and all suppliers know the location of all products, and that the information about price, quality, quantity, and availability is instantaneously available and completely correct. Thus, the entire area of negotiation which is so vital to marketing is assumed out of the picture by the economist's emphasis on a single point of equilibrium.

Perhaps the central theoretical concept of economics has been that of rationality. Economic theory holds that people behave in their decision making as though they were trying to achieve the most of some value, often called utility and often measured in money. In his definition of "economic man" the late von Neumann was careful to point out that he had no reason to believe that people behave according to the assumptions that he was making, but that these assumptions were necessary in order to develop the theory advanced in the *Theory of Games and Economic Behavior*.[1] The concept of rationality so central to economic theory appears on examination to be a very difficult concept indeed. If we define rationality as behavior designed to maximize utility and then define utility as that which behavior tends to maximize, we are not very far ahead. It can easily be shown that for any behavior there is a set of values such that the behavior is rational (maximizing) for those values.

If we pursue this argument to claim that values as well as behavior need to be rational, we are led into the impossible morass of attempting to distinguish rational values from irrational values. The present state of value theory barely enables us to investigate the problem of consistency of values let alone to establish their rationality. The only useful definition of rationality seems to be "your behavior is rational to me if I can explain it." This definition of rationality is a measure of my ability to explain and really tells me nothing about your behavior.

## THE SOCIAL AND BEHAVIORAL SCIENCES

The concept of rational and nonrational behavior leads us naturally to a consideration of the social and behavioral sciences as a source for marketing theory. If the economists have done marketing a disservice by overemphasizing the rational and economic motives of human behavior, the social scientists and, in particular, the psychologists have attempted to swing the pendulum to the opposite extreme by emphasizing irrational and psychodynamic motivations. It is true that a housewife shopping in a supermarket is not solely motivated by the dollars-and-cents consideration and does not have a small computer in her head. It is also true that her marketing behavior cannot be explained adequately by considering only the state of her psyche, the social pressures on her from friends, and the sex symbolism of the various package designs.

Although the ''economic man'' (or woman) described for us by the classical economists forms only a part of any adequate marketing description of real people, it is an essential part. The complex and perhaps confusing picture of the customer drawn for us by the behavioral sciences seems more like the kind of human beings we meet every day than does the rather pallid utility maximizer of the economists. There is more to behavioral science (and even to psychology) than Freudian psychodynamic personality theory, however, and the overall picture drawn from anthropology, political science, demography, and linguistics, etc., as well as from psychology is extremely useful. Their major contribution is more the opening up of a whole new area of exploration than the contribution of any specific set of techniques or directly usable ideas.

The behavioral sciences permit, and in fact require, that marketing science take explicit account of the human and social aspects of individuals and of groups engaged in marketing behavior. No longer is the housewife/consumer or the vice president of marketing allowed the refuge of ''human nature.'' If we are to develop an adequate science of marketing we must investigate the people and the social groups that perform the marketing actions with the same scientific care and conceptual honesty with which other scientists investigate the phenomena of interest to them. What the behavioral sciences in total offer is a method of approach and a set of techniques that enable us to design and implement that investigation. These sciences have developed a whole group of techniques that are admirably suited for use in the development of marketing theory. This is not so much because these techniques are useful for measuring marketing behavior per se, but rather that the behavioral sciences have had to deal with the problem of measuring and analyzing systems which to a large extent they cannot control.

The history of successful measurement and experimentation in the physical sciences rests largely on the development of laboratory techniques and the ability to manipulate the environment and the objects of study in very closely controlled and easily repeatable situations. With the social sciences it is almost the reverse. There has been a great deal of laboratory experimentation in psychology, but even in that science and particularly as one moves to personality theory and to clinical psychology, the laboratory becomes less appropriate and the actual world of human behavior is the arena in which the methods of science must be applied in order to develop appropriate data and to test suggested hypotheses. Many of the other social sciences have very little laboratory work behind them, such as sociology, anthropology, linguistics, and political science. Each of these disciplines has some recourse to the laboratory, and so also does marketing.

But each of these disciplines has faced squarely the problem of making measurements and testing hypotheses in the on-going world in which very few of the variables can be controlled, and the particular objects under study, i.e., human beings, have memories and cannot be put through the same procedure twice since they will remember their earlier experiences. They cannot be told to act as if they were trying to maximize their monetary return. Even in the laboratory, values are not so easily manipulated. Since marketing and marketing research are concerned with these same kind of phenomena, it is not surprising that the techniques of social survey research have been so thoroughly borrowed and amalgamated into marketing that now there is as much developmental work in this area being done by market researchers as there is by opinion research specialists.

There are two further specific conceptual notions from the behavioral sciences that should be incorporated into marketing theory. The first of these has to do with the notion of values as they affect human behavior and especially as they influence the decision-making process. In most of the formal work in statistics and decision theory, values are taken as inputs to the decision-making process. The major notion of decision theory is that the decision maker chooses among alternative courses of action so as to achieve an outcome with the highest value to him, based on the incomplete information that he has at the time of decision making. The extensive and complex developments in decision theory treat primarily the problems that arise because of different kinds and amounts of information and various kinds of available alternatives.

At first glance decision theory appears to be a very satisfactory approach to problems. People certainly do tend to choose those activities which they find rewarding and pleasant, and to avoid those which they find unpleasant and distasteful. Some of the oldest notions in psychology center around this so-called pleasure-pain principle. Yet we frequently see the reverse situation where people tend to like what they do, rather than do only what they like. A taste for avocados must be cultivated, and it is common to be indifferent to chamber music at first and only come to like and appreciate it after several hearings. The extreme proponents of this position claim that the major function and goal of society is to inculcate good taste (values) in the arts, in architecture, food, dress, music, literature, and in ethics and morals. Certainly, a person's values are as much conditioned and determined by his behavior as the other way around.

Even if we take the naive position, however, that values are fixed inputs to decision making, we are left with the extremely difficult question of where *do* the values come from and what causes them to change. There is good reason to believe that maturation plays a large part in the development and change of values. Our children look forward with eager anticipation to the time when they are old enough to stay up all night whenever they want to, or to eat as much candy as they want. They refuse to believe their elders when they are told that their values will change, and by the time they can stay up as late as they want, they will be glad to get to bed early, and that they will lose their taste for candy or at least develop tastes for some of the foods they now dislike. The seven ages of man apply no less to his psyche and his values than they do to his physical development. Of all the behavioral sciences it is the sociologists and anthropologists who have the longest history of careful attention to this problem of the generation and modification of value systems.

There are, then, three major ideas or concepts from the social and behavioral sciences that should be incorporated into the development of any science of marketing. The first of these is that there is no simple route to the explanation or understanding of human behavior. The physical and biological sciences are not adequate to explain the kinds of behavior with which marketing men are concerned. The economists have provided an approach to this type of understanding, but it requires the behavioral sciences to broaden that approach so that the human beings described are realistic ones, and behave the way the real humans we know behave.

The second important notion of interest to marketers is that our scientific research methods must be turned inwards as well as outwards. We must study marketing operators and marketing scientists and their behaviors, assumptions, and attitudes as carefully, as rigorously, and as dispassionately as we study any other aspect of the marketing system. It is always easier, as the history of science has shown, to study *things* rather than *people* and to study *other* people rather than *ourselves*. But if we are ever to understand and predict the marketing system and the culture of which it is a part, we must take the final step and study ourselves. Only after we know what we do and how we do it can we begin to do it better.

The third contribution from the behavioral sciences lies in their development of concepts and techniques for the study of on-going real systems involving people in their normal interactive environment. The development of the social sciences in large part is the development of measurement and analytic devices for studying these kinds of systems. While laboratory research has its place, the current limitations on the development of social theory are the limitations imposed by lack of resources and lack of available techniques for field research. The same is true in marketing, but there is much that marketing can learn from the successes and failures of the behavioral scientist in coping with this difficult but crucial problem.

## METHOD VS. CONTENT IN SCIENCE

When we turn our attention to the formal methodological sciences to see what they have to offer of use in marketing theory, we must first understand the essential difference between the methodological sciences and the content sciences. Any science must have two parts: it must have a philosophy and it must have content. The content refers to the various phenomena to be studied and explained by the particular science. In our case these are clearly the phenomena of marketing. The philosophy of a science refers to the *rules* by which one can *test* statements concerning the phenomena under study. Some sciences are described and named by their content area, such as chemistry, physics, aerodynamics, biology, marketing, etc. Some sciences are described and named by the kind of formalisms with which they deal. Here we have the areas of mathematics, logic, epistemology, theology, etc. To the extent that there is any unified meaning to the notion of "the scientific method" it is derived from these formal sciences rather than from the content sciences.

It is often stated that marketing will never be a science like physics and that unless it is it will not be a "real" science. Remarks of this type indicate confusion between the methodological sciences and the content sciences. Physics is a content science no less than is marketing. It has been able to employ more adequately the techniques of logic and mathematics and it is on *this* ground rather than because physics deals with material objects that it deserves accolade as an exemplary science. This distinction is brought out quite clearly in the following passages:

> As a rule [market researchers] acquire competence in conducting investigations not by mastering principles of scientific inquiry but rather by developing habits of research that are modeled on examples of sound scientific workmanship. Moreover, discussions that are intended to articulate the structure of scientific procedure usually have no direct bearing on the detailed problems with which [marketers] are normally occupied. In consequence broad issues in the logic of science are rarely matters of active concern to practicing [marketers], and most of them devote little serious thought to such "philosophical" questions as the functions a satisfactory theory must perform, how theory is related to the gross objects of familiar experience, and whether the abstract notions of a theory denote things that have some kind of ... reality.
>
> Nevertheless, questions of this sort may become pressingly relevant to the work of [market researchers], and may require careful attention from them, when new experimental discoveries or radical innovations in theoretical ideas create puzzles that profoundly challenge entrenched scientific doctrines or habitual models of analysis....[2]

The author, Ernest Nagel, is a recognized philosopher and is here distinguishing between the behavior of content scientists and the behavior of philosophers of science. However, as can be seen by the bracketed inserts in the preceding quotation, the item was quoted as though the parties concerned were market researchers and marketers. The original article, however, had the term "physicists" where we have inserted "market researchers." The author was thus talking about physics and physicists and not about marketing. The way in which marketing science *should* be like physics is in the detailed, careful, and extensive use of logic, mathematics, and the rest of the *formal* mechanisms of science. This is the same way in which marketing science should be like astronomy, biology, or any other science. Logic is useful for all sciences, and one cannot have a science without it. One *can* have a science without cyclotrons. In our borrowings from the methodological disciplines, we should not look for concepts that are directly relevant to marketing as a content area, but rather those which are relevant to the development of any science.

In summary, current marketing theory has borrowed extensively from the content area of the business disciplines, and the concept and technique area of of economic theory (marginalism, opportunity costs, economic rationality). The social and behavioral sciences have provided techniques of measurement and experimentation and concepts useful to the study of people as opposed to things. Finally, it is apparent that we shall have to look increasingly to the methodological sciences to provide concepts and structure in marketing theory.

This brief excursion into the major sources of theory in marketing is but a prelude, however, to a more central question: What are the requirements that theory in marketing should meet? We discuss this question (and the important role that the methodological sciences play in the attempt to answer it) in the concluding section of this essay.

## The Requirements of Theory in Marketing

There are many aspects of theory development and testing in marketing for which we shall make increasing demands on the methodological sciences. In this essay, however, we shall discuss only the one notion mentioned earlier—the notion of criteria for the adequacy of theory. The reason for singling out this particular aspect of philosophy for consideration is that much of the confusion in the discussion of possible and proposed theories in marketing (and in business) arises out of a lack of understanding of the *different ways* in which a theory can be inadequate.

These criteria are discussed in logic and philosophy under the names of *syntax*, *semantics*, and *pragmatics*, although the first two of those terms mean something quite different from their standard common English usage. The discussion treats each in turn. Although our attention is directed to this particular part of the philosophy of science, we should not forget that all of the material that bears on scientific method and adequate theory formulation and testing is of relevance to the design of any science and most especially so to the conscious design of a new science.

One of the earliest concerns of the science of logic has been the exploration of relations among statements. These are called formal properties and depend for their validity on the rules of logic rather than linguistics, semantics, or operational definitions—topics with which we shall deal later. In a formal deductive system there are certain terms or elements called *primitives* which are undefined within that system. It may come as a surprise to some that logic insists on primitives or undefinable terms, yet it was proved in 1931 by the German philosopher and mathematician, Kurt Godel, that no system can be designed that is completely self-contained; that is, that every term in it can be defined in the language of other terms. This came as a culmination of the fruitless search for a completely defined and probably self-consistent system of arithmetic. After the primitives have been introduced, the next step is to develop postulates and axioms which relate these primitives to each other, thus defining *operators* or terms which serve to interconnect the primitives in the deductive system. For example, in the simple statement "1 + 1 = 2" the "1's" would be primitives of the system and the "+" and "=" would be operators or relational terms.

We are all familiar with the "if ... then" type of statement such as "if all *A* is *B* and all *B* is *C*, then all *A* is *C*." This is the syllogism, the prototype of all deductive reasoning. A criticism sometimes offered against this type of deduction is that it tells you nothing about the real world; it merely says that *if* certain things are assumed, then certain consequences follow. Admittedly, this type of statement does not tell us anything about the real world. Such statements only tell us things that are logical consequences of what we already know, but this can be a most valuable source of knowledge.

There is a rather famous logical conundrum in which a student is accusing his teacher of wasting his (the student's) time. The student says, "Is what you teach me logical?" To which the teacher replies, "Yes, indeed." The student then says, "Therefore, all of the consequences are contained in that which I already know—the premises." The teacher acknowledges that this is so, and then the student asks, "If there is anything in the consequences that is not contained in the original premises, then the logic is faulty, is it not?" Again the teacher agrees, and the student can now propound the conundrum, "Then everything you teach me is either faulty or that which I already know. Why then should I study with you?"

The fallacy in this particular conundrum is rather obvious; it depends upon the meaning of the term "that which I already know." The conclusion that with only five letters to a license plate I can identify 11,881,376 different automobiles is *contained in* the structure of arithmetic and multiplication but is not *known* to me until I perform the appropriate calculations. In the statement of the conundrum, the student confuses the terms "contained in" and "already known."

## Syntactics

Many of the most fruitful theoretical systems in the history of science have been fruitful because of the richness of the conclusions that could be deduced from a very few original postulates and axioms. We shall deal later with the problem of fruitfulness and richness, but here we are concerned with the formal aspect of theory that is called *syntactics*. Syntactics has to do with the legitimacy of the operations that can be performed on the elements that form the theory. Many of the historical paradoxes in logic derive from using the same term in two different ways or from performing operations on a term that are not appropriate.

In marketing one often tries to solve problems by relating the present problem to other similar cases. This is often what is meant by using experience. Let us suppose we can adequately define "similar," so that we can tell when one situation is similar to another. (This problem will be considered when we discuss *semantics*.) The *syntactical* problem of the legitimate statements we can make about "similar" remains. There is a particular difficulty inherent in this approach that can be used to illustrate the syntactical nature of the problem. If situation *A* is similar to situation *B* and situation *B* is similar to situation *C*, then is situation *A* similar to situation *C*? The answer may be of some importance to us, since we want to know whether we can use our experience gathered, say, in test markets for *A* in assessing the probable outcome of test markets for *C*. The logician would inquire as to whether the relationship of similarity possessed the property of being transitive.[3] If it is defined so that it does, then we can safely conclude that the situation *A* is similar to situation *C*. But the definition of "similarity" that makes it transitive might restrict the term so much that *A* no longer is similar to *B*.

There is an even more powerful question that the logician might raise. Is the relationship of similarity in the *equivalence* class of relationships? This is not the place to explore these particular logical notions,[4] but it is clear that *A* may or may not be similar to *C* depending on the way we define similarity. This brings us to the major point of the illustration. Most of the use of marketing terms such as "similar situation" are not defined well enough so that these logical questions can be answered. Only as a science becomes mature and develops theoretical statements that have been accepted and used for some time does it attract the attention of methodologists and philosophers who then begin to examine the syntax of the theories and often point up extremely fundamental problems in the statement and manipulation of these theories.

The major function of the logician in this situation is to call our attention to the ambiguity in our definitions and in the use of language. This is a formal ambiguity and not the problem of operational definitions. It is the distinction between the use of language to describe relations and the use of language to describe real world phenomena. It is clear that the notion of similar is a relational notion, not an empirical one.

The problems of syntax that we have examined here are mostly trivial and rather easily solved, but many of the most serious problems in logic, whose solutions would affect the fabric of all deductive sciences, are syntactical in nature. In the development of marketing science we will need to pay attention to these problems or, in the most literal sense, we will not know what we are talking about.

## Semantics

A theory may fulfill all of the syntactical requirements with complete adequacy, and still have serious faults. The statement of the primitive notions, the operators, and the permissible manipulation of the symbols in which the theory is stated may all be complete and logically correct. The difficulties may lie with the way in which the theory is related to the real world. We have said previously that science contains two kinds of statements. Some of these statements are to be tested by an analysis of their syntax, i.e., by formal rules, and some of the statements are to be tested by experimentation, i.e., by observations made in the real world. If we are to use a theory to tell us what observations to make, then we must be clear, precise, and complete in our description of what constitutes a relevant observation and how to interpret such observations so as to test the theory. This area of the philosophy of science is called *semantics*. Unfortunately, this term has a substantially different meaning in the branch of linguistics that deals with the human response to the meaningfulness of symbols. In philosophy the notion of semantics is confined to the relationship between the elements and operators in a formal statement of theory and to operations that can be performed on real phenomena either in terms of manipulation or in terms of observation. Most of the pleas in the literature and in private discussions to define terms better are pleas for more rigorous attention to the semantics of the theory being discussed.

Logicians and general system theorists are prone to develop theories in terms of abstract symbols. Thus, some of the rigorous formulations of probablity theory define probability as a number between zero and one that can be manipulated in certain ways (i.e., that possesses certain syntactical properties). Some of the proponents of this definiton of probability act as if they are unconcerned with the ''meaning'' of probability as a measurement device or a predictive device or a descriptive term for real occurrences. Theories of this type are at least explicit about their relative unconcern with the semantic problem. A greater difficulty arises when theories use nouns and verbs from common language. Although the terms are in some cases defined syntactically by the theorist so that his manipulations are permissible, they often do not have clear definitions with reference to observations. In almost all cases, common English (or any other natural language) uses words too loosely for direct carry-over to a scientific usage.[5]

A good example of this is in the use of the term "preference" as it is used in economic utility theory and in consumer analysis. There is much discussion as to whether preferences are transitive or not, i.e., is it logically (syntactically) required that if I prefer lobster to chicken and prefer steak to lobster that I must prefer steak to chicken? Actual investigations of human preferences have revealed that in certain situations preferences are not transitive. In spite of this fact, many theoretical formulations using the concept of preference require that it be transitive. To a logician this is merely a case of using a particular term in two different ways, and if these two separate meanings are kept clearly differentiated, there is nothing but an awkward language problem; there is no logical difficulty. The logical difficulty occurs when the theorist is not specific about which meaning of preference he is using, and thus may try to describe actual consumer data on the basis of a theory that requires (in its formal sense) that preference be a transitive relationship.

As a more basic point in the discussion of the semantic requirements for theory, we can examine the requirements of an operational definition of preference. How do we measure preference? Should a person's preference be defined as the response to a verbal inquiry, or in terms of some actual behavior? If we take either of these positions we must specify the particular form of the verbal inquiry or the particular kind of behavior that we wish to observe. We also must know how to interpret the verbal response or the observation of behavior. If we examine the first possibility and say that we wish to define preference as the response given by a subject to a particularly worded question, we rapidly get into serious difficulty.

Suppose I am asked a particular question and in flippant or recalcitrant mood I answer exactly opposite to my real feelings. Do we wish to accept my response as a measurement of my preferences? If we do, then we need a theory that is useful for prediction even when the responses are from recalcitrant and flip respondents. If we do not, then we need a set of definitions that enables the interviewer to tell when I am being flip and recalcitrant and what to do about it. Since there is so much difficulty in defining preference as a verbal response, it will certainly be no easier to distinguish between a well-intentioned cooperative response and one that is designed to irritate the interviewer. It is this line of reasoning that has occasionally led psychologists to define intelligence as the score achieved on intelligence tests. If one accepts that definition seriously, the predictive power left to the concept of intelligence is the ability to predict scores on intelligence tests—not a very happy state of affairs.

If the operational definition of preferences in verbal terms is so unsatisfactory, let us examine the definition of preference in terms of real behavior. If the researcher wishes to measure my preference for lobster over chicken, and he observes me in a restaurant with a menu on which both lobster and chicken are available, and I choose chicken, is he then justified in saying that I prefer chicken to lobster? Maybe he should observe me in other restaurants at other times. Perhaps I would behave differently if the price for lobster were only half the price for chicken. Perhaps I would behave differently if I were at home rather than in a restaurant. Maybe the person with whom I am dining exerts an influence on my choice. Or perhaps I don't really care, and I pick the item that appears first on the menu. How the researcher handles these questions determines what he *means* by the term "preference." The investigation of preference in its behavioral setting has been one of the most difficult and awkward problems in psychology and in the management sciences.

Certainly a minimum requirement for the measurement of preference seems to be that the preference should be exhibited in more than one situation. If I am given a choice for President of the United States between Roosevelt and Dewey, and if one wishes to measure my preference by my voting behavior, they will have to examine a situation that occurred only once and will never occur again. Is it meaningful therefore to talk about my preference for Roosevelt or Dewey as president? If we say, "Yes, it is," we then have some extremely difficult syntactical problems related to the possibilities in terms of the predictive use of such a measurement. If we say, "No, it isn't," then we must specify how many observations *are* required for an adequate measure of preference. It is in this area of semantics that one can be arbitrary if he wishes, but the meaning of the definition of preference and of the theories using it will be greatly affected by the particular result of the arbitrary decision.

## Pragmatics

Even if a theory is adequately described in terms of its semantic and syntactic aspects, it still may not be a very good theory. The way in which it fails to be good may be because of a lack of attention to the richness or fruitfulness of the theory in terms of the needs, desires, and problems of the people who may have use for it. The aspect of the analysis of theory concerned with the *use* of theory is called *pragmatics*. We require of our theories that they be rich, fruitful, and useful and apply to important problems as well as that they be formally adequate and definitionally precise.

An investigation of the pragmatic requirements of theory takes us out of the realm of logical formalism and into the more difficult, but perhaps more vigorous, area in which philosophy is concerned with real problems of on-going human systems. If we explore seriously the pragmatic aspects of science, we are led rather directly to a concern with the problem of value. It is not enough for a theory to have a large number of deducible theorems; these theorems should apply to important problems. A theory with but a few deducible theorems that applied to the establishment of universal peace would be considered far more valuable than a theory whose outcome permitted the detailed construction of innumerable TV westerns. The difficulties of dealing in a philosophically adequate way with the problem of value, though, are far too extensive to be more than indicated in this essay. Probably the central difficulty is the decision as to *whose* values at what time should be the controlling factor. If we adopt the notion that it is always the decision maker's values, then a lawyer should make decisions based on his best interests, not his client's. This approach also makes it difficult to deal with group decision making. It is not always easy to tell whether a theory will be useful and to whom. Many theories have been developed in ''pure mathematics'' and have later proved to be of high pragmatic value. The intellectual curiosity of one generation is the practical engineering tool of another.

## IMPLICATIONS: MARKETING THEORY AND HUMAN VALUES

When we examine the goal requirements for marketing theory, we can identify at least three groups whose values must be overtly taken into account. These three groups are: the *institutions* engaged in the process of marketing (manufacturers, intermediate sellers, retailers, industrial sales groups, etc.), the *consuming public*, and the *government* policy maker. Even a cursory analysis of the goals for marketing theory and marketing science held by these three groups reveals conflicting as well as cooperative goals. Any major development of marketing science that served the goals of only one group at the expense of either of the other two would pose the same kind of ethical problem that nuclear physicists faced when almost their entire effort was devoted to harnessing the destructive energies of atomic power, rather than to a balanced development including the productive and medical uses of atomic energy.

In fact, one of the most difficult but pressing of all problems facing the development of theory in marketing is the resolution of conflict in goals. This is not only a problem for the eventual science of marketing, it is a problem for all existing sciences and disciplines, and indeed it is a problem for the individual. Every single person has to resolve conflicting demands on his time, on his resources, on his loyalties, on his emotions. That this resolution is not easy nor always satisfactory is shown by the statistics of our mental hospitals and the case records of our psychoanalysts. That it is no less satisfactory on a national and international level is shown by the state of world affairs and of the armaments race. The problem belongs to all of humanity, to philosophy, to mathematics, to politics, and even to marketing science. The requirements for theory in marketing and the problems engendered in meeting these requirements will surely tax the ingenuity and patience of the most resourceful and dogged of marketing theorists for years to come.

## ENDNOTES

1. John von Neumann and Oskar Morgenstern, *Theory of Games and Economic Behavior* (2nd ed.; Princeton, N.J.: Princeton University, 1947).
2. Ernest Nagel, "Review of *Understanding Physics Today*," by W. H. Watson, *Scientific American*, Vol. 209, No. 4 (October, 1963), pp. 145-49.
3. Let *R* be any relationship that can hold between two elements of a set (*a*, *b*, *c*, ...). The relationship is written "*aRb*." This is read, "*a* bears the relationship *R* to *b*." *R* is transitive if and only if, given *aRb* and *bRc*, we can deduce *aRc*.
4. A relationship is in the equivalence class if it is transitive, reflexive, and symmetrical. Reflexive means that *aRb* implies *aRa*. Symmetrical means that *aRb* implies *bRa*.
5. For further development of this point, see the discussion of explication in R. Carnap, *Introduction to Semantics* (Cambridge, Mass.: Harvard University Press, 1948).

# 5 —— A Prospectus for Theory Construction in Marketing

*Richard P. Bagozzi*

Reprinted from *Journal of Marketing*, published by the American Marketing Association, Vol. 48 (Winter 1984), pp. 11-29. Reprinted by permission.

## Introduction

Research is perhaps most often scrutinized in terms of the inputs that produce it and the outputs that characterize it. Typically, inputs run the gamut from the ideas and energies of researchers to the methods, prior findings, and new data of disciplines. Outputs are additions to scientific and practical knowledge. These consist of new ways of thinking about and approaching problems of interest.

The present article addresses one way that the inputs and outputs are linked. The premise is that theory construction serves an intervening role between the researcher on the one hand and knowledge production on the other hand. That is to say, the ways that theories are represented and tested are thought to entail social constructions connecting individual researchers to the body of knowledge that constitutes a discipline. It is maintained that the nature and quality of knowledge are formally dependent on theory construction. If we are to effectively influence the generation of new knowledge, we must purposely give consideration to the intermediary role of how theories should be formed.

In general, we might construe theory construction in two ways: as a *process* and as a *structure*. The process of theory construction involves the application of principles of logic, the implementation of methods and procedures (e.g., the experimental method), and the observance of standards of conduct and evaluation. To these more formal processes we must add such informal processes as creativity and decision making by individual researchers; conflict, debate, and give-and-take between researchers; and social and political processes among groups and institutions (Bagozzi 1976). The process of theory construction is a historical one, too, in that new theories are forged from older ones and are judged in relation to how well they subsume older theories, account for current anomalies, and lead to future discoveries.

At the same time, theory construction can be characterized by its structure. By structure we mean the concepts in a theory, the hypotheses made by the theory, the observations and measurements included in the theory, and the formal organization of all these elements in an overall representation. Any structure will, therefore, have semantic and syntactic dimensions.

In the present essay, discussion will focus on the structural aspects of theory construction. We will begin with an outline of one of the most highly developed and widely used frameworks in the philosophy of science: the so-called *Received View,* also known as the standard conception and more broadly as logical empiricism (Suppe 1977). Our goal will be to describe and critique the Received View with an aim toward showing how it can serve as a starting point for a new perspective more operationally oriented than earlier, abstract models. The new approach is termed the *Holistic Construal,* but it should be stressed that it is not a philosophy of science. Rather, it is a methodological programme designed to bridge the gap between the new philosophies of science (e.g., Brown 1979, Suppe 1977) and the concepts and procedures needed to implement and evaluate the conduct of research. Its philosophical roots lie primarily in the realist theory of science (e.g., Bagozzi 1980, especially pp. 19-20, 25-27, 39-40; Manicas and Secord 1983), yet it is broad enough to accommodate other viewpoints, as developed hereafter. Overall, our goal will be to lay the conceptual groundwork needed for sound theory construction in marketing. To this end, ideas from the philosophy of science are integrated with emerging views in marketing (e.g., Bagozzi 1980, 1983; Bagozzi and Fornell 1982; Bagozzi and Phillips 1982; Hunt 1976; Zaltman, LeMasters, and Heffring 1982; Zaltman, Pinson, and Angelmar 1973). By the same token, we will suggest some new ways of representing and testing theories.

Before consideration of the Received View and Holistic Construal, we should mention a caveat. The process and structure of theory construction interact with each other and jointly determine the content of both scientific and practical knowledge. Thus, in one sense it is artificial to separate them. We do so here largely for expositional purposes and because treatment of the process of theory construction is beyond the scope of this article. In addition, well-developed theories of the process are generally lacking. Toulmin's (1972) instrumentalist approach, Kuhn's (1970) notion of scientific revolutions, Hanson's (1971) ideas on the logic of discovery, Feyerabend's (1965, 1970) radical empiricism, Lakatos' (1970) research program methodology, and Shapere's (1969, 1974) work on scientific domains and rationality go a long way toward articulating the processural aspects of theory construction, but are not sufficiently formulated to be integrated with the structural dimensions developed herein. Indeed, each of the processural views contains serious shortcomings, leading one commentator to conclude that "today no single analysis ... enjoys general acceptance among most philosophers of science" (Suppe 1977, p. 119). If we can push our knowledge of a small portion of theory construction (i.e., its structure) one step further, then much will be gained along the way toward better formulation of theories. Our explication of the structure of theory is intended to tackle but one piece of the research puzzle, albeit in a modest way.

## FOUNDATIONS: THE RECEIVED VIEW

### The Canonical Formulation[1]

In abbreviated form, we may characterize the logical empiricist model of the structure of theory as follows (see Figure 1). Scientific theories are formulated in terms of a language *L* and a logical calculus *K*. The former consists of a theoretical language $L_T$ and an observational language $L_O$. The latter is comprised of formal rules of reasoning and inference and exists also in separate theoretical ($K_T$) and observational ($K_O$) modes. Within $L_T$ are theoretical (i.e., nonobservational) terms $V_T$; and within $L_O$ are empirical (i.e., observational) terms $V_O$. The $V_T$ are used to represent abstract concepts in a theory, whereas $V_O$ are used to represent empirical concepts. The *L* of a theory is expressed in sentence form, with $L_T$ capturing the central nonobservational propositions in the theory and $L_O$ reflecting empirical generalizations. The conjunction of $L_T$, $V_T$, and $K_T$ may be termed the theoretical postulates *T* of the theory; whereas the conjunction of $L_O$, $V_O$, and $K_O$ are called the implied empirical observations *O* of the theory. The empirical meaning of the theory is said to occur through the specification of the relationships between $V_T$ and $V_O$. This is accomplished through correspondence rules *C* which formally link the two. We designate the entire structure of any theory—i.e., the conjunction of *T*, *C*, and *O*—by "*TCO*."

**FIGURE 1. Elements of the Canonical Form of the Received View of Scientific Theories**

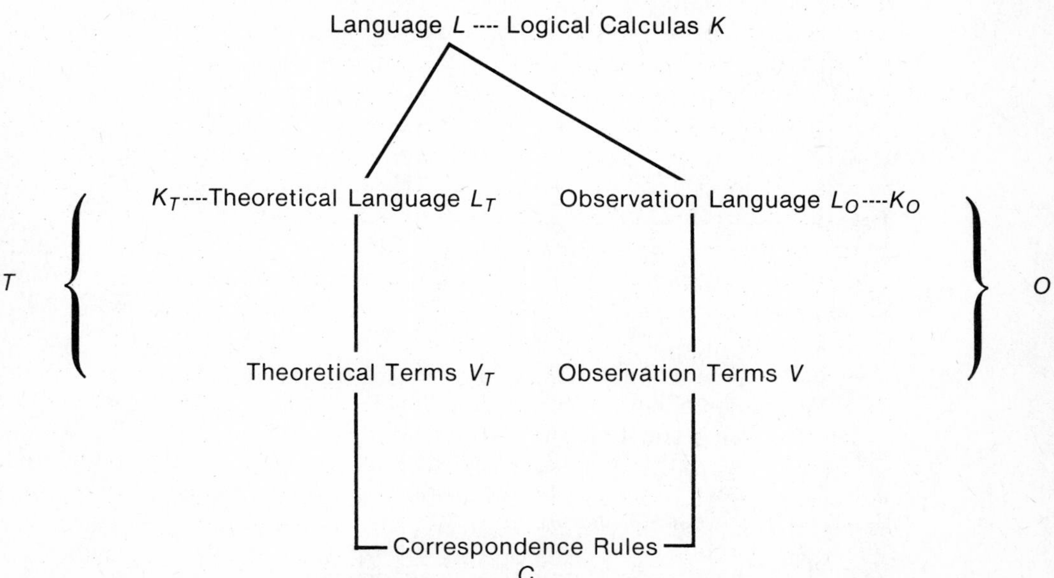

## An Illustration

To make the canonical formulation more concrete, let us illustrate it with a simple example drawn from consumer research. Consider the effect of source credibility in a persuasive communication on attitudes toward a political issue. Classical work in the communication literature suggests that greater source credibility leads to more positive attitudes. Figure 2 presents one way to pictorially represent the structure of the theory.

**FIGURE 2. Representation of the Effects of Source Credibility on Attitude under the Canonical Formulation**

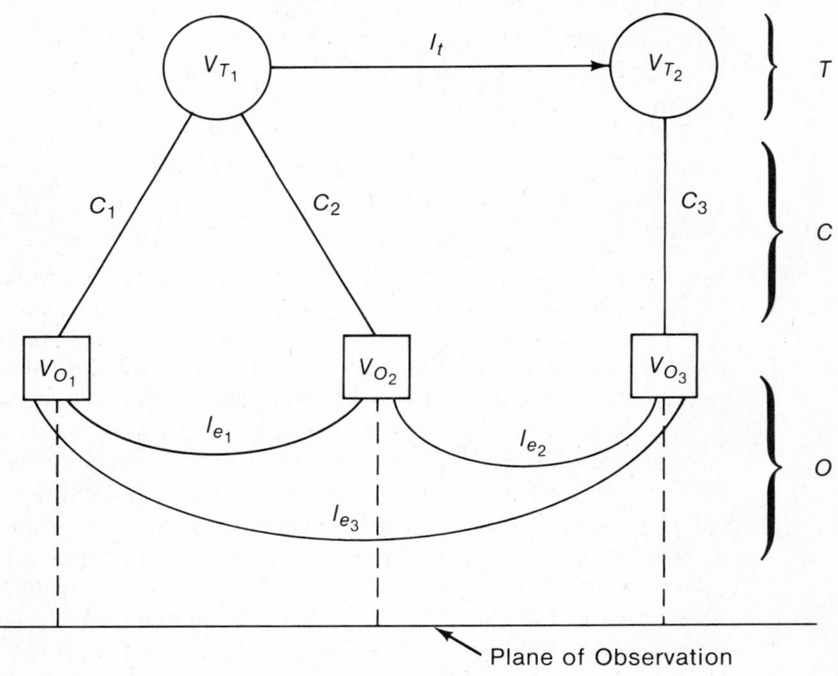


*Key*

| | |
|---|---|
| $V_{T_2}$ | source credibility |
| $V_{T_2}$ | attitude |
| $V_{O_1}$ | experimental manipulation of source credibility |
| $V_{O_2}$ | manipulation check |
| $V_{O_3}$ | operationalization of attitude |
| $l_t$ | theoretical (i.e., nonobservational) proposition: the greater the source credibility, the more favorable the attitude |
| $C_1, C_2, C_3$ | correspondence rules |
| $l_1$ | proposition of empirical association |
| $l_{e_2}, l_{e_3}$ | proposition of empirical generalization |

The central hypothesis of the theory is expressed in sentence form and depicted as $l_t$, a nonobservational proposition. Generally, nonobservational propositions are intended to be statements about actual or potential lawlike generalizations. Two theoretical terms—$V_{T_1}$ and $V_{T_2}$—are contained in $l_t$ and stand for source credibility and attitude, respectively. Although not shown in Figure 2, $V_{T_1}$ and $V_{T_2}$ would each typically be defined with primitive terms, perhaps organized in a particular way according to $K_{T_1}$ and $K_{T_2}$, respectively. For example, source credibility might be defined in terms of expertise and trustworthiness, whereas attitude might be conceptualized as particular affective responses toward the political issue in the communication. All together, $V_{T_1}$, $V_{T_2}$, $l_t$, $K_{T_1}$, $K_{T_2}$, and the primitive terms defining $V_{T_1}$ and $V_{T_2}$ constitute $T$, i.e., the theoretical postulate(s) of the effect of source credibility on attitude. In a full exposition of $T$, we might have primitive terms, definitions, axioms, theorems, and nonobservational propositions.

The $V_T$ are given empirical meaning through $C$. The most common form for correspondence rules advocated by logical empiricists is

$$Ex \rightarrow [P(x) \equiv R(x)]$$

which in words reads, "If $x$ is subjected to experimental test procedure $E$, it will exhibit theoretical property $P$ if and only if it yields result $R$" (e.g., Carnap 1956). We will discuss the implications of this form of $C$ shortly. For now, notice that $P$ corresponds to $V_T$, and $E$ and $R$ correspond to $V_O$. In Figure 2, we see that $V_{T_1}$ has, in fact, two observational terms attached to it, $V_{O_1}$ and $V_{O_2}$. The first might be the experimental manipulation(s) used to create the images of different levels of credibility. For instance, a common procedure is to employ different spokespersons for experimental and control groups such that each person possesses varying levels of knowledge, skill, experience, etc. with the issue at hand. The second observational term might be a manipulation check consisting of measures of perceived expertise and trustworthiness. Similarly, $V_{T_2}$ is shown connected to $V_{O_3}$, where the latter might be physiological, self-report, or other measures of attitude. Next, notice that the $V_O$ are shown interconnected by $l_e$, i.e., empirical propositions. These are statements linking the respective observational terms. For $V_{O_1}$ and $V_{O_2}$, the proposition (i.e., $l_{e_1}$) is expressed as an empirical association, to reflect the fact that the concepts should covary as a consequence of their common content in meaning. The remaining propositions (i.e., $l_{e_2}$ and $l_{e_3}$) are represented as empirical generalizations, to indicate that covariation here occurs as an observational consequence of underlying laws linking different concepts. Finally, notice that each $V_O$ is tied to the plane of observation with dashed lines. This is intended to stand for the actual physical sensations or sense extending data through which the empirical concepts implied by $V_O$ are monitored. This might be a visual movement noted by an experimenter, a check mark placed on a questionnaire, a deflection on a strip chart recorder, or a whole host of other types of observational recording procedures.

## Status of the Canonical Formulation in Marketing

The canonical formulation represents an ideal which, if implemented, would go far toward making our theories more explicit and subject to detailed evaluation. In practice, however, the canonical formulation seldom has been operationalized in marketing. A number of exemplars do exist that approach the ideal in terms of thoroughness of theoretical development and/or methodological rigor. A partial list of these might include Bass (1974), Howard and Sheth (1969), Little (1975), Phillips (1982), and Silk and Urban (1978). However, in general, most research in marketing is build upon theories that are expressed in incomplete forms. Overall, the practice is to address only a portion of the elements comprising the canonical formulation. Notice that we should be concerned with two issues. One is *scope,* which refers to the range of the elements of the canonical formulation that are specified in any particular theory. The second is *quality,* which signifies the adequacy to which each of the criteria included in the scope is attained.

Consideration of the quality of theory construction in marketing is beyond the scope of this essay, and no firm generalizations can be made. With respect to scope, however, at least five potential shortcomings in contemporary marketing practice may be identified.

The first issue concerns the relationships *C* between theoretical and empirical concepts. Typically, these either are not considered at all or are taken for granted. Seldom are correspondence rules specified, and even less seldom are observational implications of the correspondence rules investigated. Without consideration of the relationships between theoretical and empirical concepts, it is not possible to assess the meaning of one's terms in a theory. Closely related to this is the problem of construct validity (Bagozzi 1980, Ch. 5; Peter 1981). Construct validity is the extent to which an operationalization measures the theoretical concept which it is intended to measure. It thus depends on the definitional and theoretical meaning of the concept, the behavior of its measurements, and the semantic and syntactic relationahips between the two. Our ability to detect true empirical generalizations and interpret them as evidence of underlying nonobservational propositions is dependent fundamentally on construct validity and the relationships between theoretical and empirical concepts. Failure to specify correspondence rules and employ valid measurements of concepts in our theories not only creates a lacuna between theory construction and hypothesis testing but prevents one from addressing the degree of confirmability or falisfiability of theories. From an epistemological perspective, testability is an essential property that must be formally integrated with our theories if they are to have meaning (Popper 1959). This should be done without invoking a neutral observation language. That is, data do not exist independent of the theories we use to account for them. Swinburne (1971) discusses important paradoxes of confirmation and recent attempts to solve them.

A second issue is empirical. In addition to the degree of correspondence between theoretical and observational terms, our ability to assess and interpret theories rests on the fidelity of our measurements. The practice in marketing and the social sciences has been to focus upon $l_e$ as a representation of $l_t$ (see Figure 2). Unfortunately, to the extent that measurements are unreliable and/or that systematic methodological confounds or other biases exist, $l_e$ will deviate from $l_t$. Notice that random and systematic errors in our measurements can occur even if the latter are valid operationalizations of theoretical concepts, and we have carefully specified the correspondence rules. It has frequently been noted in marketing that the assessment of the reliability of measurements within any particular study is crucial to its evaluation, yet is seldom performed (Peter 1979, Ray 1979). To this commentary, we must add that consideration of systematic error is also a rare event.[2] Both obscure our ability to understand phenomena.

The specification of the rationale underlying a nonobservational proposition in a theory is a third important issue. No theory can be considered complete without an explication of why or how the terms in a proposition are linked. A rationale is usually based on cause and effect or functional arguments. In Figure 2, the rationale for $l_t$ was not stated explicitly. Rather, a psychological argument was implied, such as the expected effect of perceived expertise on the believability of message content. Depending on the level of specificity of the theory, the rationale as to why high source credibility should lead to favorable attitudes would either be a premise of the theory or else formally integrated into the theoretical postulates (e.g., through axioms, theorems, or intermediate propositions).

This aspect of theory construction suggests one way how new knowledge is generated. At any one point in time, any theory may provide an explanation for a phenomenon based on the content and structure of its *TCO*. But as we learn more about the specific *TCO* and gain new knowledge from other *TCO*s and areas relevant to, but separate from, the *TCO* in question, a basis may develop for deepening the rationale or revising the *TCO* in some other way. Often, the impetus for change will spring from failures of the *TCO* in prediction or the emergence of disconfirming evidence. In any case, any particular *TCO* will generally serve a transition role over time. It begins as an unproven answer to a problem or research question. Then it achieves a certain degree of success and is recognized as a valid explanation of some phenomenon. But sooner or later it will become inadequate to the tasks of explanation, prediction, and control, and must either be discarded, revised, or subsumed under a more general *TCO*. The transition might be gradual or radical, such as is reflected in Kuhn's (1970) idea of paradigm shifts and scientific revolutions.

To take an example, consider how a cognitive response rationale for the effect of source credibility on attitude might look under the canonical formulation of the Received View. Figure 3 presents an outline of a cognitive

**FIGURE 3. Expanded Canonical Representation of the Effects of Source Credibility on Attitudes (presented in abbreviated form for simplicity)**

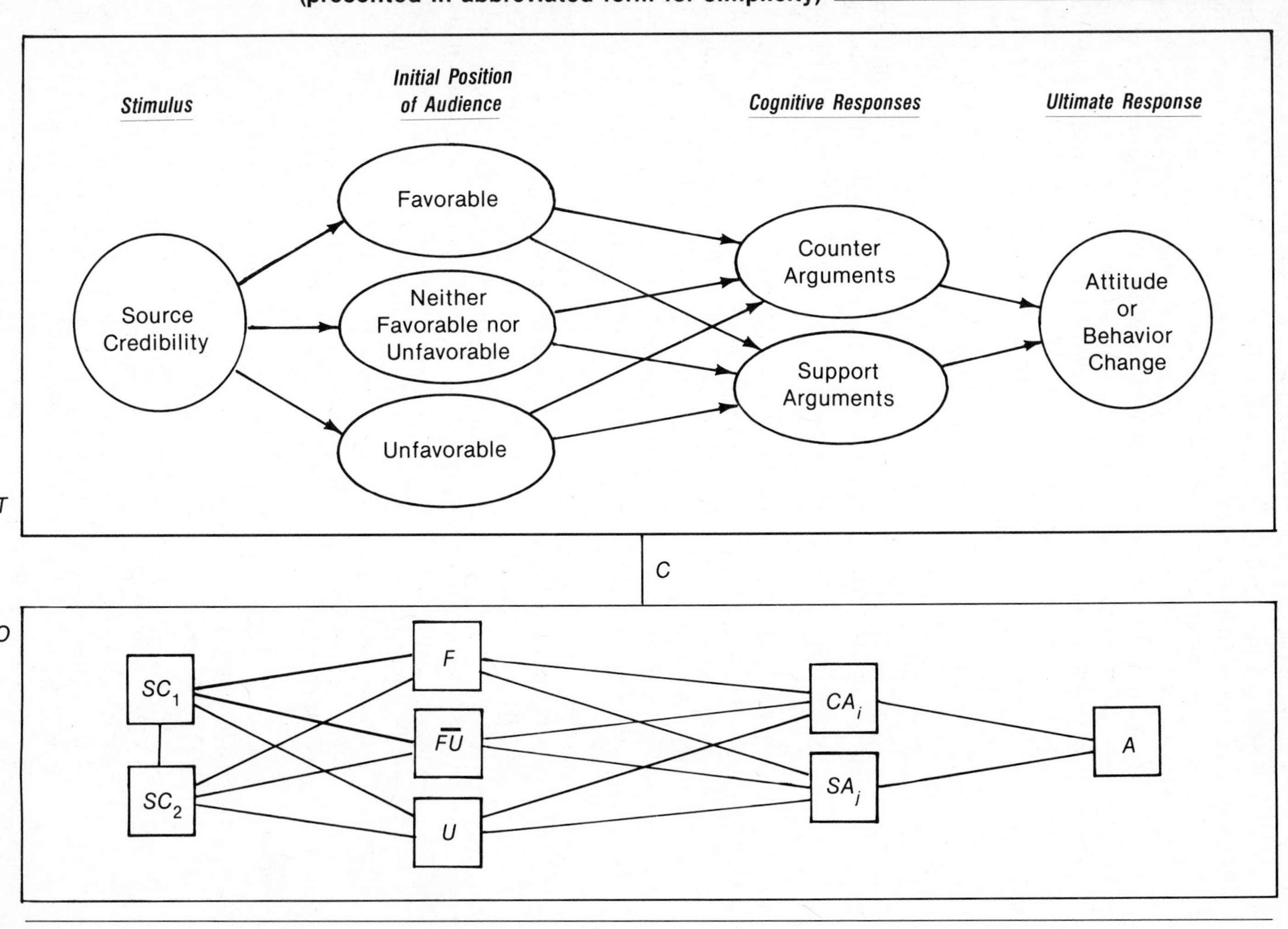

response schema which supplants the classic interpretation of Figure 2. Instead of one nonobservational proposition between source credibility and attitude, many are proposed. Moreover, the rationale is deepened. The impact of source credibility is hypothesized to be contingent on whether the audience is initially favorable, unfavorable, or neither favorable nor unfavorable toward the issue at hand. Depending on the audience's initial receptivity, source credibility will differentially affect cognitive responses. Cognitive responses, in turn, will be integrated with evaluative and decision-making processes and influence attitudes and/or behavior. One set of predictions might be:

1. Highly credible sources will be *more persuasive* than less credible sources when the receiver is *initially unfavorable* toward a message.
2. Highly credible sources will be *less persuasive* than less credible sources when the receiver is *initially favorable* toward a message.
3. Highly credible sources and less credible sources will not differ in their persuasive effects when the receiver is initially neither favorable nor unfavorable toward a message.[3]

The rationale for these theoretical predictions might be provided as follows. Consider first the prediction that highly credible sources will be more persuasive than less credible sources when the receiver is initially unfavorable toward the message. Under these circumstances, high credibility is hypothesized to inhibit counterargumentation, whereas low or moderate credibility is hypothesized to facilitate it. No change in support arguments is expected, since the receiver is unfavorable at the start. As a consequence, those receivers exposed to highly credible sources will have fewer negative evaluations to integrate and should have more favorable attitudes than those exposed to less credible sources. In contrast, highly credible sources are expected to be less persuasive than less credible sources when the receiver is initially favorable toward a message. Here it is maintained that low credibility leads to the generation of more support arguments than high credibility. This is thought to occur because low credibility threatens one's initial position, and to relieve the tension, one generates positive support for the message. However, no difference in counterargumentation between those exposed to high versus low credible sources is expected because the receivers are initially favorable. Hence, those receivers exposed to high versus low credible sources will have fewer positive evaluations to integrate and should have less favorable attitudes. Finally, for receivers neither favorable nor unfavorable toward a message, source credibility is hypothesized to have no discernable impact, as no difference in the balance of counter arguments and support arguments should arise.

Thus, returning to the issue of knowledge production, we can see that there are two ways in which new knowledge is generated. One occurs as outlined above. A given theory is refined through expansion of the number of nonobservational propositions between independent and dependent variables and/or deepening of the rationale behind the propositions. Or secondly, an older theory is replaced with a newer one. In both cases, new knowledge is not produced until the refined or new theory is found to provide a more general explanation and/or more accurate predictions.

The fourth shortcoming in theory construction in marketing is the failure to systematically consider rival hypotheses. Any test of a theory, even if performed under controlled conditions, will be subject to alternative interpretations (Popper 1959, p. 50). Sometimes this will stem from methodological inadequacies that either allow natural (but unknown) external forces to contaminate relationships of interest or else introduce artificial confounds (e.g., demand characteristics, response sets). At other times theories may be ambiguous, incomplete, or less powerful than alternatives. Generally, it is not possible to eliminate all rival hypotheses because our methodologies are imperfect and our theories are embryonic. But at a minimum, we can search and test for alternative explanations for the phenomena we study. Platt (1964) was an early person to advocate the systematic pursuit of rival explanations and suggested the following procedure:

1. Devise alternative hypotheses.
2. Formulate crucial experiments, each with multiple possible outcomes that exclude one or more of the hypotheses.
3. Execute the crucial experiments.
4. Recycle the sequence as needed to consider still other rival hypotheses for the original hypothesis and/or rival hypotheses.

It is important to stress that tests of rival hypotheses should not be reserved for separate studies but should be performed whenever possible within the context of an on-going study. In this way, because subjects, settings, instruments, etc. are held constant, we will have greater confidence in the internal validity of the rival hypotheses. The additional test of rival hypotheses in other contexts is also advocated herein and provides evidence for external validity. For examples of the use of tests of rival hypotheses as support for inferences, see Bagozzi (1981a) and Phillips (1982).

A final shortcoming of theory construction in marketing can be seen through reference to Figure 3. In practice, within the purview of any specific study, marketers have tended to emphasize either the theoretical postulates $T$ or the implied empirical observations $O$.

Examples of the former can be found in some management science models in marketing. Here elaborate networks of nonobservational propositions are specified, and while these are generally internally consistent and well-formed, tests of the theory are typically performed either on limited subsets of the network or else only on operationalizations of single theoretical variables in the network. For instance, a common practice is to use a logic regression to predict choice, where the latter is a dependent variable at the end of a long chain of premises and nonobservational propositions. The problem here is that the correpsondence between $T$ and $O$ is often a loose one, and the concatenation of assumptions and hypotheses is not really tested. It is difficult, if not impossible, to ascertain whether successful or unsuccessful predictions of the theory are meaningful. Successful predictions at best suggest that the subset of the network tested might be valid. But it also makes those assumptions and propositions not directly tested ambiguous, since many other frameworks could interface and be consistent with the tested subset. Unsuccessful predictions also produce ambiguity, in that one does not know whether (a) the subnetwork is flawed, (b) a portion of the remaining network is invalid, (c) the entire remaining network is inadequate, or (d) both the subnetwork and remaining network are at fault. To develop more valid theories, one must either reduce the size of the theoretical network to better match the observational framework, or else expand the number of observations to better conform with the theory. In either case, there is a need to better tie theoretical concepts to observations in a formal *TCO*. Chains of theoretical concepts with more than two uninterpreted concepts in a row are to be avoided. Indeed, most theoretical concepts should be directly tied to one or more observations each. Focus on a full *TCO* would shift scrutiny from sterile tautologies to testable theories.

In contrast to management science models in marketing which overemphasize *T* at the expense of *C* and *O*, consumer behavior research tends to overemphasize *O* at the expense of *T* and *C*. That is, rather than developing an overall *TCO* framework, theories are typically tested at the level of *O* only. The danger here is that research could gravitate toward a type of raw empiricism rather than achieving a balance between sound theory construction and empirical verification.

Taking the source credibility model of Figure 3 as an example, the practice has been to provide a loose theoretical discussion of *T* but to investigate hypotheses strictly at the level of *O*. Because correspondence rules are not explicitly considered, measurement error is implicitly assumed to be negligible, and focus is placed strictly upon association among measurements (i.e., on $l_e$), it is not possible to interpret findings unambiguously. Positive findings (e.g., significant *F* tests) do not rule out the possibility of interpretational confounding, i.e., *O* could correspond with many alternative *T*s, and it would not be clear what positive findings signify. Similarly, positive findings could occur because of systematic methodological confounds. Negative findings, in contrast, might indicate rejection of the (ambiguous) theoretical hypotheses, excessive random measurement error, lack of construct validity, methodological biases, or combinations of these. In any case, unless (a) measurement error in independent and dependent variables is truly low, (b) the specification and test of *O* closely corresponds to *T*, and (c) methodological confounds are absent, the research will be uninterpretable. Therefore, it is again recommended that emphasis be placed on a *TCO*. Although this will not guarantee that all biases and confounds have been accounted for or that a theoretical hypothesis is validly operationalized, it does allow one to estimate and correct for random and systematic errors and test for observational implications of correspondence rules and nonobservational propositions. The Holistic Construal presented hereafter attempts to accomplish these goals, while circumventing certain problems in the Received View. Let us consider these problems now before turning to the Holistic Construal.

## Some Fundamental Problems

Perhaps because the question of what is a scientific theory is so complex and difficult to answer, considerable ambiguity exists throughout the many facets of the Received View. We will consider only a few of the more obvious problems herein.[4]

***Theoretical and Empirical Terms.*** Many proponents of the Received View have tended to draw a sharp line between theoretical and empirical terms. Theoretical terms refer to nonobservable properties or objects, whereas empirical terms refer to observable properties or objects.[5] However, as others have pointed out (e.g., Achinstein 1968), none of the proponents has specified sound criteria for the distinction, and these may well not exist. Carnap (1966, pp. 225-226) takes the position that theoretical and empirical terms are on end points of a continuum and that differences are a matter of degree. He does not indicate how one might differentiate between theoretical and empirical terms in any one theory, however. It is necessary to have a clear meaning for unobservable and observable terms in order to determine construct validity and differentiate between lawlike generalizations on the one hand and accidental or spurious associations on the other hand. Athough no satisfactory solution seems as yet to exist in the philosophy of science, an attempt will be made later in this article to refine the meaning of terms in any theory.

***Correspondence Rules.*** Correspondence rules serve to provide empirical significance to theoretical terms, and in so doing, help us understand and validate the meaning of our theories. At least three interpretations of correspondence rules have been given under the Received View. One is that a correspondence rule is an analytic proposition between $V_T$ and $V_O$. Thus, it is believed to be true or false and to depend on the logical form of the sentence in which it is expressed and on the meaning of the terms in it. A second interpretation of a correspondence rule is that it is a convention. It functions much in the same way as a definition, wherein the meaning of a theoretical term is specified to be entailed in a given empirical concept through a priori agreement among "authorities." The problem with both the analytical and conventional interpretations of correspondence rules is that they preclude a role for empirical testing and historical development of meaning for theoretical terms. Indeed, the analytic interpretation implies that observations and experimental procedures are logical implications of a priori premises, rather than contingent assertions about the world of experience. Similarly, the conventional interpretation places empirical meaning in the realm of expert opinion. Thus, either perspective tends to exclude empirical meaning from theoretical terms, and this, in turn, leads to ambiguity as to construct validity and testability. A third interpretation is that a correspondence rule is a synthetic proposition. Its truth or falsity can be determined by factual information in the world of experience, rather than by the logical truth implied by the form in which it is expressed. This overcomes the neglect of empirical meaning by the other two approaches, but at the same time, makes it more difficult to arrive at lawlike generalizations (i.e., $l_t$) which occur between unobservable terms. In short, it appears that correspondence rules are neither analytic, conventional, nor synthetic statements. Under the Holistic Construal, we will attempt to provide a more formal and less ambiguous interpretation of correspondence rules. A final point to note here is that correspondence rules under the Received View are generally taken to supply all of the empirical (i.e., observable) meaning that theoretical terms have. The possibility for additional sources of empirical meaning will be introduced under the Holistic Construal.

***Laws and Regularities.*** Proponents of the Received View have been unclear as to the meaning of laws and how scientific theories relate to them. For many logical empiricists, the purpose of theories is to arrive at empirical laws, i.e., regularities among observations. Focus is upon $l_e$. In fact, some authors go so far as to state that the use of theoretical terms and nonobservational propositions is superfluous, and one should attempt to eliminate and replace theoretical terms with observable ones (Craig 1956; cf. Hempel 1965, pp. 210-215; Nagel 1961, pp. 134-137). One problem with this policy is that our theories would not be extendable to new contexts and time periods.

A slightly different position is offered by Carnap (1966, pp. 226-231). While acknowledging the existence of empirical laws, he notes that theoretical laws—i.e., regularities between theoretical terms—are also possible. These are thought to be more general than empirical laws and to explain the latter:

> An empirical law helps to explain a fact that has been observed and to predict a fact not yet observed. In similar fashion, the theoretical law helps to explain empirical laws already formulated, and to permit the derivation of new empirical laws. (p. 229)

Nevertheless, Carnap seems to place primary importance on empirical laws:

> The confirmation of a theoretical law is indirect because it takes place only through the confirmation of empirical laws derived from the theory.
>
> The supreme value of a new theory is its power to predict new empirical laws. (p. 231)

Because of the need to search for fundamental generalizations and causal relations and the inherent contamination present in observations (due to random and systematic error), we see a need for a shift in emphasis away from empirical laws to theoretical "laws." The Holistic Construal tries to present a new formulation of the structure of theory to accomplish this goal by focusing on the causal properties of structures.

***The Image of Science.*** The Received View sees science in a particular light. Knowledge is thought to begin with observation. This leads to empirical generalizations among observable entities. As our ideas progress, theories are formulated deductively to explain the generalizations, and new evidence is used to confirm or disconfirm the theories. Throughout the process, data are given precedence. Indeed, the entire process is viewed as essentially an inductive one. Science in general and knowledge in particular are believed to occur in an upward fashion: from data to theory to understanding. Feigl (1970, p. 7) terms this "an 'upward seepage' of meaning from the observational terms to the theoretical concepts," and it is construed in a similar way by Hempel (1952, p.36), Carnap (1939, p. 65), and others identified with the Received View.

At least two problems can be identified with this outlook. First, it does not conform well with how science is actually conducted. Science is influenced by the characteristics of individual scientists (Fisch 1977, Mahoney 1976) and social forces (Merton 1973, Mitroff 1974), and begins just as frequently with theory as it does with observations. Second, our presuppositions, biases, and cognitive faculties influence and constrain the so-called immutable data (Nisbett and Ross 1980, Thorndyke and Hayes-Roth 1979). Rather than a data-driven process, science is more and more being described as a theory-driven activity (Brown 1979, Chaps. 6 and 7; Suppe 1977, pp. 125-221). Nevertheless, it is probably more accurate to regard theory and data in an inseparable and reflexive way. In this spirit, the Holistic Construal strives to more accurately serve as a model for the structure of theory.

## AN ALTERNATIVE: THE HOLISTIC CONSTRUAL[6]

Figure 4 presents a diagram of the elements and structure of the Holistic Construal. For purposes of discussion, we will consider the Holistic Construal in three parts, but it should be stressed that the entire network is needed for a full representation and interpretation of any theory. Our pedagogical subdivision of the Holistic Construal is based on the ways of ascertaining meaning in any theory: conceptual meaning, empirical meaning, and spurious meaning. Together, the three types of meaning combine in an integrated way to form the basis for theory construction and its use in explanation, prediction, and control.

**FIGURE 4. The Elements and Structure of the Holistic Construal**

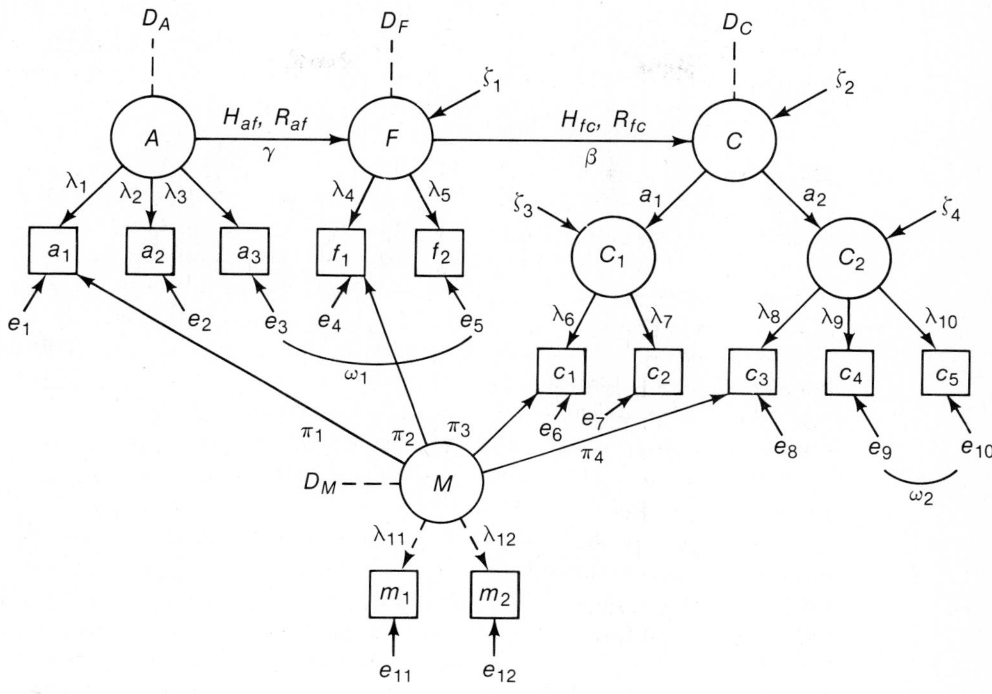


***Definition of Symbols Used in Figure 4***

***Theoretical Concepts***

- $A$ Antecedent
- $F$ Focal Concept
- $C$ Consequent
- $M$ Method Factor

***Empirical Concepts***

- $a_i$ Measurements of $A$
- $f_j$ Measurements of $F$
- $c_k$ Measurements of $C$
- $m_l$ Measurements of $M$ (if they exist)

- $D_A, D_F, D_C, D_M$ Definitions of Theoretical Concepts (expressed as attributional, structural, and/or dispositional definitions)
- $H_{af}, H_{fc}$ Nonobservational propositions relating antecedent and consequent to focal concept, respectively
- $R_{af}, R_{fc}$ Rationales for $H_{af}$ and $H_{fc}$, respectively
- $\gamma, \beta$ Inferred (i.e., estimated) representations for $H_{af}$ and $H_{fc}$, respectively
- $\lambda_m$ Inferred (i.e., estimated) implications of correspondence rules relating theoretical concepts to empirical concepts
- $\alpha_1, \alpha_2$ Inferred (i.e., estimated) derivation "definitions" for subdimensions of $C$
- $\pi_n$ Inferred (i.e., estimated) contribution of $M$ (i.e, that due to systematic error)
- $\omega_1$ Correlated error terms across constructs
- $\omega_2$ Correlated error terms within constructs
- $\zeta_o$ Errors in equations or conceptual error (i.e., unexplained variation in theoretical variables)
- $e_p$ Errors in variables or measurement error (i.e., random error)

## Conceptual Meaning

To grasp the idea of conceptual meaning, let us consider the focal concept *F* shown at the top center of Figure 4. In general, the conceptual meaning of *F* is obtained through a specification of (1) its definition, or more broadly what it is, and (2) its relation to other concepts in a larger theoretical network, that is, its relation to *A* and *C*. Notice that the meaning of *F* depends in part on other concepts in the theory.

The definition of a concept is a linguistic operation(s) that establishes a relationship(s) between a focal term and one or more other terms. Although the relationship(s) might be one of equivalence or identity, it may also be one of refinement, expansion, or partial specification, under certain conditions noted hereafter. Typically, three types of definitions can be seen to contribute to the conceptual meaning of a theoretical concept: attributional, structural, or dispositional definitions.

An *attributional definition* specifies the attributes, characteristics, or properties of a concept. An atomistic attributional definition states all of the characteristics that a concept possesses. For example, an expectancy-value model of attitude toward an act might be defined as the sum of the products of beliefs about the consequences of the act times the evaluations of those consequences. Each attribute (i.e., beliefs and evaluations) is a necessary component of the definition, and all attributes together sufficiently define attitude. Let us contrast the atomistic attributional definition to the cluster attributional definition which consists of a group of properties wherein not all, but many, must be possessed by a concept (Achinstein 1968, Chaps. 1 and 2). That is, none of the attributes in the cluster is required to be a necessary property (although one or a subset may be), and selected subsets are sufficient to define the focal concept. For instance, consider the following definition of attitude: an attitude is a learned predisposition to respond to an object in a preferential or evaluative way. Depending on one's purposes, the predispositions defining attitude might include physiological reactions, expressions of affect (e.g., like or dislike), implicit evaluative responses, beliefs, intentions, and/or approach/avoidance actions. In fact, various authors have employed one or more of these as being consistent with the ideas of "a learned predisposition to respond."

A special case of the cluster attributional definition is the law cluster concept (Putnam 1962). A law cluster concept consists of a group of laws which determine the identity of the concept. Again, not every law is needed to specify the extension of the concept, only a subset. Laws are regularities with a high degree of corroboration. Putnam (1962, p. 379) asserts that "most of the terms in highly developed science are law-cluster concepts." In physics, energy is an example; whereas in marketing, we might stretch things a bit and include the concept of perceived risk as an example because it is defined through "laws" of perception, information processing, and motivation.

A *structural definition* of a concept specifies a set of elements (e.g., properties) and relations among elements such that the concept is given meaning through the entire network. The elements might be organized in hierarchical, associative, interactive, or other patterns. An example of a structural definition can be found in Bagozzi's (1981a) representation of attitude toward donating blood. Here attitude was hypothesized to exist as a unidimensional global affective reaction connected to a three dimensional expectancy-value response consisting of perceived consequences of the act and their evaluation. Until recently, the dimensionality of concepts is a topic that has largely been ignored in marketing, as well as in the social sciences.

A third type of definition is the *dispositional definition*. The dispositional definition describes the capacities or tendencies of a concept. An attempt is made to capture the intrinsic nature of a concept through specification of either its characteristics or its internal structure, and the power and/or liability it affords for change or for influencing or being influenced by another concept. Notice that the dispositional definition is in one sense similar to the attributional or structural definitions. However, there is one important difference. The dispositional definition carries with it the implication for undergoing transformation or entering a causal relation under certain conditions. Nicosia's (1978) notion of an organization of percepts-in-tension can be regarded as a dispositional specification of cognitive structure and its emotive potential.

We thus can see that conceptual meaning of a concept is provided through its definition; i.e., though the semantic content of the terms in the definition and the syntactic significance of their organization and relation to the definiendum (i.e., the focal concept). It is important to note that this meaning is distinct from the empirical meaning provided through correspondence rules. Furthermore, conceptual meaning is also provided by the relationships a focal concept has with other concepts within the theoretical postulates in which it is embedded.

In general, in addition to its definition, the conceptual meaning of a focal concept $F$ is obtained through specification of (1) the antecedents, determinants, or causes of $F$, (2) the consequences, implications, or results of $F$, and (3) the associative (i.e., nonfunctional, noncausal) links to $F$. Let us briefly consider these.

As shown in Figure 4, some conceptual meaning of $F$ arises through its antecedents. Whereas a definition specifies what a concept is and perhaps what it is capable of becoming and doing, its antecedents supply information as to where it has been (that is, its history and development) and/or how it is formed or influenced. The meaning is supplied through the content of the hypothesis ($H_{af}$) linking $A$ to $F$ and its rationale ($R_{af}$). The content of $H_{af}$ consists of a statement of the nature of the relationship of $A$ to $F$ and is expressed in proposition form. This might entail a relatively nonspecific statement such as "the greater the magnitude or level of $A$, the less the magnitude or level of $F$," or it might entail a more specific statement as to the functional form of the relationship or even the amount of change expected in *F* as a function of *A*. The rationale for the hypothesis is needed to complete the meaning of *F* provided by *A*. In general, a rationale for a hypothesis can be obtained through specification of the mechanism by which *A* influences *F*. Typically, this will be expressed through theoretical laws and an explication of how *A* produces change in *F* (e.g., a causal explanation).

In a parallel fashion, the meaning of *F* is also determined through its relations to consequences *C* (see Figure 4). That is, the implications of *F* supply information as to where a phenomenon is going, what it can lead to, and/or what influence it has. Again, the meaning arises through delineation of the form of $H_{fc}$ and its rationale $R_{fc}$.

Finally, conceptual meaning of *F* occurs, at times, simply through associative or correlative links to other concepts (not shown in Figure 4). For example, we might interpret part of the meaning of an exchange relationship between wholesaler and retailer through other cooperative and conflictal relations connected to the parties. Associative meaning frequently arises in complex systems of concepts where equilibrating or disequilibrating forces are at work. In consumer behavior, for instance, deprivation might produce a tension or imbalance among needs, drives, and goals. Prior to deprivation, the needs, drives, and goals would be associated in a network and achieve an equilibrium. After deprivation, internal arousal spreads throughout the network as an instigator for action.

## Empirical Meaning

Empirical meaning refers herein to the observational content associated with theoretical terms. This is accomplished formally through correspondence rules.[7] Although corespondence rules also supply empirical meaning in the Received View, they function differently in the Holistic Construal. Recall that in the Received View there is a one-way and upward flow of meaning from observational terms to theoretical terms. In the Holistic Construal, the flow of meaning is basically downward from theoretical terms to observable terms. That is, theoretical terms are hypothesized to imply particular observations. Nevertheless, under certain conditions, either upward or nondirectional (i.e., associative) empirical meaning is possible. Let us consider all of these alternatives.

Table 1 presents the most common ways that correspondence rules are represented. We will look at the point forms first, which reflect the connections between experimental test operations and individual responses.[8] In the *operational definition model*, "we mean by any concept nothing more than a set of operations; *the concept is synonymous with the corresponding set of operations*" (Bridgman 1927, p. 5). One shortcoming of this model is that any new measurement operation implies a new theory. Not only does this result in a proliferation of theories and difficulty in establishing generalities, but it precludes multiple operationalization of theoretical concepts. This, in turn,

**TABLE 1. Formal Models of Correspondence Rules in Scientific Inquiry**

| Model | Point Form | Structural Form |
|---|---|---|
| The Operational Definition Model | $P(x) \equiv (E(x) \rightarrow R(x))$ "$x$ has theoretical property $P$ by definition, if and only if, when $x$ is subjected to experimental test $E$, it yields result $R$." | $P^*(x) \equiv (E(x) \rightarrow R(x))$ & $S(x)$ "$x$ has theoretical property $P^*$ by definition, if and only if, experimental test procedure $E$ is applied and result $R$ occurs and is organized in structure $S$." |
| The Partial Interpretation Model | $E(x) \rightarrow (P(x) \equiv R(x))$ "If $x$ is subjected to experimental test procedure $E$, it will exhibit theoretical property $P$, if and only if, it yields result $R$." | $P^*(y) \rightarrow (E(x) \rightarrow (P(x) \equiv R(x))$ & $S(x)$ "$y$ will have theoretical property $P^*$ if (1) experimental test procedure $E$ is applied to $x$ and its result $R$ is defined to have theoretical property $P$ and (2) $R$ is organized in structure $S$." |
| The Causal Indicator Model | $P(x) \rightarrow (E(x) \rightarrow R(x))$ "If $x$ has theoretical property $P$, then if experimental test procedure $E$ is applied, it will yield result $R$." | $P^*(y) \rightarrow (P(x) \rightarrow (E(x) \rightarrow R(x))$ & $S(x)$ "$y$ will have theoretical property $P^*$ if (1) $x$ having theoretical property $P$ implies that when experimental test procedure $E$ is applied, it will yield result $R$ and (2) $R$ is organized in structure $S$." |

prevents the determination of construct validity (Campbell 1969). For these and other reasons, the operational definition model is no longer advocated by philosophers of science. However, in marketing and the social sciences, the operational definition model has been perhaps the most frequently applied approach. Whenever a theory is tested on observations, and each observation is defined as an operationalization of a single theoretical concept (and vice versa), the operational definition model is implicitly being employed. The aforementioned shortcomings of the Received View with respect to reliability, validity, and testing issues also apply here.

The *partial interpretation model* of correspondence rules is the second point form worth consideration (see Table 1). This should be recognized as the preferred model of correspondence rules under the Received View (Carnap 1956). It is called a partial interpretation because the meaning of a theoretical term is only specified under particular test (i.e., measurement) conditions. In the absence of test conditions, the theoretical term has no meaning. One important implication of the model is that any theoretical term is permitted to have multiple operationalizations. Thus, it is meaningful to consider internal consistency reliability and construct validity, both of which require multiple measurements for their execution. Among other problems, however, the partial interpretation model does not allow theoretical terms to have semantic content over and above that provided by the rule, and any change in a measurement procedure will change the meaning of the corresponding theoretical term (Petrie 1971; Suppe 1977, pp. 102-104). Moreover, although the form of the partial interpretation model does not necessarily imply a directionality between theoretical and empirical terms, proponents of the Received View generally assert that an upward process holds.

As an alternative, the *causal indicator model* deserves scrutiny (e.g., Keat and Urry 1975). Here a causal link is specified between a theoretical term (or network of terms) and a test operation(s) and its result(s). A phenomenon or state represented by a theoretical term is thought to imply or explain observations. The correspondence rule, then, functions as a scientific law linking theoretical term to experimental test procedure to observed results (Schaffner 1969, Sellars 1961). Notice that the correspondence rule is not part of the theory or the observations to which it is linked. Rather, it is an auxiliary hypothesis concerning theoretical mechanisms existing between theoretical terms and observations. Suppes (1962) suggests that a hierarchy of theories links theoretical terms and implied observations: a physical theory (e.g., of the instrumentation), the theory of the experiment, the theory of experimental design, the theory of data, and ceteris paribus conditions. One property of the causal indicator model is that it better conforms to the image of science as a theory-driven process. It is not so much that data are ignored as it is that one's theory implies, through causal laws, certain observations. In addition, the causal indicator model permits an independent semantic interpretation to exist for theoretical terms (e.g., through definitions, analogies, iconic models), and multiple operationalizations are allowed as well. One drawback of the approach is that some observations can be produced by different or multiple theories and/or experimental procedures. Thus, a certain degree of ambiguity exists in the correspondence rule. One way to lessen the ambiguity is to examine the convergent, discriminant, concurrent, predictive, and nomological validities of measures of concepts (Bagozzi 1980, Chap. 5; 1981a).

Before we consider the structural form of the three models of correspondence rules, we should point out that the rigid dichotomy between unobservable and observable terms advocated in the Received View is rejected herein. Rather, it is proposed that three kinds of unobservables and two kinds of observables can be identified. One unobservable $V_T^{(1)}$ is unobservable in principle and includes certain primitives and theoretical terms not subject to observation in even an indirect, inferential way. Nonreductive or emergent phenomena or purely analytical concepts are examples. A second unobservable $V_T^{(2)}$ is also unobservable in principle but either implies empirical concepts or can be inferred from observations. For instance, a consumer's attitude might be reflected in his or her evaluations or choices. The third unobservable $V_T^{(3)}$ is defined in terms of observables. For example, the morale of a salesforce might be defined as the average of the observed morale scores of the individual salespersons. A definition specifies conditions that are both necessary and sufficient. The operational definition model essentially provides meaning to a $V_T^{(3)}$ through its equation to observations in this sense. The partial interpretation model provides a necessary condition and a sufficient condition for theoretical terms. Either a $V_T^{(1)}$ or a $V_T^{(2)}$ can be addressed with a partial interpretation model. The causal indicator model supplies a sufficient, but not necessary, condition for theoretical terms. As with the partial interpretation model, either a $V_T^{(1)}$ or a $V_T^{(2)}$ may be addressed. The operational definition model is a definition, whereas the partial interpretation and causal models are not true definitions.

Two types of observables are proposed. One $V_O^{(1)}$ can be directly observed with one or more of the senses, whereas the other $V_O^{(2)}$ can only be observed with sense extending instruments (e.g., physiological recording instruments, questionnaires). Either $V_O^{(1)}$ or $V_O^{(2)}$ can serve as observations in any of the correspondence rule models.

Let us now consider the structural forms of the correspondence rule models (see Table 1). We see that the operational definition model defines a theoretical term as a function of its observations. Principal components analysis is one way to implement this rule because each component is a linear function of its measurements. The shortcomings of this approach are that it assumes an upward accrual of knowledge while neglecting the possibility of a priori hypotheses, and it rests on a definitional relationship between theoretical and empirical terms. The latter characteristic introduces a conventional and analytical property to empirical meaning rather than specifying a synthetic contingency. Thus, the structural form of the operational definition model, as with its point form, is flawed.

The structural form of the partial interpretation model and the structural form of the causal indicator model both hypothesize that multiple measures can be organized in a set of subdimensions. For example, in Figure 4, consequent C is shown to have two subdimensions $C_1$ and $C_2$, and these, in turn, have two and three measurements associated with them, respectively. Of course, the two models share the aforementioned characteristics noted for the respective point forms.

Correspondence rules supply empirical meaning to theoretical terms and imply that the correspondence can be represented as a matter of of degree. In Figure 4, the empirical implications of correspondence rules are depicted as $\lambda$s. It is important to stress that we do not observe $\lambda$ but rather must infer it from data. For example, $\lambda$ might be a parameter derived from inferential statistics. When we assess the adequacy of $\lambda$, we must not only rely on statistical criteria but also on the conceptual meaning of the correspondence rule employed.

We have drawn the arrows corresponding to the $\lambda$s in Figure 4 from the theoretical concepts to empirical concepts in order to be consistent with the meaning of the causal indicator model. Factor analysis, structural equation models, and causal models most closely conform to this usage (e.g., Bagozzi 1980, Bentler 1980, Joreskog and Sorbom 1982). Nevertheless, under certain conditions, the arrowheads could have been reversed or omitted, depending on the theoretical interpretation and methodology used to operationalize the theory (e.g., Bagozzi and Fornell 1982). The operational definition model assumes that empirical concepts determine the meaning of theoretical terms and is most congruent with principal components analysis and possibly partial least squares and canonical correlation analyses. The partial interpretation model is perhaps the most flexible in terms of its relations to observations. Although it is used most often when empirical concepts determine theoretical concepts, this does not appear to be necessary, and it may be applicable when the opposite sequence is assumed or none at all. However, it still suffers the problems noted for the point form. A final caveat is that various methodologies are not mutually exclusive and sometimes can be used to solve similar problems (e.g., Bagozzi, Fornell, and Larcker 1981; Fornell and Bookstein 1982). The relationships between correspondence rules and data analytic procedures are still little understood, however, and should be approached with caution.

### Spurious Meaning

It would be ideal if our theories could be characterized solely through the representation of conceptual and empirical meaning. However, theory and measurements must be constructed in an imperfect world by imperfect human beings, and the conceptual and empirical meaning of our theoretical terms (and our nonobservational propositions) are, by necessity, contaminated by errors in observations.

In general, this contamination or ''spurious meaning'' occurs in at least two ways: as random measurement error and as systematic error. Let us examine both.

***Random Error.*** To grasp the meaning of random error, consider again Figure 4. Each measurement of an empirical concept (shown as lower case letters enclosed in boxes) can be represented as the sum of a true, theoretical concept plus random error:

$$y = T + e$$

where $y$ = observed measurement, $T$ = true-score (i.e., theoretical concept), and $e$ = random error (Lord and Novick 1968). Intuitively, what this equation means is that our measurements of theoretical concepts reflect not only the process, attributes, or phenomena underlying the theoretical concept but also a deviation around the true theoretical concept. Each attempt at measurement will typically reflect a slight over- or underestimate of the true value of the underlying concept, although in the long run, the mean of these errors will tend to cancel out. Random measurement error can be considered the outcome of the sum of many counteracting forces including, among others, chance variation, haphazard fluctuations in data gathering and instrumentation procedures, and transient changes in the phenomena being studied (e.g., random fatigue, memory, and motor vacillations).

What are the consequences of random error? In general, it may have two effects. The most direct effect is that random error will deflate the value of the parameter $\lambda$ relating a measurement to its respective theoretical concept. That is, the empirically inferred implication of a correspondence rule will indicate less agreement between concept and measurement to the extent that random error is present. Notice in Figure 4 that each measurement will have a separate amount of random error associated with it (shown as $e_i$). Thus, to the extent that random error exists, we will experience lower reliability and greater uncertainty as to the validity of what we are measuring.

The other effect of random error is upon our ability to infer relationships among theoretical concepts. For the simple model of Figure 4, the focal concept $F$ is related to antecedent $A$ through nonobservational proposition $H_{af}$ and to consequent $C$ through nonobservational proposition $H_{fc}$. The inferred estimates for these propositions are shown as $\gamma$ and $\beta$, respectively. Random errors in observations for $A$, $F$, and $C$ will generally suppress the values of $\gamma$ and $\beta$. However, procedures (e.g., structural equation models with latent variables) exist for the correction of the deleterious effects of random error (Bagozzi 1980, Bentler 1980, Joreskog and Sorbom 1982). Nevertheless, random error in measures beyond a certain point (i.e., greater than about 50%) generally leads to a poor overall goodness of fit.

***Systematic Error.*** In addition to random error, spurious meaning occurs as systematic error. Systematic error reflects patterned biases arising from response sets, evaluation apprehension, demand characteristics, methods factors, or omitted variables. These external contaminators induce regular or irregular changes in the means, variances, and/or covariances of observations. This especially becomes a problem when a subset of measurements is so affected. By suppressing or enhancing variation in selected observations in an orderly way, sources of systematic error may influence key phenomena of interest over and above the true causes and random error.

What are the specific implications of systematic error? As with random error, systematic error can influence the values of the $\lambda$s or $\gamma$ or $\beta$ shown in Figure 4. However, rather than a general suppression effect upon these parameters, systematic sources of error can either inflate or deflate parameters, depending upon their pattern and magnitude. Whereas random error tends to make it more difficult to ascertain construct validity or detect causal paths, systematic error can cause us to conclude either that a phenomenon (e.g., a causal relation) is present, when in fact it is not, or that a phenomenon is not present, when in fact it is.

From a practical modeling standpoint, there are at least three ways to detect and take into account systematic error. The simplest, but least satisfactory, is to merely represent the presence and effects of systematic error through correlated residuals in measurements. As shown in Figure 4, there are two classes of correlated residuals: correlated errors across constructs ($\omega_1$) and correlated errors within constructs ($\omega_2$). Correlated errors mean that variation in the respective measurements is produced by something in addition to the underlying theoretical concepts and random error. Unfortunately, not only is the additional cause unknown, but one or more causes could account for the correlated errors. Within the context of structural equation modeling, the use of correlated errors can correct for systematic biases. However, this will always weaken the interpretation of the meaning of the model under investigation. The correlated errors across constructs shown in Figure 4, for example, indicate either the presence of a common method bias in $a_3$ and $f_2$ or an omitted variable that serves as an antecedent (e.g., suppressor or augmentor variable) to both $A$ and $F$. In either case, our confidence that $\gamma$ represents the true relation between $A$ and $F$ will be weakened to the extent of the magnitude of $\omega_1$. Similarly, correlated errors within constructs such as $\omega_2$ in Figure 4 suggest that either $c_4$ and $c_5$ share a common method bias, or $C_2$ is not unidimensional as hypothesized. Again, this weakens the interpretability of the model.

Ideally, one would prefer that no systematic errors occur in a model. In reality, the potential exists for at least some systematic error in most studies. The use of correlated errors might then represent one way to correct for this error but should be used with caution. We suggest that correlated errors be investigated under the following conditions. First, if possible, one should have a plausible hypothesis as to why error terms should be correlated. Correlated errors are sometimes justifiable when the same variable is measured at different points in time, when a common procedure is used to record data, or when other systematic biases can be identified. Second, it is desirable that correlated errors be small in magnitude and have no or a small impact on parameter estimates in a model (i.e., on the $\lambda$s, $\gamma$, and $\beta$ in Figure 4). This would indicate that the importance of the unknown contaminator(s) is small. Along this line, it would be desirable also that the explained variance in measurements accounted for by a hypothesized underlying theoretical concept be greater than about 50% (Fornell and Larcker 1981). This implies that less than 50% of the variation is due to random and systematic errors. Third, the number of significantly correlated errors, no matter how small in magnitude, should be kept to a minimum. Correlated errors change the substantive meaning of a model, so too many correlations would result in a vastly different model. Finally, correlated errors should be employed only as a last resort and after one has explored a pure model without correlated errors and/or a model with unmeasured or measured methods factors, topics to which we will turn shortly. Even under the above conditions, correlated errors detract from the theoretical elegance and empirical interpretability of a model. Nevertheless, correlated errors can be a useful tool in exploratory research if the above safeguards are followed. Of course, cross-validation, examination of rival hypotheses, and an ongoing research program should also be employed whenever feasible to reduce the probability of false inferences.

A slight improvement over the use of correlated errors as a means for addressing systematic error is the introduction of a method factor or methods factors. A method factor is a hypothesized cause of variation in measurements in addition to that arising from random error and the contribution due to a theoretical concept. Figure 4 illustrates a method factor impinging upon the first measurement of each theoretical concept in the model. A common type of method factor is systematic bias from a measurement procedure. For example, in Figure 4, it is possible that $a_1$, $f_1$, $c_1$, and $c_3$ were all obtained from a key informant who exhibited a characteristic bias in each measurement. The remaining measurements are assumed to have been collected by other methods and to not share a common systematic bias. We might then write the causes of total variation in a measurement as follows:

$$y_i = \lambda_i T_j + \pi_i M_k + e_i$$

where $y_i$ = measurement $i$ for true score $T_j$, $M_k$ = a hypothesized method factor, $e_i$ = random error in measurement $y_i$, and $\lambda_i$ and $\pi_i$ reflect the relative contributions of $T_j$ and $M_k$, respectively. This equation proposes that the variation in a measurement can be divided into that due to an underlying theoretical concept, a method factor (i.e., systematic error), and random error (see Bagozzi and Phillips 1982). This is a hypothesis that can be tested.

Methods factors should also be used with caution and only as a last resort. One should have conceptual and/or methodological reasons for introducing a method factor, its influence should be small, few should be employed, and at least 50% variation in measurements should be accounted for by underlying theoretical concepts. Otherwise, as with correlated errors, a danger exists in overfitting or getting ambiguous findings.

The use of methods factors goes somewhat farther and is somewhat more meaningful than the use of correlated errors. In Figure 4, we have drawn the arrows associated with $\lambda_{11}$ and $\lambda_{12}$, respectively, as dashed lines to indicate that two versions of methods factors exist: one without and one with separate measurements for the factors. The version without separate measurements represents the effects of systematic error but does not explicitly identify the source of the error. The version with separate measurements represents both the source and effects of systematic error. For example, if we measured organizational properties of wholesale distributors and used key informants as sources of information (e.g., the chief executive officer, a vice president, and a middle manager within each organization), then we might expect systematic biases from each source. To account for the effects of the bias, we might merely introduce a method factor for each type of respondent. But to more specifically and accurately model the systematic error, we might use position in the organization, knowledgability, education, tenure, or other measures to operationalize the methods factors. Similarly, in consumer behavior research, we might employ different methods to measure phenomena and therefore expect systematic biases associated with each.

In sum, we see that systematic error can be represented on a continuum ranging from a partial accounting of contamination (i.e., correlated errors) to a relatively complete accounting (i.e., methods factors with explicit operationalizations). It should be stressed again that the modeling of systematic error should be done cautiously and in the light of the issues noted heretofore. Moreover, because we can never know the true state of affairs, any test of a model is at best a tentative and imperfect picture of reality. It is perhaps best to construe individual tests as a means to eliminate false hypotheses or to fail to disconfirm plausible ones. Only through research programs or accumulated knowledge over time do we approach an understanding of the workings of a phenomenon.

## Final Comments on the Holistic Construal

The Holistic Construal has its roots in both the philosophy of science and multivariate statistics. However, a number of important differences deserve mention. First, at a global level, the Holistic Construal is broader and more integrative than either philosophy of science or statistical approaches. Philosophers of science have tended to focus on logical and epistemological issues in general and to neglect specific questions as to operationalization and empirical criteria. This is understandable, given their aims and the orientation in philosophy for pursuit of general principles of knowledge and broad normative criteria. By the same token, statisticians have emphasized technical issues and ignored formal criteria of theory construction. They have taken a more mechanical orientation and been less concerned with the philosophical bases and substantive interpretation of research. The Holistic Construal constitutes an effort to bridge the philosophical and statistical traditions by being concerned with conceptual and empirical issues as they relate to a particular research problem and body of research.

The purpose of the Holistic Construal is to provide the foundation for rigorous methodological thinking. Following Kaplan (1964) we construe methodology in its broadest sense to mean concern with ''such procedures as forming concepts and hypotheses, making observations and measurements, performing experiments, building models and theories, providing explanations, and making predictions'' (p. 23). Thus, stress is placed on the formulation of a sound *TCO* and its implementation, test, and interpretation.

In contrast to the Received View, however, a number of differences should be pointed out. First, correspondence rules are not interpreted as analytical, conventional, or synthetic statements. Rather, they are taken as auxiliary hypotheses about the causal implications that theoretical postulates have for observations. Second, theoretical terms and observational terms are regarded neither as mutually exclusive categories nor as end points on a continuum. Instead, three types of theoretical terms and two types of observation terms are proposed. Third, empirical meaning of theoretical terms is not restricted to that provided through correspondence rules, but rather occurs in addition through definitions, analogies, and iconic models. Fourth, scrutiny in the Holistic Construal is upon theoretical laws. Empirical laws are regarded as error-ridden and biased reflections of theoretical laws. Finally, the image of science suggested by the Holistic Construal is one of a downward, theory-driven process. However, although theories are formulated deductively and prior knowledge and world views shape the hypotheses and outcomes, parameter estimation and hypothesis testing are generally accomplished through inductive procedures. Thus, we see a need for greater synergy between theory construction and data analysis. Overall, then, upward feedback from observations must be integrated with the downward influence of theory construction. Researchers have long advocated such a philosophy, but we have lacked a formal means to accomplish this until recently.

It is beyond the scope of this article to consider the statistical aspects of the Holistic Construal (cf. Bagozzi 1980, 1983; Bentler 1980; Bentler and Bonett 1980). But a number of differences from classical procedures commonly employed in marketing should be noted. First, structural equation models with latent variables permit the researcher the opportunity to represent both errors in variables and errors in equations. The error terms in traditional econometric models reflect an amalgam of all errors without providing for a separation and identification of the sources. In Figure 4, the *e*'s are errors in variables (i.e., random error), and the $\zeta$'s are errors in equations (i.e., unexplained variation in latent dependent variables). Not only does this modeling permit a direct assessment of random error, but the structural parameters (e.g., $\gamma$ and $\beta$ in Figure 4) are purged of random error in a manner analogous to that provided by correction for attenuation procedures. Second, the effects of systematic error can also be accounted for under certain conditions through the incorporation of correlated errors and/or methods factors. This is a consequence of the additional information provided by multiple measures of latent variables, a feature not possible with classic regression analyses. Third, structural equation models with latent variables give the researcher a powerful and straightforward means to examine reliability and various forms of validity. Heretofore, these diagnostics were based on more error ridden and arbitrary correlation procedures. Finally, the statistical tests applied to models formulated under the Holistic Construal allow one to investigate a variety of individual level and multigroup predictions in either controlled laboratory or naturalistic field settings. Of course, depending on whether one uses maximum likelihood, partial least squares, or other methods to operationalize the Holistic Construal, one must be wary of the assumptions and limitations of the techniques.

A final point to note with respect to the Holistic Construal is the importance of making any piece of research an integral part of a body of knowledge. This means drawing upon prior learning in the literature, making special efforts to develop sound measurements (e.g., Churchill 1979), and generally engaging in a research program of interlocking studies over time so that one may get as close to a phenomenon as possible and benefit from the efficiencies and serendipity that often accompanies such endeavors. Examples of early applications of the Holistic Construal can be found in Phillips (1981, 1982) and Bagozzi (1981a, b; 1982).

## Summary and Conclusions

In recent years we have witnessed a considerable degree of dissatisfaction and controversy with the way research has been done in the discipline. This is especially evident in the subareas of management science (e.g., Bass 1982 and Ehrenberg 1970) and consumer behavior (e.g., Jacoby 1978) and touches upon the adequacy and relevancy of our theories, methodologies, measurements, and findings. What accounts for this turmoil? It certainly does not appear to stem from a lack of thoughtfulness by our leaders, for many fine conceptualizations and models exist and continue to be generated. Nor does it seem to arise predominantly from a lack of sophistication in methodology or analysis, for the field is no less rigorous than the disciplines it draws upon.

This author believes that at least part of the problem is due to a failure to meld together the theoretical domain with the empirical. Up until now, at least, we have suffered from a lack of guidelines and formal means to integrate sound theory with rigorous methodology. This has been compounded by a tendency toward specialization. Substantively oriented researchers emphasize conceptual aspects of their research but sometimes place relatively less stress on methods and measures. Methodologically oriented researchers tend to focus relatively more on techniques than on theory development. At the same time, both camps spend more of their energies reading literatures and interacting with others with similar leanings. This tends to perpetuate the split. Nevertheless, probably the most important stumbling block has been the absence of a formal language to link substance with method and data.

Either the Received View or the new realist model provides a way to more purposefully conduct research. The focus of both is upon how theories can and should be constructed. This author has a preference for the realist model and has attempted, through the Holistic Construal, to develop a programme for its operationalization. By addressing the content and structure of our theories in more depth, we can make the science and art of marketing less haphazard and more subject to evaluation and control. Marketing is entering a new era that will demand of its researchers excellence in both theory and method. The irony is that as we become more explicit in our theorizing and modeling, so too will we become more vulnerble to criticism. But perhaps this is the price that must be paid if we are to renew ourselves and innovate. Rather than playing it safe and hiding behind a well-developed theory that is never really tested, or a sophisticated methodology that is applied without sound conceptual groundwork, we should demand of ourselves the best that can be offered in both substance and method. Only then will we push our knowledge to a plane truly reflective of the interplay between theory and data, which is, after all, our only valid window on reality in the marketplace.

## ENDNOTES

1. For a slightly different, but more detailed, description of the Received View, see Suppe (1977, pp. 6-61). Except for a few additions noted hereafter, the notation follows Suppe. Our interpretation of the Received View, however, departs from Suppe's in that we develop the network of implied empirical observations and integrate these with theoretical postulates and correspondence rules. Suppe's treatment focuses relatively more on the logical and nonempirical aspects of theories.
2. Bagozzi and Phillips (1982), Bagozzi and Silk (1983), and Phillips (1981) consider limited aspects of systematic error: namely, that reflected in correlated measurement residuals and in methods factors without explicit measurements. But as we develop hereafter under the Holistic Construal, more formal methods and models are needed to interpret and correct for systematic error in many cases.
3. These propositions are drawn from Sternthal, Dholakia, and Leavitt (1978).
4. For another perspective, see Suppe (1977, pp. 62-118).
5. Some authors use the idea of an "empirical term" in a broader sense to also encompass unobservables.
6. For background on the conceptual development of the Holistic Construal, see Bagozzi (1979, 1980) and Bagozzi and Fornell (1982). More methodologically oriented expositions can be found in Bagozzi (1983) and Bagozzi and Phillips (1982). Illustrations of the Holistic Construal in substantive contexts can be found in Bagozzi (1981a, b; 1982), Phillips (1981, 1982), and Bagozzi and Silk (1983). Sheth (1967, pp. 740-742) was an early scholar in marketing who recognized the need for a holistic framework based on the philosophy of science.
7. We might informally allow some empirical content to be attributed to the meaning of theoretical terms through their definitions. That is, the primitive terms or dispositional implications of the definitions might convey empirical meaning. This arises through convention and is a historical development of intersubjective agreement among scientists concerned with a particular theory. When we draw on past research in theory construction, we often implicitly assign some empirical meaning to theoretical concepts or at least their attributes. Another way that empirical meaning arises (in addition to definitional and correspondence rule sources) is through a putative iconic relation to a model (e.g., Hesse 1970; Nagel 1961, pp. 90-117). Here a physical analogy is used to represent the theory or part of it. Notice that empirical meaning in the Holistic Construal is not restricted to that provided by correspondence rules as it is in the Received View. Our expansion of the sense

of empirical meaning allows one to represent the effect on the structure of theory of historical and political processes among scientists.

8. For a discussion of the operational definition and partial interpretation point forms, see Petrie (1971). Keat and Urry (1975) discuss the causal indicator point form. To this author's knowledge, first consideration of the structural form was by Bagozzi and Fornell (1982).

## REFERENCES

Achinstein, P. (1968), *Concepts of Science*, Baltimore, MD: Johns Hopkins Press.

Bagozzi, R. P. (1976), "Science, Politics, and the Social Construction of Marketing," in *Marketing: 1776-1976 and Beyond*, K. L. Bernhardt, ed., Chicago: American Marketing, 586-592.

——— (1979), "The Role of Measurement in Theory Construction and Hypothesis Testing: Toward a Holistic Model," in *Conceptual and Theoretical Developments in Marketing*, O. C. Ferrell, S. W. Brown, and C. W. Lamb, eds., Chicago: American Marketing, 15-33.

——— (1980), *Causal Models in Marketing*, New York: John Wiley.

——— (1981a), "An Examination of the Validity of Two Models of Attitude," *Multivariate Behavioral Research*, 16 (July), 323-359.

——— (1981b), "Attitudes, Intentions, and Behavior: A Test of Some Key Hypotheses," *Journal of Personality and Social Psychology*, 39 (October), 607-627.

——— (1982), "A Field Investigation of Causal Relations among Cognitions, Affect, Intentions, and Behavior," *Journal of Marketing Research*, 19 (November), 562-583.

——— (1983), "A Holistic Methodology for Modeling Consumer Response to Innovation," *Operations Research*, 31 (January-February), 128-176.

——— and C. Fornell (1982), "Theoretical Concepts, Measurements, and Meaning," in *A Second Generation of Multivariate Analysis, Vol. II, Measurement and Evaluation*, C. Fornell, ed., New York: Praeger.

———, ———, and D. F. Larcker (1981), "Canonical Correlation Analysis as a Special Case of a Structural Relations Model," *Multivariate Behavioral Research*, 16 (October), 437-454.

——— and L. W. Phillips (1982), "Representing and Testing Organizational Theories: A Holistic Construal," *Administrative Science Quarterly*, 27 (September), 459-489.

——— and A. J. Silk (1983), "Recall, Recognition, and the Measurement of Memory for Print Advertisements," *Marketing Science*, 2 (Spring), 95-134.

Bass, F. M. (1974) "The Theory of Stochastic Preference and Brand Switching," *Journal of Marketing Research*, 11 (February), 1-20.

——— (1982), "A Discussion of Different Philosophies in the Analysis of Advertising-Sales Relationships," Dallas: University of Texas, working paper.

Bentler, P. M. (1980), "Multivariate Analysis with Latent Variables: Causal Modeling," *Annual Review of Psychology*, 31, 419-456.

——— and D. G. Bonett (1980), "Significance Tests and Goodness of Fit in the Analysis of Covariance Structures," *Psychological Bulletin*, 88 (No. 3), 588-606.

Bridgman, P. W. (1927), *The Logic of Modern Physics*, New York: MacMillan.

Brown, H. I. (1979), *Perception, Theory, and Commitment: The New Philosophy of Science*, Chicago: University of Chicago Press.

Campbell, D. T. (1969), "Definitional Versus Multiple Operationalism," *Et Al*, 2, 14-17.

Carnap, R. (1939), *Foundations of Logic and Mathematics*, Chicago, IL: University of Chicago Press.

——— (1956), "The Methodological Character of Theoretical Concepts," in *Minnesota Studies in the Philosophy of Science*, Vol. I, H. Feigl and M. Scriven, eds., Minneapolis: University of Minnesota Press, 33-76.

——— (1966), *An Introduction to the Philosophy of Science*, New York: Basic Books.

Churchill, G. A., Jr. (1979), "A Paradigm for Developing Better Measures of Marketing Constructs," *Journal of Marketing Research*, 16 (February), 64-73.

Craig, W. (1956), "Replacement of Auxiliary Expressions," *Philosophical Review*, 65, 38-55.

Ehrenberg, A. S. C. (1970), "Models of Fact: Examples from Marketing," *Management Science*, 16 (March), 435-445.

Feigl, H. (1970), "The 'Orthodox' View of Theories: Remarks in Defense as Well as Critique," in *Minnesota Studies in the Philosophy of Science*, Vol. 4, M. Radner and S. Winokur, eds., Minneapolis: University of Minnesota Press, 3-16.

Feyerabend, P. K. (1965), "Problems of Empiricism," in *Beyond the Edge of Certainty*, R. Colodny, ed., Englewood Cliffs, NJ: Prentice-Hall, 145-260.

——— (1970), "Against Method: Outline of an Anarchistic Theory of Knowledge," in *Minnesota Studies in the Philosophy of Science*, Vol. 4, M. Radner and S. Winokur, eds., Minneapolis: University of Minnesota Press, 17-130.

Fisch, R. (1977), "Psychology of Science," in *Science, Technology, and Society: A Cross-Disciplinary Perspective*, I. Spiegel-Rosing and D. deSolla Price, eds., London: Sage.

Fornell, C. and F. L. Bookstein (1982), "A Comparative Analysis of Two Structural Equation Models: LISREL and PLS Applied to Market Data," *Journal of Marketing Research*, 19 (November), 440-452.

——— and D. F. Larcker (1981), "Evaluating Structural Equation Models with Unobservable Variables and Measurement Error," *Journal of Marketing Research*, 18 (February), 39-50.

Hanson, N. R. (1971), *Observation and Explanation: A Guide to Philosophy of Science*, New York: Harper and Row.

Hempel, C. G. (1952), *Fundamentals of Concept Formation in Empirical Science*, Chicago: University of Chicago Press.

——— (1956), *Aspects of Scientific Explanation*, New York: Free Press.

Hesse, M. B. (1970), *Models and Analogies in Science*, Notre Dame, IN: University of Notre Dame Press.

Howard, J. A. and J. N. Sheth (1969), *The Theory of Buyer Behavior*, New York: John Wiley.

Hunt, S. D. (1976), *Marketing Theory: Conceptual Foundations of Research in Marketing*, Columbus, OH: Grid.

Jacoby, J. (1978), "Consumer Research: A State of the Art Review," *Journal of Marketing*, 42 (April), 87-96.

Joreskog, K. G. and D. Sorbom (1982), *Analysis of Linear Structural Relationships by the Method of Maximum Likelihood*, Chicago: National Educational Resources.

Kaplan, A. (1964), *The Conduct of Inquiry*, Scranton, PA: Chandler Publishing Company.

Keat, R. and J. Urry (1975), *Social Theory as Science*, London: Routledge and Kegan Paul.

Kuhn, T. S. (1970), *The Structure of Scientific Revolutions*, enlarged ed., Chicago: University of Chicago Press.

Lakatos, T. S. (1970), "Falsification and the Methodology of Scientific Research Programmes," in *Criticism and the Growth of Knowledge*, I. Lakatos and A. Musgrave, eds., Cambridge: Cambridge University Press, 91-196.

Little, J. D. C. (1975), "BRANDAID: A Marketing-Mix Model," Parts I & II, *Operations Research*, 23 (July-August), 628-673.

Lord, F. C. and M. R. Novick (1968), *Statistical Theories of Mental Test Scores*, Reading, MA: Addison-Wesley.

Mahoney, M. J. (1976), *Scientist as Subject*, Cambridge, MA: Ballinger.

Manicas, P. T. and P. F. Secord (1983), "Implications for Psychology of the New Philosophy of Science," *American Psychologist*, 38 (April), 399-413.

Merton, R. K. (1973), *The Sociology of Science: Theoretical and Empirical Investigations*, N. W. Storer, ed., Chicago: University of Chicago Press.

Mitroff, I. (1974), "Norms and Counter-norms in a Select Group of the Apollo Moon Scientists: A Case Study of the Ambivalence of Scientists," *American Sociological Review*, 39 (August), 579-595.

Nagel, E. (1961), *The Structure of Science*, New York: Harcourt, Brace.

Nicosia, F. M. (1978), "Brand Choice: Toward Behavioral-Behavioristic Models," in *Behavioral and Management Science in Marketing*, H. L. Davis and A. J. Silk, eds., New York: Ronald Press, 12-55.

Nisbett, R. E. and L. Ross (1980), *Human Inference: Strategies and Shortcomings of Social Judgment*, Englewood Cliffs, NJ: Prentice-Hall.

Peter, J. P. (1979), "Reliability: A Review of Psychometric Basics and Recent Marketing Practices," *Journal of Marketing Research*, 16 (February), 6-17.

——— (1981), "Construct Validity: A Review of Basic Issues and Marketing Practices," *Journal of Marketing Research*, 18 (May), 133-145.

Petrie, H. G. (1971), "A Dogma of Operationalism in the Social Sciences," *Philosophy of the Social Sciences*, 1 (May), 145-160.

Phillips, L. W. (1981), "Assessing Measurement Error in Key Informant Reports: A Methodological Note on Organizational Analysis in Marketing," *Journal of Marketing Research*, 18 (November), 395-415.

——— (1982), "Explaining Control Losses in Corporate Marketing Channels: An Organizational Analysis," *Journal of Marketing Research*, 19 (November), 525-549.

Platt, J. R. (1964), "Strong Inference," *Science*, 146 (October), 347-353.

Popper, K. R. (1959), *The Logic of Scientific Discovery*, New York: Basic Books.

Putnam, H. (1962), "The Analytic and the Synthetic," in *Minnesota Studies in the Philosophy of Science*, Vol. 3, H. Feigl and G. Maxwell, eds., Minneapolis: University of Minnesota Press, 350-397.

Ray, M. L. (1979), "Introduction to the Special Section: Measurement and Marketing Research—Is the Flirtation Going to Lead to a Romance?," *Journal of Marketing Research*, 16 (February), 1-6.

Schaffner, K. F. (1969), "Correspondence Rules," *Philosophy of Science*, 36 (September), 280-290.

Sellars, W. (1961), "The Language of Theories," in *Current Issues in the Philosophy of Science*, H. Feigl and G. Maxwell, eds., New York: Holt, Rinehart and Winston, 57-77.

Shapere, D. (1969), "Notes Toward a Post-Positivistic Interpretation of Science," in *The Legacy of Logical Positivism*, P. Achinstein and S. Barker, eds., Baltimore, MD: Johns Hopkins Press, 115-160.

——— (1974), "Discovery, Rationality, and Progress in Science: A Perspective in the Philosophy of Science," in *PSA 1972: Proceedings of the 1972 Biennial Meeting of the Philosophy of Science Association. Boston Studies in the Philosophy of Science*, Vol. 20, K. F. Schaffner and R. Cohen, eds., Dordrecht, Holland: Reidel, 407-419.

Sheth, J. N. (1967), "A Review of Buyer Behavior," *Management Science*, 13 (August), B718-756.

Silk, A. J. and G. L. Urban (1978), "Pre-Test Market Evaluation of New Packaged Goods: A Model and Measurement Methodology," *Journal of Marketing Research*, 15 (May), 171-191.

Sternthal, B., R. Dholakia, and C. Leavitt (1978), "The Persuasive Effect of Source Credibility: Tests of Cognitive Response," *Journal of Consumer Research*, 4 (March), 252-260.

Suppe, F. (1977), *The Structure of Scientific Theories*, 2nd ed., Urbana, IL: University of Illinois Press.

Suppes, P. (1962), "Models of Data," in *Logic, Methodology, and Philosophy of Science: Proceedings of the 1960 International Congress*, E. Nagel, P. Suppes, and A. Tarski, eds., Stanford, CA: Stanford University Press, 252-261.

Swinburne, R. G. (1971), "The Paradoxes of Confirmation—A Survey," *American Philosophical Quarterly*, 8 (October), 318-330.

Thorndyke, P. W. and B. Hayes-Roth (1979), "The Use of Schemata in the Acquisition and Transfer of Knowledge," *Cognitive Psychology*, 11 (January), 82-106.

Toulmin, S. (1972), *Human Understanding*, Princeton, NJ: Princeton University Press.

Zaltman, G., K. LeMasters, and M. Heffring (1982), *Theory Construction in Marketing*, New York: John Wiley & Sons.

Zaltman, G., C. R. A. Pinson, and R. Angelmar (1973), *Metatheory and Consumer Research*, New York: Holt, Rinehart and Winston.

# 6 —— "Paradigms Lost": On Theory and Method in Research in Marketing

*Rohit Deshpande*

Reprinted from *Journal of Marketing*, published by the American Marketing Association, Vol. 47 (Fall 1983), pp. 101-110. Reprinted by permission.

There has been much development in the art and science of marketing research in the past half-century or so of its formal existence. The development has been primarily in the adaptation of methodologies borrowed from other disciplines, in increased sophistication of both hardware and software for data collection and analysis, and in growth in methods of reporting and data presentation. However, one area of marketing research has not developed very much, that of theory construction. Although implicit commonsense propositions are constantly being tested in research in marketing, the formal, self-conscious specification of theoretical relationships or models that underpin research activity is of fairly recent origin. Moreover, there is one basic paradigm that is the implicit foundation of both theory specification and the methods used in current academic research—logical empiricism.

These observations may not be readily apparent to researchers in marketing. Yet as this paper will show, the impact of implicitly stressing one theoretical paradigm in the conduct of research necessarily brings with it the inherent biases associated with using that paradigm and its allied methodologies. The purposes of this paper are therefore: (1) to describe the major research paradigms used by scholars in marketing and other social sciences; (2) to show the relationships of quantitative and qualitative methods to their respective theoretical paradigms; (3) to survey recent theoretical work in marketing so as to show the reliance on a particular paradigm; and (4) to offer some thoughts on triangulating different methodologies in order to reduce possible methods bias.

## The Nature of Scientific Paradigms

Let us begin by stating what we mean by "paradigm." Probably the most commonly accepted definition among students of the philosophy of science is that proposed by Thomas Kuhn in his seminal book, *The Structure of Scientific Revolutions* (1962). As Kuhn indicates in this work and later elaborates on in Suppe (1977), a paradigm is a set of linked assumptions about the world which is shared by a community of scientists investigating that world.

Additionally, this set of assumptions provides a conceptual and philosophical framework (sometimes referred to as a weltanschaüng or "world view") for the organized study of the world.

Paradigms, according to Kuhn, are fundamental for the day-to-day work of any science. More specifically, a paradigm accomplishes the following four objectives:

> A paradigm (1) serves as a guide to the professionals in a discipline for it indicates what are the important problems and issues confronting the discipline; (2) goes about developing an explanatory scheme (i.e., models and theories) which can place these issues and problems in a framework which will allow practitioners to try to solve them; (3) establishes the criteria for the appropriate "tools" (i.e., methodologies, instruments, and types and forms of data collection) to use in solving these disciplinary puzzles; and (4) provides an epistemology in which the preceding tasks can be viewed as organizing principles for carrying out the "normal work" of the discipline. Paradigms not only allow a discipline to "make sense" of different kinds of phenomena but provide a framework in which these phenomena can be identified as existing in the first place (Filstead 1979, p. 34).

Clearly, understanding the nature of a paradigm enables a scientist to determine both what problems are worthy of exploration and also what methods are available to attack them. Yet the domain of paradigm explication has only recently been an area of inquiry for scientists. Traditionally, the issue of how a paradigm came to be accepted within a scientific community has received most attention in the field of philosophy.

One of the issues that philosophers, and in particular, philosophers of science have been concerned about relates to the process of knowing. In addressing this epistemological aspect of paradigm development, philosophers have attempted to answer the fundamental question: How do we know what we know? The answers to this basic question are not easy ones, and philosophers have been polarized into different schools of thought, based on their perceptions of how the question should be answered. For the sake of brevity, we will simplify the arguments and identify the two major schools of thought as positivism and idealism. Their adherents continue the debate today in the classic argument between quantitative and qualitative paradigms. This latter polemic is the key point of this paper. However, in order to provide the background for this controversy, it is necessary to briefly review the history of modern scientific thought.

Before we do this, however, it should be noted that in distinguishing between schools of thought, there is a tendency to categorize them in such a fashion that they seem independent and mutually exclusive. Nothing could be farther from the truth. As with any epistemic community, some of its members share certain (but not all) beliefs with members of a rival school. In the discussion that follows, therefore, it should be remembered that we are in reality dealing with a philosophical continuum ranging from positivism to idealism. In order to understand the nature of this continuum, the key characteristics of each of its two poles will be described.

## The Development of Modern Scientific Thought

The growth of marketing as a scientific discipline has followed the development of other fields of social science inquiry. All of these disciplines owe their growth to the notions of scientific method held by the founders and later contributors to each field. In order to understand how marketing developed, it is therefore useful to see how thinking in modern science has developed. This historical backdrop will provide the foundation for the later discussion on theoretical paradigms in marketing.

In the late 15th and early 16th centuries, a very strong faith in rationality existed. In fact, it was mainly because of the existence of this belief in reason that early science could develop (Holzner and Marz 1979). The faith in *reason* as a means of understanding the world was transposed into a faith in *science* as a means of understanding that world. As Francis Bacon is claimed to have said: ''I see it because I experience it.'' This experiential perspective became the cornerstone of scientific thinking. The perception of everyday scientific reality was in terms of human senses—if a phenomenon could not be seen, heard, touched, smelled, or tasted, then it could not exist. This perspective, and its subsequent reformulations, has become known as logical positivism and empiricism (Sjoberg and Nett 1966). The positivists' answer to the fundamental philosophical question mentioned earlier was: We know because of our abilities to sense phenomena.

However, major social change occurring in the late 18th and early 19th centuries led to several fundamental doubts about this response to the issue of how we know what we know. Many scholars began to question the logic and method of science as it concerned understanding human beings. In the forefront of these scholars was a group of German idealists. They were so named because although they granted the existence of a physical reality, they maintained that the mind was the source and creator of all knowledge. Rather than assuming that the social world pre-existed or was a ''given,'' idealists believed that this social world was created by the individuals who live within it (Filstead 1979).

These two basic philosophical positions of positivism and idealism can be understood by relating them to our earlier discussion of paradigms. Very simply, the logical positivist view of the world is synonymous with the quantitative paradigm, while the idealist view of the world is the qualitative paradigm (Patton 1978, 1980).[1]

As Bogdan and Taylor note in their often cited book, *Introduction to Qualitative Research Methods* (1975):

> Two major theoretical perspectives have dominated the social science scene. One [positivism] traces its origins to the great social theorists

> of the nineteenth and early twentieth centuries and especially to Auguste Comte and Emile Durkheim. The positivist seeks the *facts* or *causes* of social phenomena with little regard for the subjective states of individuals. ... The second theoretical perspective [idealism] stems most prominently from Max Weber. [The theorist in this tradition] is concerned with *understanding* human behavior from the actor's own frame of reference (p. 2).

To quote Reichardt and Cook (1979): "... the quantitative paradigm is said to have a positivistic, hypothetico-deductive, particularistic, objective, outcome-oriented, and natural science world view. In contrast, the qualitative paradigm is said to subscribe to a phenomenological, inductive, holistic, subjective, process-oriented, and social anthropological world view" (p. 9, 10).

If the above polysyllabic adjectives seem to obscure the debate, let us just reiterate the last part of Reichardt and Cook's distinction. The metaphor prevalent in the quantitative paradigm is that of natural science. As Mitroff (1974) indicates, this view of the scientific method leads its proponents to believe the natural science model is "good science" while any alternative necessarily must suffer by comparison. In criticizing this "storybook view of science" Mitroff develops another metaphor, that of anthropology, which is adopted into the qualitative paradigm. The latter view of the world assumes the importance of understanding situations from the perspective of the actors or participants in that situation. Proponents of this world view are on the opposite end of an objectivity-subjectivity continuum from those of the positivist school of thought.

In order to explain further the distinctions between the two paradigms, we present the major characteristics of each philosophical position in Table 1. As can be clearly seen from this table, there is not only a great deal of distance between these two paradigms, but also a linking of each to a preferred set of *scientific methods*. In fact, the very use of the terms *quantitative* and *qualitative* implies certain preferences in the kinds of research designs and analyses subsumed by each paradigm.

As noted earlier while discussing the nature of scientific paradigms, it is helpful while introducing characteristics of paradigms to refer to them as if they were mutually exclusive. Although Reichardt and Cook's descriptions of quantitative and qualitative paradigms in Table 1 are thus in this sense polar opposites, it should be kept in mind that individual researchers in all areas, including marketing, fall somewhere along the continuum between the two extremes. Interpretation of Table 1 should therefore be in a *relative* sense (e.g., scientists subscribing to the qualitative paradigm more frequently prefer qualitative methods to quantitative methods, and so on). It should also be noted that since our discussion here centers on the link between theory and method, other epistemological issues (such as the links between theory and the social or political aspects of knowledge) are not presented. The attributes of paradigms in Table 1 thus deal primarily with methodological issues.

**TABLE 1. Characteristics of Quantitative and Qualitative Paradigms***

| *Qualitative Paradigm* | *Quantitative Paradigm* |
|---|---|
| 1. Qualitative methods preferred. | 1. Quantitative methods preferred. |
| 2. Concerned with understanding human behavior from the *actor's* frame of reference. | 2. Seeks the facts of causes of social phenomena without advocating subjective interpretation. |
| 3. Phenomenological approach. | 3. Logical-positivistic approach. |
| 4. Uncontrolled, naturalistic observational measurement. | 4. Obtrusive, controlled measurement. |
| 5. Subjective; "insider's" perspective; close to the data. | 5. Objective; "outsider's" perspective; distanced from the data. |
| 6. Grounded, discovery-oriented, exploratory, expansionist, descriptive, inductive. | 6. Ungrounded, verification-oriented, confirmatory, reductionist, inferential, hypothetico-deductive. |
| 7. Process-oriented. | 7. Outcome-oriented. |
| 8. Validity is critical; "real," "rich," and "deep" data. | 8. Reliability is critical; "hard" and replicable data. |
| 9. Holistic—attempts to synthesize. | 9. Particularistic—attempts to analyze. |

*Adapted from Reichardt and Cook (1979).

This link between theoretical paradigm and research method is a very strong one. In recent writing in the evaluation research area where there is a continuing debate concerning preferred methods, Patton (1978) writes:

> [Evaluation] research is dominated by the largely unquestioned, natural science paradigm of hypothetico-deductive methodology. This dominant paradigm assumes quantitative measurement, experimental design, and multivariate, parametric statistical analysis to be the epitome of "good" science (p. 203).
>
> By way of contrast, the alternative to the dominant hypothetico-deductive paradigm is derived from the tradition of anthropological field studies. Using the techniques of in-depth, open ended interviewing and personal observation, the alternative paradigm relies on qualitative data, holistic analysis, and detailed description derived from close contact with the targets of study (p. 204).

Clearly it is difficult to separate theory and method, and if a scientist accepts a set of linked assumptions about the world shared by a community of scientists (to reiterate the Kuhnian notion of paradigm), then that scientist to a large extent also accepts the criteria for what the appropriate "tools" are (methodologies, instruments, and types and forms of data collection) for investigating that world. As Rist (1977) states, "the selection of a particular methodology is profoundly theoretical. ... Research methods represent different means of acting upon the environment" (p. 43).

The above premise of a strong link between research paradigm and research method may seem obvious, but its implications are perhaps not quite so clear. The following section develops these implications by reviewing the current controversy over appropriate paradigms in marketing.

## Theoretical Paradigms in Marketing

As indicated in the introductory section of this paper, self-conscious reflection on theory construction in marketing is of fairly recent origin. As yet there are only four major books dealing exclusively with metatheoretical issues in marketing and consumer behavior.[2] However, the debate concerning the relevant philosophy of marketing science appears to have begun. Consider, for example, the panel discussion on the implications of current issues in the philosophy of science for marketing at the most recent AMA theory conference. While chairing this panel discussion, Peter (1982) states:

> There has been a revolution in the philosophy of science literature in the past twenty years or so. While there are still those who cling to and attempt to shore up weakneses in the traditional view of science, much of the philosophy of science literature involves approaches which bear little resemblance to logical empiricism. While perhaps not recognized as such, logical empiricism is the dominant philosophical approach employed in marketing and it has come to us in our borrowing of theory construction and research methods from psychology and economics.
>
> With few exceptions, the revolution in philosophical thinking about science has gone unnoticed in marketing (p. 11).

There are two points concerning these statements that we wish to highlight. First, although there was a great deal of debate among panelists regarding what the appropriate philosophical posture was for marketing theory, there was no disagreement regarding Peter and other panelists positioning logical empiricism as the dominant philosophical approach employed in marketing. Second, although panel discussion ranged widely over the merits and demerits of philosophical stances ranging from logical empiricism through relativisim and historicism, there was little discussion of the implications of marketing *theory* for marketing *research method*.

Let us consider each of these issues in turn. The fact that there was no disagreement regarding logical empiricism being the mainstream paradigm in marketing is significant. This is so because panelists included both advocates of the idealist perspective as well as the positivist viewpoint. The substance of the polemic was enjoined by Brodbeck and Hunt for logical empiricism and Anderson, Lutz, Olson, Peter, Ryan, and Zaltman for the qualitative paradigm (Bush and Hunt 1982). Rather than the latter citing instances where marketing thinking exemplified the anthropological tradition, advocates of the qualitative paradigm bemoaned the preponderance of hypothetico-deductive reasoning in marketing work. As for the proponents of the quantitative paradigm, Brodbeck had previously presented a position paper reifying the core ideas of logical empiricism (1982, p. 1-6), while Hunt had delivered a paper answering in the negative the question, "Are the logical empiricist models of explanation dead?" (1982, p. 7-10).

Turning now to the second issue, as mentioned earlier, the panel discussion cited above did not concern itself with what subscription to a particular theoretical paradigm might mean in terms of preference for certain research methods. As indicated in the previous section on the nature of scientific paradigms, accepting a paradigmatic position generally leads to accepting the tools deemed appropriate for data collection. If marketers in general subscribe to a logical empiricist philosophy of how science is done, then the set of research methods used will be those characterized as objective, obtrusive, controlled, and reductionist (see Table 1). However, these methods have certain distinct limitations that make them applicable for only certain kinds of problems (which are described in detail in the next section of this paper). By excluding alternative methodologies, marketing scientists are perhaps unknowingly also constraining themselves into a set of only partially appropriate techniques for a limited subset of marketing problems. Only a few marketing scholars have recognized this fact. Sheth, for example, comments on the lack of qualitative research in consumer behavior by stating:

> We must lean toward more exploratory and qualitative research tools and tactics such as focused group interviews, projective techniques, clinical methodologies, and nonstructured surveys rather than experimental designs, construct development and measurement or laboratory studies (1981, p. 356).

This is not to say that qualitative research in marketing does not exist. On the contrary, there was tremendous interest in the topic in the fifties and sixties. Books by Dichter (1964), Ferber and Wales (1958), Murstein (1965), and Newman (1957) were widely read and referenced. But, as Bellenger, Bernhardt, and Goldstucker (1976) point out in their monograph on qualitative research techniques, very little has been written on the subject in academic journals over the past 20 years. Calder (1977), for instance, is one of the few marketing scholars to provide a philosophy of science perspective on one such qualitative technique, focus group interviews. Fern (1982), while writing on the latter subject, notes that there has been little empirical testing of focus groups, and no theory of focus group interviewing has evolved. Although a range of notions concerning why focus groups work has appeared in marketing literature, Fern indicates that agreement among authors on this issue is at the most superficial level. Clearly, there is a need for work determining the suitability of qualitative research methods for different types of marketing problems. Calder's work (1977) mentioned earlier, for instance, suggests that focus group interviewing can be of three kinds—exploratory, clinical, or phenomenological. He distinguishes between each kind, depending on what type of problem is being addressed. Similar work might look at the applicability of other qualitative research methods.

Ironically, the use of qualitative methods such as focus group interviewing is widespread in industry. A recent study by Greenberg, Goldstucker, and Bellenger (1977), for instance, reported that 47% of the firms they surveyed used focus groups. But there is a noticeable lacuna in the utilization or discussion of such techniques in academic marketing research literature. This is an area where academics have much to gain by a knowledge transfer from commercial research firms. As Sheth (1979) notes, qualitative research has become more sophisticated as more industry researchers use it repeatedly. By relying relatively exclusively on quantitative research methods, marketing scholars not only miss out on the value of such methods, but perhaps also encourage certain methods bias in their work. This might well explain why certain kinds of quantitative marketing models have been criticized for lacking validity (Sheth 1975). Let us examine some of the underlying problems in delimiting research methods.

## Methods Bias in Marketing Research

Perhaps one of the most interesting statements concerning quantitative and qualitative paradigms comes from the highly respected psychologists Charles Reichardt and Thomas Cook. While writing on the subject of evaluation research, they indicate that "the most telling and fundamental distinction between the paradigms is on the dimension of *verification* versus *discovery* ... quantitative methods have been developed most directly for the task of *verifying* or *confirming* theories and ... qualitative methods were purposely developed for the task of *discovering* or *generating* theories" (1979, p. 17; emphasis added). This distinction between quantitative and qualitative paradigms follows from the modeling of the former along the lines of natural science as we noted earlier. By adopting a "scientific method" approach scientists in the quantitative tradition assume the possibility (and perhaps even the necessity) of formally testing nomothetic propositions. Such theory verification is believed to lead toward the development of enduring theoretical structures so that eventually, as Suppes (1974) suggests, "theoretical palaces" will be erected on the foundations now being laid.

But Reichardt and Cook's statement should cause a great deal of concern to marketing scientists. As indicated in the earlier section of this paper, there is general consensus that marketing science is dominated by a logical empiricist view of social reality. This implies that the majority of marketing scholars are far more involved in theory verification than in theory generation. Moreover, the methodologies that have been developed and tested in marketing research are increasingly those suited to *confirming* propositions or hypotheses rather than to *discovering* new propositions or hypotheses.

But can there be something amiss in the logic of these last few statements? As we know, there have been several conceptual as well as methodological innovations in marketing thought which have appeared in marketing literature. Witness, for example, the recent contributions in low involvement decision making, attribution and self-perception theory, behavioral learning models, and so on. How then can we reconcile the apparent contradiction between substantive developments in marketing thought and the nature of our philosophical paradigm?

If the paradigm governing quantitative methodologies is derived from the natural sciences, then human events are assumed to be lawful, and humans and their creations are part of the natural world. The dominance of a positivist view in marketing colors our perspective of market interactions with this image. As in the natural sciences, we believe that we can objectively study market interactions while ourselves remaining distant from those interactions (in order to "increase our objectivity"). The elaboration and verification of generalizations about the marketing world become the first tasks of researchers. From that, one aspires to build up empirical generalizations which are then to be refined and restructured into more general "laws." These laws will then be woven into a coherent nomothetic theory. This is normal natural science procedure.

However, as several writers have mentioned (Arndt 1978, Jacoby 1978, Leone and Schultz 1980), the development of marketing thought has generally not followed this pattern. Rather, there have been disparate substantive contributions which have attempted to explain some small part of overall market reality. Also, attempts to develop an overarching, concatenated framework have been few and far between (Engel and Blackwell 1982, Howard and Sheth 1969).

Perhaps one of the reasons for this lack of accumulation in marketing thought is due to the nature of the paradigm in use. We have assumed that our inability to develop a body of coherent theory is due to incorrect usage of natural science methods (Leone and Schultz 1980). However, the problem may be less in the method and more in the paradigm. To restate Reichardt and Cook, we have been using methods of theory verification almost exclusively *even in situations where theory discovery was more appropriate*. This is what we mean by a "methods bias" in marketing research. If we ignore the qualitative paradigm, we also by definition exclude the principal systematic means of theory generation. Yet we attempt to make substantive contributions to marketing thought. Also, perhaps unknowingly, we use research methods more geared toward confirmation than discovery, and more toward verification than generation.

Sheth, for instance, provides an example of research on consumer information:

> Consumer information as an area of scientific research and theory is at its infancy in consumer behavior. ... It is, therefore, premature to conduct deductive research ... we must do [a] considerable amount of empirical inductive research. In short, we must learn how to crawl before we start walking or worse yet, running (1981, p. 356).

In order to know the difference between what we have been doing and what we might have been doing, we need to know a little more about the possible contributions of the qualitative paradigm to marketing research. This is the task of the following section.

## Triangulating Methods in Marketing

It is not our intention to suggest that the quantitative paradigm has no place in marketing. As noted above, theory verification is an important part of the overall growth of a body of knowledge. However, it is only one part of this growth. The other part depends on effective means for theory generation—the development of series of propositions that are rich with marketing meaning—propositions generated in some manner other than in a hypothetico-deductive linear fashion.

In contrast to quantitative approaches, qualitative methodologies assume that there is some value to analyzing both inner and outer perspectives of human behavior (Rist 1977). As one of the major texts on such methods describes the situation, the qualitative methodologist "views human behavior—what other people say and do—as a product of how people interpret their world. The task ... is to capture this *process* of interpretation. To do this requires what Weber called *verstehen*, empathic understanding or an ability to reproduce in one's own mind the feelings, motives, and thoughts behind the actions of others" (Bodgan and Taylor 1975, p. 13-14). The qualitative methodologist further believes that a complete and ultimately honest analysis can only be achieved by actively participating in the life of the subject of observation and gaining insights by means of introspection. As we mentioned earlier, this kind of methodology is based on the anthropological tradition where a strong emphasis is placed on the researcher's ability to "take the role of the other" and to grasp basic underlying assumptions of behavior by seeing the "definition of the situation" through the eyes of the participants (Rist 1977).

The qualitative procedure then is primarily inductive rather than deductive. As two of the major recent contributors to this field have commented, theory development starts with an extrapolation from "grounded events" (Glaser and Strauss 1967). Rather than beginning with hypotheses, models, or theorems, the act of building theory commences with comprehending frequently minute episodes or interactions that are examined for broader patterns and processes.

It is not the purpose of this paper to describe in detail qualitative methodological processes. Several scholars have already developed extremely valuable work in this area (Bogdan and Taylor 1975, Filstead 1970, Glaser and Strauss 1967, Schwartz and Jacobs 1979, Sjoberg and Nett 1966, Webb et al. 1966). We would, however, like to make a few more comments concerning the relevance of such methodologies for marketing research and marketing theory.

It may be helpful to consider certain metatheoretical aspects of epistemology (i.e., an appraisal of the nature and limits of knowledge). If for a moment we differentiate between the objectives of theory construction and theory testing, we may see the relative appropriateness of qualitative as well as quantitative paradigms along with their associated methods. Our discussion of the distinction between paradigms leads us to believe that qualitative methodologies are more suited for theory construction or generation and quantitative methodologies for theory verification or testing. So while attempting to build a new theory or make an innovative theory construction contribution, a marketing scientist would be well-advised to carefully study and then put into practice qualitative methods. Once the theory has been developed and grounded, the application of quantitative methods would be more appropriate.

This last point is an important one. There has been and there continues to be much controversy in several social sciences on the appropriate theoretical paradigm. Our position is that rather than becoming more and more polarized by taking paradigmatic sides, researchers would be better off realizing that *both* paradigms have a place in marketing, provided they are not being made to do each other's work. Certain scholars have noted, for instance, that quantitative methodologies emphasize reliability issues (frequently to the exclusion of validity), while qualitative methodologies emphasize validity while downplaying reliability (Deutscher 1970, Merton 1957, Rist 1977). It will only serve to further distance the advocates of each paradigm to exclude the other in their advocacy. Quantitative methodologists would criticize qualitative researchers for low reliability and the lack of work contributing toward a cumulative body of knowledge. In turn, qualitative researchers would castigate quantitative methodologists for not understanding the "shades of meaning" behind their statistical formulations. Such a polemic would be inimical to the growth of marketing knowledge. Ideally, every research endeavor needs *both* high reliability and high validity. Theory construction is *as* important as theory verification. To quote a leading psychometrician who finds fault with his own neo-positivistic scientist colleagues:

> The time has come to exorcise the null hypothesis. We cannot afford to pour costly data down the drain whenever effects present in the

> sample "fail to reach significance." ... Let the author file descriptive information, at least in an archive, instead of reporting only those selected differences and correlations that are nominally "greater than chance." Descriptions encourage us to think constructively about results from quasi-replications, whereas the dichotomy significant/nonsignificant implies only a hopeless inconsistency. The canon of parsimony, misinterpreted, has led us into the habit of accepting Type II errors at every turn, for the sake of holding Type I errors in check. There *are* more things in heaven and earth than are dreamt of in our hypotheses, and our observations should be open to them (Cronbach 1975, p. 124).

The task for marketing theorists and marketing researchers then is to understand the advantages and disadvantages of both paradigms. This implies much greater attention to the qualitative paradigm which has been neglected relative to the quantitative one. In terms of methods, the task is to triangulate procedures. This means that researchers should learn not only both quantitative and qualitative research methods, but also the strengths and weaknesses of each set of procedures. Triangulation of procedures would then lead to using an appropriate mix of both quantitative *and* qualitative methods such that the weaknesses of one set of methodologies is compensated for by the strengths of the other and vice versa.

An excellent example of such methodological triangulation is provided by Sieber (1973) who indicates how qualitative fieldwork (participant observation, informant interviewing, and using available secondary data) and quantitative survey methods can be interplayed within a research endeavor. Since we can assume that readers of this article are probably much better versed in quantitative than qualitative methodology, we will briefly summarize Sieber's arguments for the contributions that fieldwork can make to survey methods.

Many of these issues will be familiar to marketing researchers. This will be particularly true for industry practitioners. It is also true that at least some marketing scholars do use qualitative methods (for instance, in the early stages of survey design). Nevertheless, the preponderance of their attention is on the quantitative aspects of research. Our purpose here in highlighting Sieber's comments, therefore, is to serve as a reminder to marketing theorists that there is much to be gained by learning from industry practice of qualitative methods. As one observer indicates, qualitative methodology is an area which appears to be familiar to almost everybody but is really known and understood by a much smaller number of market researchers. "To the many, it is a field of market research which lacks subtlety and requires little skill. To the expert it is the complete reverse" (Sampson 1978, p. 48).

Sieber specifies three primary areas in which qualitative fieldwork can make a contribution to surveys: survey design, data collection, and analysis.

In the first case, preliminary personal interviews or participant observation on a limited sample of the subject population can help provide insights on the specific sample segments that should later be included as part of a larger survey. In this situation, qualitative fieldwork involves project investigators developing personal familiarity with a setting or group to be surveyed. This familiarity can make a major contribution to the development of a meaningful survey design by allowing the investigator to be much more specific in determining the precise sample that will be part of the survey. Much expense and later statistical data manipulation can be avoided if the initial design is the appropriate one. Let us take an illustration from organizational buying research in marketing. An investigator who was not aware that buying decisions in most large firms are made by a task group, rather than an individual, might misspecify a survey design to include only one respondent per firm, rather than all members of the buying center (Wind 1978). A preliminary set of personal interviews with a few individuals in a few organizations would have very quickly acquainted the researcher with the need for redefining survey design (Spekman and Stern 1979).

The second area where qualitative fieldwork can contribute to surveys is in data collection. Sieber indicates that exploratory interviews and qualitative observations preceding a large scale survey can yield valuable information about the receptivity, frames of reference, and span of attention of respondents. Additionally, the survey instrument can be broadened or narrowed, depending on the topics that are salient to pretest respondents. A series of focus group discussions with elderly consumers prior to a survey will, for example, reveal not only that their views concerning the efficacy of complaint behavior differ markedly from other consumers, but also that they have difficulty in reading fine print on package labels and advertisements (Phillips and Sternthal 1977; Zaltman, Srivastava, and Deshpande 1978). This first finding would greatly influence the nature of questions asked in a study of elderly consumer satisfaction and dissatisfaction behavior, and the latter finding would alert researchers to either use the telephone to collect data or have larger print on mail questionnaires.

The third contribution that qualitative fieldwork can make to survey research is in data analysis. This comment by Sieber is similar in nature to Cronbach's statement quoted earlier. Frequently, statistical results from survey data analysis can be validated by recourse to qualitative observations and informant interviews. Additionally, the entire *theoretical structure* that guides the analysis and interpretation of data can be derived wholly or largely from qualitative fieldwork. This is in keeping with our earlier discussion of the linking of qualitative methodology with theory discovery.

Sieber adds some other comments on the major contributions that fieldwork can make to survey data analysis. It can help interpret statistical relationships by reference to field observation; it can help selection of survey items in the construction of indices; and it can also help clarify puzzling or provocative responses to the survey instrument by resorting to qualitative field notes.

Much the same kind of argument can be made for the contribution of qualitative methods to other quantitative methods, such as experimentation. The opposite is also true, viz., there is a great deal that quantitative methodologies can contribute to qualitative fieldwork (Sieber 1973, pp. 1350-1357). Our aim here is not to try to be exhaustive, but rather to suggest how all aspects of market research activity can be enriched by triangulating quantitative and qualitative approaches.

## Conclusion

The basic premise of this paper is that marketing scholars have too long ignored the metatheoretical implications of reliance on a single paradigm. This paradigm has been identified as that of logical positivism. In its exclusion of a more qualitative paradigm, marketing theory has developed certain inherent methods biases. These biases come from developing new theoretical contributions while using methodologies more appropriate to theory testing than to theory generation.

The dominance of one theoretical philosophy in marketing is unfortunate, in that marketing science has grown much more rapidly in the area of hypothesis testing than in the development of new, rich explanatory theories. In order to remedy this situation two major directions have been suggested. The first is to use qualitative methods when trying to generate new theory and to use quantitative methods when attempting to test this theory.

Additionally, even theory testing can gain from a triangulation of both quantitative and qualitative methodologies. The contributions that a set of methodologies can make to one another cover all aspects of theory confirmation—research design, data collection, and data analysis.

We must reiterate that our position in this paper has been to suggest the strengths and weaknesses of both qualitative and quantitative paradigms. It is not our intention to suggest that marketing scientists can rely on one to the total exclusion of the other. However, we very strongly believe that at the current stage of knowledge development in marketing, there needs to be a far greater emphasis placed on learning about qualitative methodologies and understanding their relevance for an inquiry into the social reality of the marketplace.

## ENDNOTES

1. There have been several reformulations of both the idealist and positivist philosophies since they were first postulated. To describe the further development of these different schools of thought would be beyond the scope and

purpose of this paper. Thus, for the remainder of the discussion we will refer to the two paradigms as quantitative and qualitative.

2. These books are by Bagozzi (1980), Hunt (1983), Zaltman, LeMasters, and Heffring (1982), and Zaltman, Pinson, and Angelmar (1973).

## REFERENCES

Arndt, Johan (1978), "Comments on the Sociology of Marketing Research," in *Advances in Consumer Research*, Vol. 5, Keith Hunt, ed., 185-190.

Bagozzi, Richard P. (1980), *Causal Models in Marketing*, New York: Wiley.

Bellenger, Danny N., Kenneth L. Berhardt, and Jac L. Goldstucker (1976), *Qualitative Research in Marketing*, Chicago: American Marketing.

Bogdan, Robert and Steven J. Taylor (1975), *Introduction to Qualitative Research Methods*, New York: Wiley.

Brodbeck, May (1982), "Recent Developments in the Philosophy of Science," in *Marketing Theory: Philosophy of Science Perspectives*, Ronald F. Bush and Shelby D. Hunt, eds., Chicago: American Marketing, 1-6.

Bush, Ronald F. and Shelby D. Hunt, eds. (1982), *Marketing Theory: Philosophy of Science Perspectives*, Chicago: American Marketing.

Calder, Bobby J. (1977), "Focus Groups and the Nature of Qualitative Marketing Research," *Journal of Marketing Research*, 14 (August), 353-364.

Cronbach, Lee J. (1975), "Beyond the Two Disciplines of Scientific Psychology," *American Psychologist*, 30 (February), 116-127.

Deutscher, Irwin (1970), "Words and Deeds: Social Science and Social Policy," in *Qualitative Methodology*, William J. Filstead, ed., Chicago: Markham.

Dichter, Ernest (1964), *Handbook of Consumer Motivations: The Psychology of the World of Objects*, New York: McGraw-Hill.

Engel, James and Roger D. Blackwell (1982), *Consumer Behavior*, 4th ed., Chicago: Dryden.

Ferber, Robert and Hugh G. Wales, eds. (1958), *Motivation and Market Behavior*, Homewood, IL: Irwin.

Fern, Edward J. (1982), "The Use of Focus Groups for Idea Generation: The Effects of Group Size, Acquaintanceship, and Moderator on Response Quantity and Quality," *Journal of Marketing Research*, 19 (February), 1-13.

Filstead, William J., ed. (1970), *Qualitative Methodology: Firsthand Involvement with the Social World*, Chicago: Markham.

——— (1979), "Qualitative Methods: A Needed Perspective in Evaluation Research," in *Qualitative and Quantitative Methods in Evaluation Research*, Thomas D. Cook and Charles S. Reichardt, eds., Beverly Hills, CA: Sage, 33-48.

Glaser, Barney and Anselm Strauss (1967), *The Discovery of Grounded Theory*, Chicago: Aldine.

Greenberg, Barnett A., Jac L. Goldstucker, and Danny N. Bellenger (1977), "What Techniques Are Used by Marketing Researchers in Business," *Journal of Marketing*, 41 (April), 61-68.

Holzner, Burkhart and John Marx (1979), *Knowledge Application: The Knowledge System in Society*, Boston: Allyn and Bacon.

Howard, John A. and Jagdish N. Sheth (1969), *The Theory of Consumer Behavior*, New York: Wiley.

Hunt, Shelby D. (1982), "Are the Logical Empiricist Models of Explanation Dead?" in *Marketing Theory: Philosophy of Science Perspectives*, Ronald F. Bush and Shelby D. Hunt, eds., Chicago: American Marketing, 7-10.

——— (1983), *Marketing Theory: The Philosophy of Marketing Science*, Homewood, IL: Irwin.

Jacoby, Jacob (1978), "Consumer Research: A State of the Art Review," *Journal of Marketing*, 42 (April), 87-96.

Kuhn, Thomas (1962), *The Structure of Scientific Revolutions*, Chicago: University of Chicago Press.

Leone, Robert P. and Randall L. Schultz (1980), "A Study of Marketing Generalizations," *Journal of Marketing*, 44 (Winter), 10-18.

Merton, Robert S. (1957), *Social Theory and Social Structure*, Glencoe, IL: Free Press.

Mitroff, Ian I. (1974), *The Subjective Side of Science: A Philosophical Inquiry into the Psychology of Apollo Moon Scientists*, Amsterdam: Elsevier.

Murstein, B. I. (1965), *Handbook of Projective Techniques*, New York: Basic Books, Inc.

Newman, Joseph W. (1957), *Motivation Research and Marketing Management*, Cambridge, MA: Harvard University Press.

Patton, Michael Q. (1978), *Utilization-Focused Evaluation*, Beverly Hills, CA: Sage.

——— (1980), "Making Methods Choices," *Evaluation and Program Planning*, 3 (no. 4), 219-228.

Peter, J. Paul (1982), "Current Issues in the Philosophy of Science: Implications for Marketing Theory—A Panel Discussion," in *Marketing Theory: Philosophy of Science Perspectives*, Ronald F. Bush and Shelby D. Hunt, eds., Chicago: American Marketing, 11-16.

Phillips, Lynn W. and Brian Sternthal (1977), "Age Differences in Information Processing: A Perspective on the Aged Consumer," *Journal of Marketing Research*, 14 (November), 444-457.

Reichardt, Charles S. and Thomas D. Cook (1979), "Beyond Qualitative versus Quantitative Methods," in *Qualitative and Quantitative Methods in Evaluation Research*, Thomas D. Cook and Charles S. Reichardt, eds., Beverly Hills, CA: Sage, 7-32.

——— and ——— (1980), "Paradigms Lost: Some Thoughts on Choosing Methods in Evaluation Research," *Evaluation and Program Planning*, 3 (no. 4), 229-236.

Rist, Ray C. (1977), "On the Relations among Educational Research Paradigms: From Disdain to Detente," *Anthropology and Education Quarterly*, 8 (May), 42-49.

Sampson, Peter (1978), "Qualitative Research and Motivation," in *Consumer Market Research Handbook*, 2nd edition, Robert M. Worcester and John Downham, eds., New York: Van Nostrand.

Schwartz, H. and J. Jacobs (1979), *Qualitative Sociology*, New York: Free Press.

Sheth, Jagdish N. (1975), "Some Thoughts on the Future of Marketing Models," faculty working paper no. 232, College of Commerce and Business Administration, University of Illinois at Urbana-Champaign.

——— (1979), "The Future of Market Research Products and Markets," faculty working paper no. 554. College of Commerce and Business Administration, Univeristy of Illinois at Urbana-Champaign.

——— (1981), "Discussion" comments, in *Advances in Consumer Research*, Vol. 8, Kent Monroe, ed., Ann Arbor: Association for Consumer Research, 355-356.

Sieber, Sam D. (1973), "The Integration of Field Work and Survey Methods," *American Journal of Sociology*, 78 (May), 1335-1359.

Simon, John (1980), *Paradigms Lost: Reflections on Literacy and Its Decline*, New York: Clarkson N. Potter, Inc.

Sjoberg, Gideon and Roger Nett (1966), *A Methodology for Social Research*, New York: Harper.

Spekman, Robert E. and Louis W. Stern (1979), "Environmental Uncertainty and Buying Group Structure: An Empirical Investigation," *Journal of Marketing*, 43 (Spring), 54-64.

Suppe, Frederick, ed. (1977), *The Structure of Scientific Theories*, 2nd edition, Urbana: University of Illinois Press.

Suppes, Patrick (1974), "The Place of Theory in Educational Research," *Educational Researcher*, 3 (no. 6), 3-10.

Webb, E. J., D. T. Campbell, R. D. Schwartz, and L. Sechrest (1966), *Unobtrusive Measures: Nonreactive Research in the Social Sciences*, Chicago: Rand McNally.

Wind, Yoram (1978), "Organizational Buying Behavior," in *Review of Marketing 1978*, Gerald Zaltman and Thomas V. Bonoma, eds., Chicago: American Marketing, 160-193.

Zaltman, Gerald, Karen LeMasters, and Michael Heffring (1982), *Theory Construction in Marketing: Some Thoughts on Thinking*, New York: Wiley.

———, Christian Pinson, and Reinhard Angelmar (1973), *Metatheory and Consumer Research*, Hinsdale, IL: Dryden.

———, Rajendra Srivastava, and Rohit Deshpande (1978), "Perceptions of Unfair Marketing Practices: Consumerism Implications," in *Advances in Consumer Research*, Vol. 5, Keith Hunt, ed., Ann Arbor: Association for Consumer Research, 247-253.

# SECTION C
# Marketing and Science

Is marketing a science? This is an old question and one that is part of a broader discussion about whether business mangement is amenable to scientific rigor. Perhaps it is a more creative venture. Underlying the debate whether marketing is a science or an art, there are three issues.

The first issue is the context of marketing. If the context is nonchanging, or invariant, it is likely to be amenable to the scientific rigor associated with description, prediction, and control. On the other hand, if the context is dynamic, or highly variant, it is likely to generate only a contingency framework. We are forced to use phrases like "it depends" or "ceteris paribus" when presenting our theory. Most scholars believe that the marketing context is dynamic and, therefore, at best we can generate only contingency theories.

A second issue is the standardization of output. Hard sciences are capable of replicating outputs such as production units with precision so there is a stream of standarized outputs. The extent to which marketing can again and again generate the same sales or profit effects based on an element of the marketing mix such as advertising is highly tenuous. Indeed, no advertising agency has guaranteed a specific sales or even attitude result prior to accepting the client. To that extent marketing is much closer to other professional services such as medicine and law.

Finally, there is a third issue. Is the marketing process homogenous or highly diverse? In other words, can we offer a single solution to the practitioners for a common objective? Do our processes converge to a common outcome? Most scholars agree that marketing often tends to generate divergent rather than convergent processes, and to that extent it is more an art than a science.

So, is marketing a science or an art? Not even marketing practitioners agree on this one.

# 7 —— Marketing as a Science: An Appraisal

*Kenneth D. Hutchinson*

Reprinted from *Journal of Marketing*, published by the American Marketing Association, Vol. 16 (January 1952), pp. 286-293. Reprinted by permission.

During the past few years one of the ways in which the increased interest in marketing subjects has expressed itself is in the rather intense exploration of the field with a view to determining the exact significance of its subject matter. More explicitly, several scholars have either attempted to demonstrate that marketing should be admitted into the category of a science, or have discussed the subject as though it already were included. Interest in the project first became apparent through the appearance of an exploratory survey made by P. D. Converse in *The Journal of Marketing*.[1] However, since this particular essay had the merit of not attempting any demonstration of the thesis that marketing is a science, one can not be sure that the article really served as the foundation of future discussions on the problem.

At the time that Professor Converse wrote, regard for the application of scientific methodology to marketing problems was an increasing force, and the momentum of this interest carries on today. Three years later, Lyndon O. Brown discussed the need for the development of professional standards among marketing men in an essay which tended in the main not to regard the subject as a science, except possibly in one cloudy passage.[2] The question of the status of marketing appeared to be developing some urgency in the minds of numerous marketing scholars because in the next issue of the *Journal* there appeared a very thoughtful and searching article exploring the notion of developing a theory of marketing.[3] The authors were quite circumspect in writing this essay, omitting any direct reference to marketing as a science. Little doubt was left in the minds of the readers, however, that the authors considered marketing to be a unified body of thought; and from this one can infer that they suspect that it is a science.

At least one marketing scholar received this impression from that essay for, in the *Journal* the following spring, Roland S. Vaile wrote a communciation[4] commenting on that point of view. If anyone held illusions as to the character of marketing, Professor Vaile's article should have removed them; but marketing men apparently have great tenacity and refuse to give up easily. Although the conclusion of this essay was that marketing did not have the earmarks of a science, the question of whether this was true was to be raised again on later occasions. In 1951 a new essay was presented on the question by Robert Bartels,[5] who concluded that marketing was indeed a science and entitled to respect as such.

It would be misleading to consider this latter essay as an isolated instance; the ferment which had been started in the minds of students of marketing was working steadily and other evidences of this conclusion (that marketing is a science) can be found. The Cox and Alderson article, to which reference has been made, led to a book of essays on marketing theory;[6] in some of these further references to the science of marketing.[7] This compilation of essays affords a rather varied fare for the scholar seeking enlightenment on the true nature of marketing. Points of view differed and there were some who indicated their conviction that there was no such thing as a theory of marketing, and hence also, no science of marketing.[8]

## Reasons for Confusion

This disagreement, or confusion, in the minds of marketing students over the nature of their field arises in no small part from the comprehensive character and variety of activities embraced by the term marketing. Three distinct types of activity are discernbile. First, there is a group of activities which center around the day-to-day distribution of goods and services. Second, there are those activities which center around the interpretation of the subject in schools and colleges. Third, there is a group of activities which arises out of the explorations by market research men working on specific problems, some of which have rather broad implications. With these three different approaches to the field there would naturally arise some differences in viewpoints.

Of the first group, those whose job it is to distribute goods, almost no one would contend seriously that they are engaged in some form of scientific endeavor; wholesalers and retailers hardly fit the mold of scientists. Neither the second group, the teachers, nor the third group, the market research men, are so easily disposed of, particularly since some of them are concerned with systematizing the subject. All are interested in employing scientific methodology in the field. Members of these two groups have pressed the case most earnestly for the inclusion of marketing among the fields of science. We have seen, however, that there has been no unanimity of opinion among them. Their work with the scientific method has induced many of them to broaden their scopes, and it is to those who have attempted to demonstrate that marketing is a science that this essay is directed.

In appraising the progress which has been made in developing a science of marketing, one is tempted to make allowances for the relatively short period of time in which the issues have been under discussion. But after making whatever allowances are called for, one is likely to be somewhat disappointed over the lack of progress to date. One should expect far more in the way of results if the venture is to prove successful, and the dearth of progress to date lends the suspicion that the project is ill-advised. There seems to be little evidence to support the claim that all that is needed is time and patience until there will emerge the new and shining science of marketing.

## Two Approaches to Demonstrating That Marketing Is a Science

In attempting to demonstrate that marketing is a science, two lines of approach to the problem are discernible. The first of these might pass under the name of the semantic approach according to which the various essayists wrestle with dictionary meanings, warping them and twisting them, until at last marketing is seen to have fulfilled many, though not all, of the requisite characteristics of a science. The pseudo-precision of this method may be highly admirable even though it lacks some perspective. A somewhat fairer interpretation of such semantic exercises might reasonably lead to the conclusion merely that marketing has now become a field for human study. Since there are many fields of study, and since not all of them are sciences, such a conclusion should not be looked upon as any great step forward.[9]

To be more explicit, a homely example might be drawn; the field of carpentry could conceivably turn out to be such a field of study. There are books written on the subject; it is taught in schools; and it concerns itself with human experience. Furthermore it has empirical laws of a sort (those of gravity and leverage, for example) and perhaps some theoretical ones (whether screws or nails are preferable in certain jobs). Now all this pedantry does not create a science out of the trade of carpentry; but it illustrates how pseudo-scientific word juggling might be used to convert many humble human activities into recognized sciences. Something of this sort is now appearing in marketing literature. The function of business, however, is the economic production and marketing of goods and services; if we insist, therefore, that marketing is a science, we must be prepared to admit manufacturing and finance. Unless one wants to broaden his conception of science so as to include nearly all human activity, he is not likely to achieve success in making marketing a science through this process of distorting the meaning of words.

The second approach to the task of demonstrating the scientific character of marketing might be called the economic. Students of marketing interested in "practical" as well as academic matters seem to find the time-worn theories of neo-classical economics to be unsatisfying or downright inapplicable. This has led to a wholesale onslaught on many of the time honored concepts in which, curiously enough, they find many economists sympathetic. For some years economists themselves have been trying to free their subject from the fetters placed there by the static assumptions inherited from the classical school traditions. Some progress is being made in modernizing economic doctrines but there still remain numerous concepts which lack realism. It has been this factor which has encouraged students of marketing to pursue further the task of clarification; in fact—such work was essential.[10]

The result of such interest in economic theory is that considerable study by marketing theorists has been devoted to developing more refreshing viewpoints and more workable concepts. A review of progress to date indicates that much of it has stemmed from the practice of holding economic theories up to a critical light for re-examination. One might naturally wonder whether all this analysis is serving only to enrich current economic doctrines rather than to further the development of any independent set of marketing theories. From the standpoint of over-all human understanding, such efforts of marketing men are probably not in vain. In the long run it may well turn out that theoretical economists have derived benefits from having their concepts held up to this different type of scrutiny. Marketing students will also benefit through the possession of a better tool of analysis which this criticism may produce.

In looking over the work of marketing theorists it appears that considerable effort has been expended in attacking the generally accepted, or "orthodox," if you will, doctrines which relate to price setting. It is apparently true that much of this body of thought has been erected upon a foundation which contains some rather unrealistic assumptions, and certainly some which appear foreign to a marketer. Thus far, however, the contributions of marketing theorists to economic theory of pricing remain restricted to the field of criticism. If one were to seek evidence of constructive scholarship along these lines he would discover that no notable body of new theory has been brought forth to replace the seemingly discredited notions. An even harsher observation could be made: the probing of marketers into economic theory has tended more to becloud than to clarify the issues. In casting the light of realism upon this field such a result may well have been unavoidable. It should be interesting to inspect a few of the concepts which have had their clarity dimmed.

To the neo-classical economist the concept of price was reasonably clear, whereas to the new marketing theorists there is no great certainty as to what is meant by the term. To them price represents a wide composite of characteristics which are subject to notable variances which can conceivably differ with each transaction. Another concept which seemed to give the economist little trouble was that of a commodity. Under the new scrutiny, this also turns out to possess less clarity, varying to some extent from transaction to transaction, a fact which accounts for the varying prices. Although some attention has been directed by marketing theorists to such other concepts as competition, monopoly, market controls, and freedom of entry, it can be said with fair reliability that human comprehension of these subjects has been very little advanced. Whether one is inclined to agree with these immediate conclusions is of no great importance; what does seem to be important is the fact that marketing scholars can never expect to develop their own body of theory merely by critical appraisal of the shortcomings of another one. In time, some positive contributions must be forthcoming if the desired goal is to be achieved.

## MARKETING NOT A SCIENCE

There is a real reason, however, why the field of marketing has been slow to develop an unique body of theory. It is a simple one: marketing is not a science. It is rather an art or a practice, and as such much more closely resembles engineering, medicine, and architecture than it does physics, chemistry, or biology. The medical profession sets us an excellent example, if we would but follow it; its members are called ''practitioners'' and not scientists. It is the work of physicians, as it is of any practitioner, to apply the findings of many sciences to the solution of problems. Among the sciences which the medical man employs are biology, physiology, chemistry, physics, psychology, and many more. Engineers and architects are also practitioners who make use of chemistry, physics, psychology and other sciences. It is a characteristic of a practice that the solution of each problem faced calls for a different and distinct combination of techniques and approaches. The fact that each problem is different, however, does not deter practitioners from approaching them in the scientific manner and spirit.[11]

What constitutes a science is a question which has been settled in general for centuries, but from time to time the issues arise again as new subjects are held up for scrutiny. Within modern times the areas of social study, the socio-economic fields, have caused considerable debate over the character of science itself. The trouble with attacking this problem from a semantic point of view is that words have mutliple meanings and one is enabled to prove almost anything, and almost nothing, by careful selection of the definition which seems to fit his case. Since we are using words in this essay, we are in danger of falling into the same trap in trying to show that marketing is *not* a science that others have fallen into by trying to show that it *is* one, particularly when their demonstration has depended heavily upon the twist of word meanings. A much sounder approach to the problem would seem to be upon the ground of human experience, contrasting the place of science in human affairs with that of the arts.

Science is a word we apply to a multitude of varying activities carried on by man in his effort to understand his environment. For centuries man has attempted to comprehend the planetary processes which are all parts of the great universe of knowledge. It should be unnecessary in this age and with this group of readers to labor this particular concept; it might be more profitable to return to it after we have discussed the field of the arts.

The arts is also a comprehensive term covering human activities of a wide scope. To satisfy his wants, mankind has engaged in various practices over the centuries; as time has gone on, these practices have tended to become more complex. The various arts are those related to obtaining food, preparing clothing, and obtaining shelter, along with others which are related to aesthetic satisfactions. Man found early that he could thrive much better if he did not attempt to produce all of his commodities but instead would exchange some of his output with a neighbor who had a surplus of some other product. Early barter and later market transactions are the true predecessors of modern marketing. The forbears of modern marketing men were great merchants, not great scientists. It is the drollest travesty to relate the scientist's search for knowledge to the market research man's seeking after customers.

## Relationship Between Marketing and the Sciences

What then is the relationship existing between the sciences and marketing if indeed there be one? The answer to this query has already been indicated but perhaps should be restated. Men of science have come to develop a systematic approach to their problems which is known as the scientific method. Hypotheses are developed, facts are gathered to support or confute the hypotheses, and then tests are conducted to see if hypotheses are sound. In actual research work, the techniques employed vary with the problem at hand but the spirit of careful analysis and testing is not relaxed. Engineers and physicians are trained to approach their problems in this spirit of scientific inquiry; marketing men are learning rapidly to follow their examples. What must be realized is that the method is open for all to use and that the employment of it does not necessarily make the user a scientist nor his subject a science. A physician who studies all of his patient's symptoms before prescribing, and who keeps checking up on the progress of his treatments, is still a practitioner and not a scientist.

Such a conclusion must be inevitable or else the gates will be opened to include almost all types of human activity under the heading of sciences. Dry cleaners often approach a problem in a scientific manner but dry cleaning is not a science, nor are road building, paint mixing, poultry raising and countless other human arts. The processes which culminate in getting goods from mines, fields, and factories into the hands of consumers with the least expenditure of time, effort and money are not those that will fit into the mold of science. That many marketing problems call for extensive computations and calculations can not be denied nor can the fact that the best approach to them is through some variant of the scientific method of investigation, trial and test. In actual practice, however, many, and probably most, of the decisions in the field resemble the scientific method hardly any more closely than what is involved in reading a road map or a time table. If one remains unconvinced, he must be prepared to admit into the brotherhood of new sciences the fields of retailing, wholesaling and presumably salesmanship.

The arts and practices seem to differ from the sciences in still another respect. When problems present themselves to practitioners there is almost without exception rather serious urgency to have them solved. An engineering project must be put through immediately; a sick patient must be helped now; and a sales manager wants his analysis of the market from his research man as soon as (and usually sooner than) is possible. Any market research man who is working on a problem the answer to which may not be found for another generation, or perhaps a century, would be an exception whereas such a circumstance tends to be rather commonplace among the sciences where immediacy tends more to be the exception. At best this point of difference between the arts and the sciences is probably only a symptomatic effect rather than an underlying force separating the two.

Thinking along these lines has become confused in the minds of some individuals because of the tendency of scientists to desert their fields of research to attack some current practical problem. When a scientist leaves his field of scientific investigation to solve a difficult problem, he drops the role of a scientist seeking to expand man's grasp over the universe; he is no longer engaged in pushing out the frontiers of knowledge. At that point he becomes a practitioner in a role similar to the engineer, the physician and the architect. A physicist who leaves his pursuit of science to construct a machine (except one to further an experiment) becomes an engineer, even though one with a superior training in physics. The point being made here is not a new one, having been well settled in other fields of learning; but the truth of it seems to have been overlooked by numerous marketing men.

We do not intend to deny here that scientists should turn their attention to the solution of human problems, nor are we attempting to indicate that scientific endeavor should lack applicability. No claim is being presented here for the advantages of pure research, that form of activity which seems to do little more than satisfy the curiosity of some investigator. Science has a purpose; its function is to help mankind to understand his universe. Whether men will use the knowledge or will even misuse it is not the particular concern of the scientist. At present writing the problem of cancer is one of great concern to several fields of science and each one is developing an attack upon it. Some investigators are approaching the problem from the standpoint of the effect of behavior patterns upon its cause. Others study the structure of human cells, still others the effects of drugs, and still others the effects of radiation, and so on. This is a practical problem which science is trying to solve; but how any given patient suffering from the disease is to be treated is a problem for the practitioner.

The real dilemma of the marketing research man is not that his own field of learning is inadequate to permit proper diagnoses and prescriptions, but that the other fields upon which he should be able to lean are themselves still in somewhat beginning stages. It may seem unfair to a one hundred seventy-five year old science such as economics to classify it as "beginning," but one has only to examine the protests of marketing men over many economic concepts to learn the tenuous nature of economic principles. Sociology and psychology are also just beginning to build up a body of reliable doctrine and are far from complete tools for analysis. The market research man needs knowledge of population trends, consumer preferences, price trends, and purchasing power, merely to name a few of the concepts on which exact information is lacking. It happens to be unfortunate that marketing research has to depend upon the numerous and inexact social sciences.[12]

While we are examining the place of marketing among the various fields of learning and activity, one further point should be made. Marketing men not infrequently contribute to one of the several sciences upon which they depend. In trying to find information to solve his immediate problem he may strike upon some principle which actually enlarges the science involved. Market problems vary widely in scope. Some are of almost no social consequence, being chiefly competitive in nature; others are broader in character and depend for solution upon a wide understanding of social forces and of human behavior. It is in the pursuit of these solutions that contributions to the fields of science result. Such additions to the universal body of knowledge must be looked upon as by-products of market research, and not its chief purpose.

Beyond such small contributions, however, there is an area in which marketing scholars can produce profound results in the sciences. There is evidence that already some of this work is being done. By focusing the attention of scientists upon those concepts which are inadequately developed, the inquiring minds of marketing men can do much to give useful direction to scientific investigation. Already students of economics, sociology, and psychology are feeling the impact of this curiosity and are tending to advance knowledge along the lines demanded. Engineers and physicians have in their turn exerted powerful influences over the direction which scientific research should take. This aspect should not be overlooked in our quest for progress in the field.

## CONCLUSION

An examination of the factors involved indicates that marketing is not a science, since it does not conform to the basic characteristics of a science. A much more realistic view shows it to be an art, in the practice of which reliance must be placed upon the findings of many sciences. Marketing research men, like engineers and physicians, have to adopt a scientific approach to their problems, but their relation to the fields of science are even closer than this. Although at times they may make a contribution to some field of science, their chief contribution should be that of directing the course of scientific investigation along the lines most needed.

## ENDNOTES

1. P. D. Converse, "The Development of a Science of Marketing," *Journal of Marketing*, Vol. X, No. 1, July 1945, p. 14.
2. Lyndon O. Brown, "Toward a Profession of Marketing," *Journal of Marketing*, Vol. XIII, No. 1, July , 1948, p. 27. Brown states that there is a need for "precise raw materials which are the foundation of any science, and in turn the art of the practitioner in any field."
3. W. Alderson and R. Cox, "Towards a Theory of Marketing," *Journal of Marketing*, Vol. XIII, No. 2, October, 1948, p. 137.
4. Roland S. Vaile, "Toward a Theory of Marketing—A Comment," *Journal of Marketing*, Vol. XIII, No. 4, April, 1949, p. 520.
5. Robert Bartels, "Can Marketing Be A Science?," *Journal of Marketing*, Vol. XV, No. 3, January, 1951, p. 310.
6. R. Cox and W. Alderson, editors, *Theory in Marketing* (Chicago, Richard D. Irwin, Inc., 1950).
7. In *Theory in Marketing*, C. West Churchman, in the essay "Basic Research in Marketing," discusses market research as though the field were a science. W. Alderson, in "Survival and Adjustment in Organized Behavior," refers to "the science of marketing." E.R. Hawkins, "Vertical Price Relationships," after making some penetrating analyses of economic theory, leaves the impression that marketing is a part of the science of economics.
8. In the same work, G. L. Mehren, in the essay "The Theory of the Firm and Marketing," says that "there is no theory of marketing." E. T. Grether, in "A Theoretical Approach to the Analysis of Marketing," takes a cautious view of theorizing in the field, as does Oswald Kanuth, in "Marketing and Mangerial Enterprise."
9. Dr. Bartels recognizes this widespread characteristic of marketing in the article referred to above. After discussing the characteristics of an art, a discipline, and a science, he concludes that there is much in favor of accepting the subject of marketing as a science.
10. Evidence of this concern for clarification and modification of economic theory can be found in Cox and Alderson, *Theory in Marketing* cited above. Essays which are chiefly critiques of economic doctrines are: R. G. Gettell, "Pluralistic Competition"; E. T. Grether, "A Theoretical Approach to the Analysis of Marketing"; G. L. Mehren, "The Theory of the Firm and Marketing"; R. S. Vaile, "Economic Theory and Marketing": E.R. Hawkins, "Vertical Price Relationships"; R. Cassady, Jr., "The Time Element and Demand Analysis"; A. G. Abramson, "Public Policy and the Theory of Competition"; R. Cox, "Quantity Limits and the Theory of Economic Opportunity"; and J. Dean, "Market Competition under Uniform F.O.B. Pricing."
11. This point of view was expressed somewhat differently by R. S. Vaile in *The Journal of Marketing* article cited above.
12. We are accepting for present purposes the idea that economics and sociology are sciences, being fully aware that controversies exist over this point.

# 8 —— Is Marketing a Science?

*Robert D. Buzzell*



If you ask the average business executive what the most important agent of progress is in contemporary society, the odds are good that he will answer, "Science." There is a general respect, even awe, for the accomplishments of science. The satellites in orbit, polio vaccine, and television are tangible pieces of evidence that science conquers all.

To be against science is as heretical as to be against motherhood. Yet when executives are asked to consider the social and economic process of marketing as a science or prospective science, most confess to extreme skepticism. Is marketing a science? If not, can it ever become one? If so, what does this imply for management?

These questions are hardly new ones, but they have a special interest in light of several recent developments:

- Perhaps the most noteworthy of these is the formation, in mid 1962, of the Marketing Science Institute, an organization supported by some 29 large corporations and devoted to "fundamental research" in the field of marketing.
- At the same time, the American Marketing Association, a professional group dedicated to "the advancement of science in marketing," has re-examined its own goals and taken stock of its accomplishments to date.
- Finally, the issue of science in marketing—and especially the uses of science or of its results by executives responsible for marketing decisions—also has received considerable attention in several recently published books.

Thus, it seems appropriate at this point to pause and consider the status of science in marketing, to sift out the claims and counterclaims and to ask whether any basic changes are needed in management's approach to marketing problems.

## What Is Marketing Science?

The Marketing Science Institute is headed by Dr. Wendell R. Smith, formerly Staff Vice President for Marketing Development at the Radio Corporation of America, and before that a university teacher. Smith stated in an address delivered to the Kansas City Chapter of the American Marketing Association on July 10, 1962, that the goals of MSI were:

1. To contribute to the emergence of a more definitive science of marketing.
2. To stimulate increased application of scientific techniques to the understanding and solving of marketing problems.

It is useful to keep these two points separate. First, we can consider whether or not there is such a thing as a science *of* marketing, comparable in some sense to the sciences of physics, biology, and so on. Secondly, there is still remaining the question of how and to what extent scientific techniques can be applied *to* marketing—whether or not it is, or may be, a science in itself.

Of the two goals set forth by the MSI, certainly the first is the more ambitious. In order to qualify as a distinct science in its own right, marketing will have to meet some rather stringent requirements. For example, it is generally agreed that a science is:

- a classified and systematized body of knowledge,
- organized around one or more central theories and a number of general principles,
- usually expressed in quantitative terms,
- knowledge which permits the prediction and, under some circumstances, the control of future events.

Few believe that marketing now meets these criteria. True, there is a substantial body of classified knowledge about marketing, but there certainly is no central theory; furthermore, there are few accepted principles, and our ability to predict is limited indeed. One reason for this state of affairs is that, for most of the 50 years since the beginnings of concerted efforts to study marketing, our emphasis has been predominantly on fact-gathering.

The story of attempts to describe and understand marketing phenomena, beginning in the early 1900s, is chronicled by Robert Bartels of Ohio State University in his new book, *The Development of Marketing Thought*.[1] Bartels sees the early study of marketing as an offshoot of economics, brought about by changes in economic conditions in the late nineteenth century. These changes produced a ''growing disparity between facts and assumptions underlying prevailing [economic] theory,'' and one of the primary missions of the pioneer marketing students was to reconcile this disparity.

In particular, Bartels notes that while traditional economic theory assumed that producers could (and would) adjust to the market, by 1900 they increasingly sought to adjust the market to their own needs instead. Similarly, orthodox theory had little place for middlemen, and provided no key to understanding the growing size and diversity of such organizations as department stores and mail-order houses. In short, prevailing economic theory did not explain the observed facts about marketing, much less provide any basis for intelligent management.

Believing that economic theory was inadequate as a basis for understanding the marketing system, early students of marketing set out to describe existing institutions and practices and to discover, if possible, the rationale underlying them. Consequently, a spirit of thoroughgoing empiricism pervaded their efforts. For example, Bartels describes a project undertaken in the 1920s by the New York University School of Retailing in cooperation with a group of New York City department stores. This project culminated in the publication of the so-called ''Retailing Series,'' which described the best contemporary practices in merchandising, retail credit, and so on.[2]

This empiricism of academic investigators was strongly reinforced by the philosophy of most business executives. Recently there have been indications that some executives are becoming more receptive to the notion of ''theory.'' The willingness of its sponsors to support MSI provides an outstanding example of this. But most managers who are responsible for day-to-day decisions are still typically inclined to distrust generalizations. Charles Ramond of the Advertising Research Foundation pointed out in a paper, ''Theories of Choice in Business,'' delivered at the Annual Convention of the American Psychological Association in St. Louis on September 5, 1962:

> The businessman's practical wisdom is of a completely different character than scientific knowledge. While it does not ignore generalities, it recognizes the low probability that given combinations of phenomena can or will be repeated.... In place of scientific knowledge, then, the businessman collects lore.

Both academicians and practitioners have concentrated on the accumulation of facts about marketing. To some extent, these facts have been systematized through a process of definition, classification, and analysis. But it must be admitted that few real principles have emerged. Bartels lists a number of generalizations drawn from the literature of marketing; but some of these are actually derived from traditional economic theory, while others are merely tautologies. As an example of the first type, we are told that sellers, under pure competition, will expand output until marginal cost equals marginal revenue. An illustration of a tautology is the assertion that ''when conditions demand modification in the existing marketing structure, the change will be made.''

## Related Sciences

While marketing does not yet appear to qualify as a science in its own right, high hopes have been placed on the applications of findings and methods from other fields which are, presumably, further along the evolutionary trail. This optimism is reflected in several articles among those reprinted in a new revision of *Managerial Marketing: Perspectives and Viewpoints—A Source Book,* edited by William Lazer and Eugene Kelley.[3] First among these articles is one by Joseph W. Newman, originally appearing in HBR,[4] which asserts:

> As marketers have become increasingly aware of how much they have to learn about the nature of buying and consumption, they have turned for assistance to the behavioral sciences, which have made great progress in recent times. Much can be gained from this move.

Some of the potential benefits of adopting and applying the results of scientific inquiry in psychology, sociology, and other fields are outlined by Lazer and Kelley in another of the papers in their collection, under the formidable title of "Interdisciplinary Contributions to Marketing Management." These authors distinguish between "discovery disciplines" (i.e., those concerned with discovering regularities in specified aspects of nature) and "application disciplines" (i.e., those oriented to specific types of problems).

In these terms, marketing would appear to be primarily an area for application of findings *from* the sciences (especially behavioral sciences), and not a science in itself. Should the attempt to make it a science, then, be abandoned as a wild-goose chase?

No, it should be continued, W. J. Baumol argues in "On the Role of Marketing Theory," another article included in the Lazer and Kelley book. Baumol points out that while the problems of marketing do, in fact, fall within the spheres of such fields as economics, sociology, and psychology, it is also possible to argue that economics is merely a branch of psychology, and so on. He concludes that "marketing has its special problems and may therefore, well find it useful to develop further its own body of theory."

But what form should this theory take? Baumol warns that it is too much to expect that theory will permit *exact* predictions of the future. Theory, of necessity, involves abstraction from, and simplification of, reality. Thus, the theorist's task includes;

> ... examination of some aspect of reality and construction of a simplified small-scale model which behaves in at least some ways like the phenomena under observation. The analyst can understand and trace out the workings of his model while reality is far too complicated and chaotic for this to be possible.... This method is well established in

> the natural sciences. The physicist cannot predict just what path will be followed by a real automobile left free to roll down a real hill.... He can only tell us what will happen in the artificial circumstances described by a controlled experiment, where the elements carefully held constant in the laboratory are the aspects of reality from which his simplified model abstracts.

Has any useful theory in this sense been developed in marketing? One interesting attempt is described by Leo Aspinwall in ''The Characteristics of Goods Theory'' in the same book. Aspinwall's theory is designed ''to predict with a high degree of reliability how a product will be distributed,'' that is, to predict the marketing channels that will be used to reach ultimate consumers or other end users. Five characteristics or ''distinguishing qualities'' are defined:

1. Replacement rate—the rate at which a good is purchased and consumed.
2. Gross margin—the total cost of moving a product from point of origin to final consumer.
3. ''Adjustment''—the extent of services which must be ''applied to goods in order to meet the exact needs of the consumer.''
4. Time of consumption—durability of the product.
5. Searching time required to procure the product.

Aspinwall argues that these five characteristics are interrelated—in particular, replacement rate is inversely related to the other four, which in turn are directly related to each other. Hence, it is possible to combine the characteristics and derive a threefold classification of goods, arbitrarily designated as ''red,'' ''orange,'' and ''yellow.'' Red goods, with a high replacement rate, low gross margin, low degree of adjustment, short consumption time, and low searching time, will be characterized by ''broadcast distribution'' and relatively long marketing channels. Yellow goods, with the opposite characteristics, will be distributed direct, while orange goods occupy an intermediate position.

Now, it is possible to criticize the Aspinwall theory on several counts. First, if it is true that replacement rate is invariably related to the other four characteristics, then the whole theory could be built on this single factor; the others are redundant. In the physical sciences, the principle of ''parsimony'' is well established. William of Ockham, a fourteenth century English scholastic, laid down the rule that theories should be as simple as possible, and the reasons for this seem as compelling in marketing as anywhere else.

A second criticism of the characteristics-of-goods theory is that, to some extent, it seems circular. It can be argued that the total gross margin required to distribute a product and the searching time required to obtain it are *results* of the marketing channels used, not underlying causes. Finally, there is some ambiguity as to whether Aspinwall is trying to explain how goods *are* distributed or how they *should be* distributed. If the implication is that these are one and the same, then there is a hidden premise in the theory.

But the point is not whether or not Aspinwall's theory is correct. In either case it may well be *useful*, because it provides a way of *organizing* facts about marketing. Lazer believes that this is the ultimate value of theory. In ''Philosophic Aspects of the Marketing Discipline,'' another selection included in the book, he argues:

> Marketing thought should not proceed merely by the accumulation of observations which are unregulated by theory. It is generally accepted that fruitful observations cannot be made, nor their results arranged and correlated, without the use of hypotheses which go beyond the existing state of knowledge.

## MARKETING SCIENCE & MANAGERS

At this point, the executive may well ask: ''What has all this to do with me?'' Many feel that the whole debate about science in marketing is strictly an academic red herring, and that the quest for science is really a roundabout form of academic status-seeking. Indeed, there is a certain unintentional irony in the plaint by Lazer and Kelly that ''as a discipline, marketing is often assigned a relatively low status in the academic spectrum.''

But there is more at stake than the vanities of professors. Some very ''practical'' men feel that even the modest progress to date toward science in marketing calls for a new approach by management. On this score, Donald R. Longman, President of the American Marketing Association, said in a message to members of the association in September 1962:

> The concept of science in marketing and the idea of objective and thorough study of issues, acquisition and evaluation of relevant facts, are no longer the exclusive province in business of the researcher. The scientific approach has spread, permeating all senior levels of decision making.... This is a new thing—the marketing staff manager and decision maker as a researcher concerned with the science of marketing.

This viewpoint is strongly advocated by Edward C. Bursk in his new book, *Text and Cases in Marketing: A Scientific Approach*. Bursk states flatly that ''old-fashioned judgmental decision making must be supplanted by a more scientific approach.''

What does such an approach entail? Bursk sets forth three requirements:

1. The use of scientific theories, and techniques based on them, wherever available.
2. Increased use of experimentation.
3. The use of analysis to decide on action in a ''systematic, planned way.''

Perhaps even more important than these prescriptions is the concept of *integration* between decision making and research activities which pervades this entire book. While many executives have long recognized the need for information on which to base intelligent decisions, and have spent substantial sums on research to get such information, all to often research is not really used effectively.

Joseph W. Newman, in another HBR article,[6] has noted:

> Only in a relatively small number of companies has marketing research become a regular part of the making of important policy and operating decisions.
>
> In companies with marketing research units, a wide gap typically separates research personnel and management personnel.

What typically happens, Newman observes, is that the role of marketing ''research'' is seen purely as one of fact gathering. The manager recognizes the need for information on market shares, advertising recall, extent of distribution, and the like. But the relationships between these things and a firm's marketing policies are seldom analyzed. When they are, in some massive ''one-shot'' study, the results are usually disappointing, and the atmosphere becomes antagonistic to further investigation for several years.

Executives who distrust research per se take these failings as justification of their attitude. (Ha! You see? Even with all their formulas, they couldn't predict what would happen in Moline! What we need here is experienced judgment, not a lot of harebrained theories!)

It is probably unfortuante that the term ''research'' ever came to be used to describe the activities of most marketing research staff units. A much better designation would be ''marketing intelligence,'' since the purpose of these activities is directly analogous to those of a G-2 unit in the Army. Military intelligence personnel are not expected to develop a science of warfare. Their mission, instead, is to obtain complete, accurate, and current information.

Such concentration on detailed, particularized data is, in fact, inconsistent with real scientific inquiry. For the same reason, it is probably hopeless to expect much progress in the development of science in marketing as a result of simply stockpiling more and more current facts. This does not mean that facts are unimportant. But they should be looked on as the raw materials of research, not its end results.

All of this suggests that what is needed is a very different kind of research, together with a very different approach to it by management. This approach will require, among other things, that research specialists and management ''generalists'' know more about each others' jobs. Beyond this, Newman advocates the use of ''research generalists' who would serve as middlemen between executives and research technicians. A similar proposal has also been made by Marion Harper, Jr.[7] Finally, progress in marketing science will require a view of research as a continuous, cumulative process, with constant interaction between investigators and the decision-makers who utilize their findings.

## Development Problems

Granted for the moment that the goal of science in marketing is a desirable one, why does the task appear to be so difficult? There are essentially three schools of thought on this point.

1. That science in marketing can be achieved by continued application of the same methods used in other fields, but that results are harder to achieve because the phenomena being studied are more complex.
2. That marketing phenomena (and human behavior in general) differ in *kind* from those of the physical sciences, so that *different methods* will have to be employed in studying them.
3. That marketing (and, again, human behavior in general) can never become a science because of its inherent elusiveness. Thus, the search for science is well intentioned but doomed to failure.

Bursk subscribes to the first of these beliefs, asserting that ''the material is so intricate and intangible that hitherto it has not been tackled consciously and formally.'' His reasons for believing as he does are based on these facts:

- Buying and selling involve a ''subtle, fluid interaction,'' with actions on each side affecting actions on the other.
- The number of possible combinations of actions by a seller is very large.
- General economic conditions are continually changing, and this clouds the effects of a firm's marketing programs.
- The actions of competitors also influence marketing results.[8]

In brief, these reasons boil down to the idea that since observed behavior in marketing is influenced by *many variables*, it is very difficult to isolate the effect of any one or any small combination of variables. But is this not also true in the physical sciences? The behavior of a missile, for example, is subject to the influences of numerous factors, including some which are only dimly perceived.

In the speech referred to earlier, Charles Ramond suggested that the events studied by physical scientists are easier to understand and predict because physical systems are basically simpler than human behavior systems. First, physical systems are ''loosely coupled.'' While many variables affect an event, it is possible to study one or a few as if they were, in fact, isolated. A statistician would term this a ''low degree of interaction''; for example, while both temperature and atmospheric pressure may affect some event, it is possible to hold one of these constant and measure the effects of the other, and get good predictive results. In contrast, variables affecting human behavior interact to such an extent that the familiar ''other-things-being-equal'' assumption can lead to mistaken conclusions.

Further, according to Ramond, physical scientists have generally been able to represent real systems by *linear equations*, i.e., by relatively simple models which can readily be manipulated. But such simple models have not been found adequate to describe human behavior. For example, forecasts of sales, population growth, and so forth based on linear regression models have usually been very inaccurate.

And finally, while relationships among physical phenomena are characteristically *stable* over extended time periods, marketing is thought to be highly *dynamic*. Thus, relationships which seem to describe a system at one time may not hold at some future time.

Because marketing deals with events which are, in Ramond's phrase, ''tightly coupled, nonlinear, and dynamic,'' the progress of science is slow and painful at best. An excellent illustration of the difficulties encountered in the ''scientific approach'' is afforded by Alfred R. Oxenfeldt in ''Diary of a Research Project in the Television Set Industry.''[9] Oxenfeldt describes, blow by blow, his efforts over a five-year period to explain changes in the market shares of TV set manufacturers.

He postulated that these changes resulted from differences in product quality, prices, dealer margins, and advertising efforts. To test this hypothesis, it was first necessary to get reasonably complete information on the ''independent variables'' as well as on market-share results. But Oxenfeldt found that only partial information on any of the variables could be obtained; for instance, quality ratings by product-testing agencies were based on only one or two of the 15 or 25 models offered by a manufacturer. Worse still, many of the terms used in the industry (such as ''margin'') ''... cannot be defined rigorously or even in a manner that would insure substantial uniformity of usage.'' Finally, it was discovered that no records at all were kept of some of the most important actions taken by manufacturers.

Further investigation led Oxenfeldt to the conclusion that it would probably be impossible to discover any meaningful regularities in the TV set market as a whole. He felt that, in the end, each local market was a separate case, that each manufacturer was different from all the others, and that conditions changed significantly from one time period to the next. This, in effect, supports the notion that marketing systems are *unstable*; and this, in turn, implies that conclusions reached from the study of the past have only limited applicability to the future.

Note that the assumption of stability underlies much of what is known in the physical sciences. For example, it has been found that certain substances undergo radioactive disintegration at a constant rate relative to time. This provides the basis for the ''dating'' methods used in geology and archaeology. Suppose, however, that radioactive disintegration were *not* a stable process; indeed, there is no way to prove that it is. If the rate of disintegration does change, then all of the dates applied to various epochs in the earth's history are, in fact, wrong.

Thus, there is serious question about the belief, expressed by Harlan D. Mills in "Brand A Versus Brand B—A Mathematical Approach," that "marketing 'laws' can be derived in the same manner as the laws of physics [so that] the way is open for marketing to become, more and more, a science."[10]

If the concepts and methods of the physical sciences cannot be lifted bodily over to the study of marketing, what then? As noted earlier, one of the missions of the Marketing Science Institue is to promote the use of scientific *techniques* in marketing. Presumably this includes the development of new, special-purpose techniques. It is not possible to foresee just what form these new techniques may take.

It seems likely, however, that some of them will be based on the technology of the computer. Already some operations researchers have found that complex models of market behavior are best "solved" by simulation—that is by generating artificial experience and testing the effects of changes by simulated experimentation. Since field experiments in marketing are so costly—and sometimes downright impossible—simulation may play an increasing role in the future.

Even if a new scientific tool kit can be developed, there are some who think marketing can never be a science. E.B. Weiss, the Madison Avenue iconoclast, espouses this extreme viewpoint.[11] Weiss argues, first, that attempts to discover scientific principles over the past 40 years have been unsuccessful, and that many of them have really been hoaxes. More important, he notes that even honest efforts involve the use of such concepts as "average behavior," i.e., the use of probability theory and statistical analysis. Weiss claims that there is "no such thing as an 'average mind' or 'average behavior.' "

If this argument is meant to imply that knowledge expressed in terms of probabilities is essentially unscientific, then much of modern physics is also unscientific. The phenomenon of radioactive disintegration mentioned earlier, in fact, rests squarely on probability theory. The rate of disintegration used in dating objects is an *average* rate, and the only justification for using it is that the number of objects (atoms) involved is so large that individual deviations become unimportant.

To the extent that marketing deals with the behavior of large groups of people, the same reasoning applies to it. Certainly the notion of "average behavior" has been used effectively by insurance companies. Conclusions based on the probabilities of certain kinds of behavior among large groups cannot, of course, legitimately be applied to individuals; but predictions of individual responses may not be necessary for scientific marketing.

## ART OF USING SCIENCE

Let us suppose for a moment that the millenium does arrive, and marketing does, indeed, become a full-fledged science. What then? Will marketing decisions become routine, with computers grinding our solutions in response to the proper inputs? Not so, is the view of Theodore Levitt, as expressed in his book, *Innovation in Marketing*.[12] Levitt points out that ''management has always sought formulas and prescriptions for easier decision making.'' As a result, management has become susceptible to the ''seductions of science,'' and has fallen easy prey to the exaggerated claims of some researchers. Further, he believes that the root of the problem is that ''all too often neither the researchers nor the corporate bosses really know what it is they are trying to do.'' This is another way of saying that marketing science—even in its relatively crude present state—is concerned with means, not ends. This is equally true of the most advanced branches of knowledge. Scientists can (presumably) tell us how to get a man to the moon, but do we really *want* a man on the moon? The main theme of *Innovation in Marketing* is the need for management to define just where it is trying to go. This need will remain regardless of how much progress may be made in developing marketing as a science.

For a long time to come, it seems clear that marketing science will not advance to a stage in which the element of risk is eliminated from decisions. Bursk says that risk is an integral part of marketing management. Levitt goes even further: ''That is what management is all about—taking risks.'' While increased knowledge can help in *identifying* the risks involved in decisions, and in some cases provide *measures* of their magnitudes, it can never eliminate them altogether.

Because science is concerned with means, it does not offer any answers to the basic questions of *values* underlying marketing management. It is a commonplace that the results of science can be used rightly or wrongly. Consequently, no matter how scientific marketing may become, managers must still govern their actions, in part, by considerations of their ultimate effects on customers, employees, and society at large.

Indeed, advancements in marketing science will put ethical issues into even bolder relief than at present. To some extent, science usually implies *control*. A vision of ''the hidden persuaders,'' only this time equipped with true scientific knowledge rather than just the dubious baggage of depth interviewing, is disturbing to many observers. It can only be hoped that along with increased knowledge will come increased competence to use it wisely.

In any case, at least for a long time to come, it will remain the responsibility of the manager to evaluate the worth of alleged advances in marketing science, and to decide whether and how new knowledge is to be used in administration. As Levitt phrases it:

> The highest form of achievement is always art, never science.... Business leadership *is* an art worthy of [the manager's] own respect and the public's plaudits.

## ENDNOTES

1. Robert Bartels, *The Development of Marketing Thought* (Homewood, Illinois, Richard D. Irwin, Inc., 1962).
2. This series included more than a dozen titles by various authors, such as James L. Fri, *Retail Merchandising, Planning, and Control* (New York, Prentice-Hall, Inc., 1925) and Norris A. Brisco and John W. Wingate, *Retail Buying* (New York, Prentice-Hall, Inc., 1925).
3. William Lazer and Eugene Kelley, editors, *Managerial Marketing: Perspectives and Viewpoints—A Source Book* (Homewood, Illinois, Richard D. Irwin. Inc., 1962).
4. Joseph W. Newman, "New Insight, New Progress, for Marketing," *HBR* November-December 1957, p. 95.
5. Edward C. Bursk, *Text and Cases in Marketing: A Scientific Approach* (Englewood Cliffs, New Jersey, Prentice-Hall, Inc., 1962).
6. Joseph W. Newman, "Put Research Into Marketing Decisions," *HBR* March-April 1962, p. 105.
7. "A New Profession to Aid Marketing Management," *Journal of Marketing*, January 1961, pp. 1-6.
8. Bursk, op. cit., pp. 6-7.
9. Presented as a case in Bursk, op. cit., pp. 31-44 (adapted from "Scientific Marketing: Ideal and Ordeal," *HBR* March-April 1961, p. 51.
10. Presented as a case in Bursk, op. cit., pp. 23-30 (adapted from "Marketing as a Science," *HBR* September-October 1961, p. 137).
11. E. B. Weiss, "Will Marketing Ever Become a Science?" *Advertising Age*, August 20, 1962, pp. 64-65.
12. Theodore Levitt, *Innovation in Marketing* (New York, McGraw-Hill Book Company, Inc., 1962).

## ACKNOWLEDGEMENT

I gratefully acknowledge the assistance of Michael Halbert, who read the original version of this article and made many useful suggestions on it.

# 9 —— Marketing, Science, and Technology

*John O'Shaughnessy and*
*Michael J. Ryan*

Reprinted from *Conceptual and Theoretical Developments in Marketing*, published by the American Marketing Association, edited by Ferrell, Brown, and Lamb (1979), pp. 557-589. Reprinted by permission.

## Introduction

This paper organizes the current debate concerning the status of marketing as a science within the framework of currently accepted notions of science and technology. We propose a recognition of science *in* marketing and *in* marketing technology that forces an integration of two fields. This contrasts with current attempts to recognize ''pure'' theory and ''applied'' marketing.

## Marketing and Science

The nature of science is fuzzy as writers adopt different viewpoints. These viewpoints will be discussed, not to settle the problem as to the nature of science, but to gauge the current status of marketing as a field of study.

### A Science as Any Ordered or Teachable Body of Knowledge

In ancient Greece, any ordered and teachable body of knowledge was viewed as science. Later, in Europe, the term ''science'' came to embrace all branches of analytic and empirical study, though the word ''philosophy'' was espoused as a synonym. This view prevailed until the eighteenth century.

Marketing is a science in the original Greek sense of the word since it has a body of knowledge that can be taught.

### Science as the Natural Sciences

In the late eighteenth century, the viewpoint emerged of science as a set of empirically provable propositions to be contrasted with religion or revealed truth. Darwinism led to a more pronounced distinction and science became even more identified with the natural sciences of physics and chemistry, etc. This view was so accepted that Sir Francis Galton in 1877 moved that the section covering the so-called social sciences be excluded from the British Association for the Advancement of Science. Obviously, marketing is not a natural science.

## Science as a Method of Inquiry for Imposing Order and Testing for Truth

As those concerned with the study of animal and human behavior sought a firm basis for knowledge, they turned to the *methods* of the physical sciences. Out of this search came the "positivist movement" associated with John Stuart Mill and Auguste Comte.

What defines science is the natural science *method* of imposing order and testing for truth. Since all problems are not open to the methods of the natural sciences, this view ruled out certain subject-matter from science, e.g., ethics.

The Vienna Circle developed the "principle of verifiability" which, with later modifications (Ayer 1964) held that a statement is only factually significant when we know how to verify what it asserts. The impossibility of obtaining absolute verification led to the "principle of falsifiability" to distinguish non-scientific from scientific propositions (Popper 1965). If there were no observations that might conceivably falsify the proposition, it lay outside the realm of science. The progressive elimination of rival hypotheses was the method by which science advances.

An alternative view of how science advances was subsequently proposed by Kuhn (1962). Kuhn claimed that scientific change is either consolidatory in the sense that it occurs within the framework of an overall master-theory or *paradigm* or it is revolutionary in that some currently accepted paradigm is first challenged and then overthrown in favor of an entirely different conceptual viewpoint. This view was criticized on the ground that scientific change is never as revolutionary as Kuhn claims; the change from one paradigm to another never amounts to an entirely different world view (Toulmin 1972). Kuhn, more recently, has retreated from his central distinction between the "consolidatory" change that occurs within the boundaries of a paradigm and the "revolutionary" change that involves a complete change in paradigm. He now views change as occurring through an unending sequence of smaller "revolutions."

If science is the method of inquiry known as the scientific method then there is science *in* marketing and such a view of science is often misconceived as the science *for* marketing. Science for marketing involves both subject matter and method.

## Science as a Distinct Body of Knowledge Organized on the Basis of Explanatory Principles.

In addition to the claim that a science must use the scientific method, Hempel (1965) has made claims for the universality in science of a particular type of explanation. Hempel's approach (1965) to constructing a scientific explanation is a refinement of the so-called deductive model first elaborated by John Stuart Mill. This approach (also known as the covering law approach or the deductive-nomological type of explanation) accounts for a particular event by showing it follows from some particular law or principle. The objective of theory is to provide a set of such laws to account, as a matter of deduction, for some empirical generalization.

A more flexible view of scientific explanation than that of Hempel et al. is associated with Wisdon (1952), Toulmin (1961) and Hanson (1965). They view explanation as simply providing a network of connections between events so the explanandum is related to familiar occurrences. In either case the goal of science is the organization and classification of knowledge on the basis of explanatory principles obtained through the application of scientific method. This is the view we favor since it has general acceptance at the present time. It presupposes each science has a distinct domain and concepts.

Work currently being done in marketing contributes to the development of a science defined as the ''organization and classification of knowledge on the basis of explanatory principles.'' Whether enough has been done to constitute a science *of* marketing is doubtful. The question arises whether marketing has theoretical concepts, techniques, distinct domain, etc. from the other academic disciplines. It may be that marketing is simply the basic disciplines given a coherence by their relevance to marketing decision-making.

## Science as a Set of Distinct Problems Plus a Method of Solving Them

What distinguishes science on this view is a distinct set of problems and a method of solving them. This view had had some vogue in the social sciences but little support from philosophers of science since the solutions to problems do not always necessitate explanation.

## Applying Scientific Criteria to Marketing

There are two scientific criteria to which marketing fails to conform in the sense of an established, distinct body of knowledge organized on the basis of explanatory principles. In the first place there is no general agreement on concepts and paradigms. Secondly, there are no paradigms showing cumulative progress in the explanatory powers of the discipline.

In regard to the first criterion, academics in marketing tend to have backgrounds in related disciplines and look on marketing as an area in which to apply their area's expertise. This is evident (say) in the number of different orientations followed in empirically investigating multiattribute attitude models in marketing (Wilkie and Pessemier 1973) or the widely divergent perspectives brought in investigating distribution channels. Thus, Stern (1971) has fathered a research orientation that combines concepts from sociology, cultural anthropology, social psychology, and organizational behavior while Bucklin (1966) has promulgated an approach relying mainly on economic concepts. There seems to be no movement toward a synthesis, merger or conciliation of these approaches. Thus, as Bucklin (1978) says, the behavioral orientation has focused on power for the sake of understanding power itself rather than distribution systems. Bucklin claims the behavioral approaches do not address legitimate marketing issues, thus showing the domain issue to be controversial. There are numerous arguments concerning the legitimate subject matter of marketing (Angelmar and Pinson 1975; Arndt 1978; Bagozzi 1975, 1976; Bartels 1974; Hunt 1976a, 1976b; Kotler 1972; Kotler and Levy 1969a; Luck 1969, 1974; Sweeney 1972; Tucker 1974). Anyone reading this literature must conclude that there is disagreement concerning even the basic focus of marketing.

An observation made by Lazer (1958) some years ago is still relevant, namely, that the masterworks of marketing theory—the paradigms—have yet to be delineated. Those who believe this controversy will be resolved shortly are overly optimistic since marketing academicians are primarily engaged in technique rather than conceptual development (Longman 1971). This situation is different from that in the more advanced disciplines where theoreticians rather than technicians are exalted (Lazer 1958).

The second criterion is related to the first since explanatory power presupposes agreement as to the subject matter to be explained. It is common for diverse marketing investigations of the same phenomena to result in conceptual confusion (in spite of technological sophistication) rather than clarification. The subsequent effect is an abandonment of the area in favor of other challenges. To return to a previous example, Wilkie and Pessemier (1973) identified a number of issues that remain open despite the demise of multiattribute model research. This is unfortunate since multiattribute models frequently serve as a framework for the emerging area of information processing, which is otherwise inhibited by a lack of knowledge of the basic relationships among multiattribute variables (Ryan and Holbrook 1979). Personality research (Kassarjian 1971) provides another example of a subject being abandoned because of conceptual confusion. Psychographics is a poor replacement since it is a technique that lays no claim to theory development. The prevalence of bandwagons, referred to by one writer as "the fad of the month club" (Jacoby 1978), does not signal cumulative progess. Thus, despite a good deal of effort to develop a science of marketing, the claim to science is at present vacuous.

## MARKETING AND TECHNOLOGY

### Management as Technology

Marketing as an academic discipline seeks to apply the scientific method and to build up a body of "theory." However, marketing management is a user and not a producer of explanatory systems. Marketing *management* in fact falls under the heading of "technology" to which science contributes but does not determine.

## Science vs. Technology

Science can be distinguished from technology on the basis of its goals. Science aims at truth, better theories and explanation, while technology seeks more effective solutions to practical problems (Skolinowski 1972). Science is concerned with knowing *that* something is the case, while technology is concerned with *how* to do something.

Polanyi (1962) views technology as concerned with the design of systems that can succeed or fail. Since success/failure (effectiveness/ineffectiveness) are judgmental decisions, they are not scientifically determined. The operational principles involved are essentially "rules of rightness." Rules, unlike laws, can be effective or ineffective in terms of purpose which varies according to user, but cannot, as is the case with explanation, be judged true or false.

The rules followed in any technology are always more vague and imprecise than scientific laws. They cannot be transmitted by prescription since no complete prescription exists. Thus, the articulate contents of science are universally taught, whereas the nature of the rules for doing technological research inhibits their spread throughout the world.

As technology develops, the effect is a change in techniques, processes and other practical procedures. Such a development may or may not be initiated, accelerated or even helped by scientific theories and concepts (Toulmin 1972). In fact, different technologies depend on science to different degrees. Thus, aerodynamics is crucially dependent on science, while such activities as brewing are still very much at the art stage. In any case, technological innovations are judged on whether they work and whether they are free from objectionable side effects.

Bunge (1972) contrasts technological research with that in science. While research in science seeks "laws" to explain kinds of events, technological research seeks "stable norms" or rules, that is, the set of action-steps that should be taken if some predetermined goal is to be achieved. Bunge argues for what he calls "grounded rules," which are rules that receive some support from the findings of science. Every effort, he argues, should be made to explain why some rule is likely to be effective, as such explanation is what "distinguishes the prescriptive arts from contemporary technology" and makes for the more reliable achievement of goals. Thus, science is the basis of a "grounded technology." Bunge distinguishes "substantive" from "operative" technological theories in that the former are made up of grounded rules, while the latter are not grounded in the findings of science.

### Marketing Management as Technology

The questions we ask in marketing management are essentially "how to" questions; they are technological questions, e.g., "How do we determine what those in the market currently seek?"

Marketing management is concerned with plans or rules specifying the steps to be taken to solve such problems. Scientific findings are none the less relevant. Causal "laws," for example, link sets of antecedents to sets of consequences. Such "laws" etc. can be relevant to technology in the prediction and analysis of the various consequences arising from various strategic options.

Technology in marketing has not been the sole preserve of practitioners. Ehrenberg's "laws" (1972), for example, are technological rules and not scientific laws as they are empirical regularities unbuttressed by explanation.

Science and technolgoy form an interacting system: science gives underpinnings to technology while technology provides problems for science to solve. Of course, technological rules [e.g., the marketing concept (Keith 1960)] may be implicitly explanatory though science may still explain the conditions under which some set of consequences is more likely to arise. An understanding of the interplay and interdependence of science and technology provides the basis for understanding the synergistic relationship between the academic community and marketing practitioners. This interplay has been requested by academics (Kernan 1973) and practitioners (Cook 1974).

## Science, Technology and Marketing

### Marketing's Status

The marketing literature is only consistent in demonstrating the disagreement on the status of marketing as a science. There are those who maintain marketing is already a science (Kotler 1972); Hunt 1976a, 1976b; Bagozzi 1976; Robin 1970). There are those who believe it has the potential to be a science (Dawson 1971, Mills 1961, Bartels 1951, Taylor 1965, Alderson and Cox 1948, Levy 1976). In contrast there are those who claim marketing is not a science (Oxenfeldt 1961, Brown 1948, Sweeney 1972, Longman 1971) and will never be (Hutchinson 1952, Vaile 1949). The disagreement has been exacerbated by two major sources of confusion that are partially recognized by current writers (Hunt 1976a, 1976b; Bagozzi, 1976, Angelmar and Pinson 1975, Levy 1976).

### Marketing Can Never Be a Science

The first source of confusion arises from a failure to distinguish between:

1. Marketing as a field of human endeavor. This is marketing technology where the aim is to delineate more effective rules for achieving management's goals.

2. Marketing as a study of market and marketing phenomena. This is science in and of marketing.

Hunt (1976a, 1976b) describes normative marketing as a description of what ought to be and positive marketing as concerned with factual and explanatory propositions. He argues that those who deny marketing can ever be a science ignore this positive dimension. He claims this to be an untenable position given the abundant and visible efforts of academics to explain and predict.

Hunt's two dimensions of marketing capture a flavor of our distinction between marketing technology and science in marketing; a major distinction is his emphasis on process and our emphasis on objectives. We endorse Hunt in refuting the arguments of those who claim that marketing, when viewed as a study of market and marketing phenomena can never be a science.

## Marketing Is a Science

The second source of confusion arises over the basis for classification as a science. Though there are historical views that lend support to categorizing marketing as a science, such views corrupt the basic goals implicit in the mature sciences, namely, the development of explanatory systems regarding the phenomena of interest. They bestow title unearned and ultimately unrewarding. Still other views as to the nature of science find no support at all in the literature. Thus Robin (1970) argues for a normative science, though as Hunt point out, such a view runs counter to prevailing views of science that collectively exclude value statements.

Explanatory systems explain *classes* of phenomena or *types* of events. The question arises as to marketing's discriminative domain and focus of interest. Kotler (1972) proposes the "transaction" and Bagozzi (1975) the "exchange" as the basic phenomena of interest. Hunt (1976a, 1976b, 1978) takes the "transaction" as the base on which to build. He supports his claim for marketing as a science on the following grounds.

1. The positive dimension of marketing pursues the objectives of science.
2. Marketing has a unique focus in the "transaction."
3. The positive dimension of marketing has led to the discovery of uniformities and regularities among phenomena.
4. Positive marketing uses scientific method.

In regard to marketing having a unique focus in the "transaction" we differ with Hunt. We would also modify statement (3) to read "*explanations* of observed uniformities and regularities among *collective* phenomena" so as to capture the differentia of science to distinguish it from technology. Given Hunt's criteria and focus on the transaction, the objectives of any science of marketing must center on the the transaction and explanations must relate to the transaction. It is not clear that science has occurred or is occurring.

Kotler's and Bagozzi's proposed paradigm are basically refinements of Alderson's (1965) "Law of Exchange" which reads:

> Given that *X* is an element of assortment A1, and *Y* is an element of assortment A2; *X* is exchangable for *Y* if, and only if, three conditions are met:
>
> a. *X* is different from *Y*.
>
> b. The potency of assortment A1 is increased by dropping *X* and adding *Y*.
>
> c. The potency of assortment A2 is increased by adding *X* and dropping *Y* (p. 84).

Such a statement postulates the quasi-necessary conditions for exchange. They are *logical* pre-requisites rooted in the axioms of economics given the need to maximize some utility function. To elevate them to a "law" is to mock scientific endeavor and ignore the essential elements of scientific explanation in relating antecedents to consequents. Furthermore, to assert that this so-called law has been a major focus of empirical investigation is either to fly in the face of the facts or to stretch the meaning of exchange to be a synonym for marketing. To choose "exchange" as the central focus for study is to embrace social psychology under the rubric of marketing since the exchange of perceptions, meanings and sentiments is the essence of social psychology. In fact every type of interaction leads to some form of exchange. Of course, Alderson's law, along with so many of his ideas, has been more talked about than been the focus of empirical inquiry. Far from marketing having a building block, it is unusual to find a literature review in marketing that does not complain of the absence of a common thread.

## Marketing as a Potential Science

Although we refute the claims for marketing as a science, we do not dismiss the possibility of marketing having the potential to be a science. This is not because we endorse the arguments currently put forward in support. On the contrary, we believe many of these views are based on antiquated views of science. As a consequence, they provide easy targets. Thus, Hutchinson (1952) rejects the "potential science" claim on the ground that those making the proposal (Alderson and Cox 1948, Bartels 1951) select their own definitions of science. We agree. Taylor (1965) and Mills (1961), for example, base their claim on marketing's use of scientific method. Dawson's argument is more complex, but still misconceived. He argues that there is manifest pressure on all sides to regard marketing as a "normal science." Pressure has resulted in a disinclination to define the domain of marketing or to question its paradigms in favor of an obsessive concern with solving practical marketing problems. His own view a la Kuhn is that the current stage in marketing's development signifies a "crisis" which, in the absence of the pressure for practical results would trigger a revolution in paradigms.

This adoption of Kuhn's view of scientific advance is misapplied. It presupposes marketing is already a normal science with established paradigms. No such paradigms in fact exist.

We are sympathetic to the need (Lazer 1962, Longman 1971) to redirect our attention from a primary concern with technology to developing fruitful paradigms (Alderson 1957, Kotler 1972, Bagozzi 1975). The question arises as to where to start. The first step is to determine the central phenomenon of interest as theories, methods and other elements of a paradigm are anchored to such a base. There are rival candidates (e.g., "wants" or "adaptation" to the "transaction" and "exchange"). However, what must be borne in mind is the central distinction between science and technology. The technology of marketing cannot be ignored in the search for a central focus for the "rules of rightness" operate around a focal point.

## Conclusion

We believe that the forces working to elevate the status of marketing to that of a science will continue unabated. At this point in time claims for the current status of marketing (Hunt 1976a, 1976b) as a science are premature. Such lofty but empty claims invite ridicule rather than respect, breed complacency, and will not achieve our (Brown 1978) long sought goal. More important, such claims give rise to a comparmentalization as suggested by Levy (1976). This is dysfunctional to the overall goal of advancing both technology and science in marketing.

## REFERENCES


Alderson, W. (1965), *Dynamic Marketing Behavior*, Homewood, IL: Richard D. Irwin.

——— and R. Cox (1948), "Towards a Theory of Marketing," *Journal of Marketing*, 13 (October), 137-142.

Angelmar, R. and C. Pinson (1975), "The Meaning of 'Marketing'," *Philosophy of Science*, (June), 208-214.

Arndt, J. (1978), "How Broad Should the Marketing Concept Be?" *Journal of Marketing*, 42 (January), 101-103.

Ayer, A. J. (1964), *Language, Truth, and Logic*, London: Gollancz.

Bagozzi, R. P. (1975), "Marketing as Exchange," *Journal of Marketing*, 39 (October), 32-39.

——— (1976), "Science, Politics, and the Social Construction of Marketing," in Kenneth L. Bernhardt, ed., *Marketing: 1776-1976 and Beyond*, Chicago, IL: American Marketing Association, 586-592.

Bartels, R. (1951), "Can Marketing Be a Science?" *Journal of Marketing*, 15 (January), 319-328.

——— (1974), "The Identity Crisis in Marketing," *Journal of Marketing*, 38 (October), 73-76.

——— (1976), *The History of Marketing Thought*, 2nd edition, Columbus, OH: Grid, Inc.

Brown, L. O. (1948), "Toward a Profession of Marketing," *Journal of Marketing*, 31 (July), 27-31.

Bucklin, L. P. (1966), *A Theory of Distribution Channel Structure*, Berkeley, CA: Institute of Business and Economic Research, University of California.

——— (1978), "The New Math of Distribution Channel Control," in G. Zaltman and T. V. Bonoma, eds., *Review of Marketing*, Chicago, IL: American Marketing Association.

Bunge, M. (1972), "Toward a Philosophy of Technololgy," in C. Mitcham and R. Mackey, eds., *Philosophy and Technology*, New York: The Free Press.

Buzzell, R. (1963), "Is Marketing a Science?" *Harvard Business Review*, 41 (January-February), 32-34, 36, 40, 166, 168 & 170.

Converse, P. D. (1945), "The Development of the Science of Marketing: An Exploratory Survey," *Journal of Marketing*, 10 (July), 14-23.

Cooke, B. (1974), "Marketing—A Method in Search of Meaning," in Greer, T. V., ed., *Increasing Marketing Productivity and Conceptual and Methodological Foundation of Marketing*, Chicago: American Marketing Association, 99-103.

Dawson, L. M. (1971), "Marketing Science in the Age of Aquarius," *Journal of Marketing*, 35 (July), 66-72.

Ehrenberg, A. S. C. (1972), *Repeat-Buying: Theory and Applications*, New York: American Elsevier.

Hanson, H. R. (1965), *Patterns of Discovery*, London: Cambridge University Press.

Hempel, C. G. (1965), *Aspects of Scientific Explanation*, New York: The Free Press.

Holloway, R. J. (1969), "The Hallmark of a Profession," *Journal of Marketing*, 33 (January), 90-95.

Hutchinson, H. D. (1952), "Marketing as a Science: An Appraisal," *Journal of Marketing*, 16 (January), 286-293.

Hunt, S. D. (1978), "A General Paradigm of Marketing: In Support of the '3-Dichotomies Model'," *Journal of Marketing*, 42 (April), 107-110.

——— (1976a), *Marketing Theory*, Columbus, OH: Grid, Inc.

——— (1976b), "The Nature and Scope of Marketing," *Journal of Marketing*, 40 (July), 17-28.

Jacoby, J. (1978), "Consumer Research: A State of the Art Review," *Journal of Marketing*, 42 (April), 87-96.

Kassarjian, H. H. (1971), "Personality and Consumer Behavior: A Review," *Journal of Marketing Research*, 8 (November), 409-419.

Keith, R. J. (1960), "The Marketing Revolution," *Journal of Marketing*, 24 (January), 35-38.

Kernan, J. B. (1973), "Marketing's Coming of Age," *Journal of Marketing*, 37 (October), 34-41.

Kotler, P. (1972), "A Generic Concept of Marketing," *Journal of Marketing*, 36 (April), 46-54.

——— and S. J. Levy (1969a), "A New Form of Marketing Myopia: Rejoinder to Professor Luck," *Journal of Marketing*, 33 (July), 55-57.

——— and S. J. Levy (1969b), "Broadening the Concept of Marketing," *Journal of Marketing*, 33 (January), 10-15.

Kuhn, T. S. (1962), *The Structure of Scientific Revolutions*, Chicago, IL: University of Chicago Press.

Lazer, W. (1958), "Some Observations on the 'State of the Art' of Marketing Theory," in E. J. Kelley and W. Lazer, eds., *Managerial Marketing: Perspectives and Viewpoints*, Homewood, IL: Richard D. Irwin.

Levy, S. J. (1976), "Marcology 101 or the Domain of Marketing," in K. L. Bernhardt, ed., *Marketing: 1776-1976 and Beyond*, Chicago, IL: American Marketing Association.

Longman, K. A. (1971), "The Management Challenge to Marketing Theory," in G. Fiske, ed., *New Essays in Marketing Theory*, Boston, MA: Allyn and Bacon, 9-19.

Luck, D. J. (1969), "Broadening the Concept of Marketing—Too Far," *Journal of Marketing*, 33 (July), 53-54.

——— (1974), "Social Marketing: Confusion Confounded," *Journal of Marketing*, 38 (October), 70-72.

Mills, H. D. (1961), "Marketing as a Science," *Harvard Business Review*, (September-October), 137-142.

Oxenfeldt, A. R. (1961), "Scientific Marketing: Ideal and Ordeal," *Harvard Business Review*, (March-April), 51-64.

Polanyi, M. (1962), *Personal Knowledge*, Chicago, IL: University of Chicago Press.

Popper, K. (1965), *The Logic of Scientific Discovery*, New York: Harper.

Robin, D. P. (1970), "Toward a Normative Science in Marketing," *Journal of Marketing*, 24 (October), 73-76.

Ryan, M. J. and M. B. Holbrook (1979), "On the Relationship of Importance, Elicitation Order, and Expectancy X Value," Unpublished Working Paper, Graduate School of Business, Columbia University.

Skolinowski, H. (1972), "The Structure of Thinking in Technology," in C. Mitcham and R. Mackey, eds., *Philosophy and Technology*, New York: The Free Press.

Stainton, R. S. (1952), "Science in Marketing," *Journal of Marketing*, 7 (July), 64-65.

Stern, L. W., ed. (1969), *Distribution Channels: Behavioral Dimensions*, Boston, MA: Houghton Mifflin.

Sweeney, D. J. (1972), "Marketing: Management Technology or Social Process?" *Journal of Marketing*, 36 (October), 3-10.

Taylor, W. J. (1965), "Is Marketing a Science? Revisited," *Journal of Marketing*, 29 (July) 49-53.

Toulmin, S. (1961), *The Philosophy of Science*, London: Hutchinson.

——— (1972), *Human Understanding*, Princeton, NJ: Princeton University Press.

Tucker, W. T. (1974), "Future Directions in Marketing Theory," *Journal of Marketing*, 38 (April), 30-35.

Von Wright, G. H. (1971), *Explanation and Understanding*, Ithaca, NY: Cornell University Press.

Wilkie, W. L. and E. A. Pessemier (1973), "Issues in Marketing's Use of Multiattribute Attitude Models," *Journal of Marketing Research*, 10 (November), 428-441.

Wisdom, J. O. (1952), *Foundations of Inferences in Natural Sciences*, London: Methuen.

# 10 —— Marketing, Scientific Progress, and Scientific Method

*Paul F. Anderson*

Reprinted from *Journal of Marketing*, published by the American Marketing Association, Vol. 47 (Fall 1983), pp. 18-31. Reprinted by permission.

## INTRODUCTION

The debate concerning the scientific status of marketing is now in its fourth decade (Alderson and Cox 1948; Bartels 1951; Baumol 1957; Buzzell 1963; Converse 1945; Hunt 1976a, 1976b; Hutchinson 1952; O'Shaughnessy and Ryan 1979; Taylor 1965; Vaile 1949). During this time much heat has been generated, but relatively little light has been shed on the question of marketing's scientific credentials. The search for criteria that separate science from nonscience dates from the very beginnings of Western philosophy (Laudan 1980, 1982a). Popper labeled this question the "problem of demarcation," and asserted that its solution would be "the key to most of the fundamental problems of the philosophy of science; (1962, p. 42). Unfortunately, philosophers have been signally unsuccessful in their search for such criteria (Laudan 1982a). Indeed, there are many who consider the question to be a chimera.

The problem of demarcation is inextricably linked with the issue of scientific method. This can be seen, for example, in one of the more recent attempts to deal with the question in marketing. Hunt 1976a, 1976b) contends that the study of the positive dimensions (where the objective is explanation, prediction, and understanding) of marketing qualifies as science. He reaches this conclusion by measuring the discipline against his own set of demarcation criteria. According to Hunt, a field of inquiry is a science if (1) it has a distinct subject matter, (2) it presupposes the existence of underlying uniformities in this subject matter, and (3) it employs the "scientific method." Brief reflection will reveal, however, that Hunt's demarcation standard depends entirely on this last criterion. The first two requirements are specious since astrologers, parapsychologists and scientific creationists also study subject matters which they presuppose to exhibit regularities.

For Hunt, the key element in the scientific method is "intersubjective certification." On this view, science is epistemologically unique because different investigators with varying attitudes, opinions, and beliefs can ascertain the truth content of theories, laws, and explanations (Hunt 1976a). Elsewhere, Hunt (1983, p. 249) makes clear that his concept of scientific method is a version of positivism known as logical empiricism—an approach which has not held sway in the philosophy of science for more than a decade. During much of this century "positivism" dominated discussions of scientific method. The term was popularized by Comte, and generally refers to a strict empiricism which recognizes as valid only those knowledge claims based on experience (Abbagnano 1967, Brown 1977). In recent years, however, positivism has been challenged by insights drawn largely from the history and sociology of science. The historical and sociological perspective has revolutionized the field of science studies and has radically altered the traditional image of the scientific method.[1]

Since at least the early 1960s marketers have looked to the philosophy of science for guidance concerning scientific practice (Cox, Alderson, and Shapiro 1964; Halbert 1965; Howard and Sheth 1969; Hunt 1976b, 1983; Sheth 1967, 1972; Zaltman, Pinson, and Anglemar 1973). Indeed it is clear that this literature has informed the actual construction of theory in marketing (Howard and Sheth 1969). More recently, some of the newer approaches from the science studies field have been making their way into the discipline (Olson 1981; Peter 1982, 1983; Zaltman, LeMasters, and Heffring 1982). This article will attempt to review both the traditional and contemporary literature bearing on the questions of scientific method and scientific progress. The objective will be to demonstrate the utility of post-positivistic models of the scientific process for an understanding of marketing's scientific status. The article begins with a discussion of the two pillars of positivism: logical empiricism and falsificationism.

## LOGICAL EMPIRICISM

During the 1920s positivism emerged as a full-fledged philosophy of science in the form of logical positivism. Developed by the Vienna Circle, a group of scientists and philosophers led informally by Moritz Schlick, logical positivism accepted as its central doctrine Wittgenstein's verification theory of meaning (Brown 1977, Howard and Sheth 1969, Passmore 1967). The verification theory holds that statements or propositions are meaningful only if they can be empirically verified. This criterion was adopted in an attempt to differentiate scientific (meaningful) statements from purely metaphysical (meaningless) statements. However, logical positivism soon ran headlong into the age-old "problem of induction" (Black 1967, Hume 1911). According to the logical positivists, universal scientific propositions are true according to whether they have been verified by empirical tests—yet no finite number of empirical tests can ever guarantee the truth of universal statements (Black 1967, Brown 1977, Chalmers 1976). In short, inductive inference can never be justified on purely logical grounds (Hempel 1965).

As a result of these difficulties, Carnap (1936,1937) developed a more moderate version of positivism, which has come to be known as logical empiricism. Logical empiricism became the ''received view'' in the philosophy of science for approximately the next 20 years (Suppe 1974). Despite its decline during the 1960s, contemporary discussions of scientific method in marketing are still dominated by its influence (Hunt 1983).

Essentially, Carnap replaces the concept of verification with the idea of ''gradually increasing confirmation'' (1953, p. 48). He notes that if verification is taken to mean the ''complete and definitive establishment of truth,'' then universal statements can never be verified. However, they may be ''confirmed'' by the accumulation of successful empirical tests. This process can be illustrated with reference to Figure 1 (Savitt 1980; Zaltman, Pinson, and Angelmar 1973). According to the tenets of logical empiricism, the scientific process begins with the untainted observation of reality. This provides

**Figure 1. The Logical Empiricist Model of Scientific Method**

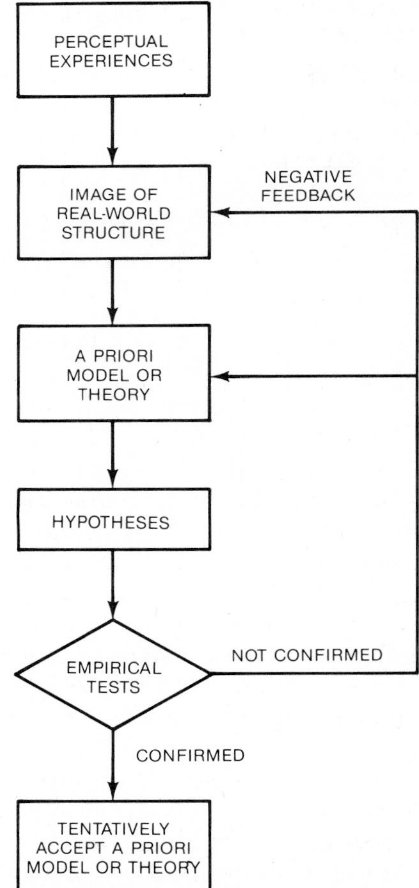

the researcher with his/her image of the real world structure from which he/she cognitively generates an a priori (i.e., untested) model of the process to be investigated. Hypotheses are derived from the model and are subjected to empirical tests. If the data are in accord with the hypotheses, a confirming instance has been identified. Thus, science progresses through the accumulation of multiple confirming instances obtained under a wide variety of circumstances and conditions.

Logical empiricism is characterized by the inductive statistical method. On this view, science begins with observation, and its theories are ultimately justified by the accumulation of further observations, which provide probabilistic support for its conclusions. Within marketing a classic example of this methodology is found in the PIMS studies. Based on observations of 57 corporations representing 620 individual "businesses,"[2] the PIMS researchers conclude that there is a positive linear relationship between market share and ROI (Buzzell, Gale, and Sultan 1975). This finding is generalized to a universal statement and is also converted into a normative prescription for business strategy.

Of course, the logical empiricist's use of probabilistic linkage between the explanans and the explanandum does not avoid the problem of induction. It remains to be shown how a finite number of observations can lead to the logical conclusion that a universal statement is "probably true" (Black 1967). Moreover, attempts to justify induction on the basis of experience are necessarily circular. The argument that induction has worked successfully in the past is itself an inductive argument and cannot be used to support the principle of induction (Chalmers 1976).

In addition to the problem of induction, logical empiricism encounters further difficulties because of its insistence that science rests on a secure observational base. There are at least two problems here. The first is that observations are always subject to measurement error. The widespread concern in the behavior sciences with reliability and validity assessments attests to this. As observational procedures and measurement technologies improve, we can minimize but never eliminate these measurement errors.[3] The second, and perhaps more significant, problem concerns the theory dependence of observation (Howard and Sheth 1969). As Hanson (1958), Kuhn (1962), Popper (1972), and others have pointed out, observations are always interpreted in the context of a priori knowledge. The history of science provides numerous examples of the fact that "what a man sees depends both upon what he looks at and also upon what his previous visual-conceptual experience has taught him to see" (Kuhn 1970, p. 113). Thus, where Tycho Brahe saw a fixed earth and moving sun, Kepler saw a stationary sun and a moving earth (Hanson 1958). Similarly, where Priestley saw dephlogisticated air, Lavoisier saw oxygen (Kuhn 1970, Musgrave 1976); and where, today, geologists see evidence of continental drift, less than 20 years ago the very same observations yielded the conclusion that the continents are fixed in place (Frankel 1979).

The fact that observation is theory laden does not, by itself, refute the logical empiricist position. It does, however, call into question the claim that science is securely anchored by the objective observation of ''reality.'' Indeed, theory dependence and fallibility of observation constitute problems for any philosophy of science which admits a role for empirical testing. However, in his development of falsificationism, Popper has offered an alternative method of theory justification which is designed to overcome some of the difficulties inherent in logical empiricism.

## FALSIFICATIONISM

Popper's alternative to the inductivist program can be illustrated with reference to Figure 2. Unlike the logical positivists, Popper accepts the fact

**FIGURE 2. The Falsificationist Model of Scientific Method**

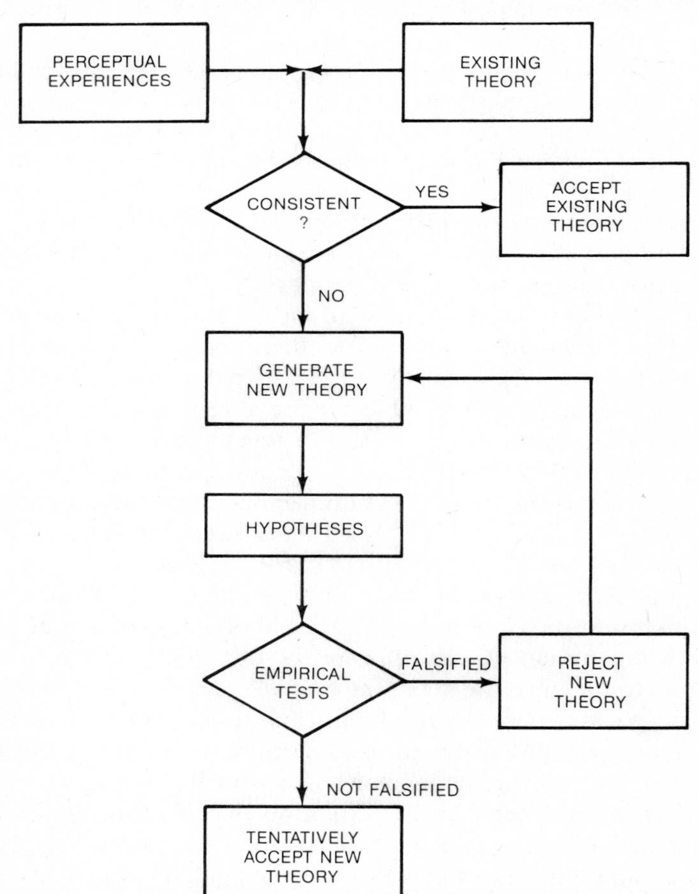

that "observation always presupposes the existence of some system of expectations" (1972, p. 344). For Popper, the scientific process begins when observations clash with existing theories or preconceptions. When this occurs, we are confronted with a scientific problem. A theory is then proposed to solve the problem, and the logical consequences of the theory (hypotheses) are subjected to rigorous empirical tests. The objective of the testing is the refutation of the hypotheses. When a theory's predictions are falsified, it is to be ruthlessly rejected. Those theories that survive falsification are said to be corroborated and are tentatively accepted.

In contrast to the gradually increasing confirmation of induction, falsificationism substitutes the logical necessity of deduction. Popper exploits the fact that a universal hypothesis can be falsified by a single negative instance (Chalmers 1976). In the Popperian program, if the deductively derived hypotheses are shown to be false, the theory itself is taken to be false. Thus, the problem of induction is seemingly avoided by denying that science rests on inductive inference.[4]

According to falsificationism, then, science progresses by a process of "conjectures and refutations" (Popper 1962, p. 46). On this view, the objective of science is to solve problems. Solutions to these problems are posed in the form of theories, which are subjected to potentially refuting empirical tests. Theories that survive falsification are accepted as tentative solutions to the problems.

Popper's program has had a significant impact, both on philosophers of science and on practicing scientists. The latter, in particular, have been attracted by falsification's image of science as a rational and objective means of attaining "truth" (Calder, Phillips, and Tybout 1981; Medawar 1979). However, despite the apparent conformity of much scientific practice with the falsificationist account, serious problems remain with Popper's version of the scientific method. For example, Duhem (1953) has pointed out that it is impossible to conclusively refute a theory because realistic test situations depend on much more than just the theory that is under investigation. Any empirical test will involve assumptions about initial conditions, measuring instruments, and auxiliary hypotheses (Chalmers 1976, Jacoby 1978, Pickering 1981). An alleged refutation of the theory can be easily deflected by suggesting that something else in the maze of assumptions and premises caused the result (Laudan 1977). Moreover, theories can be protected from falsification by ad hoc modification.

A far more serious problem for the falsificationist view is the fact that the actual history of scientific advance is rarely in agreement with the Popperian account. For example, when D. C. Miller presented overwhelming evidence of a serious experimental anomaly for relativity theory in 1925, the reaction of the physics community was one of benign disinterest (Polanyi 1958). The historical record shows that most major scientific theories have advanced *in spite* of apparent refutations by empirical data. Copernican astronomy (Kuhn 1957), the theory of oxidation (Musgrave 1976), natural selection (Gould 1977, 1980), kinetic theory (Clark 1976), and continental drift (Frankel 1979) were all, at one time or another, in danger of drowning in an ''ocean of anomalies'' (Lakatos 1974, p. 135). The Popperian program of ''conjectures and refutations'' finds it difficult to account for the actual growth of scientific knowledge in the face of historical examples such as these.

The recognition that established theories often resist refutation by anomalies while new theories frequently progress despite their empirical failures, led a number of writers in the 1950s to challenge the positivistic views of Popper and the logical empiricists (Suppe 1974). Various philosophers and historians of science noted that scientific practice is often governed by a conceptual framework or world view that is highly resistant to change. In particular, Thomas Kuhn pointed out that the established framework is rarely, if ever, overturned by a single anomaly (1962). Kuhn's model helped to initiate a new approach in the philosophy of science in which emphasis is placed on the conceptual frameworks that guide research activities. Moreover, Kuhn's work underlined the important role played by the history of science in the development and validation of philosophical analysis.

## Scientific Revolutions

Central to the Kuhnian position is the concept of a ''paradigm.''[5] Roughly, a paradigm constitutes the world view of a scientific community (Laudon 1977, Suppe 1974). The paradigm will include a number of specific theories which depend, in part, on the shared metaphysical beliefs of the community (Kuhn 1970). In addition, the paradigm will include a set of ''symbolic generalizations'' (like $E = mc^2$) and a set of shared ''values'' or criteria for theory appraisal (Kuhn 1970, 1977, p. 321). Finally, each paradigm will include ''exemplars'' or concrete problem solutions known to all members of the community (Kuhn 1970). Examples of paradigms in the natural sciences include Newtonian mechanics, Darwinian evolution, quantum theory, and place tectonics. Within the social sciences, behaviorism, Freudian psychoanalysis, diffusion of innovation, and Marxian economics have often been referred to as paradigms.

Of particular importance are Kuhn's views on the paradigm shift that takes place during scientific revolutions. He likens the process to a conversion experience, which recalls Kierkegaardian leap of faith. Some have objected that this approach implies that theory choice is essentially an irrational and subjective process (Lakatos 1974). However, this is an unfortunate misinterpretation of Kuhn's position. Kuhn argues that the actual criteria of theory appraisal are highly rational and fairly standardized within scientific communities. For example, he suggests that the requirements for accuracy, consistency, extensibility, simplicity, and fruitfulness are widely employed within most scientific disciplines (Kuhn 1977). Unfortunately, these attributes do not lead to unambiguous choices when applied to actual theories or paradigms. Thus, theory choice is said to be underdetermined by the data and the evaluative criteria.

The process of theory appraisal is further complicated by the incommensurability of paradigms (Kuhn 1970). Kuhn argues that scientists who pursue different paradigms are, in a sense, living in different worlds. They will be unable to agree on the problems to be solved, the theories to be employed, or the terminology to be used. More importantly, they will be unable to agree on any ''crucial experiments'' that would resolve their differences (Platt 1964). For example, Kuhn would argue that there is little prospect that a cognitive psychologist could be converted to a behaviorist by rational argument alone. The incommensurability of the paradigms requires too great a conceptual leap. Similar incommensurabilities exist between economics and marketing concerning the theory of consumer behavior (Becker 1971, Markin 1974), and between economics and management concerning the theory of the firm (Cyert and March 1963, Machlup 1967). Very often these paradigmatic conflicts are the result of the radically different philosophical methodologies and ontological frameworks employed by different disciplines or schools of thought (Anderson 1982). Another complication for the process of theory appraisal is the fact that new paradigms are rarely able to solve all of the problems dealt with by the established paradigm. Indeed, new paradigms are typically pursued in spite of the many difficulties with which they are confronted. Thus, in Kuhn's view, the individual scientist's decision to pursue a new paradigm must be made on faith in its ''future promise'' (Kuhn 1970, p. 158).

For Kuhn, science progresses through revolutions, but there is no guarantee that it progresses toward anything—least of all toward ''the truth'' (Kuhn 1970, p. 170). Progression, in Kuhn's view, is synonymous with problem solving. From this perspective, ''the scientific community is a supremely efficient instrument for maximizing the number and precision of the problems solved through paradigm change'' (Kuhn 1970, p. 169). But this is all that it is—there is nothing in the process of scientific revolutions that guarantees that science moves ever closer toward absolute truth. Like Darwinian evolution, science is a process without an ultimate goal.

Philosophers of science have found much to criticize in the Kuhnian model (Feyerabend 1970, Lakatos 1974, Laudan 1977, Shapere 1964). However, only two specific points will be dealt with here. First, it has been alleged that Kuhn's account is historically inaccurate (Feyerabend 1970). Of particular concern is the fact that studies of the natural sciences rarely reveal periods in which a single paradigm has dominated a discipline. As Laudan points out, ''virtually every major period in the history of [natural] science is characterized ... by the co-existence of numerous competing paradigms'' (1977, p. 74). Similarly, historical studies of the social sciences have found the Kuhnian approach lacking. For example, Leahy's (1980) study of the "cognitive revolution" in psychology concludes that the Kuhnian description of the process is deficient in almost all respects. Likewise, Bronfenbrenner (1971) and Kunin and Weaver (1971) raise serious questions concerning attempts to apply the model to economics.

The second major criticism of Kuhn has already been hinted at. Many philosophers of science object to his characterization of theory selection as an act of "faith." These writers are concerned that this seemingly removes the element of rational choice from the scientific process. As a result, alternative world view models have been developed which attempt to portray theory choice in rational decision-making terms. One such approach is the "methodology of scientific research programs" developed by Imre Lakatos (1974). Since this model is essentially a sophisticated version of falsificationism, it need not detain us here. However, more recently Laudan (1977) has proposed the "research tradition" concept, which attempts to restore rationality to theory selection by expanding the concept of rationality itself.

## Research Traditions

Following both Kuhn and Popper, Laudan argues that the objective of science is to solve problems—that is, to provide "acceptable answers to interesting questions" (Laudan 1977, p. 13). On this view, the "truth" or "falsity" of a theory is irrelevant as an appraisal criterion. The key question is whether the theory offers an explanation for important empirical problems. Empirical problems arise when we encounter something in the natural or social environment which clashes without preconceived notions or which is otherwise in need of explanation.

Unfortunately, it is not possible to discriminate among theories on the basis of solved empirical problems alone. As a result, Laudan suggests that there are two other types of problem that must enter into the appraisal process. The first of these is the "non-refuting anomaly." This is a problem which has not been solved by the theory under consideration, but which has been solved by a rival theory. Laudan maintains that theory appraisal amounts to a process of comparing the merits of one theory with those of another. Thus, an anomaly that has been explained by a rival is a more damaging problem for an extant theory than an anomaly that has not been explained at all.

The other types of problems relevant to theory appraisal are known as conceptual problems. These include logical inconsistencies within the theory itself, as well as inconsistencies between the theory under consideration and other scientific theories or doctrines. Examples of the latter include "normative" conceptual problems, in which a proposed theory clashes with the cognitive aims or philosophic methodologies of a rival theory or discipline (Anderson 1982).

Another type of conceptual problem arises when a theory clashes with an accepted world view of the discipline or the wider society. From this perspective, the decline of motivation research in marketing may be partly attributed to the fact that it assumes that "consumer behavior is triggered by subconscious motivations heavily laden with sexual overtones" (Markin 1969, p. 42). Similarly, the failure of behaviorism to gain a significant foothold in marketing may stem from the fact that it views consumer behavior as largely under the control of environmental stimuli (Nord and Peter 1980, Peter and Nord 1982, Rothschild and Gaidis 1981). Both the Freudian and Skinnerian perspectives are at variance with the established position that consumers are reasonably rational decision makers who "act on beliefs, express attitudes, and strive toward goals" (Markin 1974, p. 239). It can be seen that this "cognitive" world view constitutes a serious barrier to the acceptance of alternative theories of consumer behavior.

Thus, from Laudan's perspective, theory appraisal involves an assessment of the *overall* problem-solving adequacy of a theory. This may be determined by weighing the number and importance of the empirical problems solved by the theory against the number and significance of the anomalous and conceptual problems that the theory generates. On this view, motivational research and behavior modification are reasonably adequate theories at the empirical level. That is, they provide plausible answers to important empirical questions. However, both theories create such significant conceptual problems that it is unlikely that either will replace the cognitive orientation in the foreseeable future.

Like Kuhn and Lakatos, Laudan sees science operating within a conceptual framework that he calls a research tradition. The research tradition consists of a number of specific theories, along with a set of metaphysical and conceptual assumptions that are shared by those scientists who adhere to the tradition. A major function of the research tradition is to provide a set of methodological and philosophical guidelines for the further development of the tradition (Anderson 1982).

As in the case of its constituent theories, research traditions are to be appraised on the basis of their overall problem-solving adequacy. Thus, *acceptance* of a particular tradition should be based on a weighting of solved empirical problems versus anomalous and conceptual problems. However, it is very often the case that scientists choose to *pursue* (i.e., to consider, explore, and develop) research traditions whose overall problem-solving success does not equal that of their rivals. Moreover, there are many instances in which scientists have ostensibly accepted one research tradition while working within another.

To explain these phenomena, Laudan suggests that the context of pursuit must be separated from the context of acceptance. On this view, acceptance is a static notion. One compares the problem-solving adequacy of the tradition's existing theories with those of its competitors. Pursuit, on the other hand, is a dynamic concept. The pursuit of a research tradition should be based on its rate of problem-solving progress. Here one looks to the ability of the tradition's latest theories to solve more problems than its rivals. Very often the established tradition will have a more impressive record of overall problem solving. However, pursuit is not based on past success but rather, on future promise. From Laudan's perspective, it is perfectly rational to pursue (without acceptance) a research tradition whose recent rate of problem solving offers the hope of future progress.

For example, the early work in marketing on multiattribute attitude models seems to have been spurred by their promise as a diagnostic tool with managerial relevance (Lutz and Bettman 1977, Wilkie and Pessemier 1973). However, low coefficients of determination and questions concerning the prevalence of rational decision making by consumers (Kassarjian 1978, Sheth 1979) have raised doubts in some circles as to whether the promise has been fulfilled. Indeed, Nord and Peter (1980), Peter and Nord (1982), and Rothschild and Gaidis (1981) have recently suggested a reexamination of behaviorism by consumer researchers as an alternative to the cognitive orientation. Laudan's model implies that these writers will have to show a high rate of problem-solving progress if they wish to attract researchers to this program. In particular, they may need to demonstate through empirical studies (e.g., Gorn 1982) the ability of behaviorism to solve some of the existing anomalies in the cognitivist program. At the same time, Laudan's approach suggests that conceptual problems associated with the notions of manipulation and control and the alleged primacy of environment over cognition may be the more serious barriers to the widespread adoption of the behaviorist model.

## Epistemological Anarchy

Unfortunately, Laudan's distinction between a context of pursuit and a context of acceptance fails to provide us with a rational basis for *initial* theory selection. As Feyerabend (1981) points out, there can be no decision to pursue a research tradition on the basis of its rate of progress unless it has already been pursued by someone who has demonstrated this progress. For his own part, Feyerabend argues for a kind of epistemological anarchy in which the only universal standard of scientific method is ''anything goes.'' He claims that the historical record demonstrates, ''there is not a single rule, however plausible, and however firmly grounded in epistemology, that is not violated at some time or another'' (Feyerabend 1975, p. 23). Indeed, he believes that the violation of accepted scientific norms is essential for scientific progress.

On this view, every concrete piece of research is a potential application of a rule and a test case for the rule (Feyerabend 1978). In other words, scientists may allow standards to guide the research or they may allow the research to suspend the standards. Feyerabend argues that new appraisal criteria are introduced into research practice in piecemeal fashion. They are, in effect, partially invented in the process of carrying out research projects. For a time, new and old standards operate side by side until an alternative form of research practice (and a new rationality) is established. He believes that this process is necessary for scientific progress because conformity to rigid rules and procedures inhibits scientific imagination and creativity. He suggests that violations of conventional norms have led to some of the most significant advances in the history of thought (Feyerabend 1975).

This view suggests that there are no Universal standards of scientific practice (Feyerabend 1978). Instead, knowledge claims are unique to specific "research areas" (the rough equivalent of paradigms or research traditions). Thus, what counts as scientific knowledge is relative to the group that produces the knowledge. Each research area is immune to criticism from the outside because of the incommensurability of appraisal criteria and because of the varying programmatic commitments of different research traditions.

## The Cognitive Sociology of Science

Similar conclusions have been reached by researchers working within the cognitive tradition in the sociology of science. Traditionally, sociologists of science have restricted their inquiry largely to the institutional framework of scientific activity (Ben-David 1971, Merton 1973). It has been taken for granted that the nature of the knowledge produced by scientific communities lies outside the purview of sociological analysis. Recently, however, this assumption has been challenged by a number of sociologists including adherents of the so-called "strong program" in the sociology of knowledge developed by David Bloor (1976) and Barry Barnes (1977).

While there are differences in the programs of Bloor and Barnes (Manier 1980), both agree that the production of scientific knowledge must be viewed as a sociological process. On this view, scientific beliefs are as much a function of cultural, political, social, and ideological factors as are any beliefs held by members of a society. Bloor argues that the role of the sociologist is to build theories which explain how these factors affect the generation of scientific knowledge, including knowledge in the sociology of science itself.

Bloor and Barnes criticize philosophers like Lakatos and Laudan for asserting that rational scientific beliefs need no further explanation (Barnes 1979, Bloor 1976). They point out that rationality implies reference to norms, standards, or conventions which they view as sociologically determined and maintained. As such, rationality is not simply a cognitive process common to all but, rather, relative notion that is affected by external social factors. In particular, the strong program lays great stress upon the role of professional and class interests in affecting the nature of scientific knowledge (Barnes and MacKenzie 1979, Barnes and Shapin 1979, MacKenzie and Barnes 1979, Shapin 1981).

Of course, many philosophers and sociologists of science are understandably skeptical of explanations of this sort (Laudon 1981, 1982b; Woolgar 1981). They point out that it will always be possible to construct a plausible explanation for the social interests which might sustain a particular scientific belief. At the same time, however, more sophisticated analyses emerging from other programs in the cognitive sociology of science have revealed interesting insights into the scientific process.[6] Thus, Pickering's (1981) study of experimental work in particle physics reveals the consensual nature of theory acceptance. He argues that science is inherently a social enterprise in which theories must be argued for ''within a socially sustained matrix of commitments, beliefs and practices'' (p. 235). He demonstrates that these factors can actually impact the nature of the data produced by experimental studies because they determine, in advance, the acceptability of certain findings. This is not to suggest that the majority of scientists *consciously* adjust their apparatus and procedures to generate ''marketable'' results (Law and Williams 1982, Peter and Olson 1983). Rather, it implies that the design, implementation, and interpretation of experiments is always conducted with an eye to the acceptability of the findings.

The major implication of this sort of sociological analysis is to suggest that science is essentially a process of consensus formation. On this view, theories will be appraised not only on the basis of traditional criteria (e.g., confirmation, corroboration, novel predictions, etc.) but also on the basis of sociological criteria. These may include such factors as the conjunction of the theory with professional or class interests (MacKenzie and Barnes 1979, Shapin 1981), the social acceptability of the results (Pickering 1981), the nature of the rhetorical and presentational devices employed by scientists (Collins 1981b), the sociological ''cost'' of challenging established theory (Bourdieu 1975, Latour and Woolgar 1979), and the socially defined ''workability'' of results produced in the laboratory (Knoor-Cetina (1981, 1983).

Sociologists of science do not deny that traditional appraisal criteria appear to play a role in the process of theory acceptance. They simply argue that sociological factors may be every bit as important in determining which theories are accepted and which are rejected. The fact that science is ultimately a social activity cannot be denied. As such, it would appear fruitful to employ insights from both the philosophy and sociology of science in attempting to come to grips with the problem of scientific method within marketing.

## Implications for the Development of Marketing Science

The foregoing review would appear to warrant a number of conclusions concerning science and scientific method. First, it is clear that positivism's reliance on empirical testing as the *sole* means of theory justification cannot be maintained as a viable description of the scientific process or as a normative prescription for the conduct of scientific activities. This point is essentially noncontroversial in contemporary philosophy and sociology of science. Despite its prevalence in marketing, positivism has been abandoned by these disciplines over the last two decades in the face of the overwhelming historical and logical arguments that have been raised against it.

Second, it should also be clear that no consensus exists as to the nature or the very existence of a unique scientific method. The decline of positivism has left us with a number of competing perspectives in the philosophy and sociology of science. Each has its following of loyal supporters, but it appears unlikely that any one perspective will assert its dominance in the near future. This suggests that it is inappropriate to seek a single best method for the evaluation of marketing theory. As we have seen, appraisal standards will consist of both traditional and sociological criteria and will be subject to change over time. It is more important to ask what methodologies will convince the marketing community of the validity of a particular theory, than it is to ask what is the "correct" method.

Thus a relativistic stance appears to be the only viable solution to the problem of scientific method. Relativism implies that there are few *truly universal* standards of scientific adequacy. Instead, different research programs (i.e., disciplines subdisciplines, or collections of disciplines) will adhere to different methodological, ontological, and metaphysical commitments. These research programs are highly "encapsulated" and are immunized against attack from the outside. *Within* a program, knowledge is sanctioned largely by consensus. That is, theories are justified to the extent that they conform to programmatic commitments. However, appraisal standards as well as other programmatic entities will change over time. Indeed, it is not inconceivable that changes in cognitive aims, standards, and ontologies could lead to the eventual unification of competing programs (Laudon 1982c). Thus, research areas will tend to evolve as changes take place in methods, concepts, values, beliefs, and theories. Whether such changes can be viewed as progressive in any sense will be judged differently by different research programs.

Finally, the lack of consensus on the issue of scientific method means that there is also no agreement on the question of demarcation between science and nonscience. Since the identification of a unique methodology for science is a necessary condition for demarcation, it appears that the search for such a criterion is otiose. As Laudan has put it, "The fact that 2,400 years of searching for demarcation criterion has left us empty-handed raises a presumption that the object of the quest is non-existent" (1980, p. 275). Thus, Hunt's (1976a) assertion that "intersubjective certifiability" can serve to distinguish science from nonscience is unsupportable.[7] As Gouldner points out, "Any limited empirical generalization can, by this standard, be held to be objective, however narrow, partial, or biased and prejudiced its net impact is, by reason of its selectivity" (1974, p. 57).

Gouldner uses the concept of sample bias to illustate his point. He notes that a study using a consciously or unconsciously biased sample can easily be replicated by researchers wishing to justify a particular theory. Thus, replicability is nothing more than a "technical" definition of objectivity that does nothing to assure us that the knowledge it generates is "scientific." For example, disciplines which, by societal consensus, are taken to be non-scientific, find it possible to meet the requirement of intersubjective certifiability. Scientific creationists regularly support one another's conclusions based on investigations of the same data. Similarly, parapsychologists maintain that they are able to replicate experiments with "some consistency" (Truzzi 1980, p. 43).

More importantly, however, intersubjective certifiability is by no means as unambiguous as it would appear. For example, what sense are we to make of this criterion in light of the history of the discovery of oxygen? Both Priestley and Lavoisier conducted the same experiment, and both produced the element that we now know as oxygen (Kuhn 1970, Musgrave 1976). Yet Priestly interpreted his discovery as "dephlogisticated air," while Lavoisier eventually saw his as oxygen. Each interpreted the same experiment and the same result in terms of competing research programs. Nor is this an isolated historical case. Numerous studies have demonstrated the inherent ambiguity of the intersubjective certifiability criterion (Collins 1975, Franklin 1979, Pickering 1981, Wynn 1976). Indeed, Collins has argued that experimenters in a field actually negotiate the set of tests that will be judged as competent and, in so doing, decide the character of the phenomenon under investigation.

## Science$_1$ Versus Science$_2$

We have seen that the lack of a demarcation criterion makes it impossible to employ the term *science* unambiguously. It will be necessary, therefore, to dichotomize the term for analytical purposes. It is proposed that science$_1$ should refer to the idealized notion of science as an inquiry system which produces "objectively proven knowledge" (Chalmers 1976, p. 1). On this view, science seeks to discover "the truth" via the objective methods of observation, test, and experiement. Of course, it should be clear that no such inquiry system has ever existed—nor is it very likely that such a system will ever exist.

As a result, it will be necessary to define an alternative notion known as science$_2$. The defining element here is that of societal consensus. On this view, science is whatever society chooses to call a science. In Western cultures, this would include all of the recognized natural and social sciences. Thus physics, chemistry, biology, psychology, sociology, economics, political science, etc., all count as science$_2$. This definition bears a resemblance to Madsen's conceptualization of science as a socially organized information-producing activity whose procedures and norms are ''socially established'' (1974, p. 27). However, $science_2$ goes somewhat farther by emphasizing the importance of societal sanction. It suggests that society bestows a high epistemological status on science because it values its knowledge products, and because it believes that science *generally* functions in the best interests of society as a whole. In the remainder of this article, the terms *science* and *scientific* shall be understood in this sense, unless otherwise noted.

## The Quest for $Science_2$

The definition of science by societal consensus is not just a convenient method of avoiding the problem of demarcation. It provides us with a criterion that we can use to assess the scientific status of marketing. That is, we can compare marketing with the recognized social and natural sciences, to determine what marketing can do to become more scientific.[8] Of course, this begs the question of whether the objective is worth the effort. During the long debate over the scientific status of marketing, the desirability of becoming more scientific has never really been questioned. This is because the implicit definition of science has always been that of $science_1$. Given that the philosophy and sociology of science can no longer support the veridical status of science, how might we justify the quest for $science_2$?

One possible answer to this question recognizes that it can be in the interests of the discipline to achieve scientific status. An important goal of an area of inquiry with scientific pretensions is to ensure that its knowledge base is widely dispersed through the greater society, so that this knowledge can be used to benefit society as a whole. This is essentially a utilitarian argument (Jones et al. 1977, Reagan 1969.) It is clear that societal resources tend to flow to those disciplines that produce knowledge considered valuable for the accomplishment of societal objectives. The National Science Foundation and the National Institutes for Health are but two examples of institutional arrangements designed to allocate resources for this purpose. (In this regard, it is worth noting the NSF only recently withdrew its blanket exclusion of research in business areas from funding consideration.) Beyond the pragmatic resource issues, however, it is also obvious that many within the marketing discipline would prefer to employ their knowledge to further society's goals and to enchance its citizens' quality of life. This deontological argument assumes that knowledge producers have special obligations and responsibilities vis-a-vis society (Jones et al. 1977, Ravetz 1971, Reagan 1969).

Within the last decade, the discipline has made enormous strides in the application of its knowledge to nonprofit organizations and to the marketing of social causes (Fine 1981; Fox and Kotler 1980; Kelley 1971; Kotler 1975, 1979; Levy and Zaltman 1975; Rothschild 1981; Shapiro 1973; Sheth and Wright 1974). Much of this has come about as a result of the proselytizing activities of marketers. However, social and nonprofit marketing appear to be informed by the view that marketing is ultimately a technology for influencing the behavior of customer groups (Kotler 1972, Kotler and Zaltman 1971). Tucker has referred to this perspective as the "channel captain" orientation. That is, marketing theorists have tended to focus on the implications of their knowledge for the marketer, rather than the consumer or the larger society (Olson 1981; Sheth 1972, 1979). Thus, Tucker suggests that marketers have had a tendency to study the consumer "in the ways that fishermen study fish rather than as marine biologists study them" (1974, p. 31).

The perception that marketing is simply a technology of influence may well inhibit the flow of its knowledge to segments of society that have no interest in marketing either goods and services or social causes. Increasingly, researchers whose primary interest is in consumer behavior have been called upon by public policy officials for their expert knowledge in such areas as children's advertising, information overload, deceptive advertising, and price perception. In part, this reflects the fact that consumer behavior has been evolving into a separate discipline, with a strong orientation toward knowledge for its own sake (Sheth 1972, 1979).

This shift in emphasis within consumer behavior has enhanced its legitimacy within the academic community, and has led a number of other disciplines to borrow some of its concepts and to employ some of its research findings (Sheth 1972). Marketing has also begun to experience this process of "reverse borrowing," especially in the areas of multivariate analysis and survey research. However, the amount of borrowing from marketing is not as great as one might expect, given its level of technical and methodological sophistication. We must ask ourselves if this reflects a lack of familiarity with marketing, the dearth of marketing theory, or if it suggests a perception that a normative (i.e., marketer-oriented) discipline has little to offer in the way of useful knowledge? It would appear likely that all three factors are operative. However, this need not be the case. There is no a priori reason to believe that marketing cannot continue to reverse the knowledge flow and inform as well as be informed by more traditional academic disciplines (Sheth 1972).

It could be argued, therefore, that as marketing improves its scientific status in society, the knowledge it generates will be more acceptable within the society, and that additional resources will be made available for the further development of its knowledge base. However, this may require a reorientation within certain segments of the discipline. A focus on knowledge for its own sake (or, more appropriately, for the sake of society as a whole) may be the price which society demands before it is willing to offer full scientific legitimacy. Given the historical prejudice against marketing (Steiner 1976), this may not be too great a price to pay. Indeed, greater legitimacy in the eyes of society can only be viewed as salutary by marketing practitioners and academics alike.

## Toward Science in Marketing

If the discipline of marketing wishes to move toward scientific status, it must look to the recognized social and natural sciences for guidance. A comparison with these other fields suggests a number of action implications. First, it is clear that marketing must be more concerned with the pursuit of knowledge as knowledge. Rightly or wrongly, society tends to reserve full scientific legitimacy for those inquiry systems which are perceived to be operating in the higher interests of knowledge and general societal welfare. The perception that marketing is primarily concerned with the interests of only one segment of society will surely retard its transition to a consensus science.

Of course, marketing can point with pride to its accomplishments in improving the efficiency and effectiveness of managerial practice in the private as well as the nonprofit and public sectors. We should not gainsay the ultimate benefits this has brought to society. Nevertheless, if the discipline truly wishes to implement the broadened concept of marketing (Bagozzi 1975, Kotler and Levy 1969), it is clear that it must adopt a different set of goals and a different attitude towards its ultimate purpose. Traditionally, marketers have viewed their discipline as an applied area concerned largely with the improvement of managerial practice. However, the broadening concept makes it clear that marketing is a generic human activity, which may be studied simply because it is an intrinsically interesting social phenomenon. On this view, the exchange process itself becomes the focus of attention in much the same way that communication is the focus of communications theorists, and administration is the focus of administrative scientists. The interest must lie in understanding and explaining the phenomenon itself, rather than understanding it from the perspective of only one of the participants. Marketing's preoccupation with the concerns of Tucker's "channel captain" introduces an asymmetry into the study of the phenomenon that can only limit the discipline's perspective and inhibit its attainment of scientific status.

It should be noted that this change in focus need not create tension between academics and practioners. The knowledge produced by the discipline will still be readily available for the practical pursuits of private, nonprofit, and social marketers. The difference is that the product of marketing science will also be readily available (and perhaps more palatable) to consumers, consumer groups, other academic disciplines, and a broader range of public policy officials. As Angelmar and Pinson (1975) note, other social sciences have seen fit to institutionalize this distinction by developing subdisciplines, such as applied psychology, applied anthropology, and applied sociology.

Moreover, such a distinction already exists on a de facto basis within the fields of finance and management. As a discipline that already has an applied emphasis, marketing's task is to further develop its scientific dimensions into a fullfledged subarea whose primary focus is on basic research.

Beyond the philosophical and attitudinal changes necessary for a full transition to marketing science, a number of more pragmatic considerations must also be addressed. The recognized sciences have achieved their status, in large part, because they have something to show for their efforts. As Kuhn (1970) or Laudan (1977) would express it, the sciences have shown a remarkable ability to solve important problems. They have done so, it would seem, through a commitment to theory-driven programmatic research. History demonstrates that scientific progress has emerged out of the competition among macro-structures variously known as paradigms, reseach programs, and research traditions. The established sciences can point with pride to the scientific problems they have solved and the exemplary theories which are their solutions. Indeed, Popper has argued that a discipline should be defined not by its subject matter, but by the theories it develops to solve the problems of its domain (1962, p. 67).

In contrast, much research in marketing remains scattered and fragmented (Jacoby 1978, Sheth 1967, Wind and Thomas 1980). It is often difficult to determine what problem the research is attempting to solve, or if the solution has any real significance for the advancement of knowledge or for the design of intervention strategies. Too often the focus is on what may be termed "relationship studies." Here an attempt is made to determine if any independent and dependent variables are related, but there is little effort to link the result to an established research program or body of theory. more significantly, perhaps, it is rare that researchers engage in follow-up studies to further explore and develop the area. This approach appears to be informed by an empiricist model of science which assumes that, if enough scattered facts (relationships) are gathered, they will somehow assemble themselves into a coherent body of theory (Olson 1981). However, it should be clear that facts "do not speak for themselves" (Baumol 1957), and that the collection and interpretation of facts is always done in the light of theory.

What is required in marketing is a greater commitment to theory-driven programmatic research, aimed at solving cognitively and socially significant problems (Howard and Sheth 1969, Jacoby 1978, Olson 1981). Only in this way will marketing achieve what is taken for granted in the recognized sciences, namely, an exemplary body of theory and a collection of scientific problems which it can count as solved. These two features will go a long way toward gaining scientific recognition for marketing. It is clear that this process has already begun in such areas as consumer behavior, sales management, and channel behavior. It can only be hoped that this will continue and will soon spread to other areas of the discipline.

## ENDNOTES

1. Philosophy, sociology, and history of science are often referred to collectively under the rubric of "science studies."
2. In the best traditions of logical empiricism, the PIMS sample size has since been increased (Branch 1978, Schoeffler 1979).
3. Of course, the sample problems of measurement exist in the natural sciences. See, for example, Chalmers (1976), pp. 28-30.
4. Of course, it has been noted that Popper's notion of corroboration itself depends on an inductive inference.
5. Kuhn now refers to a paradigm as a "disciplinary matrix" (Kuhn 1970, p. 182). However, it has become conventional in discussions of his work to retain the original term.
6. In addition to the strong program, there are at least three other recognizable "schools" in the cognitive sociology of science. These include adherents of the relativist (Collins 1981a), constructivist (Knorr-Cetina 1981), and discourse (Mulkay and Gilbert 1982) programs.
7. Indeed, Hunt's demarcation standard is not even adequate on his own criteria for classification (Hunt 1983, p. 355).
8. It should be noted that the question of the extent and nature of the differences between the natural and social sciences remains a highly contentious issue (Bhaskar 1979, Keat and Urry 1975; Mill 1959, Papineau 1978, Rosenberg 1980, Thomas 1979, Winch 1958).

## REFERENCES

Abbagnano, Nicola (1967), "Positivism," *Encyclopedia of Philosophy*, 6, Paul Edwards, ed., New York: Macmillan.

Alderson, Wroe and Reavis Cox (1948), "Towards a Theory of Marketing," *Journal of Marketing*, 13 (October), 137-152.

Anderson, Paul F. (1982), "Marketing, Strategic Planning and the Theory of the Firm, " *Journal of Marketing*, 46 (Spring), 15-26.

Angelmar, Reinhard and Christian Pinson (1975), "The Meaning of Marketing," *Philosophy of Science*, 42 (June), 208-13.

Bagozzi, Richard P. (1975), "Marketing as Exchange," *Journal of Marketing*, 39 (October), 32-39.

Barnes, Barry (1977), *Interests and the Growth of Knowledge*, London: Routledge & Kegan Paul.

——— (1979), "Vicissitudes of Belief," *Social Studies of Science*, 9, 247-63.

——— and Donald MacKenzie (1979), "On the Role of Interests in Scientific Change," in *On The Margins of Science: The Social Construction of Rejected Knowledge*, R. Wallis, ed., Keele, U.K.: University of Keele, 49-66.

——— and Steven Shapin (1979), *Natural Order*, Beverly Hills, CA: Sage.

Bartels, Robert (1951), "Can Marketing Be a Science?" *Journal of Marketing*, 15 (January), 319-28.

Baumol, W. J. (1957), "On the Role of Marketing Theory," *Journal of Marketing*, 21 (April), 413-18.

Becker, Gary (1971), *Economic Theory*, New York: Knopf.

Ben-David, J. (1971), *The Scientist's Role in Society*, Englewood Cliffs, NJ: Prentice-Hall.

Bhaskar, Roy (1979), *The Possibility of Naturalism*, Brighton, U.K.: The Harvester Press.

Black, Max (1967), "Induction," *Encyclopedia of Philosophy*, 4, Paul Edwards, ed., New York: Macmillan.

Bloor, David (1976), *Knowledge and Social Imagery*, London: Routledge & Kegan Paul.

Bourdieu, Pierre (1975), "The Specificity of the Scientific Field and the Social Conditions of the Progress of Reason," *Social Science Information*, 14, 19-47.

Branch, Ben (1978), "The Impact of Operating Decisions on ROI Dynamics," *Financial Management*, 7 (Winter), 54-60.

Bronfenbrenner, Martin (1971), "The 'Structure of Revolutions' in Economic Thought," *History of Political Economy*, 3 (Spring), 136-151.

Brown, Harold I. (1977), *Perception, Theory and Commitment*, Chicago: University of Chicago Press.

Buzzell, Robert D. (1963), "Is Marketing a Science?" *Harvard Business Review*, 41 (January-February), 32-170.

———, Bradley T. Gale, and Ralph G. M. Sultan (1975), "Market Share: A Key to Profitability," *Harvard Business Review*, 53 (January-February), 97-106.

Calder, Bobby J., Lynn W. Phillips, and Alice M. Tybout (1981), Designing Research for Applications," *Journal of Consumer Research*, 8 (September), 197-207.

Carnap, Rudolph (1936), "Testability and Meaning," *Philosophy of Science*, 3, 419-71.

——— (1937), "Testability and Meaning, " *Philosophy of Science,* 4, 1-40.

——— (1953), "Testability and Meaning," in *Readings in the Philosophy of Science*, Herbert Feigel and May Brodbeck, eds., New York: Appleton-Century-Crofts, 47-92.

Chalmers, A. F. (1976), *What Is This Thing Called Science?* St. Lucia, Australia: University of Queensland Press.

Clark, Peter (1976), "Atomism versus Thermodynamics," in *Method and Appraisal in the Physical Sciences*, Colin Howson, ed., Cambridge, U.K.: Cambridge University Press, 41-105.

Collins, H. M. (1975), "The Seven Sexes: A Study in the Sociology of a Phenomenon, or the Replication of Experiments in Physics," *Sociology*, 9, 205-24.

——— (1981a), "Stages in the Empirical Program of Relativism," *Social Studies of Science*, 11, 3-10.

——— (1981b), "Son of Seven Sexes: The Social Destruction of a Physical Phenomenon," *Social Studies of Science*, 11, 33-62.

Converse, Paul D. (1945), "The Development of a Science of Marketing," *Journal of Marketing*, 10 (July), 14-23.

Cox, Reavis, Wroe Alderson, and Stanley J. Shapiro (1964), *Theory in Marketing*, Homewood, IL: Irwin.

Cyert, Richard M. and James G. March (1963), *A Behavioral Theory of the Firm*, Englewood Cliffs, NJ: Prentice-Hall.

Duhem, Pierre (1953), "Physical Theory and Experiment," in *Readings in the Philosophy of Science*, Herbert Feigl and May Brodbeck, eds., New York: Appleton-Century-Crofts, 235-52.

Feyerabend, Paul (1970), "Consolations for the Specialist," in *Criticism and the Growth of Knowledge*, Imre Lakatos and Alan Musgrave, eds., Cambridge, U.K.: Cambridge University Press, 197-230.

——— (1975), *Against Method*, Thetford, England: Lowe and Brydone.

——— (1978), "From Incompetent Professionalism to Professionalized Incompetence—The Rise of a New Breed of Intellectuals," *Philosophy of the Social Sciences*, 8 (March), 37-53.

——— (1981), "More Clothes from the Emperor's Bargain Basement," *British Journal for the Philosophy of Science*, 32, 57-94.

Fine, Seymour H. (1981), *The Marketing of Ideas and Social Issues*, New York: Praeger.

Fox, Karen F. A. and Philip Kotler (1980), "The Marketing of Social Causes: The First 10 Years," *Journal of Marketing*, 44 (Fall), 24-33.

Frankel, Henry (1979), "The Career of Continental Drift Theory," *Studies in History and Philosophy of Science*, 10, 21-66.

Franklin, Allan (1979), "The Discovery and Nondiscovery of Parity Nonconservation," *Studies in History and Philosophy of Science*, 10, 201-57.

Gorn, Gerald J. (1982), "The Effects of Music in Advertising on Choice Behavior: A Classical Conditioning Approach," *Journal of Marketing*, 46 (Winter), 94-101.

Gould, Stephen (1977), *Ever Since Darwin*, New York: Norton.

——— (1980), *The Panda's Thumb*, New York: Norton.

Gouldner, Alvin W. (1974), "Objectivity: The Realm of the 'Sacred' in Social Science," in *Values, Objectivity and the Social Sciences*, Gresham Riley, ed., Reading, MA: Addison-Wesley, 53-64.

Halbert, Michael (1965), *The Meaning and Sources of Marketing Theory*, New York: McGraw-Hill.

Hanson, Norwood R. (1958), *Patterns of Discovery*, Cambridge, U.K: Cambridge University Press.

Hempel, Carl G. (1965), *Aspects of Scientific Explanation*, New York: The Free Press.

Howard, John A. and Jagdish N. Sheth (1969), *The Theory of Buyer Behavior*, New York: Wiley.

Hume, David (1911), *A Treatise of Human Nature*, New York: Dutton.

Hunt, Shelby D. (1976a), "The Nature and Scope of Marketing," *Journal of Marketing*, 40 (July), 17-28.

——— (1976b), *Marketing Theory*, Columbus, OH: Grid.

——— (1983), *Marketing Theory*, Homewood, IL: Irwin.

Hutchinson, Kenneth D. (1952), "Marketing as a Science: An Appraisal," *Journal of Marketing*, 16 (January), 286-93.

Jacoby, Jacob (1978), "Consumer Research: A State of the Art Review," *Journal of Marketing*, 42 (April), 87-96.

Jones, W. T., Frederick Sontag, Morton O. Beckner, and Robert J. Fogelin (1977), *Approaches to Ethics*, 3rd ed., New York: McGraw-Hill.

Kassarjian, Harold H. (1978), "Anthropomorphism and Parsimony," in *Advances in Consumer Research*, 5, H. K. Hunt, ed., Chicago: Association for Consumer Research, xiii-xiv.

Keat, Russell and John Urry (1975), *Social Theory as Science*, London: Routledge & Kegan Paul.

Kelley, Eugene J. (1971), "Marketing's Changing Social/Environmental Role," *Journal of Marketing*, 35 (July), 1-2.

Knorr-Cetina, Karin D. (1981), *The Manufacture of Knowledge*, Oxford, U.K.: Pergamon.

——— (1983), "The Ethnographic Study of Scientific Work: Toward a Constructivist Interpretation of Science," in *Science Observed*, K. D. Knorr-Cetina and M. Mulkay, eds., London: Sage, 115-40.

Kotler, Philip (1972), "A Generic Concept of Marketing," *Journal of Marketing*, 36 (April), 46-54.

——— (1975), *Marketing for Nonprofit Organizations*, Englewood Cliffs, NJ: Prentice-Hall.

——— (1979), "Strategies for Introducing Marketing into Nonprofit Organizations," *Journal of Marketing*, 43 (January), 37-44.

——— and Sidney J. Levy (1969), "Broadening the Concept of Marketing," *Journal of Marketing*, 33 (January), 10-15.

——— and Gerald Zaltman (1971), "Social Marketing: An Approach to Planned Social Change," *Journal of Marketing*, 35 (July), 3-12.

Kuhn, Thomas S. (1957), *The Copernican Revolution: Planetary Astronomy in the Development of Western Thought*, Cambridge, MA: Harvard University Press.

——— (1962), *The Structure of Scientific Revolutions*, Chicago: University of Chicago Press.

——— (1970), *The Structure of Scientific Revolutions*, 2nd ed., Chicago: University of Chicago Press.

——— (1977), *The Essential Tension*, Chicago: University of Chicago Press.

Kunin, Leonard and F. Stirton Weaver (1971), "On the Structure of Scientific Revolutions in Economics," *History of Political Economy*, 3 (Fall), 391-97.

Lakatos, Imre (1974), "Falsification and the Methodology of Scientific Research Programs," in *Criticism and The Growth of Knowledge*, Imre Lakatos and Alan Musgrave, eds., Cambridge, U.K.: Cambridge University Press, 91-195.

Latour, Bruno and Steve Woolgar (1979), *Laboratory Life*, Beverly Hills, CA: Sage.

Laudan, Larry (1977), *Progress and Its Problems*, Berkeley, CA: University of California Press.

——— (1980), "Views of Progress: Separating the Pilgrims from the Rakes," *Philosophy of the Social Sciences*, 10, 273-86.

——— (1981), "The Pseudo-Science of Science?" *Philosophy of the Social Sciences*, 11, 173-198.

——— (1982a), "The Demise of the Demarcation Problem," paper presented at the Workshop on the Demarcation between Science and Pseudo-Science, Virginia Polytechnic, April 30-May 2.

——— (1982b), "More on Bloor," *Philosophy of the Social Sciences*, 12, 71-74.

——— (1982c), "*Science and Values*," Center for the Study of Science in Society, Blacksburg, VA: Virginia Polytechnic, unpublished paper.

Law, John and R. J. Williams (1982), "Putting Facts Together: A Study of Scientific Persuasion," *Social Studies of Science*, 12, 535-58.

Leahy, Thomas H. (1980), *A History of Psychology*, Englewood Cliffs, NJ: Prentice-Hall.

Levy, Sidney and Gerald Zaltman (1975), *Marketing, Society and Conflict*, Englewood Cliffs, NJ: Prentice-Hall.

Lutz, Richard J. and James R. Bettman (1977), "Multiattribute Models in Marketing: A Bicentennial Review," in *Consumer and Industrial Buying Behavior*, Arch G. Woodside, Jagdish N. Sheth, and Peter D. Bennett, eds., New York: North-Holland, 137-49.

Machlup, Fritz (1967), "Theories of the Firm: Marginalist, Behavioral, Managerial," *American Economic Review*, 57 (March), 1-33.

MacKenzie, Donald A. and Barry Barnes (1979), "Scientific Judgment: The Biometry-Mendelism Controversy," in *Natural Order*, Barry Barnes and Steven Shapin, eds., Beverly Hills, CA: Sage, 191-210.

Madsen, K. B. (1974), *Modern Theories of Motivation*, New York: Wiley.

Manier, Edward (1980), "Levels of Reflexivity: Unnoted Differences within the 'Strong Programme' in the Sociology of Knowledge," in *Proceedings of the 1980 Biennial Meeting of the Philosophy of Science Association*, P. D. Asquith and R. N. Giere, eds., East Lansing, MI: Philosophy of Science Association, 197-207.

Markin, Rom J. (1969), *The Psychology of Consumer Behavior*, Englewood Cliffs, NJ: Prentice-Hall.

——— (1974), *Consumer Behavior*, New York: Macmillan.

Medawar, P. B. (1979), *Advice to a Young Scientist*, New York: Harper.

Merton, Robert K. (1973), *The Sociology of Science*, Chicago: University of Chicago Press.

Mill, John Stuart (1959), *A System of Logic*, London: Longman, Green.

Mulkay, Michael and G. Nigel Gilbert (1982), "What is the Ultimate Question? Some Remarks in Defense of the Analysis of Scientific Discourse," *Social Studies of Science*, 12, 309-19.

Musgrave, Alan (1976), "Why Did Oxygen Supplant Phlogiston?" in *Method and Appraisal in the Physical Sciences*, Colin Howson, ed., Cambridge, U.K.: Cambridge University Press, 181-209.

Nord, Walter R. and J. Paul Peter (1980), "A Behavior Modification Perspective on Marketing," *Journal of Marketing*, 44 (Spring), 36-47.

Olson, Jerry C. (1981), "Towards a Science of Consumer Behavior," in *Advances in Consumer Research*, 9, Andrew Mitchell, ed., Association for Consumer Research, v-x.

O'Shaughnessy, John and Michael J. Ryan (1979), "Marketing, Science, and Technology," in *Conceptual and Theoretical Developments in Marketing*, O. C. Ferrell, Stephen W. Brown, and Charles W. Lamb, Jr., eds., Chicago: American Marketing, 577-589.

Papineau, David (1978), *For Science in the Social Sciences*, London: Macmillan.

Passmore, John (1967), "Logical Positivism," *Encyclopedia of Philosophy*, 5, Paul Edwards, ed., New York: Macmillan.

Peter, J. Paul (1982), "Current Issues in the Philosophy of Science: Implications for Marketing Theory—A Panel Discussion," in *Marketing Theory: Philosophy of Science Perspectives*, Ronald F. Bush and Shelby D. Hunt, eds., Chicago: American Marketing, 11-16.

——— (1983), "Some Philosophical and Methodological Issues in Consumer Research," in *Marketing Theory*, S. Hunt, Homewood, IL: Irwin, 382-94.

——— and Walter R. Nord (1982), "A Clarification and Extension of Operant Conditioning Principles in Marketing," *Journal of Marketing*, 46 (Summer), 102-7.

——— and Jerry C. Olson (1983), "Is Science Marketing?" *Journal of Marketing*, 47 (Fall), 111-25.

Pickering, Andrew (1981), "The Hunting of the Quark," *Isis*, 72 (June), 216-36.

Platt, John R. (1964), "Strong Inference," *Science*, 46 (October), 347-53.

Polanyi, Michael (1958), *Personal Knowledge*, Chicago: University of Chicago Press.

Popper, Karl (1962), *Conjectures and Refutations*, New York: Harper.

——— (1972), *Objective Knowledge* Oxford, U.K.: Clarendon.

Ravetz, Jerome R. (1971), *Scientific Knowledge and its Social Problems*, New York: Oxford University Press.

Reagan, Charles E. (1969), *Ethics for Scientific Researchers*, Springfield, IL: Charles C. Thomas.

Rosenberg, Alexander (1980), *Sociobiology and the Preemption of Social Science*, Baltimore: The Johns Hopkins University Press.

Rothschild, Michael L. (1981), *An Incomplete Bibliography of Works Related to Marketing for Public Sector and Nonprofit Organizations*, 3rd ed., Madison, WI: Graduate School of Business, University of Wisconsin.

——— and William C. Gaidis (1981), "Behavioral Learning Theory: Its Relevance to Marketing and Promotions," *Journal of Marketing*, 45 (Spring), 70-78.

Savitt, Ronald (1980), "Historical Research in Marketing," *Journal of Marketing*, 44 (Fall), 52-58.

Schoeffler, Sidney (1979), "SPI Seeks Science, Not Single 'Oversimplistic' Strategy Variable: Another Look at Market Share," *Marketing News*, 13 (February), 4.

Shapere, Dudley (1964), "The Structure of Scientific Revolutions," *Philosophical Review*, 73, 383-94.

Shapin, Steven (1981), "The History of Science and Its Sociological Reconstructions," working paper, Science Studies Unit, Edinburgh University.

Shapiro, Benson (1973), "Marketing for Nonprofit Organizations," *Harvard Business Review*, 51 (September-October), 123-32.

Sheth, Jagdish N. (1967), "A Review of Buyer Behavior," *Management Science*, 13 (August), B719-B756.

——— (1972), "The Future of Buyer Behavior," in *Proceedings of the Third Annual Conference*, M. Venkatensan, ed., Association for Consumer Research, 562-75.

——— (1979), "The Surpluses and Shortages in Consumer Behavior Theory and Research," *Journal of the Academy of Marketing Science*, 7 (Fall), 414-27.

——— and Peter L. Wright, eds. (1974), *Marketing Analysis for Societal Problems*, Urbana, IL: University of Illinois, Bureau of Economic and Business Research.

Steiner, Robert L. (1976), "The Prejudice Against Marketing," *Journal of Marketing*, 40 (July), 2-9.

Suppe, Frederick (1974), *The Structure of Scientific Theories*, Urbana, IL: University of Illinois Press.

Taylor, Weldon J. (1965), "Is Marketing a Science? Revisited," *Journal of Marketing*, 29 (July), 49-53.

Thomas, David (1979), *Naturalism and Social Science*, Cambridge, U.K.: Cambridge University Press.

Truzzi, Marcello (1980), "A Skeptical Look at Paul Krutz's Analysis of the Scientific Status of Parapsychology," *Journal of Parapsychology*, 44 (March), 35-55.

Tucker, W. T. (1974), "Future Directions in Marketing Theory," *Journal of Marketing*, 38 (April), 30-35.

Vaile, Roland S. (1949), "Towards a Theory of Marketing—Comment," *Journal of Marketing*, 13 (April), 520-22.

Wilkie, William L. and Edgar A. Pessemier (1973), "Issues in Marketing's Use of Multi-Attribute Attitude Models," *Journal of Marketing Research*, 10 (November), 428-41.

Winch, Peter (1958), *The Idea of a Social Science*, London: Routledge & Kegan Paul.

Wind, Yoram and Robert J. Thomas (1980), "Conceptual and Methodological Issues in Organizational Buying Behavior," *European Journal of Marketing*, 14, 239-63.

Woolgar, Steve (1981), "Interests and Explanation in the Social Study of Science," *Social Studies of Science*, 11, 365-94.

Wynne, Brian (1976), "C. G. Barkla and the J Phenomenon: A Case Study in the Treatment of Deviance in Physics." *Social Studies of Science*, 6, 307-47.

Zaltman, Gerald, Christian R. A. Pinson, and Reinhard Angelmar (1973), *Metatheory and Consumer Research*, New York: Holt.

———, Karen LeMasters, and Michael Heffring (1982), *Theory Construction in Marketing: Some Thoughts on Thinking*, New York: Wiley.

SECTION D

# History of Marketing Thought

The history of marketing thought is almost 75 years old. This is relatively young for a discipline in the social sciences, especially when compared to economics, psychology, sociology, and anthropology. On the other hand, marketing practice predates the Biblical age. It is surprising to note that scholars did not attempt to offer a theory for marketing practice for thousands of years.

History is fascinating, and it gives people a sense of security, pride, and motivation. Security comes from knowing that you are not alone in your endeavor to theorize, whether it is fashionable or not. Pride results from the fact that history provides a sense of fraternity with other pioneers who were as curious as you are about a phenomenon. Finally, a historical perspective gives motivation to create something new and different so that you can secure your place in history.

This section provides historical narratives of various schools of marketing thought that have emerged over the years.

# 11 — Development of Marketing Thought: A Brief History

*Robert Bartels*

*Science in Marketing*, edited by George Schwartz (New York: John Wiley and Sons, Inc., 1965), pp. 47-69. Reprinted by permission.

Two theories of art appreciation are relevant to the appraisal of marketing science. One is that a work of art is complete only when every detail of it has been finished. The other is that the completeness of a work lies in its basic conception, composition, and structure, independent of the details which embellish its fundamental outline, and that completeness is a quality inherent in every stage of its development.

By what might be called a terminal appraisal, interest is centered on the *extent* of the development of thought. Its character at different stages is compared, and a continuum is conceived ranging from incomplete to more complete and, ultimately, to complete development. Marketing thought is thus seen beginning as simple inquiry and findings, progressing to the status of a discipline, and emerging as a science. Critics differ as to the stage attained, and some doubt that marketing can be a science. Thus the picture is judged in terms of preconceptions as to what the finished product should be.

The other point of view is relative rather than absolute in its appraisal of marketing thought. A stage of thought is appraised not in relation to its past or future character but in *relation* to the concurrent circumstances which bring forth that stage of thought. Completeness is defined in terms of adequacy. Thought is appraised not as an independent variable evolving of itself but as a variable dependent on other factors for its emergence, form, and character. Thus marketing thought is depicted as relative to the world of market problems and practice. Comparability of thought at different times is a function of its inherence in a changing setting.

Actually both views are important and inseparable in understanding the evolution of marketing thought. Until recently the former was predominant. This evoked consideration of such questions as whether marketing is a science, whether there are principles of marketing, and whether there are marketing theories or ''schools'' of marketing thought. Increasingly, the other viewpoint is being adopted. This is leading to consideration of marketing as a social phenomenon, to market behavior as social behavior, and to comparative marketing studies.

Throughout this chapter both viewpoints are explored. The evolution of marketing thought through six successive periods is described. In each, the content of thought is related to the socio-economic circumstances which impelled and formed it. On the other hand, major threads of thought are traced through several periods to facilitate interpretation of the present status of marketing thought.

## The Period of Discovery

The beginnings of marketing thought might be dated at the beginning of the twentieth century, for it was between 1900 and 1910 that "marketing" was conceived or discovered and initial expression was given to ideas which became incorporated in the body of marketing thought.

Prior to 1900, market behavior and trade practice were explained mainly from the macro viewpoint, in economic theory. As the scientific study of management practice developed, attention turned from public to private economic problems, but management theory was unconcerned with distributive activity. There remained, therefore, a gap in theoretical explanation as social and economic conditions departed increasingly from the assumptions concerning the market on which existing trade theory was built. Competition no longer characterized some markets; demanders and suppliers were farther removed from each other; customary relations of demand and supply were becoming reversed; and new patterns of living were evolving. New interpretations of economic activity were needed, as were new applications of mangement science to distributive business. These needs nurtured the discovery of "marketing."

Marketing was a discovery only as "marketing" is recognized as an *idea* and not simply as an *activity*. Every conception is a discovery to the person who first perceives the concept. Until the *idea* was conceived to which the term "marketing" was applied, the simple *activity* had been called only "trade," "distribution," or "exchange." Thus early studies of market practice were titled "Distributive and Regulative Industries of the United States" or "The Distribution of Products." Use of the term "marketing" evidently began sometime soon after the turn of the century. It was found in university course titles in 1905 at the University of Pennsylvania, in 1909 at the University of Pittsburgh, and in 1910 at the University of Wisconsin. Among the men who taught such courses prior to 1906 were E. D. Jones, Simon Litman, George M. Fisk, W. E. Kreusi, H. S. Person, and James E. Hagerty.

Growing interest in trades and conception of a new meaning in economic distributive activity were not confined to any one locality or person, for the impelling circumstances were widespread. However, Ralph Starr Butler was probably among the first to articulate a concept of marketing. He has explained[1] that by "marketing" he meant to designate "everything that the promoter of a product has to do prior to his actual use of salesmen or of advertising.'' Thus from its inception ''marketing'' was conceptually different from mere selling and advertising, as well as from any other functions considered singly. Marketing originally—and continually—has meant a collective, integrative, or aggregative phenomenon. In more recent years this idea has been expressed anew in the concepts of ''managerial marketing'' and ''management of the marketing mix.''

With one exception, there seem to have been no notable general writings on marketing during the decade ending in 1910. Some economists[2] had been dealing with certain phases of trade in the new market circumstances, but none wrote as fully of it as did John Franklin Crowell in the *Report of the Industrial Commission on the Distribution of Farm Products*.[3] Drawn mainly from agricultural markets, his generalizations were not typical of all marketing practice. This publication, nevertheless, served as a general marketing reading until more integrative studies began to appear in the early 1920s.

Before general works on marketing began to appear, however, specialized studies were made prior to 1910 concerning advertising, credit, and selling, and a few writings appeared before then in each of these fields. By contrast, no writings before 1910 were concerned with sales management, retailing, wholesaling, or marketing research.

Interest in advertising increased around 1900 as a natural consequence of two circumstances—the need for promotional stimulus as buyers' markets began to replace sellers' markets and the application of new psychological findings to the motivation of consumers in this evolving marketing situation. Both psychologists and businessmen contributed to the advertising literature of that period, and prominent among the writers were W. D. Scott, E. E. Calkins, R. Holden, G. H. Powell, and T. A. DeWeese. Believing psychology to be the only stable foundation for a theory of advertising, Scott introduced into advertising such concepts as attention, association of ideas, suggestion, fusion, perception, apperception, illusions, and mental imagery.

The same circumstances which nurtured advertising also stimulated the development of personal selling—new products, new markets, and new forms of competition. Although both the ''art'' and ''science'' of selling were discussed, the subject was dealt with subjectively and, to a considerable extent, psychologically. Early writers who gained some lasting place among contributors to this field were P. L. Estabrook, H. E. Read, T. H. Russell, and L. D. H. Weld.

That the subject of credit should have been one developed during the earliest years of marketing thought was due less to market demands on credit than to financial demands. Marketing implications of the subject were slow to develop despite the fact that the financing of market and marketing activities through the use of credit had been increasing throughout the nineteenth century. Earliest writers on credit, therefore, such as W. A. Prendergast and T. J. Zimmerman, dealt with the economic and financial aspects of the subject, describing the effects of credit on social and economic institutions, the implications of distinctions between mercantile and bank credit, and the instruments then in common use in credit practice.

While roots of marketing thought were unmistakably planted in economic and conceptual developments prior to 1910, one could with imaginative hindsight easily attribute too much rather than too little to the intellectual achievements of writers of that period. It would be more accurate and just to say that between 1900 and 1910 thought began to be focused on market problems from the standpoints of agriculturists, psychologists, and financiers. New problems were arising in old fields of business practice, and some new concepts were introduced to illuminate thought in those fields. A general reaching out to know more of the facts of trade and markets was occurring. Out of all of this emerged one new term symbolizing a discovery of paramount importance—marketing.

## The Period of Conceptualization

In the second decade of this century, 1910-20, basic concepts on which the structure of marketing thought was built for the next forty or fifty years emerged and were crystalized. Advances were made both in specialized areas of marketing and in the general statement of the subject. Contributors to marketing thought during this perid were some of the estimable pioneers in this realm of applied economics of business science.

This decade was one in which the economy and the society of the United States grew in many respects. It was a period of increasing urbanization and industrialization. New industries spawned new products which called for both more sales effort and for sales effort of improved quality. Industrial practices quickened social consciousness of business and provoked establishment of the Federal Trade Commission and amendment of the Sherman Act in the Clayton Act. Labor unions pressed new claims on management. Agricultural production was increasing, as were exports. Eminence was gained by both wholesale and retail establishments.

Several of these developments had direct bearing on the study of marketing and advanced it substantially. Three lines of approach to the analysis of marketing were identified—the institutional, the functional, and the commodity approaches.

Very early, interest focused on the functional character of marketing, for it was recognized that certain activities repeatedly occurred in different marketing situations. These elemental activities became known as the "elements" of marketing, which during that decade were primarily identified as selling, buying, transporting, and storing. Various authors identified additional elements, supplementing these, which were generally acknowledged. Before 1915 Arch W. Shaw associated the "motion" of distribution with the "motion" of administration, in which he included financing, credits and collections, purchasing, employment, and accounting.

At the same time L. D. H. Weld listed the functions of middlemen as assembling, storing, risk bearing, financing, rearranging, selling, and transporting. By 1920 Paul T. Cherington elaborated the functional concept in a book entitled *The Elements of Marketing*.[4]

The institutional approach to marketing during this decade is identified with Weld and with Paul H. Nystrom. Weld, writing of wholesale middlemen engaged in distribution of agricultural products, saw merchants as specialists in handling commodities at successive stages in their distribution, economic specialists whose contribution was the reduction of distribution costs. Nystrom laid the foundations of the field of retailing thought in his *Retail Selling and Store Management*[5] and in *The Economics of Retailing*.[6] The former was essentially an operating manual, but it contained the structural elements on which the body of retailing thought was hung by subsequent writers. In the latter, he not only dealt with operating principles but also recounted the history of retailing and made comparisons between American and foreign retail establishments.

The commodity approach to marketing was, prior to 1920, confined largely to the marketing of agricultural products. Subsequently, more detailed attention was given both to this class of products and to manufactured goods.

Another concept which is found expressed in the marketing literature between 1910 and 1920 was that of the types of utilities supposedly created by marketing. Marketing was under fire during those years, for practical questions as to the economic contribution of marketing had not yet been answered logically. A concept of economic utility creation, common in economics treatises, was adopted by students of marketing. Time and place utilities had long been recognized as types of economic value, in contrast to form utility, and they were promptly claimed as part of marketing. To these were added another—possession utility—as a kind of general embodiment of all of the marketing activity which resulted in exchange, or the consummation of the market. These three utilities, later supplemented by some others, were key concepts in the economic rationalization of marketing at that time.

In the specialized fields of marketing, notable progress was made in the development of thought concerning advertising, credit, and selling. Psychologists continued to interpret new discoveries in terms of advertising applications. So specialized were the writings of some psychologists that the measurement of advertising appeals, memory, etc. were principal considerations, and no mention was made of marketing, economics, salesmanship, journalism, or advertising agencies.[7] On the other hand, divergent points of view were being focused on the subject, and by 1915 the subject was being interpreted not only from the psychological standpoint but also from that of the writer, the artist, and the advertising manager.[8] This transition of advertising practice from the application of mere psychological principles to the application of an integrated group of principles was a major development and even at that time was regarded as a ''great change'' taking place in business practice.

Advertising thought then found expression in such periodical media as *Printer's Ink, System,* and *Advertising and Selling*. Articles published in such media became the basis of Paul T. Cherington's *Advertising as a Business Force,*[9] which was one of the early integrative works on the subject.

The new use which was made of advertising following 1910 proved that it was a significant force in business. As a force, however, it was one which was directed mainly toward ultimate consumers, and relatively little attention was given the use of this medium of communication in selling to industrial or business customers. Psychologists acquainted themselves with the mental processes of individuals mainly as personal buyers.

By contrast, theory concerning the force which lay in personal selling developed along two lines, retail selling and nonretail selling. Throughout ensuing years the former unfolded along lines emphasizing storekeeping, merchandising, and techniques of informing and convincing the retail customer. The latter developed along lines of application of psychological principles to personal selling and was concerned with the enlarging responsibilities of the salesman, particularly the traveling salesman.

While psychologists were uncovering new ways of tapping the mental processes of individuals which lead to purchasing, a new philosophic note was found in some writings which represented the emerging concept of marketing. Both personal and impersonal manifestations of the selling ''force'' were found increasingly in business, but it remained to be seen whether this force was constructive or destructive, unifying or divisive. Tradition generally held selling to be successful which resulted in a sale. The fact that the buyer had to beware of sellers' taking advantage of him for centuries was not questioned in earliest treatises on selling—either advertising or personal selling. However, between 1910 and 1920 the coincidence of interests of buyers and sellers began to be recognized and expressed. Norris A. Brisco was one who pointed out in several books[10] that the notion which long associated ''trader'' with ''falsifier'' was not necessarily descriptive of modern retailing. John Wanamaker in 1876, for example, had established a policy that his salesmen were not to importune customers to buy, thus rejecting the haggling and pressure selling which had long characterized retailing.

That attitude, however, was not universally held then. Much of the literature on selling during that period emphasized the subjectivity of selling. It was regarded as an art that did not lend itself to analysis or interpretation. Difference, rather than similarity, of interest and point of view was emphasized, and selling was explained as the process whereby customers are induced to accept the seller's point of view. When it was recognized that selling could be taught and learned, it was also recognized that the best selling required the development in the salesman of the better human qualities, such as genuine interest in others, courtesy, intelligence, etc.

The increase of selling during the post-World War I years represented a demand for proficiency in a marketing activity and the progressive emergence of a harmony of economic interests which came to characterize marketing. It also called for a new type of management talent—the management of the selling function. Nothing that had been written of marketing up to that time really dealt with the managerial aspects of this process. Market considerations of which businessmen should be aware had been discussed, and techniques of advertising and credit administration had been presented, but the line of thought which was to develop into marketing management theory had its origin in what was written concerning the management of selling.

Several significant concepts of sales management came forth at that time. Popularity of Frederick W. Taylor's theories of management and work analysis led some businessmen to see sales management as supervisory behavior, as systematization and organization of salesmen's activities. Others regarded it as a more penetrating type of analysis and planning of selling. Opinions differed as to whether sales management was simply an advanced stage of selling talent or talent basically different from selling. Whichever it seemed to be, it was generally recognized to be a function indigenous to the evolving market circumstances of the time. Some individuals with broad perspective saw sales management in relation to the total marketing activity, even in relation to the entire business enterprise. J. George Frederick, for example, beheld the sales manager in an executive capacity, in a top-level position, contributing to the shaping of policies and responsible for carrying them out, concerned with qualities of the production and conditions in the factory.[11]

The force attributed to both selling and advertising was not during early years equally associated with credit. Credit was a phenomenon of finance, rather than of marketing, although it was employed in attaining marketing objectives. Moreover, credit as employed prior to 1920 pertained almost wholly to mercantile transactions involving credit; consumer credit was found in retail stores, but installment credit and cash lending to consumers were minimal. Consequently, credit thought of this decade related mainly to business uses of credit. In 1913 James E. Hagerty wrote *Mercantile Credit*,[12] which typified the practical approach to the subject taken also by most other writers of the period. The concept of the "C's" of credit—Character, Capacity, and Capital—was generally accepted, and the analysis of creditworthiness in terms of them was the principal responsibility of "credit men," as credit managers were then called.

## THE PERIOD OF INTEGRATION

The years between 1920 and 1930 marked the coming of age of the discipline of marketing. During that decade not only did all the branches of the subject attain a general or integrated statement, but two additional areas of specialization appeared—wholesaling and marketing research.

The integration and generalization of the subject of marketing were proclaimed as the "principles" of marketing. This term appeared in the general marketing writings of Paul W. Ivey, of Fred E. Clark, and of H. H. Maynard, Walter C. Weidler, and Theodore N. Beckman. It appeared also in writings on selling and on advertising. By "principles" was meant several things—that economic deductions concerning the market had in some measure been confirmed by empirical experience, that logical statements of cause and effect had been generalized among the concepts and classifications of marketing thought, and that marketing experience had become so definitized that rules of thumb could be postulated as guides to action. The principles of marketing set forth during that period were of all these types. They inspired a confidence in the knowledge and mastery of marketing which was to continue for many years.

The elements, the approaches, the concepts which emerged during previous years were blended during the 1920s in a macroanalysis of marketing which had some managerial implications. The operations of the marketing system or institutional structure were described, with increasing attention given to identification and definition of classes of phenomena, whether they be customers, products, channels, or establishments. Judging from the writings of Clark, Maynard, Weidler, Beckman, and Paul D. Converse, which became the "classical" statement of marketing, marketing was an economic activity. It was affected by the economic and social conditions of the market; it involved the performance of basic functions, mainly by marketing establishments, in the distribution of products; it was a performance in which business managers operated in a framework of social control in the form of governmental regulation and assistance. The essence of this concept was the oft-quoted definition of marketing as "all of those activities involved in the distribution of goods from producers to consumers and in the transfer of title thereto."

Among the concepts which gained a place in marketing thought at that time were the following:

> Convenience, shopping, and specialty classes of consumer products, attibuted to Melvin C. Copeland but based on a classification of products as "convenience, emergency, and shopping goods" presented about 1912 by C. C. Parlin.
>
> Buying, selling, transporting, storing, standardizing, financing, risk-bearing, and providing market information—as the "marketing functions." There were some minor variations of this list among several authorities.
>
> Wholesaling and retailing, differentiated on the basis of purchase motive of the buyer.
>
> Marketing channel—the course taken in transfer of title.
>
> The inherence, pervasiveness, and universality of the marketing functions.

Such were some of the indicators of the level of thought reached in the general statement of marketing during the 1920s.

Apart from the general development of marketing thought at that time, one of the most impressive single advancements was in retailing thought, in the form of what has been called "The Retailing Series." Imbued with confidence in the potentialities of research for improving retail management, a number of New York merchants and professors at New York University produced a series of books explaining the application of the scientific method to the solution of retailing problems. Progress in both scientific management and in statistical analysis of distribution practices contributed to this development in marketing thought. Beginning in 1925 with James L. Fri's *Retail Merchandising, Planning, and Control,*[13] the series included throughout ensuing years works on such retailing subjects as buying, credit, accounting, store organization and management, merchandising, personal relations, and salesmanship. It included also a number of works on general aspects of retailing. This series was unequaled in the marketing literature for its contribution to institutional operation and management.

It was during the 1920s also that the subject of wholesaling received its first scientific analysis and description. Perceptive of both practical and theoretical differences between retailing and wholesaling, Theodore N. Beckman undertook a study of the latter which threw new light on activity which bore much of the criticism of marketing in general. Although distinctions were commonly made between wholesalers and retailers, between wholesaling and retailing, and between wholesaling and wholesalers, more precise definition of these concepts was necessary before this branch of marketing thought could be much developed. Not only these contributions were made by Beckman throughout the successive revisions of his works on wholesaling, but wholesaling itself was depicted as an institution. Its economic service was presented, and comparisons were made with the role which wholesaling played in other nations.

Many influences wrought changes in credit during the 1920s and allied the treatment of this subject more closely to marketing. Noteworthy trends occurred both in mercantile and in consumer credit. The former was affected by the use of new terms of sale, new credit instruments, and new agencies involved in the role of credit—the Federal Reserve System, credit bureaus, and new forms of credit management assistance provided by established agencies. Economic instability and economic growth of the period evoked thought concerning better collections and the use of credit in industrial distribution.

Retail credit and consumer loan credit also experienced changes which were reflected in the body of marketing thought. With the introduction of consumer durable goods and the greater use of automobiles, impetus was given to the use of installment credit, which in fact became a promotional tool. Management rules for administration of this credit were developed by credit specialists, and economic appraisal of this credit was made, mainly by E. R. A. Seligman, whose *The Economics of Installment Selling*[14] established the critical framework by which not only consumer credit but also more general aspects of marketing were judged for some years.

The true marketing character of credit, however, was not universally appreciated, and the attitude still found expression that ''the merchant gives credit and gets nothing for it.'' Such a dark view preceded the enlightenment which was to come with a more promotional, a more marketing-oriented view of credit.

In the area of sales thought, during the 1920s perhaps the most significant trend was the reconception of salesmanship which, because of the increasing breadth given the term, led to new measures of integration of salesmen's work. The highly subjective and personal concept of selling having been superseded by objective consideration of it as a learnable technique, selling became more than the mere exchange between seller and buyer. Selling became regarded as a whole occupation requiring preparation, as for a business career. Selling included the salesman's responsibility to know pricing policies, advertising programs, distribution channels, and, above all, customer needs. Some writers saw the salesman as part of the selling team of his employer, who was responsible for coordinating his individual activity with the broader promotional program disclosed to him by the sales manager. H. K. Nixon, showing in still another manner the broadening concept of selling, spoke of it[15] as combining inspirational, psychological, economic, personal, and sociological types of activity.

With the integrative trends manifest in all other phases of marketing thought, it is understandable that those who wrote of sales management should have shared this perspective. Management of salesmen became viewed as a key role in business, for it was thought that on the success of this function depended in large measure the volume of sales of a business firm. Most important, however, was the beginning tendency to link the selling effort with the broader marketing objectives and activities of the selling organization. Excessive emphasis of specialization obscured this view, but the persistent integrative tendency of the inquiring mentality inevitably found the broader relations of selling.

Leverett S. Lyon introduced in postwar years some military concepts into sales management theory[16] and employed the term ''marketing manager'' to designate a type of management talent not then generally found. The term ''marketing strategy'' was in accord with the developments in general management theory which placed determination of business objective or end ahead of the means by which it was to be obtained. Strategy was equated with means or ''instruments''; within the over-all strategy were programs or campaigns of lesser scope. The ''instruments'' included salesmen, advertising, credit terms, price, etc. The ''ammunition'' of the marketing manager consisted of the talking points that he presents through the various instruments. Perhaps even more important than these concepts, were those of Lyon's which regarded the marketing manager as operating in ''the economic-social order of our time.'' He saw him concerned with diverse internal aspects of the business, including production and finance. He saw him in an organizational position above sales management, consumer-oriented, and having a sense of social responsibility.

Advertising thought, too, moved to a higher sense of integration during that period, and a variety of books marked ''principles'' were turned out. A useful link between advertising and marketing practice was formed by Otto Kleppner in his conception of three stages in advertising a product—pioneering, competitive, retentive. Known as the ''advertising spiral,'' this concept gave a unity to the presentation of advertising thought, a practical rallying point around which other marketing actions and decisions could be organized. Elsewhere, George B. Hotchkiss, Hugh E. Agnew, and others were refining and enlarging the technical aspects of advertising.

New to marketing thought in the 1920s was the interest which became expressed in market and marketing research. Prior to that time, scientific inquiry had been conducted with interest in findings rather than in methodology; now attention turned more to the methods and procedures of research. Urgency characterized the development of this field of knowledge at that time, not only because of the expansion of markets but because of the clyclical economic fluctuations and business postwar adjustments as well. A. W. Shaw, Paul H. Nystom, Paul T. Cherington, and C. S. Duncan had already linked marketing with systematic and scientific research, and C. C. Parlin in the years following 1912 instituted the practice of marketing research. It was not until the 1920's, however, that more formal writings on the subject began to appear under the authorship of George J. Frederick, Percival White, J. Eigelberner, W. J. Reilly, and Virgil D. Reed.

The content of marketing research during any period has depended, mainly, on the prevailing concept of marketing and the prevailing sense of marketing problems. Prior to 1910, for example, as has already been pointed out, the predominant problems of marketing were psychological or so it seemed at that time. During the following decade, because of the growing size of distributive establishments, attention turned to internal data, and research consisted largely of analysis of operating figures such as were supplied concerning department stores by university bureaus of business research. Between 1920 and 1930 attention shifted to markets, and discoveries in the use of questionnaires supplied a new technique for analyzing markets and marketing.

From the writings which have been mentioned, one might justifiably conclude that there was a growing unity in marketing thought and literature throughout the first quarter of this century. The institutional, the functional, and the commodity studies, complemented by research techniques suited to the concept of problems inherent in each, constituted the main body of marketing thought. So broad was the accepted understanding of marketing at that time that among the individual differences it would have been difficult to detect dissidences, especially any which were to have long-run significance. However, among the points of view published then were a few which in retrospect deserve some attention. They are found in the writings of W. D. Moriarity,[17] Percival White,[18] Floyd L. Vaughan,[19] and Roland S. Vaile, and Peter L. Slagsvold.[20]

In general, these authors differed from the traditional or popular statements of marketing in one or more respects. Moriarity attempted to analyze marketing in terms of classical economic theory. Inasmuch as the disappearance of many conditions underlying such theory had brought forth this new body of thought, his work did not make much of an impression. Its significance lay, however, in the fact that not everyone saw the distributive practices or the predominant marketing problem in the same light. Vaughan criticized the increasing cost of marketing. White exposed some of the "abuses" of marketing as wastes of the distributive system and proposed a system for the guidance of individual companies. Vaile and Slagsvold were concerned with certain aspects of price making and contrasted the forces at work in competitive agricultural markets with those in the manipulatable markets for manufactured goods.

## THE PERIOD OF DEVELOPMENT

By 1930 marketing thought had attained a substantial character, but the changing social and economic conditions of the next decade molded it further. Among the prominent environmental influences on marketing thought and practice between 1930 and 1940 were the following: the economic depression, expansion of urban population into suburban areas, emphasis throughout the economy on savings and low price, the vocalization of consumer attitudes known as the Consumer Movement, the trend toward government participation in as well as regulation of business activity, and severe forms of competition in distribution as a result of adoption of new marketing concepts and techniques. Among the effects of these changes during the 1930s on the distributive system were the development of large-scale retailing, the rise of countervailing institutional powers in voluntary and cooperative associations, the alteration of traditional distribution channels, the conformation of distributive activity to new social values and controls, recognition of consumer interests as the primary objective of marketing effort, and the evolution of marketing in the solution of new types of market problems.

All these circumstances had little actual effect on the structure of marketing thought which was then beginning to gain wide acceptance. Marketing continued to be viewed as a functional management area and as a form of economic production. The Clark-Converse-Maynard type of analysis which employed the commodity-functional-institutional basis for postulating marketing principles was predominant. A measure of greater attention was given to pricing theory by Charles F. Phillips in his general work *Marketing*,[21] but few other changes were made in the manner in which marketing was conceived and explained. Maturity in this line of thought was further indicated by simplifications which began to appear in its statement. Whereas elaboration and detailing of thought characterized one line of its development, reduction of the general statement of marketing to a concise, even elementary, form also occurred. The writings of H. E. Agnew, R. B. Jenkins, and J. D. Drury,[22] and of C. W. Barker and N. Anshen[23] were of this type.

Notwithstanding the satisfaction and benefits derived from this particular concept of marketing, desire to express other views of it, to formulate new views of the problems and solutions with which marketing was concerned, continued to challenge students of this subject. Thus there continued to evolve ideas which differed from the usual exposition of marketing. As in the previous decade the contributions of Moriarity and others constituted an uncommon part of marketing thought, so in the 1930s some ideas presented by Ralph F. Breyer[24] and by H. B. Killough[25] also displayed concepts of marketing to which little heed was given at that time.

The objective of those who espoused these more or less unorthodox concepts was to portray the functioning of the marketing system "as a whole." Traditionally it had been dealt with as a separate functional area in which decisions had to have an expected consistency but which was not highly integrated either with other functional areas within a business or with other aspects of the distributive system outside the business. In this emerging concept marketing was becoming viewed as a process broader than mere internal programming or even than a type of economic behavior. The full import of these new ideas, however, was not then clearly apparent.

Breyer broke with the conventional concepts of marketing, functions, channels, and system. He viewed marketing as the activity involved in fulfilling certain tasks rather than as any set list of activities or functions themselves. The tasks he identified as contactual, negotiatory, storage, measurement, quality determination, packing, transportation, payment, financing, and risk-bearing. Channels were regarded not as series of stages in which distinct and separate operations occurred but as circuits through which "flows" of events take place in opposite directions—flows of merchandise, payments, information, obligations, etc. In developing his concepts Breyer drew on theory in such fields as physics, sociology, psychology, and other social sciences.

Killough's writing was less original although it, too, was atypical. Its chief merit was in its depicting in some detail the relationship between American business and its economic and geographic setting. This was not truly a conception of business in its social setting, but compared with many other expositions it was a step in that direction.

Marketing thought became considerably more quantitative during the 1930s. That is, many of the qualitative judgments which had been formed without much factual support during preceding years were validated by evidence collected in the increasing numbers of censuses and surveys. Simple opinion surveys were superseded by complex questionnaire investigations which were concerned not only with market studies but also with research of different kinds of marketing problems. Lyndon O. Brown[26] was one who during the 1930s made significant contributions both to the adaptation of scientific research methodology to market problems and to the body of knowledge to which such methods contributed.

The increased knowledge of markets had direct application to sales management, and it influenced thought in that field in several ways. It particularly produced studies of sales quotas and distribution cost analysis. Both internal and external statistics were employed in arriving at more scientific statement of management of this portion of the marketing function.

In most of the other specialized fields of marketing thought, the developmental stage of the 1930s was evidenced in their embracing the changing business practices and in their extending the dimensions of organized thought to both new depths and new breadths. In credit, changes were occurring in uses of consumer credit. Installment plans increased with the improvement of economic conditions. Personal loan credit was stimulated by the increased number and types of agencies providing this service, especially by the entry of commerical banks into this market. However, not only were the technical aspects of credit management explored, so also were the economic aspects, inasmuch as there were several theories relating consumer credit to economic cycles, and the social aspects, considering that ethical obligations of both creditors and debtors are involved. This represented the growing concern for customer interests which was appearing in different areas of marketing.

In advertising, new dimensions were gained in technical thought through psychological discoveries, media studies, and technological advancement. Economic analyses were made in response to interest in the relation of advertising to the depression. And social studies of advertising reflected the justifiable criticism which was made of advertising uses and abuses.

## The Period of Reappraisal

The period of 1940-1950 was not a particularly fertile one for the development and expression of marketing thought. For the span of World War II, both industrial and academic activities were disrupted, and an opportunity was provided for new technologies and new lines of thought to develop. In the marketing literature, the lines of thought which were already manifest continued to find expression.

The traditional forms of marketing thought that emphasized functional and institutional concepts were projected in revisions which updated content and reinforced the type of generalizations which had come to be regarded as inherent and universal in the knowledge of marketing. Status consciousness of students of marketing was extended beyond satisfaction found in marketing principles, however, and increasing concern was felt for whether the body of marketing thought had, or could, attain the proportions and attributes of a science. Papers dealing with aspects of this question were presented as early as 1946 at meetings of the American Marketing Association.

However, concurrent with this maturation of marketing thought along one line, divergence therefrom continued to appear, both before and after the war. In 1940 a shift toward a managerial approach to the explanation of marketing was made by Ralph S. Alexander, F. M. Surface, R. F. Elder, and Wroe Alderson in their book, *Marketing*.[27] In neither its broad nor detailed character was the book revolutionary, but it was significant in that it extended lines of difference from the usual interpretation of marketing which were begun some years before, and it contained viewpoints which were to find fuller expression in the following decade. More attention was given by those authors to managerial marketing functions rather than merely to marketing functions. The planning of marketing, research, and budgetary control received more attention, and mere description was subordinated to a mangement viewpoint.

Following the war, amidst ascendent popularity of more traditional concepts, another somewhat unorthodox mold of thought was cast, entitled *Marketing, An Institutional Approach*,[28] by E. A. Duddy and D. A. Revzan. It represented not so much a managerial approach as a holistic interpretation of marketing in our economy. They undertook to explain the marketing structure as "an organic whole made up of interrelated parts, subject to growth and change and functioning in a process of distribution that is coordinated by economic and social forces." They interpreted functions as giving rise to structural organization, which is coordinated through instrumentalities of price, management, and government. Such an analysis of marketing differed from the traditional in several respects. It visualized the operation of the *whole* marketing mechanism rather than the operation of any one particular segment or establishment. It employed a conceptual framework unlike the functional-institutional-commodity analysis which had typically been made. It introduced the agency of government more as a social participant in business rather than merely as a regulator of business.

Few significant conceptual developments were made in the specialized areas of marketing thought during the 1940s, but in periodical literature and in manuscripts in preparation a number of provocative issues were being raised. Complacency with the accomplishments in marketing thought was being affronted; satisfaction with the structure, as well as with the details, of marketing thought was being shaken.

Wroe Alderson and Reavis Cox wrote in 1948:

> Students of marketing thus far have reaped from their efforts remarkably small harvests of accurate, comprehensive, and significant generalizations. Marketing literature offers its readers very few true and important "principles" or "theories".... Existing theories fail to satisfy students because they do not account for or take into consideration all of the relevant observed facts. In essence, this is today's situation in the study of marketing.[29]

At the same time E. T. Grether was saying:

> We are surfeited with knowledge in the sense of isolated facts and narrow bands of factual interpretation.... In marketing, at present,

> there is no need for "pure" theory—that is, theory ranging so widely as to take the form of a logical framework with little or no relevance to reality. In marketing, rather we need various types of "applied theory," developed out of varied interests.... [30]

Other evidences of the reappraisal of marketing thought were found at that time in the writings of several people:

Jones, F. M., "A New Interpretation of Marketing Functions," *Journal of Marketing*, Vol. VII, No. 1 (January 1943), p. 256.

Bartels, Robert, "Marketing Principles," *ibid.*, Vol. IX, No. 4 (October 1944), p. 151.

Converse, P. D., "The Development of the Science of Marketing: An Exploratory Survey," *ibid.*, Vol. X, No. 3 (July 1945), pp. 14-32.

Bartels, Robert, "Marketing Theory: Its Essential Nature," *Proceedings of the Christmas Meetings of the American Marketing Association*, 1946.

Brown, Lyndon O., "Toward a Profession of Marketing," *Journal of Marketing*, Vol. XIII, No. 3 (July 1948), p. 27.

Vaile, R. S., "Towards a Theory of Marketing: A Comment," *ibid.*, Vol. XIII, No. 2 (April 1949), p. 520.

Bartels, Robert, "Can Marketing Be A Science?" *ibid.*, Vol. XV, No. 1 (January 1951), p. 319.

Bartels, Robert, "Influences on the Development of Marketing Thought," *ibid.*, Vol. XVI, No. 3 (July 1951), p. 1.

McGarry, E. D., "The Contractual Function in Marketing," *ibid.*, Vol. XIV, No. 2 (April 1951), p. 96.

Wales, Hugh G. (ed.), *Changing Perspectives in Marketing*, University of Illinois Press, Urbana, 1951.

Still another development in thought at that time was a growing historical perspective of marketing. Evidence of this is found in the following publications:

Hagerty, James E., "Experiences of Our Early Marketing Teachers," *Journal of Marketing*, Vol. I, No. 3 (July 1936), p. 20.

Maynard, H. H., "Training Teachers of Marketing and Research Workers," *ibid.*, Vol. II, No. 2 (April 1938), p. 282.

Agnew, H. E., "The History of the American Marketing Association," *ibid.*, Vol. V, No. 2 (April 1941), p. 374.

Maynard, H. H., "Marketing Courses Prior to 1910," *ibid.*, Vol. V, No. 2 (April 1941), p. 382.

Weld, L. D. H., "Early Teachers of Marketing," *ibid.*, Vol. VII, No. 4 (October 1942), p. 158.

Converse, P. D., "Fred Clark's Bibliography as of the Early 1920's," *ibid.*, Vol. X, No. 3 (July 1945), p. 54.

Litman, Simon, ''The Beginnings of Teaching Marketing in American Universities,'' *ibid.*, Vol. XV, No. 4 (October 1950), p. 220.

Bartels, Robert, ''Influences on the Development of Marketing Thought,'' *ibid.*, Vol. XVI, No. 3 (July 1951), p. 1.

## The Period of Reconceptualization

Prior to 1950 there was little to support any claim that there were different ''schools'' of marketing thought. Marketing thought was essentially monolithic. No one would have contended that there was a theory of marketing; neither were there identifiable *theories* of marketing, nor large groups with widely differing opinions about marketing education. Yet cleavages growing out of differing concepts of marketing and of the need for marketing thought became more pronounced. Throughout the ensuing years they grew, to produce in the study of marketing the kind of period of original conceptualizing which had characterized it fifty years earlier. It was as though marketing itself were being reconceived and new meaning assigned to an old term, and new terms were being employed to convey new ideas. In this state of development it was difficult for a number of years to determine which direction the further development of marketing thought would take. Clues to dispel this uncertainty, however, might have been found in the trends of thought during the preceding years.

In general, a clear line of distinction was drawn between the traditional concept of marketing, with the form of thought which was based on it, and the conception of marketing in broader terms. The reconception of marketing, however, took several forms, most of which were embryonically present in earlier criticisms or presentations of marketing.

One development was the increased emphasis of managerial marketing. Whereas heretofore operational aspects of marketing had been stressed, sometimes from a functional standpoint, marketing management came to be seen not only as an area of decision making but also as a point of view in general management and as a coordinative management task above and beyond mere sales management. The concept of ''marketing mix'' was employed to express the fact that this was management through conscious manipulation of variables for the achievement of predetermined objectives. Leverett S. Lyon in 1926 had not only used the term ''marketing management,'' but he had glimpsed the idea of ''strategy'' and ''instruments'' being employed for the achievement of a marketing plan. In the 1950s John A. Howard[31] interpreted marketing management as the making of decisions concerning products, channels, price, promotion, and locations. Concepts of cost allocation, marginal analysis, and recent developments from the behavior sciences were woven into his fabric of marketing managment. Others also explored and amplified the new role of marketing manager, mainly as an evolution of the sales manager position. William J. Stanton and Richard H. Buskirk[32] typified the increased emphasis given to the planning function (in contrast to the selection, training, and compensation of salesmen) and to the social responsibility of marketing managers. D. Maynard Phelps and J. Howard Westing[33] showed the increased authority given to marketing executives in manufacturing concerns for product planning, market investigation, pricing, inventory control, and production scheduling.

Still another element in marketing management was the adoption of the consumer viewpoint as the starting point of all marketing planning and administration. Something of this concept, which again employed concepts that had recurred in marketing thought in earlier years, was incorporated in the writings of Hector Lazo and Arnold Corbin.[34] Thus from the time of Arch W. Shaw's writing and teaching around 1912 until the 1960s, a greater or lesser emphasis was placed on management as a principal modification of marketing thought. After 1950 this form of marketing thought was held to be increasingly important.

Traditional marketing thought was not essentially managerial in character, although it was technical and, in the specialized literatures, inclined to the level of describing "how to do it." Yet neither was it wholly firm-oriented, for it included much description of the marketing structure and of how the market mechanism and the marketing establishments function in a general way. Notwithstanding this macroaspect of marketing thought, its generalizations were not universally regarded as a truly broad, inclusive analysis of the marketing process.

A second development in marketing thought, therefore, has been the interpretation of marketing as a broad, pervasive, interrelating process. Some people visualize it as a system of "flows," somewhat after the manner that Breyer conceived it in the 1930s. Thus emphasis is given to the business policies and relationships that link all units in the channel, that make prices at all levels the concern of the manufacturer, or that make ultimate market conditions important to primary producers. Holism, or the viewing of marketing as a whole rather than as separately managed units in a complex process, has been the interest of several writers, particularly of David Revzan and of Wroe Alderson.

So long as the "whole" of marketing is a total *mechanism,* this viewpoint is still distinguishable from yet another that has found expression in this period of reexamination of the structure and concepts of marketing thought, namely, the social approach to marketing. The social interpretation of marketing, however, has itself been subject to varying interpretation as a result of the newness of this concept. To some, social approach to marketing means the adoption into marketing analysis of research methods devised and developed in other social sciences. To others, it represents recognition that the consumer market reflects not only economic and psychological factors but also social or cultural environmental factors. In addition to this, the social concept of marketing regards the whole marketing process not as a means by which *business* meets the needs of consumers but as a means by which *society* meets its own consumption needs. Thus from this standpoint sociological concepts of positional roles and theories of group behavior and interaction are brought to bear on the explanation of market and marketing behavior. This is one of the lesser developed new concepts, but it is introduced into marketing thought through some of the writings of Wroe Alderson.[35]

Akin to the social concept of marketing is another which in recent years has been gaining expression—comparative marketing. When marketing is seen to be a social phenomenon, rather than merely a mechanistic performance, it follows that cultural orientation accounts for differences in the marketing institution and process in different places and is the basis of interpreting it in any one place. This point of view is illustrated and interpreted in the book *Comparative Marketing: Wholesaling in Fifteen Countries*.[36]

## Conclusions

The history of the development of marketing thought in the United States is, in broad perspective, an account of the thinking of men in a succession of periods to solve the market problems of their day.

Both marketing and marketing thought were altered in the change of market conditions at the beginning of the twentieth century, a change which found the economic facts of life departing farther and farther from the theories which had been devised to explain economic activity and to guide entrepreneurs and government authorities in behavior concerning the market.

The principle stimulant and determinant of evolution in marketing thought was the prevailing concept of marketing itself. From its initial conception out of earliest impressions to its more recent definition, marketing has been regarded as a simple activity, as the coordination of a group of activities, as a business process undertaken from the consumers' point of view, as an economic function of production, and as a social phenomenon. It is natural that the structure of thought evolved from such differing concepts would themselves differ.

The predominant concept of marketing throughout this period was mechanistic, whereby management of the marketing process consisted of manipulation of variables within the framework of commodity, function, and institution concepts or classifications. So widely accepted and so long-standing was this concept that it became for more than a quarter of a century the usual or traditional marketing analysis.

Such a concept, however, was not all-embracing, and unsatisfied needs give rise to other lines of thought, identifiable as early as the 1920s. These lines reflected several important ideas: that the whole of marketing is greater than the sum of its parts, that the marketing system is the product of the society which it in turn influences, and that marketing is basically what *people* do rather than preconceived business processes.

A final observation returns to the proposition with which this discussion began, namely, that marketing thought may be viewed either as a continuum evolving toward a full exposition replete with details and implications or it may be viewed as a framework of thought, structured and complete at any time, to express the logic of the prevailing concept of marketing and to solve the problems of marketing as then conceived. The former is the view which leads to the expectation that marketing thought has or will attain the proportions of a science. The latter is the view which embraces the diversity of concepts of marketing which together constitute the unity of this body of knowledge and which express the role of marketing as an ever-changing function that is indigenous to its environment.

In the evolution of marketing thought since 1950, both the traditional and the orthodox forms of marketing thought are melded into an inseparable whole which must at this time, and for years to come, be understood both as separate and as allied for a proper appreciation of what marketing means as a whole.

## ENDNOTES

1. Robert Bartels, *The Development of Marketing Thought*, Richard D. Irwin, Homewood, Ill., 1962, p. 225.
2. See Frank G. Coolsen, *Marketing Thought in the United States in the Late Nineteenth Century*, Texas Tech Press, Lubbock, Texas, 1961.
3. U.S. Government Printing Office, Washington, D.C., 1901.
4. Macmillan, New York, 1920.
5. D. Appleton-Century, New York, 1913.
6. Vols. 1 and 2, Ronald Press, New York, 1915.
7. H. L. Hollingworth, *Advertising and Selling*, D. Appleton-Century, New York, 1913.
8. Harry Tipper, H. L. Hollingworth, G. B. Hotchkiss and F. A. Parsons, *Advertising: Its Principles and Practices*, Ronald Press, New York, 1915.
9. Doubleday, Page, Garden City, New York, 1913.
10. *Fundamentals of Salesmanship*, D. Appleton-Century, New York, 1916; *Retail Salesmanship*, Ronald Press, New York, 1920.
11. *Modern Sales Management*, D. Appleton-Century, New York, 1919.
12. Henry Holt, New York, 1913.
13. Prentice-Hall, New York, 1925.
14. Harper, New York, 1926.
15. *Principles of Selling*, McGraw-Hill, New York, 1931.
16. *Salesmen in Marketing Strategy*, Macmillan, New York, 1926.
17. *The Economics of Marketing and Advertising*, Harper, New York, 1923.
18. *Scientific Marketing Management: Its Principles and Methods*, Harper, New York, 1927.
19. *Marketing and Advertising*, Princeton University Press, Princeton, N.J., 1928.
20. *Marketing*, Ronald Press, New York, preliminary ed., 1929.
21. Houghton Mifflin, Boston, 1938.
22. *Outlines of Marketing*, McGraw-Hill, New York, 1936.

23. *Modern Marketing*, McGraw-Hill, New York, 1939.
24. *The Marketing Institution*, McGraw-Hill, New York, 1934.
25. *Economics of Marketing*, Harper, New York, 1933.
26. *Market Research*, Ronald Press, New York, 1937.
27. Ginn, Boston, 1940.
28. McGraw-Hill, New York, 1947.
29. "Towards a Theory of Marketing," *Journal of Marketing*, Vol. XIII, No. 4 (October 1948), p. 139.
30. "A Theoretical Approach to the Analysis of Marketing," in *Theory in Marketing*, Reavis Cox and Wroe Alderson (eds.), Richard D. Irwin, Chicago, 1949, pp. 113, 114.
31. *Marketing Management: Analysis and Decision*, Richard D. Irwin, Homewood, Ill., 1957.
32. *Management of the Sales Force*, Richard D. Irwin, Homewood, Ill., 1959.
33. *Marketing Management*, Richard D. Irwin, Homewood, Ill., 1960.
34. *Management in Marketing*, McGraw-Hill, New York, 1961.
35. *Marketing Behavior and Executive Action*, Richard D. Irwin, Homewood, Ill., 1957.
36. Robert Bartels (ed.), Richard D. Irwin, Homewood, Ill., 1963.

# 12 —— History of Marketing Thought: An Update

*Jagdish N. Sheth and*
*David M. Gardner*

Reprinted from *Marketing Theory: Philosophy of Science Perspectives*, published by the American Marketing Association, edited by Ronald Bush and Shelby Hunt (1982), pp. 52-58. Reprinted by permission.

## INTRODUCTION

Since Bartel's classic summary of history of marketing thought in the early sixties (Bartels 1962), it is somewhat surprising to find that there is no update of marketing thought even though several new schools of marketing thought have emerged in the past quarter of a century. Accordingly, the purpose of this paper is to identify various new schools of marketing thought, examine their associated causal factors, and assess their contributions toward enriching marketing theory.

Bartels (1965) provided an elegant account of the development of marketing theory in terms of the periods of discovery (1900-1910), conceptualization (1910-1920), integration (1920-1930), development (1930-1940), reappraisal (1940-1950), and finally reconceptualization (1950-1960). During these periods, early pioneers made numerous conscious efforts to evaluate marketing above selling and distribution, to link marketing as an idea rather than a group of activities so that it could be recognized as a planning function and to generate several principles of marketing so that it could be labeled as a science rather than an art. The outcome of these pioneering efforts was the development and eventual integration of the functional, the commodity and the institutional schools of marketing thought.

These conventional concepts of marketing functions, channels and goods were questioned by a number of scholars (Breyer 1934, Alexander, Surface, Elder and Alderson 1940, Grether 1949, Duddy and Revzan 1947, Lazo and Corbin 1961, Howard 1957, Alderson and Cox 1948, Bartels 1944). It resulted in reappraising marketing thought away from the functions, institutions and products and toward a more managerial and enviornmental orientation.

A closer look at the history of marketing thought including its development, integration and reappraisal during the first half of the twentieth century, however, indicates that two fundamental axioms seemed to dominate most thinking despite divergence of viewpoint.

The first axiom of consensus stemmed from the belief that marketing was essentially an economic activity, and that it was a subset of the discipline of economics. Therefore, marketing concepts (institutions, functions, products, managerial and environmental perspectives) were restricted to economic behavior of people and associated institutions. Marketing was not considered appropriate for such noneconomic domains of human behavior as fine arts, religion, politics, public services, and such intangibles as ideas.

The second axiom of consensus stemmed from the belief that the initiator of marketing activities and programs was the marketer and not the consumer in the market place. While it was recognized that understanding customer behavior through market research was desirable and even essential, it was primarily regarded as an input to the design of marketing programs and activities so that the marketer can influence, manipulate and control market behavior with greater effectiveness through his professional skills of organization and management.

It would appear to us that the genesis of more recent schools of thought since the sixties comes from questioning those two fundamental axioms of marketing thought and replacing them with more comprehensive axioms.

For example, replacement of the axiom of economic exchange with *the axiom of exchange of values* by several scholars (Drucker 1974, Kotler and Levy 1969, Kotler 1972, Levy and Zaltman 1975, Bagozzi 1975, Calman 1980) literally broadened the marketing horizons to the nontraditional areas of human behavior including religion, politics, public services, and fine arts.

Similarly, other scholars and practitioners (Katz and Kahn 1955, Howard 1963, Cyert and March 1958, Katona 1960, Rogers 1965, Simon 1957, McKitterick 1958, Mayer 1958, Starch 1958, Dichter 1964), explicityly questioned the futility of marketer as the initiator of marketing programs by suggesting that the consumer was more powerful than the marketer, that many other factors such as personal influences were more responsible for his decisions, and that it was best for the marketer to understand the *psychology* of the consumer and work backwards from the market to the factory to achieve more productivity and effectiveness out of marketing resources. In short, these scholars and practitioners encouraged *behavioral perspectives* in place of *economic perspectives* to develop a more realistic marketing theory.

The broadening of the marketing concept by the axiom of exchange of value seems to have triggered three distinct although related schools of marketing thought, all of them dealing with the issues of pervasiveness of marketing in the society. The first school of thought commonly referred to as *macromarketing*, for example, has attempted to focus on the potential and problems of marketing activities and programs from a more macro or societal perspective rather than from a more micro firm's perspective. The second school of thought, more commonly referred to as *consumerism*, emerged to provide an advocacy position in terms of developing and protecting the rights of the consumers. The third school of thought, commonly referred to as *systems approach* provided a framework for integrating both the supply and the demand factors into a single holistic theory. It argued that in an exchange of values, the customer has a more fundamental choice of self-making as a production unit, bartering it with other customers or buying in the market place which must be incorporated in any marketing thinking.

Similarly, the axiom of balance of power seems responsible for triggering another set of theory in marketing. The first and probably the most influential school of thought is commonly referred to as *buyer behavior,* which has tried to generate a behavioral theory of buying. It literally dominated the field of marketing ranging from theory to market research and practice. The second school of thought more commonly referred to as *behavioral organizations,* has focused on the behavioral aspects such as power, conflict, and interdependence among organizations and particularly among channels of distribution. The third school of thought, more commonly referred to as *strategic planning,* has focused on the balance of power issues between external environmental factors such as market values, competition, technology, resources and regulation, and the internal resource factors such as products, services, distribution and promotion.

The rest of the paper will provide a brief historical perspective on each of the six new schools of thought and at the end assess their contribution to marketing theory.

## The Macromarketing School

With the exception of the managerial school of thought put forth in the sixties, little if any consideration had been given to exogenous variables by marketing theorists. While the managerial school of thought recognized exogenous variables, the emphasis was focused on *managing* the marketing organization to plan for uncontrollable variables while manipulating those that were controllable.

The genesis of macromarketing thought is closely linked with the developing concern of the role of business in society. The negative connotations toward the ''military-industrial'' complex and the big brother philosophy generated considerable early attention and interest by marketing scholars to systematically examine the role of marketing from a societal perspective rather than from the perspective of the profit oriented firm. For the first time, it was appropriate to question that the end all and be all of marketing is company's profit maximization. It was the macromarketing school of thought which literally elevated the discussion of short term vs. long term profit maximization to a higher level of corporate vs. societal goals associated with marketing practice.

The topic was of such contemporary concern that it simultaneously attracted the attention of knowledge generators (scholars) and knowledge disseminators (popular press).

While a number of scholars helped pioneer this school of thought, two are of particular interest. Robert Holloway, in association with Robert Hancock, visualized marketing as an activity of society and consequently saw marketing as both being influenced by and influencing the society.

A "rough schema" was developed around the broad exogenous environmental variables of sociological anthropological, psychological, economic, legal, ethical, competitive, economic and technological (Holloway and Hancock 1964). Holloway was also instrumental in publishing a textbook intended to give a clear choice to those who desired a more macro view of marketing (Holloway and Hancock 1968). In his award winning article with Grether, Holloway made a clear call for studies of the impact of governmental regulation on managerial decision making and the effect of regulation on the functioning of the marketing system (Grether and Holloway 1967).

George Fisk, heavily influenced by Wroe Alderson, brought a general systems perspective to the study of marketing. His pioneering work made the distinction between microsystems and macrosystems (Fisk 1967, p. 77). This dichotomy was a springboard for his focus on social marketing. His numerous papers have shaped the present school of macromarketing thought.

Other significant contributions have been made by John Westing (1967), Richard Bagozzi (1977), James Carman (1980) and Robert Bartels (1982). Other earlier, but more popular works were contributed by Sethi with his *Up Against the Corporate Wall* (Sethi 1965).

Fortunately, the early emphasis on broad environmental issues has recently given way to a more enduring issue of how marketing can become a means to achieving national goals such as economic development, population control, and redistribution of national income and wealth. In the process, it is generating excellent conceptual thinking (Bagozzi 1977, Shawyer and French 1978). Simultaneously, many societal problems such as energy conservation, education, health care, population control and economic development are presently making use of marketing theory and practice (Kotler 1975).

The focus of this new thrust was first centered in a series of macromarketing seminars. The first seminar was held in Boulder, Colorado in 1976 with Charles Slater as its organizer. These seminars, held every year since 1976 have greatly shaped this school of thought. But as one follows these seminars, the one issue that still remains open is the boundaries of this school of thought.

Out of these seminars grew the realization, however, that the school of macromarketing thought was broad enough and unique enough to support a journal of macromarketing. This journal, under the editorship of George Fisk, has the opportunity to have a major impact on marketing theory in the next decade.

It is clear that the macromarketing school of thought has made significant contributions to marketing theory. While the exact directions of its future are not clear, it is clear that applications to marketing practice will be impacted.

## THE CONSUMERISM SCHOOL

This school of thought emerged as marketing scholars observed some obvious problems in the market place. These problems were dramatically illustrated by Ralph Nader in his book, *Unsafe at Any Speed*. However, it must be recognized that the foundation of consumer protection really rests in the concepts of welfare economics propagated by such great economists as Schumpeter, Keynes, Houthaker and Modigliani. And, it should be remembered that *Consumer Reports* as an advocacy magazine predates Ralph Nader by at least two decades.

The early writings on consumerism summarized in reading books (Aaker and Day 1971, Gaedeke and Etcheson 1972) clearly reflect the activist thinking commonly associated with people concerned with a specific cause or, social problem. Both research and theory in the area tended to be highly ad hoc and specific to problems associated with marketing practice from the advocacy perspective of the individual consumer. It included areas of research such as deceptive advertising, high pressure sales tactics, product safety, and disclosure of information. It presumed that the average consumer was both educationally ignorant and technically incompetent to make rational choices which are good for him. Hence, the need for government regulation and for voluntary organization dedicated to the protection of consumer welfare. Such elitist attitudes may be more responsible for the recent decline in the movement than any other factor.

Fortunately, consumerism as a cause has given way to more systematic and fundamental research and thinking in the area. This is manifested by the recent drive to understand and develop a theory of consumer satisfaction (Andreasen 1977, Day and Bodur 1977, Hunt 1977). Similarly, more comprehensive empirical research is undertaken to understand consumer complaining behavior as well as behavior of specialized segments such as the Blacks, the Hispanics, the handicapped, and the immigrants. A conspicuous absence of this new research trend is the lack of emotionally charged and value laden research which merely endorses prior judgments rather than become the basis for making those judgments.

This school of thought tends to overlap with both the buyer behavior and macromarketing schools. It overlaps with the buyer behavior school in that the research will often involve buyers. In that sense, the boundary between buyer behavior and consumerism is very fuzzy. For instance, the work of Bill Wilkie, sponsored by the National Science Foundation on Consumer Information Processing (Wilkie 1975) was clearly an application of well known buyer behavior research to the market place problem of consumer information.

This school overlaps with the macromarketing school in that it tends to deal with broader, more macro issues. It often focuses on regulation, market structure, education, competition and ethics.

The future of consumerism, however, is far more uncertain than macromarketing. On the one hand, there is the emergence of conservative social and political values which believes in less regulation and more personal initiatives. On the other hand, the more fundamental problems such as consumer satisfaction are getting integrated with the buyer behavior theory and marketing feedback mechanisms. It is, therefore, very likely that consumerism may not be able to survive a separate identity in marketing.

## The Systems Approach

Marketing scholars with strong quantitative interest in the early 1960s were able to bring to marketing the beginnings of a formal quantitative structure for defining and analyzing marketing problems.

The emergence of the systems approach can be directly identified with the more recent economic concepts of attribute utility (Lancaster 1971) and time as the scarce resource (Bęcker 1965). In marketing, early efforts were manifested in highly complex simulation models of marketing which were highly interdependent between the demand and the supply factors (Amstutz 1967, Kuehn and Hamburger 1963, Forrester 1959). These were replaced by more interactive modeling efforts based on the concept of adaptive control pioneered by Little (1966). The latter models exemplified by names such as Demon, Sprinter, Hendry model, Adbudg and Mediac emphasized the need to incorporate a set of demand characteristics manifested in the generic concepts of elasticity and marginal utility.

A more recent effort, however, is focused on the more fundamental options available to the consumers. These include taking upon themselves the role of producers rather than buyers in the marketing place, as well as entering into barter exchange among themselves (Sheth 1981). In the process, it has generated concepts such as household as a production unit (Etgar 1978) and economic theory of consumption behavior (Ratchford 1975).

It appears that the systems approach to marketing theory is likely to grow in the near future for several reasons. First of all, it represents a more realistic utilization of the axiom of exchange of value. Second, today more than ever, we have the computerized capabilities to model and simulate more complex interdependencies. Third, the systems approach is closer to marketing theory and practice than either the buyer behavior theory or the consumerism movement. As such, it is likely to sustain its growth and separate identity.

## Buyer Behavior Theory

No other area in marketing has had a greater dominance for such a long time period as buyer behavior. While it seems to have peaked in recent years, it is still the most dominant area of research and theory in marketing. A number of marketing scholars and their contributions can be identified as having made a major impact on this school (Bauer 1967, Howard 1963, Howard and Sheth 1969, Bliss 1963, Britt 1966, Engel, Blackwell and Kollat 1968, Nicosia 1966). While each take a different approach, the common denominator underlying their thinking was the applications of behavioral (psychological) principles to consumer behavior. This is clearly in sharp contrast to the descriptive approach of previous eras which was largely demographics and market size statistics. It is also in sharp contrast to attempts to explain buyer behavior by merely applying research findings from sociology (Martineau 1958, Levy 1963, Rogers 1965). It is the dominance of psychology which is largely responsible for bringing about a high level of scientific research traditions. It is no exaggeration to state that no other area of marketing has done so much to elevate marketing discipline from the status of professional practice to the status of scientific inquiry.

While the early buyer behavior pioneers were more interested in generating a grand theory of buyer behavior, several recent efforts have concentrated on scientific research and development of specific constructs of buyer behavior. These include brand loyalty, attitudes, intentions and information processing. At the same time, there has been increasing interest in understanding family buying decisions (Sheth 1974, Davis 1971) and industrial buying behavior (Sheth 1973, Sheth 1977, Webster and Wind 1972. Similarly, considerable degree of quantification of the area is also prevalent especially in terms of application of several mathematical models of choice behavior (McAlister 1982).

At the same time, however, buyer behavior theory has come under some criticism (Sheth 1979, Robertson and Zelinski 1982, Kassarjian 1982). It is criticized for the overemphasis of individual cognititve psychology and especially the use of multiattribute models. In our estimation, the future research in buyer behavior is likely to emerge from noncongnitive perspectives as well as from more macro sociological perspectives.

## Behavioral Organization

Concurrently with scholars in other business disciplines, marketing scholars began to see that behavioral principles that had previously been primarily identified with human group behavior, could be used to explain the behavior of organizations. In particular, drawing upon emerging thinking in management of organizations with a strong sociological perspective (Etzioni 1961, Katz and Kahn 1966, Thompson 1967, March and Simon 1958, Cyert and March 1963) several marketing scholars applied this perspective to marketing channels. They were also influenced by several emerging social psychology theories (French and Raven 1960, Thibaut and Kelley 1959). The channel of distribution came to be viewed as an organization with behavioral patterns involving all the organizations in any way dependent on a channel.

A large part of research in the area is clearly identified with Stern (1969) and Stern and El-Ansary (1977), while a few others have recently contributed to the area (Etgar 1976, Frazier 1981) relatively few marketing scholars have made significant contributions. Two reasons probably explain this lack of participation. First is the great difficulty in obtaining data. In addition to the difficulty of obtaining hard data on actual relationships, most of the relationships are heavily influenced by perceptions of power. In addition, these relationships are dynamic. Secondly, much of the existing work in organizational behavior tends to focus on the workings of a given organization which offers little in the way of a concpetual base for studying interorganizational behavior. A notable exception is the much acclaimed work of Pfeffer and Salancik which stresses and offers conceptual foundations for the study of relationships with other organizations (Pfeffer and Salancik 1978).

The importance of this school of marketing thought is almost certain to not only increase, but attract more researchers from organization behavior area who are fascinated by the dynamics of the complexities of channels of distribution.

## Strategic Planning

Planning as an activity of the firm is well established. However, in recent years, planning has moved from just another of a list of activities to one of the most important. Furthermore, strategic planning, with its twofold emphasis on analysis of the dynamic environment and dynamic adaptation, has generally had the net impact of strengthening marketing planning. This is particularly true for firms that have separated corporate planning from strategic business unit planning.

This, the newest school of marketing thought, seems to be currently suffering from the usual confusion associated with most new schools of thought. Furthermore, it is beset by two additional difficulties. The first is that the majority of contributions to this school have come from consulting firms and their clients. The names of the Boston Consulting Group, Stanford Research Institute, and General Electric, for example, are familiar to most marketing scholars as proponents and contributors to strategic planning. But the second difficulty may be more troublesome. The most well publicized approaches, for the most part, are based on either an implicit cash flow maximization basis or some form of capital asset pricing model. By their very nature then, they are not very useful for market place decisions. Rather they are most useful for corporate decisions.

So while we seemingly know much about strategic planning, we are not sure how much we know about strategic market planning. In fact, we lack competing conceptual frameworks that can be used to guide research and theory development in this area.

Nonetheless, we do have the beginnings of a school of thought. These beginnings fall into several overlapping categoreis. The first are those contributions that explicitly deal with one aspect of marketing strategy, but with a strategic reference point (Wind 1978, Pessemeir 1982, Thorelli 1977). Several texts have also appeared with a strategic focus (Hughes 1978, Constantin, Evans and Morris 1976, Luck and Ferrell 1979, Jain 1981, Cravens 1982) plus a readings book (Kerin and Peterson 1980) in addition to two monographs with strong marketing strategy implications (Hofer and Schendel 1978, Porter 1980). While these and other contributions give clear evidence that a school of thought is emerging, the real issues of what strategic marketing is and is not and what are its central concepts have not been definitely dealt with. One author, however, suggests that fine contributions will be an important part of any future list of central concepts of strategic marketing (Biggadike 1981). He lists them as the marketing concept, market segmentation, positioning, mapping and the product life cycle.

In our opinion, strategic planning is likely to continue generating additional knowledge for marketing theory for several reasons. First, marketing has become more competition oriented rather than either technology or market oriented (Kotler 1980). Second, environmental factors are changing at an ever increasing pace forcing companies to design early warning systems. Finally, foreign competition especially from Japan and Europe has generated greater emphasis on planned approach to organizing marketing resources.

## Contributions to Marketing Theory

Each of the six new schools of thought has made unique contributions to the development of marketing theory. At the same time, it would appear that some of the newer schools of thought may have directed talent and effort away from it. We will briefly assess each schools's contribution in this section.

The single biggest contribution to macromarketing school has been to redefine marketing objectives. It has clearly indicated why the unidimensional objections of profit maximization may not be appropriate for the organization. Instead, it has attempted to provide a multiobjective function for marketing effort. In addition, the macromarketing school has consistently emphasized the reality of constrained optimization of marketing objectives. These constraints relate mainly to the side effects of marketing practice from a more macro societal perspective.

A second major contribution of the macromarketing school has to do with increasing the importance and legitimacy of marketing objectives in noneconomic behaviors of society. For the first time, marketing is considered relevant to national economic and social plans in many underdeveloped countries. Similarly, it has removed the taboo associated with marketing as a commercial profit making activity in many spheres of noneconomic behaviors such as population control, energy conservation, religion and politics.

At the same time, macromarketing has also created the crisis of identity. By broadening its horizons through the concepts of exchange of value and taking broader societal perspectives, marketing is beginning to blur its boundaries with other disciplines such as business policy and public policy. It is our strong hope that macromarketing will attempt to delimit its sphere and more percisely define its boundaries in the very near future before the crisis of identity threatens the existence of marketing itself.

The consumerism school of thought has had far more impact on the marketing practice rather than on the marketing theory. Perhaps the single most important contribution can be attributed to Peter Druker (1974) who has labeled the existence of consumerism as a shame of marketing. It has also brought out the importance of market satisfaction as a far more important barometer of marketing success than either market share or profits. We believe that the concept of market satisfaction will become a major construct in the development of marketing theory.

Unfortunately, consumerism has generated more distraction from development of marketing theory. By concentrating on ad hoc and advocacy oriented issues, it has diverted attention away from the more fundamental and typical principles of marketing and toward the more atypical and isolated aspects of marketing practice.

The contribution of the sytems approach toward marketing theory is largely methodological. It has enabled scholars to think of quantification of marketing processes for simulation or optimization purposes. In the process, marketing has become more rigorous and more of a science. How much of this is illusionary and how much is real is yet to be determined. A second major contribution of the systems approach has been to provide a balance between the supply and the demand functions. It has clearly brought out the need to incorporate the mutual interdependence inherent in any economic exchange. Finally, this school of thought has enabled scholars to retain the identity of marketing despite incorporating higher levels of complexity in marketing theory. Unlike the macromarketing school, it has neither tried to broaden the horizons of marketing to noneconomic areas of behavior nor has it questioned the legitimacy of more traditional corporate objectives of profitability and market share. Finally, the systems approach has successfully integrated buyer behavior principles which are inherently at a more micro and behavioral level with the marketing principles which are inherently more macro and aggregate in scope.

In contrast, the buyer behavioral school of thought has generated more alienation and division. In fact, it has acquired a separate identity of its own as manifested by a separate organization (ARC) and a separate interdisciplinary journal (JRC). There is no question that understanding the psychology of the buyer is highly relevant to the development of a good marketing theory. Unfortunately, buyer behavior theory has been perceived as somehow more scientific and rigorous than marketing theory. Therefore, many scholars working in the buyer behavior area have consciously avoided any association with marketing practice. Indeed, it is a shame that so much knowledge generated in buyer behavior is so little used in marketing practice except perhaps in industrial selling. It is our belief that the disassociation between the two disciplines as well as existence of a separate organization and a journal are very likely to generate a divorce between marketing and buyer behavior.

At the same time, the marketing discipline owes much to buyer behavior theory. First of all, it has brought a more scientific bent to marketing theory and practice through the process of borrowing both theory and research methodology from psychology, and especially social psychology. Second, it has attracted bright young scholars to the marketing discipline because it has consciously avoided being practice driven. Finally, it has generated a number of significant constructs which are likely to become good building blocks in the development of marketing practice. These include (a) redefinition of the marketing mix from the Four P's to the dichotomy of significant and symbolic communication (Howard and Sheth 1969), (b) rules of information processing, (c) psychological market segmentation, (d) rational vs. emotional needs, and (e) reference group influences as inhibitors or enhancers of marketing influences.

The behavioral organization school of thought has the potential to contribute but it has not so far attained its potential. The primary explanation probably lies in its disassociation with the traditional marketing objectives of profitability and market share (Frazier and Sheth 1982). It has generated a significant amount of descriptive research on interdependence among organizations but at the same time it has failed to show how to utilize this knowledge in marketing practice. We are, however, confident that in due course, interorganization aspects associated with this school of thought will have strong influence in reshaping marketing theory from the traditional institutional and functional perspectives.

Finally, the contribution of the strategic planning school of thought is highly visible. First of all, it has clearly shifted attention from marketing tactics and activities to more strategic issues. Second, it has generated a more adaptive posture for marketing programs. Third, it has emphasized the concept of relative as opposed to the absolute power of marketing resources. However, the biggest impact of strategic planning school on marketing theory is likely to be the integration of market research as part of marketing practice. The interface of market research and marketing plans is likely to reshape marketing theory from a unilateral to a bilateral approach of marketing activities and programs.

## Conclusion

Two fundamental changes have generated at least six new schools of thought since Bartels' classic review of history of marketing thought up to early sixties. These are (a) replacement of economic exchange concept with the concept of exchange value, and (b) emergence of balance of power between the marketer and the customer as the initiator of marketing programs and activities.

## REFERENCES

Aaker, David A. and George S. Day (1971), *Consumerism: Search for the Consumer Interest*, New York: The Free Press.

Alderson, Wroe and Reavis Cox (1948), "Towards a Theory of Marketing," *Journal of Marketing*, 13 (October), 139.

Alexander, Ralph, F. M. Surface, R. F. Elder and Wroe Alderson (1940), *Marketing*, Boston: Ginn Publishing.

Amstutz, Arnold E. (1967), *Computer Simulation of Competitive Market Response*, Cambridge: M.I.T. Press.

Andreasen, Alan R. (1977), "A Taxonomy of Consumer Satisfaction/Dissatisfaction Measures," *Journal of Consumer Affairs*, 12 (Winter), 11-24.

Bagozzi, Richard P. (1975), "Marketing as Exchange," *Journal of Marketing*, 39 (October), 32-39.

Bagozzi, Richard P. (1977), "Marketing at the Societal Level: Theoretical Issues and Problems," in *Macro-Marketing: Distributive Processes from a Societal Perspective*, Charles C. Slater, editor, Boulder: University of Colorado, 6-51.

Bartels, Robert (1944), "Marketing Principles," *Journal of Marketing*, 9 (October), 151.

Bartels, Robert (1962), *The Development of Marketing Thought*, Homewood: Richard D. Irwin, Inc.

Bartels, Robert (1965), "Development of Marketing Thought: A Brief History," in *Science in Marketing*, George Schwartz, editor, New York: John Wiley and sons, 47-69.

Bartels, Robert (1982), "The Physics and Metaphysics of Marketing," in *Proceedings of the Eleventh Paul D. Converse Marketing Symposium*, David M. Gardner and Frederick Winter, editors, Chicago: American Marketing Association.

Bauer, Raymond A. (1967), "Consumer Behavior as Risk Taking," in *Risk Taking and Information Handling in Consumer Behavior*, Donald F. Cox, editor, Boston: Division of Research, Harvard Business School.

Becker, George (1965), "A Theory of the Allocation of Time," *Economic Journal*, 75, 493-517.

Biggadike, E. Ralph (1981), "The Contributions of Marketing to Strategics Management," *Academy of Management Review*, 6, 621-632.

Bliss, Perry (1963), *Marketing and the Behavioral Sciences*, Rockleigh, N.J.: Allyn and Bacon.

Breyer, Ralph F. (1934), *The Marketing Institution*, New York: McGraw-Hill.

Britt, Steuart Henderson (1966), *Consumer Behavior and the Behavioral Sciences*, New York: John Wiley and Sons.

Carman, James M. (1980), "Paradigms for Marketing Theory," in J. N. Sheth (ed.), *Research in Marketing*, Vol. 3, JAI Press, 1-36.

Constantin, James A., Rodney E. Evans and Malcolm L. Morris (1976), *Marketing Strategy and Management*, Dallas: Business Publications, Inc.

Cravens, David W. (1982), *Strategic Marketing*, Homewood: Richard D. Irwin, Inc.

Cyert, Richard M. and James G. March (1963), *A Behavioral Theory of the Firm*, Englewood Cliffs: Prentice-Hall, Inc.

Davis, Harry L. (1971), "Measurement of Husband-Wife Influence in Consumer Decision Making," *Journal of Marketing Research*, 8 (August), 305-312.

Day, R. L. and M. Bodur (1977), "A Comprehensive Study of Consumer Satisfaction with Services," in *Consumer Satisfaction, Dissatisfaction and Complaining Behavior*, R. L. Day, editor, Bloomington: Department of Marketing, School of Business, Indiana University, 64-74.

Dichter, Ernest (1964), *Handbook of Consumer Motivations*, New York: McGraw-Hill.

Druker, Peter A. (1974), *Management: Tasks, Responsibilities, Practices*, New York: Harper & Row.

Duddy, E. A. and D. A. Revzan (1947), *Marketing, An Institutional Approach*, New York: McGraw-Hill.

Engel, James F., David T. Kollat, and Roger D. Blackwell (1968), *Consumer Behavior*, New York: Holt, Rinehart and Winston, Inc.

Etgar, Michael (1976), "Three Models of Distributive Change," in C. C. Slater (ed.), *Macro-Marketing: Distributive Processes from a Societal Perspective*, Boulder, Colorado: Business Research Division, 85-116.

Etgar, Michael (1978), "The Household as a Production Unit," in J. N. Sheth (ed.), *Research in Marketing*, Vol. 1, JAI Press.

Etzioni, E. (1961), *A Comparative Analysis of Organizations*, Glencoe, Ill.: The Free Press.

Fish, George (1967), *Marketing Systems: An Introductory Analysis*, New York: Harper and Row, Publishers.

Forrester, Jay W. (1959), "Advertising: A Problem in Industrial Dynamics," *Harvard Business Review*, 59 (March-April), 100-110.

Frazier, Gary L. and Jagdish N. Sheth (1982), "Impact of Goal Conflicts on Interfirm Interactions, Sentiments and Compatibility," Faculty Working Paper, University of Illinois.

Frazier, Gary L. (1980), "A Conceptual Model of the Interfirm Power-Influence Process Within a Marketing Channel," in J. N. Sheth (ed.), *Research in Marketing*, JAI Press (in press).

French, J. R. P. and B. Raven (1960), "The Basis of Social Power," in D. Cartwright and A. Zander (eds.), *Group Dynamics: Research and Theory*, New York: Harper & Row, 607-623.

Grether, E. T. (1949), "A Theoretical Approach to the Analysis of Marketing," in *Theory of Marketing*, Reavis Cox and Wroe Alderson, editors, Chicago: Richard D. Irwin, 113.

Grether, E. T. and Robert J. Holloway (1967), "Impact of Government Upon the Marketing System," *Journal of Marketing*, 31 (April), 2, 1-5.

Hofer, Charles W. and Don Schendel (1978), *Strategy Formulation: Analytical Concepts*, St. Paul: West Publishing Company.

Holloway, Robert J. and Robert S. Hancock (1964), *The Environment of Marketing Behavior*, New York: John Wiley and Sons, Inc.

Holloway, Robert J. and Roberts S. Hancock (1968), *Marketing in a Changing Environment*, New York: John Wiley and Sons, Inc.

Howard, John A. (1957), *Marketing Management: Analysis and Decision*, Homewood: Richard D. Irwin.

Howard, John A. (1963a), *Marketing: Executive and Buyer Behavior*, New York: Columbia University Press.

Howard, John A. (1963b), *Marketing Management: Analysis and Planning*, Homewood: Richard D. Irwin, Inc.

Howard, John A. and Jagdish N. Sheth (1969), *The Theory of Buyer Behavior*, New York: John Wiley.

Hughes, C. David (1978), *Marketing Management: A Planning Approach*, Reading, Mass.: Addison-Wesley Publishing Company.

Hunt, H. Keith (1977), "Consumer Satisfaction/Dissatisfaction—Overview and Future Research Directions," in *Conceptualization and Measurement of Consumer Satisfaction and Dissatisfaction*, H. Keith Hunt, editor, Cambridge: Marketing Science Institute, 455-488.

Jain, Subhash C. (1981), *Marketing Planning and Strategy*, Cincinnati: South-Western Publishing Company.

Katona, George (1960), *The Powerful Consumer: Psychological Studies of the American Economy*, New York: McGraw-Hill Book Company.

Katz, Daniel and Robert L. Kahn (1966), *The Social Psychology of Organizations*, New York: John Wiley & Sons, Inc.

Kerin, Roger A. and Robert A. Peterson (1980), *Perspectives on Strategic Marketing Management*, Boston: Allyn and Bacon, Inc.

Kotler, Philip and Sidney Levy (1969), "Broadening the Concept of Marketing," *Journal of Marketing*, 33 (January), 10-15.

Kotler, Philip (1972), "A Generic Concept of Marketing," *Journal of Marketing*, 36 (April), 46-54.

Kotler, Philip (1975), *Marketing for Nonprofit Organizations*, Englewood Cliffs, N.J.: Prentice-Hall, Inc.

Kotler, Philip (1980), *Marketing Management: Analysis, Planning and Control*, 4th edition, Englewood Cliffs: Prentice-Hall, Inc.

Kuehn, Alfred A. and Morris J. Hamburger (1963), "A Heuristic Program for Locating Warehouses," *Management Science*, 9 (July), 643-666.

Lancaster, Kelvin (1971), *Consumer Demand: A New Approach*, New York: Columbia University Press.

Lazo, Hector and Arnold Corbin (1961), *Management in Marketing*, New York: McGraw-Hill.

Levy, Sidney J. (1963), "Symbolism and Life Style," in S. A. Greyser (ed.), *Toward Scientific Marketing*, Chicago: American Marketing Association, 140-150.

Levy, Sidney (1966), "Social Class and Consumer Behavior," in *On Knowing the Consumer*, Joseph W. Newman, editor, New York: John Wiley and Sons.

Levy, Sidney and Gerald Zaltman (1975), *Marketing, Society and Conflict*, Englewood Cliffs, N.J.: Prentice-Hall.

Little, John D. C. (1966), "A Model of Adaptive Control of Promotional Spending," *Operations Research*, 14 (Nov.-Dec.), 175-197.

Luck, David J. and O. C. Ferrell (1979), *Marketing Strategy and Plans*, Englewood Cliffs: Prentice-Hall, Inc.

March, James G. and Herbert Simon (1958), *Organizations*, New York: Wiley and Sons.

Martineau, Pierre (1958), "Social Classes and Spending Behavior," *Journal of Marketing*, 23 (October), 121-130.

Mayer, Martin (1958), *Madison Avenue, U.S.A.*, New York: Harper & Row.

McAlister, Leigh (1982), *Consumer Choice Theory Models*, Greenwich, Conn.: JAI Press (in press).

McKitterick, J. B. (1957), "What is the Marketing Management Concept," in *The Frontiers of Marketing Thought and Science*, Chicago: American Marketing Association.

Nicosia, Francesco M. (1966), *Consumer Decision Processes: Marketing and Advertising Implications*, Englewood Cliffs: Prentice-Hall.

Pessemier, Edgar A. (1982), *Product Management: Strategy and Organization*, 2nd edition, New York: John Wiley & Sons.

Pfeffer, J. and G. R. Salancik (1978), *The External Control of Organizations*, New York: Harper and Row.

Porter, Michael E. (1980), *Competitive Strategy*, New York: The Free Press.

Ratchford, Bryan T. (1975), "The New Economic Theory of Consumer Behavior: An Interpretive Essay," *Journal of Consumer Research*, 2 (September), 65-75.

Rogers, Everett (1965), *Diffusion of Innovations*, Glencoe: The Free Press.

Sethi, S. Prakash (1971), *Up Against the Corporate Wall*, Englewood Cliffs: Prentice-Hall, Inc.

Sheth, Jagdish N. (1973), "A Model of Industrial Buying Behavior," *Journal of Marketing*, 37 (October) 50-56.

Sheth, Jagdish N. (1974), "A Theory of Family Buying Decisions," in J. N. Sheth (ed.), *Models of Buyer Behavior*, New York: Harper and Row, 17-33.

Sheth, J. N. (1977), "Recent Developments in Organizational Buyer Behavior," in Woodside, Sheth and Bennett (eds.), *Consumer and Industrial Buying Behavior*, New York: North-Holland, 17-34.

Sheth, J. N. (1982), "Discussion," in A. Mitchell (ed.), *Advances in Consumer Behavior*, Vol. 8 (in press).

Simon, Herbert A. (1957), *Models of Man*, New York: John Wiley and Sons.

Starch, Daniel and Staff (1958), *Male vs. Female: Influence on the Purchase of Selected Products*, Greenwich, Conn.: Fawcett Publishing, Inc.

Stern, Louis W. (ed.), (1969), *Distribution Channels: Behavioral Dimensions*, Boston: Houghton Mifflin.

Stern, Louis W. and Adel El-Ansary (1977), *Marketing Channels*, Englewood Cliffs, N.J.: Prentice-Hall.

Thibaut, J. W. and H. H. Kelley (1959), *The Social Psychology of Groups*, New York: John Wiley and Sons.

Thompson, James D. (1967), *Organizations in Action*, New York: McGraw-Hill.

Thorelli, Hans B. (1977), *Strategy + Structure = Performance*, Bloomington: Indiana University Press.

Webster, Frederick E. and Yoram Wind (1972), *Organizational Buying Behavior*, Englewood Cliffs, N.J.: Prentice-Hall.

Westing, John H. (1967), "Some Thoughts on the Nature of Ethics in Marketing," in *Changing Marketing Systems*, Chicago: American Marketing Association, 161-163.

Wilkie, William L. (1975), *How Consumers Use Product Information*, Washington: National Science Foundation.

Wind, Y. (1978) "Issues and Advances in Segmentation Research," *Journal of Marketing Research*, 15 (August), 317-337.

Wind, Yoram J. (1092), *Product Policy: Concepts, Methods and Strategy*, Reading Mass.: Addison-Wesley Publishing Company.

# 13 —— Historical Research in Marketing

*Ronald Savitt*

Reprinted from *Journal of Marketing*, published by the American Marketing Association, Vol. 44 (Fall 1980), pp. 52-58. Reprinted by permission.

Will historical research in marketing continue to be undertaken mainly by nonmarketing scholars?

The question arises because marketing scholars have given little attention to this part of the discipline. More than 10 years have passed since the publication of the last major work in marketing history (Shapiro and Doody 1968), and business historians are wondering why the history of marketing has not interested marketing scholars (Hidy 1977, p. 19). Part of the void has been filled by *business* and *economic* historians who are making contributions to the marketing literature, but they are not writing marketing history. Such scholars have produced important works, such as the economic history of American wholesale middlemen in the nineteenth century (Porter and Livesay 1971). However, they do not do justice to marketing history in the way marketing scholars would.

Among the reasons advanced for the absence of historical research in marketing are the lack of appreciation of its importance and the lack of a method. The purpose of this article is to offer a rationale for such historical research and a method which can be applied in marketing. A brief sketch of the state of marketing history is presented as background.

## WHY STUDY MARKETING HISTORY?

Historical study adds a robust quality to a discipline. It enables scholars within the discipline, as well as society at large, to gain an understanding of its origins and its patterns of change. Such study relates a discipline to its own past and to other disciplines. Historical study helps to establish an identity for a discipline by providing some idea of where it is and what it is.

Historical research can also be used in the verification and synthesis of hypotheses, "the cumulative result being the promotion of theory" (Doody 1965, p. 557). It can be done at the micro level as in the case of market segmentation. The study of Josiah Wedgwood, the English porcelain manufacturer, provides new bases for understanding the origins of segmentation (McKendrick 1960). Historical research can also add to the development of macro theories such as proposed by Alderson (1965) and more recently by Bagozzi (1978). Cassady, in his studies of food retailing, argued this point. Historical studies of market behavior would provide a better understanding of how markets and competitors do behave than the current theories based on how they are supposed to behave (Cassady 1963).

## Some Basic Issues

Marketing history is defined by the content of marketing. Assume that marketing is the discipline which describes and explains the operation of markets in terms of all prepurchase and postpurchase activities related to transactions of ownership or use rights to any factor, good, or service (Narver and Savitt 1971, p. 4). Historical research in marketing is a narration of events through time in which their sequence is described. The writing of history requires the analysis and explanation of the causes and consequences of events with particular concern for change.

A historical study in marketing would focus on the elements of want satisfaction, rather than on resource allocation as in economics, or on spatial behavior as in human geography. An illustrative hypothesis for a specific study might be:

> In spite of increasing marketing abilities, merchant wholesalers in foodstuffs in Great Britain declined in importance in the nineteenth and twentieth centuries because of improvements in the transportation system which provided a closer relation between food producers and retailers.

Though the hypothesis includes concepts and ideas from other disciplines, its central thrust is within marketing. This is as it should be; however, research from other disciplines is not to be ignored. It is to be treated as complementary to the marketing issues. Good historical analysis seeks to explore and analyze the infinitely subtle relations between marketing events and economic and geographic factors. Vance, a prominent geographer who has studied wholesaling, makes this point. He says that the geographer examines the economic landscape in terms of the components and the activities that they serve, and the relations between and among the physical and social elements that are present (Vance 1970, p. 34). The marketing scholar, in contrast, must concentrate on the development of the marketing system, the factors that affect it, and most important, its management.

## The Historical Perspective

An introduction to the concept of historical perspective is required. It is defined in terms of *description* and *comparison*.

Historical research and writing are basically descriptive; they begin with the narration of events in a time sequence. Such an exercise might encompass a recognized historical period, for example, the industrial revolution.

Specific events are identified and described as to particular characteristics. Analysis addresses the questions of explanation, relationship, and consequences of the events.

Historical studies are generally not predictive although the historian does become involved in a type of prediction, sometimes called "retrodiction," in attempting to work out what might have happened in the past. The conclusions of historical study can form the basis of prediction, to the extent that extrapolation to future cases is desirable *and* realistic.

Historical studies are not deterministic in the sense of an equilibrium model. *Probable cause*, rather than deterministic cause, describes historical relationships. Moreover, unlike quantitative analysis, historical analysis does not contain the axiomatic development of mathematical theory in which inferences are certain, the theorems are absolutely determined, the axioms are given, and hence the results are deterministic (Harvey 1969, p. 232).

Comparison is also part of the historical perspective although it is important to note that comparison is only a method and not historical research itself. Events in a single place can be compared through time, and events at different places in space can be compared in the context of chronological time—at the same time, for example. The former approach is an instance of traditional, chronological historical research. The latter is no less an example of historical study. A project which examines department stores in a series of economies in 1980 would be part and parcel of historical research in marketing if emphasis were given to the time-related differences among them. What is required of the historian is recognition of the complexities in the meaning of time. This important topic is beyond the scope of the article; however, anyone undertaking historical studies should become acquainted with the problems (Whitrow 1975).

## Types of Marketing History and the State of Historical Research

The historical dimension of the discipline consists of two distinct but inextricably intertwined components. One is the historical development of the doctrines or the history of thought, the discipline's "intellectual history." The second is the history of the discipline's content. The two feed upon one another. "It may be oversimplification to contrast the body of theory in economics—whatever its deficiencies—with the absence of a corpus of marketing theory and the respective significant correlations with the presence and absence of a strong historically oriented literature, but there remains a reasonable suspicion that these factors are not unrelated" (Smalley 1964, p. 366).

There is a historical tradition in marketing, although it is not as well developed as in economics. Work has been undertaken in both components, although marketing thought has been given more attention than marketing content. The writings of Bartels (1976) and Schwartz (1963) capture the core of the history of marketing thought. Bartels concentrated on the development of marketing thought by documenting major academic contributions. His work is historical only to the extent that it is chronological. He traced the development of concepts in a number of areas. The work is not analytical because he does not attempt to explain the circumstances that affected the topics. It is not comparative because he does not evaluate the relationships between various approaches to marketing, such as functionalism or the institutional approach. The readers gain few insights into the environmental conditions and intellectual forces that produced such marketing scholars as Wroe Alderson, Reavis Cox, E. T. Grether, David Revzan, and others. Marketers, unlike economists, know little about the forces that gave direction to their intellectual development (Gray 1931).

Only a few attempts have been made to produce marketing history. The major comprehensive work is the classic *Milestones of Marketing*, published in 1938, which documents progress in marketing to that date (Hotchkiss 1938). *Readings in the History of American Marketing* falls short of an actual history although it has served as an important stimulus for encouraging historical work (Shapiro and Doody 1968). Interestingly, marketing history has not been accorded a place in the study of the history of marketing thought. Bartels includes no entry for either ''history'' or ''historical.'' In spite of his citing individuals who have contributed to marketing *thought*, he does not include their contributions to marketing *history*. For example, Frank M. Jones is acknowledged for his work in theory but not for marketing history (Jones 1937).

I do not mean to suggest that no work has been done in marketing history. The topics that have been addressed are advertising and distribution. In the former area the amount of study has led to the development of the *Journal of Advertising History* (Pollay 1977). In the latter, some work has been undertaken in retailing, most notably ''the wheel of retailing'' (Hollander 1963). More recent work by Goldman (1978) on the concept of ''trading up'' provides more hypotheses for historical study in retailing. Bucklin's comprehensive study of evolution in the distributive trades offers a broad framework for understanding growth and competition in retail and wholesale trade. Because of his reliance on economic analysis, the study is not historical in the sense developed in this article; however, it is rich in hypotheses for marketing history (Bucklin 1972).

Without condemning marketing scholars as neglectful, one can easily understand why, in general, marketing history has received little attention. As an applied discipline, marketing must cater to its client market of decision makers. Their concerns are directed toward, understandably, making better decisions in today's market. Looking backward to them is a luxury. Moreover, the discipline itself has had to absorb an ever-increasing set of new concepts and methods and then establish appropriate ways to apply them to the problems at hand. Finally, the absence of historical methodology has also limited the opportunity to reflect upon the past.

To a great degree, marketing history is a victim of the endless flood of contemporary developments and the increasing specialization of academics (Shapiro 1964, p. 569).

## METHOD FOR HISTORY IN MARKETING

The question: ''What is the correct method for historical research?'' is important and cannot be easily dismissed. All research should be based on the principles of the scientific method, although experimentation cannot be applied in history as it is applied in the biological and physical sciences or even in the social sciences. The fact that ''historical experimentation'' is impossible does not mean that historical research must be any less valid than research in those circumstances in which experimentation is used. Historical research must retain the objectivity of the scientific method, following its structure as closely as possible. The major principle is that historical research in marketing must conform in every way possible to experimental control as applied in the experimental method. It is beyond the scope of this article to argue how historical analysis might approach the structure of a well defined experiment (Marwick 1970, p. 105).

### The Formulation of Historical Research

Figure 1 is a methodological diagram for historical research in marketing which includes the essence of the scientific method. The seven elements describe the sequential pattern of activities required to do historical research. They can be examined in the context of a specific project. Assume that a marketing scholar is interested in understanding the conditions which led to the development of *fixed store retailing*, namely, the transition from journeyman merchants to continuous selling at specific locations. The results of such a study could be used to understand the problems that must be faced in a developing economy, although they would have to be considered within the limitations of the predictive nature of history as previously discussed.

***Activity 1.*** The beginning point for the researcher is to define his or her own perceptual experiences of the problem. These include, among other things, the researcher's beliefs about what has happened, perceptions about the conditions which lead to the changes, and assumptions about how the former relate to the problem at hand. This activity aims at understanding the nature and the amount of subjectivity held by the researcher which will have to be accounted for in the evaluation of the findings. Subjectivity is present in all historical research simply because of differences between

**FIGURE 1. Methodological Diagram for Historical Research in Marketing**

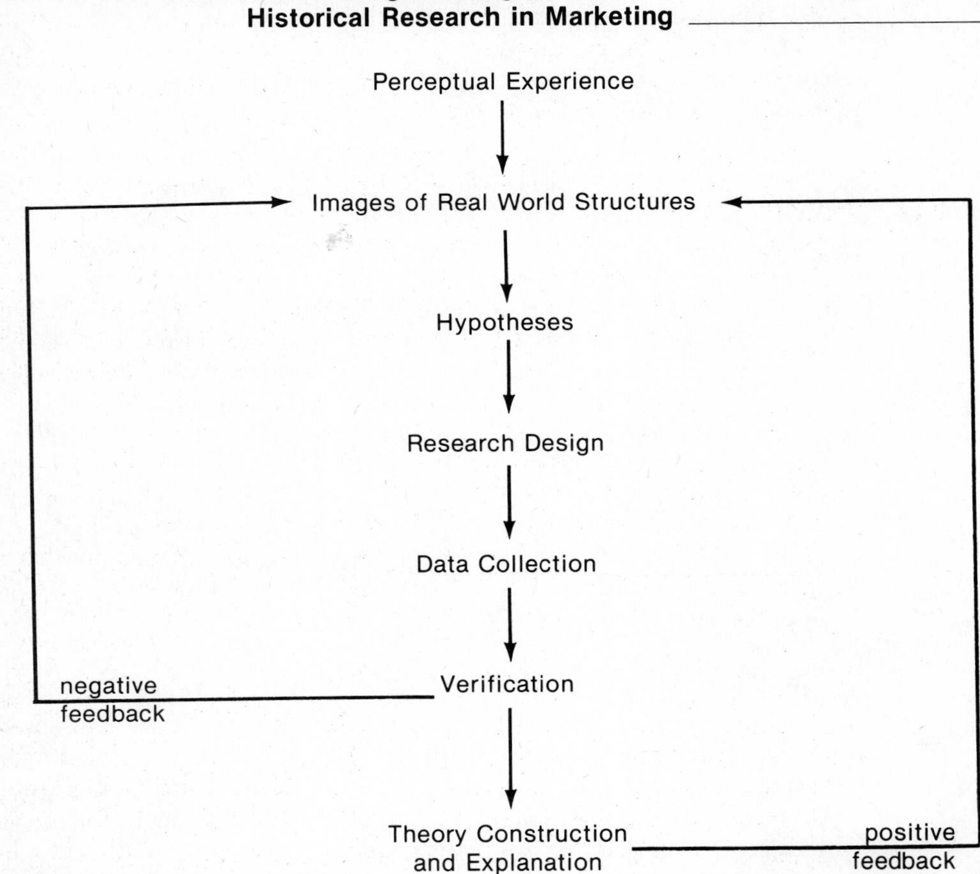


the past and the present. This gap, much as the "gap" of experimental error, must be acknowledged and accounted for.

*Activity 2.* The perceptual experiences are compared with the images of the real world as reported in the literature. This activity includes the preliminary investigation stage in which a literature search is undertaken to determine what is known about retail change of this type. In the case of marketing, the primitives, the basic functions, must be defined in a manner that allows comparison over time. For example, the contrast between fixed store retailing and journeyman merchants or peridodic markets implies something about how storage and transportation functions are performed in the economy. Hence, the characteristics of the functions as well as the factors that influence them must be understood in terms of their effects on buyers and sellers, and the effects of buyers and sellers on them.

*Activity 3.* From that exercise will develop hypotheses which are to be verified. One hypothesis for historical investigation that has evolved from the images of the real world is:

> A fixed location retailer will be established and will remain viable if the maximum range of a good exceeds the minimum range of a good, where the minimum range is defined as the distance from the fixed location incorporating sufficient demand to provide a profit and where the maximum range represents the maximum distance that buyers will travel to purchase that good (Hay and Beavon 1979, p. 27).

Within the formulation of the hypothesis, definitions of standards must be developed for the testing procedures, such as the meaning of ''viable'' and ''profitable;'' however, these do not differ from those employed in traditional research.

*Activity 4.* The research design to test the hypothesis will incorporate observation of examples of periodic markets as they operate in different environments, and surveys of the literature and individuals familiar with such markets as well as persons who possibly have seen the transition take place. The surveys will also examine materials that include descriptions of this type of transition over a variety of time periods. This activity is no different from the techniques used in traditional marketing research except in the types and sources of data found in historical research.

*Activity 5.* The sources of historical evidence differ from the traditional ones used in marketing research. Greater reliance is placed on archival materials, corporate records, and public and legal documents as well as business, economic, social, and urban histories. Artifact evidence including buildings and relics also is used.

Attention must be given to the distinction between primary and secondary sources as a means of minimizing the gap between the actor and the observer. Drawing a precise line between primary and secondary sources is difficult in historical research. Simply because a document is old does not mean that it is primary. On a spectrum from ''purely primary data'' to ''purely secondary data'' there is a greater overlap for historical data than for contemporary date. The marketing scholar can in part minimize this problem by attempting to view historical data as if he or she were a contemporary with them. This is no mean task and it requires that the researcher have some knowledge about the period of the study.

A researcher not only must understand his or her own subjectivity as previously described, but also must be prepared to understand the ways in which subjectivity can creep into primary data. Anyone who has examined legislative hearings will appreciate this problem. The verbal testimony of a witness as recorded in the hearings and the written testimony from which the oral statement is made often differ even though they are presented by the same person.

Being aware of the problems of such differences creates a degree of sensitivity which is necessary if correct statements about the validity of data are to be made. This historical researcher must closely question ''official records'' and ''first-hand reports'' in the same way that caution is exercised in accepting the information on completed mail questionnaries. In historical research, the failure to do so may be more damaging to the extent that the conclusions will often be drawn from a smaller number of observations.

First-person accounts of periodic markets will have to be evaluated in terms of the background of the writer so as to minimize the biases. A sociologist will see periodic markets in a different way than will a marketer. Because many marketing events have been reported by people who are not marketers, extra care must be exercised in the evaluation of such reports even when they are primary sources. Primary data include personal account books and ledgers, such as those used in the study of Andrew Melrose, an Edinburgh grocer. In such documents are recorded the accounts with suppliers, customers, and agents as well as banking activities (Hoh-Cheung and Muir 1973, p. 37). For the case of periodic markets, diaries, day books, public records, and the rememberances of traders will form the nucleus of primary data.

Another source of primary data is corporate records. When these are made available to the marketing historian, they can provide minute details about the development of marketing programs and activities including perceptions about the marketing activities of other firms. Access to these materials is often restricted because many corporations have had poor relationships with historians in the past. Unfortunarly, some business historians have used their studies of corporations to ridicule business practices or to support self-serving views (Williamson 1966, p. 26).

Public records and litigative proceedings also offer primary and secondary data, although they are often difficult to categorize clearly. The legal approach to the study of marketing, even though it is not well developed provides insights into what practices are acceptable and insights into the evolving legal structure which surrounds marketing decision making. The failure of a contract to meet the test of legality through litigation provides much understanding about the ways in which marketing practices evolve, though it would be incorrect to accept the test of legality as a measure of the success or failure of a specific practice. A fairly extensive literature in industrial organization and in the law offers important secondary materials (McCurdy 1978).

The question of the validity of a piece of evidence is related to the distance between the event and the user who subsequently interprets the information. Validity, or acceptability, becomes an issue when the data are drawn from studies in closely related fields. This is a precaution to the researcher in marketing so that he or she will be keenly aware of the differences in purpose of various types of historical research. Drawing upon the *business* historians, who are often interested in individual business leaders, may lead the marketing scholar to bypass marketing concepts. The problem is not that a study of a business leader contains inaccurate information, but that the information may not lead to marketing insights. Business history studies such as "The Development of the Retail Grocery Trade in the Nineteenth Century" (Blackman 1967) and "Marketing Organization and Policy in the Cotton Trade" (Lee 1968) provide interesting insights into entrepreneurial activities but they do not analyze historical developments in marketing as would be done by the marketing historian. These studies are valuable, however, because they direct the researcher to primary and secondary data.

In general, traditional statistical sources will not be available for all of the periods of historical study. What data are available may be limited in scope and may stem from sources not known to the marketing historian. For example, church records often include a listing of the names of merchants in a parish and medical records may report occupation-linked injuries. To the extent that data series in the traditional reporting form for marketing are not available and to the extent that unusual forms are not known, the work of the marketing historian will be made more difficult. The situation will be like that of the economic historian, who because of the shortage of great volumes of statistics must either muddle along with other evidence or specialize in those areas where statistics are sufficient to employ sophisticated statistical techniques (Johnson 1941, p. 46). The statistical data that are found, such as census reports, taxation reports, and transport movement documents, must be carefully scrutinzed to determine their relevance to marketing activities. They also must be tested for validity (Marburgh 1960).

## Hypothesis Verification and Theory Development

***Activity 6.*** The verification procedures are the equivalent of hypothesis testing. Verification is accomplished by comparison of qualitative factors which may or may not be associated by numerical values. The choice of the term "verification" is deliberate, to draw attention to the differences between hypothesis testing in historical research and hypothesis testing in marketing research. Most historical research involves the qualitative comparison of events over time or between different places without regard to either a known or a theoretical standard as is used in statistical inference. Unlike the test of the null hypothesis as in the case of a sample and a population, no precise process is available which allows for error estimation. Comparison itself is based on the ability of the researcher to describe a certain phenomenon in two time periods or in two areas. The process is often thwarted because of differences in the description of events. For example, in the description of periodic markets it would be important to know clearly whether they operated randomly in an area, that is, were periodic in space, or whether they are periodic in time, that is, operated at the same place but at different times. Though these differences seem obvious, great care must be taken to ensure that the proper conditions are included. As a method, comparison is characterized by the isolation of similarities and differences and by the assessment of the factors which lead to change (Boddewyn 1966).

A second verification method, which has received great attention by economic historians, is the regressive method (Marwick 1970, p. 73). This method follows the general principles of statistical analysis; obviously, its use depends on the availability of significant quantities of data.

The regressive method involves the use of evidence drawn from one period which is extrapolated either backward or forward in time in order to understand the earlier or later period. "Cliometrics," the name given the method in economic history, is an application of econometric methods to historical data. It incorporates prediction as discussed heretofore. Cliometrics has been criticized along two lines. The lack of data limits the validity of some studies, and techniques have dominated some data to give to conclusions more weight than they might have under different conditions (McCloskey 1978, p. 28). Whether this approach will be useful in historical research in marketing is unknown, although it is reasonable to suspect that the dearth of data will limit its use.

For the hypothesis describing the conditions for fixed store retailing, verification would be undertaken by the comparison of the assembled data with the constructs of the hypothesis. The researcher must subjectively apply weights to the various pieces of evidence and then reach conclusions. Because of the absence of fixed standards, close attention must be paid to the specific factors that affect the acceptance or the rejection of the hypothesis. The end product of the verification process, regardless of the outcome, will be a set of conclusions which recognize, but do not necessarily strongly endorse, alternative explanations. The precision of statistical relations which clearly link events will not be present in most cases.

***Activity 7.*** Theory development arises from the testing of the hypothesis in several environments. The development of explanatory theory is a process in which the results of positive and negative findings are merged, as shown in Figure 1. Those hypotheses which are not verified and not accepted become the negative feedback loop and are reexamined in further investigations. Those which are accepted form the basis for theory. There is no magic number of tests which signals the point when theory development can begin. Clearly, more than one case would be required.

Historical research by itself is not likely to lead to the development of predictive theory. The evidence collected and the inferences drawn can serve as the platform on which theory is built. Theory emerges when an attempt is made to predict the outcome of events. "A purely descriptive or historical treatment of marketing would not be marketing theory" (Alderson 1965, p. 23).

## Conclusions

Marketing history can show meaningful interconnections and parallels among different events. Its role will be to isolate and illustate the changes that marketing and its respective institutions have made, the factors which have been influential in effecting change, and the consequences of change. Though some scholars might choose to study the history of a firm or a single practice, greater value will come from studying marketing's role in the broader economic and social context. The history of specific events has value in itself but even more value when placed within the larger framework. Thus, if the limitations of such studies are fully recognized, marketing history might provide one avenue for preparing for the future (Carson 1978).

Because of the lack of methodological precision in historical studies, some marketing scholars may ignore them. What is lacking, however, is a full understanding of the aims of historical research. Although the development of general theory is a desired consequence of such research, more limited goals must be accepted. This fact should not detract from the search for a better knowledge of marketing's past.

## REFERENCES

Alderson, Wroe (1965), *Dynamic Marketing Behavior*, Homewood, Illinois: Richard D. Irwin, Inc.

Bagozzi, R. P. (1978), "Marketing as Exchange: A Theory of Transactions in the Marketplace," *American Behavioral Scientist*, 21, 535-56.

Bartels, R. (1976), *The History of Marketing Thought*, Columbus, Ohio: Grid, Inc.

Blackman, J. (1967), "The Development of the Retail Grocery Trade in the Nineteenth Century," *Business History*, 9, 110-117.

Boddewyn, J. (1966), "A Construct for Comparative Marketing Research," *Journal of Marketing Research*, 3 (May), 149-153.

Bucklin, L. P. (1972), *Competition and Evolution in the Distributive Trades*, Englewood Cliffs, New Jersey: Prentice-Hall, Inc.

Carson, D. (1978), "Götterdammering for Marketing?", *Journal of Marketing*, 42 (July), 11-19.

Cassady, R. Jr. (1963), "The Role of Economic Models in Microeconomic Market Studies," in *Models of Markets*, Alfred R. Oxenfeldt, ed. New York: Columbia University Press, 20-52.

Doody, A. F. (1965), "Historical Emphasis: Its Contribution to Marketing Education," in *Reflections on Progess in Marketing*, L. George Smith, ed., Chicago: American Marketing Association, 555-65.

Goldman, A. (1978), "An Updated 'Wheel of Retailing' Theory," in *Foundations of Marketing Channels*, Arch G. Woodside, J. Taylor Sims, Dale M. Lewison, and Ian F. Wilkinson, eds., Austin, Texas: Lone Star Publishers, 189-211.

Gray, S. A. (1931), *The Development of Economic Doctrine, An Introductory Survey*, New York: John Wiley & Sons, Inc.

Harvey, D. (1969), *Explanation in Geography*, London: Edward Arnold.

Hay, A. M. and K. S. O. Beavon (1979), "Periodic Marketing: A Preliminary Geographical Analysis in Part Time and Mobile Marketing," *Tijdschrift Voor Economisne en Social Geografie*, 70, 27-34.

Hidy, R. W. (1977), "Business History: A Bibliographic Essay," in *Research in Economic History Supplement I*, Robert E. Gallman, ed., Greenwich, Connecticut: JAI Press, 1-27.

Hoh-Cheung and L. H. Muir (1973), "Andrew Melrose, Tea Dealer and Grocer of Edinburgh 1812-1833," *Business History*, 9, 30-48.

Hollander, S. (1963), "The Wheel of Retailing," in *Marketing and the Behavioral Sciences*, Perry Bliss, ed., Boston: Allyn and Bacon, 311-21.

Hotchkiss, G. B. (1938), *Milestones of Marketing*, New York: The Macmillan Company.

Johnston E. A. J. (1941), "New Tools for the Economic Historian," *The Journal of Economic History, Supplement*, I, 30-38.

Jones, F. M. (1937), *Middlemen in the Domestic Trade of the United States 1800-1860*, Urbana: The University of Illinois.

Lee, C. H. (1968), "Marketing Organization and Policy in the Cotton Trade: M. Connel and Kennedy of Manchester," *Business History*, 10, 89-100.

Marburgh, T. F. (1960), "Income Originating in Trade, 1799-1869," in *Trends in the American Economy in the Nineteenth Century, Studies in Income and Wealth*, National Bureau of Economic Research, Princeton, New Jersey: Princeton University Press, 317-26.

Marwick, A. (1970), *The Nature of History*, London: The Macmillan Press.

McCloskey, D. N. (1978), "The Achievements of the Cliometric School," *Journal of Economic History*, 38, 13-28.

McCurdy, C. W. (1978), "American Law and the Marketing Structure of the Large Corporation 1875-1890," *Journal of Economic History*, 38, 631-49.

McKendrick N. (1960), "Josiah Wedgewood, An Eighteenth Century Entrepreneur in Salesmanship and Marketing Techniques," *Economic History Review*, 12, 408-31.

Narver, J. C. and R. Savitt (1971), *The Marketing Economy: An Analytical Approach*, New York: Holt, Rinehart and Winston.

Pollay, R. W. (1977), "The Importance, and the Problems of Writing the History of Advertising," *Journal of Advertising History*, 1, 3-5.

Porter, G. and H. C. Livesay (1971), *Merchants and Manufacturers, Studies in the Changing Structure of Nineteenth Century Marketing*, Baltimore, Maryland: The Johns Hopkins Press.

Schwartz, G. (1963), *Development of Marketing Theory*, Cincinnati, Ohio: South-Western Publishing Co.

Shapiro, S. J. (1964), "Marketing in America: Settlement to Civil War," in *Reflections on Progress in Marketing*, L. George Smith, ed., Chicago: American Marketing Association, 566-9.

——— and A. F. Doody (1968), *Readings in the History of American Marketing*, Homewood, Illinois: Richard D. Irwin, Inc.

Smalley, O. A. (1964), "The Empty Boxes of Marketing Organization," *Toward Scientific Marketing*, Stephen A. Greyser, ed., Chicago: American Marketing Association, 366-371.

Vance, J. E., Jr. (1970), *The Merchant's World: The Geography of Wholesaling*, Englewood Cliffs, New Jersey: Prentice-Hall, Inc.

Whitrow, G. J. (1975), *The Nature of Time*, Middlesex, England: Penguin Books Ltd.

Williamson, H. C. (1966), "The Professors Discover American Business," in *Readings in United States Economic and Business History*, Ross M. Robertson and James L. Pate, eds., Boston: Houghton Mifflin Company, 25-34.

# PART TWO
# Economic Schools of Marketing Thought

Since marketing was considered a subset of economics, it is not surprising that the early schools of marketing thought relied on the microeconomic concepts of demand theory and competition. At the same time there was a strong desire to create something unique, rather than to simply apply the economic principles to marketing phenomena. This resulted in the emergence of four separate schools of marketing thought.

The commodity school of marketing decided to focus on the *objects* of market transactions, such as products and goods. It therefore proposed a classification of goods based on some fundamental characteristics. This has resulted in the popular convenience, shopping, and specialty goods classifications.

The functional school of marketing decided to focus on the *activities* performed to achieve market transactions rather than the objects. In particular, the goal was to identify and categorize activities performed by the middlemen, such as wholesalers and retailers. This resulted in such functional categories as grading, sorting, and collecting.

The institutional school of marketing chose to focus on the *agents* of market transactions—the wholesalers and retailers—rather than the activities or objects of market transactions. In particular, the emphasis was on why and how middlemen emerge in the marketplace when production and consumption are separated by time and space. The institutional school of marketing resulted in our knowledge of channels of distribution and vertical as well as horizontal distribution arrangements.

The regional school of marketing focused on the *place* of market transactions rather than objects, institutions, or functions of market transactions. It was interested in understanding how and why geographical markets are created and what makes markets compartmentalized in terms of people's shopping patterns. Much of the interest was directly related to economic geography and the concepts of the bazaar or the marketplace.

We strongly believe that these classical schools of marketing thought have an abundance of intriguing and potentially valuable concepts that need to be rediscovered and revitalized.

# SECTION E
# Commodity School

The commodity school of marketing has focused on the objects of market transactions. It has generated a classification of all products into convenience, shopping, and specialty categories. These are still popular terms in marketing practice.

There are at least three distinct issues associated with the commodity school of marketing thought. First, is the classification exhaustive? For example, a number of scholars in more recent times have suggested a fourth category called preference goods. A related issue is whether the classification is too broad to be meaningful or managerially relevant.

A second issue is the identification of underlying dimensions on which products range from the convenience to shopping to specialty goods. While a number of attributes have been suggested, especially by Aspinwall, there is no real test or consensus among scholars about these attributes. In other words, what is the underlying theory or specific construct to which these attributes are related? Is it based on turnover, loyalty, store patronage, economic value, or physical display?

A third and even more fundamental issue is whether the traditional classification primarily developed for consumer goods is equally relevant for industrial goods and even more significantly for services. For example, is the convenience good the same as the commodity product in industrial marketing? What is the counterpart of shopping goods in industrial marketing? Is it the purchase of assets such as machinery, equipment, or computers? Finally, how do we translate the classification of goods into the classification of services? Are there also convenience, shopping, and specialty services? What about the issues of intangibility and perishability of services? The commodity school of marketing offers excellent opportunities for fresh new research and thinking.

# 14 —— Relation of Consumers' Buying Habits to Marketing Methods

*Melvin T. Copeland*



From the standpoint of consumers' buying habits, merchandise sold in retail stores can be divided roughly into three classes[1]: (1) convenience goods; (2) shopping goods; (3) specialty goods. Using this classification, one of the initial steps in laying out a sales or advertising plan is to determine whether the article to be sold will be purchased by consumers ordinarily with shopping or without shopping, at points of immediate convenience or in central trading districts, with insistence on an individual brand, with merely brand preference, or with indifference to brand.

This preliminary analysis facilitates the determination of the kind of store through which the market for the specific product should be sought, the density of distribution required, the methods of wholesale distribution to be preferred, the relations to be established with dealers, and, in general, the sales burden which the advertising must carry.

## Convenience Goods

Convenience goods are those customarily purchased at easily accessible stores; examples are canned soup, tobacco products, electric light bulbs, safety razor blades, shoe polish, laundry soap, crackers, popular magazines, confectionery, and tooth paste. The consumer is familiar with these articles; and as soon as he recognizes the want, the demand usually becomes clearly defined in his mind. Furthermore, he usually desires the prompt satisfaction of the want. The unit price for most articles in this class is too small to justify the consumer's going far out of his way or incurring the expense of a street-car fare in order to procure a special brand. It is for such reasons as these that a product subject to this type of demand gains a large sales advantage when it is purveyed in numerous stores located at points easily accessible to consumers.

The consumer is in the habit of purchasing convenience goods at stores located conveniently near his residence, near his place of employment, at a point that can be visited easily on the road to and from his place of employment, or on a route traveled regularly for purposes other than buying trips. In sparsely settled districts, to be sure, the distance a consumer must travel to reach a store carrying convenience goods necessarily is greater than in densely populated districts, but fundamentally the buying habits are the same in all districts. Convenience goods, moreover, are purchased at frequent intervals by the average consumer, and these ''repeat'' purchases enable the stores handling such wares to secure adequate patronage with reasonably small investments in stocks of merchandise.

Typical retail establishments carrying convenience goods are grocery stores, drug stores, and hardware stores. A majority of these stores are unit stores,[2] but it is in the trade in convenience goods that chain store systems have shown the greatest development. One of the essential characteristics of chain store systems is the combination of the advantages of large scale operation with those of small scale selling by locating branches at points which can be reached easily by consumers for the purchase of convenience goods. The few chains of specialty stores, which for reasons to be indicated later operate on the principle of one store in a town, constitute an exception.

Because of the desire of consumers to purchase this type of merchandise at easily accessible stores, the manufacturer of a convenience article must aim to secure distribution of his product through a large number of stores in each territory. Many of the retail outlets commonly utilized for this purpose at the present time are small unit stores; consequently, to obtain this widespread distribution it is customary for most convenience goods to be sold through wholesalers. Whenever a manufacturer of a product in this category elects to sell directly to unit stores, he must develop a large sales organization and arrange for his salesmen to visit the retailers at frequent intervals.

## Shopping Goods

Shopping goods are those for which the consumer desires to compare prices, quality, and style at the time of purchase. Usually the consumer wishes to make this comparison in several stores. Typical shopping goods are gingham cloth, women's gloves, chinaware, and novelty articles. The typical shopping institution is the department store. Shopping goods are purchased largely by women. Ordinarily a special trip is made to the shopping center for the purpose of buying such merchandise. As a rule, however, the specific store in which the purchase is to be made is not determined until after the offerings of at least two or three institutions have been inspected. The exact nature of the merchandise wanted may not be clearly defined in advance in the mind of the shopper; this is in contrast to the usual attitude in purchasing convenience goods. The purchase of shopping goods, furthermore, usually can be delayed for a time after the existence of the need has been recognized; the immediate satisfaction of the want is not so essential as in the case of most convenience goods. Because of the variety of merchandise which must be carried to satisfy the shopper and the relative infrequency of purchases of shopping articles by the average consumer, the store catering to the shopping trade must have a central location which attracts shoppers from a wide territory. In order to justify the expenses of operation in such a location, the volume of sales must be large. Conversely, it follows that the type of store which handles convenience goods ordinarily cannot carry a large enough variety and range of products to offer an attractive opportunity for shopping.

A store location suitable for trade in shopping goods usually is not adapted to the convenience goods trade; for the rental is high and the delivery interval inconvenient to consumers. It is seldom that a department store, for example, has found it possible to operate a grocery department at a profit. The factors of location, organization, and consumers' buying habits, which enable a department store to cater effectively to the shopping trade, handicap it in developing a business in convenience goods. When a manufacturer is laying out his marketing plans, therefore, he ordinarily finds it inconsistent to attempt to distribute his product through both department stores and scattered unit stores or through both department stores and chain stores. The type of store selected depends upon whether it is a shopping line, a convenience line, or a specialty line.

The number of stores selling shopping goods, furthermore, is much smaller than the number of convenience stores. The average size of the shopping store is large and its credit generally strong. This facilitates the marketing of shopping goods directly from manufacturer to retailer.

## Specialty Goods

Specialty goods are those which have some particular attraction for the consumer, other than price, which induces him to put forth special effort to visit the store in which they are sold and to make the purchase without shopping. In purchasing specialty goods, the consumer determines in advance the nature of the goods to be bought and the store in which the purchase is to be made, provided a satisfactory selection of merchandise can be effected in that store. Whereas convenience goods are purchased at stores that are easily accessible, it ordinarily is necessary for the consumer to put forth special effort to reach the store selling specialty goods. As in the case of shopping goods, the actual purchase of a specialty article may be postponed for a time after the specific need has been felt by the consumer. Examples of specialty goods are men's clothing, men's shoes, high-grade furniture, vacuum cleaners, and phonographs. Specialty goods are purchased by both men and women, but men's purchases of specialty lines are a larger proportion of the total sales of such merchandise than in the case of shopping goods.

For specialty goods the manufacturer's brand, the retailer's brand, or the general reputation of the retail store for quality and service stands out prominently in the mind of the consumer. It is because of distinctive characteristics associated with the brand or the store that the consumer is prepared to rely upon the service, quality, and prices of merchandise offered by that store as generally being fair and to accept the merchandise without shopping. In numerous lines of specialty goods, such as men's shoes and clothing, the consumer prefers to deal with a store offering an attractive variety of styles and sizes from which to select. Purchases are made by each individual customer at infrequent intervals. Consequently, a specialty store generally is located at a point to which customers can be drawn from a wide area.

From the manufacturer's standpoint, a specialty line calls for selected distribution, in contrast to the general distribution essential for convenience goods. The dealers who are to handle the specialty line must be carefully selected on the basis of their ability to attract the class of customers to whom the product will appeal. Retailers must be chosen who can be relied upon to use aggressive selling methods in attracting customers to their stores. Frequently, exclusive agencies are granted to retailers for the distribution of specialty goods. An exclusive agency is seldom, if ever, justified for any line which is not a specialty line. It is only in the marketing of specialty goods, furthermore, that manufacturers have found it practical to operate retail branches.

Because of the part which each individual retail store handling the merchandise plays in the sale of the specialty goods, the care with which these stores must be selected, and the methods of cooperation which are essential between the manufacturer and the dealer, specialty goods are especially suited to distribution by direct sale from manufacturer to retailers. The manufacturer of specialty goods who works out his plan of distribution systematically on this basis also often finds it advisable, through his national or local advertising, to assume part of the burden of focusing the demand on individual stores.

In case of several commodities, the articles tend to fall into more than one of these three categories. Staple groceries, for example, are clearly convenience goods; fancy groceries, on the other hand, are specialty goods. In each city there usually are from one to three stores which have a high reputation for specialties in groceries. Although these stores also sell staple groceries, their patronage is secured primarily on the basis of the specialties that they carry. Because of the limited market for such specialties and the volume of business necessary to justify carrying such a stock, ordinarily only one or perhaps two or three stores in a city can obtain enough business on these goods to warrant taking on a line of fancy groceries; in the same city, anywhere from one hundred to several hundred grocery stores are carrying convenience goods.

In the shoe trade, medium- and high-priced shoes for both men and women are specialty goods. Women's shoes which feature style novelties border on the shopping classification. The common grades of work shoes, on the other hand, border on the classification of convenience goods. The manufacturer of women's novelty shoes, for example, cannot advisedly leave the shopping institutions out of consideration in planning his sales program. The manufacturer of cheap work shoes, however, ordinarily must place his product in a larger number of stores than would be required were he selling medium-grade dress shoes for men.

Although women's ready-to-wear suits generally are shopping goods, a few manufacturers recently have been developing standard trade-marked lines, which tend to fall into the class of specialties. Several retail stores also have developed specialty reputations for women's ready-to-wear. In view of the conditions in the women's ready-to-wear field and also in several other fields, the averge department store now seems to be faced definitely with the question of whether its merchandising should be primarily on a shopping basis or whether at least some of its departments should be developed on a specialty basis. The piece goods departments are likely to remain shopping departments. Shoes, men's clothing, women's ready-to-wear, furniture, silverware, and numerous other departments are being developed in several department stores as specialty departments, but generally without a conscious, well-coordinated policy for a store as a whole. In these specialty departments the emphasis is shifted from comparative prices and comparative styles to the special qualities and characteristics of the merchandise carried. In other department stores the merchandising is still almost entirely on a shopping basis, with the featuring of prices and bargains that are supposed to appeal to the shopper. In so far as department stores develop specialty departments, they will afford attractive outlets for manufacturers whose distribution otherwise would be through specialty stores.

## Relation of Brands to Buying Habits

Convenience, shopping, and specialty goods are sold both branded and unbranded. Because of the differences in the buying habits of consumers in purchasing these classes of goods, brands do not play the same part in the merchandising plans for all three classes, and the advertising problems of manufacturers are quite dissimilar for shopping, convenience, and specialty merchandise.

A brand is a means of identifying the product of an individual manufacturer or the merchandise purveyed by an individual wholesaler or retailer. The real demand for any commodity is the quantity which consumers will buy at a specific price. If a product is unbranded, the volume of the demand ordinarily depends upon the quantity that consumers elect to buy, either entirely upon their own initiative or as a result of the sales efforts of the retailers by whom it is sold. When sugar was sold in bulk, for example, the demand depended upon the amount consumers wished to purchase or were induced to purchase by retailers who featured the article; sales were not directly stimulated by the sugar refiner. For an unbranded product, the individual manufacturer seldom can afford to assume the burden of stimulating demand which cannot be specifically directed to the product of his own factory. For such an unbranded product the manufacturer must rely chiefly upon his ability to produce cheaply, in order to be able to offer low prices, and he must pursue merely passive selling methods or, at most, direct his sales efforts chiefly toward wholesale and retail merchants. If the product is branded, on the other hand, the manufacturer can undertake not only to direct the active demand to his particular product, but also to arouse latent demand by stimulating a larger number of consumers to want his product or by making previous consumers desire to use more of his product at a specific price. When the American Sugar Refining Company, in 1912, for example, began to put out sugar in packages bearing the company's trademark, the company not only was in a position where it could inform the consumer regarding the merits of that particular brand, but it also could practically undertake to induce consumers to use more sugar, as, for instance, in canning fruit.

With the development of the package trade, the tendency during recent years has been for an increasing proportion of convenience goods to be branded. The increase in the sale of crackers in packages, for example, in contrast to the former bulk sales, has given greater significance to brands of crackers and has facilitated the use of aggressive sales methods by cracker manufacturers. Among shopping goods there has been some increase in the number of brands, but large quantities of merchandise in this class still are sold unbranded. Specialty goods are all branded, except in a few cases where retail stores have reputations which practically render it unnecessary for them to have brands placed on the merchandise which they sell.

When a manufacturer undertakes to focus the potential demand upon his product with brand identification, he must consider the attitude in which the consumer ordinarily approaches the purchase of such an article. The attitude of the consumer may be that of: (1) recognition, (2) preference, or (3) insistence.

## Consumer Recognition

When a brand has any significance at all, it serves primarily as a cause for recognition. If the consumer's previous acquaintance with the brand has been favorable, or if the manufacturer's or dealer's advertising has made a favorable impression, other things being equal, the recognized brand will be selected from among other unrecognized brands or from among unbranded merchandise. For some products—such as silk goods, ginghams, and women's suits—pattern, style, and price are considered by the consumer, before brand. When the selection narrows down to a choice between articles of this sort approximately equal in pattern, style, and price, the recognition of a known brand sways the choice. The manufacturer of such goods, however, cannot hope ordinarily to secure many sales merely because of brand, if his product is higher in price or less popular in pattern and style than directly competing goods shown in other stores.

Consumer recognition—an acquaintance with the general standing of the brand—probably is the only attitude toward that brand which the manufacturer of a typical shopping line ordinarily can establish in the mind of the average purchaser by means of advertising and sales efforts. If the product has some special feature, as, for example, cotton fabrics dyed in fast colors or fast-colored silk goods loaded with a minimum of tetra-chloride of tin, it occasionally is possible to arouse the interest of the consumer to a point of preference.

A family brand, by which is meant a brand or trade-mark that is applied commonly to a group of different products turned out by a single manufacturer, serves primarily to establish consumer recognition for all products in the group as soon as the consumer becomes acquainted with one article bearing the common brand. The experience of retail dealers indicates that for shopping and convenience goods the common brand aids in promoting consumer recognition. If it is a specialty line, the experience of the consumer with one article bearing the brand is likely to establish in the minds of consumers at least an attitude of preference for other articles bearing the same brand. It is unsafe, however, for the manufacturer to count upon the family brand to develop more than consumer recognition without the presentation of sales arguments for each article bearing the brand.

## Consumer Preference

Consumer recognition soon shades into consumer preference. When several brands of merchandise, which are similar in general qualities and in external appearance, are offered to the consumer by a retail salesman, the one for which previous experience, advertising, or perhaps the retailer's recommendation has created a preference, is chosen. The strength of the brand depends upon the degree of preference in the mind of the consumer. In purchasing convenience goods, for example, the consumer often approaches the retailer with the question, "Have you the X brand?" If the retailer does not have that brand in stock, another brand ordinarily is accepted by the consumer, or, if the retailer specifically urges another brand in the place of the one called for, a substitute may be taken by the consumer. This practise of asking for brands is common for many consumers in the purchase of convenience articles. The brand comes first in the consumer's mind and signifies to him the quality, style, or pattern of article, or the type of container that he wishes to obtain. In such cases the consumer has a preference for the brand asked for, but ordinarily it is not strong enough in this class of merchandise to make him insist on that brand to the point of visiting a less convenient store to make the purchase. It is because the consumer generally has merely the attitude of brand preference in purchasing convenience goods that it is essential for the manufacturer of such a product to place his wares on sale in a large number of stores in each territory.

## Consumer Insistence

The third stage in which the demand for branded articles manifests itself is consumer insistence. When the consumer approaches the purchase of an article in this attitude of mind, he accepts no substitute unless it is an emergency. This attitude of consumer insistence holds commonly in the purchase of specialty goods. To warrant undertaking to develop this attitude, the product must be so individualized in quality, in its special features, or in the service rendered by the manufacturer or retailer as to differentiate it distinctly from competing articles and to induce consumers to put forth special effort to secure that brand. The manufacturer of an electrical washing machine, for example, undertakes to present his sales arguments in such a way as to lead the consumer to insist upon the purchase of his particular make. Through advertising, the manufacturer of such a machine seeks to convince the consumer that his is the machine which should be purchased and that a store carrying this brand should be sought out.

The difference between no standing at all in the mind of the consumer, consumer recognition, consumer preference, and consumer insistence is one of the degrees to which the selling process has been carried with the consumer before he visits a retail store to make his purchase. If the consumer has no familiarity whatsoever with the brand of product to be purchased, the entire sales burden rests on the salesman in the store visited. If the consumer recognizes the brand, the manufacturer of that brand has taken the initial step in consummating the sale to the consumer. If the manufacturer has established consumer preference, the sale has proceeded one step further. If the consumer has the attitude of insistence, it remains merely for the retail salesman to close the sale.

Marketing costs generally are high. One of the first steps to be taken by a manufacturer, who is seeking to effect economies in selling his product, is to make an elementary analysis of the habits of consumers in buying articles of the sort he is producing. The formulation of an effective marketing plan must start with a consideration of the consumer; the next step is to adjust the plans of retail and wholesale distribution and the advertising program in accordance with the analysis of the buying habits of consumers among whom the market for the product is to be developed. This approach assures the maximum results from the sales efforts that are put forth.

## ENDNOTES

1. The methods of marketing goods for retail distribution are essentially different from the methods of marketing goods for wholesale consumption. In the one case it is necessary to select marketing methods whereby the goods can be parceled out in small lots to individual consumers; in the other the sales are made in wholesale lots for large scale use, as in manufacturing or in construction work.

   Mr. C. C. Parlin, manager of the Commercial Research Division of the Curtis Publishing Company, has divided merchandise for retail distribution into two classes—convenience goods and shopping goods. (*Merchandising of Textiles*, pp. 5-6.) In the case of shopping goods he made a distinction between men's shopping goods and women's shopping goods. In the classification explained in this article, convenience goods are defined to include practically the same merchandise as was included by Mr. Parlin in convenience goods. The category of merchandise included in shopping goods in this new classification, however, differs from Mr. Parlin's classification, and a new class—specialty goods—is added.
2. A unit store is a store, without an elaborate departmental organization, owned and managed as an independent unit for the sale of goods through personal salesmanship.

# 15 — The Characteristics of Goods and Parallel Systems Theories

*Leo Aspinwall*

*Managerial Marketing*, edited by Kelley and Lazar (Homewood, IL: Richard D. Irwin, Inc., 1958), pp. 434-450. Reprinted by permission.

## The Development Stages of a Science

The movement towards theory formulation in marketing follows logically the development of a science of marketing. Starting with a definition of science, we find that it consists of a classified body of knowledge. The Oxford Universal Dictionary defines science as "a branch of study which is concerned either with a connected body of demonstrated truths or with observed facts systematically classified and more or less colligated by being brought under general laws, and which includes trustworthy methods for the discovery of new truth within its own domain."

There are six generally recognized stages in the development of a science: (1) observation of phenomena; (2) collection and classification of similar phenomena for the purposes of explanation; (3) selection of several of the most reasonable explanations of these observed similar phenomena. These are called hypotheses, which are tentative theories or suppositions provisionally adopted to explain facts and to guide further investigations. (4) The most reasonable hypotheses are selected and advanced as theories. (5) When theories can, by scientifically controlled experimentation, recreate the original phenomenon, then a law is established. (6) Finally, when a body of laws is established and supported by a body of related literature, then a science emerges.

### Systematization as an Aid to Learning

The formulation of the Characteristics of Goods Theory and its closely related Parallel Systems Theory has followed exactly the process described in the foregoing paragraph. These theories are tentative suppositions, provisionally adopted to explain facts and to guide in the investigation of others. Having been charged with the responsibility of teaching marketing for over thirty years, the author has attempted to systematize marketing facts in such a way as to give students a means of relating marketing knowledge to a central thesis. Each central thesis summates in a usable way some closely related areas in marketing. Thus, when a number of such theses are integrated, we have created a model which provides a convenient means by which students can organize and systemize their understanding of marketing.

### Theory and Practical Experience

A second and equally important value that stems our of theory formulation in marketing, is the availability of a framework into which current problems of marketing can be fitted for purposes of analysis. This means that marketing theories are specialized tools which the marketing practitioner has available for use in solving day-to-day problems, but like any specialized tool, skill is acquired only by repeated use. The marketing practitioner knows full well the importance of actual experience, but to rely on experience might easily lead to serious error, since experience is closely related to conditions that were current at a certain time and which may no longer exist. Marketing theories have an element of timelessness which makes them valuable for analytical purposes: thus a combination of practical experience and marketing theories provides a sound basis for undertaking the solution of current marketing problems.

## Characteristics of Goods Theory

The characteristics of goods theory attempts to arrange all marketable goods in systematic and useful fashion. It has been tested both in the classroom and in application to business problems. It provides a perspective and frame of reference for organizing marketing facts and for weighing marketing decisions. Previous efforts included the three-way classification of products as convenience goods, shopping goods, and specialty goods. The characteristics of goods theory sets up a continuous scale rather than discrete classes and defines the criteria by which any product can be assigned to an appropirate place on the scale. All of these criteria lend themselves to objective measurement, at least potentially. By contrast, it would be rather difficult to distinguish a shopping good from a convenience good in positive, quantitative terms.

The marketing characteristics of a product determine the most appropriate and economical method for distributing it. To fix its position on the scale, representing the variation in these characteristics, is to take the first major step toward understanding its marketing requirements. To know these characteristics is to be able to predict with a high degree of reliability how a product will be distributed, since most products conform to the pattern. Serious departure from the theoretical expectations will almost certainly indicate the need for change and improvement in distribution methods. These considerations apply both to physical distribution and to the parallel problem of communications including the choice of promotional media and appeals. It follows also that goods having similar characteristics call for similar handling.

Finally, if precise weights or values could be assigned to each characteristic, their combination would determine the unique position of a product on the marketing scale.

The problem-solving process often leads into totally unfamiliar areas which sometimes bring us to a dead end. Only occasionally do these probing excursions uncover new combinations of old ideas that have some relevance to the problem in hand. When such combinations prove to be useful the mind is quick to employ such combinations again for problems of the same general type, so that repeated use tends to formulate a framework of reference which can be readily used for problem solving. Into the framework thus formulated the problem can be fitted so that the relationship of the integral parts can be observed. This may well be a mental sorting operation which seeks to classify problems into similar groups for greater efficiency in the unending task of problem solving.

The characteristics of goods theory is the result of one of these mental excursions, and its repeated use has had the effect of crystalizing the combination of old ideas into a fairly stabilized form. The theory has been revised from time to time through the constructive criticism of my colleagues, but whether it will ever be in final form is doubtful, since the dynamic character of all marketing activity is such that changes are more likely than anything else. Somehow the thought of achieving a final state of equilibrium is rather frightening.

## Characteristics of Goods

The problem of weights or values being assigned to these individual characteristics has been one of the real difficulties in giving the theory a mathematical setting. So far that objective has not been fully achieved. We have been obliged to deal with relative values which might be considered as an intermediary stage in the theory's development. The analogy of an electric circuit may eventually prove useful in formulating a mathematical approach. Getting goods distributed is not unlike moving an electric current through resistance factors, each of which takes a part of the gross margin. When the good finally reaches the consumer's hands, ready for consumption, all of the gross margin has been used. Looking at this idea from the consumer end, the amount of the gross margin the consumer has given up in order to enjoy the utilities the good provides is, in fact, the voltage that the electric current must have in order to pass through the resistance factors and finally reach the consumer.

The decision as to the number and kinds of characteristics to be used was approached by setting up tests which these characteristics should meet. These criteria are:

1. Every characteristic selected must be applicable to every good.
2. Every characteristic selected must be relatively measurable in terms of its relationship to every good.

3. Every characteristic must be logically related to all the other characteristics.

This brings us to the point of defining a characteristic. A characteristic is a distinguishing quality of a good relative to its stable performance in a market and its relationship to the consumers for whom it has want-satisfying capacity. Under this definition five characteristics have been selected, each of which must in turn be defined. These are:

1. Replacement rate.—This characteristic is defined as *the rate at which a good is purchased and consumed by users in order to provide the satisfaction a consumer expects from the product*. The replacement rate is associated with the concept of a flow or movement of units of a good from producer to ultimate consumer. The idea is somewhat akin to a turnover rate, except that our understanding of turnover is related to the number of times per year that an average stock of goods is bought and sold. Replacement rate as used here is consumer oriented. It asks how often the consumer buys shoes—once each month, once each six months, or once each year? It does not ask whether or not the shoes have been consumed, but only how often the market must be ready to make shoes available for consumers. This characteristic differentiates the rate or flow of different goods and attempts to envision the market mechanism that will meet the aggregate needs of consumers. This is marketing in motion as dictated by consumer purchasing power.

   It may be helpful to introduce a few illustrative cases and at the same time show how the idea of relative measurement is used. Loaves of bread, cigarettes, packets of matches all have high replacement rates in terms of relative measurement. Some people consume bread more often than others, yet the average frequency of all bread eaters in a consumption area determines the replacement rate for bread. In comparison with grand pianos, bread has a high replacement rate and grand pianos have a low replacement rate. Men's shirts and ready-to-wear have medium replacement rates when compared to bread and grand pianos. Here we can visualize fast-moving streams, slow-moving streams and moderately moving streams of different kinds of goods, each with its characteristically different rate of replacement.

2. Gross margin.—The definition of gross margin as used here is not different from its use in marketing generally. *The money sum which is the difference between the laid in cost and the final realized sales price* is the gross margin. It is brought to mind at once that there are several gross margins involved in moving goods from factory gates to final consumer. What is meant here is the summation of all the gross margins involved. It is that total money sum necessary to move a good from point of origin to final consumer. It might be thought

of as channel costs or as the fare a good must pay to reach its destination. If the amount of gross margin is less than the fare needed, the good will not reach destination. The calculation of the gross margin is a market-oriented function which is based, in the final analysis, on the amount of money a consumer will exchange for a particular good. If the consumer elects to pay a money fund which is less than the production cost and the necessary marketing costs, the good will not be marketed because the gross margin is too low in relation with the other characteristics. The availability of gross margin is the force that operates our marketing system. Suppose a consumer wishes to procure a pack of cigarettes from a vending machine and the machine is set to operate when a twenty-five-cent piece is inserted into the slot. Nothing would happen if a ten-cent piece were dropped into the slot, except that the ten-cent piece would be returned to the customer. The gross margin contained in the twenty-five-cent piece was large enough to bring the consumer the cigarettes he needed.

This may be the appropriate place to call attention to the fact that whenever the flow of goods is arrested for whatever reason, costs begin to take a larger share of the planned gross margin and may actually prevent a good from reaching the final market. Such losses as may have been incurred in the stoppage must be borne by someone, and the calculations made by marketing men are such that loss situations cannot be tolerated, and the flow of goods will be stopped. The secondary action in such a case is that a money flow back to the producer also stops, which in turn closes down production. While this may be oversimplified, it does emphasize the importance of gross margin to the whole economic process.

Certain types of goods are necessarily involved in storage by reason of their seasonal production. Storage assumes the availability of the needed amount of gross margin to pay these costs, otherwise such goods would not be stored. Whatever takes place during the movement of goods from producer to consumer affects gross margin.

This is the first opportunity to test these characteristics against the criteria set up for their selection. It has been shown that the replacement rate is applicable to all goods and that the replacement rate is relatively measurable. Lastly the question must be asked: Is the replacement rate related to gross margin? This is without doubt the most important relationship of all those needing demonstration in this theory. The relationship is inverse. Whenever replacement rate is high gross margin is low and, conversely, when replacement rate is low then gross margin is high. Thus, when goods move along at a lively clip the costs of moving them are decreased. This relationship brings to mind some economic laws which bear on the situation. The theory of decreasing costs seems to apply here to show that marketing is a decreasing-cost industry. This might be stated as follows: As the number of units distributed increases, the cost per unit distributed tends to decrease up to the optimum point. Mass distribution insofar as marketing is concerned has important possibilities. This is amply demonstrated in modern marketing operations. Goods handling in modern warehouses has been studied in this light and warehousing costs have been decreased, which in turn has expedited the flow of goods into consumer's hands. Here again, economic laws operate to induce the seller to pass on savings in marketing costs. Small decreases in gross margin tend to bring forth a disproportionately larger market response.

The relationship of replacement rate and gross margin has thus far been concerned with the increasing side of the relationship. When replacement rate is low and gross margin is relatively higher, it is not difficult to envision higher marketing costs. Almost at once it can be seen that selling costs will be relatively higher per unit. The gross margin on the individual sale of a grand piano or major appliance must bear the cost of direct sales, including salaries and commissions for salesmen who negotiate with prospective buyers and very often make home demonstrations. The fact that shipping costs are higher in moving pianos is well known. If carlot shipments are used there are likely to be some storage costs involved, and this additional cost must come out of gross margin. It can be shown that high-value goods such as jewelry and silverware reflect this relationship in much the same way. This inverse relationship between replacement rate and gross margin strikes a balance when goods with a medium rate of replacement are involved.

3. Adjustment.—An important characteristic which pertains to all goods and which has been named ''adjustment'' is defined as *services applied to goods in order to meet the exact needs of the consumer.* These services may be performed as the goods are being produced or at any intermediate point in the channel of distribution or at the point of sale. Adjustment as a characteristic of all goods reflects the meticulous demands of consumers that must be met in the market. Even in such goods as quarts of milk there is evidence of adjustment. Some consumers demand milk with low fat content, others require milk with high fat content, to name but one of the items of adjustment which pertains to milk. The matter of size of package, homogenized or regular, and even the matter of added vitamins come under adjustment. The services applied to milk are performed in the processing plant in anticipation of the adjustments the consumer may require. Here slight changes in the form or in size of package are adjustments performed in advance of the sale of the product. This type of adjustment imposes additional costs involving

somewhat larger inventories and the use of a greater amount of space, with all that this implies. It can be easily understood that costs are involved whenever adjustments are performed, so that additional amounts of gross margin are necessary. Adjustments made at the point of production become manufacturing costs which only mildly affect the marketing operation, so that the measured amount of adjustment in the marketing channel is relatively low.

Goods with a high replacement rate have low adjustment but the reverse is true when goods have low replacement rates. Goods with a medium replacement rate have a medium amount of adjustment. Here the inverse relationship between replacement rate and adjustment has been demonstrated, as well as the direct relationship between gross margin and adjustment.

4. Time of consumption.—Time of consumption as a characteristic of goods can be defined as *the measured time of consumption during which the good gives up the utility desired*. This characteristic is related to the replacement rate to a considerable degree, since goods with a low time of consumption are likely to have a high rate of replacement. The inverse relationship is true, but a low time of consumption does not mean that a repetitive purchasing program is maintained by the same consumer. Aspirin gives up its utility in the short period of time during which it is being consumed, but a purchase replacement may not occur until another headache needs attention. The idea of consumption time is more closely related to nondurable and durable goods both in the consumer and industrial classes.

   The time of consumption characteristic pertains to all goods, and the amount of this time is relatively measurable, which satisfies the criterion of relationship to all goods and the criterion of relative measurability. The final criterion of relationship to all other characteristics is also met in that low time of consumption is directly related to adjustment and gross margin and inversely related to the rate of replacement.

5. Searching time.—The characteristic of searching time can be defined as *the measure of average time and distance from the retail store* and hence convenience the consumer is afforded by market facilities. Suppose the need to purchase a package of cigarettes comes up for immediate attention for a consumer. The amount of effort exerted on his part to procure the needed cigarettes is correlated with the amount of searching time. In this case the amount of inconvenience suffered is usually very low since the market has reacted to the fact that there is a wide and insistent demand for cigarettes. To meet this demand, points of purchase are established wherever large numbers of potential customers are to be found. The result of such market action is that cigarettes can be purchased at many different places and in

many different institutions, and the searching time is low. The old idea expressed in another way: consumers are motivated by a drive for convenience. Out of these relationships we have come to recognize "the span of convenience" for each product. Consumers cannot easily be forced to expend an amount of time and energy that is disproportionate to the satisfaction they expect to receive from the goods in question.

It can easily be seen that for certain goods the searching time will be low, while for certain other goods the searching time will be much larger. The amount of time and energy expended by a customer in the process of furnishing a new home would be very great and, therefore, searching time would be correspondingly high. There is the need for examining the offerings of many stores, and even though these stores may be located fairly close to each other, in all probability, they will be located at some distance from the consumer's home. The reality of this situation is expressed in the characteristics of the goods. Searching time can be readily envisioned by the fact that we have many more market outlets for cigarettes than we do for grand pianos or furniture and, therefore, market availability for cigarettes is low and for pianos it is high.

Searching time is directly related to gross margin, adjustment, and time of consumption, and is inversely related to replacement rate. Searching time as a characteristic of goods pertains to all goods and for each and every good it is relatively measurable.

This information can now be fitted into a chart which will keep the relationships of the characteristics of goods in position as they pertain to all goods. This chart will show that goods with the same relative amounts of these five characteristics fall into the same broad classifications. Arbitrary names can be fitted to these broad classifications for greater convenience in conveying ideas about goods and the various ways in which they are distributed.

**CHART 1. Characteristics of Goods Theory**

| | *Color Classification* | | |
|---|---|---|---|
| *Characteristics* | *Red Goods* | *Orange Goods* | *Yellow Goods* |
| Replacement Rate | High | Medium | Low |
| Gross Margin | Low | Medium | High |
| Adjustment | Low | Medium | High |
| Time of Consumption | Low | Medium | High |
| Searching Time | Low | Medium | High |

## Color Concept

This chart introduces an additional element into the characteristics of good theory: the color classification. The idea that goods with similar characteristics are similar to each other lends itself to the establishment of three large classes of goods that can be named in such a manner as to convey the idea of an array of goods. The choice of color names may be inept in some respects, but the idea of an array of goods, based upon the sum of the relative values of characteristics of goods, is important. The length of light rays for red, orange, and yellow, in that order, is an array of light rays representing a portion of the spectrum. For our present purpose it is more convenient to use the three colors only, rather than the seven of the full spectrum. The idea of an infinite graduation of values can be envisioned by blending these colors from red to yellow with orange in between. This is the idea we wish to convey as concerning all goods.

The sum of the characteristics for each and every good is different, and the sum of characteristics for red goods is lower than the sum of the characteristics for yellow goods. The chart shows red goods to have four low values and one of a high value, while yellow goods have four high values and one low.

It is useful to stress this tension between replacement rate and the other four marketing characteristics, since they all tend to decrease as replacement rate increases. That is equivalent to saying that as demand for a product increases, marketing methods tend to develop which reflect economies in the various aspects of marketing costs. It is easily possible, of course, to transform replacement rate into its inverse for use in arriving at a weighted index of the five characteristics. If replacement rate were expressed as the average number of purchases in a year the inverse measure would be the average number of days between purchases. This measure would be low for red goods and high for yellow, like all of the other characteristics.

A schematic diagram can now be set up which represents all possible graduations in goods from red through orange to yellow. As shown in Figure 1, a simple percentage scale from 0 to 100 is laid out on both coordinates. It is true that the weighted value for any product could be laid out on a single line. Yet there is an advantage in the two-dimensional chart for the purpose of visualizing an array of goods. The scale of values thus really consists of all the points on the diagonal line in the accompanying chart. Since there is an infinite number of points on any line segment, the scale provides for an infinite array of goods. If the chart were large enough, vertical lines could be drawn with each line representing a product now on the market. Even after these lines were drawn there would still remain an infinite number of positions in between. Many of these positions might serve to identify goods which have been withdrawn from the market or others which might be introduced in the future.

**FIGURE 1. Schematic Array of a Few Selected Goods (Plotted in Terms of Yellow Goods)**

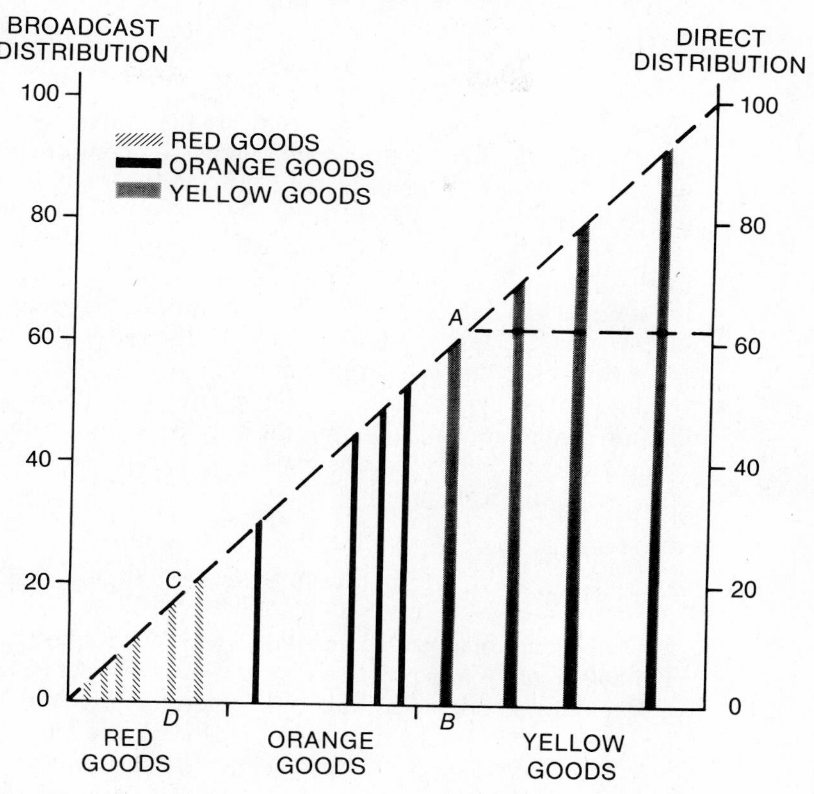


Line *AB* represents a good having an ordinate value of 63, indicating the sum of the characteristics of this good. In the general classification it has 63 percent yellow characteristics and 37 percent red characteristics. Translated into marketing terms, this good might be ladies' ready-to-wear dresses sold through department stores and shipped directly from the factory to these stores in the larger cities. The smaller cities are served by wholesalers who carry small stocks of these goods along with other dry goods items. Thus the marketing channels utilized for distributing this good would be direct to large department store accounts and semibroadcast through specialty wholesalers serving smaller city accounts.

Line *CD* in its position near the red end of the scale has a yellow characteristics value of 15 and a red value of 85, which puts this good in the large classification as a red good. The sum of the characteristics value in the scale 0 to 100 is 85 percent red. This might well be a soap product which is sold mainly by broadcast distribution using a broker, wholesaler, retailer channel. The 15 percent yellow characteristic might indicate specialty salesmen's activity involving factory drop shipments. The latter type of distribution is more direct and might account for the 15 percent of direct distribution from the factory to the retailer.

The position of a good on the color scale is not static. Most products fall in the yellow classification when they are first introduced. As they become better known and come to satisfy a wider segment of consumer demand, the replacement rate increases and the good shifts toward the red end of the scale. Thus there is a red shift in marketing which offers a rather farfetched analogy to the red shift in astronomy which is associated with the increasing speed of movement of heavenly bodies. There is also an opposing tendency in marketing, however, resulting from the constant shrinking of gross margin as a good moves toward the red end of the scale. Marketing organizations, in the effort to maintain their gross margin, may improve or differentiate a good which has moved into the red category, so that some of these new varieties swing all the way back into yellow. Thereafter the competitive drive for volume serves to accelerate the movement toward the red end of the scale again.

## Parallel Systems Theory

The sponsor of a product must decide how it is to be promoted and what channels to use for its physical distribution. He is confronted with a variety of possibilities both for stimulating demand and for moving his product to the consumer. It turns out that there is a parallel relationship between these two aspects of the marketing problem with a distribution system and its appropriate counterpart in promotion usually occurring together. This pairing of systems occurs because the promotion and distribution requirements of a product are both dependent on the marketing characteristics of the goods. The preceding material explained how goods might be arrayed according to their marketing characteristics into groups designated as red, orange, and yellow. It was further shown that this array could be translated into a numerical scale and presented in simple graphic form. The purpose of the present article is to indicate how the position of a product on this scale can be used to identify the parallel systems of promotion and distribution which should be used in marketing the product.

This set of ideas has come to be designated as the parallel systems theory. It is the kind of theory which is intended to be helpful in resolving fundamental practical issues in marketing. Theory alone cannot settle all the details of a marketing plan. It may save much time and effort by indicating the starting point for planning and the appropriate matching of systems of promotion and distribution. The gross margin earned on a product provides the fund which must cover the costs of marketing distribution and marketing promotion. The management of this fund involves many of the most critical decisions with which marketing executives have to deal. Even slight errors of judgment in this regard may spell the difference between profit and loss.

The parallel systems theory begins with a simple thesis which may be stated as follows: The characteristics of goods indicate the manner of their physical distribution and the manner of promotion must parallel that physical distribution. Thus, we have parallel systems, one for physical distribution and one for promotion. The movement of goods and the movement of information are obviously quite different processes. It was to be expected that specialized facilities would be developed for each function. The fact that these developments take place along parallel lines is fundamental to an understanding of marketing. A few special terms must be introduced at this point for use in discussing parallel systems.

A channel for the physical distribution of goods may be either a short channel or a long channel. The shortest channel, of course, is represented by the transaction in which the producer delivers the product directly to its ultimate user. A long channel is one in which the product moves through several stages of location and ownership as from the factory to a regional warehouse, to the wholesaler's warehouse, to a retail store, and finally to the consumer. The parallel concepts in promotion may be compared to contrasting situations in electronic communication. On the one hand, there is the closed circuit through which two people can carry on a direct and exclusive conversation with each other. On the other hand, there is broadcast communication such as radio and television whereby the same message can be communicated to many people simultaneously.

In general, long channels and broadcast promotion are found together in marketing while short channels and closed circuit or direct promotion are found together. The parallel systems theory attempts to show how these relationships arise naturally out of the marketing characteristsics of the goods.

## Characteristics of Goods and Marketing Systems

It will be remembered from the preceding article that goods were arrayed according to their marketing characteristics as red, orange, and yellow. Marketing systems can be arrayed in similar and parallel fashion. Red goods call for long channels and broadcast promotion. Yellow goods call for short channels and closed circuit promotion. Orange goods are intermediate as to their marketing characteristics and, hence, are intermediate as to the kind of distribution and promotion systems which they require. There is a continuous gradation from red to yellow and from broadcast to direct methods of marketing.

One of the fundamental marketing characteristics of goods is replacement rate. That is the frequency with which the average consumer in the market buys the product or replenishes the supply of it carried in his household inventory. Red goods are goods with a high replacement rate. A market transaction which occurs with high frequency lends itself to standardization and specialization of function. The movement of goods and the movement of information each becomes clearly marked and separate. Opportunity arises for a number of specialized marketing agencies to participate in distribution, and the result is what has been called the ''long channel.'' Messages to the ultimate user become as standardized as the product itself. This type of information and persuasion does not need to follow the long distribution channel from step to step in its transmission from producer to consumer. Such messages are broadcast to consumers through both electronic and printed advertising media which provide a more appropriate channel.

Yellow goods are low in replacement rate and high in other marketing characteristics such as adjustment. Requirements for this class of goods tend to vary from one user to another. Adjustment embraces a variety of means by which goods are fitted to individual requirements. The marketing process remains relatively costly and a large percentage of gross margin necessarily goes along with high adjustment. The opportunity for standardization and specialization is slight compared to that of red goods. Physical movement and promotion remain more closely associated, with a two-way communication concerning what is available and what is needed finally resulting in the delivery of the custom-made product. A transaction between a man and his tailor would illustrate this type of marketing. Many kinds of industrial equipment are specially designed for the given user and would also be at the extreme yellow end of the scale. The short channel is prevalent in such situations and all promotion or related communication moves through a closed circuit.

Many products lie in the middle range which has been designated as orange goods. They have been produced to standard specifications but with the knowledge that they will have to be adapted in greater or less degree in each individual installation. The replacement rate is high enough to offer moderate opportunity for standardization and specialization. At least one intermediary is likely to enter the picture, such as an automobile dealer buying from the manufacturer and selling to the consumer or an industrial distributor serving as a channel between two manufacturers. The car sold to customers may be of the same model and yet be substantially differentiated to meet individual preferences as to color and accessories. Broadcast media are used in promotion but not on the same scale relatively as for soaps or cigarettes. The industrial distributor is often supported in his efforts by specialty salesmen or sales engineers employed by the manufacturer. Advertising of a semibroadcast character is likely to be used. That is to say that messages are specially prepared for various segments of the market for which the appeal of the product is expected to be somewhat different. This approach lies between the standardized message to all users on the one hand the and individualized closed circuit negotiation on the other.

One qualification which may properly be suggested at this point is that marketing systems are not quite so flexible as this discussion suggests, but must conform to one type or another. Thus a channel for physical distribution could have two steps or three steps but not two and a half. Nevertheless, the picture of continuous variation along a scale is generally valid because of the combinations which are possible. A producer may sell part of his output through wholesalers who service retailers and sell the remainder direct to retailers. The proportions may vary over time so that one channel presently becomes dominant rather than the other. Similarly broadcast promotion may gradually assume greater importance in the marketing mix even though a large but declining amount of adjustment is involved in some individual sales.

## Movement of Goods and Movement of Information

The schematic relationship between goods and marketing systems is shown in Figure 2. This simple diagram depicts the parallels which have been discussed. It will be noted that the segment of the line allowed is greater for orange goods than for red goods and greater for yellow than for orange. It is a readily observable fact that the number of separate and distinct items in any stock of goods increases as replacement rate decreases. A drugstore, for example, has to sell more separate items to achieve the same volume of sales as a grocery store. An exclusive dress shop will need more variation in styles and models than a store operating in the popular price range. Paint brushes, files, or grinding wheels will be made up in a great multiplicity of specifications to serve the industrial market as compared to the few numbers which suffice for the household user. Red goods by their very nature are those in which a single item is bought frequently because it meets the requirements of many occasions for use while in the yellow goods more numerous items with less frequent sales are required for a more accurate matching of diverse and differentiated use situations.

**FIGURE 2. Relationship Between Goods and Marketing Systems**

| | | | |
|---|---|---|---|
| GOODS | RED | ORANGE | YELLOW |
| DISTRIBUTION | LONG CHANNEL | MODERATE CHANNEL | SHORT CHANNEL |
| PROMOTION | BROADCAST | SEMI BROADCAST | CLOSED CIRCUIT |

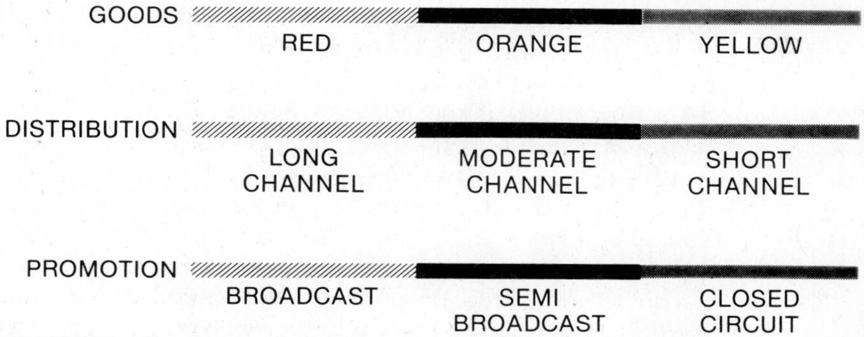

Figure 3 is intended to demonstrate the relationship between goods and the methods of distribution and promotion. It is not intended to show an accurate mathematical relationship since the data from which it is constructed are not mathematically accurate, but it does implement understanding of the problems with which marketing executives must deal. The reasoning is deductive, moving from the general to the specific and provides a quick basis for reaching an answer which can readily be adjusted to a specific case. The readings from the diagram are in complementary percentages that must be accepted as rough measurements of the kinds and amounts of distribution and promotion. Long channel distribution and broadcast promotion are grouped together as related elements of the marketing mix and designated as "broadcast" for the sake of simplicity. The line representing these two elements in combination slopes downward to the right since this type of expenditure can be expected to be relatively high for red goods and relatively low for yellow goods. Similarly short channel distribution and closed circuit communication are thrown together under the designation of "direct." The line representing direct promotion and distribution slopes upward from left to right.

## Application to a Management Problem

A short time ago a project was undertaken for a well-known manufacturer whose operation is such that the range of products his company manufactures covers the scale from red goods to yellow goods. In following the reasoning of the characteristics of goods theory and the parallel systems theory he was able to locate a certain product in its position on the base line. He drew the ordinate representing this product and found from the diagram that the distribution indicated was a modified direct distribution and that accordingly a considerable amount of direct promotion should be used. In reviewing what actually was being done with this product he knew that promotion was mostly broadcast while the distribution was a modified direct. Thus, promotion and distribution were not running parallel and such a finding for this product provided a substantial explanation of the poor performance this product was making. Research had confirmed that it was an excellent product and that it was priced correctly so that a reasonable volume of sales should have been expected. The planned sales for the product were not realized and to correct this situation a more extensive broadcast promotion program was launched, but from this program little or no increase in sales was realized. At this point the manufacturer decided that it would be worth a try to follow out the indicated promotional and distributional plan shown in the parallel systems theory analysis. A program of direct promotion was initiated and results were immediately forthcoming. The full sales expectations were realized and the manufacturer decided to establish a special division to handle the product which since that time has produced even more sales at costs considerably below the estimated costs.

**FIGURE 3. Parallel Systems Theory**

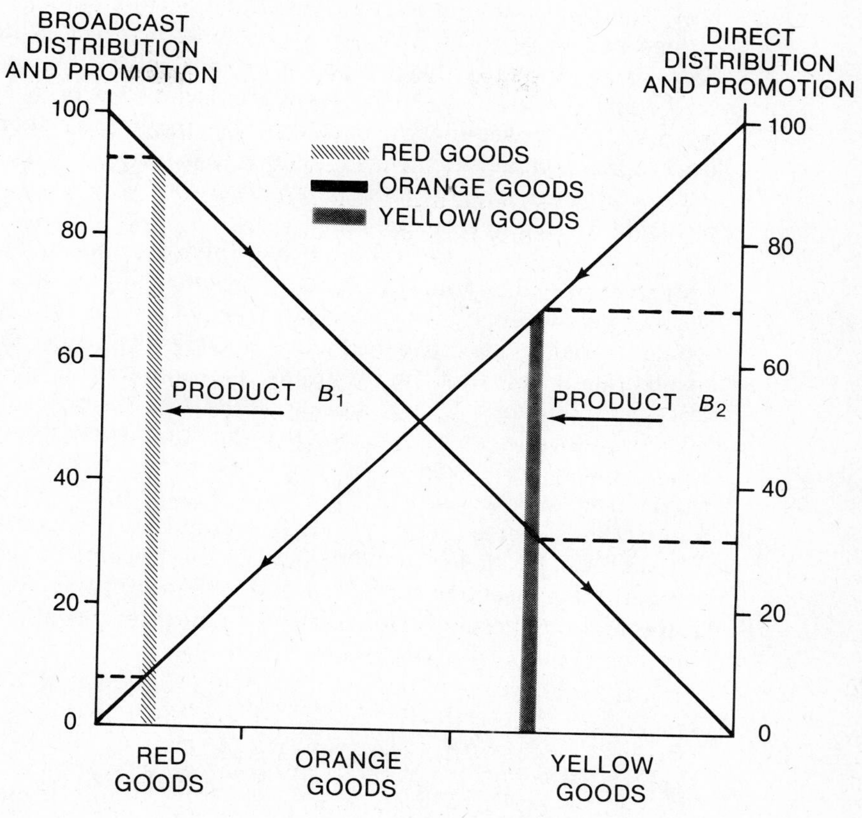


A somewhat closer look at this case revealed that broadcast promotion was reaching thousands of people who were in no way qualified users of the product and that the type of advertising message was such that qualified users were unable to specify the product even if they wished to do so. A careful study of the problem showed that the direct promotion had produced all of the sales results. Thus the cost of the broadcast promotion had to be borne by qualified users and the result was a higher price than would have been needed if direct promotional means had been employed. The final result of this operation was that prices were lowered and the profit position for the manufacturer and all institutions in the distribution channel was improved.

Product $B_1$ in Figure 3, represents the product discussed in the case above located in its correct position. Reading the ordinate value in the vertical scale shows that the product it represents should be distributed 69 percent direct and that promotion should also be 69 percent direct. The complementary

31 percent reading shown indicates that 31 percent of the distribution should be broadcast and 31 percent of the promotion should be of the broadcast type. Product $B_1$ shown on the diagram is product $B_2$ as it was incorrectly located on the base line array of goods. The incorrect location was based on a measurement of the method of promotion that was being used. Actually this product was being distributed correctly by a modified direct method, and consequently consumers who might have been influenced to use the product had no means by which to exercise their wishes; the product was not available in retail stores in such a way as to make it readily available to qualified customers.

By making analyses of products and their distribution and promotional programs, it will be found that many products are not in conformity with the parallel systems theory, and yet seem to be successful products. This would not of itself disprove the theory. Such results might indicate that better results might be had if the programs were modified in the direction indicated by the theory. This can often be done at a comparatively small cost by using test sales areas in which the adjustment can be made without affecting the national system in which the product may be operating. The results from such experimentation should confirm the analysis made under the parallel systems theory. A large amount of case material has been collected on the parallel systems theory but there seems to be an almost endless variety of cases and there is a need for constantly studying the problem in the light of the improvements in communications and distribution.

## CONCLUSION

A further definition for broadcast promotion seems to be needed as well as for direct promotion. Whenever promotional means are used, without knowledge in advance of the identity of prospective users, the promotional means is considered to be broadcast. The firm employing broadcast promotional means relies upon the chance contact with potential customers for the product or service. The broadcast distributional means for such a product are so arranged that the customer for the product who has been reached by this type of promotion can exercise his choice conveniently and quickly. Retail stores are available within a short radius of the consumer who may wish to purchase the product. Thus, the sales gap is shortened both as to time and distance and the effectiveness of the broadcast means of promotion is enhanced. The key fact that makes this type of marketing economical is that while the prospective users are unidentified, they represent a large proportion of the general public which will be exposed to the broadcast message. The opposite of broadcast promotion is direct promotion. The definition of direct promotion turns on the fact that the recipient of the direct communication is known in advance, so that the message reaches the intended purchaser by name and address or by advance qualification of the prospect as to his need and ability to purchase the product. The most direct means would be a salesman who calls upon a selected prospect whose address and name is known in advance, and where judgment has been passed upon his need for the product, and whose ability to pay for the product has been ascertained. The next in order might be a direct first-class letter or telegram sent to a prospect. Then perhaps door-to-door selling or mailing to persons found on selected mailing lists. These selected means of direct promotion used show a widening sales gap between the customer and the product. It is readily seen that broadcast promotion creates the widest sales gap. At the same time it can readily be seen that the marketing radius over which the customer may have to search for the product is increased. Compensating for this increased radius are the more intensive means of promotion that result from direct promotion, which will induce the customer willingly to undertake greater inconveniences of time and distance in order to procure the product.

These definitions relate directly back to the characteristics of goods theory. Whenever a high replacement is involved it becomes physically impossible to effect distribution by direct means. Such a situation calls for mass selling and mass movement of goods wherein all economies of volume selling and goods handling are brought into play. The low gross margin on the individual transaction requires that the aggregate gross margin resulting from mass selling be ample to get the job done. It seems ludicrous to think of fashioning cigarettes to the consumers' needs at the point of sale, putting on filters and adjusting lengths to king size. The gross margin required to do such a job would put cigarettes in the price class of silverware and the number of people who could purchase on that basis would be very small. But mounting a diamond in a special setting is not at all ludicrous, because the gross margin available is large enough to undertake such adjustment. It would be redundant to go through the whole list of characteristics since it is perfectly clear what the relationships would be.

## The Role of Theory

Theory formulation and development adds a new dimension to the understanding of our field, that of abstractions. The concept of all goods and services being arrayed simultaneously, in accordance with the standards set by the characteristics of goods, at either end of the array, is a pure abstraction. It is a thought pattern that we can conceive mentally, but which in fact does not exist. Yet, such mentally conceived abstractions provide us with an understanding of where in relation to all other goods and services, a certain good exists in the array. This alone provides a quick comparison of the distribution channels of similar goods, and if the product is a new product, suggests the most likely channels to investigate.

The concept of the migration, over a period of time, of a good to new position in the array, suggests that distribution channels change and that the reassessment of the position of a good is essential to sound marketing. Thus, when a certain good entered the field as a strictly pharmaceutical good, it was promoted and distributed in much the same manner as other pharmaceutical goods, but later as its consumer acceptance developed, it was found that its characteristics had changed and that it was necessary to change both the promotion and distribution patterns to affect economic distribution. Here, again, is an abstract idea that provides the basis for understanding the need for change in the distribution pattern of a good as it migrated from one position to another in the array. These illustrations could be carried on endlessly, since every good has its unique and distinctive position in the array, as of a point in time, and literally the variations are limited only by the imagination of the theorist. Finally, the role of theory is the stimulation of creative thinking in any field of scientific investigation. We advance only as our creative thinking pushes outward the horizons of our understanding. This is the true role of theory.

# 16 —— Retail Strategy and the Classification of Consumer Goods

*Louis P. Bucklin*

Reprinted from *Journal of Marketing*, published by the American Marketing Association, Vol. 27 (January 1963), pp. 50-55. Reprinted by permission.

When Melvin T. Copeland published his famous discussion of the classification of consumer goods, shopping, convenience, and specialty goods, his intent was clearly to create a guide for the development of marketing strategies by manufacturers.[1] Although his discussion involved retailers and retailing, his purpose was to show how consumer buying habits affected the type of channel of distribution and promotional strategy that a manufacturer should adopt. Despite the controversy which still surrounds his classification, his success in creating such a guide may be judged by the fact that through the years few marketing texts have failed to make use of his ideas.

## Controversy over the Classification System

The starting point for the discussion lies with the definitions adopted by the American Marketing Association's Committee on Definitions for the classification system in 1948.[2] These are:

> *Convenience Goods:* Those consumers' goods which the customer purchases frequently, immediately, and with the minimum of effort.
>
> *Shopping Goods:* Those consumers' goods which the customer in the process of selection and purchase characteristically compares on such bases as suitability, quality, price and style.
>
> *Specialty Goods:* Those consumers' goods on which a significant group of buyers are habitually willing to make a special purchasing effort.

This set of definitions was retained in virtually the same form by the Committee on Definitions in its latest publication.[3]

Opposing these accepted definitions stands a critique by Richard H. Holton.[4] Finding the Committee's definitions too imprecise to be able to measure consumer buying behavior, he suggested that the following definitions not only would represent the essence of Copeland's original idea, but be operationally more useful as well.

*Convenience Goods:* Those goods for which the consumer regards the probable gain from making price and quality comparisons as small compared to the cost of making such comparisons.

*Shopping Goods:* Those goods for which the consumer regards the probable gain from making price and quality comparisons as large relative to the cost of making such comparisons.

*Specialty Goods:* Those convenience or shopping goods which have such a limited market as to require the consumer to make a special effort to purchase them.

Holton's definitions have particular merit because they make explicit the underlying conditions that control the extent of a consumer's shopping activities. They show that a consumer's buying behavior will be determined not only by the strength of his desire to secure some good, but by his perception of the cost of shopping to obtain it. In other words, the consumer continues to shop *for all goods* so long as he feels that the additional satisfactions from further comparisons are at least equal to the cost of making the additional effort. The distinction between shopping and convenience goods lies principally in the degree of satisfaction to be secured from further comparisons.

## The Specialty Good Issue

While Holton's conceptualization makes an important contribution, he has sacrificed some of the richness of Copeland's original ideas. This is essentially David J. Luck's complaint in a criticism of Holton's proposal.[5] Luck objected to the abandonment of the *willingness* of consumers to make a special effort to buy as the rationale for the concept of specialty goods. He regarded this type of consumer behavior as based upon unique consumer attitudes toward certain goods and not the density of distribution of those goods. Holton, in a reply, rejected Luck's point; he remained convinced that the real meaning of specialty goods could be derived from his convenience goods, shopping goods continuum, and market conditions.[6]

The root of the matter appears to be that insufficient attention has been paid to the fact that the consumer, once embarked upon some buying expedition, may have only one of two possible objectives in mind. A discussion of this aspect of consumer behavior will make possible a closer synthesis of Holton's contribution with the more traditional point of view.

## A Forgotten Idea

The basis for this discussion is afforded by certain statements, which the marketing profession has largely ignored over the years, in Copeland's original presentation of his ideas. These have regard to the extent of the consumer's awareness of the precise nature of the item he wishes to buy, *before* he starts his shopping trip. Copeland stated that the consumer, in both the case of convenience goods and specialty goods, has full knowledge of the particular good, or its acceptable substitutes, that he will buy before he commences his buying trip. The consumer, however, lacks this knowledge in the case of a shopping good.[7] This means that the buying trip must not only serve the objective of purchasing the good, but must enable the consumer to discover which item he wants to buy.

The behavior of the consumer during any shopping expedition may, as a result, be regarded as heavily dependent upon the state of his decision as to what he wants to buy. If the consumer knows precisely what he wants, he needs only to undertake communication activities sufficient to take title to the desired product. He may also undertake ancillary physical activities involving the handling of the product and delivery. If the consumer is uncertain as to what he wants to buy, then an additional activity will have to be performed. This involves the work of making comparisons between possible alternative purchases, or simply search.

There would be little point, with respect to the problem of classifying consumer goods, in distinguishing between the activity of search and that of making a commitment to buy, if a consumer always performed both before purchasing a good. The crucial point is that he does not. While most of the items that a consumer buys have probably been subjected to comparison at some point in his life, he does not make a search before each purchase. Instead, a past solution to the need is frequently remembered and, if satisfactory, is implemented.[8] Use of these past decisions for many products quickly moves the consumer past any perceived necessity of undertaking new comparisons and leaves only the task of exchange to be discharged.

## Redefinition of the System

Use of this concept of problem solving permits one to classify consumer buying efforts into two broad categories which may be called shopping and nonshopping goods.

### Shopping Goods

Shopping goods are those for which the consumer *regularly* formulates a new solution to his need each time it is aroused. They are goods whose suitability is determined through search before the consumer commits himself to each purchase.

The motivation behind this behavior stems from circumstances which tend to perpetuate a lack of complete consumer knowledge about the nature of the product that he would like to buy.[9] Frequent changes in price, style, or product technology cause consumer information to become obsolete. The greater the time lapse between purchases, the more obsolete will his information be. The consumer's needs are also subject to change, or he may seek variety in his purchases as an actual goal. These forces will tend to make past information inappropriate. New search, due to forces internal and external to the consumer, is continuously required for products with purchase determinants which the consumer regards as both important and subject to change.[10]

The number of comparisons that the consumer will make in purchasing a shopping good may be determined by use of Holton's hypothesis on effort. The consumer, in other words, will undertake search for a product until the perceived value to be secured through additional comparisons is less than the estimated cost of making those comparisons. Thus, shopping effort will vary according to the intensity of the desire of the consumer to find the right product, the type of product and the availability of retail facilities. Whether the consumer searches diligently, superficially, or even buys at the first opportunity, however, does not alter the shopping nature of the product.

## Nonshopping Goods

Turning now to nonshopping goods, one may define these as products for which the consumer is both willing and able to use stored solutions to the problem of finding a product to answer a need. From the remarks on shopping goods it may be generalized that nonshopping goods have purchase determinants which do not change, or which are perceived as changing inconsequentially, between purchases.[11] The consumer, for example, may assume that price for some product never changes or that price is unimportant. It may be unimportant because either the price is low, or the consumer is very wealthy.

Nonshopping goods may be divided into convenience and specialty goods by means of the concept of a preference map. Bayton introduces this concept as the means to show how the consumer stores information about products.[12] It is a rough ranking of the relative desirability of the different kinds of products that the consumer sees as possible satisfiers for his needs. For present purposes, two basic types of preference maps may be envisaged. One type ranks all known product alternatives equally in terms of desirability. The other ranks one particular product as so superior to all others that the consumer, in effect, believes this product is the only answer to his need.

## Distinguishing the Specialty Good

This distinction in preference maps creates the basis for discriminating between a convenience good and a specialty good. Clearly, where the consumer is indifferent to the precise item among a number of substitutes which he could buy, he will purchase the more accessible one and look no further. This is a convenience good. On the other hand, where the consumer recognizes only one brand of a product as capable of satisfying his needs, he will be willing to bypass more readily accessible substitutes in order to secure the wanted item. This is a specialty good.

However, most nonshopping goods will probably fall in between these two polar extremes. Preference maps will exist where the difference between the relative desirability of substitutes may range from the slim to the well marked. In order to distinguish between convenience goods and specialty goods in these cases, Holton's hypothesis regarding consumer effort may be employed again. A convenience good, in these terms, becomes one for which the consumer has such little preference among his perceived choices that he buys the item which is most readily available. A specialty good is one for which consumer preference is so strong that he bypasses, or would be willing to bypass, the purchase of more accessible substitutes in order to secure his most wanted item.

It should be noted that this decision on the part of the consumer as to how much effort he should expend takes place under somewhat different conditions than the one for shopping goods. In the nonshopping good instance the consumer has a reasonably good estimate of the additional value to be achieved by purchasing his preferred item. The estimate of the additional cost required to make this purchase may also be made fairly accurately. Consequently, the consumer will be in a much better position to justify the expenditure of additional effort here than in the case of shopping goods where much uncertainty must exist with regard to both of these factors.

### The New Classification

The classification of consumer goods that results from the analysis is as follows:

> *Convenience Goods:* Those goods for which the consumer, before his need arises, possesses a preference map that indicates a willingness to purchase any of a number of known substitutes rather than to make the additional effort required to buy a particular item.
>
> *Shopping Goods:* Those goods for which the consumer has not developed a complete preference map before the need arises, requiring him to undertake search to construct such a map before purchase.
>
> *Specialty Goods:* Those goods for which the consumer, before his need arises, possesses a preference map that indicates a willingness to expend the additional effort required to purchase the most preferred item rather than to buy a more readily accessible substitute.

## Extension to Retailing

The classification of the goods concept developed above may now be extended to retailing. As the concept now stands, it is derived from consumer attitudes or motives toward a *product*. These attitudes, or product motives, are based upon the consumer's interpretation of a product's styling, special features, quality, and social status of its brand name, if any. Occasionally the price may also be closely associated with the product by the consumer.

## Classification of Patronage Motives

The extension of the concept to retailing may be made through the notion of patronage motives, a term long used in marketing. Patronage motives are derived from consumer attitudes concerning the retail establishment. They are related to factors which the consumer is likely to regard as controlled by the retailer. These will include assortment, credit, service, guarantee, shopping ease and enjoyment, and usually price. Patronage motives, however, have never been systematically categorized. It is proposed that the procedure developed above to discriminate among product motives be used to classify consumer buying motives with respect to retail stores as well.

This will provide the basis for the consideration of retail marketing strategy and will aid in clearing up certain ambiguities that would otherwise exist if consumer buying motives were solely classified by product factors. These ambiguities appear, for example, when the consumer has a strong affinity for some particular brand of a product, but little interest in where he buys it. The manufacturer of the product, as a result, would be correct in defining the product as a specialty item if the consumer's preferences were so strong as to cause him to eschew more readily available substitutes. The retailer may regard it as a convenience good, however, since the consumer will make no special effort to purchase the good from any particular store. This problem is clearly avoided by separately classifying product and patronage motives.

The categorization of patronage motives by the above procedure results in the following three definitions. These are:

*Convenience Stores:* Those stores for which the consumer, before his need for some product arises, possesses a preference map that indicates a willingness to buy from the most accessible store.

*Shopping Stores:* Those stores for which the consumer has not developed a complete preference map relative to the product he wishes to buy, requiring him to undertake a search to construct such a map before purchase.

*Specialty Stores:* Those stores for which the consumer, before his need for some product arises, possesses a preference map that indicates a willingness to buy the item from a particular establishment even though it may not be the most accessible.

## The Product-Patronage Matrix

Although this basis will now afford the retailer a means to consider alternative strategies, a finer classification system may be obtained by relating consumer product motives to consumer patronage motives. By cross-classifying each product motive with each patronage motive, one creates a three-by-three matrix, representing nine possible types of consumer buying behavior. Each of the nine cells in the matrix may be described as follows:

1. *Convenience Store—Convenience Good:* The consumer, represented by this category, prefers to buy the most readily available brand of product at the most accessible store.
2. *Convenience Store—Shopping Good:* The consumer selects his purchase from among the assortment carried by the most accessible store.
3. *Convenience Store—Specialty Good:* The consumer purchases his favored brand from the most accessible store which has the item in stock.
4. *Shopping Store—Convenience Good:* The consumer is indifferent to the brand of product he buys, but shops among different stores in order to secure better retail service and/or lower retail price.
5. *Shopping Store—Shopping Good:* The consumer makes comparisons among both retail controlled factors and factors associated with the product (brand).
6. *Shopping Store—Specialty Good:* The consumer has a strong preference with respect to the brand of the product, but shops among a number of stores in order to secure the best retail service and/or price for this brand.
7. *Specialty Store—Convenience Good:* The consumer prefers to trade at a specific store, but is indifferent to the brand of product purchased.
8. *Specialty Store—Shopping Good:* The consumer prefers to trade at a certain store, but is uncertain as to which product he wishes to buy and examines the store's assortment for the best purchase.
9. *Specialty Store—Specialty Good:* The consumer has both a preference for a particular store and a specific brand.

Conceivably, each of these nine types of behavior might characterize the buying patterns of some consumers for a given product. It seems more likely, however, that the behavior of consumers toward a product could be represented by only three or four of the categories. The remaining cells would be empty, indicating that no consumers bought the product by these methods. Different cells, of course, would be empty for different products.

## The Formation of Retail Strategy

The extended classification system developed above clearly provides additional information important to the manufacturer in the planning of his marketing strategy. Of principal interest here, however, is the means by which the retailer might use the classification system in planning his marketing strategy.

## Three Basic Steps

The procedure involves three steps. The first is the classification of the retailer's potential customers for some product by market segment, using the nine categories in the consumer buying habit matrix to define the principal segments. The second requires the retailer to determine the nature of the marketing strategies necessary to appeal to each market segment. The final step is the retailer's selection of the market segment, and the strategy associated with it, to which he will sell. A simplified, hypothetical example may help to clarify this process.

A former buyer of dresses for a department store decided to open her own dress shop. She rented a small store in the downtown area of a city of 50,000, ten miles distant from a metropolitan center of several hundred thousand population. In contemplating her marketing strategy, she was certain that the different incomes, educational backgrounds, and tastes of the potential customers in her city meant that various groups of these women were using sharply different buying methods for dresses. Her initial problem was to determine, by use of the consumer buying habit matrix, what proportion of her potential market bought dresses in what manner.

By drawing on her own experience, discussions with other retailers in the area, census and other market data, the former buyer estimated that her potential market was divided, according to the matrix, in the following proportions.

**TABLE 1. Proportion of Potential Dress Market in Each Matrix Cell**

| *Buying Habit* | *% of Market* |
|---|---|
| Convenience store—Convenience good | 0 |
| Convenience store—Shopping good | 3 |
| Convenience store—Specialty good | 20 |
| Shopping store—Convenience good | 0 |
| Shopping store—Shopping good | 35 |
| Shopping store—Specialty good | 2 |
| Specialty store—Convenience good | 0 |
| Specialty store—Shopping good | 25 |
| Specialty store—Specialty good | 15 |
| | 100 |

This analysis revealed four market segments that she believed were worth further consideration. (In an actual situation, each of these four should be further divided into submarket segments according to other possible factors such as age, incomes, dress size required, location of residence, etc.)

Her next task was to determine the type of marketing mix which would most effectively appeal to each of these segments. The information for these decisions was derived from the characteristics of consumer behavior associated with each of the defined segments. The following is a brief description of her assessment of how elements of the marketing mix ought to be weighed in order to formulate a strategy for each segment.

## A Strategy for Each Segment

To appeal to the convenience store-specialty good segment she felt that the two most important elements in the mix should be a highly accessible location and a selection of widely-accepted brand merchandise. Of somewhat lesser importance, she found, were depth of assortment, personal selling, and price. Minimal emphasis should be given to store promotion and facilities.

She reasoned that the shopping store-shopping good requires a good central location, emphasis on price, and a broad assortment. She ranked store promotion, accepted brand names and personal selling as secondary. Store facilities would, once again, receive minor emphasis.

The specialty store-shopping good market would, she believed, have to be catered to with an exceptionally strong assortment, a high level of personal selling and more elaborate store facilities. Less emphasis would be needed upon prominent brand names, store promotions, and price. Location was of minor importance.

The specialty store-specialty good category, she thought, would require a marketing mix heavily emphasizing personal selling and highly elaborate store facilities and services. She also felt that prominent brand names would be required, but that these would probably have to include the top names in fashion, including labels from Paris. Depth of assortment would be secondary, while least emphasis would be placed upon store promotion, price, and location.

## Evaluation of Alternatives

The final step in the analysis required the former dress buyer to assess her abilities to implement any one of these strategies, given the degree of competition existing in each segment. Her considerations were as follows. With regard to the specialty store-specialty good market, she was unprepared to make the investment in store facilities and services that she felt would be necessary. She also thought, since a considerable period of time would probably be required for her to build up the necessary reputation, that this strategy involved substantial risk. Lastly, she believed that her experience in buying high fashion was somewhat limited and that trips to European fashion centers would prove burdensome.

She also doubted her ability to cater to the specialty store-shopping good market, principally because she knew that her store would not be large enough to carry the necessary assortment depth. She felt that this same factor wouild limit her in attempting to sell to the shopping store-shopping good market as well. Despite the presence of the large market in this segment, she believed that she would not be able to create sufficient volume in her proposed quarters to enable her to compete effectively with the local department store and several large department stores in the neighboring city.

The former buyer believed her best opportunity was in selling to the convenience store-specialty good segment. While there were already two other stores in her city which were serving this segment, she believed that a number of important brands were still not represented. Her past contacts with resources led her to believe that she would stand an excellent chance of securing a number of these lines. By stocking these brands, she thought that she could capture a considerable number of local customers who currently were purchasing them in the large city. In this way, she believed, she would avoid the full force of local competition.

### Decision

The conclusion of the former buyer to use her store to appeal to the convenience store-specialty good segment represents the culmination to the process of analysis suggested here. It shows how the use of the three-by-three matrix of consumer buying habits may aid the retailer in developing his marketing strategy. It is a device which can isolate the important market segments. It provides further help in enabling the retailer to associate the various types of consumer behavior with those elements of the marketing mix to which they are sensitive. Finally, the analysis forces the retailer to assess the probability of his success in attempting to use the necessary strategy in order to sell each possible market.

## ENDNOTES

1. Melvin T. Copeland, "Relation of Consumers' Buying Habits to Marketing Methods," *Harvard Business Review*, Vol. 1 (April, 1923), pp. 282-289.
2. Definitions Committee, American Marketing Association, "Report of the Definitions Committee," *Journal of Marketing*, Vol. 13 (October, 1948), pp. 202-217, at p. 206, p. 215.
3. Definitions Committee, American Marketing Association, *Marketing Definitions* (Chicago: American Marketing Association, 1960), p. 11, 21, 22.
4. Richard H. Holton, "The Distinction Between Convenience Goods, Shopping Goods, and Specialty Goods," *Journal of Marketing*, Vol. 23 (July, 1958), pp. 53-56.
5. David J. Luck, "On the Nature of Specialty Goods," *Journal of Marketing*, Vol. 24 (July, 1959), pp. 61-64.
6. Richard H. Holton, "What is Really Meant by 'Specialty' Goods?" *Journal of Marketing*, Vol. 24 (July, 1959), pp. 64-67.
7. Melvin T. Copeland, same reference as note 1, pp. 283-284.

8. George Katona, *Psychological Analysis of Economic Behavior* (New York: McGraw-Hill Book Co., Inc., 1951), p. 47.
9. Same reference, pp. 67-68.
10. George Katona and Eva Mueller, "A Study of Purchase Decisions in Consumer Behavior," Lincoln Clark, editor, *Consumer Behavior* (New York: University Press, 1954), pp. 30-87.
11. Katona, same reference as note 8, p. 68.
12. James A. Bayton, "Motivation, Cognition, Learning—Basic Factors in Consumer Behavior," *Journal of Marketing*, Vol. 22 (January, 1958), pp. 282-289, at p. 287.

# 17 — Product Classification Taxonomies: Synthesis and Consumer Implications

*Ben M. Enis and Kenneth J. Roering*

Reprinted from *Theoretical Development in Marketing,* published by the American Marketing Association, edited by Lamb and Dunne (1980), pp. 186-189. Reprinted by permission.

The search for a conceptually logical and managerially useful classification of products is a continuing theme in the marketing literature. Academicians and practitioners alike are aware of the limitations of extant classification schemes, yet regularly use these classification schemes in discussing marketing theory and strategy. Accordingly, the purpose of this manuscript is to review the work on product classification schemes and synthesize that work.

## Literature Review

The first classification was suggested by Copeland (1923). He argued that products could be grouped into three categories. Twenty-five years later the American Marketing Association's Committee on Definitions (1948) incorporated his ideas in the following definitions:

> *Convenience Goods:* Those consumers' goods which the customer purchases frequently, immediately and with the minimum of effort.
>
> *Shopping Goods:* Those consumers' goods which the customer in the process of selection and purchase characteristically compares on such bases as suitability, quality, price and style.
>
> *Specialty Goods:* Those consumers' goods on which a significant group of buyers are habitually willing to make a special purchasing effort.

This categorization is based on three underlying dimensions, the amount of travel effort the consumer was willing to undertake, the amount of effort the consumer was willing to undertake in comparing available alternative products, and the amount of effort incurred to obtain a particular brand. As a result, convenience products and shopping products were frequently considered the two extremes of an effort continuum, with specialty products typically, but never very satisfactorily, in between.

In an effort to clarify this issue, Holton (1958) suggested that specialty goods are "those shopping or convenience goods which have such a limited market as to require the consumer to make a special effort to purchase them." However, Luck (1959) argued that the essence of a specialty good was not its limited market but rather the brand insistence or the willingness of the consumer to make a special purchasing effort. Holton (1959) remained convinced that specialty goods were most accurately conceptualized through the convenience-shopping continuum. In the classic article in this area, Bucklin (1963) suggested that Holton had sacrificed some of the richness of Copeland's original conceptualization and offered the following clarification.

> *Convenience Goods:* Those goods for which the consumer, before his need arises, possesses a preference map that indicates a willingness to purchase any number of known substitutes rather than to make the additional effort required to buy a particular item.
>
> *Shopping Goods:* Those goods for which the consumer has not developed a complete preference map before the need arises, requiring him to undertake search to construct such a map before purchase.
>
> *Specialty Goods:* Those goods for which the consumer possesses a preference map that indicates a willingness to expend the additional effort required to purchase the most preferred item rather than to buy a more readily accessible substitute.

This clarification by Bucklin suggests that the underlying dimensions are the degree of shopping effort and the degree of prepurchase formation. Based on these two dimensions, Holbrook and Howard (1977) have argued that the traditional classification of goods must be expanded to a four category classification. In addition to convenience, shopping and specialty goods, they add preference goods—involving low shopping effort but high brand preference. More specifically, Holbrook and Howard drew upon the work of Kaish (1967) to specify three considerations: product characteristics, consumer characteristics, and consumer responses—to form their classification of goods. They offered a two-dimensional taxonomy, in which the vertical dimension represents the degree to which the consumer exerts physical shopping effort, and the horizontal dimension refers to the timing of mental effort in arriving at a brand choice.

Enis (1974) developed a similar approach, in which the vertical axis was consumer effort and the horizontal axis was consumer loyalty. This work, influenced by Holbrook & Howard and Prasad (1975), was updated (Enis, 1979a) to reflect the notion of range of consumer satisfaction/dissatisfaction as the basis for positioning a given product on each continuum.

Bucklin (1976) suggested that the substantial developments in multivariate techniques could provide major opportunities for effectively utilizing more operational measures of the classification criteria. Using the degree of perceived brand similarity within a product class and the degree of uncertainty that the consumer feels about making choices among the brands of a given product class as the axes in a two-dimensional space, Bucklin classified goods into the following categories—convenience, specialty, shopping (low intensity) and shopping (high intensity).

Although other marketing scholars (e.g., Aspinwall, 1962; Bourne, 1956; Dommermuth, 1965; Jolson & Proia, 1976; Mayer et al., 1971; Miracle, 1965; Ramond & Assael, 1974; Weber, 1976) have focused on various aspects of the classification of goods, the preceeding discussion essentially summarizes the major developments. We propose that the value of this work to marketing scholars and practitioners can be increased by modest extension and synthesis.

## The Proposed Product Taxonomy

Classification schemes are primarily qualitative in nature and, as Hunt (1976) so convincingly suggests in his discussion of the criteria for evaluating classificational schemata, characterized by ambiguity and imprecision. But such taxonomies continue to provide a logic which is readily understood, used and appreciated in marketing. It is perhaps this pervasiveness of impact which both challenges researchers to attempt to extend knowledge in this area and causes any effort to do so to be subjected to careful scrutiny. Consequently, any attempt to contribute to understanding of product classificatory schemes should commence with a clear articulation of key concepts.

Recent treatments of the term "product" (Kotler, 1980; Levitt, 1980) suggest that the concept can be better understood by specifically recognizing its different levels. In essence, a synthesis of their thinking (see Exhibit 1) suggests four levels of the concept: core product, product offering, augmented product, and potential product. The *core product* refers to the basic want-satisfying capability of a product. The *product offering* includes the core product as well as the brand image, styling, packaging, organizational reputation, etc. The *augmented product* refers to the product offering plus the marketing program of that offering (i.e., promotion, price, delivery and installation, warranties, etc.). The *potential product* refers to possible new or extended uses to which the augmented product could be put.

The product (total bundle of tangible and intangible attributes) is offered to the buyer by the marketer in exchange for payment (Bagozzi, 1975). Logically then, a classification scheme that incorporates both the buyer's and the seller's perspective holds the greatest promise for illuminating the exchange process, since exchange only occurs when there is sufficient congruence between these perspectives. We term this search for congruence between the buyer's and seller's perspective of a product the "product discrepancy gap," a concept somewhat similar to the discrepancy of assortment idea articulated by Alderson (1957).

Incorporating both participants of the exchange process requires that the product classification scheme be comprised of two major components. Each component must reflect analogous, although not identical, dimensions fundamental to that perspective. The marketer's perspective is illustrated in Exhibit 2(a). The two dimensions are product offering differentiation and

**EXHIBIT 1. The Total Product**

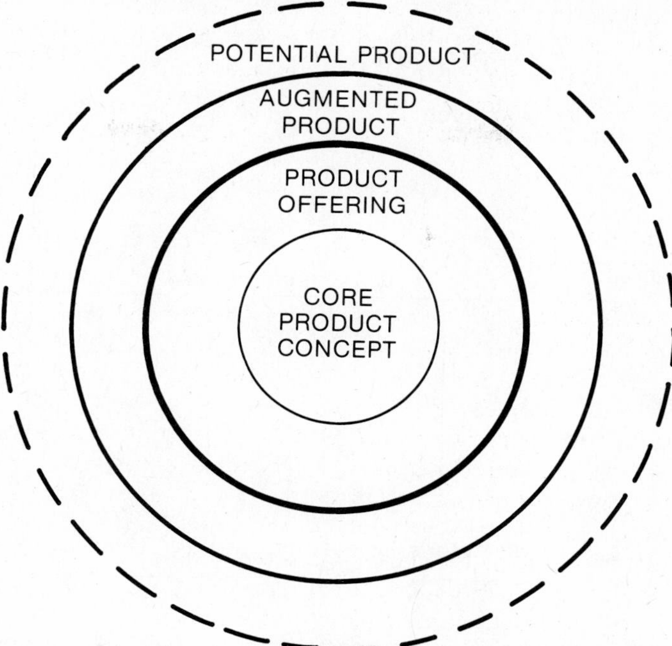


Source: Adapted and drawn by the authors form Levitt (1980) and Kotler (1980).

marketing program differentiation. Product differentiation is used in the conventional sense, that is, it refers to the capacity to develop perceived variation among products. Thus, high product differentiation connotes variety in product features, styles, quality—more ways to augment the basic product, less standardization of the product offering. This dimension is represented in Exhibit 1 as the area within the boldfaced circle.

Marketing program differentiation refers to the marketer's capacity to individualize the elements of a marketing program to better serve divergent groups within a market. That is, high marketing program differentiation connotes increased customization of the marketing mix, sharper focus on the wants and desires of individuals or small groups of buyers, and less standardization of marketing effort. This dimension is represented in Exhibit 1 as the doughnut-shaped space between the boldface and the dashed circles.

Based on these dimensions, products at the low end of the marketing differentiation continuum are characterized by mass advertising, intensive distribution, and standardized pricing. Products on the high end of the marketing program differentiation continuum are characterized by more individualized promotion appeals, selective or exclusive distribution, and negotiated pricing. Considering the horizontal dimension, one would reason that products on the low end of the product differentiation continuum are

**EXHIBIT 2. The Product Taxonomy**

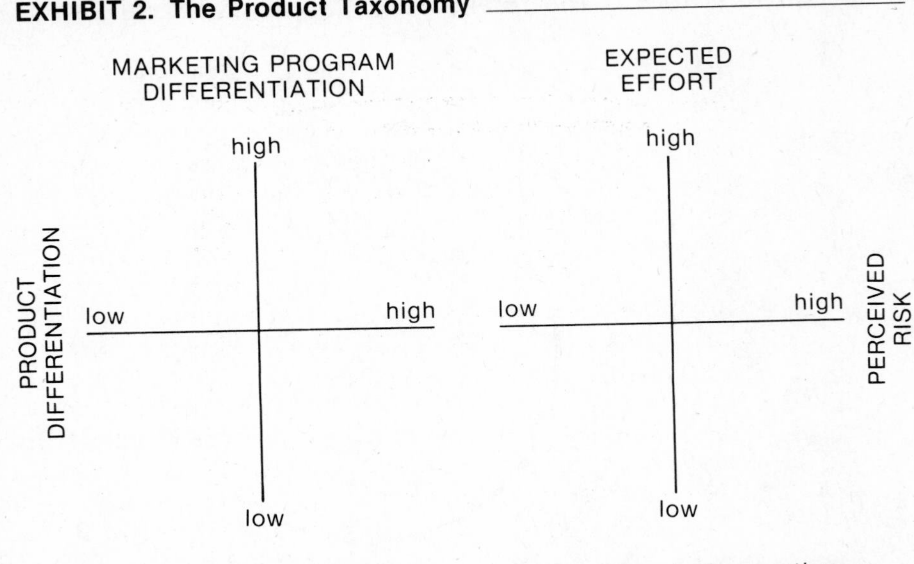


(a) The Marketer's Perspective (b) The Buyer's Perspective

characterized by dimensions normally associated with commonalities. That is, within a given product class, offerings of various marketers are quite similar in terms of physical characteristics, quality levels, grades, and performance characteristics. Highly differentiated products, on the other hand, are those which can be distinguished in terms of their form from others in the same class. The physical bases of the core product concept may be different, even though consumers may perceive these different products as capable of satisfying similar wants.

This comment suggests the need for part (b) of Exhibit 2: the product taxonomy from the buyer's perspective. In this case the two dimensions are expected effort and perceived risk. Perceived risk, the horizontal axis, refers to the belief that the consequences of a purchase decision may be more unpleasant or unfavorable than the buyer perceives them to be. Products at the low end of the perceived risk continuum are products which the buyer is confident will perform as expected and will be perceived by others in a familiar way. Products at the other end of the continuum are those for which the consumer lacks confidence regarding expected product performance. That is, the buyer is uncertain about the expected performance of the product, and/or social reaction to the product.

For products on the low end of the perceived risk continuum the buyer is rather confident of his/her ability to assess expected product performance. Thus, the pereived risk is inconsequential, even for products requiring considerable effort. Products at the high end of the risk continuum are those about which the buyer is unable to accurately discern the expected product performance.

The vertical axis of the buyer's perspective depicts the amount of effort the buyer must exert to complete the exchange transaction. Products on the high end of the expected effort continuum would typically be high in unit value and/or ego involvement, and/or purchased infrequently. As a result, the buyer is willing to exert considerable effort to acquire them. Expected effort has a number of aspects—physical, mental, affective, and temporal. Typically, significant amounts of money must be earned to purchase them, large amounts of information processed, considerable time invested. In general, such products precipitate extensive problem solving. This type of product probably follows the traditional sequence of purchase behavior: cognition, attitude change, purchase.

Products toward the low end of the effort continuum, on the other hand, are not that significant to the buyer and therefore will not precipitate such a deliberate sequence of behavior. At a given time, the desire for them may be acute, but effort expended to acquire them will not be great. These are products that are low in unit cost and/or have low ego involvement, and/or are purchased frequently and consumed quickly. Since the cost of experimentation via actual purchase is low, it may be argued that these products would follow the behavioral sequence identified in the recent literature as cognition, behavior, then attitude change (Olshavsky & Granbois, 1979).

In summary, each of the resulting quadrants is labeled respectively (I) specialty, (II) shopping, (III) convenience, and (IV) preference. Exhibit 3 provides examples.

**EXHIBIT 3. Examples of Products Classified**

| *Specialty* | *Shopping* | *Convenience* | *Preference* |
|---|---|---|---|
| Mercedes | light truck | umbrella | beer |
| machinery | computer | salt | detergent |
| museum | apartment | paper clips | grease |
| surgery | insurance | taxi | TV show |
| tax counsel | travel tour | shoeshine | airline |
| church | gambling | laborer | prostitute |
| ERA | college | police | politician |

Note that we have attempted to provide diverse examples of each type of product. Included are consumer goods, industrial goods, services desired by household consumers and organizational buyers, products that are legally exchanged and those marketed outside the law.

For exchange to occur, sufficient effort must be expended by buyer and/or marketer to bridge the product discrepancy gap. This is accomplished by seeking congruence between the marketer's product offering/marketing program and the buyer's perceived effort/expected risk evaluation of that offering (Bonoma, Bagozzi & Zaltman, 1978). That is, buyers and sellers are active participants, attempting to make satisfactory linkages betwen their respective conceptions of the product.

The two perspectives are separated in the terms of utility, (i.e., form, time, place, and/or possession) of the product. Both buyer and seller attempt to develop a logical and useful view of their product utility and that of their counterparts via the exchange flows of product configuration, information, distribution and pricing or valuation (see Kotler, 1972; Enis and Mokwa, 1979b). Where there is a joining or bridging of the two perspectives, a common understanding of product benefits and costs results and exchange is possible. The product discrepancy gap can be bridged, as shown in Exhibit 4.

**EXHIBIT 4. Bridging the Product Discrepancy Gap**

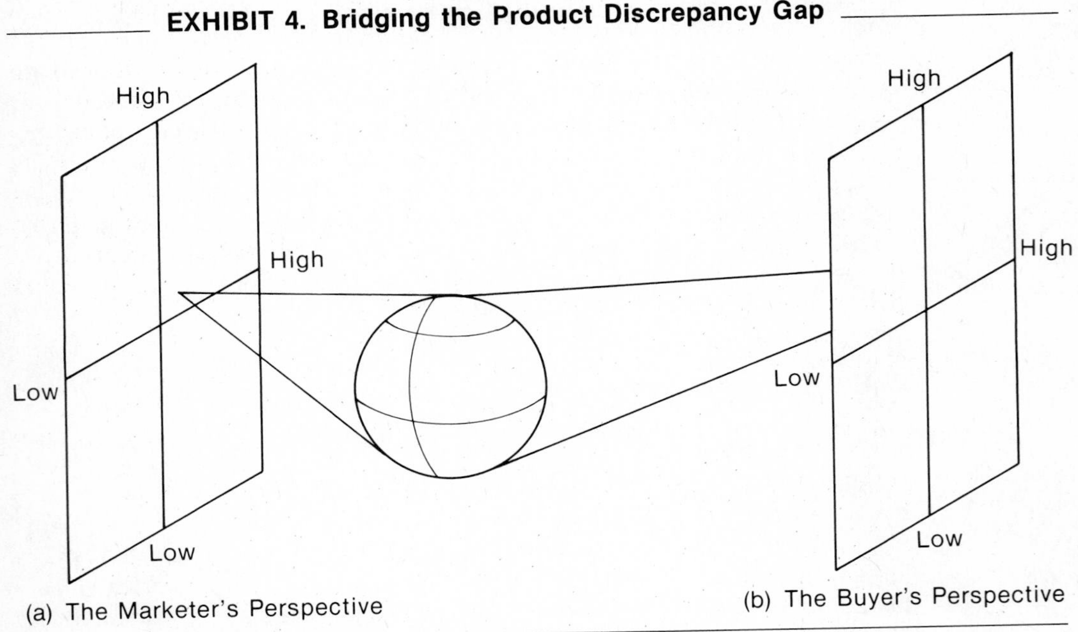


(a) The Marketer's Perspective (b) The Buyer's Perspective

## Conclusions and Research Implications

In summary, Exhibit 5 depicts the following synthesis of product classification taxonomies:

*Specialty products* are those bundles of attributes which the buyer perceives might involve high risk with respect to performance and/or interpersonal influence, and are worthy of significant shopping effort; thus the marketer of such products can differentiate both the product offering and its marketing program.

*Shopping products* are those attribute bundles which the buyer perceives are not likely to involve high performance or interpersonal risks, but are worth considerable shopping effort; thus the marketer's task is to differentiate via the marketing program a commodity—a core concept and product offering rather similar to that of competitors.

*Convenience products* are those attribute bundles perceived to be a low risk and expected to be worth little effort, thus the marketer must efficiently produce and distribute a product which is difficult to differentiate in terms of either product offering or marketing program.

*Preference products* are those attribute bundles which the buyer perceives to possibly involve high risk, but expects to exert only limited shopping effort; thus the marketer can differentiate the product offering, but must then mass market that offering efficiently.

This taxonomy has several advantages. First, it explicitly recognizes the dyadic nature of exchange relationships. Second, it appears to reconcile the debate between students of services marketing and proponents of a single general marketing strategy process for all products. The description of a product as an intangible service focuses on the core product concept, which may indeed differ from the tangible core of a good. If the total attribute bundles of the two cores are expected to yield similar benefits to buyers,

**EXHIBIT 5. The Complete Product Taxonomy**

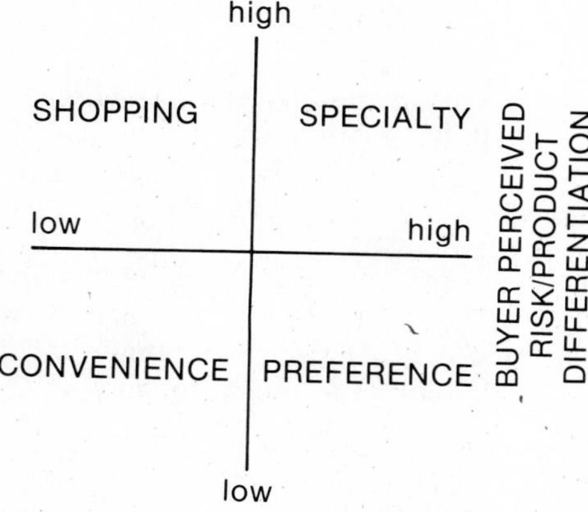

however, then the process of marketing those total products will probably also be similar. Third, the taxonomy provides at least broad guidelines for the development of macro segmentation strategies (see Wind & Cardozo, 1974) upon which specific marketing plans can profitably be based. The schema is intuitively appealing, and we believe, logically sound. Empirical verification is the next step.

This step will not be easy. A number of issues are involved. First, we recognize that not all customers view the same "product" in the same way. Some confusion exists in the marketing literature because the basic core concept is stated when total product is meant.

A second difficulty is that these perceptions and expectations vary with stage in the buying process. A buyer encountering a new purchasing situation for the first time may perceive it as quite risky. Subsequent buying decisions of the same product, however, may be based upon habitual repurchase of the same brand. This suggests that the concept of buyer loyalty may be more complex than the literature generally indicates (for an excellent review of problems here, see Jacoby & Chestnut, 1978).

A third aspect of the product taxonomy which could be tested empirically is its relationship to post-purchase satisfaction or dissatisfaction. Our hypothesis is that satisfaction/dissatisfaction is related to the quadrant in which the buyer locates a given product. It may be, for example, that shopping goods have the highest potential for buyer dissatisfaction, since we believe that buyers perceive such products to be low risk, but also expect to invest considerable effort in obtaining them. Thus, product benefits which do not meet these expectations may cause the most severe expressions of dissatisfaction.

## SELECTED REFERENCES

Alderson, W. (1957), *Marketing Behavior and Executive Action*, Homewood, IL: Richard D. Irwin, Inc.

Aspinwall, L. V. (1961), "The Marketing Characteristics of Goods," *Four Marketing Theories*, Boulder, CO: University of Colorado, 16-21.

Bonoma, T. V., R. Bagozzi and G. Zaltman (1978), "The Dyadic Paradigm with Specific Application Toward Industrial Marketing," *Organizational Buying Behavior*, Bonoma and Zaltman, eds., Chicago, IL: American Marketing Association, 49-66.

Bourne, F. S. (1956), *Group Influence in Marketing and Public Relations*, Ann Arbor, MI: Foundation for Research on Human Behavior, 1-8.

Bucklin, L. P. (1963), "Retail Strategy and the Classification of Consumer Goods," *Journal of Marketing* (January), 51-6.

——— (1976), "Retrospective Comment on Retail Strategy and the Classification of Consumer Goods," *The Great Writings in Marketing*, Howard A. Thompson, ed., Plymouth, MI: The Commerce Press, 382-8.

Copeland, M. T. (1923), "Relation of Consumer's Buying Habits to Marketing Methods," *Harvard Business Review* (April), 282-9.

Dommermuth, W. P. (1965), "The Shopping Matrix and Marketing Strategy," *Journal of Marketing Research* (May), 128-32.

Enis, B. M. (1974), *Marketing Principles*, Santa Monica, CA: Goodyear Publishing Company, 321-5.

——— (1979a), "Countering the Goods/Service Dichotomy: An Alternative Taxonomy for Product Strategy," Proceedings of Sixth International Research Seminar in Marketing, Jean-Paul Leonardi, ed., Gordes, France: Institut d' Administration Des Enterprise, A1-18.

——— and M. P. Mokwa (1979b) "The Marketing Management Matrix: A Taxonomy for Strategy Comprehension," *Conceptual and Theoretical Developments in Marketing Proceedings*, Ferrell et al., eds., Chicago, IL: American Marketing Association, 485-500.

Holbrook, M. B. and J. A. Howard (1977), "Frequently Purchased Nondurable Goods and Services," *National Science Foundation Project on Consumer Behavior*, Robert Ferber, ed., Washington, D. C.: National Science Foundation, 189-222.

Holton, R. M. (1958), "The Distinction Between Convenience Goods, Shopping Goods, and Specialty Goods," *Journal of Marketing* (July), 53-6.

——— (1959), "What is Really Meant by 'Specialty' Goods?" *Journal of Marketing* (July), 64-7.

Hunt, D. (1976), *Marketing Theory*, Columbus, OH: Grid, Inc.

Jacoby, J. and R. W. Chestnut (1978), *Brand Loyalty Measurement and Management*, New York, NY: John Wiley.

Jolson, M. A. and S. L. Proia (1976), "Classification of Consumer Goods—A Subjective Measure?" in *Marketing: 1776-1976 and Beyond*, Kenneth L. Bernhardt, ed., Chicago, IL: American Marketing Association, 71-5.

Kaish, S. (1967), "Cognitive Dissonance and the Classification of Consumer Goods," *Journal of Marketing* (October), 28-31.

Kotler, P. (1980), *Marketing Management*, 4th edition, Englewood Cliffs, NJ: Prentice-Hall, Inc., 351-4.

Levitt, T. (1980), "Marketing Success Through Differentiation—Of Anything," *Harvard Business Review* (January-February), 83-91.

Luck, D. J. (1959), "On the Nature of Specialty Goods," *Journal of Marketing* (July), 61-4.

Mayer, M. L. and J. B. Mason, and M. Gee (1971), "A Reconceptualization of Store Classification as Related to Retail Strategy Formulation," *Journal of Retailing* (Fall), 27-36.

Miracle, G. E. (1965), "Product Characteristics and Marketing Strategy," *Journal of Marketing* (January), 18-24.

Olshavsky, R. W. and D. H. Granbois (1979), "Consumer Decision Making—Fact or Fiction?" *Journal of Consumer Research* (September), 93-101.

Prasad, V. K. (1975), "Socioeconomic Risk and Patronage Preferences of Retail Shoppers," *Journal of Marketing* (July), 41-7.

Ramond, C. K. and N. Assael (1974), "An Empirical Framework for Product Classification," *Models and Buyer Behavior*, Jagdish Sheth, ed., Evanston, IL: Harper and Row, 347-362.

"Report of the Definitions Committee," (1948), *Journal of Marketing* (October), 202-17.

Weber, J. A. (1976), *Growth Opportunity Analysis*, Reston, VA: Reston Publishing Company, Ind., 118-125.

Wind, Y. and R. Cardozo (1974), "Industrial Market Segmentation," *Industrial Marketing Management* (3), 153-66.

# SECTION F
# Functional School

The functional school of thought is assumed to be the oldest school of thought in marketing. It has focused on the functions performed by institutions with which marketing was associated in the early 1900s. Although the functional school of thought probably has the most fundamental perspective, it has attracted very little attention among marketing scholars in recent years. We believe there are several reasons for this low involvement.

First, the functional school has focused on the operations of the marketing organization. As such, it is a very descriptive school that does not seem to provide any rationale for why functions are performed by institutions or for the way they are performed. In other words, it is lacking in a strategic perspective. It would be extremely important if we generated some fundamental constructs that could suggest who should perform what functions. For example, it is possible to suggest that functions should be performed by different institutions, including the consumers and the producers, based on their expertise and cost/benefit analyses. Then it would be possible to allocate functions using these two criteria to achieve an optimal distribution of various functions.

Second, the functional school of marketing has been bogged down in generating lists of functions and their groupings. While this classification scheme is good to know, it does not enable managers to decide what to do with them. Even the excellent classification of demand generation and demand satisfaction as two major objectives of the marketing function seems to be not very useful for managerial purposes.

Finally, the functional school of marketing has not borrowed any concepts from other disciplines, such as microeconomics (theory of the firm), to create a scientific basis for the theory. For example, the older concepts of value chain, recently revitalized by Michael Porter in terms of competitive advantage, can become extremely useful frameworks for enhancing the importance and image of the functional school of marketing.

# 18 — Some Problems in Market Distribution

*Arch Shaw*

Abridged from *Quarterly Journal of Economics,* Vol. 26 (August 1912), pp. 706-765.

## Introduction

The business man is concerned with the production and distribution of goods. Factory production he finds relatively well organized. The era of the rule of thumb is passing, and the progressive business man can call upon the production expert, technically trained, to assist him in solving his problems of production. But the marketing of the product has received little attention. As yet there has hardly been an attempt even to bring together, describe, and correlate the facts concerning commerical distribution. Selling is on a purely empirical basis.

The progress that has been made in organizing production is the result of systematic study. For centuries attention has been concentrated on the problems of production. Methods of study that have proven fruitful in other fields have been applied to the problems of manufacture and a body of organized knowledge is being built up.

Now the problems of market distribution are no less worthy of systematic study than are the problems of factory production. It is as essential that the finished goods be moved from the stock room of the producer to the hands of the consumer, as it is that operations be performed upon the raw material to produce the finished goods. And the problems of marketing are even more complicated than the problems of manufacturing, because the human factor is of more direct importance. Hence the rule of thumb can be less depended upon in distribution than in production.

Why has not systematic study been given to the problems of distribution? The explanation is found in a glance back in our economic history. Chief among the causes for the industrial changes leading to the establishment of the factory system in England in the eighteenth century was the constant widening of the market. It was a rapidly increasing pressure on the producer for greater quantities of staple articles for mass consumption that gave incentive to the revolution in the method of production. For a century thereafter the necessity of supplying a continually widening market, as means of transportation steadily improved and the population increased with unprecedented rapidity, made production the dominant problem. Economic conditions have put the emphasis on production.

Where the felt need is greatest, there will the organizing ability of the human race concentrate itself. The problems of production were sensed as the most pressing that faced society. He who improved methods of manufacture to increase output or reduce cost reaped a large reward. Hence the ablest minds were drawn toward the solution of those problems. The business manager gave his best thought to the difficult task of producing more goods at lower cost. The constantly widening market made selling a simple problem.

As a result we have built up a relatively efficient organization of production. While much remains to be done, the resources of modern science are being utilized to improve and organize our agencies of production. The development of producing capacity has been tremendous. New processes have been and are being introduced. New forces have been called into play. Methods are constantly being scrutinized to effect a more economical and efficient organization of production. The recent introduction in many industries of so-called ''scientific management'' is only a partial crystallization of long years of progress.

While we are but upon the threshold of the possibilities of efficiency in production, the progress thus far made has outstripped the existing system of distribution. If our producing possibilities are to be fully utilized, the problems of distribution must be solved. A market must be found for the goods potentially made available. This means, in the main, a more intensive cultivation of existing markets. The unformulated wants of the individual must be ascertained and the possibility of gratifying them brought to his attention....

The most pressing problem of the business man today, therefore, is systematically to study distribution, as production is being studied. In this great task he must enlist the trained minds of the economist and the psychologist. He must apply to his problems the methods of investigation that have proven of use in the more highly developed fields of knowledge. He must introduce the laboratory point of view. To that end, an attempt is here made to outline some of the problems of commercial distribution from the point of view of the business man, to analyze them, and to point out some methods of systematic study of these problems.

## Present Day Problem of the Distributor

The problem presented by the United States as a consuming market is a complex one. Here are ninety-odd million people distributed over an area of more than 3,000,000 square miles (excluding Alaska). Some are gathered in the large cities, where millions jostle elbows. Some are scattered over great areas with considerable distances between them and their neighbors. Some daily pass hundreds of retail stores; some must ride miles to reach the nearest store. Wide extremes in purchasing power exist. Millions have a purchasing power scarcely sufficient to obtain for themselves the barest necessities of life. A few can satisfy the most extravagant whims of the human imagination. Between these extremes lie all degrees of purchasing power, the number in each class becoming greater as you descend in the scale of purchasing power.

Their wants are as varied as their purchasing power. Environment, education, social custom, individual habits, and all the variations in body and mind tend to render human wants diverse. In each individual there are certain conscious needs being constantly gratified by the purchase of goods produced for such gratification. Then there are the conscious needs which go ungratified because of the limitations upon purchasing power and the existence of other needs of greater felt importance. And then there are the unformulated, subconscious needs which fail of expression because the individual is ignorant of the existence of goods which would gratify them....

The accepted system of distribution was built up on the satisfying of staple needs. The pressure of the market discussed above made it unnecessary for the business man to search out unformulated human needs. Only in recent years, when the development of production, potentially outstripped the available market, has shifted the emphasis to distribution, has the business man become a pioneer on the frontier of human wants. Today the more progressive business man is searching out the unconscious needs of the consumer, is producing the goods to gratify them, is bringing to the attention of the consumer the existence of such goods, and in response to an expressed demand, is transporting the goods to the consumer. The task is one of adjustment. The materials and forces of nature must be bent to human use....

## The Middleman in Distribution

The middleman is a by-product of a complex industrial organization. Chart IV shows in rough outline the evolution of the middleman from the early period when producer dealt directly with consumer to the appearance of the orthodox type of distribution (late in the eighteenth century and in the first quarter of the nineteenth century) when a complicated series of middlemen existed. It should be noted that this chart represents the typical case of the domestic product rather than that of imported commodities.

In the more primitive barter economy, the producer deals directly with the consumer, and middlemen take no part in the transaction. In the mediaeval period, as the handicrafts became specialized occupations under a town market regime, the producer is a retailer and sells directly to the consumers. Then as the market widens, a division of labor is necessary and the merchant appears as an organizer of the market. The handicraftsman becomes a steady worker, no longer concerning himself with selling. He becomes in many cases practically an employee of the merchant-retailer, who provides the stock and bears the risk. The merchant takes the finished goods from the producer and sells them to the consumer.

## CHART IV. Evolution of the Middleman

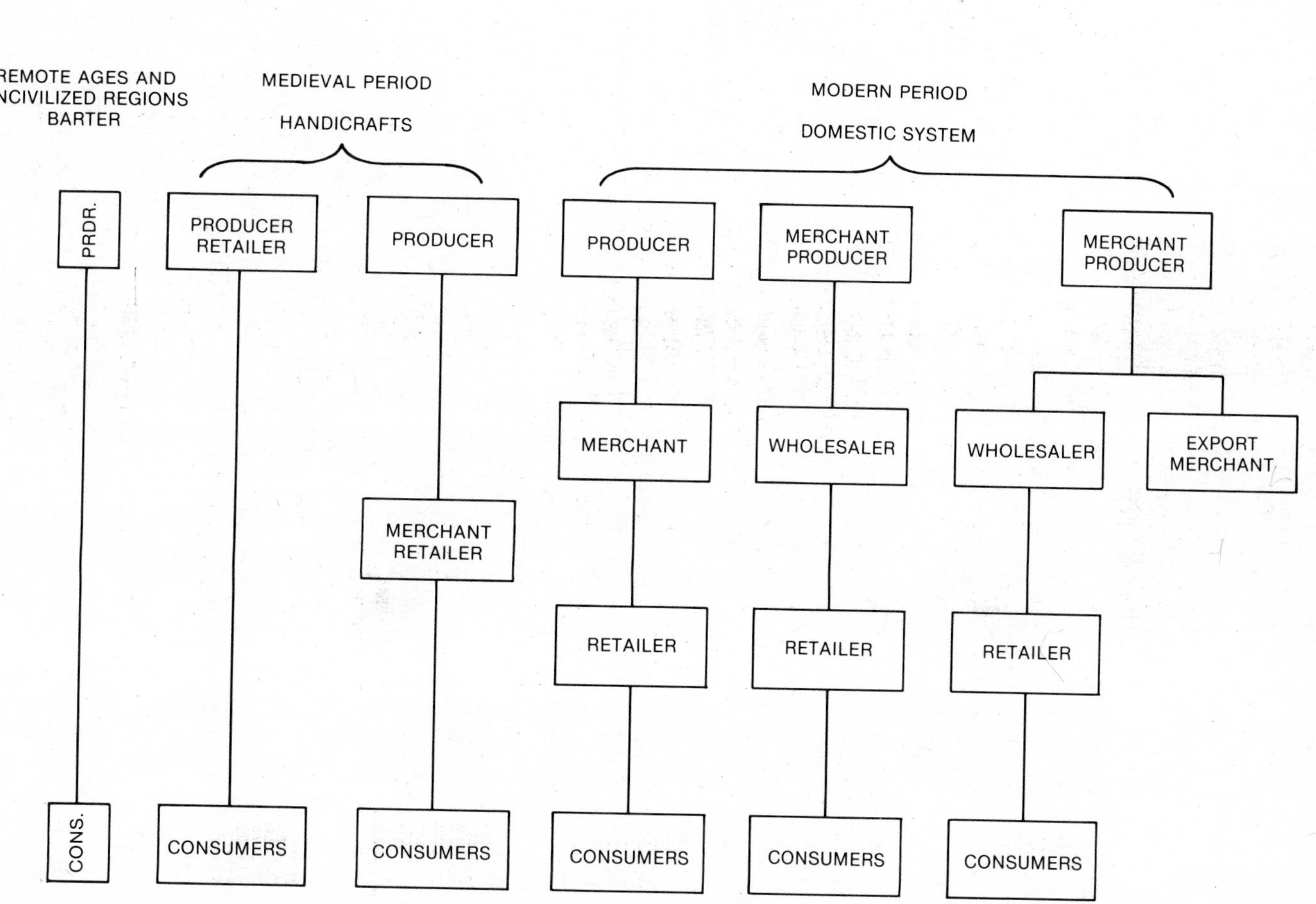

Steadily the market widens until we find a national market. The merchant is no longer a single intermediary between the producer and the consumer. The merchant who takes the goods from the producer disposes of them to retail merchants who in turn distribute them to the consumer. After a long period, we find the producers gradually strengthening their financial position, and freeing themselves from the control of a single merchant. They become merchant-producers. They assume the burden of production, and dispose of the product to various wholesalers who in turn sell to retailers, and they to the consumers. As a world market appears, the producer disposes of a part of his product to the export merchant.

In the early days of the factory system, shown in Chart V, we find that the producers have lost their character as merchants and are devoting themselves to the problems of production. The pressure on production has continued, and with the increasing intricacy of industry producers have found it necessary to concentrate their attention on production. The selling agent appears as a link in the chain of distribution to relieve the producer of the task of selling his product. The selling agent undertakes to sell the entire output of the producer, distributes it among wholesalers, who in turn distribute it to retailers, and the retailers to the consuming public.

This may be termed the orthodox type in distribution, a type almost universal in the early decades of the nineteenth century, and still common, as in the textile industry in New England.

Just as the long period of development from a system of barter economy to the early decades of the factory system showed a continuous tendency for increase in the number of middlemen intervening between the producer and the consumer, so recent years have shown a growing tendency to decrease the number of successive steps in distribution. The tendency is apparent in nearly every industry and has been clearly marked in recent years.

Under the orthodox type of distribution, with numerous middlemen intervening between the producer and the consumer, the producer is in a position of disadvantage. The fixed charges under which he operates render it necessary that he operate continuously. The outlet for his goods, however, is controlled by middlemen. Hence the middleman is able to exert pressure upon the producer and force a narrowing of his margin of profit. To free themselves from this pressure, the stronger merchant-producers seek to go around the immediate middlemen, thus decreasing the number of steps in the system of distribution.

Chart V is an attempt to show diagrammatically the development of this tendency to decrease the number of successive middlemen. By the use of salesmen going directly to the wholesaler and by advertising directed to the retailer the producer has displaced the selling agent in many cases. Sometimes the advertising is directed not only to the retailers but also to the wholesalers. To strengthen still farther his position the producer will often use advertising directed to the consumer to build up a demand for

**CHART V. Modern Tendency to Reduce Number of Successive Middlemen**

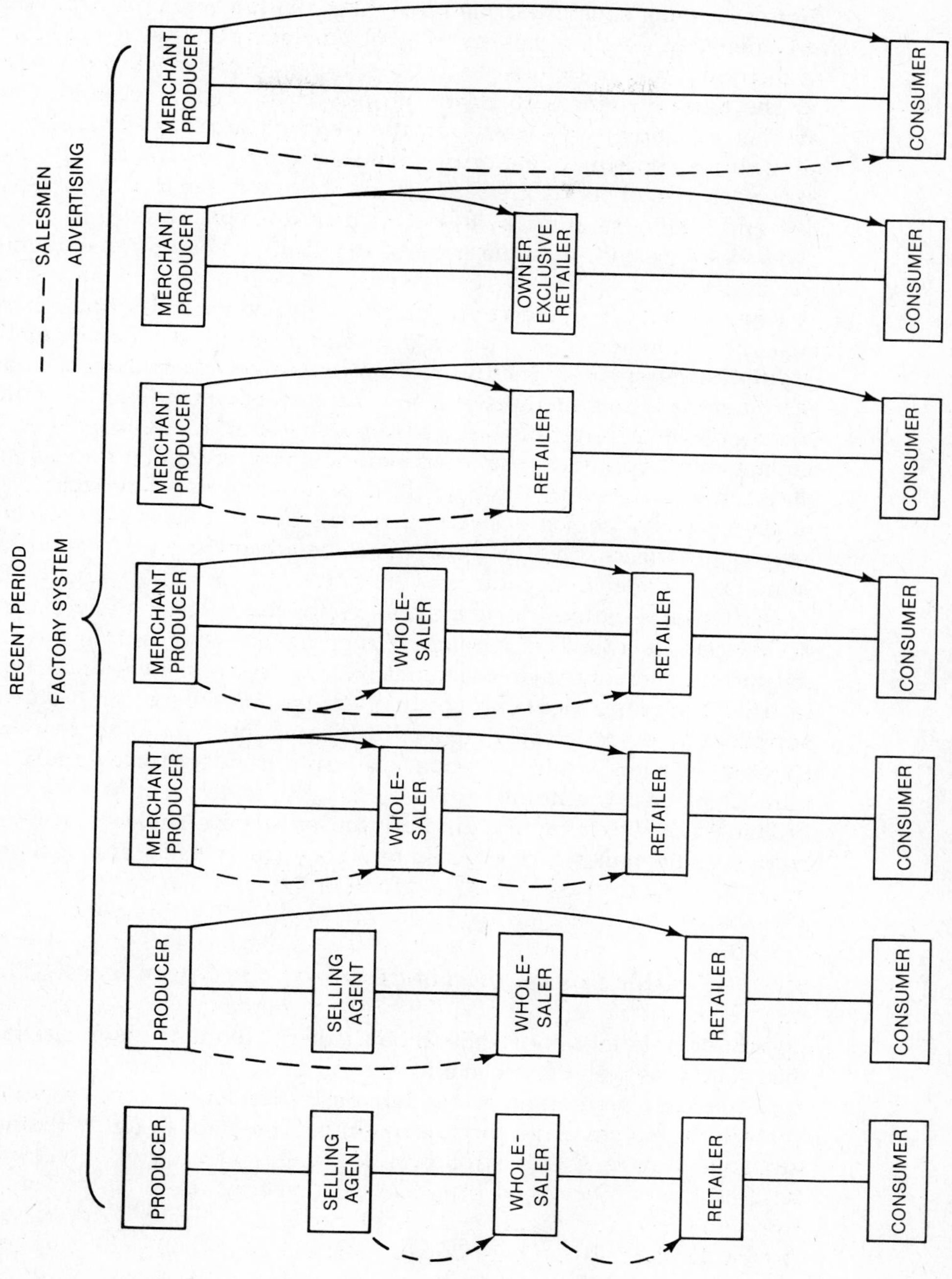

RECENT PERIOD

FACTORY SYSTEM

– – – – SALESMEN

——— ADVERTISING

PRODUCER

SELLING AGENT

WHOLE-SALER

RETAILER

CONSUMER

PRODUCER

SELLING AGENT

WHOLE-SALER

RETAILER

CONSUMER

MERCHANT PRODUCER

WHOLE-SALER

RETAILER

CONSUMER

MERCHANT PRODUCER

WHOLE-SALER

RETAILER

CONSUMER

MERCHANT PRODUCER

RETAILER

CONSUMER

MERCHANT PRODUCER

OWNER EXCLUSIVE RETAILER

CONSUMER

MERCHANT PRODUCER

CONSUMER

his product. This involves the necessity for a product differentiated by trade mark, brand, or trade name. When the producer thus directly builds up a demand among consumers, he often takes the further step of sending his salesmen to the retailer, thus omitting the wholesaler entirely from his system of distribution.

The most extreme step in the process is the complete elimination of middlemen, and the sale direct from the merchant-producer to the consumer, either by advertising alone or by salesmen supplemented by advertising. Manufacturers of specialities have largely adopted this scheme of distribution and the enormous growth of the mail order business in recent years gives evidence that in some lines of distribution there are economies in this system.

The tendency to decrease the number of middlemen is one of the most characteristic features of modern distribution. It promises to show much greater development in the future if present economic conditions substantially continue. The attempts of associations of retailers to check the growth of direct selling have thus far not been successful. In their desire to force the manufacturer to dispose of his product through regular trade channels they sometimes invoke the boycott. But our common state statutes, prohibiting combinations in restraint of trade, prevent effective agreements to boycott producers who sell direct. And the advantages of direct selling in some lines render the producer willing to incur the disfavor of the trade.

It should be noted, however, that changed conditions might give the middleman increased importance. Suppose, for instance, that the protective tariff system of the United States were to be swept away and free trade instituted. The middleman could then draw upon the foreign producer for supplies of unbranded staple goods, which might serve to increase his importance as a link in our system of distribution. While this would perhaps tend to increase the number of successive middlemen in some lines, it is probable that when the foreign producer in turn was subjected to pressure by the middleman, he, too, would tend to go around him and deal directly with the consumer.

## ANALYSIS OF THE FUNCTIONS OF THE MIDDLEMAN

To understand what seems to be a present tendency to go around the middleman as well as to consider the problem of the merchant-producer with reference to the use of middlemen in distribution, it is necessary to analyze the functions performed by the middleman. Roughly the general functions may be listed as follows:

1. Sharing the risk.
2. Transporting the goods.
3. Financing the operations.

4. Selling (communication of ideas about the goods).
5. Assembling, assorting, and re-shipping.

These functions were at first taken over by areas; that is, each successive middleman in the series took over a part of each function. Each took the risk of destruction of the goods while he held title. Each took the risk of credit losses. Each took a share in the transportation of the goods along the route from the producer's stock room to the hands of the consumers. Each took a part in financing the entire operation. Each had a part in the selling, disposing of the goods he purchased to succeeding middlemen and finally to the consumer. And each finally took a part in assembling, assorting, and re-shipping the goods to make them physically available to the consumer.

But at a relatively early date a taking over of these functions by kind instead of by area appeared. Today we have what may be termed functional middlemen in the insurance companies, direct transportation companies, and banks.

The insurance company is in a real sense a middleman in distribution. When it insures the producer against loss of goods by fire, against credit losses, and the like, it is taking over the function of risk formerly shared by successive middlemen. Today the insurance comapny will assume practically the entire element of risk. It is possible, for instance, for a large department store to insure against unseasonable holiday weather. The insurance company differs from the ordinary middleman in that it takes over one function as such rather than portions of a number of functions.

So improvements in direct transportation have enabled the producer to turn to a functional middleman to convey the goods to the consumer. The transportation companies and the express companies are in a true sense middlemen in distribution, tho they perform but one of the functions formerly shared by the successive middlemen who took over functions by area. The physical conveyance of the goods to the consumer was formerly one of the most important functions performed by a series of middlemen. Hence every improvement in the agencies of direct transportation has tended to modify existing systems of distribution. It is this fact that give enormous importance to the projected establishment of a parcels post. The innovation will, of necessity, carry with it radical readjustments in our present system of distribution.

So the function of financing the operations has largely been taken from the regular middleman. In former times the middleman took his part in the burden of finance in addition to his other functions. It is true today in the textile industry in New England that the selling agent is as much a banker as a mere agency for the sale of the goods. This is accomplished, however, by the selling agent endorsing the commerical paper of the producer, giving a two name paper acceptable by savings banks in that region, and hence making possible a lower rate of interest.

In most industries today the bank, as a functional middleman, cares for the element of finance in the operations of distribution. By advancing on goods and on commerical paper, it largely absorbs the function of finance in distribution. Legislation providing for an asset currency based on commercial paper might considerably widen the range of the banks' activity in the commercial field.

Another development has lessened the dependence of the producer upon the middleman for financial assistance. The application of the corporate form to industrial organization has made it possible to draw together larger bodies of operating capital and hence to place the producer in a stronger financial position.

As a result of the development of functional middlemen, ready to take over the functions of sharing the risk, transporting the goods, and financing the operations, the importance of middleman for these functions has diminished. There remain the function of selling (the communication of ideas about the goods) and the function of assembling, assorting, and re-shipping. It is as to these functions that the middleman is of most importance today.

Under the orthodox type of distribution which we have considered above, the producer is not in any sense a merchant. The selling agent takes upon himself the initial distribution of the entire output. He sells the goods to the wholesaler. The basis of the sale is that the wholesaler can dispose of the goods at a profit to the retailer. The wholesaler in turn sells the goods to the retailer. Again the inducement to purchase is not primarily quality or service but the opportunity to resell at a profit to the actual consumer. Only when the retailer comes to sell to the consumer does stress fall upon quality and service, as the inducement to the sale. Hence the ideas to be conveyed to the prospective purchaser to create in him a demand for the goods vary at different steps in the complicated process of distribution, because of the different points of view of those who buy for re-sale and those who buy for consumption. Price and saleability are the all important factors to the middleman; quality and service are as important to the consumer as price.

The tendency of the orthodox system of distribution of unbranded commodities is to turn the energies of the producer primarily toward lowering the cost of production and hence the price which he is able to offer the middleman. The influence of satisfaction or dissatisfaction on the part of the consumer comes to him only indirectly through a chain of middlemen. Moreover, where the goods are undifferentiated by trade mark or trade name, their identity is often completely lost in the successive stages of distribution. Even the retailer in many cases concerns himself rather with saleability than with ultimate satisfaction to the consumer. Hence, only marked defects in quality are likely to be brought to the attention of the producer. Thus the producer loses the touch with the consumer which will assist him to make improvements in quality and service in his goods. His attention is not forced upon those elements in the commodities which he manufactures. So under the orthodox type of distribution of unbranded commodities the standard of the producer tends to become saleability rather than satisfaction to the consumer.

Suppose, however, the producer does give conscious attention to elements of quality and service in his goods which render them more desirable from the standpoint of the ultimate consumer than other goods of like nature. Before the knowledge of these superior points reaches the consumer it must pass through the distorting medium of a chain of middlemen, who are not, for the most part, primarily interested in quality or service and no one of whom ordinarily gives undivided attention to the single commodity. The ideas that the retailer must communicate to the consumer to create in him a desire for the commodity are not the ideas which the wholesaler conveyed to the retailer to induce him to purchase.

Hence a producer who has added to his goods special advantages in quality or service finds it difficult to convey to the consumer through a chain of middlemen the precise ideas about those advantages that will lead the consumer to demand his goods in preference to those of another.

These considerations render the increasing communication of ideas about the goods by the producer directly to the consumer an improvement of great social significance in our scheme of distribution. The producer is forced to study the consumer's wants and to adjust his product to them. He can no longer devote his attention exclusively to cost. He realizes that the consumer's satisfaction depends on the quality of the goods and the service that they render. These become to him considerations as important as that of cost. Moreover, when he works out in his product some improvement in quality or service which more adequately adapts the commodity to the wants of the consumer, he is able to convey to the consumer precise and accurate knowledge of these improvements and to reap in increased demand for his product the reward for his efforts. Direct selling means, of necessity, a better adjustment of production to the needs of the consumer. Goods are being made to satisfy rather than to sell.

Obviously direct selling depends on a differentiation of commodities. The producer can effectively communicate ideas about his goods directly to the consumer only when the consumer is able to identify the goods. Where the physical distribution is through retail stores, the goods must be distinguished from other goods of like nature by trade mark, brand, or trade name, or the direct selling efforts of the producer are wasted.

The advantages of direct communication of ideas about the goods by the producer to the consumer as just outlined cooperate with the desire of the producer to escape pressure exerted by the middleman. As a result we find in the past half century and especially in the past decade a rapid adoption by producers of agencies for direct communciation of ideas about the goods to the consumer. This means that another function formerly divided among middlemen is being taken over as a function. The newspapers, periodicals, and other advertising agencies may hence be termed functional middlemen, as were the insurance companies, the transportation companies, and the banks. And with the rise in importance of those functional middlemen the position of the old type of middleman is again weakened.

We have still to discuss the function of assembling, assorting, and reshipping. This function is that which renders the goods physically available so that an aroused demand can be gratified. Here the middleman retains, for the most part, his importance. To be sure we find direct shipment from producer to consumer steadily increasing. This is to be expected as a consequence of the direct communication of ideas about the goods by the producer to the consumer. But in the more important lines today the consumer still depends on the retail store for the supply of the goods for which a demand has been stimulated and retail store in general turns for its supply to the wholesaler.

The problem of the distributor is two-fold: (1) to arouse a maximum of demand, and (2) to supply that demand with a minimum of leakage. The second phase of the problem involves the elements of time, convenience, and service. If the demand which has been aroused among consumers is to be fully utilized, it must be made possible for them to obtain the goods promptly when the demand arises. It must be convenient for them to obtain the goods. And in many cases, certain collateral services such as instruction, demonstration, and repairs must be given. It is here that the retailing middleman still retains this importance in most lines. If, when a conscious demand has been raised for a certain food product by the direct communication of ideas about the goods by the producer to the consumer, the latter is unable to find the product at a convenient grocery store, the aroused demand is likely to be ineffective. Hence the producer will often continue to distribute his product through the regular trade channels after taking over the selling function by directly communicating ideas about the goods to the consumer. Distribution by mail order and direct shipment by the producer have thus proven applicable only to certain commodities and in reaching certain sections and classes. The middleman is a social necessity.

When a producer begins to communicate ideas about goods directly to the consumer to arouse a demand, it is apparent that the middleman is performing only a part of the functions he previously performed. On strict economic grounds the margin of profit of the middleman should be reduced in proportion to his reduced functions.

As compensation for this reduced margin of profit on each sale, the middleman obtains a rapidity of turnover due to the selling efforts of the merchant-producer. But the middleman is often slow to see this compensating feature. He usually resists any attempt to reduce his discounts because the producer has taken over the selling function. If his compensation per sale is reduced he may refuse to handle the article. It is fair to say, however, that many progressive retailers are appreciating the possibilities of more rapid turnover of stock and are adjusting themselves to the changed conditions.

Now if the producer takes over the selling function and does not reduce the discounts allowed the middleman, the middleman is being paid for a function he no longer exercises. And ultimately this must come out of the pockets of the consumer. He is compelled to pay twice over for the exercise of a single function.

The opposition of middlemen to reduced compensation upon reduction in their functions presents a difficult problem to the producer. Often the producer postpones taking over the function of selling by direct communication of ideas to the consumer because he sees that he must continue to allow the middleman compensation for that function if he is to continue to use the middleman for the physical distribution of the goods. Sometimes the producer is forced to establish branch stores and so eliminate all middlemen from his system of distribution. This, however, is generally possible only in large centers of population and applicable only to certain classes of goods. The system of distribution through branch stores is illustrated in its application by certain large producers of trademarked shoes.

It is, however, feasible in many lines of trade-marked goods to take over the assorting, assembling, and re-shipping function of the wholesaler rather than to continue to compensate him for the selling function no longer performed. For example, one large paint manufacturer, who stimulates a demand for his branded paints and varnishes largely by direct communication of ideas about the goods to the consumer and to the retail paint dealer, found it desirable to drop out the wholesaler from his scheme of distribution. He finds in branch houses certain marked advantages. (1) He is able to obtain the entire time of trained men, devoted solely to the handling of his products. (2) He obtains a direct contact with the retail dealer, who, he finds, prefers on the whole to buy directly from the manufacturer. (3) He is enabled to carry larger and better assorted stocks than the wholesaler would be willing to carry. (4) In his experience the credit losses are less when the wholesaler is eliminated. (5) He obtains better control of general policy and prices. The larger capital required for a system of branch houses is an objection of decreasing importance owing to the rapid increase in the available capital fund andits greater fluidity. And the increased need of managerial ability is being met by improved systems of training men for managerial responsibilities.

This rather lengthly analysis of the position and functions of the middleman in distribution is still incomplete. Factors not of an economic character enter. The business man seldom faces a problem on purely economic grounds. There is always a human element to be considered, arising from the character of transactions as they exist in actual commercial life. One does not buy of a dealer solely upon narrow economic grounds. Social and personal considerations play their part. Hence, when the business man considers the position of the middleman in his own scheme of distribution, his problem is complex. Its solution is likely to be found in the rise of a class of efficient and progressive middlemen who take advantage of the producer's selling efforts in more rapid turnover of stock and provide the necessary physical distribution of the goods at a reduced percentage of profit on the unit sale with an increased annual profit....

# 19 —— Functional Elements of Market Distribution

*Franklin W. Ryan*[1]



The subject of marketing is typically presented by some half-dozen or more current books setting forth a brief and carefully selected list of marketing functions, around which the book is organized. In other words, the majority of present-day writers on marketing start out with a predetermined plan, partly derived from reading other books on marketing, with the result that when the books are completed there is a conspicuous similarity among all of them.

The present study proposes a different kind of approach, by which, instead of formulating at the start a list of functions, the first task will be to aggregate and integrate from all available sources as complete an array as possible of the elemental activities of the productive-distributive process. This proposed array of marketing elements, when completed, may then be used as a check list or working tool for various further studies,[2] or as material from which to derive new lists and combinations of marketing functions, or as a tentative foundation upon which to construct a realistic presentation of the subject of marketing.

But even more important than these possibilities, such an array of marketing elements will be of real value to executives in the marketing process—manufacturers, wholesalers, jobbers, and retailers—as a check list for purposes of studying and measuring the efficiency of their own organizations.

## Previous Attempts to List Marketing Functions

The first and original listing of marketing functions was by A. W. Shaw.[3] In discussing the functions of middlemen-specialists in the marketing process, he wrote:

> Roughly speaking, the general functions may be listed as follows:
> 1. Sharing the risk.
> 2. Transporting the goods.
> 3. Financing the operations.

4. Selling (communication of ideas about the goods).
5. Assembling, assorting, and reshipping.

After explaining that each of these functions was at first divided among a series of middlemen, the selling agent, the wholesaler, and the retailer, each assuming his part, he pointed out that at a relatively early date there began a taking over of these functions by specialists so that today the special functions of the above list are performed to a large extent by insurance companies, transportation companies, banks, and other middlemen specialists or "functional middlemen."

But Shaw had no intention of including all the activities of the marketing process under these few headings. He remarked that his "analysis of the positions and functions of middlemen in distribution is still incomplete."[4] In the same article in which appeared this brief summary of the functions taken over by middlemen specialists, he gave considerable space to several other functional elements of marketing such as pricing of goods, market analysis, and the standardization, differentiation, and branding of goods; he also mentioned inventory and stock-turn control and specially planned sales talks.[5]

Later Shaw expanded his original discussion into a book in which the following significant passage appeared:

> It appears at a glance that there are three distinct economic functions: (1) transporting the goods to create place utility, (2) storing the goods to create time utility, and (3) physical transfer of the goods to create ownership or possession utility.[6]

He also discussed what he called the facilitating functions of production and distribution, which include accounting, personnel management, credits and collections, and the administrative functions; and his final chapter goes into the problems of public relations.[7]

Another pioneer work of considerable importance was that of Ray B. Westerfield. In it he summarized the functions of marketing as follows:

> Commerce consists in the equalization and distribution of surplus goods as between persons in different places and different times. These ends are accomplished by carriage, storage, foresight, communication, and exchange. The agents of these acts are the merchants, tradesmen, and brokers.[8]

He goes on to group these functions in two classes, one of which has to do with dealing in "time-markets" and is speculative, while the other has to do with the connecting of local and distant markets, or dealing in "place-markets."

Westerfield's summarizing list seems more satisfactory than many others for the purpose intended, that of including all functions under a few heads. Furthermore, his summary comes near the end of his study, is incidental to it, and was arrived at by generalization after a careful study of historical facts. In other words, it was derived inductively rather than deductively.

In 1916 L. D. H. Weld discussed several marketing functions without presenting an enumerated list.[9] Accepting the definition of production as "the creation of utilities," this study discussed: manufacturing, to which is attributed the creation of form utilities; storage, by which time utilities are created; transportation, which operates to add place utilities to goods; and exchange (buying and selling), to which the author attributes the creation of possession utilities. The book also discussed several other marketing elements at considerable length, including financing, terms of sale, assumption of risks, shifting of risks, pricing of goods, retail-store expense control, inspection and grading, and packing.

In this work, Weld defined the field of the subject of marketing as all of the field of production, except the creation of form utilities. But, since practically all functionaries in the marketing process operate to create form utilities by various kinds of processing, conditioning, alteration, transformation, and other manufacture, the creation of form utilities, as a matter of fact, is merely one of the many elements of the marketing process. All of the different kinds of utilities (want-satisfying powers) of goods are created by the same motivation, namely, to sell goods.

Recognizing the creation of form utilities as an element of the marketing process does not confuse the subject. Manufacturing can still be studied as a separate subject, just as advertising, personnel, merchandising, and many other functions of marketing can be studied separately.

Later, in 1917, in an article by the same author, appeared the following summary of marketing functions:

> The services performed in the marketing process, including practically every item in the detailed expense account of a merchant or of the selling organization of a manufacturer, can be classified under one of the following heads: (1) assembling; (2) storing; (3) assumption of risks; (4) financing; (5) rearrangement; (6) selling; and (7) transportation. The only important exception to this classification is the expense connected with accounting and office management, or what Shaw calls "the facilitating activities" of a business. But these are purely incidental to the primary functions enumerated above, and may properly be considered as assignable to or incurred in connection with, their performance.[10]

In this same article, Weld took issue with Shaw regarding the denominating of his original list as "functions of middlemen." He claimed that they were much more; they were functions of marketing. In this he was right, but Shaw was not in error. Whereas Shaw discussed, in his two studies, nearly all the leading functional elements of marketing which can be performed profitably by middlemen-specialists. Weld's adaptation of Shaw's list into a seven-function formula for the whole marketing process was done hastily and without due consideration of many of the basic

## EXHIBIT I. Summary of Lists of Functional Categories of Market

| Name of Functional Categories | Number of Lists in Which Each Category Appears Including Author's List | *Functions of Middlemen Specialists* | | | *Functions of Middlemen in Produce Markets* | *Functions of Middlemen, Wholesalers & Jobbers* | | | *Functions of "The Marketing Institution"* |
|---|---|---|---|---|---|---|---|---|---|
| | | Shaw 1912 | Duncan 1920 | Marshall and Lyon 1921 | Nourse 1918 | Butler 1917 | Beckman 1926 | McFall and Beckman 1933 | Breyer 1934 |
| Marketing management | 1 | | | | | | | | |
| Providing facilities | 1 | | | | | | | x | |
| Accounting and recording | 3 | | | | | | x | | |
| Building a sales organization | 1 | | | | | x | | | |
| Financing | 26 | x | x | x | x | x | x | x | x |
| Credit rating | 1 | | | | | | | | |
| Handling or merchandising in general | 3 | | | | x | | | | |
| Merchandising in restricted sense | 1 | | | | | | | | |
| Trans. or carriage and delivery | 25 | x | x | x | | | x | (x) | x |
| Concentration | 2 | | | | | | | x | |
| Assembling | 16 | {x | | | | {x | | x | |
| Rearrangement or assorting | 8 | x} | | | | x} | {x | {x | |
| Inspecting | 3 | | {x | | | | | | |
| Grading | 17 | | x} | | | | x} | x} | |
| Standardization | 12 | | | | | | | | |
| Quality determination | 1 | | | | | | | | x |
| Processing, conditioning, or transformation | 5 | | | | | | | | |
| Storing | 23 | | | | | x | x | x | x |
| Warehousing | 5 | * | x | x | | | | | |
| Dispersing | 4 | | | | | | | | |
| Dividing | 1 | | | | | | | | |
| Packaging | 4 | | | | | | | | |
| Packing | 3 | | | | | | | | x |
| Distributing | 7 | | | | | x | x | x | |
| Pricing | 3 | | x | | | | | | |
| Communication | 3 | | | | | | | | |
| Publicity and advertising | 4 | † | | x | | | | | |
| Demand creation | 1 | | | | | | | | |
| Exchange | 2 | | | | | | | | |
| Contactual function | 4 | | | | | x | x | x | x |
| Negotiatory function | 1 | | | | | | | | x |
| Buying | 11 | | | | | {x | {x | {x | |
| Selling | 20 | x | (x) | x | | x} | x} | x} | |
| Measurement function | 1 | | | | | | | | x |
| Transfer of ownership | 1 | | | | | | | | |
| Payment | 1 | | | | | | | | x |
| Sales counsel | 3 | | | | | x | x | x | |
| Sales by organized exchanges | 2 | | x | | | | | | |
| Sales at auction | 1 | | | | | | | | |
| Research | 1 | | | | | | | | |
| Gathering information | 4 | | | x | | | | {x | |
| Market news | 2 | | x | | | | | | |
| Analysis of market conditions | 1 | | | | | | | x} | |
| Analysis of needs of the trade | 2 | | | | | x | | x | |
| Foresight | 2 | | | | | | | | |
| Risk-bearing or risk assumption | 15 | | | | | | | | x |
| Risk sharing or insuring | 2 | x | | x | | | | | |
| Estimating | 1 | | | | | | | | |
| Strategy | 1 | | | | | | | | |
| Cooperation with government | 1 | | | | | | | | |
| Protecting | 3 | | | x | | | | | |
| Providing an "outlet" for producer's product | 1 | | | | x | | | | |
| Equalization function | 2 | | | | x | | | | |
| Ideology | 1 | | | | | | | | |

* Shaw did not enumerate "warehousing" in his original list of 1912 but he discussed this function on page 278 of his book, *An Approach to Business Problems*. Cambridge: Harvard University Press, 1916.

† Shaw included the concept of advertising in his listed function of "selling."

## Distribution

***Functions or Activities of Marketing in General***

| Westerfield 1914 | Weld 1917 | Elsworth and Gatlin 1919 | Cherington 1920 | Ivey 1921 | Macklin 1921 | Vanderblue 1921 | Hibbard 1921 | Converse 1921, 1924, and 1930 | Clark 1922 and 1932 | Clark and Weld 1932 | White and Hayward 1924 | Brown 1925 | Black 1926 | Taylor 1931 | Pyle 1931 | Maynard, Weidler, and Beckman 1932 | Killough and Barrington Associates 1933 | Lyon 1933 | Proposed list by present author |
|---|---|---|---|---|---|---|---|---|---|---|---|---|---|---|---|---|---|---|---|
| .... | .... | .... | .... | .... | .... | .... | .... | .... | .... | .... | .... | .... | .... | .... | .... | .... | .... | .... | x |
| .... | .... | .... | .... | .... | .... | .... | .... | x | .... | .... | .... | .... | .... | .... | .... | .... | x | | |
| .... | x | x | x | x | x | x | x | x | x | x | x | x | .... | x | x | x | x | x | x |
| .... | .... | .... | .... | .... | .... | .... | .... | .... | .... | .... | .... | .... | x | | | | | | |
| .... | .... | .... | x | .... | .... | .... | .... | .... | .... | .... | .... | .... | .... | .... | .... | .... | .... | .... | x |
| .... | .... | .... | .... | .... | .... | .... | .... | .... | .... | .... | x | | | | | | | | |
| x | x | x | x | x | x | x | x | x | x | x | x | x | x | x | x | x | x | x | |
| .... | .... | .... | .... | .... | .... | .... | .... | .... | .... | .... | .... | .... | .... | .... | x | | | | |
| .... | x | x | x | x | x | x | .... | x | .... | x | x | (x) | x | x | .... | .... | x | | |
| .... | x | .... | .... | .... | .... | x | .... | .... | .... | .... | .... | {x | x | | | | | | |
| .... | .... | .... | .... | .... | .... | .... | x | .... | .... | .... | .... | | x | | | | | | |
| .... | .... | {x | x | x | {x | .... | x | {x | .... | .... | x | x | x | x | {x | {x | {x | {x | |
| .... | .... | x} | .... | .... | x} | x | .... | x} | x | x | .... | x} | x | .... | x} | x} | x} | x} | |
| | | | | | | | | | | | | | | | | | | | |
| .... | .... | .... | .... | .... | x | .... | x | .... | .... | .... | x | .... | x | x | | | | | |
| x | x | x | x | x | x | x | {x | x | x | x | x | {x | x | {x | x | x | x | x | |
| .... | .... | .... | .... | .... | .... | .... | x} | .... | .... | .... | .... | x} | .... | x} | | | | | |
| .... | .... | x | .... | .... | .... | x | .... | .... | .... | .... | .... | .... | x | x | | | | | |
| .... | .... | .... | .... | .... | .... | .... | .... | x | .... | .... | .... | .... | .... | | | | | | |
| .... | .... | .... | .... | .... | x | .... | .... | .... | .... | .... | x | .... | x | .... | .... | .... | x | | |
| .... | .... | .... | .... | .... | .... | .... | .... | x | .... | .... | .... | .... | .... | x | | | | | |
| x | .... | .... | .... | .... | x | .... | .... | .... | .... | .... | .... | (x) | .... | .... | x | | | | |
| .... | .... | .... | .... | .... | .... | .... | .... | .... | .... | .... | .... | .... | .... | .... | .... | .... | .... | x | x |
| x | .... | .... | .... | .... | .... | .... | .... | .... | .... | .... | .... | .... | x | .... | .... | .... | .... | .... | x |
| .... | .... | .... | x | .... | .... | .... | .... | .... | .... | .... | .... | .... | x | .... | .... | .... | .... | .... | x |
| .... | .... | .... | .... | .... | .... | .... | .... | .... | .... | .... | x | | | | | | | | |
| x | .... | .... | .... | .... | .... | .... | .... | .... | .... | .... | .... | .... | .... | .... | .... | .... | .... | .... | x |
| | | | | | | | | | | | | | | | | | | | |
| .... | .... | .... | .... | .... | .... | x | .... | x | x | .... | .... | x | {x | .... | x | x | x | | |
| .... | x | x | x | x | .... | x | .... | x | x | x | .... | x | x} | x | x | x | x | | |
| .... | .... | .... | .... | .... | .... | .... | .... | .... | .... | .... | .... | .... | .... | .... | .... | .... | .... | x | |
| | | | | | | | | | | | | | | | | | | | |
| .... | .... | .... | .... | .... | .... | .... | x | | | | | | | | | | | | |
| .... | .... | .... | .... | .... | .... | .... | x | | | | | | | | | | | | |
| .... | .... | .... | .... | .... | .... | .... | .... | .... | .... | .... | .... | .... | .... | .... | .... | .... | .... | .... | x |
| .... | .... | .... | .... | .... | .... | .... | .... | .... | .... | .... | .... | .... | .... | .... | .... | x | .... | x | |
| .... | .... | .... | .... | .... | .... | .... | .... | .... | .... | .... | .... | .... | x | | | | | | |
| | | | | | | | | | | | | | | | | | | | |
| x | .... | .... | .... | .... | .... | .... | .... | .... | .... | .... | .... | .... | .... | .... | .... | .... | .... | .... | x |
| .... | x | x | x | x | .... | x | .... | x | x | x | x | x | .... | x | x | x | x | | |
| | | | | | | | | | | | | | | | | | | | |
| .... | .... | .... | .... | .... | .... | .... | .... | .... | .... | .... | .... | .... | .... | .... | .... | .... | x | | |
| .... | .... | .... | .... | .... | .... | .... | .... | .... | .... | .... | .... | .... | .... | .... | .... | .... | .... | .... | x |
| .... | .... | .... | .... | .... | .... | .... | .... | .... | .... | .... | .... | .... | .... | .... | .... | .... | .... | .... | {x |
| .... | .... | .... | .... | .... | .... | .... | .... | .... | .... | .... | .... | .... | .... | .... | .... | .... | .... | x | x} |
| | | | | | | | | | | | | | | | | | | | |
| x | | | | | | | | | | | | | | | | | | | |
| .... | .... | .... | .... | .... | .... | .... | .... | .... | .... | .... | .... | .... | .... | .... | .... | .... | .... | x | |

elements of marketing which are not typically taken over by specialists.

Following the publication of these earlier treatises, many other books and articles on marketing have appeared.[11] As a general rule most of them show a tendency to express the activities of the marketing process in brief summaries of from seven to eleven categories. The lists of functions of 26 of these books and articles are indicated in Exhibit I, together with a list proposed by the present writer.

None of these books or articles, based on summarizing lists of functional categories, confines itself strictly to the few functions listed. Furthermore, the conspicuous fact that there is no unanimity among the lists reveals doubt among many of their authors as to what should be included in them. True, a few of these authors have agreed among themselves as to a standard summarizing set of marketing functions, but such an agreement seems more dogmatic than scientific. In Exhibit 1 is shown a tabulation of some 52 different concepts of functional categories taken from these various books and articles.

Shaw, the originator of the lists, did not summarize the whole marketing process, but made up only a list of functions of middlemen-specialists. He paid little attention to this list, however; and discussed in much greater detail many elements of marketing which could not logically be included in it. Being the executive head of a large business, he was primarily concerned with working out a practicable system of approach to actual business executive problems. Most of the subsequent compilers, being teachers in colleges and universities, were primarily concerned with organizing the subject of marketing for classroom presentation. Westerfield's summarizing list differs from those of later writers in that it was derived as a generalization by inductive reasoning. After studying a score or more of elemental activities of the distributive process, he presents his list as merely incidental to his conclusions. Logically it has a better claim to being all-inclusive of the marketing process than most of the others. Nourse does not attempt to summarize the whole marketing process but merely sets forth a list of functions of middlemen in produce markets.[12] Nourse was the first to see that transportation, storage, packing, grading, sorting, *etc.*, are merely elemental functions of the larger functional category of handling or merchandising. Weld, however, in his original formulation and in his recent work in collaboration with Clark, appears to hold firmly to his seven-function formula adapted from Shaw, which has become a standard for what might be called an orthodox listing of functional categories. Cherington, in his book, went through a conventional list, but used it as a point of departure, and discussed also display of goods, office functions, policing to prevent theft, and many others, apparently seeing that the formula was not adequate for the subject. Duncan, the first conspicuous heretic in contrast to the orthodox group of writers, omitted all mention of the assumption of risks, supposedly the most distinctive function of the so-called "entrepreneur," and then lapsed still further into heterodoxy by including in his list the two hitherto little-discussed functional categories of pricing of goods and the reporting and interpretation of market news. Converse, apparently once orthodox, has recently departed from the listing in his original book of 1921 so that his latest writings discuss many functions not in the original lists. A few writers have avoided the use of the word "function." Macklin presents his list as the "services" of marketing. Black presents a series of "activities" in contrast to "functions." Lyon employed the word "function" in his earlier work with L. C. Marshall, but in a letter to the present author explains that he avoids the use of it in his article on marketing in the *Encyclopedia of Social Sciences* for purposes of clarity, having in mind the general reader.

In summary, the lists of functions presented by most of these writers on marketing are usually meant to be brief summaries of functional categories and are not organized to give a complete and detailed picture of the distributive process. Most of these lists seek to find answers to two implied general questions in regard to the productive distributive process. These two implied questions are:

1. What general functions add time, place, ownership, possession, and other kinds of utilities (want-satisfying powers) to physical goods as they gradually move toward the point where they are sold to final customers?
2. What distinctive functions are performed by the entrepreneurs or business executives and their employees who carry on the work of distribution?

In answer to the first question, these books and articles typically list five functions, as follows: (1) assembling, (2) storing, (3) standardization, (4) transportation, and (5) selling. The distinctive functions of the functionaries in the productive-distributive process are usually listed as: (6) the assumption of risks, and (7) financing, which is the providing of capital for the marketing enterprise.

A general characteristic of nearly all these lists and of studies subsequent to those of Shaw and Westerfield, which have been constructed on the basis of such lists, is that although they are generally supposed to be in the field of "applied" economic science, they are predominantly deductive. There are several books which start out with lists of functions like the above and build up the entire treatment of the subject of marketing on this preconceived pattern. This is not the method of applied science.

## Method of This Study—The Place of Retailing

The present article, therefore, will be devoted to the task of building up a comprehensive list of all the functional elements of marketing, based on the actualities of the distributive process, with the objective of making it as complete as possible. This plan of aggregating and listing the actual elements of marketing on a realistic basis might well be called a "pragmatic" system of compilation, since it is fundamentally an attempt, free from preconceived formulas or traditions, to list all of the elements or activities found in the distribution of goods to the public as they are normally performed, and finally to group them under convenient headings. It is an attempt to present the facts, uncolored by previously worked-out theories or categories.[13]

But, of necessity, from the nature of the task involving, the resulting pragmatic listing of marketing elements will not be perfect. No presentation of actualities can be perfect. Perfection is found only in axioms, formulas, generalities, and other logical devices of the realm of pure ideas. There is an almost infinite variety of ways in which these functional elements and their functional categories can be listed and arranged, and the list given in Exhibit II is only one out of a great many possible lists. It was not compiled with any idea of finality but merely as a working tool. It is not a formula, not a thing of mathematical exactness, not at all like an axiom or an equation; it is merely a picture or sketch intended to express an idea.[14]

The idea of a realistic presentation of these functions is not new. Professor Taussig, in the first chapter of his *Wages and Capital* (1895) gave a very realistic sketch of the entire distributive process by which commodities pass through the hands of manufacturers, wholesalers, and retailers until they reach final purchasers.

The word ''function'' is used in this study in its ordinary meaning as the name of each of those recognizable items or elements of marketing activity, because it is the most used and most acceptable English word available. It means the normal activity of a thing, its actual performance. As used in the present inquiry, its meaning is somewhat like that of the Greek word *pragma*.

But it is necessary, for purposes of clearness, to distinguish between two uses of the word ''function.'' Where it is used for a single item or element of marketing activity, it is as an ''elemental function,'' but where a number of these are grouped together into a class for purposes of simplification, under a broader use of the term ''function,'' such classifications should be designated as ''functional categories.''

This distinction is quite necessary because some writers in this field have used the term ''function'' loosely and apparently interchangeably in both of the above senses, and have paid little attention to the elemental functions in some of the categories they have used. When some of these summarizing lists of functions or activities are examined critically, therefore, it may be found that the class names are not always of coordinate rank. Selling, for example, may be considered as a functional category, while transporting and storage are merely functional elements belonging in the category of handling or merchandising.

Of all the various successive steps in the productive-distribution process, such as the transfer of goods from extractive industries to manufacturers, from manufacturers to wholesalers and jobbers, from them to retailers, and from retailers to final customers, the ultimate transfer from retailers to final customers is admittedly the most important. All the earlier stages in the marketing process lead up to it and depend on it. If these ultimate retail sales could not be made, none of the earlier steps in the productive-distributive process would be worth while.

Furthermore, as the marketing process gradually advances by these various stages from the extractive industries through manufacturers, wholesalers and jobbers, and other middlemen toward the point of ultimate sale to final buyers,[15] the lists of marketing functional elements to be found in the various stages of selling become more and more differentiated until, in the retailing process, marketing reaches its most detailed and most complete form. All the basic functions of marketing are found in the procedure of retail stores. Consequently, in the present process of aggregating a pragmatic list of the functional elements of marketing, there need be no explanation or apology for going directly to a study of retail-store procedure, when it is obvious that this final stage of the marketing process is the most fruitful source from which to derive the various marketing elements which are the objectives of the present research.

For a considerable time there has existed a notion that the concept of a summarizing list of marketing functions is quite distinct from that of a detailed list of retailing functions; and that while the former set of seven or eight functions is valid as an explanation of all of the productive and distributive process, as far as the final stage of the retail store, from that point on less attention need by given to the abstract functional categories in general and more attention may be directed to the detailed and concrete functions connected with getting the goods into the hands of actual customers. This is substantially equivalent to an admission that although the conventional theoretical summarizing lists have not been seriously questioned in the former field, they are obviously inadequate and inapplicable from the time the goods arrive on the shelves of retailers until they are taken by final buyers. The average citizen spends a considerable amount of time shopping around and buying in various kinds of retail stores so that, in this field of knowledge, actual experience counts for more than abstract theory. Consequently, for a realistic presentation of marketing activities as actually carried on in retail stores, the only satisfactory list is one made up from actual experience.

The pragmatic list finally presented in Exhibit II is a composite aggregation of functions from the entire process of distribution, derived to a large extent by a special study of the retail trade, but not by any means limited to retailing. While clearly valid for the retailing process, it is, with a few minor qualifications, also valid for all wholesaling, jobbing, manufacturing, and extractive marketing activities as found in the productive-distributive process.

It should not be forgotten that A. W. Shaw, who was the first to study and make lists of marketing functions, defined distribution as the application of motion to materials[16] as they move from the times, places, forms, and

## EXHIBIT II. The Functional Elements of Market Distribution Classified by Convenient Groups

|  |  |
|---|---|
| I. Providing Location, Building, and Equipment | Selection and continuance of location<br>Providing and maintenance of building<br>Providing and maintenance of equipment and fixtures<br>Layout of building, equipment, and fixtures<br>Providing of heat, light, water, gas, ice, power, and sewer connections |
| II. Cooperation with Government | Obtaining the right to exist as a business by license<br>Sharing costs of government by payment of taxes<br>Conforming to city planning and zoning regulations for location of building or plant<br>Conforming to building, electrical, elevator, plumbing, and sprinkler codes, and other similar physical regulations<br>Conforming to traffic ordinances governing use of streets for the movement of goods<br>Conforming to ordinances governing the use of minor highway privileges for awnings, signs, windows, vaults, *etc.*<br>Protection of employees against disease, accidents *etc.*<br>Conforming to laws and ordinances for the protection of public health<br>Conforming to general laws for the regulation of business<br>Maintenance of standards of business ethics<br>Internal policing to protect the business |
| III. Legal Action | Use of legal devices to protect the business enterprise |
| IV. Administration of Personnel | Selection and placing of employees<br>Training employees<br>Paying employees by salary and on commission<br>Stimulation of salesforce<br>Welfare work<br>Promotion of morale; and group relations<br>Retaining special marketing counsel and other professional services |
| V. Communication | Mail correspondence and files<br>Correspondence by telegraph<br>Use of telephone<br>Messenger services |
| VI. Traveling | Traveling by executives and employees in performance of their work |
| VII. Participation in Community Affairs | Public relations<br>Sharing in local activities<br>Contributions and donations |
| VIII. Supplies | Purchase of supplies<br>Receiving of supplies<br>Use of supplies |
| IX. Disposal of Waste | Disposal of waste items such as ashes, crates, cartons, boxes, waste paper, *etc.* |
| X. Accounting and Statistical Control | Accounting<br>Expense control<br>Inventory and Stock-turn control<br>Statistical records |
| XI. Credits and Collections | Credit management<br>Collections<br>Losses from bad debts |
| XII. Administration of Cash | Receiving of cash<br>Disbursing cash<br>Depositing cash in banks<br>Obtaining special police protection in cases of large movements of cash<br>Use or armored cars |
| XIII. Merchandising and Buying | Merchandising research<br>Merchandise control<br>Style administration<br>Buying merchanise<br>Paying for merchandise<br>Transportation to store or plant<br>Receiving and assembly of merchandise<br>Storage of merchandise<br>Standardization, inspection, and grading<br>Arrangement, rearrangement, packing, and packaging<br>Processing, transformation, alteration, and other manufacture<br>Adapting goods to the market<br>Branding and trade-marking<br>Keeping goods clean and attractive |

## EXHIBIT II. The Functional Elements of Market Distribution Classified by Convenient Groups (cont.)

| | |
|---|---|
| XIV. Publicity | Advertising research<br>Newspaper advertising<br>Direct mail advertising<br>Radio advertising<br>Advertising in theaters, motion picture shows, street cars, suburban trains, and buses<br>Outdoor advertising<br>Distribution of circulars<br>Distribution of samples<br>Sales house organs<br>Overcoming unfavorable publicity<br>Other forms of building goodwill<br>Coordination of advertising with selling<br>Display of goods for sale on owned premises<br>Display of goods for sale on sidewalks and other publicly owned space |
| XV. Selling | Sales research, market analysis, and interpretation of sales statistics<br>Selecting and developing channels and methods of distribution<br>Sales planning<br>Budgeting sales, and sales operations<br>Solicitation of customers, direct<br>House-to-house selling<br>Specially planned sales talks<br>Guaranties<br>Determination of terms of sale<br>Transfer of ownership of goods<br>Measuring, weighing, counting, and checking goods sold<br>Delivery of goods to customers<br>Sales counsel to customers<br>Service in connection with certain items, such as radios, refrigerators, automobiles, *etc.*<br>Special services to customers, such as parking space, rest rooms, telephone booths, nurseries, *etc.*<br>Elevator and escalator service<br>Control of movement of people through store or plant<br>Substitution<br>Satisfying customers' complaints<br>Returns, allowances, adjustments, exchanges in connection with goods unsatisfactory to customers<br>Reselling goods to dissatisfied customers<br>Trade-in allowances on sales of new goods<br>Trading stamps<br>Sales by vending machines |
| XVI. General Management and Strategy | Building a marketing organization<br>General management of the organization<br>Departmental management and floor supervision<br>Territorial organization<br>Providing capital for use in the business<br>Financial management<br>Paying interest on borrowed capital<br>Adjustments of policies to meet condtions<br>Appraisal of current market trends from market news<br>Forecasting future market trends<br>Assumption of risks<br>Reducing risks by management<br>Shifting risks by insurance, hedging, and other devices<br>Corporation life insurance<br>Pricing of goods<br>Price maintenance<br>Membership in trade associations<br>Membership in better business bureaus<br>Meeting competition<br>Marketing strategy |

conditions in which they have no value, to the times, places, forms, and conditions where they have value; and that these final times, places, forms, and conditions, where goods can be sold to final buyers because the goods have wanted satisfying powers, are in the retail stages of marketing.

If it should be objected that a manufacturer's business is different from a wholesaler's and a retailer's because he performs the transforming function by buying goods in one form and then changing them into other forms, it can be answered that this transforming function is also performed to a considerable extent by practically all retailers, wholesalers, and jobbers.

It is generally known that wholesalers and jobbers, more than retailers, frequently buy commodities in one form and change them to other forms in various ways, and that an automobile manufacturing plant which merely assembles parts into completed automobiles is often less a manufacturer than some wholesaler or jobber who imports raw materials in one form and by various processes, as, for example, roasting, blending, and packaging of coffee, changes the product into one of a different character before it is sold. The dairy distributing companies not only buy their milk and cream from the farmers, but they also put it through a complete manufacturing process by which it is pasteurized and purified, and by which the butter-fat content of each of the different grades of milk and cream is made to conform to the accepted standards.

Nearly every type of retail store performs some manufacturing or transforming function in the course of its work. A retail jeweler sets a diamond in a ring, or strings a set of pearls, or puts a new spring in a watch; a druggist compounds a prescription; a restaurant cooks the food it sells; a clothing or gown shop makes alterations; a meat market slices its meats or removes feathers from its fowls; a grocer takes quantities of bulk material such as tub butter and packages it in pound lots, or removes the outside leaves from heads of cabbage and lettuce, or the tops from beets and carrots; a bakery bakes its bread; a liquor dealer rectifies his liquors; a radio dealer installs an aerial or a part of his own manufacture; an optometrist places lenses in frames; an automobile dealer removes a defective battery and installs a new one before he can sell a car; and finally a candy and confectionery store manufactures a chocolate nut sundae.

## Sources of This Study

There are ordinarily six main groups of sources from which to derive and compile lists of marketing functions, five of which are present-day sources while the sixth group includes all sources from previous periods of time. They are: (1) books and articles on marketing, which have been discussed above; (2) income and expense analyses of business firms; (3) statutes, ordinances, and other governmental regulations for the purpose of control of the marketing process; (4) case books and problem books on marketing and other sources of marketing cases; (5) the actual performance and procedure of business firms as revealed in their business documents, business correspondence, and by actual experience in the business; and finally, (6) the historical group of sources, which roughly includes all of the above in previous history, but which is particularly concerned with the appearance of new elemental activities from period to period. Exhibit III shows the six different methods of deriving and compiling lists of marketing elements.

**EXHIBIT III. Points of View and Methods of Deriving and Compiling the Various Elements of Market Distribution**

| | *Questions:* |
|---|---|
| 1. Books and Articles on Marketing (Deductive) | a. What activities performed in the market-distributive process add time, place, form, possession, and other utilities to physical goods as they move on the way to final purchasers?<br>b. What are the distinctive functions performed by entrepreneurs or business men in the market-distribution process? |
| 2. Analysis of Operating of Marketing Enterprises (Deductive) | What important marketing activities, under as few headings as are conveniently and logically possible, can be held responsible, for purposes of standard expense studies, for all of the money expenses of carrying on the business of a particular store or other marketing enterprise, during a given period of time? |
| 3. Government Control (Deductive-inductive) | In the exercise of police power for the general welfare of the public, what activities of the market-distributive process are properly subject to control by statutes and ordinances? |
| 4. Case Books and Problem Books on Marketing and Retailing (Inductive) | What particular activities of the marketing process, as found in actual cases, can be used to teach and illustrate the the basic principles of business success in the manufacture, wholesaling, and retailing of goods? |
| 5. Purely Pragmatic (Inductive) | What are all the activities or functions as carried on in the market-distributive process, as actually found in operation in marketing enterprises, and in what logical categories can they be classed? |
| 6. The Historical (Inductive) | a. What sets of marketing elements were actually carried on in previous important periods of history?<br>b. As between different important periods of history, what particular marketing functions have been added to the productive-distributive process to bring it to higher stages of development? |

Only in books and articles on marketing and retailing, and in income and expense analyses, can lists of functional names and words be found already compiled and aggregated. The other four sources do not furnish lists, although lists may be aggregated from them. Certain functions can be derived by analysis from statute books and municipal code books. Similarly another set may be made up from all the sources of marketing cases. But the only first-hand source, from which one is able to derive a complete pragmatic list of marketing elements, is that of the actual business world. Nevertheless, a modern marketing executive, having given little thought to the subject of the range of his various selling activities, will in the great majority of instances not be able to furnish a complete list.

## Marketing Elements Derived from Expense Analyses

If a modern retail store manager, the manager of a wholesale house, or the sales manager of a manufacturing plant should be asked for lists of all the marketing functions performed in their various establishments, there would be found a tendency on their part, since they operate from the profit motive, to think primarily in terms of income and expense, and to magnify the importance of the functions to which are attributed the different elements of income and expense. From expense analysis studies and from the pages of ledgers and cost records of marketing firms, a very good tentative list of functions may be derived, but in deriving such a list it must be continually remembered that, because of the profit motive, a retail store manager, the manager of a wholesale house, or the director of sales for a manufacturing plant recognizes the names of these functions as headings for their expense accounts only for the purpose of income and expense control, and usually not with the idea that they have listed all the functions performed in the conduct of their business.

In preparing a list of functions from income and expense analyses, the problem is like that of a geologist seeking sources of iron, which may be found in both metallic state and the form of iron ore. But the ores of iron are not iron. The headings of the income and expense accounts of a retail store, of a wholesale house, or of any other selling agency indicate or reveal an important list of marketing functions, in fact one of the most important lists that can be found, but these expense headings are not functions. They are expense classifications named from the functions. In those headings where a marketing function is mentioned, it is in the sense of an adjective modifying some element of income or expense related to the function.[17]

## Statutes and Ordinances as Sources

A third source, and historically among the oldest of manuscript sources from which to derive names of marketing functions, is that of statutes and ordinances enacted by national, state, and municipal governments. But since such statutes and ordinances to control the marketing of commodities are in the main originally designed and enacted in the exercise of the police power, to protect the life, security, safety, and comfort of the general public, a list of marketing functions derived from this source will necessarily have its limitations. A great many of the functions of marketing are ordinarily not subject to governmental control.

## Marketing Cases and Problems

The fourth source of the functional elements of market distribution is that of marketing cases and problems as derived from actual business procedure and written up in magazine articles, case books, problem books, and classroom material for the study of marketing and related subjects. The first case book in this field was that of Professor M. T. Copeland, published in 1920.

In contrast to theoretical books on marketing based on the conventional formula of a functional approach, the case book follows a method which is fundamentally inductive. The student analyzes hundreds of actual cases and problems drawn from the experience of business executives, and from them forms his own generalizations and discovers his own working principles in his own way so that they have concrete reality and meaning in his own experiences. The introduction of the business case book in business teaching marked the beginning of what might be called a pragmatic approach to business science. By this mode of procedure, the various subjects in the marketing field, such as wholesaling, retailing, sales management, and advertising, began to take on the true character of applied sciences.

In seeking and collecting cases and problems for inclusion in case books of this kind, and reference books of cases such as the *Harvard Business Reports,* they were not sought directly for the sake of marketing elements or marketing principles themselves, but rather for the principles of business management to be discovered and formulated in connection with them. But every principle of market management is a principle which is related to one or more of the elemental activities of marketing. Therefore, just as every case or problem illustrates one or more principles of management, so it also reveals a few or many of these functional elements of marketing which constitute the special field for the present research.[18]

## Pragmatic and Historical Methods of Approach

The fifth group of sources is found in the actual procedures of marketing enterprises. Although often regarded as a residential group of sources, it is of foremost importance. From this source marketing elements are derived directly and at first hand, while from all the other sources they are derived indirectly The final listing of elements in Exhibit II, while aggregated from all the different groups of sources, was checked against actual procedure to give it realistic value.

None of the six groups of sources is completely satisfactory in itself. Each has its limitations. In order to compile and integrate the most satisfactory composite array and classification of marketing elements, all six should be used together. If deduction is unsatisfactory, so is too much emphasis on the inductive method. Science proceeds by a combination of both the deductive and inductive methods. The list of functional elements derived from an expense analysis is needed as a check against the various other arrays of derived elements. The lists derived from ordinances and statutes, from books on marketing, and from marketing case books, may also be used in a similar manner. By checking all these various sets of functional elements against each other and against actual performance, a fairly representative pragmatic list of marketing functions is finally put together.

But if only the first five groups of sources are drawn upon, the resulting final listing will be without perspective. It will be merely a cross section of marketing of the present day. The enduring permanency and fundamental nature of the basic or primordial functional elements will pass unnoticed. A considerable number of the elements of marketing are discovered to be enduring in nature and are found in operation in every period of history. These elements, when aggregated together, make up a permanent or fundamental list which is valid for nearly all periods of history. A study of history also makes possible a compilation of modern marketing elements which have been introduced into the marketing process from time to time since the beginning of the modern era.[19]

This composite list of permanent marketing elements which may also serve as a basic list for nearly all periods of commercial history from the earliest Minoans, Cretans, Sumerians, Babylonians, and Egyptians to the present day, has been aggregated as shown in Exhibit III.

## Summary

The final listing and classification of functional elements of marketing (Exhibit II) was prepared after checking all the lists of functions derived from studies of actual experience in present-day marketing organizations. The list finally presented here was integrated and classified after conferences with several marketing executives, including those of three metropolitan

## EXHIBIT IV. List of Permanent or Enduring Marketing Elements Which May Serve for Nearly All Periods of Commercial History*

Accounts and records
Arrangement and rearrangement of goods
Assumption of risks
Building a marketing organization
Buying merchandise and supplies
Cash, disbursing of
Cash, receiving of
Collections
Communication
Conforming to laws, statutes, ordinances, and regulations of government
Credit management
Determination of terms of sale
Delivery
Display of goods
Financing and financial management
Forecasting market trends
General management
Layout of store or plant
Legal devices, use of
Losses from bad debts
Marketing strategy
Measuring, weighing, counting, and checking goods sold
Meeting competition
Merchandise control
Packing and packaging
Paying employees and sales people
Paying for goods bought
Paying interest on borrowed capital
Pricing of goods
Processing, conditioning, altering, transforming, and other manufacture
Providing and maintenance of building
Providing and maintenance of equipment
Providing capital for use in the business
Providing protection
Receiving and assembly of merchandise
Returns, allowances, adjustments, exchanges
Sales counsel to customers
Sales research and market analysis
Selection and development of channels of distribution
Selection and placing of employees
Sharing costs of government by paying taxes
Solicitation of customers
Standardization, inspection, and grading
Storage
Training employees
Transfer of ownership of goods sold
Transportation of goods
Traveling
Waste disposal

*The above composite list of basic or enduring marketing elements was compiled from a study of various sources, including: Homer's *Odyssey*, Book XV; the story of Joseph in *Genesis* 37-48; the laws of Moses in *Leviticus* and *Deuteronomy*; the description of the markets of the ancient Phoenician city of Tyre in *Ezekiel* 27-28; the code of Justinian (*Corpus Juris Civilis*); and confirmatory passages in various books including: Rostovtzeff, M. I., *The Social and Economic History of the Roman Empire*. Oxford: The Clarendon, Press, 1926; Abbot, Frank Frost, *The Common People of Ancient Rome*, New York: Charles Scribners Sons, 1911; Preston, Harriet Waters, and Dodge, Louise, *The Private Life of the Romans*. Boston: Benjamin H. Sanborn & Company, 1893; Calhoun, George M., *The Business Life of Ancient Athens*. Chicago: The University of Chicago Press, 1926; St. John, J. A., *History of the Manners and Customs of Ancient Greece* 3 Vols. London: Richard Bentley, 1842; Richards, Gertrude R. B., *Florentine Merchants in the Age of the Medici*. Cambridge: Harvard University Press, 1932; Ashley, W. J., *An Introduction to English, Economic History and Theory*, 2 Vols. New York: G. P. Putnams Sons, 1906; Takekoshi, Yosoburo, *The Economic Aspects of the History of the Civilization of Japan*, 3 Vols. New York: The Macmillan Company, 1930.

department stores, a representative mail-order house, a leading chain-store organization, and the managers of three unit stores, one of which was operated by a cooperative society.

As the list stands, even though it is admittedly imperfect and is only one of many possible ways of presenting the elements of marketing, it constitutes a realistic definition of marketing which will serve as the basis of approach for a considerable number of forms of analysis.

Thus, 120 different functional elements are here grouped for convenience into 16 functional categories. Whether a mercantile establishment is large or small, it will be found that these 16 functional groupings are represented. In large organizations where there is considerable division of labor, the different groups of functions will be performed by different people, but in a small one-man establishment all that are performed are performed by the one man.

The list of 16 functional categories, as shown in Exhibit II, is not set forth as a final summary of the marketing process but only tentatively, as a matter of convenience in grouping the elemental functions. With some modification and variation, they could be used for the composite basic list of the enduring or permanent elements of marketing as shown in Exhibit III.

But this list of 16 functional categories may be open to the objection that there are too many groupings. Present-day writers on marketing demand a brief summarizing list of class names. Furthermore, the above list may have too much of the appearance of finality.

Here is submitted a summarizing list of categories, by which all the elements of market distribution may be arranged in another way; it briefly answers the questions implicit in most present-day treatises on marketing. But it is set forth as a tentative generalization and not as a dogmatic formula. It is derived independently of Exhibit II, both from a study of the various other points of view, and also in an attempt to clear up the general confusion in regard to the problem of lists of functions as is revealed in Exhibit I. The list is as follows: (1) marketing management, (2) financing, (3) handling or merchandising, (4) pricing, (5) communication, (6) publicity, (7) exchange, (8) research, (9) foresight, (10) strategy, and (11) cooperation with government.[20] This list is also given in the final column of Exhibit I.

Having discussed the functional elements of marketing at considerable length, it is now possible to work up a list of functions to answer the two basic questions which are implied in books on marketing. The first question is: What general functions in the marketing process add want-satisfying power (utilities) to physical goods as they gradually progress toward the point where they are sold to final customers?

The answer to this question may now be expanded to include several functions.

**EXHIBIT V.**

| *Functions* | *Utilities Added by the Functions* |
|---|---|
| Processing, conditioning, alteration, or transforming; and keeping goods clean and attractive. | Form |
| Transportation | Place |
| Storage | Time |
| Buying and selling (transfer of title) | Ownership |
| Delivery to possession of customer | Possession |
| Measuring, weighing, counting, and checking | Measurement |
| Dividing | Size |
| Packaging | Form |
| Branding and trade-marking | Distinction |
| Standardization, inspection, and grading | Certainty |
| Pricing and price maintenance | Price |
| Building goodwill, taking part in local affairs, publicity, and advertising | Goodwill |
| Special services to customers, rest rooms, parking space, telephone booths, *etc.* | Convenience |
| Extension of credit | Credit |
| Guaranties, sales counsel to customers, and satisfying customers' complaints | Confidence and reliability |

The second question implicit in books on marketing is the following: What are the distinctive functions performed by business men in the productive-distributive process? Some of the writers on marketing, discussed above, have listed "the assumption of risks" and "financing" in answer to this question and have maintained that their total of 7 to 11 functions include the entire process.

Incidentally, if selling or the getting rid of merchandise is a function distinct from buying or the acquiring of merchandise, certainly the shifting of risks to insurance companies or by other means is a function quite distinct from the assumption of risks. Furthermore, the assumption of risks is much more an involuntary act than it is voluntary and, if predominantly involuntary, why should it be listed as one of the most important functional categories of marketing?

Why not permit business executives themselves to have a voice in naming the functions which they consider most distinctive? The assumption of risks is undoubtedly an important element in marketing, but it is not the same thing as or as important as the shifting of risks which is generally regarded as a marketing element of secondary importance.

A considerable number of marketing executives were asked to prepare lists of what they considered the 20 most important marketing elements as performed in their establishments. As a result of this analysis, the following list was taken as most representative of the choices of these men.

**EXHIBIT VI. Selected List of Marketing Elements Considered of Most Importance by Marketing Executives**

*1. Selling
*2. Merchandise control
*3. Buying
*4. Pricing
5. Inventory and stock-turn control
6. Building sales organization
7. Expense control
8. Satisying customers' complaints
9. Meeting competition
10. Display of goods
*11. Advertising and sales promotion
12. Layout
13. Delivery
*14. Use of telephone in selling
15. Credit management and collections
*16. Market analysis and research
*17. Marketing strategy
18. Building morale among employees
19. Membership in trade associations
20. Accounting

*Note that the starred items are separately recognized in the eleven-function list prepared by the present writer on page 324 except that *Buying* and *Selling* are there grouped together as *Exchange*.

Marketing executives who assisted the author in the preparation of the above list, either by submitting lists or otherwise, included: Arthur O'Keeffe, President, First National Stores, Inc., Colonel C. O. Sherrill, Vice President Kroger Grocery Company, John A. Logan, Executive Vice President, Food and Grocery Chain Stores of America, Inc., Joseph H. Appel, in charge of advertising, John Wanamaker, Inc., New York, Fred H. Tracht, Manager, University of Chicago Bookstores, George E. T. Cole, Manager, Harvard Cooperative Society, Cambridge, Mass., E. R. Sage, President, E. R. Sage & Company, Cambridge, Mass., Fred R. Lamb, Manager of the Boston branch of Sears Roebuck & Company, and H. R. Floyd, Director of Research, Wm. Filene's Sons Company, Boston.

## CONCLUSIONS

As a result of the present inquiry and examination of the various sources of marketing elements, the following conclusions may be drawn:

1. The summarizing list of seven marketing functions, apparently agreed upon by a number of present-day marketing economists, namely: (1) assembly, (2) storing, (3) standardization, (4) transportation, (5) selling, (6) assumption of risks, and (7) financing, is inadequate and does not include all the elements of marketing.

2. The underlying axiom or formula implicit in a retail-store expense analysis, that the total of all the expenses for a given period of time is caused by the total of all the marketing activities in operation during that time, is useful and valuable. But such an expense analysis demands simplification of expense headings and items, so that many elements are disregarded, and all of the expense is allocated to only the abbreviated list of expense headings in the analysis. In other words, although the basic formula is true, the method used involves a fiction in accounting theory.

3. These two deductive systems for the analysis of marketing activities, being more or less closed or preconceived as to method, have delayed the search for a complete list of all the functional elements of the marketing process. In such a situation, an unusual opportunity is presented for the use of the pragmatic method which, instead of stressing axioms, principles, formulas, and preconceived categories, seeks to find actualities, facts, consequences, and concrete things in actual experience and reality.

4. The word "function" is the most acceptable English word available for designating the activities of marketing, but it has been used loosely. Distinction should be made between functional categories or classes of functional activities and the final subdivisions of the categories which are functional elements.

5. In working up a pragmatic list of all the elements of marketing, all of the various sources should be used. But for purposes of integrating and classifying such an array of marketing elements, the summarizing lists of marketing functions prepared by orthodox marketing economists and the lists of headings of retail-store expense analyses are less useful than are the inductive methods of aggregating these elements from: (1) statutes and ordinances, (2) case books and problem books drawn from actual marketing experience, (3) actual marketing procedure, and (4) historical sources.

6. The notion that the assumption of risks is one of the outstanding and most distinctive functional categories of marketing, is misleading. True, business men assume risks, but with them risk-bearing is more involuntary than voluntary, more unconscious than conscious, more characteristic of life in general than of marketing in particular. Furthermore, the getting rid of risks, or risk-shifting, is actually a much more important functional element. But even so, risk-shifting, which is usually merely buying insurance or hedging, is not among the most important of marketing elements.

From another point of view it is unsound to regard risk assumption as one of the basic categories of marketing. Business men engage in business ventures because of foresight and not merely because they desire to take risks. Risks are risks of the unforeseen, and risk-bearing is merely one element of marketing and subsidiary to the functional category of foresight.

7. While it is desirable for purposes of teaching to distinguish between the subject of production and the subject of marketing, and while the two fields of subject matter can be very well written up in separate books for classroom purposes, no sharp line of demarcation between them can be drawn. The only scientific definition of production is "the creation of utilities or want-satisying powers." Production never stops until the goods are used up by final customers. Often, after goods are sold to customers, they have to be "sold" over again.

8. A. W. Shaw's definiton of distribution as the application of motion to materials as they progress from the times, places, forms, and conditions in which they have no value, to the times, places, forms, and conditions where they have value, is the most useful formula to use in the aggregation

and compilation of a complete list of marketing elements. Production and distribution coexist in the same field, two complementary aspects of the same phenomenon.

9. Processing or transformation, since it adds form utilities to goods, constitutes an important element in marketing. It is fallacious to say it is not an element of marketing on the ground that it is production. Nearly all the elements of the marketing process are production.

10. The notion that the concept of a list of retailing functions is different from the concept of a list of marketing functions, is not tenable. Retailing is the final step in the marketing process and, therefore, retailing is marketing. A list of marketing functions, if properly put together, is *per se* a list of retailing functions.

11. A study of historical sources reveals two different important lists of marketing elements, namely: (a) a list of enduring or permanent marketing elements which are found to be present in the marketing process in all periods of history, and (b) a list of modern marketing elements added to the process since the early American colonial period.

12. None of the various sources of marketing elements is perfect in itself. In order to compile and integrate the most satisfactory composite list of marketing elements, all sources should be used and checked against each other. By this procedure, both induction and deduction will be used together. Since science proceeds by both the inductive and deductive methods, all the different sources used together give a balanced result in the search for a better and more complete presentation of the functional elements of market distribution.

## ENDNOTES

1. EDITOR'S NOTE. This article is a collateral part of a research study of the general problem of municipal control of retail trade, which is now being undertaken by the author in cooperation with Dr. Miller McClintock, Director of the Bureau for Research in Municipal Government in Harvard University, under the general supervision of the Harvard Committee on Research in the Social Sciences. The research has been made possible through a grant from the Rockefeller Foundation. The final monograph on municipal control of retail trade, which will be published shortly, is designed to be of practical value to marketing and retailing executives in analyzing their relations to their local governments.
2. Before a scientific study of municipal control of retail business could be made, it was found necessary first to aggregate and compile a fairly complete list of the functional elements of marketing and retailing for purposes of orientation and measurement. All government control of business is control of specific elemental activities.
3. Shaw, A. W., "Some Problems in Market Distribution," *Quarterly Journal of Economics*, August, 1912, p. 371.

4. *Ibid.*, p. 739.
5. *Ibid.*, pp. 712-721, 749-754, 710-711, 740, and 761, respectively.
6. Shaw, A. W., *An Approach to Business Problems*. Cambridge: Harvard University Press, 1916, p. 278.
7. These two studies by Shaw included much more than the five listed functions of middlemen-specialists. Altogether, he discussed, either directly or indirectly, a considerable number of functional elements of marketing, as follows:
   Accounting
   Adapting goods to the market
   Advertising and sales promotion
   Assembly of goods
   Assumption of risks
   Branding and trade-marking
   Building sales organizations
   Credit management and collections
   Delivery of goods
   Expense control
   Financial management
   General management
   Government control of business
   Grading and inspection of goods
   Inventory and stock-turn control
   Layout of store or plant
   Location, selection and continuance of
   Market analysis and research
   Marketing strategy
   Merchandise control
   Personnel management
   Pricing of goods
   Processing or transformation of goods
   Providing building or plant
   Public relations
   Selection of methods of distribution
   Selling
   Specially planned sales talks
   Standardization
   Storage and warehousing
   Transfer of title
   Transportation
8. Westerfield, Ray B., *Middlemen in English Business*. New Haven: Yale University Press, 1915, p. 349.
   In the course of this study of English middlemen, the author discusses many other marketing and retailing functions as follows:
   Assumption of risks
   Communication
   Conforming to licensing regulations
   Conforming to municipal regulations
   Credit

Employing professional services
Evaluating market news and market information
Financing and relations with banks
Insurance
Packing
Personnel management
Pricing of goods
Providing capital
Reducing costs to consumers
Standardization and grading
Taking part in public life
Trade-marks
Transformation
Transportation
Traveling

9. *The Marketing of Farm Products*. New York: The Macmillan Company.
10. Weld, L. H. D., "Marketing Functions and Mercantile Organization," VII *American Economic Review* 2, June, 1917, pp. 306-307.
11. Other books and articles in which lists of marketing functions may be found, and which have been used in the compilation of Exhibit I, are as follows: Butler, Ralph Starr, *Marketing Methods*. New York: Alexander Hamilton Institute, 1917; Nourse, Edwin G., *The Chicago Produce Market*. Boston: Houghton Mifflin Company, 1918; Elsworth, Ralph, H., and Gatlin, George O., *Marketing Functions*. Washington: U.S. Department of Agriculture, 1919 (reprinted in *Readings in Marketing Principles*, edited by Wright, Ivan, and Landon, C. E. New York: Prentice-Hall, Inc.); Cherington, Paul D., *The Elements of Marketing*. New York: The Macmillan Company, 1920; Duncan, C. S., *Marketing, Its Problems and Methods*. New York: D. Appleton and Company, 1920; Macklin, Theodore, *Efficient Marketing for Agriculture*. New York: The Macmillan Company, 1921; Ivey, Paul W., *Principles of Marketing*. New York: The Ronald Press Company, 1921; Hibbard, B. H., *Marketing Agricultural Products*. New York: D. Appleton and Company, 1921; Vanderblue, H. B., "The functional Approach to the Study of Marketing," *Journal of Political Economy*, October, 1921; Marshall, L. C., and Lyon, L. S., *Our Economic Organization*. New York: The Macmillan Company, 1921; Converse, Paul D., *Marketing Methods and Policies*. New York: Prentice-Hall, Inc., 1921 and 1924, and *The Elements of Marketing*. Prentice-Hall, Inc., 1930; Clark, Fred E., *Principles of Marketing*. New York: The Macmillan Company, 1922 and 1932; Clark, Fred E., and Weld, L. D. H., *Marketing Agricultural Products*. New York: The Macmillan Company, 1932; White, Percival, and Hayward, Walter S., *Marketing Practice*. New York, Doubleday, Doran and Company, 1924; Moriarty, W. D., *The Economics of Marketing and Advertising. New York: Harper and Brothers, 1923; Brown, Edmund Jr., Marketing*. New York: Harper and Brothers, 1925; Black, John D., *Introduction to Production Economics*. New York: Henry Holt and Company, 1926; Beckman, Theodore N., *Wholesaling*. New York: The Ronald Press Company, 1926; Taylor, Henry C., *Outlines of Agricultural Economics*. New York: The Macmillan Company, 1931; Pyle, John F., *Marketing Principles, Organization and Policies*. New York: McGraw-Hill Book Company, Inc., 1931; Maynard, Harold H.,

Weidler, Walter C., and Beckman, Theodore N., *Principles of Marketing*. New York: The Ronald Press Company, 1932; Killough, Hugh B., and Barrington Associates, Inc., *The Economics of Marketing*. New York: Harper and Brothers, 1933; Lyon, Leverett S., "Marketing," an article in the *Encyclopedia of Social Sciences*, Vol. X, 1933. (Edited by Seligman, E. R. A., and Johnson, Alvin); McFall, Robert J., and Beckman, Theodore N., *Wholesale Distribution*. (Distribution, Vol. II) of the fifteenth census of the United States: 1930; Breyer, Ralph F., *The Marketing Institution*. New York: McGraw-Hill Book Company, Inc., 1934.

12. Note that Nourse and Shaw did not cover the same field. The middlemen whose functions Nourse listed are not the same as the middlemen-specialists of Shaw's lists.
13. The word "pragmatic" as used to characterize methods of thinking, was derived from the Greek word *pragma* (πραγμα), meaning a thing done, an actuality, a thing of importance, a condition as it is, a material element of a thing, an actuality of the business world. Truth, in pragmatism, is truth or actuality in experience as distinguished from the concept of absolute mathematical truth or truth in the abstract.

    "The pragmatist clings to facts and concreteness, observes truth at its work in particular cases, and generalizes. Truth, for him, becomes a class name for all sorts of definite working values in experience.... The pragmatic method means the attitude ... of looking toward last things, fruits, consequences, facts." James, William, *Pragmatism*. New York: Longmans, Green & Co., 1908, pp. 54-55, 68.
14. Another realistic presentation of the marketing-distributive process is that of Alfred Marshall in his *Industry and Trade*, published in 1919. (London: Macmillan and Company, Ltd.) In this work a considerable number of functions are discussed as follows: administration of risks, pp. 250-268, 645-651; storage, pp. 274-278; market analysis, pp. 278-280; standardization, grading, and inspection, pp. 281, 811-813; meeting competition, pp. 289-292, 423-506; packaging and branding, pp. 300-302; advertising, pp. 304-307; financing, pp. 337-349; business management and the development and training of executives, pp. 350-364; cost control, pp. 365-367; pricing, pp. 523-526; transportation, pp. 423-506. The functions of transformation (manufacture) and selling are discussed all through the book, as indicated by its title, but the author does not present a list of functions.
15. See Taussig, F. W., *Wages and Capital*, 1895, Ch. I.
16. See also Bohm-Bawerk, *The Positive Theory of Capital*, Smart's translation, p. 20.
17. Expense analyses are presented in: *Merchandising and Operating Results for Department Stores and Specialty Stores*, by H. I. Kleinhaus, General Manager, Controllers' Congress, National Retail Dry Goods Association, 1930; *Market Facts for the Retailer*, published by the Bureau of Business Standards, Inc., of the Shaw Publications; *The Hardware Store, an Intimate Study of Margins, Expenses and Profits*, and other bulletins of the National Retail Hardware Association; *Operating Expenses, Margins, Stockturns, Net Profits in Retail Business*, published by Merchants Service Bureau, National Cash Register Company, Dayton, Ohio; *Bulletins* of the National Retail Furniture Association; and *Bulletins* and *Retail Store Expense*

*Analysis* forms of the Harvard Bureau of Business Research, 1911 to 1933.

In the standard form for the analysis of retail store expenses used by the Harvard Bureau of Business Research, 1929 to 1933 inclusive, all expenses are classified under five headings as follows: (1) Administrative and General Expense, (2) Occupancy Expense, (3) Publicity Expense, (4) Buying and Merchandising Expense, (5) Selling Expense.

18. The materials available are: Copeland, M. T. *Problems in Marketing*, latest revised edition, 1931; Frederick, J. G., *Modern Sales Management*. New York: D. Appleton and Company, 1920; *Harvard Business Reports*, Volumes I to XI; Tosdal, H. R., *Problems in Sales Management*, 1921, 1925 and 1931, *Problems in Export Sales Management*, 1922, and *Introduction to Sales Management*, 1933; David, D. K., and McNair, M. P., *Problems in Retailing*, 1926; Borden, Neil H., *Problems in Advertising*, 1932; McNair, M. P., and Gragg, C. I., *Problems in Retail Distribution*, 1930, and *Problems in Retail Store Management*, 1931; Cabot, Philip, and Malott, Deane W., *Problems in Public Utility Management*, revised edition, 1930; Brown, T. H., *Problems in Business Statistics*, 1931. These books, unless stated otherwise, were published by A. W. Shaw and Company, Chicago (1921-1926) or by McGraw-Hill Book Company, Inc., New York (1930-1933).
19. These modernizing elements are found listed under the various headings in Exhibit II.
20. "Communication," "exchange," and "foresight" originally appeared in Westerfield's list. "Handling or merchandising" is from Nourse and Cherington. This category includes the handling elements of transportation, assembling, inspecting, grading, standardizing, processing, storing, packing, *etc*. The category of "pricing" comes from Duncan and is also in Lyon's list. "Publicity" is here listed as a separate functional group; this separation was recognized by Shaw and also appears in the list of Marshall and Lyon, and any marketing executive would list it as a separate group. "Research" as a category criss-crosses all the others and includes gathering information, market news, market analysis, and interpretation of market statistics. "Financing" as a functional category runs through the whole marketing process. In Exhibit I, it appears in 26 different lists of categories.

"Strategy" is here set up as a distinct category although it might well be included with marketing management as in Exhibit II. But management often fails without creative strategy. Shaw recognized strategy as an important element in market distribution. Later, J. George Frederick developed it in his book, *Modern Sales Management*. (New York: D. Appleton & Company, 1920) "Cooperation with government," another category related to management, is also clearly a separate group of elements. In primitive society, "protection" was a distinct functional category, but in the best governed modern communities, this category of "protection" may be regarded as subsidiary to "cooperation with government."

The inclusion of "foresight" as a basic functional category of marketing tends automatically to eliminate the much-discussed function of "risk-bearing" as a basic category. Foresight is the intellectual quality of business men which motivates them to engage in marketing ventures. It is naive to say that they engage in business merely to assume risks. A business risks are, more or less, risks of the unforeseen. "Risk-bearing," therefore, becomes merely an element of marketing subsidiary to the functional category of "foresight." The importance of foresight in business is developed by Wallace B. Donham in his two studies, *Business Adrift*, 1931, and *Business Looks at the Unforeseen*, 1932, both published by Whittlesey House, McGraw-Hill Book Company, New York.

The function of "equalization," discussed by Westerfield and further developed by Nourse, is not included as a basic category either in Exhibit II or in the present eleven-function selection of class names. It is not mutually exclusive of the others here listed. Furthermore, it is primarily a basic function of middlemen in the marketing process. It is not a function of the specializing middlemen studied by Shaw and by Marshall and Lyon, and not a functional category of marketing in general.

"Marketing management," a flexible term, is here used arbitrarily to include all the elements and categories in the pragmatic list of Exhibit II, not included under the other categories of the present list, and also to include the "coordination and direction" of marketing activities by marketing executives, as originally defined by Shaw.

This eleven-category list of class names may also be used for the enduring historical elements of Exhibit IV. It has already been used to classify the 52 functional concepts of Exhibit I.

# 20 —— The Functional Concept in Marketing

*Earl S. Fullbrook*

Reprinted from *Journal of Marketing*, published by the American Marketing Association, Vol. 4, No. 3 (January 1940), pp. 229-237. Reprinted by permission.

The functional approach in studying marketing is almost as old as marketing literature. Following its early introduction it received wide acceptance by writers in the field and it has continued to hold a very important place in marketing literature and teaching. Today it is the exception when any general work on marketing does not give some attention to marketing functions. Not only has the functional approach come to be common in marketing books but it is found frequently in texts used for courses in principles of economics and for introductory courses in the field of business organization and management.

In spite of the length of time the functional concept has been in use and in spite of its wide currency at the present time, it appears that little has been accomplished since the early years toward any significant refining of the concept. It is apparent from any careful survey of the material in the field that there is no very clear-cut and generally accepted interpretation of, or method of handling, marketing functions. The writer believes the functional approach can be a very useful device but contends that a great deal must be done in further developing it before its real possibilities can be realized. The following pages aim to emphasize this need and to suggest the lines along which further development should proceed.

## Origin

Credit for originally introducing the functional concept to marketing belongs to A. W. Shaw, one of the pioneers in the field of marketing literature, whose writings "mark the real beginning of the scientific analysis of marketing problems."[1] He dealt with marketing functions in his paper on "Some Problems in Market Distribution" which was published in 1912.[2] This was three years before the period of 1915 to 1917 which Converse has designated as the "first or pioneer period" in marketing literature.[3] The functional concept, therefore, extends back to the very beginning of marketing literature.

Not long after Shaw introduced the functional approach into marketing, others began to use and to develop it. Important among those using and contributing to the development of the idea in the early years were Weld, Cherington, Vanderblue, and Macklin.

## INTERPRETATIONS OF EARLY WRITERS

In introducing the subject into marketing, Shaw spoke not of functions of middlemen. Although he offered no formal definition of the term, his treatment makes it clear that he thought of functions as steps or tasks to be performed by someone in the process of marketing goods. He explained that they might be divided between middlemen on an area basis or on a functional basis or that they might be distributed on one basis at one time and on another basis at another time.[4] If functions can be allocated to distributive agencies in a variety of ways it must follow that they are tasks which can be divorced from, and treated separate from, the agencies which perform them.

Weld wrote at some length on marketing functions in 1917.[5] He defined them as: "The services that must be performed in getting commodities from producer to consumer."[6] This definition indicates that Weld regarded functions as tasks and his discussion leaves no doubt about the interpretation. He described marketing functions as essential steps involving various difficulties, which are more difficult to perform for some commodities than for others, and which require that in each case the methods of performance be adapted to the needs.

Cherington gave considerable attention to marketing functions in *The Elements of Marketing* which appeared in 1920. More definitely than any of his predecessors he stressed the need for analyzing the functions separate from their actual performance—the need "to get back of the forms of distribution to the actual functions."[7] He believed that if the functional approach was to be of much value in dealing with marketing problems, it was essential that the problems involved, not the agencies used, be given prime consideration—that attention be fixed "not upon the forms of devices which have been developed and which must be regarded as temporary and external features, but rather, upon the functions of marketing as the permanent element of the problem."[8] Functionaries, he pointed out, are constantly changing while functions cannot undergo corresponding change.[9]

The same distinction between functions and agencies was implied, at least, by Vanderblue in 1921. He believed the functional approach was the logical one "because the specialists exist to perform certain functions" and "because the problems involved in the marketing machinery and marketing process can be developed and isolated by an exposition in terms of the functions performed."[10]

Also in 1921 there was published Macklin's *Efficient Marketing for Agriculture*, which contained a discussion of marketing functions, although they were designated as marketing services. The study of marketing, he states, in order to be practical "must examine the methods of rendering these services and the agencies which provide them" and "must examine the various marketing services and determine why they are performed." The confusion of services with methods or agencies, he adds, "blurs the whole subject of marketing'' and ''has rendered futile much of the marketing criticism up to the present time.''[11]

Thus the writers who first dealt with marketing functions treated them as necessary steps or tasks to be performed in the process of getting goods from producers to consumers. They generally regarded the functional treatment as a means of analyzing what had to be done to get goods from producers to consumers and as providing a basis for determining how the job could be done best. They maintained definite distinctions between the work to be done (functions) and the means of doing it (functionaries).

## Current Treatment of Functions

Three general methods of handling marketing functions are in current use. The least effective of these, and hardly meriting recognition as a method of treatment, is to list the functions and, in a few brief statements, attempt to indicate the nature of each. Little is done to show their significance or to relate them to the rest of the material.

A second method is to list the functions and then describe them primarily by describing the ways in which they are performed. This tends to result in a description of the agencies and methods used to perform the functions—a description of marketing machinery and processes. From such a treatment there is great danger the reader will conclude that a function is an activity to be considered only in terms of how it is performed. It is the result which Macklin warned against—a confusion of services with methods or with agencies which blurs the whole subject of marketing.

The third procedure, which follows most closely the lead of those who introduced and developed the concept, is to list the functions and to explain, more or less adequately, the problems encountered in the performance of each. In this approach a function is considered as a service or task to be performed and an analysis is made to determine exactly what must be done to secure an efficient performance of each. Such an analysis tends to maintain a separation between the problems involved in the functions and the machinery used in performing them.

The above methods may easily be combined and this is what many writers tend to do. The results, however, tend to be inconsistent, in that some functions are analyzed in terms of the problems to which they give rise while the treatment of others consists of little more than a description of how they are performed in current marketing practice. Such a combination is hardly logical.

Something of the situation which exists today, at least among teachers of marketing, is indicated in the *Report of the Committee on Definitions* of the National Association of Marketing Teachers in 1935, where it is stated that:

> During the past year the Committee has attempted to deal with two marketing terms which seem to represent the ultra ultimate in

> confusing and diversity of usage. These two terms are "Marketing Function" and "Wholesaling." There is pretty general agreement as to what constitutes a satisfactory formal definition of the former of these terms. No great degree of agreement exists among those interested in marketing, however, as to the specific activities which should be classified as *marketing functions*.[12]

The wide differences of opinion existing among those interested in marketing, as to what the significant functions are, suggest that the acceptance of a formal definition does not mean a great deal, and the variations in the way the term is used in marketing discussions further suggest that the ability to agree on a formal definition does not insure a common interpretation of the term when put to use. Not only do we find significant differences in ideas as to what should be included in the list of marketing functions but there are also fundamental variations in ideas as to just what marketing functions involve. It would appear, therefore, that further study of the functional concept is needed.

## Uses of the Functional Approach

The introduction, development, and continued use of the functional approach in marketing must be due to a belief that it offers certain significant advantages. As a basis for further discussion, consideration needs to be given to these advantages, since the definition and interpretation of marketing functions should be developed with due consideration of the uses or purposes to which the concept is to be put.

To Weld, the functional approach offered a method of outlining the field of marketing and emphasizing the various and numerous activities involved in it. Because many people, even though realizing that there are functions to be performed, have no appreciation of their complexity or the difficulties of performing them, he says "a classification of marketing functions is absolutely fundamental to a study of and an understanding of the marketing machinery."[13]

To Vanderblue, the functional approach supplied a basis for analyzing marketing problems. According to his view the analysis of marketing problems along functional lines conforms with both the market structure and commercial practice and "is the logical approach in dividing the larger problem into its constituent problems, which can be considered singly, and then brought together in a consideration of the problem as a whole."[14]

In so many current treatments these same advantages of the functional approach are stressed. Clark says:

> So important are these functions to the marketing process that the best approach to many of the problems involved in marketing—whether the object is to understand general marketing processes or the processes

used in marketing particular products—is an understanding of these essential services. Such knowledge enables one to understand why middlemen exist, why marketing is costly, why certain marketing institutions and devices have developed, and often furnishes the best approach to the solution of specific marketing problems.[15]

According to Converse the:

reader who is to understand the discussion of middlemen and commodities fully, should first have some knowledge of the various marketing functions.... The reader can then have them in mind while studying middlemen and commodities, and thus be in a better position to understand and criticize the activities of the middlemen and the methods by which goods are marketed.[16]

The functional approach, Killough states:

attempts to apply to marketing, methods of analysis that have been employed with gratifying results in the scientific study of factory management. This approach breaks the subject up into processes that must be performed in the movement of goods from farm or mine to factory and from factory or farm to ultimate consumers.... Analysis of the marketing functions, one by one, contributes to a clearer understanding of the different elements of marketing cost and facilitates selection or creation of agencies which perform the functions most economically.[17]

These and many similar comments are evidence that the functional approach is thought to serve important uses. Briefly summarized, the possibilities of the functional method in studying marketing are:

1. It is a method of defining the field. Marketing is defined as including ''those business activities involved in the flow of goods and services from production to consumption.''[18] What are these activities? How can the number and variety of them best be distinguished and emphasized? It is very easy to overlook some of them and to underestimate the importance of others but the chance of doing so is materially reduced by the functional method. It affords an advantageous way of describing the ramifications and complexities of the field of distribution and of explaining the high costs of marketing.
2. Study along functional lines provides a good basis for understanding marketing agencies and processes. By analyzing them in terms of the functions they perform it is easier to determine why certain agencies exist, why certain methods are followed, and why certain costs are encountered. A full knowledge of the nature and significance of the several functions leads to a more complete understanding of all agencies and processes.
3. The functional method provides a sound basis for analyzing marketing problems. The great majority of problems in distribution cannot

be solved satisfactorily without breaking them up into their elements. Functions provide a basis for doing so, whether the problem involves general marketing processes, methods of marketing individual commodities, or individual marketing agencies and devices. Differences in the marketing of different types of commodities can be explained in terms of functions; the marketing of a single product can be planned in terms of the functions that must be performed; and the need for, and efficiency of, individual institutions may be evaluated by ascertaining if they are performing essential functions more efficiently than could be done by some other institution or combination of institutions.

These possibilities of the functional approach, however, are seldom realized and it is the writers contention that if they are to be realized to any marked degree, it is essential that we have a more adequate interpretation and treatment of the functional concept.

## Proposed Interpretation

The interpretation of marketing functions proposed here is not a new one. It is merely a proposal that an idea found in the discussions of marketing functions from the beginning be developed to its logical conclusion.

A function of marketing should be regarded strictly as a step, task, or service to be performed in getting goods from producers to consumers. This is in accord with the usual definition.[19] That the performance of a function requires activity is granted. That it is logical to regard a function as an activity to be performed is also granted. To so regard it, however, increases the probability that attention will center upon the activities performed instead of upon the nature and extent of the job which has to be done and which gives rise to the activities. If it is not in accord with the usual meaning of the word to define a function in terms of what has to be done, some other term had better be substituted. Breyer speaks of the ''elements of the marketing task''[20] and there is much in favor of some such designation.

By regarding a function solely as a task or service that requires performance, it can be analyzed entirely distinct from its actual performance and if the functional treatment is to yield signifcant results, such procedure is essential. The authors previously quoted have indicated the desirability of analyzing institutions and processes on a functional basis, but this is a productive method of attack only when, on one hand, the functions are treated as tasks to be done and, on the other, institutions and processes are recognized merely as the agencies or methods for getting the tasks done. Only after gaining a clear understanding of the nature of a task and of what its performance requires, can one evaluate agencies or methods that are used, or might be used, in doing the job.

The functions of marketing are readily adapted to such a treatment. They can be completely analyzed in terms of what the performance of each requires with little or no reference to the ways they are performed in practice. To do so results in a description of the problems encountered in getting goods from producers to consumers and affords a really sound basis for considering how these problems or tasks can be handled best.

All marketing institutions and processes have come into existence to perform marketing functions. The justification for these agencies must be that they perform essential functions. It is necessary, then, that the tasks involved be outlined separately from their actual performance. The function is what is done. The agency used to do it should be selected and shaped according to the task it has to do. In other words, first determine the problem—what has to be done—and then determine the best way of doing it. After the functions involved in a given marketing problem have been analyzed adequately attention can be turned to the best methods of performing them.

To merely indicate some of the possibilities of the method, it is applied below to two representative marketing functions.

## Examples of Proposed Treatment

The transportation function involves the movement of goods from places of production to places of consumption. It is an absolutely essential step in marketing because so few goods are consumed at the place where they are produced.

What does the performance of the transportation function involve? Is it a simple or difficult task? Will its performance add much or little to the cost of getting products to consumers? Obviously the answer varies with different commodities and even for similar commodities under different conditions. But why? What are the factors that cause these differences? It is not possible to discover a group of factors which can be used to analyze the transportation function in relation to any commodity?

While not offered as inclusive of all significant factors, the following suggests where the proposed type of analysis leads. The ease or difficutly of performing the transportation function for any commodity is determined by such elements as the distance it must be moved, its value or bulk, the degree of its perishability, the speed with which it must be moved, and the ease with which it can be handled in loading and unloading.

These factors can be applied to any commodity or group of commodities. As they are applied to different commodities in an effort to ascertain what the transportation function involves, totally different results may be secured. For some items—bulky, perishable ones that must be moved long distances—it develops that the function is an expensive one: for other items valuable, durable ones—the transportation function is far less troublesome and costly.

It should be observed that such an analysis of the transportation function steers clear of methods of performance. Applied to eggs, for instance, the analysis runs along these lines. Eggs are very perishable and must be protected from both breakage and deterioration. This requires very careful packing, protection from too cold and too warm weather, and careful handling in loading and unloading. Eggs, being somewhat bulky, require considerable shipping space. On the average they must be moved long distances. Where producers and consumers happen to be very close together the function is immensely simplified.

Other products, like coal, are very bulky and must also be moved considerable distances, but are very durable and lend themselves to easy methods of loading and unloading. In the case of still another type of good, such as jewelry, there is very small bulk and great value and, although it must be carefully packed and protected and often carried great distances, the transportation function is relatively simple and inexpensive.

From such an analysis, in which no consideration is given to methods of performance, even the beginner can easily see what the transportation function amounts to, can realize that entirely different types of transportation facilities are needed for different products, and can understand why the cost of transportation is a big factor in the prices of some products and of little importance in others.

As a second example consider buying, one of the so-called ''typical marketing functions.'' The function of buying involves having available for consumers what they want, when they want it. It includes having the right goods at the right place, at the right time, in the right quantities, and at the right prices. Since the average consumer uses so many different commodities, produced in so many and widely scattered places, the task of arranging to have each and every one available is a very important and a very complicated assignment.

What are the special phases of the buying function? As described by Converse, buying includes: (a) determining needs, (b) finding a seller, (c) negotiating price and other terms, and (d) payment, or arranging for credit.[21] This breakdown provides a satisfactory basis for starting the analysis but is only a beginning. It is desirable that each of these aspects be studied to determine what is required for its efficient performance.

If the right goods are to be at the right place, someone must do a lot of planning. In order to determine needs, markets must be carefully studied. Such factors as income, age, sex, nationality, occupations, business conditions, style movements, and price changes which affect the type and amount of goods purchased must be examined and evaluated. Some individual or institution must do it, but the job of doing it can be described advantageously without describing the agencies that do it and the methods they use. In attempting to analyze the task, why complicate it by mixing in agencies that are, or might be, engaged in performing the task? To do so tends to color the thinking and the real nature of the problem involved is not properly determined.

That striking differences are encountered in trying to determine the needs for different commodities is obvious. For a staple commodity, like salt, few difficulties are met in determining needs, whether being done for the country as a whole, for a sectional market, or for the customers of a given retailer. People continue to consume about the same kind of salt in about the same quantities. On the other hand, to anticipate the demand for a product like women's ready-to-wear gives rise to no end of difficulties. Women can be depended upon to buy something different than they purchased last time. Just what styles, colors, prices, and sizes will they want? And how much? Here the correct answers are not so easy to find. Methods of analyzing demand have to be developed.

Seeking sources of supply is the next phase of buying. An efficient performance of this step requires more than merely finding some place where the desired goods can be purchased. A careful consideration of all potential sources is called for in order that the best ones can be selected. Hence the number, nature, and location of sources will determine how difficult is the performance of this step for any particular commodity. For an item like fresh tomatoes the selection of sources is complicated because the sources may shift from week to week and month to month. First they must be obtained from one place, a little later in the season from another, and so on through the year. Furthermore the sources are not certain from year to year. A source that yields an abundant supply of fine tomatoes one year may offer only an inferior supply, or none at all, the next. Also there are so many widely scattered, small-scale producers that it is very difficult to know the possibilities of all of them. It is not surprising that many different agencies are involved in concentrating such produce in wholesale markets.

Automobiles present a contrast in respect to sources. There are only a limited number of producers. These are large, well-known, and relatively stable from year to year. Furthermore, trade names are very important and there is but a single source from which a given kind of car can be had. Here is one of the reasons why few types of middlemen are used in marketing automobiles.

The remaining phases of the buying function lend themselves to similar treatment, but it is unnecessary to go further to show that it is feasible to analyze marketing functions with little or no reference to how they are performed in practice and that doing so opens up much greater possibilities for making functions mean something and for making the functional approach serve constructive purposes.

## Conclusion

A thorough and consistent analysis of marketing functions in terms of *what has to be done* to perform them efficiently, instead of in terms of *how they are done* in practice would increase greatly the value to marketing of the functional concept. Such an analysis was suggested by those who originally introduced the idea, but too generally those who have followed in the field have not applied it. As a result the functional method has not accomplished what was expected of it and what it might accomplish if functions were adequately interpreted and analyzed.

## ENDNOTES

1. Homer B. Vanderblue, "The Functional Approach to the Study of Marketing," *Journal of Political Economy*, Vol. XXIX (October, 1921), p. 676.
2. A. W. Shaw, "Some Problems in Market Distribution," *Quarterly Journal of Economics*, Vol. XXVI (August, 1912), pp. 703-765.
3. Paul D. Converse, "The First Decade of Marketing Literature," *Natma Bulletin Supplement*, November, 1933, p. 1.
4. A. W. Shaw, *Some Problems in Market Distribution* (Cambridge, Harvard University Press, 1915), pp. 76-77.
5. L. D. H. Weld, "Marketing Functions and Mercantile Organization," *American Economic Review*, Vol. VII (June, 1917), pp. 306-318.
6. *Ibid.*, pp. 317-318.
7. Paul T. Cherington, *Elements of Marketing* (New York, The Macmillan Company, 1920), p. 44.
8. *Ibid.*, p. 56.
9. *Ibid.*, p. 50.
10. Homer B. Vanderblue, "The Functional Approach to the Study of Marketing," *Journal of Political Economy*, Vol. XXIX (October, 1921), p. 682.
11. Theodore Macklin, *Efficient Marketing for Agriculture* (New York, The Macmillan Company, 1922), pp. 29, 280-281.
12. *Report of the Committee on Definitions*, published by the National Association of Marketing Teachers, May, 1935, p. 13.
13. Weld, *op. cit.*, p. 306.
14. Vanderblue, *op. cit.*, p. 682.
15. Fred E. Clark, *Principles of Marketing* (New York, The Macmillan Company, 1932), p. 11.
16. Paul D. Converse, *The Elements of Marketing* (New York, Prentice-Hall, Inc., 1938), p. 24.
17. Hugh B. Killough, *The Economics of Marketing* (New York, Harper and Brothers, 1933), p. 101.
18. "Definitions of Marketing Terms," Consolidated Report of the Committee on Definitions, *National Marketing Review*, Vol. I (Fall, 1935), p. 156.
19. The definition of a marketing function recommended by the Committee on Definitions of the National Association of Marketing Teachers is: "A major specialized activity performed in marketing." *National Marketing Review*, Vol. I (Fall, 1935), p. 156.
20. Ralph F. Breyer, *The Marketing Institution* (New York, McGraw-Hill Book Company, 1934), p. 5.
21. Converse, *op. cit.*, p. 57.

# 21 — Marketing Functions and Marketing Systems: A Synthesis

*Richard J. Lewis and Leo G. Erickson*

Reprinted from *Journal of Marketing*, published by the American Marketing Association, Vol. 33 (July 1969), pp. 10-14. Reprinted by permission.

Several approaches have been used in the study of marketing. Among these are the commodity, institutional, managerial, functional, and systems approaches. Each has made a contribution to understanding the discipline; however, two stand out as potentially providing a theoretical framework for the discipline. They are the functional approach and the systems approach. At present the systems approach appears to be in high regard, while the functional approach seems to have lost favor to a considerable degree. This article takes the position that these two approaches have much in common and that there is considerable merit in synthesizing them.

Before a synthesis can be accomplished, it is necessary to redefine and review the functional approach.

## A Partial History of the Functional Approach

Some time ago the functional approach was voted the outstanding contribution to the development of a science of marketing.[1] Prior to that time a comprehensive definition of a marketing function existed only in the abstract. It was defined as ''a major economic activity which is inherent in the marketing process, pervades it throughout, and which through a continuous division of labor tends to become specialized.''[2] Although there was considerable disagreement as to which activities were ''major economic'' ones, the definition in itself was instructive in that it made clear that the activities were inherent, pervasive, and either specialized or likely to become so. This definition is more specific than that of the 1935 Definitions Committee of the National Association of Marketing Teachers, which defined a marketing function as ''a major specialized activity performed in marketing.''[3] Further, in an attempt to bring order to a very young discipline, this Definitions Committee provided a listing of 15 functions which were sent to some active members of the Association to determine if they would accept these functions as a semi-official list. Those surveyed could make additions to the list. Twenty-one replies were received, and the list was increased to 40 ''functions.''

Thus, as early as 1935 the functional approach to marketing was in deep trouble. The Definitions Committee was concerned about the lack of uniformity of functions being listed. It felt that under the label of the functional approach, heterogeneous and nonconsistent groups of activities were being forced into functional classifications. The Committee's concern is shown by the statement, "It is probably unfortunate that this term (marketing function) was ever developed."[4] In 1948, the Definitions Committee of the American Marketing Association reissued the 1935 definition of a marketing function and thus did not adopt the idea that a function was inherent and pervasive. However, the Committee still provided a suggested list of marketing functions.

In 1950, Edmond D. McGarry showed his concern for the state of the functional approach to marketing and attempted to clarify the meaning of the word *function*. In doing so, he stated that "The term *function* should be so defined as to meet the purpose for which it is used." To illustrate his point that function should be related to purpose, he said, "The function of the heart is not simply to beat, which is its activity, but rather to supply the body with a continuous flow of blood.... In like manner functions of marketing should denote a purposefulness in the marketing process; and the term should be used only in connection with activities that must be performed in order to accomplish the general purpose." Thus, of particular importance to this article is McGarry's attempt to relate function to purpose and also to revert to the earlier notion that the functions should be considered as inherent in the marketing process.[5]

Despite McGarry's effort to forestall the departure from the functional approach to marketing, the Definitions Committee in 1960 chose to depart even further from its restricted notion of what constitutes a marketing function. In the 1960 definitions the words *inherent* and *pervasive* were still excluded. In addition, the definition was made even less precise and less restrictive by the Committee's omission of any suggested list of marketing functions. The Committee defined a marketing function as "a major specialized activity or group of related activities performed in marketing." The comment which accompanied their definition referred to a lack of agreement on which activities are marketing functions and the lack of even a generally accepted basis for deciding what a marketing function is. The Committee concluded its definition with the statement, "Most of the lists fail sadly to embrace all the activities a marketing manager worries about in the course of doing his job,"[6] indicating that marketing functions are now to be thought of in terms of a job description for a marketing manager. If such is the case, it is understandable that no acceptable definition of marketing functions exists, for there is no definition of marketing management which is both universal and unique to marketing. Perhaps the Committee's reference to the activities of a marketing manager was a reflection of the growing trend toward the managerial approach to the study of marketing.

Therefore, at about the same time that one group of marketing scholars lauded the functional approach as the outstanding "concept or tool in the development of the science of marketing," another group of scholars said that it was unfortunate that the term *marketing function* ever appeared.

Further, the definition of a marketing function remained so loose that it led to the sort of confusion and controversy that the Definitions Committee referred to in its 1935, 1948, and 1960 reports.

## The Importance of Defining Marketing Functions

Perhaps the question should be raised as to why an accepted definition of marketing functions is of any real importance. Should an attitude of getting on with the business of marketing be adopted without worry about what functions are or are not—particularly considering the characteristics of definitions themselves?

Definitions are tautological in that they are statements of equality, saying no more on one side than on the other. Further, they are philosophically arbitrary. However, their arbitrary nature should not imply that definitions are capricious or should not exist. Unless there is agreement as to the "meaning" of a term, the result will be confusion rather than clarity and order. To encourage an arbitrary definition, such as has been done relative to functions of marketing, is to retreat from the first requirement of making a discipline scientific—that is, to provide a taxonomy within which one can classify. Since marketing is a set of activities, to abdicate responsibility for establishing its functions is to cause marketing to lose its identity.

## The Functions of Marketing

The authors agree with McGarry's definition of the term *function* and specifically with his notion that a marketing function not only relates to purpose but also is inherent in the marketing process. However, this agreement with his definition does not lead to similar agreement with his listing of marketing functions. McGarry identified the functions of marketing as contactual, merchandising, pricing, propaganda, physical distribution, and termination. The present contention is that if function is to relate to purpose in the sense of McGarry's illustration of the heart, the relationship between function and purpose must be that of identity. In order to determine what are marketing functions, the relevant questions is: what are the unique and inherent *purposes* of the marketing process? That is, what is marketing's role in the firm as distinct from that of production and finance? In this sense, it seems there are two functions (purposes) of marketing—to obtain demand and to service demand.[7] All of the activities in which we engage in marketing are means to attain these ends.

Herein lies the uniqueness of marketing's role in the firm. Obtaining and servicing demand are *inherent* in the marketing process and clearly define the purposes for which marketing activities are performed.

Historically, some of the confusion and disagreement in identifying marketing functions arose due to the labeling of many activities as functions of marketing. This is easily understood considering the lack of general acceptance of the idea of functions being *inherent* and the failure to recognize that functions are the *purposes* of marketing. When functions are regarded as inherent and as identifying the purposes of marketing, the result is the identification of what marketing does (its ends). However, to identify the activities of marketing (its means) is to determine *how* marketing accomplishes its functions. Advertising represents nonpersonal mass persuasion, personal selling represents personal individualized persuasion, sales promotion represents special promotions on a noncontinuous basis, and merchandising represents continuous adjustments to the products and services to fit changes in consumer tastes and habits. These are descriptions of marketing activities, but their common *function* is to obtain demand for the firm's goods and services.

Figure 1 outlines the functional approach described above. The two purposes of marketing—obtaining and servicing demand—are shown as its functions. In addition, three sets of activities are shown: those involved in obtaining demand, those involved in servicing demand, and those which cut across and permeate the obtaining and servicing activities. The complementary nature of these sets of activities is recognized. In fact, the firm's ability to service demand can be used as a demand-obtaining force.

## THE NATURE OF SYSTEMS[8]

In the broadest sense a system is an ongoing process. A more complete and general definition views a system as being a set of objects with a given set of relationships between the objects and their attributes. The *objects* are the parameters of a system and consist of input and output objects, process feed-back-control, and restrictions. *Attributes* are the properties of the objects in a system and allow the assignment of a value and a dimensional description.

*Relationships* are the bonds which link objects to objects, attributes to attributes, and subsystems to systems in the system process. The relationships are described as either first, second, or third order. Relationships are first order when they describe a situation where objects or subsystems to a system are functionally necessary to each other. Second order relationships are complementary to the system but are not functionally indispensable. When objects or subsystems of this type are taken together, they positively foster the system, producing a total effect greater than the sum of their independent effects. Third order effects include redundant and contradictory

**FIGURE 1. Marketing Functions and Activities**

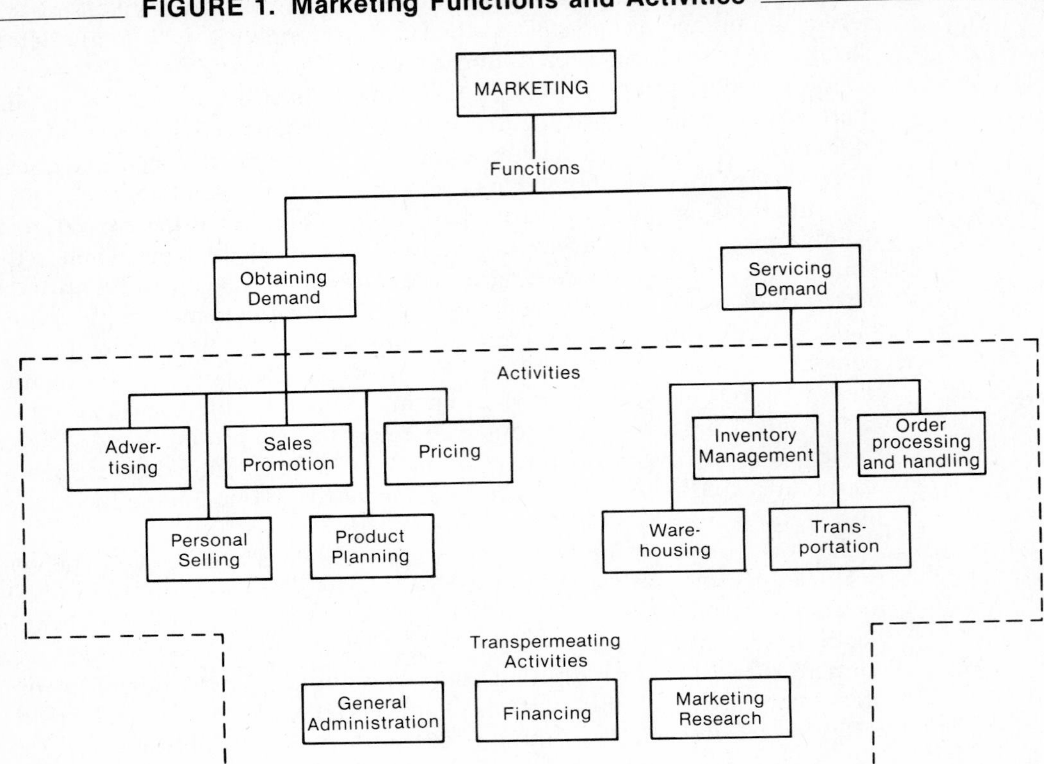


relationships. Objects or subsystems with redundant relationships have no effect on the output objects of the system. Contradictory relationships result in negative influences on the system.

The above provides a description of the elements of a general systems approach to a particular subject. It is the goal of this article to synthesize the general systems view with the functional approach to the study of marketing. The importance of using a general systems view was pointed out by Kenneth Boulding: "General Systems Theory is the skeleton of science in the sense that it aims to provide a framework or structure of systems on which to hang the flesh and blood of particular disciplines and particular subject matter in an orderly and coherent corpus of knowledge."[9] The opposite of a general system is the special system which would be used to derive a specific solution for a special purpose.

In addition to the general and special types, systems can also be described as physical versus abstract, natural versus man-made, and open versus closed. The natural category is typical of open systems in that the systems exchange their materials or energies with the environment in a predictable and understandable way. By contrast, closed systems have little exchange of energy or materials with their environment. For example, man-made systems are closed when they have a constant input and a corresponding statistically predictable output. In this connection it should be noted that in business systems the main purpose of the system object, feed-back-control, is to move the system nearer to a closed system.

In reviewing the nature of systems it can be seen that marketing is a system within the total system of a firm. It is a man-made, open system which attempts to move toward a closed system by feed-back-control. It faces internal restrictions of policy, goals, and finances from within the total system of the firm and external restrictions from the environment in such forms as governments, competitors, and customers.

## Synthesizing the Functional and Systems Approaches

Although most functional treatments of marketing have indicated an awareness of the complementary nature of marketing activities, in actuality the activities have largely been treated independently rather than interactively. A systems approach to marketing forces emphasis on the interdependent nature of marketing activities and has the further expository advantage of making *explicit* those elements inherent in the system.

Figure 2 portrays an attempt to synthesize the functional and systems approach to marketing. As shown in the figure, a marketing system is composed of objects, attributes, and relationships.

What, then, is the relationship between a functional and systems view of marketing? Referring again to Figure 2, it can be seen that the functions of marketing are synonymous with the output objects of the systems view; that is, both refer to the purposes of marketing. In addition, it shows that the three sets of activities of marketing are the input objects of a marketing system. It would be impossible to identify or design a system without first knowing what its purpose is and what the relevant activities involved are. Thus, the functional approach serves as the foundation for a systems approach to marketing. If it were not for a functional approach that clearly delineates marketing's role in the firm, as well as the means of fulfilling that role, it would be impossible to specify the output and input objects of the system.

The importance of a systems approach to marketing is that it goes beyond identifying the output and input objects. In addition, it deals with the process of combining marketing activities, the monitoring of the system through feed-back-control, and a recognition of the restrictions under which the system operates. Further, the systems approach directs attention to the description of the objects by their attributes. Of particular importance to

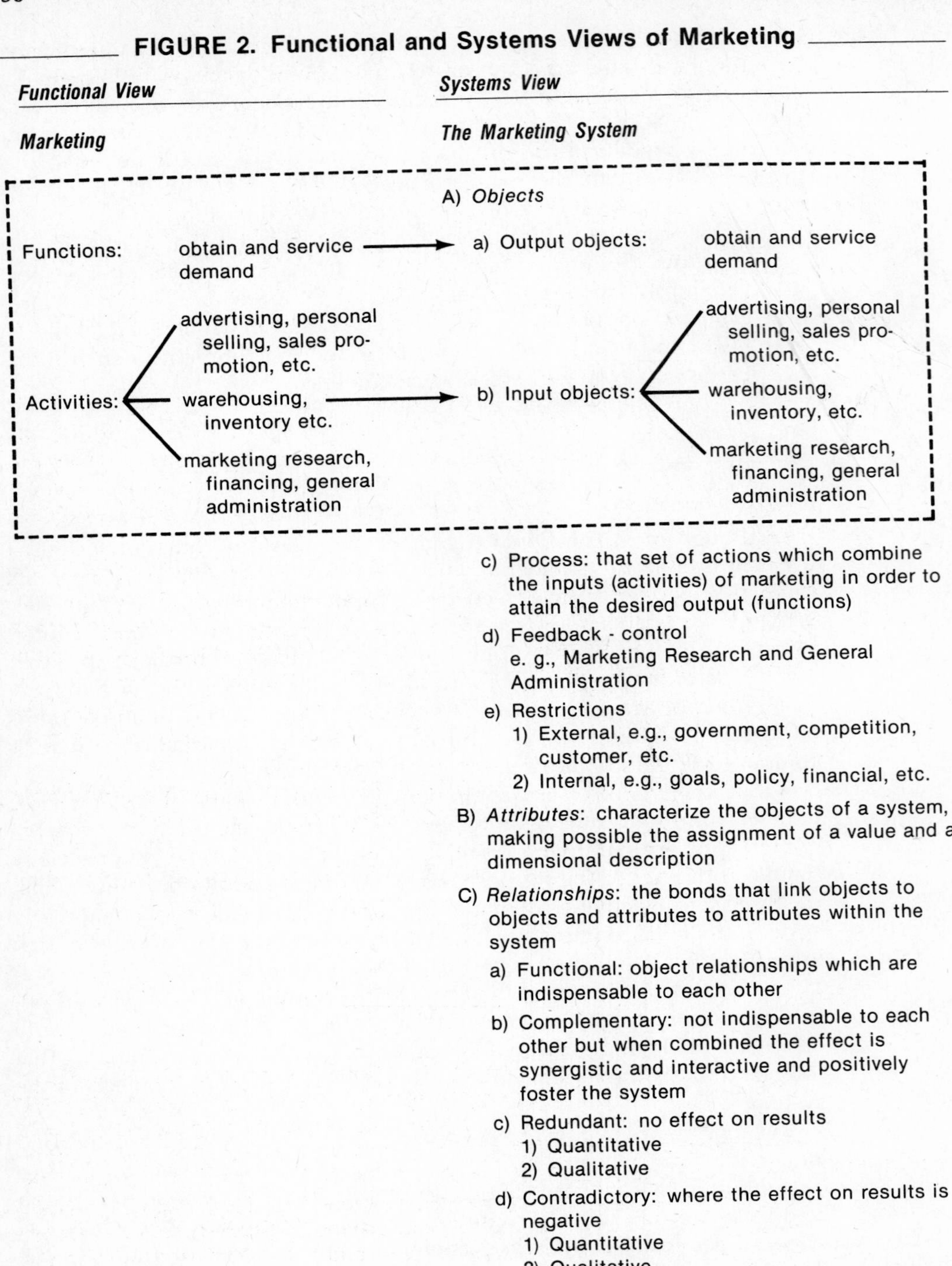
FIGURE 2. Functional and Systems Views of Marketing
Functional View
Systems View
Marketing
The Marketing System
A) Objects
Functions:
obtain and service demand
a) Output objects:
obtain and service demand
Activities:
advertising, personal selling, sales promotion, etc.
warehousing, inventory etc.
marketing research, financing, general administration
b) Input objects:
advertising, personal selling, sales promotion, etc.
warehousing, inventory, etc.
marketing research, financing, general administration
c) Process: that set of actions which combine the inputs (activities) of marketing in order to attain the desired output (functions)
d) Feedback - control
e. g., Marketing Research and General Administration
e) Restrictions
1) External, e.g., government, competition, customer, etc.
2) Internal, e.g., goals, policy, financial, etc.
B) Attributes: characterize the objects of a system, making possible the assignment of a value and a dimensional description
C) Relationships: the bonds that link objects to objects and attributes to attributes within the system
a) Functional: object relationships which are indispensable to each other
b) Complementary: not indispensable to each other but when combined the effect is synergistic and interactive and positively foster the system
c) Redundant: no effect on results
1) Quantitative
2) Qualitative
d) Contradictory: where the effect on results is negative
1) Quantitative
2) Qualitative

marketing is that portion of the systems approach concerned with identifying the nature of relationships among objects and among attributes. Herein lies the emphasis on the interactive nature of marketing activities.

## SUMMARY AND CONCLUSIONS

It is desirable to retain and to strengthen the functional approach to marketing, even if the systems approach is to be employed. The functional approach is a prerequisite to the systems approach in that it provides a definition of the input and output objects of the system. In addition, the functional approach is important in marketing for both theoretical and managerial purposes.

The essence of theory is generalization. The essence of generalization is abstraction. The functional approach's concern with activities which are *inherent* forces attention to the universal similarities of marketing regardless of culture, institution, or product. Without such an approach the result is to focus attention on differences which can lead to chaos and confusion rather than to order and clarity.

The functional approach combined with the systems approach also possesses certain managerial advantages. Perhaps the most important of these is that treatment of otherwise seemingly independent activities within a framework of interdependence and interaction is facilitated. In addition, it clearly delineates the functional centers for classifying the costs of marketing activities, thus permitting their assignment according to responsibility and accountability. Likewise, it permits a functional organization of marketing consistent with responsibility and accountability.

It seems fruitless to argue about the absolute merits of either the functional or systems approach. This article has attempted to demonstrate that the systems approach enables a more complete understanding of the marketing process in the firm. However, it requires the functional approach to provide the basic objects of the system.

## ENDNOTES

1. Paul D. Converse, Harvey W. Huegy, and Robert V. Mitchell, *The Elements of Marketing*, 5th Edition (Englewood Cliffs, N.J.: Prentice-Hall, Inc., 1952), p. 62.
2. The origin of this definition is not clear. Apparently it first appeared in Harold H. Maynard, Walter Weilder, and Theodore N. Beckman, *Principles of Marketing*, 3rd Edition (New York: The Ronald Press Co., 1939), p. 31. However, the first edition of the *Marketing Handbook* (New York: The Ronald Press Co., 1948) shows on p. 23 the definition as having originated from the A.M.A. Committee on Definitions. The 1935, 1948, and 1960 published reports of the Committee do not make reference to this definition.

3. "Definitions of Marketing Terms" (consolidated report of the Committee on Definitions), *National Marketing Review*, I (Chicago, Ill.: National Association of Marketing Teachers, Fall, 1935), p. 156.
4. Same reference as note 3.
5. Edmund D. McGarry, "Some Functions of Marketing Reconsidered," *Theory in Marketing*, Reavis Cox and Wroe Alderson, Editors (Chicago: Richard D. Irwin, Inc., 1950), Chapter 16, pp. 263-279, at page 268.
6. Ralph S. Alexander and the Committee on Definitions, *Marketing Definitions: A Glossary of Marketing Terms* (Chicago, Ill.: American Marketing Association, 1960), p. 16.
7. Richard J. Lewis, "A Business Logistics Information and Accounting System for Marketing Analysis," unpublished doctoral dissertation, Michigan State University, 1964, pp. 62-63.
8. The general framework of a system as the term is used in this article is adapted from Stanford L. Optner, *Systems Analysis for Business and Industrial Problem Solving* (Englewood Cliffs, N.J.: Prentice-Hall, Inc., 1965).
9. Kenneth Boulding, "General Systems Theory: The Skeleton of Science," *General Systems* (Ann Arbor, Mich.: Society for Systems Research, 1956), p. 17.

# SECTION G
# Institutional Structure School

The institutional school of marketing, with its emphasis on the agents of market transactions, is often considered the heart of marketing. In other words, the role of the intermediaries between producers and consumers and the flow of goods, transactions, and information through them is considered the domain of marketing. Just as product occupies much of the time and energy of the manufacturing department in a company, channel arrangements and channel management occupy much of the time and energy of the marketing department.

In recent years the channels of distribution, and therefore the institutional school of marketing, have been going through significant changes due to a number of emerging technological and social changes. First, the information age of electronics communication and electronic shopping has had an almost revolutionary impact on the channels of distribution. For example, producers have been able to reduce the time and space gaps between themselves and consumers by telemarketing and videotex technologies. This affects the importance of wholesalers and retailers who bridged the time and space gap in earlier days. In other words, direct marketing may significantly revise and even challenge the institutional school of thought.

Second, there is an increasing tendency among consumers to make their own things rather than buy them in the market place. In the industrial markets this has been true, especially in printing, chemicals, telecommunications, health care, and financial services. There is a similar trend among consumers in terms of self-help, self-service, and do-it-yourself phenomena. These are also likely to affect the institutional school of thought.

Finally, the markets are becoming international, and competition is becoming global. The institutional school of thought must incorporate the impact of internationalization of marketing. For example, who should perform the value-added functions for a product or service?

In our opinion, the institutional school of thought is likely to undergo significant changes and will therefore become an exciting area of research and theory.

# 22 — The Fundamentals of Marketing

*Louis Dwight Harvell Weld*

Chapter 1, *The Marketing of Farm Products* (New York: Macmillan, 1916), pp. 1-23.

The widespread interest in the marketing of farm products that has developed within the past few years in the United States is undoubtedly due largely to the unusual increase in prices since 1900. Computations based on statistics issued by the United States Bureau of Labor Statistics indicate that, considering the average from 1890 to 1899 as 100, retail prices of food had advanced to 154.2 in 1912, and weekly earnings of laborers to 131.6, so that the average purchasing power of wage earners in 1912 was only 85.3 per cent of what it was during the decade 1890-99.[1] Until 1907, the advance in money wages corresponded fairly closely to the increase in prices, so that wage earners practically held their own; but since 1907 wages have increased at a slower rate than have prices, with the result that purchasing power has been decreasing. It is this condition which has had much to do with the interest in the cost of marketing, and which has lent significance to the wide differences between the prices received by farmers and the prices paid by city consumers.

Although the general public has only recently become keenly interested in this subject, the farmers have long had their misgivings concerning the relation between farm prices and city retail prices. As early as during the agricultural unrest of the seventies, one of the important objects of the Patrons of Husbandry was to reduce the cost of marketing, both through cooperative purchase of supplies and disposal of products. The National Grange of to-day and many of the other farmers' organizations which followed in the wake of the remarkable Granger outburst of the seventies have had as one of their avowed purposes, the improvement of the methods of marketing.

Although the early attempts to reorganize the marketing system met with prompt and complete failure, the agitations resulted in some good through the passage of state laws, such as those governing warehouses, grain inspection, etc., in some of the Middle Western states. However, the general subject of marketing was not studied scientifically. The United States Industrial Commisssion of 1900 made a comprehensive and rather thoroughgoing investigation, and its report on this subject, though it awakened relatively little public interest at the time, stands out as a remarkable piece of work in view of the fact that so little had previously been done along this line. Aside from this, there is practically no source from which accurate information may be obtained as to the costs and methods of marketing in the past, although information on certain points may be obtained from miscellaneous sources, such as court decisions, hearings and reports of the Interstate Commerce Commission, etc. The subject of speculation had also been admirably treated prior to the present awakening of interest.

The subject of marketing deserves the attention it is now receiving, and the frequent criticism that our state agricultural colleges have devoted relatively too much energy to teaching farmers how to raise more crops, and not enough to teaching how to market them, is largely justified. The study of marketing naturally falls to the lot of the economist. To make the necessary investigations of market practices, to classify the data collected, and to draw sound conclusions as to fundamental principles is not so easy as is commonly thought. Too many speakers and writers are making glaring statements without a sufficient foundation of knowledge, and without having a broad enough point of view to include the interests of all people concerned with the marketing process. To attack the problem rationally, and with a clear and comprehensive view, it is first necessary to understand the place that marketing occupies in our general economic system and to find out what the science of economics has to offer in the way of general laws which are helpful in solving the problems involved.

## Marketing a Part of Production

Professional economists usually divide the field of economic activity into three grand divisions,—production, distribution, and consumption. When it comes to locating the subject of marketing, or market distribution as it is frequently called, in its proper division, the nomenclature used by economists is misleading, because marketing is a part of production, and not of distribution. Production is often defined as the creation of utilities; *i.e.* any process that makes a thing more useful,—either by molding it into a more desirable form in the factory, or by transporting it from one place where it is less needed to another place where it is more needed, or by storing it from one season of the year when it is less needed until another season when it is more needed,—is a productive process. Marketing clearly belongs in such a conception of production. Consumption, on the other hand, means the final using up of commodities, to satisy human wants. The term "distribution," as used by economists, means the division of wealth among those who cooperate in producing it. One phase of the problem of distribution is that of the equitable division of wealth among wage earners, capitalists, and land owners. Socialists, for example, believe that wage earners as a class get less than their rightful share and that capitalists get more. Another question on the general problem of distribution is whether each individual of a class receives his rightful share. Among wage earners, for example, are differences in wages adjusted fairly to individual ability and efficiency?

This description of what economists call ''distribution'' has been given in order to indicate clearly why marketing is not a part of that division of economics. Because of the various meanings of the word ''distribution,'' it might be better to avoid the use of the term altogether in referring to the subject with which this book deals. It is very important to realize fully that marketing, whether we call it by that name, or whether we call it ''market distribution,'' is a part of the productive process, and hence that those engaged in marketing are productive laborers, who add to the usefulness of commodities which they handle.

## Kinds of Utility

It has already been said that production may be defined as the creation of utilities. The classification of utilities into their various kinds is helpful in making clear the relation of the marketing process to other productive processes. Utilities may be divided into form, time, place, and possession utilities. Form utilities are created by changing the form of commodities, as in the manufacturing operation. Lumber is taken into a factory; it is sawed and cut into different shapes, and the shapes are fitted together into a chair or a table. Form utilities have been created, and the value of the lumber enchanced. The raising of agricultural products also falls into this class. Time utilities are created by holding or storing commodities from times that they are plentiful to times when they are scarce. The storage of ice from winter to summer is an example. Likewise the storage of eggs and butter, from times of surplus production to times of deficient production, results in an addition of usefulness, or time utility. Place utilities are created by carrying commodities from one place to another. The wheat of the American Northwest would be of little value if it could not be transported from that area of surplus production to the great centers of consumption. Possession utilities are created by the exchange of goods from the hands of one person to another.

From this analysis of utilities, it is apparent that marketing deals primarily with the creation of time, place, and possession utilities. In fact production may be roughly divided into two great divisions, viz., manufacturing or crop raising on the one hand, and marketing on the other. Marketing begins where the manufacturing process ends. When goods emerge from the factory, or have harvested on the farm, the marketing process begins. Oftentimes, manufacturing processes intervene between marketing processes. Wool is a product of sheep raising and it has to be marketed to the woolen mill. The woolen mill manufactures it into cloth, and the cloth has to be marketed to the clothing manufacturer. The latter maufactures clothing, which has to be marketed to consumers. At each step an increment of value is added by those who handle or transform the product.

Unfortunately, economists, in studying production, have had in mind primarily the creation of form utilities. Division of labor, large-scale production, and other problems of the organization and methods of production have been studied mainly in connection with the manufacturing end. Likewise, agricultural economists have concerned themselves primarily with the raising of crops, farm management, feeding of animals, etc., and not to any great extent with the marketing of the products. Some beginnings have been made along this line within the past few years, but the marketing process has never been subjected to careful scientific analysis. And yet the marketing part of production is extremely important as compared with the manufacturing or crop-growing part. Comparison of factory or farm prices with final retail prices of almost any commodity will prove this. The difference, sometimes called the ''spread'' or ''differential,'' represents the cost of marketing,—or more properly, the cost and profits of marketing. In the case of farm products, at least, the profits normally constitute such a small proportion that it involves no great error to consider that these differentials represent the costs of marketing.

## Lack of Knowledge on the Subject

The failure on the part of economists to study marketing has resulted in a serious situation. Now that nation-wide interest has been aroused in the subject, there has been no authentic source to which one might turn for definite and impartial knowledge. As a result, many mistaken notions have been spread abroad, and the general public believes that there is something radically wrong with the whole marketing system, and that it is fundamentally defective. The field has been preempted largely by individuals with no scientific training, and so many misleading and absurd statements have been allowed to pass unchallenged by men who ought to be in a position to lead and influence public opinion, that it will take some time to bring the public into a sane frame of mind with regard to this vital part of our economic system. The agitation for investigation and for state and federal legislation has been led largely by politicians, and for this reason the dealers engaged in the wholesale produce trade are inclined to believe that the movement is purely a political agitation.[1] But this is far from being the case, because as already pointed out, the general public believe that there is something fundamentally wrong.

The agitation has already resulted in definite steps to collect the information necessary to a correct understanding of the marketing problem. Many of the state universities, notably those of Minnesota and Wisconsin, have begun to make scientific investigations of the methods and costs of marketing. Many of the large cities of the country, notably New York City, have turned their attention to this problem. But the most important step is that taken by the Federal Government through the Office of Markets in the Department of Agriculture. This office had an appropriation of $200,000 for the year 1914-15, and has experts engaged in studying the methods of marketing different products. The most important source of detailed information on this subject in the future will undoubtedly be the reports issued by this office. Its activities are described more in detail in the last chapter.

## Marketing of Manufactured Products

One interesting feature of the growing interest in marketing problems is that it has centered so largely on the marketing of *agricultural products*, as distinct from ordinary *manufactured products*. The distinction is not very clear in some cases, because many staple food commodities, such as butter, flour, and live-stock products, have undergone manufacturing processes before becoming available for final consumption. In the main, however, the manufacturing processes, to which the great staples mentioned above are subjected, add increments of value which are relatively small as compared either with final retail prices or with total differentials between producers' prices and final retail prices. In discussing the costs of marketing as represented by these differentials, however, the manufacturing costs, when they occur, should not be confounded with purely marketing costs.

It is only natural that public interest should center on the marketing of farm products for two reasons: first, because of the large proportion that outlay for food constitutes of average family budgets; and second, because of the unrest that has existed among farmers for so long, as already pointed out. But the subject of marketing farm products is only one phase of the general subject of market distribution, an extremely important part of our economic system concerning which there is as yet practically no classified knowledge available. As a general proposition, manufactured products are marketed through the hands of fewer successive middlemen, but on wider differentials between factory and consumer, than are the staple farm products between farmer and consumer. It is said that the factory cost of a sewing machine is less than ten dollars as compared with a retail price of forty dollars; that a hundred-dollar typewriter costs less than twenty dollars in the factory; that the cloth cost of twenty-five dollar ready-made suit is less than five dollars, and that the retailer pays only from twelve to fifteen dollars for such a suit.

Whether or not these figures are correct, the differences between manufacturing costs and final retail prices for most manufactured goods are surprisingly great, and the focus of public interest will undoubtedly shift in the direction of this phase of the marketing problem before long. Indeed many of our universities are already beginning to realize the importance of subjecting the whole field of market distribution to dispassionate scientific research, both for the purpose of teaching college students the fundamentals of merchandising and for the purpose of gaining information that is necessary for an intelligent consideration of some of our most vital questions of governmental regulation of industry and commerce. For example, many of the most important phases of the trust problem have to do with what has come to be called "unfair competition," including such practices as price discrimination, price maintenance, restrictive sales agreements, factors' agreements, etc. These are very largely marketing problems, and their fairness or legitimacy can hardly be determined intelligently without a more adequate knowledge of the fundamental features of market distribution than now exists. The hearings and debates preceding the anti-trust legislation of 1914, and the very wording of the acts themselves (The Clayton Anti-trust and the Trade Commission laws) are conclusive proof of the uncertainty and lack of knowledge with regard to these practices. If the view expressed here is correct, the newly established Trade Commission faces a difficult task. To decide on the fairness or unfairness of any specific trade practice mentioned above with the meager stock of knowledge available at present would be analogous to attempting to decide on the reasonableness or unreasonableness of a single railroad rate without knowing anything of the fundamental considerations which govern rate making in general. In other words, a study of market distribution furnishes an important and necessary avenue of approach toward the solution of some of the most difficult phases of the trust problem.

## THE DEVELOPMENT OF MARKETS

The marketing of agricultural products becomes more and more difficult and intricate as civilization develops, as population increases, and as people tend to congregate in large cities. If the cultivators of the soil raised and made all the products that they needed, and only as much as they needed, there would be no marketing problem. In other words, if each farmer were self-sufficient, he would not have to depend on the outside world either as a source of supplies for use on the farm or as a market for his surplus products. These conditons existed in primitive economy, and in certain parts of the world, even in backward communities in the United States, a near approach to self-sufficiency may still be found.

To the extent that people live in small villages scattered throughout the agricultural regions of the world, the marketing problem is still comparatively simple, at least so far as products raised in the vicinity are concerned. To supply such people, farmers either sell direct, without the intervention of a single middleman, or more commonly through the country store, which may well be considered the first important middleman to have appeared in marketing farm products. Marketing implies both selling and buying, and although the country store developed primarily to furnish supplies for farmers to buy, yet they served—and do serve to-day to a certain extent—as an agency through which are marketed the products that farmers sell. A complete historical survey of the development of markets would necessarily include a consideration of fairs and "market days," but since these have played a relatively minor part in the development of marketing in the United States, their description adds little to an understanding of the present system.

The principle factors which mark the present organization and intricacy of the marketing organization, as compared with the primitive conditions outlined above, are the concentration of a considerable proportion of the population in large cities, and the development of specialization in agriculture whereby the farmers of each region raise certain crops in excess of their own requirements and of the requirements of the local village communities. In other words, the farming sections have surpluses of farm products which must be collected at country shipping points, transported to large centers of consumption, and there redistributed to consumers. Population is concentrated to such an extent in the large cities that the surrounding territory can furnish only a small proportion of the necessary food supply; perishable products have to be transported over great distances, and they ripen first in one section of the country and then in another as the season advances, thus complicating the problem. All this makes necessary a highly developed and complex organization without which it would be impossible to market at all certain commodities that now pass through the channels fo trade. The development of the modern transportation system is of course another factor, without which the present marketing system would be impossible. Oftentimes territorial specialization in agriculture is carried to such an extent that the quantity of a commodity raised in any one country is greater than the consumptive requirements of that country, so that there is a surplus to be exported to foreign markets.

With these considerations in mind, the marketing problem indeed appears to be one of great complexity and difficulty. The surpluses collected at country shipping points are in turn the relatively small surpluses of millions of individual farmers, which, taken together, form a mass of commodities very heterogeneous as to quality, variety, degree of ripeness, method of packing, etc. Furthermore, the great bulk of farm products is harvested and marketed during a small portion of the year, whereas city consumers desire to spread their consumption over as large a portion of the year as possible. City consumers buy these commodities in exceedingly small quantities and demand that they be made available at a moment's notice in close proximity to their residences. Add to this the fact that many commodities are highly perishable and must be handled with great rapidity and by means of special and expensive facilities, and we get a still better view of the complexity of the problem.

## Specialization in Marketing

In the evolution of the marketing system there have developed two kinds of specialization. The first is the division into separate trades, whereby each class of dealers handles a single commodity or group of commodities; and the second is the splitting up of the marketing process into a number of successive steps, or specialization by functions. The former kind of specialization apparently meets with general approval and no fault is found with it. The latter, however, is not generally understood, and the popular opinion is that subdivision of the marketing process into a number of successive steps has been carried too far,—in other words, that there are too many middlemen between producer and consumer.

## Specialization by Commodities

Specialization into separate trades according to commodities handled begins at country shipping points. Many farm products are still handled through country stores, but as a usual rule, whenever a commodity is raised in sufficient quantity to warrant it, there appears a middleman who makes a specialty of handling it,—and oftentimes a number of such specialists at a single shipping point. Thus in the grain trade there are grain elevators,—sometimes four or five in a single village; in the butter trade, there are local creameries; in the live-stock trade, cattle buyers or shipping associations; in the potato trade, potato warehouses. In the poultry and egg trade there are dealers, who are often called "cash buyers." The extent to which the marketing at any single point is specialized in this manner of course depends on the number of different products raised and the quantity of each. Where a one-crop system is in vogue, there may be only one class of local buyers.

Specialization of this character is also found in the wholesale trades. A highly specialized class of dealers exists in the grain trade, and there are even subdivisions of this class, according to the specific grains handled. In all the large live-stock markets there is a separate class of live-stock dealers. Specialists also appear in the cotton and wool trades, and in the handling of dairy and poultry products. In general, the degree of specialization in these lines depends largely on the size of the city. In the smaller or medium-sized cities, a wholesale produce dealer often handles a great variety of products, although in cities of medium size there appears a differentiation into groups, such as one handling butter, eggs, and poultry, one handling fruits, and one handling vegetables; although the two last named are commonly combined.

In the largest cities, these groups become even more differentiated, according to commodities handled. Butter and eggs are commonly handled by the same dealers, but poultry is frequently handled by a separate class of merchants. In New York the poultry trade is even divided between live poultry and dressed poultry. In the vegetable trade, there is also considerable subdivision. Potatoes are very commonly handled by a separate class of traders, even in the smaller cities, and there may be found dealers who specialize in certain vegetables, such as onions or cabbages, although they commonly handle a few other commodities in addition.

Specialization has also developed in the retail trade, but not to the extent as in the wholesale trade. The grocery store usually handles a great variety of farm products. Meats are sold by butcher shops, but these are often found in connection with grocery stores. Fruits, although sold by grocery stores, are handled in great quantities by the corner fruit stands. There has been a tendency for butter and eggs to be sold by a separate class of dealers, who also commonly sell tea and coffee in addition. A special class of dealers also handles hay and feed, and tobacco is also sold by a separate class of shop keepers. Complications in such an analysis as this arise as soon as we begin to consider agricultural products that are radically changed in form by manufacturing, and in our study of marketing farm products it is best to carry the products only so far as they retain at least approximately their natural state.

## Specialization by Functions

Ordinarily the marketing process may be divided roughly into four successive steps, viz., country shippers, transportation companies, wholesale dealers, and retail stores. In passing through the wholesale trade, there may be two or three successive middlemen, such as a commission man and a jobber, or a broker and a jobber, or a broker, an auction company, and a jobber. The cold-storage warehouse may enter as an additional middleman, or a drayman may enter between railroad company and commission man, or between wholesaler and cold-storage plant. The functions of these various middlemen will be described in subsequent chapters; we are concerned in this place with the mere fact of subdivision.

It will be remembered that marketing is a part of production. Specialization into successive steps is a form of division of labor, and division of labor is commonly praised as a phenomenon that reduces the cost of production or that makes possible the production of a greater amount of wealth with the same amount of effort. We praise division of labor in the packing plant whereby each workman performs a single task and becomes an expert at that task. We also praise that form of specialization whereby the manufacturing process is subdivided among separate plants. In the steel industry, for example, one plant makes nothing but pig iron; another makes the pig iron into crude steel; another rolls the steel into bars; another takes the bars and makes structural forms, or machinery. In the worsted industry, the tendency is towards a greater subdivision of tasks among separate plants. The combing of wool into "tops" is usually performed by the same mills that spin yarn, but there is a tendency for tops to be made in a separate set of mills, as in England, where the worsted industry has reached a high degree of development, and where combing is usually performed in a separate set of combing mills. In both the steel and worsted industries the plants performing successive steps are sometimes separately owned, or they may be under a single ownership, in which case we have ''integration'' of industry; in either case there is specialization.

It is difficult to understand why this division of labor or specialization argument should not apply to the marketing part of production as well as to the manufacturing part of production. Those who have really made a first-hand intensive study of the wholesale produce trade realize that there are certain necessary functions to be performed, and that these functions are much more difficult and complex than is commonly supposed. Each successive middleman specializes on one particular set of functions. For example, in New York city a large part of the butter reaching that city passes through the hands of two different middlemen before reaching the retail stores. The first is a wholesale receiver, who receives butter in large quantities and in great variety from a large number of country creameries. He sends out solicitors to get in touch with the creameries, and he often finances them by allowing them to draw drafts on day of shipment. He provides a store or warehouse with adequate refrigeration, assembles the miscellaneous shipments from different parts of the country, weighs them and makes returns to shipper and sorts them out roughly according to quality. In this particular trade the wholesale receiver does not have delivery equipment, but has an independent drayman (really another middleman) haul the goods from the freight sheds to his warehouse.

These functions of the receiver form a business in themselves. He sells in lots of from twenty to fifty or more tubs to jobbers, who in turn send salesman to the thousands of retail stores, delicatessens, restaurants, hotels, etc., and deliver one tub at a time from day to day, as the needs of the retail outlets demand. It is common for a jobber to specialize on some particular class of retailers who require certain qualities and amounts of butter, and he makes his purchases from the receivers according to the class of trade he serves. Furthermore, he finances the retailer by giving him credit, and maintains an accounting department to care for innumerable small accounts. In other words, the jobber specializes in steering the carloads of butter that arrive every day into innumerable small channels according to quality and quantity desired.

The extent to which this subdivision of processes is carried out varies in different trades according to the characteristics of the commodity handled, and according to the size of the city which is being supplied. In the butter trade, the organization outlined above does not exist to any great extent outside of New York, Chicago, and Philadelphia. In other cities, the wholesale receivers commonly sell direct to the retail trade. In fact there has been a tendency in recent years in New York City for these two branches of the trade to consolidate, although there will probably always be a need for a separate class of jobbers. In the fruit trade it is the usual rule for goods to pass through the hands of at least two classes of middlemen, analogous to those described above, and oftentimes a broker or an auction company comes in as a third step, even in the smaller cities.

It is sometimes thought that these various middlemen arbitrarily divide the trade among themselves, each clinging to one definite set of functions, and leaving other functions to other middlemen. It is true that in some trades these divisions are very clear cut and that the various dealers sometimes definitely protect each other by refusing to overlap into each other's field of activity. But as a rule an adjustment or readjustment of this division of functions is going on all the time, and traders are continually experimenting, unconsciously perhaps, in extending or restricting their functions, irrespective of the desires of other traders on whose territory they may be encroaching. Sometimes an extension of functions on the part of a wholesale receiver, for instance, into the jobbing field, results in a lower cost of marketing and hence a permanent readjustment of the trade. Such an adjustment usually comes about gradually without causing much friction.

When one dealer undertakes to combine and to perform functions formerly performed by two or more successive middlemen, we have what might be called integration of marketing processes, similar to what is called integration of industry. The United States Steel Corporation offers perhaps the best illustration of integration through the ownerhsip of mines, steamers, railroads, blast furnaces, open-hearth furnaces, etc. But, as mentioned before, such integration does not mean any smaller degree of specialization. The chain-store company is an illustration of such integration in merchandising, because it takes over the functions of the jobber and the retailer with resulting economies, but specialization by functions still exists because the business is divided into departments, each department having a definite set of duties.

But the tendency in many trades has been for dealers to restrict their operations by specializing on a narrower and narrower set of functions, thus bringing about a greater subdivision of processes and a larger number of successive middlemen. Such a reorganization is impossible, however, unless economies result. Instances of the introduction of new middlemen who facilitate distribution and lower the total cost of marketing are common; the auction company is a good illustration; the entrance of the broker in some trades furnishes another example; the specialist who does nothing but cut bulk butter into prints has brought about certain economies in the butter trade; a cooperative or centralized delivery system which would do away with the vast duplication of delivery equipment and the covering and recovering of the same territory, is an illustration of this principle which may develop in the future.

## ARE THERE TOO MANY MIDDLEMEN?

When the statement is made that there are too many middlemen, it may mean one of two things: either that the process of subdivision already described has gone too far so that there are too many successive steps, or that there are too many of each class, such as too many country buyers, too many wholesalers, or too many retailers.

The discussion in the preceding paragraphs bears directly on the question as to whether there are too many successive steps, and this is what most people mean when they glibly state that there are too many middlemen. It was pointed out that such subdivision is merely an example of the well-known doctrine of division of labor, and that economies may result from specialization by functions. Although it is perhaps impossible to say definitely whether there are too many middlemen in this sense, it is at least true that there is ample economic justification for a subdivision of the marketing process among specialized classes of dealers; that in some cases lower cost and greater efficiency may be gained by further specialization; and that in other cases it may be possible to reduce the cost by combining the functions of two or more middlemen into the hands of one single middleman. The functions of marketing have to be performed, however many separate middlemen there are; the problem is to find the most economical combination of functions.

This is a matter that can be determined only by careful investigation in each separate trade. Those who have really made first-hand studies of the marketing system in an impartial and unprejudiced way realize that on the whole the system of marketing that has developed is efficient, rather than "extremely cumbersome and wasteful," and that there are very good practical reasons for the form of organization that has developed. It is necessary to realize these fundamental facts before the reader can approach a study of the marketing problem with a sane point of view. That is why such an important conclusion is stated in the first chapter of this book. It may be claimed that this conclusion has been reached largely by *a priori* reasoning, but the reader will perhaps agree that facts brought out in subsequent chapters substantiate the validity of this point of view.

Whether there are too many middlemen of each class is also a more difficult question to answer than is commonly believed. While the subdivision of processes into successive steps is a problem in division of labor or specialization, the question as to whether there are too many country buyers, too many wholesalers, or too many retailers, is principally a problem in large-scale production, or proper size of business units. As for local shipping units, such as creameries, elevators, etc., there are many places where shipping facilities are inadequate; at other places there are often more buyers than necessary, as frequently occurs in the live-stock business, or in the cotton trade, or in the grain business. The larger the shipping unit, the lower the cost of handling, as in the case of grain elevators in Minnesota, but this applies principally to forms of marketing which require considerable investment of capital in warehouse or other facilities.

In the wholesale trade we already have fairly large business units, and it is questionable whether much would be gained by a further concentration.

The principal question in this connection is in the retail trade, and most writers and speakers on the subject feel perfectly safe in stating that there are too many retail stores. This also is a complicated question, however, and its consideration will be deferred to the chapter devoted to the retail trade.

## ENDNOTES

1. Rubinow, "The Recent Trend of Real Wages," *American Economic Review*, December, 1914, p. 811.
2. This view was expressed again and again, for example, at the Annual Convention of the National League of Commission Merchants held at Detroit in January, 1915.

# 23 — Postponement, Speculation and the Structure of Distribution Channels

*Louis P. Buckline*

Reprinted from *Journal of Marketing Research*, published by the American Marketing Association, Vol. 2 (February 1965), pp. 26-31. Reprinted by permission.

## The Concept of Substitutability

Underlying the logic of the principle to be developed is the hypothesis that economic interaction among basic marketing functions, and between these functions and production, provides much of the force that shapes the structure of the distribution channel. These interactions occur because of the capability of the various functions to be used as substitutes for each other within certain broad limitations. This capability is comparable to the opportunities available to the entrepreneur to use varying ratios of land, labor, and capital in the production of his firm's output. The substitutability of marketing functions may occur both within the firm and among the various institutions of the channel, *e.g.*, producers, middlemen, and consumers. This substitutability permits the work load of one function to be shrunk and shifted to another without affecting the output of the channel. These functional relationships may also be seen to be at the root of the "total cost" concept employed in the growing literature of the management of the physical distribution system [3,9].

A familiar example of one type of substitution that may appear in the channel is the use of inventories to reduce the costs of production stemming from cyclical demand. Without the inventory, production could only occur during the time of consumption. Use of the inventory permits production to be spread over a longer period of time. If some institution of the channel senses that the costs of creating a seasonal inventory would be less than the savings accruing from a constant rate of production, it would seek to create such a stock and to retain the resulting profits. The consequence of this action is the formation of a new and alternate channel for the production.

The momentum of change, however, is not halted at this point. Unless there is protection against the full brunt of competitive forces, the institutions remaining in the original, and now high-cost channel, will either be driven out of business or forced to convert to the new system as well. With continued competitive pressure the excess profits, initially earned by the institutions which innovated the new channel, will eventually be eliminated and total channel costs will fall.

In essense, the concept of substitutability states that under competitive conditions institutions of the channel will interchange the work load among functions, not to minimize the cost of some individual function, but the total costs of the channel. It provides, thereby, a basis for the study of distribution channels. By understanding the various types of interactions among the marketing functions and production that could occur, one may determine the type of distribution structure that should appear to minimize the total channel costs including those of the consumer. The principle of postponement-speculation, to be developed below, evaluates the conditions under which one type of substitution may occur.

## POSTPONEMENT

In 1950, Wroe Alderson proposed a concept which uniquely related certain aspects of uncertainty and risk to time. He labelled this concept the ''principle of postponement,'' and argued that it could be used to reduce various marketing costs [2]. Risk and uncertainty costs were tied to the differentiation of goods. Differentiation could occur in the product itself and/or the geographical dispersion of inventories. Alderson held that ''the most general method which can be applied in promoting the efficiency of a marketing system is the postponement of differentiation ... postpone changes in form and identity to the latest possible point in the marketing flow; postpone change in inventory location to the latest possible point in time.'' [1] Savings in costs related to uncertainty would be achieved ''by moving the differentiation nearer to the time of purchase,'' where demand, presumably, would be more predictable. Savings in the physical movement of the goods could be achieved by sorting products in ''large lots,'' and ''in relatively undifferentiated states.''

Despite its potential importance, the principle has received relatively little attention since it was first published. Reavis Cox and Charles Goodman [4] have made some use of the concept in their study of channels for house building materials. The Vaile, Grether, and Cox marketing text [10] also makes mention of it. As far as can be determined, this is the totality of its further development.

As a result, the principle still constitutes only a somewhat loose, and possibly misleading, guide to the study of the distribution channel structure. The major defect is a failure to specify the character of the limits which prevent it from being applied. The principle, which states that changes in form and inventory location are to be delayed to the latest possible moment, must also explain why in many channels these changes appear at the earliest. As it stands, the principle of postponement requires modification if it is to be applied effectively to the study of channels.

### Postponement and the Shifting of Risk

If one views postponement from the point of view of the distribution channel as a whole, it may be seen as a device for individual institutions to shift the risk of owning goods to another. The manufacturer who postpones by refusing to produce except to order is shifting the risk forward to the buyer. The middleman postpones by either refusing to buy except from a seller who provides next day delivery (backward postponement), or by purchasing only when he has made a sale (forward postponement). The consumer postpones by buying from those retail facilities which permit him to take immediate possession directly from the store shelf. Further, where the consumer first contacts a number of stores before buying, the shopping process itself may be seen as a process of postponement—a process which advertising seeks to eliminate.

From this perspective it becomes obvious that every institution in the channel, including the consumer, cannot postpone to the latest possible moment. The channel, in its totality, cannot avoid ownership responsibilities. Some institution, or group of institutions, must continually bear this uncertainty from the time the goods start through production until they are consumed.

Since most manufacturers do produce for stock, and the ownerhsip of intermediate inventories by middlemen is characteristic of a large proportion of channels, it is clear that the principle of postponement can reach its limit very quickly. As a result, it provides no rationale for the forces which create these inventories. Hence, postponement is really only half a principle. It must have a converse, a converse equally significant to channel structure.

## Speculation

This converse may be labelled the principle of speculation. It represents a shift of risk to the institution, rather than away from it. The principle of speculation holds that changes in form, and the movement of goods to forward inventories, should be made at the earliest possible time in the marketing flow in order to reduce the costs of the marketing system.

As in the case of postponement, application of the principle of speculation can lead to the reduction of various types of costs. By changing form at the earliest point, one makes possible the use of plants with large-scale economies. Speculation permits goods to be ordered in large quantities rather than in small frequent orders. This reduces the costs of sorting and transportation. Speculation limits the loss of consumer good will due to stock outs. Finally, it permits the reduction of uncertainty in a variety of ways.

This last point has already been well developed in the literature. It received early and effective treatment from Frank H. Knight [6]. He held that speculators, by shifting uncertainty to themselves, used the principle of grouping, as insurance, to transform it into the more manageable form of a relatively predictable risk. Further, through better knowledge of the risks to be handled, and more informed opinion as to the course of future events, risk could be further reduced.

## The Combined Principle

From the point of view of the distribution channel, the creation of inventories for holding goods before they are sold is the physical activity which shifts risk and uncertainty. Such inventories serve to move risk away from those institutions which supply, or are supplied by, the inventory. Such inventories, however, will not be created in the channel if the increased costs attending their operation outweigh potential savings in risk. Risk costs, according to the substitutability hyopthesis, cannot be minimized if other costs increase beyond the savings in risk.

This discussion shows the principle of speculation to be the limit to the principle of postponement, and vice versa. Together they form a basis for determining whether speculative inventories, those that hold goods prior to their sale, will appear in distribution channels subject to competitive conditions. Operationally, postponement may be measured by the notion of delivery time. Delivery time is the number of days (or hours) elapsing between the placing of an order and the physical receipt of the goods by the buyer [9, p. 93]. For the seller, postponement increases, and costs decline, as delivery time lengthens. For the buyer, postponement increases, and costs decline, as delivery time shortens. The combined principle of postponement-speculation may be stated as follows: A speculative inventory will appear at each point in a distribution channel whenever its costs are less than the net savings to both buyer and seller from postponement.

## Operation of the Principle

The following hypothetical example illustrates how the postponement-speculation principle can be applied to the study of distribution channels. The specific problem to be considered is whether an inventory, located between the manufacturer and the consumer, will appear in the channel. This inventory may be managed by the manufacturer, a consumer cooperative or an independent middleman.

Assume that trade for some commodity occurs between a set of manufacturers and a set of customers, both sets being large enough to insure active price competition. The manufacturers are located close to each other in a city some significant distance from the community in which the customers are situated. All of the customers buy in quantities sufficiently large to eliminate the possibility of savings from sorting. Manufacturing and consumption are not affected by seasonal variations. Assume, further, that production costs will not be affected by the presence of such an intermediate inventory.

To determine whether the intermediate inventory will appear, one must first ascertain the shape of the various relevant cost functions with respect to time. In any empirical evaluation of channel structure this is likely to be the most difficult part of the task. For present purposes, however, it will be sufficient to generalize about their character.

The costs incurred by the relevant functions are divided into two broad categories. The first includes those costs originating from activities associated with the potential inventory, such as handling, storage, interest, uncertainty, and costs of selling and buying if the inventory is operated by a middleman. It also includes those costs emanating from transportation, whether the transportation is direct from producer to consumer or routed through the inventory. All of these costs will, in turn, be affected by the particular location of the inventory between the producer and the consumer. In the present instance, it is assumed that the inventory will be located in the consumer city.

In general, this first category includes all the relevant costs incurred by the producer and intermediary, if any. These are aggregated on Diagram 1. In this diagram, the ordinate represents the averge cost for moving one unit of the commodity from the producer to the consumer. The abscissa measures the time in days for delivery of an order to the consumer after

**DIAGRAM 1. Average Cost of Distributing One Unit of a Commodity to a Customer with Respect to Delivery Time in Days**

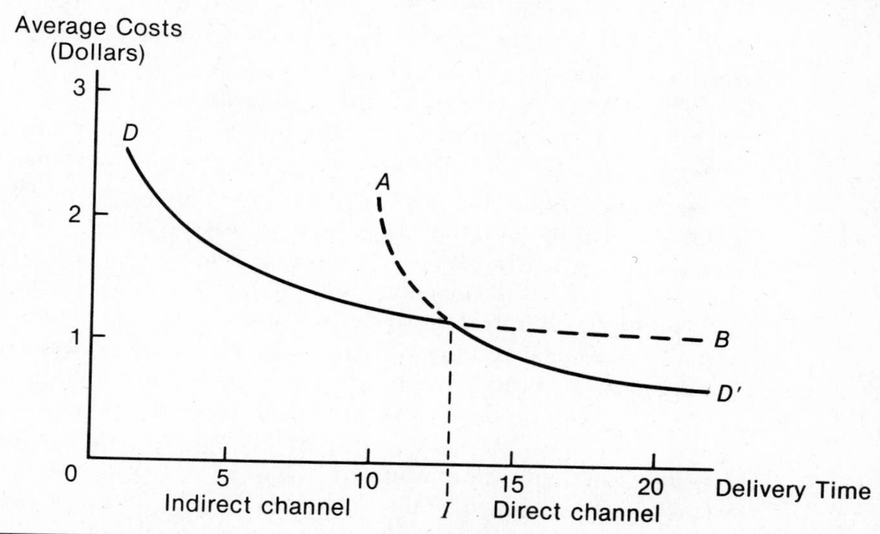

it has been placed. The curve *DB* measures the cost of using the speculative inventory to supply the consumer for the various possible delivery times. Curve *AD′* shows the cost of supplying the consumer direct without use of such an inventory. *DD′* is the minimum average cost achievable by either direct or indirect distribution of the commodity.

The diagram shows that *DD′* declines as the delivery time is allowed to increase [7]. With very short delivery times the intermediate inventory is absolutely necessary because only in this way can goods be rushed quickly to the consumer. Further, when virtually immediate delivery is required, the safety stock of the inventory must be kept high in order to prevent temporary stockouts from delaying shipment. Also, delivery trucks must always be available for short notice. These factors create high costs.

As the delivery time to be allowed increases, it becomes possible to reduce the safety stocks, increase the turnover and reduce the size of the facilities and interest cost. Further increases permit continued savings. Eventually a point will be reached, *I* in Diagram 1, where the delivery time will be sufficiently long to make it cheaper to ship goods directly from the factory to the consumer than to move them indirectly through the inventory. This creates the discontinuity at *I* as the costs of maintaining the inventory and the handling of goods are eliminated.

In part, the steepness of the slope of *DD′* will be affected by the uncertainties of holding the inventory. Where prices fluctuate rapidly, or goods are subject to obsolescence, these costs will be high. The extension of delivery time, in permitting the intermediate inventory to be reduced in size, and eventually eliminated, should bring significant relief.

The second category of costs involves those emanating from the relevant marketing functions performed by the customer. Essentially, these costs will be those of bearing the risk and costs of operating any inventory on the customer's premises. These costs are shown as *C* on Diagram 2, with the ordinate and abscissa labelled as in Diagram 1.

The shape of *C* is one that increases with delivery time. The longer the delivery time allowed by the customer, the greater the safety stock he will have to carry. Such stock is necessary to protect against failures in transport and unpredictable surges in requirements. Hence, his costs will increase. The greater the uncertainty cost of inventory holding, the steeper will the slope of this function be.

Determination of the character of the distribution channel is made from the joint consideration of these two cost categories, *C* and *DD′*. Whether an intermediate inventory will appear in the channel depends upon the relationship of the costs for operating the two sets of functions and how their sum may be minimized. Functions *DD′* + *C* on Diagram 3 represents the sum of functions *DD′* and *C*. The diagram reveals, in this instance, that costs of postponement are minimized by use of a speculative inventory as the minimal cost point, *M*, falls to the left of *I*. If, however, the risk costs to the customer had been less, or the general cost of holding inventories at

**DIAGRAM 2. Average Inventory Cost for One Unit of a Commodity to a Customer with Respect to Delivery Time in Days**

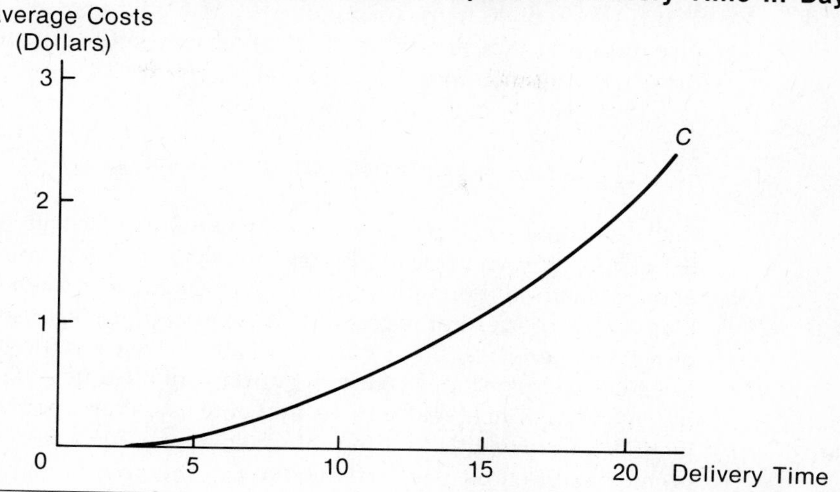


**DIAGRAM 3. Total of Average Distributing and Customer Inventory Costs with Respect to Delivery Time in Days**

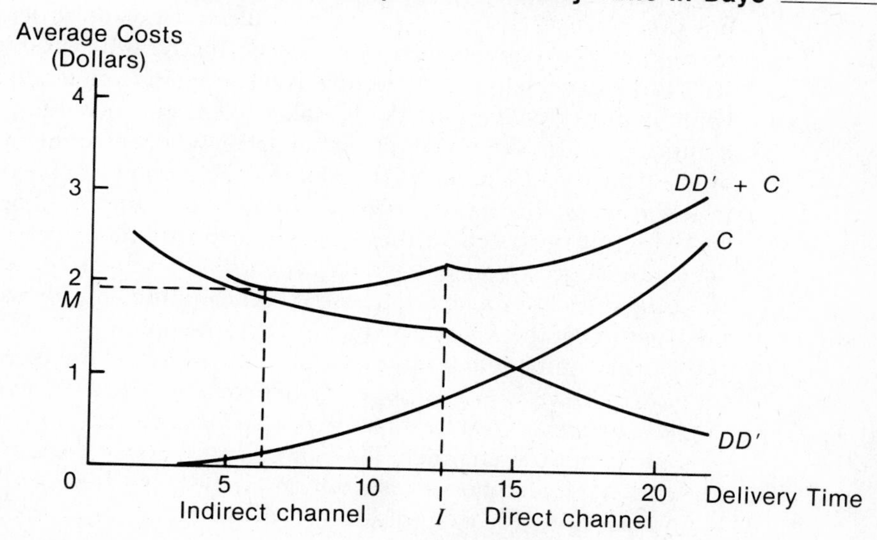

the customer's home (or plant site, as the case may be) had been lower, then *C* would be farther to the right. *M* would also shift to the right. With a sufficient reduction in consumer cost, *M* would appear to the right of the discontinuity, indicating that direct shipment in the channel would be the means to minimize postponement cost.

## Significance of the Principle

As developed, the principle of postponement-speculation provides a basis for expecting inventories to be present in channels because of production and distribution time requirements. In particular, it treats the role of speculative inventories in the channel. The concept, as a consequence, extends beyond the physical flow of the goods themselves to the flow of their title. Speculative inventories create the opportunity for new institutions to hold title in the channel. Without such inventories, there may be little economic justification for a title holding intermediary to enter the channel. The economic need to have such an inventory in the physical flow opens the door to a middleman to show whether he is capable of reducing the risk cost of that inventory below the level attainable by either the producer or some consumer cooperative.

The presence of an inventory in the channel for either collecting, sorting, or dispersing does not create the same type of opportunity for a title-taking intermediary to appear in the channel. Such inventories are not speculative in character. They do not need to hold uncommitted stocks of goods available for general sale in order to fulfill their purpose. For example, the REA Express, the parcel post system, freight forwarders, and even the Greyhound Bus Corporation's freight system sort a substantial volume of goods through many nonspeculative type inventories each day. Milk producers establish handling depots where bottled milk is transferred from large, long-distance vehicles to city delivery trucks. Catalogue sellers discharge full truck shipments upon the post offices of distant cities where customers reside. None of these inventories involves the risk of unsold goods. None of these inventories provides the basis for the emergence of a title-holding middleman.

From this perspective, the principle of postponement-speculation may be regarded as a concept which broadens the channel analyst's understanding of the intimate relationship between title and physical flows. The intertwining of the roles of ownership and the holding of speculative stocks provides a fundamental rationale for the position of the merchant middleman. The principle of postponement-speculation, as a consequence, can be employed to provide at least part of the explanation for the number of ownership stages in the channel. This, of course, is one of the basic questions toward which traditional distribution analysis is directed [5].

In this light, for example, the principle may be of use in explaining the emergence of an ''orthodox channel of distribution.'' This concept, developed by Shaw [8], was used to characterize the nature of the distribution channel through which a large proportion of products traveled, to wit: the manufacturer-wholesaler-retailer route. That such a concept should emerge to characterize products, whose sorting needs are different because of diverse physical characteristics and market reach, is of extreme interest. Similarities among channels for different products implies that forces, which may not vary significantly among many types of goods, should be sought as explanatory variables of channel structure. Since many groups of consumer goods generate similar temporal types of risk, the principle of postponement-speculation may provide a major explanation for this phenomenon.

## Testing the Principle

The principle of postponement-speculation will not be easy to test for a number of reasons. First of all, it is normative. It is derived from assumptions of profit maximization and predictions are based upon what firms should do. Second, it approximates the real world only when the channel environment is sufficiently competitive to produce a variety of price-product-delivery time offers. Finally, it cannot predict the necessary time delays that occur in the channel for new facilities to be built or old ones abandoned.

Despite these problems, a number of hypotheses may be generated from the model and subjected to evaluation by surveys of existing channels. These surveys would locate any intermediate, speculative inventory in the channel and measure the time elapsing between the placing of an order by, and its delivery to, the customer. Use of industrial or commodity channels would undoubtedly be the best initial subjects for the surveys. The confounding effects of collecting, sorting, and dispersing in consumer channels will make the impact of the principle of postponement-speculation more difficult to isolate.

Six hypotheses which could be tested in this manner follow:

1. The shorter the delivery time, the greater the probability the channel will include an intermediate, speculative inventory.
2. The shorter the delivery time, the closer any speculative stock will be to the consumer.
3. The shorter the distance between a customer and a speculative stock, the greater the probability of a second such inventory in the channel.
4. Products which are heavy, bulky, and inexpensive are likely to flow through channels with more intermediate, speculative inventories than products with the opposite characteristics.
5. Products which consumers find expensive to store on their premises, but whose use is both urgent and difficult to forecast, have a greater probability of passing through an intermediate, speculative inventory than products with the opposite characteristics.

6. The greater the inelasticity of consumer and/or producer cost with respect to changes in delivery time, the greater the stability of the most efficient channel type over time.

All of these hypotheses are subject to the *ceteris paribus* limitation. Tests, as a result, should include only those channels operating under reasonably similar economic conditions. This is particularly important with respect to the distance between the producer and the consumer. Variations in this factor will affect the cost of providing any given delivery time. Channels which traverse longer distances, in other words, are likely to require more speculative inventories than those which move goods less extensively.

The *ceteris paribus* limitation also contains an important implication beyond that of the problems of testing. Consideration of this limitation provides the rationale for the presence of several different types of channels supplying the same type of product to a given group of customers. Producers, for example, provisioning some market from a distance, may be forced to use channels distinct from their competitors located adjacent to the customers. This diversity of channels may also be produced by imperfections in competition as well as variations in the urgency of demand among consumers in the market. Those who can easily tolerate delays in delivery are likely to use a different channel from those patronized by customers with dissimilar personalities or capabilities.

## Implications of the Principle

The principle of postponement-speculation, in addition to providing a basis for devloping hypotheses for empirical testing, makes it possible to do some *a prior* generalizing concerning the type of channel structure changes one may expect to see in the future. Any force, or set of forces, which affects the types of costs discussed may be sufficient to move the balance from speculation to postponement, or vice versa.

One type of change, already occurring and which may be expected to spread in the future, rests upon the relationship between the cost of transportation and speed. Rapidly evolving methods of using air transport economically and efficiently are serving to narrow the spread between the cost of high-speed transportation and low-speed transportation. This has the effect of reducing the relative advantage of speculation over postponement. Hence, intermediate inventories will tend to disappear and be replaced by distribution channels which have a direct flow.

The increasing proliferation of brands, styles, colors, and price lines is another type of force which will affect the balance. This proliferation increases the risk of inventory holding throughout the entire channel, but particularly at those points closest to the consumer. Retailers will attempt to minimize this risk by reducing the safety stock level of their inventories and relying more upon speedy delivery from their suppliers. The role of the merchant wholesaler, or the chain store warehouse, will become increasingly important in this channel. Indeed, there will probably be increasing efforts on the part of retailers to carry only sample stocks in those items where it is not absolutely necessary for customers to take immediate delivery. General Electric, for example, is experimenting with wholesaler-to-consumer delivery of large appliances. Drugstores, where the role of the pharmacist appears to be slowly changing from one of compounding prescriptions to inventorying branded specialties, will become further dependent upon ultra-fast delivery from wholesalers.

Those stores, such as discount houses, which are successfully able to resist the pressure toward carrying wide assortments of competing brands are likely to utilize channels of distribution which differ significantly from their full-line competitors. Large bulk purchases from single manufacturers can be economically delivered directly to the discount house's retail facilities. Where warehouses are used in discount house channels they can serve stores spread out over a far greater geographical area than would be normally served by a wholesaler. Such stores are also apt to find their market segments not only in middle income range families, but also among those consumers who tend to be heavily presold by manufacturer advertising, or who simply are less finicky about the specific type of item they buy.

A final possible trend may spring from consumers who find that their own shopping costs represent too great an expenditure of effort with respect to the value received from postponement. As a result, such consumers are likely to turn more and more to catalogue and telephone shopping. Improved quality control procedures by manufacturers and better means of description in catalogues could hasten this movement. The acceptance of Sears telephone order services in large cities testifies that many individuals are prone to feel this way. If the movement were to become significantly enlarged, it could have a drastic effect upon the existing structure of distribution.

## Summary

The study of distribution channels, and why they take various forms, is one of the most neglected areas of marketing today. Part of the neglect may be due to the absence of effective tools for analysis. The principle of postponement-speculation is offered in the hope that it may prove useful in this regard and stimulate work in the area.

The principle directly treats the role of time in distribution and, indirectly, the role of distance as it affects time. The starting point for the development of the constructs of the principle may be found in the work of Alderson and Knight [2, 3, 7]. Postponement is measured by the change of delivery time in the shipping of a product. Increasing the delivery time decreases postponement costs for the seller, increases them for the buyer and vice versa.

Justification and support for the relationships suggested between the costs of marketing functions and delivery time may be found in the recent literature of physical distribution.

The principle reveals the effect upon channel structure of the interaction between the risk of owning a product and the physical functions employed to move the product through time. It holds that, in a competitive environment, the costs of these functions be minimized over the entire channel, not by individual function. The minimum cost and type of channel are determined by balancing the costs of alternative delivery times against the cost of using an intermediate, speculative inventory. The appearance of such an inventory in the channel occurs whenever its additional costs are more than offset by net savings in postponement to the buyer and seller.

## REFERENCES

1. Wroe Alderson, *Marketing Behavior and Executive Action*, Homewood, Illinois: Richard D. Irwin, Inc., 1957, 424.
2. ———, "Marketing Efficiency and the Principle of Postponement," *Cost and Profit Outlook*, 3 (September 1950).
3. Stanley H. Brewer and James Rosenweig, "Rhochematics," *California Management Review*, 3 (Spring 1961), 52-71.
4. Reavis Cox and Charles S. Goodman, "Marketing of Housebuilding Materials," *The Journal of Marketing*, 21 (July 1956), 55-56.
5. William R. Davidson, "Channels of Distribution—One Aspect of Marketing Strategy," *Business Horizons*, Special Issue—First International Seminar on Marketing Management, February, 1961, 85-86.
6. Frank H. Knight, *Risk, Uncertainty and Profit*, Boston: Houghton Mifflin Company, 1921, 238-39, 255-58.
7. John F. Magee, "The Logistics of Distribution," *Harvard Business Review*, 38 (July-August 1960), 97-99.
8. Arch W. Shaw, "Some Problems in Market Distribution," *The Quarterly Journal of Economics*, (August 1912), 727.
9. See Edward W. Smykay, Donald J. Bowersox, and Frank J. Mossman, *Physical Distribution Management*, New York: Macmillan Company, 1961, Ch. IV.
10. Roland S. Vaile, Ewald T. Grether, and Reavis Cox, *Marketing in the American Economy*, New York: Ronald Press Company, 1952, 149-50.

# 24 —— Functional Spin-Off: A Key to Anticipating Change in Distribution Structure

*Bruce Mallen*

Reprinted from *Journal of Marketing*, published by the American Marketing Association, Vol. 37 (July 1973), pp. 18-25. Reprinted by permission.

The purpose of this article is to suggest to anyone interested in understanding distribution channel change an approach whereby the channel designer may anticipate distribution change in his industry *before* such change has developed into an obvious trend. The channel designer would then be in a position to incorporate this information in planning his distribution strategy and in adapting to his distribution environment.

To successfully complete his task, the channel designer must closely analyze five factors:[1]

1. The selected target markets
2. The rest of his marketing mix: price, product, promotion, physical distribution, etc.
3. His company's resources
4. Competition and other external forces
5. Current and anticipated distribution structures in his industry

Perhaps the most difficult of these factors to analyze is the future changes in distribution structure—those that have not yet developed into obvious trends. Typically, the channel designer must limit himself to reading futuristic type articles on distribution trends[2] and/or to surveying a cross-section of opinions in his industry. The problem with the first information source is that such articles are usually too general to be of direct benefit to the reader and are extrapolations of current obvious trends rather than anticipations of changes which have not yet developed into trends. The problem with an opinion study is that the consensus may be completely wrong—nothing more than the reflection of a common pool of ignorance.

This article does not attempt to provide a comprehensive explanation of distribution structure based on empirical research. Rather it presents a sequence of relationships which can be used to aid in anticipating change.

## The Conceptual Approach

For approximately 60 years, economic and marketing scholars have recognized the concept of marketing functions and have related them in a more and more exact fashion to the determination of channel structure. Early contributions were made by Butler, Shaw, Weld, Cherington, Clark, Breyer, and Converse. More recently Stigler, Vaile, Grether, Cox, Alderson, and Bucklin have been major contributors to functionalism as it relates to channel structure.[3]

The basic message of all channel functionalists is as follows:

1. Marketing functions are the various types of job tasks which channel members undertake.
2. These functions can be allocated in different mixes to different channel members.
3. The functional mixes will be patterned in a way which provides the greatest profit either to the consumer (in the form of lower prices and/or more convenience) or the channel members with the most power (which depends on market structure).
4. Should one or more channel members (or potential members) see an opportunity to change the functional mix of the channel in order to increase his profits, he will attempt to do so.
5. Should the attempt be successful, and if the functional mix change is big enough, it will (by definition) change the institutional arrangement in the channel, i.e., the channel structure.

Thus, the channel functionalist attempts to answer two basic questions: What is the most efficient functional mix in a given situation, and how will this functional mix affect the channel structure?

There are four dimensions of distribution structure in which change can be anticipated:

1. The number of channel levels
2. The number of channels or whether one, two (dual), or more (multi) channel types will be used
3. The types of middlemen that will evolve
4. The number of middlemen that will develop at each level

Although the goal to attain market power and to manipulate demand is an important consideration in understanding structural change, the drive for efficiency is also of primary importance. The fundamental premise of this paper is that given a specific level of demand, firms will try to maximize profits by designing or selecting a channel which will generate the lowest total average costs for their organizations.

This drive for efficiency and its anticipated effects on the four dimensions of channel structure can be evaluated through the concept of "functional spin-off."

## The Basic Concept of Functional Spin-off

The basis for the functional spin-off concept is a 1951 article by Stigler.[4] In this article, Stigler provides a most important conceptual framework for measuring and anticipating channel structural arrangements. His approach to isolating the reasons why firms will ''subcontract'' some functions is to analyze or break down the average total cost curve of the firm by function rather than by the normal category of expense calculations such as salaries and interest. Included would be costs associated with functions such as ownership, promotion, information gathering, risk taking, negotiation, and so on. Each function will then have its own cost curve, and the sum of the cost curves for each function will be the total average cost curve of the firm.

These functional cost curves will have various shapes, and each may differ from the other to some degree. Average cost curves for some functions will increase with increasing volume whereas others will decrease with increasing volume. The average cost curves for some functions will assume a U-shaped design: they decrease with increasing volume and at some point start to increase with increasing volume. (Stigler assumes a U-shaped design for the total average cost curve.)

*Functional spin-off and the number of channel levels.* It is economically beneficial to spin off to marketing specialists those distributive functions which have a decreasing curve as volume increases when the firm has a relatively small volume. When a firm enters or creates a new market, it typically produces a small volume in that market. Assuming the middleman specialist faces the same cost curve as the producer, the individual producer at this low volume will have a higher average cost for performing a function with a decreasing cost curve than the specialist who can combine the volumes of a number of producers and thus benefit from the economies that the performance of this particular function generates at higher volumes. If the middleman specialist passes on all or some of the lower costs, the producer's total average cost will decline as a result of this spin-off of the distribution function. In effect, the middleman has generated the basic *raison d'etre* for his own existence by providing external economies to producer firms.

Although the falling functional cost curve is of most interest because it is probably the most common situation, the reverse curve also has implications for channel structure. With a rising functional cost curve, it would make sense economically to spin off certain functions to small specialists when the firm has achieved a high volume. These small specialists can perform the rising cost function at lower costs if they stay small and do not combine the volumes of too many producers. If they are competitive (a more likely event than in the falling cost functional curve situation) such savings will be passed on to the producer.

*Some qualifications.* At the beginning of the development of a new market, there may not be enough volume for a middleman to enter the market since there may not be enough producers from which the middleman can draw supplies to create the large volume required for a profitable operation. In this case, the producer will not have any middleman to whom he may spin off a high cost function. The situation may also occur during the declining stage of the product life cycle when industry volume has decreased to a point where insufficient total sales exist to justify a functional specialist. In the second case, vertical reintegration becomes necessary as middlemen leave the market.

As the market develops, more producers enter, industry volume increases, and it becomes viable for middlemen to operate. It is possible that with even greater volume, a given spin-off function will in turn be broken down into several subfunctions, some of which may be spun off by existing middlemen to even narrower specialists; for example, import distributors might spin off certain types of selling to domestic wholesalers. Thus several levels and other types of middlemen may be added to the structural arrangement.

It should be noted that even if the middleman is a monopolist, he cannot exploit his situation completely. A producer will distribute directly if a middleman attempts to charge more for his services than the producer would have to pay with direct distribution. In other words, the middleman faces an elastic demand curve for his services. At most, he can take all of the efficiencies that he provides in the form of his own profits, but no more. The middleman monopolist is more likely to be present at the beginning of a new market situation, where volume does not warrant the entry of competitive middlemen. Eventually, however, with increasing volume and no artificial barriers to entry, competitive middlemen will enter the market.

It should also be noted that functions are not independent but are interrelated. Therefore, the spin-off of one function could have repercussions, up or down, for the cost of one or more other functions. For example, coordination costs may fall with the spin-off of a function. That is, if a given function is not being performed in a company, there is no longer the need for internal company communication between the people that would have been performing the function and the rest of the company.

## Extensions of the Functional Spin-off Concept as Related to Channel Levels

*U- or L-Shaped average cost function*. There are a number of important implications for industrial structure and, more specifically, channel structure on which Stigler did not elaborate. Perhaps the most important are the implications arising from a functional average cost curve which initially declines and then at some point starts to increase (really a U-shaped curve) or even flattens out.

If the cost curve does not continue to fall, at a high level of volume a point will be reached at which that producer can retake the function without losing economies. For example, in Figure 1 at volumes up to $Q_1$ it will pay the producer to spin off to middlemen the function shown by the cost curve. Between $Q_1$ and $Q_2$, performance by the producer or spinning it off will provide the same economies. After volume $Q_2$, however, it would be beneficial for the producer to resume performance of the function (unless middlemen

**FIGURE 1. A U-shaped Average Cost Curve for a Given Function Faced by an Individual Producer or Marketing Middleman**

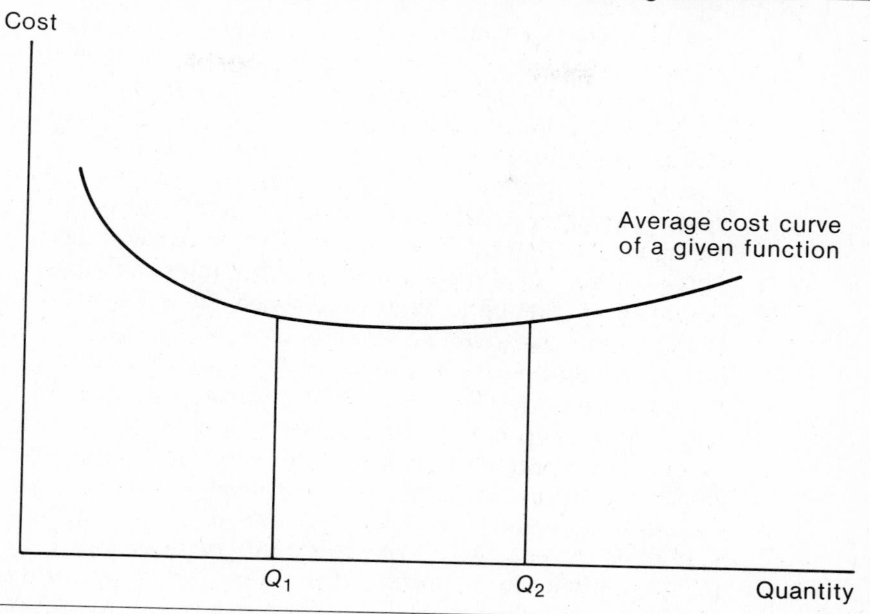


split themselves up and form smaller firms or smaller middlemen are available in the market, so that a very large volume can be distributed among them). The resumption process can apply to any function. For example, the resumption of the ownership function removes the task from a merchant middleman and results in the producer selling direct to the market; self-performance of the advertising function means a producer will not use an advertising agency but relies completely on his own personnel, and so on.

*Functions with continually decreasing average cost curves.* Another extension of the Stigler model is that if the functional cost curve continually falls, the middleman industry, and perhaps individual middleman firms which result from this situation, will become bigger and bigger.

Stigler's model can also be reconstructed into a dynamic rather than a static one. If the channel's costs fall, prices fall; so that given an elastic demand curve, volume will increase, In other words, the market situation propels itself further along the various functional cost curves, with the implications depending on the shapes of these curves. For falling functional cost curves, another round of functional spin-offs, falling costs and prices, and increasing volume will take place. An implication of this last situation is that the middleman industry would become very large, perhaps creating extremely large firms. This process may have facilitated the rise of the mass merchandiser.

## Extensions of the Functional Spin-off Concept as Related to Other Structure Dimensions

*Multi-channel structures*. The concepts employed here can also be useful in explaining the rationale behind dual-channel or multi-channel distribution systems. If the functional cost curves are analyzed by larger retail versus small retailer markets, it is possible for the same function to have different shapes in each market. For example, for the small retail market the producer's functional cost curve at a given quantity may fall with increasing volume; whereas for the large retailer market the cost curve for that same function at the same given quantity may be flat or even increase with volume. This would occur if there were few economies associated with increasing volume in marketing to big retailers once any reasonable amount was sold to them; e.g., the selling effort and cost per unit which is required to sell X units to big retailers is the same as to sell 2X units.

If the above situation held true in a given case, it would be economically beneficial for the producer to spin off to a middleman the particular function involved in selling to the small retailer market and to sell directly to the large retailer market. Even if the shapes of the cost curves in each market were identical, say declining and then leveling off, the spin-off in the small retailer market would be beneficial if the quantity being sold was still small enough to be on the declining portion of the curve. Of course, if the situation was reversed, i.e., selling the small quantity to the large retailer market and large (flat portion of curve) quantity to the small retailer market, the spin-off would take place in the large retailer market. This would lead to indirect distribution to large retailers and direct distribution to small retailers.

Figure 2 portrays the possible situations. $Qs$ ($_1$ or $_2$) is assumed to be the quantity sold to the small retailer market and $Qb$ ($_1$ or $_2$) is the quantity assumed to be sold to the large retailer market by a given producer. In the cost curves shown in this figure, the reason for selling directly to retailers (large or small) at high volumes is shown, i.e., leveling cost curves at $Qs_2$ or $Qb_2$; as well as the reason for selling indirectly, i.e., falling cost curves at $Qs_1$ or $Qb_1$.

Assume four possible volume situations:

a. $Qs_1$ and $Qb_2$
b. $Qs_2$ and $Qb_1$
c. $Qs_2$ and $Qb_2$
d. $Qs_1$ and $Qb_1$.

In the first situation, if the producer is selling $Qs_1$ and $Qb_2$ it can be seen that lower average costs for a given marketing function to small retailers can be obtained at higher volumes (e.g., $Qs_2$). Hence, it makes economic sense for the producer to spin off the function of selling to small retailers to middlemen who, by combining the volume of two or more producers, can achieve these economies and, if competitive, pass them on to the producer.

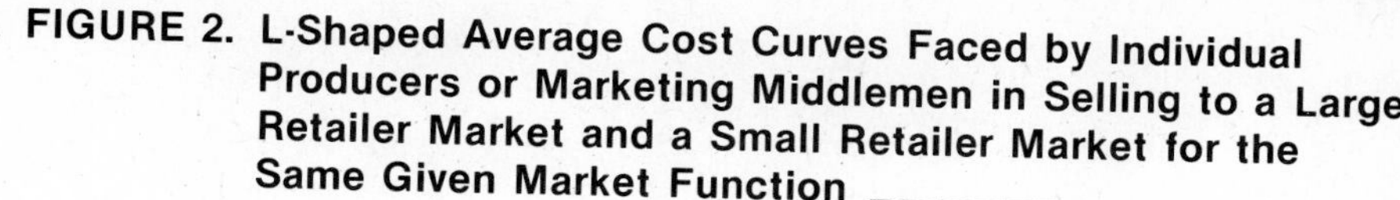
**FIGURE 2. L-Shaped Average Cost Curves Faced by Individual Producers or Marketing Middlemen in Selling to a Large Retailer Market and a Small Retailer Market for the Same Given Market Function**

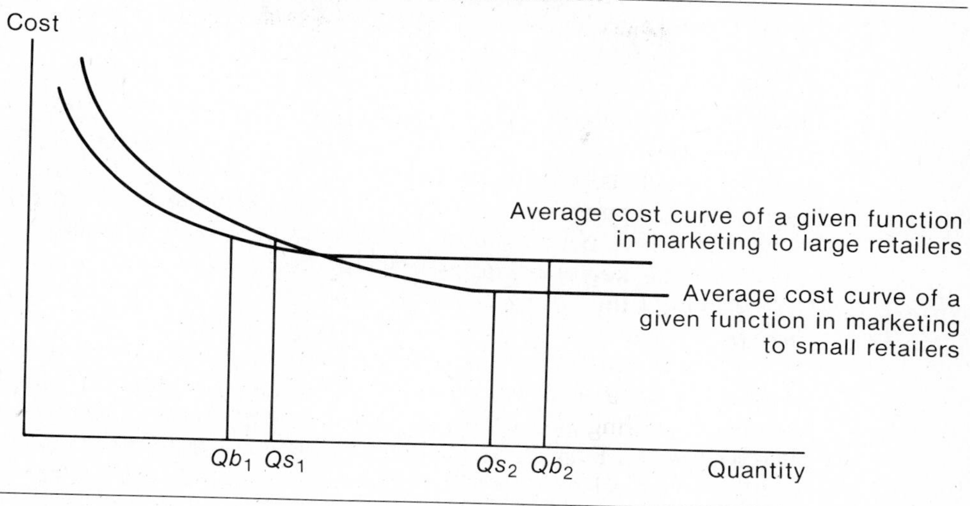


At $Qb_2$ it is obvious that no further economies (or diseconomies) are available at this and higher volumes to the firm. Therefore, it would not be reasonable to spin off the function to middlemen in marketing to large retailers at that point.

In another situation, if a producer is selling $Qb_1$ and $Qs_2$ the reverse channel structure would result. The function would be spun off to middlemen in selling to large retailers and would be retained on a direct basis for small retailers.

Should the relevant volumes be $Qb_2$ and $Qs_2$, there would not be any multi-channels, i.e., there would be only direct distribution. Should the relevant quantities be $Qb_1$ and $Qs_1$, there would be spin-offs in both cases; and should the middlemen be the same firms in both cases, there would not be any multi-channel distribution, but simply indirect single-channel distribution. If, on the other hand, distribution to the large retailer market and the small retailer market required different types of middlemen, there would still be multi-channel distribution although of a different nature.

*Middlemen types*. The types of marketing intermediaries that are created will be directly determined by the mix of functions spun off to them, inasmuch as part of the definition of a middleman depends on the functions he performs. For example, if part of the ownership function is spun off, then merchants are created; if a negotiation function is spun off, then agents are created; if advertising only, then advertising agencies; if marketing research only, then marketing research agencies; and so on.

*Horizontal channel structure*. Up to this point the discussion has dealt with only three of the four dimensions of structure listed earlier: the number of levels; the determination of the number of patterns of distribution—single-, dual-, or multi-channels; and their type (as defined by functions performed). Insight into the determination of one other channel dimension—horizontal structure, or the number of middlemen at each channel level—may also be provided by the functional spin-off concept. However, integration of certain concepts from the field of industrial organization with the spin-off concept is necessary.

The basic force which will determine the number of channel members at a given level appears to be the size of the market in relation to the optimum scale of the firm.[5] The greater the market size is in relation to the optimum scale size, the greater the number of channel members that will evolve, and vice versa. The optimum scale size will itself change from industry to industry and over time as technology changes.

In addition to this fundamental determining relationship, there are a number of other factors. Most of these factors are closely associated with scale and market size, which also help to determine how many members will exist at a channel level. The forces which tend to create more firms at a given channel level include: diseconomies of medium or large scale plants and firms, only small inefficiencies at smaller than optimum scale of operation, growth of market size, high profit potentials, inability to agree on merger terms, legal barriers on merger or monopolization, and buyers wishing the convenience of many outlets.

The forces which tend to create fewer firms at a given channel level include: no diseconomies of large scale operations or diseconomies commencing at only extremely high output of plants and firms; only small inefficiencies at a larger than optimum scale of operations; decline in market size; low profit potential; monopolization practices brought about through collusion, predatory behavior, or barriers to entry; and ''outside'' financial considerations in effecting mergers.

Although most theoretical discussions normally view diseconomies as starting almost immediately after the optimum scale is reached, in practice there appears to be a rather broad range of possible scales—from a minimum optimum scale to some maximum (which in some cases could accommodate a monopoly)—which could provide the same optimum efficiencies.

> We will seldom if ever find firms with a single unique optimal scale. Diseconomies of very large scale are typically encountered, if at all, only at scales substantially greater than the minimum optimal scale of a firm. This is in spite of the fact that a priori theories of pricing and market structure have usually represented the scale.... [6]
>
> ... the bulk of evidence is consistent with the hypothesis that the gigantic firms are in general neither more nor less efficient than firms which are simply large.[7]

Hence, since diseconomies come slowly, if at all, a basic underlying trend could be toward fewer firms and, at the extreme, one (monopoly) channel member at a given level of a channel. In other words, it is conceivable that a channel level not only can be an oligopoly, duopoly, or even a monopoly and still operate, but *must* have that market structure in order to operate at an optimum scale.

This concept of a wide range of optimum scales when combined with the concept of functional spin-off has important implications for channel structure. It suggests the possibility of a structure which consists of all producers using direct channels, all using indirect channels, or some using direct and some using indirect. The first case is probable when all producers reach the minimum optimum point; the second is probable when none reach the minimum optimum point. The last case (of mixed structure) is most probable when some do and some do not reach this point; it is also optimally compatible when all reach the minimum optimum point, as in the first case.

Consider a hypothetical example of a market having a total volume of $10 million and a minimum optimum scale for distribution functions (whether undertaken by the producer or a middleman) of $1 million, with no diseconomies up to the total market. If no producer reaches this minimum, then it is probable that all will distribute indirectly with a total of one to ten middlemen in the market. If one producer reaches 100% of the market, he can distribute directly with no middlemen in the market, he can distribute completely through one to ten middlemen, or he can distribute directly in part and indirectly in part through one to nine middlemen (nine, if he lets $9 million go indirectly). If only one producer reaches $1 million in output, he may distribute directly or indirectly. If he distributes indirectly, then the other producers, who will probably distribute indirectly in any case, will do so through one to nine middlemen. If there are ten producers, and eight producers each reach at least $1 million in sales for a total of $9 million, some of the eight may distribute directly and others indirectly, or all may distribute one way or the other. If all decide to distribute directly, then the remaining two producers will probably distribute indirectly through one middleman.

Thus the minimum optimum scale point only indicates the maximum number of channel members that are compatible with maximum efficiency, and so leaves room for a number of other forces (not discussed here) which will determine the actual point in the optimum range that will be utilized by the firms in the industry, i.e., the actual outcome in terms of number of channel members at different levels. Further, firms may not even choose to (or cannot) operate within the optimum range because of some of the factors listed earlier. These factors include: only small inefficiences at nonoptimum scales, a decline in market size, a high profit potential even without optimum operation, monopolization practices, inability to merge, and a desire for outlet convenience. In spite of these possibilities, one cannot ignore what is a very key determinant of the number of channel members that will exist at each level—market size in relation to the optimum scale of firm and the spin-off ability.

## Hypotheses

The key hypotheses generated by the functional spin-off and industrial organization concepts for distribution structure are as follows:

*As Related to "Number of Levels" Dimension*

1. A producer will spin off a marketing function to a marketing intermediary(s) if the latter can perform the function more efficiently than the former. This will logically be the case when economies can be effected for that function by a change in volume from that of the producer. The greater the economies, the greater will be the incentive to spin off. If the majority of producers in a given industry are in or will be in a similar position, then the use of marketing intermediaries will characterize, or come to characterize, that industry.
2. If there are continual economies to be obtained within a wide range of volume changes, the middleman portion of the industry (and perhaps individual middlemen) will become bigger and bigger.
3. A producer will keep or resume a marketing function from a marketing intermediary(s) if the former can perform the function at least as efficiently as the latter. This will logically be the case when no economies can be effected for that function by a change in volume from that of the producer. If the majority of producers in a given industry are in, or will be in, a similar position, then the nonuse of marketing intermediaries (direct distribution) will characterize, or come to characterize, that industry.
4. If in performing a marketing function a marketing intermediary finds that for a part of that function (i.e., a subfunction) another perhaps more specialized marketing intermediary can perform it more efficiently, then he will spin off that subfunction to the latter. This will occur for the same reasoning presented in hypothesis 1 above. Similarly, the first marketing intermediary will keep or resume a subfunction if there are no economies to be effected by a spin-off.

*As Related to "Number of Channels" Dimension*

5. If a producer finds that in marketing to one (or more) of his markets a middleman can perform a given marketing function more efficiently for the reasons noted in hypothesis 1 above and for another (or others) of his markets he can perform the same function at least as efficiently for the reasons noted in hypothesis 3 above, he will spin off that function in marketing to the first market(s) and keep

or resume the function in marketing to the second. If the majority of producers in a given industry are in, or will be in, a similar position; then the use of dual- or multiple-channels will characterize, or come to characterize, that industry.

*As Related to "Middlemen Types" Dimension*

6. If marketing intermediaries characterize an industry, their nature will be determined by the mix of functions and subfunctions spun off. For example, if the ownership function is a prevalent spin-off function, then the merchant will be a prevalent type of marketing intermediary in the industry.

*As Related to "Number of Middlemen" Dimension*

7. The greater the market size is in relation to optimum scale size (at each channel level), the greater the number of channel members that will come into being. With the growth of market size, and especially if there exist diseconomies or only very small economies of larger scale, more firms may be expected to enter the channel. With a decline in market size, and especially if there exist economies of larger scale, firms may be expected to leave the channel.
8. With a change in technology and the growth of optimum scale size, firms may be expected to leave the channel if there is no corresponding change in market size and vice versa.

## Implications

Using the eight relationships hypothesized above, the channel planner is in a better position to anticipate trends in his industry by estimating relevant cost and market data (It is beyond the scope of this article to describe a program of data collection or to suggest how to overcome the admittedly difficult, but not impossible, task of collecting competitive cost information.)

The channel planner must estimate the present and future total market volume, new technological changes which affect the optimum firm scale, and the volume and shape of the average cost curve for the key marketing functions of a representative sample of firms (producers and marketing intermediaries) in his industry. Fortunately, because his purpose is to gauge broad underlying trends, the data can be fairly rough without losing its usefulness. Trade associations often collect competitive cost data for use by their members. However, further estimates of different types of marketing costs by market being served would probably have to be made from such sources. He then can apply to his findings the structural results predicted by the eight hypotheses listed above.

For example, if he finds that producing firms in his industry in general have faced a declining average cost curve for the ownership function in the past but are now approaching a flat portion of the curve where no economies of scale are forthcoming, and further he predicts an increase in total market volume, he will anticipate in his channel strategy a general move by his industry to more direct ownership channels (see hypothesis 3 above). He will also anticipate more firms entering the market at the producer level (see hypothesis 7 above: note in this case that the market size may actually decline at the merchant middleman level because of the first conclusion). The exact change in number of channel members will depend on factors discussed earlier under the subtitle "horizontal channel structure." If, in the same example, the channel planner also finds that with the same volume increase the negotiation function cost curve declines sharply, he will also anticipate an increase in the number of agent middlemen.

The possible combination of cost and market size changes are numerous. The channel planner by collecting the data and applying the concepts discussed here should be able to anticipate distribution structure changes before they become obvious trends.

The functional spin-off concept is a powerful conceptual tool for the marketer in understanding many of the aspects of channel structure (which itself is one of the most and perhaps *the* most fundamental contribution of marketing as a discipline)[8] and in predicting structural outcomes in specific industries. It is also useful, in a micro or managerial sense, to the channel selector or designer who is seeking to conceptually organize and understand the framework of underlying economic forces within which he must operate and make his decisions and to which he must adapt.

## ENDNOTES

1. For a detailed description of the selection process, see Bruce Mallen, "Selecting Channels of Distribution for Consumer Products," in *Handbook of Modern Marketing*, Victor P. Buell, ed. (New York: McGraw-Hill, 1970), pp. 4-15 to 4-30.
2. See, for example, William R. Davidson, "Changes in Distribution Institutions," *Journal of Marketing*, Vol. 34 (January 1970), pp. 7-10; and Philip B. Schary, "Changing Aspects of Channel Structure in America," *British Journal of Marketing*, Vol. 4 (Autumn 1970), pp. 133-147.
3. Ralph S. Butler, *Selling and Buying*, Part II, *Advertising, Selling and Credits of Modern Business*, Vol. IX (New York: Alexander Hamilton Institute, 1911), pp. 276-277; Ralph S. Butler, H. F. Debower, and J. G. Jones, *Modern Business*, Vol. III, *Marketing Methods and Salesmanship* (New York: Alexander Hamilton Institute, 1914), pp. 8-9; Arch W. Shaw, *Some Problems In Market Distribution* (Cambridge, Mass.: Harvard University Press, 1915), pp. 4-28; L. D. Weld, "Marketing Functions and Mercantile Organization," *American Economic Review*, Vol. 7 (June 1917), pp. 306-318; Paul T. Cherington, *Elements of Marketing* (New York: MacMillan, 1920), pp. 44, 56-59; Fred E. Clark, *Principles of Marketing* (New York: Macmillan, 1922); Ralph F. Breyer, *The Marketing Institution* (New York: McGraw-Hill, 1934); P. D. Converse, *Essentials of*

*Distribution* (New York: Prentice-Hall, 1936); George J. Stigler, "The Division of Labor is Limited by the Extent of the Market," *Journal of Political Economy,* Vol. 54 (June 1951), pp. 185-193; R. S. Vaile, E. T. Grether, and R. Cox, *Marketing in the American Economy* (New York: Ronald Press, 1952), pp. 121-133; Wroe Alderson, *Marketing Behavior and Executive Action* (Homewood, Ill.: Richard D. Irwin, 1957); Louis P. Bucklin, *A Theory of Distribution Channel Structure* (Berkeley, Calif.: Institute of Business and Economic Research, University of California, 1966).

4. Stigler, same reference as note 3.
5. For an excellent detailed discussion of this concept (though not interpreted in a channel context) see, Joe S. Bain, *Industrial Organization* (New York: John Wiley and Sons, Inc., 1968), Chapter 6.
6. Same reference as note 5, p. 175.
7. Same reference as note 5, p. 173.
8. R. Ferber, D. Blankertz, and S. Hollander, *Marketing Research* (New York: Ronald Press Company, 1964), p. 471. See also, Michael Halbert, *The Meaning and Sources of Marketing Theory* (New York: McGraw-Hill, 1965), p. 10.

# 25 —— Alternative Explanations of Institutional Change and Channel Evolution

*Bert C. McCammon, Jr.*

Reprinted from *Toward Scientific Marketing*, published by the American Marketing Association, edited by S. Greyser (1963), pp. 477-490. Reprinted by permission.

## Introduction

Marketing channels and institutions must adapt continuously to their environment in order to avoid "economic obsolescence." Most of the required adaptations are tactical in nature. Channel alignments, for example, can usually be maintained over an extended period of time by effecting a series of minor, though necessary, revisions in marketing practices. Individual firms, under normal conditions, can also maintain their competitive position without significantly altering prevailing policies and procedures. Thus, institutional change in marketing tends to be a process in which firms and channels maneuver for short-run advantage and in which they adapt almost imperceptibly to environmental disturbances.

Periodically, however, a firm's or channel's existence is threatened by a *major* change in marketing practices. The sudden appearance of new products, new methods of distribution, new types of competitors, and new sales approaches, may imperil existing institutional relationships. These abrupt departures from the *status quo* can disrupt prevailing patterns of competition, alter cost-price relationships, and "enforce a distinctive process of adaptation"[1] on the part of threatened organizations.

Schumpeter, earlier, and Barnet and Levitt, later, argue that this type of competition, usually called innovative competition, is a prerequisite for economic growth.[2] Despite general acceptance of this position, very little is known about the innovative process in marketing. More specifically, we lack a body of theory that explains how new marketing practices are originated and diffused throughout the structure of distribution.

The emergence and acceptance of new practices is a complex process which has been analyzed extensively in the agricultural sector of our economy,[3] and in the medical profession.[4] For example:

> The farmers participating in the diffusion process are relatively easy to identify. Beal and Rogers have classified such participants as innovators (the developers or initial accepters of new ideas), early adopters, majority adopters, and laggards. "Indirect" participants, who occupy

important positions in the communications network, are classified as key communicators, influentials, and skeptics. Each of these decision makers has a distinctive socio-economic profile and a differentiated mode of behavior. Researchers, by analyzing interaction patterns, can predict the rate at which a new farm practice will be accepted, and they can forecast the probable impact of this innovation on non-adopters.[5]

Unfortunately, comparable analysis has not been undertaken in retailing or wholesaling. The distinguishing characteristics of innovators, early adopters, and other participants in the diffusion process have not been identified, nor have the factors which inhibit or encourage change been isolated. Consequently, the explanation and prediction of institutional change in marketing tends to be a tenuous intellectual exercise.

The diffusion process in marketing is more complex than it is in agriculture because the counter strategies of non-adopters have to be considered as well as the spread of the innovation itself. The phenomenon of transient and selective adoption has to be recognized too. Individual firms may emulate an innovator in the short-run while devising long-run strategies, or alternatively these firms may adopt new practices on a limited or modified basis. Conventional department stores, for example, have recently emulated the discounter by opening self-service branches. This may be an interim strategy in the sense that the branches may change over time so that they eventually bear little resemblance to the original innovation. With respect to selective adoption of new practices, many supermarkets prepack meat but not produce, and numerous department stores operate self-service drug and toy departments while merchandising other lines on a full-service basis. Consequently, it appears that a complex model is needed to analyze the emergence and diffusion of new practices in the marketing structure.

The purposes of this paper are (1) to explore the barriers to change in the marketing structure, (2) to evaluate the sources of innovation within the structure, and (3) to suggest some hypotheses about the factors which determine rate at which new practices are accepted.

## Barriers to Change Within The Marketing Structure

Conventional economic analysis provides a useful frame of reference for explaining institutional change. The firm, in economic theory, attempts to maximize its profits and thus accepts technological improvements as soon as they appear. Innovations under these circumstances are absorbed quickly and the diffusion process is completed in a relatively short period of time. Shifts in channel alignments are also susceptible to economic analysis. Client firms utilize intermediaries because the latter can perform specific functions (in a given location) at a lower cost per unit than can the former. Intermediaries, in this context, are sources of external economies to their clientele. Such economies are possible because intermediaries, by aggregating user requirements, can perform the designated function(s) at an optimum scale, or alternatively, intermediaries, by aggregating user requirements, can more fully utilize existing (though non-optimum) facilities.[6]

As output expands or as *technology changes*, the client firms reach a point at which they can perform the delegated functions at an optimum scale. When this point is reached, functions tend to be reabsorbed, and the channel becomes more completely integrated. This process of reintegration is not necessarily frictionless. The intermediary attempts to avoid being "integrated out" of the channel by changing his method of operation so that it more closely conforms to the client's requirements. Manufacturer's agents in the electronics field, for example, have retained their principals by carrying inventory, and building supply wholesalers continue to sell to large developers by offering goods on a cash and carry basis.

Economic analysis of institutional change can be and has been carried much further.[7] This type of analysis, however modified, inevitably assumes that the firm's behavior is determined by cost/revenue considerations, and thus it leaves unanswered some or all of the following questions:

- Why is change resisted by marketing institutions even though it appears to offer economic advantages?
- Why do "uneconomic channels of distribution" persist over extended periods of time?
- Why do some firms accept change rapidly, while others lag in their adaptation or refuse to change at all?

Answers to these and related questions depend upon an analysis of sociological and psychological barriers to change, some of which are discussed below.

## Reseller Solidarity[8]

Resellers in many lines of trade often function as a highly cohesive group, bargaining with suppliers and adjusting to their environment collectively as well as individually. Resellers "organized" on this basis must maintain internal harmony and a workable consensus. Consequently, they tend to support traditional trade practices and long established institutional relationships.

Several factors are apparently conducive to group action. Resellers tend to act as a unit when the firms involved are relatively homogeneous. Each of the entrepreneurs in this situation tends to be confronted by similar problems and has comparable expectations. Thus he identifies with the other members of the trade and is willing to work cooperatively with them.

Resellers also tend to engage in collective action when the entrepreneurs have common backgrounds. The owner-managers of drugstores, for example, are often "highly organized" because most of them are pharmacists and are often alumni of the same universities. Business conditions affect reseller solidarity too. There is likely to be more group action during periods of adverse business conditions than during periods of prosperity. Finally, the degree of reseller solidarity that prevails is conditioned by the intensity and complexity of competition. A line of trade, confronted by unusually aggressive competition from outside sources, is more likely to engage in group action than would be the case if this threat did not exist.

The presence of a strong professional or trade association tends to reinforce conservative group behavior. Retail druggists, as an illustration, support long established professional associations which defend existing trade practices. Carpet retailers, on the other hand, are not represented by a trade association, and for this reason, as well others, their industry is characterized by unstable retail prices and by constantly changing institutional arrangements.

To summarize, the presence of group solidarity within the structure of marketing tends to inhibit the rate at which innovation is accepted and thus slows down the diffusion process.

## Entrepreneurial Values

The entrepreneur's reaction to change is conditioned by his value hierarchy. Large resellers, as a group, are growth oriented and their decisions are based upon economic criteria. Innovations that promote growth are regarded as being desirable, and technological alternatives are evaluated on the basis of "profitability" analysis.[9] Consequently, the large reseller, given sufficient time to adjust, tends to be responsive to innovation and will either accept it or otherwise react to it on the basis of cost-revenue relationships.

Small resellers often have a markedly different set of values. Wittreich, on the basis of his research, argues that small retailers tend to have relatively static expectations.[10] That is, they are interested in reaching and *maintaining* a given scale of operation, and reject opportunities for growth beyond this point. Such retailers tend to view their demand curve as being relatively fixed. Thus, they are inclined to resist innovation because it presumably cannot improve their position and could conceivably disrupt a reasonably attractive *status quo*.

Vidich and Bensman, in their study of life in a small community, reach essentially the same conclusions about the small merchant's behavior.[11] Furthermore, they argue that small retailers are extremely reluctant to invest additional funds in their businesses, almost irrespective of the profits involved. Instead they prefer "secure" investment outlets such as real estate and securities. The small retailers studied by Vidich and Bensman also believed that they had suffered a decline in status during the past three decades, and they resisted any institutional arrangements that would further depress their relative position within the community. This latter condition may partially explain why voluntary and cooperative groups have not been more successful. Retailers participating in these programs sacrifice some of their autonomy, and the loss of this autonomy may be perceived as a loss of status. Wroe Alderson, in another context, has argued that a behavior system will survive as long as it fulfills the status expectations of its participants.[12] Since the small retailer's status is a function of "being in business for himself," the desire to maintain independence may partially explain both the rejection of contractual integration and the persistence of "uneconomic channels."

To summarize, recent research indicates that the small retailer (and presumably other small businessmen) will resist innovation, because they "value" stability more highly than growth.[13] They will also resist innovations that require a substantial investment of funds or that result in a perceived loss of status.

## Organizational Rigidity

A well established firm is an historical entity with deeply entrenched patterns of behavior. The members of the organization may resist change because it violates group norms, creates uncertainty, and results in loss of status. Customers may also resent change and threaten to withdraw their patronage. Furthermore the firm has "sunk" costs in training programs, in office systems, and in equipment which it prefers to recover before instituting major revisions in its procedures. Consequently most firms absorb innovation gradually, or react to innovative competition through a series of incremental adjustments.[14] Because of these factors, the diffusion of an innovation through an industry and the distinctive pattern of adaptation it enforces take considerable time.

The firm's reaction to change is also a function of the extent to which the innovator has penetrated the firm's core market. Most firms appeal to a specific group of customers who are uniquely loyal. These customers may patronize the firm for a variety of reasons, but the attraction is such that their patronage is virtually assured. As long as this core market remains intact, the firm can usually maintain sufficient sales to continue operations until it matures strategies to counteract the innovator.[15] If the core market is infringed, however, the firm must either emulate the innovator or develop immediate counter strategies.

To summarize, a firm, because of organizational rigidities, prefers to respond incrementally to innovation. It will gradually imitate the innovating firm or develop counter strategies over an extended period of time. If the innovator has penetrated the firm's core market, however, it must respond quickly to this challenge in order to ensure continued operation.

## The Firm's Channel Position[16]

There is a dominant channel of distribution for most lines of merchandise. This channel, as compared with other institutional alignments, has the greatest prestige and often handles the bulk of the industry's output. Behavior within the channel is regulated by an occupational code which "controls" pricing policies, sales promotion practices, and other related activities. Deviation from the code's prescriptions are punished in a variety of ways, ranging from colleague ostracism to economic sanctions.

Individual firms can be classified in terms of their relationship to the dominant channel of distribution and in terms of their adherence to the occupational code. The *insiders* are members of the dominant channel. They have continuous access to preferred sources of supply, and their relatively high status in the trade is a byproduct of channel membership. The insiders, as a group prescribe the contents of the occupational code and enforce it. They are desirous of the respect of their colleagues, and recognize the interdependency of the firms in the system. In short, the insider has made an emotional and financial commitment to the dominant channel and is interested in perpetuating it.

The *strivers* are firms located outside the dominant channel who want to become a part of the system. These firms have discontinuous access to preferred resources, and during periods of short supply, they may be "short ordered" or not shipped at all. The striver, since he wants to become a member of the system, is responsive to the occupational code and will not engage in deviate behavior under normal economic conditions. Thus he utilizes the same marketing practices as the insider.

The *complementors* are not part of the dominant channel, nor do they desire to obtain membership. As their title suggests, these firms complement the activities undertaken by members of the dominant channel. That is, the complementors perform functions that are not normally performed by other channel members, or serve customers whose patronage is normally not solicited, or handle qualities of merchandise the dominant channel doesn't carry. Thus the complementors are marginally affiliated with the dominant channel and want to see it survive. Their expectations are of a long-run nature and they respect the occupational code.

The *transients* also occupy a position outside the dominant channel and do not seek membership in it. Many transients are mobile entrepreneurs who move from one line of trade to another; other transients are firms that owe their allegiance elsewhere, i.e., they consider themselves to be members of a channel other than the one in question. Therefore they utilize the latter channel's product as an "in and out" item or as a loss leader, since it is not their market "that is being spoiled" by such activity. All of the transients have short-run expectations and the occupational code is not an effective constraint.

Classification of firms into these four categories explains some of the competitive patterns which have emerged in the ready-to-wear field, in the toy industry, and in the TBA market. Transient firms, in all of these merchandise lines, have disrupted the *status quo* by engaging in deviate competitive behavior. Significantly, none of the four types of firms described above are likely to introduce major marketing innovations. The insiders and the strivers are primarily interested in maintaining existing institutional arrangements. The complementors also have a vested interest in the *status quo*, and the transients are not sufficiently dependent on the product line to develop an entirely new method of distribution. Thus the above analysis suggests that a firm completely outside the system will introduce basic innovations, and historically this has often been the case. Consequently, a fifth category for *outside innovators* is required to explain major structural realignments.

### Market Segmentation

As market segments emerge and/or as they are recognized by entrepreneurs, firms that formerly competed directly with each other begin to compete in a more marginal sense. That is, former rivals begin to appeal to different types of customers, and as a result the tactics adopted by one firm may have a negligible potential impact on other firms. Competition, under these circumstances, becomes more fragmented, and the compulsion to accept or react to innovation declines—a condition that slows down the diffusion process.

The discount supermarket, for example, has not increased in importance as rapidly as many of its proponents initially believed, and the bantam supermarket has experienced much the same fate. It appears that these innovative methods of operation appeal to a limited number of market segments, and conventional supermarkets, appealing to other market segments, have not been compelled to react to these new forms of competition.

## Sources of Innovative Activity

### The Channel Administrator

An individual firm usually controls a given marketing channel in the sense that it directs the allocation of resources for all channel members. Manufacturers, farm marketing cooperatives, voluntary groups, and chain store buying offices are illustrations of organizations that direct the activities of other channel members. These decision makers do not set goals for the other firms in the channel, but they do decide what kind of firms shall be combined to form the distribution network for the systems they organize.[17]

The channel administrator often is an innovator, particularly when a new product is being marketed. Manufacturers of new fabricated materials, for example, often have to develop unique institutional arrangements to distribute their products,[18] and the Singer Sewing Machine Company pioneered the use of a franchise agency system and installment credit when it began to market sewing machines during the 1850's.[19] Furthermore channel administrators can be quite responsive to *procedural* innovations. During the last decade, channel administrators have taken the initiative in developing new physical distribution techniques, and they have accepted rather rapidly such innovations as merchandise management accounting, PERT cost analysis, stockless purchasing arrangements, and value analysis.

Channel administrators, however, tend to be well established firms, and thus they are subject to the organizational constraints described above. More specifically, they tend to resist an innovation that involves a major restructuring of the firm's relationship with its customers, since they have the most to lose by such restructuring and the least to gain.

Large firms can overcome their tendency to maintain the *status quo* by underwriting *elite* activities. The elite members of an organization engage in projects that have problematic, long-run payouts rather than certain, short-run yields. The ratio of professional personnel to high status administrators is a rough measure of the use of elite personnel within an organization. The higher the proportion of professional personnel to proprietors, managers, and officials, the more likely is the existence of staff departments preserving long-run interests against the pressure of immediate problems. Stinchcombe, and Hill and Harbison have analyzed the relationship between innovation and the proportion of elite personnel employed.[20] Their findings indicate that innovating industries employ proportionately more professionals than do noninnovating industries.

Furthermore, within a given industry, the firms with proportionately more professionals innovate more rapidly than those with fewer. Significantly, wholesaling and retailing are classified as "stagnant" industries, and the payrolls of these types of firms contain significantly fewer professional employees per hundred administrators than is the case in "progressive" industries. Admittedly, the definitions of "progressiveness" and "stagnation" can be somewhat arbitrary, as can the definition of a "professional" employee. Consequently, the data just cited should be regarded as being suggestive rather than definitive, but the suggestion is unambiguous—retailers and wholesalers could effect economies and develop more productive institutional arrangements if they engaged in additional research and underwrote more elite activities.

## The "Outsider"

Institutional innovation, particularly in retailing, has historically occurred *outside* of the established power structure. The retail innovator, in fact, has tended to resemble Eric Hoffer's "The True Believer."[21] J. C. Penney, Richard Sears, King Cullen, and others were discontented "outsiders" who believed that they had discovered a technique of irresistible power. They had an extravagant conception of the potentialities of the future, minimized the problems of managing a large enterprise, and promulgated their merchandising doctrines with an almost evangelical fervor. The premise that the institutional innovator is likely to come from outside the established power structure is also inherent in the wheel of retailing concept which is the most comprehensive theory of innovation yet developed in marketing.[22] Silk and Stern, in their recent study, also conclude that the marketing innovator has traditionally been an "outsider," but they additionally argue that recent innovators have tended to be much more deliberate in their choice processes and much more methodical in their analyses than were their predecessors of several decades ago.[23] In any case, if we accept the assumption that significant innovation tends to occur outside the existing system, then it is important from a social point of view to create a marketing environment in which entry is relatively easy.

## Analyzing Institutional Change

There is a tendency in marketing to refine analysis beyond the point of maximum usefulness, and this is particularly true when the phenomena under investigation are relatively complex. Quite obviously, many of the changes that have occurred in the structure of distribution during the past 50 years can be explained in terms of a relatively simple challenge and response model. The emergence and rapid growth of voluntary and cooperative groups in the food field is a logical response to the expansion of corporate vertical integration, and the rise of the cash and carry wholesaler in the building supply industry is a natural response to the growing importance of the large developer. Thus, if the marketplace is viewed as an area in which firms constantly search for differential advantage and/or react to it, much of what appears to be rather complex behavior can be reduced to fairly simple terms.

### Hypotheses

Systems theorists and sociologists have selectively investigated the diffusion of new ideas and practices. The hypotheses that have emerged from this research serve as useful points of origin for subsequent exploration in marketing. More specifically, *marketing analysts should consider the following hypotheses when attempting to explain institutional change:*

1. The rate of diffusion depends upon the innovation itself. Innovations that involve a substantial capital investment, a major restructuring of the firm's relationship with its customers, and a sizable number of internal realignments are more likely to be accepted slowly than those that involve relatively minor intra- or inter-firm changes.
2. The innovator is likely to be an "outsider" in the sense that he occupies a marginal role in a given line of trade and is on the outskirts of the prevailing sociometric network. Such individuals are interested in innovation because they have the most to gain and the least to lose by disrupting the status quo.
3. A firm will respond incrementally to innovation unless its core market is threatened. If the latter is the case, the response to

innovation will proceed swiftly. That is, the firm will parry the innovator's thrust by developing a counter strategy or it will emulate the innovator on a partial or total basis.

4. The higher the entrepreneur's aspirations, the more likely he is to initiate or accept innovation. Alternatively, the lower the entrepreneur's aspirations, the less likely he is to accept innovation, particularly when such acceptance conflicts with his other values.
5. The acceptance of innovation is not always permanent. A firm may emulate an innovator as a part of a transitional strategy. When the firm develops an ultimate strategy, the emulating features of its behavior will be discarded.
6. Innovation will be accepted most rapidly when it can be fitted into existing decision-making habits. Innovations which involve an understanding of alien relationships or which involve new conceptual approaches, tend to be resisted. Many small retailers, for example, have difficulty in accepting the supermarket concept, because it involves a fairly sophisticated understanding of cost-volume relationships.
7. Influentials and innovators are not always the same firms. Institutional innovators, since they tend to be "outsiders," have relatively little influence among their entrepreneurial colleagues. Other firms, occupying central positions in a given line of trade, possess considerable influence, and an innovation will not be adopted widely until these influential firms accept it.
8. Greater energy is required to transmit an innovation from one channel to another than is required to transmit it within a channel. The diffusion of innovation therefore tends to be confined to a given line of trade, before it is adopted by another. The supermarket, as an illustration, became dominant in the food field, before this method of operation was employed by ready-to-wear retailers.

The above hypotheses represent only a small sampling of those developed in other fields. They deserve careful consideration by researchers interested in explaining and predicting institutional change in marketing.

## ENDNOTES

1. Joseph Schumpeter, *Business Cycles*, McGraw-Hill, New York, 1939, p. 10.
2. Joseph Schumpeter, *Capitalism, Socialism, and Democracy*, Harper's, New York, 1947; Edward M. Barnet, *Innovate or Perish*, Graduate School of Business, Columbia University, New York, 1954; Theodore Levitt, *Innovation in Marketing*, McGraw-Hill, New York, 1962.
3. See for example, E. M. Rogers and G. M. Beal, *Reference Group Influence in The Adoption of Agricultural Technology*, Iowa State University, Ames, 1958.

4. See for example, J. Coleman, E. Katz, and H. Menzel, "The Diffusion of an Innovation among Physicians," *Sociometry*, December, 1957, pp. 253-270.
5. S. C. Dodd, "Diffusion is Predictable: Testing Probability Models for Laws of Interaction," *American Sociological Review*, August, 1955, pp. 392-401.
6. The latter source of economies is often called the "blending principle."
7. See, for example, R. H. Coase, "The Nature of the Firm," *Economica*, New Series, Volume IV, 1937, pp. 386-405; George J. Stigler, "The Division of Labor Is Limited by the Extent of the Market," *The Journal of Political Economy*, June, 1951, pp. 185-193; R. Artle and S. Berglund, "A Note on Manufacturers' Choice of Distribution Channel," *Management Science*, July, 1959, pp. 460-471; Edward H. Bowman, "Scales of Operations: An Empirical Study," *Operations Research*, May-June, 1958, pp. 320-328; Louis B. Bucklin, "The Economic Structure of Channels of Distribution," *Marketing: A Maturing Discipline* (Martin L. Bell, Editor), American Marketing Association, 1960, pp. 379-385; and F. E. Balderston, "Theories of Marketing Structure and Channels," *Proceedings, Conference of Marketing Teachers from Far Western States*, University of California, Berkeley, 1958, pp. 135-145.
8. The discussion in this section is based on the analyses contained in J. C. Palamountain, Jr., *The Politics of Distribution*, Harvard University Press, Cambridge, Massachusetts, 1955, and in E. T. Grether, "Solidarity in The Distribution Trades," *Law and Contemporary Problems*, June, 1937, pp. 376-391.
9. See Bert C. McCammon, Jr. and Donald H. Granbois, *Profit Contribution: A Criterion for Display Decisions*, Point-of-Purchase Advertising Institute, Inc., New York, 1963.
10. Warren J. Wittreich, "Misunderstanding the Retailer," *Harvard Business Review*, May-June, 1962. pp. 147-159.
11. Arthur J. Vidich and Joseph Bensman, *Small Town in Mass Society*, Doubleday and Company, Garden City, New York, 1960, pp. 73 and 91-93.
12. Wroe Alderson, "Survival and Adjustment in Behavior Systems," *Theory in Marketing* (Edited by Reavis Cox and Wroe Alderson), Richard D. Irwin, Homewood, Illinois, 1950, p. 80.
13. For additional confirmation of this hypothesis, see Louis Kriesberg, "The Retail Furrier, Concepts of Security and Success," *American Journal of Sociology*, March, 1952.
14. For an interesting discussion of incremental adjustments to innovation, see Alton F. Doody, "Historical Patterns of Marketing Innovation," *Emerging Concepts in Marketing* (William S. Decker, Editor), American Marketing Association, Chicago, 1962, pp. 245-253.
15. Alderson, *op. cit.*, p. 81.
16. The discussion in this section is based on the analysis that appears in Louis Kriesberg, "Occupational Controls Among Steel Distributors," *The American Journal of Sociology*, November, 1955, pp. 203-212.
17. For a more complete discussion of the channel administrator concept, see George Fisk, "The General Systems Approach to the Study of Marketing," *The Social Responsibilities of Marketing* (Edited by William D. Stevens), American Marketing Association, Chicago, 1961, pp. 207-211.
18. See E. Raymond Gorey, *The Development of Markets for New Materials*, Division of Research, Graduate School of Business Administration, Harvard University, Boston, 1956.

19. Andrew B. Jack, "The Channels of Distribution for an Innovation: The Sewing-Machine Industry in America, 1860-1865," *Explorations in Entrepreneurial History*, February, 1957, pp. 113-141.
20. Arthur L. Stinchcombe, "The Sociology of Organization and the Theory of the Firm," *The Pacific Sociological Review*, Fall, 1960, pp. 75-82. Samuel E. Hill and Frederick Harbison, *Manpower and Innovation in American Industry*, Princeton University Press, 1959, pp. 16-27.
21. Eric Hoffer, *The True Believer*, New American Library, New York, 1951, pp. 13-20.
22. For a careful analysis of the wheel of retailing concept, see Stanley C. Hollander, "The Wheel of Retailing," *Journal of Marketing*, July, 1960, pp. 37-42.
23. Alvin J. Silk and Louis William Stern, "The Changing Nature of Innovation in Marketing: A Study of Selected Business Leaders, 1852-1958," *Business History Review*, Fall, 1963, pp. 182-199.

# SECTION H
# Regional School

The regional school of marketing thought has focused on the *place* of market transactions. It has generated such concepts as retail gravitation, wheel of retailing, and one-stop shopping.

The regional school is also likely to undergo significant changes as a consequence of technological, competitive, and market changes. First, it will become increasingly difficult to define a market or trading area based on geographical or spatial considerations. This is due to the emerging capability of customers to order from their homes through electronic shopping technologies. As the boundaries for market and home become blurred by technology, the concepts of retail gravitation, one-stop shopping, and wheel of retailing are likely to be revised.

Similarly, as markets become international, the definition of what constitutes the market and who competes in that market also become more difficult. Once again, the spatial foundation of the regional school is likely to be rocked as we extend beyond the domestic markets.

Finally, it is becoming very difficult to pinpoint who competes with whom. For example, with the announcement that Sears will provide financial and health care services in the shopping malls, it becomes difficult to define the customers and competitors, and hence the marketplace.

We believe the regional school will become extremely critical for physical distribution and logistics functions but less and less relevant for defining markets. Furthermore, additional considerations such as traffic patterns, parking, and other support services will become marginally more important than distance and population density as the determinants of retail gravitation.

# 26 —— Trading Areas

*Jac Goldstucker*

Abridged from *Science in Marketing*, edited by George Schwartz (New York: John Wiley and Sons, Inc., 1965), pp. 281-320, by permission.

## Introduction

A firm's location is a significant ingredient for generating sales. The American business executive is seldom, if ever, satisfied with his firm's present sales volume. A strong feeling exists within the business community "that permanent injury is being done to a business that permits its total sales volume to decline sharply (even though all of its rivals are experiencing the same decline) and that it is desirable to expand sales even at the sacrifice of profits ..."[1] This statement suggests that there are more than material returns involved in many executive decisions. Perhaps more important is the egotistic satisfactions which accrue to the executive from his identifiction with a large and powerful enterprise.[2]

The impetus for growth and power is present within the executive. However, he must develop a strategy to translate this drive into action. Merchandising, in its broadest meaning, is the strategic weapon on which executives can rely to increase a firm's sales. Astute buying, forceful and well-timed promotion and provisions for service are among the factors which comprise the firm's strategy for growth and power.

The merchandising strategy influences customers to patronize one firm rather than another. In many cases (such as retail stores) the pressure is to persuade the customer to travel from his base to a given store location. In other circumstances, a firm sends salesmen to seek out potential patrons. The salesmen hope to find a receptive audience already favorably conditioned by the firm's strategy.

Growth stimulates growth. Therefore, as a firm increases in size, it tends to seek sales over larger and larger geographic expanses. It is apparent that beyond some point geographic distances become so great that buyers and sellers lose contact. It is then that vendors—manufacturers, wholesalers, and retailers—attempt to narrow the breach. Firms which operate branch plants, branch warehouses, and multiple stores use the approach of multiple unit operation toward the end. They recognize that customers will endure only limited inconveniences in seeking a vendor, particularly when alternatives are available. Therefore the executive must in the long run locate his branches so that they are convenient to the customers. However, this decision also involves cost considerations.

Size, growth, and power are no doubt valued for reasons not fully explained by material gain. Nevertheless, material gain, in the form of profit, assures that resources will be available to perpetuate and expand the enterprise. Therefore, location decisions are inextricably enmeshed with costs. The costs involve physical effort by the seller in supplying the consumer and physical effort and inconvenience on the part of the consumer to secure the products. These costs are generally expressed as utility or satisfaction from the point of view of the consumer and profit from the businessman's point of view. *Thus, a "natural" trading area might be defined as an area in which the costs of contact between buyers and sellers are minimal.* Where contact costs are minimal, the satisfactions of both consumers and businessmen must be optimal.

For decades trading area analysts have tried to define, in general terms, the greatest geographic area over which buyers and sellers can maintain contact while still optimizing their respective satisfactions and profit. This goal requires that analysts identify variables affecting consumer satisfaction and businessman's profit. Then, it is necessary to develop yardsticks in order to measure optimum profit and optimum satisfaction. For only through such measures can the appropriate intensive and extensive limits of a trading area be set.

The task is difficult as it presents a two-faced problem. One of the problems is that thus far no one has discovered all the variable components of consumer utility or satisfaction. In addition, while some variables are known, means of measuring and weighting them are unavailable. The second problem concerns businessmen's profits. This problem is also one of identifying and measuring variables comprising costs of contacting the consumer. Accountants find that marketing or distribution cost components—advertising, personal selling, packaging—are difficult to measure.[3] Therefore, with respect to quantifying consumer utility and marketing costs, the difficulty involved in developing yardsticks to measure trading areas has not yet been overcome.

This chapter is devoted to a survey of the available knowledge concerning the dimensions of retail, wholesale, manufacturing and extractive trading areas. The purpose is to focus attention on what we know about trading areas, what gaps exist in our knowledge, and the direction which further inquiry might take to fill in these gaps. This in turn should advance understanding of trading areas and hence contribute to their more efficient coverage with benefits accruing both to business and to consumers.

## Location of Economic Activity

The location and development of economic activity have long been of interest to geographers and sociologists, who developed a general principle which is the basis for trading area concepts. They pointed to the natural tendency toward the centralization of human activities and institutions. The result is that the "central place" dominates the activities of the surrounding population.[4]

The establishment and growth of towns and central places, between the lower Rhine and Seine in the Middle Ages, were the result of the relationship between defense and trade.[5] Merchants did not realize enough business in one place to sustain themselves. Hence, they moved from place to place. As they traveled, they needed resting places and storage facilities for their stock of goods. This was particularly important during winter months. The greatest safety was under the protection of an abbey or fortress; traders attached themselves to such a complex, not unlike a present-day suburb. Artisans attached themselves to the community to provide the traders with wares to sell. Tavernkeepers joined the group to supply food and drink. Groups of boatmakers, longshoremen, and others who provided transport vehicles and facilities also gathered together. Eventually the economic power of the trading complex grew and attracted larger and larger populations. Soon this economic power exceeded that of the abbey and fortress so that their positions became subservient to the needs of the larger community.

A combination of religion, refuge, and a rich consumer fostered the development of towns. In order to grow, however, a town must possess economic or geographic advantage. If the town had a strategic defense position, a dominant location with respect to trade routes, and agricultural or mineral resources, its growth and effectiveness could be favorably predicted almost with certainty. The town's economic importance was dependent upon its location and its site....

The factors just mentioned fostered the location of a town in a certain district but did not determine the actual site of the town within that district. Deciding the site was a function of its suitability for defense and of its command over roads and waterways. Towns developed where trade routes crossed, where natural transshipment points existed, or on the highest point that ships could reach on navigable streams.

This centralization of people into central places resulted in considerable industrial development. Areas which had surplus ore, for example, did more than simply accommodate local demand. Incentive for greater returns encouraged metal fabricators to expand output and to supply deficient areas. Monasteries, taking advantage of natural resources, produced surplus wines, leather goods, and other commodities and engaged in trade of these surpluses. Industry and trade were established and grew....

An economic region is defined as follows: (1) one center of economic control, (2) greater internal homogeneity than would be the case if it merged with contiguous areas, (3) a characteristic group of import products, and (4) a characteristic group of export products.[6] Located within each economic region are cities, towns, and villages. As the population has become increasingly urbanized, the resulting agglomerations have been the bases for the Standard Metropolitan Areas concept used by the Bureau of the Census.[7]

These metropolitan areas frequently provide an environment for centers of economic control.

The total economic activity within one region is made up of a wide variety of firms and industries which are most likely located within the regions's metropolitan areas. These retail, wholesale, and manufacturing firms view the geographic expanse as a trading area. The extent of a firm's trading area depends on a variety of things which will be discussed later. Nevertheless, there is an idea that a given firm (and a given community as well) has a ''natural'' trading area which it *should* serve. This area is not necessarily consistent with its *actual* trading area.

Given the proper set of assumptions, one can safely theorize about the most likely shape of trading areas. A good beginning is to consider Marshall's definition of a ''market'':

> Thus the more nearly perfect a market is, the stronger is the tendency for the same price to be paid for the same thing at the same time in all parts of the market: but, of course, if the market is large, allowance must be made for the expense of delivering the goods to different purchasers; each of whom must be supposed to pay, in addition to the market price, a special charge on account of delivery.[8]

Marshall focuses attention on price and geographic outreach in a perfectly competitive market. He implies that the geographic area of a market depends on the price of the goods plus the cost of transporting them. The higher the price (including the price of the transportation), the smaller will be the area of demand and the wider the area of supply. Secondly, by focusing attention on the geographic expanse of the trading area, it is practical to apply this type of definition to many marketing problems. For example, in the marketing of a homogeneous product like cement, geography is a prime consideration.[9]

If firms operated in a perfect market, they would tend toward equal size and the market for each firm would be a circle.[10] Until all space was occupied, new firms would find it profitable to enter. With all space finally occupied, the trading area of each firm would be hexagonal.[11] These hexagons, absorbing all space, would take on the appearance of a honeycomb as illustrated in Figure 1.[12]

These assumptions of symmetry obviously do not apply in the real world. Firms are not the same. Their offerings differ. In the real world, the determinants of the dimensions of trading areas are believed to be (1) the extent of product differentiation and the relative effectiveness of brand promotion, (2) the range of choice in administered pricing made possible by product differentiation, oligopoly, and other influences, (3) the ratio of fixed to total costs, (4) the economies of scale of production at each center, (5) the burden of transfer costs in total delivered prices to customers, and (6) the availability of adequate markets within a radius of economical outreach.[13]

These factors can be applied to explain the pattern of trading area coverage by manufacturers, wholesalers, and retailers. They influence decisions with

FIGURE 1. Honeycomb Markets

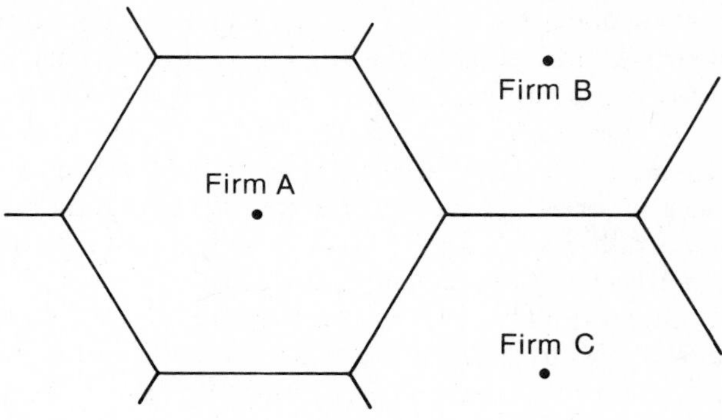


respect to branch merchandising, chain store location and multiregion establishments by manufacturers, distributors, and retailers. They explain why some types of products are sold over limited geographical expanses while others are sold over vast areas. They explain why some firms in the same industry are local and others are regional.

These brief comments on some of the theories of location provide sufficient background for an examination of the available trading area knowledge. Products are made either to be consumed directly or are made to facilitate the production of goods used to produce consumer goods. Therefore, it seems logical to begin with a discussion of retail trading areas. The discussion then moves to considerations of wholesale, manufacturing, and extractor trading areas.

## Retail Trading Areas[14]

The retailer who understands (knows) certain characteristics of his trading area is in a position to make more accurate business decisions with respect to sales forecasting, financing, and budgeting activities. Merchandising and promotion policies are more likely to reflect the tastes and preferences of consumers. Indeed, such knowledge aids in determining when and where to open new branches as well as their most appropriate nature and characteristics. Finally, familiarity with the many facets of the trading area is of benefit to the entire community. Merchants can organize cooperative activities directed at known rather than unknown or fancied objectives, the result being progress and development within the community.

### Factors Influencing Retail Trading Areas[15]

***Product.*** The class of product influences retail trading areas. By definition, there are fewer substitutes for specialty goods than there are for convenience and shopping goods, and the demand is more limited and diffused. As a result, trading areas for specialty goods are typically more extensive than they are for convenience and shopping goods. Hence within a community the trading area for retail firms handling one class of goods differs from that of firms selling other classes.[16]...

***Variations within a Store.*** Variations within a given store also influence the store's trading area. For example, a department store which stocks convenience, shopping, and specialty goods might find that its trading area varies for each class of good. Furthermore, the extent of the trading area for each class is influenced by the others. A store noted for its specialty goods offerings may have a greater trading area for its convenience and shopping goods than is typical. Customers coming from afar to buy the specialty goods are likely to buy other types of goods as well.

***Comparative Prices.*** A retailer can expand his selling area by reducing price on nationally recognized brands of merchandise if rivals do not retaliate. Thus one finds that large retailers, buying large quantities of merchandise at a discount, can sell at lower prices and over greater distances than can their smaller competitors....

***The Automobile.*** The automobile has had both a centralizing and decentralizing effect on the extent of retail trading areas. It has enabled people, urban and rural, to reach the central business district with greater facility. This extended the outreach of larger centers at the expense of the small country villages. Thus, the automobile along with improved highways contributed to the centralization of trading areas.

The increased number of automobiles in use has generated traffic congestion in central areas. This has encouraged consumers to seek more accessible areas in which to shop. Suburban shopping centers with branches of major central city retailers and containing ample parking have developed to meet these needs. The result is decentralization within a retailing trading area. This decentralization process might be viewed as a source for new small trading areas.[17]

***Growth of Metropolitan Areas.*** The increase in population plus the movement from rural to urban areas have resulted in the marked growth of cities and their suburbs. In most cases, while both cities and suburbs have grown, suburban increases have been at a faster rate. This has given further impetus to decentralization of retail trading areas.[18]

***Flow of Goods and of Traffic.*** The flexibility and growth of transportation facilities have enabled downtown stores to deliver goods over wide areas from decentralized warehouses. Furthermore, traffic flow analysis has facilitated the location and relocation of stores and additional units of chain stores and of branches.

***Geography.*** The geographic location of a retail center influences the extent of its market. For example, the mountains to the west of Denver limit the city's trading area in that direction. The same barriers limit Salt Lake City's area to the east. Chicago and Milwaukee are limited on the east by Lake Michigan.

***Miscellaneous Factors.*** There are additional factors which influence consumer purchasing habits. Outstanding merchandising institutions such as Neiman-Marcus of Dallas exert a greater than average influence on trading areas. The extent of group action also influences outreach. For example, Chicago's State Street Council engages in continuous concerted action to attract customers from the city and suburbs into the Loop shopping area. Cities with convention facilities, artistic and sports activities, and other such attractions are able to draw large transient groups, many of whom buy merchandise while in the center. Finally, Weigand makes the point that the tendency for individuals "to live in one area, work in a second, worship in a third, and recreate in a fourth means that the consumer may shop in any one or more of these areas; or he may confuse the situation by shopping in yet a different one."[19] The point is that different areas have diverse "pulls" on a family, complicating retail trading area analysis.

While it is generally believed that these variables influence the extent of the retail trading area, tools to measure their influence are not available. Furthermore, the list probably is not entirely exhaustive. The uncertainty is reflected in such statements as "not too much is known about the whole subject of retail trading areas."[20] The lack of knowledge may be related to the fact that there is a lack of agreement among marketing people as to the precise meaning of the term. The absence of a universally accepted definition hinders formulation of a standard research methodology and of principles universally applicable to trading area analysis.

Some who use the term "retail trading area" do not define it at all. Others define it, but the definitions differ. Each reflects the particular frame of reference or point of view of the user. A review of only a few of the varying concepts will serve to emphasize the point.

One definition is formulated in terms of the commodities being sold."(A trading area) is a district whose boundaries are usually determined by the economical selling range for a commodity or group of commodities sold by a middleman or a group of middlemen located in the district."[21]

Another concept is of a store trading area. "Markets usually contain stores of different types and sizes. Each store has its own trading area."[22] "Store trading areas are the joint product of many simultaneous interacting factors so numerous that they defy generalization."[23] Defined in terms of an individual retail establishment, a trading area is "that geographic area from which the particular station draws the majority of its business."[24]

Definitions also are framed in terms of a retail trading area of a community. For example, Larson and Poteat state "Trading areas may be defined as those areas in which a seller may reasonably expect to vend a profitable volume of his goods or services. From the viewpoint of the buyer, a trading area is that region inside which he may reasonably expect to find goods and services at competitive and prevailing prices. There are, of course, many refinements to these definitions."[25] Fine defines a community retail trading area as "the area surrounding the community from which it secures approximately 90 per cent of its sales of a representative group of commodities."[26]

It is well recognized that definitions and research methodology with respect to retail trading areas vary widely. Nevertheless, many studies of particular trading areas have been undertaken over the past years by Chambers of Commerce, university research bureaus, private firms, and governmental agencies.[27]...

## Methods Used to Measure Retail Trading Areas[28]

One method is based on an audit of *automobile license numbers*. By identifying the residences of the owners of cars (from state motor vehicle license records) parked at a store, a shopping center, or the central business district of a community, one could determine from where the particular retail complex draws its customers. These points, plotted on a map, define the particular retail trading area....

Another method is based on *circulation of newspapers* from competing centers. The assumption is that the newspapers draw consumers into the trading center. There is a positive correlation between the sale of shopping goods and newspaper circulation.[29] However, it is not quite clear whether readership leads to buying or whether buying leads to readership.[30]...

A widely used method of defining retail trading area limits is to determine where customers make their purchases. This can be done indirectly by examining the *customers' addresses*.[31] Addresses of credit and cash customers of important stores in competing centers are collected and plotted on a map. The method is used primarily to check shopping goods sales for a limited time period. A direct method of determining where consumers buy is to contact them either by *personal interview* or *mailed questionnaire*.[32]

Batcher used bank checks as a basis for defining the extent of a trading area.[33] Checks used to pay retail accounts are noted as to addresses of the writers as they are given to the retailer and cleared through local banks. These points are mapped and become the basis for determining retail trading areas.

Nelson suggests a method of retail trading area analysis to determine approximate store or shopping center location. This is referred to as the *microanalysis technique*.[34] It requires that the analyst "think deliberately and specifically about small areas that he can more easily understand."[35] Trading areas are first divided into small areas. The amount of business available from each one is determined. Customers in the areas are interviewed to see where they live, what their income is, and what their buying patterns are with respect both to where they buy and how much. Nelson indicates that the microanalysis technique has the following advantages:[36]

1. The analyst thinks in units small enough for human comprehension.
2. The detailed study uncovers unusual situations.
3. In this kind of research a multiplicity of judgments does not result in errors that are cumulative.
4. In the process of detailed study, a great deal of information can be uncovered about the trading area and the people in it which will be useful in the design of the store and its promotional activities....

Pfanner discusses a statistical method for determining the power which a city has for attracting retail trade. He makes the assumption that a state is a self-contained trading area. Then, by multiple correlation analysis and by using income-tax returns and automobile registrations as independent variables, he estimates from census data the per capita sales of furniture, jewelry, women's apparel, and automobile accessories in 90 cities and by counties for the state of Ohio. "The difference between the estimated sales figure (as reported in the Census of Retail Trade) for that city is the estimate of the amount of trade in a particular commodity group that the city draws from outside its boundaries. This figure, expressed as a percentage of actual sales of a city, is the drawing power of that city." The study also reveals variations among product areas and among cities.[37]

Huff has proposed a method for estimating the "trade potential of prospective shopping developments."[38] He developed a model and deduced mathematical conclusions from it. Next, he used the empirical data gathered from a suburban community in the Los Angeles Metropolitan Area. When he compared the expected consumer behavior with the empirically determined behavior, he found a high positive correlation. This led Huff to conclude that on the basis of his pilot study the model can be used successfully "to estimate demand for agglomeration of retail firms."

## Reilly's Law

By far the most widely and consistently used, tested, and discussed technique for measuring retail trading areas is W. J. Reilly's law of retail gravitation. Reilly attempted to formulate a principle which would explain how boundaries of trading areas are determined. The principle can be expressed as a mathematical formula to facilitate the delineation of a center's retail trading area with respect to a competing center in the same geographic area. The law was formulated to apply principally to fashion and shopping goods. It states that "two cities attract retail trade from any intermediate city or town in the vicinity of the breaking point, approximately in direct proportion to the populations of the two cities and in inverse proportion to the square of the distances of these two cities to the intermediate town."[39]

The formula which expressed this relationship is as follows:

$$\frac{B_a}{B_b} = \left(\frac{P_a}{P_b}\right)\left(\frac{D_b}{D_a}\right)^2$$

where $B_a$ is the proportion of the trade from the intermediate city attracted by City *A*
$B_b$ is the proportion attracted by City *B*
$P_a$ is the population of City *A*
$P_b$ is the population of City *B*
$D_a$ is the distance from the intermediate town to City *A*
$D_b$ is the distance from the intermediate town to City *B*

Reilly recognized that about a dozen factors influence retail trade. However, he believed population and distance to be reliable indices of the behavior of other factors. Reilly then applied his "law." To test the formula he conducted field studies of pairs of trading centers. The result was sufficient to prove to Reilly that his law worked—that customers between the two cities generally gravitate to the larger city.[40]...

Converse made major contributions when he undertook research to verify the Reilly formula.[41] He used Urbana-Champaign and five other competing primary centers as a basis for his research. Thirteen other towns located between Urbana-Champaign and the five primary centers were studied. Converse, using Reilly's formula, predicted the division of trade between Urbana-Champaign and each of the five primary centers. Then, through field research, he surveyed families to determine where they made their shopping goods purchases. He concluded that "on the whole, it (Reilly's law) works rather accurately."[42]

In a later study, Converse tested the law. He again found that the law was substantially accurate. Nevertheless, he cautioned against its indiscriminate use, stressing that his empirical studies included primary trading centers which were substantially larger than the intermediate towns. He suggested that perhaps if the size of the primary and intermediate towns had been more nearly comparable, Reilly's "law" might be less accurate.[43]...

Converse developed his "breaking point formula" also to measure the flow of shopping goods trade. It is as follows:

$$\text{Breaking point} - \text{miles from } B = \frac{\text{Miles between } A \text{ and } B}{1 + \sqrt{\dfrac{\text{Population of } A}{\text{Population of } B}}}$$

The author suggests that Reilly's formula aids in determining how trade between two trading centers should be divided. The "breaking point" formula, on the other hand, can be used to determine a town's normal trading area without performing any field work.[44]

Converse also developed the ''new law of retail gravitation,'' which states that ''a trading center and a town in or near its trade area divide the trade of the town approximately in direct proportion to the population of the two towns and inversely as the squares of the distance factors, using 4 as the distance factor of the home town.''[45] The formula is:

$$\frac{B_a}{B_b} = \left(\frac{P_a}{H_b}\right)\left(\frac{4}{d}\right)^2$$

where $B_a$ is the proportion of trade going to the outside town
$B_b$ is the proportion of trade retained by the home town
$P_a$ is the population of the outside town
$H_b$ is the population of the home town
$d$ is the distance to the outside town
4 is the inertia factor[46]

Converse suggested that the ''new law'' has several uses. ''It can be applied to satellite towns or other towns inside the trade area of a larger town. It gives an appropriate measure of how the trade is divided without making a survey. Surveys can be made to check actual results against predicted or 'average' results.''[47]...

Finally, Schwartz synthesized the empirical studies of the Reilly and Converse laws and concluded that ''available information does not offer evidence for a rejection of the laws.'' However, he questioned ''whether the formulas can yet be regarded as marketing *laws*.''[48]

The purpose of this rather comprehensive survey of Reilly's and Converse's ''laws'' and of the literature pertaining to them has been to emphasize the contribution of these two men to retail trading area analysis. The ''laws'' have certain acknowledged limitations: the primary criticisms are that they are not precise; they should not be called ''laws''; and that they apply primarily to shopping and to style or specialty goods rather than to convenience goods. The formula considers distance and population as proxy variables in influencing the division of retail trade between two primary centers. It has already been noted that other factors exert influences causing deviations from ''normal'' as postulated by Reilly. Distance alone should not be the measure. In this modern day, distance and time are usually related. The important factor may be the time which is required to travel a distance. Specifically, where population depends on public transportation, retailers tend to locate in areas serviced by the public facilities. Customers then will be attracted from large areas, and the extent will depend in part on accessibility. Reilly recognized these possibilities and others as well. However, he concluded that ''other factors are either so closely related to, or so directly dependent upon these two primary factors that the effects of the dependent factors tend to balance out when cities are compared on the basis of population and distance.'' However, this writer is of the opinion that these assumptions cannot be accepted as reducing the need to identify, test, and measure other variables which influence the extent of retail trading areas....

### Retail Trading Areas—A Synthesis

This review of the literature points up the fact that as yet no principles have been developed which can be universally applied in the analysis of trading areas. Retail trading areas are a particularly complex aspect of spatial economics. That is due to the multiplicity of variables involved—the large number and varied types of retail stores, the classes and variety of goods handled, the location and accessibility of the community, and perhaps others. Furthermore, the human behavior variable is still difficult to measure and predict, advances made by the sociologists and psychologists notwithstanding. The mores of a population, the community's policy with respect to growth and development, the inertia of the shoppers plays a part in retail trading area determination. Each one of these—and there are undoubtedly many others—is a component of this human behavior variable.

Man, more than perhaps any other living organism, is able to adjust quickly to environmental changes. The direction which the adjustment may take is usually predictable only with a very wide range and in a short time interval. Hence, given the present level of knowledge with respect to human behavior, developing theories which give both precise and consistent results, is much more difficult in the social sciences than in the physical sciences where variables, once identified, are more readily controllable. Such factors must explain at least partially the shortcomings of such theories as Reilly's ''law.''...

This synthesis suggests areas where further research might be profitably pursued to develop the theories, principles, and yardsticks needed to augment our understanding of retail trading areas. These suggested areas for additional research are discussed in detail in the final section of the chapter.

## WHOLESALE TRADING AREAS[49]

When urban areas became large enough to support many retail outlets, wholesale establishments arise to supply them. Thus, one finds wholesale centers, large and small, throughout the entire United States. Wholesale activities are essentially of two kinds: (1) those that assemble the products of primary producers and disperse the products to the market, and (2) those concerned with collecting, sorting, and dispersing finished goods. The market for wholesalers engaged in these latter activities consists of retail and industrial users who are frequently located over a large geographic area.

However, firms at each location are faced with a problem of the distances over which they can economically operate. Costs, competition, and prices influence their outreach.

Although there are many wholesale centers, about 44 percent of the wholesale sales volume is concentrated in the ten largest of the present 212 Standard Metropolitan Areas.[50] With few exceptions (notably the heavily populated East and California), each economic region has a wholesale center which is dominant in that region.

The Bureau of Census divides the United states into nine regions or geographic areas which approximate the ''natural'' economic regions as described on page 408. Within each region are several Standard Metropolitan Areas, and each has its own wholesale trade. There are four characteristics common to a wholesale center: ''(1) a large population whose consumption needs must be met, (2) a great deal of manufacturing and processing, (3) a wealth of agencies for transporting, warehousing, financing, and trading, and (4) enterprises and facilities for handling and reshipping goods into domestic and foreign commerce.''[51]

## Factors Influencing Wholesale Trading Areas[52]

If wholesalers handling the same kind of goods operated in a perfect market, the territory which each served would in the long run be hexagonal just as would be the case with retail trade territories (see page 410). The wholesale market is, however, imperfect; in fact, one can make a logical case that it is an oligopoly.[53] In other than the very largest wholesale centers, the number of wholesale firms is small.[54]

Wholesalers, operating in an imperfect market and selling differentiated products, employ various marketing strategies to influence their market shares. Depending on the degree of success of these strategies, market areas vary among firms in the industry and among product lines within the firm. Through research and observation, certain factors which are thought to influence wholesale trading areas have been noted. Some of these are the class of goods, the kind of firm, relative prices among firms, transportation costs, selling costs, geography, and the characteristics of a firm's management.

***Product and Firm Differences.*** Trading areas for wholesalers are partly a function of the classes of products they sell. Lewis found that even within one city, wholesalers handling the same line of products have vastly different territories.[55] This is partially a reflection of the marketing functions or services extended to customers....

Territorial coverage of firms marketing products which are staple and relatively undifferentiated is usually localized. When a wholesaler of this type of goods is located in a large city, his area of coverage may be no more than a single section of that city. These city wholesalers are not likely to operate in small secondary centers. As a result, small wholesalers are able to operate from secondary centers and service them with little competition from large city wholesalers.[56]...

Specialty wholesalers generally have larger trading areas than do staple wholesalers, although both are usually concentrated in a few metropolitan areas.[57] Geographic concentration of sources of supply provides both width and depth of assortment, which is of great importance to retail buyers in selecting merchandise for their stores. This wide assortment, along with other types of differentitation, enables a given firm to extend its outreach relative to other competitive firms, the extent depending on relative differentiation among firms. While specialty goods are normally sold over wider areas than are staples, a general-line wholesaler with a wide assortment may extend his trading area far beyond that of his specialty goods rivals located in the same center....

***Price.*** Price exerts an important influence on market outreach. It is generally accepted that those who buy for business use are more objective and unemotional in making their purchases than are household consumers. They are fairly expert and are concerned with the price of the products which they must buy. Since wholesalers deal with businesses, institutions, and governmental agencies, it is reasonable to assume that a given vendor is able to sell farther from his home location when his price is lower than that of his local competition and that of competition located in other centers. If products were homogeneous and transfer costs were proportional to distance, lower prices at one wholesale center would enable firms located there to press farther out toward competing centers. But staple and nationally branded products being relatively homogeneous, the prices and terms are usually uniform between competing wholesale centers. Hence each wholesale center is somewhat insulated from the competition of other nearby centers, and one finds that markets for staples are fairly narrow....

Many wholesalers have integrated their operations with the hope that resulting economies of scale will enable the enterprise to follow price policies which will broaden its market outreach. On the other hand, since firms of different size survive, it may be assumed that size is not the sole determinant of survival. Since there is little quantitative evidence of the effects of economics of scale in wholesaling, any conclusions in this area must depend on the assumptions which are made.[58]

***Transportation Costs.*** Transportation costs are usually an important consideration in determining the boundaries of wholesale trading areas, since variations in freight rates are associated with price differences. The landed cost of goods to the wholesaler affects the prices he must charge for his merchandise. Hence, the freight rate structure influences the extent of a trading area because of its bearing on selling price.[59]

Transportation costs also influence the shape of a trading area. The major source of supplies of most types of products is in the eastern part of the United States. As a result, the wholesale trading area of any center is wider toward the west than toward the east. Expressed differently, this means that any given wholesaler generally sells farther to this west than to his east. This is related to the backhaul cost in selling east of the center.[60]...

The expansion of motor trucking over the past decades has introduced greater flexibility into transport service. The rates of motor trucks are usually as low or lower than the LCL rates of the railroads. Many localities, formerly isolated because of lack of rail facilities, are now served by highways and can therefore be serviced easily and economically by trucks. This service has tended to enable large wholesalers to extend their trading areas. At the same time, local jobbers are able to operate profitably.[61]

***Selling Costs.*** Another factor influencing trading areas is the cost of soliciting business by personal salesmen. Other things being equal, selling costs will increase rapidly on a percentage basis as the enterprise reaches farther out. Expenses incurred when a firm elects to keep a salesman on the road and time spent traveling rather than selling will affect outreach. These costs increase as population density decreases. It should be noted, however, that the selling function can be performed in many different ways. Some of these methods are less expensive than others....

***Geography.*** A regions's physical characteristics affect the extent of wholesale trading areas. The geographic location of major wholesale centers in the United States has one of two general characteristics. Some are located on or near waterways, rivers, or oceans and function in both foreign and domestic commerce. Others are located in the interior but are transportation junction points. Most major wholesale centers have one or both of these characteristics. This is true of New York, Chicago, Denver, Minneapolis, Salt Lake City, and many others....

## Methods Used to Measure Wholesale Trading Areas

In spite of manufacturers' and distributors' interest in wholesale trading areas, there are relatively few published studies in this field. Those available are in the nature of atlases of trading areas for particular goods (see notes 56 and 57) or deal with specific wholesale markets. These latter studies are concerned, primarily, with the geographic extent of the trading area of wholesale firms located within a particular community or region.[62]

In most of the studies cited, interest centers on the extent of a wholesale trading area. The method used to delimit the territories is primarily that of mapping the location of each wholesaler's customers. By interviewing the wholesaler, checking his records (such as sales invoices or call reports), and contacting his customers, the researcher determines the trading area. Then by summing the customers of the entire agglomeration of wholesalers in a given center, the magnitude of the wholesale trading areas is determined. If the trading area for a particular product is desired, only wholesalers selling that product line are considered.[63]...

D. J. Bowersox has developed a mathematical technique to determine the optimum location of a food distribution center. He states that "The basic goal in selecting a distribution center location is to achieve one-day delivery to each supermarket at the lowest possible distribution cost. Therefore, the optimum location solution is one which determines that geographic point from which all supermarkets can be replenished at least cost. The critical costs stem from local delivery to supermarkets."[64]...

### Summary Comments Concerning Wholesale Trading Areas

A survey of wholesaling literature leads one to a basic conclusion. Little has been done to develop research techniques and tools with which to analyze and measure wholesale trading areas. Although it is generally recognized that the wholesaling industry arises primarily to meet the needs of retail trade, it is also clear that retailing and wholesaling trading areas are not coextensive.

What a firm's wholesale trading area should be in order for it to be covered efficiently cannot be determined without appropriate yardsticks. Indeed, what the territory actually is depends primarily on a highly subjective evaluation of what executives *feel* that their particular territory should be. The evaluation is frequently based on incomplete knowledge of the marginal cost and marginal revenue relations at the periphery of the firm's trading area.

Fundamentally, there are no empirically tested yardsticks to measure wholesaling trading areas.... Perhaps the lack of research and methodology means that enough information is available to fit the present needs of wholesalers and other marketing people. This writer doubts that such is the case.

## Primary Producers' Trading Areas[65]

The theoretical area determination under the assumption of pure competition can be applied to primary products, both agricultural and extractive, with a minimum of alteration. Obviously, however, no markets are purely competitive. Still, primary products have at least some of the characteristics of such a market structure: (1) the products tend to be relatively homogeneous, at least within grades; (2) the products are usually supplied by many small, independent producers; (3) the relatively low specific value of the products mean that transportation costs weigh heavily on final market price thus influencing trading area outreach; and (4) supply and demand conditions exert a relatively strong pressure on determining market price.[66]

The importance of transportation costs explains why agricultural products tend to be produced, processed, and consumed locally. The exception is when production is highly concentrated and the demand is diffused, such as for sea foods, citrus fruits, redwood lumber, and some types of ore.

## Factors Determining Trading Areas for Primary Products

***Freight Rate Structures.*** If markets were perfectly competitive and transportation costs varied proportionately and directly with distance, the extent of the trading area for producers of primary products would depend on transportation costs and demand elasticity. However, freight rate structures reflect a wide variety of built-in discriminations. Interstate truck lines are faced with size and weight limits and tax loads which limit the scope of the truck operations and, therefore, the extent of trading areas.[67]...

***Quality.*** Variations in the quality of primary and extractive products effect trading areas. Differences in quality of wheat, even though of the same grade, differences in quality of southern soft woods and western hard woods contribute to the extent of trading areas. These quality differences affect price and market flows.

***Areas of Surplus and Deficit Production.*** A section in the *Year Book of Agriculture*, 1954, includes maps of surplus production areas by commodity.[68] Examination of these maps reveals principal directions of the flows which the commodities take from production to consumption areas. The shape of the trading area depends on the relative size of the surplus and deficit areas which in turn affects market price. For example, a major surplus area producing in large quantities at low cost may penetrate greater distances than areas with only minor surpluses and higher cost.

***Interstate Trade Barriers.*** Interstate barriers are also frictions which distort trading areas. Some states ban or restrict out-of-state agricultural products. The intent is to reduce competition and enable local producers to sell for higher prices even though a variety of seemingly valid arguments are made to support such restrictive behavior. For example, oleomargarine taxes in dairy-producing states serve this purpose. Consequently, the trading areas for such products are distorted.

The factors discussed are among the more important ones in influencing the trading areas for primary producers, agricultural and extractive. Each class of primary products is relatively homogeneous and in most cases is produced by many firms. The buyers are usually well informed with respect to product quality, availability, and prevailing price. Hence, in general terms, the theory of perfectly competitive models is useful in defining trading areas limits for such products as these. Using the model as a basis for analysis, one is able to identify many of the so-called market frictions, hereby explaining the actual shape of the trading areas as opposed to its theoretical shape.

## Manufacturers' Trading Areas

Manufacturers typically are able to sell their products over a wider area than are retailers, wholesalers, or producers of primary products. Several factors make this possible:

1. Opportunity for successful product differentiation.
2. Pricing alternatives.
3. Opportunity for integration and economies of scale.
4. Ratio of transfer costs to total value of the product.
5. Ratio of fixed to total costs.
6. Dispersion of consumers in the market.
7. Management's desire and opportunity for expansion and control.

***Opportunity for Successful Product Differentiation.*** Chamberlin points out that:

> A general class of products is differentiated if any significant basis exists for distinguishing goods (or services) of one seller from those of another. Such a basis may be real or fancied so long as it is of any importance whatever to buyers and leads to a preference for one variety of the product over another.[69]

Successful differentiation reduces the number of substitutes for a product. Hence manufacturers with highly differentiated products, real or imagined, are more likely to extend their trading areas. On the other hand, successful differentiation results in overlapping trading areas. If the products were homogeneous among manufacturers, the market of each would resemble a hexagon. Each producer would sell in his own area. With differentiation, several manufacturers sell in the same area. The share of the market which each obtains depends on how effectively each differentiates his product.

***Transfer Costs, Prices, and Economies of Scale.*** These three factors are important determinants of trading area coverge. If transfer costs are great relative to the price of the product, market outreach is limited. Transfer costs are a part of total costs. The price of the product must be high enough to defray all costs. As manufacturers attempt to extend their trading areas, transfer costs increase more than proportionately to other costs. A higher price will compensate for the added costs. However, ability to increase price depends on competititve conditions, structure of transportation rates, and elasticity of demand....

Economies of scale also affect market outreach. If economies result in lower at-the-plant costs, the product can bear a proportionately heavier transfer cost for any given price. Thus, the product can be marketed at a distance further than would be possible in the absence of economies of scale.

If fixed costs are a relatively great proportion of total costs, then the impetus to expand output and extend trading areas is also great. Essentially, it is the spreading of large fixed costs over greater output which yields economies of scale. This relationship of fixed to total costs stimulates the search for distance markets.[70]

***Dispersion of Customers.*** Selling costs influence both the size of a trading area and the manner in which it will be covered. Selling effort will be less costly when customers are highly concentrated because the time spent reaching the customers is negligible. On the other hand, selling costs tend to increase when customers are widely dispersed. Salesmen must spend time traveling to reach these buyers. As a result, less time is available to devote to selling....

***Concentrated Manufacturing with Widespread Demand.*** It should be noted briefly that when customers for a product are widely dispersed and when manufacturing facilities of an industry are highly concentrated, manufacturers' trading areas tend to be large. For example, demand for photographic equipment is spread throughout the entire United States. Yet manufacture of the goods is highly concentrated.

We have suggested that the trading area which a manufacturer is able to serve depends on a number of variables, such as degree and success of product differentiation, pricing policies, burden of transfer costs, economies of scale, demand elasticity, and others. These factors are not mutually exclusive in exerting influence on the extent of a trading area. However, since we are unable to weight these variables, we are unable to determine what influence each has or what influence various combinations exert on manufacturers' trading area coverage.

## Conclusions and Suggestions for Further Research

This chapter has been devoted to a survey of the available information pertaining to the analysis of trading areas of retailers, wholesalers, manufacturers, and primary producers. Techniques and theories for determining actual and potential trade territories have been examined. Synthesizing past and present research, the available information leads one to conclude that trading area analysis is as yet an art—not a science. In selecting locations, in selling and servicing territories, in comparing actual with potential sales, executives rely primarily on their experience and judgment, seeking corroboration from their associates. There is much to be done if the goal is to develop and practice a *science* of trading area analysis and that, indeed, appears to be the goal. The work of Reilly and Converse, the attempts by others to test and improve the pioneering methods of these two men, and current efforts to develop mathematical models with universal predictive properties indicate continuing interest in discovering a scientific method of dealing with trading area problems.

Business managers are continually selecting sites, building stores and plants, defining their trading areas, and making provisions to serve them. These activities initially must have been based primarily on improvisation. However, the accumulated experience from such actions, along with some aid from the theoreticians, has developed within management a more sophisticated judgment. Nevertheless the decisions are being made, and without universal principles, theories, or models.

This survey of trading area research and literature suggests some topics into which further investigations offers promise of fruitful results. One such topic is that of consumer behavior with respect to purchasing decisions. While much has been learned in recent years about the consumer, there is still a void in our knowledge. I have defined a ''natural'' trading area as one where the cost of contact between sellers and buyers is minimal. Buyers' costs involve the physical effort, inconvenience, and actual dollar outlay incurred in securing goods. The buyer will buy a good so long as the utility or satisfaction resulting from possessing that good is greater than the cost of obtaining it. For such concepts as buyer cost and utility to be of use in helping to set limits to trading areas, one must be able to identify the components of both cost and utility. That being done, the need is then to measure each, weigh it in relation to the other variable components, and, finally, to determine the degree and direction of variability of each in relation to the others.

Another topic for further investigation has to do with motives and motivation of business executives. The lack of dependable yardsticks for trading area analysis is due partially to the fallacy of some of the assumptions on which the research in the field rests. Location theory, Reilly's law, and other concepts which have been examined are all concerned with profit maximizing behavior. If, as many behavioral scientists point out, business executives act to maximize a wide variety of nonmaterial gains, then trading area theory is perhaps seeking answers to the wrong questions. This suggests the need to augment our understanding of factors which move business executives to value power, size, and growth. These motivations may more fully explain policies with respect to trading area coverage than do the assumptions related to profit maximization and economic incentive.

One must recognize, however, that it is through profits that the so-called nonmaterial satisfaction can be realized. Size, growth, and power often are long-run consequences of a profitable operation. Therefore, those activities which contribute to profit help maximize nonmaterial gains. As a consequence, factors which are economic in nature should also be examined. This suggests yet another area in which continued research might make an important contribution to trading area analysis, and that is factors affecting costs. Accounting has developed adequate understanding of direct production costs. Available techniques provide a rather rigorous basis for their allocation. On the other hand, the allocation of indirect and joint costs is still a cause of some concern. As a result, continuing attention is being devoted to improving indirect and joint costing methods.

Distribution costs should be of greater concern than production costs to marketing people and their accountants. Although some attention has been devoted to the study of distribution costs and to developing means whereby they can be analyzed and allocated, progress in the area lags far behind the need for understanding. As pointed out previously, this is a reflection of the difficulty associated with costing nonproduction activities. For example, the purpose of newspaper advertising by a retail store is to generate sales. An advertisement is run which appears to yield few immediate results. However, the cumulative effect of that and other advertisements plus other promotional activities may in the long run generate a sales volume far greater than the sum of that resulting from each advertisement taken singly. Yet management has no way of knowing what long-run sales would have been had the advertisement not been run. Therefore, the cost of that particular advertisement cannot be allocated on a per sale basis with an adequate degree of objectivity. The same reasoning is applicable in assessing the effects of personal selling, delivery, and various other service functions sustained as a part of a firm's marketing activities.

Without adequate tools to measure the costs of these marketing activities, a firm suffers disadvantage in attempting to assess the costs associated with serving a particular trading area. Thus, what "natural" trading area firm can most efficiently serve is indeterminate. Hence, accelerated research in distribution cost analysis is inevitable if trading area analysis is to become less subjective and more scientific.

This overview suggests that the enrichment of trading area analysis is hampered by a dearth of empirically validated theories and principles necessary in order to advance understanding in the field. The barriers are the problems involved in identifying, measuring, and weighting the variables which determine the dimensions of trading areas. These barriers must be surmounted before real progress is made. Until then, determining the "natural" trading area of a firm or a community will continue to be an art, not a science.

## ENDNOTES

1. A. R. Oxenfeldt, *Industrial Pricing and Market Practices*, Prentice-Hall, Englewood Cliffs, New Jersey, 1951, pp. 178-179.
2. The entire subject of size, growth, and prestige as management incentives is explored in W. G. Scott, *Human Relations in Management*, Richard D. Irwin, Homewood, Ill., 1962, Ch. 17.
3. C. T. Horngren, *Cost Accountancy*, Prentice-Hall, Englewood Cliffs, New Jersey, 1962, p. 517.

4. W. Christaller, *Die Centralen Orte In Suddeutschland* Erlangen, 1933.
5. This discussion is based on H. Heaton, *Economic History of Europe*, Harper, New York, 1948.
6. See R. L. Vaile, E. T. Grether, and R. Cox, *Marketing in the American Economy*, Ronald Press, New York, 1952, pp. 488 ff.
7. Bureau of the Budget, Executive Office of the President, *Standard Metropolitan Areas*, July 28, 1950.
8. A. Marshall, *Principles of Economics*, 8th ed., 1956 reprint, Macmillan, London, pp. 270-271.
9. G. J. Stigler, *The Theory of Price*, revised ed., Macmillan, New York, 1952, pp. 55-56.
10. Market boundaries are also discussed by F. A. Fetter, "The Economic Law of Market Areas," *Quarterly Journal of Economics*, Vol. XXXVIII (May 1924), pp. 520-530; also A. Losch. *op. cit.*, pp. 105-108.
11. The theory of hexagonal trading areas assumes that the firms in the industry are symmetrical with respect to buyers as well as to each other. See. A. Losch, *op. cit.*, Ch. 10 and E. Ullman, "A Theory for the Location of Cities," *American Journal of Sociology*, Vol. XLVI (May 1941), pp. 853-864.
12. S. Valavanis, "Losch on Location," *American Economic Review*, Vol. XLV (September 1955), p. 640, and E. S. Mills and M. R. Lav, "A Model of Market Areas with Free Entry," *The Journal of Political Economy*, Vol. LXXII (June, 1964), pp. 278-288.
13. R. S. Vaile, E. T. Grether, and R. Cox, *op. cit.*, pp. 525-526.
14. Several basic texts in marketing and in retailing discuss retail trading areas. See W. R. Davidson and P. L. Brown, *Retailing Management*, 2nd ed., Ronald Press, New York, 1960, Chs. 3 and 4; D. J. Duncan and C. F. Phillips, *Retailing, Principles and Methods*, 6th ed., Richard D. Irwin, Homewood, Ill., 1963, Ch. 4; E. A. Duddy and D. A. Revzan, *Marketing, An Institutional Approach*, 2nd ed., McGraw-Hill, New York, 1953, Ch. 23; and R. S. Vaile, E. T. Grether, and R. Cox, *op. cit.*, Ch. 27.
15. The list of factors and the discussion from R. S. Vaile, E. T. Grether, and R. Cox, *op. cit.*, pp. 557-567, where they are discussed in greater detail.
16. See R. Cassady, Jr. and H. Ostlund, *The Retail Distribution Structure of the Small City*, The University of Minnesota Press, Minneapolis, 1935.
17. See W. K. Bowden and Ralph Cassady, Jr., "Decentralization of Retail Trade in the Metropolitan Market Area," *Journal of Marketing*, Vol. V, No. 3 (January 1941), pp. 270-275; and Ralph Cassady, Jr. and W. K. Bowden, "Shifting Retail Trade Within the Los Angeles Metropolitan Market," *Journal of Marketing*, Vol. VIII, No. 4 (April 1944), pp. 398-399.
18. See R. Cox "Impact of Changes in the Size and Structure of Cities," in *Explorations in Retailing*, Stanley C. Hollander (ed.), Bureau of Business and Economic Research, College of Business and Public Service, Michigan State University, East Lansing, 1961, pp. 15-22.
19. R. E. Weigand, "Exclusive Dealerships—A Different View," *Journal of Retailing*, Vol. XXXVIII, No. 1 (Spring 1962), p. 17.
20. E. A. Duddy and D. A. Revzan, *op. cit.*, p. 401.
21. National Association of Marketing Teachers, "Definition of Marketing Terms," *National Marketing Review* (Fall 1935), p. 166.

22. W. Applebaum and S. B. Cohen, "Store Trading Areas in a Changing Market," *Journal of Retailing*, Vol. XXXVI, No. 3 (Fall 1961), p. 14.
23. *Ibid.*, p. 16.
24. W. S. Penn, Jr., "Measurement of Service Station Trading Areas," API Publication No. 1546, *Case Histories in Petroleum Marketing*, American Petroleum Institute, New York.
25. G. E. Larson and M. N. Poteat, "Selling the United States Market," *Domestic Commerce Series No. 29 (New Series)*, U. S. Department of Commerce, Government Printing Office, Washington, D. C., 1951, p. 13.
26. I. V. Fine, "Retail Trade Area Analysis," *Wisconsin Commerce Papers*, Vol. I, No. 6, University of Wisconsin, Bureau of Business Research and Service, Madison (January 1954), pp. 10-12. The use of 90% "tends to hold overlap of trading areas between competing centers to a minimum...."
27. A few such studies are *Retail and Wholesale Trading Areas of Minneapolis and St. Paul*, revised 1951, prepared by the Economic Research Department, Minneapolis Chamber of Commerce; "How to Make a Local Area Trade Survey," Domestic Distribution Department, U. S. Chamber of Commerce, Washington, D. C. (June 1940); *Water for the Future*, Vol. I. "Resources of the Texas Gulf Basin," Bureau of Business Research, The University of Texas, Austin, Texas, 1959. This study consists of several volumes. Volume I indicates that "To facilitate analysis the survey area was divided into sub-areas called 'trading areas'." (p. 2); F. G. Coolsen and W. S. Myers, *Kentucky Retail Market Areas and Trading Centers*, Bureau of Business Research, University of Kentucky, Frankfort, Kentucky, 1953. G. E. Larson and M. N. Poteat, *op. cit.*, and W. S. Penn, Jr., *op. cit.*
28. From E. A. Duddy and D. A. Revzan, *op. cit.*, Ch. 23.
29. A. S. Donnahoe, "Can Advertising Markets Be Defined Or Measured As Geographical Areas?" *Journal of Marketing*, Vol. XVII, No. 2 (October 1953), p. 121.
30. V. W. Bennett, "Consumer Buying Habits in a Small Town Located Between Two Large Cities," *Journal of Marketing*, Vol. VIII, No. 4 (April 1944), p. 414.
31. W. J. Reilly plotted retail trading areas from charge accounts of department and specialty stores as a basis against which he could compare other methods in checking the operation of his "law." See W. J. Reilly, "Methods for the Study of Retail Relationships," *Bureau of Business Research Monograph No. 4*, University of Texas, Austin (November 22, 1929).
32. This method is used by V. W. Bennett, *op. cit.*
33. A. S. Batcher, *A Method of Delineating Retail Trading Zones*, School of Business and Public Administration, University of Arizona, Tucson, 1939.
34. R. L. Nelson, *The Selection of Retail Locations*, F. W. Dodge Corporation, New York, 1958, p. 148.
35. *Ibid.*, p. 153.
36. *Ibid.*, pp. 153-154.
37. J. A. Pfanner, "A Statistical Study of the Drawing Power of Cities for Retail Trade," *Studies in Business Administration*, Vol. X, No. 3, University of Chicago, 1940, p. 14.
38. This and the quotation that follows are from D. L. Huff, "A Probabilistic Analysis of Consumer Spatial Behavior," *Emerging Concepts of Marketing*, W. S. Decker (ed.), American Marketing Association, Chicago, 1963, pp.

443-461; also, D. L. Huff, "Defining and Estimating a Trading Area." *Journal of Marketing*, Vol. XXVIII (July 1964), pp. 34-38.
39. W. J. Reilly, *The Law of Retail Gravitation*, 1st ed., The University of Texas, Austin, 1931.
40. From W. J. Reilly, "Methods for the Study of Retail Relationships," *op. cit.*
41. P. D. Converse, *A Study of Retail Trade Areas in East Central Illinois*, University of Illinois Press, Urbana, 1943.
42. *Ibid.*, pp. 44-48.
43. P. D. Converse, *Retail Trade Areas in Illinois*, University of Illinois, Urbana, 1946.
44. P. D. Converse, "New Laws of Retail Gravitation," *Journal of Marketing*, Vol. XIV, No. 3 (October 1949), pp. 379-380.
45. *Ibid.*, p. 382. (October 1953), pp. 170-171, and 172-174.
46. *Ibid.* The method of testing this formula is discussed in the article, pp. 380-382.
47. *Ibid.*
48. G. Schwartz, "Laws of Retail Gravitation: An Appraisal," *University of Washington Business Review*, Vol. XXII, No. 1 (October 1962), p. 69.
49. A basic text in wholesaling is T. N. Beckman, N. H. Engle, and R. D. Buzzell, *Wholesaling*, 3rd ed., Ronald Press, 1959. Also see *Journal of Marketing*, Vol. XIV, No. 2 (September 1949). The entire issue is devoted to various aspects of wholesaling.
50. Derived from the *Census of Business, Wholesale Trade*, 1958.
51. Vaile, Grether, and Cox, *op. cit.*, p. 537.
52. This discussion is taken in part from Vaile, Grether, and Cox, *op. cit.*, pp. 540-548.
53. "In its simplest form oligopoly is found in an industry in which the competing firms (producing either close or perfect substitute outputs) are several, but few enough and large enough so that each controls enough of the total industry output that a moderate extension of its output will reduce the sales of rivals by a noticeable amount." J. S. Bain, *Pricing, Distribution, and Employment*, revised ed., Holt, New York, 1953, p. 70.
54. Derived from the *Census of Business, Wholesale Trade, and Retail Trade*, 1958. There are more than six times as many retail outlets in the United States as there are wholesale firms.
55. E. H. Lewis, *Marketing Patterns of Philadelphia Wholesalers*, published by the author, Philadelphia, 1948.
56. *Ibid.*
57. *Atlas of Wholesale Dry Goods Trading Areas*, Department of Commerce, Washington, D. C., 1941.
58. Stigler, *op. cit.*, p. 144 and p. 223.
59. E. M. Hoover, *op. cit.*
60. E. M. Hoover, *op. cit.*, pp. 51-53, especially the map on page 52 derived from the *Atlas of Wholesale Dry Goods Trading Areas, op. cit.*
61. For a discussion of transport costs as they affect trading areas, see D. P. Locklin, *Economics of Transportation*, 5th ed., Richard D. Irwin, Homewood, Ill., 1960, Ch. 4.
62. A number of such studies are "Major Trade Areas in Eleven Western States," *University of Denver Business Review*, Vol. VII, No. 4, The University of

Denver (April 1931); E. A. Petersen, *op. cit.*; C. D. Harris, *Salt Lake City, A Regional Capital*, University of Chicago Press, 1940; E. G. Rasmussen, "Hardware Trading Centers and Trading Territories in Nine Southeastern States," *Journal of Marketing*, Vol. VIII, No. 2 (October 1943); R. D. Tousley and R. F. Lanzillotti, "The Spokane Wholesale Market," *Economic and Business Studies*, Bulletin No. 18, The State College of Washington, Pullman, 1951; and E. H. Lewis, *Wholesaling in the Twin Cities*, University of Minnesota Press, Minneapolis, 1952.

63. For example, see R. D. Tousley and R. F. Lanzillotti, *op. cit.*, for a map of the wholesale trading area of Spokane, p. 809; in the same volume are more than a dozen wholesale trade area maps by product.
64. D. J. Bowersox, "Food Distribution Center Location: Technique and Procedure," *Marketing and Transportation Paper No. 12*, Bureau of Business and Economic Research, Graduate School of Business Administration, Michigan State University, East Lansing, 1962. The food distribution center may be either an independent food wholesaler or a warehouse of a retail food chain. Also see "Evaluating Delivery Operations of Wholesale Food Distributions," *Marketing Research Report No. 502*, United States Department of Agriculture, Washington, D. C. (October 1961), and R. M. Hiel, "Techniques of Measuring Market Potential for Wholesalers," *Bureau of Business Management Bulletin No. 820*, College of Commerce and Business Administration, University of Illinois, Urbana (March 1962).
65. Much of this secion is based on R. S. Vaile, E. T. Grether, and R. Cox, *op. cit.*, Ch. 25.
66. Where price supports exist, this statement is true only if the support price is below equilibrium price.
67. "Highway Transportation Barriers in 20 States," *Marketing Research Report No. 157*, United States Department of Agriculture, Washington, D. C. (March 1957), p. 36; and "Effects of State and Local Regulations in Interstate Movement of Agricultural Products by Highway," *Marketing Research Report No. 496*, United States Department of Agriculture, Washington, D. C. (July 1961).
68. "An Atlas," *Year Book of Agriculture*, United States Department of Agriculture, Washington, D. C., 1954, pp. 402-490.
69. E. H. Chamberlin, *The Theory of Monopolistic Competition*, 8th ed., Harvard University Press, Cambridge, Mass., 1962, p. 56.
70. Basing-point pricing was an instrument devised to increase the market outreach of high fixed-cost producers.

## BIBLIOGRAPHY

Anderson, T. Hart, "Wholesale Areas Found Elliptical," *New York Times* (October 27, 1929).

Applebaum, W. and S. B. Cohen, "Store Trading Areas in a Changing Market," *Journal of Retailing*, Vol. XXXVI, No. 3 (Fall 1961).

"An Atlas," *Year Book of Agriculture*, United States Department of Agriculture, Washington, D. C., 1954.

*Atlas of Wholesale Dry Goods Trading Areas*, Department of Commerce, Washington, D. C., 1941.

Bain, J. S., *Pricing, Distribution, and Employment*, Holt, New York, 1953.

Batcher, A. S., *A Method of Delineating Retail Trading Zones*, School of Business and Public Administration, University of Arizona, Tucson, 1939.

Beckman, T. N., N. H. Engle, and R. D. Buzzell, *Wholesaling*, Ronald Press, 1959.

Bennett, V. W., "Consumer Buying Habits in a Small Town Located Between Two Large Cities," *Journal of Marketing*, Vol. VIII, No. 4 (April 1944).

Bowden, W. K. and R. J. Cassady, Jr., "Decentralization of Retail Trade in the Metropolitan Market Area," *Journal of Marketing*, Vol. V, No. 3 (January 1941).

Bowersox, D. J., "Food Distribution Center Location: Technique and Procedure," *Marketing and Transportation Paper No. 12*, Bureau of Business and Economic Research, Graduate School of Business Administration, Michigan State University, East Lansing, Michigan, 1962.

Canoyer, H. G., "Selecting a Store Location," *Economic Series No. 56*, Department of Commerce, Washington, D. C., 1946.

Cassady, R. J., Jr. and W. K. Bowden, "Shifting Retail Trade Within the Los Angeles Metropolitan Market," *Journal of Marketing*, Vol. VIII, No. 4 (April 1944).

Cassady, R. J., Jr. and H. S. Ostlund, *The Retail Distribution Structure of the Small City*, University of Minnesota Press, Minneapolis, 1935.

*Census of Business, Wholesale Trade, and Retail Trade*, 1958.

Chamberlin, E. H., *The Theory of Monopolistic Competition*, 8th ed., Harvard University Press, Cambridge, Mass., 1962.

Christaller, W., *Die Centralen Orte in Suddeutschland*, Erlangen, 1933.

"City Told Taxes Drive Out Trade," *New York Times*, Vol. 602, No. 38 (May 17, 1963).

Converse, P. D., "Comment on Movement of Retail Trade in Iowa," *Journal of Marketing*, XVIII, No. 2 (October 1953).

———, "New Laws of Retail Gravitation," *Journal of Marketing*, Vol. XIV, No. 3 (October 1949).

———, *Retail Trade Areas in Illinois*, University of Illinois Press, Urbana, 1946.

———, *A Study of Retail Trade Areas in East Central Illinois*, University of Illinois Press, Urbana, 1943.

Coolsen, F. G. and W. S. Myers, *Kentucky Retail Market Areas and Trading Centers*, Bureau of Business Research, University of Kentucky, Frankfort, 1953.

Cox, R., "Impact of Changes in the Size and Structure of Cities," *Explorations in Retailing*, Stanley C. Hollander (ed.), Bureau of Business and Economic Research, College of Business and Public Service, Michigan State University, East Lansing, 1961.

Davidson, W. R. and P. L. Brown, *Retailing Management*, 2nd ed., Ronald Press, New York, 1960.

"Definition of Marketing Terms," *National Marketing Review*, National Association of Marketing Teachers (Fall 1935).

Donnahoe, A. S., "Can Advertising Markets Be Defined or Measured as Geographical Areas?" *Journal of Marketing*, Vol. XVIII, No. 2 (October 1953).

Douglas, E., "Measuring the General Retail Trading Area—A Case Study," *Journal of Marketing*, Vol. XIII (April 1949) and Vol. XIV (July 1949).

Duddy, E. A. and D. A. Revzan, *Marketing, An Institutional Approach*, McGraw-Hill, New York, 1953.

Duncan, D. J. and C. F. Phillips, *Retailing, Principles and Methods*, 6th ed., Richard D. Irwin, Homewood, Ill., 1963.

"Effects of State and Local Regulations in Interstate Movement of Agricultural Products by Highway," *Marketing Research Report No. 496*, United States Department of Agriculture, Washington, D. C. (July 1961).

"Evaluationg Delivery Operations of Wholesale Food Distributors," *Marketing Research Report No. 502*, United States Department of Agriculture, Washington, D. C. (October 1961).

Fetter, F. A., "The Economic Law of Market Areas," *Quarterly Journal of Economics*, Vol. XXXVIII (May 1924).

Fine, I. V., "Retail Trade Area Analysis," *Wisconsin Commerce Papers*, Vol. 1, No. 6, University of Wisconsin, Bureau of Business Research and Service, Madison (January 1954).

"A Five Percent Sales Tax Rate Looms for Pennsylvania," Tax Report of the *Wall Street Journal*, Vol. 53, No. 154 (May 22, 1963).

Goldstucker, J. L., "A Study of Wholesale Trading Areas," *Journal of Marketing*, Vol. XXVI, No. 2 (April 1962).

Harris, C. D., *Salt Lake City, A Regional Capital*, University of Chicago Press, 1940.

Hartsough, M. L., *Twin Cities as a Metropolitan Market*, University of Minnesota Press, Minneapolis, 1925.

Heaton, H., *Economic History of Europe*, Harper, New York, 1948.

Hiel, R. M., "Techniques of Measuring Market Potential for Wholesalers," *Bureau of Business Management Bulletin No. 820*, College of Commerce and Business Administration, University of Illinois, Urbana, 1962.

"Highway Transportation Barriers in Twenty States," *Marketing Research Report No. 157*, United States Department of Agriculture, Washington, D. C. (March 1962).

Hoover, E. M., *The Location of Economic Activity*, McGraw-Hill, New York, 1948.

Horngren, C., *Cost Accountancy*, Prentice-Hall, Englewood Cliffs, N. J., 1962.

"How to Make a Local Area Trade Survey," *Domestic Distribution Department,* United States Chamber of Commerce, Washington, D. C. (June 1940).

Huff, D. L., "A Probablistic Analysis of Consumer Spatial Behavior," *Emerging Concepts of Marketing*, W. S. Decker (ed.), American Marketing Association, Chicago, 1963.

———, "Defining and Estimating a Trading Area," *Journal of Marketing*, Vol. XXVIII (July 1964).

Isard, W., *Location and Space Economy*, Wiley, New York, 1956.

Jones, F. M., "A Survey of a Retail Trading Area," *Bureau of Business Research Bulletin No. 44*, College of Commerce and Business Administration, University of Illinois, Urbana, 1932.

Jung, A. F., "Is Reilly's Law of Retail Gravitation Always True?" *Journal of Marketing*, Vol. XXIV, No. 2 (October 1959).

Larson, G. E. and M. N. Poteat, "Selling the United States Market," *Domestic Commerce Series No. 29 (New Series)*, United States Department of Commerce, Government Printing Office, Washington, D. C., 1961.

Lewis, F. H., *Marketing Patterns of Philadelphia Wholesalers*, published by the author, Philadelphia, 1948.

———, "Wholesale Market Patterns," *Journal of Marketing*, Vol. XII, No. 3 (January 1948).

———, *Wholesaling in the Twin Cities*, University of Minnesota Press, Minneapolis, 1952.

Locklin, D. P., *Economics of Transportation*, 5th ed., Richard D. Irwin, Homewood, Ill., 1960.

Losch, A., *Economics of Location*, Yale University Press, New Haven, Conn., 1954.

"Major Trade Areas in Eleven Western States," *University of Denver Business Review*, Vol. VII, No. 4, The University of Denver (April 1931).

Marshall, A., *Principles of Economics*, 8th ed., 1956 reprint, Macmillan and Company, Ltd., London, 1956.

Mills, E. S. and M. R. Lav, "A Model of Market Areas with Free Entry," *The Journal of Political Economy*, Vol. LXXII (June 1964).

Muller, A., *Die Elemente der Staatskunst*, 3 Berlin 1809.

Nelson, R. L., *The Selection of Retail Locations*, F. W. Dodge Corporation, New York, 1958.

Oxenfeldt, A. R., *Industrial Pricing and Market Practices*, Prentice-Hall, New York, 1951.

Penn, W. S., Jr., "Measurement of Service Station Trading Areas," API Publication No. 1546, *Case Histories in Petroleum Marketing*, American Petroleum Institute, New York.

Petersen, E. A., *Market Analysis of the Denver Wholesale Trade Territory*, University of Colorado Press, Boulder, 1936.

Pfanner, J. A., "A Statistical Study of the Drawing Power of Cities for Trade," *Studies in Business Administration*, Vol. No. 3 University of Chicago, 1940.

Read, E. V. W., "Analysis of Retail Trading Relationships of Elgin, Illinois, A Satellite City," *Journal of Business*, Vol. IX, No. 1, University of Chicago, 1938.

Reilly, W. J., *The Law of Retail Gravitation*, 1st ed., University of Texas, Austin, 1931.

———, "Methods for the Study of Retail Relationships," *Bureau of Business Research Monograph No. 4*, University of Texas, Austin (November 22, 1929).

*Retail and Wholesale Trading Areas of Minneapolis and St. Paul*, Economic Research Department, Minneapolis Chamber of Commerce, 1951.

Reynolds, R. B., "A Rejoinder to P. D. Converse's 'Comment on Movement of Retail Trade in Iowa'," *Journal of Marketing*, Vol. XVIII, No. 2 (October 1953).

———, "A Test of the Law of Retail Gravitation," *Journal of Marketing*, Vol. XVII, No. 3 (January 1953).

Rasmussen, E. G., "Hardware Trading Centers and Trading Territories in Nine Southeastern States," *Journal of Marketing*, Vol. VIII, No. 2 (October 1943).

Schwartz, G., "Laws of Retail Gravitation: An Appraisal," *University of Washington Business Review*, Vol. XXII, No. 1 (October 1962).

Scott, W. G., *Human Relations in Management*, Richard D. Irwin, Homewood, Ill., 1962.

*Standard Metropolitan Areas*, Bureau of the Budget, Executive Office of the President, Washington, D. C. (July 28, 1950).

Stigler, G. J., *The Theory of Price*, revised ed., Macmillan, New York, 1952.

Tousley, R. D. and R. F. Lanzillotti, "The Spokane Wholesale Market," *Economic and Business Studies*, Bulletin No. 18, The State College of Washington, Bureau of Economic and Business Research, Pullman, Wash. (November 1951).

Ullman, E., "A Theory for the Location of Cities," *American Journal of Sociology*, Vol. XLVI (May 1941).

Vaile, R. L., E. S. Grether, and R. Cox, *Marketing in the American Economy*, Ronald Press, New York, 1952.

Valavanis, S., "Losch on Location," *American Economic Review*, Vol. XLV, No. 4 (September 1955), pp. 637-644.

Von Thunen, J. H., *Der Isolierte Staat in Befiehung auf Landwirtschaft und Nationalokonomie*, Hamburg, 1826.

Weber, A., *Ueber den Standort der Industrien*, Part I, Reine Theorie des Standorts, Tubingen, 1909.

Weigand, R. E., "Exclusive Dealerships—A Different View," *Journal of Retailing*, Vol. XXXVIII, No. 1 (Spring 1962).

# 27 — Regional-Spatial Analysis in Marketing

*E. T. Grether*

Reprinted from *Journal of Marketing*, published by the American Marketing Association, Vol. 47 (Fall 1983), pp. 36-43.
Reprinted by permission.

Marketing scholars continue to press forward in their efforts to strengthen the foundations of marketing as an academic discipline. A widely ranging literature is evolving in which issues related to "marketing theory" are being thrashed out, both at the micro and macro levels. Running through and in the background of these discussions are the increasing number of papers intended to improve the techniques and tools of analysis.

No endeavor will be made in this paper to depict or interpret the full play except as necessary to provide perspective on the single issue of the nature and role of regional-spatial analysis. For the most part, a search of the current textbooks and literature discloses very little. Either regional analysis is dead or dying from lack of interest among marketing scholars, or it has been lost temporarily in the urgencies of other, more interesting matters and fashions, especially consumer behavioral studies and improvement in research techniques.[1] Given time and some amount of scholarly leadership, the balance may be restored. An important reason for this belief is that regional-spatial analysis is important to marketing, both in relatively traditional industries and settings and in new guises in the high technology and service industries of the emerging postindustrial society.

This writer became involved in a regional type of analysis largely in reaction to very active interests, pressures, and concerns of business enterprises and governmental agencies in California and the far west, beginning in the late 1920s. Regionalism was not only an economic, political, and marketing set of conditions and forces but reflected a deeply rooted general consciousness. The setting, of course, was ideal for this type of manifestation. A population of highly individualistic persons had become clustered on the western rim of the United States, separated from the other parts of the country by a wide, sparsely populated area of mountains and desert and from the Pacific basin countries by the Pacific Ocean. All of these regional forces peaked in California, the state with the most rapid growth. The heritage of the famous 1849 gold rush period provided not only an idealized aura to the region, but also capital and rapid population growth.

## The Influence of B. Ohlin and E. H. Chamberlin

Two books that appeared almost simulataneously in the 1930s provided the basis for a more realistic analysis of regional forces than had been available in classical and neoclassical economics. The first was Bertil Ohlin's *Interregional and International Trade* in 1931. The other was Edward H. Chamberlin's *Theory of Monopolistic Competition* in 1933. The stimulus of these two volumes led to the introduction of a course in economics entitled "Theory of Domestic Trade" by the writer in the 1930s, at the University of California, Berkeley, which paralleled the introductory course in marketing. At that time, this was a useful combination of approaches because the course related to the basic work in economics and provided a framework of analysis for the more highly descriptive and managerial work in marketing.

Ohlin's view was that it is artificial to separate the analyses of domestic and international trade—hence the title *Interregional and International Trade*. He based his approach upon the concept of economic region in which he related to the existent general localization theory, on the one hand, and to the mutual interdependence theory of pricing on the other, then universally accepted. But he was also concerned about adding a dynamic content to accepted static equilibrium analysis in order to relate time and space to each other. In this regard he was building upon a problem noted already by Alfred Marshall which continues to arise in the literature of economics, marketing, and other disciplines, such as geography, and which still holds great opportunities for creative scholarship. But Ohlin was most concerned with "the space element" which he felt had been almost completely neglected, partly because the "general theory of pricing is almost exclusively a *one market* theory wherein the idea of space hardly figures at all" (Ohlin 1931, p. 4). In any event, the great internal free trade area of the United States provided a beautiful opportunity for applying Ohlin's approach within the bounds of one national market and relating to the regionalism of the far west.

The fortunate appearance of Chamberlin's *Theory of Monopolistic Competition* provided the framework and tools for more realistic economic analysis and for relating to the interests of students in marketing. Chamberlin's stress on product heterogeneity and product differentiation, upon sales expenditures to influence demands, and quality of product variations by the individual sellers, were exceedingly revelatory and helpful to those unhappy with the limitations of accepted formal models, especially the model of pure competition. As the years moved along, Chamberlin's product differentiation was expanded by the concept of enterprise differentiation which led directly into entrepreneurship. It was unfortunate that Chamberlin used the term *monopolistic competition* with its opprobrious connotation. It would have been preferable if he had used the term *differential advantage*, following the usage of H. J. Davenport in *The Economics of Enterprise* in 1925. The important point is that Chamberlin provided the basis and thrust in economic analysis for managerial applications in the literature of marketing in recent years. Chamberlin originally felt that his chief contribution was to "the large group case"—to the explanation of why so many small sellers are able to survive in competition. His "tilted demand curve" explanation became the classic way of explaining the presence of, say, numerous small gasoline service stations. Actually, he contributed even more to the oligopolistic analysis of small groups. Chamberlin (1951) restated his position in a paper which somehow or other has been overlooked. In this restatement he indicated that "the present formulation ... begins with the individual seller and uses the spatial example to illustrate how the entire economic system may be viewed as an elaborate network of interrelated firms.... The importance of oligopolistic relations in the whole system emerges with greater force.... The theory emerges now as a general one, designed to replace that of pure competition for analyzing the whole economy" (p. 72).

In any event, the combination of Ohlin's regional and interregional framework, with its emphasis upon space, and Chamberlin's active intervention of aggressive sellers into the marketing mix provided the framework for a much more realistic analysis directly applicable to marketing management. Case materials were readily available from regional sources to add realistic content. In the teaching and subsidiary research processes, regionalism came to life in a truly revelatory manner, not only to students but to business and governmental agencies. The economic and marketing relations between California and the far west and the other parts of the U.S. and world trade in general were illumiated in ways impossible without the footing in regional analysis.

But in the case of the writer, the regional aspects reflected not only the reactions to and demands in the regional environment, but also the firm belief that interregional analysis contributes to greater understanding in marketing as well as in other disciplines, especially economic and geographic analysis. In other words, for scholarship in general and for the purposes of any given business enterprise, interregional conditions and relations are so basic that they must be included in analyses and interpretations, especially in the great internal free trade area of the United States. Space will not be taken here to follow along with this concept in its various applications. An excellent brief review and interpretation is available in Savitt (1981a).

Two publications of the writer indicate the nature of the interregional analysis. The first was an essay contained in the first volume of papers assembled by Reavis Cox and Wroe Alderson (Grether 1950), in which it was suggested that the regional approach has enough to offer "in general and especially under current trends and needs to attract the vigorous attention of a proportion of the scholars in this field" (p. 121). It was further stated, "The behavior of the firm should be investigated not only in a price and marketing sense, but under the conditions of its physical and social environment in its determination of its location, its spatial outreach in selling and buying, and its relationship in the marketing channel with suppliers on the one hand and buyers on the other'' (p. 117).

The second publication was part 5 of Vaile, Grether, and Cox (1952), in which the nature and patterns of regional and interregional marketing were interpreted, followed by discussions of the marketing areas of primary producers and manufacturers, wholesalers, and finally of retailers.[2] The general approach was in terms of *marketing in the American economy*.

## Developments Since 1950

Since these two publications appeared, the literature of marketing has expanded enormously and has become exceedingly diversified. Three interacting aspects are especially significant for this discussion, viz.:

1. the introduction and wide application of the so-called *marketing concept*;
2. the application of the behavioral sciences in marketing research and writings;
3. the general stress on marketing management.

During the nascent period of marketing's academic growth, its nearest established academic discipline was economics. In fact, marketing was considered by many to be applied economics and not unreasonably so, in view of the central role of markets in economics. Despite numerous crosscurrents, it is probably a safe generalization that the behavioral sciences, especially the applications in consumer behavior analysis, are now in the ascendancy. And this has important implications for our problem of regional analysis since it was initially based on combined economic-locational writings. The increased stress on managerial applications has accentuated this role of the behavioral sciences, as well as other noneconomic disciplines and tools.

It would appear that much of the groundwork was prepared just prior to the turbulent 1960s in the two studies of American business education sponsored by the Carnegie Corporation and the Ford Foundation, and the subsequent specific programs of the Ford Foundation in support of the behavioral sciences and quantitative analysis, including mathematics and statistics (Gordon and Howell 1959, Pierson 1959). It was stated in the Gordon-Howell study, ''of all the subjects which he might undertake to study formally, none is more appropriate for the businessman-to-be than human behavior.... The very nature of the firm and of the manager's role in the firm suggests that every person anticipating a responsible position in a modern business enterprise needs a substantial amount of knowledge about human behavior'' (p. 167). By human behavior was meant the subject matter of the field of psychology, sociology, and (cultural) anthropology. It should be emphasized that these ''behavioral sciences'' recommendations were *not in lieu of economics but in addition*. A problem for the future is to reestablish an appropriate set of working relations, integration, and perhaps even synthesis between the behavioral sciences and economics and other disciplines, including geography.

But new syntheses arise very slowly, if at all, out of planned formal scholarly interdisciplinary interactions. It would appear that interdisciplinary breakthroughs are more likely to arise out of the leadership of creative individuals and their disciples (as in the case of Wroe Alderson), or perhaps out of regional clusterings engendered by a strong regional consciousness. Regional clusterings seem to be a very basic aspect of the recent sensational developments in the high technology area. All things considered, however, among academicians, professional peer recognition and pressures typically tend to support established disciplines or current fashions. Consequently, the more likely result is for the members of an established professional group to reach out into other domains rather than to join forces in grand efforts to establish new syntheses. Instead of new interdisciplinary bodies of knowledge, there tend to be overlappings or combined efforts which produce outputs in which the contributions of each discipline are clearly demarcated. The writer has participated in support of, promoted, and observed several such efforts at the University of California, Berkeley.

For some time, there seemed to be a possibility that relatively footloose scholars with newer tool kits in linear programming, management science, operations research, statistics, econometrics, etc., aided by computers, might become a means for creative crossfertilization. But by now these tools have become absorbed into the established disciplines, as have their pioneer users, for the most part. In these processes the established disciplines and their pockets of subarea have become strengthened and modified in ways that have introduced some flexible adaptation instead of basic reorientation. At any given moment of time a cross-sectional view will not in itself disclose the likely long run drift. Such may well be the state of the discipline of marketing today.

But there may be another set of influences at work. Since the turbulent 1960s there appears to be a general tendency to leap from the individual market participant as consumer buying unit or business enterprise, to society, social responsibility, societal marketing, and so on. All of us, of course, colloquially tend to speak easily and glibly about society, the environment, the market, as we also do of the channel. But common parlance is one thing—scholarly analysis and writing should be quite another!

In the leap from the individual market participant to society and social responsibility there appears to be a tendency also to overlook, disregard, or underemphasize competition analysis. One can get the impression that if business enterprises practice the marketing concept with an awareness of social or societal responsibilities, while churches, governmental agencies, educational and charitable insitutions, and so on are also engaged in marketing, that somehow it will all end up beneficially for society in a manner that will minimize the necessity for an effective rule of competition or detailed governmental or other interventions. Along these lines, socially responsible marketing management may well be on the way to providing the basis for a grand apologetic for modern managerialism which classical economics performed for 19th century capitalism (Mason 1958) and which Marx, Engels, and Lenin developed for communist "democratic centralism."

Nowhere in the literature of marketing is this ambition or hope expressed so baldly. But if a business enterprise can largely disregard the rule of market competition and its setting in federal, state, and local regulations, then we are indeed well into or about to enter a brave new world which will require a grand rationalization.

Most likely, and more modestly and realistically, what is occurring is some extension of forces not fully recognized by classical economists but which began to be understood by neoclassicists. That is, markets or the so-called market mechanisms often were not merely passive and neutral mechanisms through which the underlying basic supply and demand relations were focused, but were, to an important degree, in themselves positive forces affecting the nature of the expression of these relations. The literatures of monopolistic and imperfect competition and of industrial organization reflected this increasing awareness, as did the discussions and governmental interst in administrative pricing.

Even so, until recently economists for the most part disregarded or overlooked vertical and channel organization and relations, except for vertical ownership integration, perhaps on the assumption that these relations would more or less automatically reflect and interact to basic supply factors in production and to consumer sovereignty in consumer demand. Consequently, for years this entire area was left open for scholars in marketing who have filled the void with a variety of channel studies—one of the brightest areas of marketing scholarship. It is worth noting, too, that these studies also use behavioral science tools and materials in addition to economic analysis. In Grether (1950) it was noted that "the analysis of hierarchies in the market channel takes on new meaning in the perspective of a distinction between local and home marketing and interregional marketing" (p. 120). That is, channel and regional-spatial analysis should be interlinked, and particularly so as enterprises expand beyond their home market locations. David A. Revzan's (1971) and (1981) analysis and interpretation of the inherent interrelations of vertical and spatial-geographical aspects of channel organizations is classic.

## Market Competition as the Basic Force

In western societies and especially in the United States, one must still assume that competition is the driving regulative force which is being nurtured and maintained by governmental and private actions, and powerfully undergirded in law and history, despite the inconsistencies and paradoxes of much enforcement activity. Even the most successful American corporations cannot and do not operate on the assumption that they can disregard active, latent, and potential competition, local, regional, national, or worldwide. Certainly, the current competitive state of some American industries and corporations would appear to make further comment unnecessary. It could be suicidal indeed for any well-established enterprise to assume that it is so competition free that it can and should address itself only to social responsibilities of its own choosing. Actually, all enterprises enter the great arena of dynamic competition with its complexities through a variety of interpretive devices, even as does formal economic analysis. The manager even of a small enterprise should not plump him/herself too casually into the fray. And all of this becomes tremendously magnified for large diversified enterprises, especially multinationals. Always there is the analysis of the industry—if one is clearly definable (as steel or tires). Within the industry concept or separately, if there is no clearly recognizable, say S.I.C., grouping, is the analysis of recognized near and potential competititors. Then there are the suppliers and the nature of these relationships, and the customers in the ultimate consumer, business, governmental, or other markets.

Marketing scholars have responded to the opportunities and needs of this environment in diverse ways, most important of which have been the improvements in research conceptualizations and techniques. An excellent example is market segmentation analysis. For the most part these procedures have had their largest application in consumer studies.[3] But a recent Marketing Science Institute study also relates to the industrial area, which has been relatively overlooked (Bonoma and Shapiro 1983).

Segmentation analysis, whether at the consumer, industrial, or other level, is an exceedingly complex and useful set of procedures for dealing with the variety, heterogeneity, and diversity in markets through processes of aggregation and disaggregation. These procedures obviously are in sharp contrast to the simple models of competition analysis, and are very helpful in coming to grips with the actualities of real world markets. The needs and potentialities are so tremendous that they suggest almost unlimited horizons of opportunity for research and should be helpful to management in both private and public sectors.

Another example of the transitional impact of the increasing emphasis on marketing management is in the broad area of physical distribution management (PDM). The physical handling, storage, transportation, and movement of goods is as old as trade itself, and has left many glamorous deposits that have come down into our modern period, including branding and, hence, brand promotion. During the period when classical economics thrived, the costs of physical distribution undoubtedly were relatively higher than they are now because staple products of relatively low specific values dominated trade.

Physical distribution management or logistics is especially important to regional analysis because academically and theoretically it is rooted in locational theory and the spatial movements of goods. The new specialized literature which has broken out of the original approaches clearly shows both the historical nexus and the break with this nexus. Thus in Symkay, Bowersox, and Mossman (1961) there is discussion of plant location theory and of location factors in general in relation to transfer costs. There is also some adaptation to the theories of monopolistic and oligopolistic competition in the setting of geographical variations and evolving legal structures. But the authors considered their volume a pioneering interdisciplinary effort to bring together techniques developed in mathematics, statistics, transportation, marketing, and economics. Subsequent updates of this work enhance the managerial orientation and focus.

In 1964 another volume appeared which also had a strong interdisciplinary footing and managerial orientation, viz. Heskett, Ivie, and Glaskowsky's *Business Logistics*. This volume also relates clearly to the economic analysis of location theory and to market area analysis of location theory and to market area analysis (see especially chapter 6).

Two more recent textbooks are not only larger in size and contents but are more clearly micromanagerial in approach. Johnson and Wood (1982) was first published in 1977. The authors state that "physical distribution/logistics is a classic example of the systems approach to business problems" (1982, p. 8). For the most part, traditional economic and locational theory and analysis do not appear except in a minor way in a discussion of warehouse and plant locations.

The most recent publication is that by Lambert and Stock (1982), a micromanagerial text with very little reference to historical and theoretical materials, especially theoretical literature on location. The publisher's announcement states that the volume "has a pragmatic, applied approach with a unique managerial emphasis. Examples of corporate application of concepts are included in each chapter as are how-to-do-it appendixes." The analysis definitely reflects the impact of the marketing concept and clearly relates physical distribution to marketing management by the firm. Although there is a strong interest in and awareness of broader macro relations, the stress is clearly micromanagerial in the perspective of strategic planning by the enterprise.

But in macro terms, regional and spatial factors for both economic and managerial analysis should be at the same level as that of the industry and near and potential competition. Often the identity, number, and importance of the competitors vary as between regions. This factor alone may assist in the delineation of regions for purposes of analysis and control. And demands, whether ultimately those of consumer, business, or government, despite the alleged homogenization of markets, can and do vary widely between regions. For many years Revzan has stressed the "myth of the national market." It is not that enterprises do not sell throughout the national market or world markets, but that the results often vary widely between regions and even subregions. From the standpoint of a given enterprise, this in itself may be a reasonable basis for regional delineation. Planning marketing strategy is tremendously improved when related to regional breakdowns of both competition and demand. The same observation applies also to the exercise of community-social responsibility. And it applies most sharply of all in any application of market structure analysis as a basis for planning and implementing competition policy in relation to antitrust or other laws. The definition of the relevant geographic market in antitrust enforcement requires the foundation of detailed regional and subregional analysis. Market shares and competitive adjustments often are highly variable between regions and subregions or sections of the country. But most important, interregional competition is undoubtedly one of the most important forces in the maintenance of effective competition, especially in the great internal free trade area of the United States.

Recently a very important structural change seems to be occurring within the U.S. and throughout the industrial world. The traditional basic industries—agriculture, steel, automotive, petroleum, coal, and so on—appear to be following paths of relative decline in terms of contributions to GNP and to employment. In agriculture the processes are well-recognized and have been noted for years. At the moment, the processes of adjustment and transition are striking deep into some of our major industries, within the United States and abroad. Consequently, a new regionalism has emerged as, for example, the political alignment of New England and the midwestern factory belt in relation to the so-called sunbelt. Within this broad realignment there are many and diverse expressions that vary by industries and especially with growth patterns of the regions, industries, and individual enterprises. The repercussion throughout the international trading world for the time being is to sharpen the distinctions between so-called underdeveloped and developing countries and areas and more mature industrial countries such as the United States, western Europe, and Japan. In international trade the play of economic, business, and marketing forces is being expressed in regional groupings based on some homogeneity of economic interests. Regionalism is a powerful political, economic, and marketing force which cannot be disregarded by multinational corporations (McCarthy 1981).

Analysis is further confounded by overlappings of diversified corporations able to seek out and serve demands not related to their initial and traditional patterns. In general the patterns of diversification historically were based on supply side raw materials, technologies, expertise, and connections. This is no longer true, as many corporations have followed demand-side opportunities into highly variable patterns of diversification, including regional, geographical-international diversification (cf. Peters and Waterman 1982). Strategic market planning and strategies should not and do not remain at general levels, however, but must be related to the analysis of regional and sectional differences. This is not only true in traditional basic industries, in which costs of movement over distance are often controlling considerations, but in the emerging high technology and service industries of the post-industrial world.

It is too soon to speak with confidence regarding regionalism in the worlds of high technology, but it appears that there are regional clusterings such as the Silicon Valley in the San Francisco area, route 128 in the Boston area, and North Carolina's Research Triangle. Recent news reports suggest that Austin, Texas, is about to join the front ranks also, through the establishment of an advanced computer research consortium. Such clusterings provide networks of communication, cooperation, and crossfertilization along with competition. Undoubtedly as experience lengthens and deepens, it will become necessary to distinguish between ''cultural'' or breeding centers and various types of outputs engendered. It may develop that cultural anthropologists could have important interpretive roles, along with economists and geographers.

Undoubtedly differentiation and heterogeneity will be magnified in the emerging world of high technology and services, in contrast with the industrial conditions that existed when classical economics took form. Most likely there will be counteracting forces such as greatly improved information technologies. The basic forces, however, will arise out of increasing differentiation and heterogeneity, which will undoubtedly change the patterns of regionalism and subregionalism.

## Concluding Observations

On June 8-11, 1976, a Nobel symposium was held in Stockholm on ''The International Allocation of Economic Activity.'' Economists and a few economic geographers were brought together for an exchange of ideas.

In the concluding remarks by W. Max Corden and Ronald E. Findlay (*International Allocation* 1977), they noted that:

> [L]ess than ten years separate the publication dates of Ricardo's *Principles* and von Thunen's *Isolated State*, the two great works from which modern trade theory and modern location theory trace their descents. However, it would seem that trade theory established itself as a unified and comprehensive body of analysis much earlier than location theory, as a result of the systematic development of Ricardian doctrine by J. S. Mill, Marshall, Edgeworth, and many others, whereas von Thunen's work, as Isard has pointed out, was relatively neglected during the nineteenth and earlier twentieth centuries. Consequently, when Alfred Weber, the next major figure in location theory, began writing in the first decades of this century, he had to contend with a very influential body of doctrine on international trade and commercial policy that for the most part ignored the *spatial* dimensions of economic activity ... *only Bertil Ohlin appears to have been willing to attempt a genuine integration of trade and location theory* (emphasis added).

The discipline of marketing also needs a scholar able and willing to attempt a genuine integration of regional-spatial analysis into the framework.[4] Such an endeavor would provide helpful and appropriate gathering points enroute to the full portrayal of the basic heterogeneity and entrepreneurship of modern markets and marketing. This approach should help interpret the brilliant understandings of Wroe Alderson, well recognized as the leading marketing theorist of recent times. Alderson's greatest insight may well have been the recognition of heterogeneity in contrast with the general acceptance of homogeneity. He clearly recognized and stated his indebtedness to Chamberlin. They both had the same weltanschauung, especially the stress on the basic drive towards differentiation. But Chamberlin was and remained an economist to the end, whereas Alderson wished to relate the micro organized behavior system of the business enterprise to a much broader set of sociobehavioral environmental relations.[5]

The high relative stress in the literature of marketing upon consumer-behavioral studies and the behavioral sciences in general has provided the foundation for the integration of economic analysis and the behavioral sciences, broadly conceived, in three ways. First, marketing literature, perhaps almost subconsciously (certainly not by direct reference), may reflect the differentiation and heterogeneity of Chamberlinian theory, especially in terms of his (1951) restatement. Lee Preston (1976) stated that "... the great bulk of marketing literature that has anything at all to do with product differentiation, pricing, advertising, and other management variables, has become ... Chamberlinian in character. The Chamberlin model is, in fact, the dominant model of the marketing textbooks and classrooms." To illustrate, Preston refers to Kotler's *Marketing Management*, 1972 edition. Second, the consumer-behavioral studies by marketing scholars may add content to fill a large void in Chamberlin's theory. J. S. Bain [1967], in a brilliant exposition and review of Chamberlin's work, stated, "He contributed very little, however, to the theory of consumer choice even though his theories of the firm and of markets cried out for such a contribution. Partly, in consequence, the notable deficiency of these theories was their comparative lack of normative content."

Third, it should also be a creative means of bringing scholars of various disciplines—economics, geography, behavioral sciences, planners, and so on—into more systematic relationships. The rise and decline of the Regional Science Association under the dynamic, resourceful leadership of Walter Isard reflects to some degree the shift away from classical and neoclassical economics nexus towards broader sets of relations. For example, economic geographers are no longer tied closely to classical, economic locational analysis, but are much more pluralistic and are also employing behavioral science tools. They have a very strong interest in the analysis of space and time relations (see Allan R. Pred article in *International Allocation* (1977), Cox and Golledge (1981), Pipkin (1981)). And economists in recent years are making more realistic assumptions, both about firm behavior and consumer choice behavior. Economists and marketing scholars together may well be filling the void in Chamberlinian theory noted by Bain (1967). These combined efforts undoubtedly presage broader sets of interrelationships that bode well for the future of scholarship.[6]

## ENDNOTES

1. Professors L. L. Sammet of the Berkeley faculty and Gordon H. King of the Davis campus of the University of California advise me that a somewhat similar decline has occurred in agriculture; for example, Bressler and King (1970) has not been reprinted by the publisher. In a letter received from King he says, "currently the emphasis is on trying to build models that are more 'realistic' than the spatial equilibrium models."
2. Word and space constraints do not allow an updating in this paper. Fortunately, an excellent review is available. See Savitt (1981b).
3. See, for example, the special section on market segmentation research in the August 1978 issue of *Journal of Marketing Research*.
4. Ronald Savitt's published and unpublished writings suggest that he could well provide this service to the profession. Fortunately, too, he was assistant to Wroe Alderson during Wroe's final year. Readers will find his paper (Reekie and Savitt 1982) very insightful.
5. For a more complete discussion, see Grether (1967).
6. The literature that might be cited is enormous. A good short cut is available in Ratchford (1982).

## REFERENCES

Bain, J. S. (1967), "Chamberlin's Impact on Microeconomic Theory," in *Monopolistic Competition Theory, Studies in Impact*, R. Kuenne, ed., New York: John Wiley, 174.

Bonoma, Thomas V. and Benson P. Shapior (1983), *Industrial Market Segmentation: A Nested Approach*, Cambridge, MA: Marketing Science Institute (February).

Bressler, R. G., Jr., and R. H. King (1970), *Markets, Prices, and Interregional Trade*, New York: John Wiley.

Chamberlin, E. H. (1933), *The Theory of Monopolistic Competition*, Boston, MA: Harvard University Press.

——— (1951), "Monopolistic Competition Revisited," *Economica*, 18 (November), 72.

Cox, K. and R. Golledge (1981), *Behavioral Problems in Geography Revisited*, New York: Macmillan.

Cox, Reavis and Wroe Alderson, eds. (1950), *Theory in Marketing*, V. 1, Homewood, IL: Irwin.

Gordon, R. A. and J. E. Howell (1959), *Higher Education for Business*, New York: Columbia University Press.

Grether, E. T. (1950), "A Theoretical Approach to the Study of Marketing," in *Theory in Marketing*, R. Cox and W. Alderson, eds., Homewood, IL: Irwin.

——— (1967), "Chamberlin's Theory of Monopolistic Competition and the Literature of Marketing," in *Monopolistic Competition Theory: Studies in Impact*, R. Kuenne, ed., New York: John Wiley, 313-21.

Heskett, J. L., R. M. Ivie, and U. A. Glaskowsky, Jr. (1964), *Business Logistics: Management of Physical Supply and Distribution*, New York: Ronald.

*The International Allocation of Economic Activity* (1977), proceedings of a Nobel symposium held at Stockholm; New York: Holmes & Meier.

Johnson, James C. and Don F. Wood (1977), *Comtemporary Physical Distribution*, Tulsa: Pennwell Publishers.

——— and ——— (1982), *Contemporary Physical Distribution and Logistics*, Tulsa: Pennwell Publishers.

Lambert, D. M. and J. R. Stock (1982), *Strategic Physical Distribution Management*, Homewood, IL: Irwin.

Mason, Edward S. (1958), "The Apologetics of 'Managerialism,' " *Journal of Business*, 31 (January), 1-11.

McCarthy, E. J. (1981), *Basic Marketing: A Managerial Approach*, Homewood, IL: Irwin.

Ohlin, Bertil (1931), *Interregional and International Trade*, Boston, MA: Harvard University Press.

Peters, Thomas J. and Robert Waterman, Jr. (1982), *In Search of Excellence: Lessons from America's Best-Run Companies*, New York: Harper.

Pierson, Frank et al. (1959), *The Education of American Businessmen*, New York: McGraw-Hill.

Pipkin, B. (1981), "Cognitive Behavioral Geography and Repetitive Travel," in *Behavioral Problems in Geography Revisited*, K. Cox and R. Golledge, New York: Macmillan, 145-81.

Preston, Lee (1976), *Public Policy and Marketing Thought*, in *Proceedings of the Ninth Converse Symposium*, A. Andreason and S. Sudman, eds., Chicago: American Marketing Association, 141-42.

Ratchford, Brian T. (1982), "Economic Approaches to the Study of Market Structure and Their Implications for Marketing Analysis," in *Analytic Approaches to Product and Marketing Planning: The Second Conference Proceedings*, R. Srivastava and A. Shocker, eds., Cambridge, MA: Marketing Science Institute, 60-78.

Reekie, W. D. and R. Savitt (1982), "Marketing Behavior and Entrepreneurship: A Synthesis of Alderson and Austrian Economics," *European Journal of Marketing*, 16 (no. 7), 55-68.

Revzan, David A. (1971), *A Marketing View of Spatial Competition*, Berkeley, CA: Institute of Business and Economic Research, University of California.

——— (1981), *A Geography of Marketing: Integrative Statement*, Berkeley, CA: Institute of Business and Economic Research, University of California.

Savitt, Ronald (1981a), "The Theory of Interregional Marketing," in *Regulation of Marketing and the Public Interest*, F. Balderston, J. Carman, and F. Nicosia, eds., New York: Pergamon, 229-38.

——— (1981b), "Review of Trading Area Studies, Marketing Economic Analysis," in *The Definition of Trade Areas and Their Boundaries: A Literature*

*Review and Annotated Bibliography*, R. G. Ironside et al., eds., section 3, Alberta: University of Alberta, Dept. of Geography (March).

Smykay, E. W. (1973), *Physical Distribution Management*, 3rd edition, New York: Macmillan.

———, N. J. Bowersox, and F. H. Mossman (1961), *Physical Distribution Management: Logistic Problems of the Firm*, New York: Macmillan.

Vaile, Roland, E. T. Grether, and Reavis Cox (1952), "Marketing Within and Between Regions, in *Marketing in the American Economy*, part 5, New York: Ronald.

# 28 —— The Theory of Interregional Marketing

*Ronald Savitt*

Reprinted with permission from *Regulation of Marketing and the Public Interest*, edited by F. Balderson, et al. (New York: Pergamon Press, 1981), pp. 229-238.

Although E. T. Grether is best known for his work in the area of marketing and public policy, some of his earlier work represented important contributions to the development of marketing theory. The writings in marketing theory integrated concepts from economics and helped to develop the burgeoning marketing literature. These ideas have been valuable in understanding the marketing system, especially the nexus between marketing and public policy.

As an economist, Grether has always been interested in the functioning of markets and the performance of firms. His analysis of market forces has concentrated on understanding the barriers which affect competition among firms. Underlying his analysis of competition has been the theoretical perspective of interregional marketing. There is a common theme in much of his writing which shows a great understanding of the multidimensional nature of firms. The problems of marketing organization from the standpoint of microanalysis, he has remarked, consist of three substantive issues:

> (1) how to obtain and maintain effective access to the materials, supplies, capital, labor, etc., essential for the operation of the enterprise; (2) how to gain and maintain access to the customers whom it supplies; and (3) which of the complex relationships and activities essentially should it bring within direct control and operation of the enterprise itself, and which should it leave to the spontaneous process of the market. (Grether, 1966, *Marketing and Public Policy*, p. 80)

The theory of interregional marketing which pervades his analysis of public policy issues was put forward in two separate works. The first discussion is found in ''A Theoretical Approach to the Analysis of Marketing'' (Grether, 1950); the second is found in *Marketing in the American Economy* (Vaile, Grether, and Cox, 1952). The present discussion extends the theory and applies it to a specific problem in public policy, the definition of ''relevant geographic market.'' The paper proceeds by stating the integrated theory and then proposing how it might be used to fully understand the spatial dimensions of firms and regions.

## Interregional Marketing

### Background

The theory of interregional marketing is at the same time a theory of trade and a theory of location. It explains why a firm locates at a specific point in time and space, why trade takes place between that point and other points, and what the market boundaries (the region) are for that firm. It provides management with direction with regards to trade potential and location possibilities (Douglas, 1975, p. 44). Further, interregional marketing offers new dimensions for those concerned with antitrust and regulation to better understand marketing behavior in so far as any definition of market based on the theory demands the inclusion of a wide range of variables.

The theory of interregional marketing has been greatly influenced by the work of Edward Hastings Chamberlin and Bertil Ohlin and the environment in which Grether found himself in California in the 1930s and 1940s. The regional elements in the theory are based on Ohlin's work in interregional trade; the issues of competitive behavior stem from Chamberlin's basic ideas regarding monopolistic competition. The theory, however, is more than the integration of the concepts of these two economists in so far as Grether brought his own analytic powers to bear on the issues of marketing organization.

From Ohlin, Grether drew upon the wider concept of ''the market'' than that had pervaded the earlier economic literature. Ohlin clearly suggested the degrees to which such analysis must go:

> ... the geographical distribution of productive factors is important. Industrial activity must be adapted to the varying supply of such factors in different places; for only to a limited extent can the supply itself be adapted to the demands of various industries.... This fact alone would necessitate a general analysis of the space aspect of the price mechanism.
>
> The one-market doctrine evidently needs a superstructure for the consideration of the geographical or territorial aspects of pricing, i.e., the location of industry, and of trade between places and districts of various types. (Ohlin, 1933, p. 4)

Hence, the spatial dimensions of a market are not solely limited to something approaching the ''sales territory'' but include buying as well and, as shall be developed later, potentially the entire set of marketing functions. As Grether argued, the essence of interregional marketing ''takes the form of specific goods and services bought and sold by individual enterprises under the conditions of their environment. The device of economic region allows one to focus attention upon resource utilization and other factors that lie at the basis of our whole structure of production and marketing.'' (Grether, 1950, *Theory in Marketing*, p. 118)

Within the concept of the region, Grether refined and then applied Chamberlin's monopolistic competition and developed it as enterprise differentiation (Alderson, 1965, p. 197). Basically, it stated that the spatial and temporal behavior of firms within a region, between regions, or among regions, is a function not only of the transport gradient assumptions of pure competition, but also a function of the degree to which Chamberlinian selling costs affect behavior. Grether's approach is to clearly examine what might be termed ''active behavior,'' the differentiation in products, services, and space, rather than accept the passive assumptions of economics. The firm is described as a dynamic, competitive entity; ''Its 'variation' may refer to an alteration in the quality of the product itself—technical changes, a new design, or better materials; it may mean a new package or container; it may mean more prompt or courteous service, a different way of doing business, or perhaps a different location.'' (Chamberlin, 1933, p. 71)

## The Core of the Theory

The core of the theory is an attempt to understand the behavior of the firm in a marketing perspective; it could almost be considered a theory of marketing strategy.

> The behavior of the firm should be investigated not only in a price and marketing sense, but under the conditions of its physical and social environment, in its determination of its location, its spatial out reach in selling and buying, and its relationship in the marketing channel with suppliers on the one hand and buyers on the other. (Grether, 1950, *Theory in Marketing*, p. 117)

The existing economic structures can not be taken as given to explain marketing organization and behavior. ''Because the marketing system is an integral part of that economic structure—both determining and determined—it must be explained in terms of the broad economic function as well as in terms of its relationship to a given economic organization.'' (Grether, *Theory in Marketing*, 1950, p. 117) All of the factors which affect a firm's behavior must be understood; as Ohlin stated: ''Nothing less than a consideration of all the elements that constitute the price mechanism—the system of mutual interdependence—can adequately explain the nature of interregional trade.'' (Ohlin, 1933, p. 29)

Ohlin's definition or statement of the region is at the core of Grether's: a region is defined as a relatively large geographic area with the following characteristics: (1) it has more than one center of economic control; (2) it has greater internal homogeneity than would be present if merged with other contiguous areas; (3) it exports a characteristic group of products to other areas; and (4) it imports the characteristic products of other areas (Vaile, Grether, and Cox, 1952, p. 488). The purpose of defining a region is to focus ''analysis on the products and services characteristic of the region in export and import trade.'' (Grether, 1950, *Theory in Marketing,* p. 119)

The intensity of interregional marketing, the focus on the active behavior in the performance of all the marketing functions, depends primarily on four elements. These are the relative inequality of the regions with respect to supplies of factors of production, the relative prosperity of regions, the strength of reciprocal demands among regions, and the relative effectiveness of internal competition within regions. When competition is active and effective, there should normally be a stronger basis for interregional marketing than when competition is docile (Vaile, Grether, and Cox, 1952, p. 509). Competition is active to the extent that firms engage in rivalry which leads to enterprise differentiation. Because marketing goes beyond the conditions of pure competition, new assumptions had to be taken into consideration. Under pure competition, firms will only engage in interregional trade if they can recover their transport costs. Under Grether's assumptions, sellers will be willing to absorb such costs; implicitly, the economies of larger sales resulting from greater market opportunities will allow these costs to be covered. To the extent that demand elasticities vary among firms, regions, or nations, then price discrimination arising from enterprise differentiation will allow them to cover costs.

Interregional marketing takes into consideration the effects of numerous factors in the determination of market areas. While it concentrated primarily on the definition of market areas for the individual firm by incorporating buying and selling functions, the level of analysis can be shifted to other functions as well as to the regions themselves. Grether, as Ohlin, did not accept the proposition that specialization was the cause of interregional trade (marketing). Rather, ''trade is caused by the uneven distribution of the factors and their lack of divisibility, and it tends to reduce the disadvantages caused thereby.'' (Ohlin, 1933, p. 58) Further, the vertical dimension of the marketing channel was incorporated; ''The essence of marketing and hence marketing organization and the unique area of professional marketing literature is found in vertical, internal relationships and transactions.'' (Grether, 1966, *Marketing and Public Policy,* p. 81) This becomes especially important since ''The analysis of hierarchies in the marketing channel takes on new meaning in the perspective of a distinction between local and home marketing and interregional marketing.'' (Grether, 1950, *Theory in Marketing,* p. 120)

## The Theory's Importance

The theory is important for four major reasons. First, the theory is an important integration of the works of two major economists whose ideas might not have been taken into marketing. By doing this, Grether created a framework for the emerging discipline of marketing and a boundary between economics and marketing which allowed for the ''possibility for the development of 'theory in marketing' by an extension of both micro- and macroeconomic theory.'' (Grether, 1967a, p. 320) Secondly, the theory introduced in a systematic fashion geographic analysis into marketing. Marketing theory should analyze ''the behavior of the firm (or the region as a trading unit) as it adjusts to horizontal spatial relationships to industrial, regional, and national groups.'' (Lockley, 1964, p. 53) Thirdly, the theory provides an expansive, comprehensive view of the firm which is the basis of general marketing strategy especially in the area of diversification and growth. Finally, the theory adds considerble dimension to the definition of ''relevant geographic market'' in antitrust and regulation matters. This aspect is discussed in greater detail in the next section.

## Interregional Marketing and Public Policy

The theory of interregional marketing is implicitly applied in much of Grether's writings on public policy. It can be seen in the systematic approach to the evaluation of cases and specific decisions. This section of the paper provides an extension of the theory to the problem of defining ''relevant geographic market'' which comes to the front in many areas, especially mergers. The discussion begins with a brief review of the links between interregional marketing and competition; the theory is extended by developing propositions which are consistent with the basic framework. This latter serves as the basis for considering alternative approaches to present definitions of ''relevant geographic market.''

### Interregional Marketing and Competition

It is fair to state that the theory provides more than a powerful taxonomy for understanding marketing behavior because of the focus on the linkages between marketing and the environment. Within it is found a normative direction for the nature of competition. ''In doing this he (Grether) obviously has in mind the idea that by the means of a rational marketing structure uninhibited by trade barriers and other entrenched trade practices a much stronger economy could be developed.'' (McGary, 1953) This point is clearly made by Grether:

> A critical issue to the maintenance of a strong pro competitive policy is the extent to which competitive forces are effective over geographical areas. The high relative wealth of the United States is often explained in terms of effective competition in our great, internal free trade area. Undoubtedly, this model has been the most important single economic influence behind the European Common Market conceptualization. (Grether, 1967b, p. 238)

The degree to which firms and regions engage in rivalry is the determinant of the benefits of competition. Namely, as firms more actively pursue markets, the larger markets should provide lower costs at the same time that consumers are provided with greater choice. Barriers which are constructed to eliminate rivalry—that is, eliminate the expansion of markets—should be eliminated. That does not mean that firms should have unbridled power at all times in the exploitation of markets. The absence of artificial barriers should encourage the type of competitive process that Grether develops.[1] He argues that the geographic marketing under monopolistic competition has a special, critical significance in the national endeavor to maintain and promote competition. There are dangers that systematic price structures, for example, established ''overtly, or implicitly under competition among the few, could subvert or even stifle the basic forces and adjustments of surplus and deficit ... between regions. Clearly, this outcome could not and should not be tolerated in the name of preserving competition.'' (Grether, 1966, *Marketing and Public Policy*, p. 73) In order to know about such effects, substantial analysis as directed by the theory is required. ''Marketing decisions and therefore the significance of government constraints vary greatly, depending on whether the interests are merely local, regional, national, or international.'' (Grether, 1966, *Marketing and Public Policy*, p. 94)

How the market might be defined using Grether's approach and views of the competitive process is taken up in a subsequent section. Before that discussion is presented, however, some elaboration of the theory of interregional marketing is introduced.

## The Theory Extended

Instead of viewing the firm as a relatively simple element in the interaction of supply and demand, the firm can be related to the market transaction in more complex terms. In order for exchange to take place, all of the marketing functions must be performed by some combination of agencies that are located in some orderly space and time relationship. For simplicity, assume the case of a single buyer and seller. Instead of describing the geographic extent of the market in terms of only the sales function, the ''sales territory,'' consider the extent of the market for all of the marketing functions. As in Figure 1, the geographic areas of each of the functions can be described. In that figure, three areas for three separate functions are shown. What is important to note is that each has its own space and that none of them are congruent. The locational patterns for each of the functions varies; hence, there is already a more complex and realistic definition of the market than the ''sales territory'' approach.

This approach illustrates only one dimension; more must be included. Recall that the theory is also concerned with the inclusion of vertical relationships; that is, those which have a temporal dimension as well as spatial. The traditional illustration of the channel in the marketing literature is to show the flow characteristics between and among various members of the channel. That description is somewhat unfortunate because it often implies

**FIGURE 1. Geographic Areas of Marketing Functions**

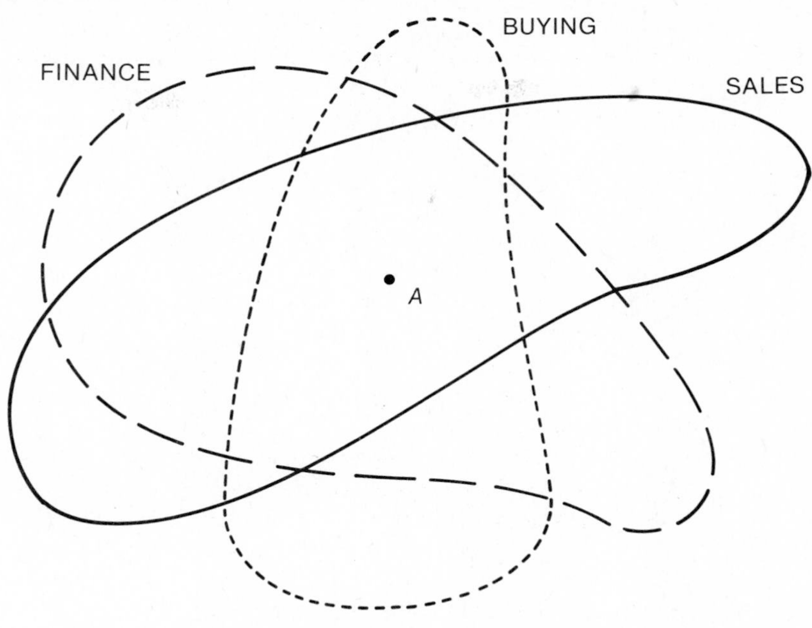


a difference in the spatial location of the various agencies. Channel members or agencies performing different functions may be located at the same point in space or they may be located at very different places. Regardless of their location in time or in space, they are part of the out-reach of any firm and, as shown earlier, the performance of the functions by a firm has an important effect on the boundaries for the firm. The center principle of this argument is that a firm's market cannot be defined solely by a single function which is based on the location of customers in regard to a location of the firm. Of course, the problem becomes more complex when a firm has several branches, because it is all too easy to accept the simple fitting descriptions like a jig-saw puzzle. The individual pieces fit together, but none alone gives a good idea of the total.

The problem is not of conceptual complexity but of the ability to fully illustrate the dimensions of the region for a firm. Figure 2 attempts to give some insights into this. The planes at each end of the three-dimensional figure represent the out-reach of selected marketing functions. The distance between them represent time or vertical dimensions. It is clear that the figure shows a fairly regular set of characteristics which may be unreal; however, it does show one more level of complexity. More analytical exercises using n-dimension space are required but beyond the scope of the present discussion.

**FIGURE 2. Regional Dimensions for a Firm**

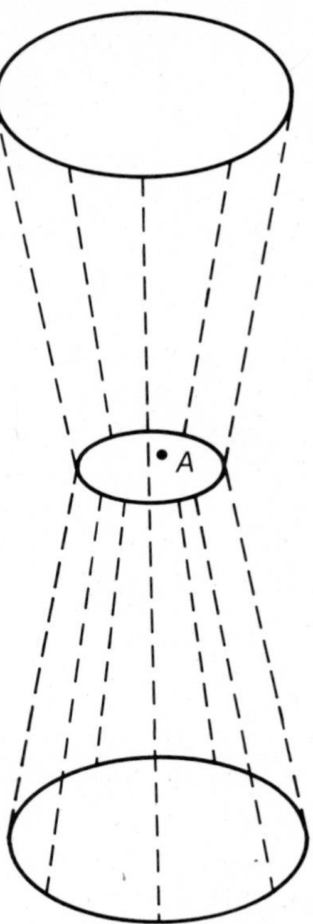


A composite figure of the regions for competing firms for each of the marketing functions, or at least for the important ones, could be constructed. That would be a highly fluid figure over time as firms engage in competition with one another. This differentiation will not only have the spatial characteristics of shifting the physical location; that is, more branches, but also by readjusting the performance of the various functions. Time can be affected to the extent that changes are made in vertical relationships—integration by merger or contract, for example.

## The "Relevant Geographic Market"

The concept of "relevant geographic market" takes new and grander dimensions under the theory of interregional marketing. It allows a more detailed analysis than presently considered—one, as Grether has noted, that "should involve the total pattern of competitive relationships in relation to the given sub-market under scrutiny." (Grether, 1967b, p. 240) The market is thus defined in multidimensional terms including time and space.

The definition of the "relevant geographic market" in economic or legal terms certainly does not meet the criteria suggested previously. Carl Kaysen and Donald F. Turner, in their important book on antitrust policy, indicated the difficulties that are present in such analysis. They began their definition using the traditional economic proposition regarding the cross-elasticities; namely, "Two products belong to the same market if a small change in price or (product) causes a significant diversion in relatively short time of the buyers' purchases or the sellers' production from one product to another." (Kaysen and Turner, 1959, p. 27) They go on to point out how difficult it was to develop geographic market definitions from Department of Commerce data. They employed relatively simple rules which required quantum leaps in faith. They assumed that firms were in national markets when all of the production of the product was concentrated geographically, "and thus all sellers are capable of operating in national markets so far as the geographic structure of industry goes." (Kaysen and Turner, 1959, p. 28)

A less satisfactory approach was given by the United States' Supreme Court when, in effect, Justice Black suggested that there was no critical element in defining the "relevant geographic market." In the *Pabst* case, he suggested that:

> The language of this section requires merely that the Government prove the merger has substantial anticompetitive effect somewhere in the United States—"in any section" of the United States. This phrase does not call for the delineation of a "section of the country" by meters and bounds as a surveyor would lay off a plot of ground.[2]

In one sense, the concept of geographic market is not to be considered relevant as it relates to any specific market. While it is expected that business management, economists, and policy makers will have different interests and viewpoints about behavior, it seems unreasonable to suggest "relevant geographic market" can be accepted in such terms. The nature of the element which is to be preserved, namely competition, loses all meaning in that approach.

## Will It Work?

The critical issue is whether an extended view of "relevant geographic market" will be accepted. The answer is that some change should be considered. A likely candidate for a basis for reformulation of the concept is the theory of interregional marketing. It will not be an easy task. The theory is a complex one. Much work is required just to formalize the measures to be used in operationalizing the theory and its application to the study of competition in a vertical, interregional channel system. However, it is a beginning theoretical structure that takes into consideration a wider set of elements than any of the available approaches.

## NOTES

1. Grether has written extensively on artificial price barriers. See: *Resale Price Maintenance in Great Britain*, University of California Press, 1935; *Price Control Under Fair Trade Legislation*, Oxford University Press, 1939; *Price Control Under Fair Trade Legislation; Report of The Federal Trade Commission on Resale Price Maintenance, U.S. Government Printing Office*, 1945.
2. *United States* v. *Pabst Brewing Co. et. al.*, 384 U.S. 547 (1966), p. 549.

# PART THREE
# Behavioral Schools of Marketing Thought

Soon after World War II, marketing began to search for disciplines other than microeconomics and sociology in order to borrow and adopt concepts. To some extent, this was a reflection of similar changes taking place in microeconomics. For example, there was the emergence of the behavioral theory of the firm, which attempted to displace the classical theory of the firm. Similarly, demand theory was also increasingly threatened by the emerging discipline of economic psychology, which was based on consumer expectations.

At the same time, there was a significant shift in the marketing concept. It began to emerge as understanding customers and working backwards into production as opposed to the older marketing concept of working forward from the factory to the marketplace. Indeed, this began to be labeled as the difference between marketing and selling.

These factors encouraged marketing to borrow concepts and theories from psychology, including social, clinical, and general psychology. Also, the focus of research and understanding shifted from marketers to consumers. Part three identifies several schools of thought that are highly influenced by the behavioral sciences.

## SECTION I

# Consumer Buyer Behavior School

The consumer behavior school has attempted to understand and theorize the buying behavior of consumers, especially with respect to brand loyalty and brand choice behavior. There are several important aspects related to this school of marketing thought.

First, consumer behavior theory gave marketing a clear push toward a discipline and away from practice. A number of theories developed for understanding consumer behavior and their testing by scientific procedures raised the respect of marketing in the eyes of allied disciplines. Market research became highly analytical, and operations research techniques as well as multivariate methods began to be used in marketing.

Second, consumer behavior theory began to shift the focus of marketing away from the marketer and toward the consumer. Indeed, it became fashionable to suggest that consumers must be researchers. Scholars became more interested in theory for its own sake rather than for the managerial purposes of marketing. This led to a schism in the discipline, and it culminated in the formation of a separate academic organization, the Association for Consumer Research (ACR), and the creation of a separate journal, *The Journal of Consumer Behavior* (JCR).

Finally, consumer behavior theory also shifted its focus away from understanding the aggregate markets and began to focus on individual consumers. This has resulted in the development of numerous theories of consumer behavior, probably to explain the complexity and diversity of individual consumers. Unfortunately, this has also resulted in a void for a theory of market behavior. What we need very urgently is a behavioral theory of markets.

# 29 — Rational Behavior and Economic Behavior

*George Katona*

*Psychological Review,* Vol. 60, No. 5 (1953), pp. 307-318.

While attempts to penetrate the boundary lines between psychology and sociology have been rather frequent during the last few decades, psychologists have paid little attention to the problems with which another sister discipline, economics, is concerned. One purpose of this paper is to arouse interest among psychologists in studies of economic behavior. For that purpose it will be shown that psychological principles may be of great value in clarifying basic questions of economics and that the psychology of habit formation, of motivation, and of group belonging may profit from studies of economic behavior.

A variety of significant problems, such as those of the business cycle or inflation, of consumer saving or business investment, could be chosen for the purpose of such demonstration. This paper, however, will be concerned with the most fundamental assumption of economics, the principle of rationality. In order to clarify the problems involved in this principle, which have been neglected by contemporary psychologists, it will be necessary to contrast the most common forms of methodology used in economics with those employed in psychology and to discuss the role of empirical research in the social sciences.

## Theory and Hypotheses

Economic theory represents one of the oldest and most elaborate theoretical structures in the social sciences. However, dissatisfaction with the achievements and uses of economic theory has grown considerably during the past few decades on the part of economists who are interested in what actually goes on in economic life. And yet leading sociologists and psychologists have recently declared ''Economics is today, in a theoretical sense, probably the most highly elaborated, sophisticated, and refined of the disciplines dealing with action'' (15, p. 28).[1]

To understand the scientific approach of economic theorists, we may divide them into two groups. Some develop an *a priori* system from which they deduce propositions about how people *should* act under certain assumptions. Assuming that the sole aim of businessmen is profit maximization, these theorists deduce propositions about marginal revenues and marginal costs, for example, that are not meant to be suited for testing. In developing formal logics of economic action, one of the main considerations is elegance of the deductive system, based on the law of parsimony. A wide gap separates these theorists from economic research of an empirical-statistical type which registers what they call aberrations or deviations, due to human frailty, from the norm set by theory.

A second group of economic theorists adheres to the proposition that it is the main purpose of theory to provide hypotheses that can be tested. This group acknowledges that prediction of future events represents the most stringent test of theory. They argue, however, that reality is so complex that it is necessary to begin with simplified propositions and models which are known to be unreal and not testable.[2] Basic among these propositions are the following three which traditionally have served to characterize the economic man or the rational man:

1. The principle of complete information and foresight. Economic conditions—demand, supply, prices, etc—are not only given but also known to the rational man. This applies as well to future conditions about which there exists no uncertainty, so that rational choice can always be made. (In place of the assumption of certainty of future developments, we find nowadays more frequently the assumption that risks prevail but the probability of occurrence of different alternatives is known; this does not constitute a basic difference.)
2. The principle of complete mobility. There are no institutional or psychological factors which make it impossible, or expensive, or slow, to translate the rational choice into action.
3. The principle of pure competition. Individual action has no great influence on prices because each man's choice is independent from any other person's choice and because there are no ''large'' sellers or buyers. Action is the result of individual choice and is not group-determined.

Economic theory is developed first under these assumptions. The theorists then introduce changes in the assumptions so that the theory may approach reality. One such step consists, for instance, of introducing large-scale producers, monopolists, and oligopolists, another of introducing time lags, and still another of introducing uncertainty about the probability distribution of future events. The question raised in each case is this: Which of the original propositions needs to be changed, and in what way, in view of the new assumptions?

The fact that up to now the procedure of gradual approximation to reality has not been completely successful does not invalidate the method. It must also be acknowledged that propositions were frequently derived from unrealistic economic models which were susceptible to testing and simulated empirical research. In this paper we shall point to a great drawback of this method of starting out with a simplified *a priori* system and making it gradually more complex and more real—by proceeding in this way one tends to lose sight of important problems and to disregard them.

The methods most commonly used in psychology may appear at first sight to be quite similar to the methods of economics which have just been described. Psychologists often start with casual observations, derive from them hypotheses, test those through more systematic observations, reformulate and revise their hypotheses accordingly, and test them again. The process of hypotheses-observations-hypotheses-observations often goes on with no end in sight. Differences from the approach of economic theory may be found in the absence in psychological research of detailed systematic elaboration prior to any observation. Also, in psychological research, findings and generalizations in one field of behavior are often considered as hypotheses in another field of behavior. Accordingly, in analyzing economic behavior[3] and trying to understand rationality, psychologists can draw on (*a*) the theory of learning and thinking, (*b*) the theory of group belonging, and (*c*) the theory of motivation. This will be done in this paper.

## Habitual Behavior and Genuine Decision Making

In trying to give noneconomic examples of "rational calculus," economic theorists have often referred to gambling. From some textbooks one might conclude that the most rational place in the world is the Casino in Monte Carlo where odds and probabilities can be calculated exactly. In contrast, some mathematicians and psychologists have considered scientific discovery and the thought processes of scientists as the best examples of rational or intelligent behavior.[4] An inquiry about the possible contributions of psychology to the analysis of rationality may then begin with a formulation of the differences between (*a*) associative learning and habit formation and (*b*) problem solving and thinking.

The basic principle of the first form of behavior is repetition. Here the argument of Guthrie holds: "The most certain and dependable information concerning what a man will do in any situation is information concerning what he did in that situation on its last occurrence" (4, p. 228). This form of behavior depends upon the frequency of repetition as well as on its recency and on the success of past performances. The origins of habit formation have been demonstrated by experiments about learning nonsense syllables, lists of words, mazes, and conditioned responses. Habits thus formed are to some extent automatic and inflexible.

In contrast, problem-solving behavior has been characterized by the arousal of a problem or question, by deliberation that involves reorganization and "direction," by understanding of the requirements of the situation, by weighing of alternatives and taking their consequences into consideration and, finally, by choosing among alternative courses of action.[5] Scientific discovery is not the only example of such procedures; they have been demonstrated in the psychological laboratory as well as in a variety of real-life situations. Problem solving results in action which is new rather than repetitive; the actor may have never behaved in the same way before and may not have learned of any others having behaved in the same way.

Some of the above terms, defined and analyzed by psychologists, are also being used by economists in their discussion of rational behavior. In discussing, for example, a manufacturer's choice between erecting or not erecting a new factory, or raising or not raising his prices or output, reference is usually made to deliberation and to taking the consequences of alternative choices into consideration. Nevertheless, it is not justified to identify problem-solving behavior with rational behavior. From the point of view of an outside observer, habitual behavior may prove to be fully rational or the most appropriate way of action under certain circumstances. All that is claimed here is that the analysis of two forms of behavior—habitual versus genuine decision making—may serve to clarify problems of rationality. We shall proceed therefore by deriving six propositions from the psychological principles. To some extent, or in certain fields of behavior, these are findings or empirical generalizations; to some extent or in other fields of behavior, they are hypotheses.

1. Problem-solving behavior is a relatively rare occurrence. It would be incorrect to assume that everyday behavior consistently manifests such features as arousal of a problem, deliberation, or taking consequences of the action into consideration. Behavior which does not manifest these characteristics predominates in everyday life and in economic activities as well.
2. The main alternative to problem-solving behavior is not whimsical or impulsive behavior (which was considered the major example of ''irrational'' behavior by nineteenth century philosophers). When genuine decision making does not take place, habitual behavior is the most usual occurrence: people act as they have acted before under similar circumstances, without deliberating and choosing.
3. Problem-solving behavior is recognized most commonly as a deviation from habitual behavior. Observance of the established routine is abandoned when in driving home from my office, for example, I learn that there is a parade in town and choose a different route, instead of automatically taking the usual one. Or, to mention an example of economic behavior: Many businessmen have rules of thumb concerning the timing for reorders of merchandise; yet sometimes they decide to place new orders even though their inventories have not reached the usual level of depletion (for instance, because they anticipate price increases), or not to order merchandise even though that level has been reached (because they expect a slump in sales).

4. Strong motivational forces—stronger than those which elicit habitual behavior—must be present to call forth problem-solving behavior. Being in a "crossroad situation," facing "choice points," or perceiving that something new has occurred are typical instances in which we are motivated to deliberate and choose. Pearl Harbor and the Korean aggression are extreme examples of "new" events; economic behavior of the problem-solving type was found to have prevailed widely after these events.
5. Group belonging and group reinforcement play a substantial role in changes of behavior due to problem solving. Many people become aware of the same events at the same time; our mass media provide the same information and often the same interpretation of events to groups of people (to businessmen, trade union members, sometimes to all Americans). Changes in behavior resulting from new events may therefore occur among very many people at the same time. Some economists (for instance, Lord Keynes, see 9, p. 95) argued that consumer optimism and pessimism are unimportant because usually they will cancel out; in the light of sociopsychological principles, however, it is probable, and has been confirmed by recent surveys, that a change from optimistic to pessimistic attitudes, or vice versa, sometimes occurs among millions of people at the same time.
6. Changes in behavior due to genuine decision making will tend to be substantial and abrupt, rather than small and gradual. Typical examples of action that results from genuine decisions are cessation of purchases or buying waves, the shutting down of plants or the building of new plants, rather than an increase or decrease of production by 5 or 10 percent.[6]

Because of the preponderance of individual psychological assumptions in classical economics and the emphasis placed on group behavior in this discussion, the change in underlying conditions which has occurred during the last century may be illustrated by a further example. It is related—the author does not know whether the story is true or fictitious—that the banking house of the Rothschilds, still in its infancy at that time, was one of the suppliers of the armies of Lord Wellington in 1815. Nathan Mayer Rothschild accompanied the armies and was present at the Battle of Waterloo. When he became convinced that Napoleon was decisively defeated, he released carrier pigeons so as to transmit the news to his associates in London and reverse the commodity position of his bank. The carrier pigeons arrived in London before the news of the victory became public knowledge. The profits thus reaped laid, according to the story, the foundation to the outstanding position of the House of Rothschild in the following decades.

The decision to embark on a new course of action because of new events was then made by one individual for his own profit. At present, news of a battle, or of change of government, or of rearmament programs, is transmitted in short order by press and radio to the public at large. Businessmen—the manufacturers or retailers of steel or clothing, for instance—usually receive the same news about changes in the price of raw materials or in demand, and often consult with each other. Belonging to the same group means being subject to similar stimuli and reinforcing one another in making decisions. Acting in the same way as other members of one's group or of a reference group have acted under similar circumstances may also occur without deliberation and choice. New action by a few manufacturers will, then, frequently or even usually not be compensated by reverse action on the part of others. Rather the direction in which the economy of an entire country moves—and often the world economy as well—will tend to be subject to the same influences.

After having indicated some of the contributions which the application of certain psychological principles to economic behavior may make, we turn to contrasting that approach with the traditional theory of rationality. Instead of referring to the formulations of nineteenth century economists, we shall quote from a modern version of the classical trend of thought. The title of a section in a recent article by Kenneth J. Arrow is "The Principle of Rationality." He describes one of the criteria of rationality as follows: "We can imagine the individual as listing, once and for all, all conceivable consequences of his actions in order of his preference for them" (1, p. 135). We are first concerned with the expression "all conceivable consequences." This expression seems to contradict the principle of selectivity of human behavior. Yet habitual behavior is highly selective since it is based on (repeated) past experience, and problem-solving behavior likewise is highly selective since reorganization is subject to a certain direction instead of consisting of trial (and error) regarding all possible avenues of action.

Secondly, Arrow appears to identify rationality with consistency in the sense of repetition of the same choice. It is part and parcel of rational behavior, according to Arrow, that an individual "makes the same choice each time he is confronted with the same set of alternatives" (1, p. 135).[7] Proceeding in the same way on successive occasions appears, however, a characteristic of habitual behavior. Problem-solving behavior, on the other hand, is flexible. Rationality may be said to reflect adaptability and ability to act in a new way when circumstances demand it, rather than to consist of rigid or repetitive behavior.

Thirdly, it is important to realize the differences between the concepts action, decision, and choice. It is an essential feature of the approach derived from considering problem-solving behavior that there is action without deliberate decision and choice. It then becomes one of the most important problems of research to determine under what conditions genuine decision and choice occur prior to an action. The three concepts are, however, used without differentiation in the classical theory of rationality and also, most recently, by Parsons and Shils. According to the theory of these authors, there are "five discrete choices (explicit or implicit) which every actor makes before he can act" (15, p. 78); before there is action "a decision must always be made (explicitly or implicitly, consciously or unconsciously)" (15, p. 89).

There exists, no doubt, a difference in terminology, which may be clarified by mentioning a simple case: Suppose my telephone rings; I lift the receiver with my left hand and say, "Hello." Should we then argue that I made several choices, for instance, that I decided not to lift the receiver with my right hand and not to say "Mr. Katona speaking"? According to our use of the terms decision and choice, my action was habitual and did not involve "taking consequences into consideration."[8] Parsons and Shils use the terms decision and choice in a different sense, and Arrow may use the terms "all conceivable consequences" and "same set of alternatives" in a different sense from the one employed in this paper. But the difference between the two approaches appears to be more far-reaching. By using the terminology of the authors quoted, and by constructing a theory of rational action on the basis of this terminology, fundamental problems are disregarded. If every action by definition presupposes decision making, and if the malleability of human behavior is not taken into consideration, a one-sided theory of rationality is developed and empirical research is confined to testing a theory which covers only some of the aspects of rationality.

This was the case recently in experiments devised by Mosteller and Nogee. These authors attempt to test basic assumptions of economic theory, such as the rational choice among alternatives, by placing their subjects in a gambling situation (a variation of poker dice) and compelling them to make a decision, namely, to play or not to play against the experimenter. Through their experiments the authors prove that "it is feasible to measure utility experimentally" (14, p. 403) but they do not shed light on the conditions under which rational behavior occurs or on the inherent features of rational behavior. Experiments in which making a choice among known alternatives is prescribed do not test the realism of economic theory.

## Maximization

Up to now we have discussed only one central aspect of rationality—means rather than ends. The end of rational behavior, according to economic theory, is maximization of profits in the case of business firms and maximization of utility in the case of people in general.

A few words, first, on maximizing profits. This is usually considered the simpler case because it is widely held (*a*) that business firms are in business to make profits and (*b*) that profits, more so than utility, are a quantitative, measurable concept.

When empirical research, most commonly in the form of case studies, showed that businessmen frequently strove for many things in addition to profits or in place of profits, most theorists were content with small changes in their systems. They redefined profits so as to include long-range profits and what has been called nonpecuniary or psychic profits. Striving for security or for power was identified with striving for profits in the more distant future; purchasing goods from a high bidder who was a member of the same fraternity as the purchaser, rather than from the lowest bidder—to cite an example often used in textbooks—was thought to be maximizing of nonpecuniary profits. Dissatisfaction with this type of theory construction is rather widespread. For example, a leading theorist wrote recently:

> If *whatever* a business man does is explained by the principle of profit maximization—because he does what he likes to do, and he likes to do what maximizes the sum of his pecuniary and non-pecuniary profits—the analysis acquires the character of a system of definitions and tautologies, and loses much of its value as an explanation of reality (13, p. 526).

The same problem is encountered regarding maximization of utility. Arrow defines rational behavior as follows: "... among all the combinations of commodities an individual can afford, he chooses that combination which maximizes his utility or satisfaction" (1, p. 135) and speaks of the "traditional identification of rationality with maximization of some sort" (2, p. 3). An economic theorist has recently characterized this type of definition as follows:

> The statement that a person seeks to maximize utility is (in many versions) a tautology: it is impossible to conceive of an observational phenomenon that contradicts it.... What if the theorem is contradicted by observation: Samuelson says it would not matter much in the case of utility theory; I would say that it would not make the slightest difference. For there is a free variable in his system: the tastes of consumers.... Any contradiction of a theorem derived from utility theory can always be attributed to a change of tastes, rather than to an error in the postulates or logic of the theory (16, pp. 603 f.).[9]

What is the way out of this difficulty? Can psychology, and specifically the psychology of motivation, help? We may begin by characterizing the prevailing economic theory as a single-motive theory and contrast it with a theory of multiple motives. Even in case of a single decision of one individual, multiplicity of motives (or of vectors or forces in the field), some reinforcing one another and some conflicting with one another, is the rule rather than the exception. The motivational patterns prevailing among different individuals making the same decision need not be the same; the motives of the same individual who is in the same external situation at different times may likewise differ. This approach opens the way (*a*) for a study of the relation of different motives to different forms of behavior and (*b*) for an investigation of changes in motives. Both problems are disregarded by postulating a single-motive theory and by restricting empirical studies to attempts to confirm or contradict that theory.

The fruitfulness of the psychological approach may be illustrated first by a brief reference to business motivation. We may rank the diverse motivational patterns of businessmen by placing the striving for high immediate profits (maximization of short-run profits, to use economic terminology; charging whatever the market can bear, to use a popular expression) at one extreme of the scale. At the other extreme we place the striving for prestige or power. In between we discern striving for security, for larger business volume, or for profits in the more distant future. Under what kinds of business conditions will motivational patterns tend to conform with the one or the other end of the scale? Preliminary studies would seem to indicate that the worse the business situation is, the more frequent is striving for high immediate profits, and the better the business situation is, the more frequent is striving for nonpecuniary goals (see 8, pp. 193-213).

Next we shall refer to one of the most important problems of consumer economics as well as of business-cycle studies, the deliberate choice between saving and spending. Suppose a college professor receives a raise in his salary or makes a few hundred extra dollars through a publication. Suppose, furthermore, that he suggests thereupon to his wife that they should buy a television set, while the wife argues that the money should be put in the bank as a reserve against a "rainy day." Whatever the final decision may be, traditional economic theory would hold that the action which gives the greater satisfaction was chosen. This way of theorizing is of little value. Under what conditions will one type of behavior (spending) and under what conditions will another type of behavior (saving) be more frequent? Psychological hypotheses according to which the strength of vectors is related to the immediacy of needs have been put to a test through nationwide surveys over the past six years.[10] On the basis of survey findings the following tentative generalization was established: Pessimism, insecurity, expectation of income declines or bad times in the near future promote saving (putting the extra money in the bank), while optimism, feeling of security, expectation of income increases, or good times promote spending (buying the television set, for instance).

Psychological hypotheses, based on a theory of motivational patterns which change with circumstances and influence behavior, thus stimulated empirical studies. These studies, in turn, yielded a better understanding of past developments and also, we may add, better predictions of forthcoming trends than did studies based on the classical theory (see note 10). On the other hand, when conclusions about utility or rationality were made on an *a priori* basis, researchers lost sight of important problems.[11]

## Diminishing Utility, Saturation, and Aspiration

Among the problems to which the identification of maximizing utility with rationality gave rise, the measurability of utility has been prominent.

At present the position of most economists appears to be that while interpersonal comparison of several consumers' utilities is not possible, and while cardinal measures cannot be attached to the utilities of one particular consumer, ordinal ranking of the utilities of each individual can be made. It is asserted that I can always say either that I prefer *A* to *B*, or that I am indifferent to having *A* or *B*, or that I prefer *B* to *A*. The theory of indifference curves is based on this assumption.

In elaborating the theory further, it is asserted that rational behavior consists not only of preferring more of the same goods to less ($2 real wages to $1, or two packages of cigarettes to one package, for the same service performed) but also of deriving diminishing increments of satisfaction from successive units of commodity.[12] In terms of an old textbook example, one drink of water has tremendous value to a thirsty traveler in a desert; a second, third, or fourth drink may still have some value but less and less so; an *n*th drink (which he is unable to carry along) has no value at all. A generalization derived from this principle is that the more of a commodity or the more money a person has, the smaller are his needs for that commodity or for money, and the smaller his incentives to add to what he has.

In addition to using this principle of saturation to describe the behavior of the rational man, modern economists applied to one of the most pressing problems of contemporary American economy. Prior to World War II the American people (not counting business firms) owned about 45 billion dollars in liquid assets (currency, bank deposits, government bonds) and these funds were highly concentrated among relatively few families; most individual families held no liquid assets at all (except for small amounts of currency). By the end of the year 1945, however, the personal liquid-asset holdings had risen to about 140 billion dollars and four out of every five families owned some bank deposits or war bonds. What is the effect of this great change on spending and saving? This question has been answered by several leading economists in terms of the saturation principle presented above. "The rate of saving is ... a diminishing function of the wealth the individual holds" (5, p. 499) because "the availability of liquid assets raises consumption generally by reducing the impulse to save."[13] More specifically: a person who owns nothing or very little will exert himself greatly to acquire some reserve funds, while a person who owns much will have much smaller incentives to save. Similarly, incentives to increase one's income are said to weaken with the amount of income. In other words, the strength of motivation is inversely correlated with the level of achievement.

In view of the lack of contact between economists and psychologists, it is hardly surprising that economists failed to see the relevance for their postulates of the extensive experimental work performed by psychologists on the problem of levels of aspiration. It is not necessary in this paper to describe these studies in detail. It may suffice to formulate three generalizations as established in numerous studies of goal-striving behavior (see, for example, 12):

1. Aspirations are not static, they are not established once for all time.
2. Aspirations tend to grow with achievement and decline with failure.
3. Aspirations are influenced by the performance of other members of the group to which one belongs and by that of reference groups.

From these generalizations hypotheses were derived about the influence of assets on saving which differed from the postulates of the saturation theory. This is not the place to describe the extensive empirical work undertaken to test the hypotheses. But it may be reported that the saturation theory was not confirmed; the level-of-aspiration theory likewise did not suffice to explain the findings. In addition to the variable "size of liquid-asset holdings," the studies had to consider such variables as income level, income change, and savings habits. (Holders of large liquid assets are primarily people who have saved a high proportion of their income in the past!)[14]

The necessity of studying the interaction of a great number of variables and the change of choices over time leads to doubts regarding the universal validity of a one-dimensional ordering of all alternatives. The theory of measurement of utilities remains an empty frame unless people's established preferences of *A* over *B* over *C* provide indications about their probable future behavior. Under what conditions do people's preferences give us such clues, and under what conditions do they not? If at different times *A* and *B* are seen in different contexts—because of changed external conditions or the acquisition of new experiences—we may have to distinguish among several dimensions.

The problem may be illustrated by an analogy. Classic economic theory postulates a one-dimensional ordering of all alternatives; Gallup asserts that answers to questions of choice can always be ordered on a yes—uncertain (don't know)—no continuum; are both arguments subject to the same reservations? Specifically, if two persons give the same answer to a poll question (e.g., both say "Yes, I am for sending American troops to Europe" or "Yes, I am for the Taft-Hartley Act") may they mean different things so that their identical answers do not permit any conclusions about the similarity of their other attitudes and their behavior? Methodologically it follows from the last argument that yes-no questions need to be supplemented by open-ended questions to discern differences in people's level of information and motivation. It also follows that attitudes and preferences should be ascertained through a multi-question approach (or scaling) which serves to determine whether one or several dimensions prevail.

## On Theory Construction

In attempting to summarize our conclusions about the respective merits of different scientific approaches, we might quote the conclusions of Arrow which he formulated for social science in general rather than for economics:

> To the extent that formal theoretical structures in the social sciences have not been based on the hypothesis of rational behavior, their postulates have been developed in a manner which we may term *ad hoc*. Such propositions ... depend, of course, on the investigator's intuition and common sense (1, p. 137).

The last sentence seems strange indeed. One may argue the other way around and point out that such propositions as "the purpose of business is to make profits" or "the best businessman is the one who maximizes profits" are based on intuition or supposed common sense, rather than on controlled observation. The main problem raised by the quotation concerns the function of empirical research. There exists an alternative to developing an axiomatic system into a full-fledged theoretical model in advance of testing the theory through observations. Controlled observations should be based on hypotheses, and the formulation of an integrated theory need not be delayed until all observations are completed. Yet theory construction is part of the process of hypothesis-observation-revised hypothesis and prediction-observation, and systematization should rely on some empirical research. The proximate aim of scientific research is a body of empirically validated generalizations and not a theory that is valid under any and all circumstances.

The dictum that "theoretical structures in the social sciences must be based on the hypothesis of rational behavior" presupposes that it is established what rational behavior is. Yet, instead of establishing the characteristics of rational behavior *a priori*, we must first determine the conditions $a_1$, $b_1$, $c_1$ under which behavior of the type $x_1$, $y_1$, $z_1$ and the conditions $a_2$, $b_2$, $c_2$ under which behavior of the type $x_2$, $y_2$, $z_2$ is likely to occur. Then, if we wish, we may designate one of the forms of behavior as rational. The contributions of psychology to this process are not solely methodological; findings and principles about noneconomic behavior provide hypotheses for the study of economic behavior. Likewise, psychology can profit from the study of economic behavior because many aspects of behavior, and among them the problems of rationality, may be studied most fruitfully in the economic field.

This paper was meant to indicate some promising leads for a study of rationality, not to carry such study to its completion. Among the problems that were not considered adequately were the philosophical ones (rationality viewed as a value concept), the psychoanalytic ones (the relationships between rational and conscious, and between irrational and unconscious), and those relating to personality theory and the roots of rationality. The emphasis was placed here on the possibility and fruitfulness of studying forms of rational behavior, rather than the characteristics of *the* rational man. Motives and goals that change with and are adapted to circumstances, and the relatively rare but highly significant cases of our becoming aware of problems and attempting to solve them, were found to be related to behavior that may be called truly rational.

## ENDNOTES

1. The quotation is from an introductory general statement signed by T. Parsons, E. A. Shils, G. W. Allport, C. Kluckhohn, H. A. Murray, R. R. Sears, R. C. Sheldon, S. A. Stouffer, and E. C. Tolman. The term "action" is meant to be synonymous with "behavior."
2. A variety of methods used in economic research differ, of course, from those employed by the two groups of economic theorists. Some research is motivated by dissatisfaction with the traditional economic theory; some is grounded in a systematization greatly different from traditional theory (the most important example of such systematization is national income accounting); some research is not clearly based on any theory; finally, some research has great affinity with psychological and sociological studies.
3. The expression "economic behavior" is used in this paper to mean behavior concerning economic matters (spending, saving, investing, pricing, etc.). Some economic theorists use the expression to mean the behavior of the "economic man," that is, the behavior postulated in their theory of rationality.
4. Reference should be made first of all to Max Wertheimer who in his book *Productive Thinking* (17) uses the terms "sensible" and "intelligent" rather than "rational." Since we are mainly interested here in deriving conclusions from the psychology of thinking, the discussion of psychological principles will be kept extremely brief (see 6 and 8, Chaps. 3, 4).
5. Cf. the following statement by a leading psychoanalyst: "Rational behavior is behavior that is effectively guided by an understanding of the situation to which one is reacting" (3, p. 16). French adds two steps that follow the choice between alternative goals, namely, commitment to a goal and commitment to a plan to reach a goal.
6. Some empirical evidence supporting these six propositions in the area of economic behavior has been assembled by the Survey Research Center of the University of Michigan (see 8 and also 7).
7. In his recent book Arrow adds after stating that the economic man "will make the same decision each time he is faced with the same range of alternatives: The ability to make consistent decisions is one of the symptoms of an integrated personality" (2, p. 2).
8. If I have reason not to make known that I am at home, I may react to the ringing of the telephone by fright, indecision, and deliberation (should I lift the receiver or let the telephone ring?) instead of reacting in the habitual way. This is an example of problem-solving behavior characterized as deviating from habitual behavior. The only example of action mentioned

by Parsons and Shils, "a man driving his automobile to a lake to go fishing," may be habitual or may be an instance of genuine decision making.

9. The quotation refers specifically to Samuelson's definiton but also applies to that of Arrow.
10. In the Surveys of Consumer Finances, conducted annually since 1946 by the Survey Research Center of the University of Michigan for the Federal Reserve Board and reported in the *Federal Reserve Bulletin*. See also 8 and a forthcoming publication of the Survey Research Center on consumer buying and inflation during 1950-52.
11. It should not be implied that the concepts of utility and maximization are of no value for empirical research. Comparison between maximum utility as determined from the vantage point of an observer with the pattern of goals actually chosen (the "subjective maximum"), which is based on insufficient information, may be useful. Similar considerations apply to such newer concepts as "minimizing regrets" and the "minimax."
12. This principle of diminishing utility was called a "fundamental tendency of human nature" by the great nineteenth century economist, Alfred Marshall.
13. The last quotation is from the publication of the U. S. Department of Commerce, *Survey of Current Business*, May 1950, p. 10. This quotation and several similar ones are discussed in 8, pp. 186 ff.
14. The empirical work was part of the economic behavior program of the Survey Research Center under the direction of the author. See (8) and also (10) and (11).

## REFERENCES


1. Arrow, K. J., "Mathematical Models in the Social Sciences," in D. Lerner & H. D. Lasswell (eds.), *The Policy Sciences*, Stanford: Stanford University Press, 1951, pp. 129-155.
2. Arrow, K. J., *Social Choice and Individual Values*, New York: Wiley, 1951.
3. French, T. M., *The Integration of Behavior*, Vol. I, Chicago: University of Chicago Press, 1952.
4. Guthrie, E. R., *Psychology of Learning*, New York: Harper, 1935.
5. Haberler, G., *Prosperity and Depression*, (3rd ed.), Geneva: League of Nations, 1941.
6. Katona, G., *Organizing and Memorizing*, New York: Columbia University Press, 1940.
7. Katona, G., "Psychological Analysis of Business Decisions and Expectations," *American Economic Review*, 1946, 36, 44-63.
8. Katona, G., *Psychological Analysis of Economic Behavior*, New York: McGraw-Hill, 1951.
9. Keynes, J. M., *The General Theory of Employment, Interest and Money*, New York: Harcourt, Brace, 1936.
10. Klein, L. R., "Assets, Debts, and Economic Behavior," in *Studies in Income and Wealth*, Vol. 14, New York: National Bureau of Economic Research, 1951.
11. Klein, L. R., "Estimating Patterns of Savings Behavior from Sample Survey Data," *Econometrica*, 1951, 19, 438-454.

12. Lewin, K., *et al*, "Level of Aspiration," in J. McV. Hunt (ed.), *Personality and the Behavior Disorders*, New York: Ronald, 1944.
13. Machlup, F., "Marginal Analysis and Empirical Research," *American Economic Review*, 1946, 36, 519-555.
14. Mosteller, F. and P. Nogee, "An Experimental Measurement of Utility," *Journal of Political Economy*, 1951, 59, 371-405.
15. Parsons, T. and E. A. Shils (eds.), *Toward a General Theory of Action*, Cambridge, Mass.: Harvard University Press, 1951.
16. Stigler, G. J., "Review of P. A. Samuelson's *Foundations of Economic Analysis*," *Journal of American Statistical Association*, 1948, 43, 603-605.
17. Wertheimer, M., *Productive Thinking*, New York: Harper, 1945.

# 30 —— Theory of Buyer Behavior

*John A. Howard and J. N. Sheth*

Reprinted from *Changing Market Systems*, published by the American Marketing Association, edited by R. Moyer (1967), pp. 253-262. Reprinted by permission.

In the last fifteen years, considerable research on consumer behavior both at the conceptual and empirical levels has accumulated. This can be gauged by reviews of the research.[1] As a consequence we believe that sufficient research exists in both the behavioral sciences and consumer behavior to attempt a comprehensive theory of buyer behavior. Furthermore, broadly speaking, there are two major reasons at the basic research level which seem to have created the need to take advantage of this opportunity. The first reason is that a great variety exists in today's effort to understand the consumer, and unfortunately there is no integration of this variety. The situation resembles the seven blind men touching different parts of the elephant and making inferences about the animal which differ, and occasionally contradict one another. A comprehensive theory of buyer behavior would hopefully not only provide a framework for integrating the existing variety but also would prepare the researcher to adopt appropriate research designs which would control sources of influences other than those he is immediately interested in. The difficulty of replicating a study and the possibility of getting contradictory findings will be minimized accordingly.

The second major basic research reason for a comprehensive theory is the potential application of research in buying behavior to human behavior in general. In asserting the need to validate psychological propositions in a real world context Sherif has repeatedly and eloquently argued for applied research.[2] Also, McGuire argues that social psychology is moving toward theory-oriented research in *natural settings* because a number of forces are encouraging the movement away from laboratory research, and he cites the current work in buyer behavior as one of these forces.[3]

Again, one way that we can contribute to ''pure'' areas of behavioral science is by attempting a comprehensive theory which would help to identify and to iron out our own inconsistencies and contradictions. Such an attempt looks ambitious on the surface, but after several years of work and drawing upon earlier work,[4] we are confident that it can be achieved.

## A Brief Summary of the Theory

Before we describe each component of the theory in detail, it will be helpful to discuss briefly the essentials of our view of the consumer choice process.

Much of buying behavior is more or less repetitive brand choice decisions. During his life cycle, the buyer establishes purchase cycles for various products which determine how often he will buy a given product. For some products, this cycle is very lengthy, as for example in buying durable appliances, and, therefore, he buys the product quite infrequently. For many other products, however, the purchase cycle is short and he buys the product frequently as is the case for many grocery and personal care items. Since there is usually the element of repeat buying, we must present a theory which incorporates the dynamics of purchase behavior over a period of time if we wish to capture the central elements of the empirical process.

In the face of repetitive brand choice decisions, the consumer simplifies his decision process by storing relevant information and routinizing his decision process. What is crucial, therefore, is to identify the elements of decision making, to observe the structural or substantive changes that occur in them over time due to the repetitive nature, and show how a combination of the decision elements affect search processes and the incorporation of information from the buyer's commercial and social environment.

The buyer, having been motivated to buy a product class, is faced with a brand choice decision. The elements of his decision are: (1) a set of motives, (2) several courses of action, and (3) decision mediators by which the motives are matched with the alternatives. Motives are specific to a product class, and they reflect the underlying needs of the buyer. The alternative courses of actions are the purchase of one of the various brands with their potential to satisfy the buyer's motives. There are two important notions involved in the definition of alternatives as brands. First, the brands which are alternatives of the buyer's choice decision at any given time are generally a small number, collectively called his "evoked set." The size of the evoked set is only two or three, a fraction of the brands he is aware of and a still smaller fraction of the total number of brands actually available in the market. Second, any two consumers may have quite different alternatives in their evoked sets.

The decision mediators are a set of rules that the buyer employs to match his motives and his means of satisfying those motives. They serve the function of ordering and structuring the buyer's motives and then ordering and structuring the various brands based on their potential to satisfy these ordered motives. The decision mediators develop by the process of learning about he buying situation. They are, therefore, influenced by information from the buyer's environment and even more importantly by the actual experience of purchasing and consuming the brand.

When the buyer is just beginning to purchase a product class such as when a purchase is precipitated by a change in his life cycle, he lacks experience. In order, therefore, to develop the decision mediators, he *actively seeks information* from his commercial and social environments. The information that he either actively seeks or accidentally receives, is subjected to perceptual processes which not only limits the intake of information (magnitude of information is affected) but modifies it to suit his own frame of reference (quality of information is affected). These modifications are significant since they distort the neat ''marketing stimulus-consumer response'' relation.

Along with active search for information, the buyer may, to some extent, generalize from past similar experiences. Such generalization can be due to physical similarity of the new product class to the old product class. For example, in the initial pruchases of Scotch whiskey, the buyer may generalize his experiences in buying of gin. Generalization can also occur even when the two product classes are physically dissimilar but have a common meaning such as deriving from a company-wide brand name. For example, the buyer could generalize his experiences in buying a refrigerator or range to his first purchase of a dishwasher of the same brand.

Whatever the source, the buyer develops sufficient decision mediators to enable him to choose a brand which seems to have the best potential for satisfying his motives. If the brand proves satisfactory, the potential of that brand to satisfy his motives is increased. The result is that the probability of buying that brand is likewise increased. With repeated satisfactory purchases of one or more brands, the buyer is likely to manifest a routinized decision process whereby the sequential steps in buying are well structured so that some event which triggers the process may actually complete the choice decision. Routinized purchasing implies that his decision mediators are well established, and that the buyer has strong brand preferences.

The phase of repetitive decision making, in which the buyer reduces the complexity of a buying situation with the help of information and experience is called the *psychology of simplification*. Decision-making can be divided into three stages and used to illustrate the psychology of simplification: Extensive Problem Solving, Limited Problem Solving and Routinized Response Behavior. The further he is along in simplifying his environment, the less is the tendency toward active search behavior. The environmental stimuli related to the purchase situation become more meaningful and less ambiguous. Furthermore, the buyer establishes more cognitive consistency among the brands as he moves toward routinization and the incoming information is then screened both with regard to its magnitude and quality. He becomes less attentive to stimuli which do not fit his cognitive structure and he distorts those simuli which are forced upon him.

A surprising phenomenon, we believe, occurs in many instances of frequently purchased products such as in grocery and personal care items. The buyer, after attaining routinization of his decision process, may find himself in too simple a situation. He is likely to feel the monotony or boredom associated with such repetitive decision-making. It is also very likely that he is satisfied with even the most preferred brand. In both cases, he may feel that all existing alternatives including the preferred brand are unacceptable. He therefore, feels a need to *complicate* his buying situation by considering new brands, and this process can be called the *psychology of complication*. The new situation cause him to identify a new brand, and so he begins again to simplify in the manner described earlier. Thus with a frequently-purchased item buying is a continuing process with its ups and downs in terms of information seeking analogous to the familiar cyclical fluctuations in economic activity.

## ELEMENTS OF THEORY

Any theory of human behavior needs some means for explaining individual differences. The marketing manager also is interested in differentiated masses of buyers. He wants to understand and separate individual differences so that he can classify or segment the total market based upon individual differences. By understanding the psychology of the individual buyer we may achieve this classification. Depending on the internal state of the buyer, a given stimulus may result in a given response. For example, one buyer who urgently needs a product may respond to the ad of a brand in that product class by buying it whereas another buyer who does not need the product may simply notice the ad and store the information or ignore the ad. A construct such as ''level of motivation'' will then explain the divergent reactions to the same stimulus. Alternatively, two buyers may both urgently need a product, but they buy two different brands. This can be explained by another construct: predispositon toward a brand.

Figure 1 represents the theory of buyer behavior. The central rectangular box isolates the various internal state variables and processes which combined together show the state of the buyer. The inputs to the rectangular box are the stimuli from the marketing and social environments. The outputs are a variety of responses that the buyer is likely to manifest based on the interaction between the stimuli and his internal state. Besides the inputs and outputs, there are a set of seven influences which affect the variables in the rectangular box.[5] These variables appear at the top of the diagram and are labelled ''exogeneous variables.'' Their function is to provide means of adjusting for the interpersonal differences discussed above. The variables within the rectangular box serve the role of endogeneous variables in the sense that changes in them are explained but they are something less then endogeneous variables. They are not well defined and hence are not measurable. They are hypothetical constructs. Their values are inferred from relations among the output intervening variables. Several of the exogeneous variables such as personality, social class and culture have traditionally been treated as part of the endogeneous variables. We believe that they affect more specific variables, and by conceptualizing their effect as via the hypothetical constructs, we can better understand their role.

Thus it will be seen that the theory of buyer behavior has four major components: the stimulus variables, the response variables, the hypothetical constructs and the exogeneous variables. We will elaborate on each of the components below both in terms of their substance and their interrelationships.

**FIGURE 1. A Theory of Buyer Behavior**

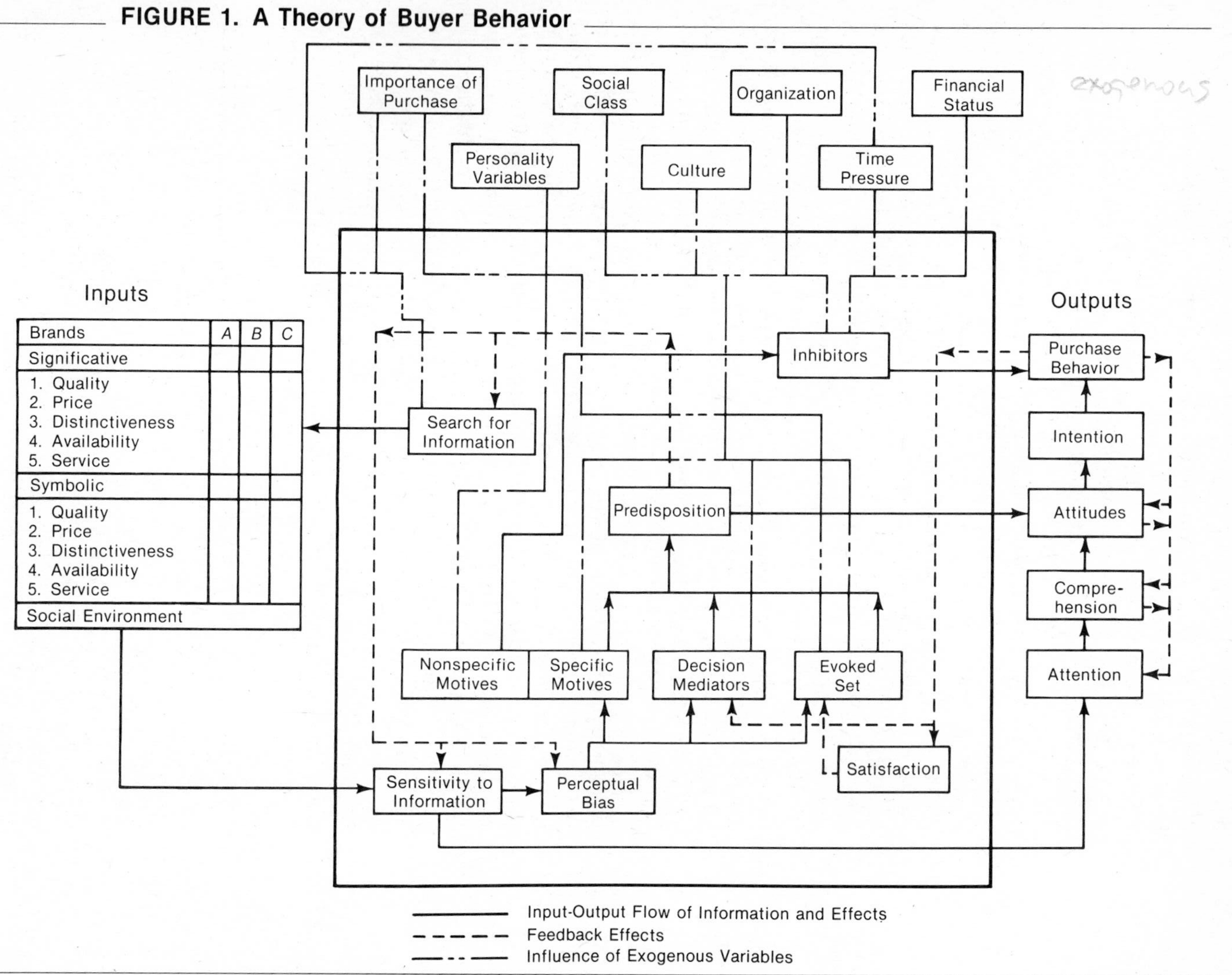

## Stimulus Variables

At any point in time, the hypothetical constructs which reflect the buyer's internal state are affected by numerous stimuli from the environment. The environment is classified as Commerical or Social. The commercial environment is the marketing activities of various firms by which they attempt to communicate to the buyer. From the buyer's point of view, these communications basically come either via the physical brands themselves or some linguistic or pictorial representations of the attributes of the brands. If the elements of the brands such as price, quality, service, distinctiveness or availability are communicated through the physical brands (significates) then the stimuli are defined and classified as significative stimuli. If, on the other hand, the attributes are communicated in linguistic or pictorial symbols such as in mass media, billboards, catalogs, salesmen, etc. then the stimuli from commercial sources are classified as symbolic stimuli. We view the marketing mix as the optimum allocation of funds between the two major channels of communication—significative or symbolic—to the buyer.

Each commercial input variable is hypothesized to be multivariate. Probably the five major dimensions of a brand—price, quality, distinctiveness, availability and service—summarize the various attributes. The same dimensions are present in both significative or symbolic communication which become the input stimuli for the buyer. However, certain dimensions may be more appropriately conveyed by significative rather than symbolic communication and vice versa. For example, price is easily communicated by both channels; shape may best be communicated by two-dimensional pictures rather than verbal communication. Finally, size may not be easily communicated by any symbolic representation: the physical product (significate) may be necessary.

The third stimulus input variable is social stimuli. It refers to the information that the buyer's social environment provides regarding a purchase decision. The most obvious is word of mouth communication.

The inputs to the buyer's mental state from the three major sources are then processed and stored by their interaction with a series of hypothetical constructs, and the buyer may react immediately or later.

## Hypothetical Constructs

The hypothetical constructs and their interrelationships are the result of an integration of Hull's learning theory,[6] Osgood's cognitive theory,[7] and Berlyne's theory of exploratory behavior[8] along with other ideas.

We may classify the constructs into two classes: (i) those that have to do with perception, and (ii) those having to do with learning. Perceptual constructs serve the function of information processing while the learning constructs serve the function of concept formation. It is interesting that, after years of experience in advertising, Reeves has a very similar classification:[9] his "penetration" is analogous to perceptual variables and his "unique selling propositions'' is analogous to learning variables. We will at first describe the learning constructs since they are the major components of decision making; the perceptual constructs which serve the important role of obtaining and processing information are more complex and will be described later.

## Learning Constructs

The learning constructs are labeled as: (1) Motives—Specific and Nonspecific, (2) Brand Potential of Evoked Set, (3) Decision Mediators, (4) Predisposition toward the brands, (5) Inhibitors, and (6) Satisfaction with the purchase of the brand.

*Motive* is the impetus to action. Motives or goals may be thought of as constituting a means-end chain and hence, as being general or specific depending upon their position in the chain. Motives can refer to the buyer's specific goals in purchasing a product class. The buyer is motivated by the expectation or anticipation due to past learning of outcome from the purchase of each of the brands in his evoked set.

The specific motives—lower level motives in the means-end chain—are very closely anchored to the attributes of a product class and in this way they become purchase criteria. Examples of specific motives for buying a dietary product such as Metrecal or Sego are low calories, nutrition, taste, and value.

Very often, several specific motives are nothing more than indicators of some underlying more general motive, that is, some motive that is higher in the means-end chain. In the above example, the specific motives of nutrition and low calories might be merely indicators of the common motive of good health.

Motives also serve the important function of raising the buyer's general motivational state or arousal and thereby tuning up the buyer, causing him to pay attention to environmental stimuli. Examples of nonspecific motives are probably anxiety, fear, many of the personality variables such as authoritarianism, exhibitionism, aggressiveness, etc., and social motives of power, status, prestige, etc. Although they are nonspecific, they are not innate, but rather learned, mostly due to acculturation. The nonspecific motives also possess a hierarchy within themselves. For example, anxiety is considered to be the source of another motive, that of the need for money.[10]

*Brand Potential of Evoked Set* is the second learning construct. A buyer who is familiar with a product class has an evoked set of alternatives to satisfy his motives. The elements of his evoked set are some of the brands that make up the product class. The concept is important because for this buyer the brands in his evoked set constitute competition for the seller.

A brand is, of course, a class concept like many other objects or things. The buyer attaches a *word* to this concept—a label—which is the brand name such as "Campbell's Tomato Soup". Whenever he sees a can of Campbell's Tomato Soup or hears the phrase, the image conveys to him certain satisfactions, procedures for preparation, etc. In short, it conveys certain meaning including its potential to satisfy his motives.

Various brands in the buyer's evoked set will generally satisfy the goal structure differently. One brand may possess potential to the extent that it is an ideal brand for the buyer. Another brand, on the other hand, may satisfy motives just enough to be part of his evoked set. By the process of learning the buyer obtains, and stores knowledge regarding each brand's potential and then rank orders them in terms of their want-satisfying potential. The evoked set, in short, is a set of alternatives with each alternative's payoff. Predisposition mentioned below enables the buyer to choose one among them.

*Decision Mediator* is the third learning construct and it brings together motives and alternatives. The brand potential of each of the brands in his evoked set are the decision alternatives with their payoffs. Decision mediators are the buyer's mental rules for matching the alternatives with his motives, for rank-ordering them in terms of their want-satisfying capacity. As mental rules, they exhibit reasoning wherein the cognitive elements related to the alternatives and the motives are structured. The words that he uses to describe these attributes are also the words that he thinks with and that he finds are easy to remember. The criterial attributes are important to the manufacturer because if he knows them, he can deliberately build into his brand and promotion those characteristics which will differentiate his brand from competing brands.

The decision mediators thus represent enduring cognitive rules established by the process of learning, and their function is to obtain meaningful and congruent relations among brands so that the buyer can manifest goal-directed behavior. The aim of the theory of buyer behavior is not just the identification of motives and the respective brands but to show their structure as well. It is the decision mediators which provide this structure.

In view of the fact that decision mediators are learned, principles of learning become crucial in their development and change over time. There are two broad sources of learning: (1) actual experience, and (2) information. Actual experience can be either with the *same* buying situation in the past or with a *similar* buying situation. The latter is generally labelled as generalization as discussed earlier. Similarly, information as a source of learning can be from: (1) the buyer's commercial environment, or (2) his social environment. Later, we will elaborate on each of the sources of learning.

*Predisposition*, the fourth construct, is the summary effect of the previous three constructs. It refers to the buyer's preference toward brands in his evoked set. It is, in fact, an aggregate index which is reflected in attitude which, in turn, is measured by attitude scales. It might be visualized as the "place" where brands in Evoked Set are compared with Mediator's choice criteria to yield a judgment on the relative contribution of the brands to the buyer's motives. This judgment includes not only an estimate of the value of the brand to him but also an estimate of the confidence with which he holds that position. This uncertainty aspect of Predisposition can be called "brand ambiguity," in that the more confident he holds it, the less ambiguous is the connotative meaning of the brand to the buyer and the more likely he is to buy it.[11]

*Inhibitors*, the fifth learning construct, are forces in the environment which create important disruptive influences in the actual purchase of a brand even when the buyer has reasoned out that that brand will best satisfy his motives. In other words, when the buyer is both predisposed to buy a brand, and has the motivation to buy some brand in the product class, he may not buy it because several environmental forces inhibit its purchase and prevent him from satisfying his preferences.

We postulate at least four types of inhibitors. They are: (1) high price of the brand, (2) lack of availability of the brand, (3) time pressure on the buyer, and (4) the buyer's financial status. The first two are part of the environmental stimuli, and therefore, they are part of the input system. The last two come from the two exogeneous variables of the same name. It should be pointed out that social constraints emanating from other exogeneous variables may also create temporary barriers to the purchase of a brand.

An essential feature of all inhibitors is that they are *not internalized* by the buyer because their occurrence is random and strictly situational. However, some of the inhibitors may persist systematically over time as they concern a given buyer. If they persist long enough, the buyer is likely to incorporate them as part of his decision mediators and thus to internalize them. The consequence is that they may affect even the structure of alternatives and motives.

*Satisfaction*, the last of the learning constructs, refers to the degree of congruence between the actual consequences from purchase and consumption of a brand and what was expected from it by the buyer at the time of purchase. If the actual outcome is adjudged by the buyer as *at least* equal to the expected, the buyer will feel satisfied. If, on the other hand, the actual outcome is adjudged as less than what he expected, the buyer will feel dissatisfied and his attitude will be less favorable. Satisfaction or dissatisfaction with a brand can exist with respect to any one of the different attributes. If the brand proves more satisfactory than he expected, the buyer has a tendency to enhance the attractiveness of the brand. Satisfaction will, therefore, affect the reordering of the brands in the evoked set for the next buying decision.

## Relations Among Learning Constructs

Underlying Predisposition toward the brands and related variables, several important notions are present. The simplest way to describe them is to state that we may classify a decision process as either Extensive Problem Solving, Limited Problem Solving or Routinized Response Behavior depending on the strength of Predisposition toward the brands. In the early phases of buying, the buyer has not yet developed decision mediators well enough: specifically his product class concept is not well formed and predisposition is low. As he acquires information and gains experience in buying and consuming the brand, Decision Mediators become firm and Predisposition toward a brand is generally high.

In Extensive Problem Solving, Predisposition towards the brands is low. None of the brands is discriminated enough based on their criterial attributes for the buyer to show greater brand preference toward any one brand. At this stage of decision making, brand ambiguity is high with the result that the buyer actively seeks information from his environment. Due to greater search for information, there exists a greater *latency of response*—the time interval from the initiation of a decision to its completion. Similarly, deliberation or reasoning will be high since he lacks a well-defined product class concept which is the denotative aspect of mediator. He is also likely to consider many brands as part of Evoked Set, and stimuli coming from the commercial environment are less likely to trigger any immediate purchase reaction.

When Predisposition toward the brands is moderate, the buyer's decision process can be called Limited Problem Solving. There still exists brand ambiguity since the buyer is not able to discriminate and compare brands so that he may prefer one brand over others. He is likely to seek information but not to the extent that he seeks it in Extensive Problem Solving. More importantly, he seeks information more on a relative basis to compare and discriminate various brands rather than to compare them absolutely on each of the brands. His deliberation or thinking is much less since Decision Mediators are tentatively well defined. Evoked Set will consist of a small number of brands, each having about the same degree of preference.

In Routinized Response Behavior, the buyer will have a high level of Predisposition toward brands in his evoked set. Furthermore, he has now accumulated sufficient experience and information to have little brand ambiguity. He will in fact discriminate among brands enough to show a strong preference toward one or two brands in the evoked set. He is unlikely to actively seek any information from his environment since such information is not needed. Also, whatever information he passively or accidentally receives, he will subject it to selective perceptual processes so that only congruent information is allowed. Very often, the congruent information will act as "triggering cues" to motivate him to manifest purchase behavior. Much of impulse purchase, we believe, is really the outcome of a strong predisposition and such a facilitating commercial stimulus as store display. The buyer's evoked set will consist of a few brands toward which he is highly predisposed. However, he will have greater preference toward one or two brands in his evoked set and less towards others.

As mentioned earlier, Predisposition is an aggregate index of decision components. Thus, any changes in the components due to learning from experience or information imply some change in Predisposition. The greater the learning, the more the predisposition toward the brands in the evoked set. The exact nature of learning will be described later when we discuss the dynamics of buying behavior.

## Perceptual Constructs

Another set of constructs serve the function of information procurement and processing relevant to a purchase decision. As mentioned earlier, information can come from any one of the three stimulus inputs—significative commercial stimuli, symbolic commercial stimuli, and social stimuli. Once again we will here only describe the constructs; their utilization by the buyer will be explained when we discuss the dynamics of buying behavior. The perceptual constructs in Figure 1 are: (a) Sensitivity to information, (b) Perceptual Bias, and (c) Search for Information.

A perceptual phenomenon implies either ignoring a physical event which could be a stimulus, seeing it attentively or sometimes imagining what is not present in reality. All perceptual phenomena essentially create some change in quantity or quality of objective information.

*Sensitivity to information* refers to the opening and closing of sensory receptors which control the intake of information. The manifestation of this phenomenon is generally called perceptual vigilance (paying attention) or perceptual defense (ignoring the information). Sensitivity to Information, therefore, primarily serves as a gate keeper to information entering into the buyer's mental state. It thus controls the quantity of information input.

Sensitivity to information, according to Berlyne[12], is a function of the degree of ambiguity of the stimuli to which the buyer is exposed. If the stimulus is very familiar or too simple, the ambiguity is low and the buyer will not pay attention unless he is predisposed to such information from past learning. Furthermore, if ambiguity of the stimulus continues to be low, the buyer feels a sense of monotony and actually seeks other information, and this act can be said to *complicate* his environment. If the stimulus is very complex and ambiguous, the buyer finds it hard to comprehend and, therefore, he ignores it by resorting to perceptual defense. Only if the stimulus is in the moderate range of ambiguity is the buyer motivated to pay attention and to freely absorb the objective information.

In a single communication, the buyer may at first find the communication complex and ambiguous and so he will resort to perceptual defense and tend to ignore it. As some information enters, however, he finds that it is really at the medium level of ambiguity and so pays attention. On the other hand, it might be that the more he pays attention to it, the more he finds the communication too simple and, therefore, ignores it as the process of communication progresses.

A second variable which governs Sensitivity to Information is the buyer's predisposition toward the brand about which the information is concerned. The more interesting the information, the more likely the buyer is to open up his receptors and therefore to pay attention to the information. Hess has recently measured this by obtaining the strength of pupil dilation.

*Perceptual Bias* is the second perceptual construct. The buyer not only selectively attends to information, but he may actually distort it once it enters his mental state. In other words, quality of information can be altered by the buyer. This aspect of the perceptual process is summarized in Perceptual Bias. The buyer may distort the cognitive elements contained in information to make them congruent with his own frame of reference as determined by the amount of information he already has stored. A series of cognitive consistency theories have been recently developed to explain how this congruency is established and what the consequences are in terms of the distortion of information that we might expect.[13] Most of the qualitative change in information arises because of feedback from various decision components such as Motives, Evoked Set and Decision Mediators. These relations are too complex, however, to describe in the summary.

The perceptual phenomena described above are likely to be less operative if the information is received from the buyer's social environment. This is because: (i) the source of social information, such as a friend, is likely to be favorably regarded by the buyer and therefore proper, undistorted reception of information will occur, and (ii) the information itself is modified by the social environment (the friend) so that it conforms to the needs of the buyer and, therefore, further modification is less essential.

*Search for Information* is the third perceptual construct. During the total buying phase which extends over time and involves several repeat purchases of a product class, there are stages when the buyer *actively* seeks information. It is very important to distinguish the times when he passively receives information from the situations where he actively seeks it. We believe that perceptual distortion is less operative in the latter instances, and that a commercial communication, therefore, at that stage has a high probability of influencing the buyer.

The active seeking of information occurs when the buyer senses ambiguity of the brands in his evoked set. As we saw earlier, this happens in the Extensive Problem Solving and Limited Problem Solving phases of the decision process. The ambiguity of brand exists because the buyer is not certain of the outcomes from each brand. In other words, he has not yet learned enough about the alternatives to establish an expectancy of potential of the brands to satisfy his motives. This type of brand ambiguity is essentially confined to initial buyer behavior which we have called Extensive Problem Solving. However, ambiguity may still exist despite knowledge of the potential of alternative brands. This ambiguity is with respect to his inability to discriminate between alternatives. The buyer may be unable to discriminate because his motives are not well structured: he does not know how to order them.

He may then seek information which will resolve the conflict among goals, a resolution that is implied in his learning of the appropriate product class aspect of decision mediators that we discussed earlier.

There is yet another stage of total buying behavior in which the buyer is likely to seek information. It is when the buyer has not only routinized his decision process but he is so familiar and satiated with repeat buying that he feels bored. Then, all of the existing alternatives in his evoked set including the most preferred brand become unacceptable to him. He seeks change or variety in that buying situation. In order to obtain this change, he actively searches for information on other alternatives (brands) that he never considered before. At this stage, he is particularly receptive to any information about new brands. Incidentally, here is an explanation for advertising in a highly stable industry. This phenomena has long baffled both the critics and defenders of the the institution of advertising. Newcomers to the market and forgetting do not provide a plausible explanation.

We have so far described the stimulus input variables and the hypothetical constructs. Now we proceed to describe the output of the system—the responses of the buyer.

## Response Variables

The complexity of buyer behavior does not stop with the hypothetical constructs. Just as there is a variety of inputs, there exist a variety of buyer responses which becomes relevant for different areas of marketing strategy. This variety of consumer responses can be easily appreciated from the diversity of measures to evaluate advertising effectivness. We have attempted to classify and order this diversity of buyer responses in the output variables. Most of the the output variables are directly related to some and not other constructs. Each output variable serves different purposes both in marketing practice and fundamental research. Let us at first describe each variable and then provide a rationale for their interrelationships.

## Attention

Attention is related to Sensitivity to Information. It is a response of the buyer which indicates the magnitude of his information intake. Attention is measured continuously during the time interval when the buyer receives information. There are several psychophysical methods of quantifying the degree of attention that the buyer pays to a message. The pupil dilation is one.

## Comprehension

Comprehension refers to the store of knowledge about the brand that the buyer possesses at any point in time. This knowledge could vary from his simply being aware of a single brand's existence to a complete description of the attributes of the product class of which the brand is an element. It reflects the denotative meaning of the brand and in that sense it is strictly in the cognitive realm. It lacks the motivational aspects of behavior. Some of the standard measures of advertising effectiveness such as awareness, aided or unaided recall, and recognition may capture different aspects of the buyer's comprehension of the brand.

### Attitude Toward a Brand

Attitude toward a brand is the buyer's evaluation of the brand's potential to satisfy his motives. It, therefore, includes the connotative aspects of the brand concept; it contains those aspects of the brand which are relevant to the buyer's goals. Attitude is directly related to Predisposition and so it consists of both the evaluation of a brand in terms of the criteria of choice from Mediator and the confidence with which that evaluation is held.

### Intention to Buy

Intention to buy is the buyer's forecast of his brand choice some time in the future. Like any forecast, it involves assumptions about future events including the likelihood of any perceived inhibitors creating barriers over the buyer's planning horizon. Intention to buy has been extensively used in the purchases of durable goods with some recent refinements in terms of the buyer's confidence in his own forecast; these studies are in terms of broadly defined product classes.[14] We may summarize this response of the buyer as something short of actual purchase behavior.

### Purchase Behavior

Purchase Behavior refers to the overt act of purchasing a brand. What becomes a part of company's sales or what the consumer records in a diary as a panel member, however, is only the terminal act in the sequence of shopping and buying. Very often, it is useful to observe the complete movement of the buyer from his home to the store and his purchase in the store. Yoell, for example, shows several case histories where a time and motion study of consumer's purchase behavior have useful marketing implications.[15] We think that at times it may be helpful to go so far as to incorporate the act of consumption into the definition of Purchase Behavior. We have, for example, developed and used the technique of sequential decision making where the buyer verbally describes the sequential pattern of his purchase behavior in a given buying situation. Out of this description a "flow chart" of decision making is obtained which reveals the number and the structure of the decision rules that the buyer employs.

Purchase Behavior is the overt manifestation of the buyer's Predisposition in conjunction with any Inhibitors that may be present. It differs from Attitude to the extent that Inhibitors are taken into consideration. It differs from

Intention to the extent that it is the actual manifestation of behavior which the buyer only forecasted in his intention.

Several characteristics of Purchase Behavior become useful if we observe the buyer in a repetitive buying situation. These include the incidence of buying a brand, the quantity bought, and the purchase cycle. Several stochastic models of brand loyalty, for example, have been developed in recent years.[16] Similarly, we could take the magnitude purchased and compare light buyers with heavy buyers to determine if heavy buyers are more loyal buyers.

## Interrelationship of Response Variables

In Figure 1, it will be seen that we have ordered the five response variables to create a hierarchy. The hierarchy is similar to the variety of hierarchies used in practice such as AIDA (Attention, Interest, Desire and Action), to the Lavidge and Steiner hierarchy of advertising effectiveness,[17] as well as to the different mental states that a person is alleged by the anthropologists and sociologists to pass through when he adopts an innovation.[18] There are, however, some important differences which we believe will clarify certain conceptual and methodological issues raised by Palda and others.[19]

First, we have added a response variable called Attention which is crucial since it reflects whether a communication is received by the buyer. Secondly, several different aspects of the cognitive realm of behavior such as awareness, recall, recognition, etc. are lumped into one category called Comprehension to suggest that they all are varying indicators of the buyer's storage of information about a brand which can be extended to *product class*, and in this way we obtain leverage toward understanding buyer innovation. Third, we have defined Attitude to include both affective and conative aspects since any one who wants to establish causal relations between attitude and behavior must bring the motivational aspects into attitude. Furthermore, we separate the perceptual and the preference maps of the buyer into Comprehension and Attitude respectively. Fourth, we add another variable, Intention to Buy, because there are several product classes in both durable and semi-durable goods where properly defined and measured intentions have already proved useful. To the extent that Intention incorporates the buyer's forecast of his inhibitors, it might serve the useful function of informing the firm how to remove the inhibitors before the actual purchase behavior is manifested.

Finally, and most importantly, we have incorporated several feedback effects which were described when we discussed the hypothetical constructs. We will now show the relations as direct connections among response variables but the reader should bear in mind that these "outside" relations are merely the reflection of relations among the hypothetical constructs. For example, Purchase Behavior via Satisfaction entails some consequences which affect Decision Mediators and brand potential in Evoked Set; any change in them can produce change in Predisposition. Attitude is related to Predisposition and, therefore, it can also be changed in the period from pre-purchase to post-purchase. In incorporating this feedback, we are opening the way to resolving the controversy whether attitude causes purchase behavior or purchase behavior causes attitude. Over a period of time, the relation is interdependent, each affecting the other. Similarly, we have a feedback from Attitude to comprehension and Attention, the rationale for which was given when we described the perceptual constructs.

## Dynamics of Buying Behavior

Let us now explain the changes in the hypothetical constructs which occur due to learning.

The learning constructs are, of course, directly involved in the change that we label "learning." Since some of the learning constructs indirectly govern the perceptual constructs by way of feedbacks, there is also an indirect effect back upon the learning constructs themselves. As mentioned earlier, learning of Decision Mediators which structure Motives and Evoked Set of Brands which contain brand potentials, can occur from two broad sources: (i) past experience and (ii) information. Experience can be further classified as having been derived from buying a specified product or buying some similar product. Similarly, information can come from the buyer's commercial environment or his social environment, and if commercial, it can be significative or symbolic.

We will look at the development and change in learning constructs as due to: (i) generalization from similar buying situations, (ii) repeat buying of the same product class, and (iii) information.

### Generalization from Similar Purchase Situations

Some decision mediators are common across several product classes because many motives are common to a wide variety of purchasing activity. For example, a buyer may satisfy his health motive from many product classes by looking for nutrition. Similarly, many product classes are all bought at the same place which very often leads to spatial or contiguous generalization. The capacity to generalize provides the buyer with a truly enormous range of flexibility in adapting his purchase behavior to the myraid of varying market conditions he faces.

Generalization refers to the transfer of responses and of the relevance of stimuli from past situations to new situations which are similar. It saves the buyer time and effort in seeking information in the face of uncertainty that is inevitable in a new situation. Generalization can occur at any one of the several levels of purchase activity, but we are primarily interested in generalization of those decision mediators which only involve brand choice behavior in contrast to store choice or choice of shopping time and day. In other words, we are concerned with brand generalization.

## Repeat Purchase Experiences

Another source of change in the learning constructs is the repeated purchase of the same product class over a period of time.

In Figure 1 the purchase of a brand entails two types of feedbacks, one affecting the decision mediators and the other affecting the brand potential of the evoked set. First, the experience of buying with all its cognitive aspects of memory, reasoning, etc. has a learning effect on the decision mediators. This occurs irrespective of which specific brand the buyer chooses in any one purchase decision because the decision mediators like the motives are product-specific and not limited to any one brand. Hence every purchase has an incremental effect in firmly establishing the decision mediators. This is easy to visualize if we remember that buying behavior is a series of mental and motor steps while the actual choice is only its terminal act.

Purchase of a brand creates certain satisfactions for the buyer which the consumer compares with his expectations of the brand's potential and this expectation is the basis on which he made his decision in the first place. This comparison of expected and actual consequences causes him to be satisfied or dissatisfied with his purchase of the brand. Hence, the second feedback from Purchase Behavior to Satisfaction changes the attractiveness of the brand purchased. If the buyer is satisfied with his consumption, he enhances the potential of the brand and this is likely to result in greater probability of its repeat purchase. If he is dissatisfied, the potential of the brand is diminished, and its probability of repeat purchase is also similarly reduced.

If there are no inhibitory forces which influence him, the buyer will continue to buy a brand which proves satisfactory. In the initial stages of decision-making he may show some tendency to oscillate between brands in order to formulate his decision mediators. In other words, he may learn by trial-and-error at first and then settle on a brand and thereafter, he may buy the brand with such regularity to suggest that he is brand loyal. Unless a product is of very high risk, however, there is a limit as to how long this brand loyalty will continue: he may become bored with his preferred brand and look for something new.

## Information as a Source of Learning

The third major source by which the learning constructs are changed is information from the buyer's (i) commercial environment consisting of advertising, promotion, salesmanship and retail shelf display of the competing companies, and (ii) his social environment consisting of his family, friends, reference group and social class.

We will describe the influence of information at first as if the perceptual constructs were absent. In other words, we assume that the buyer receives information with perfect fidelity as it exists in the environment. Also, we will discuss separately the information from the commercial and social environments.

## COMMERCIAL ENVIRONMENT

The company communicates about its offerings to the buyers either by the physical brand (significates) or by symbols (pictorial or linguistic) which represent the brand. In other words, significative and symbolic communication are the two major ways of interaction between the sellers and the buyers.

In Figure 1, the influence of information is shown on Motives, Decision Mediators, Evoked Set, and Inhibitors. We believe that the influence of commercial information on motives (specific and nonspecific) is limited. The main effect is primarily to *intensify* whatever motives the buyer has rather than to create new ones. For example, physical display of the brand may intensify his motives above the threshold level which combined with strong predisposition can result in impulse (unplanned) purchase. A similar reaction is possible when an ad creates sufficient intensity of motives to provide an impetus for the buyer to go to the store. A second way to influence motives is to show the *perceived instrumentality* of the brand and thereby make it a part of the buyer's defined set of alternatives. Finally, to a very limited extent, marketing stimuli may change the *content of the motives*. The general conception both among marketing men and laymen is that marketing stimuli change the buyer's motives. However, on a closer examination it would appear that what is changed is the *intensity* of buyer's motives already provided by the social environment. Many dormant or latent motives may become stimulated. The secret of success very often lies in identifying the change in motives created by social change and intensifying them as seems to be the case in the recent projection of youthfulness in many buying situations.

Marketing stimuli are also important in determining and changing the buyer's evoked set. Commercial information tells him of the existence of the brands (awareness), their identifying characteristics (Comprehension plus brand name) and their relevance to the satisfaction of the buyer's needs (Attitude).

Marketing stimuli are also important in creating and changing the buyer's decision mediators. They become important sources for learning decision mediators when the buyer has no prior experience to rely upon. In other words, when he is in the extensive problem solving (EPS) stage, it is marketing and social stimuli which are the important sources of learning. Similarly, when the buyer actively seeks information because all the existing alternatives are unacceptable to him, marketing stimuli become important in *changing* his decision mediators.

Finally, marketing stimuli can unwittingly create inhibitors. For example, a company feels the need to emphasize price-quality association, but it may result in high-price inhibition in the mind of the buyer. Similarly, in emphasizing the details of usage and consumption of a product, the communication may create the inhibition related to time pressure.

## Social Environment

The social environment of the buyer—family, friends, reference groups—is another major source of information in his buying behavior. Most of the inputs are likely to be symbolic (linguistic) although at times the physical product may be shown to the buyer.

Information from his social environment also affects the four learning constructs: Motives, Decision Mediators, Evoked Set and Inhibitors. However, the effect on these constructs is different from that of the commercial environment. First, the information about the brands will be considerably modified by the social environment before it reaches the buyer. Most of the modifications are likely to be in the nature of adding connotative meanings to brand descriptions, and of the biasing effects of the communication's perceptual variables like Sensitivity to Information and Perceptual Bias. Second, the buyer's social environment will probably have a very strong influence on the content of his motives and their ordering to establish a goal structure. Several research studies have concentrated on such influences.[20] Third, the social environment may also affect his evoked set. This will be particularly true when the buyer lacks experience. Furthermore, if the product class is important to the buyer and he is technically incompetent or uncertain in evaluating the consequences of the brand for his needs, he may rely more on the social than on the marketing environment for information. This is well documented by several studies using the perceived risk hypothesis.[21]

## Exogenous Variables

Earlier we mentioned that there are several influences operating on the buyer's decisions which we treat as exogenous, that is, we do not explain their formation and change. Many of these influences come from the buyer's social environment and we wish to separate the effects of his environment which has occurred in the past and not related to a specific decision from those which are current and directly affect the decisions that occur during the period the buyer is being observed. The inputs during the observation period provide information to the buyer to help his current decision-making. The past influences are already imbedded in the values of the perceptual and learning constructs. Strictly speaking, therefore, there is no need for some of the exogenous variables which have influenced the buyer in the past. We bring them out explicitly, however, for the sake of research design where the researcher may control or take into account individual differences among buyers due to such past influences. Incorporating the effects of these exogenous variables will reduce the size of the unexplained variance or error in estimation which it is particularly essential to control under field conditions. Figure 1 presents a set of exogenous variables which we believe provide the control essential to obtaining satisfactory predictive relations between the inputs and the outputs of the system. Let us briefly discuss each of the exogenous variables.

*Importance of Purchase* refers to differential degrees of ego-involvement or commitment in different product classes. It, therefore, provides a mechanism which must be carefully examined in inter-product studies. Importance of Purchase will influence the size of the Evoked Set and the magnitude of Search for Information. The more important the product class, the larger the Evoked set.[22]

*Time Pressure* is a current exogenous variable and, therefore, specific to a decision situation. It refers to the situation when a buyer feels pressed for time due to any of several environmental influences and so must allocate his time among alternative uses. In this process a re-allocation unfavorable to the purchasing activity can ocurr. Time pressure will create Inhibition as mentioned earlier. It will also unfavorably affect Search for Information.

*Financial Status* refers to the constraint the buyer may feel because of lack of financial resources. This affects his purchase behavior to the extent that it creates a barrier to purchasing the most preferred brand. For example, a buyer may want to purchase a Mercedes-Benz but lacks sufficient financial resources and therefore, he will settle for some low-priced American automobile such as a Ford or Chevrolet. Its effect is via Inhibitor.

*Personality Traits* take into consideration many of the variables such as self-confidence, self-esteem, authoritarianism and anxiety which have been researched to identify individual differences. It will be noted that these individual differences are ''topic free'' and, therefore, are supposed to exert their effect across product classes. We believe their effect is felt on: (i) non-specific Motives and (ii) Evoked Set. For example, the more anxious a person, the greater the motivational arousal; dominant personalities are more likely by a small margin to buy a Ford instead of a Chevrolet; the more authoritarian a person, the narrower the category width of his evoked set.

*Social and Organizational Setting* (Organization) takes us to the group, to a higher level of social organization than the individual. It includes both the informal social organization such as family and reference groups which are relevant for *consumer behavior* and the formal organization which constitutes much of the environment for *industrial purchasing*. Organizational variables are those of small group interaction such as power, status and authority. We believe that the underlying process of intergroup conflicts in both industrial and consumer buying behavior are in principle very similar, and that the differences are largely due to the formalization of industrial activity. Organization, both formal and social, is a crucial variable because it influences all the learning constructs.

*Social Class* refers to a still higher level of social organization, the social aggregate. Several indices are available to classify people into various classes. The most common perhaps is the Warner classification of people into upper-upper, lower-upper, upper-middle, lower-middle, upper-lower, and lower-lower classes. Social class mediates the relation between the input and the output by influencing: (i) specific Motives, (ii) Decision Mediators, (iii) Evoked Set, and (iv) Inhibitors. The latter influence is important particularly in the adoption of innovations.

*Culture* provides an even more comprehensive social framework than social class. Culture consists of patterns of behavior, symbols, ideas and their attached values. Culture will influence Motives, Decision Mediators, and Inhibitors.

## CONCLUSIONS

In the preceding pages we have summarized a theory of buyer brand choice. It is complex. We strongly believe that complexity is essential to adequately describe buying behavior, from the point of view of both marketing practice and public policy.

We hope that the theory can provide new insights into past empirical data and to guide future research so as to instill with coherence and unity current research which now tends to be atomistic and unrelated. We are vigorously pursuing a large research program aimed at testing the validity of the theory. The research was designed in terms of the variables specified by the theory, and our most preliminary results causes us to believe that it was fruitful to use the theory in this way. Because it specifies a number of relationships, it has clearly been useful in interpreting the preliminary findings. Above all, it is an aid in communication among the researchers and with the companies involved.

Finally, a number of new ideas are set forth in the theory, but we would like to call attention to three in particular. The concept of evoked set provides a means of reducing the noise in many analyses of buying behavior. The product class concept offers a new dimension for incorporating many of the complexities of innovations and especially for integrating systematically the idea of innovation into a framework of psychological constructs. Anthropologists and sociologists have been pretty much content to deal with peripheral variables in their investigations of innovation. The habit-perception cycle in which perception and habit respond inversely offers hope for explaining a large proportion of the phenomenon that has long baffled both the critics and defenders of advertising: large advertising expenditures in a stable market where, on the surface, it would seem that people are already sated with information.

## ENDNOTES

1. Theodore Levitt *Innovation in Marketing: New Perspectives for Growth* (New York: McGraw-Hill Book Company, 1962).
2. Jack B. McKitterick "What is the Marketing Management Concept?" in Frank M. Bass (ed.) *The Frontiers of Marketing Thought and Science* (Chicago: American Marketing Association, 1957), pp. 71-82.
3. George Katona *The Powerful Consumer* (New York: McGraw-Hill Book Company, 1960).
4. John A. Howard *Marketing Theory* (Boston: Allyn and Bacon, 1965), Chapter 1.
5. Lester Guest "Consumer Analysis" *Annual Review of Psychology* Vol. 13 (1962), pp. 315-344; Frederick May, "Buying Behavior: Some Research Findings" *Journal of Business* (October 1965), pp. 379-396; Dik Warren Twedt, "Consumer Psychology" *Annual Review of Psychology* Vol. 16 (1965), pp. 265-294; Jagdish N. Sheth, "A Review of Buyer Behavior" *Management Science* Vol. 13 (August 1967), pp. B718-B756.
6. Jagdish N. Sheth, *op. cit.*, p. B 742.
7. Musafer Sherif and Carolyn Sherif "Interdisciplinary Coordination as a Validity Check: Retrospect and Prospects" in M. Sherif (ed.) *Problems of Interdisciplinary Relationships in the Social Sciences* (Aldine Publishing Company, to be published in 1968).
8. William J. McGuire "Some Impending Reorientations in Social Psychology" *Journal of Experimental Social Psychology* Vol. 3 (1967), pp. 124-139.
9. Patrick Suppes *Information Processing and Choice Behavior* (Technical Paper No. 9: Institute for Mathematical Studies in the Social Sciences, Stanford University, January 31, 1966), p. 27.
10. John A. Howard *Marketing Management* (Revised edition ,R. D. Irwin, Inc., 1963); J. A. Howard, *Marketing: Executive and Buyer Behavior* (Columbia University Press, 1963).
11. James G. March and Herbert A. Simon *Organizations* (New York: John Wiley & Sons, 1958).
12. Terminology in a problem area that cuts across both economics and psychology is different because each discipline has often defined its terms differently from the other. We find the economist's definitions of oxogenous versus endogenous, and theory versus model more useful than those of the psychologist. The psychologists's distinction of hypothetical constructs and intervening variables, however, provides a helpful breakdown of endogenous variables. Finally, for the sake of exposition we have often here not clearly distinguished between the theory and its empirical counterparts. Although this practice encourages certain ambiguities, and we lay ourselves open to the charge of reifying our theory, we believe that for most readers it will simplify the task of comprehending the material.
13. Clark C. Hull *Principles of Behavior* (New York: Appleton-Century-Crofts, Inc., 1943); Clark C. Hull *A Behavior System* (New Haven: Yale University Press, 1952).
14. Charles E. Osgood "A Behavioristic Analysis of Perception and Meaning as Cognitive Phenomena" in *Symposium on Cognition, University of Colorado,*

*1955* (Cambridge, Harvard University Press, 1957), pp. 75-119; Charles E. Osgood "Motivational Dynamics of Language Behavior" in J. R. Jones (ed.) *Nebraska Symposium on Motivation*, 1957 (Lincoln: University of Nebraska Press, 1957), pp. 348-423.

15. D. E. Berlyn "Motivational Problems Raised by Exploratory and Epistemic Behavior" in Sigmund Koch (ed.) *Psychology: A Study of a Science* Vol. 5 (New York: Mc-Graw-Hill Book Company, 1963).
16. Rosser Reeves *Reality in Advertising* New York (Alfred A. Knopf, Inc., 1961).
17. J. S. Brown *The Motivation of Behavior* (New York: Mc-Graw-Hill Book Company, 1961).
18. George S. Day "Buyer Attitudes and Brand Choice Behavior" (unpublished Ph. D. Dissertation, Graduate School of Business, Columbia University, 1967).
19. Berlyne, *op. cit.*
20. S. Feldman (ed.) *Cognitive Consistency: Motivational Antecedents and Behavioral Consequents* (Academic Press, 1966); Martin Fishbein (ed.) *Readings in Attitude Theory and Measurement* (New York: John Wiley & Sons, 1967).
21. Thomas F. Juster *Anticipations and Purchases: An Analysis of Consumer Behavior* (Princeton University Press, 1964).

# 31 —— Theory Development in Consumer Buying Behavior

*Peter D. Bennett*

Reprinted by permission of the publisher from Chapter 1, "Theory Development in Consumer Buying Behavior," by Peter D. Bennett, *Consumer and Industrial Buying Behavior,* edited by Woodside, Sheth, and Bennett, pp. 3-15. Copyright 1977 by Elsevier Science Publishing Co., Inc.

Scientific disciplines, like people, can be found in a wide variety of ages and stages of development. A field of study that aspires to be a scientific discipline, however, must be guided by an approach to scientific inquiry upon which scholars in the field are in significant agreement. The philosophy of science abounds with valuable guides to such inquiry (cf. Popper 1961; Kaplan 1964; Nagel 1961).

Most science philosophies are "handed down" from the advanced disciplines (predominantly physics) to the less mature ones. The developing disciplines rightly adjust and adapt procedures and methods to fit their own field of inquiry, in light of its specific needs, stage of development, and phenomena under investigation. This chapter presents a brief version of such an adaptation to the domain of consumer behavior.

In recent years, others (e.g., Zaltman *et al.*, 1973; Hunt 1976) have produced treatises on theory development in marketing or consumer behavior, often under the rubric of "metatheory." This chapter presents a somewhat different approach. It is both a loving and critical comment on the thought-provoking presidential address by Jacoby (1976) at the fall 1975 conference of the Association for Consumer Research.

Anyone treating the subject would agree that its central importance to our discipline lies largely in the fact that theory is enormously practical. So when scholars engage in theory building, they are being quite practical. The term theory building is chosen from Dubin (1969, p. 3) because

> ... It symbolizes the always present goal of scientists' activities. Their task is to build viable models of the empirical world that can be comprehended by the human mind. These theoretical models are intensely practical, for the predictions derived from them are the grounds on which modern man is increasingly ordering his relationships with the environing universe.

For centuries, time, effort, energy and even lives were expended trying to build flying machines that flapped their wings like birds. But shortly after we developed a dependable theory with its ''law of aero-dynamics lift over an air-foil'' man was able to fly.

## The Purposes of Theory

Although there are various purposes, or goals, of theory that we could all agree on and others which we would not, the essence of theory may be captured by recognizing that it has two legitimate end (or ultimate) goals—*prediction* and *understanding*. Theories are of value because they provide us with an understanding of the phenomena in question. Dubin has referred to what he calls ''the power paradox'' of theories. This paradox is well illustrated in two sets of theories familiar to most scholars of consumer behavior. The Bush and Mosteller (1955) type learning theory, may be compared to the learning theory of Clark Hull (1943); or, compare Kuehn's (1958) theory of brand choice with that of Howard and Sheth (1969).

''The power of paradox may be summarized as follows: A theoretical model that focuses on the analysis of process of interaction,'' such as that of Hull or of Howard and Sheth, ''may contribute significantly to understanding.'' But ''understanding of process when achieved does not *necessarily* provide the basis for accuracy of prediction about the reality being modeled by the theoretical system'' (Dubin 1969, p. 23).

On the other hand, the theory may have relatively high predictive power, as with Bush and Mosteller or Kuehn, and this high may be independent of any understanding of the process producing the outcome forecast. In short, powerful understanding does not guarantee precision in prediction, and precision in prediction may be possible without any real understanding of the process.

I am convinced that consumer behavior has recently been challenged by a serious alternative to much of our theory building in Frank Bass's (1974) stochastic theory of consumer behavior. We must admit that much of what Bass says about our attempts to build deterministic theories contains some validity and calls for a better response than we have seen thus far.

Bass argues that there is a significant stochastic element in consumer choice behavior, and he is correct. Yet his use of predictive power as a criterion for judging deterministic theory, at the expense of understanding the phenomena we are studying, must be questioned. There are several ways that theory which explains or adds understanding has value even if its predictive power is rather poor.

First, it serves to limit the domain, by distinguishing a realm of phenomena. A theory of primary group behavior has value in not explaining secondary group behavior. A theory of consumer behavior has value in drawing the limits of its domain, such as omitting sexual behavior. A two-person zero sum game tells us we need to look further for an explanation of n-person or nonzero sum games.

The second value of theory is that it serves to simplify or reduce the complexity of the phenomena in question. By turning realistic but mysterious chaos into unrealistic but understandable order, the theory provides understanding even though it may simultaneously limit its predictive value. Third, a theory may provide understanding of a full range of phenomena that may never be directly observable because they never actually exist. An example of this is the extreme case of disconfirmation of consumer expectations recently reported by Olson and Dover (1976). Although their manipulation of expectations and subsequent disconfirmation rarely, if ever, exist in the real world of consumer marketing, they demonstrate how theory can deal with broad ranges of such variables. Much of the work on fear appeals provides another such example.

## THE STRUCTURE OF THEORY

It is perhaps most instructive to define theory as consisting both of a *morphology* (or form) and a *mechanism*. Its morphology is an inclusive list of *constructs*, which may be variables, or constants, or simply nominal categories. Its mechanisms are its lists of *functional relationships* among the constructs.

Before exploring these two central aspects for understanding the structure of theory, it might be useful to redefine theory. The logical rules of both theory and theology are very similar. The crucial difference between the two lies in the attitude toward truth content. A theological model is presented as fixed, absolute, true, and therefore not requiring tests of its truth. To attempt to test a theological model is properly labeled blasphemy because it is a form of implicit or explicit rejection of faith in the truth of the model. Thus the truth of a theological model rests on the faith of those who accept it. Even the most modern theologians of the existential school agree with Kierkegaard that their theology requires a leap of faith. A theory, on the other hand, is clothed in uncertainty about those who act according to its predictions. Such individuals are not taken wholly by surprise when the theory does not work out in practice.

The morphology of a theory is the constructs it contains. A legitimate, even necessary, first step in theory building is the taxonomical one: the specification and classification of the constructs of which the theory is built. When Rostow (1962) invented the classification scheme delineating the levels of economic development, for example, he was creating the morphology of a theory. Freud did the same thing when he distinguished the ego from the id and both of them from the superego. Cohen and Barban (1970) were doing this when they developed a taxonomy of consumer types and a taxonomy of products on the basis of consumer responses to them.

In the process of theory building, we may find it useful to divide and subdivide, and yet further subdivide, as when we separate male from female, or young from old, or married from single, and wind up with a typology of units such as "young married males," "old single females," and so on.

An important thing to remember, especially as it affects workers in the behavioral disciplines, is that we typically do not focus on the thing itself, but rather on properties of the thing. The thing itself, the person, is simply too complex to comprehend in its totality; simplification results from dealing with its properties. When these properties are expressed in various degrees, they are called variables. An obvious example is a person's age. When it is not meaningful to express the property in degree but rather as either existing or not existing, they are simply termed attributes. To categorize situations as "straight rebuys," "modified rebuys" and "new tasks" (Webster & Wind 1972) is to deal with attributes of the industrial purchasing process. Both variables and attributes have their legitimate place in theory.

There are a number of possible schemes for classifying the constructs that make up the morphology of a theory. It is especially valuable to distinguish among *real, nominal* and *summative* constructs (Dubin 1969). Real constructs are those for which we either have or are able to create measurement devices, or empirical indicators.

Nominal constructs, on the other hand, are those for which we do not presently, have empirical indicators. They may be quite valuable, however, because they have meaning and can be useful in tying together the theory as a whole. They also have the potentital to become real constructs. For example, from its first appearance in 1963, a crucial and intriguing concept in Howard's theory of buyer behavior (Howard, 1963) is that of the "evoked set." Although the evoked set was once a nominal construct for which there did not appear to be any ready measuring device, it was not less important to the theory. Subsequently, of course, empirical indicators have been developed so that we may count the evoked set among the real constructs (cf. Campbell 1967).

A third type, the summative construct, is a global unit that stands for an entire complex of things. If a sociologist speaks of "the mass society," or an economist of an "underdeveloped economy," they are using summative units. Theory builders have, at times, attempted to construct entire theories from this kind of unit, although they have no legitimate place in theory. Yet they may be useful as frames of reference, that is, as an educational device designed to orient a layman or a student to a field of inquiry. Although they may be legitimate for pedagogical purposes, frames of reference are not theories.

All the foregoing involves operationalism. Consider the following familiar quotation attributed to Lord Kelvin:

> When you cannot measure what you are speaking about; when you cannot express it in numbers; your knowledge is of a meagre and unsatisfactory kind.

This statement, regardless of its popularity, is both wrongheaded and potentially dangerous. It makes the mistake of confusing precision of the constructs employed in theory with their analytical power. As was stated earlier, attributes can be as powerful as variables, sometimes even more so. Nominal constructs, likewise, may be as useful as real constructs.

Bergmann's (1957) perspective is most instructive. He emphasizes that when a model is being tested empirically, those constructs composing the model and involved in the proposition being tested must be measured by some kind of empirical indicator to determine their value. He insists, however, that empirical indicators are only necessary when the proposition is subjected to the test; not before. The central importance of operationalism relates to the empirical test of a proposition and not to the formulation of a model from which the proposition is derived. It is quite legitimate that our theories retain constructs such as "choice criteria," "perceptual bias," "evaluative criteria," "internal search," and even "problem recognition." There is no logic that insists that only those models whose propositions are all testable should be employed in our theories.

In summary, the issue for the working researcher is not to insist that theories contain only real constructs. It is rather to require that the structure of theories be clearly understood so that the functions of nominal constructs in them will be readily recognized. It is true that empirical tests are made only of real units and their interactions. It is equally true that in order to be complete, theories often contain nominal units that are presently beyond empirical approach, but are essential to the theory. Their importance is that knowledge about the real constructs and their behavior increases when the nominal constructs are included in the theory.

## Functional Relationships

Let us turn now to the mechanism of theory. Constructs are not theories, and the complete list of concepts that contains the subject matter of a discipline does not constitute the theory of that discipline. It is only when these units are combined into models of the perceived world that we have theories. In Bergmann's (1957, p. 50) view, there is a difference between truth and significance.

> A concept is neither true nor false, only propositions are. A concept is neither valid nor invalid, only arguments are. Yet there is distinction of "good" and "bad" among defined descriptive concepts. To have a name for it I shall say that a concept either is or is not *significant*. A concept is significant if and only if it occurs, together with others, in statements of lawfulness which we have reason to believe are true.

These "statements of lawfulness," or functional relationships, are the mechanism of a theory. They stand in contrast to the constructs, or concepts which are the morphology of a theory. For the sake of brevity we will use the word "law," despite the semantic confusion in the various philosophies of science, to mean the specification of interaction among units of theory.

Laws, like constructs, are of various kinds, and it will be useful to describe three kinds of laws employed in theory building. The first is a *categoric law* of interaction, which simply states that values of one unit are associated with values of another. The association is in the form of the presence or absence of the respective values of the two units. These laws say little more than that two units are related in some way.

Categoric laws are typically of the lowest efficiency level. Lawlike statements can be made about consumers' counterarguing behavior (Bither and Miller 1969) in the presence or absence of inoculation, or in the Howard and Sheth theory of the relationship between the constructs "motive" and "perceptual bias."

For this reason, categoric laws are symmetrical. It does not matter whether one or the other of the units comes first in the statement of the law. Thus we are able to deal with these lawlike relationships without getting into the issue of causality. We need not be overly concerned with whether the state of our motives causes certain perceptual biases or whether certain perceptual biases cause certain changes in motives to say they are related.

A second type of lawlike relationship between the units of a theory is a *sequential law*. This is a law of interaction that always includes a time dimension. A statement concerning consumer attitude change following a disconfirmation of expectations is a clear example. Again, referring to Howard and Sheth as a source for an example, there is a unit in that theory called "purchase" and another termed "satisfaction," and these are related by lawlike statements, or functional relationships that are examples of what is meant by sequential law. These are closely analogous to special cases of the relationships of the reinforcement learning theories from which they borrow heavily. In Howard and Sheth, purchase always precedes satisfaction; in Hull, response precedes reinforcement. It should be stressed again that there is no particular claim in this case to cause and effect, only that the two units are related in a time-determined fashion. Thus, sequential laws are asymmetrical; the asymmetry being time determined.

The third kind of law is *determinant law*. This associates determinant values of one construct with determinant values of another. Reilly's Law of Retail Gravitation (Reilly 1929) is a form of determinant law. This law states that the limit of one city's trading area in miles toward another city is equal to the distance between the two cities divided by one plus the square root of the population ratio of the two cities. Boyle's law states that under conditions of constant temperature the volume of a gas is inversely proportional to the pressure bearing upon the gas. The essential feature is that the values of the two units are paired, so that for each value of the first unit we have a corresponding value of the second unit (or of other units if we are dealing with more than two) and that these associated values are invariantly linked. The most common characteristic of a determinant law is that it may be drawn as a line, a curve, a plane, a surface, and is generally subject to the full range of the laws of logic or mathematics.

While categoric laws remain typically at the lowest efficiency levels, sequential and determinant laws may reach any level of efficiency. Dubin (1969) states: "By efficiency of a law is meant the range of variability of the values of one unit when they are related by a law to values of another unit" (p. 110). Or, in how narrow a range can we estimate the parameters of a model?

These laws can increase in efficiency above the presence/absence statement of categoric laws to a higher level of directionality. For example, the level of affect or cohesiveness of a group increases with the frequency of interaction of the group. Or brand loyalty increases with increased ego involvement in the product class. An even higher level is a law that claims that directionality follows a particular shape, as that encountered in classical learning curves or stochastic theories of brand choice. At the highest level of efficiency, laws are expressed in the rate of change in the values of one variable and the associated rate of change in the values of another.

## A Note on Causality

The notion of cause and effect is a particularly knotty issue in the philosophy of science. In his recent address, Jacoby (1976) exhorted us toward work to demonstrate causality as a justification for his own bias toward experimental as opposed to correlational methodologies. He pointed out that "no matter how highly correlated the rooster's crow is to the sun rising, the rooster does not cause the sun to rise" (Jacoby 1976, p. 5). Assistance from some colleagues in a rather remote sister discipline, Poultry Science, can help us see both the value and the danger in such a concern for developing causal laws in our theories.

Cocks crow when the sun comes up. Without further research, experimental or otherwise, we would all agree that the cock's crow does not cause the sun to rise. It helps to add that cocks do not crow in the dark, but that they will crow in the middle of the night when subjected to artificial light. Research also shows that when exposed to light, after a period of darkness, the cock's pituitary gland secretes a hormone associated with the crowing behavior. Further, artificial methods of getting that hormone into the system are also related to the same behavior. Since the invention of the alarm clock, the practical significance of all this is not apparent. However, a similar process exists in the female. When exposed to light, the hen's body secretes a similar hormone, and the presence of that hormone is associated with egg-laying behavior. A consumer concerned about the price of eggs or a chicken farmer concerned with production rates, knows that a theory of egg-laying behavior can be practical.

Some philosophers of science (e.g., Dubin) would go so far as to argue that there is no value at all in being able to call a law that connects two constructs (sunrise and crowing behavior) a causal law rather than simply a law of interaction. Their central argument is that laws are not measured, constructs are measured. Surely laws can reach higher levels of efficiency and become sequential laws, but it is dangerous to label them causal laws.

They argue, rightly it seems, that labeling laws in this fashion does not improve the predictive value of the theory. They are on weaker ground when we consider the explanatory value of theory. So while it is difficult to agree with that extreme position, we should be aware of one crucial danger, jumping too soon to a causal law, as in saying that the rising sun causes crowing or laying behavior. Perhaps the danger lies in not separating the light of the sunrise from constructs such as heat or ultraviolet rays. Or it might have prohibited us from isolating the pituitary from other glands, or the particular hormone from others. In short, thinking we have found a causal law may halt the search for meaningful intervening variables. Actually, there may be additional intervening variables between the hormone and the crowing/laying behavior. In the early stages of theory development (where consumer behavior students now find themselves), this danger may far outweigh the value of calling a law causal.

## The Task of Consumer Behavior Scholars

Finally, to deal with two parallel issues, I will present an admittedly incomplete set of important tasks for consumer behavior scholars, and comment on how this community of scholars has responded to such tasks. The latter discussion is offered in the same spirit as Jacoby's (1976)—''as I see it.''

### Build Theoretical Models

One obvious task is to build and clearly articulate theoretical models of the phenomena that comprise the subject matter of our discipline. Such models appear to live on different levels of comprehensiveness. At one extreme are global models, which usually have two major characteristics: they have almost boundless domains and are built largely with summative constructs which, we have argued, have no legitimate place in theory building.

At the other extreme are the fragments of theory, which have highly proscribed domains and limited numbers of constructs and laws of interaction. Somewhere between these extremes are what Merton (1949) calls ''theories of the middle range,'' which he described as having neither too few nor too many boundary determining criteria (leaving it to our judgment in consumer behavior what ''too few'' and ''too many'' mean, although he presented such judgments for sociology).

We are fortunate not to have been cursed with too many global models which, with their profusion of nonoperational summative constructs, do little to advance the field. True, what we do know about cognitive structure may rate a construct like "brand comprehension" the summative label, but that is more the exception than the rule.

There are several, perhaps too many, theories of the middle range. A couple of these (e.g., Howard & Sheth 1969; Hansen 1972) are fairly well formed and meet the usual criteria for such theories, given the stage of the development of our young discipline. There are also some poorly formed "theories" that seem to have been spurred on by the writing of an undergraduate textbook rather than the kind of theory building suggested here.

At this stage of consumer behavior theory development, we should lean toward tolerance in the development of theories of much narrower domain. Although these "fragments" (as Merton refers to them) may involve a modest number of constructs and perhaps only a single law of interaction, they may become the building blocks of more comprehensive theories. The reader need only peruse this book to encounter examples of these mini-theories.

## Attitude Toward Theory

Our attitude toward theory is extremely important. This applies to theory in general and to consumer behavior theory specifically. Karl Popper said it best: "The proper expectation of scientific research is to disconfirm a theory so that it may be replaced by a better one" (quoted in Dubin 1969, p. viii). Let us look at what happens when we try to prove a theory and when we try to improve it.

The problem with setting about to prove a theory is that certain covert influences may operate on the researcher. Not only may he or she do the obvious and reject experimental results that do not conform to the hypothetical prediction of the theory, but a greater danger exists that he will collect data solely for the constructs incorporated in the original model. Yet another danger is that by attempting to prove the model, either by the research design or by discarding data, values on any given unit used in the study that are beyond the ranges predicted by the model may be excluded from attention.

If, on the other hand, the intent is to improve the model, then opposite influences may operate on the researcher. He is likely to focus particular attention on the deviant cases and on the nonconforming results that do not accord with the predictions made by the model. Insights are derived from the evidence on these deviant cases and later become the basis for improving the extant theory by reformulating it to encompass all cases, even those originally considered deviant.

Another problem with our attitudes toward theory seems especially prevalent in our discipline—to consider theories as belonging to persons, not to the discipline. Unfortunately we are guilty as a group of believing that theories belong to Howard and Sheth, Nicosia, Engel and his associates, Hansen, and so on. It is similar to thinking that macroeconomic theory belongs to Keynes or that the theory of monopolistic competition belongs to Chamberlain or Robinson. Until we outgrow these attitudes, our egos will doom us either to proliferate dozens of theories or to our present reluctance to test and improve our theory. Either of these conditions will only retard our development.

## Communicate with Theory

In addressing this issue recently, under a section titled "Look Ma—No Theory," Jacoby (1976, p. 2) said:

> Despite the availability of theory and the necessity for theory in any scientific endeavor, [we don't use it]. Little reliance is placed on theory either to suggest which variables and aspects of consumer behavior are of greatest importance and in need of research, or as a foundation around which to organize and integrate findings ... While most of us talk a good game about the value and need for theory, it is clear that we would rather be caught dead than using theory.

This problem can be divided into two parts: communication from the theory to the research, and communication from the research results back to the theory. As regards the former, Muzafer Sherif's comments are instructive: "The pious contention, 'Let the facts speak for themselves,' is an absurdity which cannot occur in actual practice, even in the case of empiricism in the raw. Facts are *there*, all right, whether they are studied or not. This is one thing. It is altogether another thing to claim that facts speak for themselves. Without exception, there is always a *selective process* in the collection of data" (Sherif 1966, p. 49). Theory should contribute to that selective process.

Jacoby (1976) quotes a 1972 paper by Kollat and his colleagues, which said, in referring to the major theoretical models of consumer behavior, "... it is rare to find a published study that has utilized, been based on, or even influenced by, any of the models mentioned above" (Kollat et al. 1972). Jacoby then went on to say, "Unfortunately, not much has changed since then."

Now I would like to temper that a bit. My own conclusions toward the end of 1969 (Bennett 1970) were identical, and I might also have used the word "rare" in 1972, but I would have been kinder by fall, 1975. What this is all about, of course, is the *generative* value of theory. That value depends largely on how clearly the constructs and the laws of interaction among them are specified. Much of the improvement that has occurred in recent years can be attributed largely to the improved generative value of Howard and Sheth (1969), Hansen (1972), and the revised version of Engel and coworkers (1973) over the previously published theories.

To avoid any misunderstanding, let me hasten to add that I am referring here to an improvement, rather than a solution, to the problem of basing our research firmly on the theory from which it springs. The substance of the charge still holds. While it cannot be proved, it is probably a safe bet that not one out of five of us who have jumped on the "Fishbein wagon" (Wilkie & Pessemier 1973; Ryan & Bonfield 1975) have ever bothered to go back to read Dulaney (1968).

The other half of the communication process is much worse. Even when research has "utilized, been based on, or influenced by" theory, it is rare indeed to find the researcher reversing the process and speaking about what the research results mean to the theory. We have been particularly lax in this contribution to theory.

There are various ways researchers may contribute to theory. We will mention a few of these kinds of contributions and indicate some examples. Except in very few cases, however, the authors have not stated explicitly how their research has modified and improved the theoretical models they discuss.

## Discovery of Constructs

One contribution to theory is the discovery of new units. There is no more devastating condemnation of another scholar's work than to say it is "purely descriptive." This is nonsense. In every discipline, but particularly in its early stages of development, purely descriptive research is indispensable. A host of true landmark studies have been crucial in delineating the constructs of which theories have been built. Examples are Gunnar Myrdal's *An American Dilemma* (1962), Walt Rostow's *Stages of Economic Growth* (1962), Stouffer's *The American Soldier* (1949), Sherif's work on the autokinetic effect (1935), and Bales's categorization of interactions within small groups (1955). Within our own discipline in the last few years, for example, are the taxonomical work on prepurchase information seeking (Claxton et al. 1974), on situational variables (Belk 1975; Lutz & Kakkar 1975), and on the attitude acquisition process (Olson & Mitchell 1975).

## Construct Validation

Another contribution to theory is the validation of constructs. From among many, we could cite the work on attitudes (Bettman et al. 1975), on confidence (Howard 1973), and on intention (Granbois & Summers 1975).

A third contribution involves converting nominal constructs into real constructs by developing empirical indicators where such indicators do not exist, or by improving the present ones. This may be achieved through selecting the most useful one from among a number of these indicators. For example, morale might be measured by the rate of absenteeism or by using turnover rates. A contribution is made to theory when a researcher is able to indicate which of these two empirical indicators is the most useful measure of the construct, morale. Such improvement may occur when the researcher is able to develop a standard, or broadly applicable empirical indicator for a particular unit or concept. A grave danger lies in the researcher becoming inextricably bound to his measurement instrument—when he contends, for instance, that "intelligence *is* what my test measures." The effect of this conclusion is to insist that the theoretical construct be determined by the empirical indicator, rather than the other way around. It is surprising how frequently this is done in both the behavior sciences and in consumer behavior theory.

Recent examples of this kind of contribution exist in the development of empirical indicators in the consumer behavior domain for such constructs as prepurchase information seeking (Newman & Lockeman, 1975), personality, social class (Jain 1975), innovativeness (Leavitt & Walton 1975), self-actualization (Brooker 1975), and of decision nets in the consumer choice process (Bettman 1974).

The researcher can contribute to theory building by broadening the domain of the theory. Frequently, researchers append to their results the caveat that the empirical conclusions derived apply only to a model with boundary conditions they have specified. This is not an expression of modesty. "It is an affirmative declaration that the empirical investigation extended only up to the boundaries of the theory, or theoretical model, being investigated" (Dubin 1969, p. 137). The domain of a model is the territory over which we are able to make truth statements about the theory and about the constructs composing the theory. It follows that it is useful to extend the domain over which such truth statements can be made. One major domain-extending activity is replication. Kuehn's (1958) model would be of limited usefulness if it held true only for Snow Crop orange juice. The fact that such a model has been replicated has been useful in extending its domain. An editorial in a recent issue of the *Journal of Marketing Research* says in part, "Too often manuscripts tend to replicate earlier studies ..." (Boyd, 1976). This can only serve to discourage a tradition of replication when we should be spurring it on.

Encouraging examples of extending the domain of consumer behavior theory are its carryover into another culture (Farley et al. 1974), into store choice behavior (Monroe & Guiltman 1975) and into voting behavior (Nakanishi et al. 1974).

Yet another thing we can do is to evaluate the theory we have and attack it directly in an attempt to test its unsupported propositions. They are nearly always there and are necessary to the internal consistency of the theory, but are quite often unsupported by available evidence. One *could* go about this process extensively by simultaneously testing all the presently unsupported hypotheses or propositions in a theory. Farley and Ring (1970) have undertaken this approach with the Howard and Sheth theory with limited success.

It is more appropriate to approach this task in an intensive manner by concentrating attention on one or a few strategic propositions in which the particular researcher may have a special interest. For example, a proposition in the Howard-Sheth theory states that prepurchase information-seeking behavior is an inverse function of the learning of brand choice. Being particularly interested in that proposition, which was unsupported by empirical evidence at the time, I began to test it (Bennett & Mandell 1969). It is not immodest to claim that the theory is better for that effort, and an accumulation of many such efforts will result in a much more completely supported theory of buyer behavior.

Other examples of this kind of contribution are another test of the learning-information-seeking hypothesis (Sheth & Venkatesan 1968), of the influence of fear appeals on the attitude-intention linkage (Sternthal & Craig 1974), of the ambiguity-arousal hypothesis derived from Berlyne (1960), (Venkatesan 1973; Copley & Callum 1971), and of the influence of confidence on attitudes and preference (Bennett & Harrell 1975; Olson & Dover 1976).

Although the examples cited above are not exhaustive, to continue longer would tire the reader. In reference again to Jacoby's speech, where he said, "Perhaps those with a new theory or model should treat it like a new product: either stand behind it and give it the support it needs (i.e., test it and refine it as necessary) or take the damn thing off the market!" (Jacoby 1976, p. 3) That seems too harsh. Since the theory of our discipline belongs not to individuals but to the community of scholars, the task of standing behind it, testing it, and refining it as necessary is a task for us all.

This is only one among many prescriptions to which scholars in our community have been exposed. It has attempted to lay out a positive path for those who wish to participate in the development of consumer behavior theory. Its optimistic note stands in contrast to some of the more recent comments on the same subject, asserting that progress is being made in theory development in consumer behavior. The road is long and difficult, but there are signs that some of us are on the road and no longer in the ditch.

# 32 — The Surpluses and Shortages in Consumer Behavior Theory and Research

*Jagdish N. Sheth, Ph.D.*

*Journal of Academy of Marketing Science*,
Vol. 7, No. 4 (Fall 1979), pp. 414-426.
Reprinted by permission.

## Introduction

The purpose of this paper is to take an inventory of consumer behavior theory and research as we end the decade of the seventies. There is no question that consumer behavior as a discipline has displayed a spectacular growth in borrowing concepts from the behavioral and quantitative sciences, in broadening its horizons from traditional marketing problems to social problems, and in generating a body of knowledge about consumers as buyers, users and decision makers (Sheth, 1972; Jacoby, 1975). It is simply a matter of time before consumer behavior will divorce itself from marketing and stand on its own as a distinct discipline relevant to many other constituents besides marketers and many other disciplines beside marketing. Thus, it appears to be an opportune time to take stock of consumer behavior theory and research and assess its surpluses and shortages.

Perhaps the most difficult part of taking an inventory of a growing discipline is to decide on where to begin and how to plan assessing the surpluses and shortages in consumer behavior. After some thinking, I have come up with the following three aspects which seem to provide a simple yet comprehensive approach:

1. *What* has been the focus of understanding in consumer behavior and what should be the future focus?
2. *How* have we researched the consumer behavior phenomenon in the past, and where should we go from here?
3. *Why*, in the past, did we choose to study consumer behavior and what should be the future motivation for our continued interest in the area?

Each of the above three aspects will be examined in some depth which hopefully will reveal what we have sufficiently done and where the deficiencies exist in consumer behavior theory and research.

## Focus of Consumer Behavior Theory and Research

While consumer behavior theory and research may look very eclectic at first glance, two aspects stand out as the common underlying dimensions with which most research efforts seem to be bonded together. The first aspect is the dominance of focus on the *individual consumer* in many of his roles such as shopper, buyer, decision maker and the user. The second aspect is the dominance of decision making process and the consequent implicit, if not explicit presumption that the buying behavior is a rational problem-solving process (Howard and Sheth, 1969; Sheth, 1976). Accordingly, we seem to have abundance of research studies about the individual consumer and about theories of consumer behavior which are based on decision making processes. This is particularly evident in the recent proliferation of multiattribute attitudes, information processing and brand choice models.

By the same token, research studies on dyads and small groups such as families and organizations are limited. Even larger groups such as market segments, social classes and ethnic groups have been studied more in terms of *aggregates* of individual consumers rather than as distinct group entities.

The situations seems to be decidedly worse with respect to analyzing and understanding those consumers and areas of consumer behavior which do not lend themselves to decision making process approaches. For example, the deviant consumer behavior such as shoplifting, the obsessive consumer behavior such as obesity, alcoholism and drug addiction, and the fads and fashion patronage behavior have not been very successfully understood by the rational problem-solving approaches of the decision making tradition.

It is fairly obvious even to a naive observer that not all consumers or all consumer behavior phenomena can be fully explained or understood by a single perspective especially as elegant and rational as the decision making perspective. I believe that we need to bring at least three additional perspectives to fully comprehend the consumer behavior phenomenon. These are (1) habit and conditioning; (2) situationalism; and the (3) novelty-curiosity or epistemic perspective. Hopefully, the three mutually exclusive perspectives will be exhaustive enough to encompass the diversity of consumers and consumer behavior phenomena. It would be most fascinating to generate hard measures of consumer behavior realities with respect to the frequency and magnitude of prevalence of each perspective. My *a priori* hunch is that the decision making perspective may account for a relatively smaller proportion of total consumer behavior phenomena.

Table 1 represents an attempt to summarizing the surpluses and deficiencies with respect to what we have versus what we should focus on in consumer behavior theory and research. What seems to be enough is the decision making framework applied to explain and predict individual consumer

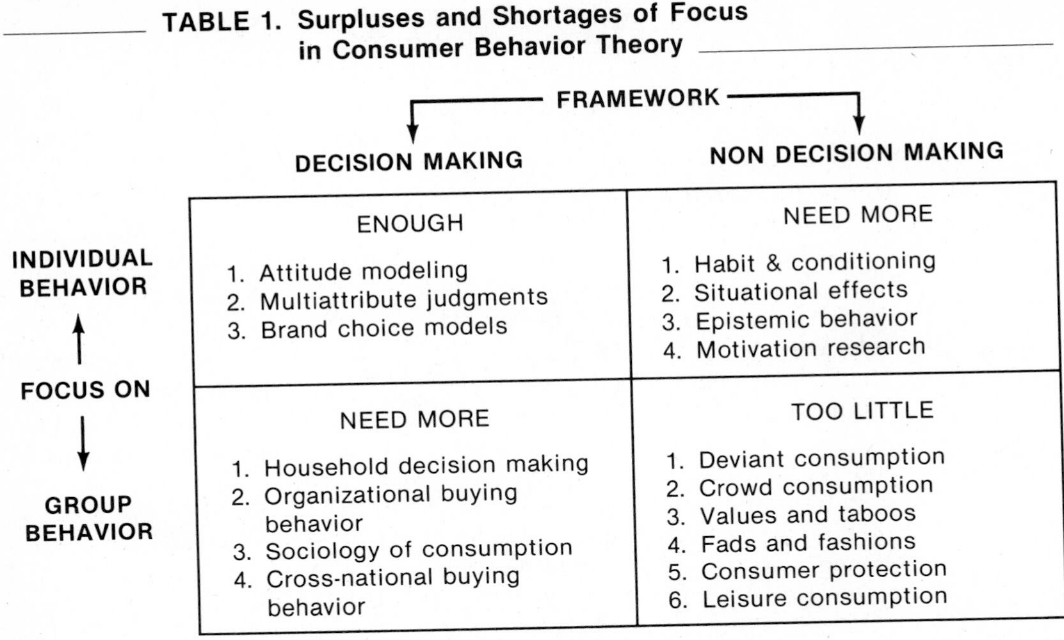

**TABLE 1. Surpluses and Shortages of Focus in Consumer Behavior Theory**

| FOCUS ON \ FRAMEWORK | DECISION MAKING | NON DECISION MAKING |
|---|---|---|
| INDIVIDUAL BEHAVIOR | ENOUGH<br>1. Attitude modeling<br>2. Multiattribute judgments<br>3. Brand choice models | NEED MORE<br>1. Habit & conditioning<br>2. Situational effects<br>3. Epistemic behavior<br>4. Motivation research |
| GROUP BEHAVIOR | NEED MORE<br>1. Household decision making<br>2. Organizational buying behavior<br>3. Sociology of consumption<br>4. Cross-national buying behavior | TOO LITTLE<br>1. Deviant consumption<br>2. Crowd consumption<br>3. Values and taboos<br>4. Fads and fashions<br>5. Consumer protection<br>6. Leisure consumption |

behavior. Two classes of research in this interactive combination are the multiattribute judgments and brand choice models. My own view is what these models now need is more usage and applications by the marketing practitioners and policy makers rather than further theoretical development. Perhaps the applications in real world may provide us insights about the robustness of these models better than deductive reasoning given that the world of social science is more contingent and less absolute to be reduced to some invariant laws of social, economic or consumer behavior.

What we need most because too little consumer research or theory effort has been devoted so far is the opposite interactive combination: understanding group behavior which are likely to be based on non-problem solving processes. Examples of such areas of focus for consumer research include crowd consumption, deviant consumption, fads and fashions and understanding values, taboos, and similar clinical mass motivations. This research should be directed at the *macro* (group) rather than at the *micro* (individual) level.

Of course, the above statements do not imply that there is no further need to study the individual consumers or that the decision making framework has outlived its utility. As the Table indicates, we still need more research and theory about the individual consumer but in the non-decision making domains of his epistemic behavior, impact of situational effects on his choice behavior, the formation, endurance and utilization of habits (affective predispositions to behave) which may or may not have any underlying cognitive structure, and the whole area of motivation research which was disreputed prematurely in the early days of consumer behavior.

Similarly, there are many areas of group behavior which can be understood by the decision making framework, and where more research and theory are clearly needed. These include the more traditional areas of household decision making, organizational buying behavior, and the newer areas of sociology of consumption and cross-national buying behavior. The important point to come in mind is that we need to develop or borrow more *macro* decision making frameworks rather than simply extend the micro decision making frameworks used in understanding individual consumers. For example, recent literature on cultural aggregates, game theory, jury decision processes, and interorganizational conflict, power and coalitions may prove more relevant than the tenets of social psychology.

## Process of Consumer Behavior Theory and Research

The process of theorizing and researching consumer behavior seems to be at least two dimensional. The first dimension reflects the heavy reliance on, and the consequent dominance of descriptive as opposed to normative processes. This is understandable and seems to be due to two reasons. First, we are dealing with very pervasive human or social issues in consumer behavior where it is difficult to impose a common set of normative value-laden judgments or perspectives without being criticized or at least questioned by others. In other words, the descriptive process of finding out how and why consumers behave the way they do and making policy or practice decisions based on these findings seems most reasonable, humanistic, less subject to criticism, and compatible with our belief in the democratic processes. Second, social behavior is too complex and contingent to reduce down to an exact science. It is, therefore, more difficult to generate normative or axiomatic propositions to which all agree and subscribe as they seem to do in biological and physical sciences. While these two factors explain why we might have leaned toward the descriptive processes in consumer behavior, they cannot justify it.

The second dimension related to how we have gone about researching and theorizing the consumer behavior area is the dominance of borrowed concepts and constructs as opposed to generating our own concepts and constructs unique to consumer behavior. The dominance of borrowed versus self-generated constructs can be attributed to several factors. First, the early pioneers in the discipline of consumer behavior made a fundamental presumption that consumer behavior is not unique but part of a larger syndrome of human and social behavior. It is interesting to note that economics did not make a similiar presumption and consequently ended up developing its own constructs and axioms. Second, when a discipline begins to emerge without a formally defined boundary or at best an ill-defined boundary, it is easier to borrow constructs than create them. This seems very much true of consumer behavior; we still do not precisely know what to include and what to exclude from consumer behavior to make it a distinct discipline. Third, pervasiveness of the phenomenon itself may have been a contributing factor: It attracted many scholars from a variety of disciplines such as economics, behavioral sciences, social sciences, marketing, and the quantitative sciences. Consequently, there was no single thrust or driving force comparable to what has been true in the pioneering days of economics and psychology. Multitudes of viewpoints and processes were simultaneously applied to understanding consumer behavior as evidenced from reviews of earlier literature (Sheth, 1967). While this was great for the discipline to get off the ground faster and mature quickly, it ended up in the dominance of using borrowed constructs at the expense of self-generating constructs uniquely suited to the discipline.

Having identified the two process dimensions (descriptive vs. normative and borrowed vs. self-generated constructs), the task of taking inventory of how we developed consumer behavior theory and research is made much easier: There is a clear surplus of borrowed constructs and a critical shortage of self-generating constructs in consumer behavior. Similarly, there is a surplus of descriptive constructs and a shortage of normative constructs. In Table 2, I have provided some examples of the types of research and theory processes in consumer behavior which we must discourage and other types which we must encourage to create a balance of processes of researching in consumer behavior.

First of all, I think we have borrowed enough constructs from several descriptive disciplines. This includes social psychology, personality research, diffusion of innovations, econometric models as well as stochastic models. On the other hand, we badly need to generate our own constructs related to several normative aspects of consumer behavior. These include devloping normative theories of market segmentation, what should be the strategy mix to impact on the consumers without generating negative side effects, how should we protect the consumer *and* which types of consumers, designing anti-consuming policies for certain goods and services, and developing an audit system for measuring consumption indicators which go beyond the recently popular economic and social indicators. The most radical of the proposed areas of future research and theory is the development of marketing policy which would outline rights and obligations of the marketers.

Again, the above analysis does not mean that we should discard descriptive processes altogether or that we should totally stop borrowing constructs from other disciplines. As Table 2 indicates, there are a number of exciting areas of research and theory in consumer behavior which can and should rely upon the descriptive processes. These include self-generating a unique

**TABLE 2. Surpluses and Shortages in the Process of Consumer Behavior Theory & Research**

| | PROCESS: DESCRIPTIVE | PROCESS: NORMATIVE |
|---|---|---|
| BORROWED CONSTRUCTS | ENOUGH<br>1. Social psychology<br>2. Personality research<br>3. Diffusion theories<br>4. Demographics<br>5. Reference Groups<br>6. Stochastic models<br>7. Econometric models | NEED MORE<br>1. Strategies of planned change<br>2. Game Theories<br>3. Mathematical modeling<br>4. Axiomatic modeling |
| ↑ CONSTRUCTS ↓ | | |
| SELF-GENERATED CONSTRUCTS | NEED MORE<br>1. Typology of consumption needs<br>2. Consumption styles<br>3. Consumption life style<br>4. Theory of search behavior<br>5. Stimulus-as-coded<br>6. Product life cycle<br>7. Brand/suplier loyalty<br>8. Consumer satisfaction | TOO LITTLE<br>1. Normative market segmentation<br>2. Strategy mix models<br>3. Consumerism and consumer welfare<br>4. Anti-consuming<br>5. Consumption indicators<br>6. Marketing policy |

typology of consumption needs/wants, a typology of consumption life styles as opposed to general life styles, and consumption life cycle based on the time dependent covariances of preselected and representative goods and services. It also includes more research on self-generated constructs of brand/supplier loyalty, product life cycle theory, and consumer satisfaction/dissatisfaction research. Finally, we badly need self-generated constructs for the phenomena of information search and the process by which marketing stimuli get internalized in the consumer's mind both in the short and in the long-term memory functions. In this last category of research areas, I am more and more convinced that we need to generate our own constructs rather than borrow from cognitive, perceptual and/or neuropsychology. My conviction is based more on the strong differences in definition, size and character of information units between borrowed constructs and what is relevant in consumer behavior.

Lastly, there are several normative disciplines from which we have neglected to borrow in the past, even though they appear to be useful to consumer behavior. These include the policy literature in sociology related to strategies of planned social change, game theory and normative decision theory, mathematical modeling such as queing theory, inventory control theory and critical path analysis for educating and upgrading the household consumer so that he can better optimize his scarce resources of time, effort and money, and finally axiomatic disciplines such as metatheory, microeconomics, and logic. My own forecast is that this type of borrowing of normative constructs from other disciplines will be slow not because we don't need them but because we don't know what they mean due to lack of educational training in this area within marketing, social psychology and consumer behavior which typically generate scholars in our field.

## Purpose of Consumer Behavior Theory and Research

Looking at the issue of why we have generated consumer behavior knowledge, it would appear that there are at least two underlying dimensions. The first is the dominance of satisfying the managerial as opposed to the disciplinary (meta theory) needs. The second is the dominance of acquiring empirical knowledge (facts and figures) about the consumer as opposed to the theoretical foundations of consumer behavior.

The dominance of managerially oriented research on consumer behavior is clearly due to the following factors. First and foremost, consumer behavior was, and to a large extent it still is, a part of marketing theory and practice. The earliest studies in consumer behavior were undertaken for the marketing managers who wanted to know more about the consumer before deciding on specific marketing strategies. Hence, market research has such a strong overlap with consumer research in content and methodology. Second, research funding by governmental agencies or foundations to study the consumer in a disciplinary mode has been practically nonexistent until very recently. Without such funding it has been necessary to rely on commercial or applied research, and consequently, the purpose has been more managerial and less disciplinary. Finally, as I mentioned earlier, in the early days of the discipline, most scholars were trained and possessed expertise in other disciplines. To them, consumer behavior was an interesting extension and application area of their pet theories and ideas. Many of them had no strong commitment or loyalty. In that regard, consumer behavior at that time looked like what international business looks like today. As would be expected, without such commitment and full time migration, it is difficult to produce disciplinary research.

Similarly, the dominance of acquiring empirical knowledge rather than theoretical elegance can be attributed to several factors. First, the inductive approach, by and large, dominates a discipline in its infancy and growth phases which results in generating more empirical observations (facts and figures). Interest is more on description and reporting of a specific event or behavior rather than on its explanation, and the method of inquiry is less experimental and more survey research. This tends to generate the bias in favor of the empirical as opposed to theoretical richness. Sadly, this bias is still prevalent as indicated by the hesitation of the scholarly journals to publish theoretical papers. Second, the managerial purpose underlying consumer research has also tended to intensify the bias. The manager has a pet theory of consumer behavior specific to his task and he is often looking toward research findings to support his own theory. It is, therefore, no wonder when he says "give me facts about the consumer and don't confuse me with *your* theories!" A third and related factor is the extreme difficulty to prove or disprove competing theories of consumer behavior. This is mostly due to the contingent nature of the phenomenon, and somewhat due to our ability to transalate theories into testable hypotheses and to effectively cope with consequent operationalization and analysis problems.

What we have then as a surplus in the why aspect of consumer behavior is the managerial purpose and the empirical knowledge, and what we have as a shortage is the disciplinary (metatheory) purpose and the theoretical knowledge. Table 3 summarizes this point and offers several examples of surpluses and shortages in consumer behavior so far as the purpose of researching and theorizing the area are concerned.

It is obvious that empirical knowledge on an ongoing basis for managerial purposes is probably sufficient by now. In fact, some scholars have openly complained that both the government and the industry collects too much information by way of surveys and audits, consumer demographics, life

**TABLE 3. Surpluses and Shortages in the Purpose of Consumer Behavior Theory & Research**

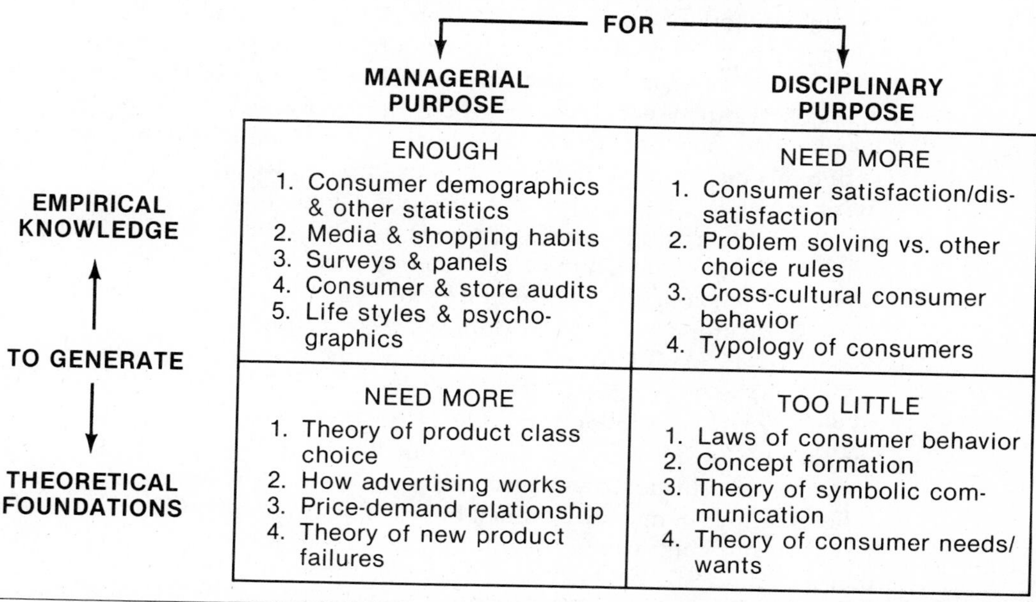

| FOR → | MANAGERIAL PURPOSE | DISCIPLINARY PURPOSE |
|---|---|---|
| EMPIRICAL KNOWLEDGE | ENOUGH<br>1. Consumer demographics & other statistics<br>2. Media & shopping habits<br>3. Surveys & panels<br>4. Consumer & store audits<br>5. Life styles & psychographics | NEED MORE<br>1. Consumer satisfaction/dissatisfaction<br>2. Problem solving vs. other choice rules<br>3. Cross-cultural consumer behavior<br>4. Typology of consumers |
| ↑ TO GENERATE ↓ | | |
| THEORETICAL FOUNDATIONS | NEED MORE<br>1. Theory of product class choice<br>2. How advertising works<br>3. Price-demand relationship<br>4. Theory of new product failures | TOO LITTLE<br>1. Laws of consumer behavior<br>2. Concept formation<br>3. Theory of symbolic communication<br>4. Theory of consumer needs/wants |

styles and psychographics as well as his media and shopping habits especially since the start of the age of electronic computers and other electronic devices. It would appear to me that the next progressive step is data analysis. For it is a sad commentary that probably eighty to ninety percent of the information about the consumer goes unanalyzed or at least underanalyzed. In short, data analysis and not data collection should be the further direction in the area of generating empirical knowledge for managerial purposes.

On the other side of the equation, what seems to be in most acute shortage are the theoretical foundations of the discipline itself. While we do have several nice and rich hypotheses (e.g., perceived risk, buyer attitudes, and stochastic preferences) and some good comprehensive theories in consumer behavior, unfortunately most of them are developed for the managerial perspective. We need discipline-oriented theoretical foundation, especially in the areas of concept formation, symbolic communciation and a good theory of consumer needs/wants.

Above all, it would be superb if we can evolve toward some commonly agreed upon and scientifically validated laws of consumer behavior. I might add that in my search for such laws of consumer behavior, I have so far discovered two laws: (1) Those who don't need a product or information, consume or use it; and (2) Those who need a product or information, do not consume or use it! Seriously, there is some validation to these two laws of consumer behavior as one scans the literature of why consumer protection efforts have failed as well as examines the vast amount of consumption behavior data in conjunction with the socioeconomic-demographic profiles of the consuming populations. If this is true, we might provide a far better explanation for imperfect competition and social welfare disequilibrium than what has been proposed in the theory of firms in microeconomics.

This analysis does not mean that we should ignore or even discard the managerial purpose in consumer behavior. However, what the manager needs much more critically are the theoretical foundations of how the marketing mix does or does not work. For example, it would be nice if scholars in consumer behavior can provide him with a single agreed upon explanation as to how advertising works; or provide rich theoretical foundations for the price-demand relationship; or offer a good theory of new product failures. So far as I am concerned, I think it would be not only nice but seems also possible to offer a good theory of product class choice behavior with which the manager can understand who competes and compliments with his products in the market place.

Finally, the discipline itself needs further empirical knowledge on a number of substantive issues. These include the degree and character of consumer satisfaction/dissatisfaction; prevalence of problem solving versus other methods of making product, brand or store choices; and cross-cultural parallels and contrasts in magnitudes and types of products and services consumed on our planet.

## Summary and Conclusions

This paper is an attempt to take an inventory of consumer behavior theory and research in order to identify surpluses and shortages of concepts, information and body knowledge we face today as we say goodbye to the decade of the seventies.

The inventory was taken with respect to the three areas of focus, process and purpose in generating the body of knowledge we call consumer behavior theory and research. The following conclusions were derived in the process:

1. We have focused too much on the individual consumer as opposed to group behavior and similarly too much on the rational models of problem solving (decision making) as opposed to other non-problem solving models of choice behavior. The interaction of these two focus factors has resulted in abundance of attitude models, multi-attribute judgments, and brand choice models. What we need most is understanding of group phenomena such as crowd consumption, fads and fashions, deviant consumption behavior, and obsessive consumer behavior with the use of more macro and non-problem solving hypotheses and theories of choice behavior.
2. The process of theorizing and researching consumer behavior has been dominated by descriptive as opposed to normative constructs, and by constructs borrowed from other disciplines rather than self-generated constructs unique to consumer behavior. In the process, we seem to have surplus of social psychology, diffusion theory, reference groups, as well as econometric and stochastic modeling of consumer behavior. What we need now are more normative and self-generated hypotheses and theories related to market segmentation strategy mix models, consumerism and consumer welfare theories, anti-consuming models and a normative marketing policy which defines the rights and obligations of the marketers.
3. Most of the consumer behavior research and theory has been for managerial purposes in contrast to the disciplinary (metatheory) purposes. Similarly, it has been more empirical rather than theoretical. This has resulted in generating lots of facts and figures about the consumer himself, how much does he buy, his media and shopping habits and his demographics, life styles and psychographics. In the process, market research and consumer research have become almost synonymous. What we need, however, are rich theoretical foundations of the discipline itself with respect to many areas such as concept formation, symbolic communication and a theory of consumer needs/wants.

It would be simply exhilarating if we can evolve some agreed upon and properly validated laws of consumer behavior. So far, it seems that we have discovered only two obvious laws of consumer behavior: those who don't need the product, consume it, and secondly those who need it, do not consume it! While these laws may go a long way in explaining the phenomena of imperfect competition and social welfare disequilibrium as compared to the traditional micro-economic theory of the firm, we can do much better if we decide to change our focus, process and purpose in understanding consumer behavior.

## REFERENCES

Howard, J. A., and J. N. Sheth (1969) *The Theory of Buyer Behavior*, Wiley & Sons.

Jacoby, J. (1975), "Consumer Psychology as a Social Psychological Sphere of Action," *American Psychologist*, 30, October, 977-987.

Sheth, J. N. (1967) "A Review of Buyer Behavior," *Management Science*, 13, B718-B756.

Sheth, J. N. (1972), "The Future of Buyer Behavior Theory," in *Proceedings of the Third Annual Conference*, Association for Consumer Research, 562-575.

Sheth, J. N. (1976) "Howard's Contributions to Marketing: Some Thoughts," in A. Andreasen and S. Sudman (eds.) *Public Policy and Marketing Thought*, Proceedings of the Ninth P. D. Converse Symposium, American Marketing Association, 17-26.

## SECTION J

# Industrial Buyer Behavior School

Understanding industrial customers became increasingly more relevant and important as consumer behavior theory limited its function to consumer goods and services. Industrial buying behavior is contrasted with consumer buying behavior in several ways. First, industrial buying behavior is more formal and procedural. It requires a significant amount of formal communication and coordination within the buying organization as well as a considerable amount of paperwork.

Second, industrial buying behavior is often subjected to corporate politics. This often results in vendor choices on factors that are not based on economic or technical considerations. For example, reciprocity relationships and personal favors are very prevalent in industrial buying behavior.

Finally, industrial buying behavior is an organized function and revolves around the concept of a buying center. This results in joint decision making among members of the buying center, but members often have conflicting goals and perceptions related to procurement issues. The consequence is conflict and conflict resolution strategies such as bargaining and politicking. Although consumer buying behavior also often involves joint decision making, such as for vacations, home purchases, and automobiles, it is seldom organized into a buying center.

We believe that there are more similarities than differences between industrial and consumer buying behavior. Therefore, each can learn from the other.

# 33 — A General Model for Understanding Organizational Buying Behavior

*Frederick E. Webster, Jr.*
*and Yoram Wind*

Reprinted from *Journal of Marketing*, published by the American Marketing Association, Vol. 36 (April 1972), pp. 12-19. Reprinted by permission.

Industrial and institutional marketers have often been urged to base their strategies on careful appraisal of buying behavior within key accounts and in principal market segments. When they search the available literature on buyer behavior, however, they find virtually exclusive emphasis on consumers, not industrial buyers. Research findings and theoretical discussions about consumer behavior often have little relevance for the industrial marketer. This is due to several important differences between the two purchase processes. Industrial buying takes place in the context of a formal organization influenced by budget, cost, and profit considerations. Furthermore, organizational (i.e., industrial and institutional) buying usually involves many people in the decision process with complex interactions among people and among individual and organizational goals.

Similar to his consumer goods counterpart, the industrial marketer could find a model of buyer behavior useful in identifying those key factors influencing response to marketing effort. A buyer behavior model can help the marketer to analyze available information about the market and to identify the need for additional information. It can help to specify targets for marketing effort, the kinds of information needed by various purchasing decision makers, and the criteria that they will use to make these decisions. A framework for analyzing organizational buying behavior could aid in the design of marketing strategy.

The model to be presented here is a *general* model. It can be applied to all organizational buying and suffers all the weaknesses of general models. It does not describe a specific buying situation in the richness of detail required to make a model operational, and it cannot be quantified. However, generality offers a compensating set of benefits. The model presents a comprehensive view of organizational buying that enables one to evaluate the relevance of specific variables and thereby permits greater insight into the basic processes of industrial buying behavior. It identifies the *classes* of variables that must be examined by any student of organizational buying, practitioner, or academician. Although major scientific progress in the study of organizational buying will come only from a careful study of specific relationships among a few variables within a given class, this general model can help to identify those variables that should be studied. It can be useful in generating hypotheses and provides a framework for careful interpretation of research results that makes the researcher more sensitive to the complexities of the processes he is studying.

## Traditional Views

Traditional views of organizational buying have lacked comprehensiveness. The literature of economics, purchasing, and, to a limited degree, marketing has emphasized variables related to the buying task itself and has emphasized "rational," economic factors. In these economic views, the objective of purchasing is to obtain the minimum price or the lowest total cost-in-use (as in the materials management model[1]). Some of the models focusing on the buying task have emphasized factors that are not strictly economic such as reciprocal buying agreements[2] and other constraints on the buyer such as source loyalty.[3]

Other traditional views of organizational buying err in the opposite direction, emphasizing variables such as emotion, personal goals, and internal politics that are involved in the buying decision process but not related to the goals of the buying task. This "nontask" emphasis is seen in models which emphasize the purchasing agent's interest in obtaining personal favors,[4] in enhancing his own ego,[5] or in reducing perceived risk.[6] Other nontask models have emphasized buyer-salesman interpersonal interaction[7] and the multiple relationships among individuals involved in the buying process over time.[8] The ways in which purchasing agents attempt to expand their influence over the buying decision have also received careful study.[9] These views have contributed to an understanding of the buying process, but none of them is complete. To the extent that these models leave out task or nontask variables they offer incomplete guidelines for the industrial market strategist and researcher. The tendency in interpreting research results based on these simple models is to overemphasize the importance of some variables and to understate or ignore the importance of others.

## An Overview of a General Model

The fundamental assertion of the more comprehensive model to be presented here is that organizational buying is a decision-making process carried out by individuals, in interaction with other people, in the context of a formal organization.[10] The organization, in turn, is influenced by a variety of forces in the environment. Thus, the four classes of variables determining organizational buying behavior are *individual, social, organizational,* and *environmental*. Within each class, there are two broad categories of variables: Those directly related to the buying problem, called *task* variables;

and those that extend beyond the buying problem, called *nontask* variables. This classification of variables is summarized and illustrated in Table 1.

**TABLE 1. Classification and Examples of Variables Influencing Organizational Buying Decisions**

| | *Task* | *Nontask* |
|---|---|---|
| Individual | desire to obtain lowest price | personal values and needs |
| Social | meetings to set specifications | informal, off-the-job interactions |
| Organizational | policy regarding local supplier preference | methods of personnel evaluation |
| Environmental | anticipated changes in price | political climate in an election year |

The distinction between task and nontask variables applies to all of the classes of variables, and subclasses, to be discussed below. It is seldom possible to identify a given set of variables as exclusively task or nontask; rather, any given set of variables will have both task and nontask dimensions although one dimension may be predominant. For example, motives will inevitably have both dimensions—those relating directly to the buying problem to be solved and those primarily concerned with personal goals. These motives overlap in many important respects and need not conflict; a strong sense of personal involvement can create more effective buying decisions from an organizational standpoint.

Organizational buying behavior is a complex *process* (rather than a single, instantaneous act) and involves many persons, multiple goals, and potentially conflicting decision criteria. It often takes place over an extended period of time, requires information from many sources, and encompasses many interorganizational relationships.

The organizational buying process is a form of problem-solving, and a *buying situation* is created when someone in the organization perceives a problem—a discrepancy between a desired outcome and the present situation—that can potentially be solved through some buying action. Organizational buying behavior includes all activities of organizational members as they define a buying situation and identify, evaluate, and choose among alternative brands and suppliers. The *buying center* includes all members of the organization who are involved in that process. The roles involved are those of user, influencer, decider, buyer, and gatekeeper (who controls the flow of information into the buying center). Members of the buying center are motivated by a complex interaction of individual and organizational goals. Their relationships with one another involve all the complexities of interpersonal interactions. The formal organization exerts its influence on the buying center through the subsystems of tasks, structure (communication, authority, status, rewards, and work flow), technology, and people. Finally the entire organization is embedded in a set of environmental influences including economic, technological, physical, political, legal, and cultural forces. An overview of the model and a diagrammatic presentation of the relationships among these variables are given in Figure 1.

## Environmental Influences

Environmental influences are subtle and pervasive as well as difficult to identify and to measure. They influence the buying process by providing information as well as constraints and opportunities. Environmental influences include physical (geographic, climate, or ecological), technological, economic, political, legal, and cultural factors. These influences are exerted through a variety of institutions including business firms (suppliers, competitiors, and customers), governments, trade unions, political parties, educational and medical institutions, trade associations, and professional groups. The nature of these institutional forms will vary significantly from one country to another, and such differences are critical to the planning of multinational marketing strategies.

As Figure 1 illustrates, environmental influences have their impact in four distinct ways. First, they define the availability of goods and services. This function reflects especially the influence of physical, technological, and economic factors. Second, they define the general business conditions facing the buying organization including the rate of economic growth, the level of national income, interest rates, and unemployment. Economic and political forces are the dominant influences on general business conditions. Some of these forces, such as economic factors, are predominantly (but not exclusively) task varibles whereas others such as political variables may be more heavily nontask in nature. Third, environmental factors determine the values and norms guiding interorganizational and interpersonal relationships between buyers and sellers as well as among competitors, and between buying organizations and other institutions such as governments and trade associations. Such values and norms may be codified into laws, or they may be implicit. Cultural, social, legal, and political forces are the dominant sources of values and norms. Finally, environmental forces influence the information flow into the buying organization. Most important here is the flow of marketing communications from potential suppliers, through the mass media and through other personal and impersonal channels. Information flows reflect a variety of physical, technological, economic, and cultural factors.

**FIGURE 1. A Model of Organizational Buying Behavior**

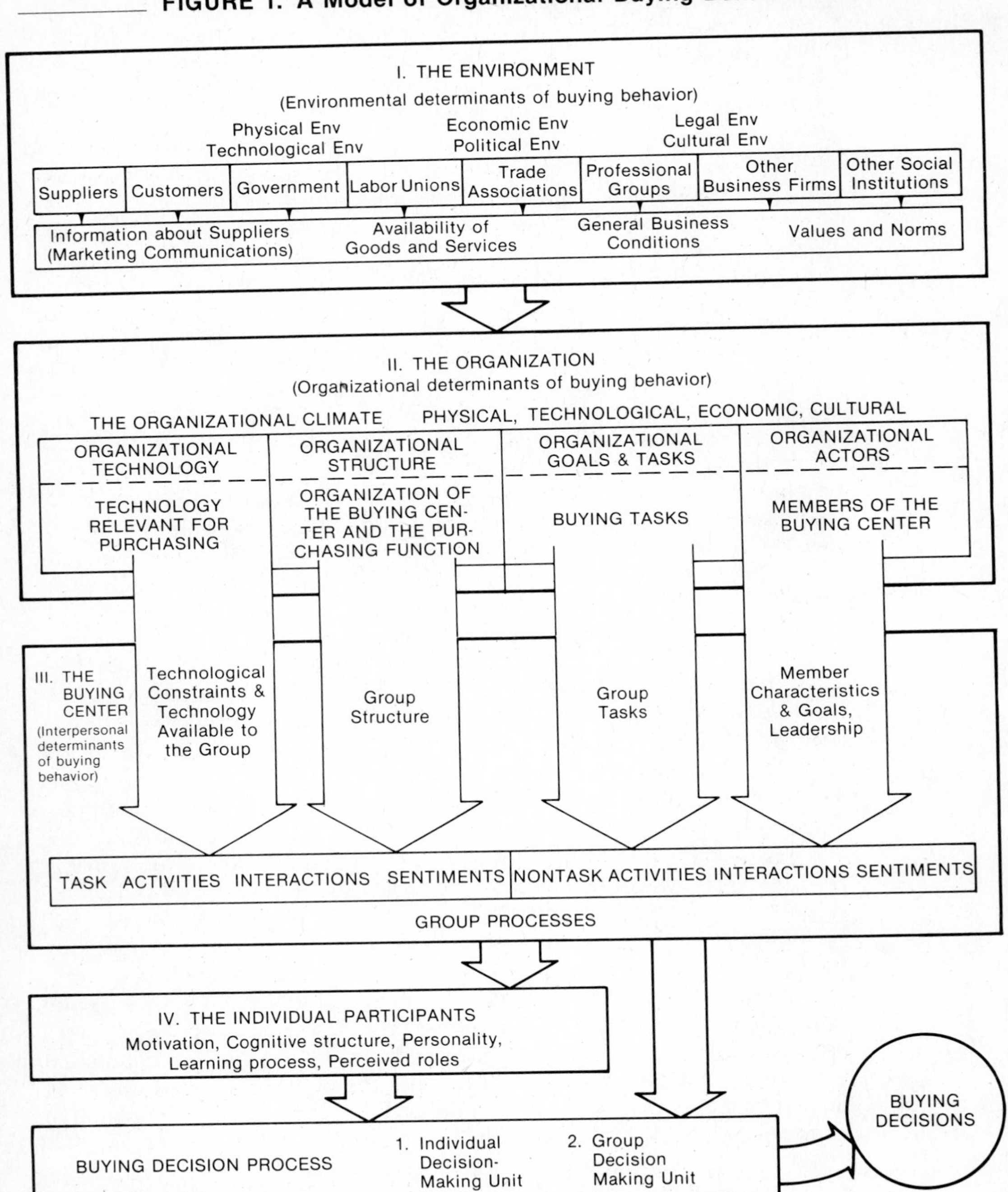

The marketing strategist, whose customers are organizations, must carefully appraise each set of environmental factors and identify and analyze the institutions that exert those influences in each of the market segments served. This kind of analysis is especially important in entering new markets. For example, economic factors as revealed in measures of general business conditions must be continually assessed where market prices fluctuate and buyers make decisions to build or reduce inventories based on price expectations. Similarly, the impact of technological change in markets served must be considered as the basis for strategic decisions in the areas of product policy and promotion. The necessity of analyzing institutional forms is most readily apparent when markets are multinational in scope and require specific consideration of government policies and trade union influences. Environmental factors are important determinants of organizational buying behavior, but they can be so basic and pervasive that it is easy, and dangerous, to overlook them in analyzing the market.

## Organizational Influences

Organizational factors cause individual decision makers to act differently than they would if they were functioning alone or in a different organization. Organizational buying behavior is motivated and directed by the organization's goals and is constrained by its financial, technological, and human resources. This class of variables is primarily task-related. For understanding the influence of the formal organization on the buying process, Leavitt's classification of variables is most helpful.[11] According to Leavitt's scheme, organizations are multivariate systems composed of four sets of interacting variables:

*Tasks*—the work to be performed in accomplishing the objectives of the organization.

*Structure*—subsystems of communication, authority, status, rewards, and work flow.

*Technology*—problem-solving inventions used by the firm including plant and equipment and programs for organizing and managing work.

*People*—the actors in the system.

Each of these subsystems interacts with, and is dependent upon, the others for its functioning. Together, these four interacting sets of factors define the information, expectations, goals, attitudes, and assumptions used by each of the individual actors in their decision making. This general model defines four distinct but interrelated sets of variables that must be carefully considered in the development of marketing strategies designed to influence that process: buying tasks, organization structure, buying technology, and the buying center.

## Buying Tasks

Buying tasks are a subset of organizational tasks and goals that evolves from the definition of a buying situation. These are pure task variables by definition. The specific tasks that must be performed to solve the buying problem can be defined as five stages in the buying decision process: (1) identification of need; (2) establishment of specifications; (3) identification of alternatives; (4) evaluation of alternatives; and (5) selection of suppliers.[12] Buying tasks can be further defined according to four dimensions:

1. The *organizational purpose* served—e.g., whether the reason for buying is to facilitate production, or for resale, or to be consumed in the performance of other organizational functions.
2. The *nature of demand*, especially whether demand for the product is generated within the buying organization or by forces outside of the organization (i.e., ''derived'' demand) as well as other characteristics of the demand pattern such as seasonal and cyclical fluctuations.
3. The *extent of programming*; i.e., the degree of routinization at the five stages of the decision process.
4. The *degree of decentralization* and the extent to which buying authority has been delegated to operating levels in the organization.

Each of these four dimensions influences the nature of the organizational buying process and must be considered in appraising market opportunities. At each of the five stages of the decision process, different members of the buying center may be involved, different decision criteria are employed, and different information sources may become more or less relevant. Marketing strategies must be adjusted accordingly. There are rich research opportunities in defining the influence of different members of the buying center at various stages of the buying process.[13]

## Organizational Structure

The formal organizational structure consists of subsystems of communication, authority, status, rewards, and work flow, all of which have important task and nontask dimensions. Each of these subsystems deserves careful study by researchers interested in organizational buying. The marketing literature does not include studies in this area. A beginning might be several rigorous observational or case studies.

The *communication* subsystem performs four essential functions: (1) information; (2) command and instruction; (3) influence and persuasion; and (4) integration.[14]

The marketer must understand how the communication system in customer organizations *informs* the members of the buying center about buying problems, evaluation criteria (both task and nontask related), and alternative sources of supply. He must appraise how *commands and instructions* (mostly task-related) flow through the hierarchy defining the discretion and latitude of individual actors. The pattern of *influence and persuasion* (heavily nontask in nature) defines the nature of interpersonal interactions within the buying center. Organizational members may differ in the extent to which they prefer either commands and instructions or more subtle influence and persuasion to guide the actions of subordinates. The *integrative* functions of communication become critical in coordinating the functioning of the buying center and may be one of the primary roles of the purchasing manager.

The *authority* subsystem defines the power of organizational actors to judge, command, or otherwise act to influence the behavior of others along both task and nontask dimensions. No factor is more critical in understanding the organizational buying process because the authority structure determines who sets goals and who evaluates (and therefore determines rewards for) organizational performance. The authority structure interacts with the communication structure to determine the degree of decentralization in the decision process.

The *status* system is reflected in the organization chart and defines the hierarchical structure of the formal organization. It also expresses itself in an informal structure. Both the formal and the informal organization define each individual's position in a hierarchy with respect to other individuals. Job descriptions define positions within the organization and the associated dimensions of responsibility and authority. Knowing the responsibility, authority, and the position in the internal status hierarchy of each member of the buying center is a necessary basis for developing an account strategy for the organizational customer. A complete theory of organizational buying will permit accurate predictions of an organizational actor's influence based upon his position and role.

The *rewards* system defines the payoffs to the individual decision maker. It is intimately related to the authority system which determines the responsibilities of organizational actors for evaluating other individuals. Here is the mechanism for relating organizational task accomplishment to individual nontask objectives. Persons join organizations in anticipation of the rewards given by the organization and agree to work toward organizational objectives in return for those rewards. A careful analysis of the formal and social reward structure of the organization as it affects and is perceived by the members of the buying center can be most helpful in predicting their response to marketing effort. The key fact is that people work for organizations in order to earn rewards related to personal goals, both economic and noneconomic.[15]

Every buying organization develops task-related procedures for managing the *work flow* of paperwork, samples, and other items involved in the buying decision process. The flow of paperwork also has nontask aspects which reflect the composition of the buying center as well as the authority and communication subsystems of an organizational structure. Needless to say, marketers must understand the mechanical details of buying procedures.

Such procedures also provide documentation of the buying process that can provide useful data for the academic researcher.

### Buying Technology

Technology influences both what is bought and the nature of the organizational buying process itself. In the latter respect, technology defines the management and information systems that are involved in the buying decision process, such as computers and management science approaches to such aspects of buying as "make or buy" analysis. More obviously, technology defines the plant and equipment of the organization, and these, in turn, place significant constraints upon the alternative buying actions available to the organization. It is a common failing of industrial marketing strategy, especially for new product introductions, to underestimate the demands that will be placed upon existing technology in customer organizations.[16] A new material, for example, may require new dies and mixing equipment, new skills of production personnel, and substantial changes in methods of production.

### Buying Center

The buying center is a subset of the organizational actors, the last of the four sets of variables in the Leavitt scheme. The buying center was earlier defined as consisting of five roles: users, influencers, deciders, buyers, and gatekeepers. Since people operate as part of the total organization, the behavior of members of the buying center reflects the influence of others as well as the effect of the buying task, the organizational structure, and technology.

This interaction leads to unique buying behavior in each customer organization. The marketing strategist who wishes to influence the organizational buying process must, therefore, define and understand the operation of these four sets of organizational variables—tasks, structure, technology, and actors—in each organization he is trying to influence. The foregoing comments provide only the skeleton of the analytical structure for considering each of these factors and its implications for marketing action in a specific buying situation. The marketer's problem is to define the locus of buying responsibility within the customer organization, to define the composition of the buying center, and to understand the structure of roles and authority within the buying center.

## Social (Interpersonal) Influences

The framework for understanding the buying decision process must identify and relate three classes of variables involved in group functioning in the buying center. First, the various roles in the buying center must be identified. Second, the variables relating to interpersonal (dyadic) interaction between persons in the buying center and between members of the buying center and ''outsiders'' such as vendors' salesmen must be identified. Third, the dimensions of the functioning of the group as a whole must be considered. Each of these three sets of factors is discussed briefly in the following paragraphs.

Within the organization as a whole only a subset of organizational actors is actually involved in a buying situation. The buying center includes five roles:

*Users*—those members of the organization who use the purchased products and services.

*Buyers*—those with formal responsibility and authority for contracting with suppliers.

*Influencers*—those who influence the decision process directly or indirectly by providing information and criteria for evaluating alternative buying actions.

*Deciders*—those with authority to choose among alternative buying actions.

*Gatekeepers*—those who control the flow of information (and materials) into the buying center.

Several individuals may occupy the same role; e.g., there may be several influencers. Also, one individual may occupy more than one role; e.g., the purchasing agent is often both buyer and gatekeeper.

To understand interpersonal interaction within the buying center, it is useful to consider three aspects fo role performance: (1) Role *expectations* (prescriptions and prohibitions for the behavior of the person occupying the role and for the behavior of other persons toward a given role); (2) role *behavior* (actual behavior in the role); and (3) role *relationships* (the multiple and reciprocal relationships among members of the group). Together, these three variables define the individual's *role set*. An awareness of each of these dimensions is necessary for the salesman responsible for contacting the various members of the buying center. It is especially important to understand how each member expects the salesman to behave toward him and the important ongoing relationships among roles in the buying center.

As illustrated in Figure 1, the nature of group functioning is influenced by five classes of variables—the individual members's goals and personal characteristics, the nature of leadership within the group, the structure of the group, the tasks performed by the group, and external (organizational and environmental) influences. Group processes involve not only activities but also interactions and sentiments among members, which have both task and nontask dimensions. Finally, the output of the group is not only a task-oriented problem solution (a buying action) but also nontask satisfaction and growth for the group and its members.

In analyzing the functioning of the buying center, it helps to focus attention on the buyer role, primarily because a member of the purchasing department is most often the marketer's primary contact point with the organization. Buyers often have authority for managing the contacts of suppliers with other organizational actors, and thus also perform the "gatekeeper" function. While the buyer's authority for selection of suppliers may be seriously constrained by decisions at earlier stages of the decision process (especially the development of specifications), he has responsibility for the terminal stages of the process. In other words, the buyer (or purchasing agent) is in most cases the final decision maker and the target of influence attempts by other members of the buying center.

In performing their task, purchasing agents use a variety of tactics to enhance their power which vary with the specific problems, the conditions of the organization, and the purchasing agent's personality. The tactics used by purchasing agents to influence their relationships with other departments can be viewed as a special case of the more general phenomenon of "lateral" relationships in formal organizations—those among members of approximately equal status in the formal organizational hierarchy.[17] These include *rule-oriented* tactics (e.g., appealing to the boss for the enforcement of organizational policy; appealing to rules and formal statements of authority); *rule-evading* tactics (e.g., complicance with requests from users that violate organizational policies); *personal-political* tactics (e.g., reliance on informal relationships and friendships to get decisions made and an exchange of favors with other members of the buying center); *educational* tactics (e.g., persuading other members of the organization to think in purchasing terms and to recognize the importance and potential contribution of the purchasing function); and finally *organizational-interactional* tactics (e.g., change the formal organizational structure and the pattern of reporting relationships and information flows).

Buyers who are ambitious and wish to extend the scope of their influence will adopt certain tactics and engage in bargaining activities in an attempt to become more influential at earlier stages of the buying process. These tactics or bargaining strategies define the nature of the buyer's relationships with others of equal organizational status and structure the social situation that the potential supplier must face in dealing with the buying organization. An understanding of the nature of interpersonal relationships in the buying organization is an important basis for the development of marketing strategy.

## The Influence of the Individual

In the final analysis, all organizational buying behavior is individual behavior. Only the individual as an individual or a member of a group can define and analyze buying situations, decide, and act. In this behavior, the individual is motivated by a complex combination of personal and organizational objectives, constrained by policies and information filtered through the formal organization, and influenced by other members of the buying center. The individual is at the center of the buying process, operating within the buying center that is in turn bounded by the formal organization which is likewise embedded in the influences of the broader environment. It is the specific individual who is the target for marketing effort, not the abstract organization.

The organizational buyer's personality, perceived role set, motivation, cognition, and learning are the basic psychological processes which affect his response to the buying situation and marketing stimuli provided by potential vendors. Similar to consumer markets, it is important to understand the organizational buyer's psychological characteristics and especially his predispositions, preference structure, and decision model as the basis for marketing strategy decisions. Some initial attempts to develop categories of buying decision makers according to characteristic decision styles (''normative'' and ''conservative'') have been reported.[18] Cultural, organizational, and social factors are important influences on the individual and are reflected in his previous experiences, awareness of, attitudes and preference toward particular vendors and products and his particular buying decision models.

The organizational buyer can, therefore, be viewed as a constrained decision maker. Although the basic mental processes of motivation, cognition, and learning as well as the buyer's personality, perceived role set, preference structure, and decision model are uniquely individual; they are influenced by the context of interpersonal and organizational influences within which the individual is embedded. The organizational buyer is motivated by a complex combination of individual and organizational objectives and is dependent upon others for the satisfaction of these needs in several ways. These other people define the role expectations for the individual, they determine the payoffs he is to receive for his performance, they influence the definition of the goals to be pursued in the buying decision, and they provide information with which the individual attempts to evaluate risks and come to a decision.

## Task and Nontask Motives

Only rarely can the organizational buyer let purely personal considerations influence his buying decisions: In a situation where ''all other things are equal,'' the individual may be able to apply to strictly personal (nontask) criteria when making his final decision. In the unlikely event that two or more potential vendors offer products of comparable quality and service at a comparable price, then the organizational buyer may be motivated by purely personal, nontask variables such as his personal preferences for dealing with a particular salesman, or some special favor or gift available from the supplier.

The organizational buyer's motivation has both task and nontask dimensions. Task-related motives relate to the specific buying problem to be solved and involve the general criteria of buying "the right quality in the right quantity at the right price for delivery at the right time from the right source." Of course, what is "right" is a difficult question, especially to the extent that important buying influencers have conflicting needs and criteria for evaluating the buyer's performance.

Nontask-related motives may often be more important, although there is frequently a rather direct relationship between task and nontask motives. For example, the buyer's desire for promotion (a nontask motive) can significantly influence his task performance. In other words, there is no necessary conflict between task and nontask motives and, in fact, the pursuit of nontask objectives can enhance the attainment of task objectives.

Broadly speaking, nontask motives can be placed into two categories: achievement motives and risk-reduction motives. Achievement motives are those related to personal advancement and recognition. Risk-reduction motives are related, but somewhat less obvious, and provide a critical link between the individual and the organizational decision-making process. This is also a key component of the behavioral theory of the firm[19] where uncertainty avoidance is a key motivator of organizational actors.

The individual's perception of risk in a decision situation is a function of uncertainty (in the sense of a probabilistic assessment) and of the value of various outcomes. Three kinds of uncertainty are significant: Uncertainty about available alternatives; uncertainty about the outcomes associated with various alternatives; and uncertainty about the way relevant other persons will react to various outcomes.[20] This uncertainty about the reaction of other persons may be due to incomplete information about their goals or about how an outcome will be evaluated and rewarded.

Information gathering is the most obvious tactic for reducing uncertainty, while decision avoidance and lowering of goals are means of reducing the value of outcomes. A preference for the status quo is perhaps the most common mode of risk reduction, since it removes uncertainty and minimizes the possibility of negative outcomes. This is one explanation for the large amount of source loyalty found in organizational buying and is consistent with the "satisfying" postulate of the behavioral theory of the firm.

The individual determinants of organizational buyer behavior and the tactics which buyers are likely to use in their dealings with potential vendors must be clearly understood by those who want to affect their behavior.

## SUMMARY

This article suggested the major dimensions and mechanisms involved in the complex organizational buying process. The framework presented here is reasonably complete although the details clearly are lacking. It is hoped that these comments have been sufficient to suggest a general model of the organizational buying process with important implications for the development of effective marketing and selling strategies as well as some implicit suggestions for scholarly research. The model is offered as a skeleton identifying the major variables that must be appraised in developing the information required for planning strategies. Hopefully, the model has also suggested some new insights into an important area of buying behavior presently receiving inadequate attention in the marketing literature.

## ENDNOTES

1. Dean S. Ammer, *Materials Management* (Homewood, Illinois: Richard D. Irwin, Inc., 1962), pp. 12 and 15.
2. Dean S. Ammer, "Realistic Reciprocity," *Harvard Business Review*, Vol. 40 (January-February, 1962), pp. 116-124.
3. Yoram Wind, "Industrial Source Loyalty," *Journal of Marketing Research*, Vol. 7 (November, 1970), pp. 450-457.
4. For a statement of this view, see J. B. Matthews, Jr., R. D. Buzzell, T. Levitt, and R. Frank, *Marketing: An Introductory Analysis* (New York: McGraw-Hill Book Company, Inc., 1964), p. 149.
5. For an example, see William J. Stanton, *Fundamentals of Marketing*, Second Ed. (New York: McGraw-Hill Book Company, Inc., 1967), p. 150.
6. Theodore Levitt, *Industrial Purchasing Behavior: A Study of Communications Effects* (Boston: Division of Research, Graduate School of Business Administration, Harvard University, 1965).
7. Henry L. Tosi, "The Effects of Expectation Levels and Role Consensus on the Buyer-Seller Dyad," *Journal of Business*, Vol. 39 (October, 1966), pp. 516-529.
8. Robert E. Weigand, "Why Studying the Purchasing Agent is Not Enough," *Journal of Marketing*, Vol. 32 (January, 1968), pp. 41-45.
9. George Strauss, "Tactics of Lateral Relationship," *Administrative Science Quarterly*, Vol. 7 (September, 1962), pp. 161-186.
10. The complete model is presented and discussed in detail in Frederick E. Webster, Jr. and Yoram Wind, *Organizational Buying Behavior* (Englewood Cliffs, New Jersey: Prentice-Hall, Inc., in press).
11. Harold J. Leavitt, "Applied Organization Change in Industry: Structural, Technical, and Human Approaches," in *New Perspectives in Organization Research*, W. W. Cooper, H. J. Leavitt, and M. W. Shelly, II, eds. (New York: John Wiley and Sons, Inc., 1964), pp. 55-71.
12. A modified version of this model is presented in P. J. Robinson, C. W. Faris, and Y. Wind, *Industrial Buying and Creative Marketing* (Boston: Allyn & Bacon, Inc., 1967), p. 14.
13. For research on the influence of organizational actors and information sources at various stages of the decision process, see Urban B. Ozanne and Gilbert A. Churchill, "Adoption Research: Information Sources in the Industrial Purchasing Decision," in *Marketing and the New Science of Planning*, Robert L. King, ed. (Chicago, Ill: American Marketing Association,

Fall, 1968), pp. 352-359; and Frederick E. Webster, Jr., "Informal Communication in Industrial Markets," *Journal of Marketing Research*, Vol. 7 (May, 1970), pp. 186-189.

14. Lee Thayer, *Communication and Communication Systems* (Homewood, Ill,: Richard D. Irwin, Inc., 1968), pp. 187-250.
15. Yoram Wind, "A Reward-Balance Model of Buying Behavior in Organizations," in *New Essays in Marketing Theory*, G. Fisk ed. (Boston: Allyn & Bacon, 1971).
16. Frederick E. Webster, Jr., "New Product Adoption in Industrial Markets: A Framework for Analysis," *Journal of Marketing*, Vol. 33 (July, 1969), pp. 35-39.
17. Same reference as note 9.
18. David T. Wilson, H. Lee Mathews, and Timothy W. Sweeney, "Industrial Buyer Segmentation: A Psychographic Approach," paper presented at the Fall, 1971 Conference of the American Marketing Association. See also Richard N. Cardozo, "Segmenting the Industrial Market," in *Marketing and the New Science of Planning*, Robert L. King ed. (Chicago: American Marketing Association, 1969), pp. 433-440.
19. Richard M. Cyert and James G. March, *A Behavioral Theory of the Firm* (Englewood Cliffs, N. J.: Prentice-Hall, 1963).
20. Donald R. Cox, ed., *Risk Taking and Information Handling in Consumer Behavior* (Boston: Division of Research, Graduate School of Business Administration, Harvard University, 1967).

# 34 —— A Model of Industrial Buyer Behavior

*Jagdish N. Sheth*

Reprinted from *Journal of Marketing*, published by the American Marketing Association, Vol. 37 (October 1973), pp. 50-56. Reprinted by permission.

The purpose of this article is to describe a model of industrial (organizational) buyer behavior. Considerable knowledge on organizational buyer behavior already exists[1] and can be classified into three categories. The first category includes a considerable amount of systematic empirical research on the buying policies and practices of purchasing agents and other organizational buyers.[2] The second includes industry reports and observations of industrial buyers.[3] Finally, the third category consists of books, monographs, and articles which analyze, theorize, model, and sometimes report on industrial buying activities.[4] What is now needed is a reconciliation and integration of existing knowledge into a realistic and comprehensive model of organizational buyer behavior.

It is hoped that the model described in this article will be useful in the following ways: first, to broaden the vision of research on organizational buyer behavior so that it includes the most salient elements and their interactions; second, to act as a catalyst for building marketing information systems from the viewpoint of the industrial buyer; and, third, to generate new hyoptheses for future research on fundamental processes underlying organizational buyer behavior.

## A Description of Industrial Buyer Behavior

The model of industrial buyer behavior is summarized in Figure 1. Although this illustrative presentation looks complex due to the large number of variables and complicated relationships among them, this is because it is a generic model which attempts to describe and explain all types of industrial buying decisions. One can, however, simplify the actual application of the model in a specific study in at least two ways. First, several variables are included as conditions to hold constant differences among types of products to be purchased (product-specific factors) and differences among types of purchasing organizations. These exogenous factors will not be necessary if the objective of a study is to describe the process of buying behavior for a specific product or service. Second, some of the decision-process variables can also be ignored if the interest is strictly to conduct a survey of static measurement of the psychology of the organizational buyers.

**FIGURE 1. An Integrative Model of Industrial Buyer Behavior**

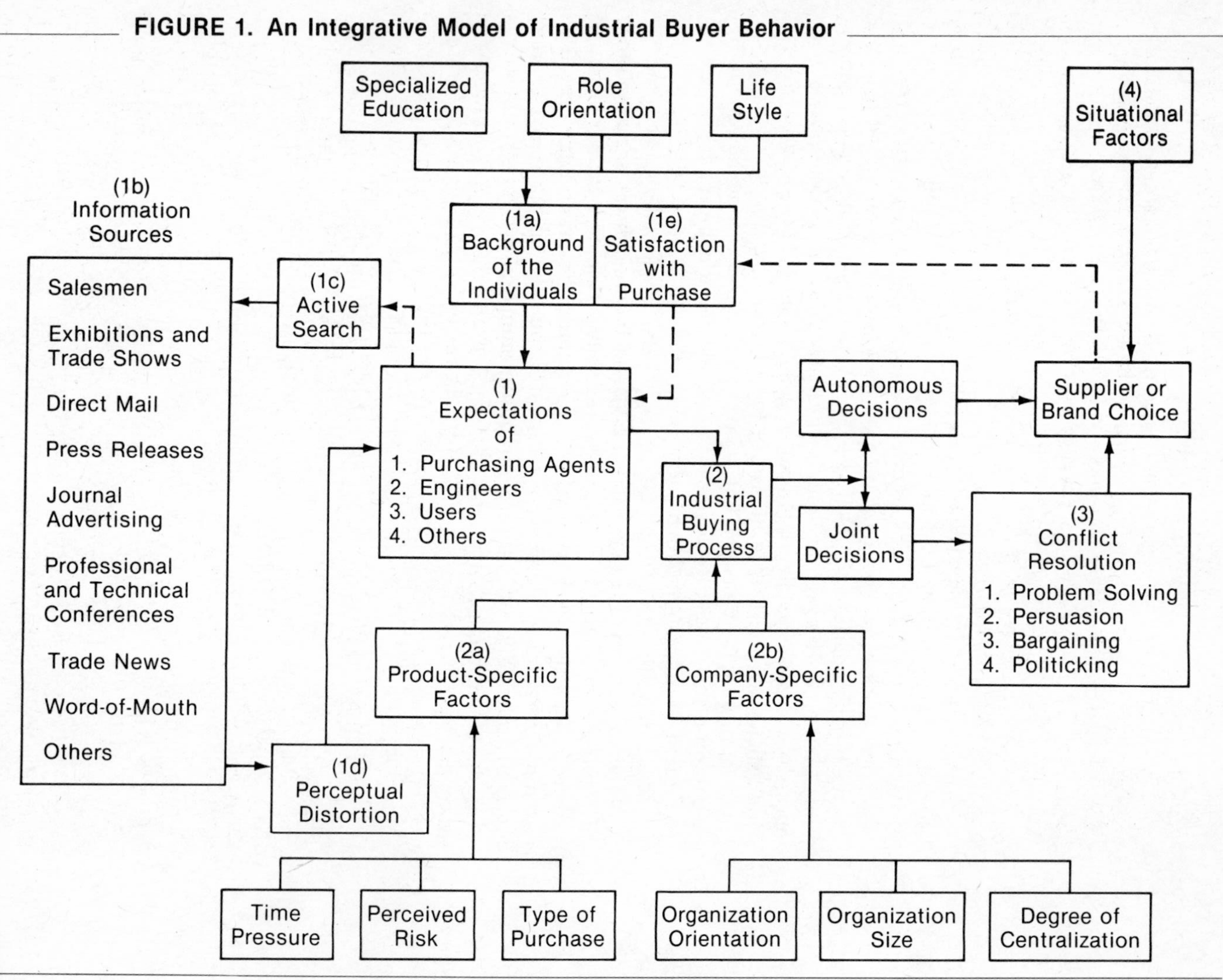

For example, perceptual bias and active search variables may be eliminated if the interest is not in the process of communication to the organizational buyers.

This model is similar to the Howard-Sheth model of buyer behavior in format and classification of variables.[5] However, there are several significant differences. First, while the Howard-Sheth model is more general and probably more useful in consumer behavior, the model described in this article is limited to organizational buying alone. Second, the Howard-Sheth model is limited to the individual decision-making process, whereas this model explicitly describes the joint decision-making process. Finally, there are fewer variables in this model than in the Howard-Sheth model of buyer behavior.

Organizational buyer behavior consists of three distinct aspects. The first aspect is the psychological world of the individuals involved in organizational buying decisions. The second aspect relates to the conditions which precipitate joint decisions among these individuals. The final aspect is the process of joint decision making with the inevitable conflict among the decision makers and its resolution by resorting to a variety of tactics.

## Psychological World of the Decision Makers

Contrary to popular belief, many industrial buying decisions are not solely in the hands of purchasing agents.[6] Typically in an industrial setting, one finds that there are at least three departments whose members are continuously involved in different phases of the buying process. The most common are the personnel from the purchasing, quality control, and manufacturing departments. These individuals are identified in the model as purchasing agents, engineers, and users, respectively. Several other individuals in the organization may be, but are typically not, involved in the buying process (for example, the president of the firm or the comptroller). There is considerable interaction among the individuals in the three departments continuously involved in the buying process and often they are asked to decide jointly. It is, therefore, critical to examine the similarities and differences in the psychological worlds of these individuals.

Based on research in consumer and social psychology, several different aspects of the psychology of the decision makers are included in the model. Primary among these are the *expectations* of the decision makers about suppliers and brands [(1) in Figure 1]. The present model specifies five different processes which create differential expectations among the individuals involved in the purchasing process: (1a) the *background of the individuals,* (1b) *information sources,* (1c) *active search,* (1d) *perceptual distortion,* and (1e) *satisfaction with past purchases.* These variables must be explained and operationally defined if they are to fully represent the psychological world of the organizational buyers.

## Expectations

Expectations refer to the *perceived* potential of alternative suppliers and brands to satisfy a number of explicit and implicit objectives in any particular buying decision. The most common explicit objectives include, in order of relative importance, product quality, delivery time, quantity of supply, after-sale service where appropriate, and price.[7] However, a number of studies have pointed out the critical role of several implicit criteria such as reputation, size, location, and reciprocity relationship with the supplier; and personality, technical expertise, salesmanship, and even life style of the sales representative.[8] In fact, with the standardized marketing mix among the suppliers in oligopolistic markets, the implicit criteria are becoming marginally more and more significant in the industrial buyer's decisions.

Expectations can be measured by obtaining a profile of each supplier or brand as to how satisfactory it is perceived to be in enabling the decision maker to achieve his explicit and implicit objectives. Almost all studies from past research indicate that expectations will substantially differ among the purchasing agents, engineers, and product users because each considers different criteria to be salient in judging the supplier or the brand. In general, it is found that product users look for prompt delivery, proper installation, and efficient serviceability; purchasing agents look for maximum price advantage and economy in shipping and forwarding; and engineers look for excellence in quality, standardization of the product, and engineering pretesting of the product. These differences in objectives and, consequently, expectations are often the root causes for constant conflict among these three types of individuals.[9]

Why are there substantial differences in expectations? While there is considerable speculation among researchers and observers of industrial buyer behavior on the number and nature of explanations, there is relatively little consensus. The five most salient processes which determine differential expectations, as specified in the model, are discussed below.

***Background of Individuals.*** The first, and probably most significant, factor is the background and task orientation of each of the individuals involved in the buying process. The different educational backgrounds of the purchasing agents, engineers, and plant managers often generate substantially different professional goals and values. In addition, the task expectations also generate conflicting perceptions of one another's role in the organization. Finally, the personal life styles of individual decision makers play an important role in developing differential expectations.[10]

It is relatively easy to gather information on this background factor. The educational and task differences are comparable to demographics in consumer behavior, and life style differences can be assessed by psychographic scales on the individual's interests, activities, and values as a professional.

***Information Sources and Active Search.*** The second and third factors in creating differential expectations are the source and type of information each of the decision makers is exposed to and his participation in the active search. Purchasing agents receive disproportionately greater exposure to commercial sources, and the information is often partial and biased toward the supplier or the brand. In some companies, it is even a common practice to discourage sales representatives from talking directly to the engineering or production personnel. The engineering and production personnel, therefore, typically have less information and what they have is obtained primarily from professional meetings, trade reports, and even word-of-mouth. In addition, the active search for information is often relegated to the purchasing agents because it is presumed to be their job responsibility.

It is not too difficult to assess differences among the three types of individuals in their exposure to various sources and types of information by standard survey research methods.

***Perceptual Distortion.*** A fourth factor is the selective distortion and retention of available information. Each individual strives to make the objective information consistent with his own prior knowledge and expectations by systematically distorting it. For example, since there are substantial differences in the goals and values of purchasing agents, engineers, and production personnel, one should expect different interpretations of the same information among them. Although no specific research has been done on this tendency to perceptually distort information in the area of industrial buyer behavior, a large body of research does exist on cognitive consistency to explain its presence as a natural human tendency.[11]

Perceptual distortion is probably the most difficult variable to quantify by standard survey research methods. One possible approach is experimentation, but this is costly. A more realistic alternative is to utilize perceptual mapping techniques such as multidimensional scaling or factor analysis and compare differences in the judgments of the purchasing agents, engineers, and production personnel to a common list of suppliers or brands.

***Satisfaction with Past Purchases.*** The fifth factor which creates differential expectations among the various individuals involved in the purchasing process is the satisfaction with past buying experiences with a supplier or brand. Often it is not possible for a supplier or brand to provide equal satisfaction to the three parties because each one has different goals or criteria. For example, a supplier may be lower in price but his delivery schedule may not be satisfactory. Similarly, a product's quality may be excellent but its price may be higher than others. The organization typically rewards each individual for excellent performance in his specialized skills, so the purchasing agent is rewarded for economy, the engineer for quality control, and the production personnel for efficient scheduling. This often results in a different level of satisfaction for each of the parties involved even though the chosen supplier or brand may be the best feasible alternative in terms of overall corporate goals.

Past experiences with a supplier or brand, summarized in the satisfaction variable, directly influence the person's expectations toward that supplier or brand. It is relatively easy to measure the satisfaction variable by obtaining information on how the supplier or brand is perceived by each of the three parties.

## Determinants of Joint vs. Autonomous Decisions

Not all industrial buying decisions are made jointly by the various individuals involved in the purchasing process. Sometimes the buying decisions are delegated to one party, which is not necessarily the purchasing agent. It is, therefore, important for the supplier to know whether a buying decision is joint or autonomous and, if it is the latter, to which party it is delegated. There are six primary factors which determine whether a specific buying decision will be joint or autonomous. Three of these factors are related to the characteristics of the product or service (2a) and the other three are related to the characteristics of the buyer company (2b).

### Product-Specific Factors

The first product-specific variable is what Bauer calls *perceived risk* in buying decisions.[12] Perceived risk refers to the magnitude of adverse consequences felt by the decision maker if he makes a wrong choice, and the uncertainty under which he must decide. The greater the uncertainty in a buying situation, the greater the perceived risk. Although there is very little direct evidence, it is logical to hypothesize that the greater the perceived risk in a specific buying decision, the more likely it is that the purchase will be decided jointly by all parties concerned. The second product-specific factor is *type of purchase*. If it is the first purchase or a once-in-a-lifetime capital expenditure, one would expect greater joint decision making. On the other hand, if the purchase decision is repetitive and routine or is limited to maintenance products or services, the buying decision is likely to be delegated to one party. The third factor is *time pressure*. If the buying decision has to be made under a great deal of time pressure or on an emergency basis, it is likely to be delegated to one party rather than decided jointly.

### Company-Specific Factors

The three organization-specific factors are *company orientation, company size,* and *degree of centralization*. If the company is technology oriented, it is likely to be dominated by the engineering people and the buying decisions will, in essence, be made by them. Similarly, if the company is production oriented, the buying decisions will be made by the production personnel.[13] Second, if the company is a large corporation, decision making will tend to be joint. Finally, the greater the degree of centralization, the less likely it is that the decisions will be joint. Thus, a privately-owned small company with technology or production orientation will tend toward autonomous decision making and a large-scale public corporation with considerable decentralization will tend to have greater joint decision making.

Even though there is considerable research evidence in organization behavior in general to support these six factors, empirical evidence in industrial buying decisions in particular is sketchy on them. Perhaps with more research it will be possible to verify the generalizations and deductive logic utilized in this aspect of the model.

## Process of Joint Decision Making

The major thrust of the present model of industrial buying decisions is to investigate the process of joint decision making. This includes initiation of the decision to buy, gathering of information, evaluating alternative suppliers, and resolving conflict among the parties who must jointly decide.

The decision to buy is usually initiated by a continued need of supply or is the outcome of long-range planning. The formal initiation in the first case is typically from the production personnel by way of a requisition slip. The latter usually is a formal recommendation from the planning unit to an ad hoc committee consisting of the purchasing agent, the engineer, and the plant manager. The information-gathering function is typically relegated to the purchasing agent. If the purchase is a repetitive decision for standard items, there is very little information gathering. Usually the purchasing agent contacts the preferred supplier and orders the items on the requisition slip. However, considerable active search effort is manifested for capital expenditure items, especially those which are entirely new purchase experiences for the organization.[14]

The most important aspect of the joint decision-making process, however, is the assimilation of information, deliberations on it, and the consequent conflict which most joint decisions entail. According to March and Simon, conflict is present when there is a need to decide jointly among a group of people who have, at the same time, different goals and perceptions.[15] In view of the fact that the latter is invariably present among the various parties to industrial buying decisions, conflict becomes a common consequence of the joint decision-making process; the buying motives and expectations about brands and suppliers are considerably different for the engineer, the user, and the purchasing agent, partly due to different educational backgrounds and partly due to company policy of reward for specialized skills and viewpoints.

Interdepartmental conflict in itself is not necessarily bad. What matters most from the organization's viewpoint is *how* the conflict is resolved (3). If it is resolved in a rational manner, one very much hopes that the final joint decision will also tend to be rational. If, on the other hand, conflict resolution degenerates to what Strauss calls "tactics of lateral relationship,"[16] the organization will suffer from inefficiency and the joint decisions may be reduced to bargaining and politicking among the parties involved. Not only will the decision be based on irrational criteria, but the choice of a supplier may be to the detriment of the buying organization.

What types of conflict can be expected in industrial buying decisions? How are they likely to be resolved? These are some of the key questions in an understanding of industrial buyer behavior. If the inter-party conflict is largely due to disagreements on expectations about the suppliers or their brands, it is likely that the conflict will be resolved in the *problem-solving* manner. The immediate consequence of this type of conflict is to actively search for more information, deliberate more on available information, and often to seek out other suppliers not seriously considered before. The additional information is then presented in a problem-solving fashion so that conflict tends to be minimized.

If the conflict among the parties is primarily due to disagreement on some specific criteria with which to evaluate suppliers—although there is an agreement on the buying goals or objectives at a more fundamental level—it is likely to be resolved by *persuasion*. An attempt is made, under this type of resolution, to persuade the dissenting member by pointing out the importance of overall corporate objectives and how his criterion is not likely to attain these objectives. There is no attempt to gather more information. However, there results greater interaction and communication among the parties, and sometimes an outsider is brought in to reconcile the differences.

Both problem solving and persuasion are useful and rational methods of conflict resolution. The resulting joint decisions, therefore, also tend to be more rational. Thus, conflicts produced due to disagreements on expectations about the suppliers or on a specific criterion are healthy from the organization's viewpoint even though they may be time consuming. One is likely to find, however, that a more typical situation in which conflict arises is due to fundamental differences in buying goals or objectives among the various parties. This is especially true with respect to unique or new buying decisions related to capital expenditure items. The conflict is resolved not by changing the differences in relative importance of the buying goals or objectives of the individuals involved, but by the process of *bargaining*. The fundamental differences among the parties are implicitly conceded by all the members and the concept of distributive justice (tit for tat) is invoked as a part of bargaining. The most common outcome is to allow a single party to decide autonomously in this specific situation in return for some favor or promise or reciprocity in future decisions.

Finally, if the disagreement is not simply with respect to buying goals or objectives but also with respect to *style of decision making,* the conflict tends to be grave and borders on the mutual dislike of personalities among the individual decision makers. The resolution of this type of conflict is usually by *politicking* and back-stabbing tactics. Such methods of conflict resolution are common in industrial buying decisions. The reader is referred to the sobering research of Strauss for further discussion.[17]

Both bargaining and politicking are nonrational and inefficient methods of conflict resolution; the buying organization suffers from these conflicts. Furthermore, the decision makers find themselves sinking below their professional, managerial role. The decisions are not only delayed but tend to be governed by factors other than achievement of corporate objectives.

## Critical Role of Situational Factors

The model described so far presumes that the choice of a supplier or brand is the outcome of a systematic decision-making process in the organizational setting. However, there is ample empirical evidence in the literature to suggest that at least some of the industrial buying decisions are determined by ad hoc *situational factors* (4) and not by any systematic decision-making process. In other words, similar to consumer behavior, the industrial buyers often decide on factors other than rational or realistic criteria.

It is difficult to prepare a list of ad hoc conditions which determine industrial buyer behavior without decision making. However, a number of situational factors which often intervene between the actual choice and any prior decision-making process can be isolated. These inlcude: temporary economic conditions such as price controls, recession, or foreign trade; internal strikes, walkouts, machine breakdowns, and other production-related events; organizational changes such as merger or acquisition; and ad hoc changes in the market place, such as promotional efforts, new product introduction, price changes, and so on, in the supplier industries.

## Implications for Industrial Marketing Research

The model of industrial buyer behavior described above suggests the following implications for marketing research.

First, in order to explain and predict supplier or brand choice in industrial buyer behavior, it is necessary to conduct research on the psychology of other individuals in the organization in addition to the purchasing agents. It is, perhaps, the unique nature of organizational structure and behavior which leads to a distinct separation of the consumer, the buyer, and the procurement agent, as well as others possibly involved in the decision-making process. In fact, it may not be an exaggeration to suggest that the purchasing agent is often a less critical member of the decision-making process in industrial buyer behavior.

Second, it is possible to operationalize and quantify most of the variables included as part of the model. While some are more difficult and indirect, sufficient psychometric skill in marketing research is currently available to quantify the psychology of the individuals.

Third, although considerable research has been done on the demographics of organizations in industrial market research—for example, on the turnover and size of the company, workflows, standard industrial classification, and profit ratios—demographic and life-style information on the individuals involved in industrial buying decisions is also needed.

Fourth, a systematic examination of the power positions of various individuals involved in industrial buying decisions is a necessary condition of the model. The sufficient condition is to examine trade-offs among various objectives, both explicit and implicit, in order to create a satisfied customer.

Fifth, it is essential in building any market research information system for industrial goods and services that the process of conflict resolution among the parties and its impact on supplier or brand choice behavior is carefully included and simulated.

Finally, it is important to realize that not all industrial decisions are the outcomes of a systematic decision-making process. There are some industrial buying decisions which are based strictly on a set of situational factors for which theorizing or model building will not be relevant or useful. What is needed in these cases is a checklist of empirical observations of the ad hoc events which vitiate the neat relationship between the theory or the model and a specific buying decision.

## ENDNOTES

1. For a comprehensive list of references, see Thomas A. Staudt and W. Lazer, *A Basic Bibliography on Industrial Marketing* (Chicago: American Marketing Assn., 1963); and Donald E. Vinson, "Bibliography of Industrial Marketing" (unpublished listing of references, University of Colorado, 1972).
2. Richard M. Cyert, et al., "Observation of a Business Decision," *Journal of Business*, Vol. 29 (October 1956), pp. 237-248; John A. Howard and C. G. Moore, Jr., "A Descriptive Model of the Purchasing Agent" (unpublished monograph, University of Pittsburgh, 1964); George Strauss, "Work Study of Purchasing Agents," *Human Organization*, Vol. 33 (September 1964), pp. 137-149; Theodore A. Levitt, *Industrial Purchasing Behavior* (Boston: Division of Research, Graduate School of Business, Harvard University, 1965); Ozanne B. Urban and Gilbert A. Churchill, "Adoption Research: Information Sources in the Industrial Purchasing Decision," and Richard N. Cardozo, "Segmenting the Industrial Market," in *Marketing and the New Science of Planning*, R. L. King, ed. (Chicago: American Marketing Assn., 1968), pp. 352-359 and 433-440, respectively. Richard N. Cardozo and J. W. Cagley, "Experimental Study of Industrial Buyer Behavior," *Journal of Marketing Research*, Vol. 8 (August 1971), pp. 329-334; Thomas P. Copley and

F. L. Callom, "Industrial Search Behavior and Perceived Risk," in *Proceedings of the Second Annual Conference, the Association for Consumer Research*, D. M. Gardner, ed. (College Park, Md.: Association for Consumer Research, 1971), pp. 208-231; and James R. McMillan, "Industrial Buying Behavior as Group Decision Making," (paper presented at the Nineteenth International Meeting of the Institute of Management Sciences, April 1972).

3. Robert F. Shoaf, ed., *Emotional Factors Underlying Industrial Purchasing* (Cleveland, Ohio: Penton Publishing Co., 1959); G. H. Haas, B. March, and E. M. Krech, *Purchasing Department Organization and Authority*, American Management Assn. Research Study No. 45 (New York: 1960); *Evaluation of Supplier Performance* (New York: National Association of Purchasing Agents, 1963); F. A. Hays and G. A. Renard, *Evaluating Purchasing Performance*, American Management Assn. Research Study No. 66 (New York: 1964); Hugh Buckner, *How British Industry Buys* (London: Hutchison and Company, Ltd., 1967); *How Industry Buys/1970* (New York: Scientific American, 1970). In addition, numerous articles published in trade journals such as *Purchasing and Industrial Marketing* are cited in Vinson, same reference as note 1, and Strauss, same reference as note 2.
4. Ralph S. Alexander, J. S. Cross, and R. M. Hill, *Industrial Marketing*, 3rd ed. (Homewood, Ill.: Richard D. Irwin, 1967); John H. Westing, I. V. Fine, and G. J. Zenz, *Purchasing Management* (New York: John Wiley & Sons, 1969); Patrick J. Robinson, C. W. Farris, and Y. Wind, *Industrial Buying and Creative Marketing* (Boston: Allyn & Bacon, 1967); Frederick E. Webster, Jr., "Modeling the Industrial Buying Process," *Journal of Marketing Research*, Vol. 2 (November 1965), pp. 370-376; and Frederick E. Webster, Jr., "Industrial Buying Behavior: A State-of-the-Art Appraisal," in *Marketing in a Changing World*, B. A. Morin, ed. (Chicago: American Marketing Assn., 1969), p. 256.
5. John A. Howard and J. N. Sheth, *The Theory of Buyer Behavior* (New York: John Wiley & Sons, 1969).
6. Howard and Moore, same reference as note 2; Strauss, same reference as note 2; McMillan, same reference as note 2; *How Industry Buys/1970*, same reference as note 3.
7. Howard and Moore, same reference as note 2; *How Industry Buys/1970*, same reference as note 3; Hays and Renard, same reference as note 3.
8. Howard and Moore, same reference as note 2; Levitt, same reference as note 2; Westing, Fine, and Zenz, same reference as note 4; Shoaf, same reference as note 4.
9. Strauss, same reference as note 2.
10. For a general reading, see Robert T. Golembiewski, "Small Groups and Large Organizations," in *Handbook of Organizations*, J. G. March, ed. (Chicago: Rand McNally & Company, 1965), chapter 3. For field studies related to this area, see Donald E. Porter, P. B. Applewhite, and M. J. Misshauk, eds., *Studies in Organizational Behavior and Management*, 2nd ed. (Scranton, Pa.: Intext Educational Publishers, 1971).
11. Robert P. Abelson, et al., *Theories of Cognitive Consistency: A Source Book* (Chicago: Rand McNally & Company, 1968).
12. Raymond A. Bauer, "Consumer Behavior as Risk Taking," in *Dynamic Marketing for a Changing World*, R. L. Hancock, ed. (Chicago: American Marketing Assn., 1960), pp. 389-400. Applications of perceived risk in industrial

buying can be found in Levitt, same reference as note 2; Copley and Callom, same reference as note 2; McMillan, same reference as note 2.

13. For some indirect evidence, see Strauss, same reference as note 2. For a more general study, see Victor A. Thompson, "Hierarchy, Specialization and Organizational Conflict," *Administrative Science Quarterly*, Vol. 5 (March 1961), p. 513; and Henry A. Landsberger, "The Horizontal Dimension in Bureaucracy," *Administration Science Quarterly*, Vol. 6 (December 1961), pp. 299-332, for a thorough review of numerous theories.
14. Strauss, same reference as note 2.
15. James G. March and H. A. Simon, *Organizations* (New York: John Wiley & Sons, 1958), chapter 5; and Landsberger, same reference as note 13.
16. George Strauss, "Tactics of Lateral Relationship: The Purchasing Agent," *Administrative Science Quarterly*, Vol. 7 (September 1962), pp. 161-186.
17. Same reference as note 16.

35 — Conceptual and Methodological Issues in Organisational Buying Behaviour

*Yoram Wind and Robert J. Thomas*

*European Journal of Marketing*, Vol. 14, No. 5/6 (1980), pp. 239-263. Reprinted by permission.

## Introduction

Advances in our knowledge of organisational buying behaviour and in the utilisation of findings from organisational buying behaviour studies depend on two key factors: (a) close collaboration between users of such information (e.g., industrial marketing managers) and the basic and applied researches involved in organisational buying research, and (b) resolution of the major conceptual and methodological issues involved in the study of organisational buying behaviour.

Whereas the key to the first factor is the recognition that such collaboration is essential for the development of usable information on organisational buying behaviour, the second factor requires closer examination and specification. It is the objective of this paper to highlight some of the major conceptual and methodological issues involved in organisational buying behaviour. Specifying these issues could help avoid some of the pitfalls involved in the utilisation of research and, more importantly, could stimulate research aimed at the resolution of these issues.

The paper is divided into four parts. First, a brief review of the current status of the organisational buying behaviour literature is offered. This is followed by the identification of five potential groups of users of information or organisational buying behaviour. Their idiosyncratic research needs are identified and serve as a backdrop against which to evaluate the relevance of current organisational buying research. The last two sections of the paper focus on the conceptual and methodological issues involved in organisational buying research. Embedded throughout the discussion are suggestions for new research directions which, if implemented could help advance the relevance and quality of organisational buying research.

## Current Status of Organisational Buying Behaviour

Typical academic and industry-based research on organisational buying behaviour can be classified into five types; these are summarised in Figure 1.

**FIGURE 1. Classification of Organisational Buying Research Efforts by Orientation and Scope**

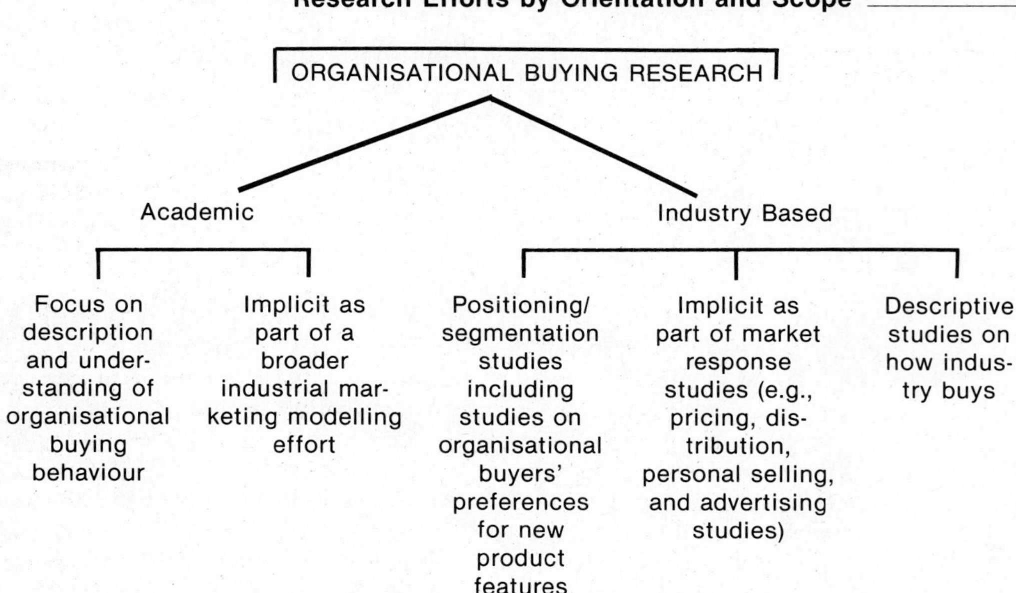


With the exception of the "How Industry Buys ..."studies, most of the industry-based research is proprietary and has not been published. Any review of organisational buying behaviour, therefore, is predominantly based on published academic studies. Given that some of the more sophisticated and innovative organisational buying research projects are undertaken by (or for) industrial firms, a review of the published literature offers only a partial view of the current state of knowledge concerning organisational buying behaviour. Our brief review focuses on academic studies, but our conclusions concerning the conceptual and methodological issues of organisational buying behaviour tend to incorporate our experience with the other types of research.

The subset of academic studies which is directly concerned with a better understanding of organisational buying behaviour can be classified as falling into one of three areas:

1. the buying centre (the least studied area),
2. the organisational buying process, or
3. the factors affecting the organisational buying center and process.

These three concepts can provide the basis for organising much of the diverse research efforts in organisational buying behaviour. Illustrative findings from each of these areas are briefly reviewed in the following sections.

## The Buying Centre

There is widespread agreement that organisational buying involves multiple participants. Yet, despite the acceptance of the "buying centre" concept (Wind, 1978; Spekman and Stern, 1979), little is known about the composition of the buying centre, the determinants of the specific buying centre composition and changes in it, and the nature of influence patterns among its members. Table I summarises some illustrative studies relating to the identification of the buying centre, the roles in the buying centre, and the influence patterns within it.

The general findings on the composition of the buying centre suggest that it varies by organisation and even within a given organisation, by buying situation and other idiosyncratic characteristics. The functioning of buying committees, group versus individual choice models employed in reaching buying decisions, the buying centre's organisational environment, and changes in composition and activities in response to changing conditions are emerging to describe further the structure and process which characterise organisational buying centres.

The illustrative role studies suggest that organisational members vary in their perceptions. Furthermore, these roles are likely to vary throughout the buying process. From a managerial perspective, McAleer's (1974) study, which reveals differences in responses to advertising stimuli, and other studies (such as Wind, 1979), which identified considerable intra-organisational heterogeneity, suggest the need to re-examine the conventional approach to segmentation of industrial markets.

Studies concerned with purchase influence are very sensitive to the measurement approach used. For example, Spekman (1979), using an attributional approach, found "expert" power to be relevant to the purchasing agents' ability to influence others. This finding was confirmed by Thomas (1980) when using a similar research approach. However, when an experimental approach (on the same subjects) was used, other bases of power were found to be more important than expertise, and the specific base further varied by organisational position and nature of conflict within the buying centre.

## The Buying Process

From the time at which a need arises for a product or service, to the purchase decision and its subsequent evaluation, a complex myriad of activities can take place. The continual conceptual reformulation of this process is evidence of the difficulty in its modelling. A number of illustrative models are suggested in Table II.

The models vary in complexity from Bradley's (1977) four stages of a governmental purchase decision, to Wind's (1978) twelve stages for the purchase of scientific and technical information services. This variation suggests that the organisational buying process is complex, it may vary by

**TABLE I. Illustrative Findings from Unit of Analysis Studies**

| *Issue* | *Study* | *Major Finding* |
|---|---|---|
| Identifying the composition of the buying centre | Wind (1978) | Decisions to purchase industrial components are carried out by members of a "buying centre" whose composition changes depending on the organisation (centralised versus decentralised) and buying situation. |
| | Harding (1966); *How Industry Buys* (1969); "Who Makes Purchasing Decisions?" (1974); LAP Report 1042.2 (1977). | Multiple persons at different managerial levels involved in organisational buying decisions. |
| | Spekman & Stern (1979) | The composite profile of buying group structure tends to reflect a bureaucratic orientation. |
| | Wind (1979) | The size and composition of buying centres for the purchase of STI vary by organisation size and buying situation. |
| | "How Industry Buys Chemicals" (1979) | The purchase decision is a team project in which *all* functional groups participate to a significant degree. |
| Roles in the buying centre. | Gorman (1971) | Buying roles are multidimensional, with little consensus on purchase-related criteria among purchasing, functional and top managers. |
| | McAleer (1974) | Architects and contractors differ in their response to promotional stimuli. |
| | Pingry (1974) | Found more similarities than differences between purchasing agents and engineers on several criteria. |
| | Calder (1977) | Characterised buying centre roles by seven persons, eight positions, and ten tasks. |
| | Wind (1978) | The importance of different organisational roles (positions) varies by the phase of the buying process; size of organisation is a relevant factor. |
| Influence in the buying center | Strauss (1962) | Purchasing agents engage in lateral intra-organisational relationships ("power struggles") to enhance their studies. |
| | Wind (1971) | Buying center members tend to respond to the formal and social rewards of other buying centre members in interpersonal relationships. |
| | McMillan (1973) | Non-purchasing personnel (scientists and managers) had more perceived influence on vendor selection decision than purchasing agents. |
| | Grashof and Thomas (1976) | There was a high degree of self-inflation of perceived influence; however, it was consistent throughout the buying process. |
| | Cooley, Jackson, and Ostron (1977) | Differences in relative power of engineering versus purchasing functions. |
| | Spekman (1979) | As buying centre members perceived greater environmental uncertainty, greater power is attributed to the purchasing agent. |
| | Thomas (1980) | A decision maker's evaluations of a product are affected by the authority, stature, or expertise of others, but depend on the decision maker's position, the degree of conflict, and specific product features. |

**TABLE II. Illustrative Formulation of the Organisational Buying Process**

| *Robinson & Faris (1967)* | *Ozanne & Churchill (1971)* | *Webster & Wind (1972)* | *Kelly (1974)* | *Bradley (1977)* | *Wind (1978)* |
|---|---|---|---|---|---|
| (1) Problem (need) recognition | (1) Awareness | (1) Identify needs | (1) Recognise need | (1) Purchase initiation | (1) Identification of needs |
| (2) Determine characteristics | | (2) Establish specifications | | | (2) Establish specifications |
| (3) Describe characteristics | | | | | |
| (4) Search for sources | (2) Interest | (3) Identify alternatives | (2) Information search | (2) Survey of alternatives | (3) Search for alternatives |
| (5) Acquire proposals | | | | | (4) Establish contact |
| (6) Evaluate proposals | (3) Evaluation | (4) Evaluate alternatives | (3) Evaluate alternatives | (3) Supplier short-listing | (5) Set purchase and usage criteria |
| | | | | | (6) Evaluate alternatives |
| | | | (4) Approval of funds | | (7) Budget availability |
| | | | | | (8) Evaluate specific alternatives |
| | | | | | (9) Negotiate |
| (7) Select order routine | (4) Trial | (5) Select supplier | (5) Decision | (4) Award contract | (10) Buy |
| | (5) Adoption | | | | (11) Use |
| (8) Performance feedback | | | | | (12) Post-purchase evaluation |

product/industry and buying situation (straight rebuy, modified rebuy, or new task), it is difficult to model, and, most critical, it is difficult to validate empirically since the order in which these steps typically are presented to the respondent can affect his/her response.

Much of the research on organisational buying behaviour is conducted on various stages of the process. Table III lists some illustrative studies for some of the key buying process stages.

**TABLE III. Illustrative Findings from Buying Process Studies**

| *Issue* | *Study* | *Finding* |
|---|---|---|
| Overall buying process | Cyert, Simon & Trow (1956)<br>Robinson & Faris (1967)<br>Wind (1968)<br>Ozanne & Churchill (1971)<br>Brand (1972)<br>Saleh and LaLonde (1972)<br>Kelly (1974)<br>Bradley (1977)<br>Wind (1978) | Buying Process is:<br>- complex<br>- difficult to model<br>- different by product/industry<br>- different across buying situations |
| Identification of needs | von Hippel (1978) | Customer requests may lead to more successful products than formal study of organisation needs. |
| Identification of alternatives (search process) | Levitt (1965) | Vendor's reputation and quality of presentation are important. |
| | Ozanne & Churchill (1968) | Use same sources throughout adoption process. |
| | Webster (1970) | Use personal sources; salespersons are important. |
| | Morrill (1970) | Advertising improves buyers' attitudes toward seller. |
| | A.D. Little Inc. (1971) | An evaluation of 1100 research studies on the effectiveness of industrial advertising suggested that industrial advertising, as a partner to personal selling, can generate sales. |
| | Kelly and Hensel (1973) | Personal sources are more credible and useful than nonpersonal sources. |
| | Lehman & Cardozo (1973) | Institutional advertisements more effective than product advertisements among organisational buyers. |
| | Stiles (1973) | Information processing varies by task complexity. |
| | Schiffman, Winer & Gaccione (1974) | Mass communication sources more important in awareness stage; sales personnel more important at latter stages. |
| | San Augustine, Foley, & Freidman (1977) | Overt searchers (inquiries about product) more aware of advertising campaign, but poorer recall. |
| | Patti (1977) | Buyers perceive trade advertisements as important as salespersons; sellers believe sales personnel most important source. |
| | Beardon *et al.* (1978) | Consumer magazines were found to be more cost efficient than trade publications. |
| Set purchase and usage criteria | Lazo (1960) | The greater the similarity of products on an objective basis, the more likely the buyer's decision will be based on subjective factors. |
| | Dickson (1966) | Quality, delivery, and performance history are important attributes; price is less important for complex products. |
| | Wind, Green & Robinson (1968) | Assessed the relative importance of ten purchase (vendor selection) criteria. |
| | Lehmann & O'Shaughnessy (1974) | Of 17 attributes, reliabiliy of delivery is most important; differences in attribute importance according to variations in buying perceptions of procedure and performance problems related to product. |

**TABLE III. Illustrative Findings from Buying Process Studies (cont.)**

| *Issue* | *Study* | *Finding* |
|---|---|---|
| | Kelly & Coaker (1976) | Choice ceiteria varied in importance across organisations. |
| | Kiser & Rao (1977) | Of 65 attributes, reliability, costs, management capabilities, and service are most important for hospitals and industrial firms. |
| | Evans (1980) | Replicated findings of Lehmann & O'Shaughnessy study. |
| Evaluate alternative buying actions | Wildt & Bruno (1974) | Predicted preferences for capital equipment purchases with linear compensatory attitude model. |
| | Scott & Wright (1976) | Found multiple regression estimation weights buyers give in evaluations to be reliable. |
| | Wind, Grashof, & Goldhar (1978) | Product design based on results of conjoint analysis approach. |
| Purchase decision | "How Industry Buys Chemicals" (1979) | The decision to buy is not a judgement made solely at the time the purchase order is issued. Rather, each decision evolves over a time span in which most functional groups participate. |
| Post-purchase evaluation | Lambert, Dornoff & Kernan (1977) | Feedback critical of choice produced a positive effect on attitude toward rejected alternatives and no effect on attitude toward actual choice. |

In addition to these types of studies, recent years have witnessed an increasing number of unpublished industrial studies on the *criteria used by industrial firms to make purchase decisions*. Many of these studies have utilised a conjoint analysis design coupled with a computer simulation (Green and Wind, 1975) or, more recently, some optimisation procedure such as the one developed by Green as part of the POSSE system (Rogers National Research, 1979). Conjoint analysis studies have been conducted for over 300 industrial products and services including copying machines, printing equipment, data transmission, diagnostic x-ray equipment, other medical equipment, automotive styling, information retrieval services, ethical drugs, freight train operations, financial services, car rental services, telephone services, airline services and others.

## Factors Affecting the Buying Decision Process

The organisational buying process and the composition of the buying centre tend to vary depending on two sets of factors: the buying situation (whether the purchase is a new task, a modified rebuy, or straight rebuy) and the idiosyncratic personal, interpersonal, organisational, and environmental, conditions.

The importance of the buying situation has long been recognised in both organisational buying behaviour studies (Robinson and Faris, 1967; Webster and Wind, 1972) and consumer behaviour (Howard and Sheth,

1969; Howard, 1977). The two classifications proposed by the above authors are extremely similar:

new task .....extensive problem solving;

modified rebuy .....limited problem solving;

straight rebuy .....routinised response behaviour;

and both formulations suggest that different decision processes are followed under these three situations (buyers have different information needs, levels of risk, propensities to search for new suppliers, etc.). The composition of the buying centre also reflects different buying situations.

Other organisational buying situations have been studied. For example, in a binational study of industrial purchasing agents, Lehmann and O'Shaughnessy (1974) identified routine order products, procedural problem products, performance problem products, and political problem products. They found that the importance of product attributes is significantly related to the type of product or buying situation. Similarly, Cardozo and Cagley (1971) found that industrial buyers' choices varied between high and low risk buying situations.

More recently other buying situations have been proposed to explain consumer behaviour—low versus high involvement (Krugman, 1965) and low versus high imagery products (Wind, 1980)—which can be applied also to the organisational buying context.

The second set of factors, those affecting the composition of the organisational buying centre and its buying process, includes four subsets of factors: personal, interpersonal, organisational, and inter-organisational. A few illustrative findings concerning these factors are summarised in Table IV.

In addition to these factors, there are three other sets of factors that should be included in comprehensive studies of organisational buying behaviour:

1. the effect of the firm's marketing variables (product design, positioning, price, advertising, promotion, distribution, etc.);
2. the effect of the marketing strategies of competitors;
3. the effect of environmental forces (other than those reflected in the interorganisational factors) including the economic, political, legal, technological, and social/cultural forces and trends.

The focus on factors explaining and predicting organisational buying behaviour has dominated most of the US studies of organisational buying behaviour. It has also been the focal point of most of the theoretical modelling work in this area. General organisational buying behaviour models such as those proposed by Webster and Wind (1972) and Sheth (1973) have

### TABLE IV. Illustrative Findings from Studies on Factors Affecting the the Buying Decision Process

| *Factor* | *Study* | *Finding* |
|---|---|---|
| Personal factors | Cardozo & Cagley (1971) | Individual differences (job responsibility and background) in response to risk in buying situations. |
| | Wilson (1971) | Need for certainty is an important determinant of choice. |
| | Peters & Venkatesan (1973) | Perceived risk, specific self-confidence, education, computer experience, and number of jobs held were associated with adopters versus non-adopters. |
| | Baker & Abu-Ismail | Early adoption is a function of economic, behavioural, and managerial variables rather than economic variables alone. |
| Inter-personal factors | Evans (1963) | Similarity of attributes within the dyad appears to increase likelihood of sale. |
| | Tosi (1966) | Role consensus between buyer and seller not significant in explaining salesperson's effectiveness. |
| | Farley & Swinth (1967) | Support for balance theory versus exchange theory; i.e., buyer had warmer feeling toward salesperson regardless of message. |
| | Martilla (1971) | Interpersonal communication was found to be an important element *within firms*, while its importance *between* firms depended on the type of product and geographic market factors. |
| | Mathews, Wilson & Monoky (1972) | Perceived buyer-seller similarity increased number of co-operative responses. |
| | Schiffman, Winer & Gaccione (1974) | Opinion leaders have greater interpersonal interaction with administrative personnel in other firms. |
| | Busch & Wilson (1976) | Expertise is more effective than referent power in producing customer changes. |
| | Sweitzer (1976) | Empathy was found to explain buyer-seller responses (as opposed to similarity). |
| | Huppertz, Arenson, & Evans (1978) | Buyers can perceive inequity in buyer-seller relationship and may exit from situation. |
| | Weitz (1978) | Explained 20 per cent of field sales performance with a model based on industrial salespersons's perceptions of customer evaluation and decision processes. |
| Organisational factors | Webster (1968) | Innovative firms characterised by aggressive management, high rate of product development, and capability of evaluating new products. |
| | Hayward (1972) | Group mills adopt innovations earlier than independent mills. |
| | O'Neal, Thorelli, & Utterback (1973) | Adoption was related to technical change in industry, positive information, and advantage and compatibility of innovation. |
| | Hakansson & Wootz (1975) | Location of organisation and price/quality of product were important supplier selection factors. |
| | Czepiel (1976) | Early adopting decision groups (buying centres) were smaller and had greater experience than later adopters. |
| | Gronhaug (1976) | Product-dependent organisations (those whose income is dependent on product markets) are more likely to perceive budget constraints than product-independent organisations (e.g., those whose income is controlled by regulatory groups). |

**TABLE IV. Illustrative Findings from Studies on Factors Affecting the Buying Decision Process (cont.)**

| *Factor* | *Study* | *Finding* |
|---|---|---|
| | Robertson & Wind (1980) | Knowledge of organisational climate (organisational psychographics) adds significantly to our ability to explain (and predict) the adoption of innovative medical equipment. |
| Inter-organisational factors | Pruden & Reese (1972) | Power, authority, and status interactions were found to differentiate high- versus low- performing salespeople. |
| | Czepiel (1974) | Informal communications network linked firms involved in diffusion process. |
| | Hunt & Nevin (1974) | There is a significant relationship between the power of a channel member and the sources of power available to him/her. |
| | Etgar (1976) | Power of a channel leader is related to his/her power sources, dependency of other channel members on him/her, and counter-vailing power of channel members. |
| | Ford (1978) | Buyer-seller relations are a function of channel relationships within which they are involved. |

attempted to provide primarily a framework for classifying (and explaining) the myriad of factors affecting organisational buying behaviour. These models suffer, however, from the same problems which confront their consumer behaviour counterparts (such as the models of Howard and Sheth, 1969; Engel, Kolat, and Blackwell, 1968, and their more recent revisions). More recent work has focused, therefore on more specific theoretical constructs and has included conceptualisations of the organisational buying behaviour process along the lines of the social influence process (Bonoma and Zaltman, 1978) a dyadic buyer-seller interaction process (Sheth, 1975; Wilson, 1978; Bonoma, Bagozzi, and Zaltman, 1978), exchange, social judgment, and action models (Bagozzi, 1978), balance theory (Wind, 1971), the behavioural theory of the firm (Wind, 1968), and various individual and group choice paradigms which centre on the criteria used by the key members of the buying centre in making the organisational buying decisions (e.g., Wind, 1973).

These and other specific theoretical constructs have provided much of the impetus to academic research in organisational buying behaviour over the last decade. Some of this work, especially the focus on the choice criteria used by key members of the organisational buying center (relative importance of the criteria is viewed as an operational summary measure of the various influences on the buying decision), has been adopted in many commercial-based and sponsored organisational buying studies. (Note, for example, the increased incidence of conjoint analysis type studies for industrial product design, positioning, pricing, and segmentation.)

## Users of Information on Organisational Buying Behaviour

Industrial marketing managers typically have been considered as the primary users of information on organisational buying behaviour. Despite the importance of this ''user market,'' four other groups can and should be considered as users. These include scholars interested in organisational behaviour in general, and organisational buying behaviour in particular; scholars interested in the better understanding of consumer behaviour; other managerial decision makers (including managers of the procurement function who can benefit directly from a better understanding of organisational buying behaviour, and marketing managers on consumer goods companies who can get ideas from organisational buying findings, concepts, and approaches, for example); and public policy decision makers. The value of research on organisational buying behaviour depends on the degree to which it helps meet the needs of these five heterogeneous user groups.

The different motivations of the five user groups can be presented as a series of research questions relating to the major oganisational buying concepts: the buying centre, the buying process, and the factors affecting them. By crossing the research questions from each perspective with the three sets of concepts, a table can be created which helps define the scope of the problems and opportunities in organisational buying behaviour. Such an illustrative table is presented as Table V.

The findings concerning organisational buying behaviour can help the various users in formulating the right questions, in suggesting specific hypotheses, and in offering various research approaches. Generalisable findings and theories which could provide specific guidelines for action are not offered, however, by the current literature. In this respect, the organisational buying behaviour area is not unlike its current behaviour counterpart. Additional research linking specific decisions (such as allocating resources between advertising and sales personnel which has to be addressed by industrial marketing managers) to organisational buying behaviour (and, hence, the market response) has to be established empirically in each case.

The interest in, and research on, organisational buying have been increasing over the past two decades. Yet few empirical generalisations have emerged which can provide specific guidelines for action. This was clearly stated in the review of organisational buying behaviour in the first *Review of Marketing* (Wind, 1978 (a)): ''We are still lacking in substantive generalisations as to which variables would have what effects under what conditions.'' This conclusion still holds, due in part to the fragmented nature of much of the published organisational buying research, the lack of a replication tradition, and the relatively small and non-representative samples of most academic studies.

Furthermore, there appears to be no general direction or implicit research programme guiding much of the organisational buying research. Whether

## TABLE V. User Perspective on Organisational Buying Behaviour

| | | *Major Buying Concepts* | | | |
|---|---|---|---|---|---|
| *User perspective* | *Illustrative research questions* | *Buying centre* | *Buying decision process* | *Factors affecting buying centre & buying process* | *Outcome to the user* |
| Industrial marketing management | (a) Who participates in the decision to buy? | ✓ | | | Input to the critical marketing decisions (market segmentation, product positioning, product design, pricing, sales force, promotion and advertising) and strategic planning decisions concerning the product/market portfolio of the firm. |
| 1 | (b) What is the kind and amount of influence of those involved in buying? | ✓ | | | |
| | (c) How do (a) and (b) vary throughout the buying decision process? | | ✓ | | |
| | (d) What is the response to marketing stimuli (product design, price, promotion, advertising and distribution) of those involved in buying? | | | ✓ | |
| | (e) How should a market of organisations be semented, if at all? Etc | ✓ | ✓ | ✓ | |
| Students of organisational buying behaviour | (a) Same as 1(a) through 1(e) above; however, concern is to generalise across industries. | ✓ | ✓ | ✓ | Better understanding of organisational buying behaviour. |
| 2 | (b) How should the unit of analysis be defined? | ✓ | | | |
| | (c) Is there a generalised buying process, or will it vary by industry and other conditions? | | ✓ | | |
| | (d) Are the findings on the relative importance of various factors generalisable under various buying situations? | | | ✓ | |
| | (e) What are the appropriate methodologies for researching organisational buying behaviour? Etc. | ✓ | ✓ | ✓ | |

## TABLE V. A User Perspective on Organisational Buying Behaviour (cont.)

| | | *Major Buying Concepts* | | | |
|---|---|---|---|---|---|
| *User perspective* | *Illustrative research questions* | *Buying center* | *Buying decision process* | *Factors affecting buying centre & buying process* | *Outcome to the user* |
| Students of consumer behaviour<br>3 | (a) Do family buying centres behave similarly to organisational buying centres? What can be transferred from one discipline to another & | ✓ | | | Hypotheses and approaches to the study of consumer behaviour |
| | (b) Are family buying decision processes similar to organisational buying situations? | | ✓ | | |
| | (c) Are there similarities in the extent to which specific personal, inter-personal, social, and environmental factors affect organisational versus family buying processes? Etc. | | | ✓ | |
| Other managerial decision makers<br>4 | (a) How can the procurement process be best managed? | ✓ | ✓ | ✓ | |
| | (b) Can industrial marketing strategies and methods based on organisational buying behaviour be applied to consumer markets and vice-versa?<br>—Are consumer-based concept evaluation methods applicable to organisational markets? | | | ✓ | |
| | —Can team selling be applied to family buying centres? | ✓ | | | |
| | (c) Is a two-step segmentation approach useful in consumer markets? Etc. | ✓ | ✓ | ✓ | |
| Public policy decision makers<br>5 | (a) Are organisational buyers susceptible to deceptive advertising? Is deception a problem in industrial advertising and selling? | | | | Input to public policy related to or based on organisational buying. |
| | (b) How competitive is a market; i.e., what are the organisational buyers' perceptions of the market structure? | | | ✓ | |
| | (c) To what extent is price discrimination prevalent in organisational buying processes? Etc. | | | ✓ | |

this is due to legitimate idiosyncratic research interests, the varied scope of consulting assignments, available research grants, or some other motivation, it would be helpful if research on organisational buying behaviour came to grips with the key issues necessary for the advancement of the field. A few of the key issues which constitute the major problems facing research in this area and suggest tremendous opportunities for advancement of the field are discussed next.

## CONCEPTUAL ISSUES

Three conceptual issues which continually plague the advancement of organisational buying research are the unit of analysis, the relationship between the buying and selling organisations, and the conceptual (and operational) specification of variables and relationships hypothesised in the construction of organisational buying behaviour models.

### The Unit of Analysis

One of the unique aspects of organisational buying behaviour is the organisational buying centre (Wind, 1978), the varying number of individuals, groups, and organisations involved in the buying process.

***Methodological versus Managerial Considerations.*** The methodological unit of analysis is the one selected by researchers for data collection and analysis. The managerial unit of analysis, on the other hand, is one selected by the marketing decision maker as the basis for his/her marketing plans. The extent to which these units are compatible, or *need* to be compatible, is the first issue. For example, if two organisational positions (e.g., purchasing agent and R & D engineer) are the methodological unit (which is often the case), and their preferences and perceptions are the basis for a product positioning study, is it legitimate for mangers to interpret the average product-space as being characteristic of the ''organisation''? Or should the individual views be retained and dealt with as such at the managerial level? What guidelines should be used to make such translations from the methodological to the managerial units of analysis?

While this issue may be dismissed as being a ''practical'' research issue, enough examples exist in the literature which indicate that academic researchers are often tempted to offer managerial implications for a unit of analysis which is incompatible with the methodological unit used.

***Identifying the Unit of Analysis.*** There are three categories of units of analysis which are relevant to defining buying centres: individual, multiple, and interactional units. An *individual* unit refers to the kind of behavioural or living system being observed. It can vary from a person to a culture or some larger ecological environment. However, for our purposes we can limit it to persons (e.g., purchasing agents), *P*, departments (e.g., purchasing department), *D*, and organisations (e.g., a division, a strategic business unit, or the whole company), *O*.

While at first glance it may seem unreasonable to view departments or organisations as units of analysis, it only reflects the bias (at least in the literature reviewed) for a social-psychological view of organisational buying behaviour. Few studies employ, for example, a sociological approach in which measures describing a social unit (e.g., departmental cohesiveness, organisational climate) are related to organisational decisions.

A *multiple* unit of analysis includes two or more ''individual'' units—the definition of most buying centres. An alternative view of a buying centre would be two or more organisational departments involved in buying. Such a definition may better explain purchase decisions than the characteristics of individual persons, but has been rarely employed. The extent to which multiple organisations can define a buying centre may be less frequent, although not unrealistic. For example, five or six hospitals in a region may jointly buy a CT scanner.

The *interactional* unit of analysis is depicted by the relationship between (among) two (or more) individual units of analysis. Recent theoretical discussions have begun to focus on such interactional or relational approaches (e.g., Bonoma and Johnston, 1978; Hakansson and Ostber, 1975; Nicosia and Wind, 1977), although usually in the context of buyer-seller interactions or exchanges. The concern here is to recognise the importance of interactions within a buying centre.

A buying centre, therefore, can be defined in a variety of ways, including:

Individual unit: e.g., *P; D; O*

Multiple units: e.g., *PPP; DD; OO; PPD ...*

| Interactional units: e.g., | $P \times P$; | $P \times D$; | $O \times O$; | $P \times D$ |
|---|---|---|---|---|
| | *Inter-personal* | *Inter-depart-mental* | *Inter-organisa-tional* | *Mixed* |

***Selecting the Unit of Analysis.*** The unit of analysis selected for methodological and managerial purposes should depend on the objectives of the user of the anticipated information. From the researcher's point of view, if the problem is formulated as identfying the factors which explain organisational purchase decisions, then the dependent variable should clearly reflect an organisational unit of analysis. The independent variables, however, may be selected at all levels—person, department, or organisation. While it may be desirable for the researcher to define variables at all three levels, this greatly complicates the research process and requires several methodological ''decisions'' for which there are few guidelines. These include determining the units of analysis for sampling of variables and respondents, data collection, and data analysis and interpretation. To the extent that the researcher opts for mixing these units, error in explanation may result. For example, sampling organisations, interviewing individuals, and making conclusions about the buying centre require several transformations from one unit to another. Further study of these transformations, e.g., when they are or are not appropriate, is essential if progress in organisational buying research is to be achieved.

## Inter-Organisational Relationships

While occasionally a buying centre may be composed of a number of organisations and their inter-organisational relations, the primary concern of the inter-organisational relationship issue is with the relationship between buying and selling organisations—a relationship which has long been recognised as much more complex than that of a simple dyadic relationship between a seller and buyer (Wind, 1967). Yet, most of the current studies in this area do focus on buyer-seller dyads (see, for example, Matthews, Wilson, and Monaky, 1972 and Woodside and Davenport, 1974). Improvement in our understanding of organisational buying behaviour requires, however, better concepts and approaches to the study of inter-organisational relationships. This has been recognised by Nicosia and Wind (1977), Sheth (1975), Stern (1971), Webster and Wind (1972), Zaltman, Duncan, and Holbek (1973), and others.

A useful foundation for the inter-organisational relation issue is the organisational-set approach (Evan, 1966). According to this approach, any inter-organisational system is composed of any input organisation-set, a focal organisation-set, and an output organisation-set. A buying organisation may be viewed as the focal unit of interest surrounded by input and output organisation-sets.

| *Input Organisation-Set* | *Focal Organisation-Set* | *Output Organisation-Set* |
|---|---|---|
| Suppliers | | Wholesalers |
| Labour Unions | Buying | Retailers |
| Advertising Agencies | Organisation | Customers |
| Government Agencies | | Regulatory Agencies |
| R&D Organisations | | Communities |
| Marketing Research | | |
| Firms | | |
| Etc. | | Etc. |

The questions related to the buying decisions of the focal organisation may involve the size, diversity, and network configuration of the input and output sets. For example, will a larger number of suppliers result in less source loyalty than fewer suppliers? Will the mix of domestic versus international suppliers alter the purchasing function and structure? Will a focal organisation with a large number of diverse input organisations have a more formal buying process than organisations with fewer and less diverse input organisations? One might expect that large and diverse input set may force a firm better to structure its activities to cope with the diversity.

Will buying organisations with large output sets (e.g., long channels of distribution) have larger and more formalised buying centres? Does the size of the output set change the function performed by the buying organisation (e.g., more concern for packaging and logistics)?

The formal and informal and personal and impersonal interaction patterns among members of the organisation-sets and the focal organisation raise further issues and offer opportunities for creative conceptualisation and analysis. It may be possible to map networks of relations with directed graphs, as Czepiel (1974) has done. Alternatively, the ''boundary'' roles of the members of the organisation-sets can be studied. Corresponding to input and output organisation-sets, input and output boundary roles can be identified. Such boundary personnel as purchasing agents, top executives, lawyers, personnel officers, etc., interact on a regular basis with members of other organisations. For example, Pruden and Reese (1972) studied the role-set relationship between sales personnel and their customers. From an organisation buying behaviour perspective, one must ask who are the relevant boundary personnel in buying situations? Will larger input organisation-sets have more boundary personnel in the focal organisation than smaller input sets? How do boundary roles in the buying centre relate to other buying centre roles? Do boundary roles with large input role-sets have more status within their focal organisation than those with smaller input role-sets?

## Selection of Variables and Hypotheses for Model Construction

The great variability in the composition of the correct unit of analysis in organisational buying behaviour studies, which can include individuals, departments, organisations, and any relationships among them, imposes severe conceptual difficulties on the selection of dependent and independent variables and the hypothesised relationships among them. For individual units, many of the standard personnel, departmental, and organisational variables can suffice and, in fact, many organisational buying behaviour studies focus on a single respondent (ignoring the other possible members of the buying centre) and use individually based variables such as the ones listed on the upper panel of Table VI.

In the case of multiple and interactional units, the variables are less well developed. Consider, for example, a four-person buying centre; aggregated individual measures may not be sufficient to depict buying centre behaviour—or, if they are used, what aggregation procedures should be used? For example, how should the age of each person be handled to describe the

## TABLE VI. Illustrative Variables Used in Organisational Buying Behaviour Studies

*Individual Variables*

—Age
—Education
—Position in organisation
—Salary level
—Work experience
—Work experience in particular organisation
—Work experience in present position
—Work performance level (e.g., promotions)
—Perceived risk
—Self confidence (specific and general)
—Attitudes
—Motivations
—Perceived role obligations
—Social organisation membership
—Professional organisation membership
—Personality inventories
—Locus of control
—Interpersonal values
—Cosmopolitan versus local
—Life Style
—Decision making style
—Importance of criteria used in making purchase decisions
—Etc.

*Organisational Characteristics*

—SIC Code
—Performance trend (rising, falling)
—Financial (sales, assets, profits)
—Structure (centralised, decentralised)
—Centralisation
—Communication
—Complexity
—Consensus
—Co-ordination
—Dispersion
—Effectiveness
—Formalisation
—Innovation
—Mechanisation
—Routinisation
—Span of control
—Purchase policy
—Purchase pattern
—Etc.

''age'' of the buying centre? Should it be summed or averaged to indicate the buying centre ''age''? Or should the differences in age among the members be the descriptive measure of the buying centre's age?

To the extent that individual level variables may be unsatisfactory, the analyst may opt to shift to other units, or even to mix the units. For example, a four-person buying centre may involve two engineers from the same department, a production manager, and perhaps a purchasing agent. It may be feasible to consider the engineering department, the production department, and the purchasing agent (i.e., $D_E$, $D_P$, $I$) as the relevant buying centre. This would require the definition of appropriate departmental variables (e.g., purchase policies and process, size, location or other variables such as the ones listed in the lower panel of Table VI).

To describe interactional units, the problems become more difficult. Research on interaction among buying centre units is sparse. An exploratory study by Calder (1977), based on Oeser and Harary's (1962 and 1964) studies, uses structural role analysis to depict relations among buying centre members. Interpersonal influence, personal assignment, authority, and task specialisation are four relations specified to represent a role in this approach. Additional work in this direction should prove fruitful since the approach is suitable to mathematical formulation and, subsequently, the testing of hypotheses.

Kelley and Thibaut (1978) provide the basis for an alternative approach of evaluating interpersonal relations. Their analysis centres around types of interpersonal relationships which are differentiated by their ''interdependence.'' The pattern or taxonomy of interdependencies characterising a relationship is defined by an ''outcome matrix.'' By identifying the components of a matrix for the parties involved, determining their relative magnitude, and specifying their orientations (concordance versus correspondence), an analytical framework is available for mathematical formulation and hypotheses testing. Attributions, negotiation, and coalition formation are important relational processes which can have an effect on the outcome matrices. Whether or not such an approach is useful in describing, explaining, and predicting organisational buying behaviour remains to be seen. Nevertheless, it does provide an alternative framework at least to begin to explore some of the difficulties of describing and studying interactional units of analysis.

An important component of all organisational buying studies is the construction of an explicit and well specified model. The selection of an appropriate model of ''organisational'' behaviour and the determination of the relevant dependent and independent variables is not an easy task, conceptually or operationally. A major issue involved in developing a conceptual model of organisational buying behaviour is the specification of hypotheses linking the various independent variables to the desired dependent variable. A second concern is defining the scope of the problem to be investigated, the expected cost, and the value of the information to be gained from the study.

From a practical perspective, how much should a company spend for organisational buying research? What is the value of such research; or more appropriately, what criteria or measures of effectiveness are available to determine its value? How should the size and allocation of the research budget be determined?

A major concern in the development of appropriate organisational buying behaviour models is the relationship between the model and the concepts and findings of other related disciplines. Further exploration of these possible interdisciplinary relationships is among the most fruitful directions for future organisational buying behaviour models and studies. More specifically, one can consider an increased interdependency between organisational buying behaviour and the following.

1. Industrial marketing strategy and the emerging discipline of strategic planning. To date, despite some excellent initial efforts such as the recent industrial marketing strategy book by Webster (1979) and the Choffray and Lilien book (1980), little attention has been given by organisational buying researchers to the information needs of industrial corporate planners and marketing strategies. In this latter context, a most encouraging development in recent years has been the increased attention to the modelling of industrial marketing decisions such as the ADVISOR project (Lilien, 1979).
2. The sales force management literature and its natural but yet missing link to industrial buying behaviour.
3. The procurement literature, especially the increasing segment devoted to procurement research and the sourcing abroad issues.
4. The consumer behaviour literature and its obvious relevance as a source of concepts and research approaches.
5. The organisational behaviour literature and its concern for organisational design.

The interdependencies with other disciplines are not a one-way street. Most of the other disciplines would also benefit from such research efforts as were illustrated, for example, in the case of the consumer-organisational buying behaviour interface (Wind, 1977).

## Methodological Issues

Associated with the conceptual issues are a number of methodological issues relating to the identification and analysis of multi-person or group buying units, the measurement of inter-organisational relationships, and the operational definitions and analysis or variables relating to a number of individuals and groups within a buying centre. The conceptual and methodological issues of a buying centre are the most serious obstacle to current progress in organisational buying research, but they also offer some of the greatest opportunities for the improvement of our understanding of organisational buying behaviour and, at the same time, for the advancement of the measurement and analysis of multi-person data—an advancement which could help most of the management and behavioural sciences.

The specific methodological issues involved in organisational buying research are organised along the problems and opportunities of: research design, sampling and data collection, and data analysis.

## Research Design

A number of research designs frequently used (and found useful) in consumer marketing research may or may not be appropriate for industrial marketing problems. For example, is "test market" feasible in industrial marketing research? Are longitudinal study designs practical? Are panels of industrial buyers feasible? How can relationships among key variables be measured? How valid are laboratory experiments? Does "motivation research" have any utility in industrial marketing research? If so, can the analysis of individual motivations be aggregated to the organisational level, etc.?

A variety of designs should be considered, and of special importance is the development of a continuous research programme which integrates the results of previous studies, experiences, and available inter-company and external data sources. A critical design issue involves the selection of an appropriate unit of analysis and the determination of the desired respondent selection procedure. Who are the appropriate respondents in an organisational marketing study? Should one individual, two or more individuals, or a number of individuals occupying particular roles be selected as respondents? If the unit of analysis is the buying centre, how does one identify relevant buying centre members as respondents? Is it sufficient to use salespersons' information, or should some other key informant be selected? Which members of the buying centre should be respondents—buyers, decision makers, users, gatekeepers, etc?

## Sampling and Data Collection

The central sampling problem in research on organisational buying behaviour is the inability to select an individual respondent as an independent unit. It is necessary to select the individual in reference to the organisational structure. Consequently, the "organisation" is most often the relevant initial sampling unit and this has to be followed with a second sampling scheme of individual respondents within the sampled organisation. In the case where the unit of analysis is one or more of well-defined organisational positions (e.g., comptroller, president, head of purchasing, etc.), there is little choice in the matter. However, if the concern is to sample organisational "users" of a product, there may be several respondents making up this subuniverse. Should they be selected randomly?

The complexity of these sampling issues is further complicated by the frequent constraints on the universe (a limited number of firms) and the high cost of data collection which tends to lead to rather small samples. These issues suggest the range of options facing the researcher in considering sample size (large versus small), representatives (random versus purposive), and unit (organisation versus individuals). In the case where a sample of organisations is drawn first followed by a sample of individuals from each organisation, 16 sampling strategies are possible (such as large random sampling of organisations followed by large random sampling of respondents within each organisation), each requiring different assumptions for parameter estimation and data analysis.

For this illustrative strategy, classical hypothesis testing and parameter estimation procedures may be appropriate. Yet for the strategy at the other extreme (small, purposive sample of organisations followed by a small, purposive sample of individuals from each organisation), classical statistical assumptions are violated, making it necessary to consider nonparametric procedures for estimation and hypothesis testing. Clearly, the other 14 strategies require careful consideration by the researcher so as not unwillingly to violate critical statistical assumptions. The typical studies of organisational buying behaviour rarely recognise such sampling related issues.

Although there are few guidelines (Coleman, 1958) for successive samplings of social units, some practical approaches have evolved which may spark the consideration of more creative sampling procedures. These include census sampling (everyone in the organisation is selected as respondents); within organisation cluster sampling; sequential, multi-stage, random sampling (e.g., successive random samples drawn from SIC codes, organisations within SIC codes, departments or positions within each organisation, and individuals from each department); circular sampling (in which an accessible member of the organisation is interviewed and asked to indicate other organisational members who may be involved in the purchase of the product; these other members are then interviewed and asked about still others, and so on, until the recommendations become ''circular'', that is, the same names or positons keep appearing as persons involved in the purchase); and interpersonal-linkage sampling (a variant on circular sampling, focusing on interpersonal relationships among the members of the organisation).

***Data Collection.*** The data collection procedures used depend on the research design employed (especially the nature of the respondent task) and the sample selection procedure. If circular sampling is used, for example, one would be limtied to personal or telephone interviews within the organisation. While personal interviews and mail questionnaires are probably the most popular data collection procedures, telephone interviewing and, more recently, computer assisted data collection procedures have considerable potential.

### Data Analysis

The small samples of most organisational buying studies place severe restrictions on the use of many statistical techniques associated with parametric hypothesis testing. Should more emphasis be given, therefore, to nonparametric statistics and descriptive statistics?

The use of current data analysis techniques varies across studies. Both commerical and academic studies range from the most sophisticated approaches (of multivariate statistical techniques coupled with computer simulation and optimisation programmes such as in the various industrial applications of the POSSE methodology) to the conventional and often unimaginative use of cross tabs. The quality of data analysis can be enhanced by applying selected multivariate techniques.

Yet, advances in organisational buying behaviour research require more than a straightforward application of multivariate data analysis. Attention should be given to the multi-response problem and to creative and innovative ways of analysing multi-personal data. Initial efforts in this direction have been made (see, for example, Wind, 1978), but considerably more attention should be given.

The interpretation of organisational buying data requires special care in projecting from small samples to larger populations. Conceptual, measurement, and analytic limitations should be recognised and taken into consideration when interpreting the results. For example, if only three of a potential six or seven buying centre members are interviewed from a large sample of organisations, statements may only be relevant about the three members selected and not the whole buying centre.

## Conclusions

The issues discussed in this paper, although not all inclusive, are suggestive of directions for future research efforts. It is apparent that basic (published) research in organisational buying behaviour must do some "catching up" to begin to resolve some of the problems faced by users of such information. Similarly, the day-to-day research in industrial marketing (although often more advanced than the published material) can benefit from incorporating and addressing some of the conceptual and methodological issues discussed here.

Much of the development of organisational buying research is likely to derive from existing techniques and methods in consumer and marketing research. However, caution must be used in these applications since the nature of organisations as consumers is different from that of individuals as consumers. To this end, new developments in organisational buying concepts and research approaches, coupled with additional borrowing from sociology, organisational behaviour, political science, and other related behavioural sciences, would be helpful.

The organisational buying behaviour area, although plagued with issues, offers a challenging area for conceptual and methodological growth with opportunities for innovative research programmes which could be of great value and relevance to the five user groups of organisational buying behaviour information.

## REFERENCES

Baker, M. J. and Abu-Ismail, F., "The Diffusion of Innovation in Industrial Markets," in *Educators' Proceedings*, Chicago, American Marketing Association, 1977, pp. 498-501.

Bagozzi, R. P., "Exchange and Decision Processes in the Buying Centre," in Bonoma, T. V. and Zaltman, G., eds., *Organizational Buying Behaviour*, Chicago, American Marketing Association, 1978, pp. 100-25.

Beardon, W. O., Teel, J. E., Williams, R. H. and Durand, R. M., "Exposing Organizational Buyers to Consumer Magazine Advertisements," *Industrial Marketing Management*, Vol. 7, December 1978, pp. 379-86.

Bonoma, T. V., Bagozzi, R. and Zaltman, G., "The Dyadic Paradigm with Specific Application Toward Industrial Marketing," In Bonoma, T. V. and Zaltman, G., eds., *op. cit.*, pp. 49-66; Bonoma, T. V., Johnson, W. J., "The Social Psychology of Industrial Buying and Selling," *Industrial Marketing Management*, Vol. 7 August, 1978, pp. 213-24, Bonoma, T. V., and Zaltman, G., eds., *Organizational Buying Behaviour*, Chicago, American Marketing Association, 1978.

Bradley, M. F., "Buying Behaviour in Ireland's Public Sector," *Industrial Marketing Management*, Vol. 6, August, 1977, pp. 251-8.

Brand, G. T., *The Industrial Buying Decision*, New York, John Wiley & Sons, 1972.

Busch, P. and Wilson, D. T., "An Experimental Analysis of a Salesman's Expert and Referant Bases of Social Power in the Buyer-Seller Dyad," *Journal of Marketing Research*, Vol. 13, February, 1976, pp. 3-11.

Calder, B. J., "Structural Role Analysis of Organizational Buying: A Preliminary Investigation," in Woodside, A., Sheth, J. N. and Bennett, P. D., (eds.), *Consumer and Industrial Buyer Behaviour*, New York, American Elsevier, 1977.

Cardozo, R. N. and Cagley, J. W., "Experimental Study of Industrial Buyer-Behaviour," *Journal of Marketing Research*, Vol. 8, August, 1971, pp. 329-34.

Choffray, J. M. and Lilien, G. L., *Marketing Planning for New Industrial Products*, mimeographed, 1980.

Coleman, J. S., "Relational Analysis: The Study of Social Organizations with Survey Methods," *Human Organization*, Vol. 16, Summer, 1958, pp. 28-36.

Cooley, J. R., Jackson, D. W. and Ostrom, L. L., "Analyzing the Relative Power of Participants in Industrial Buying Decisions," in Greenberg, B. A. and Bellender, D. N., (eds.), *Contemporary Marketing Thought*, Chicago, American Marketing Association, 1977, pp. 243-6.

Cyert, R. M., Simon, H. A. and Trow, D. B., "Observation of a Business Decision," *Journal of Business*, Vol. 29, October, 1956, pp. 237-48.

Czepiel, J. A., "Word-of-Mouth Process in the Diffusion of a Major Technological Innovation," *Journal of Marketing Research*, Vol. 11, May, 1974, pp. 172-80;

"Decision Group and Form Characteristics in an Industrial Adoption Decision," in Bernhardt, K. (ed.), *Marketing: 1776-1976 and Beyond*, Chicago, American Marketing Association, 1976, pp. 340-3.

Dickson, G. W., "An Analysis of Vendor Selection Systems and Decisions," *Journal of Purchasing*, Vol. 2, February, 1966, pp. 5-17.

Engel, J. R., Kollat, D. T. and Blackwell, R. D., *Consumer Behaviour*, 2nd edition, New York, Holt, Rinehart and Winston, 1973.

Etgar, M., "Channel Domination and Countervailing Power in Distributive Channels," *Journal of Marketing Research*, Vol. 13, August, 1976, pp. 254-62.

Evan, W. M., "The Organization-Set: Toward a Theory of Interorganizational Relations," In Thompkins, J., (ed.), *Approaches to Organisational Design*, Pittsburgh, University of Pittsburgh Press, 1966, pp. 175-91.

Evans, F. G., "Selling as a Dyadic Relationship—A New Approach," *The American Behavioral Scientist*, Vol. 6, May 1963, pp. 76-9.

Evans, R. K., "Choice Criteria Revisited," *Journal of Marketing*, Vol. 44, Winter, 1980, pp. 55-56.

Farley, J. U. and Swinth, R. C., "Effects of Choice and Sales Message on Customer-Salesman Interaction," *Journal of Applied Psychology*, Vol. 51, April, 1967, pp. 107-10.

Ford, I. D., "Stability Factors in Industrial Marketing Channels," *Industrial Marketing Management*, Vol. 7, December, 1978, pp. 410-22.

Gorman, R. H., "Role Conception and Purchasing Behavior," *Journal of Psychology*, Vol. 7, February, 1971.

Green, P. E. and Wind, Y., "New Way to Measure Consumers' Judgment," *Harvard Business Review*, Vol. 53, July-August, pp. 107-17.

Gronhaug, K., "Exploring Environmental Influences in Organizational Buying," *Journal of Marketing Research*, Vol. 13, August, 1976, pp. 225-9.

Grashof, J. F. and Thomas, G. P., "Industrial Buying Center Responsibilities: Self versus Other Members' Evaluation of Importance," in *Marketing: 1776-1976 and Beyond*, Chicago, American Marketing Assocation, 1976, pp. 340-3.

Hakansson, H. and Ostberg, C., "Industrial Marketing: An Organizational Problem?" *Industrial Marketing Management*, Vol. 4, June, 1975, pp. 113-23. Hakansson, H. and Wootz, B., "Supplier Selection in an International Environment—An Experimental Study," *Journal of Marketing Research*, Vol. 12, February, 1975, pp. 46-53.

Harding, M., "Who Really Makes the Purchasing Decision?" *Industrial Marketing*, Vol. 51, September, 1966, pp. 76-81.

Hayward, G., "Diffusion of Innovation in the Flour Milling Industry," *European Journal of Marketing*, Vol. 6, July, 1972, pp. 195-202.

"How Industry Buys/1970," New York, Scientific American Inc., 1969.

"How Industry Buys Chemicals," Wesport, Conn., SENTCOM, Ltd., 1979.

Howard, J. A., *Consumer Behaviour: Application of Theory*, New York, McGraw-Hill, 1977; Howard, J. A., and Sheth, J. N., *The Theory of Buyer Behavior*, New York, Wiley, 1969.

Hunt, S. D. and Nevin, J. R., "Power in a Channel of Distribution: Sources and Consequences," *Journal of Marketing Research*, Vol. 11, May, 1974, pp. 186-93.

Huppertz, J. W., Arenson, S. J. and Evans, R. H., "An Application of Equity Theory to Buyer-Seller Exchange Situations," *Journal of Marketing Research*, Vol. 15, May, 1978, pp. 250-60.

Kelly, P., "Functions Performed in Industrial Purchase Decisions with Implications for Marketing Strategy," *Journal of Business Research*, Vol. 2, October, 1974, pp. 421-33; Kelly, P. and Coaker, J. W., "Can We Generalize about Choice Criteria for Industrial Purchasing Decisions?" in *Educators' Proceedings*, Chicago, American Marketing Association, 1976, pp. 330-3; Kelly, P. and Hensel, J. W., "The Industrial Search Process: An Exploratory Study," *Proceedings of the American Marketing Association*, Series #35, Chicago, 1973, pp. 212-6; American Marketing Assocation, Kelly, P. and Thibaut, J. W., *Interpersonal Relations: A Theory of Interdependence*, New York, John Wiley & Sons, 1978.

Kiser, G. E. and Rao, C. P., "Important Vendor Factors in Industrial and Hospital Organizations: A Comparison," *Industrial Marketing Management*, Vol. 6, August, 1977, pp. 289-6.

Krugman, H. E., "The Impact of Television Advertising: Learning Without Involvement," *Public Opinion Quarterly*, Vol. 29, Fall, 1965, pp. 239-56.

Lambert, D. R., Dornoff, R. J. and Kernan, J. B., "The Industrial Buyer and the Postchoice Evaluation Process," *Journal of Marketing Research*, Vol. 14, May, 1977, pp. 246-51.

LAP Report 1042.2., "Industrial Sales People Report 4.1—Buying Influences in Average Company," New York, McGraw-Hill Research, 1977.

Lazo, H., "Emotional Aspects of Industrial Buying," in Hancock, R. (ed.), *Dynamic Marketing for a Changing World*, Chicago, American Marketing Association, 1960, pp. 258-65.

Lehman, M. A. and Cardozo, R. N., "Product or Industrial Advertisements?" *Journal of Advertising Research*, Vol. 13, April, 1973, pp. 43-6.

Lehmann, D. R. and O'Shaughnessy, J., "Difference in Attribute Importance for Different Industrial Products," *Journal of Marketing*, Vol. 38, April, 1974, pp. 36-42.

Levitt, T., *Industrial Purchasing Behavior: A Study of Communications Effects*, Boston, Graduate School of Business Administration, Harvard University, 1965.

Lilien, G. L., "ADVISOR 2: Modelling the Marketing Mix Decision for Industrial Products," *Mangement Science*, Vol. 25, February, 1979, pp. 191-204.

A. D. Little Inc., *An Evaluation of 1100 Research Studies on the Effectiveness of Industrial Advertising*, report to American Business Press, Inc., May 1971.

Martilla, J. A., "Word-of-Mouth Communication in the Industrial Adoption Process," *Journal of Marketing Research*, Vol. 8, May, 1971, pp. 173-8.

Mathews, L. H., Wilson, D. T. and Monoky, J. F. Jr., "Bargaining Behavior in a Buyer-Seller Dyad," *Journal of Marketing Research*, Vol. 12, February, 1972, pp. 103-5.

McAleer, G., "Buying Influence—A Verified Basis for Segmentation within an Industrial Market," *Proceedings*, Southern Marketing Assocation, 1974, pp. 71-5.

McMillan, J. R., "Role Differentiation in Industrial Buying Decisions," in *Proceedings of the American Marketing Assocation*, Series #35, Chicago, American Marketing Assocation, 1973, pp. 207-11.

Morrill, J. E., "Industrial Advertising Pays Off," *Harvard Business Review*, Vol. 48, March-April, 1970, pp. 4-14.

Nicosia, F. M. and Wind, Y., "Emerging Models of Organizational Buying Process," *Industrial Marketing Management*, Vol. 6, October, 1977, pp. 353-69.

Oeser, O. and Harary, F., "A Mathematical Model for Structural Role Theory, I,"*Human Relations*, Vol. 15, 1962, pp. 89-109; "A Mathematical Model for Structural Role Theory, II," *Human Relations*, Vol. 17, 1964, pp. 3-17.

O'Neal, C. R., Thorelli, H. B. and Utterback, J. M., "Adoption of Innovations by Industrial Organizations," *Industrial Marketing Management*, Vol. 2, June, 1973, pp. 235-50.

Ozanne, U. B. and Churchill, G. A., "Adoption Research: Information Sources in the Industrial Purchasing Decision," in King, R. L. (ed.), *Marketing and the New Science of Planning*, Chicago, American Marketing Association, pp. 352-9; "Five Dimensions of the Industrial Adoption Process," *Journal of Marketing Research*, Vol. 8, August, 1971, pp. 322-8.

Patti, C. H., "Buyer Information Sources in the Capital Equipment Industry," *Industrial Marketing Management*, Vol. 6, August, 1977, pp. 259-64.

Peters, M. P. and Venkatesan, M., "Exploration of Variables Inherent in Adopting an Industrial Product," *Journal of Marketing Research*, Vol. 10, August, 1973, pp. 312-5.

Pingry, J. R., "The Engineer and Purchasing Agent Compared," *Journal of Purchasing*, Vol. 10, November, 1974, pp. 33-45.

Pruden, H. O. and Reese, R. N., "Interorganization Role-Set Relations and the Performance and Satisfaction of Industrial Salesmen," *Administrative Science Quarterly*, Vol. 17, December, 1972, pp. 601-9.

Robertson, T. S. and Wind, Y., "Organizational Psychographics and Innovativeness," *Journal of Consumer Research*, June, 1980 (forthcoming).

Robinson, P. J. and Faris, C. W. (eds.), *Industrial Buying and Creative Marketing*, Boston, Allyn & Bacon, 1967.

Rogers National Research, 1979.

Saleh, F. and LaLonde, B. J., "Industrial Buying Behaviour and the Motor Carrier Selection Decision," *Journal of Purchasing*, Vol. 8, February, 1972, pp. 18-33.

San Augustine, A. J., Foley, W. F. and Friedman, H. H., "Overt Searchers Responses to Advertising," *Industrial Marketing Management*, Vol. 6, June, 1977, pp. 193-6

Schiffman, L. G., Winer, L. and Gaccione, V., "The Role of Mass Communication, Salesmen, and Peers in Industrial Buying Decisions," in *Proceedings*, Chicago, American Marketing Assocation, 1974, 4870492.

Scott, J. E. and Wright, P., "Modelling an Organizational Buyer's Product Evaluation Strategy: Validity and Procedural Considerations," *Journal of Marketing Research*, Vol. 13, August, 1976, pp. 211-24.

Sheth, J. N., "A Model of Industrial Buyer Behaviour," *Journal of Marketing*, Vol. 37, October 1973, pp. 50-6; "Buyer-Seller Interaction: A Framework," *Proceedings of the Association for Consumer Research*, Winter, 1975, pp. 382-6.

Spekman, R. E., "Influence and Information: An Exploratory Investigation of the Boundary Role Person's Basis of Power, " *Academy of Management Journal*, Vol. 22, March, 1979, pp. 104-17; Spekman, R. E. and Stern, L. W., "Environmental Uncertainty and Buying Group Structure: Empirical Investigation," *Journal of Marketing*, Vol. 43, Spring, 1979, pp. 54-64.

Stern, L. W., "Potential Conflict Management Mechanisms in Distribution Channels: An Interorganizational Analysis," in Thompson, D. N. (ed.), *Contractual Marketing Systems*, Boston, D. C. Heath, 1971.

Stiles, G. W., "An Information Processing Model of Industrial Buyer Behaviour," *Proceedings*, Chicago, American Marketing Association, 1973, pp. 534-5.

Strauss, G., "Tactics of Lateral Relationship: The Purchasing Agent," *Administrative Science Quarterly*, Vol. 7, September 1962, pp. 161-86.

Sweitzer, R. W., "Interpersonal Information Processing of Industrial Buyers," in *Marketing: 1776-1976 and Beyond*, Chicago, American Marketing Association, 1976, pp. 334-339.

Thomas, R. J., "Interpersonal Correlates of Purchase Influence in Organizations," unpublished Ph.D. dissertation, The Wharton School, University of Pennsylvania, 1980.

Tosi, H. L., "The Effects of Expectation Levels and Role Consensus of the Buyer-Seller Dyad," *Journal of Business*, Vol. 39, October, 1966, pp. 516-29.

von Hippel, E., "Successful Industrial Products from Customer Ideas," *Journal of Marketing*, Vol. 42, January, 1978, pp. 39-49.

Webster, F. E. Jr., "Word-of-Mouth Communication and Opinion Leadership in Industrial Markets," *Proceedings of Fall Conference*, Chicago, American Marketing Association, 1968, pp. 455-9; *Industrial Marketing Strategy*, New York, Wiley, 1979; Webster, F. E. Jr. and Wind, Y., *Organizational Buying Behaviour*, Englewood Cliffs, N. J., Prentice-Hall, 1972.

Weitz, B. A., "Relationship Between Salesperson Performance and Understanding of Consumer Decision Making," *Journal of Marketing Research*, Vol. 15, November, 1978, pp. 501-16.

"Who Makes Purchasing Decisions?" *Hospitals*, Vol. 48, December 16, 1974, pp. 78-9.

Wildt, A. R. and Bruno, A. V., "Prediction of Preference for Capital Equipment Using Linear Attitude Models," *Journal of Marketing Research*, Vol. 11, May, 1974, p. 203-5.

Wilson, D. T., "Industrial Buyers' Decision-Making Styles," *Journal of Marketing Research*, Vol. 8, November, 1971, pp. 433-6.

Wind, Y., "The Determinants of Industrial Buyers' Behaviour," in Robinson, P. J. and Faris, C. (eds.), *Industrial Buying and Creative Marketing*, Boston, Allyn & Bacon, 1967, pp. 151-80. "Applying the Behavioural Theory of the Firm to Industrial Buying Decisions," *The Economic and Business Bulletin*, Vol. 20, Spring, 1968, pp. 22-8; "A Reward-Balance Model of Buying Behaviour in Organizations," in Fisk, G. (ed.), *New Essays in Marketing Theory*, Boston, Allyn & Bacon, 1971; "Recent Approaches to the Study of Organizational Buying Behaviour," in Greer, T. (ed.), *Increasing Marketing Productivity*, Chicago, American Marketing Association, 1973, pp. 203-206; "On the Interface Between Organizational and Consumer Buying Behaviour," in Hunt, H. K. (ed), *Advances in Consumer Research*, ACR, 1977, pp. 657-62; "The Boundaries of Buying Decision Centers," *Journal of Purchasing and Materials Management*, Vol. 14, Summer, 1978, pp. 23-9; "Organizational Buying Behaviour," in Zaltman, G. and Bonoma, T. (eds.), *Review of Marketing, 1978*, Chicago: American Marketing Association, 1978(a), pp. 160-93; "Industrial Market Segmentation Under Conditions of Intra-Organizational Heterogeneity," Wharton School Working Paper, 1979; *Product Policy*, Reading,

Mass., Addison-Wesley, 1980 (forthcoming); Wind, Y., Grasof, J. F. and Goldhar, J. D., "Market-Based Guidelines for Design of Industrial Products," *Journal of Marketing*, Vol. 42, July, 1978, pp. 27-37; Wind, Y., Green, P. E. and Robinson, P. J., "The Determinants of Vendor Selection: The Evaluation Function Approach," *Journal of Purchasing*, Vol. 4, August, 1968, pp. 29-41.

Woodside, A. G. and Davenport, J. W. Jr., "The Effect of Salesman Similarity on Consumer Purchasing Behavior," *Journal of Marketing Research*, Vol. 11, May, 1974, pp. 198-202.

Zaltman, G., Duncan, R. and Holbeck, J., *Innovations and Organizations*, New York, Wiley Interscience, 1973.

## ACKNOWLEDGEMENT

This paper is part of a project on "Organization Buying and Usage Behaviour of Scientific and Technical Information," funded under Grant SIS 75-12928 by the Office of Scientific and Technical Information Services, National Science Foundation.

# SECTION K
# Buyer-Seller Interactions School

Buyer-seller interaction is the heart of marketing. It represents the market transaction with its inherent issues of exchange and values. Surprisingly, buyer-seller interaction has not been well studied in marketing. We have research and theory on personal selling and sales management, but only limited knowledge on the interaction between the buyers and the sellers. Except for the classical thinking of Evans, only recently have buyer-seller interactions become interesting to marketing scholars. This interest is further enhanced by more recent interest in negotiations and bargaining.

There are several important aspects to the buyer-seller interaction process. First, it is usually not very clear who the buyer is, especially in the industrial setting. It is a major intelligence task to find out the true decision makers in industrial buying because buying is often performed by a committee or by the buying center. It is also challenging in many consumer choices. For example, it is very desirable for the salesperson for a car or a house to identify which member of a family is the buyer or whether the family is out there primarily to recreate.

Second, it is not only the substance of the transaction but also the style that is important. It is possible that the seller offers the merchandise or service the buyer wants at that price but that the manner in which the transaction is carried out is not compatible between the two sides. Unfortunately, there is not much research on this style dimension except perhaps on the importance of atmosphere in retailing.

A third important area of understanding in the buyer-seller interaction process involves the issues of relationship, friendship, and reciprocity. It is not uncommon to find that a long-term personal relationship among corporate executives is often the critical factor in successful buyer-seller interactions. There is a similar phenomenon prevalant in consumer behavior as witnessed by party selling and pyramid marketing practices.

# 36 —— Selling as a Dyadic Relationship—A New Approach

*F. B. Evans*

F. B. Evans, ''Selling as A Dyadic Relationship—A New Approach,'' *American Behavioral Scientist*, Vol. 6, No. 9 (May 1963), pp. 76-79. 

Very little is known about what takes place when the salesman and his prospect meet. The two parties meet in a highly structured situation, and the outcome of the meeting depends upon the resulting interaction. In this sense, the ''sale'' is a social situation involving two persons. The interaction of the two persons, in turn, depends upon the economic, social, physical, and personality characteristics of each of them. To understand the process, however, it is necessary to look at both parties to the sale as a dyad,[1] not individually. Specifically the hypothesis is: the sale is a product of the particular dyadic interaction interaction of a given salesman and prospect rather than a result of the individual qualities of either alone. This approach to the selling situation is quite different from the ones typically found in business practice.

## The Traditional View of Selling

Although salesman selection and evaluation cannot be undertaken with any significant degree of certainty (in spite of the large investments made in psychological test procedures), the emphasis in business is still placed upon finding ideal sales types. The salesman is thought of as outgoing, bluff, hardy, and aggressive.[2] Salesmen, themselves, feel that the stereotype fits. Raymond W. Mack has suggested that salesmen are ''money'' oriented as opposed to technical people who are ''work'' oriented.[3] There is very little commitment to the job and no fixed behavior patterns. Mack further suggests that selling is an occupation one enters for status maintenance; a job into which are filtered the sons of managers, professionals, and proprietors who are unable to keep up with the standards set by their fathers.[4] It is also said that unlike many other professions even moderate success in selling depends upon a real liking for the job.[5]

Literally thousands of books and articles have been written about sales techniques but invariably these deal only with the salesman's point of view. Three approaches are common to these works. They are:

1. *The Sales Personality*—what the salesman must be. The salesman must develop a ''sales personality'' by self-appraisal and self-development.[6] The salesman must be mentally tough but he must have more tact, diplomacy, and social poise than most other employees. He must be ambitious, self-confident, like people, thrive on responsibility, like to travel and want to be his own boss.[7]
2. *The Persuasive Salesman*—how to persuade or manipulate prospects. Some writers suggest a general approach, for example: a. Establish need for the product. b. Believability. c. Make materials attractive and positive. d. Repetition. e. Offer a variety of products or services.[8] Other writers concentrate on finding different ways to handle the various kinds of prospects. For example: regardless of type, all true prospects will buy from someone. Will it be you? It could be if you learn to classify prospects and then use the methods, principles, and techniques that will permit you to handle the various prospects in the most profitable manner.[9]
3. *The Adaptable Salesman*—be whatever the prospect wants. For example: the good salesman is a chameleon and likes being one. He must be what the client wants, to make the client feel that he (the salesman) understands him,[10] and, the salesman must find a man's wave length and tune in.[11]

## Interaction Studies

### Business Studies

Two sociological studies have dealt with retail saleswomen and restaurant waitresses. Both have recognized the importance of the interaction between the client and the salesperson. Lombard studied twenty saleswomen in the children's clothing department of a large department store.[12] He found that salesgirls perceive customers who reject the merchandise as rejecting them and vice versa,[13] that customers in a hurry perceive salesgirls as not being interested in them,[14] and that the salesgirl who feels secure in beliefs about herself perceives the customer as someone who needs help.[15] She feels she has done her best when she helps the customer.

Whyte similarly pointed out the importance of the interaction between the restaurant waitress and her customers, and the waitress and the cook.[16] He found that the behavior of the waitress varies with the social status of the customer she serves.[17] The higher the social status of the restaurant's clientele, the less friendly and personal the waitress must act. The well adjusted waitress did not react to her customer's moods, etc. She controlled her behavior.[18] Whyte also noted,'' if the cook and waitress have a fight or if the waitress clashes with her supervisor, then that waitress is likely take out her aroused feelings on the customer through poor service or discourtesy....''[19]

## Interviewing

As opposed to selling, most studies of interviewing in social research have dealt with the interaction problems of interviewer and respondent. The general assumption is that the more freely the information is given the more valid it is likely to be.[20] Anything that hinders the communication may bias the answers. The fewer such characteristics as age, sociometric status, and education the interviewer and respondent have in common, the more difficult the interview.[21] Similarly the interviewer's role expectations of the interviewee can bias the survey results.[22] The interviewer may record the answers that he thinks the respondent should (wants to) give rather than the correct one.

The September, 1956 issue of the *American Journal of Sociology* was devoted to the problems of interviewer and respondent interaction. It showed that the relative ages and sex of the respondent and the interviewer affect the answers to questions used.[23] The least inhibited communication took place between young people of the same sex, the most inhibited between people of the same age but different sex.[24] Similarly a study of over 2,400 interviews showed that 90% of the respondents reacted favorably to being interviewed and found pleasure in the relationship with the interviewer.[25]

It has also been shown that interview results can be biased by many other factors. Hyman has said that excessive social orientation of the interviewer is not conducive to superior performance.[26] In other words, too much rapport with the respondent is as bad as too little. And a study of 40 telephone interviews showed that the results were biased if the interviewer said ''good'' after certain answers as opposed to saying ''mm-hmm.''[27]

## Medicine and Psychotherapy

A doctor's speech and manner are often an important part of his treatment of patients. Many patients are susceptible to *iatrogenicity*, doctor-induced illness.[28] In medical school the prospective doctor is taught the importance of not communicating his own anxieties to the patient.[29] What the doctor says and what the doctor *is* is an important part of the pattern of treatment.[30]

In psychotherapy, communication with the patient *is* the treatment, and every action of the therapist is an important part of the pattern. There is, accordingly, considerable discussion of the interaction situation in the psychoanalytic literature.[31]

## Other Interaction Studies

Besides the areas of interviewing and medicine, many other studies in sociology and social psychology have dealt with variables which are important to two-person interaction systems.

It is a common psychological assumption that the average person will often forego a wanted article if he has to face a negative emotional situation to get it, and if the emotional situation is pleasing and gratifying to him, he is likely to purchase articles which he would not otherwise buy.[32] Homans has pointed out that the more frequent the interaction between people, the stronger in general their affection or liking for one another, provided the relationship is mutually rewarding.[33] Similarly, studies have shown that an individual will prefer to interact with someone like himself rather than different if the interaction situation allows for mutual gain.[34]

Studies of military personnel have shown that there is less intense aggression directed towards an instigator of higher status (rank) than toward one of lower status.[35] And in social case work it has been noted that when the client's problems arouse anxiety in the caseworker, there is a risk that the worker will respond in relation to his own anxiety, and not to the client's needs.[36]

## Selling Life Insurance

Life insurance selling is considered to be one of the higher types of ''creative'' selling. It is highly rated among sales occupations. The life insurance agent is better liked and thought to be better trained, more honest, less aggressive, and less high pressured than the automobile or real estate salesman.[37]. It is also an occupation where relatively few succeed in the long run; less than quarter of the new inexperienced agents last through the first four years.

Rarely does the life insurance purchaser seek out either the agent or the company. The agent must locate the prospect and sell him upon his need for (more) insurance. Also, few people discriminate among the major life insurance companies in the United States. The typical view is that all the large companies are equally good and that their prices and services are identical.[38] The particular life insurance agent who contacts a prospect is the critical factor in determining whether or not a sale is made. Little life insurance would be sold without the actions of the salesman.

## Dyadic Interaction in Life Insurance Selling

In spite of the recognized importance of the relationship between the life insurance agent and his prospect almost no research has been done which focuses upon them as an interacting pair.[30] A study is now being conducted to examine the interaction situation of particular salesman-prospect dyads. The sample consists of approximately 125 established and successful salesmen and some 500 of their particular prospects, half of whom purchased from the agents and half of whom did not. The analysis will focus upon the dyads, successful outcomes versus unsuccessful outcomes.

The main hypothesis of this study is that the interaction in the dyad determines the results. The more similar the parties in the dyad are, the more likely a favorable outcome, a sale. The areas being studied include the social, economic, physical, personality, and communicative characteristics of both parties. Also included are the salesman's role and the prospect's view of it, sales techniques, product and company knowledge, and the influence of third parties to the selling situation.

Although this study is only about one-third completed at this time, comparisons of the sold and unsold prospects (alone) indicate the importance of their reactions to the particular salesman who called upon them. Table 1 shows that prospects who purchase insurance know more about the salesman and his company and feel more positively towards them than prospects who do not buy.

**TABLE 1. Comparison of Sold and Unsold Prospects' Recall and Attitudes Towards Sales Agent Who Called on Them**

| *Interaction Indicator* | *Sold (Percentage)* | *Unsold (Percentage)* |
|---|---|---|
| Consider salesman a friend | 31 | 6 |
| Consider salesman an expert | 67 | 55 |
| Salesman liked me as a person | 78 | 60 |
| Salesman enjoys his job | 95 | 75 |
| Salesman enjoyed talking to me | 98 | 71 |
| Prospect knew salesman's name | 76 | 32 |
| Would introduce salesman to my business friends | 92 | 78 |
| Would introduce salesman to my social friends | 89 | 79 |
| Salesman represents the best company | 20 | 10 |
| Denied agent's call | 0 | 20 |
| Company A, not represented by salesman, is best | 18 | 17 |
| Total Dyads | (45) | (104) |

The salesmen in this study have shown a high degree of role involvement. Most feel that they are salesmen 24 hours a day, not just for working hours; they feel they work no harder than people with office jobs, and are satisfied with the way their lives have turned out. They enjoy talking to prospects and typically discuss things other than insurance with the prospects.

Half of the agents view their job as being like that of a minister; the other half think it is more like a teacher's. None believe it is like other sales jobs. They say that they hold clients' interests higher than either a lawyer or tax accountant does. They do not feel that they are intruders upon the prospect's privacy and they claim not to be personally upset by a prospect's refusal to buy. Also they conform to rigid standards of dress which they think the role requires.

In spite of their role involvement these salesmen exhibited many conflicting attitudes. Less than 10% of them would like to see their sons follow in their footsteps. They claimed that they enjoyed meeting new people, yet over two-thirds of them said they would quit selling if they had to make only cold canvas calls. They say they need introductions or referrals from past clients. Three-quarters of the agents indicated no interest in the professional C.L.U. degree, nor did they believe it would in any way help their selling.

Although the agents realize that they must please their prospects, they tend to deny the importance of the interpersonal relations. They say that their prospects are the kind of people they'd like to know better as friends, the kind they'd invite to a family party or to their church's picnic. Still they claim that a prospect's age, religion, ethnic background, appearance, or whether he has children makes no difference to them. It seems quite unselective. The agents in the study are all married men with children, and the majority do not smoke.

The agents equate hard work with success. They want to tell the prospect what's best for him. They prefer to call on prospects at home, in the evening, and to talk to them in either the dining room or kitchen. A table is a handy sales tool. Some agents like to have the wife present when the sales presentation is made but most are indifferent on this point. In carrying out his role the salesman believes he knows the expectations and reactions of his prospects. In this he is only partially right.

The agent's training and his job expectations make him believe (or want to believe) that he can sell everyone. The agents tend to deny the importance of their interaction with particular kinds of prospects. However, analysis of the dyads available so far in this study points to the importance of certain similarities between the salesman and his prospect. Table 2 indicates that the successful dyads are more alike internally than the unsuccessful ones. The differences are small, but they are consistent.

The more alike the salesman and his prospect are, the greater the likelihood for a sale. This is true for physical characteristics (age, height), other objective factors (income, religion, education) and variables that may be related to personality factors (politics, smoking). It is also important to note that the perceived similarity for religion and politics is much higher and of greater importance to the sales than the true similarity.

## Summary and Conclusion

Life insurance selling is commonly conceived of as depending upon the relationship between the salesman and his prospect yet the salesman-prospect dyad has rarely been studied. The traditional marketing approach to

**TABLE 2. Internal Pair Similarity of Sold and Unsold Dyads**

| *Characteristic* | *Sold Dyads (Percentage)* | *Unsold Dyads (Percentage)* | *Total (Percentage)* |
|---|---|---|---|
| Salesman same height or taller than Prospect | 32 | 68 | 100 |
| Salesman shorter than Prospect | 28 | 72 | 100 |
| Salesman same or better educated than Prospect | 35 | 65 | 100 |
| Salesman less educated than Prospect | 23 | 77 | 100 |
| Salesman and Prospect less than nine years apart in age | 33 | 67 | 100 |
| Salesman and Prospect more than nine years apart in age | 25 | 75 | 100 |
| Salesman earns same or more than Prospect | 33 | 67 | 100 |
| Salesman earns less than Prospect | 20 | 80 | 100 |
| Salesman and Prospect either both smokers or both non-smokers | 32 | 68 | 100 |
| Salesman and Prospect have different smoking habits | 26 | 74 | 100 |
| Salesman and Prospect have same religion | 32 | 68 | 100 |
| Salesman and Prospect have different religions | 28 | 72 | 100 |
| Salesman and Prospect have same political party | 35 | 65 | 100 |
| Salesman and Prospect have different political party | 27 | 73 | 100 |
| Prospect perceives Salesman's religion the same as his own | 36 | 64 | 100 |
| Prospect perceives Salesman's religion different from his own | 28 | 72 | 100 |
| Prospect perceives Salesman's political party the same as his own | 48 | 52 | 100 |
| Prospect perceives Salesman's political party different from his own | 20 | 80 | 100 |
| Total Dyads | 30(45) | 70(104) | 100(100) |

selling has been contrasted with interaction studies in sociology and medicine. Research is now being done on the salesman-prospect dyad. Some early results of this study indicate differences in the ways sold and unsold prospects viewed the particular salesman who called upon them, how the salesman views his role, and differences in pair similarity between sold and unsold dyads. Similarity of attributes within the dyad appears to increase the likelihood of a sale.

Much more basic research into various aspects of the selling situation will be needed before any definitive and practical results may be expected.

## NOTES AND REFERENCES

1. For a general discussion of dyad analysis, see M. W. Riley, *et al., Sociological Studies in Scale Analysis* (New Brunswick, N.J.: Rutgers University, 1954).
2. W. K. Kirchner and M. D. Dunnette, "How Salesmen and Technical Men Differ in Describing Themselves," *Personnel Journal*, 37, No. 11 (April, 1959), p. 418.
3. Raymond W. Mack, Northwestern University, in an unpublished speech, "Who is the Salesman?," 1955.
4. *Ibid*.
5. Anne Roe, *The Psychology of Occupations* (New York: John Wiley & Sons, 1956), pp. 178-79.
6. R. W. Husband, *The Psychology of Successful Selling* (New York: Harper & Brothers, 1953), pp. 260-270.
7. W. J. Stanton and R. H. Bushkirk, *Management of the Sales Force* (Homewood, Ill.: Richard D. Irwin, 1959), p. 126ff.
8. W. E. Robinson, President, The Coca-Cola Company, "Fundamental Factors in Persuasion," *Industrial Medicine and Surgery*, June, 1956, pp. 269-72.
9. J. W. Thompson, "A Strategy of Selling," *Salesmanship*, edited by S. J. Shaw and J. W. Thomson (New York: Henry Holt, 1960), p. 18.
10. H. J. Leavitt, "Selling and the Social Scientist," *Journal of Business*, XXVII (April, 1954), pp. 41-43.
11. H. S. Bell, *Championship Selling* (Englewood Cliffs, N.J.: Prentice Hall, 1959), p. 45.
12. George F. F. Lombard, *Behavior in a Selling Group* (Boston: Harvard, 1955).
13. *Ibid*., p. 207.
14. *Ibid*., p. 209.
15. *Ibid*., p. 227.
16. William F. Whyte, *Human Relations in the Restaurant Industry* (New York: McGraw-Hill, 1948).
17. *Ibid*., p. 92.
18. *Ibid*., p. 109.
19. *Ibid*., p. 18.
20. Mark Benny and Everett C. Hughes, "Of Sociology and the Interview," *American Journal of Sociology*, LXII (September, 1956), p. 139.
21. Robert L. Kahn and Charles F. Cannell, *The Dynamics of Interviewing* (New York: John Wiley, 1957), p. 11.
22. Herbert Hyman, *et al., Interviewing in Social Research* (Chicago: University of Chicago, 1954), pp. 83-117.
23. Mark Benny, David Reisman, and Shirley A. Star, "Age and Sex in the Interview," *American Journal of Sociology*, LXII (September, 1956), pp. 143-52.
24. *Ibid*., p. 152.

25. Charles F. Cannell and Morris Axelrod, "The Respondent Reports on the Interview," *American Journal of Sociology*, LXII (September, 1956), p. 177.
26. Hyman, *et al., op. cit.*, p. 282.
27. Donald C. Hildam and Roger W. Brown, "Verbal Reinforcement and Interviewer Bias," *Journal of Abnormal and Social Psychology*, 53 (1956), p. 111.
28. Robert P. Goldman, "Do Doctors Make You Sick?" *Custom and Crises in Communication*, edited by Irving J. Lee (New York: Harper, 1954), pp. 257-61.
29. Brian Bird, *Talking with Patients* (Philadelphia: J. B. Lippincott, 1955), p. 63.
30. Fillmore H. Sanford, "Interpersonal Communication" *Industrial Medicine and Surgery*, 25 (June, 1956), pp. 261-65.
31. Harry Stack Sullivan, *The Psychiatric Interview* (New York: W. W. Norton, 1954); Dominick A. Barbara, "The Value of Non-Verbal Communication in Personality Understanding," *The Journal of Nervous and Mental Diseases*, 123, No. 3 (March, 1956); and H. L. Lennard, *et al., The Anatomy of Psychotherapy: Systems of Communication and Expectation* (New York: Columbia University, 1960).
32. Charles Berg, *The First Interview* (London: George Allen and Unwin, 1955), p. 31.
33. George C. Homans, *Social Behavior: Its Elementary Forms* (New York: Harcourt, Brace & World, 1961), pp. 186-187.
34. Selwyn Becker (unpublished research report, Stanford University, 1959).
35. John W. Thibaut and Henry W. Riecken, "Authoritarianism, Status, and the Communication of Aggression," *Human Relations*, No. 8 (May, 1955), p. 119.
36. Francis B. Stark, "Barriers to Client-Worker Communication at Intake," *Social Case Work*, XL, No. 4 (April, 1959), p. 183.
37. R. K. Bain, "The Process of Professionalization: Life Insurance Selling" (unpublished doctoral dissertation, University of Chicago, 1959, p. 342).
38. Unpublished data, by the writer, 1959.
39. Research on life insurance selling is commonplace but it has followed the traditional marketing methodologies. *Supra*.

# 37 — Buyer-Seller Interaction: A Conceptual Framework

*Jagdish N. Sheth*

*Advance in Consumer Research,* edited by Anderson, Vol. 3, B (1976), pp. 382-386. Reprinted by permission.

## Abstract

This paper attempts to provide a comprehensive conceptualization of the buyer-seller interaction process. The basic postulate under the conceptualization is that the quality of interaction is a function of the compatibility between the buyer and the seller with respect to both the style and the content of communication. After defining the dimensionalities of style and content, a number of personal, organizational and product-specific factors are described as determinants of style and content of communication in buyer-seller interaction process.

## Introduction

A review of the literature in the area of buyer-seller interaction process points out at least three dimensions of the state of the art (See Evans, 1963; Davis and Silk, 1972; Hulbert and Capon, 1972; O'Shaughnessy, 1972; and Webster, 1968 for summaries and reviews of the knowledge in the area).

First, the extent of empirical research on the buyer-seller interaction process is relatively sparse suggesting considerably less interest in this area at least among the academic researchers. While there is considerable talk about the mysteries of the super-salesman and some good research in the area of selection and training of sales representatives in industrial marketing, the vital linkage of the buyer-seller interaction process remains yet to be systematically researched.

Second, whatever empirical research one finds in the area is highly sporadic and ad hoc. Most of it consists of attempts to extend specific hypotheses borrowed from the behavioral sciences to describe and explain process of buyer-seller interaction. These consist of several similarity hypotheses related to the backgrounds and physical characteristics of the buyer and the seller, and the reliance on the Yale School of thought on personal communication including impact of source, message and channel factors (Howard and Sheth, 1969; Capon, Holbrook and Hulbert, 1975). Consequently, the area of buyer-seller interaction is replete with numerous hypotheses, interesting observations and considerable degree of contradictory or unrelated research findings.

Third, there is a conspicuous absence of any comprehensive conceptualization or theory of buyer-seller interaction. It seems no one has as yet attempted to go beyond reviewing the literature in order to sort out existing evidence and to reconcile inconsistent or contradictory findings by offering a comprehensive or holistic perspective to the problem area.

A comprehensive perspective of the buyer-seller interaction process seems timely and can serve several useful functions. It will encourage more systematic and realistic research which takes into account many interdependent phenomena relevant to understanding the buyer-seller interaction process; it will probably point out new areas of research by providing insights which can only come from a comprehensive perspective; finally it is likely to discourage research in what may prove to be irrelevant or less useful subareas. Often, research in a growing area tends to localize in a very narrow issue losing sight of the many other unexplored and more useful aspects within it. Witness the recent experience in the area of attitude structures and specifically the controversy about the judgmental rules a person utilizes in processing multiattribute information.

Accordingly, the purpose of this paper is to attempt a comprehensive conceptualization of the buyer-seller interaction process. It is hoped that such a conceptualization will generate additional insights into the problem area and encourage more selective and concerted research.

## Overview

The conceptual framework suggested in this paper is comprehensive and abstract enough to include buyer-seller interactions in both household and organizational marketing. In other words, it is capable of explaining the process of buyer-seller interaction which takes place at the retail outlets for consumer goods as well as between sales representatives and purchasing agents of formal organizations.

It is also comprehensive enough to include all types of buyer-seller interactions. These can be interpersonal (face to face), written or even telecommunication in nature. It is surprising to note how written and telecommunication buyer-seller interactions have been ignored in past research activities.

The conceptual framework developed in this paper has consciously avoided extending any particular well-known theory of interpersonal communication from the behavioral sciences. Often, such blind extensions have proved less useful in the past (Sheth, 1974b). Instead, attempt is made to conceptualize the area from a managerial perspective and selectively choose as many theories and hypotheses from behavioral sciences as seem relevant to provide insights into why and how some buyer-seller interactions work to the satisfaction of both the parties and others don't.

The basic postulate underlying the conceptual framework summarized in Figure 1 is that whether a specific buyer-seller interaction will or will not work is a function of two distinct dimensions of interaction. The first dimension is the *content of communication* representing the substantive aspects of the purposes for which the two parties have got together. It entails suggesting, offering, promoting or negotiating a set of product-specific utilities and their expectations.

While the dimensions of product-specific utilities will be described in detail later in the paper, it is sufficient to note here that often the expectations offered by the seller and desired by the buyer for a specific product or service do not match resulting in failure of the interaction transaction to be consummated successfully and satisfactorily.

A second dimension of buyer-seller interaction determination is the *style of communication*. It represents the format, ritual or mannerism which the buyer and the seller adopt in their interaction. The style of interaction reflects the highly individualistic preferences and normative expectations of the buyer and the seller about the process of interaction itself. Much of the search for the supersalesman is often localized in identifying the style of interaction of highly successful salesman in organizational marketing.

The buyer-seller interaction process itself is treated as a transaction which can have multiple effects or consequences. Comparable to the impact of advertising (Sheth, 1974a), the buyer-seller interaction is presumed to perform any of the following five functions: (a) increase awareness of each other's expectations about the product or service; (b) remind each other's past satisfactory transactions and their behavioral outcomes; (c) reinforce each other's behavior related to the sale of the product or service; (d) precipitate behavioral actions on each other's part by intensifying expectations; (e) persuade each other to change their respective expectations.

Whatever the objective, a satisfactory interaction transaction between the buyer and the seller will occur if and only if they are compatible with respect to *both* the content and style of communication. In all other situations, the interaction transaction is presumed to be less than ideal. In Figure 1, a two by two classification of interaction transaction is provided as a very simple framework to understand the impact of incompatibility with respect to style and content of communication. For example, if the buyer and the seller are compatible with respect to style but not with respect to content of communication, it is argued that while a dialogue will continue between the two parties, the actual sale may not be consummated due to difference in product expectations. Either the interaction process will be terminated or negotiations will take place to change each other's product expectations. On the other hand, if the buyer and the seller are compatible with respect to content but not the style of communication, it is argued that either the process will be terminated or even if the sale is consummated there will be negative feelings about each other's style or manner of interaction resulting in an unsatisfactory transaction. Finally, when both the style and the content are incompatible between the buyer and the seller, not only will there be no transaction culminating in a sale, but there are likely to be negative

**FIGURE 1. A Conceptual Framework of Buyer Seller Interaction**

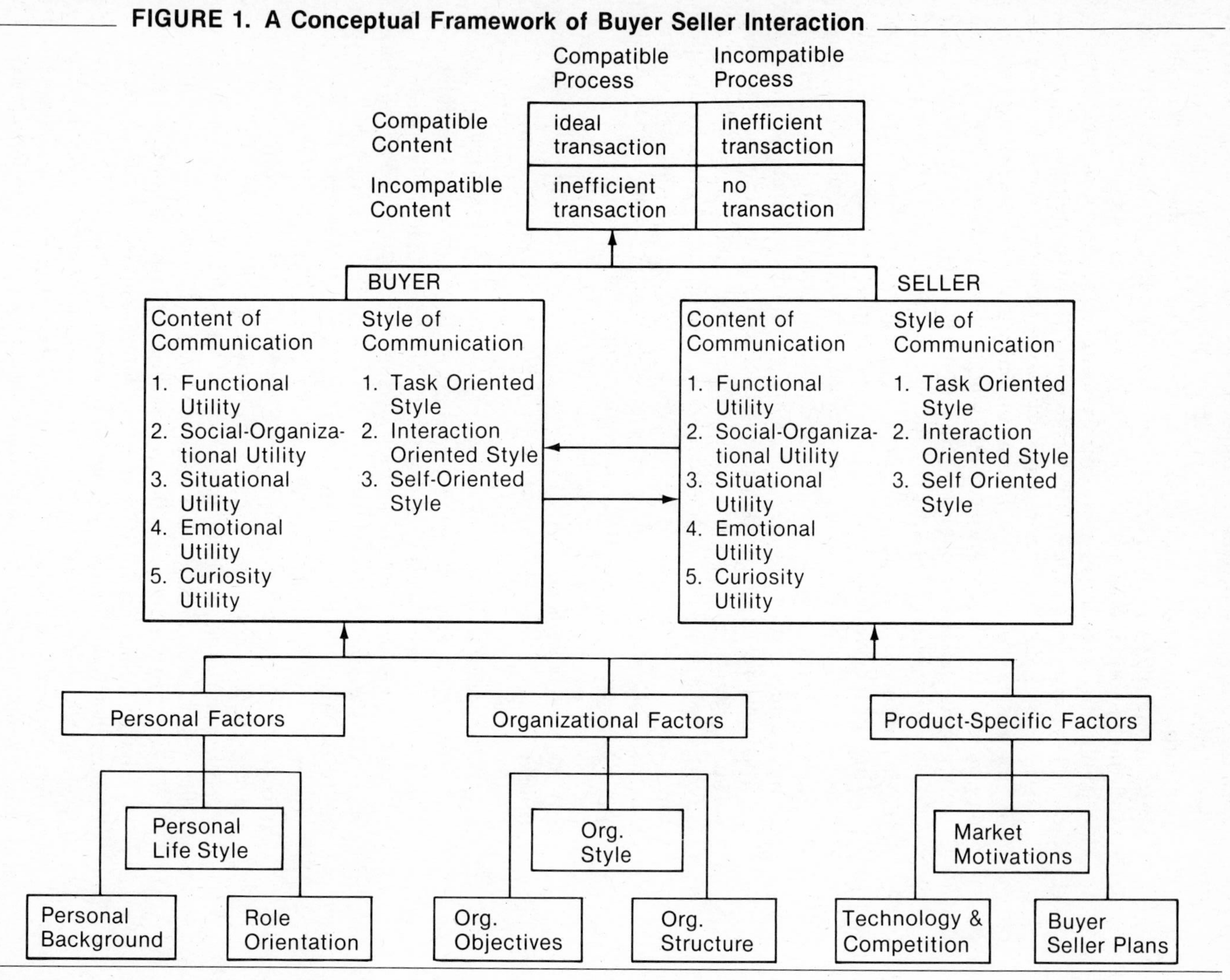

side effects of complaints, bad word of mouth about each other, and distrust of each other.

Both the style and content of buyer-seller communication are determined by a number of personal, organizational and product-related factors. For example, the personal life styles and backgrounds will often determine the style of communication the buyer or the seller chooses to engage in. Similarly, organizational training and orientation will also mould the buyer or the seller with respect to the style of communication he is expected to engage in. Finally, the content of communication is likely to be determined by product-related variables such as market motivations, buyer and seller plans and technology or competitive structure of industry.

## Content of Communication

While it is obvious that any incompatibility with respect to what the buyer wants and what the seller offers in a product or service will be detrimental to consummating a sale, it is more interesting and useful to identify dimensions and sources of content incompatibility. Based on a recent model of individual choice behavior (Sheth, 1975), it is proposed that underlying buyer-seller expectations about a product or service, there lies a five dimensional utility space. The five dimensions represent different types of product-related utilities which the buyer desires and the seller offers to each other. Each type of utility is briefly described below:

1. ***Functional Utility***. It represents product's utility which is strictly limited to its performance and which defines the purpose of its existence and classification as a type of good or service. For example, the functional utility associated with an instant breakfast can be described in terms of taste, convenience, nutrition and calories. Similarly, the functional utility associated with a passenger car tire can be defined in terms of mileage, blow out protection, traction, handling and ride. The functional utility is often measured in terms of a person's expectations on a number of product-anchored attributes or evaluative criteria. It is presumed to be a complex function of positive and negative expectations on multiattribute profiles. In this paper, we treat functional utility as one dimension of product utility and ignore for a moment the question of its own dimensionality.
2. ***Social-Organizational Utility***. Sometimes a product or service acquires social-organizational connotations or imageries indepenent of its performance or functional utility. This is due to its consistent identification with a selective set of socioeconomic, demographic or organizational types. Such identification with a selective cross-section of household or organizational buyers tends to impute certain utilities or disutilities in the product or service producing an

imagery or a stereotype. For example, cigarettes are often consumed due to their social imagery even though they may be functionally harmful. Certain products are, therefore, used for their prestige and not so much their performance. The existence of social-organizational utility in a product or service is also prevalent in organizational buyer behavior especially with respect to those products and services which are directly associated with the organization man. This is not surprising in view of the fact that there exists an organizational stratification of people working in organizations comparable to social stratification of households based on organization structure, hierarchy, and power distribution.

3. ***Situational Utility.*** It represents a product's utility which is *derived* from existence of a set of situations or circumstances. The product or service has no intrinsic or independent utility and will not be offered or bought without the presence of circumstances which create its need. The situational utility is often strong among those products or services which are consumed on an ad hoc basis rather than on a continuous basis. For example, the utilization of the services of the priest for marriage ceremony or the lawyer for divorce proceedings tend to be nonrepetitive by and large. Similarly, a housewife may buy a product or service as a gift item due to a very specific situation or occasion such as graduation or marriage. Organizations often tend to use the services of professionals on an ad hoc basis because of a specific project. Many of the capital expenditure items and highly specialized professional skills have greater degree of situational utility in them. It is extremely important to identify situations and activities which add to the utility of the product or service.

4. ***Emotional Utility.*** Sometimes a product or service evokes strong emotive feelings such as respect, anger, fear, love, hate or aesthetics due to its association with some other objects, events, individuals or organizations. The strong emotive feelings are therefore generalized to the product or service resulting in a different type of utility or disutility. For example, some Jewish buyers tend to refrain from buying German products because of strong emotional feelings they arouse as reminders of the German Nazi movement. Similarly, many Hindus refrain from eating beef due to strong emotive feelings anchored in religious tenets. While one would expect less prevalence of emotive utility in organizational products or services than in household products or services, this is not borne out by empirical research. Organizations also tend to manifest emotive behavior as is evidenced in international trade and cross-national negotiations.

5. ***Curiosity Utility.*** The fifth type of utility often present in both household and organizational products or services is related to

novelty, curiosity and exploratory needs among individuals. Based on the assumption that man constantly seeks out new, different things due to either satiation with existing behavior or due to boredom inherent in highly repetitive tasks, certain *new* products or services acquire additional utilities which are not intrinsic to their performance. These products or services are both offered and sought largely due to their novelty and to satisfy a person's curiosity arousal. They have a very short life cycle and often degenerate as fads or fashions.

Each product or service has a vector of the five types of utilities described above. Furthermore, both the buyer and the seller will have certain expectations about the product or service on these five types of utilities. It is not at all uncommon both in household and organizational marketing to learn that the specific utility expectations of the buyer and the seller do not match resulting in some form of incompatibility with respect to content of interaction.

The degree of incompatibility can be measured by performing a dimensional analysis of the vectors of buyer- seller expectations. For example, we can locate the vectors of buyer and seller expectations in a five dimensional space, and measure the degree of incompatibility as a function of the distance between the buyer and the seller points located in the space. The greater the distance between the buyer and the seller point in space, the greater the incompatibility with respect to the content of communication. Presuming the equivalence between Euclidian distance and psychological incompatibility, the degree of incompatibility can be measured as follows:

$$D_{BS} = \sqrt{\sum_{j=1}^{5} (b_{B_j} - b_{S_j})^2} \tag{1}$$

where $D_{BS}$ = Distance or incompatibility between Buyer and Seller
$b_{B_j}$ = Buyer's expectations with respect to $j$th type of utility
and $b_{S_j}$ = Seller's expectations with respect to $j$th type of utility

The distance between the buyer and the seller will determine to what extent they are matched with respect to content of communication. Since the buyer in a free enterprise system has the economic buying power it is presumed that the seller will often adapt or change his offerings in such a way as to minimize the distance. However, it is often not true in reality because the seller also attempts to change the location of buyer expectations in the space by persuasive communication strategies or sales tactics.

Who will make the adjustment is clearly a function of who has the greater power in the buyer-seller relationship. While the buyer has the economic power, the seller often has greater technical expertise to offset buyer's power. As a very broad generalization, it is likely that in a buyer's market, the seller is more likely to change in the long run. In the seller's market it is more likely that the buyer will change or adapt. In all other cases, tactics of persuasion, negotiations and bargaining are likely to emerge as consequences of buyer-seller interaction.

## Style of Communication

The vast literature on group dynamics and interpersonal relationships in small groups (Bass, 1960; Heider, 1958; Homans, 1961), provides an excellent source to discuss the concept of style of interaction. As mentioned before, it refers to the format, ritual and mannerism involved in buyer-seller interaction. While we will rely heavily on research in group dynamics, it is important to keep in mind that the dimensionalities of style of interaction discussed here are common to nonpersonal interactions such as via telecommunication or postal systems. The style of interaction is presumed to be three dimensional. The specific dimensions are described below:

1. ***Task-Oriented Style.*** This style of interaction is highly goal oriented and purposeful. The individual is most interested in the efficiency with which the task at hand can be performed so as to minimize cost effort and time. Any activity during the interaction process which is either not task-oriented or inefficient is less tolerated by the individual who prefers the task-oriented style. The buyer or the seller who prefers this style of interaction often tends to be mechanistic in his approach to other people.
2. ***Interaction-Oriented Style.*** The buyer or the seller who prefers this style of interaction believes in personalizing and socializing as an essential part of the interaction process. In fact, preference for this style of interaction is often manifested at the loss or ignoring of the task at hand. The buyer or the seller motivated by the interaction oriented style is often compulsive in first establishing a personal relationship with the other person and then only getting involved in the specific content of interaction.
3. ***Self-Oriented Style.*** This style reflects a person's preoccupation with himself in an interaction situation. He is more concerned about his own welfare and tends to have less empathy for the other person. He is often unable to take the other person's perspective and views all aspects of interaction from his own selfish point of view. The concepts of self-preservation, self-survival and self-emulation tend to dominate this style of interaction.

It is also not uncommon to find situations in which the buyer and the seller are incompatible with respect to style of interaction. Given a three-dimensional vector of style of interaction, it is possible to measure the extent of incompatibility with the following Euclidian distance:

$$D_{BS} = \sqrt{\sum_{j=1}^{3} (C_{B_j} - C_{S_j})^2} \tag{2}$$

where $D_{BS}$ = Distance between Buyer and Seller on style of interaction
$C_{B_j}$ = Buyer's orientation with respect to $j$th type of style of interaction
$C_{S_j}$ = Seller's orientation with respect to $j$th type of style of interaction

The greater the distance between the buyer and the seller points in the style space, the more incompatible they will be with respect to style of interaction.

Unlike content of interaction, it is more difficult to change or adapt with respect to style of interaction. This is largely because the style orientations of individuals are often deep rooted in personality variables, early socialization processes and personal life styles. It is, therefore, difficult to discuss who should make changes in what situation in the buyer-seller interaction process. If the style of interaction is highly incompatible between the buyer and the seller, it is probably best to terminate interaction and attempt to link the right types of sellers with the buyers in the interaction process.

## Determinant Factors

Both the style and the content of buyer-seller interaction are determined by a set of exogeneous factors. These are classified into three categories: (a) personal factors anchored to the individuals involved in the interaction; (b) organizational factors anchored to the respective organizations the buyer and the seller belong to. Even in household marketing, we believe there are organizational factors not only associated with the seller but also with the buyer in so far as a typical household has some organizational structure, no matter how implicit it may be; (c) product-related factors anchored to market motivations, competive structure and buyer-seller plans. We will briefly describe some of the more salient variables in each category. However, it is beyond the scope of this paper to treat them exhaustively or even attempt to specify their causal influences on the style and content of interaction.

1. ***Personal Factors.*** The personal factors are likely to determine the style of interaction each individual prefers. Among many personal factors, there seems to be some consensus among the researchers with regard to the following specific variables. The first one is the

demographic, socioeconomic and organizational background of the individual. These include physical characteristics such as sex, race, height, weight etc. as well as both generalized education and special skills acquired by the individual. A second specific variable is the individual's life style. It reflects the molding of the individual over time as a function of socialization and personality development. The third specific variable is the role orientation of the individual with respect to the interaction process. It includes expectations and performance of specific roles on the part of the salesman such as a consultant, order taker, informer, persuader, etc.

2. ***Organizational Factors.*** Organizational factors often determine both the style and the content of interaction. The organization often recruits, selects, trains and prepares the buyer or the seller with respect to both the content and style of communication. The organizational factors which account for variability among organizations in their degree of controlling the content and style of interaction are organization objectives, organization style and organization structure. The content will be heavily influenced by organization objectives and to some extent by organization structure. Similarly, each organization has an explicit or implicit style of management often dictated by the top man in the organization. The organization style is likely to influence the personal style of communication of the seller or the buyer.
3. ***Product-Specific Factors.*** The product-specific factors are more likely to determine the content rather than the style of interaction. While there are many specific factors one can include in the list, we will isolate three specific factors which seem more relevant and interesting. The first factor, of course, relates to market motivations. It refers to the generalized needs, wants and desires customers have for which the specific product is more or less relevant. The second factor relates to buyer and seller plans. The buyer has certain plans in his mind about the specific use he is likely to make use of the product. Similarly, the seller has certain plans with respect to market differentiation and customer segmentation. The product expectations of the buyer and the seller are likely to be heavily determined by their respective plans. The third factor is anchored to the supply side of the product. It refers to the technological and competitive leadership the seller has in that product category. The product expectations and utilities especially in regard to functional, situational and curiosity utilities are more likely to be determined by technology and competition prevalent in the industry.

The three types of determinants of style and content of interaction are extremely relevant to isolate individual differences among buyers and sellers, product differences for the same buyer or seller, and organizational differences for the same product. They essentially serve the function of reducing all the buyer-seller interactions to a common base by partialing out the effects of personal, organizational and product differences.

## CONCLUSION

This paper has attempted a comprehensive conceptualization of the buyer-seller interaction process based on the presumption that whether or not there will be a satisfactory interaction will depend on whether the buyer's and the seller's style as well as content of interaction match. To the extent they do not match, the interaction is likely to be either terminated or will entail negative side effects.

Knowledge of mismatch between the buyer and the seller either with respect to style or with respect to content will require managerial corrective actions. These actions may take the form of modifying sales appeals, retraining salespeople, reassignment of salesmen as well as changes in recruiting and selection of personnel.

## REFERENCES

Bernard M. Bass, *Leadership, Psychology and Organizational Behavior* (New York: Harper & Brothers, 1960).

Noel Capon, Morris Holbrook and James Hulbert, "The Selling Process: A Review of Research," (unpublished paper, 1975).

Franklin B. Evans, "Selling as a Dyadic Relationship-A New Approach," *The American Behavioral Scientist*, 6 (May, 1963), 76-79.

Harry L. Davis and Alvin J. Silk, "Interaction and Influence Process in Personal Selling," *Sloan Management Review*, 13 (Winter, 1972), 54-56.

Fritz Heider, *The Psychology of Interpersonal Relations* (New York: John Wiley & Sons, 1958).

George Homans, *Social Behavior: Its Elementary Forms* (New York: Harcourt, Brace & World, 1961).

John A. Howard and Jagdish N. Sheth, *The Theory of Buyer Behavior* (New York: John Wiley & Sons, 1969).

James Hulbert and Noel Capon, "Interpersonal Communication in Marketing: An Overview," *Journal of Marketing Research*, 9 (February, 1972), 27-34.

John O'Shaughnessy, "Selling as an Interpersonal Influence Process," *Journal of Retailing*, 47 (Winter, 1971-72), 32-46.

J. N. Sheth, "Measurement of Advertising Effectiveness: Some Theoretical Considerations," *Journal of Advertising*, 3 (January, 1974), 6-11.

J. N. Sheth, "The Future of Buyer Behavior Theory," in J. N. Sheth (ed.) *Models of Buyer Behavior* (New York: Harper & Row, 1974).

J. N. Sheth, "Toward a Model of Individual Choice Behavior," paper presented at the ESOMAR Seminar on Modeling, June 11, 1975.

Frederick E. Webster, Jr., "Interpersonal Communication and Salesman Effectiveness," *Journal of Marketing*, 32 (July, 1968), 7-13.

# 38 —— Effectiveness in Sales Interactions: A Contingency Framework

*Barton A. Weitz*

Reprinted from *Journal of Marketing*, published by the American Marketing Association, Vol. 45 (Winter 1981), pp. 85-103. Reprinted by permission.

In 1978, the average expenditure for training each industrial salesperson was over $15,000 (*Sales and Marketing Management* 1979). Even though annual sales training expenses are well over one billion dollars, there is only limited knowledge about which selling behaviors are most effective in customer interactions. A conceptual framework for exploring this issue is presented in this paper.

To demonstrate the focus of this framework, a scheme for classifying variables related to salesperson performance is shown in Figure 1. The initial classification is based on whether the variable relates to the salesperson's macroenvironment or microenvironment. Macroenvironmental variables include territorial characteristics such as potential and workload and the level of effort expended by the salesperson in covering the territory. However, the objective of the framework presented in this paper is to delineate factors related to the effectiveness of salespeople in influencing customers during interpersonal interactions. Thus, the framework focuses on the effectiveness of sales behaviors in the microenvironment of the sales interaction.

Variables related to effectiveness in the microenvironment are further classified into those related to the sales situation and those related to the salesperson. Variables related to the salesperson's effort during customer interactions are not treated in the framework. Thus, the framework focuses on the shaded areas in Figure 1.

The fundamental idea behind the framework is that effectiveness in sales interactions can be understood best by examining the interactions between sales behaviors, resources of the salesperson, the nature of the customer's buying task, and characteristics of the salesperson-customer relationship. This framework provides a mechanism for integrating previous research and a direction for future research.

In the next section, the shortcomings of prior research on effectiveness in sales interactions are discussed. These shortcomings suggest the need for a contingency approach. After presenting the nature and applications of a contingency approach, the approach is expanded into a framework. The basic postulate of the framework is stated, constructs in the framework are defined, and a set of propositions is developed. These propositions are

**FIGURE 1. Variables Related to Salesperson Performance**

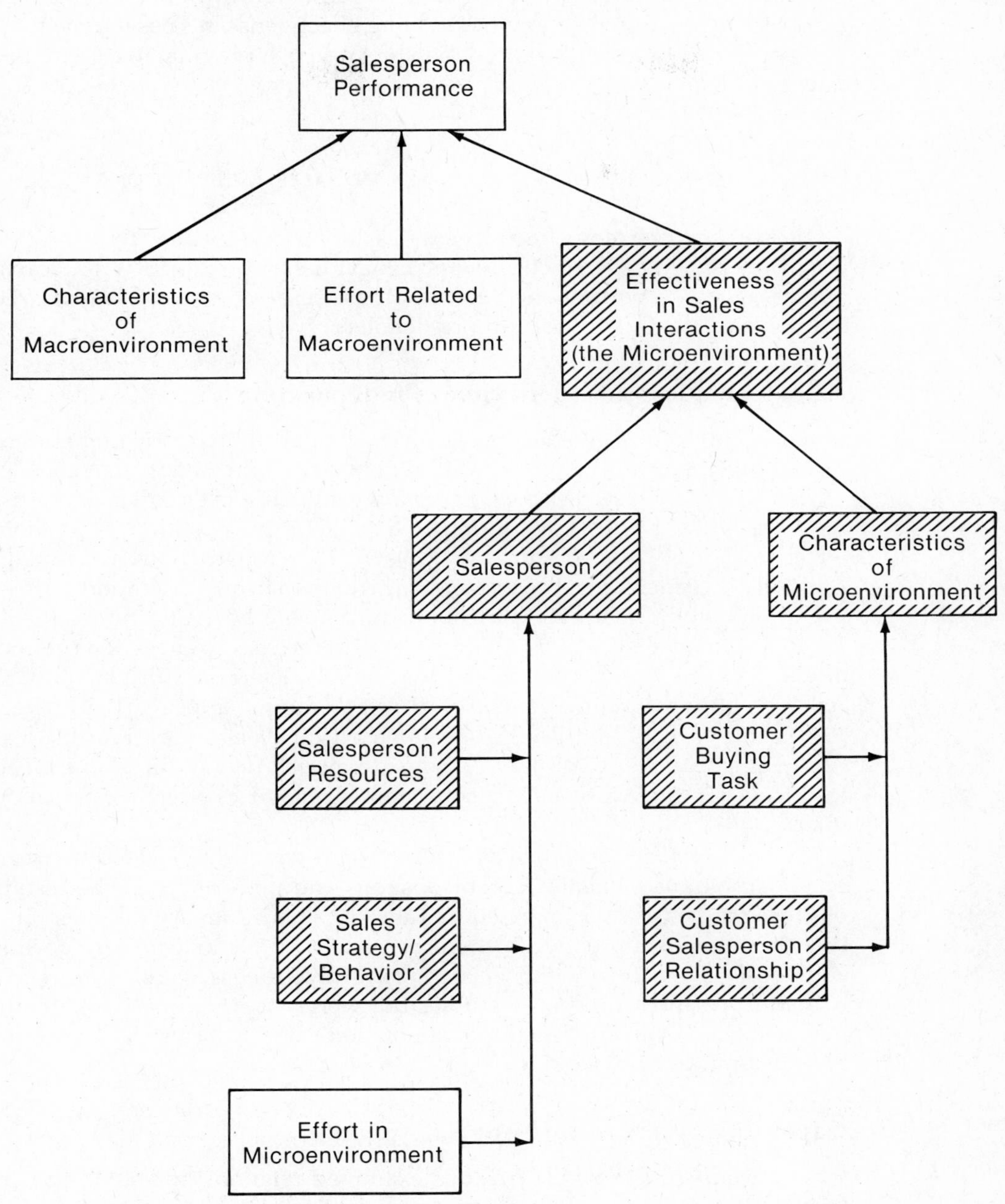

supported by research in leadership, bargaining, social psychology, and personal selling. Further research is needed to complete the framework; however, the portions of the framework presented in this paper suggest a potentially fruitful direction for studying effectivenss in sales interactions. The paper concludes with a discussion of a research program to explore this new direction.

## Research on Effectiveness in Sales Interactions

Research concerning effectiveness in sales interactions has concentrated on uncovering salesperson behaviors, behavioral predispositions, and capabilities related to performance. Each of these research streams is reviewed below. (See Weitz 1979 for a more detailed review.)

### Sales Behaviors and Behavioral Predispositions

The study of sales behaviors has been limited to experimental studies examining the effectiveness of different types of messages delivered by salespeople.[1] These studies have found little difference in effectiveness across message types. Levitt (1965) found that a ''good presentation'' was more effective than a ''poor presentation.'' Jolson (1975) reported that a ''canned'' presentation generated more purchase intention than an ''extemporaneous'' presentation but the universality of this finding has been questioned (Reed 1976). There were no significant differences in the effectiveness of a product oriented-versus a personal-oriented message (Farley & Swinth 1967); ''hard sell,'' emotional appeals versus ''soft-sell,'' rational appeals (Reizenstein 1971); and six different sales appeals based on Bales Interaction Process Analysis categories (Capon 1975). Thus, experimental studies have failed to uncover influence strategies consistently related to effectiveness in an interaction.

Correlational studies have attempted to uncover relationships between personality traits/behavioral predispositons and performance. The results of these studies are summarized in Table 1.[2] This summary demonstrates that the relationship between these personality traits and performance is equivocal. Characteristics associated with forcefulness were significantly related to performance in ten studies but were not significantly related to performance in four studies. Social orientation was significant in two studies and insignificant in six studies.

### Capability and Resources of Salespeople

A second stream of research has examined relationships between performance and the salesperson's resources and capabilities. Several studies have examined the relationship between performance and specific abilities

**TABLE 1. Behavioral Predispositions and Performance**

| *Significantly Related to Performance* | *Not Significantly Related to Performance* |
|---|---|
| *Forcefulness* | |
| oil company (Harrell 1960) | oil company (Miner 1962) |
| life insurance (Merenda & Clarke 1959, Greenberg & Mayer 1964) | life insurance (Zdep & Weaver 1967) |
| retail/trade (Howells 1968) | retail (Howells 1968) |
| technical rep (Howells 1968) | stockbroker (Ghiselli 1973) |
| commodities (Howells 1968) | |
| mutual fund (Greenberg & Mayer 1964) | |
| automobile (Greenberg & Mayer 1964) | |
| trade (Dunnette & Kircher 1960) | |
| stockbroker (Ghiselli 1973) | |
| food, appliance wholesaler (Mattheiss et at. 1977) | |
| *Sociability* | |
| life insurance (Merenda & Clarke 1959) | oil company (Miner 1962, Harrell 1960) |
| technical rep (Howells 1968) | industrial (Pruden & Peterson 1971) |
| retail (Howells 1968) | real estate (Scheibelhut & Albaum 1973) |
| retail/trade food (Howells 1968) | utility (Scheibelhut & Albaum 1973) |
| | industrial (Bagozzi 1978) |
| | food, appliance wholesaler (Mattheiss et al. 1977) |

conceptually related to interpersonal persuasion. These studies indicate that effectiveness in sales interactions is related to the salesperson's ability to develop accurate impressions of customer beliefs about product performance (Weitz 1978); the salesperson's ability to use these impressions in selecting influence strategies (Weitz 1978), and the salesperson's ability to detect the impact of influence strategies and make adaptations (Grikscheit and Crissey 1973).

The results of studies that have examined more general measures of capabilities are summarized in Table 2. This summary indicates that the relationship between capabilities and performance, like the relationship between performance and behavioral predispositions, is quite *inconsistent*, and in some cases, even *contradictory*. In some cases these inconsistencies may be due to variations in methodology across studies. However, several studies have used the same methodology across different sales forces and reported inconsistent results (Dunnette and Kirchner 1960; Howells 1968; Mattheiss et al. 1977; Scheibelhut and Albaum 1973). Even variables that can be assessed with high accuracy and reliability, such as age, education, and sales experience, are related to performance in some studies and unrelated in others.

**TABLE 2. Salesperson Capabilities and Performance**

| *Significantly Related to Performance* | *Not Significantly Related to Performance* |
|---|---|
| *Age* | |
| industrial (Kirchner et al. 1960)<br>retail (Mosel 1952, Weaver 1969) | household durable (Cotham 1969)<br>life insurance (Tanofsky et al. 1969; Meranda and Clarke, 1959)<br>industrial (Lamont & Lundstrom 1977)<br>retail (French 1960) |
| *Education* | |
| life insurance (Merenda & Clark 1959)<br>retail (Mosel 1952, Weaver 1969) | speciality food manufacturer (Baehr & Williams 1968)<br>insurance (Tanofsky et al. 1969)<br>industrial (Lamont & Lundstrom 1977)<br>household durable (Cotham 1969)<br>retail (French 1960) |
| *Sales Related Knowledge, Sales Experience, Product Knowledge, Training* | |
| Life insurance (Baier & Dugan 1957) | life insurance (Tanofsky et al. 1969, Meranda & Clarke 1959)<br>speciality food manufacturer (Baehr & Williams 1968)<br>household durable (Cotham 1969)<br>retail (French 1960) |
| *Intelligence* | |
| stockbroker (Ghiselli 1973)<br>oil company (Miner 1962, Harrell 1960)<br>industrial (Bagozzi 1978)* | oil company (Harrell 1960)<br>trade (Dunnette & Kirchner 1960)<br>appliance wholesaler (Mattheiss et al. 1977) |
| *Empathy* | |
| new automobile (Tobolski & Kerr 1952)<br>automobile (Greenberg & Mayer 1964)<br>life insurance (Greenberg & Mayer 1964)<br>mutual fund (Greenberg & Mayer 1964) | used automobile (Tobolski & Kerr 1952)<br>industrial (Lamont & Lundstrom 1977) |

*significant but negatively related.

## Customer Characteristics—The Dyadic Approach

The disappointing results from prior research on sales behaviors, behavioral predispositions, and general salesperson capabilities have led to a growing interest in dyadic research approaches. While there are a wide variety of studies associated with the dyadic approach, the unifying theme of these studies is that characteristics of the customer as well as those of the salesperson are considered. This approach is consistent with a contingency approach because it suggests that effectiveness in sales interactions is moderated by or dependent upon characteristics of both the salesperson and the customer.

Dyadic similarity studies have not demonstrated a meaningful relationship between similarity and effectiveness. Several correlational studies have either not supported the relationship (Doreen, Emery, and Sweitzer 1979) or found similarity explains a low percentage of the variance (Churchill, Collins, and Strang 1975). In addition, the correlation studies (Churchill et al. 1975; Evans 1963; Riordan, Oliver and Donnelly 1977) have not controlled for the plausible rival hypothesis that customers who made purchases perceived that they were more similar to the salespeople than customers who did not make purchases (Davis and Silk 1972). While experimental studies found that similarity is a significant factor in determining sales performance, it has not been as important as expertise (Bambic 1978; Busch and Wilson 1976; Woodside and Davenport 1974).[3]

Research exploring the effectiveness of dyadic similarity has not provided the new approach needed for studying effectiveness in sales interactions. These dyadic studies have focused on a single, static property and have not considered the interaction between sales behavior and dyadic characteristics. The contingency framework presented in this paper expands upon the dyadic approach by describing the relationship between effectiveness, sales behaviors, and a variety of salesperson and customer characteristics.

## Contingency Factors and Personal Selling Effectiveness

Past research efforts have attempted to uncover universal characteristics or behaviors that enable salespeople to perform successfully across a wide range of situations. Interactions between sales behaviors and aspects of the sales situation have not been considered. This research has ignored the unique advantage of personal selling in a company's marketing communication mix. Salespeople have the opportunity to match their behavior to the specific customer and situation they encounter. They can consider each interaction individually and present themselves and their product so as to be maximally effective in that interaction. In some interactions salespeople might find it more advantageous to present themselves as similar to their customers, while in other interactions salespeople might find it more advantageous to be perceived as an expert.

### Prior Considerations of Contingency Factors

The impact and managerial significance of examining the interaction between sales behaviors and sales environment is not a novel idea. Thompson (1973, p. 8) states that "every contact a salesman has ... involves different human problems or situations. In brief, *there is no one sales situation and no one way to sell.''* Gwinner (1968) proposed that four traditional approaches to selling have advantages and drawbacks that make each suitable in particular selling environments. In addition, it has been suggested that different approaches and salesperson characteristics are needed to be effective in selling new business versus selling to established customers (Kahn and Shuchman 1961), selling to purchase-oriented versus salesperson-oriented customers (Blake and Mouton 1970), and selling to customers who vary on the dimensions of dominance-submissive and hostile-warm (Buzzota, Lefton, and Sherberg 1972).[4]

Although little empirical research has explicitly considered interactions between environmental variables and sales behaviors, several researchers have demonstrated empirically that the relationship between performance and behavioral predispositions varies across sales circumstances. Differences in the relationship between personality traits and effectiveness have been found for industrial/trade salespeople and retail sales clerks (Ghiselli 1969), trade and industrial salespeople (Dunnette and Kirchner 1960; Howells 1968), real estate and private utility salespeople (Scheibelhut and Albaum 1973), and new and used car salespeople (Tobolski and Kerr 1952). Chapple and Donald (1947) found that the relationships between communication styles and performance differed across retail selling situations. For example, speech initiation behavior was related to the performance of salespeople operating in an open floor environment but not related to salespeople working behind a counter.

## Contingency Factors in Leadership Research

The leadership research illustrates the benefits to be gained by considering interactions between behaviors and moderating variables. The analogy between personal selling and leadership is particularly appropriate due to the similarity in behaviors considered and the similarity in historical development. Personal selling can be defined as the process by which a salesperson attempts to influence a customer to purchase his/her product, while leadership is defined as the ''process whereby one person exerts social influence over the members of a group'' (Filley, House, and Kerr 1976, p. 211). Thus, the salesperson directs influence behaviors toward customers just as the leader directs influence behaviors toward group members.

Three approaches have been used to study leadership effectiveness (Filley et al. 1976). The first approach looked for personality traits that differentiate effective and ineffective leadership. These studies were followed by attempts to identify behavior patterns associated with effective leadership. The inability to find universally effective behaviors has led researchers over the past twenty years to direct their attention toward studying the interaction between leader characteristics, leader behaviors, and characteristics of the work situation (Filley et al. 1976). Theories based on these interactions are referred to as contingency theories since the relationship between performance and leader behavior is contingent upon or moderated by characteristics of the leader, the subordinates, and the work situation.

A contingency approach also provides a promising framework for studying the effectiveness of interpersonal influence behaviors in sales situations. Such a framework is developed in the next section. After stating a basic postulate, each construct is defined and propositions describing the relationship between the constructs are presented.

## A Contingency Framework for Sales Effectiveness Across Interactions

A contingency framework for investigating the effectiveness of sales behaviors across interactions is shown in Figure 2. The basic elements of the framework for (a) the behavior of the salesperson in customer interactions, (b) the salespersons' resources, (c) the customer's buying task, and (d) the customer-salesperson relationship. The following basic postulate describes the interrelationship of these elements:

| Basic Postulate | The effectiveness of sales behaviors across customer interactions is contingent upon or moderated by (a) the salesperson's resources, (b) the nature of the customer's buying task, (c) the customer-salesperson relationship and interactions among (a), (b), and (c). |
|---|---|

This framework for personal selling specifies that effectiveness is related to the first-order interaction between behaviors and characteristics associated with the salesperson, the customer, and the dyad. Potential higher-order interactions are anticipated in the basic postulate. Based on this postulate it is not surprising that previous research on personal selling has failed to find consistent, main effect relationships between performance and individual elements such as behavioral tendencies (forceful or sociable personality traits), behaviors (hard sell versus soft sell or establishing referent versus expertise influence bases), salesperson resources (intelligence, empathy), and characteristics of customer-salesperson relationships (dyadic similarity).

Each of the constructs associated with the framework is discussed in the next section, followed by some propositions derived from past research. The elements and propositions discussed in this paper were selected on the basis of past research in personal selling and leadership. They are not intended to exploit completely the potential set of propositions that can be developed from the framework.

**FIGURE 2. A Contingency Model of Salesperson Effectiveness**

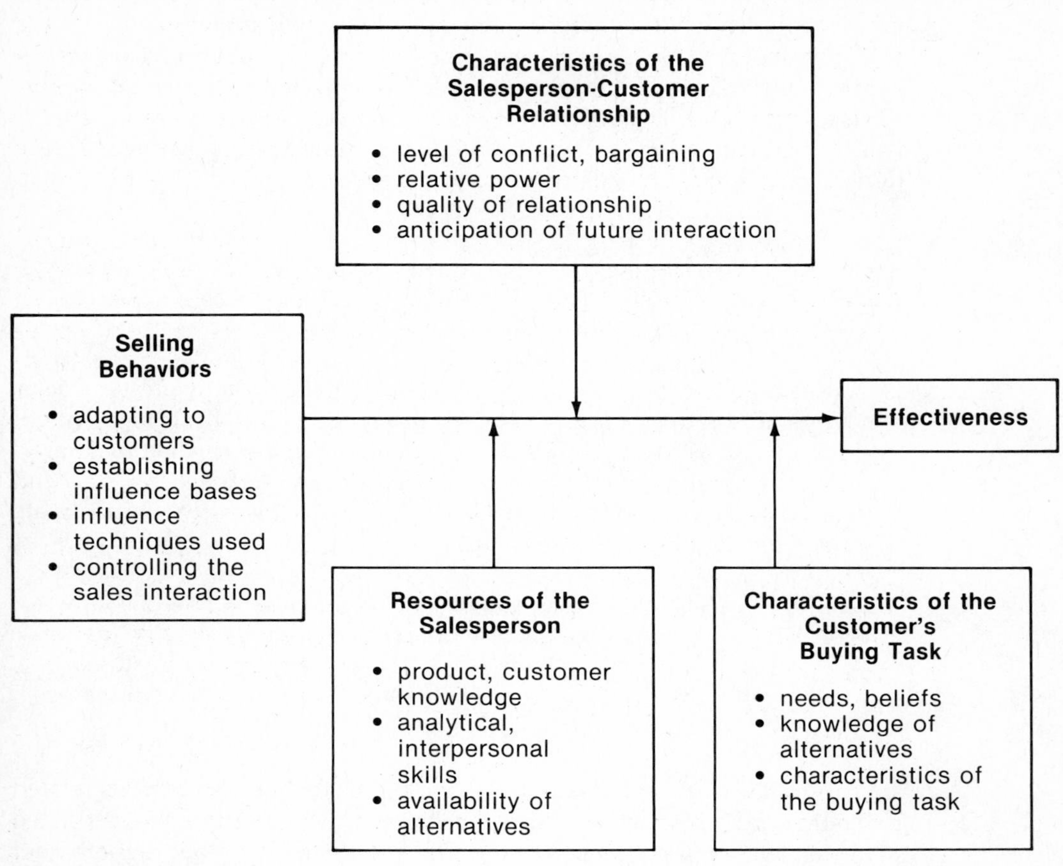


## Constructs in a Contingency Framework

### Salesperson Effectiveness

Effectiveness is defined from the perspective of the salesperson rather than the salesperson-customer dyad. This perspective differs from a conceptualization of the salesperson-customer interaction as a problem solving activity in which two parties attempt to reach a mutually beneficial solution (Willett and Pennington 1966). The problem solving perspective is not used because it does not consider the inherent advocacy nature of the salesperson's activities. While salespeople are somewhat interested in searching for a solution to the customer's problem that maximizes customer satisfaction, they and their managers strongly prefer solutions that incorporate the purchase of the products or services they are selling.

Consistent with the salesperson and sales management perspective, effectivness in sales interaction is defined by the degree in which the ''preferred solutions'' of salespeople are realized *across their customer interactions*.[5] This definition of effectiveness incorporates the fundamental interest of management in the performance of salespeople and selling behaviors across the entire set of interactions in which salespeople engage. The outcome of a specific interaction is of secondary interest.[6]

Even though this definition of effectiveness does not explicitly consider customer satisfaction, customer satisfaction is considered implicitly because effectiveness is defined across customer interactions. The following illustration demonstrates the implications associated with an effectiveness measure based on performance across interactions rather than during one interaction. Suppose a salesperson made a sale by using a deceptive influence strategy. From the salesperson's perspective, this influence strategy would have been effective in the interaction. However, the customer might not be satisfied with the product, and realizing the deception, would not buy products from the salesperson in the future. Thus, the use of deceptive influence strategies would not be effective for the salesperson across interactions with the customer, even though it was effective in one specific interaction.

Adopting a salesperson perspective does not mean that the customer's characteristics and needs are not considered. Customer characteristics and needs are considered in the framework, but only in terms of their moderating influence on the effectiveness of a salesperson's behavior.

## Salesperson Behaviors

While marketers have described salesperson orientations (Blake and Mouton 1970) or general sales approaches (Gwinner 1968), most empirical research on salesperson behaviors have considered microbehaviors such as the effectiveness of specific sales messages. Little though has been directed toward identifying underlying dimensions in which a salesperson's behavior can be assessed. In the remaining portion of this section, some of these dimensions are discussed.

***Adapting to the Customer.*** The behavior of salespeople can be characterized by the degree to which they adapt their behavior to the interaction. At one extreme, salespeople are nonadaptive when they deliver the same ''canned'' presentation (Jolson 1975) to all customers. In contrast to this nonadaptive behavior, salespeople can engage in a unique behavior pattern oriented to each customer.

Dimensions on which sales behavior can be adapted are discussed in following sections. It seems reasonable to assume that the effectiveness of influence bases, influence techniques, specific messages and formats, and the degree of control exerted varies across a salesperson's customers. Thus a salesperson could increase effectiveness in a specific interaction by altering behavior along the above mentioned dimensions (Weitz 1980).

Measures of adaptivity in sales behavior have not been developed; however, there are some personality measures that indicate a predisposition to engage in adaptive behaviors. For example, one would expect dogmatism and authoritarianism to be negatively related to adaptivity while tolerance for ambiguity would be positively related to adaptivity. A dispositional measure that appears to be closely related to adaptive behavior is self-monitoring. Synder (1974) has developed a scale to measure the degree to which people monitor their environment and use these environmental cues to alter their behavior. One would expect that high self-monitors would be more adaptive in sales situations.

***Establishing a Base of Influence.*** Another dimension of salesperson behavior is attempting to establish a base of influence. Wilson (1975) suggests that salespeople need to develop source credibility and legitimacy during the initial stages of an interaction. Without such a base of influence, salespeople cannot effectively influence their customers.

In a review of the use of influence bases in organizational setting, McCall (1979) concluded that "the relevance of a given power base, the appropriateness of various tactics, and the likely impacts of power use are intimately linked with each other and with the situation at hand" (p. 205). Thus, given a set of possible influence bases (French and Raven 1959), salespeople need guidance as to which bases are most effective in specific circumstances. Propositions concerning variables that moderate the effectiveness of these influence bases are presented in the next section.

***Influence Techniques Used.*** Salesperson behaviors can be classified in terms of the influence techniques used. Several studies have been directed toward defining and analyzing a wide variety of influence techniques (Capon and Swasy 1977; Falbo 1977; Spiro and Perreault 1979). These studies suggest that influence techniques can be classified using the following dimensions: (a) open/direct v. closed/indirect and (b) business/product-related v. emotional/person-related. When open/direct influence attempts are used, the purpose of the influence attempt is not hidden. Closed influence techniques involve the use of deception and hidden purposes. (See Yalch 1979 for a discussion of closed sales techniques used in finalizing a sale.)

Product-related influence techniques are defined as business or task oriented messages—information messages directed toward the product and the purchase decision. In contrast, emotional messages are directed toward the customer with the intent of appealing to psychological needs and improving customer-salesperson relations. Emotional messages attempt to reduce risks associated with the social consequences of the purchase decision, while product messages attempt to reduce risks associated with product performance (Newton 1967).

Influence techniques can also be classified by the target and format of the messages delivered. The target can be defined as the specific cognitive element, belief, or value toward which the message is directed. Message formats include comparative v. noncomparative messages and one-sided v. two-sided appeals.

***Controlling the Interaction.*** The final dimension of sales behavior to be considered is the extent to which the salesperson controls the sales interaction. This behavioral dimension is closely related to the dominant-submissive dimension proposed by Buzzota, Lefton, and Sherberg (1972), the salesperson-oriented dimension proposed by Blake and Mouton (1970), and the traditional salesperson behavior of using high or low pressure. The use of control or pressure is a method of aggressively directing the flow of the interaction toward making a sale. Several researchers have attempted to assess the degree of control exercised by salespeople by analyzing recordings of sales interactions (Willett and Pennington 1966, Olshavsky 1973).

Some insights into control behaviors of salespeople can be gained by examining leader control behaviors. Autocratic and ''initiating structure'' leader behaviors are associated with a high degree of leader control. In the context of a sales interaction, autocratic behavior is related to the use of high pressure tactics. Initiating structure behavior is related to the salesperson aggressively structuring the customer's problem so that the solution involves purchasing the salesperson's product.

## Moderating Variables

A wide variety of moderating variables are suggested by personal selling and leadership research. In the contingency framework shown in Figure 2 moderating variables are organized into the following three categories: (a) the customer's buying task, (b) the salesperson's resources, and (c) the customer-salesperson relationship. These categories parallel the following moderating variables used in Fiedler's leadership studies (Fiedler and Chemers 1974): the structure of the group's task, the leader's resources (position power), and the leader-member relations.

***Customer's Buying Task.*** Several researchers have suggested that sales behaviors should vary depending on the buying task confronting the customer. Robinson, Farris, and Wind (1967) defined three types of buying tasks—new buy, modified rebuy, and straight rebuy. The new buy task begins as an ill-structured problem that the customer has not confronted in the past, while the straight rebuy is a highly structured, routinized decision. Since these tasks differ in amount of information needed and level of uncertainty or risk associated with the purchase decision, one would expect that different sales behaviors would be appropriate for each situation. The different sales behaviors required in these situations have led Kahn and Shuchman (1961) to suggest that salespeople should specialize in either selling new customers (new buy or modified rebuy situations) or existing customers (straight rebuy situations).

Hakansson, Johanson, and Wootz (1977) and Newton (1967) have classified purchase decision in terms of the risk associated with decision outcomes. They have defined specific types of risks and suggested appropriate sales behaviors for each risk type. While the Robinson et al. (1967) classification scheme has received wide acceptance in the marketing literature, measures of the underlying dimensions have not been developed. In Fiedler's leadership research, task structure is also an important moderating variable. Task structure is operationalized by examining the following task characteristics: (a) goal clarity, (b) goal-path multiplicity, (c) decision verifiability, and (d) decision specificity. These characteristics in a buying task context represent the degree to which the product requirements are known by the customer, the degree to which a variety of products could satisfy the customer's needs, and the degree to which the customer is able to evaluate the performance of the product after the sale.

***The Salesperson's Resources.*** The salesperson enters a customer interaction with a set of skills or abilities, a level of knowledge about the products and the customer, and a range of alternatives that can be offered to the customers. These factors can amplify the effectiveness and/or constrain the range of behaviors in which the salesperson can act effectively. The inclusion of salesperson resources as moderating variables is related to the notion that salespeople should "lead from strength." It is reasonable to assume that salespeople are more effective when they engage in behaviors related to the skills, abilities, and personal characteristics they possess. For example, a highly trained salesperson would be more effective at establishing an expert base on influence and delivering highly informational communications.

In addition to personal resources, the company which the salesperson represents provides resources that can moderate the effectiveness of sales behaviors. Some of these company-provided resources are company reputation, the range of alternatives the salesperson can offer, and the degree to which the salesperson can alter characteristics of the extended product (price, delivery, terms, etc.) to satisfy customer needs. Levitt (1965) demonstrated that the effectiveness of the quality of a sales presentation is moderated by the reputation of the salesperson's company. Saxe (1979) found that the effectiveness of customer-oriented sales behaviors (assessing customer needs, offering products that will satisfy those needs, describing products accurately, avoiding high pressure, etc.) is moderated by the salesperson's ability to help the customer. Ability to help was operationalized as the match between the salesperson's products and the customers needs, the time available to the salesperson, and the support provided by the salesperson's company.

***The Customer-Salesperson Relationship.*** As mentioned previously, dyadic similarity is the only variable associated with the customer-salesperson relationship that has been considered in sales effectiveness research. This research, reviewed above, indicates that the dyadic similarity is, at best, weakly related to effectiveness.[7]

Two characteristics of the customer-salesperson relationship that have not been considered in sales effectiveness research are the relative power and the level of conflict between the members of the dyad. Both power and conflict have received considerable attention in social psychology (Raven and Rubin 1976), organizational behavior (McCall 1979; Thomas 1976) and channels of distribution (Reve and Stern 1979).

*Relative power* can be defined in terms of dependency (Emerson 1962). The relative power of a salesperson over a customer is related to the degree to which the salesperson mediates the customer's achievement of a goal and the importance the customer places on achieving the goal. Thus, a salesperson possessing unique information concerning a solution to a customer's problem would have power over the customer. The more important the problem is to the customer, the more power the salesperson possesses. Conversely, if the salesperson's rewards (income) are dependent upon the customer's business, the customer has power over the salesperson. Thus, the relative power in an interaction could be measured in terms of the importance of each party's goals related to the purchase decision and the degree to which each party affects the other party's achievement of those goals.

*Conflict*, like relative power, has not been considered in personal selling research. Conflict includes a wide variety of phenomena such as:

> (1) *Antecedent conditions* (for example, scarcity of resources, policy differences) of conflict behavior, (2) *affective states* (e.g., stress, tension, hostility, anxiety) etc., (3) *cognitive states* of individuals (i.e., their perception of awareness of conflict situations), and (4) *conflictful behavior*, ranging from passive resistance to overt aggression (Pondy 1967, p. 268).

In a salesperson-customer relationship, the level of conflict is reflected in the quality of the relationship, the amount of negotiating or bargaining associated with making a sale, the level of competition the salesperson faces, and the degree to which the salesperson's offerings can satisfy the customer's needs.

In addition to relative power and conflict, the *nature of the present customer-salesperson relationship* and the *anticipation of future interactions* can moderate the effectiveness of sales behaviors. One important aspect of the salesperson-customer relationship is whether the salesperson represents an ''in'' or an ''out'' supplier. An ''in'' salesperson is presently selling the product to the customer, while an ''out'' salesperson is attempting to make an initial sale. Both Kahn and Shuchman (1961) and Robinson et al. (1967) have suggested that ''in'' and ''out'' salespeople need to perform different functions. Thus, one would expect that different sales behaviors would be appropriate in each situation.

A final characteristic of the customer-salesperson relationship is the anticipation of future interactions. Research has shown that this characteristic influences the bargaining behavior undertaken by two parties (Rubin and Brown 1975) and presumably the effectivenes of sales behaviors. For example, one would expect that effective retail and industrial salespeople typically engage in different behaviors because industrial salespeople typically have continuing relationships with customers, while the retail salespeople do not.

## Contingency Propositions

Some propositions incorporating the previously defined constructs are presented in this section. These propositions are stated so that testable hypotheses can be derived to direct future research efforts.

### Propositions Concerning Adaptive Behavior

Proposition 1: Engaging in adaptive sales behaviors across interactions is positively related to effectiveness in the following circumstances:

Salesperson resources—the salesperson has the resources, both personal abilities and product alternatives, to engage in adaptive sales behaviors.

Customer buying tasks—the salesperson's customers typically are engaged in complex buying tasks that could result in large orders.

Customer-salesperson relationship—the salesperson has a good relationship with the customer characterized by a low level of conflict and the salesperson anticipates future relationships with the customer.

In general, the salesperson who adapts his/her behavior to the specific interaction situation will be better at presenting a product as a solution to the customer's problem. Thus, one would expect the degree of adaptive behavior to be positively related to effectiveness in a specific interaction.

However, a salesperson's effectiveness across a series of interactions may not be positively related to adaptiveness because there is a cost associated with adaptive sales behavior. The salesperson must spend time during the interaction to collect information from the customer. This information is used to adapt the sales presentation to the specific customer. The time spent collecting information about the customer is not directly related to the salesperson's effectiveness across customers. The salesperson's effectiveness might be higher if more time were spent selling the customer or calling on other customers.

Thus, one would hypothesize that adaptive sales behavior is positively related to sales performance when the benefits outweigh the costs of adapting. Such circumstances are likely to occur when the benefits of adapting are high (large potential orders, opportunity to use information in anticipated future interaction, high probability of securing an order because of a wide range of alternatives that can be offered) or the costs of adapting are low (low expected cost of collecting information due to good relationships with customers). In contrast, one would hypothesize no relationship between adaptivity and performance when the costs typically equal or outweigh the benefits. This circumstance is likely to occur when the expected benefits are low (small orders with no potential for future orders) or the expected costs are high (a conflicting relationship that makes it difficult to collect information). Some empirical support for this proposition is provided by Saxe (1979). He found that a salesperson's resources in terms of capabilities in satisfying customer needs moderated the relationship between effectiveness and the practice of customer-oriented, adaptive behaviors.

Support for these contingency hypotheses concerning adaptive behavior also can be found in the various sales approaches used in industry. Gwinner (1968) indicates that highly qualified and paid salespeople are needed to implement adaptive approaches like problem solution and need satisfaction. These approaches are typically used in industrial sales situations. The least adaptive approach, stimulus response, is limited to ''very simple selling situations (low product complexity), to very low priced products, or to buyer-seller relationships wherein time is an important factor'' (Gwinner 1968, p. 39). Thus the stimulus-response approach has been used primarily in door-to-door selling of household products. The mental states approach, a more adaptive approach, is used ''in those situations where the product or service is complicated and difficult to understand. In addition, this strategy may be employed when repeat calls on a long-run basis are required. A salesman representing a multiproduct line can effectively use this strategy since the method allows him to vary his sales presentation within the framework of an established plan'' (Gwinner 1968, p. 40).

## Propositions Concerning the Establishment of an Influence Base

Proposition 2: Attempting to establish an expertise base of influence is positively related to effectiveness in the following circumstances:

Salesperson resources—the salesperson has a high level of knowledge about the product and the customer's applications.

Customer buying tasks—the salesperson's customers typically are engaged in high risk, complex buying tasks.

Customer-salesperson relationship—the salesperson is typically an ''out'' supplier.

To establish an expertise base of influence or social power, salespeople need to create the impression that they possess superior skills or knowledge related to the purchase decision. It is reasonable to assume that salespeople who actually possess greater knowledge will be more effective in assuming the role of an expert.

The effectiveness of an expertise base of influence is related to the customer's need to make a correct decision. Thus, this base of influence will be more appropriate when customers are enaged in complex, high risk purchase decisions (new buy or modified rebuy tasks). In these purchase decisions, customers have a great need for information that will help in making a good decision. Salespeople who are perceived as experts or as possessing unique skills at reducing the risks associated with the customer's decision will be able to exert substantial influence on the customer's decision.

Wilson (1975) has suggested that the initial stage of customer encounters should be devoted to establishing "credibility and legitimation. Unless this basic acceptablility is developed, further communication is likely to become quite ineffective if not impossible" (p. 394). Thus, establishing credibility by creating the impression of expertise would be most effective when an "out" salesperson makes initial contact with a customer.

Proposition 3: Attempting to establish similarities with a customer as a base of influence is positively related to effectiveness in the following circumstances:

Salesperson resources—the salesperson is actually similar to the customer in terms of characteristics related to the purchase decision.

Customer-buying task—the salesperson's customers typically are engaged in simple, low risk purchase decisions or in purchase decisions with high psychological or social risks.

Customer-salesperson relationship—the salesperson is typically an "in" supplier.

Wilson and Ghingold (1980) found that salespeople feel establishing rapport with customers is a critical aspect of effectiveness in sales interactions. One method for establishing rapport is for the salesperson to create a link with the customer by identifying similarities—characteristics they have in common. Establishing similarities may increase the trustworthiness of salespeople, facilitate the exchange of information about salespeople and customers, and lead customers to feel their needs and problems are well understood. Salespeople who actually are similar to their customer will be in a better position to establish this base of influence.

When customers are making simple purchase decisions, their information needs are not great. In these situations, an influence base associated with getting the customers to identify with the salesperson will be more effective than an expertise base of influence. Capon and Swasy (1977) provides some support for this proposition. In a role playing situation, students felt that messages directed at establishing a similarity influence base would be more effective when selling to consumers as opposed to purchasing agents. Presumably consumers typically engage in simpler decision processes with higher psychological risks than purchasing agents.

It may be particularly important for the "in" salesperson to maintain good relations with a customer over a long time period by establishing a similarity base of influence. In support of this proposition, Bambic (1978) found that purchasing agents indicate the greatest preference for an attitudinally similar salesperson when the salesperson represents a qualified "in" supplier.

## Proposition Concerning the Use of Influence Techniques

Proposition 4: The use of closed as opposed to open influence techniques is more effective under the following circumstances:

Customer-salesperson relationships—

a. The salesperson typically is more powerful than his/her customers.
b. The level of conflict between the customers and the salesperson is high.
c. The salesperson typically does not anticipate future interactions with the customer.

The use of closed influence techniques suggests that salespeople are willing to sacrifice a customer's long-term satisfaction so that they can make an immediate sale. This type of behavior would be most effective when customers do not have the opportunity to sanction the salesperson if they discover that they have been manipulated or deceived. If the customers will not be encountering the salesperson in the future, they will not have the opportunity to invoke sanctions such as not considering the salesperson's products in future applications. If the salespeople are more powerful than the customers, the customers will have to forego invoking sanctions because the salespeople control the degree to which the customers can satisfy their needs.

Salespeople might decide to sacrifice future sales to make an immediate sale. This would occur if the immediate sale is very large, larger than potential future sales. In this circumstance, salespeople would risk the long-term consequences associated with closed influence techniques to seek a short-term benefit.

Spiro and Perreault (1979) found that salespeople use closed influence techniques when engaging in difficult sales situations—situations characterized by poor customer-salesperson relationships, low customer interest, and routine purchase decisions involving undifferentiated products. Open influence tactics were used when there was a high level of buyer/seller involvement—situations characterized by good customer-salesperson relationships and purchase decisions that were important to both parties. Assuming that, on average, salespeople engage in appropriate sales behaviors, these findings indicate that closed influence tactics are most effective in sales situations with negotiating obstacles and open influence tactics are more effective in high involvement situations.

## Proposition Concerning Control of the Sales Interactions

Proposition 5: Attempting to exert control over the sales interaction is related to effectiveness in the following circumstances:

Customer's buying task—customers are engaged in ambiguous purchase decisions.

Customer salesperson relationship—

a. future interactions between customers and the salesperson are not anticipated.
b. the salespeople typically are more powerful than the customers.

Salespeople who exert a high level of control in a sales interaction frequently direct the interaction toward an outcome that is more compatible with the needs of the salespeople than the needs of the customers. This behavior would be most effective when the customers are confronting an ambiguous problem and do not have adequate information to solve the problem. Since the exertion of control might sacrifice customer satisfaction, this behavior would be more effective when the salesperson has a goal of making an immediate sale. When future interactions with a customer are anticipated, the salesperson's long-term effectiveness will be more closely related to satisfying the customer's needs. Under these circumstances, salespeople might be less effective when they control the interaction towards an outcome desired by them. These conclusions are consistent with Bursk's (1947) description of situations in which low pressure selling is more effective than high pressure selling. Bursk suggests that low pressure selling (low control of the sale interaction) is most appropriate when the customer is knowledgeable and when continued goodwill is at stake.

The leadership research also provides support for this proposition. This research indicates that autocratic, ''initiating structure'' behaviors (high control behaviors) are most appropriate when the group is engaged in an ambiguous, stressful, and nonroutine task. In addition, the more the group members perceive that they possess the abilities to accomplish a task, the less willing they are to accept directive or coaching behavior from their leader (Filley et al. 1976, p. 255). Supportive, participative, consideration leader behaviors (low control behaviors) are most effective when group members possess information about the task and when the task is routine. Based on these research findings, salespeople will be more effective if they attempt to control sales situations when customers are engaged in routine buying decisions (straight rebuys).

Since little personal selling research has considered the effect of moderating variables, the previously stated propositions are quite speculative. Little empirical support can be provided at this time. A research program for developing and testing contingency hypotheses follows.

## Developing and Testing Contingency Proposition

In this section, a research program is outlined for developing and testing contingency hypotheses. The three stages of this program are hypothesis generation, hypothesis testing in a laboratory environment, and hypothesis testing in a field setting. These stages parallel the general framework suggested by Ray (1978) for examining communication phenemona.[8] In discussing the hypothesis testing stage, contingency research approaches are contrasted with the traditional research approach used in personal selling.

### Generating Contingency Hypotheses

In the preceding section, a number of contingency propositions are presented. These propositions were developed by reviewing the limited amount of research in personal selling that has considered moderating variables and by translating relevant leadership research into a personal selling context. However, these propositions represent only a portion of the contingency ''theories'' used by salespeople in their customer interactions.

The everyday use of contingency influence strategies is illustrated in a recent study by Falbo and Peplau (1980). When asked to write open-ended essays on the topic ''how I get my way,'' many subjects indicated that their power strategies varied depending on the target. Thus, the existence of contingency influence strategies arises naturally without prompting from researchers.

Methodologies for uncovering rules or ''theories'' employed by practitioners are reviewed in Zaltman, Lawther, and Heffring (1980). (See Wilson and Ghingold 1980 for an example of a ''theories in use'' approach used in a personal selling context.) These ''theories in use'' methodologies involve observing and questioning salespeople.

One approach for uncovering ''theories in use'' is to investigate how salespeople organize their knowledge and experience. A richer taxonomy of moderating variables can be developed by determining what characteristics salespeople use to classify customers and sales situations. (See Canto and Mischel 1979 for a review of the research on social classification schemes used by people.)

Schank and Abelson (1977) proposed that part of knowledge is organized around hundreds of stereotypical situations and activities. The implications of these scripts (stereotypic-action sequences) have been empirically investigated by Bower, Black, and Turner (1979). Salespeople probably possess contingency selling scripts that guide their behavior in customer interactions. One might access these scripts by asking salespeople to describe their behavior in specific sales situations. The nature of the differences in scripts across sales situations should be useful in developing contingency propositions.

Theories in use also can be uncovered by using a cognitive response methodology. Salespeople can be asked to describe their thoughts during specific customer encounters. These thoughts can be collected directly after the encounter or during a replay of a recording of the encounter. A more structured format can be used to collect these cognitive responses by asking salespeople to indicate their thoughts when observing a standardized recording of a customer-sales encounter (Grikscheidt 1971).

In contrast to these open-ended methods for collecting information, salespeople can be asked to answer questions concerning the appropriate behavior when confronting a sales scenario (Capon and Swasy 1977) or questions concerning their behavior during a specific past sales encounter (Spiro and Perreault 1979). Vroom and Yetton (1973) have developed a method for soliciting contingency leader responses and describing relevant situational variables.

## Experimental Testing of Contingency Propositions

Having developed contingency hypotheses, the next step is to test these hypotheses in a laboratory environment using an experimental design. Laboratory experiments are quick and effective ways for testing behavioral propositions. The control achieved in a laboratory allows the researcher to determine causal relationships between variables and eliminate potential alternative explanations.

The experimental approach has been used in several studies previously reviewed; however, these studies have not been designed to examine contingency hypotheses. Only main effect relationships between effectiveness and salesperson characteristics or behavior were considered in these studies. For example, Woodside and Davenport (1974) manipulated two sales behaviors (establishing an expertise base of influence, and establishing a similarity base of influence) and tested whether differences in these behaviors had an effect on purchasing behavior.

In contrast to these past studies, contingency propositions are tested in an experimental setting by examining the interaction between a sales behavior and a moderating variable. Thus, the second part of proposition 2 would be tested by manipulating the level of expertise expressed by the salesperson and the complexity of the buying decision confronting the subject (customer), and testing for a significant interaction between these two factors.

Levitt's (1965) classic study on industrial selling is the only study in which the effectivensss of a behavior-sales circumstance interaction was investigated. In this study, a behavior (quality of presentation) and a resource of the salesperson (company reputation) were manipulated. Unfortunately, there were methodological problems in examining the contingency (interaction) hypotheses (Capon et al 1972).

While laboratory experiments are an excellent method for testing theories and determining causality, there are two problems with laboratory experiments for testing hypotheses concerning personal selling. First, laboratory experiments typically sacrifice external validity to insure high internal validity. To insure homogeneous treatments, the salesperson frequently is removed from the experiment. In some experiments, the salesperson is replaced by a videotape (Busch and Wilson 1976), a film (Levitt 1965), or a paper and pencil description (Bambic 1978). In these experiments, the phenomenon under study is more closely related to impersonal, mass communication than interpersonal influence.

Second, laboratory experiments are most readily adapted to testing the effectiveness of sales behaviors in one-shot, selling situations. It is difficult to create laboratory situations that examine the effects of behaviors across sales interactions. This arises because some behaviors such as adaptation and the use of close influence techniques have ''carry over'' effects. Both adaptation and the close influence techniques can lead to increased effectiveness in one interaction but decreased effectiveness in subsequent interactions. These ''carryover effects'' are difficult to manipulate and measure in an experimental design. Due to this problem, some propositions can be tested only in field studies. In addition, field tests offer a method for assessing the impact of behavior across actual selling interactions.

## Field Testing of Contingency Hypotheses

The steps in testing contingency hypotheses in the field are shown in Figure 3. When contingency hypotheses are tested in the field across interactions, the first step is to develop reliable and valid measures of typical sales behaviors and sales situations (moderator variables) in which salespeople engage.

Few measures of sales behaviors exist; however there are paper and pencil measures to determine influence techniques typically used (Arch 1979), the degree to which a customer-oriented behavior is employed (Saxe 1979), and behavioral predispositions such as self-monitoring. Although studies have postulated moderating variables in the sales situation, no measures of circumstances encountered in sales situations have been developed. Thus, research must be directed toward developing measures of sales behaviors and moderating variables before contingency hypotheses can be tested in field settings.

When behavior and situation measures have been developed, contingency hypotheses can be tested by getting measures of typical behavior patterns from salespeople, typical situation measures from independent sources such as sales managers or customers, and then relating these measures to salesperson effectiveness using techniques for examining moderator variable relationships (Allison 1973; Zedeck 1971). While traditional measures of sales

**FIGURE 3. Steps in Correlational Test of Contingency Hypotheses**

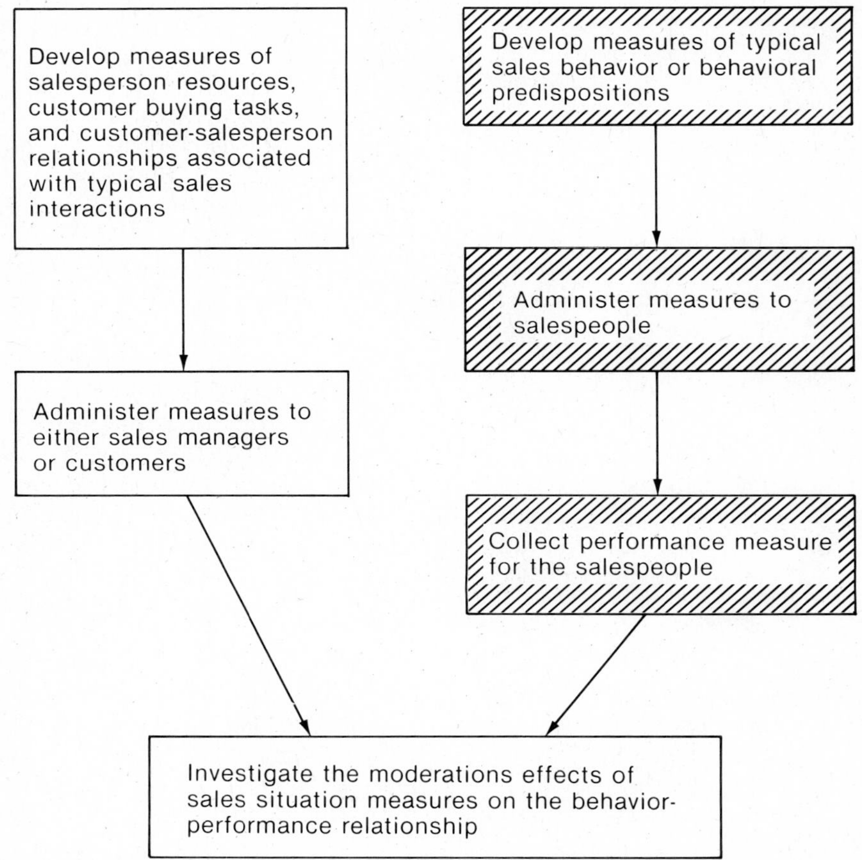


performance such as sales or sales to quota can be used as measures of effectiveness, care must be taken to control for sources of variance unrelated to effectiveness in sales interactions (see Figure 1).

The difference between testing contingency hypotheses in the field and traditional correlational studies of salesperson effectiveness is illustrated by the shaded areas in Figure 3. Traditional correlational studies have considered only the shaded steps. In these studies, measures of salesperson behavioral predispositions and performance are collected. No measures are made of the typical sales situations encountered by the salesperson. Hypotheses are tested by correlating performance with behavioral predispositions.

Contingency studies necessitate the inclusion of the unshaded steps—the collection of situational measures. In addition, the test of contingency hypotheses requires the use of moderator variable regressions so that interactions can be examined.

## CONCLUSION

Most empirical research on salesperson performance has been based on the implicit assumption that a universal set of characteristics or behaviors is associated with successful sales performance across all sales situations. It is reasonable to investigate such parsimonious propositions in the early stages of studying a problem, but more complex propositions are warranted if simple propositions fail to explain the phenomenon of interest. The review of the research of personal selling effectiveness at the beginning of this paper illustrates the lack of support for simple universal propositions. These universal propositions have been of some value, but few have consistently explained a significant propositon of the variance in performance. Thus, it is appropriate, at this time, to investigate the more complex propositions in which circumstances of the sales situation moderate the relationship between the salesperson behavior and effectiveness.

To provide a direction for this research approach, some salesperson behaviors and moderating variables were defined and propositions suggested concerning the effectiveness of these behaviors in different sales interaction circumstances. The group of behaviors and moderating variables considered is intended to be suggestive rather than exhaustive. Little research has been directed toward developing a taxonomy of sales behaviors or characteristics of the salesperson-customer interaction. When descriptive research on classifying sales behaviors and interaction characteristics is more advanced, many additional and richer contingency propositions can be developed and tested.

Even though the propositions presented in this paper are limited, some new and potentially significant variables for understanding personal selling effectiveness have been introduced. Sales behaviors related to adapting to the customer and controlling the sales interaction have not been investigated empirically, even though practitioners view these behaviors as critical to sales effectiveness. Dyadic research has focused on similarity, a dyadic characteristic which appears to have little relationship to effectiveness. Characteristics of the customer-salesperson relationship such as relative power, level of conflict, and the anticipation of future interactions have played an important role in interpersonal influence research in social psychology and organizational behavior, but have been ignored in personal selling research. While this new research direction suggests more complex propositions and research designs, it is anticipated that the effort expended on this new approach will lead to a substantial improvement in our understanding of personal selling effectiveness.

## ENDNOTES

1. Several descriptive studies (Olshavsky 1973; Pennington 1968; Taylor and Woodside 1968; Willett and Pennington 1966) have examined sales behavior but have not explicitly considered the effectiveness of sales behaviors.
2. In this table, personality traits indicating a predisposition toward forceful behavior in interpersonal relations (such as dominance, ego drive, achievement motivation, and aggressiveness) have been combined under sociability. To facilitate comparisons across studies, the performance measure used to report the results shown in Tables 1 and 2 is the most objective measure considered in the study. Thus, relationships with sales and sales to quota are reported rather than relationships to sales manager's evaluations.
3. The expertise conditions explained more variance than the similarity conditions. These differences may be due to the weaker relationship between similarity and effectiveness, but they may also be due to differences in the strengths of the manipulations.
4. While Blake and Mouton (1970) and Buzzota et al (1972) recognize that the effectiveness of sales behaviors varies across customers, their conceptualizations on personal selling are not contingency approaches of the type suggested in this paper. Both of these conceptualizations contend that one sales behavior, either warm-dominant (Q4 type in Buzzota et al.) or problem-solving oriented (9-9 type in Blake and Mouton), is most effective across all sales situations. A contingency approach is based on the notion that the most effective sales behavior varies across sales situations.
5. An interaction is defined as beginning when a salesperson first contacts a customer in an attempt to make a sale. The interaction concludes when the salesperson makes the sale or decides to discontinue efforts in this direction. An interaction may be concluded during one face-to-face encounter or may continue over a sequence of encounters.
6. This framework focuses on individual differences in effectiveness across interactions that are due to interpersonal influence behavior. However, traditional measures of performance across interactions such as sales or sales-to-quota incorporate other important sources of variance in effectiveness (see Figure 1). These factors must be controlled when testing propositions developed from this framework.
7. This lack of a meaningful relationship may be due to the definition of similarity used in the studies. In an extensive review on source credibility, Simons et al. (1970) concluded that only relevant similarities between the communicator and the recipient of the communications have significant impact on attitude change. Relevancy is defined in terms of beliefs or experiences pertaining to the object of the attitude. Thus, one would expect that only similarity of beliefs and experiences with respect to the product and the buying decision would influence effectiveness. Dyadic studies in personal selling have operationalized the similarities in terms of physical characteristics, demographics and irrelevant attitudes.
8. The microtheoretical notions discussed by Ray (1978) are similar to the contingency propositions developed from the framework presented in this paper.

## REFERENCES


Allison, P. D. (1973), "Testing for Interaction in Multiple Regression," *American Journal of Sociology*, 83 (July), 144-153.

Arch, David (1979), "The Development of Influence Strategy Scales in Buyer-Seller Interactions," in *1979 Educators' Conference Proceedings*, N. Beckwith et al., eds., Chicago: American Marketing Association.

Baehr, Melany E. and G. Williams (1968), "Prediction of Sales Success from Factorially Determined Dimensions of Personal Background Data," *Journal of Applied Psychology*, 52 (April), 98-103.

Bagozzi, Richard P. (1978), "Salesforce Performance and Satisfaction as a Function of Individual Difference, Interpersonal, and Situational Factors," *Journal of Marketing Research*, 15 (November), 517-531.

Baier, Donald and Robert D. Dugan (1957), "Factors in Sales Success," *Journal of Applied Psychology*, 41 (February), 37-40.

Bambic, Peter (1978), "An Interpersonal Influence Study of Source Acceptance in Industrial Buyer-Seller Exchange Process: An Experimental Approach," unpublished Ph.D. dissertation, Graduate School of Business, Pennsylvania State University.

Blake, Robert R. and J. S. Mouton (1970), *The Grid for Sales Excellence*, New York: McGraw-Hill Book Co.

Bower, Gordon H., John B. Black and Terrence J. Turner (1979), "Scripts in Memory for Text," *Cognitive Psychology*, 11 (April), 177-220.

Boyd, Harper W., Michael L. Ray, and Edward C. Strong (1972), "An Attitudinal Framework for Advertising Strategy," *Journal of Marketing*, 36 (April), 27-33.

Brock, Timothy C. (1965), "Communicator-Recipient Similarity and Decision Change," *Journal of Personality and Social Psychology*, 1 (June), 650-654.

Bursk, Edward C. (1947), "Low Pressure Selling," *Harvard Business Review*, 25 (Winter), 227-242.

Busch, Paul and David T. Wilson (1976), "An Experimental Analysis of a Salesman's Expert and Referent Bases of Social Power in the Buyer-Seller Dyad," *Journal of Marketing Research*, 13 (February), 3-11.

Buzzotta, V. R., R. E. Lefton, and Manual Sherberg (1972), *Effective Selling Through Psychology*, New York: John Wiley & Sons.

Cantor, N. and W. Mischel (1979), "Prototypes in Person Perception," in *Advances in Experimental Social Psychology*, L. Berkowitz, ed., Vol. 12, New York: Academic Press, 3-52.

Capon, Noel (1975), "Persuasive Effects of Sales Messages Developed from Interaction Process Analysis," *Journal of Business Administration*, 60 (April), 238-244.

———, Morris Holbrook, and John Hulbert (1972), "Industrial Purchasing Behavior: A Reappraisal," *Journal of Business Administration*, 4, 69-77.

——— and John Swasy (1977), "An Exploratory Study of Compliance Gaining Techniques in Buyer Behavior," in *Contemporary Marketing Thought*, B. Greenberg and D. Bellenger, eds., Chicago: American Marketing Association.

Chapple, Eliot and Gordon Donald, Jr. (1947), "An Evaluation of Department Store Salespeople by the Interaction Chronograph," *Journal of Marketing*, 112 (October), 173-185.

Churchill, Gilbert A., Jr., Robert H. Collins, and William A. Strang (1975), "Should Retail Salespersons be Similar to Their Customers?" *Journal of Retailing*, 51 (Fall), 29-42 +.

Cotham, James C., III (1969), "Using Personal History Information in Retail Salesman Selection," *Journal of Retailing*, 45 (Summer), 31-38 +.

Davis, Harry L. and Alvin J. Silk (1972), "Interaction and Influence Processes in Personal Selling," *Sloan Management Review*, 13 (Winter), 56-76.

Doreen, Dale, Donald R. Emery, and Robert W. Sweitzer (1979), "Selling as a Dyadic Relationship Revisited." Paper presented at the 1979 AIDS Conference, New Orleans.

Dunnette, Marvin D. and Wayne K. Kirchner (1960), "Psychological Test Differences between Industrial Salesmen and Retail Salesmen," *Journal of Applied Psychology*, 44 (April), 121-125.

Emerson, Richard M. (1962), "Power-Dependence Relations," *American Sociological Review*, 27 (February), 31-41.

Evans, Franklin (1963), "Selling as a Dyadic Relationship—A New Approach," *American Behavioral Scientist*, 6 (May), 76.

Falbo, Toni (1977), "Multidimensional Scaling of Power Strategies," *Journal of Personality and Social Psychology*, 35 (August), 537-547.

——— and Letitia Peplau (1980), "Power Strategies in Intimate Relationships," *Journal of Personality and Social Psychology*, 38 (June), 618-628.

Farley, John and R. Swinth (1967), "Effects of Choice and Sales Message on Customer-Salesman Interaction," *Journal of Applied Psychology*, 51 (April), 107-110.

Fiedler, Fred E. and Martin M. Chemers (1974), *Leadership and Effective Management*, Glenview, Il: Scott, Foresman and Company.

Filley, Alan C., Robert J. House, and Steven Kerr (1976), *Managerial Process and Organizational Behavior*, 2nd ed., Glenview, Il.: Scott, Foresman and Company.

French, Cecil L. (1960), "Correlates of Success in Retail Selling," *American Journal of Sociology*, 66 (April), 128-134.

French, John R. P. and Bertram Raven (1959), "The Bases of Social Power," in *Studies in Social Power*, D. Cartright, ed., Ann Arbor: University of Michigan, Institute for Social Research, 150-167.

Gadel, M. S. (1964), "Concentration by Salesmen on Congenial Prospects," *Journal of Marketing*, 28 (April), 64-66.

Ghiselli, Edwin E. (1969), "Prediction of Success of Stockbrokers," *Personnel Psychology*, 22 (Summer), 125-130.

——— (1973), "The Validity of Aptitude Tests in Personnel Selection," *Personnel Psychology*, 26 (Winter), 461-477.

Greenberg, Herbert and David Mayer (1964), "A New Approach to the Scientific Selection of Successful Salesmen, *Journal of Psychology*, 57 (January), 113-123.

Grikscheit, Gary M. (1971), "An Investigation of the Ability of Salesmen to Monitor Feedback," Ph.D. dissertation, Michigan State University.

——— and William J. E. Crissy (1973), "Improving Interpersonal Communication Skill," *MSU Business Topics*, 21 (Autumn), 63-68.

Gwinner, Robert (1968), "Base Theory in the Formulation of Sales Strategy," *MSU Business Topics*, 16 (Autumn), 37-34.

Hakansson, Hakan, Jan Johanson, and Bjorn Wootz (1977), "Influence Tactics in Buyer-Seller Processes," *Industrial Marketing Management*, 5 (Fall), 319-332.

Harrell, Thomas W. (1960), "The Relation of Test Scores to Sales Criteria," *Personnel Psychology*, 13 (Spring), 65-69.

Howells, G. W. (1968), "The Successful Salesman: A Personality Analysis," *British Journal Of Marketing*, 2, 13-23.

Jolson, Marvin A. (1975), "The Underestimated Potential of the Canned Sales Presentation," *Journal of Marketing*, 39 (January), 75-78.

Kahn, George N. and Abraham Shuchman (1961), "Specialize Your Salesmen!" *Harvard Business Review*, 39 (January/February), 90-98.

Kirchner, Wayne K., Carolyn S. McElwain, and Marvin D. Dunnette (1960), "A Note on the Relationship between Age and Sales Effectiveness," *Journal of Applied Psychology*, 44 (April), 92-93.

Lamont, Lawrence M. and William J. Lundstrom (1977), "Identifying Successful Industrial Salesmen by Personality and Personal Characteristics," *Journal of Marketing Research*, 14 (November), 517-529.

Levitt, Theodore (1965), *Industrial Purchasing Behavior: A Study in Communications Effects*, Boston, MA: Division of Research, Harvard Business School.

McCall, Morgan W., Jr. (1979), "Power, Authority, and Influence," in *Organizational Behavior*, S. Kerr, ed., Columbus, OH: Grid Publishing Company, 185-206.

Mattheiss, T. H., Richard M. Durnad, Jan R. Muczyk, and Myron Gable (1977), "Personality and the Prediction of Salesmen's Success," in *Contemporary Marketing Thought*, B. Greenberg and D. Bellenger, eds., Chicago: American Marketing Association, pp. 499-502.

Merenda, Peter F. and Walter V. Clarke (1959), "Predictive Efficiency of Temperament Characteristics and Personal History Variables in Determining Success of Life in Insurance Agents," *Journal of Applied Psychology*, 43 (December), 360-366.

Miner, John B. (1962), "Personality and Ability Factors in Sales Performance," *Journal of Applied Psychology*, 46 (February), 6-13.

Mosel, James N. (1952), "Prediction of Department Store Sales Performance from Personnel Data," *Journal of Applied Psychology*, 36 (February), 8-10.

Newton, Derek A. (1967), "A Marketing Communication Model for Sales Management," in *Risk Taking and Information Handling in Consumer Behavior*, Donald F. Cox, ed., Boston: Division of Research, Graduate School of Business Administration, Harvard University.

Olshavsky, Richard W. (1973), "Customer-Salesmen Interaction in Appliance Retailing," *Journal of Marketing Research*, 10 (May),208-212.

Pasold, Peter W. (1975), "The Effectiveness of Various Modes of Sales Behavior in Different Markets," *Journal of Marketing Research*, 12 (May), 171-176.

Pennington, Alan (1968), "Customer-Salesmen Bargaining Behavior in Retail Transactions," *Journal of Marketing Research*, 8 (November), 501-504.

Pondy, Louis R. (1967), "Organizational Conflict: Concepts and Models," *Administrative Science Quarterly*, 12 (September), 296-320.

Pruden, Henry O. and Robert A. Peterson (1971), "Personality and Performance-Satisfaction of Industrial Salesmen," *Journal of Marketing Research*, 8 (November), 501-504.

Raven, B. H. and J. Z. Rubin (1976), *Social Psychology: People in Groups*, New York: John Wiley & Sons.

Ray, Michael L. (1978), "The Present and Potential Linkages between the Microtheoretical Notions of Behavioral Science and the Problems of Advertising: A Proposal for a Research System," in *Behavioral and Management Science in Marketing*, Harry L. Davis and Alvin Silk, eds., New York: Ronald Press, 99-141.

Reed, Jim D. (1976), "Comments on 'The Underestimated Potential of the Canned Sales Presentation,' " *Journal of Marketing*, 40 (January), 67-68.

Reizenstein, Richard C. (1971), "A Dissonance Approach to Measuring the Effectiveness of Two Personal Selling Techniques through Decision Reversal," *Proceedings*, Fall Conference, Chicago: American Marketing Association, 176-180.

Reve, T. and L. Stern (1979), "Interorganizational Relations in Marketing Channels," *Academy of Management Review*, 4 (July), 80-91.

Riordan, Edward A., Richard L. Oliver, and James H. Donnelly, Jr. (1977) "The Unsold Prospect: Dyadic and Attitudinal Determinants," *Journal of Marketing Research*, 14 (November), 530-537.

Robinson, P. J., C. W. Farris, and Y. Wind (1967), *Industrial Buying and Creative Marketing*, Boston: Allyn and Bacon.

Rubin, Jeffrey Z. and Bert R. Brown (1975), *The Social Psychology of Bargaining and Negotiation*, New York: Academic Press.

*Sales and Marketing Management* (1979), "1979 Survey of Selling Costs," 124 (February 26).

Saxe, Robert (1979), "The Customer Orientational Salespeople," unpublished Ph.D. dissertation, Graduate School of Management, University of California at Los Angeles.

Schank, R. C. and R. P. Abelson (1977), *Scripts, Plans, Goals and Understanding*, Hilldale, NJ: Lawrence Erlbaum Associates.

Scheibelhut, John H. and Gerald Albaum (1973), "Self-Other Orientations Among Salesmen and Non-Salesmen," *Journal of Marketing Research*, 10 (February), 97-99.

Simons, Herbert W., Nancy N. Berkowitz, and R. John Moyer (1970) "Similarity, Credibility and Attitude Change: A Review and A Theory," *Psychological Bulletin*, 73 (January), 1-16.

Snyder, Mark (1974), "The Self-Monitoring of Expressive Behavior," *Journal of Personality and Social Psychology*, 30 (October), 526-537.

Spiro, Rosann L. and William D. Perreault, Jr. (1979), "Influence Used by Industrial Salesmen: Influence Strategy Mixes and Situational Determinants," *Journal of Business*, 52 (July), 435-455.

Tanofsky, Robert, R. Ronald Shepps, and Paul J. O'Neill (1969), "Pattern Analysis of Biographical Predictors of Success as an Insurance Salesman," *Journal of Applied Psychology*, 53 (April), 136-139.

Taylor, James L. and Arch G. Woodside (1968), "Exchange Behavior Among Life Insurance Selling and Buyer Centers in Field Settings," Working paper no. 72, Center for Marketing Studies, Research Division, College of Business Administration, University of South Carolina.

Thomas, Kenneth W. (1976), "Conflict and Conflict Management," in *Handbook of Industrial and Organizational Psychology*, M. Dunnette, ed., Chicago: Rand McNally.

Thompson, Joseph W. (1973), *Selling: A Managerial and Behavioral Science Analysis*, New York: McGraw-Hill Book Co.

Tobolski,Francis P. and Willard A. Kerr (1952), "Predictive Value of the Empathy Test in Automobile Salesmanship," *Journal of Applied Psychology*, 36 (October), 310-311.

Vroom, V. H. and P. W. Yetton (1973), *Leadership and Decision Making*, Pittsburgh: University of Pittsburgh Press.

Walker, O. C., Jr., G. A. Churchill, and W. M. Ford (1977), "Motivation and Performance in Industrial Selling: Existing Knowledge and Needed Research," *Journal of Marketing Research*, 14 (May), 156-168.

Weaver, Charles N. (1969), "An Empirical Study to Aid in the Selection of Retail Salesclerks," *Journal of Retailing*, 45 (Fall), 22-26.

Weitz, Barton A. (1978), "The Relationship Between Salesperson Performance Understanding of Customer Decision Making," *Journal of Marketing Research*, 15 (November), 501-516.

——— (1979), "A Critical Review of Personal Selling Research: The Need for a Contingency Approach," in *Critical Issues in Sales Management: State-of-the-Art and Future Research Needs*, G. Albaum and G. Churchill, eds., Eugene, OR: University of Oregon, College of Business Administration.

——— (1980), "Adaptive Selling Behavior for Effective Interpersonal Influence," paper presented at AMA Conference on Theoretical and Empirical Research on Buyer-Seller Interactions, Columbia, South Carolina.

Willett, Ronald P. and Alan L. Pennington (1966), "Customer and Salesman: The Anatomy of Choice and Influence in a Retail Setting," in *Science, Technology, and Marketing*, Raymond M. Hass, ed., Chicago: American Marketing Association, 598-616.

Wilson, David T. (1975), "Dyadic Interaction: An Exchange Process," in *Advances in Consumer Research*, B. Anderson, ed., Cincinnati, OH: Association for Consumer research, 394-397.

———, and Ghingold, Morry (1980), "Building Theory from Practice: A Theory-in-Use Approach," in *Theoretical Developments in Marketing*, C. Lamb, Jr. and P. Dunne, eds., Chicago: American Marketing Association, 236-239.

Woodside, Arch G. and William J. Davenport (1974), "The Effect of Salesman Similarity and Expertise on Consumer Purchasing Behavior," *Journal of Marketing Research*, 11 (May), 198-202.

Yalch, Richard F. (1979), "Closing Sales: Compliance-Gaining Strategies for Personal Selling," in *Sales Management: New Developments from Behavioral and Decision Model Research*, R. Bagozzi, ed., Cambridge, MA: Marketing Science Institute.

Zaltman, Gerald, Karen Lawther, and Michael Heffring (1980), *Theory Construction in Marketing*, New York: John Wiley & Sons Inc.

Zdep, S. M. and H. B. Weaver (1967), "The Graphoanalytic Approach to Selecting Life Insurance Salesman," *Journal of Applied Psychology*, 51 (June), 295-299.

Zedeck, Sheldon (1971), "Problems with the Use of 'Moderator' Variables," *Psychological Bulletin*, 76 (October), 295-310.

# SECTION L
# Interorganizational Behavior School

The interorganizational school of marketing has focused on the relationships between channel members in distribution, such as retailers and wholesalers. Unlike the institutional school of marketing, the emphasis here has been on the behavioral explanations for the channel relationships instead of the economic explanations.

The key issue in the interorganizational behavior school is the balance of power between channel members. This power can come from many sources. First, is the product or service a monopoly business? If it is, one would expect greater power in the hands of the manufacturers or providers of the service. Thus, in a seller's economy such as the Third World countries, the manufacturer often has absolute powers over the distributors and customers.

Second, what is the value added function performed by the middleman? The greater the value added in the value chain, the greater is the power in the hands of the channel members.

Third, what is the degree of forward or backward integration? The possibility of forward integration generates more power to the manufacturer, whereas the backward integration possibly will generate more power to the distributors and the dealers.

Finally, the size of the respective channel members is also likely to be a major factor in balancing the power of channel members. For example, if manufacturing is highly oligopolistic but retailing is unorganized, it is likely that manufacturers will have more power. On the other hand, if retailing is organized into national chain stores but manufacturing is highly fragmented, it will generate more power for the retailer.

# 39 —— A Theory of Retailer-Supplier Conflict, Control, and Cooperation

*Bruce Mallen*

*Journal of Retailing*, Vol. 39 (Summer 1963), pp. 24-32 and 51. Reprinted by permission.

The bulk of consumer goods passes through a channel of distribution with retailers standing at one end and various types of suppliers placed at one or more earlier stages in the channel. The more common channels are either manufacturer-to-wholesaler-to-retailer or, more directly, manufacturer-to-retailer.

Channels in this paper involve only those firms that take title or negotiate title for merchandise. As such it includes all kinds of producers, wholesalers, middleman agents, and retailers. It excludes transportation and storage companies. Those firms involved in a channel may be called "channel members."

This paper will show that between channel members a dynamic field of conflicting and cooperating objectives exists; also that if the conflicting objectives outweigh the cooperating ones, the effectiveness of the channel will be reduced. Thus, the efficient distribution of consumer goods will be impeded.

The channel members can meet this problem in three distinct ways. First, they can have a leader (one of the channel members) who "forces" members to cooperate; this is an autocratic relationship. Second, they can have a leader who "helps" members to cooperate, creating a democratic relationship. Finally they can do nothing, and so have an anarchistic relationship. Lewis B. Sappington and C. G. Browne, writing on the problem of internal company organizations, state:

> The first classification may be called "autocracy." In this approach to the group the leader determines the policy and dictates or assigns the work tasks. There are no group deliberations, no group decisions....
>
> The second classification may be called "democracy." In this approach the leader allows all policies to be decided by the group with his participation. The group members work with each other as they wish. The group determines the division and assignment of tasks....
>
> The third classification may be called "anarchy." In anarchy there is complete freedom of the group or the individual regarding policies or task assignments, without leader participation.[1]

If anarchy exists, there is a great chance of the conflicting dynamics destroying the channel. If autocracy exists, there is less chance of such happening. However, the latter method creates a state of cooperation based on power and control. This controlled cooperation is really subdued conflict and makes for a more unstable equilibrium than does voluntary democratic cooperation.

## Conflict

### The Exchange Act

The act of exchange is composed of two elements: a sale and a purchase. It is to the advantage of the seller to obtain the highest return possible from such an exchange, and the exact opposite is the desire of the buyer. This exchange act takes place between any kind of buyer and seller. If the consumer is the buyer, then that side of the act is termed shopping; if the manufacturer, purchasing; if the government, procurement; and if a retailer, buying. Thus, between each level in the channel an exchange will take place (except if a channel member is an agent rather than a merchant).

One must look to the *process* of the exchange act for the basic source of conflict between channel members. This is not to say the exchange act itself is a conflict. Indeed, the act or transaction is a sign that the element of price conflict has been resolved to the mutual satisfaction of both principals. Only along the road to this mutual satisfaction point or exchange price do the principals have opposing interests. This is no less true even if they work out the exchange price together, as in mass retailers' specification buying programs.

It is quite natural for the selling member in an exchange to want a higher price than the buying member. The conflict is subdued through persuasion or force by one member over the other, or it is subdued by the fact that the exchange act or transaction does not take place, or finally as mentioned above, it is eliminated if the act does take place.

Suppliers may emphasize the customer aspect of a retailer rather than the channel member aspect. As a customer the retailer is somebody to persuade, manipulate, or even fool. Conversely, under the marketing concept, the view of the retailer as a customer or channel member is identical. Under this philosophy he is somebody to aid, help, and serve. However it is by no means certain that even a large minority of suppliers have accepted the marketing concept.

To view the retailer as simply the opposing principal in the act of exchange may be channel myopia, but this view exists. On the other hand, failure to recognize this basic opposing interest is also a conceptual fault.

When the opposite principals in an exchange act are of unequal strength, the stronger is very likely to force or persuade the weaker to adhere to the former's desires. However, when they are of equal strength, the basic conflict cannot so easily be resolved. Hence, the growth of big retailers who can match the power of big producers has led to possibly greater open conflict between channel members, not only with regard to exchange, but also to other conflict sources.

## Conflict Areas

The conflict not only lies in the exchange act, which is essentially a pricing problem, but it can permeate all areas of marketing. Thus a manufacturer may wish to promote a product in one manner or to a certain degree while his retailers oppose this. Another manufacturer may wish to get information from his retailers on a certain aspect relating to his product, but his retailers may refuse to provide this information. A producer may want to distribute his product extensively, but his retailers may demand exclusives. A supplier may force a product onto its retailers, who dare not oppose, but who retaliate in other ways, such as using it as a loss leader. Large manufacturers may try to dictate the resale price of their merchandise; this may be less or more than the price at which retailers wish to sell it. Occasionally a local market may be more competitive for a retailer than is true nationally. The manufacturer may not recognize the difference in competition and refuse to help this channel member. There is also conflict because of the desire of both manufacturers and retailers to eliminate the wholesaler.

Retailers complain of manufacturers' special price concessions to competitors, and rebel at the attempt of manufacturers to control resale prices. Manufacturers complain of retailers' deceptive and misleading advertising, nonadherence to resale price suggestions, bootlegging to unauthorized outlets, seeking special price concessions by unfair methods, and misrepresenting offers by competitive suppliers.

Other points of conflict are the paper-work aspects of pricing. Retailers complain of delays in price change notices and complicated price sheets.

One very basic source of channel conflict is the possible difference in the primary business philosophy of channel members. Writing in the *Harvard Business Review,* Wittreich says:

> In essence, then, the key to understanding management's problem of crossed purpose is the recognition that the fundamental [philosophy] in life of the high-level corporate manager and the typical [small] retail dealer in the distribution system are quite different. The former's [philosophy] can be characterized as being essentially dynamic in nature, continuously evolving and emerging; the latter, which are in sharp contrast, can be characterized as being essentially static in nature, reaching a point and leveling off into a continuously satisfying plateau.[2]

While the big members of the channel may want growth, the small retail members may be satisfied with stability and a "good living."

### Conflict Summary

There is a continuing struggle among channel members for leadership of the channel, and such rivalry leads to the constantly changing patterns of distribution. The struggle for power over distribution can lead to the autocratic or anarchic patterns. If there is a definite defeat amongst a level of channel members there is ''aristocracy.'' If there is only a stalemate between two giants for leadership, there is ''anarchy.''[3]

## COOPERATION

### Cooperation Introduction

But despite some of the conflict dynamics, channel members usually have more harmonious and common interests than conflicting ones. A team effort to market a producer's product will probably help all involved. All members have a common interest in selling the product; only in the division of total channel profits are they in conflict. They have a singular goal to reach, and here they are allies. If any one of them fails in the team effort, this weak link in the chain can destroy them all. As such, all members are concerned with each other's welfare (unless a member can be replaced easily).

### Organizational Extension Concept

This emphasis on the cooperating rather than the conflicting objectives of channel members has led to the concept of the channel as simply an extension of one's own internal organization. Conflict in such a system is to be expected even as it is to be expected within an organization. However, it is the common or ''macro-objective'' that is the center of concentration. Members are to sacrifice their selfish ''micro-objectives'' to this cause. For by increasing the profit pie they will all be better off than squabbling over pieces of a smaller one. The goal is to minimize conflict and maximize cooperation. This view has been expounded in various articles by Peter Drucker, Ralph Alexander, and Valentine Ridgeway.

> Together the manufacturer with his suppliers and/or dealers comprise a system in which the manufacturer may be designated the primary organization and the dealers and suppliers designated as secondary organizations. This system is in competition with similar systems in the economy, and in order for the system to operate effectively as an integrated whole there must be some administration of the system as a whole, not merely administration of the separate organizations within that system.[4]

Peter Drucker[5] has pleaded against the conceptual blindness that the idea of the legal entity generates. A legal entity is not a marketing entity. Since half of the cost to the consumer is added on after the product leaves the producer, the latter should think of his channel members as part of his firm. General Motors is an example of an organization which does this.

> Both businessmen and students of marketing often define too narrowly the problem of marketing channels. Many of them tend to define the term channels of distribution as a complex of relationships between the firm on the one hand, and marketing establishments exterior to the firm by which the products of the firm are moved to market, on the other.... A much broader more constructive concept embraces the relationships with external agents or units as part of the marketing organization of the company. From this viewpoint, the complex of external relationships may be regarded as merely an extension of the marketing organization of the firm. When we look at the problem in this way, we are much less likely to lose sight of the interdependence of the two structures and more likely to be constantly aware that they are closely related parts of the marketing machine. The fact that the internal organization structure is linked together by a system of employment contracts, while the external one is set up and maintained by a series of transactions, contracts of purchase and sale, tends to obscure their common purpose and close relationship.[6]

## Cooperation Methods

But how does a supplier project its organization into the channel? How does it make organization and channel into one? It accomplishes this by doing many things for its retailers that it does for its own organization. It sells, advertises, trains, plans, and promotes for these firms. A brief elaboration of these methods follows.

Missionary salesmen aid the sales of channel members, as well as bolster the whole system's level of activity and selling effort. Training of retailers' salesmen and executives is an effective weapon of cooperation. The channels operate more efficiently when all are educated in the promotional techniques and uses of the products involved.

Involvement in the planning functions of its channel members could be another poignant weapon of the supplier. Helping resellers to set quotas for their customers, studying the market potential for them, forecasting a member's sales volume, inventory planning and protection, etc., are all aspects of this latter method.

Aid in promotion through the provision of advertising materials (mats, displays, commercials, literature, direct-mail pieces) ideas, funds (cooperative advertising), sales contests, store layout designs, push money (PM's or spiffs), is another form of cooperation.

The big supplier can act as management consultant to the members, dispensing advice in all areas of their business, including accounting, personnel, planning, control, finance, buying, paper systems or office procedure, and site selection. Aid in financing may include extended credit terms, consignment selling, and loans.

By no means do these methods of coordination take a one-way route. All members of the channel, including supplier and retailer, see their own organizations meshing with the others, and so provide coordinating weapons in accordance with their ability. Thus, the manufacturer would undertake a marketing research project for his channel, and also expect his retailers to keep records and vital information for the manufacturer's use. A supplier may also expect his channel members to service the product after sale.

A useful device for fostering cooperation is a channel advisory council composed of the supplier and his retailers.

Finally, a manufacturer or retailer can avoid associations with potentially uncooperative channel members. Thus, a price conservative manufacturer may avoid linking to a price-cutting retailer.

E. B. Weiss has developed an impressive, though admittedly incomplete list of cooperation methods. (See page 640.) Paradoxically, many of these instruments of cooperation are also weapons of control to be used by both middlemen and manufacturers. However, this is not so strange if one keeps in mind that control is subdued conflict and a form of cooperation—even though perhaps *involuntary* cooperation.

## Extension Concept Is the Marketing Concept

The philosophy of cooperation is described in the following quote:

> The essence of the marketing concept is of course customer orientation at all levels of distribution. It is particularly important that customer orientation motivate all relations between a manufacturer and his customer—both immediate and ultimate. It must permeate his entire channels-of-distribution policy.[7]

This quote synthesizes the extension-of-the-organization system concept of channels with the marketing concept. Indeed, it shows that the former is in essence "the" marketing concept applied to the channel area in marketing. To continue:

> The characteristics of the highly competitive markets of today naturally put a distinct premium on harmonious manufacturer-distributor relationships. Their very mutuality of interest demands that the manufacturer base his distribution program not only on what he would like from distributors, but perhaps more importantly, on what they would like from him. In order to get the cooperation of the best distributors, and thus maximum exposure for his line among the various market segments, he must adjust his policies to serve their best interest and, thereby, his own. In other words, he must put the principles of the marketing concept to work for him. By so doing, he will inspire in his customers a feeling of mutual interest and trust and will help convince them that they are essential members of his marketing team.[8]

### Methods of Cooperation as Listed by E. B. Weiss[9]

1. Cooperative advertising allowances
2. Payments for interior displays including shelf-extenders, dump displays, "A" locations, aisle displays, etc.
3. P.M.'s for salespeople
4. Contests for buyers, salespeople, etc.
5. Allowances for a variety of warehousing functions
6. Payments for window display space, plus installation costs
7. Detail men who check inventory, put up stock, set up complete promotions, etc.
8. Demonstrators
9. On certain canned foods a "swell" allowance
10. Label allowance
11. Coupon handling allowance
12. Free goods
13. Guaranteed sales
14. In-store and window display material
15. Local research work
16. Mail-in premium offers to consumer
17. Preticketing
18. Automatic reorder systems
19. Delivery costs to individual stores of large retailers
20. Studies of innumerable types, such as studies of merchandise management accounting
21. Payments for mailings to store lists
22. Liberal return privileges
23. Contributions to favorite charities of store personnel
24. Contributions to special store anniversaries
25. Prizes, etc., to store buyers when visiting showrooms—plus entertainment, of course
26. Training retail salespeople
27. Payments for store fixtures
28. Payments for new store costs, for more improvements, including painting
29. An infinite variety of promotion allowances
30. Special payments for exclusive franchises
31. Payments of part of salary of retail salespeople
32. Deals of innumerable types
33. Time spent in actual selling on retail floor by manufacturer, salesmen
34. Inventory price adjustments
35. Store name mention in manufacturer's advertising

## Channel Domination

The usual pattern in the establishment of channel relationships is that there is a leader, an initiator who puts structure into this relationship and who holds it together. This leader controls, whether through command or cooperation, *i.e.*, through an autocratic or democratic system.

Too often it is automatically assumed that the manufacturer or producer will be the channel leader and that the middlemen will be the channel followers. This has not always been so, nor will it necessarily be so in the future. The growth of mass retailers is increasingly challenging the manufacturer for channel leadership, as the manufacturer challenged the wholesaler in the early part of this century.

### Disagreement Among Scholars

No topic seems to generate so much heat and bias in marketing as the question of who should be the channel leader, and more strangely, who *is* the channel leader. Depending on where the author sits, he can give numerous reasons why his particular choice should take the channel initiative.

Authors of sales management and general marketing books say the manufacturer is and should be the chief institution in the channel. Retailing authors feel the same way about retailers, and wholesaling authors (as few as there are), though not blinded to the fact that wholesaling is not "captain," still imply that they should be, and talk about the coming resurrection of wholesalers. Yet a final and compromising view is put forth by those who believe that a balance of power rather than a general and prolonged dominance of any channel member is best.

### Pro-Manufacturer

The argument for manufacturer leadership is production oriented. It claims that they must assure themselves of increasing volume. This is needed to derive the benefits of production scale economics, to spread their overhead over many units, to meet increasingly stiff competition, and to justify the investment risk they, not the retailers, are taking. Since retailers will not do this job for them properly, the manufacturer must control the channel.

Another major argumentative point for maunufacturer dominance is that neither the public nor retailers can create new products even under a market oriented system. The most the public can do is to select and choose among those that manufacturers have developed. They cannot select products that they cannot conceive. This argument would say that it is of no use to ask consumers and retailers what they want because they cannot articulate abstract needs into tangible goods; indeed, the need can be created by the goods rather than vice-versa.

This argument may hold well when applied to consumers, but a study of the specification buying programs of the mass retailers will show that the latter can indeed create new products, and need not be relegated to simply selecting among alternatives.

### Pro-Retailer

This writer sees the mass retailer as the natural leader of the channel under the marketing concept. The retailer stands closest to the consumer; he feels the pulse of consumer wants and needs day in and day out. The retailer can easily undertake consumer research right on his own premises and can best interpret what is wanted, how much is wanted, and when it is wanted.

An equilibrating state in the channel conflict may come about when small retailers join forces with big manufacturers in a manufacturer leadership channel to compete with a small manufacturer-big retailer leadership channel.

## Methods of Domination

How does a channel leader dominate his fellow members? What are his tools in this channel power struggle? A manufacturer has many domination weapons at his disposal. His arsenal can be divided into promotional, legal, negative, suggestive, and ironically, cooperative compartments.

### Promotional

Probably the major method that manufacturers have used is the building of a consumer franchise through advertising, sales promotion, and packaging of their branded products. When he has developed some degree of consumer loyalty, the other channel members must bow to his leadership. The more successful this identification through the promotion process is, the more assured is the manufacturer of his captaincy.

### Legal

The legal weapon has also been a poignant force for the manufacturer. It can take many forms such as, where permissible, resale price maintenance. Other contractural methods are franchises, where the channel members may become mere shells of legal entities.

Through this weapon the automobile manufacturers have achieved an almost absolute dominance over their dealers.

Even more absolute is resort to legal ownership of channel members, called forward vertical integration. Vertical integration is the ultimate in manufacturer dominance of the channel. Another legal weapon is the use of consignment sales. Under this method the channel members must by law sell the goods as designated by the owner (manufacturer). Consignment selling is in a sense vertical integration; it is keeping legal ownership of the goods until they reach the consumer, rather than keeping legal ownership of the institutions which are involved in the process.

## Negative Methods

Among the "negative" methods of dominance are refusal to sell to possibly uncooperative retailers or refusal to concentrate a large percentage of one's volume with any one customer.

A spreading of sales makes for a concentrating of manufacturer power, while a concentrating of sales may make for a thinning of manufacturer power. Of course, if a manufacturer is one of the few resources available and if there are many available retailers, then a concentrating of sales will also make for a concentrating of power.

The avoidance and refusal tactics, of course, eliminate the possibility of opposing dominating institutions.

## Suggestives

A rather weak group of dominating weapons are the "suggestives." Thus, a manufacturer can issue price sheets and discounts, preticket and premark resale prices on goods, recommend, suggest, and advertise resale prices.

These methods are not powerful unless supplemented by promotional, legal, and/or negative weapons. It is common for these methods to boomerang. Thus a manufacturer pretickets or advertises resale prices, and a retailer cuts this price, pointing with pride to the manufacturer's suggested retail price.

There is one more group of dominating weapons, and these are really all the cooperating weapons mentioned in a previous section. The promise to provide these, or to withdraw them, can have a "whip and carrot" effect on the channel members.

## Retailers' Dominating Weapons

Retailers also have numerous domination weapons at their disposal. As with manufacturers, their strongest weapon is the building of a consumer franchise through advertising, sales promotion, and branding. The growth of private brands is the growth of retail dominance.

Attempts at concentrating a retailer's purchasing power are a further group of weapons and are analogous to a manufacturer's attempts to disperse his volume. The more a retailer can concentrate his purchasing, the more dominating he can become; the more he spreads his purchasing, the more dominated he becomes. Again, if the resource is one of only a few, this generalization reverses itself.

Such legal contracts as specification buying, vertical integration (or the threat), and entry into manufacturing also can be effective. Even semiproduction, such as the packaging of goods received in bulk by the supermarket can be a weapon of dominance.

Retailers can dilute the dominance of manufacturers by patronizing those with excess capacity and those who are "hungry" for the extra volume. There is also the subtlety, which retailers may recognize, that a strong manufacturer may concede to his wishes just to avoid an open conflict with a customer.

## SUMMARY

Figure I summarizes this whole paper. Each person within each department will cooperate, control, and conflict with each other (notice arrows). Together they form a department (notice department box contains person boxes) which will be best off when cooperating (or cooperation through control) forces weigh heavier than conflicting forces. Now each department cooperates, controls, and conflicts with each other. Departments together also form a higher level organization—the firm (manufacturer, wholesaler, and retailer). Again, the firm will be better off if department cooperation is maximized and conflict minimized. Finally, firms standing vertically to each other cooperate, control, and conflict. Together they form a distribution channel that will be best off under conditions of optimum cooperation leading to consumer and profit satisfaction.

1. A channel relation was found to consist of conflict, and cooperation or control. An autocratic relationship exists when one channel member controls conflict and forces the others to cooperate. A democratic relationship exists when all members agree to cooperate without a power play. An anarchistic relationship exists when there is open conflict, with no member able to impose his will on the others. This last form could destroy or seriously reduce the effectiveness of the channel.
2. The process of the exchange act where one member is a seller and the other is a buyer is the basic source of channel conflict. There are, however, many other areas of conflict, such as differences in business philosophy or primary objectives.
3. Reasons for cooperation, however, usually outweigh reasons for conflict. This has led to the concept of the channel as an extension of a firm's organization.
4. This concept drops the facade of "legal entity" and treats channel members as one great organization with the leader providing each with various forms of assistance. These are called cooperating weapons.

**FIGURE I. Organizational Extension Concept**

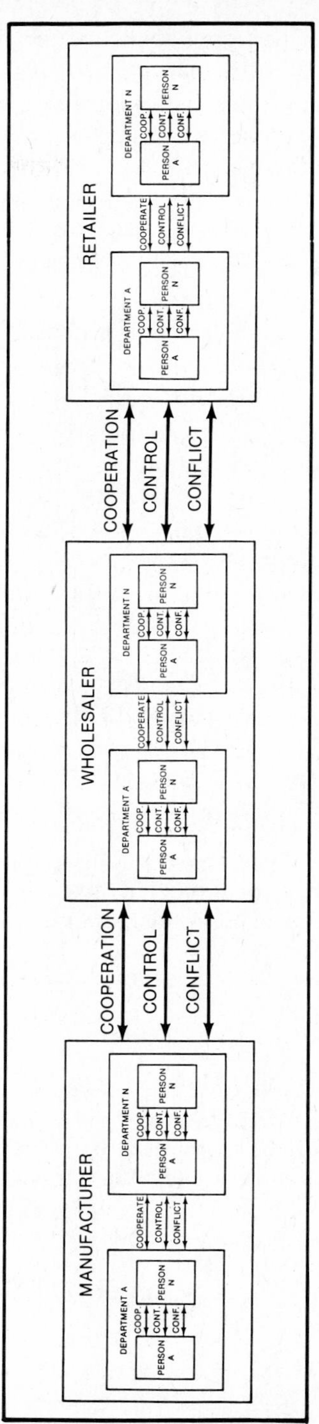


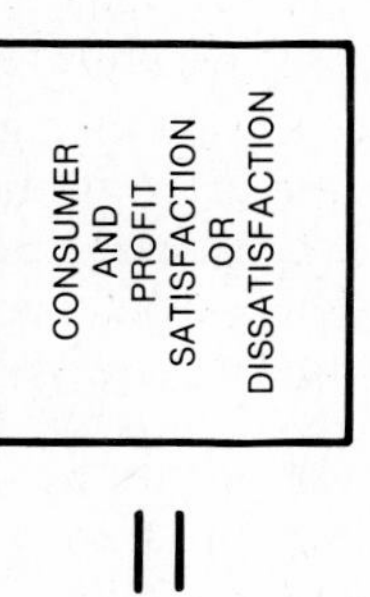

5. It is argued that this concept is actually the marketing concept adapted to a channel situation.
6. In an autocratic or democratic channel relationship there must be a leader. This leadership has shifted and is shifting between the various channel levels.
7. The wholesaler was the leader in the last century, the manufacturer now, and it appears that the mass retailer is next in line.
8. There is much disagreement on the above point, however, especially on who should be the leader. Various authors have differing arguments to advance for their choice.
9. In the opinion of this writer, the mass retailer appears to be best adapted for leadership under the marketing concept.
10. As there are weapons of cooperation so are there weapons of domination. Indeed the former paradoxically are one group of the latter. The other groups are promotional, legal, negative, and suggestive methods. Both manufacturers and retailers have at their disposal these dominating weapons.
11. For maximization of channel profits and consumer satisfaction, the channel must act as a unit.

## ENDNOTES

1. Lewis B. Sappington and C. G. Browne, "The Skills of Creative Leadership," in *Managerial Marketing*, rev. ed., Lazer and Kelley (eds.) (Homewood, Ill.: Richard D. Irwin, Inc., 1962), p. 350.
2. Warren J. Wittreich, "Misunderstanding The Retailer," *Harvard Business Review* XL, No. 3 (May/June 1962), p. 149.
3. The term "anarchy" as used in this paper connotates "no leadership" and nothing more.
4. Valentine F. Ridgeway, "Administration of Manufacturer-Dealer Systems," Lazer and Kelley, p. 480.
5. Peter Drucker, "The Economy's Dark Continent," *Fortune* (April 1962), pp. 103 ff.
6. Ralph S. Alexander, James S. Cross, Ross M. Cunningham, *Industrial Marketing*, rev. ed. (Homewood, Ill.: Richard D. Irwin, Inc., 1961), p. 266.
7. Hector Lazo and Arnold Corbin, *Management in Marketing* (New York: McGraw-Hill Book Company, Inc., 1961), p. 379.
8. Ibid.
9. Edward B. Weiss, "How Much of a Retailer Is the Manufacturer," in *Advertising Age*, XXIX No. 29 (July 21, 1958), p. 68. Reprinted with permission from the July 21, 1958 issue of *Advertising Age*. Copyright 1958 by Crain Communications, Inc.

# 40 —— Distribution Channels as Political Economies: A Framework for Comparative Analysis

*Louis W. Stern and Torger Reve*

Reprinted from *Journal of Marketing*, published by the American Marketing Association, Vol. 44 (Summer 1980), pp. 52-64. Reprinted by permission.

Published studies related to distribution channels present, collectively, a rather disjointed collage. This is due, in part, to the absence of a framework which can accommodate the various paradigms and orientations employed in performing research on distribution channel phenomena. What is needed is a comprehensive mapping of the field which depicts the various paths one could follow, the likely places where one might end up, and the boundaries of the various places within the entire conceptual space. If this mapping were successfully accomplished, then those individuals already within the field would have a better understanding of where their work stood relative to others' and would, hopefully, be encouraged to seek out complementary paradigms to those which they have adopted. The mapping would also indicate to many of those who perceive themselves as standing outside the field that much of what they are doing could easily have relevance to the substance of the field. They might even be motivated to advance the field themselves. And, most importantly, the mapping would be helpful to prospective scholars who, to a large extent, do not have a very solid understanding of the research opportunities avialable within the field. While no single article is ever likely to accomplish such a comprehensive mapping, there is clearly a strong need to make a beginning. If a meaningful start at ordering the field can be undertaken, then this will likely encourage others to pursue the completion and refinement of the ordering process.

Despite the centrality of distribution channels in marketing, there exist three major deficiencies in the current status of distribution channel theory and research. *First*, analyses of distribution channels have largely focused on the technologies (e.g., sales force incentive systems, pricing procedures, and the like) employed by individual organizations in their efforts to structure and control channel activities (cf., Gattorna 1978; McCammon and Little 1965; McCammon, Bates, and Guiltinan 1971). These analyses have adopted a *micro* orientation in keeping with traditional problem-solving approaches in marketing management. Little attention has been given to questions of the maintenance, adaptation, and evolution of marketing channels as competitive entities.

*Second,* channel theory is fragmented into two seemingly disparate disciplinary orientations: an *economic* approach and a *behavioral* approach. The former attempts to apply microeconomic theory and industrial organization analysis to the study of distribution systems and has been essentially "efficiency" oriented, focusing on costs, functional differentiation, and channel design (cf., Baligh and Richartz 1967; Bucklin 1966; Bucklin and Carman 1974; Cox, Goodman, and Fichandler 1965). The latter borrows heavily from social psychology and organization theory and has been essentially "socially" oriented, focusing on power and conflict phenomena (cf., Alderson 1957; Stern 1969). Rarely have there been attempts to integrate these two perspectives. Indeed, they should be viewed as complementary, because the former deals mainly with economic "outputs" while the latter is concerned with behavioral "processes."

*Third,* empirical studies of distribution networks have been extremely limited in their scope and methodological sophistication. The vast majority of empirical works in the channels area has been purely descriptive in nature, with little or no testing of formal hypotheses derived from theory (cf., McCammon and Little 1965). Although more recent studies evidence a trend toward more systematic testing of theoretical relationships, these investigations have typically been confined to an analysis of a single distribution channel within a particular industry (exceptions include Etgar 1976a, 1978; Hunt and Nevin 1974; Porter 1974; Weik 1972).[1] Future channel research must focus on making systematic *comparisons* of different distribution networks within and between various environmental conditions, irrespective of whether the different networks are found in the same industry or across industries.

A promising framework for addressing these issues is provided by the *political economy* approach to the study of social systems (Benson 1975; Wamsley and Zald 1973, 1976; Zald 1970a, 1970b). Basically, the *political economy approach views a social system as comprising interacting sets of major economic and sociopolitical forces which affect collective behavior and performance.* The purpose of this article, therefore, is to present a political economy framework which can be applied to gain deeper understanding of the *internal* functioning of a distribution channel. Such a framework also permits comprehension of the processes where distribution channels are influenced by and adapt to environmental conditions. It is, however, recognized that this framework is only one of many that might be suggested. It has been selected because of its strong potential for comprehensively mapping this area of marketing inquiry.

The political economy framework outlined here should be viewed as the first step in the direction of identifying and dimensionalizing the major variables influencing and ordering channel structure and behavior. A premise of the framework as initially formulated is that complex socioeconomic interrelations involve multilateral interactions as opposed to "simple" cause-effect mechanisms, such as those between power use and conflict or between channel design and costs. Given the present state of channel theory development, the initial task to be performed in accomplishing methodological and interpretive rigor is to lay out the relevant channel dimensions in terms of "fields," e.g., external-internal; economic-sociopolitical; structural-process. Otherwise, theoretical research in the area will continue to suffer from ad hoc operationalizations, where researchers select independent measures and globally hypothesize some dependent outcome without indicating or even being aware of which other interacting variables are being held or assumed constant. Hence, the political economy framework should be seen as an attempt to *chart out* or classify the total field of channel interaction. The political economy perspective as an organizing framework impels the generation of significant research questions and, therefore, has the potential for producing new theoretical insights.

As an aid to exploring the promise of the framework, a number of *illustrative* propositions have been generated throughout this article. They should be helpful in stimulating future research because they provide some insights into the kinds of meaningful relationships among core concepts which are motivated by employing the framework. However, it should be noted that there has been no attempt to specify research designs to "test" the propositions. This is because the propositions can be operationalized in a variety of ways. Given the existing state of knowledge in the channels area, it might be misleading for us to suggest specific operationalizations and would, almost certainly, deflect attention from the main purpose of the article due to the controversy they might evoke. As an aid to the reader, we have provided an appendix which conceptually defines a few of the key constructs used. This "glossary" only serves to suggest the conceptual boundaries of the constructs; it is not intended to provide operation allegations.

In the following section, the full political economy framework is broadly outlined. Then, the remainder of the paper explores, in considerable detail, the *intra*-channel variables included in the framework.

## The Political Economy Framework

The political economy framework is capsulized in Figure 1. As indicated, there are two major systems: (I) the *internal political economy*, i.e., the internal structuring and functioning of the distribution channel, and (II) the *external political economy*, i.e., the channel's task environment. Both systems are divided into two component parts: an *economy* and a *polity*. The major relationships which need to be explored are indicated by arrows with capital letter notations (see Figure 1).

### The Internal Political Economy

Distribution channels are interorganizational "collectivities" of institutions and actors simultaneously pursuing self-interest and collective

**FIGURE 1. A Political Economy Framework for Distribution Channel Analysis**

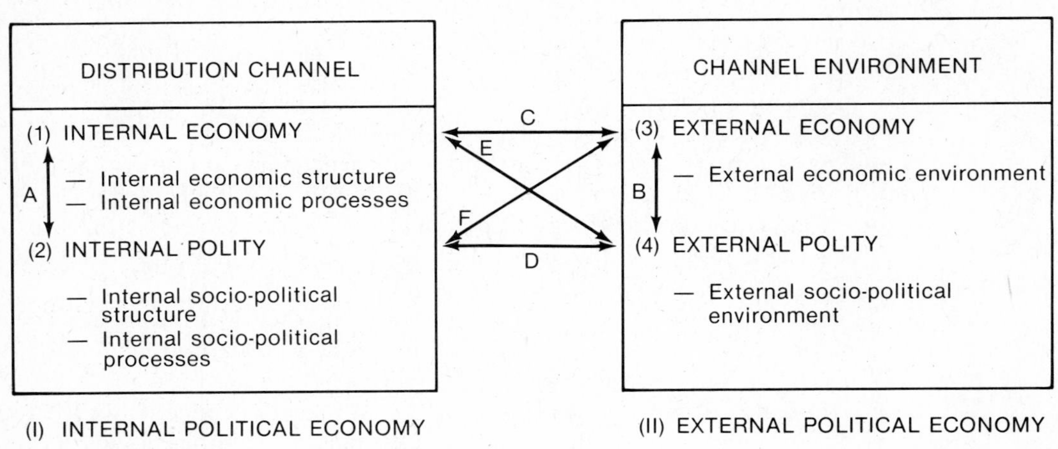


goals (Reve and Stern 1979; Van de Ven, Emmett, and Koenig 1974). As such, the actors interact in a socioeconomic setting of their own, called an internal political economy. To comprehend fully the relevant internal dimensions and interactions, the framework suggests that a channel be analyzed in relation to its (1) *internal economy*, i.e., the internal economic structure and processes and its (2) *internal polity*, i.e., the internal sociopolitical structure and processes.

The internal economic structure is described by the type of transactional form linking channel members, i.e., the vertical economic arrangement within the marketing channel, while the internal economic processes refer to the nature of the decision mechanisms employed to determine the terms of trade among the members. On the other hand, the internal sociopolitical structure is defined by the pattern of power-dependence relations which exist among channel members, while the internal sociopolitical processes are described in terms of the dominant sentiments (i.e., cooperation and/or conflict) within the channel.

Identifying that marketing channels consist of an internal economy and an internal polity is not a major departure from prior approaches to channel research. The contribution of the political economy framework is the explicit insistence that economic and sociopolitical forces not be analyzed in isolation. By considering the interactions between the economy and the polity, it is possible to understand and explain the internal structuring and functioning of distribution systems and to derive a number of illustrative propositions for channel research.

### The 'External' Political Economy

Organizations always operate within an environment. The environment of a distribution channel is a complex of economic, physical, cultural, demographic, psychological, political, and technological forces. In the political economy framework, such forces are, as shown in Figure 1, incorporated in (3) *the external economy,* i.e., the prevailing and prospective economic environment and (4) *the external polity,* i.e., the external sociopolitical system in which the channel operates. The external economy of a distribution channel can be described by the nature of its vertical (input and output) and horizontal markets. The external polity can be described by the distribution and use of power resources among external actors (e.g., competitors, regulatory agencies, and trade associations) (cf., Palamountain 1955; Pfeffer and Salancik 1978; Thompson 1967; Yuchtman and Seashore 1967). An analysis of the external sociopolitical environment entails specification of the type of actors exercising power in the environment (Evan 1965), the power relations and means of control used between the external actors and the focal channel (Thompson 1967), the power relations between external actors (Terreberry 1968), and the extent to which the activities of channel members are actually controlled by environmental forces (Benson 1975).

The external economic and sociopolitical forces interact and define environmental conditions for the channel. The external political economy thus influences the internal political economy through adaptation and interaction processes (Aldrich 1979). Furthermore, channels not only adapt to their environments, but also influence and shape them (Pfeffer and Salancik 1978). The arrows in Figure 1 which indicate interactions between the component systems therefore point in both directions.

Attention is now turned to an elaboration of the internal political economy of distribution channels. The focus on intra-channel variables is a natural starting point, given that virtually all existing channel research has dealt with internal channel phenomena. Knowledge of environmental variables and their impact is fragmentary at best (Etgar 1977). Future examinations of the political economy framework must, however, focus on environmental variables and on the interactions between the internal and external economies.

## The Internal Political Economy of Distribution Channels: An Elaboration of the Framework

In this section the major internal economic and sociopolitical forces at work in distribution channels are described. These forces interact in shaping channel arrangements and in affecting marketing channel behavior and performance.

## Internal Economy of Distribution Channels

Distribution channels are primarily set up to perform a set of essential *economic* functions in society, bridging the gap between production and consumption. Thus, it is no surprise that a substantial proportion of channel research, especially the earlier studies, has focused on an analysis of the *internal economy* of distribution channels (see Gattorna 1978; McCammon and Little 1965 for reviews).

As already indicated, the internal economy of a distribution channel may be divided into two components. The *internal economic structure* refers to the vertical economic arrangements or the transactional form in the channel. These arrangements range from a series of independently owned and managed specialized units which transact exchanges across markets to complete vertical integration where exchanges between wholly-owned units are conducted within a hierarchy (Williamson 1975). Whereas market transactions rely primarily on the use of the price mechanism, hierarchical transactions rely on administrative mechanisms. Between these two extreme economic arrangements lies a wide variety of structures in which the market mechanism is modified through some kind of formal or informal contractual arrangements between the parties involved (Blois 1972; Liebeler 1976).

Operating within each internal economic structure of a channel are certain *internal economic processes* or decision mechanisms. Thus, agreement on the terms of trade and the division of marketing functions among channel members may be reached in impersonal, routine, or habitual ways; through bargaining; or via centralized planning processes. The type of processes used to allocate resources in any given channel is likely to conform to or, at least, be constrained by the transactional form of the channel. Typically, competitive, price-mediated mechanisms are dominant in those market transactions where information is relatively complete and products are undifferentiated, as in soybean trading, while centralized planning is dominant in most hierarchical transactions. But competitive, price-mediated mechanisms have also been simulated in hierarchical structures through mathematical programming models using computed shadow prices as terms of transfer (Jennergren 1979). For other transactions which fall in between the two structural extremes, the allocation of many marketing activities is largely determined through bargaining among the parties.

Of critical importance for channel analysis is the need to compare the efficiency and effectiveness of various transactional forms or structures across each of the three decision-making mechanisms. It is also important to consider cases where a specific economic process is employed across economic structures. For example, an illustrative proposition dealing with centralized planning processes might be:

P1. The more centralized planning processes predominate, irrespective of the transactional form, the more efficient and effective the marketing channel for a product or service is likely to be.

In this sense, efficiency could be defined in terms of output to input ratios (e.g., sales per square foot) and effectiveness could be some external market referent (e.g., market share). A number of theoretical rationales underlie P1: (1) the likely constraints on suboptimization within the channel derived from joint decision making, (2) the exploitation of potential scale economies, (3) the possible cost advantages gained via increased programming of distributive functions, and (4) the reduction of transaction costs due to reduced uncertainties and lessened opportunism (cf., Etgar 1976a; Gronhaug and Reve 1979).

There are, however, a number of rationales working against P1's central premise: (1) the satisficing modes which operate when centralized planning processes predominate, (2) the danger of bureaucratization and loss of cost consciousness, and (3) the curbing of initiative at "lower" levels. Therefore, P1 demands investigation in concert with a second, counter proposition.

P2. The more centralized planning processes predominate, irrespective of the transactional form, the less likely is the marketing channel to be able to react quickly to external threats.

This proposition has its roots in the criticism which has often been directed at vertically integrated systems (cf., Arndt and Reve 1979; Sturdivant 1966). However, it may also apply to market transactions, because the more that the exchange process among channel members is organized, the more severe become trade-offs between efficiency and adaptiveness. On the other hand, while fast and specific adaptation to localized threats will likely be slow when centralized planning processes are prevalent, the adoption of such processes may permit better environmental scanning, more opportunities to influence external actors, and more ability to absorb shocks over the long run than those channels which are typified by bargaining or by routine or habitual decision making.

Analysis is also required within transactional forms across the various decision making mechanisms. Especially significant are the issues which Williamson (1975) raises in his markets and hierarchies framework. He shows how market transactions may become very costly due to human factors, such as bounded rationality and opportunism, coupled with environmental factors, such as uncertainty and economically concentrated input or output markets (i.e., small numbers bargaining). When information is unequally possessed, opportunistic behavior is likely to prevail, and exchange may be commercially hazardous. An illustrative proposition drawn from this line of reasoning is:

P3. Market transactions in oligopsonistic situations are likely to lead to information imbalances, opportunistic behavior, and high transaction costs. Impersonal, routine, or habitual decision making mechanisms in such situations will not suffice to overcome opportunistic behavior within the channel.

For example, when the members of atomistic industries, such as those found in the manufacture of maintenance, operating, and repair items, rely on open market forces to determine the terms of trade between themselves and the members of oligopolies, such as in the aerospace or automotive industries, the latter may withhold relevant information regarding demand projections and manipulate the exchange process by distorting any information passed along in order to achieve inequitable advantages from their fragmented suppliers. Extensive theoretical rationales underlying P3 are provided by Williamson (1975), Arrow (1974), and Lindblom (1977). Empirical research, using this internal economy perspective, is required to test the large number of Williamsonian hypotheses dealing with why channel structures based on market transactions may tend to fail.

## Internal Polity of Distribution Channels

As has been noted by several channel analysts (e.g., Alderson, Palamountain), distribution channels are not only economic systems but also social systems.[2] This observation has led to research on the behavioral aspects of distribution channels and the intrachannel sociopolitical factors (Stern 1969; Stern and El-Ansary 1977). In a political economy framework, these forces are referred to as the *internal polity* of distribution channels. The economy and the polity of channels are basically allocation systems, allocating scarce economic resources and power or authority, respectively. Both the economy and polity of channels can also be viewed as coordination systems (Hernes 1978) or ways of managing the economics and politics of interorganizational systems.

The polity of a marketing channel might be seen as oriented to the allocation and use of authority and power within the system. Similar to the internal economy, there are also structural and process variables which describe the working of the internal polity. Adopting Emerson's (1962, 1972) notion of power relationships as the inverse of the existing dependency relationships between the system's actors, the *internal sociopolitical structure* is given by the initial pattern of power-dependence relations within the channel. The limiting cases of dependence are minimal power and completely centralized power. Power is a relational concept inherent in exchange between social actors (Emerson 1962, 1972). There will always be *some* power existing within channels due to mutual dependencies which exist among channel members, even though that power may be very low (El-Ansary and Stern 1972). However, power can also be fully concentrated in a single organization which then appears as the undisputed channel administrator (e.g., Lusch 1976). Such a power constellation can be referred to as a unilateral power system (Bonoma 1976). Because of the numerous marketing flows which tie the channel members together, the more common case is a mixed power situation where different firms exercise control over different flows, functions, or marketing activities (e.g., Etgar 1976b). The latter can be referred to as a mixed power system (Bonoma 1976).[3] Careful analysis is required to assess correctly the power-dependency patterns in a marketing channel (cf., El-Ansary and Stern 1972; Etgar 1976b; Frazier and Brown 1978; Hunt and Nevin 1974; Wilkinson 1973), because sociopolitical structures alter over time. Changing bases of power, coalition formations, and evolving linkages with external actors are among the factors causing such dynamism and creating measurement problems.

The various patterns of power-dependence relationships in a distribution channel are thought to be associated with various *sociopolitical processes*. The sociopolitical processes primarily refer to the dominant sentiments and behaviors which characterize the interactions between channel members. Although channel sentiments and behaviors are multidimensional constructs, two major dimensions in channel analysis are cooperation and conflict. Cooperation can be represented as joint striving towards an object (Stern 1971)—the process of coalescing with others for a good, goal, or value of mutual benefit. Cooperation involves a combination of object- and collaborator-centered activity which is based on a compatibility of goals, aims, or values. It is an activity in which the potential collaborator is viewed as providing the means by which a divisible goal or object desired by the parties may be obtained and shared. Conflict, on the other hand, is opponent-centered behavior (Stern 1971) because in a conflict situation, the object is controlled by the opponent while incompatibility of goals, aims, or values exists. The major concern in such situations is to overcome the opponent or counterpart as a means of securing the object. Conflict is characterized by mutual interference or blocking behavior.[4]

While they are highly interrelated, cooperation and conflict are separate, distinguishable processes. Exchange between social actors generally contains a certain dialect varying between conflictual and cooperative behavior (Guetzkow 1966). A common example is found in customer-supplier relationships ordered by long-term contracts. They reflect basically cooperative sentiments, but conflicts regularly take place regarding the interpretation of contractual details and problem-solving approaches.

At one extreme, dysfunctional conflict processes—those aimed at injuring or destroying another party—will severly impede any existing or potential cooperative behaviors among the parties. However, the absence of confrontation will not necessarily produce maximal joint-striving, because the complacency and passivity which may be present in the relationship may cause the parties to overlook salient opportunities for coalescing (cf., Coser 1956; Thomas 1976). Indeed, because of the mutual dependencies which exist in channels, it is likely that conflict, in some form, will always be present (Schmidt and Kochan 1972; Stern and El-Ansary 1977; Stern and Gorman 1969). In addition, channels cannot exist without a minimum level of cooperation among the parties. Thus, conflictual and cooperative processes will exist simultaneously in all channels.

Having specified major structure and process variables in the internal polity, it now is possible to examine their interactions for illustrative propositions. For instance, there exists a relatively large number of situations in distribution where power is somewhat balanced, e.g., when department store chains deal with well-known cosmetic manufacturers, when large plumbing and heating wholesalers deal with major manufacturers of air conditioning equipment, and when supermarket chains deal with large grocery manufacturers. Drawing from political science theory, it can be proposed that:

P4. In marketing channels typified by balanced power relationships, interactions will be predominantly cooperative as long as the balance of strength is preserved (e.g., Kaplan 1957). However, the potential for dysfunctional conflict is higher than it would be if power were imbalanced (Gurr 1970).

The first part of P4 is primarily drawn from balance of power theories of international politics which predict peaceful coexistence as long as balance of strength remains. This position is congruent with the insights offered by bilateral oligopoly and duopoly theories in economics (Scherer 1970) which forecast the development of informal or formal interfirm agreements regarding pricing and competitive actions. The second part of P4 draws on relative deprivation theories of collective conflict (Gurr 1970) which predict that conflict potential and the magnitude of manifest dysfunctional conflict will be highest in balanced power situations.

Even though P4 is intuitively appealing, counter propositions can be offered which indicate that empirical verification is required. For example, Korpi (1974), a political scientist, argues that conflict potential is higher in slightly imbalanced than in balanced power constellations while Williamson (1975), an economist, posits that a centralized power pattern—the extreme form of imbalanced power—will tend to exhibit predominantly cooperative modes of exchange when compared to a more balanced pattern. Furthermore, in an imbalanced situation, ideology is often used as a unifying and cooperation-inducing force by the more powerful party. The seeming cooperation in a balanced power constellation may be of a deterrent nature. Thus, there is a need to distinguish between detente-type cooperation and ideologically-induced cooperation.

As with the variables specified for the internal economy, there is clearly a need to compare structural sociopolitical conditions across processes and vice versa in order to generate propositions which can permit predictions for channel management. At the same time, it is important to understand that conflict and cooperation processes are activities conducive to some economic end; they are not ends in themselves. Furthermore, the way in which power is used within a channel will clearly affect the sociopolitical processes. For example, it may be proposed that:

P5. In marketing channels characterized by imbalanced power, the use of coercive power will produce a dysfunctional level of conflict.

Additionally,

P6. Marketing channels characterized by imbalanced power and dominated by coercive influence strategies will be inherently unstable, resulting in decreased competitive viability.

To some extent, the works of Raven and Kruglanski (1970); Stern, Schulz, and Grabner (1973); and Lusch (1976) examining the relation between bases of power and resulting conflict point in the direction of these propositions.

Alternately, in line with findings generated by Wittreich (1962), Kriesberg (1952), and Weik (1972), it is possible to propose that:

P7. Marketing channels characterized by minimal power will exhibit low levels of cooperation.

This is supported by McCammon (1970) who has argued that conventional marketing channels, comprised of isolated and autonomous decision making units, are unable to program distribution activities successfully. If power is low, so is dependence. Thus, two or more relatively independent entities may not be motivated to cooperate.

The above propositions indicate a few of the expected relations within the internal polity of distribution channels. As mentioned, they are merely illustrative of the meaningful insights for channel theory and management available in this kind of analysis.

## Interaction Between Internal Economy and Internal Polity of Distribution Channels

The essence of the political economy framework for the analysis of marketing systems is that economic and sociopolitical forces are not analyzed in isolation. Therefore, it is imperative to examine the interactions between the economy and the polity. To illustrate the potency of the combination, it is again possible to generate a series of propositions. Each of these propositions draws upon the variables enumerated previously.

The constellation of a given economic structure with a certain sociopolitical structure within a marketing channel will influence the economic and sociopolitical processes which take place. Considered first is the intersection between various power structures and economic structures typified by market transactions.

P8. In marketing channels in which market transactions are the predominant mode of exchange and in which power is centralized, centralized planning processes will emerge.

A relative power advantage within a channel is often used to program channel activities, and in such situations, decision making with respect to at least certain functions (e.g., promotion, physical distribution) tends to be centralized. Indicative of these types of channel arrangements are those found in the food industry where manufacturers, such as Nabisco and Kraft, develop shelf or dairy case management plans for supermarket chains; in the automotive aftermarket where warehouse distributors, such as Genuine Parts Company, evoke inventory management programs for jobbers (e.g., NAPA); in lawn care products where manufacturers, such as O. M. Scott, engage in detailed merchandise programming with the various retailers of their products; and in general merchandise retailing where retailers, such as Sears, Wards, and Penneys, preprogram the activities of their private label suppliers.

In addition to economic efficiency considerations, several behavioral considerations underlie P8. Thus, following Williamson (1975), some form of organizing process (in this case, centralized planning or programming) is required in order to overcome the tendencies toward opportunistic behavior present in market transactions and to cope with the bounded rationality of each channel member. The means to achieve centralized planning may be centralized power, although this is not always likely to be the case. For example, even in cases where there are balanced power structures in channels, centralized planning processes have emerged. This was the case when the Universal Product Code was developed jointly by retailers and manufacturers operating through their food industry trade associations.

P8 can be elaborated by considering the sociopolitical processes which are likely to prevail in market transactions with centralized planning.

P9. Under the conditions specified by P8, marketing channels will exhibit a relatively high level of conflict, but they will also exhibit highly cooperative processes. Such channels will tend to be more competitively effective than others where market transactions are also the predominant mode of exchange.

Following Korpi's (1974) reasoning, P9 predicts that conflict potential will be high due to the imbalanced power situation. The expectation with respect to cooperation is based on the ability of the channel administrator to mitigate opportunistic tendencies among the units in the channel and to establish superordinate goals. The overall effect of the combination of interacting variables in P9 will be to produce effective channel systems in which programmed merchandising is likely to be the rule rather than the exception. Such channels are likely to be more successful in improving their market shares relative to other channels typified by market transactions.

Anecdotal evidence supporting P8 and P9 can be found in the construction and farm equipment industries. In these industries, market transactions are the predominant means of exchange between the various manufacturers and their dealers. However, Caterpillar and Deere have gained sizable leads over their rivals by developing highly efficient and effective systems of distribution through the use of their considerable power in their channels. They have achieved an unusual amount of success by programming their networks and by managing conflict within them.

Another proposition in line with the discussion above is that:

P10. In marketing channels in which hierarchical transactions are the predominant mode of exchange and in which power is centralized, conflict processes are more likely to be effectively managed, superordinate goals are more likely to be established, and efficiency is more likely to be achieved relative to any other marketing channel.

The underlying rationale for this proposition is supplied by Williamson (1975):

> Unlike autonomous contractors, internal divisions that trade with one another in a vertical integration relationship do not ordinarily have preemptive claims on their respective profit streams. Even though the divisions in question may have profit center standing, this is apt to be exercised in a restrained way. For one thing, the terms under which internal trading occurs are likely to be circumscribed. Cost-plus pricing rules, and variants thereof, preclude supplier divisions from seeking the monpolistic prices to which their sole supply position might otherwise entitle them. In addition, the managements of the trading divisions are more susceptible to appeals for cooperation. Since the aggressive pursuit of individual interests redounds to the disadvantage of the system and as present and prospective compensation (including promotions) can be easily varied by the general office to reflect noncooperation, simple requests to adopt a cooperative mode are more apt to be heeded. Altogether, a more nearly joint profit maximizing attitude and result is to be expected. (p. 29)

However, it should be noted that, even within a vertically integrated channel, opportunism and bounded rationality may still be found. In addition, the large size of many vertically integrated organizations often creates problems of bureaucratization and inflexibility. Thus, P10 isolates centralized, as opposed to decentralized, power. For example, the power which Sears' field operations held with regard to inventory levels within its stores was one of the major reasons for the disastrous inventory situation the company faced in 1974. In order to reduce the opportunistic behavior which existed among Sears' various divisions (e.g., the retail stores refused to hold their rightful share of the inventories which were building to abnormal levels in Sears' distribution centers), the entire company was reorganized and power was centralized more firmly in its Chicago headquarters. Now it remains to be seen whether Sears' management is equal to the task of successfully controlling the organization. Clearly, the advantages of such an internal political economy can dissipate as increasing degrees of vertical integration lead to more complex organization, more impersonal relationships, less perception of the relationships between actions and results, less moral involvement, generally more self-serving behavior, and greater toleration for substandard performance.

It should be noted that the political economy framework also encourages the examination of more narrowly focused propositions than those already stated. Given the difficulties associated with researching channel issues (due primarily to the lack of accessibility to and the sensitivity of the data involved), it is likely that research using the political economy framework should start with relatively manageable tasks. Illustrative of such propositions are:

P11. The more that relationships between channel members are characterized by cooperative behavior, the greater the level of profits attainable to the channel as a whole.

P12. The greater the proportion of relative power possessed by any channel member, the greater the proportion of the channel's profits that member will receive.

Central issues in political economies are (1) how surpluses are generated and (2) how they are distributed among the members. These ''processes'' provide critical links between the ''political'' and ''economic'' aspects of the system. P11 suggests a positive relationship between the level of cooperation within the channel and the joint profits obtained by it. The rationale is that cooperative behavior facilitates coordination and programming of activities within the channel which, in turn, provides potential cost advantages and improved competitive strength. In some cases, cooperation is likely to be informal, requiring a minimum of interaction. In these cases, environmental factors such as professional or trade norms, the role of trade associations, and the impact of government regulations may play significant roles in encouraging joint striving behavior. In other cases, cooperation may take the form of ad hoc consultations, the formation of committees, the establishment of federative coordination bodies, or the construction of bilateral contracts, joint ventures, or other types of formal long-term agreements (Pfeffer and Salancik 1978).

P12 addresses the critical issue of the allocation of joint profits within the marketing channel. The division of returns clearly is a matter of relative power and bargaining skill. Thus, the benefits obtained in the economic arena are divided in the political arena, a situation which is analogous to the income reallocation problem in welfare economics. Porter (1974) has found some empirical support for P12 using mainly secondary data.

Focusing on the interaction between the economy and polity of marketing channels may also produce insights into the evolution and adaptation of channel institutions. Innovative distributive institutions, such as limited line-limited service grocery stores (e.g., Aldi) and catalogue showrooms (e.g., McDade), may emerge due to differential cost advantages achieved by improved logistical systems or sharper positioning relative to specific consumer segments. The initiative for such innovations often comes from ''outsiders'' who are at odds with traditional channel norms and practices (Kriesberg 1955; McCammon and Bates 1965). Thus, the innovations result, at least in part, because of functional conflicts within existing channels. As the new institutions mature, they tend to hire personnel from competitors, thereby gradually changing their professional orientation. At the same time, they bcome preoccupied with quality, add services, and begin to cater to broader market segments, thus moving towards the same practices as their competitors. The functional conflicts with other channel members tend to disappear, and opportunities for new outsiders to innovate emerge. Such scenarios as the ''wheel of retailing'' simply illustrate how sociopolitical circumstances often influence economic activities within a marketing channel. In turn, the economic form influences the sociopolitical sentiments surrounding the emerging transactions which lead, in turn, to further changes in economic activities.

## Conclusion

Analysis of distribution channels as political economies provides a framework in which to incorporate and integrate the variety of approaches and findings found in the existing channel literature. More importantly, the emergent framework provides a basis for future research by isolating the critical dimensions determining transactional effectiveness and efficiency in distribution. It also provides a conceptual mapping which may be useful to anyone with an interest in channel relationships.

The framework, including the illustrative propositions developed from it, presents a preliminary, general look at distribution channel structuring and functioning. In particular, the propositions advanced above serve to underscore the caveat that the economy and the polity of such systems are inseparably linked and cannot be studied in isolation (Frey 1978; Lindblom 1977; Thorelli 1965; Tivey 1978). Choosing an internal economic structure for a channel seems to have clear implications for the internal sociopolitical structure involved. The constellations formed by the intersection of the various economic and sociopolitical structures also have implications for the type of sociopolitical processes to be expected within channels. An internal economic structure may have certain benefits in terms of the economic performance and the competitive effectiveness of the channel. On the other hand, the sociopolitical processes associated with a given internal economy may vary both in the transaction costs and in the rationality of decision making for the channel as a whole. All of these factors directly influence channel performance. Another general implication which may be drawn from this type of analysis is that the various political economies of channels require different interorganizational management strategies for maintaining and expanding channel operations and for dealing with channel conflicts.

Clearly, factors in the external political economy will have a profound influence on a channel's internal political economy. Any propositions generated by adopting the political economy framework, including those outlined here, need to be modified by circumstances in the external economy and polity. A description of the impact of external forces and internal-external interactions then emerges as a topic for future work. However, this directive must be kept in proper perspective. In the only published empirical research focusing directly on the latter topic, Etgar (1977) has indicated that certain aspects of the internal political economy of channels can be expected to explain more of the variance in channel behavior than environmental factors. Following his findings, the strongest emphasis in future research should probably remain focused on achieving a deeper understanding of the internal political economy. The framework provided in this article should, hopefully, be of some assistance in this respect.

## Appendix

### Definitions of Key Concepts in the Political Economy Framework (See Fig. A-1)

*Political economy* = collectivity comprised of an economic system (economy) and a sociopolitical system (polity) which jointly influence collective behavior and performance.

I. *Internal political economy* = the internal structuring and functioning of an organized collectivity (e.g., marketing channel) analyzed in terms of an internal economy and an internal polity and their interactions.

II. *External political economy* = the task environment of an organized collectivity (e.g., marketing channel) analyzed in terms of an external economy and an external polity and their interactions.

I.1. *Internal economy* = the internal economic allocation system analyzed in terms of the internal economic structure and processes.

I.2. *Internal polity* = the internal sociopolitical allocation system analyzed in terms of the internal sociopolitical structure and processes.

II.1. *External economy* = the economic task environment of an organized collectivity (e.g., marketing channel) described by the nature of its vertical (input and output) and horizontal markets.

II.2. *External polity* = the sociopolitical task environment of an organized collectivity (e.g., marketing channel) described by the distribution and use of power resources among external actors and their prevailing sentiments.

I.1.1. *Internal economic structure* = the economic arrangements or transactional form within an organized collectivity (e.g., marketing channel) set up to complete internal exchanges.

I.1.2. *Internal economic processes* = the decision making processes within an organized collectivity (e.g., marketing channel) which determine the terms of trade and the divisions of labor, functions, and activities among the internal actors.

**FIGURE A-1. Key Concepts in the Political Economy Framework**

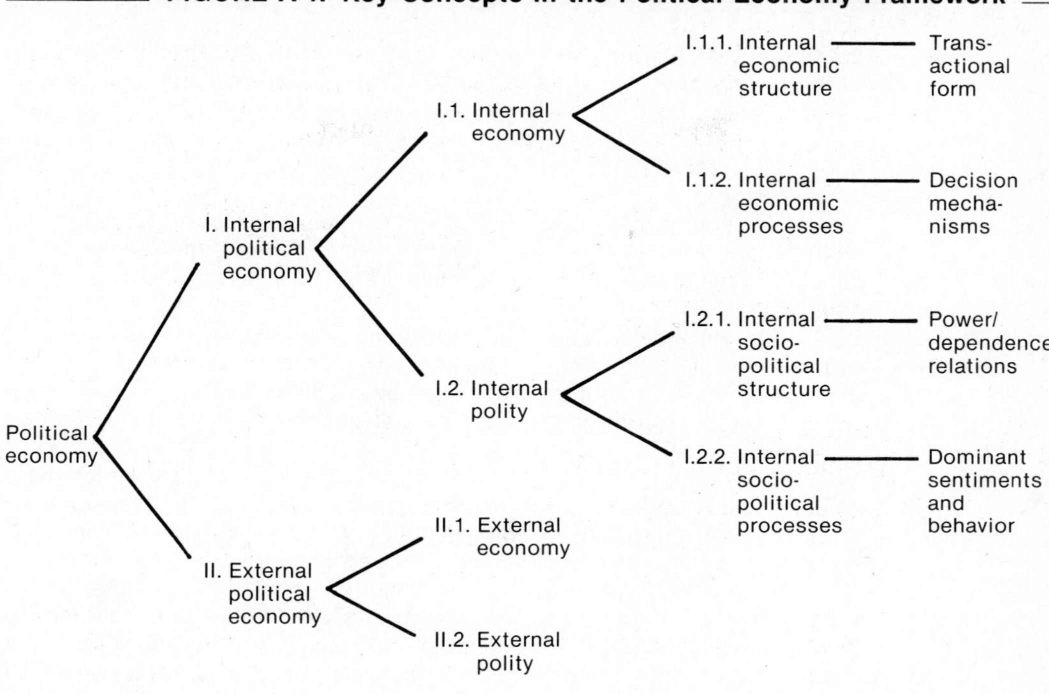


*I.2.1. Internal sociopolitical structure* = the pattern of power/dependence relations within an organized collectivity (e.g., marketing channel).
*I.2.2. Internal sociopolitical processes* = the dominant sentiments and behaviors which characterize the interactions between actors within an organized collectivity (e.g., marketing channel).
*I.1.1. Transactional form* = internal economic arrangements ranging from markets to hierarchies (e.g., vertical integration).
*I.1.2. Decision making processes* = internal collective choice processes ranging from impersonal determination of terms of trade through the price mechanism, through bargaining processes, to centralized planning processes.
*I.2.1. Power/dependence relations* = internal power/dependence pattern ranging from minimal power (low dependence), through mixed power constellations of balanced and imbalanced power (mutual dependence), to centralized power (unilateral dependence).
*I.2.2. Dominant sentiments and behaviors* = internal sentiments and behaviors of cooperation and functional or dysfunctional conflict characterizing internal exchange, ranging from minimal cooperation, high dysfunctional conflict to maximal cooperation, functional conflict.

## ENDNOTES

1. Methodologically, many of the studies fall short due to the incorrect use of informant methodologies as well as insufficient and often single-item operationalizations of constructs, thus not allowing for reliability checks and construct validation. For an excellent critique, see Phillips (1980). Thus, more emphasis needs to be given to careful research designs and improved measurement.
2. Simply observing that many marketing channels are loosely aligned (e.g., McVey 1960) does not invalidate their systemic nature. For argumentation supporting the perspective that channels are social action systems, see Reve and Stern (1979).
3. Bonoma (1976) also proposes a third power constellation—the bilateral power system—in which the interactants are in a unit relation jointly determining unit policy for individual and group action. Such systems, which are held together by social altruism, have not yet been examined in distribution channel settings.
4. In the social sciences in general and the conflict literature in particular, there has been a considerable amount of controversy surrounding the distinction between conflict and competition. We believe that competition is distinguishable from conflict. Competition can be viewed as a form of opposition which is object-centered; conflict is opponent-centered behavior. Competition is indirect and impersonal; conflict is very direct and highly personal. In competition, a third party controls the goal or object; in conflict, the goal or object is controlled by the opponent. A swim meet is competition; a football game is conflict. For a discussion of the distinction between the two terms in a distribution channel context, see Stern (1971). For an excellent comprehensive review of the controversy, see Fink (1968).

## REFERENCES

Alderson, W. (1957), *Marketing Behavior and Executive Action*, Homewood, IL: Irwin.

Aldrich, H. A. (1979), *Organizations and Environments*, Englewood Cliffs, NJ: Prentice-Hall, Inc.

Arndt, J. and T. Reve (1979), "Innovativeness in Vertical Marketing Systems," in *Proceedings of Fourth Macro Marketing Conference*, P. White & G. Fisk, eds., Boulder CO: University of Colorado Press.

Arrow, K. J. (1974), *Limits of Organizations*, New York: John Wiley and Sons.

Baligh, H. H. and L. E. Richartz (1967), *Vertical Market Structures*, Boston: Allyn and Bacon.

Benson, J. K. (1975), "The Interorganizational Network as a Political Economy," *Administrative Science Quarterly*, 20 (June), 229-249.

Blois, K. (1972), "Vertical Quasi-Integration," *Journal of Industrial Economics*, 20 (July), 253-260.

Bonoma, T. V. (1976), "Conflict, Cooperation and Trust in Three Power Systems," *Behavioral Science*, 21 (November), 499-514.

Bucklin, L. P. (1966), *A Theory of Distribution Channel Structure*, Berkeley, CA: Institute of Business and Economic Research, University of California.

——— and J. M. Carman (1974), "Vertical Market Structure Theory and the Health Care Delivery System," in *Marketing Analysis of Societal Problems*, J. N. Sheth and P. L. Wright, eds., Urbana-Champaign, IL: Bureau of Economic and Business Research, 7-41.

Coser, L. A. (1956), *The Functions of Social Conflict*, Glencoe, IL: Free Press.

Cox, R., C. Goodman and T. Fichandler (1965), *Distribution in a High Level Economy*, Englewood Cliffs, NJ: Prentice-Hall, Inc.

El-Ansary, A. and L. W. Stern (1972), "Power Measurement in the Distribution Channel," *Journal of Marketing Research*, 9 (February), 47-52.

Emerson, R. M. (1962), "Power-Dependence Relations," *American Sociological Review*, 27 (February), 31-41.

——— (1972), "Exchange Theory, Part II: Exchange Relations and Network Structures," in *Sociological Theories in Progress*, J. Berger, M. Zelditch Jr., and A. Anderson, eds., Boston: Houghton Mifflin.

Etgar, M. (1976a), "The Effect of Administrative Control on Efficiency of Vertical Marketing Systems," *Journal of Marketing Research*, 13 (February), 12-24.

——— (1976b), "Channel Domination and Countervailing Power in Distribution Channels," *Journal of Marketing Research*, 13 (August), 254-262.

——— (1977), "Channel Environment and Channel Leadership," *Journal of Marketing Research*, 14 (February), 69-76.

——— (1978), "Differences in the Use of Manufacturer Power in Conventional and Contractual Channels," *Journal of Retailing*, 54 (Winter), 49-62.

Evan, W. M. (1965), "Toward a Theory of Inter-Organizational Relations," *Management Science*, 11 (August), B-217-230.

Fink, C. F. (1968), "Some Conceptual Difficulties in the Theory of Social Conflict," *Journal of Conflict Resolution*, 12 (December), 412-460.

Frazier, G. L. and J. R. Brown (1978), "Use of Power in the Interfirm Influence Process," in *Proceedings*, Eighth Annual Albert Haring Symposium, Indiana University, 6-30.

Frey, B. S. (1978), *Modern Political Economy*, Oxford, England: Martin Robertson.

Gattorna, J. (1978), "Channels of Distribution," *European Journal of Marketing*, 12, 7, 471-512.

Gronhaug, K. and T. Reve (1979), "Economic Performance in Vertical Marketing Systems," *Proceedings of Fourth Macro Marketing Conference*, P. White and G. Fisk, eds., Boulder: University of Colorado Press.

Guetzkow, H. (1966), "Relations Among Organizations," in *Studies in Organizations*, R. V. Bowers, ed., Athens, GA: University of Georgia Press, 13-44.

Gurr, T. R. (1970), *Why Men Rebel*, Princeton, NJ: Prenceton University Press.

Hernes, G., editor (1978), *Forhandlingsokonomi og Blandingsadministrasjon*, Bergen, Norway: Universitetsforlaget.

Hunt, S. D. and J. R. Nevin (1974), "Power in a Channel of Distribution: Sources and Consequences," *Journal of Marketing Research*, 11 (May), 186-193.

Jennergren, L. P. (1979), "Decentralization in Organizations," to appear in *Handbook of Organizational Design*, P. G. Nystrom and W. H. Starbuck, eds., Amsterdam: Elsevier.

Kaplan, M. A. (1957), "Balance of Power, Bipolar and Other Models of International Systems," *American Political Science Review*, 51 (September), 684-695.

Korpi, W. (1974), "Conflict and the Balance of Power," *Acta Sociologica*, 17, 2, 99-114.

Kriesberg, L. (1952), "The Retail Furrier: Concepts of Security and Success," *American Journal of Sociology*, 58 (March), 478-485.

——— (1955), "Occupational Control Among Steel Distributors," *American Journal of Sociology*, 61 (November), 203-212.

Liebeler, W. J. (1976), "Integration and Competition," in *Vertical Integration in the U.S. Oil Industry*, E. Mitchell, ed., Washington, DC: American Enterprise Institute for Public Policy Research, 5-34.

Lindblom, C. E. (1977), *Politics and Markets*, New York: Basic Books.

Lusch, R. F. (1976), "Sources of Power: Their Impact on Intrachannel Conflict," *Journal of Marketing Research*, 13 (November), 382-390.

McCammon, B. C. Jr. (1970), "Perspectives for Distribution Programming," in *Vertical Market Systems*, L. P. Bucklin, ed., Glenview, IL: Scott, Foresman, 32-51.

——— and A. D. Bates (1965), "The Emergence and Growth of Contractually Integrated Channels in the American Economy," in *Economic Growth, Competition, and World Markets*, P. D. Bennett, ed., Chicago: American Marketing Association, 496-515.

——— and R. W. Little (1965), "Marketing Channels: Analytical Systems and Approaches," in *Science in Marketing*, G. Schwartz, ed., New York: John Wiley and Sons, 321-384.

———, A. D. Bates and J. D. Guiltinan (1971), "Alternative Models for Programming Vertical Marketing Networks," in *New Essays in Marketing Theory*, G. Fisk, ed., Boston: Allyn and Bacon, 333-358.

McVey, P. (1960), "Are Channels of Distribution What the Textbooks Say?" *Journal of Marketing*, 24 (January), 61-65.

Palamountain, J. C. Jr. (1955), *The Politics of Distribution*, Cambridge, MA: Harvard University Press.

Pfeffer, J. and G. R. Salancik (1978), *The External Control of Organizations*, New York: Harper & Row.

Phillips, L. (1980), *The Study of Collective Behavior in Marketing: Methodological Issues In the Use of Key Informants*, unpublished doctoral dissertation, Evanston, IL: Northwestern University.

Porter, M. (1974), "Consumer Behavior, Retailer Power, and Market Performance in Consumer Goods Industries," *Review of Economics and Statistics*, 56 (November), 419-436.

Raven, B. H. and A. W. Kruglanski (1970), "Conflict and Power," in *The Structure of Conflict*, P. Swingle, ed., New York: Academic Press, 69-109.

Reve, T. and L. W. Stern (1979), "Interorganizational Relations in Marketing Channels," *Academy of Management Review*, 4 (July), 405-416.

Scherer, F. M. (1970), *Industrial Market Structure and Economic Performance*, Skokie, IL: Rand McNally.

Schmidt, S. M. and T. A. Kochan (1972), "Conflict: Toward Conceptual Clarity," *Administrative Science Quarterly*, 17 (September), 359-370.

Stern, L. W., editor (1969), *Distribution Channels: Behavioral Dimensions*, Boston: Houghton Mifflin.

——— (1971), "Antitrust Implications of a Sociological Interpretation of Competition, Conflict, and Cooperation in the Marketplace," *The Antitrust Bulletin*, 16 (Fall), 509-530.

——— and A. I. El-Ansary (1977), *Marketing Channels*, Englewood Cliffs, NJ: Prentice-Hall, Inc.

——— and R. H. Gorman (1969), "Conflict in Distribution Channels: An Exploration," in *Distribution Channels: Behavioral Dimensions*, L. W. Stern, ed., Boston: Houghton Mifflin, 156-175.

———, R. A. Schulz and J. R. Grabner (1973), "The Power Base-Conflict Relationship: Preliminary Findings," *Social Science Quarterly*, 54 (September), 412-419.

Sturdivant, F. D. (1966), "Determinants of Vertical Integration in Channel Systems," in *Science, Technology and Marketing*, R. M. Hass, ed., Chicago: American Marketing Association, 472-479.

Terreberry, S. (1968), "The Evolution of Organizational Environments," *Administrative Science Quarterly*, 12 (March), 590-613.

Thomas, K. (1976), "Conflict and Conflict Management," in *Handbook of Industrial and Organizational Psychology*, M. D. Dunnette, ed., Chicago: Rand McNally, 889-935.

Thompson, J. D. (1967), *Organizations in Action*, New York: McGraw Hill.

Thorelli, H. B. (1965), "The Political Economy of the Firm: Basis for a New Theory of Competition?" *Schweizerische Zeitschrift fur Volkwirtschaft und Statistik*, 101, 3, 248-262.

Tivey, L. (1978), *The Politics of the Firm*, Oxford: Martin Robertson.

Van de Ven, A., D. Emmett and R. Koenig, Jr. (1974), "Framework for Interorganizational Analysis," *Organization and Administrative Sciences*, 5 (Spring), 113-129.

Wamsley, G. and M. Zald (1973), "The Political Economy of Public Organizations," *Public Administration Review*, 33 (January-February), 62-73.

——— and ——— (1976), *The Political Economy of Public Organizations*, Bloomington, IN: Indiana University Press.

Weik, J. (1972), "Discrepant Perceptions in Vertical Marketing Systems," in *1971 Combined Proceedings*, F. Allvine, ed., Chicago: American Marketing Association, 181-188.

Wilkinson, I. (1973), "Power in Distribution Channels," *Cranfield Research Papers in Marketing and Logistics*, Cranfield, England: Cranfield School of Management.

Williamson, O. E. (1975), *Markets and Hierarchies: Analysis and Antitrust Implications*, New York: Free Press.

Wittreich, W. (1962), "Misunderstanding the Retailer," *Harvard Business Review*, 40 (May-June), 147-155.

Yuchtman, E. and S. Seashore (1967), "A System Resources Approach to Organizational Effectiveness," *American Sociological Review*, 33 (December), 891-903.

Zald, M. (1970a), "Political Economy: A Framework for Comparative Analysis," in *Power in Organizations*, M. Zald, ed., Nashville: Vanderbilt University Press, 221-261.

——— (1970b), *Organizational Change: The Political Economy of the YMCA*, Chicago: University of Chicago Press.

# 41 — The Theory of Power and Conflict in Channels of Distribution

*John F. Gaski*

Reprinted from *Journal of Marketing*, published by the American Marketing Association, Vol. 48 (Summer 1984), pp. 9-29. Reprinted by permission.

For about a decade the phenomena of power and conflict in channels of distribution have been given rather regular, empirical attention in the marketing literature, both separately and as a joint occurrence (e.g., Brown and Frazier 1978; Dwyer 1980; El-Ansary 1975; El-Ansary and Stern 1972; Etgar 1976b, 1978b; Hunt and Nevin 1974; Lusch 1976a, 1977; Rosenberg and Stern 1971; Stern, Sternthal, and Craig 1973; Walker 1972; Wilkinson 1974, 1979). Each published article on the subject, naturally, has developed a different aspect of what may be called ''channel power and conflict theory.'' For instance, the relationship between power and conflict, especially the impact of one channel member's power on the amount of intrachannel conflict that is present, seems to be of particular interest. Based on reported findings, it apears that the nature and sources of the power possessed by a channel entity may affect the presence and level of conflict (as well as other behavioral variables) within the channel (Brown and Frazier 1978; Dwyer 1980; Hunt and Nevin 1974; Lusch 1976a, 1977; Walker 1972).

While it is arguable whether the relationships among power, conflict, and other channel constructs have been refined enough to qualify this research stream for location in the maturity phase of its ''theoretical life-cycle'' (see Bettman, Kassarjian, and Lutz 1978, pp. 194-5), even if channel power and conflict theory is merely approaching maturity, this may be an appropriate time to take inventory of what has been done in the area. For this purpose, the following review provides (1) an exposition of the pertinent conceptual background, (2) an integrated presentation of empirical results from the channel literature, and (3) some proposals for theoretical refinement.

## Power: Definition and Elaboration

Although many behavioral scientists express despair about the arcane nature of power and the difficulty encountered in attempting to define it, understanding of the concept actually seems to be fairly consistent throughout the literature. Consider the following:

> *A* has power over *B* to the extent that *A* can get *B* to do something that *B* would not otherwise do (Dahl 1957).
>
> The power of actor *A* over actor *B* is the amount of resistance on the part of *B* which can be potentially overcome by *A* (Emerson 1962).
>
> When an agent, *O*, performs an act resulting in some change in another agent, *P*, we say that *O* influences *P*. If *O* has the capability of influencing *P*, we say that *O* has power over *P* (Cartwright 1965).

Clearly, there is considerable agreement among the authors of these frequently cited definitions of power. As an expression of the underlying theme, ''the ability to evoke a change in another's behavior'' is hereby proposed. In other words, power is the ability to cause someone to do something he/she would not have done otherwise. Essential concurrence is offered by others who define power as

> ... an asymmetrical relation between the behavior of two persons ... how a change in the behavior of one (the influencer) alters the behavior of the other (the influencee) (Simon 1953).
>
> ... anything that establishes and maintains the control of man over man (Morgenthau 1960).

Naturally, all the conceptualizations of power listed above are not identical. But if the ability to get someone to do something he/she would not have done otherwise is allowed as the central essence of the power phenomenon (actually social power, since humans are the designated targets), agreement can be and has been reached concerning application of the concept to a marketing context:

> Power refers to the ability of one channel member to induce another channel member to change its behavior in favor of the objectives of the channel member exerting influence (Wilemon 1972).
>
> [P]ower can be regarded as the ability of a firm to affect another's decision making and/or overt behavior (Wilkinson 1974).

Finally, according to El-Ansary and Stern (1972):

> ... the power of a channel member [is] his ability to control the decision variables in the marketing strategy of another member in a given channel at a different level of distribution. For this control to qualify as power, it should be different from the influenced member's original level of control over his own marketing strategy.

It is the El-Ansary and Stern version that will be operative throughout the following discussion.

## Some Perspectives on Power

The nature of power has been illuminated greatly by the contributions of a number of authors, particularly Emerson (1962) and French and Raven (1959). Emerson has called attention to the relationship between power and dependence:

> ... the power of *A* over *B* is equal to, and based upon, the dependence of *B* upon *A*.... The dependence of actor *B* upon actor *A* is (1) directly proportional to *B*'s motivational investment in goals mediated by *A*, and (2) inversely proportional to the availability of those goals to *B* outside of the *A-B* relation (1962, pp. 32-3).

Thus, not only is the connection between dependence and power suggested, but the components of dependence are specified as well.

More specificity is added by French and Raven in what has become a popular classification of the bases, or sources, or power. The sources of *A*'s power over *B* are the relationships between *A* and *B* from which power is derived. According to French and Raven (1959, pp. 155-65), these are (1) *B*'s perception that *A* has the ability to mediate rewards for *B*; (2) *B*'s perception that *A* has the ability to mediate punishments for *B*; (3) *B*'s perception that *A* has a legitimate right to prescribe behavior for *B*; (4) *B*'s identification with *A*; and (5) *B*'s perception that *A* has some special knowledge or expertness. Reward, coercive, legitimate, referent, and expert are the designations given to each of these power sources, respectively. The perceptions of the one who is subject to the power are obviously of critical importance, and this dictates a brief digression.

Power, like the sources of power, has been described as a relationship (Bachrach and Baratz 1969, p. 101; Cartwright 1959, p. 213; Dahl 1957, p. 202, 1963, p. 40; Emerson 1962, p. 32; Nagel 1975, p. 29; Simon 1953, pp. 501-16)—a relationship defined by the perception of the party over whom power is held. The centrality of such perception has been recognized by many authors, including Bacharach and Lawler (1976, pp. 123-34); Beier and Stern (1969, p. 94); Raven (1965, p. 373); Simon (1953, pp. 510-2); Tedeschi and Bonoma (1972, pp. 3, 32); and Thibaut and Kelley (1959, pp. 101, 122). Representative expressions of the position are as follows:

> ... the power of *O* depends on the perceptions of *P* in terms of *O*'s ability to satisfy *P*'s desires ... (Beier and Stern 1969, p. 94).
>
> (P)erson *A*'s promise of reward to *B* will be effective in changing *B*'s behavior only if he perceives that *A* can truly deliver the promised outcomes (Thibaut and Kelley 1959, p. 101).

Accordingly, power is considered a function of the perception of power bases (e.g., "ability to satisfy *P*'s desires," "promise of reward," per Beier and Stern, Thibaut and Kelley) on the part of the one subjected to the power, or the influencee. Indeed, it may be more correct to regard the perception itself as the source of power. This interpretation of a perceptual basis of power is widely accepted in the marketing channel literature (Beier and Stern 1969, p. 94; El-Ansary and Stern 1972, p. 48; Hunt and Nevin 1974, p. 188; Lusch 1976a, pp. 384-6; Wilkinson 1974, p. 16, 1979, p. 84) and will be accepted here as well, subject to the following qualification.

There is another manifestation of power which is not dependent on the influencee's perception. this may be called ''manipulative power'' or ''ecological control,'' and is based on such methods as control of information, restriction of alternatives, conditioning, or in any way modifying the influencee's environment. Tedeschi and Bonoma provide a good description of the phenomenon:

> When *P* has the ability to control critical aspects of *W*'s environment in such a way that the new environment will bring about a desired change in *W*'s behavior, then *P* has ''ecological'' control over *W* (1972, p. 15).

Obviously, this is not the type of power that has been considered in the marketing channel literature. The omission may or may not represent a serious deficiency. If it is conceivable that one channel member's control over another's information, alternatives, environment, etc., could be extensive and effective enough to amount to a significant source of power, then the perception-based power commonly examined in marketing represents only a subset of power rather than the complete domain of the construct. In any case, the extent of manipulative power may never be known, since it is not clear how it could be measured. The intent here is simply to recognize the existence of the phenomenon, acknowledgment of which has not yet occurred in the marketing channel literature.

## Conflict: Definition and Elaboration

Conflict, according to one authoritative definition, is ''tension between two or more social entities (individuals, groups, or larger organizations) which arises from incompatibility of actual or desired responses'' (Raven and Kruglanski 1970, p. 70). The distinction made between actual and desired responses is suggestive of the common taxonomic practice of separating conflict into two or more categories of phenomena, usually representing a behavioral and a perceptual/attitudinal dimension. Raven and Kruglanski, for instance, refer to ''manifest'' and ''underlying'' conflict (1970, p. 71; also Deutsch 1969), with *manifest conflict* meaning overt actions and *underlying conflict* meaning that which involves interpersonal attractions, interests, and desires.

Others, too, identify both psychological and behavioral levels of conflict without attempting to designate either as ''true'' conflict. Thomas, for instance, specifies a ''frustration-conceptualization-behavior-outcome'' sequence (1976, pp. 894-912), while Pondy classifies conflict into five "stages":

(1) latent conflict: underlying sources of conflict;
(2) perceived conflict: perception only, when no conditions of latent conflict exist;
(3) felt conflict: tension, anxiety, disaffection in addition to the perception;
(4) manifest conflict: behavior which blocks another's goal achievement;
(5) conflict aftermath: post-conflict conduct, either resolution or suppression (1967, pp. 300-305).

Obviously, some minor partitioning can approximate Pondy's or Thomas' terms to the underlying-manifest or perceptual/attitudinal-behavioral dichotomy. It is not being suggested that all the conflict schemata reported above represent the same conceptual dichotomization, but there does seem to be a recurrence of underlying factors.

Definition of conflict in a marketing channel setting has been provided by Lusch (1976a, p. 383), who accepts the "latent-affective-manifest" framework, Rosenberg (1974, p. 69), Firat, Tybout, and Stern (1975, pp. 435-6), Brown (1977, p. 385), and also Stern and El-Ansary (1977):

> *Channel conflict* is a situation in which one channel member perceives another channel member to be engaged in behavior that is preventing or impeding him from achieving his goals (p. 283).

According to Stern and Gorman (1969, p. 156) and Etgar (1979), channel conflict is present:

> ... when a component (channel member) perceives the behavior of another component to be impeding the attainment of its goals or the effective performance of its instrumental behavior patterns (pp. 61-62).

Adopting the consensus, channel conflict will be considered to be the perception on the part of a channel member that its goal attainment is being impeded by another, with stress or tension the result. Terms such as *manifest conflict* and *affective* or *felt conflict* can be applied to the impeding of goal attainment and stress or tension, respectively, but the view here is that "conflict" refers only to the perception that another is being obstructive, with tension the implicit accompaniment.

It has been suggested that conflict is virtually inevitable in marketing channels. Most agree that this condition is due primarily to the functional interdependence between channel members (e.g., Assael 1968; Cadotte and Stern 1979, p. 134; Lusch 1976a; Mallen 1963; Pondy 1967; Reve and Stern 1979; Stern and El-Ansary 1977, pp. 282-84). However, channel conflict may have its origin in an even more fundamental relationship. Mallen (1963) points out the ineluctable conflict of interest embedded in the very act of exchange:

> The act of exchange is composed of two elements: a sale and a purchase. It is to the advantage of the seller to obtain the highest return possible from such an exchange, and the exact opposite is the desire of the buyer... This is not to say the exchange act itself is a conflict. Indeed, the act or transaction is a sign that the element of price conflict has been resolved to the mutual satisfaction of both principals. Only along the road to this mutual satisfaction point or exchange price do the principals have opposing interests (p. 25).

Therefore, since exchange characterizes relations between channel members, so too will conflict.

## Power, Conflict, and the Current Status of Theory

Of those who have recognized a connection between power and conflict, not all share the same perspective. Power has been designated as both the independent and dependent variable in the relationship. Raven and Kruglanski (1970, pp. 87-90) describe the tendency for coercive power to provoke increased conflict in a dyad. Pondy claims, ''Vertical conflicts in an organization usually arise because superiors attempt to control the behavior of subordinates, and subordinates resist such control'' (1967, p. 314). Others focus on power as a result of, or response to, conflict:

> Let one person frustrate the other in the pursuit of his goals, and you already have the germ of a political system. For the one may then try to change the behavior of the other. If he does so by creating the expectation of sizable rewards or deprivations, then relations of power come into existence (Dahl 1963, p. 72).

Some even suggest that power requires the preexistence of conflict:

> In order for a power relation to exist there must be a conflict of interests or values between two or more persons or groups. Such a divergence is a necessary condition of power because ... if *A* and *B* are in agreement as to ends, *B* will freely assent to *A*'s preferred course of action (Bachrach and Baratz 1969, p. 101).

Also see Nagel (1975, pp. 154-56). But there is fairly widespread acknowledgment that the causal sequence between power and conflict can, and does, proceed in either direction. The position is adequately summarized by Stern and Gorman:

> [T]he exercise of power is a major conflict response as well as a cause of conflict.... The issuance of threats, ... usually of an economic nature

> in the case of intra-channel friction, is generally a pathological response to conflict, because threats tend to elicit threats, thus increasing the degree of conflict.... [W]hen one party establishes the use of coercion, the other is likely to respond in kind, intensifying conflict rather than resolving it (1969, pp. 161-2).

Curiously, empirical work in the area of marketing channels, generally of cross-sectional nature (see Table 1), has consistently assumed power to be the causative factor with respect to conflict, as well as other variables. To trace development of the theory of power and conflict in marketing channels, a review of the major contributions to this stream of research is now presented.

## Empirical Contributions

The empirical genesis of channel power theory was the El-Ansary and Stern (1972) attempt to specify the determinants of power. Remarkably prominent considering the absence of significant results, this study failed to establish a relationship between a channel member's power and its presumed antecedents, dependence and sources of power. Attributing the conclusive findings to the lack of a clear power structure in the particular

**TABLE 1. Empirical Studies of Power and/or Conflict in Marketing Channels**

***Cross-Sectional Surveys****

| | |
|---|---|
| Assael, *ASQ* 1969 | Kelly and Peters (AMA) 1977 |
| Rosenberg and Stern, *JMR* 1971 | Lusch, *IJPD* 1977 |
| El-Ansary and Stern, *JMR* 1972 | Brown and Frazier (AMA) 1978 |
| Pearson, *JP* 1973 | Etgar, *JM* 1978b |
| Hunt and Nevin, *JMR* 1974 | Michie (AMA) 1978 |
| Porter, *RES* 1974 | Wilkinson and Kipnis, *JAP* 1978 |
| Wilkinson, *JMRS* 1974 | Etgar, *JR* 1979 |
| El-Ansary, *JR* 1975 | Wilkinson, *JR* 1979 |
| Etgar, *JMR* 1976a | Guiltinan, Rejab, and Rodgers, *JR* 1980 |
| Etgar, *JMR* 1976b | Phillips, *JMR* 1981 |
| Lusch, *JMR* 1976a | Wilkinson, *IJPD&MM* 1981 |
| Lusch, *JR* 1976b | Lusch and Brown, *JMR* 1982 |
| Etgar, *JMR* 1977 | |

***Laboratory Experiments***

| | |
|---|---|
| Walker (AMA) 1972 | Hunger and Stern, *AMJ* 1976 |
| Stern, Sternthal, and Craig, *JMR* 1973, *JAP* 1975 | Roering, *JBR* 1977 |
| | Dwyer, *JR* 1980 |

*All citations are issued in References at end of article.

channel sampled (heating and cooling equipment distributors, a conventional channel), El-Ansary and Stern did provide some guidance, in terms of hypotheses and measures, from which further research could proceed. (For instance, El-Ansary (1975), in another look at elemental constructs, performed a factor-analytic verification of Emerson's ''motivational investment'' and ''availability of alternatives'' as determinants of channel-member dependence.)

Noting El-Ansary and Stern's complaint about the peculiarities of their sample, Hunt and Nevin (1974) investigated a channel with a more explicitly-defined power structure, i.e., a franchise system. They found franchisor power to be a function of the sources of power available, and also reported that franchisee satisfaction is increased when noncoercive sources of power, as opposed to coercive sources, are used. (Noncoercive sources of power were operationalized as rewards, or assistances; coercive, as punishments.) This latter result was replicated by Lusch (1977) and Michie (1978) in automobile channels, and by Wilkinson (1981) in a beer channel. Lusch and Brown (1982) found noncoercive power sources to be inversely related to power, but acknowledged that this result could have been due to problems with their attributional power measure.

In other power-related work, Wilkinson (1974) produced results indicating a weak relationship between power and sources of power in a distribution channel for household durable goods. Etgar (1978b) showed reward and coercive power sources to be positively related to channel power. Brown and Frazier (1978), adopting a different perspective, argued that their finding of an inverse relationship between manufacturer power and certain power sources (reward, coercive, legal, which they called ''influence strategies'') indicates that the more manufacturer power is perceived by dealers, the less those power sources need to be used. Walker (1972), in a laboratory setting, found power to be evocative of dissatisfaction on the part of those who are subject to it, and Wilkinson (1979) developed limited evidence that power can increase a channel member's own satisfaction, but was unable to establish a relationship between an entity's satisfaction and the power to which it is subject. Also, Etgar's (1976a) finding that an administratively coordinated channel produces superior operational efficiency to a noncoordinated system may be interpreted to mean that power has a positive effect on channel performance.

In an effort to extend Hunt and Nevin's findings to a noncontractual channel, Etgar (1976b) surveyed independent insurance agents in a conventional channel arrangement and reported a strong correlation between insurers' power sources and their power over agents' business practices. Other results were a significant, but weak, positive relationship between agents' dependence (on insurers) and insurers' power, and an inverse relationship between agents' countervailing power and insurer's power. The operational distinction offered by Etgar between power sources and agent dependence was, in effect, one between nonmonetary assistances (power sources) and overall financial reliance (dependence). Measures of countervailing power featured insurer dependence-surrogates such as "degree of customer loyalty" and "agent's premium volume," which, presumably, could serve as bases for threats and rewards. Phillips (1981) reinforced Etgar's principal results by reporting a positive association between wholesaler dependence on suppliers (and customers) and supplier (customer) power over the wholesaler. Phillips also identified an inverse relationship between supplier/customer power and wholesaler countervailing power, as well as an inverse relationship between wholesaler countervailing power and wholesaler dependence on supplier/customers. In a somewhat related finding, Porter (1974) found dealer countervailing power to be inversely related to performance from the supplier's perspective.

In another study Etgar(1977) found environmental factors explained very little of the variance in channel member power, which may support (or at least not falsify) the proposition that sources of power and dependence are the principal determinants of power in a channel. Finally, again on the subject of countervailing power, Wilkinson and Kipnis (1978) found a wide variety of business organizations less likely to use coercive sources of power and more likely to use noncoercive sources as the target of influence was considered to be more powerful.

The first to explicitly incorporate conflict into the analysis of channel power was Lusch (1976a). (Walker's previously cited experiment (1972) did reveal that powerful bargainers were capable of securing agreements unfavorable to less powerful bargainers, which is compatible with the hypothesis that the existence of power produces dyadic conflict, though this conclusion was not explicitly expressed. There was also an experimental study by Stern, Schultz, and Grabner (1973) which provided very limited evidence of a relationship between the use of power bases and conflict. However, it is arguable whether this study can legitimately be included in the channel literature since the authors did not couch it in a channel context and, unlike the few other experiments cited, there was no attempt to simulate a channel setting.) In the distributive system for automobiles, Lusch found a significant positive association between intrachannel conflict as perceived by dealers and coercive sources of franchisor power, with conflict negatively related to noncoercive sources of power. Lusch interpreted these results to mean that coercive sources of power increase conflict in the channel, while noncoercive sources reduce conflict. In response to Etgar (1978a), Lusch (1978) acknowledged that the causal direction could well have been the opposite. In addition, Wilkinson (1981), while reporting the same essential relationships as Hunt and Nevin (1974) and Lusch (1976a), suggested that much of the presumed causal sequencing of channel constructs may be erroneous.

In one other study on the subject, Brown and Frazier (1978) also observed that the use of particular power sources by manufacturers ("influence strageties" in their terms) were positively correlated with channel conflict and inversely related to dealer satisfaction.

There has been some other research of note relating channel conflict to other variables. Rosenberg and Stern (1971) reported ''the greater one member's dissatisfaction with another's performance, the higher the conflict level between them,'' referring to distributors' and dealers' dissatisfaction with dealers and manufacturers, respectively. Although based on measures of association, the authors postulated a causal role for conflict. Their principal contribution, however, remains the progress made toward operationalization of channel conflict.

Stern, Sternthal, and Craig (1973, 1975) attempted to test experimentally the efficacy of different conflict management strategies such as personnel exchange and the adoption of superordinate goals. Results were inconclusive regarding the superordinate goal approach, but exchange-of-persons did achieve some reduction in between-group conflict, measured perceptually and behaviorally. Hunger and Stern (1976) in a similar experiment found the superordinate goal to be effective in reducing felt conflict.

Lusch (1976b) produced modest evidence that in some cases, channel conflict tends to reduce dealer operating performance, measured as return on assets and asset turnover, while Pearson (1973) was unable to establish any relationship between conflict and performance, which he measured as order-filling success and turnover. Kelly and Peters (1977) developed evidence comparable to Lusch's, i.e., limited, and Assael (1969), in an exploratory study, found that in the presence of special conditions, conflict may have a salutary effect on dealer satisfaction and channel performance.

More recently, Dwyer (1980) reported experimental results showing a channel member's satisfaction to be strongly correlated with its perception of a channel partner's cooperativeness. If cooperation is accepted to be the reciprocal of conflict (and it is not suggested that such acceptance is universal), then this can be construed as further evidence of an inverse relationship between conflict and satisfaction. Dwyer's other findings, that channel member *A*'s satisfaction is positively related to (a) perceived self-control over decision variables and (b) channel member *B*'s perception of *A*'s power bases, support the proposition that countervailing power ''is a chief contributor to satisfaction'' (pp. 55-7). Finally, recognizing the commonality between cooperativeness and noncoercive power sources, Dwyer's results may also be interpreted to indicate a positive relationship between the use of such power sources and the satisfaction of a channel member subject to them (since cooperation and satisfaction are positively correlated).

Two other recent studies have touched on important aspects of power in marketing channels. Roering (1977), in an experiment, found dependence was directly related to bargaining agreement and inversely related to competitive bargaining behavior. Guiltinan, Rejab, and Rodgers (1980) reported that a franchisee's perceived influence over a franchisor, uncertainty reduction, and provision of helpful information by a franchisor explain a significant amount of channel work coordination. However, since these studies do not directly examine the central relationships of channel power theory as shown in Figure 1, they are not represented there.

### The Composite Model

The above compilation of research findings permits construction of a model of the relationships among power, conflict, and selected other variables based entirely on empirical evidence. Such a model is depicted in Figure 1. (Only findings of statistically significant relationships are included in the model; e.g., El-Ansary and Stern (1972) is not depicted for this reason, in spite of its importance.) The model reflects the uncritical nature of the review, with the validity of all measures and conclusions accepted for the purpose of exposition. It is a representation, then, of the present state of channel power and conflict theory. Some issues relating to the theory will now be raised.

## Methodological Problems

Table 2 is a compact portrayal of the character and deficiencies of existing channel power and conflict research. Some of the more serious of these deficiencies are summarized below.

### Poor Operationalizations

In a majority of the studies that have contributed "substantive" findings to power and conflict theory, i.e., those listed in Figure 1 and Table 2, it is debatable whether some key measures are really measuring what they are supposed to (see Table 2 for details). Power is an especially troublesome construct. Of course, power may be an inherently difficult attribute to measure, but many of the reported operationalizations clearly do not capture the idea of "ability to alter behavior," the consensus definition. Wilkinson (1974) seems to be on the right track, if only his measure of "maximum possible effect" on policies could be accurately assessed and reported by respondents, which is questionable.

### Insufficient Evidence of Reliability and Validity

Most of the reported research in this area seems to be fairly conscientious in providing "content" validity where applicable, such as the lengthy listings of issues pertaining to the domains of power sources, power, or conflict. But there is little beyond this. Aside from the Phillips (1981) paper (which has the construct validation problem as its focus), of the 18 studies incorporated into prevailing theory (Figure 1, Table 2), probably only the Lusch work (1976a, 1976b, 1977) gives adequate attention to construct validation by today's standards. Of course, Walker (1972) was primarily measuring manipulable or observable variables, and much of the work cited above was done before the field acquired such heightened concern over construct validity.

**FIGURE 1. The Theory of Channel Power and Conflict**

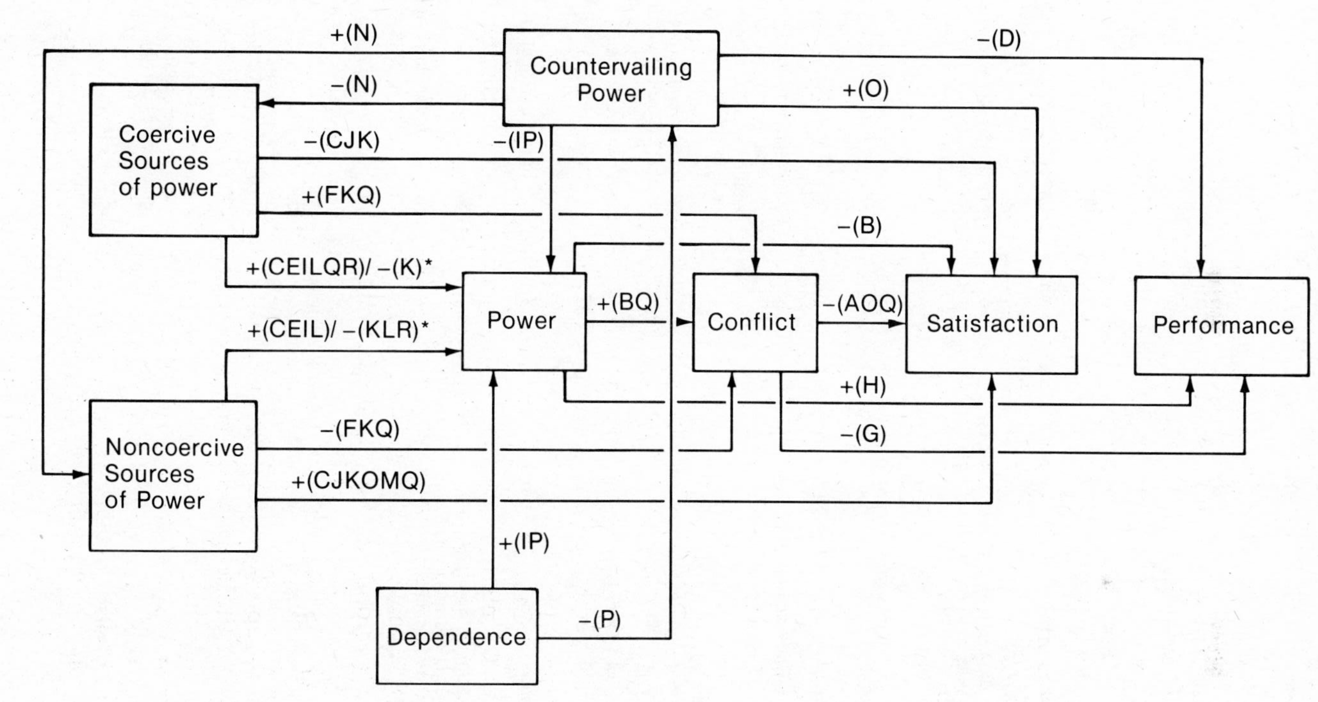


\+ = positive relationship; − = inverse relationship
Letters in parentheses refer to empirical grounds for each relationship:

A. Rosenberg and Stern (1971)
B. Walker (1972)
C. Hunt and Nevin (1974)
D. Porter (1974)
E. Wilkinson (1974)
F. Lusch (1976a)
G. Lusch (1976b)
H. Etgar (1976a)
I. Etgar (1976b)
J. Lusch (1977)
K. Brown and Frazier (1978)
L. Etgar (1978b)
M. Michie (1978)
N. Wilkinson and Kipnis (1978)
O. Dwyer (1980)
P. Phillips (1981)
Q. Wilkinson (1981)
R. Lusch and Brown (1982)

*There is conflicting empirical evidence concerning the direction of some relationships.

## TABLE 2. Summary of Major Power and Conflict Research

| | *Rosenberg and Stern 1971* | *Walker 1972* | *Hunt and Nevin 1974* |
|---|---|---|---|
| 1. Research design | Survey (mail questionnaire and personal interview) of 110 manufacturers, distributors, and dealers of household durables. | Laboratory simulation of manufacturer-retailer bargaining, 76 student subjects. | Mail survey of 815 fast food franchises. |
| 2. Constructs included[a] | Conflict, satisfaction. | Power, conflict, satisfaction. | Power sources, power, satisfaction. |
| 3. Measurement | *Conflict:* Perceptual, self-report. Algebraic difference between mean Likert scale responses regarding perceptions of 32 issues by respondents at different levels in channel, e.g., "Distributor's prime goal is to always increase sales" (strongly agree-strongly disagree). *Satisfaction:* Single-item measure of degree of satisfaction with other channel member's performance (5-point scale from "very satisfied" to "very dissatisfied"). | *Power:* Manipulated experimentally. Balanced power condition—one manufacturer, one retailer; unbalanced power—one manufacturer, two retailers. *Conflict:* Payoffs ($6.00 maximum). Inference can be made that low payoff represents goal impediment, therefore conflict. *Satisfaction:* Semantic differential scale regarding attitude toward partner. | *Noncoercive power sources:* Franchisee perceptions of quality of franchisor assistances (5-point scale, 14 items). *Coercive power sources:* Franchisee perceptions of potential for franchisor to impose punishments (3 dummy variables, 3 5- or 6-point scales). *Power:* Franchisee perception of franchisor control over 7 decision areas (6-point scale). *Satisfaction:* Dummy variable. Whether or not franchisee would "do it over again," i.e., be a franchisee. |
| 4. Validity, reliability evidence | *Conflict:* Content validity.[b] No alpha reported, although Likert scale used. *Satisfaction:* Low convergent validity with alternate measure. | None. | *Power, noncoercive power sources:* Content validity. *Coercive power sources, satisfaction:* None. |
| 5. Statistical analysis | t-test, correlation. | t-test. | Multiple classification. |
| 6. Major strengths | Measures taken from multiple loci in channel; initial progress toward operationalization of constructs. | Internal validity; measures taken from both sides of dyad. | New dichotomization of power sources; initial attempt to test fundamental hypothesis. |
| 7. Major weaknesses | Questionable validity and legitimacy of conflict measure, i.e., absolute difference between scale responses of different subjects; inadequate validity, reliability evidence in general; low response rate; small sample size; no grounds for causal inference. | Highly questionable external validity due to unrealistic setting (severe seller's market with price discrimination allowed); student subjects. | Measures: Power measure does not necessarily measure the "ability to alter behavior," but may measure "actual alteration" of behavior; coercive power sources measure not even face valid; no validation of single-item satisfaction measure. No validation of sample representativeness; no grounds for causal inference. |

a. (of those in the Figure 1 model).
b. adequate sampling of domain of issue.

## TABLE 2. Summary of Major Power and Conflict Research (cont.)

| | *Porter 1974* | *Wilkinson 1974* | *Etgar 1976a* |
|---|---|---|---|
| 1. Research design | Cross-sectional survey of 42 consumer goods industries (19 convenience, 23 nonconvenience). | Survey (personal interview) of 50 suppliers, manufacturers, and retailers in a household durable channel. | Comparison of coordinated and noncoordinated channels within the same industry. Mail survey of 53 direct-writing insurance dealers (coordinated channel), 63 independent agents (noncoordinated channel). |
| 2. Constructs included[a] | Countervailing power, performance. | Power, power sources. | Power, performance (if inference can be made that these are fair equivalents of Etgar's variables "central coordination" and "efficiency," respectively). |
| 3. Measurement | Retailer *countervailing power:* (1) "Convenience store" retailers defined as low in bargaining power because of (a) low contribution to product differentiation through sales assistance, and (b) locational density. "Nonconvenience store" retailers defined as high in bargaining power because of (a) high contribution to product differentiation through sales assistance, and (b) locational selectivity. (2) Within the set of nonconvenience outlets, size of establishment assumed inversely related to dealer bargaining power (because smaller stores sell specialized lines, hence, more contribution to differentiation). *Performance:* Manufacturer rate of return (net profit after taxes as a percent of stockholders' equity). | Perceptual, attributed. *Power sources:* Seven-point scale, from "nil" to "very great" regarding other channel member's "maximum possible" effect on several (5-7) policy areas. *Power:* Same scale relating to effect on policies in general. | *Power:* Direct writing channel assumed high in central coordination, independent agent channel assumed low. *Performance:* Nine technological exchange and behavioral indices: Contact intensity, duplication of activities, activity standardization, product line specialization, speed of flows, communication quality, risk, adoption of advanced technologies, productivity (premium volume per employee). |
| 4. Validity, reliability evidence | *Countervailing power:* (1) Pragmatic/discriminant validity. Multiple regression model unadjusted for dealer contribution to differentiation predicts performance better for convenience channels than for nonconvenience channels. (2) None. | *Power sources:* Content validity discriminant validity (factor analysis). *Power:* None. | Performance indices are observables. |
| 5. Statistical analysis | Multiple regression, correlation, t-test. | ANOVA, t-test, correlation, multiple regression. | Multiple regression, discriminant analysis, t-test. |
| 6. Major strengths | Use of objective measures. | Measures taken from multiple loci in channel; comparison of self-perceived and attributed power (found to be discrepant). | Objective representation of independent and dependent variables; good sampling of domain of dependent variable; attempt to control for extraneous factors such as size, product mix, age of dealership. |
| 7. Major weaknesses | Possibility of other systematic differences associated with independent variable; questionable validity of secondary countervailing power measure. | Less than optimal statistical tests used, e.g., univariate rather than multivariate t-tests; dubious validity of direct comparison of subjective ratings across individuals; extremely small sample; nonprobability sampling renders all statistical tests suspect; no grounds for causal inference. | Possibility of other confounding factors systematically related to independent variable; questionable external validity, i.e., results may be peculiar to insurance industry in California. |

a. (of those in the Figure 1 model).

## TABLE 2. Summary of Major Power and Conflict Research (cont.)

| | *Etgar 1976b* | *Lusch 1976a* | *Lusch 1976b* |
|---|---|---|---|
| 1. Research design | Mail survey of 113 independent insurance agents. | Mail survey of 567 auto dealers. | Mail survey of 567 auto dealers. |
| 2. Constructs included[a] | Power, power sources, dependence, countervailing power. | Power sources, conflict. | Conflict, performance. |
| 3. Measurement | *Power:* Agent's perception of insurer's actual control over 3 policy areas, treated as dummy variables. *Power sources:* Agent's self-report of 4 indicators: Reliance on training (5-point scale), importance of insurer's advertising (7-point scale), speed of underwriting service, speed of claim settlement. *Dependence:* Agent's self-report of 4 indicators of financial reliance on insurer. *Countervailing power:* Agent's self-report of 3 objective indicators (premium volume, number of agencies bought within 5 years, advertising to sales ratio) and 2 perceptual measures (customer loyalty, strength of trade association). | *Noncoercive power sources:* Perceptual, attributed. Dealer perceptions of quality of manufacturer assistances (16 items, 5-point scale from "excellent" to "not provided"). *Coercive power sources:* Perceptual, attributed. Dealer perceptions of "perceived likelihood" of application of punishments by manufacturer (6 items, 7-point scale). *Conflict:* Perceptual, self-report. Frequency of disagreement (index summed across 20 issues). | *Conflict:* Perceptual, self-report. Frequency of disagreement (index summed across 20 issues). *Performance:* Objective measures—return on assets, asset turnover—obtained from dealers. |
| 4. Validity, reliability evidence | Modest content validity. | *Power sources:* Content validity; convergent, discriminant validity via factor analysis. *Conflict:* Content validity; weak convergent validity (.50 correlation with unspecified, single-item alternate measure); .89 alpha. | *Conflict:* Content validity, .89 alpha. |
| 5. Statistical analysis | Canonical correlation. | Multiple regression. | Simple and multiple regression. |
| 6. Major strengths | Introduction of countervailing power construct; attempt to use objective measures. | Large sample, representativeness verified; more attention to construct validity than most other studies; improvement on Hunt-Nevin operationalization of coercive power sources. | Large, representative sample; introduction of an objectively-measured variable; some attention to validity, reliability. |
| 7. Major weaknesses | Invalid power measure (measures *achieved* control rather than *ability* to control); inattention to construct and even content validity; redundant measures of dependence and power sources, i.e., overlapping conceptual domains; no sample validation; no basis for causal inference. | Ignores intensity dimension of conflict, instrumentality dimension of power sources; no grounds for causal inference. | Weak results; no grounds for causal inference. |

a. (of those in the Figure 1 model).

## TABLE 2. Summary of Major Power and Conflict Research (cont.)

| | *Lusch 1977* | *Brown and Frazier 1978* | *Etgar 1978b* |
|---|---|---|---|
| 1. Research design | Mail survey of 567 auto dealers. | Pilot study. Personal interviews with 26 auto dealers. | Survey (personal interview) of 99 retailers of beer, liquor, gasoline, boats, cars, motorcycles, organs, swimming pools. |
| 2. Constructs included[a] | Power sources, satisfaction. | Power sources, power, conflict, satisfaction. | Power sources, power. |
| 3. Mesaurement | *Power sources:*Same as 1976a measure, weighted by perceived instrumentality. *Satisfaction:* Index across 16 items in domain, 4-point scale. | *Power sources:* Dealer reports of percentages of contacts in which each power source used. *Power:* Indicant of dealer dependence—dealer perception of importance-weighted manufacturer performance across 4 decision issues (11-point scale) *multiplied by* dealer report of percentage of agreements to total contacts *multiplied by* dealer attribution of manufacturer cooperation (11-point scale from "no" to "high"). *Conflict:* Dealer perception of importance-weighted frequency of disagreements with manufacturer across 8 issues. *Satisfaction:* Perceptual rating. Seven-point scale from "very dissatisfied" to "very satisfied." | *Power sources:* Index of dealer perception of supplier potency over 8 "economic" and 6 "noneconomic" variables (7-point Likert scales). *Power:* Index of dealer perception of supplier control over 12 policy areas (7-point Likert scales). |
| 4. Validity, reliability evidence | *Power sources:* Content validity; convergent discriminant validity via factor analysis. *Satisfaction:* Content validity; .653 correlation with single-item alternate measure (convergent validity); .87 alpha. | Questionable content validity, i.e., only 4 decision issues? | None. |
| 5. Statistical analysis | Multiple regression. | Correlation. | Multiple regression. |
| 6. Major strengths | Large, representative sample; validity and reliability evidence; incorporation of instrumentality dimension in measures of power sources. | Slightly different classification of power sources; innovative attempt to measure power; incorporation of importance weights in measures. | Multi-channel setting; attempt to re-partition power sources. |
| 7. Major weaknesses | Self-reports of instrumentality of questionable validity; no grounds for causal inference. | Pilot study methodology: Small convenience sample, lack of construct validation. Highly dubious validity of power measure, i.e., one component measures conflict, one measures satisfaction, so naturally it will correlate with conflict and satisfaction measures. Self-reports of importance weights of dubious authenticity; no grounds for causal inference. | Small, nonvalidated sample; questionable discriminant validity between independent variables (economic and noneconomic power sources), therefore, possible multicollinearity; invalid power measure; no grounds for causal inference. |

a. (of those in the Figure 1 model).

## TABLE 2. Summary of Major Power and Conflict Research (cont.)

| | *Michie 1978* | *Wilkinson and Kipnis 1978* | *Dwyer 1980* |
|---|---|---|---|
| 1. Research design | Mail survey of 161 automobile dealers. | Personal interviews with 67 evening graduate students (lower level executives, professionals, accountants, engineers, supervisors) who described critical incidents between their organizations and others. | Laboratory simulation of channel setting (bilateral duopoly) using 80 student subjects. |
| 2. Constructs included[a] | Power sources, satisfaction. | Power sources, countervailing power. | Power sources, conflict, satisfaction, countervailing power. |
| 3. Measurement | *Noncoercive power sources:* Dealer's perceived quality rating (5-point scale) across 17 assistances. *Coercive power sources:* Dealer's perception of "likelihood of use" (5-point scale) across 7 coercive sources. *Satisfaction:* 5-point scale representing "level of gratitude" with respect to 15 warranty-related policies, averaged across the 15 items. | *Power sources:* Content analysis. Ex post facto classification by researchers of incidents reported as "strong" or "weak" influence tactics (interpretable as coercive and noncoercive power sources). *Countervailing power:* (1) Subject's report of relative size of other organization (smaller, same, or larger). (2) Subject's perception of "the effect the target organization could have on their organization's plans, operations, and success" (7--point scale from "very little" to "very great"). | *Power sources:* Perceptual, attributed. Graphic rating scales to express perceptions of capabilities across 5 French and Raven power bases. *Conflict:* Multi-item semantic differential scale (offered as measure of cooperation). *Satisfaction:* Multi-item semantic differential scale. *Countervailing power:* Same as power sources but from opposite perspective. |
| 4. Validity, reliability evidence | *Power sources:* Content validity; discriminant validity via factor analysis, i.e., coercive/noncoercive sources load on different factors. *Satisfaction:* Content validity; convergent validity (.515 correlation with alternate measure); alpha of .93. | Convergent validity for countervailing power measures (both correlate positively with a third variable). | Alphas of .94 and .95 for satisfaction and conflict scales, respectively. |
| 5. Statistical analysis | Multiple regression, ANOVA. | Chi-square, correlation, multiple regression. | Correlation, partial correlation, path analysis. |
| 6. Major strengths | Replication of earlier work in specific-issue context, i.e., examines power sources and satisfaction with respect to *warranty*. | Novel data collection method; sample includes variety of organizations. | Setting more realistic than other experiments; causal modeling attempted. |
| 7. Major weaknesses | Lack of distinction between independent and dependent variables renders results trivial, i.e., power source and satisfaction scales measure the same thing. | Small, nonrepresentative sample; only basis for causal inference is subjects' retrospective reports of order of events. | Still, a lab experiment with student subjects, so an external validity problem; no real basis for causal inference because analysis involves simple measures of association between postexperiment perceptual measures, as opposed to pre- and post-treatment measures. |

a. (of those in the Figure 1 model).

**TABLE 2. Summary of Major Power and Conflict Research (cont.)**

| | *Phillips 1981* | *Wilkinson 1981* | *Lusch and Brown 1982* |
|---|---|---|---|
| 1. Research design | Mail survey of 506 wholesale executives. | Personal interview of 60 hotel retailers of bulk beer, examining 75 brewer-hotel dyads (i.e., some hotels dealt with 2 breweries). | Mail survey of 567 automobile dealers. |
| 2. Constructs included[a] | Power, dependence, countervailing power. | Power sources, power, conflict, satisfaction. | Power sources, power. |
| 3. Measurement | *Power:* Distributor perception of supplier (or customer) "control" over decision variables (global measure). *Dependence:* Distributor self-report of "substitutability of suppliers" (1-item, 5-point scale). *Countervailing power:* Distributor self-report: What percentage of business could be shifted if dropped by supplier (or customer). Also, self-report of "amount of bargaining power" (1-item, 7-point scale). | *Noncoercive power sources:* Respondent rating of quality of supplier assistance (5-point scale) across 8 items. *Coercive power sources:* Respondent rating of likelihood of supplier use of coercive tactics (5-point scale) across 4 items. *Power:* Respondent rating of "how much influence the brewery has on their hotel's decision-making" (5-point scale) across 7 policy areas. *Conflict:* Respondent rating of frequency of disagreement with supplier (5-point scale) across 14 issues. *Satisfaction:* Respondent rating of degree of satisfaction (5-point scale) averaged across 8 aspects of supplier performance. | *Noncoercive power sources:* Dealer perceptions of quality of manufacturer assistances (5-point scale from "excellent" to "not provided") *multiplied by* evaluation of importance (4-point scale from "highly important" to "below averge importance") summed over 16 items. *Coercive power sources:* Dealer perceptions of "perceived likelihood" of application of punishments by manufacturer (7-point scale) *multiplied by* evaluation of importance (4-point scale from "very damaging" to "of little damage") summed over 6 items. *Power:* Dealer rating of "extent of manufacturer control" (4-point scale) across 15 decision variables, decomposed into four power factors. |
| 4. Validity reliability evidence | Strong test of validity using multitrait-multimethod analysis and LISREL analysis of covariance methodology. Convergent, discriminant validity present only when "methods factors" (informant position) modeled. | Cronbach's alpha reported for each scale: *Noncoercive power sources*, .82; *coercive power sources*, .60; *power*, .70; *conflict*, .85; *satisfaction*, .82. | *Power sources:* Content validity; convergent, discriminant validity via factor analysis. *Power:* Content validity; split-half reliability of power factors; alphas of .82, .70, .56, and .46 for power factors. |
| 5. Statistical analysis | Correlation (for purposes of testing relationships among power constructs). | Correlation, stepwise regression, multiple regression (presented as quasi-path analysis). | Multiple regression, correlation, multiple classification. |
| 6. Major strengths | Demonstration of invalidity of informant reports of channel constructs. | Replication of previous work; calling attention to possible alternative causal ordering of variables. | Large sample, inclusion of evaluative component in power source measure and examination of its explanatory contribution; acknowledgment of invalidity of power measure and attempt to explain inverse relationship between noncoercive power sources and power. |
| 7. Major weaknesses | Poor measures. Power operationalized ambiguously as "control" which allows interpretation as either "power" or "exercised power" (see *Power: The Exercised-Unexercised Dimension* section). | Small sample; poor measures (once again, power scale may be measuring *exercised* power, even if respondents capable of assessment); no evidence of validity; weak analysis; no real grounds for causal inference with either alternative model. | Face-invalid power measure: "Extent of control" may capture *actual* alteration of behavior (exercised power) rather than *ability* to alter behavior (power). Also questionable whether respondents are capable of accurate answers. |

a. (of those in the Figure 1 model).

## Informant Bias

Nearly all the research reviewed here has utilized what is known as "key informant" data collection methodology, in which "the social scientist obtains information about the group under study through a member who occupies such a role as to be well-informed" (Campbell 1955). Some limited justification for the technique is found in Campbell and also Seidler (1974).

Unfortunately, as Phillips (1981) has shown, such methodology is extremely undependable and may have produced biased results all along. In a seminal study, Phillips demonstrated that key informant reports of organizational characteristics such as power (operationalized as "control"), dependence, and countervailing power are highly dependent on the position of the respondent in the organization. Therefore, "informant reports on organizational characteristics often fail to serve as highly valid indicators of the concepts they intend to represent" (pp. 408-9). This may be the most serious of the methodological indictments of channel power and conflict research.

## Inadequate Statistical Analysis

In most of the studies cited there has been little reluctance to presume the causal ordering of variables, in spite of the fact that the predominant method of analysis has been simple measures of association with survey data. (The only occasions in which variables were manipulated experimentally, Walker (1972) and Dwyer (1980), suffer from greater than usual problems of external validity due to the enormous gulf between laboratory and channel settings.) Other than Dwyer's (1980, pp. 58-61) and Wilkinson's (1981) modest efforts at path analysis (the former involving a gross leap of faith regarding the temporal sequence of variables), there has been no attempt to apply causal modeling techniques to channel power and conflict research. (Phillips, as cited above, did employ the LISREL structural equation program, but not for the purpose of isolating causal relationships among constructs.) Considering the revolution that is taking place in causal inference methodology in marketing research (see Bagozzi 1980, *Marketing News* 1981), if this development also represents the wave of the future in channel research, perhaps this area will also be revolutionized.

## Conclusion

In view of the severe methodological shortcomings permeating channel power and conflict research to which none of the work cited, even the most central and seminal, has been immune, serious questions must be raised concerning just what can be legitimately concluded about the subject. As an anonymous *JM* reviewer succinctly expressed it: "All fields go through a shake-out period and the mistakes we have made have their parallels in many other fields, [but] if one sums up all these weakneses, there is some question as to whether we really know *anything* about power and conflict in distribution'' (italics added). This is an unfortunate commentary on the past decade of research in the area. But every scientific void has a silver lining: As the deficiencies in this area are recognized, perhaps more marketing researchers will regard channel theory as an opportunity and be attracted to it.

## Conceptual Issues

In addition to the numerous methodological problems, channel power and conflict research has revealed the need for some clarification and specification regarding the nature of the constructs involved. The following section is a conceptual discussion, with methodological overtones, of these components of channel power and conflict theory, proceeding from left to right in Figure 1.

### Sources of Power: The Exercised-Unexercised Dimension

Some of the most prominent work in this area is undermined by deficient conceptualization of the construct ''power sources,'' a lapse that may have resulted in grossly misleading findings.

Among the most central relationships of channel power and conflict theory are those developed by Hunt and Nevin (1974) and Lusch (1976a) regarding the impact of sources of power on conflict and satisfaction. In particular, Hunt and Nevin found that noncoercive sources of power increase satisfaction, while coercive sources of power reduce satisfaction within the marketing channel. Lusch reported that noncoercive sources of power reduce intrachannel conflict and coercive sources increase conflict. These results, of course, are perfectly consistent with the intuitive sense that coercive power sources (punishments) would tend to increase conflict and reduce satisfaction on the part of channel members subject to them, while noncoercive sources (rewards, as operationalized by Hunt and Nevin and Lusch) would do the opposite. However, the relationships identified were somewhat weaker than might be expected, and this may have been due to the operationalization of the independent variables in a way that did not distinguish betwen exercised (or activated) and unexercised (or latent) sources of power. If sources of power are present but application is withheld, the consequences may be far different from, or perhaps the opposite of, what would occur if the sources were actively exercised. For instance, the imposition of harsh sanctions upon channel members (exercised coercive sources of power) seems certain to cause dissatisfaction and conflict, while the dormant presence of the potential to invoke such sanctions (unexercised coercive sources) could conceivably be regarded by franchisees or dealers as benevolent restraint. Likewise, the granting of beneficial assistance (exercised noncoercive sources) should be favorably received, but withholding of such benefits (unexercised noncoercive sources) may not be (see Baldwin

1971, pp. 23-7). The Hunt and Nevin and Lusch operationalizations of coercive and noncoercive sources of power, which do not specify whether these are exercised or not, appear to allow the inclusion of such separate phenomena, with potentially divergent effects on the dependent variables, within the same independent variable categories. In other words, the effects attributed to the various sources of power may actually represent the combined impact of exercised and unexercised power sources.

In related research, the Wilkinson and Kipnis (1978) and Brown and Frazier (1978) operationalizations of power sources actually measure only their exercise or application; therefore, no one has yet attempted to specify both exercised and unexercised power sources at the same time. Doing so would allow determination of whether these clearly distinct phenomena have the differential consequences suggested by these propositions and depicted in Figure 2(a):

P1: Exercised coercive power sources will decrease satisfaction (of the target channel member) and increase intrachannel conflict.

P2: Unexercised coercive power sources will increase satisfaction and decrease intrachannel conflict.

P3: Exercised noncoercive power sources will increase satisfaction and decrease intrachannel conflict.

P4: Unexercised noncoercive power sources will decrease satisfaction and increase intrachannel conflict.

It should be of interest to determine whether these predicitons are accurate or if the presence of power sources is all that matters, which is the impression left by the research cited.

## Sources of Power: The Coercive-Noncoercive Distinction

In their operationalizations of power sources, channel researchers have frequently adopted the convention of dichotomizing the French and Raven framework as coercive (punishments) and noncoercive (rewards) (Hunt and Nevin 1974; Lusch 1976a, 1977; Wilkinson and Kipnis 1978).[1] Apart from the possibility of insufficient attention to the other sources of power, i.e., legitimate, expert, and referent, this seems to be a straightforward approach. However, considering the critical element of exercise discussed in the previous section, the matter may be somewhat more complicated. For example, in designing a research instrument to be administered to a channel participant, should the item *providing service* be included to represent a reward power source, or should *withholding service* be used to identify a punishment? Should *prompt delivery* be used as a manifestation of reward, or should the item read *slow delivery* to express a punishment? As Baldwin (1971) says, Is withholding a reward ever a punishment? Always a punishment? Is withholding a punishment ever a reward? Always a reward? (p. 23). He suggests resolution in terms of the subject's ''baseline

**FIGURE 2(a). Hypothesized Effects of Exercised and Unexercised Power Sources**

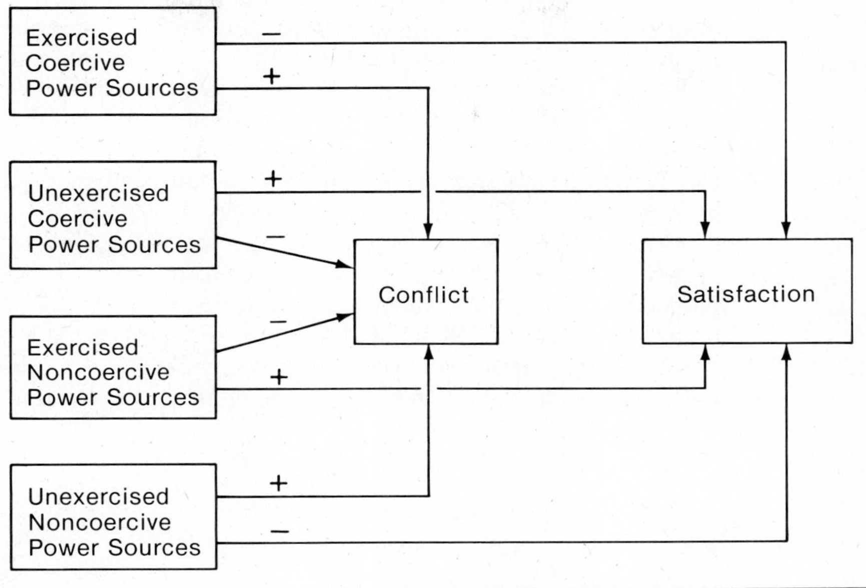


**FIGURE 2(b). Hypothesized Effects of Exercised and Unexercised Power**

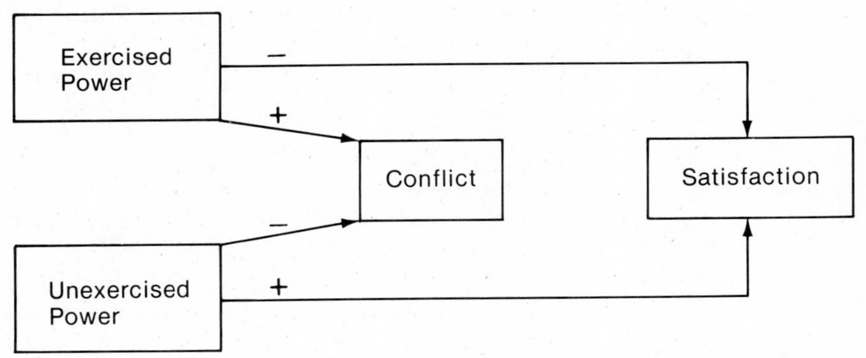


of expectations'': That which improves the value position relative to the baseline of expectations is a reward (a positive sanction in Baldwin's lexicon); a deprivation relative to this baseline is a punishment, or negative sanction.

Obviously, implementation of this approach, which would involve the collection of data on channel members' prior expectations, would also add an additional complication to any research instrument. A more objective, and workable, classification method may be to distinguish coercive and reward power sources on the basis of *latitude for deviation* in a favorable or unfavorable direction. Coercive power sources can be defined as those potential actions with a natural limit in the positive or favorable direction, but great latitude for deviation in the negative direction. For example, delivery can only be so prompt (the natural limit would be instantaneous delivery), but there is an unlimited degree of delay possible. Therefore, the managerial action expressed as ''slow delivery'' or ''delay of delivery'' is a coercive power source. On the other hand, reward power sources are those actions naturally limited in the negative or unfavorable direction, but with much latitude for favorable deviation. An example of this would be the provision of service. The absence of service is the negative limit, but there is indefinite potential for the provision of service. Therefore, ''providing service'' is the proper expression of this reward power source. Some other examples, which should help clarify this taxonomy, appear in Figure 3.

## The Sources of Power-Dependence Redundancy: A Conceptual Refinement

Contrary to expectations, there is little evidence to support a strong relationship between power and dependence in marketing channels. El-Ansary and Stern (1972) found none, and Etgar (1976b, pp. 259-60) saw dependence (by his measure) contributed very little to the explanation of power beyond

**FIGURE 3. Illustration of Taxonomic Distinction of Power Sources**

*Coercive Power Sources*

| | *Unfavorable Deviation* | | *Natural Favorable Limit* |
|---|---|---|---|
| Delay delivery | Infinite delay possible | ← | Instantaneous delivery |
| Take legal action | Infinite amount of legal action possible | ← | Absence of legal action |
| Charge high prices | Unlimited potential for high prices | ← | Free goods |

*Reward Power Sources*

| | *Natural Unfavorable Limit* | | *Favorable Deviation* |
|---|---|---|---|
| Provide service | No service | → | Unrestricted amount of service possible |
| Provide advertising support | No advertising support | → | Unlimited advertising support |
| Train personnel | No training | → | Unlimited training |

what was accounted for by power sources. A possible explanation for this apparent refutation of Emerson is that channel member dependence and sources of power in marketing channels are conceptually inseparable. Simply, any content-valid selection of channel member *A*'s power sources, especially reward sources, should adequately cover the domain of what channel member *B* is dependent upon for ultimate success. Rewards, assistances, and also the absence of punishments, as commonly operationalized in the channel literature, identify the conditions that underlie a channel entity's financial well-being. After all, national and local advertising, salesperson training, sales promotion, pricing assistance, site location, and product line deletions and additions (Etgar 1976b, p. 257; Hunt and Nevin 1974, pp. 188-91; Lusch 1976a, pp. 385-7) comprise a big part of the marketing mix. And although this has rarely appeared in the channel literature (see Lusch 1977), an appropriate importance weighting procedure for these power sources should capture the dimensions of ''motivational investment'' and ''availability outside the *A-B* relation'' specified by Emerson (1962). For example, indications by a channel member (as in survey responses) of ''how important it is *to him/her* for *this supplier* to provide these assistances'' could accomplish this purpose. While such a procedure may be criticized as a combined measure of sources of power and dependence, if it is considered reasonable to operationalize power sources as importance-weighted, then it is also reasonable to conclude that dependence is a component or dimension of these power sources rather than a separate phenomenon.

The following proposition is offered, therefore:

P5: With valid measurement, global or general dependence measures will continue to add significantly to power sources in the prediction of channel power, although dependence alone should be a reasonably adequate predictor of power.

## Power: The Exercised-Unexercised Dimension

That there is a conceptual distinction between *the ability to alter* another's behavior and *the actual alteration* of another's behavior should be beyond dispute. Unfortunately, researchers of power in marketing channels, while generally accepting the former as its definition, have tended to measure the construct as though it were defined as the latter (Dwyer 1980; El-Ansary and Stern 1972; Etgar 1976b, 1978b; Hunt and Nevin 1974; Phillips 1981), or at least employed measures subject to ambiguous interpretation, i.e., asked a channel respondent to identify who has ''control'' over marketing decision variables. Although a powerful channel entity may have the ability to control another's marketing decisions, he/she may *allow* the other to make those decisions, and this may be the phenomenon such a measure is capturing.

While there seems to be a consensus that the term *power* be used to designate the potential or ability to change another's behavior, it is hereby proposed that the term *exercised* (or activated or achieved) *power* refers to the actual alteration of behavior (see Wrong 1968, pp. 677-9). Terms such as *influence* or *control* have been offered for this purpose in the past, but such usage promotes unnecessary confusion. Rather than arbitrarily selecting terms so commonly used as synonyms to designate such vastly distinct constructs, surely it would be preferable to employ more self-explanatory language, such as *power* for *the ability* and *exercised* or *activated power* for *the actual changing*. It is hoped that clearer designation of these constructs will contribute to a greater awareness of the divergent consequences that may follow from exercised as opposed to possessed, but unexercised, power. Analogous to the argument in the section on exercised and unexercised power sources, the following propositions, shown in Figure 2(b), would be worthy of test:

P6: Exercised power, i.e., actually altering a channel member's behavior, will decrease the satisfaction of that channel member and increase intrachannel conflict.

P7: Unexercised power will increase satisfaction and decrease intrachannel conflict.

One distinction needs to be made between the exercise of power and the exercise of power *sources*. The exercise of power sources refers to an activity: the granting of rewards or imposition of punishments. The exercise of power refers to a result or outcome: the alteration of another's behavior, irrespective of the means used to accomplish it. For this reason, the language *activated* or *achieved power* may be preferred to represent the construct.

A natural question at this point is: What exactly is the sequence of events by which power becomes exercised power, by which the potential becomes actualized? The process may be visualized as involving a communication mediator, typically a request or command (Figure 4(a)), which has conventionally been known as an "influence attempt." (Incidentally, there will typically be a communication variable intervening between power sources and their exercise as well, as depicted in Figure 4(b). See Angelmar and Stern (1978) for an elaboration of these intrachannel communications.) Frazier (1980, p. 16) has pointed out that these communication mediators can be implicit, rather than overtly expressed.

It may also be recognized that exercised power represents not only an outcome but a successful outcome. So a further question is: What of an unsuccessful attempt to exercise power, or an unsuccessful influence attempt? How shall that be designated; what are its consequences?

To this, the answer is emphatic: There is no such thing as an unsuccessful attempt to exercise power *when power is present*. Power means the *ability*, not the inability, to alter behavior. Its exercise is at the discretion of the power holder. If an attempt to exercise power is unsuccessful, it is merely confirmation that the power did not exist in the first place. The attempt at exercise, therefore, is revealed as an attempt to exercise nonpower. (Those

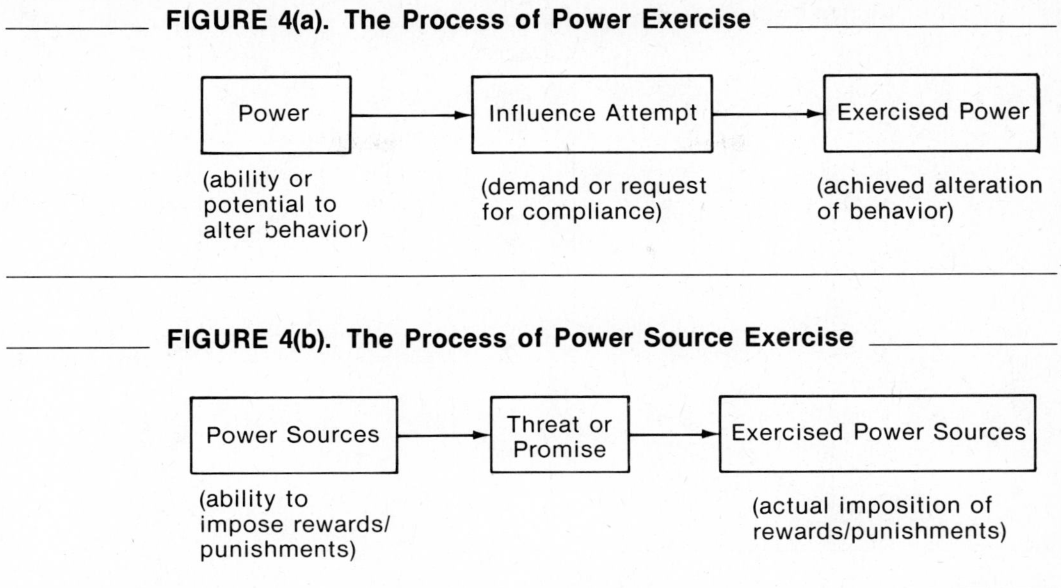


**FIGURE 4(a). The Process of Power Exercise**

**FIGURE 4(b). The Process of Power Source Exercise**

who regard power as a force vector subject to the offsetting influence of ''countervailing'' power, rather than the net of the two forces, will not accept this interpretation. But to those who do regard power as only one force vector, consider that this position is incompatible with the prevailing definition of power as the ability to alter behavior. This ability is a net result of a number of forces, including the power sources of the power holder, the countervailing power of the power subject, and perhaps environmental forces. So if power is a force vector, subject to offsetting forces, then a new definition will have to be found because the force vector could be present without the ability, due to these offsetting forces.)

This point can be visualized with the assistance of Figure 5. Power can be thought of as the ability to alter the behavior of a designated target over a certain set of decision variables, to various degrees, at certain points in time (adding some specificity to the Dahl treatment (1957, pp. 202-3)). Given these dimensions, power can be expressed as a ''volume.'' The fact that $X$ is actually a discrete variable should not impair the analysis. Also, the ''degree'' dimension can be considered to incorporate an importance or instrumentality component.

If channel member $A$ had the ability to alter any of channel member $B$'s decisions to any extent desired at any time, channel member $A$'s ''volume of power'' over $B$ would be the cube $XYZ$. But if $A$ can only alter some of $B$'s decisions ($x$) to a limited degree ($y$), some of the time ($z$), his/her power volume is actually only $xyz$. Within $xyz$, $A$ has power over $B$; outside $xyz$, $A$ does not. If $A$ attempts to alter $B$'s behavior and does not succeed,

**FIGURE 5. "Volume" of Power**

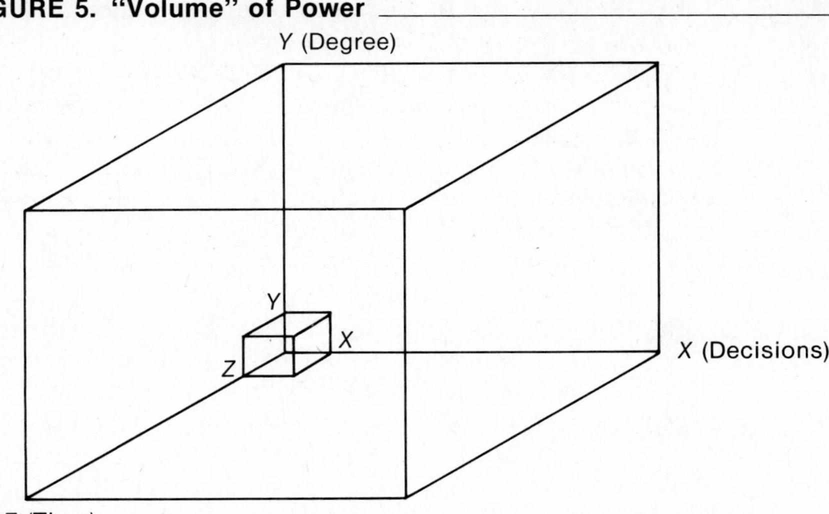


obviously *A* is attempting to operate outside of *xyz*, to influence a decision over which he/she has no power, at least at that time, to that degree. To illustrate, consider any point in the space directly above *xyz*. For *A* to attempt to exercise power over *B* there would result the successful change of the intended decision variable, but only to degree *y*. *A* would be unsuccessful in altering *B*'s behavior beyond *y*. Since *A* was attempting to exercise power or change *B*'s behavior to a degree beyond *y*, this is an unsuccessful attempt to exercise power, actually nonpower, since *A* had no power at that degree in excess of *y*.

At any point directly to the right of *xyz*, *A* cannot influence *B*'s decisions to any degree, and points directly in front of *xyz* represent times, or occasions, when *A* has no power over *B*.

At the least, the foregoing discussion should emphasize that the nature and expression of power in marketing channels is somewhat more complex than has been suggested in the literature so far, and that the current state of research has been inadequate to deal with it.

## Countervailing Power

In the interest of developing better operational measures of countervailing power, better conceptualization of the construct is advisable. An attempt to provide it follows.

Power refers to the ability of channel member *A* to control the decision variables of channel member *B*. Countervailing power is channel member *B*'s ability to inhibit channel member *A*'s power over *B*'s decision variables (perhaps a better term than "countervailing power" would be "countervailing of power").[2] Countervailing power does not refer to *B*'s ability to control *A*'s decison variables. That is *B*'s *power* over *A* and represents a parallel structure (Figure 6(a)). There may be some overlap between the two sets of decision variables, but they are unlikely to be identical for entities at two different levels in a channel.

However, countervailing power does represent power. *B*'s ability to get *A not* to do something *A* would otherwise have done (countervailing power) is formally equivalent to *B*'s ability to get *A* to do something *A* would *not* otherwise have done (power), since both involve potential alteration of behavior. The only operational difference is the target decision variable set. In Dahl's terms, different segments of the "scope" of power would be involved (1957, pp. 202-3; see also Wrong 1968, pp. 673-4).

**FIGURE 6(a). The Parallel Structure of Power in a Channel Dyad**

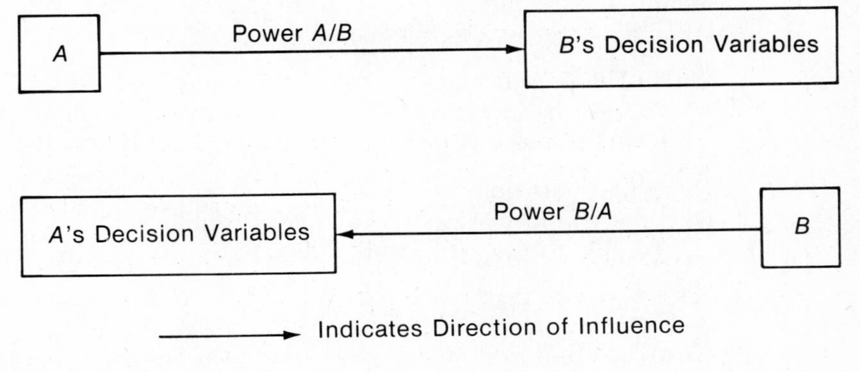


**FIGURE 6(b). Sources of Power/Countervailing Power**

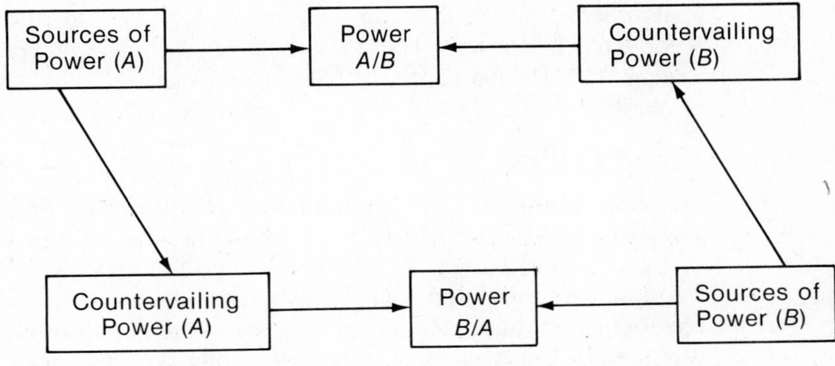

It is also proposed that the sources of a channel member's countervailing power will be the same as the sources of his/her power (see Figure 6(b)). However, in most manufacturer-dominated channels, the range of power sources for a dealer is likely to be much narrower than what is available to the manufacturer.

Since manufacturer or supplier power is typically and correctly measured by the perceptions of the dealer (not that the measures are valid, only the perspective), it is suggested that dealer countervailing power be measured by the perceptions of the supplier. Considering the enormous difficulty in measuring power, as seen in previous sections, perhaps the best approach to the operationalization of countervailing power, as well as power, would be the use of proxy measures such as power sources. Etgar's (1976b) operationalization of countervailing power was actually a surrogate based on sources of countervailing power.

Regarding testable propositions, the Mack and Snyder (1957, p. 212) argument that more diffused power in a system leads to more dysfunctional interaction suggests the following:

> P8: The presence of countervailing power in a channel will increase intrachannel conflict and decrease the satisfaction of the channel entity possessing the countervailing power.

Of course, disconfirmation of such a hypothesis would be consistent with the contrary view that a channel entity with countervailing power will be able to thwart goal impediment and, therefore, increase its satisfaction.

## Conflict, Satisfaction, and Performance

Fortunately, perhaps by their nature, conflict, satisfaction, and performance have caused less conceptual difficulty than some of the other constructs of channel theory. Beyond the affective/manifest issue, most measures of conflict in use seem to capture the idea and domain of "perceived goal impediment." Satisfaction is a straightforward construct, although there has been a disturbing use of single-item scales to measure it (Brown and Frazier 1978; Hunt and Nevin 1974; Rosenberg and Stern 1971). Performance is a variable subject to quantitative specification (Etgar 1976a; Lusch 1976b; Pearson 1973). Although different measures of performance have been employed (see Porter 1974, Lusch 1976b, and Etgar 1976a entries in Table 2), they tend to utilize objective or observable indices that represent, in some way, financial success or factors related to it.

One possible issue to be resolved concerning these constructs which have frequently been related theoretically to power is: which perspective in the channel dyad should they be measured from, power holder or power subject? Conflict and satisfaction are generally represented by perceptions of the power subject (distributor or dealer); performance usually reflects the viewpoint of the power holder (manufacturer or supplier). It would be of interest to also take measures of these constructs from alternate positions in the channel, as has been done on occasion (Dwyer 1980; Rosenberg and Stern 1971; Walker 1972; Wilkinson 1979). This would permit testing of the speculative hypothesis:

> P9: In a channel dyad, one entity's perception of conflict, satisfaction, and performance will be inversely related to the perceptions reported by the other channel entity.

Furthermore, the behavioral consequences of such perceptual disparities could also be examined. For instance, would differences in satisfaction level between a supplier and dealers adversely affect channel performance?

## Conclusion

Based on the belief that channel power and conflict theory is at a pivotal stage of development, this paper has attempted to outline the conceptual foundations and empirical content of the subject area, and to point up some issues that remain to be resolved. The hope is that this effort contributes to a much needed process of refinement by which channel power and conflict theory finally arrives at a mature stage of development, in which the relationships posited are supportable enough to be, among other things, useful to channel managers.

## ENDNOTES

1. Recently (see Etgar 1978b, Lusch and Brown 1982) there has been an attempt to reclassify the sources of power into an economic/noneconomic dichotomy. However, the distinction between these categories of power bases may not be as clear as first appears. Some of Etgar's so-called "noneconomic" power bases (e.g., selection of products, back-up by advertising) are as closely linked to economic results as those designated as "economic" (help in retail advertising, assistance in store management, etc.). And provision of information (one of Lusch and Brown's "noneconomic power sources") can certainly have as direct an economic impact as any other "reward." A dichotomization given to more logical and definite distinction should be preferred, and for this reason the rationale outlined in Figure 3 is proposed.
2. This interpretation is highly compatible with Galbraith's original definition of countervailing power as "restraints on power" (1956, p. 111).

## REFERENCES


Anglemar, Reinhard and Louis W. Stern (1978), "Development of a Content Analytic System for Analysis of Bargaining Communication in Marketing," *Journal of Marketing Research*, 15 (February), 93-102.

Assael, Henry (1968), "The Political Role of Trade Associations in Distributive Conflict Resolution," *Journal of Marketing*, 32 April, 21-28.

——— (1969), "Constructive Role of Interorganizational Conflict," *Administrative Science Quarterly*, 14 (December), 573-582.

Bacharach, Samuel B. and Edward J. Lawler (1976), "The Perception of Power," *Social Forces*, 55 (September), 123-134.

Bachrach, Peter and Morton S. Baratz (1969), "Decisions and Non-Decisions: An Analytical Framework," in *Political Power: A Reader in Theory and Research*, Roderick Bell, David V. Edwards, and R. Harrison Wagner, eds., New York: Free Press.

Bagozzi, Richard P. (1980), *Causal Models in Marketing*, New York: Wiley.

Baldwin, David A. (1971), "The Power of Positive Sanctions," *World Politics*, 24 (October), 19-38.

Beier, Frederick J. and Louis W. Stern (1969), "Power in the Channel of Distribution," in *Distribution Channels: Behavioral Dimensions*, Louis W. Stern, ed., Boston: Houghton Mifflin, 92-116.

Bettman, J. R., H. H. Kassarjian, and R. J. Lutz (1978), "Consumer Behavior," in *Review of Marketing 1978*, G. Zaltman and T. Bonoma, eds., Chicago: American Marketing, 194-195.

Brown, James R. (1977), "Toward Improved Measures of Distribution Channel Conflict," in *Contemporary Marketing Thought*, Barnett A. Greenberg and Danny N. Bellenger, eds., Chicago: American Marketing, 385-389.

——— and Gary L. Frazier (1978), "The Application of Channel Power: Its Effects and Connotations," in *Research Frontiers in Marketing: Dialogues and Directions*, Subhash C. Jain, ed., Chicago: American Marketing, 266-270.

Cadotte, Ernest R. and Louis W. Stern (1979), "A Process Model of Interorganizational Relations in Marketing Channels," *Research in Marketing*, 2, 127-158.

Campbell, Donald T. (1955), "The Informant in Quantitative Research," *American Journal of Sociology*, 60 (January), 339-342.

Cartwright, Dorwin (1959), "A Field Theoretical Conception of Power," in *Studies in Social Power*, Dorwin Cartwright, ed., Ann Arbor: University of Michigan Press.

——— (1965), "Influence, Leadership, Control," in *Handbook of Organizations*, James G. March, ed., Chicago: Rand McNally, 1-47.

Dahl, Robert A. (1957), "The Concept of Power," *Behavioral Science*, 2 (July), 201-218.

——— (1963), *Modern Political Analysis*, Englewood Cliffs, NJ: Prentice-Hall.

Deutsch, M. (1969), "Conflicts: Productive and Destructive," *Journal of Social Issues*, 25 (January), 7-42.

Dwyer, F. Robert (1980), "Channel-Member Satisfaction: Laboratory Insights," *Journal of Retailing*, 56 (Summer), 45-65.

El-Ansary, Adel I. (1975), "Determinants of Power-Dependence in the Distribution Channel," *Journal of Retailing*, 51 (Summer), 59-74, 94.

——— and Louis W. Stern (1972), "Power Measurement in the Distribution Channel," *Journal of Marketing Research*, 9 (February), 47-52.

Emerson, Richard M. (1962) "Power-Dependence Relations," *American Sociological Review*, 27 (February), 31-41.

Etgar, Michael (1976a), "Effects of Administrative Control on Efficiency of Vertical Marketing Systems," *Journal of Marketing Research*, 13 (February), 12-24.

——— (1976b), "Channel Domination and Countervailing Power in Distributive Channels," *Journal of Marketing Research*, 13 (August), 254-262.

——— (1977), "Channel Environment and Channel Leadership," *Journal of Marketing Research*, 14 (February), 69-76.

——— (1978a), "Intrachannel Conflict and Use of Power," *Journal of Marketing Research*, 15 (May), 273-274.

——— (1978b), "Selection of an Effective Channel Control Mix," *Journal of Marketing*, 42 (July), 53-58.

——— (1979), "Sources and Types of Intrachannel Conflict," *Journal of Retailing*, 55 (Spring), 61-78.

Firat, Fuat A., Alice M. Tybout, and Louis W. Stern (1975), "A Perspective on Conflict and Power in Distribution," in *1974 Combined Proceedings*, Ronald C. Curhan, ed., Chicago: American Marketing, 435-439.

Frazier, Gary L. (1980), "Vertical Power Relationships in Channels of Distribution: An Integrated and Extended Conceptual Framework," faculty working paper #686, College of Commerce and Business Administration, University of Illinois at Urbana-Champaign.

French, John R. P. and Bertram Raven (1959), "The Bases of Social Power," in *Studies in Social Power*, Dorwin Cartwright, ed., Ann Arbor: University of Michigan Press.

Galbraith, John K. (1956), *American Capitalism*, Boston: Houghton Mifflin.

Guiltinan, Joseph P., Ismail B. Rejab, and William C. Rodgers (1980), "Factors Influencing Coordination in a Franchise Channel," *Journal of Retailing*, 56 (Fall), 41-58.

Hunger, J. David and Louis W. Stern (1976), "An Assessment of the Functionality of the Superordinate Goal in Reducing Conflict," *Academy of Management Journal*, 19 (December), 591-605.

Hunt, Shelby D. and John R. Nevin (1974), "Power in a Channel of Distribution: Sources and Consequences," *Journal of Marketing Research*, 11 (May), 186-193.

Kelly, J. Steven and J. Irwin Peters (1977), "Vertical Conflict: A Comparative Analysis of Franchisees and Distributors," in *Contemporary Marketing Thought*, Barnett A. Greenberg and Danny N. Bellenger, eds., Chicago: American Marketing, 380-384.

Lusch, Robert F. (1976a), "Sources of Power: Their Impact on Intrachannel Conflict," *Journal of Marketing Research*, 13 (November), 382-390.

——— (1976b), "Channel Conflict: Its Impact on Retailer Operating Performance," *Journal of Retailing*, 52 (Summer), 3-12, 89-90.

——— (1977), "Franchisee Satisfaction: Causes and Consequences," *International Journal of Physical Distribution*, 7 (February), 128-140.

——— (1978) "Intrachannel Conflict and Use of Power: A Reply," *Journal of Marketing Research*, 15 (May), 275-276.

——— and James R. Brown (1982), "A Modified Model of Power in the Marketing Channel," *Journal of Marketing Research*, 19 (August), 312-323.

Mack, Raymond W. and Richard C. Snyder (1957), "The Analysis of Social Conflict—Toward an Overview and Synthesis," *Journal of Conflict Resolution*, 1 (June), 212-248.

Mallen, Bruce (1963), "A Theory of Retailer-Supplier Conflict, Control, and Cooperation," *Journal of Retailing*, 39 (Summer), 24-32, 51.

*Marketing News* (1981), "*JMR* Seeks Causal Modeling Papers for '82 Special Issue," 15 (May 15), sect. 2, 18.

Michie, Donald A. (1978), "Managerial Tactics: An Alternative Explanation of Warranty Satisfaction in a Channel of Distribution," in *Research Frontiers in Marketing: Dialogues and Directions*, Subhash C. Jain, ed., Chicago: American Marketing, 260-265.

Morgenthau, H. (1960), *Politics Among Nations*, New York: Knopf.

Nagel, Jack, H. (1975), *The Descriptive Analysis of Power*, New Haven: Yale University Press.

Pearson, Michael M. (1973), "The Conflict-Performance Assumption," *Journal of Purchasing*, 9 (February), 57-69.

Phillips, Lynn W. (1981), "Assessing Measurement Error in Key Informant Reports: A Methodological Note on Organizational Analysis in Marketing," *Journal of Marketing Research*, 18 (November), 395-415.

Pondy, Louis R. (1967), "Organizational Conflict: Concepts and Models," *Administrative Science Quarterly*, 12 (September), 296-320.

Porter, Michael E. (1974), "Consumer Behavior, Retailer Power, and Market Performance in Consumer Goods Industries," *The Review of Economics and Statistics*, 56 (November), 419-436.

Raven, Bertram H. (1965), "Social Influence and Power," in *Current Studies in Social Psychology*, Ivan D. Steiner and Martin Fishbein, eds., New York: Holt, 371-382.

——— and Arie W. Kruglanski (1970), "Conflict and Power," in *The Structure of Conflict*, Paul Swingle, ed., New York: Academic Press, 69-109.

Reve, Torger and Louis W. Stern (1979), "Interorganizational Relations in Marketing Channels," *Academy of Management Review*, 4 (no. 3), 405-416.

Roering, Kenneth J. (1977), "Bargaining in Distribution Channels," *Journal of Business Research* 5 (March), 15-26.

Rosenberg, Larry J. (1974), "A New Approach to Distribution Conflict Management," *Business Horizons*, 17 (October), 67-74.

——— and Louis W. Stern (1971), "Conflict Measurement in the Distribution Channel," *Journal of Marketing Research*, 8 (November), 437-442.

Seidler, John (1974), "On Using Informants: A Technique for Collecting Quantitative Data and Controlling Measurement Error in Organization Analysis," *American Sociological Review*, 39 (December), 816-831.

Simon, Herbert (1953), "Notes on the Observation and Measurement of Political Power," *Journal of Politics*, 15 (November), 500-516.

Stern, Louis W. and Adel I. El-Ansary (1977), *Marketing Channels*, Englewood Cliffs, NJ: Prentice-Hall, Inc.

——— and Ronald H. Gorman (1969), "Conflict in Distribution Channels: An Exploration," in *Distribution Channels: Behavioral Dimensions*, Louis W. Stern, ed., Boston: Houghton Mifflin, 156-175.

———, Robert A. Schulz, Jr., and John R. Grabner, Jr. (1973), "The Power Base-Conflict Relationship: Preliminary Findings," *Social Science Quarterly*, 54 (September), 412-419.

———, Brian Sternthal, and C. Samuel Craig (1973), "Managing Conflict in Distribution Channels: A Laboratory Study," *Journal of Marketing Research*, 10 (May), 169-179.

———, ———, and ——— (1975), "Strategies for Managing Interorganizational Conflict: A Laboratory Paradigm," *Journal of Applied Psychology*, 60 (August), 472-482.

Tedeschi, James T. and Thomas V. Bonoma (1972), "Power and Influence: An Introduction," in *The Social Influence Process*, James T. Tedeschi, ed., Chicago: Aldine-Atherton, Inc., 1-49.

Thibaut, J. W. and H. H. Kelley (1959), *The Social Psychology of Groups*, New York: Wiley.

Thomas, Kenneth (1976), "Conflict and Conflict Management," in *Handbook of Industrial and Organizational Psychology*, Marvin D. Dunnette, ed., Chicago: Rand McNally, 889-935.

Walker, O. C., Jr. (1972), "The Effects of Learning on Bargaining Behavior," in *1971 Combined Proceedings*, F. C. Allvine, ed., Chicago: American Marketing, 194-199.

Wilemon, David L. (1972), "Power and Negotiation Strategies in Marketing Channels," *The Southern Journal of Business*, 7 (February), 12-32.

Wilkinson, I. F. (1974), "Researching the Distribution Channels for Consumer and Industrial Goods: The Power Dimension," *Journal of the Market Research Society*, 16 (no. 1), 12-32.

——— (1979), "Power and Satisfaction in Channels of Distribution," *Journal of Retailing*, 55 (Summer), 79-94.

——— (1981), "Power, Conflict, and Satisfaction in Distribution Channels—An Empirical Study," *International Journal of Physical Distribution and Materials Management*, 11 (no. 7), 20-30.

——— and David Kipnis (1978), "Interfirm Use of Power," *Journal of Applied Psychology*, 63 (no. 3), 315-320.

Wrong, Dennis H. (1968), "Some Problems in Defining Social Power," *The American Journal of Sociology*, 73 (May), 673-681.

42 — Interorganizational Exchange Behavior in Marketing Channels: A Broadened Perspective

*Gary L. Frazier*

Reprinted from *Journal of Marketing*, published by the American Marketing Association, Vol. 47 (Fall 1983), pp. 68-78. Reprinted by permission.

## INTRODUCTION

Sheth (1976) maintains that without a comprehensive conceptual perspective, empirical research in an area tends to localize on a limited set of research issues, thereby ignoring processes, constructs, and relationships of primary importance. This characterizes very well what has transpired to date in the marketing channels area. As Sheth and Gardner (1982) indicate, progress in understanding interorganizational behavior in marketing channels has been held back by an inadequate and incomplete conceptual framework. Empirical research in the channels literature has been very limited in scope, as noted by Stern and Reve (1980), centering primarily on how firms acquire and use power, the causes and consequences of intrachannel conflict, the interrelationship between power and conflict, and channel member satisfaction (see Reve and Stern 1979 for a review).

This article provides channel researchers with a broadened perspective of what research issues need to be addressed in improving our understanding of interorganizational exchange behavior in marketing channels. A framework of interorganizational exchange behavior is developed that attempts to describe and explain the initiation, implementation, and review of ongoing channel relationships. Only the implementation (coordination) of ongoing channel relationships has received any empirical attention thus far. In describing the framework, a variety of research issues are raised and propositions made that must be addressed in future theoretical and empirical research.

## THE FRAMEWORK

Figure 1 exhibits the framework of interorganizational exchange behavior. Previous research on exchange relationships within the marketing literature and related behavioral science disciplines, as well as personal interviews with members from the automobile, medical supply and equipment, and industrial supply channels guided its construction. However, deductive

**FIGURE 1. A Framework of Interorganizational Exchange Behavior in Marketing Channels**

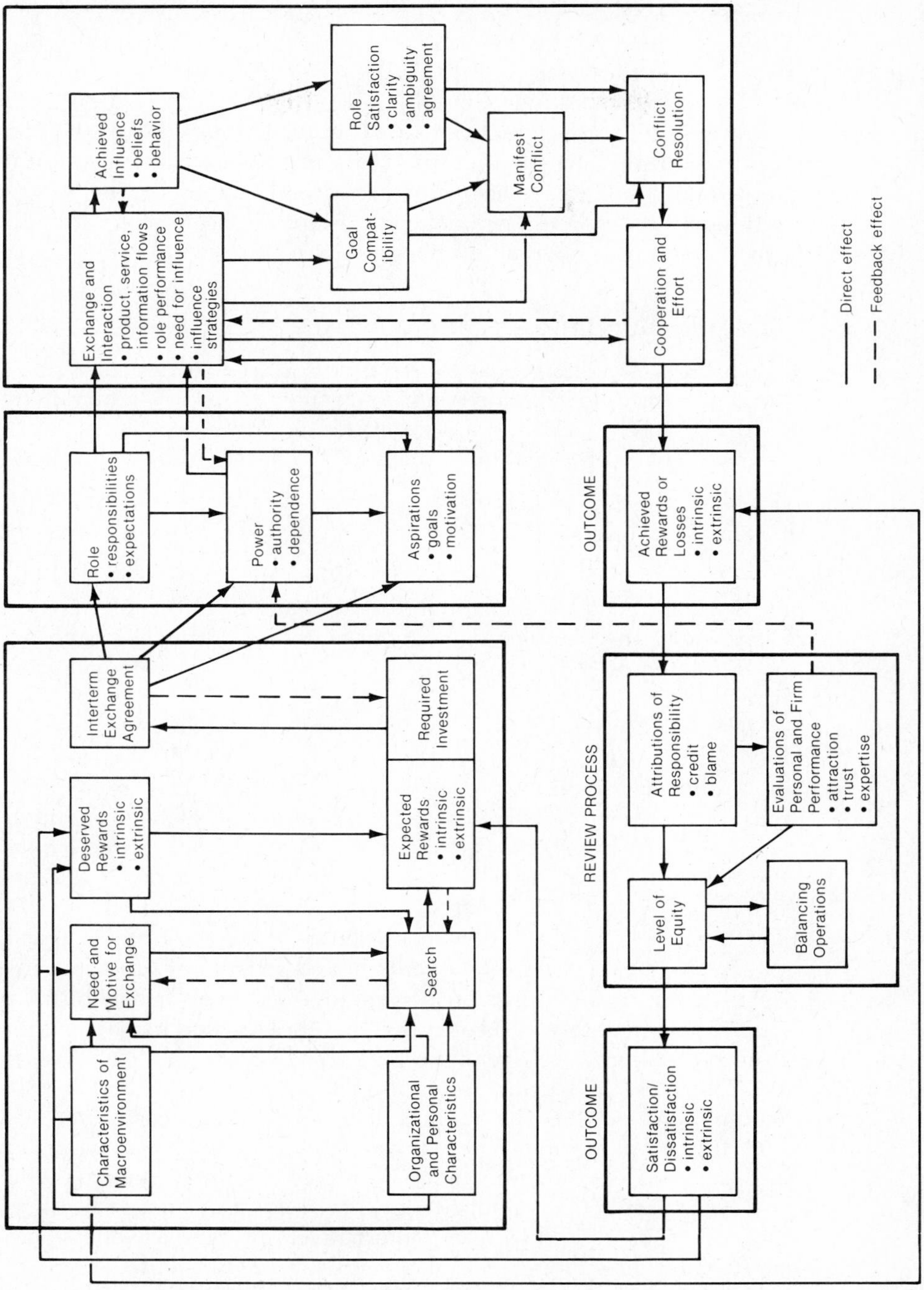

reasoning primarily guided the framework's development in terms of the constructs included within each process and the nature of their proposed interrelationships. For descriptive purposes, the framework will be discussed from the viewpoint of a representative of one firm, referred to as the "source," initiating, implementing, and reviewing an exchange relationship with a representative of another firm, referred to as the "target."[1] While the framework is presented in a sequential fashion, the initiation, implementation, and review processes are highly interactive. What occurs within any one process will have important implications for the other two processes and the overall exchange relationship over time.

## The Initiation Process

This process focuses on why and how firms seek to initiate exchange relationships within marketing channels at times. It begins when members of a firm perceive a *need* and have a *motive* to form an exchange relationship (Foa and Foa 1974). This could involve (1) replacing a current exchange partner that is perceived to be unsatisfactory, (2) adding an additional exchange partner who offers healthy product margins or increased volume, or (3) starting a new business or going into a new geographical region where no exchange relationships currently exist. While the source can become aware of the firm's need for additional resources and form the specific motive for establishing an exchange relationship him-/herself, this awareness can also be facilitated by external agents such as sales representatives from other firms or current customers.

When the firm's need is perceived to be intense enough, the source will institute a *search* for viable exchange partners (Etgar 1976b). Initially, "general" information on rewards associated with alternative exchange partners may need to be assembled, possible sources of such information being salespeople and personal friends. This is used in forming an "evoked set," the alternatives that the source sees as potentially acceptable and on whom he/she will collect more specific information (Howard and Sheth 1969). The source will personally contact representatives of the firms in question (or vice versa) and discuss the benefits of an exchange relationship in greater detail. From these discussions, the source will form beliefs of the *expected rewards*, extrinsic as well as intrinsic, that the firm and he/she would receive from each alternative over time (Bagozzi 1975; Etgar 1976b; Foa and Foa 1974; Sheth 1973). Extrinsic rewards include increases in market share, sales volume, and profits. The amount of psychological pleasure received from entering and managing an exchange relationship as well as gaining approval and status within the industry are examples of intrinsic rewards. The source will also form beliefs about the level of *required investment* in time, effort, and money associated with each alternative. The persuasiveness of the alternatives' representatives will play a crucial role in the development of the source's belief structure (cf., Hunt and Nevin 1976).

*Deserved rewards* represent the level of rewards the source feels the firm and he/she ''should'' receive from an exchange relationship, given their involvement and participation therein. As suggested by equity theory, the source will use them as a standard in both forming an evoked set and deciding whether or not the expected rewards from an alternative are adequate (Homans 1974, Lawler and Porter 1967). If the expected rewards from each alternative turn out to be below the level of deserved rewards, the source will usually attempt to find other more attractive alternatives in an extended search.

*Organizational and personal factors,* such as the firm's financial resources and authority structure, and the source's background (e.g., education, business experience) and personality (e.g., need for achievement, tolerance for uncertainty), will influence (1) when the need for an exchange relationship is recognized, (2) the content and strength of the motive, (3) the extent of search and the composition of the evoked set, and (4) the level of deserved rewards (cf., Bucklin 1973; Granbois, Summers, and Frazier 1977; Pfeffer and Salancik 1978; Sheth 1973; Triandis 1977). For example, when organizational time and financial constraints present themselves, the source may need to limit the search and perhaps lower deserved rewards, while seriously considering establishing an exchange relationship with the ''best'' alternative identified thus far. In cases where a source has considerable experience and expertise, he/she may already have a well-formed evoked set and belief structure, making an extended search unnecessary.

*Characteristics of the macroenvironment* can also dramatically influence this process as well as the others (Foa and Foa 1974; Pfeffer and Salancik 1978; Stern and Reve 1980). For example, if competition is strong and the national economy weak, a firm's need for rewards may not be met by its present business. Its motive, therefore, could be to transform its product lines and align with new suppliers, requiring an extended search process on the part of the source. The level of deserved rewards may be lower than in a prosperous company. The availability of alternatives and information, as well as the distinctiveness of the image presented to the marketplace by each alternative, will influence the source's search process and the composition of the evoked set.

When the final decision must be made, the source will choose the alternative that offers the firm and him-/herself the highest level of ''valued rewards'' at acceptable investment and risk levels, risk being reflected by the perceived variation in the level of expected rewards over time (Anderson 1982, Van Horne 1980). This prediction represents an integration of expectancy theory, exchange theory, and financial investment theory. Some alternatives may provide a high level of expected rewards that are very valuable to the source and the firm, but at a very high risk and a high investment in terms of time, effort, and money. The source may be risk averse and the firm may lack the necessary resources to begin such a relationship.

Once the source decides on a given alternative, discussions and bargaining will take place on the specific conditions of an exchange relationship. If the target also decides the source's firm is desirable (for a "matching process" is definitely in play) and negotiations do not break down, an *interfirm exchange agreement* will be formed (Bagozzi 1975, Foa and Foa 1974). It can range from a mere verbal agreement to a formal legal contract that stipulates conditions of exchange and termination (e.g., a franchise agreement). If unresolvable disagreements arise, negotiations will terminate, forcing the source to either attempt to form a relationshp with the next best alternative, continue the search, or reevaluate the firm's need and motive for forming an exchange relationship at this time. This is reflected by the feedback loops within the initiation process in Figure 1. In many cases the initiation process can terminate without the successful completion of any exchange agreement.

***Outcomes.*** When an interfirm exchange agreement is formed, three outcomes result that will influence the ongoing relationship (see Figure 1). Each firm will agree whether implicitly or explicitly to assume a *channel role* with all of its accompanying responsibilities (Stern and El-Ansary 1977). The source and target will also form role expectations about the level of each firm's performance on these inherent responsibilities (Gill and Stern 1969). For example, if the target perceived the source's firm to have a competitive advantage in its industry because of product technology and effective mass advertising, the target's expectations of its performance on these two responsibilities will be relatively high. Role expectations will be highly related to expected rewards in a positive fashion.

A level of *power*, a "potential for influence" on another's beliefs and behavior (cf., El-Ansary and Stern 1972), will be generated for each firm based on two primary factors: (1) authority, and (2) dependence (Frazier 1984).[2] As defined by Robicheaux and El-Ansary (1975), a firm's authority represents its prescribed right to influence or specify certain behaviors that are accepted by the other firm. It is a source of power because merely possessing authority does not guarantee achieved influence on another's behavior if it is not used or not used effectively (Kotter 1977). Any conditions in the exchange agreement that provide certain rights for one firm or obligations for the other will lead to a level of authority for the former. Additionally, based on the channel position of each firm, certain norms or rules of conduct can exist in the industry (e.g., price maintenance) that contribute to each firm's authority.

Dependence theory (Emerson 1962) predicts that one firm's power in a two-firm relationship is based on the other's dependence therein, its need to maintain the relationship in order to achieve desired goals. The higher the level of valued rewards anticipated in the relationship relative to those available in alternative relationships, the higher a firm's dependence (Aldrich 1979, Emerson 1962). Furthermore, the investment the firm needs to put into the relationship in terms of time, effort, and money as well as the perceived costs of switching to and starting another exchange relationship can also contribute to its dependence on the other firm (Cadotte and Stern 1979).

Finally, each firm will develop *aspirations* in terms of goals for the coming year and general motivation levels. The higher the expected rewards and the required investment, the higher a representative will set the firm's goals and the higher the motivation for making the relationship a success (Homans 1974; Vroom 1964; Walker, Churchill, and Ford 1977). This may be particularly true where a firm is basing its entire livelihood on this one exchange relationship. Furthermore, a firm's aspirations will tend to be high when it possesses a high level of power and its personnel are comfortable and content with its role in the exchange.

## The Implementation Process

This process begins when *exchanges* of products, services, and associated information begin between the two firms, ongoing *interactions* taking place between each firm's representatives.[3] In a short time the source and target will begin forming perceptions of the other firm's role performance, how well it is carrying out its channel role. Role performance will influence each firm's dependence on the relationship, as it will influence the level of expected rewards and the rewards actually achieved from the exchange (Frazier 1983). Where the role performance of the source's firm is seriously below prior role expectations, the dependence of the target's firm will be lessened from its initial level.

Because the firms must take each other's efforts into account if they are to accomplish their goals, each firm will have a need for influence in the exchange, an interest in shaping the direction of the relationship through the use of its power (Reve and Stern 1979). The intensity of this need will vary, based on a variety of factors. The higher the level of ideological agreement between the personnel of each firm on the nature of the tasks confronted by the organizations and the appropriate approaches to these tasks, the less need will exist for frequent influence attempts (Aldrich 1975, Cadotte and Stern 1979). The existence of conflicting goals will lead to a greater number of influence attempts than if all goals were compatible. The source will have little need to increase the target's effort if the target's motivation to make the exchange successful is already high. When a firm's personnel possess a high level of ability, aptitude, and managing experience, they will need less assistance leading to a lower number of required influence attempts (Walker, Churchill, and Ford 1977). Pfeffer and Salancik (1978) predict that a firm that shows high vulnerability at one time will face increased influence attempts in the future. Finally, empirical results in Dwyer and Walker (1981) suggest that in "balanced power" relationships, the frequency of overall influence attempts will be increased.

When an influence attempt is necessary, the source will make use of varying influence strategies, i.e., means of communication used in applying a firm's power (Angelmar and Stern 1978, Stern and Heskett 1969). On one hand, the source can attempt to change the target's beliefs concerning the inherent desirability of performing the behavior(s) in question. This is the most appropriate form of influence to seek when a common goal exists for each firm, but where confusion exists as to the best means of attaining it (Frazier and Summers 1984). On the other hand, circumstances frequently arise where the source requires prompt compliance from the target or needs to influence the target to take an action that is not inherently in his/her firm's best interests. Perhaps the target exhibits considerable perceptual biases or shows a general lack of motivation. In such cases the source may try to directly alter the target's behavior without a corresponding change in beliefs. Such behavioral change can be attempted by requesting a special favor, offering special incentives (e.g., a promise strategy), or using coercion and pressure (e.g., a threat, a legalistic reference) (Kelman 1961, Raven and Kruglanski 1970). In general, the strategies used in a direct attempt to obtain a behavior change are relatively pressurized and costly. Where the use of power reduces the level of rewards the target perceives his/her firm to receive from the exchange and/or increases its costs, the target will tend to retaliate and the firm's dependence in the relationship will be reduced (Bacharach and Lawler 1980, Beier and Stern 1969, Foa and Foa 1974). Pfeffer and Salancik (1978) describe possible reactions to influence attempts:

> Organizations attempt to avoid influence and constraint by restricting the flow of information about them and their activities, denying the legitimacy of demands made upon them, diversifying their dependencies, and manipulating information to increase their own legitimacy (p. 261).

*Achieved influence* on a channel member's beliefs and/or behavior results when the firm is successful in its influence attempt. Empirical evidence in Hunt and Nevin (1974), Etgar (1976a), Pfeffer and Salancik (1978), and Dwyer and Walker (1981) suggests that a firm with a high level of power in both an absolute and relative sense will be relatively successful in reaching high levels of achieved influence with associated firms. The selection of appropriate influence strategies and their effective utilization will contribute significantly to levels of achieved influence. Personal characteristics of both the source and target will affect the success of the source's influence attempts (Goodstadt and Hjelle 1973). For example, Triandis (1977), summarizing a number of empirical studies on influence in social psychology, reports that individuals are more likely to conform to influence attempts when they are less self-confident, less intelligent, less original, lower in the need for achievement, and higher in the need for affiliation. Characteristics of the macro and channel environment can also dramatically influence the success of a firm's influence attempts (Pfeffer and Salancik 1978); empirical results in Etgar (1977) indicate that channel leaders exercise more control in their channel when their product is in the maturity or postmaturity stage, its demand is unstable, interchannel competition is high, and servicing customers is of great importance (also see Assael 1968, Lusch 1976).

Whatever the source's influence approach and general intent, it is the target's interpretation of the source's use of power that is of primary importance (Kelley 1972, Regan 1978). If the source is seen to use power in striving for collective goals and does not impede the other firm's progress in attaining desired rewards, a high level of *goal compatibility* will be seen to exist (Etgar 1979). Furthermore, empirical results in Rosenberg and Stern (1971), Lusch (1976), and Brown and Day (1981) suggest that ideological agreement on business and marketing strategy is positively related to goal compatibility. Contrarily, if a firm is seen to frequently pressure the other into taking actions against its best interests, an adverse impact on goal compatibility will result, contributing to the target's frustration (Foa and Foa 1974). High levels of disagreement on appropriate strategy and tactics can arise in such cases, leading to high levels of perceived and affective conflict.

The manner in which the firms are seen to interact will also have a significant impact on *role satisfaction* (Aldrich 1979, Deutsch 1973). If communications between the firms are poor and the source frequently pressures the target into taking actions against his/her firm's best interests, the target can become confused as to the activities the firm must perform and in what manner, and its level of autonomy. Role clarity will be low as a result (Walker, Churchill, and Ford 1977). If the target feels his/her firm does not have enough information and advice to adequately perform its responsibilities, and the source's firm has not provided anticipated assistances, role ambiguity will be high (Walker, Churchill, and Ford 1977). Finally, if the source and the target disagree on the activities under their respective domains, the level of agreement on their roles (domain consensus) will be low (Assael 1968). All of the above will lead to low levels of overall role satisfaction and high levels of perceived and affective conflict.

*Manifest conflict* is characterized by mutual goal interference where one party perceives the other to be blocking its goal attainment and reacts accordingly to block the other's goal attainment (Stern, Sternthal, and Craig 1973). Low levels of role performance relative to role expectations, ideological agreement, goal compatibility, and role satisfaction can lead to frustration and aggression on the part of one or both parties and, therefore, manifest conflict (Homans 1974). In partial support of this, Etgar (1979) found ideological agreement and role clarity to be inversely related to levels of manifest conflict.

*Conflict resolution* is most effective before conflict reaches its manifest state (Sheth 1973). However, even when manifest conflict does arise, its consequences can be functional overall if it is resolved in such a way as to enhance perceptions of goal compatibility, improve role clarity, and lessen role ambiguity and role disagreement. Furthermore, if manifest conflict developed over one member's low aspirations and rigidity, and in its aftermath, his/her motivation and cooperativeness improves, positive consequences can result (Cadotte and Stern 1979, Deutsch 1973). On the other hand, if manifest conflict is not resolved effectively, nonfunctional consequences will predominate. Personal relations can be disrupted; empirical results in Stern, Sternthal, and Craig (1973) suggest that the other firm will be perceived as greedy, rigid, hostile, unfair, deceptive, unrealistic, uncooperative, and lacking in empathy in high conflict situations. Members may resist further influence attempts and try to enhance their power at the expense of the other (Raven and Kruglanski 1970, Triandis 1977). The scope of conflict can expand so it becomes a matter of general principle.

*Cooperation* reflects the firms' ability to collaborate and work together in a joint fashion toward their respective goals (Stern and Reve 1980). *Effort* concerns how much each firm puts into the relationship, their drive to reach goals and make the relationship successful. If the aspirations and role performance of each firm are both high, their cooperation and effort should also be high (cf., Dwyer 1980, Hall and Clark 1975). In such cases, each firm should see value in collaborating on issues of joint concern and show an intense drive to reach desired goals. Guiltinan, Rejab, and Rodgers (1980) show empirically that cooperation and coordination tend to be high when (1) interfirm communications are perceived to be effective in reducing uncertainty, and (2) participative decision making is perceived to take place. Furthermore, the same constructs that contribute to low levels of conflict should contribute to high levels of cooperation and effort; that is, high levels of ideological agreement, goal compatibility and role satisfaction, and the use of power in a nonpressurized fashion (Hall and Clark 1975, Kelley and Grzelak 1972). This is not to say that cooperation and conflict cannot coexist in the same relationship, especially where expected rewards and role performance are high, no alternative relationship is perceived to exist that offers the same level of rewards, and each firm sees value in cooperating with the other. However, in general, cooperation and effort will show inverse relationships with conflict, especially manifest conflict.

Levels of cooperation and effort will feed back to affect the future course of the exchange. High levels of cooperation and effort at one point in time will contribute to a relatively low need for influence, the use of indirect, nonpressurized strategies when an influence attempt is required, and perceptions of goal compatibility and role satisfaction in the future. In cooperative exchange relationships, the chances of serious manifest conflicts surfacing will be relatively low.

***Outcome.*** *Achieved rewards* or *losses* represent the outcome of the implementation process. Each firm's role performance, the effectiveness of its influence attempts, level of effort, and ability to cooperate will significantly affect the level of achieved rewards (losses) (cf., Gill and Stern 1969, Stern and Reve 1980). Constructs such as ideological agreement, role satisfaction, and manifest conflict will have indirect effects on extrinsic rewards or losses while having direct effects on intrinsic rewards achieved from the exchange. Of course, characteristics of the macroenvironment (e.g., state of the economy, competition) will play a major role in driving achieved reward or loss levels.

## The Review Process

This process concerns an evaluation of the rewards or losses achieved by each firm from the exchange. Both the source and target will make *attributions of responsibility* for achieved rewards or losses (Heider 1958, Kelley and Michela 1980). Credit for achieved rewards will be assigned to one or both firms, and perhaps the situation. Blame will be assigned if losses occur or if achieved rewards do not meet prior expectations and goals. The source and target will use these attributions as cues to ascribe characteristics to each firm, thereby influencing *evaluations of personnel and firm performance* (Staw 1975, Varela 1971).

If the target attributes a good deal of credit to the source's firm for achieved rewards, evaluations of its role performance can be enhanced (Kelley and Michela 1980). The target's attraction to and trust in the source and the source's firm can increase, as can their perceived expertise. This will serve to reinforce if not heighten the dependence of the target's firm on the source's firm. On the other hand, if the target assigns most of the credit to his/her firm, that it is successful largely due to its personnel's abilities, resources, and managerial expertise, it can serve to lessen its dependence on the source's firm. The target's attraction to the source can diminish somewhat, and he/she may feel the firm can make a success of any exchange relationship, minimizing the importance of the source's firm's role performance. However, even in situations where the target takes most of the credit, if it is felt that there exists no other exchange relationship where the firm could be as successful, the firm's dependence level would not be affected greatly, if at all. The target will tend to take a large part of the credit when success is achieved (cf., Miller and Ross 1975, Zuckerman 1979). Finally, when the target assigns a large part of the credit for achieved rewards to the situation or external environment, future rewards will be seen as relatively unstable and uncertain; future effort levels can be adversely affected as a result (Weiner et al. 1972).

In relationships where losses occur or achieved rewards are considered inadequate, where the target assigns the blame will have a critical impact. If losses or inadequate rewards are blamed on the situation, but it is seen to be improving shortly, dependence, aspiration, and cooperation levels can remain largely unchanged (Kelley 1972, Phares 1957). If the source's firm is largely blamed, perceptions of its role performance will be adversely affected, lessening the target's attraction to the source and his/her firm's dependence in the relationship. The level of cooperation in the subsequent relationship may be relatively low. A target will tend to blame an exchange partner or the situation for adverse conditions (cf., Assael 1968; Doyle, Corstjens, and Michell 1980; Wortman, Costanzo, and Witt 1973). In situations where the target's firm does largely assume the blame and its managers feel it futile to attempt to remedy its poor performance, the firm's aspirations in the exchange relationship can drop. Personal characteristics will influence the target's reaction to adverse conditions (Triandis 1977).

The *level of equity* perceived to exist in the exchange will be based on two comparisons, each facilitated by the attribution process. First, the target will consider whether or not the firm's ratio of rewards (losses) to contributions is out of balance (Adams 1963, Blumstein and Weinstein 1969). If the firm has put in a good deal of time, money, and effort into the relationship, but achieved rewards do not meet deserved and expected rewards and goals, the target will perceive that an injustice exists. Second, the target will also evaluate the other firm's ratio of rewards (losses) to contributions (inputs) and compare it to his/her firm's ratio (Adams and Freedman 1976). When the ratios are seen to be similar, the level of equity will be relatively high. On the other hand, if the source's firm is seen to reap an undue level of rewards from the exchange, given its contributions (e.g., effort, products, personnel), the target will perceive the exchange to be inequitable. In such cases, the target will typically seek to reduce the disparity in rewards relative to contributions (Blumstein and Weinstein 1969; Huppertz, Arenson, and Evans 1978). This is reflected in Figure 1 by the *balancing operations* component. The target can take direct actions on his/her own and may lower the firm's level of contributions to the relationship or attempt to reduce the rewards received by the source's firm by resisting subsequent influence attempts. Alternatively, the source can attempt to balance the exchange by increasing his/her firm's contributions and/or offering special rewards and incentives to the target (e.g., increased cooperation on product allocation).[4] The source can also attempt to alter target perceptions of what is fair, or stress that the injustice will be remedied by the rewards received in the next period (Pfeffer and Salancik 1978). In most cases, due to rationalization, the target will not perceive his/her firm as receiving more rewards than justified. Those firms lacking alternatives and, hence, being in a high dependence situation, will likely have less equity concerns than those in low dependence situations (Blalock and Wilkin 1979).

***Outcome.*** *Satisfaction/dissatisfaction* with the overall exchange relationship reflects a party's cognitive state of feeling adequately or inadequately rewarded for the sacrifice undergone in facilitating that relationship (Howard and Sheth 1969). It will be influenced by a variety of factors. If achieved rewards (losses) compare poorly to deserved and expected rewards, the target will be relatively dissatisfied with the exchange because it has not provided the firm with what he/she expected and feels it deserves. However, members of firms that possess large amounts of financial resources will be relatively less frustrated and dissatisfied when achieved rewards are lower than expected (Foa and Foa 1974). Attributions of responsibility must be considered. For example, if achieved rewards are poor, but most of the blame is placed on the situation, the target should be less dissatisfied than if the blame were placed on either firm (Kelley 1972). If the situation is seen to be improving, an even lower level of dissatisfaction will result. If blame is placed on the participants to the exchange, but the primary reasons why low rewards were achieved can be remedied, dissatisfaction again can be relatively low. Where rewards are high and much of the credit is taken by the target, his/her satisfaction in the relationship will be relatively high (Kelley and Michela 1980, Weiner et al. 1972). Perceived equity in the exchange will lead to greater satisfaction (Foa and Foa 1974). Furthermore, empirical results in Hunt and Nevin (1974) and Lusch (1977) suggest a target's satisfaction is positively related to the other firm's role performance, while inversely related to the source's use of power in a coercive, pressurized fashion. Based on a laboratory study, Dwyer (1980) found satisfaction to be positively correlated to the channel member's level of autonomy and the perceived cooperativeness of the firms. Brown and Day (1981) found that satisfaction is inversely related to conflict in their field study. Goal compatibility and role satisfaction will also contribute to the target's overall satisfaction.

Generally, high levels of satisfaction will have positive consequences for the relationship. As consistency theory suggests, when satisfied the target should exhibit greater attraction to the relationship and, as a result, agreement on decision strategy and the firm's dependence level should increase (Blau 1964). Because expectancy levels tend to change in the direction of the reinforcement received in the past (Blau 1964, Chadwick-Jones 1976), a high level of satisfaction will reinforce if not heighten levels of deserved and expected rewards. As a result, the target's effort and cooperation in the relationship should increase in the immediate future (Hunt and Nevin 1974, Luetgert 1967). On the other hand, dissatisfaction will serve to depress the target's expectations; less activity will be exerted in the relationship, as a result (Homans 1974). Dissatisfaction based on blame attributed to the source's firm and inequity can lead to or heighten perceptions of goal incomaptibility and role dissatisfaction, high levels of manifest conflict, and low cooperation. Continued dissatisfaction with achieved rewards, along with the perceived availabilty of a more desirable exchange partner who also wants the target as an exchange partner, will lead to a dissolution of the relationship. The number of alternatives in the target's evoked set, and the expected rewards and investments associated with each, will significantly influence when and if the target decides a change is warranted in exchange partners.

## Discussion

Previous research in the marketing channels literature has focused on the implementation or coordination of interorganizational exchange relationships and the constructs of interfirm power and conflict. The framework presented herein clearly suggests that a broadening of research effort is required to aid future progress and understanding in the marketing channels area. Attention is especially warranted on why and how exchange relationships are initiated, and how the rewards or losses from the exchange are reviewed and evaluated by each channel member. Indeed, because constructs within the initiation, implementation, and review processes are so highly interrelated with one another, a clear understanding of attempts to coordinate ongoing exchange relationships, including the constructs of power and conflict, is not possible without some understanding of the other two processes, and vice versa. This suggests it would be beneficial for channel researchers to examine both distal and immediate antecedents of existing exchange relationships, analyzing the "history of each exchange" so to speak, in examining and explaining their current nature. For example, where channel members receive an unrealistic picture of expected rewards and required investments in beginning exchange relationships, problems will typically arise later on. Role expectations will be high, and actual role performances will not meet them. When achieved rewards fail to meet expected rewards, and investments are higher than anticipated, the channel members will become frustrated, attribute blame, and perceive the exchange to be inequitable. Dissatisfaction will arise, leading to decreased cooperation and effort levels in the future. An acknowledgment and inspection of this flow of events would lead to a greater understanding of current attempts to coordinate such exchange relationships.

The broadened perspective offered by this article should prove useful in three primary ways. First, it should promote further theoretical development in the channels area. The framework presented herein has integrated a variety of ideas and empirical findings from the channels literature. Furthermore, it has refined and extended the existing conceptual framework on interorganizational exchange relationships by bringing in important theories, ideas, and findings from related behavioral science disciplines, and developing an internally consistent set of construct definitions. New ground has been broken in bringing framework constructs together in a systematic manner, as part of an organized whole. For example, to date the important distinctions between the constructs of power, influence strategies, and achieved influence have not been clearly made in the channels literature; these distinctions must be made to promote further progress. Altogether, this provides the basis for new theoretical insights and a foundation upon which future reseachers must build. Eventually, the development of models and middle range theories to explain interorganizational exchange behavior may result from the framework of processes and relationships presented in Figure 1.

Second, the broadened perspective offered herein should serve to guide empirical research in the marketing channels area. Specific propositions were made throughout the article, both in regard to processes and construct relationships that require empirical testing in a variety of marketing channel contexts. Due to little, if any, empirical attention to date, especially valuable would be tests of propositions dealing with intraorganizational and personal characteristics that influence interorganizational exchange behavior, channel member expectations (e.g., deserved and expected rewards), cooperation and effort levels, achieved rewards or losses, including the effects of learning and reinforcement over time, attributions of responsibility, and equity judgments. Researchers should not attempt to test the entire framework of relationships exhibited in Figure 1 at one time, as this would be impractical and beyond the scope of any one empirical study.[5] The framework should help researchers to evaluate and interpret the mediating effects of constructs not included in their studies.

Finally, the broadened perspective offered herein should prove useful to practitioners, promoting their interest in more effective distribution channel management. The article provides them an organized framework for viewing and analyzing interorganizational exchange behavior, thereby aiding their evaluations of current exchange policies and practices.

## LIMITATIONS

This article has two major limitations. First, by design, the framework in Figure 1 is very broad in nature, providing a general mapping of research issues relating to interorganizational exchange behavior. Only major constructs and interrelationships were considered. As a result, because of its breadth, some specification error will exist in the framework that must be remedied in the future by concentrating in greater depth on each individual process.

Second, many of the article's propositions show a rationality bias to some degree, assuming a highly structured decision and interfirm interaction process. As a result, the general framework of relationships may have most applicability where channel members are *highly involved* in their exchange relationships. For instance, it may apply fairly well in a franchise channel system where franchisors have field sales representatives oversee each of their exchange relationships, and the typical franchisee has, at most, two or three suppliers, each very important to the firm's overall welfare. However, where independent industrial distributors have a large number of suppliers, distributor personnel may not follow the structured approach espoused herein with each exchange relationship, especially with their minor suppliers. As a result, some propostions are likely to be both true and false under different conditions. On one hand, if interest is generated and empirical tests of propositions are made, even if some are not borne out, the purpose of this article will have been largely achieved. However, contingency propositions and theories will eventually need to be developed to adequately explain exchange behavior across (as well as within) conventional, administered, contractual, and corporate channel systems.

## Conclusion

This article has provided channel researchers with a broadened perspective of what research issues need to be addressed in improving our understanding of interorganizational exchange behavior. It should serve to guide future research developments in the marketing channels area. The framework outlined herein provides a general overview of interorganizational exchange behavior; it should be looked upon as a first step along the path toward adequate models and theories of exchange behavior in marketing channels. Based on empirical tests of the propositions developed herein within various marketing channel contexts and further theoretical development, situations where the general framework applies and where it does not can be formally investigated and evaluated in the future.

## ENDNOTES

1. This terminology is not used to suggest that the flow of influence in channel relationships is one-sided. Even in ongoing relationships where one firm dominates, the other will make some influence attempts over time, if not achieve some concessions. Additionally, at least in reasonably large, decentralized firms, a group of individuals or sometimes coalitions will be involved in its exchange relationships, either in interacting with its exchange partners, or in influencing those personnel who do (Pfeffer and Salancik 1978, Phillips 1981). Therefore, in such cases underlying many of the components within Figure 1 would be intraorganizational interaction and political processes necessary to arrive at a need and motive for an exchange, an overall level of satisfaction or dissatisfaction with the exchange relationship, etc. Only in situations where one individual primarily monitors and directs a firm's exchange relationship can this be ignored.
2. French and Raven's (1959) bases of power approach has also been used to explain the source of a firm's power. It was not utilized in this study because each base of power appears better conceptualized as a means of applying power, rather than as a source of power. See Bacharach and Lawler (1980) and Frazier (1984) for critical reviews.
3. Whereas in the initiation process the boundary personnel of each firm were responsible for some creative selling, as well as deciding with whom to begin an exchange relationship, their primary responsibility changes in the implementation process to managing and coordinating the ongoing exchange relationship.

4. While federal law prohibits the offering of special incentives or privileges on a discriminative basis in the distribution channel without adequate cost justification, differential inducements, especially relating to personal favors and levels of cooperation, are still given in many distribution channel relationships (cf., Stephenson, Cron, and Frazier 1979).
5. Researchers should choose a segment of the framework that interests them the most and test the propositions made herein regarding it (e.g., equity judgments and their correlates). Furthermore, researchers should further develop conceptually the segments in question, generating additional propositions on their own in the process.

## REFERENCES

Adams, J. Stacy (1963), "Wage Inequities, Productivity, and Work Quality," *Industrial Relations*, 3 (October), 9-16.

——— and Sara Freedman (1976), "Equity Theory Revisited: Comments and Annotated Bibliography," in *Advances in Experimental Social Psychology*, Vol. 9, L. Berkowitz and E. Walster, eds., New York: Academic Press, 43-90.

Aldrich, Howard (1975), "An Organization-Environment Perspective on Cooperation and Conflict between Organizations in the Manpower Training System," in *Interorganization Theory*, Anant Negandhi, ed., Kent, OH: Kent State University Press.

——— (1979), *Organizations and Environments*, Englewood Cliffs, NJ: Prentice-Hall.

Anderson, Paul (1982), "Marketing, Strategic Planning, and the Theory of the Firm," *Journal of Marketing*, 46 (Spring), 15-26.

Angelmar, Richard and Louis Stern (1978), "Development of a Content Analytic System for Analysis of Bargaining Communication in Marketing," *Journal of Marketing Research*, 15 (February), 93-102.

Assael, Henry (1968), "The Political Role of Trade Associations in Distributive Conflict Resolution," *Journal of Marketing*, 32 (April), 21-28.

Bacharach, Samuel and Edward Lawler (1980), *Power and Politics in Organizations*, San Francisco: Jossey-Bass.

Bagozzi, Richard (1975), "Marketing as Exchange," *Journal of Marketing*, 39 (October), 32-39.

Beier, Frederick and Louis Stern (1969), "Power in the Channel of Distribution," in *Distribution Channels: Behavioral Dimensions*, Louis Stern, ed., Boston: Houghton-Mifflin.

Blalock, Hubert and Paul Wilkin (1979), *Intergroup Processes: A Micro-Macro Perspective*, New York: The Free Press.

Blau, Peter (1964), *Exchange and Power in Social Life*, New York: Wiley.

Blumstein, Philip and Eugene Weinstein (1969), "The Redress of Distributive Injustice," *American Journal of Sociology*, 74 (January), 408-418.

Brown, James and Ralph Day (1981), "Measures of Manifest Conflict in Distribution Channels," *Journal of Marketing Research*, 18 (August), 263-274.

Bucklin, Louis (1973), "A Theory of Channel Control," *Journal of Marketing*, 37 (January), 39-47.

Cadotte, Ernest and Louis Stern (1979), "A Process Model of Interorganizational Relations in Marketing Channels," in *Research in Marketing*, Vol. 2, Jagdish Sheth, ed., Greenwich, CT: JAI Press.

Chadwick-Jones, John (1976), *Social Exchange Theory*, New York: Academic Press.

Deutsch, Morton (1973), *The Resolution of Conflict*, New Haven, CT: Yale University Press.

Doyle, Peter, Marcel Corstjens, and Paul Michell (1980), "Signals of Vulnerability in Agency-Client Relations," *Journal of Marketing*, 44 (Fall), 18-23.

Dwyer, F. Robert, (1980), "Channel Member Satisfaction: Laboratory Insights," *Journal of Retailing*, 56 (Summer), 59-74, 94.

——— and Orville Walker, Jr. (1981), "Bargaining in an Asymmetrical Power Structure," *Journal of Marketing*, 45 (Winter), 104-115.

El-Ansary, Adel and Louis Stern (1972), "Power Measurement in the Distribution Channel," *Journal of Marketing Research*, 4 (February), 47-52.

Emerson, Richard (1962), "Power-Dependence Relations," *American Sociological Review*, 27 (February), 31-41.

Etgar, Michael (1976a), "Channel Domination and Countervailing Power in Distribution Channels," *Journal of Marketing Research*, 13 (August), 254-262.

——— (1976b), "Effects of Administrative Control on Efficiency of Vertical Marketing Systems," *Journal of Marketing Research*, 13 (February), 12-24.

——— (1977), "Channel Environment and Channel Leadership," *Journal of marketing Research*, 15 (February), 69-76.

——— (1979), "Sources and Types of Intrachannel Conflict," *Journal of Retailing*, 55 (Spring), 61-78.

Foa, Uriel and Edna Foa (1974), *Societal Structures of the Mind*, Springfield, IL: Charles C. Thomas.

Frazier, Gary (1983), "On the Measurement of Interfirm Power in Channels of Distribution," *Journal of Marketing Research*, 20 (May), 158-166.

——— (1984), "The Interfirm Power-Influence Process Within a Marketing Channel," in *Research in Marketing*, Vol. 7, J. Sheth, ed., Greenwich, CT: JAI Press, forthcoming.

——— and John Summers (1984), "Interfirm Influence Strategies and Their Application Within Distribution Channels," *Journal of Marketing*, 48, forthcoming.

French, John and Bertram Raven (1959), "The Bases of Social Power," in *Studies in Social Power*, D. Cartwright, ed., Ann Arbor: Univeristy of Michigan Press, 150-167.

Gill, Lynn and Louis Stern (1969), "Roles and Role Theory in Distribution Channel Systems," in *Distribution Channel: Behavioral Dimensions*, Louis Stern, ed., Boston: Houghton-Mifflin.

Goodstadt, Barry and Larry Hjelle (1973), "Power to the Powerless: Locus of Control and Use of Power," *Journal of Personality and Social Psychology*, 27 (August), 190-196.

Granbois, Donald, John Summers, and Gary Frazier (1977), "Correlates of Consumer Expectation and Complaining Behavior," in *Consumer Satisfaction, Dissatisfaction, and Complaining Behavior*, Ralph Day, ed., Bloomington, IN: Indiana University Press.

Guiltinan, Joseph, Ismail Rejab, and William Rodgers (1980), "Factors Influencing Coordination in a Franchise Channel," *Journal of Retailing*, 56 (Fall), 41-58.

Hall, Richard and John Clark (1975), "Problems in the Study of Interorganizational Relationships," in *Interorganization Theory*, Anant Negandhi, ed., Kent, OH: Kent State University Press.

Heider, Fritz (1958), *The Psychology of Interpersonal Relations*, New York: Wiley.

Homans, George (1974), *Social Behavior: Its Elementary Forms*, rev. ed., New York: Harcourt.

Howard, John and Jagdish Sheth (1969), *The Theory of Buyer Behavior*, New York: Wiley.

Hunt, Shelby and John Nevin (1974), "Power in a Channel of Distribution: Sources and Consequences," *Journal of Marketing Research*, 11 (May), 186-193.

——— and ——— (1976), "Full Disclosure Laws in Franchising: An Empirical Investigation," *Journal of Marketing*, 40 (April), 53-62.

Huppertz, John, Sidney Arenson, and Richard Evans (1978), "An Application of Equity Theory to Buyer-Seller Exchange Situations," *Journal of Marketing Research*, 15 (May), 250-260.

Kelley, Harold (1972), *Causal Schemata and the Attribution Process*, Morristown, NJ: General Learning Press.

——— and Janusz Grzelak (1972), "Conflict between Individual and Common Interest in an N-person Relationship," *Journal of Personality and Social Psychology*, 21 (February), 190-197.

——— and John Michela (1980), "Attribution Theory and Research," *Annual Review of Psychology*, 31, 457-501.

Kelman, Herbert (1961), "Processes of Opinion Change," *Public Opinion Quarterly*, 25 (Spring), 57-78.

Kotter, John (1977), "Power, Dependence, and Effective Management," *Harvard Business Review*, 55 (July-August), 125-136.

Lawler, Edward and Lyman Porter (1967), "The Effect of Performance on Job Satisfaction," *Industrial Relations*, 7 (October), 20-28.

Luetgert, J. (1967), "Generalized Effects of Social Reinforcement on Paired-Associate Learning by Grade School Achievers and Under-achievers," Ph.D. dissertation, Indiana University.

Lusch, Robert (1976), "Sources of Power: Their Impact on Intrachannel Conflict," *Journal of Marketing Research*, 13 (November), 382-390.

——— (1977), "Franchisee Satisfaction: Causes and Consequences," *International Journal of Physical Distribution*, 7 (no. 3), 128-140.

Miller, Dale and Michael Ross (1975), "Self-serving Biases in the Attribution of Causality: Fact or Fiction?" *Psychological Bulletin*, 82 (March), 213-225.

Pfeffer, Jeffrey and Gerald Salancik (1978), *The External Control of Organizations: A Resource-Dependence Perspective*, New York: Harper.

Phares, E. Jerry (1957), "Expectancy Changes in Skill and Chance Situations," *Journal of Abnormal Social Psychology*, 54 (May), 339-342.

Phillips, Lynn (1981), "Assessing Measurement Error in Key Informant Reports: A Methodological Note on Organizational Analysis in Marketing," *Journal of Marketing Research*, 18 (November), 395-415.

Raven, Bertram and Ari Kruglanski (1970), "Conflict and Power," in *The Structure of Conflict*, Paul Swingle, ed., New York: Academic Press, 69-109.

Regan, Dennis (1978), "Attributional Aspects of Interpersonal Attraction," in *New Directions in Attribution Research*, Vol. 2, J. Harvey, W. Ickes, and R. Kedd, eds., Hillsdale, NJ: Erlbaum, 207-233.

Reve, Torger and Louis Stern (1979), "Interorganizational Relations in Marketing Channels," *Academy of Management Review*, 4 (July), 405-416.

Robicheaux, Robert and Adel El-Ansary (1975), "A General Model for Understanding Channel Member Behavior," *Journal of Retailing*, 52 (Winter), 13-30, 90-94.

Rosenberg, Larry and Louis Stern (1971), "Conflict Measurement in the Distribution Channel," *Journal of Marketing Research*, 8 (November), 437-442.

Sheth, Jagdish (1973), "A Model of Industrial Buyer Behavior," *Journal of Marketing*, 37 (October), 50-56.

——— (1976), "Buyer-Seller Interaction: A Conceptual Framework," working paper #292, Bureau of Economic and Business Research, University of Illinois.

——— and David Gardner (1982), "History of Marketing Thought: An Update," in *Marketing Theory: Philosophy of Science Perspectives*, R. Bush and S. Hunt, eds., Chicago: American Marketing, 52-58.

Staw, Barry (1975), "Attributing the Causes of Performance: An Alternative Interpretation of Cross-sectional Research on Organizations," *Organizational Behavior and Human Performance*, 13 (June), 414-432.

Stephenson, P. Ronald, William Cron, and Gary Frazier (1979), "Delegating Pricing Authority to the Sales Force: The Effects on Sales and Profit Performance," *Journal of Marketing*, 43 (Spring), 21-28.

Stern, Louis and James Hesket (1969), "Conflict Management in Interorganizational Relations: A Conceptual Framework," in *Distribution Channels: Behavioral Dimensions*, Louis Stern, ed., Boston: Houghton-Mifflin.

———, Brian Sternthal, and Samuel Craig (1973), "Managing Conflict in Distribution Channels: A Laboratory Study," *Journal of Marketing Research*, 10 (May), 169-179.

——— and Adel El-Ansary (1977), *Marketing Channels*, Englewood Cliffs, NJ: Prentice-Hall.

——— and Torger Reve (1980), "Distribution Channels as Political Economies: A Framework for Comparative Analyses," *Journal of Marketing*, 44 (Summer), 52-64.

Tedeschi, James, Barry Schlenker, and Thomas Bonoma (1973), *Conflict, Power, and Games*, Chicago: Aldine.

Triandis, Harry (1977), *Interpersonal Behavior*, Monterey, CA: Brooks/Cole.

Van Horne, James (1980), *Financial Management and Policy* 5th ed., Englewood Cliffs, NJ: Prentice-Hall.

Varela, Jacob (1971), *Psychological Solutions to Social Problems*, New York: Academic Press.

Vroom, Victor (1964), *Work and Motivation*, New York: Wiley.

Walker, Orville, Gilbert Churchill, Jr., and Neil Ford (1977), "Motivation and Performance in Industrial Selling: Present Knowledge and Needed Research," *Journal of Marketing Research*, 15 (May), 156-168.

Weiner, B., I. Frieze, A. Kukla, L. Reed, S. Rest, and R. Rosenbaum (1972), "Perceiving the Causes of Success and Failure," in *Attribution: Perceiving the Causes of Behavior*, E. Jones et al., eds., Morristown, NJ: General Learning Press, 95-120.

Wortman, Camille, Philip Costanzo, and Thomas Witt (1973), "Effect of Anticipated Performance on the Attribution of Causality to Self and Others," *Journal of Personality and Social Psychology*, 27 (September), 372-381.

Zuckerman, Miron (1979), "Attribution of Success and Failure Revisited, or: The Motivational Bias Is Alive and Well in Attribution Theory," *Journal of Personality*, 42 (June), 245-287.

# SECTION M
# Systems School

There is a growing interest in a systems perspective of marketing. There are three fundamental concepts underlying the systems school. First, this school advocates strong interdependence among the components of the system to the extent that change in one component can result in a domino effect on the total system. It also includes the concepts of reciprocal relationship, or circular relationship, among the constructs or the components of the system.

Second, the perspective of this school generally assumes a dynamic system that is evolutionary rather than revolutionary or invariant. In other words, a systematic change is inherent in the system but is not a radical shift or discontinuity. For example, the catastrophe theory will be counter to the systems perspective.

Finally, the systems approach tends to be comprehensive. It believes in developing a grand theory that is generic enough to accommodate all aspects of marketing. Of course, this may result in too much generality, and its applicability or situation-specific relevance may be lost.

The systems school is in its infancy. In our opinion, unless there is strong empirical testing and validation, it is not likely to become popular even though it seems to be most relevant to marketing.

# 43 —— A Normative Theory of Marketing Systems

*Wroe Alderson*

Reprinted from *Theory in Marketing*, published by the American Marketing Association, edited by Cox, Alderson, and Shapiro (1964), pp. 92-108. Reprinted by permission.

Marketing as a phase of group activity appeared rather late in the history of human culture. Despite some tentative beginnings in village societies, the flowering of trade was coincidental with the rise of cities in the great river valleys of Egypt and Asia. Marketing from the first has been an extremely dynamic culture component, accelerating the differentiation of other activities and the functional specialization of both individuals and groups. Human behavior in the marketplace is an essential aspect of human behavior in general. Marketing theory may eventually be recognized as part of the theoretical framework for a general science of behavior.

Theory in the behavioral field is both descriptive and normative. In an earlier treatment of behavior systems[1] the author proposed several survival theorems as descriptive generalizations concerning the behavior of systems. The intent in this essay is to formulate some normative principles of system behavior which will be consistent with the rational self-interest of those who control a system or participate in its activities. It will then be argued that these principles provide the basis for a normative theory of marketing which is relevant for the decision maker. Some marketing developments will be cited in which the question may well be raised as to whether these basic normative principles are being violated.

## The Ecological Framework

Pending the more comprehensive formulation of a general science of human behavior, the available starting points for the marketing theorist include economics and cultural ecology. Economics and ecology are two ways of looking at the relations between living things and the resources which sustain their activities. Marketing as a field of study does not rest comfortably under the label of applied economics. There is an overlap between the tools and concepts of general economics and the analytical needs of the marketing specialist, but far from a perfect fit. The broader framework of ecology holds greater promise for the development of marketing science in both descriptive and normative terms. The term "ecology," borrowed from biology, has been applied to human societies with several distinct shadings of meanings.

The sense intended here lies close to that of cultural ecology, a term introduced by the anthropologist, Julian Steward.[2] A crucial aspect of culture, says Steward, is the technololgy through which the culture-bearing society accomplishes adaptation to its environment. The ecology of human societies is one which recognizes culture change rather than biological evolution as the major instrument of adaptation within the relevant time span.

Marketing specialists are working in an applied segment of what may eventually become a general science of human behavior. Every attempt to market a new product or to distribute an old product more efficiently is actually an effort to modify patterns of behavior. Every active marketing program endeavors to accelerate culture change or to delay it. Marketing is directly concerned with the material culture embodied in exchangeable products. In order to understand exchange, the specialist must also try to understand the changing aspirations of individuals and groups in the culture and to assess the opportunities and constraints arising in the social and physical environment.

The behavioral and cultural approach to marketing processes largely falls outside the scope of economics, at least as defined by some of its most distinguished exponents. Economics as the mathematical logic of scarcity is invaluable for marketers but not sufficient. Its abstract theorems concerning allocation of scarce resources have application to marketing activities although the general economist has usually dealt with applications to production. But the level of taste, the technological functions, and the flows of information which the economist *qua* economist takes for granted are the primary business of a science of marketing. The marketing specialist observes how marketing systems work and recommends ways of making them work better. This functionalist approach must take account of the structure of the behavior systems through which men seek their goals and once again requires a perspective which cannot be derived from economics alone.

Cultural ecology, like animal ecology, is concerned with the adjustment of a population to its environment. Steward regards population per square mile as a fundamental parameter of any ecological setting. Emphasis is placed, however, on group behavior and the technology available to a tribe or a larger society in exploiting its resources. Various conditions may exist as to the degree of adjustment between a culture-bearing society or group and its environment. In static equilibrium there is little change in the size of the population, in its aspirations, or in its technology. In a state of disequilibrium, resources are steadily depleted by destructive technologies. Increasing population pressure on the remaining means for sustaining life results in even more reckless exploitation and still more destructive competition. What may be called the habitability of the environment, or its ability to sustain a desired level of living, moves steadily downward. In dynamic equilibrium the technology employed produces both an increasing surplus of consumable goods and advances in the technology itself. The society is encouraged to raise its aspirations and to adopt technologies which will meet its expanding requirements without destroying the long-run habitability of the environment. Contemporary societies, both East and West, hope to maintain the conditions for dynamic ecological equilibrium.

The marketing function plays a vital role in the dynamic process of matching goods and needs and in organizing institutions and processes to serve this ultimate purpose. The ecological perspective offers criteria for marketing performance which transcend the limited measures of economic efficiency. Indeed, marketing ideally connects separate production centers or operating systems in such a way as to optimize the outputs of the whole society. It is concerned with the external relations of individual units or organized behavior systems. These relations involve that peculiar amalgam of competition and cooperation which is so well recognized in ecology and so difficult to accommodate within the framework of received economic theory.

Since marketing is a function of organized behavior systems, and since these systems are the agencies through which a society exploits its environment, marketing theory is necessarily concerned with the structure and nature of organized behavior systems. The internal structure and operation of a system has a vital bearing on such external functions as marketing. Some years ago the author asserted the need for recognizing three levels of equilibrium in organized human activities and relating these levels to each other.[3] First there is market equilibrium, which pertains to the network of external relations among organized behavior systems. Secondly, there is organizational equilibrium, which is a form of internal balance within an individual system. Finally, there is the more embracing concept of ecological equilibrium pertaining to the adjustment between a society and its environment.

The notion of survival is crucial and is relevant at all three levels with distinct but related meanings. At the ecological level there is no doubt about the individual's goal of biological survival. Obviously he also has a personal stake in avoiding a state of disequilibrium in which the whole population could be wiped out. With respect to the behavior system to which he belongs, an individual may survive or fail to survive as a member. Generally he will struggle to retain his status as a participant so long as it promises satisfactions greater than those he would expect as a nonmember. Finally the problem of survival for the organized behavior system is of critical importance.

## Control of Adaptive Processes

The three-level equilibrium scheme will be reduced to a two-level scheme in searching for the roots of normative theory. This approach looks at the internal state of the system and the adjustment of the system to its external environment and considers the ways in which they affect each other. The proximate environment may be defined as the external domain with which the system is in direct and continuous contact and interaction. Most narrowly defined, the proximate environment for a marketing organization would correspond to the markets in which it buys and sells and competes with other marketing organizations.

A more comprehensive concept might be called the ultimate environment. It would embrace the social and physical environment and any external factors which might appear relevant to the survival and success of the organization and which in turn might be critically affected by the organization's actions.

The internal structure might be examined further with respect to the control of the adaptive processes by which the system is related to is environment. An organized behavior system, such as a business firm, normally behaves as if survival were a goal of the system. The underlying objectives are those of the participants in the system. Their expectations of benefits from the system can only be realized if the system survives. To act so as to perpetuate the system is consistent with the power principle which states that rational man will act in such a way as to promote the power to act. The argument does not hold that the goal of survival takes the place of more immediate objectives such as business profits. Rather, the desire of participants to preserve the system is reflected in modifications of the system's behavior in seeking more specific objectives.

Growth is a closely related goal of an organized behavior system. The desire to grow springs partly from a feeling that survival is threatened at the lower scale of operation. Present participants seek growth to attract other participants whose special competence gives greater assurance of system survival. Growth now becomes mandatory in order to satisfy the expectations of more numerous and more ambitious participants. The behavior system struggles for survival and growth within the ecological web consisting of the whole collection of systems through which the society exploits its environment. It will fail to survive if it cannot attract the cooperation or meet the competition of other systems within the web. It will fail if it does not achieve the internal organizational equilibrium which is essential to effective and continuous adaptation. It will fail most irretrievably if the entire society fails and can no longer survive in its environment. A crucial factor in success or failure is to be found in the nature of the system's control processes.

The foregoing may suggest that a system can adapt without conscious or deliberate intent in pursuing its goals of survival and growth. Adaptation without deliberate control does take place in small organizations with a low level of aspiration and a simple static technology. In more advanced systems successful adaptation involves strategic decisions which can only emanate from an effective control center. Internal balance in a system with many human participants is revealed as an extremely complex state in any attempt to analyze it fully. The expectations of participants are interdependent but not identical, and there are often rival attempts to control the system to serve the interests of rival groups or individuals. Even in a well-ordered system of large magnitude there is the complication of numerous subordinate control centers linked more or less effectively with the central command post. In the present analysis the problem of internal balance will be considered in the simplest terms, dealing with the relations of a central group to all other participants as a group.

The resulting model of the adaptive system consists at the minimum of four elements. Internally the participants are divided into the control group $P_c$ and the subordinate participants, $P_s$. The two groups of participants are related to each other through a power structure and a communication structure. Externally there is the proximate environment $E_i$ and some broader domain in which the system might aspire to operate, $E_a$. At the limit $E_a$ approaches the ultimate environment $E_u$. The system is related to the environment through its technology and the aspirations of its participants. The control group makes crucial decisions as to the aspiration level translated into operating goals and as to the technology to be employed in achieving the goals of the system.

The power structure in the system determines whether the control group can compel or persuade the subordinante participants to accept and implement the strategic decisions. The communication structure determines whether there will be effective coordination in carrying out the common effort. Most of the impact on the external environment is delivered through the subordinate participants, and most of the information about the environment is fed back through the same subordinates or some specialized investigatory group. There is an obvious parallel to the behavior of the human body. The decision reached in the brain to move a certain object is effected by the hand. Information that the act has been satisfactorily accomplished comes back from the sensory nerves in the finger tips or through a specialized sensory organ, the eye.

A powerful control group may be able to set a level of aspiration which diverges sharply from the level of activity at which the system is currently operating. To choose a level of aspiration is equivalent to defining the relevant environment $E_a$ which is relevant for any program pursuing these aspirations. In marketing terms, the definition of the environment may reflect a decision to reach more consumers, to market selectively only to preferred consumers, or to market goods and services not now in the line. In broader management terms, the environment may be defined to include all who are affected directly or indirectly, whether they are users of the product or not. Rational self-interest requires the broader definition if there is a serious threat to the survival of the system in this broader domain. Questions of survival always arise when the system is viewed in the setting of the ultimate environment. These questions are so fundamental that the control group in every large system is obliged to give some thought to the ultimate ecological sanctions which our society faces today.

It has been said that the control group sets operational goals which are the projection of some level of aspiration. Goals specify the outputs to be obtained or the changes to be wrought in dealing with the environment.

The control group has a second strategic decision to make. It must specify the optimal technology for reaching the stated goals. All but the most rudimentary systems have some repertoire of behavior patterns allowing a choice among alternative courses of action. A critical choice is often that between a customary or habitual behavior pattern and a modified pattern which the control group believes will be more effective. In a period of rapid technological changes the control group may exert constant pressure for improved procedures as well as for more ambitious goals.

## The Pathology of Systems

The several basic elements will be in precise adjustment if the system is in equilibrium. There are several ways in which such a system can go into a state of disequilibrium. The pathology of systems is somewhat analogous to the pathology of the human body. A system may suffer a slight indisposition which is easily remedied. It can drag along at a fraction of its potential efficiency as if it suffered from a chronic disease. Maladjustment can be so severe that the system seems fated to decline steadily toward final extinction in the manner of a human being with a terminal illness.

Several of the more serious maladies of systems will be described in terms of the system model. The control group may fail to exercise direction or influence over subordinates. The latter persist in customary patterns of behavior or improvise their own adjustments at their points of contact with the environment. Such a system is running out of control, and unless control can be reestablished it will eventually disintegrate as a system. A system may possess considerable momentum as the result of past successes, but without effective control it will lose this thrust through collision with obstacles in the environment.

In another form of maladjustment the control may be in effective command for the time being but without adequate communication from below to register the aspirations and attitudes of subordinates. A decline of morale may follow, resulting in apathy and inefficiency. In other cases there is covert or overt rebellion. Conflict can result in attrition of the subordinate group through elimination of its leaders and the flight of others. It can force a change of leadership in the control group. A new state of adjustment may be achieved if the new leadership projects goals which are more acceptable to the subordinate groups and a technology which is efficient in achieving these goals.

Finally there is the situation in which control group and subordinate group work together but in apparent disregard of salient features of the environment. Quite often the environmental facts are not actually known or their significance for the operation of the system is not correctly appraised. Sometimes there seems to be a tacit conspiracy among all participants to ignore obvious but unpleasant facts. With a system, as with an individual, there seems to be some inherent bias toward believing those things which are consistent with the way in which participants would like to see the system operate.

A form of maladjustment of special interest for marketing and some other aspects of economic and political behavior is the condition which may be called the extinction mode. Once a system is in this condition, the probability of transition to some other state approaches zero and the degree of maladjustment tends to increase rather than lessen, regardless of any action taken. This type of situation is sometimes described as a vicious circle or, more precisely, as a vicious spiral, since a system caught in such a state seems destined to run down. Some concrete examples will be given of systems in the extinction mode.

## Systems in the Extinction Mode

The Swedish economist, Gunnar Myrdal, has been a leading exponent of the self-perpetuating adverse trend. In a study of the race problem in the United States, Myrdal documented the existence of a self-perpetuating trend with respect to the condition of the Negro population over a period of many years.[4] The low social status and poor living conditions of the Negro was taken by many whites as indicative of native inferiority and lack of capacity for progress. This judgment was used to justify the denial of opportunities for education and economic advancement. Illiteracy and lack of income tended to perpetuate a life of squalor and other symbols of low social status. The extinction mode is characterized by such adverse interactions but in an extreme form. The self-perpetuating trend steadily depletes the capabilities of the system and finally threatens its very existence.

A prime example of a system in the extinction mode is found in the southern society based on one-crop agriculture before the Civil War. Slave labor was controlled by the threat of force, and no attempt was made to induce cooperation by taking account of the aspirations of the slaves. The poor whites were partially disfranchised by various devices and did not aspire to match the standard of living of the planter class. Existing largely through subsistence agriculture, the poor whites were secure in their intermediate social status so long as the Negroes remained enslaved.

With a monolithic power structure it was possible for the control group to enforce compliance with its choice of goals and technology. Soil fertility was rapidly depleted in many areas where the slave economy prevailed. There was a progressive concentration of slave labor in the deep South which accelerated the depletion of the shrinking base of fertile soil. While many realized the seriousness of their plight they could see no way out since neither planter nor poor white could face the prospect of emancipation of a huge mass of Negroes who had deliberately been kept in a retarded stage of development.

Southern leaders were still striving in the decade before the Civil War to retain their traditional dominance in the power structure of the country as a whole. Many forces were against them, including population increase and technological advance in the North, the lack of new lands suitable for slave agriculture, and the growth of worldwide opinion demanding an end to slavery. The only solution appeared to be secession which would leave the control group in command at least in its own region. If the South could withdraw from the Union without federal opposition it might carry out its military designs on Mexico, Cuba, and Central America and then return in far greater strength to the task of dominating the North American continent. The act of secession, however, inevitably transformed the long struggle for political power into military conflict. Despite the added strain of war, the control group in the South continued to pursue infeasible goals with an obsolete technology to the point of final exhaustion. This instance has been cited, not for the lack of marketing examples but because it is such a complete and dramatic illustration of a system in the extinction mode.[5]

Numerous marketing examples could be found in the bankruptcy records: the old line grocer who did not believe that the supermarket was here to stay and refused to adopt self-service; the wholesaler who wanted to remain independent while his customers were joining voluntary chains or setting up retailer-owned cooperatives; the manufacturer who would sell only to wholesalers in the face of the steady trend in his industry toward direct distribution. In the cases which will be described briefly here, the firms involved still survive, either because they found a way out of what appeared to be a trapped state or because the process of extinction has not yet run its course.

Some years ago Mead, Johnson & Company sold its baby food, Pablum, only to wholesale druggists even though consumers bought the product mainly in grocery stores rather than drugstores. Retail grocers bought it from wholesale grocers who in turn bought it from wholesale druggists. Since Pablum had to carry two wholesale margins rather than one, it became increasingly difficult for it to compete with other baby food lines sold through the grocery trade. Mead, Johnson also had a line of ethical drug products moving through wholesaler druggists. It felt that it could not engage in an overt and protracted effort to correct the situation on Pablum for fear of the loss it might sustain on its other products. The solution was found in doing something which no one previously had thought possible—namely, to create a nationwide organization of food brokers in a single week's time.

In 1920 a federal court placed the meat-packers known as the Big Five under consent decree and set them on the road to extinction. Since then one of the five has gone out of business; two others have been through one or more incidents with bankruptcy and financial reorganizations; a fourth lost money nearly every year for a long term of years until management undertook a drastic curtailment of its operations; the fifth may have enjoyed some relief from pressure because of the troubles of its competitiors, but in recent years has had increasing difficulties of its own. The trapped competitive group created by the consent decree was barred from entering many areas of enterprise, such as grocery retailing, while the chains were entirely free to enter meat-packing. The Big Five could not initiate competitive moves against anyone except each other. Meanwhile they were faced with the competition of newcomers, particularly in cured meats and prepared meat products, the only profitable part of the business. As recently as 1959 the large meat-packers made one more effort to have the consent decree lifted, but it is doubtful whether legal relief would provide a real solution for them at this late date.

About fifteen years ago the author made a study which was financed jointly by the large tire manufacturers who were known as the Big Four. One of these companies seemed to be in strong position because it had the largest share of original equipment business, that is, tires sold to automobile manufacturers for new cars. While the margin on this volume was slim, it was thought that being strong in original equipment was the surest way of getting a substantial portion of the more profitable replacement business.

A decade later this apparent advantage seemed all at once to act as a handicap. Pressed into premature innovation on the tubeless tire, the company experienced a rise in complaints and claims for adjustment. The rise in the adjustment rate seemed particularly sharp to the dealers who handled complaints on original equipment tires as well as on replacement tires. With some loss of dealer confidence in the line the quality of dealer sales effort deteriorated. Some dealers went out of business or switched to other brands of tires. As the dealer base continued to shrink, the ratio of original equipment business rose correspondingly. Thus the adverse conditions which threatened the dealer organization were further aggravated. Outside surveys show a sharp decline in the company's volume of business in replacement tires. Heroic measures would be required for this company to recapture its former position in the tire business, and it is not yet clear whether management will accept the large risks which are inherent in these measures. It is well entrenched in other types of rubber products and might even be well advised, so far as tires are concerned, to accept its extinction as inevitable.

## Keeping a System Healthy

One of the writer's colleagues at the University of Pennsylvania continues to be unhappy about the notion of survival as a system goal. Recently he said, "Do you really expect the head of an organization to take a shot of survival every morning along with his orange juice?" One might reply that he would not expect the executive to take a shot of profit maximization either, but the critic's case is somewhat better than that. Profit is a quantitative variable which can be maximized, at least theoretically, by meeting specified conditions for an optimal value. In their attempt to develop a more realistic form of analysis, Herbert Simon and his associates abandon the notion of profit maximization. They assume that the executive will try to satisfice, achieving a profit that equals or exceeds a minimum requirement.

Survival as a goal does not fit neatly into either perspective. The executive can neither optimize nor satisfice with respect to survival since it is not a quantitative variable. A biological organism is either living or dead; it either survives or perishes. If one insisted in assigning numerical values, survival might be given a value of one and failure to survive a value of zero.

The best analogy for the capacity of a system to survive is the health of a biological organism. In either case it is rational to exercise proper care to keep the body or the system healthy. The prime strategy in either case is a strategy of avoidance. The individual tries to avoid infection or other conditions which might cause illness. Through occasional medical examinations he hopes for early detection of what might otherwise become an incurable and ultimately fatal disease. The executive watches for maladjustment in the system and attempts to apply prompt remedies. Above all, he should try to prevent the system from falling into the condition which has been called the extinction mode. At best the issue of survival is fraught with uncertainty just as the person who worries most about his health may still die of cancer. The point is that there are some rational steps for the executive to take if he is concerned about the goal of survival for his organization.

Executive action, prompted by survival motives, is not entirely limited to passive or preventive measures. Although survival cannot be quantified, it may be possible to identify a quantifiable variable which could be called capacity to survive. The obvious parallel would be the vitality of a living organism. Of two live individuals, one might have greater vitality or capacity to stay alive in the face of stress or exposure. The rational individual, however, would scarcely seek to maximize vitality or survival potential. Rather he would hope to maintain a sufficient reserve of survival potential so that the system could meet any conditions with which it is likely to be confronted. The interesting but difficult problem of measuring survival potential is not germane to the present discussion.

## Survival in the Wider Perspective

The discussion of survival so far would be consistent with a perspective limited to the interests of the single firm. The executive might preserve the health of the firm so that he would then be able to maximize or satisfice. But the rational executive extends his vision and concern to the healthfulness of the setting in which the firm must operate. In addition to survival of the firm he might consider the survival of his immediate community, the survival of the American economy, the survival of free enterprise, the survival of western culture, or the survival of mankind. As businessman, citizen, or student of affairs he may well be aware of survival issues at all levels.

His organization might perish because of a catastrophic event in one of these larger systems. If he directs a very large organization, the survival of a larger system might be significantly affected by his decisions.

J. M. Clark[6] has argued that our modern economy cannot work except through the development of a high sense of responsibility among the executives who direct large enterprises. Competition, in his opinion, imposes limits on business conduct but does not control and determine executive decision as postulated in the theory of pure competition. There is an area of discretion which allows room for values which transcend the immediate welfare of the individual firm. Survival values at the broadest reach are still rooted in rational self-interest. These values are supported by ecological sanctions. Environmental constraints are controlling in the long run with severe penalties attached to their violation.

Many firms encounter ecological sanctions in the immediate environment of the communities in which their plants are located. If the industry is engaged solely in the extraction of raw materials, the habitability of the environment is depleted as mineral deposits or forests are mined out. The nature of the activity may make the environment unsightly and unpleasant even while it produces income for the resident population. As the process of depletion continues the responsible executive will certainly give some consideration to the stranded population which may be left behind when the natural resource is gone. Some have taken effective steps to stimulate alternative forms of economic activity in their own interest and that of the community. Conservation of resources has received increasing recognition in both public and private policy. The doctrine of conservation is a clear departure from the philosophy of pure and perfect competition in the direction of acknowledging responsibility for maintaining the habitability of the environment.

There are other and subtler ways in which the marketing and management practices of a company can affect the quality of life in its community. It is possible that the conservative attitudes of Philadelphia business in the nineteenth century and its failure to employ aggressive promotion was a factor in the relatively static economy of the city today. Apparently there was a tendency to feel that quality should speak for itself and to cling to traditional definitions of quality. A famous hat company in Philadelphia almost went broke making a high-quality, high-priced hat after mass demand had shifted. A new management finally brought the company to a more prosperous state by realizing that the typical customer was interested in a greater variety of apparel and would prefer two hats for the same money even though of less durability.

Many American business executives regard the antitrust laws as essential to the maintenance of free enterprise. Their desire to conform may be reinforced by this belief more than by the rather moderate legal penalties which usually apply. Similarly they accepted an American policy which looked favorably on the development of the common market in Europe even though the exports of some American products might be affected unfavorably. The ultimate sanction today is the prospect of atomic warfare. The threat of atomic missiles is not merely that they would kill millions of people but that they would destroy the habitability of large regions of the earth for centuries to come. This continual threat creates an awareness of ecological sanctions of greater intensity than ever before. The dangers inherent in man's powers to control or modify his environment are seen in the damaging side effects of pesticides, synthetic detergents, and powerful drugs. Whatever the discount to be taken on the public reaction to Rachel Carson's *Silent Spring,* she has called attention to survival issues which cannot be ignored by the responsible executive.

It will be more difficult to find satisfactory solutions for some of these problems than it is to write a persuasive criticism. Modern drugs, for example, are dangerous precisely because they are powerful enough to bring about specified physiological effects in the body. Presumably no one wishes to put a stop to the introduction of new drugs even though some individuals with idiosyncracies may suffer from them. It would not be advantageous to return to the drugs of thirty years ago which had little potency for either help or harm. The responsible executive is required by both private and public considerations to seek further safeguards without slowing the pace of fundamental progress.

There is some evidence that one or more self-perpetuating adverse trends exist with respect to advertising, although this primary marketing institution is certainly not in the extinction mode. The total volume of advertising steadily increases, but it is not likely that the capacity of consumers to pay attention to advertising increases at the same rate. In fact, the more intensive that advertising becomes the larger may be the number of people who deliberately try to avoid it. Determined advertisers may then step up the pressure in the hope of gaining the amount of attention as before. A still greater number of people begin to feel that the volume of advertising has exceeded a tolerable level and they attempt to avoid exposure as much as possible.

Consumer surveys in recent years have indicated a decline in the credence given to advertising. The clamor of conflicting claims has become so raucous in some fields (for example, headache remedies) that consumers might suspect that no one is telling the truth. The remedy for consumer sales resistance, according to exponents of the hard sell, is to make even more sweeping claims and engage in more violent attacks on competitive products. The very features of advertising which created skepticism are carried to further extremes, and the adverse effect on believability is compounded.

For advertising to become corrupt and ineffective could be a crippling blow to a free-market economy. This type of economy feeds on innovation, and the sponsor must communicate with consumers to induce acceptance of innovation. The prospective purchaser does not evaluate the new product in isolation but relates it to other products and eventually to his vision of the good life. He really wants help from the advertiser in putting the product in perspective, in picturing it in the setting in which he is expected to use it and enjoy it. But what if the way of life suggested by the advertisement is shoddy and unattractive? Who wants to live in a hypochondriac's world in which the greatest joy is quick relief from headache? Who wants to live in a fool's paradise in which smokers believe that they can indulge in nicotine and yet escape all the hazards of indulgence? Who really wants the dullard's cuisine in which bland and tasteless foods are touted as the gourmet's delight? The consumer cannot believe in the product if the advertiser could not possibly believe in the kind of world he projects as a setting for his product.

Marketing attempts to alter the patterns of contemporary culture and advertising is its primary instrument for this purpose. Some critics charge that advertising is an active agency in the debasement of public taste. It is more likely that advertising has contributed to cultural confusion. Advertising itself is a public art, and as an art it deserves and must expect criticism. The *Saturday Review* has made a beginning in establishing annual awards for advertising. But advertising is not only art but prophecy. Its practitioners set themselves up in the business of dreaming dreams and seeing visions. They must embrace more exalted standards of virtue than being good providers for their families and voting the straight Republican ticket. Like Jeremiah, each man must live with the fearful chance that he may be numbered among the false prophets.

Not only advertising but marketing in general is in the business of making promises. The manufacturer promises the consumer that she will derive superior satisfaction from his product and promises dealers and distributors that they will make money handling it. There will always be some disappointment since these promises must be fulfilled in a world of diverse and uncertain circumstances. But what about promises concerning which there is substantial doubt that they can ever be fulfilled? Look at the down time on appliances which were sold with the implied promise that they were trouble-free, and without adequate provision for repair services. Try purchasing three items from three different departments in your city's leading store and see whether the transaction can be concluded without some error or failure in performance. Remember the glorious vision of carefree driving which came with your new automobile as you sit in a hopeless traffic jam somewhere on an inadequate street and highway system—or as you ponder the statistics showing that traffic accidents are the principal cause of death in the active years from fifteen to thirty.

Nearly everyone is engaged in marketing in the sense of offering goods or his own services in the market and in buying the goods and services of others. Everyone makes promises of performance and payment, and individuals live up to their promises in varying degrees. The promises made as an aspect of mass marketing are different. Here we are promising each other through our industrial leaders a better way of life, the fruits of technology and enterprise, the physical means and instruments for supporting desired patterns of activity. These reciprocal pledges add up to a Promised Land which we know is not quite attainable. We make some allowance for what the economist Frank Knight once called industrial poetry. But if the channels of communication are largely filled with misinformation and deliberate deception, the system cannot survive. The writer does not believe that this is true of marketing messages, but the damage would be done if the majority of consumers suspected that it was true. At a minimum, the marketer must believe in what he is doing if he is to convince anyone else. He, at least, should be prepared to live in the kind of world his efforts seem calculated to produce.

## Functionalism: Descriptive and Normative

The writer has characterized his theoretical position as functionalism and has accepted the implied commitment to the total systems approach.[7] The functionalist in marketing engages in the study of systems with the aim of understanding how they work and how they can be made to work better. As a theorist he devises descriptive generalizations of marketing activities and institutions and finds a useful tool in the systems concept. He discovers a number of organized behavior systems in the world of marketing and finds that this recognition of systems of interacting forces aids him in explaining what is going on. He might note, for example, that systems have a tendency to persist over time, behaving as if they pursued a goal of survival.

This descriptive theory does not imply that systems are necessarily efficient in seeking any goal, including the goal of survival. It recognizes that systems cease to exist despite the efforts of participants to perpetuate them. The theory stresses environmental change and maladjustment which often occurs because of the lag in the adaptive processes of the system. In order to adapt, the control group in the system must be aware of the change which requires adjustment and must make the right choice among possible adaptations. The descriptive theory presents a picture of a number of systems occupying the same or an overlapping environment, all seeking goals including that of survival but with varying degrees of adjustment to their opportunities and their problems. In each system there are decisions to be made about the level of aspiration and the technology employed. The decisions taken will vary with factors in the problem situation and with the characteristics of the decision makers.

The normative theory sketched in this essay deals with the question of how systems should operate to achieve goals. It emphasizes the goal of survival as the means of relating the problem of adaptation in a given system to the larger systems of which it is a part. It recognizes that freedom of choice exists at each level except for the economic sanctions of the market, the social sanctions imposed by a system on its subsystems or individual participants, and the ecological sanctions inherent in the limitations of the ultimate environment. If a system fails because it violates some of these sanctions, then all of its subsystems must fail. The theory does not make the decision maker in a subsystem responsible for the success of the larger system since its management is not under his control. It does hold him responsible for avoiding actions which threaten the survival of the larger system, since this obligation is a corollary of his role in perpetuating his own system.

Functionalism draws a sharper distinction between descriptive and normative theory than is customary among general economists. Some years ago a leading economist was asked whether he regarded his abstract model of the economy as descriptive or normative. More specifically, he was asked whether he regarded it as presenting an ideal of how the market economy should work or the best available description of how it actually works. He answered without the slightest reservation that the model was obviously both. He was not quite saying that the world we live in is the best of all possible worlds. He was asserting that economic activity is determined by market forces with only slight deviation from the pattern expressed in the model. The model should be taken as the norm, and the aim of policy should be to eliminate these deviations from the norm. Under this view there is very little difference between descriptive theory and normative theory.[8]

Functionalism opens a much wider gap between descriptive theory and normative theory, between things as they are and things as they should be according to criteria of rational conduct. There will always be room for improvement in marketing under the functionalist view of marketing theory. The policy maker at any level will be choosing among alternatives in the face of uncertainty generated by change and complexity. He may take account of ethical and esthetic considerations beyond anything which has been presented here. He may choose an action because it is right according to some social norm and not merely advantageous for his organization. His choice must be made within a set of limitations which rest on the fact that he must work through a system and act on behalf of a system. If he endeavors to promote his rational self-interest through a system, he is obliged to take account of the factors which affect the health of the system and its chances for survival.

The greater divergence between descriptive theory and normative theory asserted here with respect to functionalism is also observed in recent developments in dynamic economics. Samuelson and others have asserted that for any system with a goal of growth there is an optimal growth path over time. It does not follow that the control group in the system will discover this growth path or that it will be able to manage the system effectively in pursuing this path. Martin Shubik[9] has given a formal treatment of games of survival among oligopolistic competitors. He shows that a wide range of choice is available to the players in such a game and the formulation of normative rules for the players is by no means simple. He stresses the factor of incomplete information in making the outcome indeterminate.

The proposed normative theory of marketing systems may be contrasted with Churchman's approach to a scientific ethics presented in a recent book.[10] He formulates four imperatives which he feels show determinate decisions taken by the executive. The normative theory proposed here is probably most closely related to Churchman's discussion of the prudential imperative. The decision maker is advised to take this action or avoid that action in the pursuit of rational self-interest. The basic difference is the emphasis on sanctions rather than imperatives. Sanctions limit the scope of action rather than prescribing specific action. In this respect the normative theory is more in the spirit of J. M. Clark than of Churchman. Clark recognizes that the test of the market imposes constraints on competitors but that further constraints are necessary to the adequate functioning of a competitive system.

One of the editors of this book, after reading a draft of this essay, said that it appeared to be an attempt to formulate ethical standards for marketing behavior. The author denies such an intention, but the denial rests on his own special conception of what constitutes an ethical choice. He holds that an ethical problem arises only at the point where the accepted rules no longer serve and the decision maker is faced with the responsibility for weighing values and reaching a judgment in a situation which is not quite the same as any he has faced before. If there is a rule which tells him precisely what to do or a sanction which compels him to do it, he may be confronted with a moral or legal issue but not with an ethical problem.

Churchman as a scientist is inclined to believe that every decision would be completely determined if we knew enough to provide the decision maker with adequate rules. He readily admits that we are far from having such rules today. For the present he is obliged to employ such sweeping principles as his ethical imperative which suggests that we should behave in the way that future generations would wish us to behave. The view presented here is more libertarian, resting on a deep conviction of the reality of choice. It relies on constraints imposed by the market, by organized society, and by the ecological structure of the environment. Within these constraints some area of free choice remains. One would hope that the responsible executive will use this freedom creatively. He is behaving ethically when he makes creative choices on behalf of the organization he directs and the culture to which he belongs. The sanctions discussed in this version of normative theory are presumed to operate through rational self-interest. Hopefully the theory can support some normative judgments about marketing goals as well as marketing means without taking on the momentous task of creating a science of ethics.

## ENDNOTES

1. Wroe Alderson, "Survival and Adjustment in Organized Behavior Systems" in Reavis Cox and Wroe Alderson (eds.), *Theory in Marketing* (Homewood, Ill.: Richard D. Irwin, Inc., 1950).

2. Julian Steward, *Theory of Culture Change* (Urbana, Ill.: University of Illinois Press, 1955). The same general view, without the term "cultural ecology," is more fully documented by Ralph Linton in such books as *The Tree of Culture*, (New York: Alfred A. Knopf, Inc., 1955).
3. Wroe Alderson, "Conditions for a Balanced World Economy," *World Economics*, May, 1944.
4. Gunnar Myrdal, *The American Dilemma* (New York: Harper & Bros., 1944).
5. The author has derived this interpretation of the Civil War as a power struggle largely from the multivolumed history of Allan Nevins.
6. J. M. Clark, *Alternative to Serfdom* (New York: Alfred A. Knopf, Inc., 1948).
7. Wroe Alderson, *Marketing Behavior and Executive Action* (Homewood, Ill.: Richard D. Irwin, Inc., 1957).
8. George J. Stigler, *The Theory of Price* (New York: The Macmillan Co., 1952).
9. Martin Shubik, *Strategy and Market Structure* (New York: John Wiley & Sons, Inc., 1959).
10. C. West Churchman, *Prediction and Optimal Decision* (Englewood Cliffs, N.J.: Prentice-Hall, Inc., 1961).

# 44 — General Living Systems Theory and Marketing: A Framework for Analysis

*R. Eric Reidenbach and*
*Terence A. Oliva*

Reprinted from *Journal of Marketing*, published by the American Marketing Association, Vol. 45 (Fall 1981), pp. 30-37. Reprinted by permission.

In 1950, E. T. Grether recognized that for the continued development of marketing science two things were needed: better tools for analyzing the facts of marketing, and the development of a conceptual framework that will assist in asking the right questions about marketing phenomena and "in fitting facts into an orderly pattern with enlarged and significant meaning." (Schwartz 1963, p. 68). A short time later, Halbert described the state of theory development in marketing as lacking in a major theoretical framework (Halbert 1965, p. 17). More recently Bartels (1974, 1976) and Hunt (1976) have also tried to define and explain the nature of marketing and thus echo the earlier calls for an analytical framework. The failure to develop such a framework is due, in part, to the fact that marketing theory tends to lag behind marketing practice. From a pedagogical viewpoint we have had to develop explanatory devices like the four P's, which while helping to annunciate our tentative ideas, still fall short as building blocks for true theory development that could lead to marketing science. Furthermore, they tend to lead to a reductionistic focus where we lose sight of the holistic perspective. For example, we perform pricing or promotion studies, and the results tell us something about pricing or promotion as discrete variables but ignore their interactive potential. While there have been some significant gains in the form of operating heuristics, such approaches have not helped true theory development. Marketing's traditional approaches work, just as any number of reductionistic scientific and engineering approaches work, in a limited arena. The problem occurs when we try to generalize to all systems (organizations that market) or when the system's interactions become very complex.

The most diehard functionalist would have to agree that even in small firms, marketing involves more than the four P's and that it is hard to separate the marketing functions from other functions such as management and accounting. Yet from a theoretical perspective, this is precisely what we do, and it is not just limited to marketing. Theory development in other organizational areas has evolved in a similar manner, for example, management's P.O.D.C. (Plan, Organize, Direct, and Control). While such approaches have merit, they restrict our ability to deal with and to develop a more comprehensive theoretical analysis, which is becoming critically necessary in our increasingly complex world.

We believe there is a way out of the dilemma of dealing with the complexities of modern organizations that will provide a strong base for developing marketing theory; and, at the same time, will allow us still to use the time tested functional approaches that have served well in the past. It is our contention that Miller's (1978) General Living Systems Theory (GLST) offers that much needed framework.

## General Living Systems Theory

James Grier Miller in his monumental work, *Living Systems* (1978) has outlined a general theory that focuses on concrete systems from the cell through supranational levels. What Miller has attempted, then, is to develop a complete description of the structure, process, and behavior of all living systems whether they are organisms (plants, animals, humans) or organizations (groups, families, cities, nations). Miller explicitly identifies those key characteristics that all living systems must have to live. These are:

Living Systems—those systems that are:

- open—i.e., have permeable boundaries and require matter/energy and information transfers across those boundaries for survival
- negentropic—i.e., energy renewing
- complex above a minimum level
- contain a blueprint of their structure and process from the moment of origin
- contain organic compounds
- have a decision-making unit controlling the entire system
- have 19 critical subsystems or are in parasitic or symbiotic relationships with systems that provide the missing functions
- subsystems are integrated, self regulating, and act as a whole with a purpose
- can exist only in a given environment

Every living system must have these nine characteristics and must contain, in some form, the nineteen critical subsystems specified in Table 1. These critical subsystems are not identified as management, marketing, or finance but are identified by the critical system's function(s) they perform. By specifying them in this manner, there is less likelihood of drawing artificial boundaries that either do not correspond with actual living system functions or inappropriately divide a function. In short, it tends to avoid the procrustean approach of fitting the organizations to the preestablished disciplines rather than developing disciplines based on the object of inquiry.

## TABLE 1. The 19 Critical Subsystems of a Living System

***Subsystems Which Process Both Matter-Energy and Information***

1. *Reproducer*, the subsystem capable of giving rise to other systems similar to the one it is in.
2. *Boundary*, the subsystem at the perimeter that holds together the components making up the system, protects them from environmental stresses, and excludes or permits entry to various sorts of matter-energy and information.

***Subsystems Which Process Matter-Energy***

3. *Ingestor*, the subsystem that brings matter-energy across the system boundary from the environment.
4. *Distributor*, the subsystem that carries inputs from outside the system or outputs from its subsystem around the system to each component.
5. *Converter*, the subsystem that changes certain inputs to the system into forms more useful for the special processes of that particular system.
6. *Producer*, the subsystem that forms stable associations that endure for significant periods among matter-energy inputs to the system or outputs from its converter, the materials synthesized being for growth, damage repair, or replacement of components of the system, or for providing energy for moving or constituting the system's outputs of products or information markers to its suprasystem.
7. *Matter-energy storage*, the subsystem that retains in the system, for different periods of time, deposits of various sorts of matter-energy.
8. *Extruder*, the subsystem that transmits matter-energy out of the system in the forms of products or wastes.
9. *Motor*, the subsystem that moves the system or parts of it in relation to part or all of its environment or moves components of its environment in relation to each other.
10. *Supporter*, the subsystem that maintains the proper spatial relationships among components of the system, so that they can interact without weighting each other down or crowding each other.

***Subsystems Which Process Information***

11. *Input transducer*, the sensory subsystem that brings markers bearing information into the system, changing them to other matter-energy forms suitable for transmission within it.
12. *Internal transducer*, the sensory subsystem that receives from subsystems or components within the system, markers bearing information about significant alterations in those subsystems or components, changing them to other matter-energy forms of a sort that can be transmitted within it.
13. *Channel and net*, the subsystem composed of a single route in physical space or multiple interconnected routes, by which markers bearing information are transmitted to all parts of the system.
14. *Decoder*, the subsystem that alters the code of information input to it through the input transducer or internal transducer into a "private" code that can be used internally by the system.
15. *Associator*, the subsystem that carries out the first stage of the learning process, forming enduring associations among items of information in the system.
16. *Memory*, the subsystem that carries out the second stage of the learning process, storing various sorts of information in the system for different periods of time.
17. *Decider*, the executive subsystem that receives information inputs from all other subsystems and transmits to them information outputs that control the entire system.
18. *Encoder*, the subsystem that alters the code of information input to it from other information processing subsystems, from a private code used internally by the system into a public code that can be interpreted by other systems in its environment.
19. *Output transducer*, the subsystem that puts out markers bearing information from the system, changing markers within the system into other matter-energy forms that can be transmitted over channels in the system's environment.

What Miller gives us then, is a tool for understanding the nature, processes, and behavior of living systems. Yet, it is done as a result of the observations about all levels of living systems, not from a particular point of view. Hence it tends to avoid the biases and omissions that creep in as a result of viewing organizations from the reductionist perspective of a given discipline. Miller's theory unravels the complexity of living systems in a manner with which we can deal. This means that when we identify a set of processes as marketing, we can see how those processes relate to those processes identified with the other academic disciplines. Simply put, the interrelationships and overlappings among the disciplines are made manifest.

Similarly, we can see how a given process within an organization can function in one way for marketing and another for management or accounting. Many so-called marketing activities may have managerial components and vice versa, and pricing is a good example. It would be difficult to argue that price, while being one of the four P's, is in actual practice solely under the domain of marketing. We are dealing with complex, interrelated operations accomplished within a systemic context. Therefore, our theoretical simplifications miss the mark when dealing with complex organizations, even though they are appropriate as preliminary pedagogical tools or for dealing with less complex situations.

## Marketing: A Set of Critical Subsystems

In this section we focus on critical subsystems (see Table 1) that perform traditional marketing functions. This narrowing of perspective allows us to move from the familiar ground of traditional marketing functions to Miller's critical subsystems, and, subsequently, to a more systemic view. However, it must be kept in mind that when we identify a given critical subsystem as marketing, we are also explicitly recognizing that the subsystem identified performs activities viewed as management, accounting, finance, and/or any other nonmarketing business activities. Furthermore, this narrowing of focus, while necessary, is done at the expense of ignoring other critical nonmarketing organizational subsystems and, consequently, ignoring their interactive nature. Examples of the multifunctional nature of these subsystems are included to give the reader a flavor of their interactive nature.

### Subsystems That Primarily Process Information

Nine of the 19 critical subsystems (see Table 1) are involved in the processing of information, attesting to the paramount importance of information to any living system (organization). One of the major functions of marketing is that of providing information, both from the environment to the firm and from the firm back to the environment. The critical subsystem bringing information into the organization from the environment is

11. *The Input Transducer*: The sensory subsystem that brings markers bearing information into the system, changing them to other matter-energy forms suitable for transmission within it.

This is an important function that coincides with the monitoring of the many uncontrollable and controllable environments in which the firm operates. These environments include the economic, social-cultural, technological, competitive, distributive, political, and legal (McCarthy 1978, p. 94). Changes in these environments represent either an opportunity or a threat to the firm. The history of business is replete with cases of firms that have not properly developed this subsystem or have ignored the information provided by it. Such was the situation with the railroads (Levitt 1960) and the automobile industry (Vanderwicken 1975) to name two outstanding topical examples. In both cases industry growth was retarded due in part to a breakdown either within the input transducer or between that critical subsystem and the decider subsystem. Such, however, is not the case with Procter and Gamble, whose goal with respect to product introduction is to be 90% sure of product success prior to test marketing (Vanderwicken 1974). This high level of confidence is based on information gathered through their input transducer subsystem(s) and conveyed to other critical organizational subsystems.

In addition to the marketing activities, the input transducer provides information for the other nonmarketing functions. The input transducer is an integral component in any management information system, where, in addition to collecting market information, the organization is concerned with collecting information to make technological and sociopolitical forecasts (Roman 1970). Overall a major concern of the decider subsystem is to establish a strategic database of aid in assessing current situations as well as future opportunities (King and Cleland 1977).

14. *The Decoder*: The subsystem that alters the code of information input to it through either the input transducer or internal transducer into a private code that can be used internally by the system.

The structure of this subsystem will vary according to the orientation of the organization's decider unit. For example, in highly centralized organizations, this subsystem may consist of a small committee acting in an advisory capacity, serving a single decider unit (no. 17, Table 1). In more decentralized organizations, the decoder subsystems may consist of several project teams, each responsible to its own decider subsystem acting somewhat independently. This is the basis for Sheth's model of industrial buying behavior (Sheth 1973). Regardless of the structure, the output of the decoder subsystem (no. 14, Table 1) consists of specific organizational reports and communications transmitted to the decider for subsequent action. The decider subsystem then develops forecasts, budgets, plans, and makes decisions that guide the organization towards its predetermined objectives. Notice this is a traditional management function, yet realistically it cannot be divorced from other nonmanagerial activities.

Those subsystems providing information from the firm back to the environment are:

18. *The Encoder*: The subsystem that alters the code of information input to it from other information processing subsystems, from a private code used internally by the system into a public code that can be interpreted by other systems in its environment.
19. *Output Transducer*: The subsystem that puts out markers bearing information from the system, changing markers within the system into other matter energy forms that can be transmitted over channels in the system's environment.

It is through the encoder subsystem that target market communication is developed. Private codes (i.e. objectives, strategies, and tactics) are converted into a public code (i.e., ad campaigns, displays, and promotional messages). This public code is then physically communicated to the various pertinent audiences in the environment by means of the output transducer subsystem. Channels take the form of television, radio, magazines, billboards, etc. These audiences most obviously consist of consumers in the markets being serviced. However, wholesalers, distributors, and other distribution channel members also represent important audiences, as well as other concerned publics (Kotler 1980, pp. 50-53).

An interesting proposition arises with respect to these critical subsystems. It will be recalled that the criteria of a living system require that these critical subsystems be either incorporated within the system or exist in either a parasitic or symbiotic relationship with it. Depending on the size or level of sophistication of the organization, these information processing subsystems will either exist as a part of the organization (the advertising department, research department, etc.), or exist in a symbiotic relationship in the form of advertising agencies, research firms, or consultants. In the latter case, both systems (the firm and the agency) benefit from this relationship, hence the symbiosis.

The input transducer, decoder, encoder, and output transducer are the four critical subsystems providing the requisite information flows from the organization to generate the demand necessary for survival. Again, these subsystems do not only deal with demand creation but process and convey other nonmarketing information within and throughout the organization. There are four critical subsystems that process matter/energy and are involved with the important task of servicing demand. These are discussed next.

## Subsystems That Primarily Process Matter-Energy

The first two subsystems involved in the service function are:

3. *Ingestor*: The subsystem that brings matter-energy across the boundary from the environment.
4. *Distributor*: The subsystem that carries inputs from outside the system or outputs from its subsystem around the system to each component.

These two subsystems, in essence, describe the concern of purchasing and material management, the primary focus of which is to ''assure an orderly flow of materials into the corporation'' (Staudt, Taylor, and Bowersox 1976, pp. 315-517). Concerned with the task of procurement, these two subsystems secure components, parts, raw materials, and equipment from outside suppliers existing in the organization's environment. In so doing they are concerned with attempting to optimize the input mix that is dependent upon the optimal output mix.

Once in the system, the necessary materials must be conveyed to the proper components of the converter subsystems (no. 5, Table 1) that transforms inputs into meaningful outputs of the system. Because of the need to reconcile flows between the various demand servicing subsystems, a matter-energy subsystem is instrumental.

7. *Matter-Energy Storage*: The subsystem that retains in the system, for different periods of time, deposits of various sorts of matter-energy.

This is the inventory function of the firm permitting the collecting of finished goods and inputs that have not yet been converted. This subsystem assures an orderly flow of input into the coverter and an orderly flow out of the converter. Again, this subsystem may exist in a symbiotic relationship with the organization. Independent warehouses and channel members act as depositories for both unprocessed materials and finished products. Clearly, this subsystem interfaces with production management and accounting.

17. *Decider*: The executive subsystem that receives information inputs from all other subsystems and transmits to them information outputs that control the entire system.

The functions of this critical subsystem correspond to those performed by marketing management, although other aspects of organization management, are carried out by this subsystem. As mentioned before, the decider system receives information inputs from the input transducer and decoder subsystems. These inputs are acted upon and become strategic plans directing the functioning of the other critical subsystems involved in marketing and nonmarketing functions. The decider subsystem occupies a key position between the two generic functions of demand identification/creation and demand servicing. This enables an interface and reconciliation of input to output or demand creation and demand servicing.

Figure 1 shows in schematic form how traditional marketing activities can be mapped into Miller's framework. It is the necessary starting point of moving from traditional marketing to the systemic and integrated approach needed to develop a theory of marketing. The multiplicity of activities (from a disciplinary standpoint) by a given subsystem leads us to suggest the need for an integrated approach to the study of marketing. The input transducer, for example, cannot be understood from a marketing, management, or accounting standpoint only. It must be understood as a required process of a living system, and therefore, requires a multidimensional viewpoint.

In summary, what has happened in the past is the development of a number of disciplines, each of which yields a single view. What is needed is a single discipline with a multiplicity of views. Some of the more salient implications of these statements for marketing are examined in the next section.

## Implications for Marketing Theory

What implications does GLST hold for marketing theorists and writers? First and foremost, GLST makes explicit that no real understanding (hence, theory development) of organizations can be gained from the perspective of a single discipline or even a patchwork quilt of several disciplines. What is required is an integrated approach. More specifically, marketing, as well as other business disciplines, should be analyzed, studied, and taught in an integrated fashion. This means that team teaching might be a more effective and appropriate approach. Research might be taught by a combined team from marketing, management, psychology, consumer behavior, and statistics. Obviously, this would call for a restructuring of current business curricula, not just in marketing but throughout the entire business school.

Is such a restructuring unrealistic? We think not. The truth is that in the real world such integration actually exists. What we have not had is a theory of integrated wholes. GLST provides a theoretical framework that focuses on the integration that actually exists. Furthermore, the increasing complexity of organizational systems is such that they are having to become more integrated and to develop hybrid structures to meet new organizational demands. An interesting example of this comes from management, where the traditional rule had been that each subordinate should have only one boss. Operationally this has proved to be inappropriate in high technology organizations (e.g., the electronics industry), which have had to move to matrix structures where subordinates have no fewer than two bosses. The point is that GLST indicates that organizations must and will adapt to survive and that the rules for this do not depend on preestablished disciplines, but rather on the rules of living systems. The result is that if we are to move

**FIGURE 1. Marketing Subsystems Within the Organization**

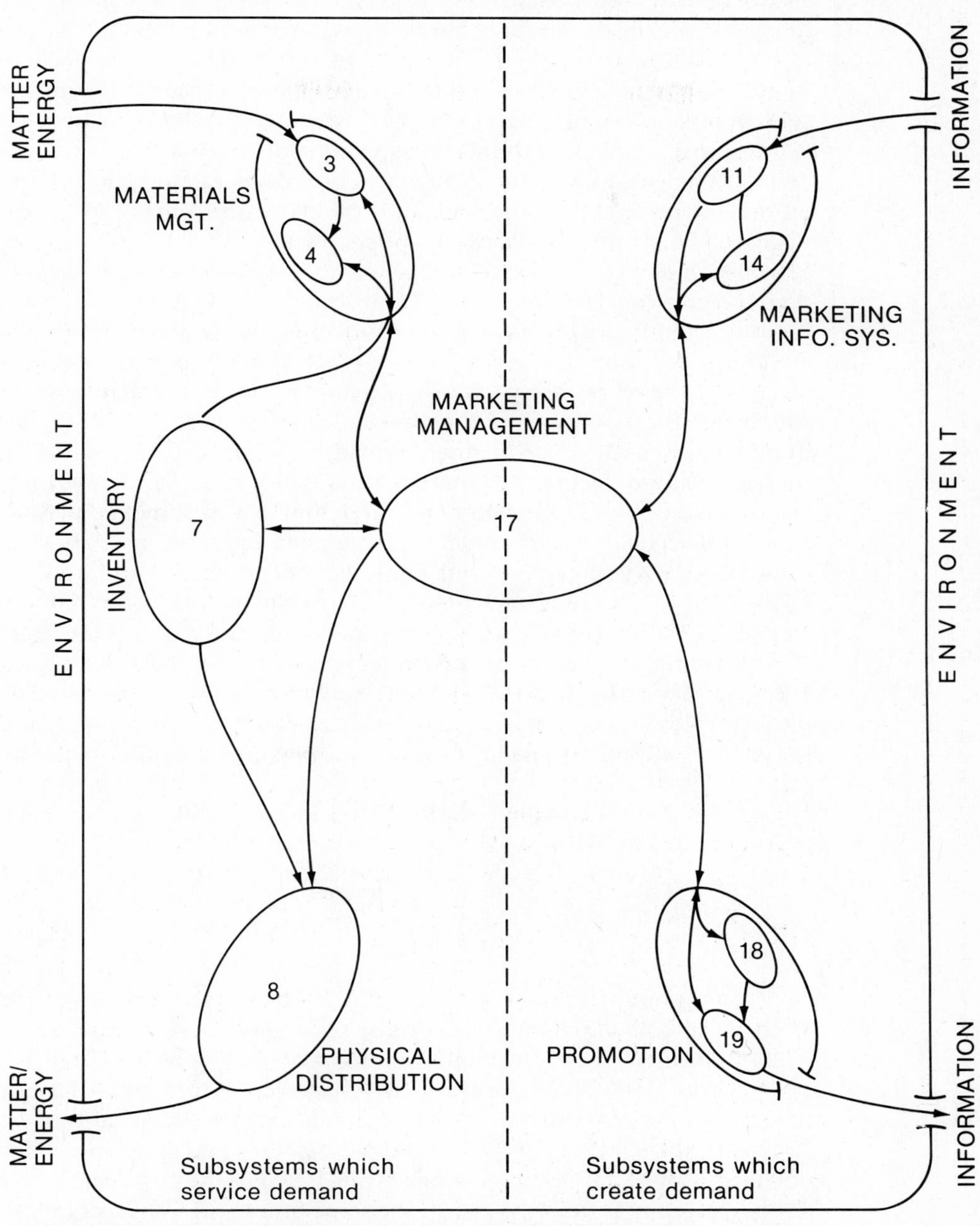


LEGEND: Numbers represent subsystem function in Miller's paradigm.
Arrowheads represent matter/energy and/or information flow directions.

toward a complete theory of marketing, it will have to be within the broader theory of living organizations (i.e., GLST), just as subatomic particle physics must fall within the more general theory of relativity.

This leads us to our second implication for marketing, one closely related to that mentioned above. A comprehensive theory of marketing must represent an integration of disciplines. Team research like team teaching is going to be a must. Marketing draws heavily on fields like psychology, sociology, and economics, and what is needed is a common paradigm which provides a framework for analyzing the constituent fields comprising the social sciences. Realistically, one individual cannot hope to know everything in a given field. This becomes even more critical when we are looking at the class of all demand creating and servicing organizations. GLST provides the direction for interdisciplinary teams of researchers to work toward a common understanding. Without such a framework we will continue to develop reductionistic, categorical perspectives such as the four P's which work only in simplistic situations, while at the same time being aware of the complications that actually exist in the business world.

The third implication for marketing is that it must be defined within a GLST context. Some of the more recent definitions have moved in this direction. Kotler (1980, p. 19) evidenced this need by defining marketing as a "human activity directed at satisfying wants and needs through exchange processes." His definition represents a broadened view of marketing that encompasses the application of marketing techniques to nontraditional areas of activity, e.g., charitable organizations, police forces, the army, etc. (Kotler 1980, pp. 680-687). This broadening, however, has been accomplished at the expense of specificity (Bartels 1974, p. 76), and it can be argued that Kotler's definition also includes such maintenance functions as breathing, a trivial application.

GLST offers an equally broadened yet more specific view of marketing at the organizational level as:

> That system activity which is performed by a subset of nine critical subsystems directed at the identification, creation, and servicing of demand.

Several points in this concept merit mention. First, marketing functions are performed by an identifiable and specific set of subsystems. This facilitates a study of their individual nature and, of equal importance, their systemic nature. GLST specifies this systemic nature by indicating the necessary interrelationships between and among these critical subsystems. Secondly, focusing on the identification, creation, and servicing of demand delineates trivial applications of marketing (such as the breathing argument) as one descends systems levels. At the same time, a GLST view of marketing does not preclude its application to marketing's newfound arenas of activity. That is, marketing is accomplished by organisms and organizations that create and service demand. This also applies to churches, government, etc.

Thirdly, as with any true extension of a field, the new definition does not obviate the traditional conceptualizations. Rather, it shows how they fit within the next context. Just as economic theory has built on its initial model of purely competitive economies, so too must marketing extend itself from its functional perspective to a systemic one. We cannot stress too highly that we are not suggesting that the traditional functional approach be discarded. Instead we envision it viewed within a newer and broader system context. Figure 2 indicates how this may be accomplished. Traditionally we have tended to develop and study the universal marketing functions as distinct categories. GLST shows how the functional processes fit within the living system, which critical subsystem(s) performs them, and how they relate to one another within the living processes. That is, Figure 2 flows into Figure 1. The result is that we still have pedagogical and theoretical simplicity at those levels where it is appropriate, while at the same time retaining the complex richness of the organismic whole. This is critical if we are ever to move away from merely knowing that buying, for example, is not just a marketing function. We must be able to show how it is an integral part of the organizational life process.

**FIGURE 2. Marketing Functions Related to the Critical Subsystems**

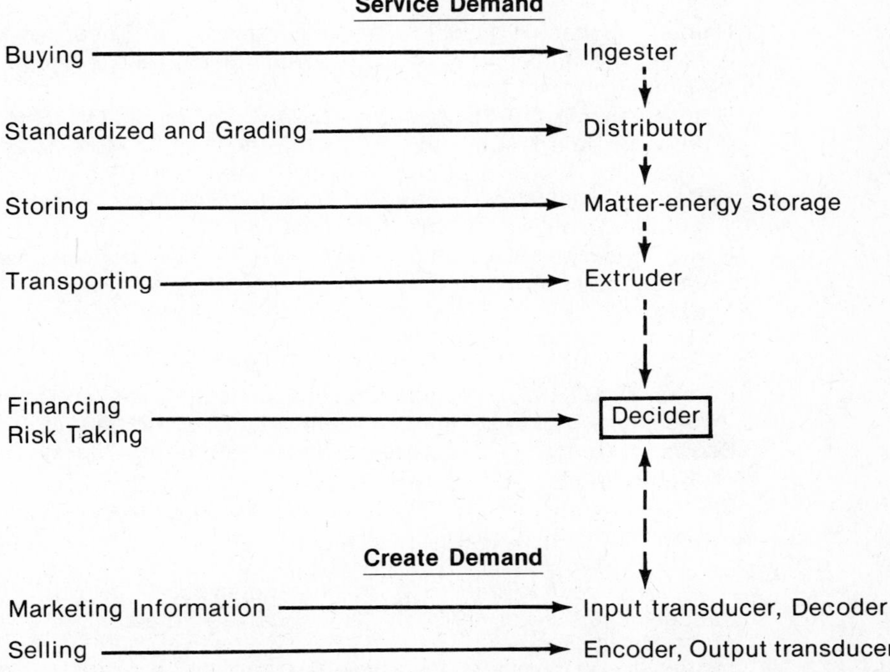

## Summary

This paper has endeavored to examine marketing in light of Miller's general living systems theory. We have looked at the marketing functions in light of the critical subsystems that comprise all living systems. It is not our intent to suggest that what has been presented is complete and/or beyond criticism but to present a framework for analyzing marketing that will allow us to extend the traditional functional analysis to a systemic analysis. Miller has given us a starting point. His GLST provides us with the analytic framework to start an integrated attempt at analyzing the marketing function and, hence, move toward a true theory of marketing.

However, no such attempt can be successful unless we recognize the need for integrated team-oriented research. We cannot retreat into a single discipline and expect to produce a viable theoretical analysis about an organizational entity. GLST points out clearly that academic reductionism will simply lead to sterility of thought and theory, leaving us even further removed from the complexities of the real world.

## REFERENCES

Bartels, Robert (1974), "The Identity Crisis in Marketing," *Journal of Marketing*, 38 (October), 73-76.

——— (1976), *The History of Marketing Thought*, 2nd ed., Columbus, OH: Grid Inc.

Halbert, Michael H. (1965), "The Requirements for Theory in Marketing," in *Theory in Marketing*, Reavis Cox, Wroe Alderson and Stanley J. Shapiro, eds., Homewood, IL: Richard D. Irwin, Inc., 17-36.

Hunt, Shelby D. (1976), *Marketing Theory*, Columbus, OH: Grid Inc.

King, W. R. and D. Cleland (1977), "Information for More Effective Strategic Planning," *Journal of Long Range Planning*, 10 (February), 59-64.

Kotler, Philip (1980), *Marketing Management: Analysis, Planning and Control*, 4th ed. Englewood Cliffs, NJ: Prentice-Hall, Inc.

Levitt, Theodore (1960), "Marketing Myopia," *Harvard Business Review*, 38 (July-August), 45-56.

McCarthy, E. Jerome (1978), *Basic Marketing: A Managerial Approach*, 6th ed. Homewood, IL: Richard D. Irwin, Inc.

Miller, James G. (1978), *Living Systems*, New York: McGraw-Hill.

Roman, D. D. (1970), "Technological Forecasting in the Decision Process," *Academy of Management Journal*, 13 (June), 127-138.

Schwartz, George (1963), *Development of Marketing Theory*, Cincinnati, OH: South Western Publishing Company.

Sheth, Jagdish N. (1973), "A Model of Industrial Buyer Behavior" *Journal of Marketing*, 37 (October), 50-56.

Staudt, Thomas A., Donald, A. Taylor, and Donald J. Bowersox (1976), *A Managerial Approach to Marketing*, 3rd ed., Englewood Cliffs, NJ: Prentice-Hall Inc.

Vanderwicken, Peter (1974), "P & G's Secret Ingredient," *Fortune*, 42 (July), 75-79, 164-166.

——— (1975), "What's Really Wrong at Chrysler," *Fortune*, 43 (May), 176-179, 214-216.

# 45 ___ Marketing Theory of the Firm

*John A. Howard*

Reprinted from *Journal of Marketing*, published by the American Marketing Association, Vol. 47 (Fall 1983), pp. 90-100. Reprinted by permission.

The large multidivisional company faces the problem of bringing its available functional skills to bear on the decision-making process at the right time and place. The problem is perhaps sharpest in making decisions involving product innovation where marketing has many of the needed skills: basic research, technology, product development, and introduction. It has been aggravated by the changing role of marketing over the past two decades. For instance, marketing's role has diminished at the higher levels, as that of financial managers and lawyers has increased (Hayes and Abernathy 1980).

From intensive discussions with CEO's, professional board members, and high level consultants over the past three years, the author is convinced that a major reason for this decline is that marketing mangers have not had a systematic body of knowledge, or worse yet, have focused their attention upon the sales subfunction. Such knowledge is needed to support their functioning effectively at the top level where a rationale—a good logic—is so essential to explain and justify action that is unfamiliar to the other functions.

Almost exactly coinciding with this decline has been the emergence of a solid body of basic knowledge of the customer. But, like the output of most basic research, it comes in bits and pieces. To be useful to managers, a superstructure of descriptive concepts is required to focus these bits and pieces upon strategic planning.

True, progress has been made in strategic planning (Day 1977, 1981b). The mere discussion of the concept has been useful in endowing marketing thinking with the need for and potential of a longer-term planning horizon. But as Wind (1981, p. 22) has emphasized, marketing has contributed little to the understanding of corporate strategy: "Yet, conceptually, a closer interface between marketing and corporate strategy would be beneficial to both areas." Wind and Robertson (1982) present a proposal for bringing it about.

The major barrier to this interface is the lack of a well-articulated structure for accomplishing it. The objective of this article is to describe a superstructure of descriptive concepts and to relate it to prescriptive concepts to provide a normative theory to guide management.[1] The theme is that marketers have a resource—their understanding of the customer—that is not yet fully utilized in their effort to plan strategically.

## Approach to Theory

Since subtle ideas are involved in theory building, it will be helpful to specify the approach being taken. The superstructure is a descriptive system, but both descriptive and prescriptive concepts are necessary.[2] A manager needs a systematic way of describing the environment as input to the prescriptive concepts to achieve specific objectives. Figure 1 displays this descriptive-prescriptive dichotomy combined with the philosophical dichotomy of empirical versus axiomatic to form a four-celled table. Obviously, in the current state of marketing knowledge, it is necessary to rely largely on an empirical approach. The field has not yet built much analysis from an axiomatic foundation where the basic assumptions are stated mathematically. However, the logic of marketing would be much surer if an axiomatic approach so well-exemplified by economic theory were available.

As shown in the upper left of Figure l, most descriptive concepts of the customer are empirical. For example, in recent years customer research has drawn much more heavily from psychology, where axiomatization is not common. However, because of the splendid work in industrial organization by economists in the last 30 years, there is an axiomatic basis for describing competition, as indicated in the lower left cell in Figure 1. This will be discussed below.

The upper left cell of Figure 1 is familiar territory to marketers. Prescriptive concepts for relating the various functions in the planning process are necessary. A key characteristic of a prescriptive concept is that it is related to objectives to be accomplished. Concepts are needed for integrating the functional fields around the product development process. These tend not to be well-formulated and, of course, are empirical. Anderson (1982) has carefully designed a descriptive theory of these interfaces, but in this author's judgment it focuses upon the symptoms instead of the disease.

**FIGURE 1. Intellectual Foundations**

| Logical Foundation | Purpose: Descriptive | Purpose: Prescriptive |
|---|---|---|
| Empirical | customers | marketing<br>organization<br>financial<br>manufacturing<br>R&D |
| Axiomatic | competition | contribution<br>present value |

In the lower right is the familiar profit contribution tool which has been widely used in marketing teaching and practice. Also, the present value concept first introduced into marketing by Howard (1963a) in the Ford Foundation study of marketing knowledge has come increasingly into current marketing thinking, as an orientation toward the long-term has become common. Both of these are axiomatic, having developed out of economic theory.

Four descriptive concepts are essential elements of the normative theory: demand and supply cycle, product hierarchy, competitive structure, and customer decision model.

## Demand and Supply Cycle

The demand and supply cycle (D&SC) describes customer and supplier behavior over the life cycle, as seen in Figure 2. On the left a set of specifications about customer information needs and other characteristics are described. To put stages of the customer decision process on the life cycle may seem questionable, since individual customers may not conform precisely to the mode. However, it is a useful device analogous to Alfred Marshall's ''representative firm'' of almost a hundred years ago (Marshall 1961). These specifications imply a series of first-cut, parameter-setting but general questions faced by the manager in planning product development. On the right of Figure 2 is a corresponding set of specifications and implied questions about how the five functional areas of a company—marketing, organization, financial control, manufacturing, and R&D—change over the life cycle in carrying out that planning. The concept of a life cycle is not meant here to be rigorous, such as a logistic curve. Rather, it is merely that an innovation—a new product class—typically grows slowly for awhile, then more rapidly, and finally levels off. For a very useful discussion of the life cycle, see Day (1981a).

The central theoretical point here is that for a company to be successful, customers *should* be the dominant driving force. To support this contention, two unrelated strands of basic research are combined. First, Abernathy and Utterback (1978), using the terminology on the right side of Figure 2, have shown from a long program of research that successful product innovators exhibit a particular pattern of behavior over the life cycle. However, the purpose here is not to discuss the prescriptive aspects of these features, as implied in Figure 1, but to describe the management subprocesses that operate in successful companies during the innovation process.

Second, customers are described as the basis for showing their role. Since the splendid work of Abernathy and Utterback on the supply side is weak on the demand side, this gap is filled by customer behavior research. As seen in Figure 2, it has become increasingly evident that customers exhibit the pattern of behavior described there largely in terms of information requirements (Howard 1983), as postulated two decades ago (Howard 1963b).

## FIGURE 2. Demand and Supply Cycle

***INDUSTRY VOLUME***

***A—Customer Response***

***Routinized Response Behavior***

1. Limited information required
2. Information *content*
   a) reminder
   b) some brand performance
3. Information *form* irrelevant
4. Almost no time necessary
5. Price elasticity <1; cross elasticity high

***Limited Problem Solving***

1. Substantial amount of information necessary
2. Information *content* is brand only
   a) how brand identified
   b) how brand performs
   c) brand distinctiveness, information consistency, and peer consensus
3. Information *form* requirements loose
4. Not much time required
5. Price elasticity >1; cross-elasticity low
6. Segments develop

***Extensive Problem Solving***

1. Great amount of information essential
2. Information *content*
   a) how product is used, relation to other products
   b) identifying and evaluative attributes
   c) position of brand on attributes
      1) how brand identified
      2) how brand performs
      3) brand distinctiveness, information consistency, and peer consensus
3. Information *form*; small pieces, ordered as listed, concrete, kernel sentences
4. Substantial time necessary
5. Price elasticity <1; cross-elasticity = 0

***INTRODUCTION***

***GROWTH***

***MATURITY***

***B—Supplier Response***

***Stable—Operations dominated***

1. Price competition and cost reduction
2. Cost reduction and quality improvement pressures cause process innovation
3. Incremental process change increases quality and productivity
4. Production is capital intensive and rigid
5. Organization control by structure, goals, and rules

***Transition—Product dominated***

1. Compete on product variation, dominant design emerges
2. Reduced customer and technical uncertainty stimulates R&D increases
3. Major process changes required by rising volume and emerging market niches
4. Production more rigid and changes only in major steps
5. Organization control through liaison, project, and task groups

***Fluid—Market dominated***

1. Innovation springs from customer's needs
2. Compete on product performance
3. Frequent major changes in product
4. Production flexible and inefficient
5. Organization information informal entrepreneurial

***TIME***

When the two patterns are compared in terms of the processes implied in those two descriptions, a persuasive case is presented that successful companies are dominantly customer-driven. If a pattern of supplier behavior was designed under typical conditions to best serve the customer needs, as specified in Figure 2, it would probably closely match the supplier behavior described there. Further, recent evidence from analysis of the PIMS data indicates that profitable companies tend to be substantially more "customer-driven" than "competitor-driven" (Carpenter 1983).

This hypothesis is not surprising for the introductory stage. However, it also applies at the growth stage because a company can enter only by means of an improved product, and so it, too, should be customer-driven. Finally, in the mature stage it still should be customer-driven, which is shown by Wierenga's research (1974). Four-fifths of a large panel of consumers of three frequently-purchased mature products over a two-year period reported periods of shifting brands with varying degrees of frequency, and thus periodically became ready targets of company promotional activity. Marketing did not cause them to shift, but once they considered shifting, marketing could influence them to shift to a particular brand. Thus, an appropriate way to define routinized response behavior is that it exists when the customer has developed an evoked set of brands among which he/she chooses and periodically cycles out of a pattern of repeat purchase and back again to that pattern.[3] The remaining one-fifth of the sample regularly bought the same brand.

Rather than accepting the principle here that the customer (left side of Figure 2) causes supplier behavior (right side of Figure 2), one might argue that the two sides are mutually interdependent. However, as long as there is competition among suppliers, those suppliers who best meet the customers' needs will best survive.

## Significance of Customer-Driven

What is the significance to a normative theory of a firm being customer-driven? Abernathy and Utterback emphasize that for a company to innovate successfully with a product by serving customer requirements, it must undergo a series of management *process* innovations necessary to carrying out the product innovation. These are implied in the changing behavior pattern over the life cycle on the right side of Figure 2. These process innovations have to do with marketing, organization, financial planning and control, manufacturing, and R&D, the areas of management listed in the upper right cell of Figure 1.

The marketing decisions are clearly implied. Information and other conditions must be provided to fit the customer's needs if he/she is to buy. Organizational decisions are less obvious. At the bottom, a collegial organization is desirable, while at the top a hierarchical structure is more effective. Correspondingly, financial planning and control plays less of a role at the bottom than at the midpoint and much more than at the top, where the emphasis must be on efficiency. Research and development is strongest in the growth stage, as noted on the right of Figure 2. It might seem that it should be the introductory stage. However, as a product ascends the life cycle, the opportunity for incremental product improvement increases as each company strives to have its product be the dominant design for the industry. In fact, Abernathy and Utterback point out that often the sum of these incremental improvements is greater than the original and stimulates R&D expenditures. Marketing has been severely criticzed for not paying enough attention to R&D (Bennett and Cooper 1981). Finally, manufacturing decisions are also implied. References to cost, for example, imply manufacturing, since production is often the major cost element of a product. More specifically, the great flexibility, both in product design and volume needed at the uncertain bottom of the cycle, requires a highly inefficient factory. At the top, a standardized product design, high volumes, and emphasis on cost reduction encourages a highly efficient factory. The CAD-CAM concept and the supporting technology leads to a major integration of marketing, engineering, and manufacturing (Morgan 1982) which can greatly reduce the design-production cycle and improve product quality. Marketing becomes better integrated because in the new system, both engineering and manufacturing become more aware of the necessity to introduce the customer's needs into design and planning.

The D&SC with its time and cross-functional perspective is a natural starting point for a manager to begin planning his/her strategy. At a minimum it is a checklist of the questions for which he/she should have the answers. The analysis can be carried as far as current knowledge will permit. Having exhausted this knowledge, the manager must turn to the product hierarchy. Then, as information is received from each of the three descriptive concepts, necessary changes can be made in the management of the functions, and beginning strategy formulated.

## Product Hierarchy

The product hierarchy (PH) is an empirical descriptive concept which ties together all four descriptive concepts. It is a static view, a snapshot, of an individual customer, whereas the D&SC is growth oriented, a moving picture of an aggregation. Figure 3 describes a typical customer's mental picture or memory of a particular product, of its competing products, and more general aggregations of these and of relations among them (Rosch 1978). Current practice, however, sometimes mistakenly creates the PH in terms of technology. Even though it is a picture of only one customer's mind, the person's culture—especially language—forces substantial commonality upon its dimensions. Finally, it is an old concept with a new label.[4]

## Definition

Technically, the PH is a taxonomy of products by which categories are related to one another by class inclusion. The greater the inclusiveness of a category within a taxonomy, the higher the level of abstraction. More specifically, it is that portion of the semantic memory which pertains to a particular product and its related products, including all the associations with these products in the customer's mind, such as how to identify each one, how good, and how available each one is.[5] That the concept exists in people's minds has been clearly shown by Rosch and others, but the methodology used by these researchers like most basic research is too slow and expensive for marketing practice. Effort has long been made to infer a type of brand hierarchy by stochastic modeling, but only recently has the attempt been made to integrate it into behavioral theory (Vanhonacker 1980). Consequently, as yet it is not a well-measured concept. It is something like attitude was two decades ago, but even without knowing the precise content, managers find it highly useful in organizing their thinking.

## Contribution of Product Hierarchy

The product hierarchy suggests why a customer is able to respond to an unknown product concept in a concept test as well as he/she does. The PH provides a framework—a "map" for buying—within which the customer can attempt to match the new concept to a variety of products and levels of product groupings in memory. Having found the "closest fit," the customer then has a wealth of information to draw upon in beginning to form a concept of that new thing. The PH orders the market so that he/she can make a reasonably rational decision.

It provides the marketer with a static picture of what the customer "knows." By comparing this static picture, $PH_t$, with what it should look like at some designated future time, $t + 1$, the marketer can then define the marketing task as that which will move the customer from $PH_t$ to $PH_{t+1}$.

Before discussing other management contributions of the PH, more elaboration of Figure 3 will help. Figure 3 is a representation of the way General Motors thought a typical customer looked at the automobile market in 1968 when it was planning the introduction of the Vega. The Vega was viewed as a new brand in the subcompact car class, competing especially with the VW, and, therefore, would be filling the dotted box on that level. However, since the Vega was heavier and more expensive, it might have been viewed by the customer as a compact or as a whole new product class filling the second level dotted box. Thus the PH provides the vital information of whether a product is an innovation or a new brand in an established product class. This process suggests that how a customer categorizes a product determines what it is—just another brand, an innovation, or a radical innovation. In this way the customer determines the life cycle of a product,

**FIGURE 3. Product Hierarchy for Automobiles**

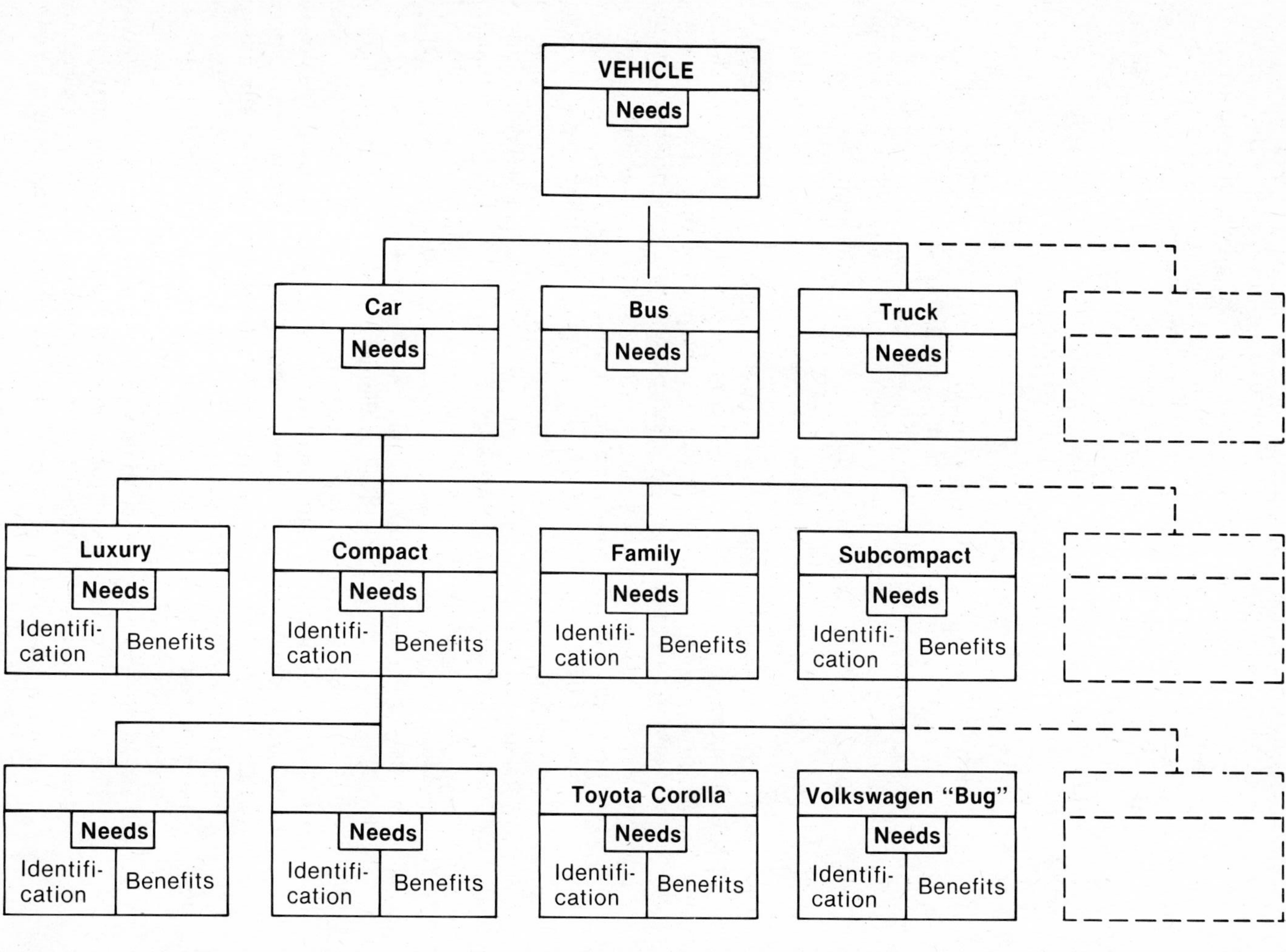

a major market constraint upon the manager. This evidence of customer power adds further support to the hypothesis that a successful company is likely to be customer-driven.

The term *needs* in Figure 3 refers to general descriptions of the role the product can play in the customer's life. For example, the VW could be used to take your kids to school, drive to the station, etc. Miller (1978) has called this general kind of information needed by a prospective buyer "practical knowledge" as contrasted with the more precise "lexical knowledge." Lexical or word knowledge are the two overall sets of attributes by which a customer conceptualizes a brand or product class. For example, the lexical knowledge for the Vega was the identifying characteristic ("body style") and evaluative characteristics (benefits, e.g., "durability"). Finally, market segments are indicated by the position of this customer's preferred brand in relation to a "prototype" as described by Mervis and Rosch (1981), the prototype being the typical position in the array of brands making up the product class. He/she compares anything new with this prototype to decide in which category it belongs and what the characteristics of the new thing are. When the preferred brand is to the extreme right or left of the prototype, a market segment is suggested.

With this background, two additional and important functions of the PH can now be appreciated. First, it feeds customer-appropriate vocabulary—as in Figure 3, a noun labels the basic level (car) and another noun labels the subordinate level (subcompact), respectively—into the demand side of the D&SC. These nouns are not only important in themselves in explaining an innovation to a customer, but the order in which they appear in the product hierarchy is also important as shown in the extensive problem solving stage of the left side of Figure 2. However, marketing may early influence these nouns. Second, it specifies who the competitors are at each level. However, because of the direct influence of competition on strategy, it is dealt with next as a separate concept.

## Competitive Structure

As was seen in the PH, what the customer categorizes as equivalent brands determines who competes, which is the major input to competitive structure (CS). Thus, the customer is not only the source of the life cycle but also the source of competition, the second major constraint upon the manager. This indication of customer power lends further credence to the hypothesis that successful companies are customer-driven.

Three key dimensions determining competitive intensity, as shown in Figure 4, are the number of competitors (on an inverse scale), size distribution of those competitors (degree of domination), and degree of product differentiation. Sellers are shown on the right and buyers on the left.

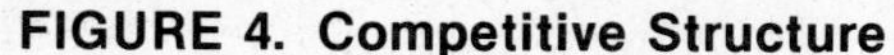
FIGURE 4. Competitive Structure

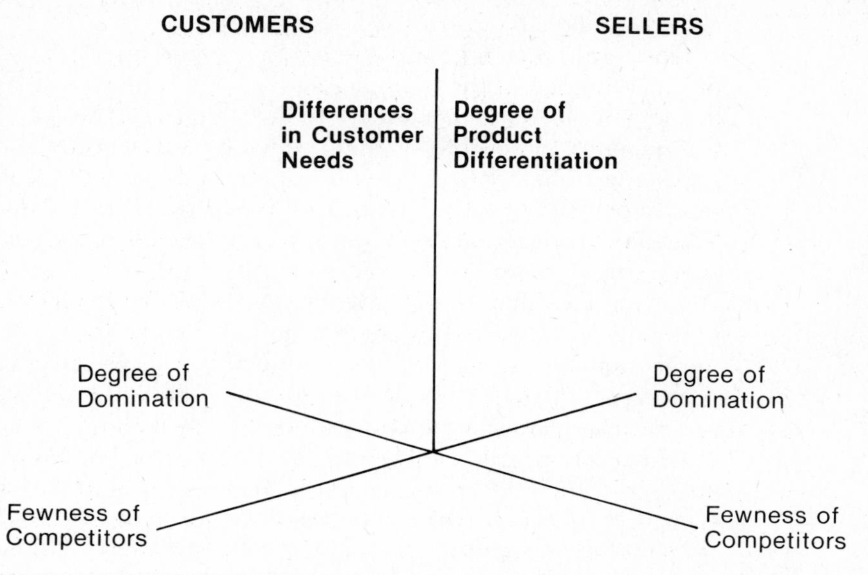


When selling to a consumer market, the "Scarcity of Competitors" and "Degree of Domination" axes on the left are irrelevant because the customers are thousands, if not millions, and none exercises any degree of market domination except in the case of buying groups, for example. However, the vertical dimension can be quite relevant for consumer markets in terms of "Differences in Customer Needs," which indicates potential segments. In industrial markets, the buying side may be quite concentrated and powerful.

These three determinants cover much the same ground as does Porter (1980). This is not surprising since both evolved from the same basic source, industrial organization research. The analysis here to simplify is less detailed than Porter's, but the emphasis in this paper is on the customer where his work is less complete.

The three determinants of competition provide a strategic picture. It represents the market power of an industry versus its customers or suppliers, either of whom can influence the profit margins of the companies in an industry. An element of this strategic picture is the price elasticity measure referred to in Figure 2 because it tells the manager whether it is advisable to use price and how.

## Market Structures

Within this industry framework, the individual company strives to achieve its own ends. But, as a part of the strategic orientation, it still must often be concerned about the welfare of the industry as a whole. One way to think about this is Figure 5, showing five competitive structures in terms of only two dimensions to simplify.

When the innovation is first introduced, the innovator is obviously a monopolist. As new companies enter the market, typically a monopolistic competitive structure develops. Later, a ''shake-out'' occurs and the industry is reduced to an oligopoly, but a differentiated oligopoly. It occurs through acquisitions and mergers, with the end result a substantially decreased number. It is estimated, for example, that since 1976 the personal computer industry has increased to about 150 companies in the U.S. It is expected that within three to five years the number will be reduced to a dozen or so. As one observer put it, ''A lot of people haven't been to business school, and don't realize that products get old, markets settle down, and things shake out'' (*Business Week* 1982). However, as the product is standardized, the industry moves toward a pure oligopoly structure. The intensity of competition varies sharply among these structures.

An individual company's industry responsibility increases in oligopoly structures. If the company has a large share of the market, it will be expected to be concerned about the welfare of the industry and to serve as a price leader that others will follow, and to price accordingly. Within the constraints of this industry responsibility, the marketer can then proceed to behave tactically in such a way as to achieve his/her goal by striving for share to get costs down and attain a long-term profitable position.

## Customer Decision Model

What the customer thinks has been shown to determine two of the major market constraints upon the manager, life cycle and competition. Here, the third constraint, the customer, is seen to be largely determined by how the customer thinks and processes information, which is described by Figure 6, the customer decision model (Howard 1983). That the customer is the source of this power adds still further support for the hypothesis that a company should be customer-driven.

**FIGURE 5. Possible Competitive Structures**

| Degree of Product Differentiation | One | Many | Few | |
|---|---|---|---|---|
| | (1) Monopoly | Pure Competitive | (4) Pure Oligopoly | **Undifferentiated** |
| | | Monopolistic Competitive (2) | Differentiated Oligopoly (3) | **Differentiated** |

**FIGURE 6. Customer Decision Model**

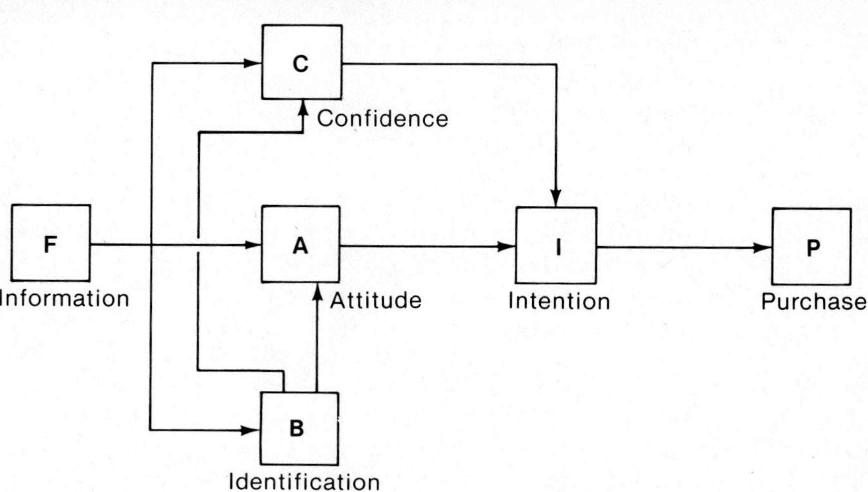


Knowledge about the customer has increased substantially over the past two decades. The purpose of the customer decision model (CDM) is to help focus that knowledge upon practice. Without some such focusing superstructure, that knowledge, which is bits and pieces, is only teasingly useful. The CDM is a bare-bones structure that can be amplified and strengthened by incorporating additional complexities which add substantially to the manager's understanding of the market (Howard 1983).

As Figure 6 indicates, CDM is made up of an information input (F), brand identification (B), confidence (C), an intention to buy (I), and purchase (P). Arrows show the causal links. When used for modeling, the CDM first provides both estimates of current relations and projections into the future required in answering "what if" questions, so useful in providing the specific customer information implicitly asked for in the customer side of the D&SC. It also includes specific information about both content and form of customer information. Finally, it tells the manager where a product is on the life cycle. This is valuable information because the author's experience indicates that an innovator is frequently not aware of innovating.

## Integration of Information Flows

The CDM is the foundation upon which the other three descriptive concepts rest. Figure 7 portrays the information flows among the four descriptive concepts and, among other things, shows the central role of the CDM. First, as the arrow from Figure 6 indicates, a major task of the CDM is to provide much of the information required on the customer side of the D&SC.

## FIGURE 7. Marketing Theory of the Firm

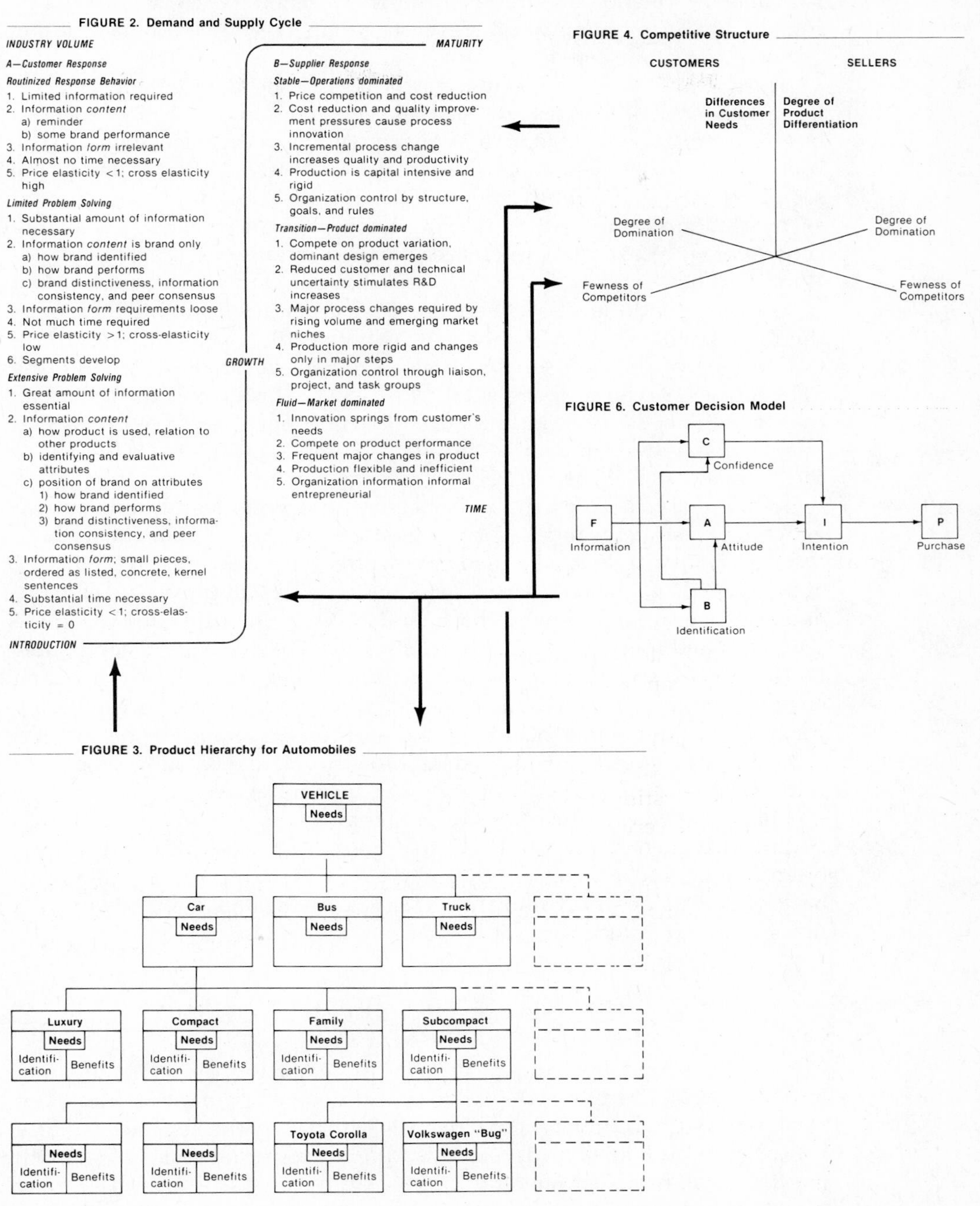

Second, especially in the current state of measurement of the PH, considerable information about the customer is needed for it which the CDM can supply, for example, where each product is rated on identifying characteristics and benefits.

Third, the CDM can transmit information to the CS correcting market segmentation. For instance, the market segmentation now being practiced by the suppliers (the right side of Figure 4) may be inconsistent with the preferences of the customers (the left side of Figure 4). If so, one of the suppliers may gain an advantage, either by discontinuing an irrelevant segmentation attempt and/or devising a new segmentation approach more consistent with customer preferences. For discussions of segmentation, see Wind (1978).

Going beyond the CDM, there are three other arrows in Figure 7. First the PH tells the left side of the D&SC whether the product is an innovation, extensive problem solving. It also provides vocabulary. Second, the PH tells the CS who the competitors are, which, of course, is the basic data that the CS needs to begin to be useful. Third, once the CS receives that information and a competitive analysis is complete, the results are fed to the supplier side of the D&SC.

In summary, the descriptive superstructure provides information for generating a strategy and its supporting financial data. This is the input to the prescriptive system. The manager, within the framework of the D&SC and triggered by it, raises all necessary questions. From his/her own memory and using the input from the PH, CS, and CDM, the manager answers these questions and formulates a potential strategy. That strategy is compatible with all three elements of the D&SC: the life cycle stage, the corresponding customers' informational and other requirements, and the corresponding functional requirements including interfaces among them. The next step is to feed the supporting financial data into a normative decision process to estimate the payoff in terms of the company's objectives.

This linear view of the process assumes away the interactive complexity and misses much of the richness of the process. For example, the manager often will set a tentative strategy and try it in a test market. Thus, a feedback of marketing effort into the CDM is created, and the results give a measure of the effectivenss of his/her tentative strategy.

## Management Decision

Figure 7 shows how the descriptive pieces of the theory fit together into a rationale for designing strategy to lead the company in a market. However, the prescriptive piece that deals with the criteria by which strategy should be chosen must be developed. And, the *process* of that choice which implies a criterion also remains.

The criterion is the firm's objective. Financial theory describes it as maximization of shareholder wealth as measured by the market price of the common stock (Van Horne 1980). Maximization of profits is not as inclusive. For example, total profits are not as important because the company can always increase its profits by issuing stock and using the proceeds to buy treasury bills. Even maximization of earnings per share is not as good because it does not specify timing or duration of expected returns. Neither does it consider the risk or uncertainty of the expected earnings stream. In this definition, management is viewed as an agent of the owners that must be given adequate incentives and monitored to ensure performance, which does not come without cost, as Anderson (1982) has pointed out.

Maximization is not an adequate description of what management behavior should be because of management's current inability to compute optimal choices. However, maximization can be accepted as an ideal toward which management strives. Sheth and Frazier (1982) make an interesting proposal. As decision making tools, such as new mathematical tools for computing optimal decisions, become available and computers become more powerful, the ideal can more nearly be approached (Simon 1978, 1979).

To implement shareholder wealth as a criterion, the financial concepts of present value are necessary but not sufficient. The marketer has the best understanding of the market needed to prepare the estimated cash flows for the given period required as input to the financial models which estimate the effect of that cash flow upon the company's current stock values. Marketing must be prepared, however, to link marketing models to financial models and to use a much longer planning horizon. This will require long-term forecasting of potential sales.

As the organization becomes more hierarchical, such as over the life cycle, the issue of consistency of lower goals with this higher level objective becomes increasingly important. The lower level goals should be adequately constrained to prevent inconsistency.

## Conclusions

The structure proposed here is a marketing theory of the firm. It consists of interlinked descriptive concepts that provide information input to prescriptive concepts in formulating strategic plans to serve the firm's objective. First, a basic premise is that customer-driven firms are more likely to be successful. Two sources of empirical evidence for this are provided. Also, that the customer is the source of three major constraints—life cycle, competition, and the customer—him/herself indicates the power of the customer and adds support to the hypothesis. Finally, current strategic planning approaches, e.g., Porter (1980), focus upon the competitive element. The conclusion here is that the focus should instead be upon the customer.

Second, to carry out product innovation successfully, substantial process innovation must also occur. This causes the nature of each of the functions to change in predictable ways and, consequently, the nature of their interfacing with each other to change. The theory gives marketers a rationale for their planning which facilitates their interfacing with other functions in the design and implementation of strategy.

Third, the theory specifies the objective—the central ingredient of a normative approach—against which to evaluate strategic plans and part of the process for carrying out the evaluation.

## Contribution of Theory

First, the theory describes the process of how a firm should behave in bringing together the five functional areas of a firm around planning for a product in a division or unitary firm. Second, it deals with both goods and services; for example, both buyer and supplier behavior of the D&SC applies to services as well.

Third, by providing an extensive rationale, it can enable marketing to play a greater role in leading the corporation, thereby answering Mr. Welch's question, "Where is marketing, now that we really need it?" Welch (1981), as CEO of the General Electric Company, has displayed remarkable insight into marketing's ability to deliver on the essential marriage of marketing and technology. "Frankly, I'm more confident about technology's capability in this marriage than I am about marketing's.... Technology has its own imperative ... its own inner drive. I'm not concerned about the engine room ... there's plenty of horsepower there. My concern is with the helm. With marketing." Science, supported by the scientific method with its own value system, will probably prove him correct on the technology side. Marketing theory provides a partial affirmative answer; a later extension of it to the multidivisional firm can supply a more complete affirmative answer.

Fourth, the theory is a framework for obtaining mutual understanding of and encouraging consensus among "warring" functional departments that often seriously handicap a company, especially in its attempt to innovate.

Fifth, the contribution of the graphic form of the theory to management problem solving should not be underestimated. Problem solving is often no more than a change in the way we represent things. Simon (1981) has long emphasized the role of representation in problem solving and recommends it be one of the seven areas of study that should be required in any professional school, including management.

Finally, the theory has truly enormous implications for basic research. Space permits only mention of some areas. Measurement deserves high priority, e.g., the product hierarchy. Axiomatizing our systems would strengthen the logic; e.g., Newell and Simon (1972, p. 53) emphasize how effective economics has been. However, in achieving this rigor, we must be careful not to lose relevant content. Management information processing needs careful attention, especially with developing computer systems (Simon 1978). The potential of management decision heuristics is suggested by Yavitz' observations of product portfolio analysis (Howard 1981). Fundamental description and classification of strategies would help; e.g., Capon, Farley, and Hulbert (1983) are systematically investigating 113 large U.S. manufacturing firms. Organizational buying, such as multiple buyers, deserves attention (Scott and Keiser 1983).

## ENDNOTES

1. Here only those features of the superstructure that are relevant to the division or unitary, usually small, company are dealt with.
2. Another set of labels for the same dichotomy is, of course, positive and normative. Also, empirical vs. axiomatic instead of inductive vs. deductive is intended to sharpen the distinction and emphasize rigor. The author is indebted to J. U. Farley and D. R. Lehmann for discussions on this issue.
3. I am indebted to Morris B. Holbrook for emphasizing this point.
4. Howard and Sheth (1969) called it a "conceptual structure." Howard (1977) refers to it as "semantic structure." Rosch (1978) and other category researchers have called it "a taxonomy of categories," and to Miller and Johnson-Laird (1976), it is a "semantic field."
5. Information-processing researchers have increasingly found it useful to distinguish between semantic and episodic memories. Semantic memory refers to the knowledge of the psychological meanings of words and the processes that operate on them, while episodic memory refers to knowledge associated in time and place.

## REFERENCES


Abernathy, W. J. and J. M. Utterback (1978), "Patterns of Industrial Innovation," *Technology Review*, 10 (June-July), 41-47.

Anderson, P. F. (1982), "Marketing, Strategic Planning, and the Theory of the Firm," *Journal of Marketing*, 46 (Spring), 15-26.

Bennett, R. and R. Cooper (1981), "The Misuse of Marketing: An American Tragedy," *Business Horizons*, 24 (January), 51-61.

*Business Week* (1982) (November 22), 72.

Capon, N., J. U. Farley, and J. M. Hulbert (1983), "The 'Strategicness' of Planning," unpublished working paper, New York: Strategy Research Center, Graduate School of Business, Columbia University.

Carpenter, G. (1983), "Product Quality, General Promotion and Profitability," unpublished working paper, Los Angeles: Center for Marketing Studies, UCLA.

Day, G. S. (1977), "Diagnosing the Product Portfolio," *Journal of Marketing*, 41 (April), 29-38.

——— (1981a), "The Product Life Cycle: Analysis and Applications Issues," *Journal of Marketing*, 45 (Fall), 60-67.

——— (1981b), "Strategic Market Analysis and Definition: An Integrated Approach," *Strategic Management Journal*, 2 (July-September), 281-300.

Hayes, R. H. and W. J. Abernathy (1980), "Managing Our Way to Economic Decline," *Harvard Business Review*, 58 (July-August), 67-77.

Howard, J. A. (1963a), *Marketing: Executive and Buyer Behavior*, New York: Columbia University Press.

——— (1963b), *Marketing Management*, 2nd edition, Homewood, Il: Irwin, Chapters 3 and 4.

——— (1977), *Consumer Behavior: Application of Theory*, New York: McGraw-Hill.

——— (1981) "The Empirical Theory of Managing the Market," in *Review of Marketing 1981*, B. Enis and K. Roering, eds., Chicago: American Marketing, 235-50.

——— (1983), "Applied Buyer Behavior," unpublished working paper, New York: Columbia University, chapter 6.

——— and J. N. Sheth (1969), *The Theory of Buyer Behavior*, New York: Wiley.

Marshall, A. (1961), *Principles of Economics*, 9th edition, New York: Macmillan, Vol. 1.

Mervis, C. B. and E. Rosch (1981), "Categorization of Natural Objects," *Annual Review of Psychology*, 32, 89-115.

Miller, G. A. (1978), "Practical and Lexical Knowledge" in *Cognition and Categorization*, E. Rosch and B. Lloyd, eds., Hillsdale, NJ: Lawrence Erlbaum Associates, 305-319.

——— and P. N. Johnson-Laird (1976), *Language and Perception*, Cambridge, MA: Harvard University Press.

Morgan, L. A. (1982), "The GE Quality Culture," address to the Engineering Mangement Conference, New York, NY, April 15.

Newell, A. and H. Simon (1972), *Human Problem Solving*, Englewood Cliffs, NJ: Prentice-Hall.

Porter, M. E. (1980), *Competitive Strategy*, New York: The Free Press.

Rosch, E. (1978), "Principles of Categorization," in *Cognition and Categorization*, E. Rosch and B. Lloyd, eds., Hillsdale, NJ: Lawrence Erlbaum Associates, 27-48.

Scott, J. E. and S. K. Keiser (1983), "Forecasting Acceptance of New Industrial Products with Judgment Modeling," unpublished working paper, Newark: University of Delaware.

Sheth, J. N. and G. L. Frazier (1982), "An Earnings-Return Model for Strategic Market Planning," Urbana, IL: faculty working paper No. 869, Bureau of Business and Economic Research, University of Illinois.

Simon, H. A. (1978), "On How to Decide What to Do," *Bell Journal of Economics*, 9, (Autumn), 494-513.

——— (1979), "Rational Decision Making in Organizations," *American Economic Review*, 69 (no. 4), 498-99.

——— (1981), *Sciences of the Artificial*, 2nd edition, Cambridge, MA: MIT Press.

Vanhonacker, W. R. (1980), "Cross-validation of Three Customer-based Market Structure Analysis Procedures: Complementarity vs. Substitutibility," research working paper 287A, New York: Graduate School of Business, Columbia University.

Van Horne, J. C. (1980), *Financial Management and Policy*, 5th edition, Englewood Cliffs, NJ: Prentice-Hall, 7-11.

Welch, J. F., Jr. (1981), "Where is Marketing Now That We Really Need it?" address given at marketing conference, New York: The Conference Board, October 28.

Wierenga, B. (1974), *An Investigation of Brand Choice Processes*, Rotterdam: The University of Rotterdam, 156-184.

Wind, Y. (1978), "Issues and Advances in Segmentation Research," *Journal of Marketing Research*, 15 (August), 315-405.

——— (1981), "Marketing and Corporate Strategy: Problems and Perspectives," unpublished working paper, Philadelphia: University of Pennsylvania.

——— and T. S. Robertson (1982), "Strategic Marketing: New Directions for Theory and Research," unpublished working paper, Philadelphia: University of Pennsylvania.

# SECTION N
# Exchange School

As one would expect, the fundamental concept of the exchange school is exchange between the buyer and the seller. Although the concept of exchange seems simple, it has generated more controversy in marketing than most other concepts.

The basic issues related to this controversy include the following: First, how broadly we define the domain of marketing depends on the breadth of exchange definitions. For example, if exchange is defined in its broadest sense, one must include all interpersonal interactions such as friendship, kinship, and work activities as part of marketing. If it is limited to exchange of values, it becomes more restricted and excludes such things as friendship and kinship. Even here one can argue that both friendship and kinship include exchange of values.

In our opinion, marketing must limit itself to exchanges of economic values. If it does not, it is likely to be blurred with other disciplines, such as social psychology and group dynamics.

Second, whether the exchange is dyadic or multiparty is a separate issue. Although most of the research and thinking has been limited to the dyadic exchange between two parties, it is pointed out that many marketing transactions, especially in international trade, involve exchanges of economic values among many parties to complete a transaction.

A third area of concern within the exchange school is the object of exchange. Is it limited to products and services, or can it include exchanges of ideas? In other words, what is the unit of analysis? Is it the values or the objects that generate those values?

Although exchange is a fundamental concept in both marketing and economics, it is likely to remain problematic unless these issues are resolved.

# 46 —— A Conceptual Approach to Marketing

*William McInnes*

Reprinted from *Theory in Marketing*, published by the American Marketing Association, edited by Cox, Alderson, and Shapiro (1964), pp. 51-67. Reprinted by permission.

Although the practice of marketing is as old as civilization itself, efforts to evolve a theory or a science of marketing are relatively new. It is, in fact, only in the present century that the term "marketing" as well as concepts surrounding that term have received any widespread acceptance.[1] The activity of the marketplace has far outstripped the reflections of the theorists.

While the marketing system has expanded to colossal dimensions, the development of marketing thought—through concepts, hypotheses, theories, or principles—has proceeded at no such rapid pace. The promise of the early conceptual work of pioneers such as Ralph Starr Butler, Arch Shaw, and Louis Weld did give birth in the twenties—"the Golden Decade in the development of marketing thought"—to integration, classification, and some "principles."[2] This was followed in the thirties by a new emphasis on text writing, course elaboration in the universities, and the introduction of consumer considerations. The forties witnessed an offsetting interest in the managerial aspects of marketing and marketing policy. But when the first book to be devoted entirely to marketing theory was about to appear, there was general agreement that even at mid-century "there is a plethora of individual facts and a dearth of conceptual schemes which would relate these facts in meaningful generalizations."[3] There had been some attempts to form generalized theories but these "fail to satisfy students because they do not account for or take into consideration all of the relevant observed facts."[4]

The publication of the first edition of *Theory in Marketing* brought to the dynamic field of marketing fresh concepts borrowed from such disparate areas as physics, psychology, vector analysis, behavior systems, and regional trade.[5] But 12 years later, Bartels, in summing up the progress of 60 years, could still write that although marketing thought has devoted much attention to describing prevailing practices, to classifying activities and institutions, and even to developing some basic generalizations, "relatively little use has been made of theoretical analysis, of concepts from related social sciences, or of experimental hypotheses in the construction of systems of marketing thought."[6] The task, therefore, remained "for someone to present an acceptable integration of marketing that will serve as an introduction upon which more specialized study could be built or as a comprehensive explanation of marketing for both specialist and nonspecialist in the field."[7]

Apparently, ''a box of tools for analyzing the facts and events''—to borrow a phrase from Schumpeter—is still required, and, hence, there is still room for a different conceptual approach to the problem. This essay is one such attempt.

Many concepts in marketing, particularly the more generalized ones, have been brought in from other fields such as economics, psychology, or the physical sciences. Such an approach, extremely popular today, has the advantage of widening perspectives and of fitting the model into more generally known streams of thought or behavior patterns. But a widened perspective has been accompanied by a blurring of focus. Marketing tends to become only applied psychology, or applied economics, analogical biology, or a specialized behavior system. In the search for general princples from which marketing action can be deduced, the specific role and functions of marketing are too easily lost.

An alternative is to start with the most concrete and specific phenomenon observed by both the practical businessman and the theorist. That phenomenon is the market. Most theorists and practitioners would agree that marketing has something to do with ''dealing in a market,'' and while this does not tell very much about marketing, it does at least give focus to the problem. The primary observable phenomenon for any theory of marketing is the hard practical fact of the market itself.

Nor is the acceptance of this fact of the market merely the starting point for businessman or theorist. It is also the ultimate criterion for either action or theory. A businessman is successful only when he succeeds in the market; a theorist has advanced theory only when he says something about the market. Though the theorist or research director may utilize tools from several different disciplines, the basic model must spring from the phenomenon of the market. The market is not only the point of communication between practice and theory, it is the ultimate judge of both.

This essay, then, will begin with observations of market phenomena. Next, it will generalize from these observations, isolating the dimensions of the market. Finally, after specifying these dimensions and relating them to the tasks of marketing, it will propose a model of a marketing system.

## What Is a Market?

Markets result from the social intercourse of men when the makers and users of economic goods and services seek to satisfy their needs and wants through exchange. But what specifically is a market? To practical businessmen, markets are often considered to be places—Wall Street, Covent Garden, or Pike Street—where an exchange occurs. They are ''determinate areas and times for intercourse between buyers and sellers.''[8] This inexact notion, arising out of the traffic of traders in the marketplace, may not be scientific, but it does emphasize contact and geographic location as requisites for exchanges. In our modern world of electronic communication, however, it is hard to conceive how the extent of the market is entirely congruent with a determinate geographical area.

The interregional trade theory of E. T. Grether is an application of the geographical concept of markets and marketing.[9] His explanation of the "business activities involved in directing the flow of goods and services from producer to consumer or user"[10] centers around multiple geographical markets. Marketing theory analyzes the behavior of the firm (or the region as a trading unit) as it adjusts its horizontal spatial relationships to industrial, regional, and national groups.

A second conceptual approach is institutional rather than geographical. In this view, leaning heavily on John R. Commons, it is patterns of collective action in control of individual action which make markets, and, hence, theory should center on institutions rather than on individual actions.[11] One of the first writers to apply the institutional approach to marketing was Ralph Breyer.[12] With his natural aptitude for seeking the wholeness and order in marketing phenomena,[13] he saw marketing as "primarily a physical function made necessary because of the separation of production and consumption,"[14] and the main institutions of the market to be supply and demand, space, time, and competition. Reavis Cox's concept of marketing as a combination of flows through organizations which "takes place between entire channels rather than between individual entities along the channel" is also an institutional approach to marketing.[15]

With its emphasis on group behavior, the institutionalist approach broadens the perspective of marketing theory. But it tends to overlook the individual forces that, collectively, make up institutional behavior; nor does it explain the relationship between the two. Besides, it highlights interactions rather than causes, and, hence, it tends to description rather than analysis. The institutional approach has been perhaps the most adaptable to the importing of tools from other areas, but caution must be exerted lest in the assimilation process the distinctive characteristics of market phenomenon be obliterated.

A third stream of marketing thought flows from the headwaters of economic theory. A market is treated as a process "actuated by the interplay of the actions of the various individuals cooperating under the division of labor."[16] The basic conception is one of equilibrium of supply and demand under varying conditions of pure or (more recently) imperfect competition.[17] The process of objective exchange valuation becomes the center of attention for the economists with some (e.g., classical school) focusing on the supply side of the process, and others (e.g., the Austrians) on the demand side. The difficulty that arises from any attempt to make marketing a direct application of economic theory is that the basic premise of valuation limits too closely the multiple dimensions of the market. Such precison aids economic analysis but only at the expense of marketing analysis. Although market facts may be translated into costs and prices, they are not synonymous with either. Economic theory brings to the study of the market a strong central concept—valuaton. But this is by no means the only concept for an integrated theory of marketing.

A final approach, especially associated with Edmund D. McGarry, is the functional, a classification of those activities which constitute "the *sine qua non* of marketing, those things without which marketing would not exist."[18] Though there has never been any general agreement on how many tasks make up marketing, the functional approach tries to isolate what is essential to the field and so it has advanced marketing thought.[19] What is lacking, however, is an explicit relation to the market itself as the criterion or what is an essential task and what is not.

All of the above approaches—geographical, institutional, process, and functional—have contributed to the progress of marketing thought. The next step would appear to be to make more explicit the concept of a market and then to relate marketing directly to that concept. An adequate conceptualization, like the geographical approach, should include the physical flow of goods between regions—but it should also include the multiple flows of negotiation, ownership, and information. Like the institutional approach, this integrated concept should touch on collective patterns of behavior and institutions—but it should also investigate the individual forces from which institutions emerge. With the process approach, it should analyze valuation—but it should explore the physical, psychological, and perceptional dimensions assumed in economic theory. With the functional approach, it should be able to classify and segregate the essential tasks from the nonessential—but it should also be able to make more explicit the market criterion for classification. The approach may be widened in scope so that it can borrow the tools of psychology, sociology, mathematics, and economics—but the model should be based on a concept of the market that will preserve its distinctiveness as a marketing theory. In addition, it should be capable of analyzing not only existing situations but also opportunity in the market system. Ideally, it should be general enough to include the marketing mechanism of Russia as well as of the United States.

## The Market and Marketing

In a social economy, where the maker of economic goods does not use them and the provider of economic services does not benefit from them, there is a real separation between producers and consumers. But while they are separated, they are also necessarily related. Hence, the separation is accompanied by an interdependence which is very real. As soon as a person (or firm) produces a good or service, he is in the market for a consumer.[20] As soon as a person (or institution) develops the capacity to consume, he is in the market for a producer. There is a mutual, necessary attraction between the parties. Another name for this real, interdependent relationship betwen producer and consumer is a market. The market is the gap which separates producer and consumer. As the separation of producer and consumer grows greater under an expanding division of labor and increasingly differentiated consumer wants, the relationship becomes no less real but only more complex. Thus, more people, higher incomes, more sophisticated desires mean—almost paradoxically—bigger markets even with increasing separation of consumer and producer. The market is made from two elements: separation and relationship.

In an exchange economy, the relationship of producer and consumer—i.e., the market—is a universal fact. The mere fact of relationship, however, is insufficient to generate an exchange.[21] The existence of a market relation is the foundation for exchange not a substitute for it. Producers of wheat in Kansas City by the very fact of planting wheat become related economically to consumers of bread in Boston. But there is no exchange, even when objective exchange valuation is identical, until several intermediate steps are taken. From a marketing point of view, the market relation is both an obstacle and an opportunity. It is real enough and yet it is not fully realized. It is not actual but rather potential. It has the real elements needed to generate exchange, but these elements are not presently actualized. An analogy may be helpful in illustrating this relation. Hydrogen and oxygen bear a definite and real relation to the compound known as water. When joined together, they form water rather than anything else. But while they both bear a definite and real relation to water, they remain only potentially water until they are combined, usually with the aid of a catalyst. Similarily, producers and consumers are related by a market, but no exchange occurs until some force or agent brings them into actual contact. This force, making a potential market contact into a real market contact, is what is generally known as marketing.

Marketing is any "motion"[22] or activity that actualizes the potential relation of producer and consumer. The essential task of marketing is, therefore, always related primarily to the market. The work of marketing always begins with the discovery of market potential. Its function is, as Cherington realized over forty years ago, "the establishment of ... a contact."[23] A concept of marketing in its widest sense, therefore, is *any activity which actualizes the potential market relationship between the makers and users of economic goods and services*. A science of marketing would attempt to analyze and form testable hypotheses about this actualization; the practice of marketing would exploit the actualization process to generate sales.

## Dimensions of Market Potential

The concept of marketing given above is wide. This is necessarily so because the market on which it is based is wide, and marketing is coextensive with the market. Hence, it is only when we determine the dimensions of the market that we can determine the corresponding dimensions of the marketing task. Marketing task and market potential are inseparably linked, for marketing makes contact from separation and bridges the gap between producer and consumer. The next step, then, is to try to specify the dimensions of the market, i.e., we must determine the modes of separaton between producers and consumers.

The most visible dimension of a market is the *spatial separation* of the parties to an exchange. That is why markets are frequently associated with a specific meeting place. Only when the parties get together in some way can an exchange occur. The greater the physical separation of the parties, the wider the physical dimensions of the market and the greater the potentiality in their relationship; the nearer they come together, the narrower that dimension and the smaller the spatial market potential.

But geographic separation carries as a necessary consequence a time lapse. There must be a time lag betwen production and consumption of at least the time necessary for the movement of goods through the intervening space. Thus, the second dimension of the market is *separation in time*. Every market situation includes a time factor. The greater the time lapse between production and consumption, the greater the time dimension of the market potential; the shorter the time lapse, the smaller the time market potential.

Following closely upon space and time dimensions is the separation of information and persuasion. Customers don't know about supply sources; producers don't know where customers are. There is always a *perceptional separation* between producers and consumers in a market.[24] The fewer consumers who know or are interested in that product, the greater is the market potential.[25] When customers are well informed and highly motivated, the smaller is the remaining market potential. If a large majority of customers know about razor-blade brands and are sold on a particular brand, there is little market potential remaining for other manufacturers of razor blades unless these latter manufacturers can provide new information and new motivation that will switch brand loyalty.

Even when fully informed and motivated makers and users of economic goods are brought together, no exchange is completed—at least in a private property system—until the title of ownership is conveyed. The market relation has an inherent *separation of ownership* that makes up one of its dimensions.

Allied to this separation of ownership in the market structure is the *separation of values* placed upon the product by producer and consumer. The producer measures his sacrifice in terms of costs and competition and sets an offering price. The consumer measures his want satisfaction in terms of utility and ability to pay. The greater the separation of valuation, the greater is the market potential; the closer the valuation, the smaller the market potential. Because of the high price of color TV sets today and the growing desire of customers for such sets, there is a large market potential. Because this potential represents a separation of valuation rather than an agreement on an acceptable price, we conclude that there is a large market potential for color TV, even though there has been little marketing until recent years to exploit that market potential. It is important to remember that the existence of a market is not the same as a sale. But even without a sale, it cannot be denied that the market somehow exists, and one of its dimensions is valuation. If consumer capacity and willingness to pay and producer capacity and willingness to offer differ greatly, this fact does not obliterate a market. It only makes the separation between the two parties that much wider.

Thus, the basic model of a market consists of a set of real but potential relationships in five dimensions: space, time, perception, valuation, and ownership. The streams of power structures affecting a market enter through these limits; the actions of behavior systems filter into the market through these dimensions. Underlying social and economic changes on either the producer or consumer side of the market—births, deaths, rising incomes, new plant locations—not only change the market terminals but also affect the market potential. Since market potentiality is measured by the extent of separation of the parties to an exchange in each of these five dimensions, the greater the separation, the greater the market potential. Every underlying change, however, is always specified in the market relation as a change in the degree of separation of space, time, perception, valuation, or ownership. Thus, while the market is not a closed system apart from the real world, it does have its distinctiveness guaranteed by its five dimensions. These dimensions form the basic pattern that makes a market; they are the five dimensions of market potential that confront every marketing agent and determine every marketing institution.

To convert a five-dimensional concept of market potential into a working model requires some tools for measuring its quantitative aspects. The task is not simple, but neither does it appear entirely impossible. There are generally acceptable standards for measuring space potentials (miles,feet, etc.) and time potential (hours, minutes, etc.). The economists have provided the units of money costs and prices to measure values.

To measure in some way the separation of ownership would seem to call for a combination of legal as well as physical units. To measure perceptional separation requires the borrowing of sophisticated tools from psychology and sociology, and at our present stage of knowledge, would yield far from perfect results. But the inadequacy of the tools does not seem to invalidate the basic market model. The search should be for sharper tools rather than for a modification of the model if the market itself is real.

An economist or businessman might well reduce all the measurements of market potential to dollar costs. This would be both convenient and practical. But it should be remembered that such an effort looks at the market institution purely as an economic activity through the narrow medium of dollar costs. It is easy to overlook opportunity when the range of vision is too narrow. A market planner might find a wider perspective by studying markets in terms of spatial and time units before translating these units into economic costs. A social historian might want to evaluate a market in terms of the more original units of space, time, perception, and ownership as well as valuation. The preservation of the five dimensions allows appraisal of a market as a social organization as well as a managerial tool. To consider only costs is to lose something of the multiple dimensional structure that is a market.

Statistical data can provide the raw material for quantification of the model. But it should be kept in mind that statistics are always historical and so can never reveal a completely current situation. Besides, they are often not available in sufficient detail to apply to specific products, especially where branding has developed high product differentiation. Statistical resumes of past sales of a firm provide merely an indicator of market potential. They reveal only that part of the market potential that has been exploited, not the total potential that remains. Yet, it is precisely in this latter area that opportunity exists. Hence, records of sales must be used with caution as indicators of potential, and they should be supplemented with other data for effective measurement.

Sometimes, when an accurate measure of the dimensions of a market potential cannot be attained, it is possible to measure relative changes in any of the dimensions. Although such an operation cannot find absolute values, it can reveal relative rates of change of potential. The rate of increase in transportation facilities, the rate of change of crop output, the relative increase in consumer expectations and intentions to buy, all give some indication of the change in market potentials even while not requiring knowledge of the underlying absolute figures. With increasingly sophisticated mathematical tools, the difficulty resulting from lack of absolute figures is not as great as it used to be.

For some products, market potential is more determinate than for others. Natural resources have a more definite location on the production side of the market than do services. Doctors' fees have, through custom, a more definite valuation potential than does scrap steel. On the consumption side of the market, industrial users are generally easier to locate than users in the consumer market, since many industrial firms cluster together geographically. But in all cases, potentials exist. They represent, simultaneously, both an obstacle and an opportunity for the businessman: an obstacle because they require effort to be overcome; an opportunity because it is through the removal of an obstacle that reward can be earned.

## Marketing and Market Potentials

If a market represents a separation—in space, time, perception, valuation, and ownership—between makers and users of economic goods, then some force is required to bridge the gap and realize the opportunity latently existing in the market potential. That force, or activity, we call marketing.

And since its one job is to convert market potentials into actual markets, it is convenient to call the process of marketing, *actualization*. By its effort, marketing actualizes what is merely potential in the market relation. It generates—from a preexisting situation—an exchange.

## Actualization

The five potentials of space, time, ownership, valuation, and perception are important because they circumscribe the field of marketing. They are the bases from which springs all marketing activity, the opportunities which confront all marketing agents. They reveal the only possibilities of successful marketing action. But though they are important to marketing, they do not represent marketing itself. Marketing is the creative force which reacts on these potentialities as material. Hence, it is necessary to analyze marketing activity, an activity which in its essential and generic meaning is actualization. Marketing *is* actualization—the force which actualizes the potentialities of the market relation. It is the motion which closes the gap caused by the separation of makers and users in a social economy and defined by market potentials. Thus, actualization is a central concept for a science of marketing.

The actualization of the space potential can have its origin only in the space potential existing between producer and consumer. It embraces all those motions needed to bring the product from the geographical point where it is produced to the point where the consumer wants it.

The motions of space actualizaton may assume different forms which are limited only by the primary principle of directness of route between terminals. A firm may shorten the distance between production and consumption by branch plants using local resources. Shopping centers may move into the centers of populations. Or a firm may find a more direct route from its plant to its consumers. It may move goods by rail instead of water, or by plane instead of truck. Directness, of course, must always be related to the consumption and production terminals of the market. If consumers are shifting, then the most direct route is the one which shifts with them.

Out of space actualization arise three motions which must be performed, though they may be shifted among agencies. They are: assembly, transportation, and dispersion. Goods must be gathered together; they must be shipped; they must be broken down into consumable units. For specific products, the importance of each of these motions varies, but none can be dismissed entirely. In some instances, it is possible to shift the tasks to the consumer himself, but even this cannot be considered as having eliminated the movement. When a shopper carries her groceries home in her own car, she is performing the marketing activity of transportation. The customer who, on the other hand, calls in for one pound of butter to be delivered to her leaves both the transportation and dispersion task to the retailer.

Time actualization is the marketing motion which places the goods a customer wants before him at the moment he wants them. If the consumer is willing to take the product as soon as it comes off the production line, time actualization is of small importance in the marketing picture. But if the producer is compelled to hold the goods for a long period, then actualization of the time potential is very significant.

The primary principle of time actualization is speed. The product should move in the shortest time possible between the consumption and production terminal of the market. But speed also must be considered as a relative quantity. It must be related to the production possibilities and to the desires of the consumer. Time actualization is successful only when it places before the consumer the goods he wants when he wants them. It does not determine that moment but only attempts to meet that deadline when the consumer has determined the moment for himself. If the interval between production and consumption can be shortened, or if the two terminals can be better synchronized, then time actualization will decline, but otherwise the tasks which flow from this actualization must be assumed by someone.

Time actualization is manifested in what can be called the *chronologizing functions*. These chronologizing functions are the activities which close the time gap. They are of three types: financing, risk management, and storage. Financing supports the investment while it is in the channel of distribution; risk management pays for the costs of the uncertainties involved in the time lag; storage provides the means for holding physical quantities of the product until wanted by consumers.

Ownership actualization embraces all the motions of conveying title from producer to consumer. It is extremely important because even though buyers and sellers may be in the same place at the same time, no exchange will take place until title has been transferred. Only when this step is taken is the transaction complete. This phase of actualization is the traffic management of the market relation.

The major manifestations of ownership actualization appear in the negotiating functions of contact and termination. Contactual negotiation embraces finding a market, making a market, and creating a market. Terminating negotiation embraces all those activities which facilitate the transaction and bring it to a full conclusion, e.g., drawing up contracts, keeping records, maintaining standardized procedures. Each of these activities assists in the transfer of title, though they have nothing to do with the physical or temporal distribution of goods. Hence, they are forms of ownership actualization.

Valuation actualization is made up of all those motions necessary to align sellers' bids and buyers' offers. Its range or movement is circumscribed on the one side by the consumer's ability and willingness to offer. The motion itself, when not effected by the equilibrium forces of competition, must be carried out by some marketing agent. It is usually expressed in what is called price policy, either lowering producers' offers or raising buyers' bids in order to bring about the contact which generates an exchange. This may be done by adjusting terms of sales, varying terms of shipment, quoting discounts off list, setting odd prices or price lining. All of these actions stem from the fundamental motion of valuation actualization. Through this actualization, the imperfections which keep automatic pricing from clearing the market are not removed from the market, but transactions can be realized in spite of the imperfections.

Perceptional actualization brings within the perceptional range of consumers the goods that are available for sale. It adjusts the consumer to the product. It is manifested in the activities of disseminating information and of persuasion, the former to overcome the ignorance of the perceptional potential, the latter to overcome the inertia of that potential. Through these activities, users are adjusted to the product. They are given ideas and motives. The ideas may be transmitted through several different types of media; persuasion is carried to the consumer through the use of appeals. Ordinarily, the work of perceptional actualization is carried out by the seller. However, in periods of shortage and in some parts of the industrial market, this task has been successfully shifted to the buyer. What is important to realize is not that this or that agent carries out a marketing task but, even more fundamentally, that the marketing tasks must be carried out by someone. The function is more basic than the institution.

It is by relating the activity of marketing to the corresponding market potentials from which that activity must flow that a list of marketing functions become possible. It is of secondary importance, then, as to how long the list is; what matters is that under this conceptual system, a criterion of selection is known.

The existence of producers and consumers provides the raw material for a market relation. As soon as a manufacturer is in business, he is automatically drawn to the market. As soon as a consumer exists, he is in the market for some goods, and every change in his capacity or willingness to consume is reflected in the market in some way. The very existence of these two groups and their mutual interdependence sets up the relationship that is the market.

The potentiality of the market relation, on the other hand, springs not from the appearance of producers and consumers on the scene but from the extent of their separation as specified in five dimensions. The greater the separation of the agents, the greater the potential.

The market, therefore, is a complex phenomenon consisting of both relationship and of potentiality. The former represents a power of attraction; the latter, a power of separation. Nor are these opposing powers equally offsetting. In a dynamic economy, the separations increase more rapidly, and the whole market system of relationships grows very complex and more rigid. A catalyst is needed to effect the actualization of market potentials, an activity not disturbing the basic relationships of the market but adjusting the product to the individual consumer. Under conditions of mass production, it is frequently impossible to adjust to change by retooling or redesigning the product. But this does not necessarily mean the end of exchange itself. There are other means of meeting the individual preferences of as many consumers as possible without substantially remaking the product. This is what is generally referred to as merchandising.[26] It is the catalyst that adapts standardized products to individual consumer preferences. It adds to the product some incidental feature which will make the finished article more attractive to individual buyers. The purpose of this addition is to bring into the market buyers who would otherwise be indifferent to the product, because of some incidental whim or preference. Merchandising in this sense takes five forms: incidental changes in the product itself; package changes; service changes; changes in methods of offering where neither space nor time is the prime consideration; and the offering of a premium with the product. Substantial change of the product would not be marketing but production adaptation and so is not included under merchandising activities. Merchandising is the catalyst of the marketing system necessary to facilitate actualization under conditions of the mass market. It gives the individual in a mass market *what* he wants.

The five marketing tasks, corresponding to the five dimensions of the market and facilitated by the catalyst of merchandising activity, when carried out by some marketing agent, fulfill all the conditions for actualizing a market potential and generating an exchange. It should be noted, however, that though each mode of actualization may be analyzed separately, they present themselves as a total force to the marketing executive. All of them must be carried out by someone before any exchange can take place. The marketing manager must, therefore, consider the total dimensions of space, time, perception, ownership, and valuation as well as weigh the merchandising activities which will maximize sales. Marketing tasks can be taken on or sometimes shifted to others—but they cannot be ignored.

Besides, all phases of marketing actualization are interrelated. The appearance of specialized agencies to handle parts of the actualization may add to the efficiency of the motions, but this also adds to the interdependence of the institutions involved. Faster express service provided by railroads improves the performance of time actualization, but it may add to the problems of price actualiztion because it costs more. Decentralization of agricultural markets adds to the efficiency of space and time actualization, but it is possible to decentralize only when communication facilities permit a wider dissemination of market news and prices.

The end result of actualization is a market transaction and the satisfaction of consumer wants. Actualization allows the consumer to know about a product and to obtain it for himself where he wants it, at the price he is willing to pay, in a form suited to his individual preferences. If the motions involved use up a minimum of resources to achieve this goal, then marketing efficiency is at a maximum. Marketing institutions appear and disappear in the market, but behind them are the permanent forces of actualization working on market potentials to close the gap in the market relation.

## Significance and Application of the Concept of Actualization

Perhaps the most convenient way to suggest the applications of this concept of market potentials and marketing is to propose some generalized hypotheses that should follow from the original premises. This can be done under four headings: institutions, management activities, the role of marketing in the social economy, and the relation of the concept to further research.

If the concepts of market potential and marketing actualization are valid, market institutions are primarily the effects rather than the causes of marketing functions. The distinct lines of identification between wholesale, retail, and service institutions should be expected to be more blurred in real life than they are in the tests. Institutions, therefore, would be the products of change more than the innovators. The real force of change would result from the underlying social conditions that affect market potentials together with the marketing actualization performed in response to the changes in the market potentials. The institutions should reflect these changes even more than they cause them, and there should be evidence of countervailing power in market potentials as opposed to producer institutions. The existence of an institution should depend ultimately on the functions it performs in relation to the market potential it faces rather than on any other factor.

This conceptual approach also opens the door to considering the consumer as a marketing agent capable of assuming market functions herself and, therefore, capable by her impact of altering marketing institutions. The functions would still exist; it is only the agent performing them that changes. There still has to be transportation, storage, financing, merchandising, assembly, etc. But these may, and have been, shifted to parties other than producers, wholesalers, or retailers. Marketing theory would suggest to the economist that if he desires to study the implications of such a shift in responsibility, he should include some measure of the cost of the function performed by whatever agent assumes that function. To the sociologist, marketing theory would point out that all five dimensions of marketing actualization must be considered before a complete sociological analysis can be made of either market institutions or marketing functions.

The concept of marketing actualization would, at first glance, frighten a practical businessman. This is not surprising, since theory is not the coin of the marketplace. But it would not be as frightening if the concept were translated into the concrete phrase: if you wish to be successful as a marketing agent, you must first determine when, where, who, and at what price consumers want your product, and then you must arrange to tell people about your product, motivate them to buy it, get it to the right parties where and when they want it and in the way they want it. This phraseology lacks the formality of theoretical speech—but it does make communication possible. And it does preserve in substance the concept itself.

It suggests, too, that a strong marketing orientation is required of a business manager, an orientation which reflects a respect for both market potentials and marketing actualization possibilities. Since a continuing knowledge of market potentials is essential for rational marketing action, some provision in every firm for keeping abreast of the market should be made. The more complex and diffuse the market grows, the greater the need for this function. The more sophisticated and generally available the tools for measuring markets in specific dimensions of time, space, consumer information and motivation, valuation, and ownership become, the greater the precision that can be obtained in determining the location of markets. Statistics can shadow market potentials (though never circumscribe them, for they are data from the past) and suggest a useful way of filling out the skeletons of market dimensions. Sales statistics, however, would have to be used with caution. They would show the strength of past activity but not the full scope of present or future possibility.

Market potentials, however, form in this approach only the raw material for marketing. It is not research information but action based on correct information that can yield results. Marketing orientation in a firm, therefore, would imply a strong line marketing organization with research as a staff function whose effectiveness is always to be measured in terms of the action results it produces. The ability to actualize market potentials is the criterion for judging a marketing organization. Respect for market forces is but one of the qualifications to be expected in a marketing executive. Equally important for actualization are the qualities of force and imagination through which the manager uses that knowledge.

If rational marketing action requires both knowledge of market potential and imagination in responding with marketing action, it seems to follow that marketing can never be completely scientific. Creativity, in fact, would grow increasingly vital where there is a great quantity of knowledge, but little response in action. There could never be a complete resolution of the problem of science versus art in marketing management, only a tension with some attempt at balance. Marketing in the present view is a responsive action to a market situation. It does not by itself create demand nor any of the dimensions of the market. It rather must exploit what it can discover by chance, intuition, or research. No theory, therefore, of such phenomena can be strictly scientific. "The logic of marketing has rested upon variations of a simple mechanistic concept of marketing," complains Bartels.[27] Any such beginning assumption of a mechanistic concept is doomed to failure if markets and marketing are not purely quantitative. This does not, of course, deny the possibility of measurement; it only limits its scope. Measurement must follow the model, not determine it.

The present concept of marketing looks at the market not only as a business activity but also as a social phenomenon. The data may be translated into terms of costs, at least approximately, but this is not always necessary. Some studies, depending on their purpose, might profit more by dealing in original units than in economic costs. Even a marketing manager might find it more helpful, at least initially, to talk in terms of the distances to be covered, the time lapses involved, the legal titles to be conveyed, and the amount of paper work included. Marketing is more than a management tool; it is an element of the social structure.

The implication for future research springs from the fact that the concept, rooted in market phenomena, offers a general framework within which data can be gathered, hypotheses ventured, and measurement refined. Quantification will require many contributions from related sciences—from demography, motion and time studies, economics, mathematics and probability analysis, psychology, law, biology, and sociology. Much interest has, in fact, been aroused in assimilating these tools to solve marketing problems, even to the point of almost obliterating the field of marketing itself. This seems to do a disservice to the progress of marketing thought, which must always be rooted in the market if it is to remain a distinctive area for investigation. Research should be fitted to the problem, not the problem to research.

At the present stage, the above approach offers only a concept. The tasks of hypothesis formulation and verification lie ahead. But one assurance remains: no matter how inadequate or unreal the mental constructs proposed by theorists, one solid, baffling, yet intriguing fact remains to give impetus and direction to all marketing speculation. That fact is the starting point and checkpoint for all theory. That fact is the market.

## ENDNOTES

1. For the widest historical treatment of the development of marketing thought, cf. Robert Bartels, *The Development of Marketing Thought*, (Homewood, Ill.: Richard D. Irwin, Inc., 1962), pp. 1-3, 10-12.
2. *Ibid*., p. 174.
3. Edmund D. McGarry, "Some Viewpoints in Marketing," *Journal of Marketing*, Vol. 18 (July, 1953), p. 33.
4. Wroe Alderson and Reavis Cox, "Towards a Theory of Marketing," *Journal of Marketing*, Vol. 13 (October, 1948), p. 139.
5. Wroe Alderson and Reavis Cox (eds.), *Theory in Marketing* (Homewood, Ill.: Richard D. Irwin, Inc., 1950).
6. Bartels, *op. cit.*, p. 207.
7. *Ibid*, p. 182.
8. "Market as a Place of Sale," *Palgrave's Dictionary of Political Economy*, Vol. II, 1923 ed. Marshall defines a market as "a district, small or large, in which there are many buyers and many sellers all so keenly on the alert and so well acquainted with one another's affairs that the price of a commodity is always practically the same for the whole of the district" (*Principles of Political Economy* [3d ed.; London: Macmillan & Co., Ltd., 1895], p. 188). It can be seen on analysis that this definition applies only to the unrealistic condition of perfect competition.

9. E. T. Grether, "A Theoretical Approach to the Analysis of Marketing," in Cox and Alderson (eds.), *op. cit.*, p. 118.
10. This is the nominal definition of marketing proposed by the Definitions Committee of the American Marketing Association in 1948. Cf. *Journal of Marketing*, Vol. 13 (October, 1948), p. 209.
11. Cf. John R. Commons, *The Economics of Collective Action* (New York: The Macmillan Co., 1951), pp. 120-44.
12. Cf. Ralph Breyer, *The Marketing Institution* (New York: McGraw-Hill Book Co., Inc., 1934).
13. Ralph Breyer, letter to Robert Bartels in 1940 (Bartels, *op. cit.*, p. 224).
14. Bartels, *op. cit.*, p. 184.
15. Reavis Cox, "Quantity Limits and the Theory of Economic Opportunity," in Cox and Alderson (eds.), *op. cit.*, p. 240.
16. Ludwig von Mises, *Human Action* (New Haven: Yale University Press, 1949), p. 258.
17. To Adam Smith, the market was synomymous with the power to exchange. The source of this power he located in the costs of production. Cost of production created value, and value made a market. The Austrian and marginal utility schools in later years shifted the discussion of the sources of value to the demand side of the market. In their opinion, it was utility, and not costs of production, which created value. Alfred Marshall combined the work of his predecessors and made the market the consequence of both supply and demand mutually interacting and determining each other. Marshall's market was like the intersection in an electrical circuit of alternating current. With Say, he agreed that supply created demand; with the Austrians, he agreed that demand also acted on supply. Then he combined both. The forces interacted. One explained the other. But what of the intersection itself? What of the market? What was that? It remained, like the pointer on a scale, an abstraction: an indicator but not something real. Chamberlin found this approach a "complete misfit" (Edward Chamberlin, *The Theory of Monopolistic Competition* [Cambridge, Mass.: Harvard University Press, 1936], p. 10) for modern conditions because the theories of value had been formulated independently of institutional factors. He introduced the elements of elasticity of the demand curve, product differentiation, and selling costs which have an impact on marginal revenue and marginal costs and so affect the valuation process by destroying the automaticity of equilibrium assumed by earlier writers. However, he did not explore factors other than value which also tend to break down the automatic working of the exchange process.
18. Edmund D. McGarry, "Some Functions of Marketing Reconsidered," in Cox and Alderson (eds.), *op. cit.*, p. 268.
19. A tabular presentation of marketing functions proposed by several authors is given in Franklin Ryan, "Functional Elements of Market Distribution," *Harvard Business Review*, Vol. 13 (January, 1935), pp. 208-9. Even though the classification is twenty-eight years old, the modern listing has not seen many substantial changes. This is probably due to the failure to develop a clear criterion of selection rather than to any historical stagnation of marketing activity.

20. The modern development of "the marketing concept" is a recognition of this dependence of the manufacturer, financier, banker, retailer, etc., on the market as the vital source of their existence and activity.
21. A market concept limited to analyzing existing reality would not be particularly useful. A concept, or theory, must be dynamic, not static. It must embrace opportunity as well as present conditions. The basic argument here is that the market must be considered in a wider perspective than any present evidence of exchange. Otherwise, there would appear to be no possibility of explaining development of markets.
22. This concept was first suggested by Arch Shaw in 1912 (*Some Problems in Market Distribution* [Cambridge, Mass.: Harvard University Press], 1915). While it may appear too abstract, it does have a convenient relationship to market potential and market actualization, particularly to the philosophically inclined theorist.
23. Paul Cherington, *The Elements of Marketing* (New York: The Macmillan Co., 1920), p. 12.
24. The term "perception" is used here to connote both ignorance and inertia; i.e., a lack of knowledge *and* interest. Neither producers nor consumers of economic goods are concerned only with the speculative knowledge of a product. It is only motivated knowledge leading to an exchange that is pertinent.
25. At first sight, this hypothesis seems to suggest a paradox that the greater the disparity of the relation between makers and users of goods, the greater the market—i.e., that the market for a product is better when consumers and producers don't get together rather than when they do. But it should be remembered that the basis of the relationship between the parties is a connecting link so that no matter how greatly these parties are separated, the very fact that they are producers and consumers involves a necessary mutual interest. It is not stated that a market equals an exchange. But it does suggest that a market is a bigger phenomenon than some marketing people would admit. This implies, of course, that the marketing task is greater—but it also leaves room for admitting the possibility of marketing activity wherever there is a market.
26. Merchandising has been defined elsewhere as "the planning involved in marketing the right merchandise or service at the right place, at the right time, in the right quantities, and at the right price" (AMA Definitions Committee, *op. cit.*, p. 26). This seems, however, far too broad and, in fact, makes merchandising and marketing synonymous. Here the term is used in a much stricter sense—as indicated in the text—as but one component in the whole marketing structure. Merchandising results, strictly, not from the separation of producers and consumers but from the rigidity that arises from mass markets and inflexible mass-production requirements. It is the response of marketing to the particular difficulties of size rather than of separation. It acts not so much to make a sale as to maximize a sale when the basic conditions for an exchange have been created.
27. Bartels, *op. cit.*, p. 207.

# 47 ___ Toward a Formal Theory of Marketing Exchanges

*Richard P. Bagozzi*

Reprinted from *Conceptual and Theoretical Developments in Marketing,* published by the American Marketing Associaion, edited by Ferrell, Brown, and Lamb (1979), pp. 431-447. Reprinted by permission.

The idea of exchange is central to the meaning of marketing. Indeed, marketing scholars generally agree that the fundamental phenomenon to be explained, predicted, and controlled in the marketplace is the exchange relationship (Kotler, 1972; Hunt, 1976). Disagreements surrounding the role of the idea of exchange in marketing primarily center on the scope or breadth of the concept rather than on its content (cf., Ferrell and Zey-Ferrell, 1977; Bagozzi, 1977). Nevertheless the discipline lacks both a coherent conceptualization of exchange and a well-developed theory for explaining exchange.

This article has two objectives. The initial goal is to outline the substance of exchange and discuss a number of dimensions not treated before in the marketing literature. A second purpose is to present a formal theory of exchange in the marketplace. The theory is an elaboration and extension of a model proposed earlier by the author (Bagozzi, 1978a).

## THE CONCEPT OF EXCHANGE

The notion of exchange is universal and as ancient as man himself. Unfortunately, this aspect of the concept has lead marketers to take it for granted and regard it as a primitive concept, not requiring further definition. Reliance on the common-sense, every day idea of exchange has prevented the development of the concept itself and its role in marketing theory. In order to understand, explain, and influence exchanges, it will be necessary to begin with an abstraction of what it is and means.

### Existing Conceptualizations

Nearly every behavioral science studies exchange as an accepted domain of its respective discipline. Well-developed ideas on exchange exist in economics, sociology, psychology, and anthropology. The pervasiveness of the concept in different academic circles suggests its fundamental character, placing it in the company of other key ways of representing human behavior such as functionalism, structuralism, or general systems theory. A by-product of this state of affairs is the apparent overlap in subject matter between marketing and the various behavioral sciences. To better understand the implications of this overlap for marketing theory, it will prove useful to examine its nature and extent.

Five points deserve mention as to the nature of the commonality in subject matter. First, no single, systematic exchange paradigm can be identified across the behavioral sciences. Rather, each discipline has conceived of exchange in a narrow, specialized way. Typically, the conceptualization found in a particular discipline is tied implicitly or explicitly to the *Weltanschauung* of that discipline. To economists, exchange entails a transfer of money for a product or service. The motivation for trade is one of self-gain; the process is rational; and the most well-developed theory applies to exchanges in perfectly competitive markets. Economic theories of exchange are asocial in the sense that the actual processes of interaction among actors are not modeled. Rather, the outcomes of exchanges are predicted, and the social process is presumed operative. Further, as exemplified in bilateral monopoly and other forms of economic exchange, the exact outcome of any transaction is left indeterminate, given the theory. Finally, economic models of exchange focus on two actors who each possess only a single physical entity desired by the other, and the relationship between actors is regarded as an impersonal, one-shot affair.

To psychologists and some sociologists, exchange is regarded as the joint outcome in a relationship resulting when both parties choose from among two or more actions potentially affecting each other (e.g., Thibaut and Kelley, 1959). The exchange is defined to occur in relatively restricted and contrived settings such as the prisoner's dilemma game. The vast majority of research has examined exchanges wherein two actors interact, only two mutually exclusive actions by each are allowed, the actors cannot leave the relationship, the range and domain of choices are identical for both actors, choices are made simultaneously, communication with the other actor is not allowed, only four possible outcomes exist, and the motivation and/or rewards for transacting are limited to monetary gain. Unlike economic exchange, however, the possibility exists for the development of on-going transactions, and various interpersonal processes such as social influence, conflict, and bargaining can be modeled.

Finally, to anthropologists and many sociologists, the defining characteristic of exchange is its social nature. That is, rather than focusing on the objects of exchange, the decision calculus of the actors, or the actual transfer, per se, emphasis is placed on the function of exchanges for a specific group or society at large. The functions of exchange are typically symbolic and often reflect normative constraints on actors or positions in a social system. Exchange, then, is used metaphorically to refer to implicit transactions. Some anthropologists even stress that apparent one-way transfers constitute instances of exchange (e.g., gift-giving, theft) and that psychic or social entities are often more important than physical ones to the relationship (cf., Sahlins, 1965; Firth, 1973).

In sum, no uniform notion of exchange exists in the behavioral sciences, and many narrow, idiosyncratic viewpoints can be identified. This is, perhaps, to be expected, given the different histories and purposes of each discipline. However, the commonality of subject matter is a surface one—in name only—in that the substance of the overlap is minimal.

A second, related point to note about the overlap is that seldom is a formal definition of exchange provided. Many theorists use the term in a loose, descriptive sense to refer to any relationship in which tangible things change hands. Others use the term, as noted above, metaphorically. More often than not, the meaning of exchange is taken for granted. In addition, some researchers use the term in titles to their articles but then proceed to ignore it and investigate other phenomena such as power (cf., Cook and Emerson, 1978). On balance, it is difficult to say in what sense and to what degree the overlap in subject matter is genuine, given the vague and ambiguous use of the term.

Third, it should be noted that the study of exchange constitutes only part of the entire realm of the subject matter in each respective behavioral science. In some disciplines, the concept of exchange represents one of a number of ways for examining more basic or more general phenomena. In this sense, exchange constititutes a methodology or conceptual orientation. Sociologists, for example, investigate social behavior from the viewpoints of conflict theory, structural-functionalism, or role-theory, as well as exchange ''theory.'' In other instances, exchange, itself, is the dependent variable for study, but only one of many others to be found in a discipline. Thus, in addition to social exchanges, psychologists study attitudes, small group processes, and decision-making, among other subjects.

A fourth point to stress is that many disciplines examine exchange behaviors but do so primarily to shed light on other issues. The study of exchange plays a subordinate role. For example, some anthropologists investigate the meaning that exchange has for kinship systems or other aspects of primitive societies. Similarly, sociologists studying macrosocial phenomena often use structural concepts as explanatory variables, but simultaneously employ exchange concepts as assumed *premises* with which to build their theories (e.g., Blau, 1964). Anthropologists and sociologists are typically interested more in the larger question of social order and not so much in the exchanges between individuals or institutions.

Finally, it should be noted that no discipline in the behavioral sciences claims exchange as its fundamental subject matter. Given this fact and the fact that exchange performs a limited, varied, subordinate, and vaguely defined role in the behavioral sciences, the opportunity exists for marketers to develop a relatively unique, general, and fundamental phenomenon for study. Already, the weight of historical precedence and an emerging consensus among marketing scholars recognizes exchange as the core of the discipline. The task remains for marketers to identify general characteristics and principles of exchange and to explain variation in exchange behavior with a general theory or theories.

## The Elements of Exchange

We know very little about exchange behavior and lack a formal conceptualization of its parts. Alderson (1965) does provide a "law of exchange" and suggests the centrality of the concept in marketing. But he never defines what he means by exchange. Kotler (1972) presents certain axioms describing exchanges, Bagozzi (1975) discusses the types of exchange and their meaning, and Hunt (1976) helps us to view the discipline as "the science of transactions." But none of these authors has examined the content of exchange in great depth. Although such an examination is beyond the scope of this article, an attempt will be made to point out several key aspects of the concept that deserve further attention.

All exchanges involve a transfer of something tangible or intangible, actual or symbolic, between two or more social actors. For purposes of analysis, social actors might include actual persons, positions in a social network (e.g., roles), groups, institutions, or organizations, or any social unit capable of abstraction. The thing or things exchanged may be physical (e.g., goods, money), psychic (e.g., affect), or social (e.g., status). Rather than entailing a give-and-take of one thing for another, most exchanges are probably characterized by the transfer of bundles of physical, psychic, and social entities. The social actors may or may not be fully aware of all dimensions of what is exchanged or even their own motives or purposes for transacting. Usually, however, the things exchanged will be rewarding or punishing in some way to the parties involved. The values of things exchanged may be sought as ends in themselves or as means to ends.

The determinants of exchange are varied. Often they arise out of the volition of individual social actors who function more or less as rational decision makers. Sometimes exchanges emerge out of compulsion, coercion, or habit. They may also result as a social response to norms or the expectations or pressures of others. One factor affecting the origin or course of an exchange is the availability of alternative sources for satisfaction. Whether one will enter or remain in an exchange and what and how much one will give and get will depend on what the market will bear. Alternative sources of satisfaction act as constraints on the relationship as well as bargaining ploys. In different degrees, any social actor in an exchange will have alternative sources for the same object or for substitute sources of satisfaction. All of the above determinants of exchange will be discussed more fully later in the article.

If the concept of exchange is to be used in an explanatory—as opposed to a purely descriptive—sense, then it will have to be conceptualized as a phenomenon capable of variation in one or more ways. This author believes that exchanges might be fruitfully conceived as a threefold categorization of *outcomes, experiences*, and *actions*, each varying in degree and occurring to the actors as individuals, jointly or shared, or both. Outcomes in an exchange refer to physical, social, or symbolic objects or events accruing to the actors as a consequence of their relationship. Each person might receive separate outcomes such as a buyer and seller obtain in a consummated exchange. Or the parties might achieve mutual, shared rewards, as well as individual gains. The increase in sales connected to a new promotion campaign and resulting from give-and-take between the marketing and sales departments would be an example of joint outcomes. Individuals in both departments might share in the direct profit and social prestige of the successful campaign, as well as the salary regularly ear-marked for them for performing their respective everyday roles. In any event, outcomes in an exchange refer to the things the actors get, either as individuals, a unit, or both.

Another important variable representing an exchange is the experiences the actors feel. Experiences are psychological states and consist of affective, cognitive, or moral dimensions. They typically are conveyed symbolically through the objects exchanged, the functions performed by the exchange, or the meanings attributed to the exchange. Again, experiences can be felt by each actor individually, as well as jointly. Joint experiences entail what sociologists term ''social constructions,'' in that both actors in the exchange are thought to produce a mutual, shared understanding as a consequence of their interchanges. The common joy or feeling of accomplishment felt by a husband and wife as they interact in a consumer decision-making process would be an example of a joint experience in this sense.

The final variable with which to represent an exchange is the actions performed by the actors as a product of their interchange. Actions might represent individual choices and responses or joint commitments. Examples include the degree of cooperation, competition, or conflict in the dyad; and the intensity, duration, and timing of actions. For instance, one measure of the conflictual nature of exchange between wholesaler and retailer might be the number of threats transmitted between them in a period of time.

The goal of conceptualizing exchanges as specific outcomes, experiences, or actions is to provide a set of dependent or endogenous variables for study. With these as the subject matter of marketing, efforts can be made to specify explanatory variables and relate these to exchange in an overall theory.

## THE ANTECEDENTS TO EXCHANGE

To explain exchange (i.e., variation in individual or joint outcomes, experiences, or actions), four classes of determinants are hypothesized: social influence, social actor characteristics, third party effects, and situational contingencies (see Figure 1). Each is briefly described below.

**FIGURE 1. The Determinants of Exchange**

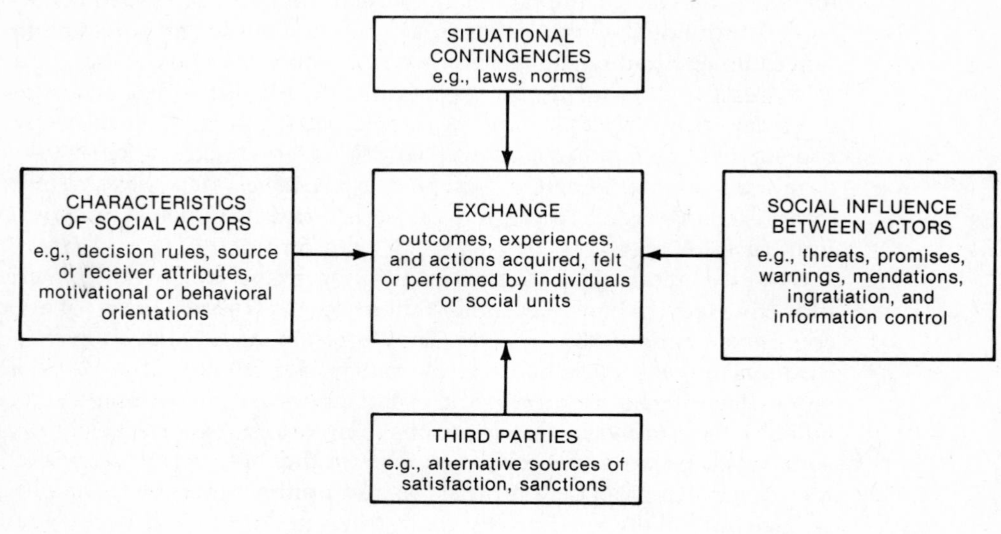


## Social Influence Between the Actors

It is hypothesized that the parties to an exchange satisfy individual needs and reach mutual accommodations through a process of social negotiation. This process involves a give-and-take wherein the parties communicate their desires, intentions, and purposes; and adjustments in offers, counteroffers, and standards of acceptability are made throughout the process until an agreement to exchange or not is made. The process occurs both covertly and overtly, and the parties may or may not be fully aware of its dynamics or their role and outcomes during the negotiations.

The process of social negotiation entails a communication of rewarding or punishing stimuli through one or more of four modes of influence: threats, promises, warnings, or mendations (Tedeschi, Schlenker, and Bonoma, 1973). A threat is made when one social actor sends a message conveying a punishment to the other social actor and the message is conveyed under conditions wherein the sender can actually mediate the punishment and no attempt is made to conceal the influence. For example, if a manufacturer were to state in a communication to a retail customer, "if you reduce the shelf space devoted to brand *X*, then we will discontinue our promotion credit to you," then he or she would be employing a threat mode of influence. In contrast, a promise is made when one social actor sends a rewarding message to another such that the sender actually mediates the reward and no attempt is made to conceal the influence. The statement by a manufacturer, "we will give you a promotion credit of 5 percent of sales," would be an example of a promise in the above sense.

Threats and promises (and all modes of social influence) can be contingent/noncontingent, request-specific/nonspecific, and consequences-specific/nonspecific. A contingent message uses the if-then implicative form to specify what will happen to the receiver of the message under certain conditions. The noncontingent message omits the conditions and relies solely on an assertion of intent or opinion on the part of the sender. The threat example in the previous paragraph is a contingent one, while the promise example is noncontingent. Further, the threat example is relatively specific as to its request and consequences.

A warning is said to occur when a sender communicates that a punishment will befall a target under certain conditions. The sender does not attempt to conceal his or her influence attempt under this mode; however, unlike the threatener, the sender of a warning does not directly mediate the punishing stimulus. Rather, either an external agent is involved and/or the punishment is contingent on the action or inaction of the target. The use of fear advertisements by the Heart Association is perhaps the best example of a warning in the sense defined here. A mendation is said to occur when a sender implies that a reward will accrue to a target should he or she act or fail to act. Again, the sender does not attempt to conceal his or her influence attempt; however, unlike the promiser, the sender of a mendation does not directly mediate the reward but a third party and/or the target does. An example of the mendation mode of influence might be the following statement made by a salesperson to a potential customer: "if you buy machine *Y* before July 1, when the law changes, then you will be able to realize the special income tax credit."

Threats and promises usually imply the potential for the exercise of power by one actor over another. Warnings and mendations, in contrast, are, perhaps, best exemplified by the general mode of influence termed "persuasion," where the element of force or coercion is presumed absent and the ideal of "free choice" is approached. Behavior in the marketplace is, of course, characterized by all four modes in varying degrees. These modes share the attribute that influence attempts are not concealed. Influence can also be employed when the source of communication desires to hide his or her attempts. Under these conditions, the clandestine influence takes on a distinct manipulatory flavor. Reinforcement control, information control, and ingratiation are three types of influence in this sense. A final point to note with respect to the use of social influence between actors in an exchange is that the impact of any mode depends on the characteristics of the social actors as well as the situation surrounding the exchange. It is to these that we now turn.

## Characteristics of the Social Actors

The starting point for any exchange is the needs of the individual actors, the values of things that can be exchanged, and the give-and-take reflected in the social influence comprising the negotiations. The exact course of any exchange, including its final outcome, will depend, in part, on the unique interface of the characteristics of the actors.

Two kinds of characteristics seem salient. The first is termed source/receiver characteristics and has been studied extensively by communication researchers (cf., McGuire, 1969, 1972). Source characteristics include such variables as attraction, expertise, credibility, prestige, trustworthiness, or status. Receiver characteristics comprise such variables as self-confidence, background attributes, cognitive styles, and certain personality traits. In general, source and receiver characteristics influence exchanges through their ability to authenticate or deauthenticate the subjective expected utility associated with communicated threats, promises, warnings, or mendations (e.g., Tedeschi, et al., 1973: 65-83). For example, one study indicates that the greater the perceived similarity of a salesperson (a source characteristic akin to attraction), the greater the probability of purchase (Brock, 1965). The premise is that mendations from a similar salesperson were believed more, while those from the dissimilar salesperson were discounted. In a similar manner, other source/receiver characteristics interact with the modes of social influence to affect evaluative behavior and compliance.

A second kind of social actor characteristic influencing exchanges is the interpersonal orientation of the actors. Interpersonal orientations refer to the degree of motivational predispositions or behavioral tendencies the actors bring to an exchange. Research in bargaining and negotiation suggests that the conduct and outcomes of the exchange depend on the degree to which the parties (1) have a positive interest in the welfare of the other as well as one's own, (2) are oriented toward equitable or joint gain as opposed to doing better than the other or maximizing individual gain, regardless of what or how the other does, and/or (3) are sensitive to interpersonal aspects of relationships with the other (e.g., Rubin and Brown, 1975). Some individuals come to an exchange with cooperative, competitive, malevolent, rigid, responsive, etc., orientations, and these dispositions constrain the course of give-and-take by dictating the conditions for trade. One way in which interpersonal orientations are manifest is through the decision rules followed independently or jointly by the actors. Decision rules include, among others, maximize one's own gain; maximize the gain of the other; maximize the joint gain; from each according to one's ability, to each according to one's need; and balance outcomes over inputs (equity). A second way interpersonal orientations function is through affective processes such as is reflected in empathy, altruism, and charity motivated decisions.

## Third Party Effects

Exchanges are also influenced by the constraints or opportunities afforded by third parties, i.e., social actors outside an exchange but with an actual or potential interest in activities or outcomes of the exchange. Following Thibaut and Kelley (1959), two standards held by the actors in an exchange seem salient. First, the parties to an exchange evaluate potential offers in light of their comparison level (*CL*) which represents the degree of satisfaction required or desired by the parties. The *CL* will be a function of the needs of the actors; their history of reinforcement, satiation, or deprivation; and their expectations tempered by the rewards that relevant others receive. Although the *CL* indicates the amount of benefits the parties would like to obtain in an exchange relationship, the acceptable amount may be less than this, particularly if the rewards available from other sources of satisfaction are lower yet. Thus, each party to an exchange also has a comparison level for alternatives ($CL_{alt}$) which represents the amount of rewards potentially accessible from a third party. The hypothesis is that, if the level of outcomes actually received by an exchange partner is below one's $CL_{alt}$, then he or she will leave the relationship for the more satisfying alternative.

Third parties also serve as influences on exchanges in two other respects. First, through social comparison processes with third parties, the actors in an exchange arrive at standards of equity with which they evaluate their actual and anticipated outcomes. Second, third parties use social influence (e.g., persuasion, coercion) to affect the outcome of exchanges. Over the years, for example, the executive branch of the federal government has used moral persuasion to induce manufacturers to limit their price increases. Similarly, environmentalists use influence tactics to alter the exchange relationship between polluters and consumers.

## Situational Contingencies

Situational contingencies represent another class of determinants facilitating or constraining exchanges. Four categories may be identified: the physical environment, the psychological climate, the social milieu, and the legal setting. The physical environment places limitations on the actions the parties to an exchange can make. Time pressures; the structure and content of issues, alternatives, and actions; and the quantity and quality of lighting, air, and noise are all instances of physical environment constraints affecting exchanges. Closely related to this factor is the psychological environment which encompasses the level of emotional (e.g., anxiety provoking) and cognitive (e.g., informational) stimuli surrounding an exchange and potentially disrupting it. The social milieu also influences exchanges and includes social class, peer group, and reference group pressures. This aspect of situational contingencies differs from third party influences in that the former deals with generalized expectancies that the parties feel and do not necessarily attribute to specific social actors, while the latter refers to relatively specific, felt pressures identified with particular social actors. Further, the social milieu typically entails internalized compulsions in the form of norms, morals, or ethics, while third party influences are more external and tied to the actions of others. Nevertheless, the force of the social milieu is backed often by incentives or sanctions, should one stray from social expectations. Finally, the legal setting constitutes a particularly potent type of influence on exchange. Laws govern, in part, how, when, where, what, and why parties exchange.

## Toward a Formal Theory

### Overview of an Earlier Theory

In another article (Bagozzi, 1978a), the author derived a theory which hypothesizes that marketing exchanges are a social process functioning under economic and psychological constraints. The unit of analysis was the dyadic relationship between two actors, and the dyad was also assumed to interact with other buyers and sellers. To explain exchanges, a utility function for the dyad was hypothesized, and a budget constraint and production functions were specified. In this sense, the theory is similar in form to that proposed by economists in "the new theory of consumer behavior," although the unit of analysis in this latter tradition is the individual decision maker rather than the exchange relationship itself (cf., Becker, 1965; Lancaster, 1971; Rosen, 1974). The nature of that part of the theory based on the new theory of consumer behavior may be summarized in words as follows:

> In order to achieve desired levels of satisfaction from the consumption of goods and services, the [actors in an exchange relationship] are assumed to interact with each other and the providers of goods and services. Through decision-making processes and interpersonal influence within the dyad and similar exchanges between the dyad and outsiders, it is hypothesized that the [actors] combine time and market goods and services to produce [a] theoretical construct termed "subjective satisfaction" which represents the joint, negotiated outcome of decision-making and exchange for the [dyad]. The entire exchange process occurs subject to the constraints on the dyad's resources of time and wealth (Bagozzi, 1978a, 545-546).

Two important departures from the new theory of consumer behavior should be noted. First, unlike economists who have not conceptualized the arguments to the utility function very well and who have failed to operationalize these, the theory proposed by Bagozzi (1978a) explicitly models the arguments as theoretical constructs consisting of affective, cognitive, and moral mental events shared by the actors. Further, correspondence rules and measurements are suggested and integrated with the theory in an overall model. Second, the theory developed by Bagozzi formally introduces psychic and social costs in the budget constraint equation, rather than allowing these to remain as strictly mathematically, assumed "shadow prices," as done in the economic theory. Operationalizations and correspondence rules are also proposed within the context of the overall model.

The modified theory was then extended to encompass social psychological processes such as those listed in Figure 1. This was accomplished through the use of a structural equation model. In this model, subjective satisfaction from goods, psychic and social costs, and the perceived resources of the dyad (e.g., permanent income) are endogenous variables, while social influence, situational contingencies, characteristics of the actors, and third party effects are exogenous determinants.

## Extension of the Theory

In their interactions with each other and with other social actors, the parties to an exchange are presumed to maximize

$$U_d = U(Z_a, Z_c, Z_{mb}) \tag{1}$$

where $U_d$ is the utility for the dyad, and the $Z_i$'s represent the joint, subjective "satisfactions" produced by the actors through their interdependencies and actions. The subjective satisfactions are hypothesized to occur as three basic, shared mental events:[1] affect ($Z_a$), cognitions ($Z_c$), and moral beliefs ($Z_{mb}$). Using an argument somewhat similar to that made in the new theory of consumer behavior (e.g., Becker, 1965), each dyad is posited to possess a set of production functions that determine in what way and in what amount the $Z_i$'s are "produced" by certain inputs such as market goods and services ($x_j$), time ($t_k$), psychological characteristics of the actors ($pc_l$), and social-forces ($s_m$):

$$Z_i = Z(x_j, t_k, pc_l, s_m, \ldots) \tag{2}$$

Notice that the $Z_i$'s and the variables on the right-hand side of equation (2) constitute theoretical concepts which may be operationalized. The exact forms for the production functions are thus amenable to theoretical development and testing. Although this is a necessary prerequisite for the attainment of an explanatory theory, the conditions are not met by current conceptualizations in the new theory of consumer behavior.

To complete the development of the theory, the utility of the dyad, $U_d$, must be maximized subject to both the production functions and psychological and social constraints on the dyad.[2] Rather than assuming that social influence, situational contigencies, psychological characteristics, and third party effects are exogenous as done in Bagozzi (1978a), however, these variables may be treated as endogenous processes by introducing them into the production functions.

As a simple example, consider the case where a single satisfaction ($Z_a$) is produced with a single good ($x$) and a single social-force construct ($s$). Thus, maximizing $U_d$ is equivalent to maximizing the output of $Z_a$:

$$U_d^* = Z_a(x, s) \tag{3}$$

Following a logic paralleling Becker (1974), it is possible to represent the social-force influencing the exchange as the following additive function:

$$s = d + e \tag{4}$$

where $d$ represents the social-force due to the interaction within the dyad (e.g., through the modes of social influence), and $e$ stands for the amount of social-force from other factors and not as a function of the dyad (e.g., situational contingencies, third party effects).

The income constraint for this situation can then be written as

$$p_x x + p_s d = I \tag{5}$$

where $p_x$ is the price of a unit of $x$; $p_s$ is the expenditure on social influence between the parties to an exchange; and $I$ is money income. Combining equations (4) and (5) yields:

$$p_x x + p_s s = I + p_s e = S \tag{6}$$

where $S$ represents "social" income.

Thus maximizing equation (3) subject to equation (6), produces the following marginal utilities for an equilibrium:

$$\frac{\dfrac{\partial U_d^*}{\partial x}}{\dfrac{\partial U_d^*}{\partial s}} = \frac{p_x}{p_s} \tag{7}$$

That is, the parties in the dyad, as a producing and consuming unit, equate the ratio of the marginal utilities for $x$ and $s$ to their respective marginal costs. Similarly, following Becker (1974: 1070), it is possible to show that

$$w_x \eta_x + (1 - w_x)\eta_s = 1 - \alpha \tag{8}$$

where $w_x = p_x x / S$, i.e., the total expenditure on $x$ expressed as a fraction of $S$; $\eta_x$ is the own-income elasticity of $x$; $\eta_s$ is the own-income elasticity of $s$; and $\alpha = p_s e / S$, i.e., the share of $e$ in $S$. Thus an increase in income—holding prices constant—would increase the demand for $x$ and $s$. However, given equation (8), a one percent change in income will produce a change of less than one percent in $x$ and $s$. The exact change will be equal to $1 - \alpha$; i.e., the change due to an increase in income will be reduced by the percentage share of social-forces from outside the dyad (e.g., due to situational contingencies and third party effects). As a result, the relative impact of a change in income on utility will be mitigated the more potent are external social-forces.

### Suggestions for Future Research

The theory outlined above provides a framework for modeling social exchange, including the impact of individual differences and social and environmental factors. A number of issues deserve further consideration, however. First, the topic of decision rules demands study. Rather than relying solely on a joint maximization rule, it would be useful to examine such alternatives as reciprocity, altruism, distributive justice, status consistency, or competitive advantage (cf., Meeker, 1971). Second, the nature of temporal constraints deserves scrutiny. Although the new theory of consumer behavior is innovative in this regard, it does not go far enough. By relying on a fixed physical conceptualization of time, it fails to recognize the subjectivity and malleability of temporal concerns. Third, the theory is too shortsighted in that it models decision making in a static sense. Because situations change and people's tastes and demands ebb and flow, a dynamic theory would have more face validity. Finally, to make the theory testable, operationalizations and correspondence rules need to be specified. Some recommendations in this regard have been proposed by Bagozzi (1978a).

## CONCLUSIONS

Marketing thought is at a crossroads. For most of its history, marketing has existed as a technology for solving problems of the manager. The small amount of conceptual work found in the literature has either addressed narrow methodological concerns or else regarded the discipline in an applied sense as an appendage of business, management, or economics. Very little effort has been expended toward the goal of examining the philosophical and theoretical bases of the discipline. Yet such a step is necessary if a theory of marketing is to grow and flourish. Presently, an undercurrent of interest and enthusiasm exists for the subject matter of marketing. Rather than focusing exclusively on the boundaries of the discipline, however, it is perhaps time to redirect our intellectual energies toward the development of a general theory of marketing. The ideas proposed in this article are designed to provoke debate with the ultimate goal of stimulating a dialogue among theoretically concerned marketers.

## ENDNOTES

1. Three generic kinds of subjective satisfactions are chosen here because these are the ones suggested by social psychologists as fundamental to most, if not all, human behavior. For a discussion of the meaning of affect,

cognitions, and moral beliefs from a philosophical and social psychological perspective, see Bagozzi (1980). It should be recognized that other satisfactions might exist, and thus, the number of arguments in equation (1) should be left as an open question.

2. Traditional budget and time constraints are assumed to influence the psychological and social constraints which are regarded as more fundamental.

## REFERENCES


Alderson, Wroe (1965), *Dynamic Marketing Behavior: A Functionalist Theory of Marketing*, Homewood, IL: Richard D. Irwin, Inc.

Bagozzi, Richard P. (1975), "Marketing as Exchange," *Journal of Marketing*, 39 (October), 32-39.

——— (1978a), "Marketing as Exchange: A Theory of Transactions in the Marketplace," *American Behavioral Scientist*, 21 (March/April), 535-556.

——— (1977), "Is All Social Exchange Marketing? A Reply," *Journal of the Academy of Marketing Science*, 5 (Fall), 315-326.

——— (1980), *Causal Models in Marketing*, New York: John Wiley & Sons, forthcoming.

Becker, Gary S. (1965), "A Theory of the Allocation of Time," *The Economic Journal*, 75 (September), 493-517.

——— (1974), "A Theory of Social Interactions," *Journal of Political Economy*, 82 (November/December), 1063-1093.

Blau, Peter (1964), *Exchange and Power in Social Life*, New York: John Wiley & Sons.

Brock, Timothy C. (1965), "Communicator-recipient Similarity and Decisions Change," *Journal of Personality and Social Psychology*, 1, 650-654.

Cook, Karen S. and Richard M. Emerson (1978), "Power, Equity, and Commitment in Exchange Networks," *American Sociological Review*, 43 (October), 721-739.

Ferrell, O. C. and Mary Zey-Ferrell (1977), "Is All Social Exchange Marketing?" *Journal of the Academy of Marketing Science*, 5 (Fall), 307-314.

Firth, Raymond (1973), *Symbols: Public and Private*, Ithaca, New York: Cornell University Press.

Hunt, Shelby D. (1976), "The Nature and Scope of Marketing," *Journal of Marketing*, 40 (July), 17-28.

Kelley, Harold H. and John W. Thibaut (1978), *Interpersonal Relations: A Theory of Interdependence*, New York: John Wiley & Sons.

Kotler, Philip (1972), "A Generic Concept of Marketing," *Journal of Marketing*, 36 (April), 46-54.

Lancaster, Kelvin (1971), *Consumer Demand: A New Approach*, New York: Columbia University Press.

McGuire, William J. (1969), "The Nature of Attitudes and Attitude Change," in G. L. Lindzey and E. Aronson (eds.), *Handbook of Social Psychology*, Vol. 3, Reading, Mass.: Addison-Wesley, 136-314.

——— (1972), "Attitude Change: The Information-Processing Paradigm," in C. G. McClintock (ed.), *Experimental Social Psychology*, New York: Holt, Rinehart and Winston, 108-141.

Meeker, Barbara F. (1971), "Decision and Exchange," *American Sociological Review*, 36 (June), 485-495.

Rosen, Sherwin (1974), "Hedonic Prices and Implicit Markets: Product Differentiation in Pure Competition," *Journal of Political Economy*, 82 (January/February), 34-55.

Rubin, Jeffrey Z. and Bert R. Brown (1975), *The Social Psychology of Bargaining and Negotiation*, New York: Academic Press.

Sahlins, Marshall (1965), "On the Sociology of Primitive Exchange," in M. Banton (ed.), *The Relevance of Models for Social Anthropology*, A. S. A. Mon. I, London: Tavistock, 139-236.

Tedeschi, James T., Barry R. Schlenker, and Thomas V. Bonoma (1973), *Conflict, Power and Games*, Chicago: Alldine.

Thibaut, John W. and Harold H. Kelley (1959), *The Social Psychology of Groups*, New York: John Wiley & Sons.

# 48 —— An Inquiry into Bagozzi's Formal Theory of Marketing Exchanges

*O. C. Ferrell and J. R. Perrachione*

Reprinted from *Theoretical Developments in Marketing,* published by the American Marketing Association, edited by Lamb and Dunne (1980), pp. 158-161. Reprinted by permission.

## Abstract

The purpose of this inquiry is to systematically analyze Richard Bagozzi's attempts to develop a formal theory of marketing exchanges. We attempt to stimulate debate and further creative effort by pointing out what we believe are the contributions and deficiencies in Bagozzi's published works on marketing exchange.

## Introduction

There has been a growing interest in and acceptance of exchange theory as a conceptual framework for the marketing discipline. Alderson (1965), Alderson and Martin (1965), Kotler (1972), Levy and Zaltman (1975), and more recently Bagozzi have developed the concept of marketing as exchange. But until very recently there has been relatively little debate or discussion of exchange theory as a framework for marketing. Over the past five years Richard Bagozzi has published at least eight papers on exchange theory (1974a, 1974b, 1975a, 1975b, 1976, 1977, 1978, and 1979), and yet only two articles critiquing his work have been published (Ferrell and Zey-Ferrell 1977; and Robin 1978). More recently, Bagozzi has published "Toward a Formal Theory of Marketing Exchanges" (1979), which earned him an award for the most outstanding paper at the American Marketing Association's First Semi-Annual Theory Conference. This paper has been developed against that backdrop.

Our intention (as the word "inquiry" suggests) is to analyze systematically Bagozzi's attempts to develop a formal theory of marketing exchanges. We feel that exchange is a theoretical area of much relevance and importance to the discipline of marketing, and deserves as much attention as can be engendered. Richard Bagozzi has been the most active writer in this area in the past five years, and for that fact alone deserves special praise.

Our specific objectives are threefold: (1) to trace the development of Bagozzi's formal theory of marketing exchanges (Appendix); (2) to note the contributions of Bagozzi's work; and (3) to stimulate debate and further creative effort by pointing out what we believe are deficiencies and contradictions in Bagozzi's theorizing.

## Bagozzi's Development of a Marketing Exchange Framework

The Appendix briefly outlines chronologically the stated goals and content of Bagozzi's publications on exchange theory. We have included in the Appendix some brief comments on each publication.

Bagozzi's use of terminology and conceptualizations is fairly (although not entirely) consistent within his work, and (to a lesser extent) between his work and other disciplines from which he borrows; however, there is a noticeable lack of structure or logic in the progression of his conceptualizing from article to article. As Bagozzi has mentioned repeatedly (1975a), a more thorough description of exchange is needed to include all (or more) types of marketing transactions. If marketing does need its own theory of exchange (whether it be as a definition of marketing, or a central core of marketing, or simply an area of marketing)—as assuredly it does—equating marketing exchange with all exchange (social or otherwise) can only be self-defeating. For example, Bagozzi has defined social marketing as ''the answer to a particular question: Why and how are exchanges created and resolved in social relationships?'' (1975a, p. 38). If *all* exchange is relevant to marketing, then no need for marketing as a separate discipline exists. Conversely, if marketing is to advance as a unique field of inquiry, it does need *its own* theory of marketing exchange. This is one of the most significant shortcomings of Bagozzi's theory-building—he has neglected or failed to start at the most basic level by defining and delimiting the area or concept of marketing exchange.

Bagozzi repeatedly poses a set of questions about exchange, be it economic exchange or social exchange or marketing exchange—(1) Why do people and organizations engage in exchange relationships, and (2) how are exchanges created, resolved, or avoided? While Bagozzi at various points (1975a) claims to have defined social exchange, marketing exchange, social marketing, and to have provided a fledgling theory of marketing exchange, he has never managed to answer, nor provide the means for answering, these questions.

Bagozzi has failed to develop a systematic approach to developing a theory of marketing exchanges. He has talked about many discrete variables, but has done so in a disjointed and fragmented manner, and has not really unified them in a model that will be useful to analyze and predict exchanges.

One of Bagozzi's criticisms of exchange theory was that—even as the concept of exchange exists in other fields after years of attention—one of the shortcomings of exchange is that it does not meet the philosophy of science criteria for theories, in that it exists as "only a set of loosely related propositions" (1975b). Bagozzi likewise will have to tighten his theoretical formulation significantly before it is exempt from the same criticism. Bagozzi's articles are most notable for their restatement of the exchange theories of other disciplines; but if exchange is to serve as a central part of a definition of marketing, a unique and innovative approach to exchange is necessary, and Bagozzi's models do not provide this. If marketing is unique as a discipline, what is unique about it? Bagozzi assumes marketing is quite broad, encompassing all activities involving "exchange" and the cause-and-effect phenomenon associated with it (Bagozzi 1975a, p. 32). If so, then how can marketing be a discipline in and of itself? And if marketing is not a unique discipline, why does it need its own theory of exchange?

## Bagozzi's Formal Theory

This aspect of the inquiry focuses on a section in Bagozzi's paper (1979) subtitled "Toward a Formal Theory" in which he attempts to place his conceptual exchange framework in a structural equation model. In general we question if this section of the paper actually relates to his conceptual framework. The model he presents in "Toward a Formal Theory ..." relies on standard economic equations that few, if any, economists have ever been able to empirically test.

Bagozzi's formal theory uses a series of economic equations to illustrate the exchange dyad. The equations are standard economic manipulations and there are no errors or mistakes relating to the economic principles in the equations. Bagozzi's formal theory is not acceptable as a formal theory of marketing because it is not testable and the current model does not operationalize the determinants of exchange as outlined by Bagozzi (1979). More specifically, the following criticisms of his functional and structural equations seem appropriate:

1. The utility function in equation (1) is for utility of the dyad, that is, utility the dyad receives from everything; it is not the exchange utility.
2. Can the affective, cognitive and moral beliefs presented in equation (2) be operationalized for testing?
3. Equation (3) is not realistic. It provides only two variables, a single good ($x$) and a single social-force construct ($s$). In a real transaction according to Bagozzi, other variables and substitute products would influence the exchange. Therefore, a multi-equation model is needed. We doubt if even the simple equation presented can be operationalized. Equation (4) represents social forces and we question if $e$ (social forces from other factors and not as a function of the dyad) could ever be measured or used as a variable.

4. Equations (5) (6) (7) (8) are standard economic manipulations found in economic theory. The logic or theory behind a maximizing equation of exchange is based on the Edgeworth Exchange Box (Alchian and Allen, 1969). Throughout these equations utility is based on rational maximization of the dyad, not maximization of individual utility. Also there is confusion as to what variables are held constant.

Bagozzi's "Toward a Formal Theory of Marketing Exchanges" in our judgment does not produce a theory in the sense that we assume a theory is "a set of interrelated propositions which describes, explains and predicts" (Turner 1978). What Bagozzi has developed is a conceptual framework and some loosely related functional equations that may be criticized for the same shortcoming of exchange principles in the field of economics. Bagozzi's conceptual framework appears to be internally consistent and useful in describing some aspects of marketing exchanges. Bagozzi's application of standard economic principles and operations to depict the exchange framework does not move toward a formal theory of marketing exchange. Based on his conceptual framework, a dynamic constellation of situational contingencies, third party effects, characteristics of social actors and social influence between actors are the determinants of exchange. Where are these forces in his attempt to move toward a formal theory of marketing exchange?

It is our opinion that the major flaws in Bagozzi's attempt to develop a formal theory are an over-reliance on economic equations, its basic assumption concerning the economic (i.e., rationally maximizing) nature of the exchange process, its limitation to dyads as functional units, its static rather than dynamic nature, and its failure to clearly and relevantly define its concepts and to tie them together sufficiently to go beyond piecemeal description to explanation. One of Bagozzi's recurring goals or self-imposed criteria is to construct a theory that will go beyond description to explanation (and eventually prediction and control) (1974, pp. 77, 78; 1979, pp. 431, 434). Yet the model(s) he has proposed, in spite of their frequent descriptive richness, are consistently insufficient when measured against the explanation criterion.

Bagozzi states (1977, p. 39) that marketing is a very generalized discipline that can be applied generally, and yet offers structured and static models with significantly less than universal applicability to explain/define marketing. One of the possible causes of Bagozzi's overly static and structural formal theory may be that he "fell back" on rigor, structure, and overemphasis on the criteria of the philosophy of science before he was really ready to do so. This may in turn be attributable to, and/or may have contributed to, the lack of a clear and concise definition of marketing exchange as a concept.

In his 1978 article, Bagozzi states that social influence variables are possibly the most important determinant(s) of exchange outcomes (p. 539), and that exchange is very much a dynamic process (p. 540). In the conclusion of the 1978 article he further states that ''exchange behaviors exhibit a dynamism that risks being obscured by static analyses'' (p. 554). By the 1979 presentation of his theory, he has managed to obscure that dynamism and to almost lose it entirely.

The concept of the totally rational, maximizing, utilitarian, ''economic man'' is obsolete: basing a formal theory of marketing exchange (especially one that would be appropriately and necessarily dynamic) on such a concept does not provide a clear picture of the true state of the world. Bagozzi's attempts to integrate psychological and sociological variables into static economic equations does not do justice to his excellent conceptual framework. While static, structural equations can and do serve a useful purpose, they are not sufficient in and of themselves to explain the dynamic nature of exchange relations in marketing. In the future, we hope that Bagozzi will examine other approaches in transforming his conceptual framework into a formal theory.

## Conclusion

Bagozzi has restated the exchange theories of other disciplines. He has also drawn many potentially useful and relevant concepts from other disciplines. Thus, what he has accomplished is not enough to qualify as a formal theory (or even the basis for a formal theory) of marketing exchanges.

It is dangerous to borrow exchange theory concepts from economics and psychology and sociology, and apply them directly in marketing. It was their inadequacy that gave rise to the development of a distinct discipline of marketing in the first place. A return to these theories and concepts can at best be only of limited utility in developing a formal theory of exchange for marketing, and reliance on them to the extent Bagozzi does may well be counter-productive. Many aspects of a marketing exchange theory will and must borrow from and/or be related to those areas; a good theory will have to be eclectic. We do not believe that what Bagozzi gives us is sufficiently eclectic enough to provide the necessary bridge between marketing and related disciplines. Our intention is not to castigate Bagozzi's work unduly; the marketing discipline needs more people of his caliber attempting exactly what he has been attempting to accomplish. We do not question Bagozzi's competence as a marketing scholar; we do challenge Bagozzi to clarify and improve his formal theory. By examining criticism and then more firmly committing himself to a position and taking a more definite stand in that regard, Bagozzi is most likely to maximize his contributions to the area of marketing exchange theory. The clarity of his statement of his general goals and objectives in his 1977 reply to Ferrell and Zey-Ferrell vis-à-vis his earlier articles should be adequate evidence of this. Indeed, it is to that end alone that this inquiry has been directed.

## APPENDIX

### Tracking the Development of Bagozzi's Formal Theory of Marketing Research

| *Article* | *Stated Goal(s)* | *Synopsis* | *Comments* |
|---|---|---|---|
| 1974a "Marketing as Organized Behavioral System of Exchanges" (*JM*) | Define core concepts of exchange and marketing as exchange | Exchange is people interacting to maximize rewards & minimize costs<br>Reviews exchange (a la Alderson) and marketing as exchange (a la Kotler) and states that "exchange per se has very little utility beyond pure description." (p. 78) | Primarily review, highly descriptive, beginnings of a foundation for theory of exchange<br>Describes concept of exchange system that will appear in many of his subsequent articles |
| 1974b "What Is a Marketing Relationship" (*Der Markt*) | Define what is a marketing relationship<br>State four criteria for a marketing relationship | Marketing relationship is seen as an intersection of four criteria, socio-cultural sanctions, aspects of social relationships, purposes and values of the social actors in the relationship and philosophy of science criteria | Article is similar to 1974a in that it is a descriptive review of foundations of exchange theory<br>Implies that marketing relationships are a subset of all social relationships but later contradicts this in 1975a |
| 1975a "Marketing as Exchange" (*JM*) | Show that traditional marketing exchange is only a specific case of general exchange theory<br>Discuss media and meaning of exchange | Marketing is defined as all exchange plus associated cause-effect and describes marketing as "a general function of universal applicability: it is the discipline of exchange behavior ..." (p. 39). Concludes: exchange is a central concept in marketing, and may serve as foundation for general theory of marketing | Seems to be a manifesto advocating social marketing (which he undefines)<br>Primarily descriptive; may be drifting off course he set for himself of establishing a basis for a theory of marketing exchange |
| 1975b "Social Exchange in Marketing" (*JAMS*) | Review of economic and social exchange models<br>Expand and extend each model of exchange | Discusses exchange models and describes deficiencies of current models<br>Describes the exchange system: actors, relationships, and causes (endogenous and exogenous) | Good review of exchange models<br>Most comprehensive review of economic and social exchange models in any of his articles<br>Only article where more than passing mention of the specific shortcomings of exchange models |

## Tracking the Development of Bagozzi's Formal Theory of Marketing Research (cont.)

| *Article* | *Stated Goal(s)* | *Synopsis* | *Comments* |
|---|---|---|---|
| 1976 "Science, Politics and the Social Construction of Marketing" (AMA EP) | Defense of marketing as a social construction consisting of a scientific product, social product and human product | Marketing processes are interrelated in a structure of dialetical relationships, exchange theory viewed as a foundation of the discipline without imposing rigidity or narrowness and subject matter of marketing is assumed to be exchanges or systems of exchange among social actors | Paper calls for marketing to construct its identity as the discipline that claims exchange behavior and the theory(ies) explaining how and why people engage in exchanges because "no discipline claims exchange as its defining characteristic"—somewhat imperialistic in his approach |
| 1977 "Is All Social Exchange Marketing? A Reply" (*JAMS*) | Response to a critique of his work by Professors Ferrell and Zey-Ferrell | Focuses on fallacies of logic in Ferrell and Zey-Ferrell's critique; implies that no problems exist in his work and provides more insight in his goals in developing an exchange framework | This is his first really clear statement of what he is trying to do in his series of articles concerning marketing exchanges but he failed to deal with or clarify contradictions in 1975a and 1975b |
| 1978 "Marketing as Exchange: A Theory of Transactions in the Marketplace" (*ABS*) | To present a formal theory of exchange | Discusses structure of exchange: phenomenon to be explained in terms of outcomes, shared effect, and actions; by studying: social actor variables, influence variables, and situational variables, and presents "a self-contained, deductive—axiomatic theory of exchange behavior expressed as a system of causal relationships" (p. 543) | Best statement of formal theory, but several major shortcomings: too much reliance on static economic model (via structural equations); primarily descriptive (rather than explanatory, predictive, etc.); too limited in its dyadic approach to exchange; a good start in developing a formal theory |
| 1979 "Toward a Formal Theory of Marketing Exchanges" (*AMA Theory Proceedings*) | Develop a formal theory of exchange | Briefly discusses exchange as used in various behavioral sciences and describes the elements of exchange in terms of outcomes, experiences, and actions<br>The antecedents of exchange are: social influence between actors, actor characteristics, third party effects (social comparison), situational contingencies | This paper is a regression from the theory presented in the 1978 article because different terminology is used to say essentially the same thing; the conceptual framework appears to be useful and internally consistent but the equations used in the formal theory do not relate to the conceptual framework and there is an over-reliance on economic equations |

## REFERENCES

Alchion, Arman A. And William R. Allen (1969), *Exchange and Production Theory in Use*, Belmont, CA: Wadsworth Publishing Company, Inc.

Alderson, Wroe (1965), *Dynamic Marketing Behavior: A Functionalist Theory of Marketing*, Homewood, IL: Richard D. Irwin.

Alderson, W. and Miles W. Martin (1965), "Toward a Formal Theory of Transactions and Transvections," *Journal of Marketing Research*, Vol. II (May), 117-127.

Bagozzi, Richard P. (1974a), "Marketing as an Organized Behavioral System of Exchange," *Journal of Marketing*, 38 (October), 77-81.

Bagozzi, Richard P. (1974b), "What is a Marketing Relationship?" *Der Markt*, 51, 64-69.

Bagozzi, Richard P. (1975a), "Marketing as Exchange," *Journal of Marketing*, 39 (October), 32-39.

Bagozzi, Richard P. (1975b), "Social Exchange in Marketing," *Journal of the Academy of Marketing Science*, 3 (Fall), 314-327.

Bagozzi, Richard P. (1976), "Science, Politics and the Social Construction of Marketing," in *Marketing: 1776-1976 and Beyond*, K. L. Bernhardt, ed., Chicago: American Marketing Association, 586-592.

Bagozzi, Richard P. (1977), "Is All Social Exchange Marketing? A Reply," *Journal of the Academy of Marketing Science*, 5 (Fall), 315-325.

Bagozzi, Richard P. (1978), "Marketing as Exchange," *American Behavioral Scientist*, 21 (March/April), 535-536.

Bagozzi, Richard P. (1979), "Toward a Formal Theory of Marketing Exchanges," in *Conceptual and Theoretical Developments in Marketing*, O. C. Ferrell, Stephen Brown and Charles Lamb, eds., Chicago: American Marketing Association, 431-447.

Ferrell, O. C. and Mary Zey-Ferrell (1977), "Is All Social Exchange Marketing?" *Journal of the Academy of Marketing Science*, 5 (Fall), 307-314.

Kotler, Philip (1972), "The Generic Concept of Marketing," *Journal of Marketing*, 36 (April), 46-54.

Levy, Sidney J. and Gerald Zaltman (1975), *Marketing and Conflict in Society*, Englewood Cliffs, NJ: Prentice-Hall, Inc.

Robin, Donald E. (1978), "A Useful Scope for Marketing," *Journal of the Acaddemy of Marketing Science*, 6 (Summer), 228-238.

Turner, Jonathan H. (1978), *The Structure of Sociological Theory*, Homewood, IL: The Dorsey Press.

# PART FOUR
# The Holistic School of Marketing Thought

For several reasons the desire to create a grand theory that can explain everything in a discipline seems universal across disciplines. First, there is often the fear that various scholars in the discipline may be like the seven blind men trying to describe an elephant. Unless someone has the full vision, it is likely that we may make wrong inferences about the nature and scope of the discipline.

Second, it is only natural that in the presence of building blocks, someone will be tempted to create a house out of them. Synthesis creates the excitement of discovery and creativity in which we all take pride if we declare ourselves as being in the knowledge-creation business.

Finally, it seems to be a personality trait. Some scholars like depth, others like breadth. Those who like depth tend to stay in one area of specialization and consciously ignore its relationship to other areas in the same disciplines. Those who like breadth tend to wander beyond the areas of the discipline and attempt to link parallel concepts across disciplines.

In Part Four we provide some examples of marketing scholars who have attempted to create general theories of marketing. As would be expected, there is more than one theory of marketing. Indeed, to suggest a universal theory of marketing is feasible is likely to generate some skeptical smiles.

# SECTION O
# General Theories of Marketing

The interest in developing a general theory of marketing dates back almost to the origins of marketing. Each school of thought can be regarded as an attempt to provide one general viewpoint on the nature and scope of marketing.

This section provides a sample of such general theories of marketing. They are included here because they transcend any one school of thought. Indeed, all of them attempt to integrate various schools of marketing thought.

It is interesting to note that consumer behavior has generated several well-known general theories, but marketing has tended to focus more on middle-range theories. Perhaps substantive knowledge has finally reached a stage when it will be possible to develop a well-respected general theory of marketing.

# 49 —— Towards a Theory of Marketing

*Wroe Alderson and Reavis Cox*

Reprinted from *Journal of Marketing*, published by the American Marketing Association, Vol. 13 (October 1948), pp.137-152. Reprinted by permission.

## The Lively Interest in Marketing Theory

Conspicuous in the professional study of marketing in recent years has been a lively and growing interest in the theory of marketing, i.e., the general or abstract principles underlying the body of facts which comprise this field. Perhaps the best overt evidence of this interest lies in the enthusiasm with which members of the American Marketing Association and its chapters respond to invitations that they attend meetings or prepare papers concerned with theoretical topics. This interest in theory seems to have arisen spontaneously and independently in a number of places at the same time.

Courses in marketing theory are now being given in several universities. Theory is assuming increasing prominence in books and articles written by men whose primary background is in marketing. Theory of marketing was emphasized initially in the establishment of the Parlin memorial Lecture. Sections on theory have been regularly scheduled at the national conferences of the association beginning with the Pittsburgh meeting in 1946. The Philadelphia chapter of the American Marketing Association has held monthly luncheon meetings on this subject for the past two years. The Board of Directors of the association has approved the idea that the association establish an annual award in the theory of marketing. A symposium on the theory of marketing is now in preparation which is to be published as a special supplement to the *Journal of Marketing*.

The interest in theory expressed at one place or another and in one way or another by both the academic men and the practitioners of commercial research is real and substantial enough to merit careful attention. The time seems ripe to evaluate its significance—i.e., to determine as precisely as possible the nature of the interest, to survey the reasons for its appearance, and to consider the sort of intellectual discipline into which it is likely to mould the study of marketing if, as seems probable, it continues to grow in depth and scope during the years immediately ahead.

## The Nature of the Interest in Marketing Theory

Data do not exist upon which to base a detailed description of the nature of this interest in theory among marketing men. Some part of it no doubt represents simple curiosity at a relatively high intellectual level. Part of it is a variety of follow-the-leader. When some people become avidly and outspokenly interested in anything, others will take a look to see what is going on. A few will act interested because they think they ought to be.

The central core of the foundation that underlies the interest in a new theoretical approach to marketing is, however, much more substantial than this. Apparently it consists of two principal parts. One is a very widespread and generally justified conviction that students of marketing thus far have reaped from their efforts remarkably small harvests of accurate, comprehensive and significant generalizations. Marketing literature offers its readers very few true and important "principles" or "theories." The other part is an evident belief among some observers that students of marketing have achieved too little even in setting fundamental and significant problems for themselves, to say nothing of working out procedures for solving such problems once they have been formulated.

At first glance the lively interest of marketing men in the theoretical aspects of their subject may seem to spring chiefly from the first source—dissatisfaction with the numbers and kinds of generalization thus far achieved through sedulous accumulation of innumerable facts. A second look suggests that what marketing men really seek is not an immediate statement of the generalizations to which effective study will in due course lead them, but a better statement of the problems to be solved and more ingenious methods to be applied in solving them. The multitude of facts thus far assembled seems to add up to very little. One must conclude that something has gone wrong with the method of attack—that a new and creative analysis is required.

Northrop, in his stimulating study of the logic of research,[1] holds that the most difficult part of an inquiry usually is its initiation. As he sees matters, inquiry begins with a problem circumstances have called to someone's attention. Ordinarily the problem arises because newly discovered facts upset accepted explanations.

The first step is to analyze the problem imaginatively, since its nature will dictate the methods that must be used to solve it. From the analysis of the problem springs an understanding of the sorts of fact that must be assembled to answer it and of the methods by which they can be assembled. After this come the actual assembly of the facts required, description and classification of these facts, derivation from them of fruitful and relevant hypotheses, and verification of the hypotheses thus deductively derived by inductive appeal to further facts.

Apparently what marketing men now seek in their appeal to theory is imaginative guidance into such a creative analysis of the problems of marketing. This can be put another way. Events in recent years have forced students of marketing to put a heavy emphasis upon problems of private management and public policy. One result has been to reveal the inadequacy of the earlier years of study in the field, which proceeded by almost haphazard accumulation of facts. It has become evident that if the difficulties raised by events in the areas of public and private policy as applied to marketing are to be solved, they must be put into a framework that provides a much better perspective than is now given by the literature. Only a sound theory of marketing can raise the analysis of such problems above the level of an empirical art and establish truly scientific criteria for setting up hypotheses and selecting the facts by means of which to test them.

## Specific Reasons for the Interest in Marketing Theory

The nature of the demand students of marketing are making upon their would-be theorists can be clarified further by considering some of the specific problems they feel to be treated inadequately in the existing literature. Northrop, as we have seen, suggests that a problem calling for the initiation of some systematic inquiry usually makes its appearance when existing theories fail to satisfy students because they do not account for or take into consideration all of the relevant observed facts. In essence, this is today's situation in the study of marketing.

Conclusions as to policy and procedure in the field of marketing, and particularly those derived from the so-called principles stated in manuals of mangement or in the great body of general economic theory, often seem not to jibe with the observable facts. Furthermore, a good many such problems are thrown at marketing men where the facts have not been collected or, even more important, where no one has a clear understanding of the sorts of fact that must be assembled and analyzed. A few illustrations will serve to make clear the present less-than-satisfactory position of marketing theory.

### Problems of Price Discrimination

Difference in the prices competing buyers pay for goods bought from a common supplier or in the prices they receive from a common buyer raise critical problems of managerial and public policy. Here, as in other aspects of economic life, we come up against the twentieth century's version of an ancient problem—that of the just or fair price. Laws have been enacted and the courts have rendered judgments under these laws that alter profoundly prevailing views as to what is socially desirable in pricing and what is not.

Among marketing men there exists an uneasy feeling that at least some of the policies thus being established would be substantially different if the facts of marketing as they ought to be known to marketing men were included in the supporting theories. In particular, it seems to be felt that the policy decisions rest upon a careless acceptance of mere conventions as objective facts. Thus the conventional definition of price in narrow terms as a ratio between quantities of money and quantities of goods, rather than in terms of completely negotiated sales transactions, is taken to denominate price in connotations where only the broader definition can be valid.[2] Yet marketing men have done virtually nothing to correct the situation by defining a completely negotiated sales transaction and proceeding to work out theories based upon it.

## Spatial Aspects of Marketing

Students of the economics of land utilization have given much attention to problems raised by the location of various kinds of economic activity. Students of marketing have made very little contribution to that discussion. This is true despite the fact that repeatedly they must give attention to related managerial problems. For example, they often help business men determine how large a trading area is served by a particular store or by a particular cluster of stores. They advise operators as to where within a particular trading area a retail or wholesale enterprise should locate its physical facilities.

Neither the marketing man nor the analyst of land utilization has received much help from the general economist, with his theories of pure rent and his tendency simply to assume rather than to explain the existence of a spatial distribution of marketing activities such that forces of supply and demand can in some significant sense be brought to a focus in price. Hence, it appears that marketing men should assume the task of working out concepts that have true significance in analyzing the nature of the distributive space through which goods and services are marketed and the nature of the forces that have brought the existing distributive pattern into existence.

## Temporal Aspects of Marketing

Economic theory has sometimes evaded problems raised by time through analyzing instantaneous relationships instead of utilizing period analysis. This procedure in effect reduces the economy to a timeless universe in which other problems become more amenable to analysis. A market becomes an organization existing in full maturity at a given instant of time, rather than an organism growing and changing through time. Price becomes a unit of behavior taken at a particular instant and resulting from the interplay of forces that work themselves out instantaneously, rather than a structure or pattern extending over time. Consumption becomes an instantaneous process rather than one that requires appreciable periods of time.

Under some circumstances these distortions of fact do no harm and may be very helpful; but they also lead to erroneous results when the economist forgets to drop his rigid assumptions as he works with problems for which the passage of time is critically important, such as the negotiation of transactions, trading in futures and the consumption of consumers' durables.

Unfortunately, many marketing people have themselves accepted uncritically conclusions resting upon such misleading assumptions. Only now are they coming to realize that theories built upon this kind of foundation fail to conform to what they know concerning the facts of price structures and price policies, of commodity exchanges, and of the use of consumer credit to finance the purchase of durables. It is clear that new concepts and new analyses based on new and more realistic assumptions are required if the nature and significance of market phenomena involving the passage of appreciable periods are to be explored thoroughly.

## Economic Entities

For purposes of economic analysis it is conventional to work with entities that are not always readily observable or measurable in the flesh. They are arbitrarily assumed to exist as identifiable units that make decisions and engage in economic behavior. They consequently are extremely important in analyses of the ways in which economic decisions are reached. The firm, the market, and the economy are excellent illustrations.

Exposure to day-to-day problems and processes in marketing has suggested to some students that there are purposes for which other entities may be more meaningful. Thus in working with the problems raised by marketing functions and the costs of performing them, perhaps the marketing channel is a more meaningful concept than any of these others. Again, the dispersion market may be singled out for meaningful analyses. Yet again, marketing men know that for some purpose the most meaningful analysis emerges when, contrary to the most usual custom among economists, emphasis is put upon cooperative rather than upon competitive behavior. Economics as a pattern of mutually interacting and supporting activities consciously directed toward accomplishing a common, over-all task, is a concept as valid as the one that emphasizes rivalry and competition in efforts to gain individual advantage. For an understanding of marketing as a social instrument, it may be the essential concept.

Despite the need, marketing men have made little progress toward setting up new fruitful concepts of economic entitites derived from their experiences of economic activity or toward working out theoretical formulations based upon such concepts. In particular, they have done little toward working out a theory of cooperation in the broad sense, although they have given much attention to formally organized enterprises that describe themselves as cooperatives rather than as competitive businesses.

## Limitations upon the Alternatives Open to Economic Entities

Much of the prevailing economic theory and many of the public policies based upon it proceed upon the assumption that business management and the management of consumption both operate by making decisions intended to maximize results under a continuous function. Little or no weight is given to the fact that decisions are really discontinuous (made in "lumps" or "bundles," as it were) and that real choices must be made from specific alternatives of quite limited number and scope. Marketing men know these facts, yet they have done very little toward setting up alternative formulations based upon what they know concerning the limitations within which managers and consumers operate.

## Attitudes and Motivations of Buyers and Sellers

Every theory of management as well as every theory of economic behavior must rest upon some concept of human motivations and attitudes. The concepts, implicit or explicit, that underlie much of economic theory, clearly fall far short of conforming to the facts of human behavior. Although one turns first to psychologists for correctives, students of marketing themselves have a better opportunity than anyone else to observe human beings in action as buyers and sellers. With the aid of psychologists, sociologists and statisticians, they are developing increasingly effective ways to observe and measure. They cannot expect to reap the full harvest of their efforts, however, until they have worked out more meaningful concepts, problems, hypotheses and, eventually, theories into which they can fit their stores of fact concerning what people do.

## The Development of Market Organization

Characteristic of much economic analysis is the underlying assumption that the complex of human behavior required to set up, operate and continuously remodel a going market has already done its work. The going market simply exists. Little thought (perhaps none) is given to the fact that this assumption is not tenable—that someone has to exert great effort continuously if there is to be the intricate organization required to inform potentital buyers and sellers, to bring them together in the actual negotiation of a transaction, and to make it possible for them to carry out all transactions negotiated.

Much of the criticism of marketing as wasteful stems fundamentally from taking this assumption as a statement of observed fact. It is self-evident that if we assume an effective market organization to be in existence and operating, any further effort to organize and operate it is by definition unnecessary. Students of marketing need to work out a theory built upon the assumption that the development, continuous adjustment, improvement, and steady operation of the machinery of marketing is an economic function as real and as important as any of the more familiar economic functions that can be performed only when the market organization as we know it, or some acceptable substitute for it, has been devised and set up and is kept in operation.

## Sources for a Theory of Marketing[3]

It would be a mistake to assume that the interest in marketing theory springs solely from a growing realization that the study of marketing must remain fragmentary, superficial and inaccurate in the absence of valid and profound theoretical formulations. Equally important, perhaps, is the dawning of a realization that here and there in the literature of several intellectual disciplines are appearing the elements from which an adequate theory of marketing will be constructed. Many of these elements are little more than vague ideas and suggestions. Only the barest start has been made toward refining them into really meaningful concepts and procedures that will serve as guides to hypothesis making and fact gathering. They are nevertheless numerous enough and suggestive enough to support a belief that a theory of marketing is becoming feasible as well as desirable. The appearance of feasibility has played a part in arousing interest no less important than that played by the realization of need.

The accumulating elements for at least a rudimentary theory of marketing are scattered throughout the literature of the social sciences. Many of them are isolated ideas, often little more than flashes of inspiration to be found in longer discussions of entirely different matters. Some of them are indirect suggestions concerning concepts and methodology that can be derived from the efforts of workers in economic fields other than marketing. Some exist only in the unpublished and partially formulated notes of scholars who have shared their ideas with others in talks before technical meetings, discussions before classes, or private conversations and correspondence.

Under such circumstances it is not to be expected that anyone can present a definitive bibliography of possible sources for a theory of marketing. All that will be attempted here is to list some of the ideas the present writers have picked up in their own cogitations and investigations. Enriched by the analogous discoveries of others, they should provide inspiration, stimulation and cross-fertilization of concept and procedure. Out of these in due course will come a comprehensive and valid theory of marketing.

### Contributions from Economic Theory

An obvious possible source for contributions to a meaningful theory of marketing is general economic theory itself. Since a theory of marketing must be in part a revision and correction of economic theory, it would perhaps be fair to say that the principal contribution economic theorists can make to its development is to work out economic theories that stimulate a search by specialized students of marketing for something that explains the known facts more fully. In so far as economic theorists work out doctrines that meet the needs and conform to the experience of marketing specialists, they will, of course, render the development of a specialized theory of marketing unnecessary.

In practice, starting points for a theory of marketing maybe found in the work of theorists who have developed concepts that are readily adaptable to this field. Some of these are ideas accepted by the great body of orthodox theorists; others represent offshoots that have achieved only limited acceptance.

Institutional economics, for example, provides marketing theorists with a particularly useful set of concepts and formulations. As we shall see shortly, one of the most promising possible approaches to a theory of marketing is through the study of what we shall call group behaviorism. The sociologist's concept of institutions as patterns or configurations of group behavior provides the basic approach that has been applied by the institutionalists (with only limited success so far, it must be admitted) to the study of economic problems. Marketing men, much of whose work consists of seeking out general patterns of group behavior, should find this approach particularly fruitful.

It should be remembered that marketing men call one of their traditional approaches to the study of marketing the institutional approach. As used by most marketing men (the recently published text by Edward A. Duddy and David A. Revzan being a conspicuous exception), the term has been restricted to efforts to describe what goes on in marketing by classifying, describing and analyzing the operations of the two million or so individual establishments that particicpate in marketing. This approach is not institutional in the sociologist's sense. It is nevertheless adaptable to a more fundamental and far-reaching approach that would treat retailers, wholesalers and other entities active in marketing as institutions in the true sociological usage of the term. In this view, the agencies of marketing would become patterns of human behavior and communication clustered about some physical facility, such as a store or warehouse, that can be identified and located for counting and measurement. Similarly the economic entities discussed above could be viewed as clusters or patterns of group behavior.

Individual economists of the institutional school also offer specific fruitful ideas for the development of marketing theory. Thus John R. Commons provides the basic inspiration for dividing transactions into routine and fully negotiated ones. Upon this idea can be built a meaningful analysis of changes in the ways buyers and sellers do business and of the significances of these changes for costs of marketing.

Von Neumann and Morgenstern have taken the fully negotiated transaction as their point of departure in a book that brings a new mathematical approach to the analysis of market behavior. This may turn out to be the genuine revolution in economic theory which has been presaged by such diverse developments as Keynes' challenge to Says' Law of Markets and the recasting of competitive theory of Chamberlin and others. Starting from an exhaustive analysis of the negotiated transaction they offer hope of a fresh attack on such problems as efficiency in distribution and monopolistic restriction.

Clark's pioneer work on overhead costs provided a source from which stems directly or indirectly, much of the fruitful effort of marketing men to work out definitions of cost and of the relations between cost and price from which in time will almost certainly come significant contributions to the theory of marketing.

Marketing is of necessity involved with competition and price. Therefore the core of marketing theory might well be modern price theory with its stress on different types of competitive situations.

The work of E. H. Chamberlin, Joan Robinson, Robert Triffin as well as such men as Bain and others in analyses of non-perfect competition, offers an especially vital challenge to marketing theorists. Marketing men will certainly follow their lead in questioning the validity as statements of fact of the assumptions underlying much traditional economic theory. At the same time, marketing men have every opportunity to advance monopolistic competition theory in providing alternative assumptions and hypotheses drawn from experience in the market.

Certainly the last word has not been said on product differentiation as a factor in what Triffin calls heterogeneous competition—a term, incidentally, which well might replace "monopolistic competition" as being more descriptive and not so weighted with objectionable connotations. Economic discussions tend to assume that product differentiation always represents a departure from uniformity but the reverse may be true with respect to units produced by the firm which differentiates. Suppose there is a field in which each producer is making a great many varieties of the same article in accordance with the diverse specifications demanded by purchasers. Then one enterprising firm has an opportunity to steal a march on competition by manufacturing only identical units. By adopting a standard formula within its own business it may achieve substantial advantages in mass production economies and be obliged to use only a part of the savings in sales and advertising expenses to attract to itself the buyers who are willing to accept its standardized product.

More broadly it may be said that differentiation is a basic function of the market which is carried out primarily through the channels of distribution and which is intimately related to the problem of efficiency in marketing. Chamberlin recognizes time and place utility and all specialzied services as aspects of product differentiation but does not treat the subject exhaustively. For marketing theory a crucial problem is the point in the flow at which differentiation does or should take place. As a general principle it seems clear that it should be avoided as long as possible to maximize the proportion of the distribution job which can enjoy the economies of minimum differentiation.

The relation of sales cost to competition has been touched upon by many writers but remains an item of unfinished business for marketing theory. The general assumption appears to be that the effect of competition in imperfect markets is to raise sales costs. This assumption needs to be tested against an analysis which starts from the negotiated sale transaction as the norm and recognizes that there may be many ways of achieving the relative economy of routine sales transactions. Advertising may help to perform for one class of products the simplification of transactions achieved through commodity exchanges in another. It is not likely that distribution can ever achieve the economies which arise from the use of power machinery in production. It is well to remember, however, that specialization and routinization provide the original basis for improving efficiency in both production and distribution.

One of the most profound questions with respect to the heterogeneous competition which prevails in our economy today is whether we can develop a theory of competition which has any real relevance for public policy on such matters as the regulation of marketing policy. The apparent willingness of many influential economists to throw over the benefits of mass production in order to achieve a closer approach to atomistic competition is surely unrealistic. Following J. M. Clark and Robert Triffin, a radical revision of competitive theory may revolve around overhead costs and differentiated market position in a heterogeneous economy. Empirical studies of competition indicate that these two factors can provide the basis for dynamic equilibrium.

The direction for advance which is indicated here is an analysis of the process of price negotiation and the conditions for a balance of economic forces achieved through bargaining. Ordinarily there are limits observed by either side and principles by which their bargaining activities are guided which may result in a long-run outcome with respect to prices which is not too different from the long-run outcome under the supposition of pure competition. In a mass production economy the central consideration in negotation may generally be expected to be the endeavor to balance access to markets through diversified channels against the need for enough volume to reach the breaking point in production costs.

The devlopment of the so-called macroeconomics in recent years largely under the influence of Keynes has concentrated the attention of economists on national aggregates such as total consumer income, the level of employment, consumer expenditures, and capital formation. The results which may be hoped for in more reliable estimates and predictions of these aggregates have great practical significance for marketing research, which is quite generally concerned with evaluating the outlook for individual concerns or products. The theoretical significance of Keynes for marketing lies in other directions, as for example in underscoring the importance of market organization by advancing the thesis that the automatic functioning of the market mechanism cannot be taken for granted.

Work such as that exemplified in Bertil Ohlin's analysis of inter-regional trade has already provided the conceptual basis for one course in the theory of marketing.[4] It has also provided foundations for more meaningful analyses than have been widely attempted as yet of the economics of trading areas, economic regions within a national economy, and the various sections of a metropolitan community. Beginnings have been made toward these sorts of analyses; but they offer fruitful opportunities for more penetrating studies than have yet been made.

## Contributions from Systematic Studies of Group Behavior

A second possible source for contributions to the evolving theory of marketing will be found in studies of group behavior made by social scientists in fields other than economics, and notably in the work of anthropologists, sociologists and social psychologists. George Lundberg's application to marketing in his Parlin lecture of his concepts of measurable patterns and clusters of communication, is an example of what can be done with ideas borrowed directly from sociology. It offers a promising device to be used in analyzing the economic significance of such entities as cities, towns, trading centers, trading areas and individual retailers with their customers and their sources of supply; of advertising media and those they reach; and of the multitude of other patterns of communication through which human wants are converted into economic demand, information is distributed among sellers and buyers, and transactions are negotiated and carried into effect.

Kenneth Boulding speculates in a recent article on the limitations of the principle of maximization of returns as the foundation of the theory of the individual business enterprise. He suggests that the principle of organizational preservation may turn out to be more fruitful. One of the authors of this article has pointed out that organizations act as if they had a will to survive and that this drive arises from the individual's struggle for socio-economic status.[5]

Among psychologists, the topological concepts developed by the late Kurt Lewin and expounded in somewhat simpler form by his former student Robert W. Leeper, offer some promise of setting up procedures that may lead to a more effective understanding of human motivation than has thus far been achieved. In the field of industrial relations, Elton Mayo at Harvard and E. W. Bakke at Yale have developed promising concepts and procedures for inquiries into the factors that determine how human beings behave in the relations of employer to employee and in the development of trade unions. Such concepts and procedures give some evidence of being applicable to problems of marketing with good effect.

Students of public opinion and consumer attitudes, among whom Hadley Cantril may be mentioned, are virtually within the field of marketing; but they have drawn heavily upon other disciplines in their work.

## Contributions from Ecological Studies

Research by a wide variety of students into problems of human geography, population, traffic and city planning has offered many opportunities for enriching the theory of marketing. R. M. Haig's early essay on the economic functions of the metropolis and Harold Mayer's classification and analysis of the patterns of growth exhibited by secondary shopping centers in Chicago, are examples of useful analyses derived from the work of city planners.

W. J. Reilly's law of retail gravitation probably fits best into the ecological classification although it could also be placed in the next section among the examples of work done in marketing research that is leading to a more fundamental understanding of the nature and function of marketing. Long neglected, Reilly's law has again begun to attract notice. After some revisions, it has provided the basic procedure used by Paul D. Converse to determine the directions and distances people go to shop for certain types of goods in Illinois. Still further revised, it has provided a system worked out in detail by the Curtis Publishing Company for dividing the entire country into trading areas for shopping goods. Although the immediate application has thus been made to the problems faced by individual merchants and individual communities in building their trade, this law as revised provides one starting point for a theory of the relationships of individual retailers or clusters and their customers.

Even more significant have been the efforts of John Q. Stewart to apply to the distribution of the population, and to the influences individual people and clusters of people exert upon each other at a distance, concepts much like those he has used in his work as a physicist and astronomer. His method, which he has summed up under the term social physics, may well lead to the clearest understanding yet attained and the most precise measurement thus far made of the forces that determine how people assemble themselves into markets and the ways in which they exert influence upon each other. It may thus provide a procedure for reducing to quantitative measurement the concept of patterns of social communication or influence devised by the sociologists.

## Contributions in Marketing Literature Itself

Tentative beginnings toward a meaningful theory of marketing may also be found scattered through the literature of marketing itself. It is impossible to make a complete listing here of the many significant contributions; but a few names may be mentioned so as to indicate the nature of these beginnings:

Melvin T. Copeland's early work in the classification of commodities on the basis of shopping methods used by the consumers who acquire them.

The work done in defining and describing the functions of marketing by such men as A. W. Shaw, Paul T. Cherington, Fred E. Clark, and, more recently, E. D. McGarry.

E. T. Grether's use, noted above, of the concept of interregional trade as a frame upon which to build a theory of marketing, and his work with price discrimination and price structures.

The effort by Charles F. Phillips, since widely copied, to work the ideas and principles of value developed by neoclassical and monopolistic-competition economists into the body of marketing principles.

Robert W. Bartels' attempt to cull out of the literature of marketing all the principles or theories it contains.

Ralph W. Breyer's pioneer effort to struggle with the problems of space and time in marketing, with the concept of marketing as a social institution, and with the influence of changes in costs imposed at one level of the channel upon costs incurred at other levels.

The work done by John Paver, Victor H. Pelz, and others in using traffic flows and pedestrian movements as indicators of the structure of markets and trading areas.

Ralph Cassady's analyses of price discrimination and its legal significance, and the work done by Cassady and others with problems of decentralization in the retail trade of large cities.

The work of Roland S. Vaile and, more recently, Neil H. Borden in the study of the economic effects of advertising. Thus is supplemented by William B. Ricketts' work with procedures for evaluating the business effects of advertising.

Many other examples could be given; but these will suffice for present purposes. They make it clear that students who undertake to build a systematic theory of marketing will find stones at hand for the purpose. The stones must be dug out of the existing literature, reshaped, and supplemented by many others that remain to be discovered. They nevertheless provide material for a start.

## A Possible Approach to an Integrated Theory of Marketing

Any comprehensive approach to the development of a marketing theory would need to meet several tests:

1. It should give promise of serving the variety of needs that have created the current interest in marketing theory.
2. It should be able to draw in a comprehensive way upon the starting points for theory already available in the literature, such as those listed above.

3. It should provide a consistent theoretical perspective for the study of all the major classes of significant entities in marketing.

Such a viewpoint would appear to be available in what may be called group behaviorism as it has been developing in the social sciences. This view differs from the narrower use of the term behaviorism by Pavlov and Watson in that it gives a sociological rather than a physiological emphasis to the analysis. The basic concept of group behaviorism is the organized behavior system.

Marketing theory may be said to consist of making clear what we mean by behavior, what we mean by system, and what we mean by organization, all as applied to marketing. Application to marketing implies that principles pertaining to these basic concepts should be given specific form and content in relation to all of the types of organized behavior systems that are significantly involved in the marketing process. These types of behavior system include, as we have seen, the firms engaged in buying or selling, the family as an earning and consuming unit, the local dispersion market, the channel of distribution, the industry supplying a phase of consumer or industrial need, and the economic system as a whole.

Group behaviorism differs from institutionalism in that it is basically concerned with the concrete entities that interact within a behavior system. It differs from the approach to systems that has generally been followed in mathematical economics in that it takes account of the patterns of group behavior developed within specific systems as qualifying their operation. Thus, while it may make use of equilibrium concepts, it does not depend primarily on analogies drawn from the equilibrium systems discussed in physics.

Group behaviorism has the further distinction that it emphasizes those aspects of individual behavior that tend to perpetuate organized behavior systems and thus to render them at least semiconservative in the technical sense. Economic theory tends to assume that the systems under consideration do not obey the laws of conservation.

The approach through group behaviorism is most closely allied to what is usually called the functional approach in marketing. It would undertake to analyze marketing processes by taking primary account of the objectives they are designed to serve. Thus it retains the emphasis of the general economists on the forces of supply and demand but must go further in order to throw light on specific problems and situations in marketing. Eventually it should enable the market analyst to formulate the way in which market forces interact at any point in the system he has under investigation.

Marketing is still in what Northrop described as the first stage of scientific study, namely that of the gathering of vast compilations of fact. It was Francis Bacon, at the very beginning of modern scientific awakening, who felt that all problems would be solved if only enough facts were accumulated. Economic theory in the main has remained one step further back in a prescientific or metaphysical stage. It has occupied itself with the effort toward logical deductions from assumptions.

Neither economics nor marketing can lay much claim to being scientific until they attain the stage of continuous interaction between theory and research. The assumptions on which theory rests must more and more spring from careful empirical generalization. The facts which research gathers must more and more be relevant to hypotheses adopted on theoretical grounds.

## An Application of Group Behaviorism to Marketing Research

The feasibility and significance of approaching a theory of marketing through group behaviorism will be tested in an exploratory survey of the productivity of marketing in Philadelphia being organized this summer (1948). For purposes of this survey, the economic entity chosen is the Philadelphia dispersion market. Tentatively this has been defined as an organized behavior system embracing a group of people to whom goods and services flow through points of entry located within the Philadelphia area in so far as they do not originate within the area itself; the formal organizations, agencies or entities that do the work required to effectuate the flow in so far as the consumers do not do it for themselves; and the patterns of social communication, physical flow and movement through time by means of which the work is arranged and effectuated. For purposes of quantitative analysis, some arbitrary departures from the details of this definition doubtless must be made because of limitations upon the sorts of data to be had within limits of feasible financial expenditure. These concessions to practical difficulties will be held to the narrowest possible limits.

The specific objective of the project is to test the feasibility and significance of a long list of tentative formulas devised by one of the authors. These formulas are intended to serve as indicators of degrees of efficiency in dispersion marketing. The project will also give some indications, however, as to whether the basic theoretical approach being made is valid. In so doing it will, if it succeeds, meet the first of the tests suggested in the preceding section for the validity of approaches to the development of a marketing theory. That is, it will help satisfy the two basic needs underlying the demand for such a theory: First, it will provide a way of stating theoretical problems in marketing that, in the terms used by Northrop, permits the initiation of really meaningful inquires. Second, it will make possible the drawing up of generalizations that have meaning and significance because they can be subjected to the test of relevant facts.

The project, if it succeeds, will also satisfy the test of making comprehensive drafts upon the literature for approaches, concepts and procedures. For example, the frame of reference that treats the dispersion market as the unit for observation comes from the developing realization already noted that new types of economic entities must be visualized. The treatment of any such entity as an organized system of group behavior derives from the sociological concept of institutuions as patterns of social communication. Emphasis will be placed upon the cooperative, as contrasted with the competitive aspects of the market, the objective being to determine what the market as a whole accomplishes for the people who compose it.

In setting up the formulas, which are essentially ratios between units of input and units of output, heavy reliance has been placed upon the functional approach to a study of marketing. "Functions" have been redefined for the purposes of analysis at this particular level; but the survey will hold closely to the basic concept of measuring the output or product of marketing in units of work defined by reference to the functions the dispersion market is supposed to perform.[6] A kind of equilibrium analysis will be achieved through establishing a concept of unit or optimum efficiency for each task the market performs. Against this unit efficiency, taken as a goal, the actual performance of the market in each particular can be evaluated. Instead of being looked upon as a device to introduce imperfections into an otherwise perfect market, the behavior system under analysis will be taken as designed to reduce the degree of imperfection already present.

The specific measures to be used derive in the last analysis from the numerous studies of which a few examples were given above under the headings "Ecological Studies" and "Marketing Literature Itself." Present indications are that the ecological studies will be particularly useful. In order to measure some aspects of effort expended and work done, reliance can best be put upon concepts of movement or flow through some one or more varieties of space and time against the resistance of some one or more varieties of obstacle. To use these concepts effectively, clear definitions will be required of distributive space and time, location or position, and flow or movement. The definitions will have to be so set up that the terms lend themselves to quantitative measurement. For these purposes, studies of the sort illustrated above by reference to Lundberg, Paver, Pelz, Reilly, Converse and Stewart will be particularly helpful. For the analysis of other aspects of effort expended and work done, reliance can perhaps best be made on other sources illustrated by Commons' suggestion of the contrast between fully negotiated and routine transactions, various studies of retail mortality, and struggles by many economists with problems of price differentiation and price structure.

There is every likelihood that this sort of comprehensive analysis of any entity such as the dispersion market will lead to significant formulations of theory, as this term has been defined above; that is, this sort of study should provide clear, detailed and specific statements of what is meant by behavior in marketing, what is meant by a system or pattern of behavior, and what is meant by organized or group patterns. It should be particularly useful in so far as it provides a procedure for reducing these various matters to quantitative measurement.

Furthermore, there are good prospects that what is worked out in this sort of survey will provide a theoretical perspective applicable to the study of other identifiable and significant entities in marketing. Thus it gives promise of meeting the third test suggested above. It bids fair to be not merely an isolated empirical study but a unit in something much larger. Should it prove successful, it will contribute substantially to creating the general theory so earnestly wanted by students of marketing.

## Marketing Theory and Economic Theory

An issue requiring the most careful consideration is whether the marketing field can satisfy its needs for a marketing theory until reformulation of economic theory has progressed further. Any market analyst who sees his role as that of facilitating adjustments of private and public policy in a world of change must grow impatient with the faltering attempts of economic theorists to deal with the dynamic aspects of an enterprise economy. The most acute marketing problems are precipitated by the facts of technological change. The market analyst is bound to wonder how the economists can expect to cope with change so long as he is so generally inclined to consider technology outside his proper field of interest.

The market analyst does not have the luxury of choice as to whether he will adopt a dynamic view. At the very least he must take account of technological change in marketing. Progressive changes in the technology of distribution, in the methods and channels of marketing, are surely significant for economic theory. They are of the essence of any perspective which might be distinguished as marketing theory. Thus the marketing theorist is obliged to break the economist's taboo on the discussion of technology at least as it applies to the techniques of marketing.

There is another aspect of the dynamics of market organization which is fundamental for marketing theory and eventually inescapable, it would appear, for economic theory. That is the fact that an organized behavior system is not a neutral framework or container for the actions and evaluations which take place within it. That is to say that a market changes day by day through the very fact that goods are bought and sold. While evaluation is taking place within a marketing structure, the structure itself is being rendered weaker or stronger and the changes in organization which follow will have an impact on tomorrow's evaluations. Marketing theory will not provide an adequate approach if it ignores this interaction between the system and the processes which take place within it. Whether economic theory can dispense with such considerations is another question.

## ENDNOTES

1. F. S. C. Northrop, *The Logic of the Sciences and the Humanities*, Macmillan Co., New York, 1947.
2. Some aspects of this problem were considered in an earlier article by one of the present authors: Reavis Cox, "Non-Price Competition and the Measurement of Prices," *Journal of Marketing*, Vol. X, No. 4, April, 1946, pp. 370-383.
3. Formal references to the sources cited in this section will be found in the bibliography at the end of the article.
4. This is a course in the theory of domestic commerce organized by E. T. Grether at the University of California. So far as the present writers have been able to discover, only three courses are currently given in the colleges of the country that specifically undertake a systematic presentation of a theory of marketing. In addition to Dean Grether's course, there is one given by E. D. McGarry at the University of Buffalo that builds upon an analysis of the functions of marketing. The third, given by Reavis Cox at the University of Pennsylvania, is built around analyses of the meaning and measurement of location in and flow through distributive space and time, problems of human behavior, patterns of social communication, prices and price structure, and problems of efficiency, waste and productivity.
5. Wroe Alderson, "Conditions For a Balanced World Economy," *World Economics*, Vol. II, No. 7, October, 1944, pp. 3-25.
6. For a statement of some views held by the present writers concerning ways of measuring productivity in marketing, see Reavis Cox, "The Meaning and Measurement of Productivity in Marketing," and Wroe Alderson, "A Formula for Measuring Productivity in Distribution," *Journal of Marketing*, Vol. XII, April, 1948, pp. 433-448.

## BIBLIOGRAPHY

The ideas credited to the various authors mentioned in Section IV may be found in the following sources:

1. Joe S. Bain, "Market Classifications in Modern Price Theory," *The Quarterly Journal of Economics*, LVI, No. 4, August, 1942, pp. 560-574.
2. E. W. Bakke, *Mutual Survival: The Goal of Unions and Management* (New Haven: Yale University Labor and Management Center, 1946).
3. E. W. Bakke, *Principles of Adaptive Human Behaviour*. (A mimeographed preliminary draft privately circulated.)
4. Robert W. Bartels, "Marketing Principles," *Journal of Marketing*, Vol. IX, No. 2, October, 1944, pp. 151-157.
5. Neil H. Borden, *The Economic Effects of Advertising* (Chicago: Richard D. Irwin, Inc., 1942).
6. Kenneth E. Boulding, "Samuelson's *Foundations*: The Role of Mathematics in Economics," *Journal of Political Economy*, Vol. LVI, No. 3, June, 1948, pp. 187-199.
7. William K. Bowden and Ralph Cassady, Jr., "Decentralization of Retail Trade in Metropolitan Market Area," *Journal of Marketing*, Vol. V, No. 3, January, 1941, pp. 270-275.

8. Ralph F. Breyer, *Bulk and Package Handling Costs* (New York: American Management Association, 1944).
9. Ralph F. Breyer, *The Marketing Institution* (New York: McGraw-Hill Book Co., 1934).
10. Hadley Cantril and others, *Gauging Public Opinion* (Princeton: Princeton University Press, 1944).
11. Ralph Cassady, Jr., "Some Economic Aspects of Price Discrimination Under Non-Perfect Market Conditions" and "Techniques and Purposes of Price Discrimination," *Journal of Marketing*, Vol. XI, No. 1, July, 1946, pp. 7-20, and No. 2, October, 1946, pp. 135-150.
12. Ralph Cassady, Jr., and William K. Bowden, "Shifting Retail Trade Within the Los Angeles Metropolitan Market," *Journal of Marketing*, Vol. VIII, No. 4, April, 1944, pp. 398-404.
13. Edward H. Chamberlin, *The Theory of Monopolistic Competition: A Re-orientation of the Theory of Value* (Cambridge: Harvard University Press, 1st ed., 1933, frequently revised since then).
14. Paul T. Cherington, *The Elements of Marketing* (New York: Macmillan Co., 1920).
15. Fred E. Clark, *Principles of Marketing* (New York: Macmillan Co., 1st ed., 1922, revised at intervals since).
16. J. M. Clark, *Studies in the Economics of Overhead Costs* (Chicago: University of Chicago Press, 1923).
17. John R. Commons, *Institutional Economics* (New York: Macmillan Co., 1934).
18. Paul D. Converse, *Retail Trade Areas in Illinois* (Urbana: University of Illinois, 1946).
19. Melvin T. Copeland, "Relation of Consumers' Buying Habits to Marketing Methods," *Harvard Business Review*, April, 1923, pp. 282-289.
20. Richard P. Doherty, "The Movement and Concentration of Retail Trade in Metropolitan Areas" and "Decentralization of Retail Trade in Boston," *Journal of Marketing*, Vol. V, No. 4, April, 1941, pp. 395-401, and Vol. VI, No. 3, January, 1942, pp. 281-286.
21. Edward A. Duddy and David A. Revzan, *Marketing: An Institutional Approach* (New York: McGraw-Hill Book Co., 1947).
22. E. T. Grether, "Geographical Price Policies in the Grocery Trade, 1941," *Journal of Marketing*, Vol. VIII, No. 4, April, 1944, pp. 417-422.
23. E. T. Grether, *Price Control Under Fair Trade Legislation* (New York: Oxford University Press, 1939).
24. Robert Murray Haig, "Toward an Understanding of the Metropolis," *Quarterly Journal of Economics*, Vol. XL, February and May, 1926, pp. 179-208 and 402-434.
25. J. M. Keynes, *The General Theory of Employment, Interest and Money* (New York: Harcourt, Brace & Co., 1936).
26. Robert W. Leeper, *Lewin's Topological and Vector Psychology: A Digest and a Critique* (Eugene: University of Oregon, 1943).
27. Kurt Lewin, *Principles of Topological Psychology* (New York: McGraw-Hill Book Co., 1936).
28. Kurt Lewin, "The Conceptual Representation and the Measurement of Psychological Forces," *Contributions to Psychological Theory*, Vol. I, No. 5 (Durham: Duke University Press, 1938).

29. George Lundberg, *Marketing and Social Organization* (Philadelphia: Curtis Publishing Co., 1945).
30. George Lundberg and Mary Steele, "Social Attraction Patterns in a Village," *Sociometry*, Vol. I, January-April, 1938, pp. 375-419.
31. Harold M. Mayer, "Patterns and Recent Trends of Chicago's Outlying Business Centers," *Journal of Land and Public Utility Economics*, Vol. XVIII, No. I, February, 1942, pp. 4-16.
32. Elton Mayo, *Human Problems of an Industrial Civilization* (Boston: Harvard University, Division of Research, 2nd ed., 1946).
33. Edmund D. McGarry, *The Functions of Marketing*. (Manuscript).
34. Bertil Ohlin, *Interregional and International Trade* (Cambridge: Harvard University Press, 1935).
35. John Paver and Miller McClintock, *Traffic and Trade* (New York: McGraw-Hill Book Co., 1935).
36. Charles F. Phillips, *Marketing* (Boston: Hougton Mifflin Co., 1938).
37. William J. Reilly, *Methods for the Study of Retail Relationships* (Austin: University of Texas, 1929).
38. William B. Ricketts, *Testing and Measuring Advertising Effectiveness* (Manuscript).
39. Joan Robinson, *The Economics of Imperfect Competition* (London: Macmillan Co., 1933).
40. A. W. Shaw, "Some Problems in Market Distribution," *Quarterly Journal of Economics*, August, 1912, pp. 703-765.
41. John Q. Stewart, "Concerning 'Social Physics'," *Scientific American*, May, 1948, pp. 20-23.
42. John Q. Stewart, "Empirical Mathematical Rules Concerning the Distribution and Equilibrium of Population," *Geographical Review*, Vol. XXXVII, No. 3, July, 1947, pp. 461-485.
43. Frank Strohkarck and Katherine Phelps, "The Mechanics of Constructing a Market Area Map," *Journal of Marketing*, Vol. XII, No. 4, April, 1948, pp. 493-496. (A description of the method used by the Curtis Publishing Company in constructing its map, "Market Areas for Shopping Lines".)
44. Traffic Audit Bureau, *Methods for the Evaluation of Outdoor Advertising* (New York: Traffic Audit Bureau, 1946. This study was done under the direction of Victor H. Pelz.)
45. Robert Triffin, *Monopolistic Competition and General Equilibrium Theory* (Cambridge: Harvard University Press, 1940).
46. Roland S. Vaile, *Economics of Advertising* (New York: Ronald Press Co., 1927).
47. John Von Neumann and Oskar Morgenstern, *Theory of Games and Economic Behavior* (Princeton: Princeton University Press, 1944).
48. Chester I. Barnard, *Organization and Management* (Harvard University Press, 1948).
49. J. M. Clark, *Alternative to Serfdom* (Alfred A. Knopf, 1948).
50. Oswald Kanuth, *Managerial Enterprise* (W. W. Norton, 1948).

# 50 — Alderson's General Theory of Marketing: A Formalization

*Shelby D. Hunt, James A. Muncy, and Nina M. Ray*

Reprinted from *The Review of Marketing: 1981*, published by the American Marketing Association, pp. 267-272. Reprinted by permission.

## Abstract

Wroe Alderson is one of three marketers to attempt a general theory of marketing. Substantial controversy exists concerning this general theory, partially because few understand Alderson and his work. The authors attempt to clarify Alderson's work by "formalizing" his theory.

## Introduction

There have been several attempts to develop a general theory of marketing: Bartels (1968), El-Ansary (1979), and Alderson (1965). Bartels (1968) proposed that a general theory of marketing consisted of the following seven component subtheories: 1) the theory of social initiative; 2) the theory of economic separations; 3) the theory of market roles, expectations, and interactions; 4) the theory of flows and systems; 5) the theory of behavior constraints; 6) the theory of social change and marketing evolution; and 7) the theory of the social control of marketing.

Hunt (1971) analyzed the seven subtheories proposed by Bartels, found them to be lacking in lawlike generalizations, and concluded that the seven subtheories were not theories at all but were "an assemblage of classificational schemata, some intriguing definitions, and exhortations to fellow marketing students to adopt a particular perspective in attempting to generate marketing theory." Further evaluations of Bartels' "general theory" were conducted by Pinson, Angelmar, and Roberto (1972) which concluded that more specific criteria for evaluating theoretical constructions were needed. A reply by Hunt (1973) provided further explication of criteria for evaluating theories and concluded that Bartels' conceptualization was "neither a theory of marketing nor a general theory of marketing."

El-Ansary (1979) proposed that, by definition, the general theory of marketing should be the "broadest theory" explaining marketing phenomena. Further, the general theory of marketing should be the "central theory" or the culmination of all other theories, and should ''logically integrate'' all other theories in marketing. Although El-Ansary did not specifically develop a general theory of marketing, he proposed an outline, which if developed, would comprise a general theory of marketing. El-Ansary suggested that a general theory of marketing would be composed of subtheories involving the following areas: consumer behavior, organizational buyer behavior, interorganizational management, channel member behavior, channel system behavior, channel institutions, micromarketing, macromarketing, and strategic marketing. The conceptualization of a general theory of marketing put forth by El-Ansary has not yet been subjected to critical analysis.

The works of Wroe Alderson constitute the third approach to developing a general theory of marketing. Although Alderson authored numerous articles, two books summarize the major points of his theory: *Marketing Behavior and Executive Action* (1975) and *Dynamic Marketing Behavior* (1965). The present article will focus on and attempt to formalize Alderson's general theory of marketing.

## Background

Substantial controversy exists concerning Alderson's general theory of marketing and its contribution to marketing thought. An early review by Nicosia (1962) suggested that Alderson's theory ''merits consideration as a frame of reference.'' Similarly, Schwartz (1963) concluded that ''on the whole, Alderson's concept of an organized behavior system and his theory of market behavior represent a significant contribution to marketing theory.'' As evidence of continued interest in the works of Alderson, one need only to observe that there were four articles on Alderson in the proceedings of the 1979 American Marketing Association special conference on marketing theory, and three articles on Alderson in the 1980 theory conference. Finally, Blair and Uhl (1976) point out:

> marketing theorists of the 1950s and 1960s hailed Wroe Alderson as a leader in their field. Time has substantiated their judgement; Alderson's works are among the few writings of their period accorded anything more than historical esteem ... Alderson was the most powerful author immediately preceeding what Kotler has called marketing's shift from applied economics to applied behavioral science ... Alderson's writings offer perhaps the most recent general theory of marketing. Also, Alderson was an author of great insight. These facts contribute to Alderson's continued major significance in modern marketing thought.

Nevertheless, many authors have seriously questioned the importance and usefulness of Alderson's theoretical work. Dawson and Wales (1979) examined the status of Aldersonian theory in current literature. They concluded that ''almost none of the concepts pioneered by this leading marketing theorist appear in any of the leading (selling) marketing principles texts.'' Barksdale (1980) also observed that few marketing books include references to Alderson's work. Barksdale also concluded that Alderson's concepts were ''not well developed,'' his ideas were ''not closely reasoned'' and his theoretical system never became the organizing concept for the mainstream of marketing thought.

Why are there such widely divergent views on Alderson's general theory of marketing? The thesis of this paper is that a substantial amount of the controversy can be attributed to differences in interpreting Alderson's work. These different interpretations have led to substantial misunderstandings concerning Alderson's theory of marketing. It is sad, but true, that Alderson was a notoriously nonsystematic writer. As Hostiuck and Kurtz (1973) point out ''even recognized scholars of marketing groan at the mere mention of Alderson and intimate that they never really understood him.''

## Purpose

The purpose of this paper is to clarify the issues concerning Alderson's work by reconstructing and rigorously stating in propositional format Alderson's entire general theory of marketing. In the philosophy of science this process is referred to as the ''formalization'' of a theory (Rudner 1965). The complete formalization of a theory consists of a formal language system that has been axiomatized and appropriately interpreted. Such a fully formalized theory would include: elements, definitions, formation rules for elements, axioms, transformation rules for axioms, rules of interpretation. Although very few theories are ever completely formalized, the process of partially formalizing theories is a key step in theory development. As has been observed (Hunt 1976), ''the partial formalization theory is an absolutely necessary precondition for meaningful analysis of the theory.'' The remainder of this paper will attempt to rigorously reconstruct, that is, partially formalize, Alderson's general theory of marketing.

## A Partial Formalization of Alderson's Theory of Marketing

A. *Definition of key terms*

1. There are three primitive elements in marketing: *sets, behaviors,* and *expectations* (1965), p. 25).
    a. sets are aggregates containing some class of components such as points in a line, physical objects of human beings (1965, p. 47)
    b. behavior is activity occupying time (1965, p. 48)
    c. expectations are attached to what the individual thinks may happen and the favorable or unfavorable results of these future events (1965, p. 50)

2. Collections are sets which can be taken as inert with no interaction among the components (1965, p. 47).
3. Conglomerates are collections as they occur in a state of nature (1965, p. 57).
4. Assortments are collections which have been assembled by taking account of human expectations concerning future action (1965, p. 47).
5. Systems are sets in which interactions occur that serve to define the boundaries of the set (1965, p. 47).
6. There are four kinds of behaviors (1965, p. 48).
   a. normal behavior is that which is an end in itself or a means to an end,
   b. symptomatic behavior is that which is not functional in that it is neither an end nor a means to an end,
   c. congenial behavior is that which is chosen because it is presumed to be an end in itself and is directly satisfying, and
   d. instrumental behavior is that which is regarded as a means to an end.
7. A behavior system is a system in which persons are the interacting components (1965, p. 47).
8. An organized behavior system is one with these minimum characteristics:
   a. a criterion for membership,
   b. a rule or set of rules assigning duties, and
   c. a preference scale for outputs (1965, p. 48).

B. *Marketing is the exchange which takes place between consuming groups and supplying groups* (1957, p. 15).

1. Exchange in a society results from specialization of the production function (1965, p. 39).
2. Marketing is fundamentally instrumental behavior (1965, p. 261).
3. Marketing is fundamentally a phenomenon of group behavior (1957, p. 13).
4. Marketing is conducted by organized behavior systems which have the following four subsystems (1975, p. 35):
   a. a power system,
   b. a communication system,
   c. a system of inputs and outputs, and
   d. a system of internal and external adjustments.
5. The potency of an assortment is the expected value of an assortment or its anticipated effectiveness in marketing contingencies (1965, p. 50).

6. The Law of Exchange states: if $x$ is an element in the assortment $A$, and $y$ is an element of the assortment $B$, then $x$ is exchangeable for $y$ if, and only if, the following three conditions hold:
   a. $x$ is different from $y$,
   b. the potency of the assortment $A$ is increased by dropping $x$ and adding $y$ and
   c. the potency of the assortment $B$ is increased by adding $x$ and dropping $y$ (1965, p. 84).
7. An exchange is optimal if both parties to the exchange prefer the exchange when compared to the set of all other available exchanges (1965, p. 85).
8. A set of exchanges in a series can replace direct sales by the supplier to the ultimate consumer if the exchanges are optimal at each step (1965, p. 85).

C. *The household is one of the two principal organized systems in marketing* (1965, p. 37).
1. The household persists over time because the behavior system offers a surplus to its participants that they would not expect to enjoy outside the system (1965, p. 37).
2. The household purchasing agent enters the market to replenish or extend the assortment of goods needed to support expected patterns of the future behavior (1965, p. 144).
3. Household buying behavior is a form of instrumental behavior (1965, p. 146).
4. The household purchasing agent engages in search behavior (1965, p. 50).
   a. Search is defined as the sorting of information (1965, p. 50).
   b. Searching for goods is largely a mental process involving movement on the part of the consumer but not involving movement on the part of the consumer but not involving physical movement of the goods (1965, p. 36).
5. The household purchasing agent is guided by two principles in making decisions:
   a. the conditional value of the good if used, and
   b. the probability of use or the estimated frequency of use (1965, p. 38).
6. Household demand is heterogeneous, that is, households have differences in tastes, desires, incomes, locations, and the uses for goods (1965, p. 193).

D. *The firm is the second primary organized behavior system in marketing* (1965, p. 38).
1. Firms evolve in a society when specialization of labor results in removing the production function from the household (1965, p. 39).

2. Firms act as if they had a primary goal of survival (1957, p. 54).
   a. The survival goal results from members of the firm believing that they can obtain more in terms of goods and status by working towards the survival of the system than by acting individually or by becoming a member of another system (1957, p. 54).
   b. The goal of growth is sought because of the conviction that growth is necessary for survival (1957, pp. 103-108).
3. In order to survive, firms compete with other firms in seeking the patronage of households (1957, p. 103-108).
4. A firm can be assured of the patronage of a group of households only when the group has reasons to prefer the output of the particular firm over the output of competing firms (1957, pp. 103-108).
   a. Therefore, each firm will seek some advantage over other firms to assure the patronage of a group of households.
   b. Such a process is called ''Competition for differential advantage'' (1957, pp. 103-108).
5. Competition consists of the constant struggle of firms to develop, maintain, or increase their differential advantages over other firms (1957, p. 106). Competition for differential advantage is the primary force leading to innovation in marketing (1957, p. 102).
6. New firms enter a field because of an expectation of enjoying some differential advantage (1957, p. 102). The success of the new firm creates opportunities for other firms to enter the field through:
   a. simulation, that is, copying the marketing strategy of the original entrant,
   b. deviation, that is, developing a marketing strategy which deviates in some significant way from the marketing strategy of the original entrant, and
   c. complementation, that is, serving as a supplier to the original entrant (1965, pp. 198-200).
7. The bases of differential advantages are:
   a. market segmentation,
   b. selection of appeals,
   c. transvection,
   d. product improvement,
   e. process improvement, and
   f. product innovation (1965, p. 185).
8. Through time competitors will attempt to neutralize the differential advantage of an entrant (1965, p. 204).
   a. The time for neutralization must be sufficiently long to provide an expected reward for innovation (1965, p. 206).
   b. The time for neutralization must not be *too long* or firms will take unfair advantage of households (1965, p. 206).

   c. Instantaneous neutralization occurs only in the case of price reductions on homogeneous or very closely competitive products with few sellers (1965, p. 204).

9. The existence of a differential advantage gives the firm a position in the marketplace known as an ''ecological niche'' (1957, p. 56).
   a. The ''core'' of a firm's ecological niche consists of the group of households for which the firm's differential advantage is most completely suited (1957, p. 56).
   b. The ''fringe'' of a firm's ecological niche consists of the group of households for which the firm's differential advantage is satisfactory but not ideal (1957, p. 56).
   c. Firms can withstand (survive) attacks by competitors on its ''fringe'' as long as its ''core'' remains intact (1957, p. 56).
   d. Firms can survive attacks by competitors on its ''core'' as long as they exhibit ''plasticity,'' which is the will and ability to find another differential advantage and another core (1957, p. 57).

10. Given heterogeneity of demand and competition for differential advantage, there will be ''heterogeneity of supply,'' that is, firms will produce:
   a. a variety of different goods and
   b. many variations of the same generic kind of goods (1957, p. 103).

E. *Given heterogeneity of demand and heterogeneity of supply, the fundamental purpose of marketing is to effect exchanges by matching segments of demand with segments of supply* (1957, pp. 195-199).

1. The matching process comes about as a result of a sequence of sorts and transformations (1965, p. 26).

2. A sort is the assignment of goods, materials or components to the appropriate facilities (1965, p. 27). The four kinds of sorts are:
   a. sorting out, the breaking down of a heterogeneous collection into smaller homogeneous collections; and
   b. accumulation, the building up of a large homogenous collection into several smaller homogeneous collections; and
   c. allocating the breaking down of a large homogeneous collection into several smaller homogenous collections; and
   d. assorting, the building up of a large heterogeneous collection from several homogeneous collections (1957, pp. 202-210) (1965, p. 34).

3. The sortability of a collection can be measured by the sortability scale (1965, p. 32).
   a. Sortability equals: $\frac{(\text{number of classes}) - 1}{(\text{number of items}) - 1}$
   b. A perfectly homogeneous collection would have a sortability of ''zero'' (1965, p. 32).

c. A perfectly heterogeneous collection would have a sortability of ''one'' (1965, p. 32).

4. Transformations are changes in the physical form of a good or its location in time or space (1965, p. 49).
5. A transvection is the unit of action by which a single end product is placed in the hands of the consumer after moving through all the intermediate sorts and transformations from the original raw materials in the state of nature (1965, p. 86).
6. In any transvection the sorts and transformations must alternate, that is, a sort always intervenes between any two transformations (1965, p. 93).
7. A transvection has the optimal number of steps if costs cannot be decreased either by increasing or decreasing the number of sorts or transformations (1965, p. 94).
8. The sum of all transvections during a given period, allowing for time lags, is equivalent to the marketing process (1965, p. 35).
9. Heterogeneous markets may be ''discrepant'' (1965, p. 27).
   a. There may be goods desired by consumers but not produced. This kind of discrepancy is ''cleared'' by innovation (1965, p. 27).
   b. There may be goods produced by firms but not desired by consumers. This kind of discrepancy is ''cleared'' by information (1965, p. 27).
   c. Discrepant markets result from failures in communication 1965, p. 29).
   d. A major problem for marketing is determining the optimal amount of information to clear markets (1965, p. 30).
10. Homogeneous markets may be discrepant. Homogeneous discrepant markets are not ''cleared'' by innovation, but rather, by adjusting:
    a. price and
    b. quantity (1965, p. 28).
11. In heterogeneous markets the role of price is reduced to a datum which is included in the information that households need to know about a good (1965, p. 31).
12. In a perfectly heterogeneous market each small segment of demand could be satisfied by just one unique segment of supply (1965, p. 29). In real world markets there are always partial homogeneities, that is:
    a. groups of households desiring essentially the same product and
    b. groups of firms supplying essentially the same product (1965, p. 26).

F. *A third organized behavior system in marketing is the channel of distribution.*
   1. The channel of distribution does not qualify as a *primary* organized behavior system in marketing.

a. This is, because in contrast with firms and households, not *all* channels of distribution are organized behavior systems (1965, p. 44).
b. Only those channels of distribution where all participants have a common stake in the survival of the channel should be considered organized behavior systems (1965, p. 44).

2. Indications of whether a particular channel can be considered to be an organized behavior system are:
   a. whether there is a control group which develops a marketing plan of operation for the channel and
   b. whether there is cooperation among the members of the channel in adhereing to the plan (1965, p. 252).
3. A primary cause of conflict in channels of distribution is the distribution of rewards among the channel members (1965, p. 253).
4. Both large manufacturers and large retailers attempt to be the control group which develops the marketing plan for the channel and turns it into an organized behavior system (1965, p. 257).
5. Marketing intermediaries (and therefore, channels) come into existence because they can effect economies in sorting (1957, p. 211).
   a. One major economy is the reduction of contactual costs (1965, p. 250).
   b. The number of contacts between $n$ manufacturers and $m$ retailers is $n$ times $m$ (1965, p. 250).
   c. The number of contacts between $n$ manufacturers and $m$ retailers, given one wholesaler, is $n$ plus $m$ (1965, p. 250).
6. The assortment of goods which is optimal for any particular manufacturer to produce is seldom the same as the assortment of goods which is optimal for an intermediary to carry. The difference between these two optimal assortments is called the "discrepancy of assortments" (1965, p. 78).
7. The discrepancy of assortments is a major inhibiting factor within channels of distribution.
   a. It inhibits the forward integration of manufacturers and the backward integration of retailers (1975, p. 217).
   b. This explains why the successive stages in marketing are so commonly operated as independent agencies (1957, p. 217).
8. A wholesaler is most vulnerable if it purchases only a small part of what the manufacturer supplies and sells to retailers only a small portion of what their customers demand (1965, p. 80). Therefore, wholesalers need to be strongly anchored either to their manufacturers or to their retailers.
9. There are four problem areas calling for decisions in retailing:
   a. store location and size;
   b. the assortment;

c. store image; and
d. form of promotion (1965, p. 212).

10. Every retail store is truly unique in at least one of its fundamental characteristics, namely, location (1965, p. 211).

G. *Given heterogeneity of demand, heterogeneity of supply, and the requisite institutions to effect the sorts and transformations necessary to match segments of demand with segments of supply, the marketing process will take conglomerate resources in the natural state and bring about meaningful assortments of goods in the hands of consumers* (1965,p. 26).

## Conclusion

Readers will note that the term ''functionalism'' does not appear in the preceding formalization of Alderson's general theory of marketing. This absence is by design, not accident. Functionalism is a procedure or perspective which one can adopt in attempting to create theory. Functionalism is not, of itself, a part of the final theoretical structure. In general, functional analysis seeks to understand a behavior pattern or sociocultural institution by determining the role it plays in keeping the given system in proper working order or maintaining it as a going concern (Hempel 1965). Unfortunately, Nicosia (1962) and others have continued to refer to ''Alderson's functionalism'' as if functionalism were an inherent part of the theory itself. It is not.

The preceding formalization of Alderson's general theory of marketing explains at least some of the variance in the differing evaluations of Alderson's work. For example, Blair and Uhl conclude that ''Alderson's functionalism will not characterize enlightened efforts in future marketing theory construction.'' However, their conclusion is based in part on attributing to Alderson such positions as the following: ''organized behavior systems were defined through Barnard's model, as collectivities whose organizing glue is economic advantage, and whose members *all act to maximize organizational acheivement*'' (emphasis added). As can be clearly seen in the formalization, Alderson did not state that the members ''act to maximize organizational achievement.'' Alderson states that members of an organized behavior system *pursue their own goals* while attempting to insure the survival of the organized system.

In order to effectively evaluate the theoretical efforts of an author, it is absolutely imperative to be accurate and precise as to exactly what the theorist's positon is/was. It is the belief of the present authors that the definitive evaluation of Alderson's general theory of marketing has yet to be undertaken. We hope and believe that the preceding formalization will assist theoretical analysts in their efforts to evaluate Alderson's work.

Assuming that the preceding formalization accurately characterizes Alderson's general theory of marketing, is it, or is it not, a good ''general theory?''

What is needed are some criteria for evaluating "general" theories. Both Hunt (1976) and Zaltman (1972) have explored the issue of evaluating theoretical construction. For example, Zaltman (1972) suggests that there are four classes of criteria for evaluating theoretical constructions: 1) formal criteria, 2) semantical criteria, 3) methodological criteria, and 4) epistemological criteria. Nevertheless, these works and criteria do not address the issue of whether there are *specific* criteria which should be applied to "general" theories as compared to ordinary, "garden variety" theoretical constructions. Intuitively, it would seem that the adequacy of a "general" theory of marketing would depend in large part on precisely delimiting the exact nature of marketing phenomena and the marketing discipline. The definitive evaluation of Alderson's general theory of marketing must await the complete explication of the characteristics of a general theory.

## REFERENCES

Alderson, Wroe (1957), *Marketing Behavior and Executive Action*, Homewood, IL: Richard D. Irwin, Inc.

______ (1965), *Dynamic Marketing Behavior*, Homewood, IL: Richard D. Irwin Inc.

Alwater, Thomas V. (1979), "Lost or Neglected Components of A General Equilibrium Theory of Marketing," *Conceptual and Theoretical Developments in Marketing*, Ferrell, Brown, and Lamb, eds., Chicago: American Marketing Association, 184-196.

Barksdale, H. C. (1980), "Wroe Alderson's Contributions to Marketing Theory," *Theoretical Developments in Marketing*, Lamb and Dunne, eds., Chicago: American Marketing Association, 1-4.

Bartels, Robert (1968), "The general Theory of Marketing," *Journal of Marketing*, 32 (January), 29-33.

Blair, Edward and Kenneth P. Uhl (1976), "Wroe Alderson and Modern Marketing Theory," *Distributive Processes From A Societal Perspective*, Charles C. Slater, ed., Boulder: Business Reseach Division, Graduate School of Business Administration.

Dawson, Lyndon E., Jr. and Hugh Wales (1979), "Consumer Motivation Theory in Historical Persepctive," *Conceptual and Theoretical Developments in Marketing*, Ferrell, Brown and Lamb, eds., Chicago: American Marketing Association, 210-221.

El-Ansary, Adel (1979), "The General Theory of Marketing Revisited," *Conceptual and Theoretical Developments in Marketing*, Ferrell, Brown and Lamb, eds., Chicago: American Marketing Association, 399-407.

Hempel, Carl (1965), *Aspects of Scientific Explanation*, New York: The Free Press.

Hostuick, K. Tim, and David L. Kurtz (1973), "Alderson's Functionalism and the Development of Marketing Theory," *Journal of Business Research*, 1 (Fall), 141-156.

Hunt, Shelby D. (1971), "The Morphology of Theory and the General Theory of Marketing," *Journal of Marketing*, 35 (April), 65-68.

——— (1973), "Lawlike Generalizations and Marketing Theory," *Journal of Marketing*, 37 (July), 69-70.

——— (1976), *Marketing Theory: Conceptual Foundation of Research in Marketing*, Columbus: Grid, Inc.

Lusch, Robert (1980), "Alderson, Sessions, and the 1950's Manager," *Theoretical Developments in Marketing*, Lamb and Dunne, eds., Chicago: American Marketing Association, 4-6.

Monieson, David D. and Stanley J. Shapiro (1980), "Biological and Evolutionary Dimensions of Aldersonian Thought: What He Borrowed Then and What He Might Have Borrowed Now," *Theoretical Developments in Marketing*, Lamb and Dunne, eds., Chicago: American Marketing Association, 7-12.

Nicosia, Francisco (1962), "Marketing and Alderson's Functionalism," *Journal of Business*, 35 (October), 403-413.

Pinson, Christian R. A., Anglemar Reinhard and Edwardo L. Roberto (1972), "An Evaluation of the General Theory of Marketing," *Journal of Marketing*, 36 (July), 66-69.

Rethans, Arno J. (1979), "The Aldersonian Paradigm: A Perspective for Theory Development and Synthesis," *Conceptual and Theoretical Developments in Marketing*, Ferrell, Brown and Lamb, eds., Chicago: American Marketing Association.

Rudner, Richard (1966), *Philosophy of Social Science*, Englewood Cliffs, New Jersey: Prentice Hall, Inc.

Wales, Hugh and Lyndon E. Dawson, Jr. (1979), "The Anomalous Qualities Between Present-Day Conferences and Alderson's Marketing Theory Seminars," *Conceptual and Theoretical Developments in Marketing*, Ferrell, Brown and Lamb, eds., Chicago: American Marketing Association, 222-227.

Zaltman, Gerald, Christian R. A. Pinson and Reinhard Anglemar (1972), *Metatheory and Consumer Research*, New York: Holt, Rinehart and Winston, Inc.

# 51 —— The General Theory of Marketing: Revisited

*Adel I. El-Ansary*

Reprinted from *Conceptual and Theoretical Developments in Marketing*, published by the American Marketing Association, edited by Ferrell Brown, and Lamb (1979), pp. 399-407. Reprinted by permission.

Is a general theory of marketing possible? What should it be? The purpose of this paper is to examine these important issues proposed for discussion at this Special AMA Conference on Conceptual and Theoretical Developments of Marketing. To examine these issues background notes on Bartels' ''General Theory of Marketing'' and ensuing debates by Hunt ''The Morphology of Theory and the General Theory of Marketing'' and Pinson et al. ''An Evaluation of the General Theory of Marketing'' are in order.

## The General Theory of Marketing

### What Is a General Theory?

Robert Bartels espoused ''The General Theory of Marketing,'' in 1968 (Bartels 1968). According to Bartels, the broadest statement of marketing thought in any period is the ''general theory'' of that day and place (Bartels 1968, p. 30). Furthermore, Bartels indicates that a contemporary general theory of marketing is implicit in a sufficiently broad concept or definition of marketing.

### The Need for a General Theory

Marketing theory began as a single, rather general theory. As time passed, marketing practice and viewpoints have changed, and marketing concepts and approaches proliferated. All these changes have altered both the content and the form of marketing thought producing greater diversity of theories. The proliferation of facts, concepts, theories is forcing integration of knowledge on higher planes of unification and abstraction. A general theory of marketing is needed to unify the diverse theories of marketing.

## What Is Bartels' General Theory?

Bartels proposed the general theory ''of the time, 1968'' consisting of seven component subtheories:

1. Theory of social initiative
   - society, not the business entrepreneur, is the basic undertaker of all activities
   - ecological orientation is the starting point in marketing analysis
2. Theory of economic (market) separations
   - producers and consumers are separated
   - marketing activities contribute to the removal of market separations
   - the character of market separations influence marketing activities
3. Theory of market flows, expectations, and interactions
   - people who engage in marketing behavior have expectations
   - sometimes expectations are not realized
   - when expectations are not realized, people may change their behavior
4. Theory of flow and systems
   - elements of marketing can be classified into those that flow and those that do not flow
   - flowing elements of marketing can be classified by type, series, parallel, reciprocal and duplicatory
   - relationships among these flows are complex and these flows should be studied by marketing students
5. Theory of behavior constraints
   - marketing behavior is constrained
   - some constraints—economic, social, ethical, and technical are imposed by society
6. Theory of social change and marketing evolution
   - marketing systems change
   - a theory of marketing must account for such change
7. Theory of social control of marketing
   - society evaluates, regulates, and sets standards for the appraisal of marketing

Bartels proposes a definition of marketing consistent with the outline of his general theory. ''Marketing is the process whereby society, to supply its consumption needs, evolves distributive systems composed of participants, who, interacting under constraints—technical (economic) and ethical (societal)—creates the transactions or flows which resolve market separations and result in exchange and consumption'' (Bartels 1968, p. 32).

## THE MORPHOLOGY OF THEORY: AN EVALUATION OF BARTELS' GENERAL THEORY

Hunt subjected Bartels unified theoretical structure for marketing to an evaluation utilizing the criteria and specifications of a theory (Hunt 1971).

1. A theory is a systematically related set of statements.
2. A theory includes law-like generalizations specifying relationships among variables.
3. These statements and law-like generalizations should be empirically testable.

The purpose of theory is to increase scientific understanding through a systemized structure capable of both explaining and predicting phenomena (Ruder 1966, p. 10).

Hunt's application of these criteria demonstrates that "the seven component subtheories are not theories, and thus the collection of seven components cannot be referred to as 'a general theory of marketing.' They represent an assemblage of classificational schemata, some intriguing definitions, and exhortations to fellow marketing students to adapt a particular perspective in attempting to generalize marketing theory ..." (Hunt 1971, p. 68).

Pinson et al. describe Hunt's evaluation as superficial and inadequate. However, their rigorous analysis led to similar conclusions about Bartels' general theory (Pinson et al. 1972). Indeed, all the seven subtheories failed to meet one or more of the criteria for theoretical structures.

This author is in complete agreement with Hunt's conclusion. A general theory of marketing cannot be merely a broad statement about marketing at the time. According to the broad statement concept of a general theory we have so many of these theories. For example, Hunt's "The Nature and Scope of Marketing" (Hunt 1976) and Sweeney's "Marketing Management Technology or Social Process?" (Sweeney 1972) are general theories of marketing à la Bartels. Indeed, a general theory and its components should only qualify as theoretical structures if they meet the criteria for a theory. The remainder of this paper is a presentation of an alternative design for a general theory in marketing.

## THE DESIGN FOR A GENERAL THEORY OF MARKETING

### Definition and Requirements for a General Theory

A general theory of marketing can be defined as:

- A logically interrelated and completed set of theories that explain marketing phenomena.
- The general theory is the broadest and most central theory of the set of theories specified above.

- The interrelationships among the component theories can be explicitly stated as law-like generalizations.
- The interrelationships are empirically testable.
- Selected component theories that are logical leads into and linkages with broad theories of corporate management strategy, economic, behavioral, and quantitative science.

## Is It Possible?

Applying the first criterion, a general theory of marketing is only possible if all component subtheories that explain marketing phenomena are complete. A general theory of marketing cannot be stated for the time being since its component theories are in the developmental stages. However, it is desirable to develop a design incorporating its component theories and their interrelationships. Such design provides guidelines for theory development in marketing.

## Component Theories of a General Theory

Component theories of a general theory, and the interrelationships are shown in Figure 1. The premises and interrelationships of component theories are explained below.

1. A vertical marketing system, distribution channel, is a key integrative concept in marketing.
2. Vertical marketing systems are composed of consumers and commercial organizations. A theory of consumer behavior and a theory of organizational buyer behavior are essential to understand and predict consumer and organizational buyer behavior. In turn, consumer and organizational buyer behavior theories are a natural lead into and linkage with theories of economics and other behavioral sciences.
3. In addition to organizational buyer behavior, channel member conflict, power, communication and role behavior have to be understood and predicted. Therefore, a theory of channel member behavior is necessary.
4. A theory of interorganization management integrates the theories of organizational buyer behavior and channel member behavior. Meanwhile a theory of aggregate consumption integrates the theories of consumer behavior and organization buyer behavior. Similarly, a theory of channel system behavior integrates the planning, organization, and control of a channel system. A theory of interorganization management is a natural lead into and linkage with broader theories of management.
5. The theories of consumer behavior and interorganization management combined are inputs to the theory of channel system behavior.

**FIGURE 1. Components of a General Theory of Marketing**

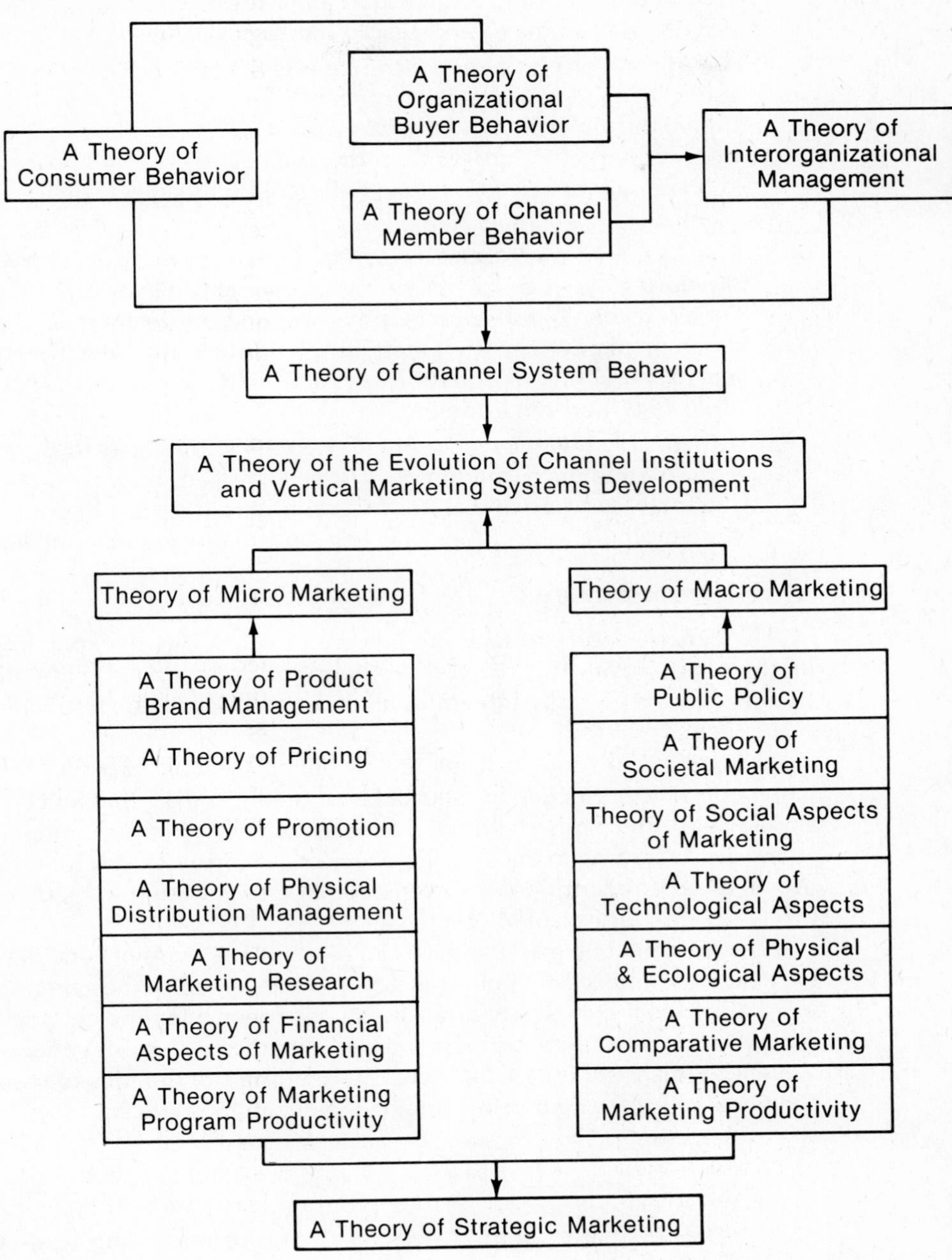

6. The theory of channel system behavior is in part an input theory of the evolution of channel institutions and vertical marketing system development. Other inputs to the evolution theory include the theories of micro and macro marketing.
7. The theory of micro marketing emerges from a set of theories of product brand management, pricing, promotion, physical distribution management, marketing research, financial aspects of marketing and marketing program productivity. The theory of micro marketing is a natural lead into and linkage with theories of quantitative science.
8. The theory of macro marketing emerges from a set of theories of public policy, societal marketing, social/cultural aspects of marketing, technological aspects, physical and ecological aspects, comparative marketing, and marketing productivity. The theory of macro marketing is a natural lead into and linkage with theories of ecology and environment.
9. A theory of strategic marketing management integrates the theories of macro and micro marketing. The theory of strategic marketing is a natural lead into and is an integral part of a theory of corporate strategy integrating other business and management functions.

### The General Theory

The general theory of marketing is the broadest theory explaining marketing phenomena. It is the central theory or the culmination of all other theories, i.e., it logically integrates all other theories and is a substitute for all of them.

This definition and concept of the general theory capitalizes on the correspondence principle in theory development stating that a new theory should substitute older theories it means to include as it incorporates all their elements. According to this concept of general theory, a theory for the evolution of channel institutions and vertical marketing systems development is the general theory of marketing.

Alternatively, one may conceive of a sequence of levels of general theory. For example, a theory of interorganization management is the general theory integrating the theories of organizational buyer behavior and channel member behavior. A theory of higher order is the theory of channel system behavior which is the general theory integrating the theories of consumer behavior and interorganization management.

## Conclusion

A critical review of Bartels' general theory of marketing leads to the conclusion that it is at best an assemblage of classificational schemata, definitions, and exhortations to fellow marketing students. Bartels' definition and concept of general theory is found to be inadequate if the requirements for theoretical structure are applied.

Adhering to the criteria for theoretical structures, an alternative concept of a general theory was presented. The concept presented specifies that:

1. A general theory is composed of logically interrelated and complete sets of theories that explain marketing phenomena.
2. The general theory is the broadest and most central theory of the set specified above. According to the correspondence principle, this central theory should substitute for other components of the set in the design.
3. A general theory should encompass the interrelationships and linkages of the component theories stated in a law-like, empirically testable generalization.
4. Selected component theories are logical leads into and linkages with broad theories of other disciplines contributing to or borrowing from marketing theory.

The proposed design of the components of a general theory is tentative. Alternative equally logical and comprehensive designs can be acceptable. Alternative designs may incorporate different component theories, suggest a different central theory and/or alter the interrelationships among component theories in the current design. It is stressed here, however, that the specification of a design and the selection of a concept of a general theory is important as they serve as guidelines for the development of marketing theory.

## REFERENCES

Bartels, Robert (1974), "The Identity Crisis in Marketing," *Journal of Marketing*, 38 (October), 73-76.

Bartels, Robert (1968), "The General Theory of Marketing," *Journal of Marketing*, 32 (January), 29-33.

Hunt, Shelby D. (1976), "The Nature or Scope of Marketing," *Journal of Marketing*, 40 (July), 17-28.

Hunt, Shelby D. (1971), "The Morphology of Theory and the General Theory of Marketing," *Journal of Marketing*, 35 (April), 65-68.

Martinelli, Patrick A. (1969), "Can Marketing Theory Be Developed Through the Study of Social Institutions?," *Journal of Marketing*, 33 (April), 60-62.

Mount, Peter P. (1969), "Exploring the Commodity Approach in Developing Market Theory," *Journal of Marketing*, 33 (April), 62-64.

Pinson, Christian R. A., Reinhard Englemar, and Eduardo L. Roberto (1972), "An Evaluation of the General Theory of Marketing," *Journal of Marketing*, 36 (July), 66-69.

Ruder, Richard (1966), *Philosophy of Social Science*, Englewood Cliffs, N.J.: Prentice-Hall, Inc.

Shuptrine, Kelly F. and Frank A. Osmanski (1975), "Marketing's Changing Role: Expanding and Contracting?," *Journal of Marketing*, 39 (April), 58-66.
Sweeney, Daniel J. (1972), "Marketing: Management Technology or Social Process?," *Journal of Marketing*, 36 (October), 3-10.

# 52 —— General Theories and the Fundamental Explananda of Marketing

*Shelby D. Hunt*

Reprinted from *Journal of Marketing*, published by the American Marketing Association, Vol. 47 (Fall 1983), pp. 9-17. Reprinted by permission.

After a flurry of articles and books on marketing theory in the 1950s and 1960s, a hiatus occurred in the development of the theoretical foundations of marketing. Marketing turned toward other directions, as Lutz, (1979) has observed:

> For the most part, I believe that we have been experiencing a technological revolution of sorts, with most of our energies being devoted to the discovery and application of increasingly sophisticated mathematical and statistical procedures. This revolution has been a necessary step forward for the discipline, but it has perhaps diverted out attention away from similarly important inquiry into the conceptual foundations of marketing (p. 3).

Evidence abounds that the hiatus is over and that interest in developing marketing theory is increasing. For example, there have now been three special conferences on marketing theory sponsored by the American Marketing Association (Bush and Hunt 1982; Ferrell, Brown, and Lamb 1979; and Lamb and Dunne 1980). These conferences have played a particularly significant role in encouraging marketing researchers to develop marketing theory. There have also been several books on marketing theory (Bagozzi 1980; Hunt 1976a, 1983; Zaltman, LeMasters, and Heffring 1982; Zaltman, Pinson, and Angelmar 1973). The works of Zaltman et al. and Hunt explore the philosophy of science foundations of marketing theory, while Bagozzi's work attempts to integrate metatheoretical criteria with mathematical modeling techniques.

In addition to the special conferences and books on marketing theory, theorists have devoted significant attention to the conceptual domain of the marketing discipline (Ferber 1970; Hunt 1976b; Kotler 1972; Kotler and Levy 1969; Kotler and Zaltman 1971; Luck 1969, 1974). These debates on the nature of marketing concluded that (1) the primary focus of marketing is the exchange relationship, (2) marketing includes both profit sector and nonprofit sector organizations, and (3) all the problems, issues, theories, and research in marketing can be analyzed using the three categorical dichotomies of profit sector/nonprofit sector, micro/macro, and positive/normative (Arndt 1981a).

Consistent with the preceding writers, Bagozzi (1974) concurs that the basic subject matter that marketing science attempts to explain and predict is the exchange relationship. He proposes the foundations for a formal theory of marketing exchanges and suggests that "it is perhaps time to redirect our intellectual energy toward the development of a general theory of marketing" (Bagozzi 1979, p. 455). Is it time? This article addresses the question, "What would be the characteristics of a general theory of marketing if we had one?" In order to answer this question, it will be necessary (1) to examine briefly the nature of theory in marketing, (2) to explore the characteristics of general theories in the philosophy of science, (3) to propose what a general theory of marketing would attempt to explain and predict, (4) to delineate the structure of general theories in/of marketing, and (5) to evaluate the status of general theories in/of marketing.

## The Nature of Marketing Theory

What is the nature of scientific theory? A concensus conceptualization of the characteristics of a theory is:

> Theories are systematically related sets of statements, including some law-like generalizations, that are empirically testable. The purpose of theory is to increase scientific understanding through a systematized structure capable of both explaining and predicting phenomena.

This conceptualization of theory (originally proposed by Rudner (1966) and first introduced into the marketing literature by Hunt (1971)) is characterized as consensus since it is consistent with the writings of (1) philosophers of science, (2) philosophers of social science, and (3) marketing theorists.

### Philosophy of Science Perspectives on Theory

The stream of thought that dominated twentieth-century philosophy of science has been logical (or modern) empiricism, which owes its origins to the logical positivists of the 1920s. In fact, the perspectives of the logical empiricists have been dubbed the "received view" of philosophy of science (Suppe 1977). Logical empiricism proposes that the "distinctive aim of the scientific enterprise is to provide systematic and responsibly supported explanations" (Nagel 1961, p. 15). Theories play a central role in explaining phenomena, since a theory is "a system of hypotheses, among which law formulas are conspicuous" (Bunge 1967, p. 381). Similarly, Bergman (1957, p. 31) notes that "a theory is a group of laws deductively connected." Finally, Braithwaite (1968, p. 22) suggests that "a scientific theory is a deductive system in which observable consequences logically follow from the conjunction of observed facts with the set of the fundamental hypotheses of the system." Note that the views of all these received view philsophers of science are consistent with the previously suggested perspective. For a formal statement of the received view of theory, see Suppe (1977, pp. 16-53).

In recent years, the proponents of logical empiricism have been vigorously attacked (for a discussion of the complete nature of these attacks, see Bush and Hunt 1982, Keat and Urry 1975, Suppe 1977). Although critics fail to speak with a single voice, most of these attacks have not centered on whether theories contain systematically related statements of law-like generalizations, or even on whether theories should be empirically testable. Rather, the attacks have focused on issues like "what are the requirements for a generalization to be considered law-like?" Proponents of the received view are content with the (essentially Humean) notion that *law-like* denotes nothing more than the observed regularity in the occurrence of two or more phenomena. Critics of logical empiricism, such as the scientific realists, insist that regularity is not enough; a kind of causal necessity must be shown (Harre and Madden 1975, p. 8). As Keat and Urry (1975, p. 44) have pointed out, both proponents and opponents of the received view hold that there are "general standards of scientificity, of what counts as an adequate explanation, of *what it is that we must try to achieve by scientific theories*, and of the manner in which *empirical evidence* should be used to assess their truth or falsity" (emphasis added). Thus, although they may differ as to technical details, both advocates and critics of the received view basically concur as to the general characteristics of theory.

## Marketing and Philosophy of Social Science Perspectives

Both philosophers of social science and marketing theorists also agree on the nature of theory. Thus, Kaplan (1964, p. 297) indicates that "a theory is a system of laws" and that "the laws are altered by being brought into systematic connection with one another, as marriage relates two people who are never the same again." Blalock (1969, p. 2) suggests that "theories do not consist entirely of conceptual schemes or typologies but must contain law-like propositions that interrelate the concepts or variables two or more at a time." The marketing theoretician Wroe Alderson (1957, p. 5) concludes that a "theory is a set of propositions which are consistent among themselves and which are relevant to some aspect of the factual world." Zaltman, Pinson, and Angelmar (1973, pp. 77-79) propose that a theory is a set of propositions, some of which are nonobservational, from which other propositions that are at least testable in principle can be deduced. Other contemporary writers in marketing theory use the same or similar conceptualization (Bagozzi 1980, pp. 63-65; El-Ansary 1979, p. 401; Ryan and O'Shaughnessy 1980, p. 47; Shoostari and Walker 1980, p. 100; and Solomon 1979, p. 377).

Starting from the perspective that theories are systmatically related sets of statments, including some law-like generalizations, that are empirically testable, how do general theories differ from the ordinary kind? In short, what is it that makes a general theory "general"?

## THE NATURE OF GENERAL THEORIES

There are several ways that one theory can be more general than another. Recalling that the purpose of theories is to explain and predict phenomena, general theories can be more general by explaining more phenomena. That is, general theories have a large extension or domain. Dubin (1969, p. 41) proposes that ''the generality of a scientific model depends solely upon the size of the domain it represents.'' Zaltman, Pinson, and Agelmar (1973, p. 52) concur: ''A second formal syntactical dimension of a [theoretical] proposition is its *degree of generality*. All propositions purport to refer to a particular segment of the world, their universe of discourse.''

As an example of how the extension of a theory affects its generality, consider the ''hierarchy of effects'' model. As originally proposed by Lavidge and Steiner (1961), and later developed by Palda (1966), the hierarchy of effects model attempts to explain how consumers respond to advertising through the hierarchy of cognition (thinking), affect (feeling), and conation (doing). Some empirical studies, such as those by Assael and Day (1968) and O'Brien (1971), have found support for the hierarchy of effects model.

Next consider the low involvement model originally proposed by Krugman (1965). The low involvement model suggests that for trivial products, the consumers interests are so low that they will respond to advertising through a hierarchy of cognition, conation, and affect (rather than cognition, affect, and conation). Empirical studies by Ray (1973), Rothschild (1974), and Swinyard and Coney (1978) have supported the low involvement hierarchy. The point here is that, according to the extension criterion, the low invovlement model is more general than the traditional hierarchy of effects model, since there are many more ''low involving'' products than there are ''highly involving'' products. That is, the domain of the low involvement model is larger than the domain of the original hierarchy of effects model.

A second way that theories can be more general is by systematically relating a larger number of law-like generalizations. Farber (1968, p. 173) suggests that in psychology ''comprehensive theories, i.e., those serving to organize a *considerable number* of laws, depend on the state of knowledge in a given area'' [emphasis added]. Similarly, Brodbeck (1968) proposes that:

> The more comprehensive a theory is, the more it unifies phenomena by revealing apparently different things to be special cases of the same kind of thing. The classic example of a comprehensive, unifying theory is Newton's. From the Newtonian theory of gravitation it was possible to derive Galileo's laws for the free fall of bodies on earth, Kepler's laws about the motions of the planets around the sun, the laws about the tides, and a host of other previously known but disparate phenomena. It explained all these and predicted new laws not previously known (p. 457).

The preceding example suggested that the low involvement model was more general than the traditional hierarchy of effects model because it explained more phenomena. A recent model developed by Smith and Swinyard (1982), referred to as the "integrated information response model," attempts to unify both the traditional and low involvement models. It draws upon the expectancy value model developed by Fishbein and Ajzen (1975), and proposes that the key distinction between purchases for "trial" and for "commitment" has been largely overlooked. Our purpose here is not to evaluate this new model, but rather, to point out that, to the extent that the model is validated by empirical testing, it represents a step forward in developing a more general theory of consumer behavior. This more general theory is brought about by incorporating into one theory all the law-like propositons of both the low involvement and hierarchy of effects models.

A third way that theories can be general is that their constructs may have a high level of abstraction. Blalock (1969) states:

> The general theory will be stated in highly abstract terms, with as few assumptions as possible as to the form of the equations, the values of the parameters, or (in the case of statistical theory) the specific distributions of the error terms. It will often be found that this very general theory cannot yield useful theorems, and so additional assumptions will be made in order to study important special cases...the principle value of a highly general theoretical formulation is that it enables one to place the various special cases in perspective and to prove general theorems appropriate to them all (p. 141).

Howard and Sheth (1969) were cognizant of the relationship between "level of abstraction" and "level of generalization." Thus, they indicate "first, the theory is said to be at a moderate level of abstraction, because it deals only with buying behavior, but nevertheless to be abstract enough to encompass consumer buying, institutional buying, distributive buying, and industrial buying" (p. 391).

Unfortunately, the phrase "high level of abstraction" does not have perfect antecedent clarity, and at least three different meanings seem possible. First, high level of abstraction may indicate "more encompassing." This seems to be the usage suggested by Howard and Sheth when they propose that their theory of buyer behavior encompasses not only consumer buying, but other forms of buying as well. This meaning of level of abstraction would make it consistent with the notion that a general theory encompasses and explains a large number of phenomena.

A second possible meaning of high level of abstraction might be that the terms in the theory are "far removed" from directly observable phenomena. Thus, empirical referents or operational definitions for the "highly abstract" constructs may be difficult, if not impossible, to develop. Given the requirement that all theories must be empirically testable, there appears to be a significant danger in developing theories that are too abstract, or too far removed from observable reality. Even marketing theorists who have recently moved away from strict logical empiricism still hold empirical testing in high regard. Thus, Zaltman, LeMasters, and Heffring (1982) propose:

> Once a general theoretical statement has been made, the next step is to make a deduction and translate it into an *empirical* statement so that observations can be made and the ''truth'' of the statement tested. This testability of a statement is of extreme importance to logical deductive analysis (p. 107).

The original logical positivist positon required all terms or constructs in a scientific theory to have direct empirical referents, i.e., be ''observable.'' Recognizing that this position was untenable, the logical empiricists required all abstract or ''theoretical'' terms to be linked to directly observable terms via devices known as ''correspondence rules.'' Current analysis in the philosophy of science suggests that even the logical empiricist position may be too stringent. Keat and Urry (1975) propose that attention be focused on the testability of statements rather than the observability of all terms in statements. Thus, they propose the following: ''A statement is scientific only if it is possible to make observations that would count in some way for or against its truth or falsity'' (p. 38). This principle suggests that the constructs in a theory cannot be allowed to become so abstract (so far removed from reality) that they render the theory incapable of generating hypotheses capable of being empirically tested, since such a theory would necessarily be explanatorially and predictively impotent.

There is a third possible meaning for high level of abstraction. Sometimes it seems that the relationships among constructs in highly abstract general theories are very loosely specified. Consider the problem of a researcher attempting to test the general theory of consumer behavior proposed by Engel, Kollat, and Blackwell (1973). The researcher wishes to include in the experiment the construct *environmental influences*. Unfortunately for the researcher, the model gives little guidance as to specifically which environmental influences should be included and how each should be related to other key constructs. When high level of abstraction means that the relationships between many of the key constructs in the ''general'' theory are very loosely specified, empirical testing is hindered and explanatory power is reduced. Therefore, it has been suggested elsewhere (Hunt 1976a) that many of these highly abstract general models may play their most significant role in what is referred to as the ''context of discovery.'' That is, these kinds of general models or theories may be most useful in suggesting fruitful avenues for researchers to explore in generating or discovering theories that have direct explanatory power.

How then do general theories differ from ordinary theories? We may conclude that general theories explain a large number of phenomena and serve to unify the law-like generalizations of less general theories. Theorists concerned with developing general theories should be alert to the problems involved in empirically testing their theoretical constructions. When key constructs in the theory become highly abstract, in the sense of being too far removed from observable reality or in the sense that relationships among key constructs become too loosely specified, then empirical testability suffers, predictive power declines, and explanatory impotence sets in. Despite these limitations, such theories or models might still serve the useful purpose of "road maps" for guiding the theoretical efforts of others.

## The Fundamental Explananda of Marketing

If general theories in/of marketing have a broad domain and unify many law-like generalizations, what are the phenomena that these general theories would seek to explain and predict? In philosophy of science terminology, what are the fundamental explananda of marketing science? Alternatively, in experimental design terms, what are the fundamental dependent variables? Consistent with the perspective of most marketing theorists (Alderson 1965; Bagozzi 1974, 1978, 1979; Kotler 1972), this writer has proposed that the basic subject matter of marketing is the exchange relationship or transaction (Hunt 1976b). The discipline of marketing has its normative or applied side which is technology, rather than empirical science. The purpose of marketing technology is to assist marketing decision makers by developing normative decision rules and models. Such rules and models are often based on the findings of marketing science and various analytical tools (such as statistics and mathematics). The basic or positive side houses the empirical science of marketing (Hunt 1976b).

The preceding discussion implies that *marketing science is the behavioral science that seeks to explain exchange relationship*. Given this perspective of marketing science, and adopting the customary (albeit somewhat arbitrary) convention of designating one party to the exchange as the "buyer" and one party as the "seller," the fundamental explananda of marketing can be logically derived. The four interrelated sets of fundamental explananda of marketing science are:

- The behaviors of buyers directed at consummating exchanges
- The behaviors of sellers directed at consummating exchanges
- The institutional framework directed at consummating and/or facilitating exchanges
- The consequences on society of the behaviors of buyers, the behaviors of sellers, and the institutional framework directed at consummating and/or facilitating exchanges

As illustrated in Figure 1, the first set of fundamental explananda indicates that marketing science seeks to answer *why do which buyers purchase what they do, where they do, when they do, and how they do*? The "which buyers" seeks to explain why certain buyers enter into particular exchange relationships

**FIGURE 1. The Nature of Marketing Science**

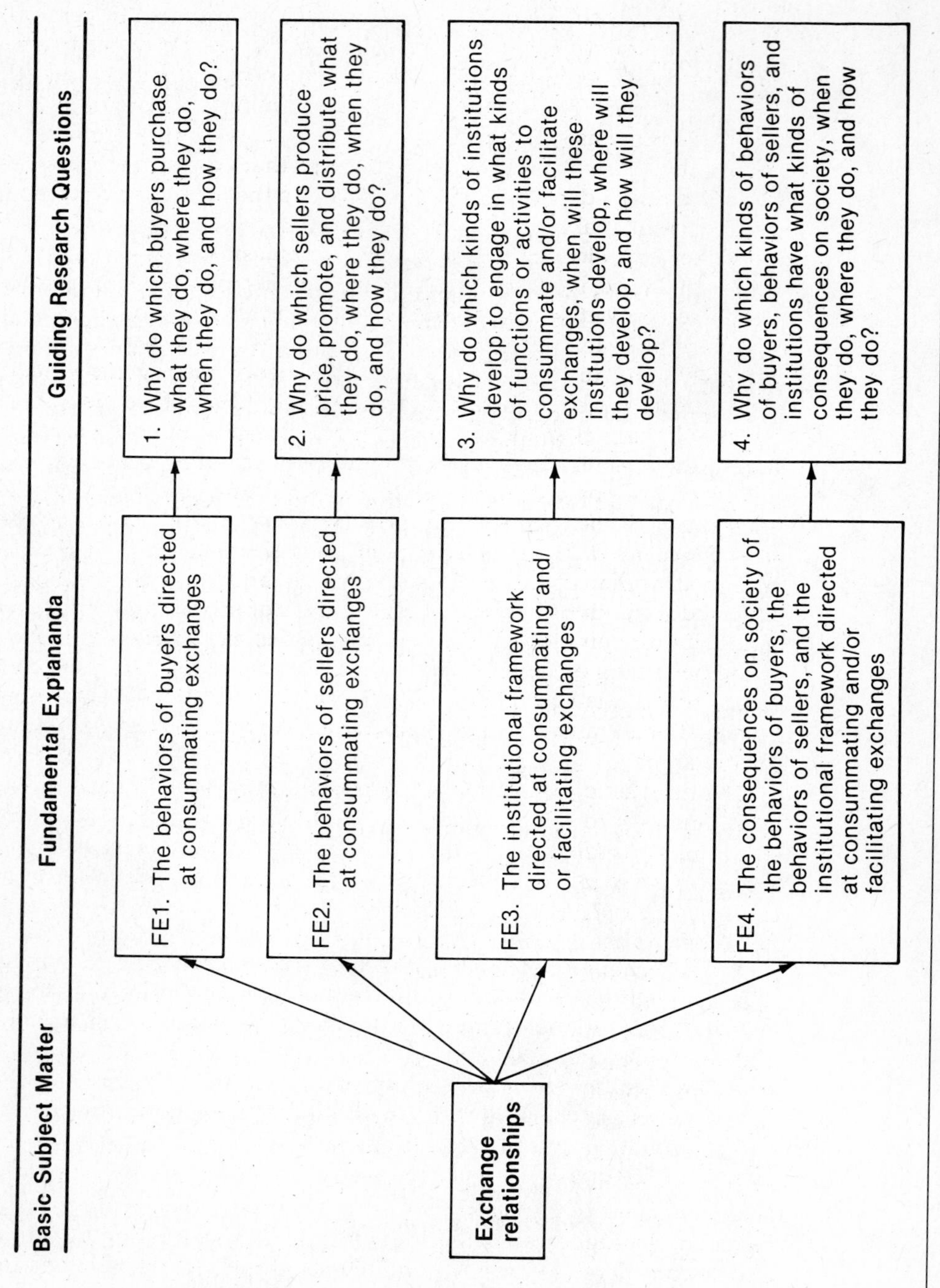

and others do not. The "what" indicates that different buyers have different product/service mixes that they purchase. The "where" is the institutional/locational choice of buyers. That is, why do some buyers purchase at discount department stores and others at full service department stores, and why do some buyers purchase in neighborhood stores and others in shopping centers? The "when" refers to the timing decisions of buyers. Why do buyers purchase differently in different stages in the family life cycle? Finally, the "how" refers to the processes that consumers use in making their purchasing decisions. That is, what are the identifiable stages in consumer decision making? The "how" also refers to any organizational systems that buyers develop to accomplish the purchasing task—for example, the sharing of buying responsibilities among various members of the household.

The second set of fundamental explananda of marketing concerns the behaviors of sellers. As Lutz (1979, p. 5) has pointed out, "It has been extremely unfortunate that the vast bulk of theory-based behavioral research in marketing has been on consumer behavior." He then concludes that "if we truly believe that exchange is the fundamental building block of marketing, then, we have virtually ignored (in a scientific sense) the behavior of the party selling to the consumer." The guiding question is *why do which sellers produce, price, promote, and distribute what they do, where they do, when they do, and how they do*? The "which" points out that not all sellers participate in all exchanges. The "what" seeks explanations for the kinds of products produced, kinds of prices charged, kinds of promotions used, and kinds of distributors employed. The "when" seeks explanations for the timing of the behaviors of sellers. The "where" refers to the locations chosen by sellers to do business. The "how" refers to the processes involved and organizational frameworks developed by sellers when engaging in exchange relationships.

The third set of fundamental explananda suggests that marketing science seeks answers to the question, *why do which kinds of institutions develop to engage in what kinds of functions or activities to consummate and/or facilitate exchanges, when will these institutions develop, where will they develop, and how will they develop*? The "which" points out that not all kinds of institutions participate in the consummation and/or facilitation of all kinds of exchanges, and seeks to identify the kinds of institutions and "what" specific kinds of activities (functions) will be performed by each. The "when" refers to the evolution or changing of the kinds of institutions through time and "where" these changes will take place. The "how" refers to the processes that bring about these institutional changes.

As used here, the term *institution* refers both to the intermediaries that either take title to the goods or negotiate purchases or sales, such as wholesalers and retailers, and also to purely facilitating agencies such as those solely engaged in transportation, warehousing, advertising, or marketing research. As suggested by Arndt (1981b, p. 37), marketing institutions can also be considered as "sets of conditions and rules for transactions and other interactions.'' Note that the study of marketing systems can be considered the study of collections of interacting marketing institutions. In short, the third set of explananda seeks to explain the nature and development of all kinds of marketing systems.

The fourth set of fundamental explananda concerns the consequences of marketing on society. The guiding question is, *why do which kinds of behaviors of buyers, behaviors of sellers, and institutions have what kinds of consequences on society, when they do, where they do, and how they do*? The ''which'' directs the theorists to focus on specific kinds of behaviors and/or institutions and explain ''what'' kinds of consequences these behaviors or institutions will have on society. Again, the ''when'' refers to the timing of the consequences, and the ''where'' focuses on whom the consequences will fall. For example, will the consequences fall disproportionately on the disadvantaged members of society? Finally, the ''how'' focuses on the processes and mechanisms by which various parts of society are impacted by marketing activities. The study of the kinds of consequences discussed here are generally subsumed under the term *macromarketing*.

The preceding four sets of explananda are proposed as fundamental in the sense that every phenomenon that marketing science seeks to explain can ultimately be reduced to a phenomenon residing in one of the four sets. A general theory in marketing would seek to explain all, or substantially all, the phenomena in a single set. For example, a theory that purports to explain all the behaviors of buyers directed at consummating exchanges would be characterized as a general theory in marketing. In contrast, a general theory *of* marketing would purport to explain all the phenomena in all four sets.

## General Theories: Structure and Status

General theories can have two different structural forms, a hierarchical form or a collection of subtheories form. A hierarchical theory is one whose component laws are deductions from a very small subset of basic principles or axioms (Kaplan 1964, p. 298). The work of Bagozzi (1978) is an example of one attempt to develop a general theory from a very limited set of assumptions concerning exchange behaviors.

The second way to develop a general theory is to take several smaller theories and combine them in a systematic fashion. This is the approach taken by Bartels (1968) when he proposed that a general theory of marketing could be developed by combining the following seven subtheories: social initiative, market separations, expectations, flows, behavioral constraints, marketing evolution, and social control. This is also the approach taken by El-Ansary (1979), who suggested that the central organizing element for a general theroy of marketing would be the channel of distribution. El-Ansary then identified 23 subtheories which, if combined in a systematic fashion, would comprise a general theory of marketing.

The position adopted here is that the development of a general theory of marketing along strict hierarchical lines would be extraordinarily difficult, and the possibility for its success would be remote. Much more likely to be successful would be the procedure of developing a general theory for each of the four sets of fundamental explananda, and then integrating each of the four theories into one comprehensive schema. Although we are not close to developing a general theory of marketing at this time, progress is being made. There have been several attempts to develop a general theory of buyer behavior. Although the works of Engle, Kollat, and Blackwell (1973), Howard and Sheth (1969), and Nicosia (1966) have received the most attention, there have been other efforts at developing a comprehensive model of buyer behavior (Andreasen 1965, Bettman 1979, Hansen 1972, Markin 1974, Wind and Webster 1972). Some of these models have received empirical support; others remain to be tested. Note that most of these models were developed in the late 1960s and early 1970s; perhaps the time is right for a new integrative model, which would combine the best aspects of the various general models proposed to date.

As noted earlier, marketing has generally neglected theory concerning the behaviors of sellers directed at consummating exchanges. A notable exception was the work of Alderson (1965) on competition for differential advantage. This theoretical construction purports to explain the forces motivating firms in the marketplace by noting that in order to survive, firms compete with other firms for the patronage of households. A firm can be assured of the patronage of a group of households only when the group has reasons to prefer the output of the particular firm over the output of competing firms. Therefore, each firm will seek some advantage over other firms to assure the patronage of a group of households, a process known as ''comnpetition for differential advantage.'' Competition consists of the constant struggle of firms to develop, maintain, or increase their differential advantages over other firms. Unfortunately, very little has been done with the theory since the middle 60s.

Several scholars have made major attempts to develop a general theory of marketing institutions. Using a microeconomic/functionalist approach, Bucklin (1966) has developed a ''theory of distribution channel structure.'' He identifies the outputs of the channel distribution as delivery time, lot size, and market decentralization, and then proposes that the channel functions necessary to produce these outputs are transit, inventory, search, persuasion, and promotion. After determining the interrelationships among outputs and functions, Bucklin postulates the existence of a ''normative channel'' which the existing channel will tend toward in long run equilibrium.

A second theoretical work by Baligh and Richartz (1967) builds a mathematical model of the channel of distribution, drawing upon the original work by Balderston (1958). The Baligh and Richartz model is based on the key concepts of cooperation, competition, and their impact on ''contactual'' costs. The fundamental premise underlying their theory is that ''exchange transactions are not costless and that in consequence there exists the possibility that these costs can be reduced'' (Baligh and Richartz 1967, p. 6). Lastly, Robicheaux and El-Ansary (1975) have developed a general model for channel member behavior. The focal point of the model is the total performance of the channel of distribution, which is postulated to be determined by both structural and individual characteristics. Shoostari and Walker (1980) evaluate the model and conclude that ''the model has the potential of becoming a highly valuable theory of channel performance'' (p. 102).

To the best of this writer's knowledge, none of the three general models concerning marketing institutions has been subjected to empirical tests. As with the general models of consumer behavior, most of the attempts to generate general theories concerning marketing institutions were developed in the 1960s. Again, as with consumer behavior, perhaps it is time to take a fresh look at the entire area and attempt to integrate the works of such authors as Baligh, Bucklin, El-Ansary, Richartz, and Robicheaux into a comprehensive model.

Unlike buyer behavior, seller behavior, and marketing institutions, there have been no attempts to develop a general theory of the consequences of marketing on society. The work of Beckman (1957) proposes that we can use ''value added'' as a measure of the total output of marketing activities. Similarly, the work of Bucklin (1978) postulates procedures for determining the efficiency with which marketing institutions perform their assigned tasks. A theory by Steiner (1973) explains the consequences on consumer prices of heavy advertising by national firms. Finally, Slater (1968) developed a model explaining the role of marketing in inducing economic development. Nevertheless, none of these theories in name or in fact constitutes a general theory of the consequences of marketing activities and institutions on society. No one has even attempted a ''general theory of macromarketing.''

Two scholars have attempted to develop general theories of marketing. In 1968 Bartels suggested that a general theory of marketing should consist of seven subtheories: social initiative, economic (market) separations, market flows, interactions and expectations, flows and systems, behavior constraints, social change and marketing evolution, and social control of marketing. An evaluation of these subtheories (Hunt 1971) pointed out their lack of law-like generalizations and concluded that the collection could not, therefore, be a general theory of marketing. This conclusion was also reached in the subsequent analysis by El-Ansary (1979).

Alderson (1965) also suggested that his work constituted a general theory of marketing. Although his efforts at developing a general theory have never been evaluated using the criteria contained herein, his work has been partially formalized and rendered amenable to systematic investigation (Hunt, Muncy, and Ray 1981). It is noteworthy that the partial formalization reveals that Alderson at least touched upon each of the four sets of fundamental explananda that a general theory of marketing would have to contain. In an attempt to explain the behavior of buyers, Alderson used the twin concepts of (1) the conditional value of a good, if used, and (2) the probability of use or the estimated frequency of use (Alderson 1965, p. 38). He used competition for differential advantage to explain seller behavior and the ''discrepancy of assortments'' to explain the rise of intermediaries (Alderson 1965, p. 78). Finally Alderson's normative theory of marketing systems explores some of the effects of marketing systems on society (Alderson 1965, pp. 301-321). Although Alderson addressed each of the fundamental explananda of marketing, research in each separate area has gone well beyond the theoretical work of Alderson. For example, Alderson's theory of buyer behavior would be considered a somewhat naive approach today. Thus, although Alderson's efforts must be considered extraordinary for his time, they cannot be considered a satisfactory general theory of marketing for today.

## SUMMARY AND CONCLUSION

In summary, this article has attempted to explore the nature of general theories in/of marketing. Since theories are systematically related sets of statements, including some law-like generalizations that are empirically testable, general theories should have these characteristics and more. The extra dimension of general theories is that they should explain more phenomena and unify more laws. General theories *in* marketing would explain all the phenomena within one of the four sets of fundamental explananda of marketing: (1) the behaviors of buyers directed at consummating exchanges, (2) the behaviors of sellers directed at consummating exchanges, (3) the institutional framework directed at consummating and/or facilitating exchanges, and (4) the consequences on society of the behaviors of buyers, the behaviors of sellers, and the institutional framework directed at consummating and/or facilitating exchanges. A general theory *of* marketing would explain all phenomena of all four sets. Such a general theory would probably be comprised of an integrated collection of subtheories, rather than a hierarchical theory.

Is a general theory of marketing possible? Given the progress that is being made on at least three of the four sets of fundamental explananda, and given the increased emphasis being placed on theory development in marketing, there are grounds for optimism. There certainly is no logical reason for believing that it is impossible to develop such a general theory. Nevertheless, even if marketing should never generate a general theory of its total subject matter, the pursuit of such a general theory, like the pursuit of truth in general would still be a worthy quest.

## REFERENCES

Alderson, W. (1957), *Marketing Behavior and Executive Action*, Homewood, Ill: Irwin.

——— (1965), *Dynamic Marketing Behavior*, Homewood, IL: Irwin.

Andreasen, A. R. (1965), "Attitudes and Customer Behavior: A Decision Model," in *New Research in Marketing*, L. Preston, ed., Berkeley, CA: Institute of Business and Economic Research, University of California, 1-16.

Arndt, Johan (1981a), "The Conceptual Domain of Marketing: Evaluation of Shelby Hunt's Three Dichotomies Model," *European Journal of Marketing*, 14 (Fall), 106-121.

——— (1981b), "The Political Economy of Marketing Systems: Reviving the Institutional Approach," *Journal of Macromarketing*, 1 (Fall), 36-47.

Assael, J. and G. S. Day (1968), "Attitudes and Awareness as Predictors of Market Share," *Journal of Advertising Research*, 8 (October), 3-12.

Bagozzi, R. P. (1974), "Marketing as an Organized Behavioral System of Exchange," *Journal of Marketing*, 38 (October), 77-81.

——— (1978), "Marketing as Exchange," *American Behavioral Scientist*, 21 (March/April), 535-536.

——— (1979), "Toward a Formal Theory of Marketing Exchanges," in *Conceptual and Theoretical Developments in Marketing*, O. C. Ferrell, S. Brown, and C. Lamb, eds., Chicago: American Marketing, 431-447.

——— (1980), *Causal Models in Marketing*, NY: Wiley.

Balderston, F. E. (1958), "Communication Networks in Intermediate Markets," *Management Science*, 4 (January), 154-171.

Baligh, H. H. and L. E. Richartz (1967), *Vertical Market Structures*, Boston: Allyn and Bacon.

Bartels, R. (1968), "The General Theory of Marketing," *Journal of Marketing*, 32 (January), 29-33.

Beckman, T. N. (1957), "The Value Added Concept as a Measurement of Output," *Advanced Management* (April), 6-8; reprinted in *Managerial Marketing: Perspectives and Viewpoints*, W. Lazer and E. J. Kelley, eds., Homewood, IL: Irwin, 1962.

Bergman, G. (1957), *Philosophy of Science*, Madison: University of Wisconsin Press.

Bettman, James R. (1979), *An Information Processing Theory of Consumer Choice*, Reading, MA: Addison-Wesley.

Blalock, H. M. (1969), *Theory Construction*, Englewood Cliffs, NJ: Prentice-Hall.

Braithwaite, R. B. (1968), *Scientific Explanation*, Cambridge: Cambridge University Press.

Brodbeck, M. (1968), *Readings in the Philosophy of the Social Sciences*, New York: Macmillan.

Bucklin, L. P. (1966), *A Theory of Distribution Channel Structure*, Berkeley, CA: University of California, Institute of Business and Economic Research.

——— (1978), *Productivity in Marketing*, Chicago, IL: American Marketing.

Bunge, M. (1967), *Scientific Research I: The Search for System*, New York: Springer-Verlag.

Bush, R. F. and S. D. Hunt (1982), *Marketing Theory: Philosophy of Science Perspectives*, Chicago: American Marketing.

Dubin, R. (1969), *Theory Building*, New York: The Free Press.

El-Ansary, A. (1979) "The General Theory of Marketing: Revisited," in *Conceptual and Theoretical Developments in Marketing*, O. C. Ferrell, S. W. Brown, and C. Lamb, eds., Chicago: American Marketing, 399-407.

Engel, J., D. B. Kollat, and R. Blackwell (1973), *Consumer Behavior*, 2nd ed., New York: Holt.

Farber, I. E. (1968), "Personality and Behavioral Science," in *Readings in the Philosophy of the Social Sciences*, M. Brodbeck, ed., New York: Macmillan.

Ferber, R. (1970), "The Expanding Role of Marketing in the 1970s," *Journal of Marketing*, 34 (January), 29-30.

Ferrell, O. C., S. W. Brown, and C. W. Lamb, Jr., eds. (1979), *Conceptual and Theoretical Developments in Marketing*, Chicago: American Marketing.

Fishbein, M. and I. Ajzen (1975), *Belief, Attitude, Intention and Behavior: An Introduction to Theory and Research*, Reading, MA: Addison-Wesley.

Hansen, F. (1972), *Consumer Choice Behavior*, New York: The Free Press.

Harre, R. and E. H. Madden (1975), *Causal Powers*, Totowa, NJ: Rowman and Littlefield.

Howard, J. A. and J. N. Sheth (1969), *The Theory of Buyer Behavior*, New York: Wiley.

Hunt, S. D. (1971), "The Morphology of Theory and the General Theory of Marketing," *Journal of Marketing*, 35 (April), 65-68.

——— (1976a), *Marketing Theory: Conceptual Foundations of Research in Marketing*, Columbus, OH: Grid.

——— (1976b), "The Nature and Scope of Marketing," *Journal of Marketing*, 40 (July), 17-28.

——— (1983), *Marketing Theory: The Philosophy of Marketing Science*, Homewood, IL: Irwin.

———, J. A. Muncy, and N. M. Ray (1981), "Alderson's General Theory of Marketing: A Formalization," in *Review of Marketing 1981*, B. M. Enis and K. J. Roering, eds., Chicago: American Marketing.

Kaplan, A. (1964), *The Conduct of Inquiry*, Scranton, PA: Chandler Publishing.

Keat, R. and J. Urry (1975), *Social Theory as Science*, London: Routledge and Kegan Paul.

Kotler, P. (1972), "A Generic Concept of Marketing," *Journal of Marketing*, 36 (April), 46-54.

——— and S. J. Levy (1969), "Broadening the Concept of Marketing," *Journal of Marketing*, 33 (January), 10-15.

——— and G. Zaltman (1971), "Social Marketing: An Approach to Planned Social Change," *Journal of Marketing*, 35 (July), 3-12.

Krugman, H. E. (1965), "The Impact of Television Advertising: Learning without Involvement," *Public Opinion Quarterly*, 29, 349-356.

Lamb, C. W. and P. M. Dunne, eds. (1980), *Theoretical Developments in Marketing*, Chicago: American Marketing.

Lavidge, R. C. and G. A. Steiner (1961), "A Model for Predictive Measurements of Advertising Effectiveness," *Journal of Marketing*, 25 (October), 59-62.

Luck, D. (1969), "Broadening the Concept of Marketing—Too Far," *Journal of Marketing*, 33 (July), 53-55.

——— (1974), "Social Marketing: Confusion Compounded," *Journal of Marketing*, 38 (October), 70-72.

Lutz, R. J. (1979), "Opening Statement," in *Conceptual and Theoretical Developments in Marketing*, O. C. Ferrell, S. W. Brown, and C. W. Lamb, eds., Chicago: American Marketing, 3-6.

Markin, R. J. (1974), *Consumer Behavior: A Cognitive Orientation*, New York: Macmillan.

Nagel, E. (1961), *The Structure of Science*, New York: Harcourt.

Nicosia, F. W. (1966), *Consumer Decision Processes*, Englewood Cliffs, NJ: Prentice-Hall.

O'Brien, T. (1971), "Stages of Consumer Decision Making," *Journal of Marketing Research*, 8 (August), 283-289.

Palda, K. S. (1966), "The Hypothesis of a Hierarchy of Effects: A Partial Evaluation," *Journal of Marketing Research*, 3 (February), 13-24.

Ray, M. (1973), "Marketing Communications and the Hierarchy of Effects," in *New Models for Mass Communications Research*, Vol. 2, P. Clark, ed., Beverly Hills, CA: Sage.

Robicheaux, R. and A. El-Ansary (1975), "A General Model for Understanding Channel Member Behavior," *Journal of Retailing*, 52 (Winter), 13-30, 90-94.

Rothschild, M. L. (1974), "The Effects of Political Advertising on the Voting Behavior of a Low-Involvement Electorate," Ph.D. dissertation, Stanford University, Graduate School of Business.

Rudner, R. (1966), *Philosophy of Social Science*, Englewood Cliffs, NJ: Prentice-Hall.

Ryan, Michael and John O'Shaughnessy (1980), "Theory Development: The Need to Distinguish Levels of Abstraction," in *Theoretical Developments in Marketing*, Charles W. Lamb, Jr. and Patrick M. Dunne, eds., Chicago: American Marketing, 47-50.

Shoostari, Nader and Bruce Walker (1980), "In Search of a Theory of Channel Behavior," in *Theoretical Developments in Marketing*, Charles W. Lamb, Jr. and Patrick M. Dunne, eds., Chicago: American Marketing, 100-103.

Slater, C. C. (1968), "Marketing Processes in Developing Latin American Societies," *Journal of Marketing*, 32 (July), 50-55.

Smith, R. E. and W. R. Swinyard (1982), "Information Response Models: An Integrated Approach," *Journal of Marketing*, 45 (Winter), 81-93.

Solomon, Paul (1979), "Marketing Theory and Metatheory," in *Conceptual and Theoretical Developments in Marketing*, O. C. Ferrell, Stephen W. Brown, and Charles W. Lamb, Jr., eds., Chicago: American Marketing, 374-382.

Steiner, R. L. (1973), "Does Advertising Lower Consumer Prices?" *Journal of Marketing*, 37 (October), 19-26.

Suppe, F. (1977), *The Structure of Scientific Theories*, 2nd ed., Chicago: University of Illinois Press.

Swinyard, W. R. and K. A. Coney (1978), "Promotional Effects on a High- versus Low-Involvement Electorate," *Journal of Consumer Research*, 5 (June), 41-48.

Wind, Y. and F. E. Webster (1972), "Industrial Buying as Organizational Behavior: A Guideline for Research Strategy," *Journal of Purchasing*, 8 (August), 5-16.

Zaltman, Gerald, Karen LeMasters, and Michael Heffring (1982), *Theory Construction in Marketing*, New York: Wiley.

———, Christian R. A. Pinson, and Reinhard Angelmar (1973), *Metatheory and Consumer Research*, New York: Holt.